NEW PERSPECTIVES ON

HTML5, CSS3, and JavaScript

6th Edition

Patrick Carey

CENGAGE

Australia • Brazil • Mexico • Singapore • United Kingdom • United States

New Perspectives on HTML5, CSS3, and JavaScript
6th Edition
Patrick Carey

SVP, GM Science, Technology & Math: Balraj S. Kalsi

Senior Product Director: Kathleen McMahon

Product Team Manager: Kristin McNary

Associate Product Manager: Kate Mason

Senior Director, Development: Julia Caballero

Senior Content Development Manager: Leigh Hefferon

Associate Content Developer: Maria Garguilo

Development Editor: Pam Conrad

Product Assistant: Jake Toth

VP, Marketing for Science, Technology, & Math: Jason Sakos

Marketing Director: Michele McTighe

Marketing Manager: Stephanie Albracht

Production Director: Patty Stephan

Senior Content Project Manager: Jennifer K. Feltri-George

Art Director: Diana Graham

Manufacturing Planner: Fola Orekoya

Cover image(s): iStockPhoto.com/moncsicsi

Compositor: GEX Publishing Services

For product information and technology assistance, contact us at
**Cengage Customer & Sales Support, 1-800-354-9706
or support.cengage.com.**

For permission to use material from this text or product, submit all requests online at **www.cengage.com/permissions.**

Library of Congress Control Number: 2017939432
Softcover ISBN: 978-1-305-50392-2
Loose-leaf ISBN: 978-1-337-68576-4

Cengage
20 Channel Street
Boston, MA 02210
USA

Cengage is a leading provider of customized learning solutions with employees residing in nearly 40 different countries and sales in more than 125 countries around the world. Find your local representative at: **www.cengage.com.**

Cengage products are represented in Canada by Nelson Education, Ltd.

To learn more about Cengage platforms and services, register or access your online learning solution, or purchase materials for your course, visit **www.cengage.com.**

Some of the product names and company names used in this book have been used for identification purposes only and may be trademarks or registered trademarks of their respective manufacturers and sellers.

Disclaimer: Any fictional data related to persons or companies or URLs used throughout this book is intended for instructional purposes only. At the time this book was printed, any such data was fictional and not belonging to any real persons or companies.

Microsoft and the Windows logo are registered trademarks of Microsoft Corporation in the United States and/or other countries. Cengage Learning is an independent entity from Microsoft Corporation and not affiliated with Microsoft in any manner.

Printed at CLDPC, USA, 03-21

Preface

The New Perspectives Series' critical-thinking, problem-solving approach is the ideal way to prepare students to transcend point-and-click skills and take advantage of all that HTML5, CSS3, and JavaScript have to offer.

In developing the New Perspectives Series, our goal was to create books that give students the software concepts and practical skills they need to succeed beyond the classroom. We've updated our proven case-based pedagogy with more practical content to make learning skills more meaningful to students. With the New Perspectives Series, students understand *why* they are learning *what* they are learning, and they are fully prepared to apply their skills to real-life situations.

"I love this text because it provides detailed instructions and real-world application examples. It is ideal for classroom and online instruction. At the end of the term, my students comment on how much they've learned and put to use outside the classroom."
—Bernice Howard
St. Johns River Community College

About This Book

This book provides thorough coverage of HTML5, CSS3, and JavaScript, and includes the following:
- Up-to-date coverage of using HTML5 to create structured websites.
- Instruction on the most current CSS3 styles to create visually-interesting pages and captivating graphical designs.
- Working with browser developer tools to aid in the creation and maintenance of fully-functioning websites.

New for this edition!
- Coverage of responsive design techniques to create website designs that can scale to mobile, tablet, and desktop devices.
- Hands-on study of new HTML elements and CSS styles including layouts using flexboxes and grid frameworks.
- Exploration of CSS3 styles for graphic design, including image borders, drop shadows, gradient fills, 2D and 3D transformations, and graphic filters.
- Exploration of responsive design for web tables.
- Coverage of CSS styles for animation and transitions.
- Coverage of JavaScript arrays, program loops, and conditional statements.
- Coverage of JavaScript methods for form validation and e-commerce.
- Coverage of custom objects, properties, and methods used in object-based programming.

System Requirements

This book assumes that students have an Internet connection, a text editor, and a current browser that supports HTML5 and CSS3. The following is a list of the most recent versions of the major browsers at the time this text was published: Internet Explorer 11, Microsoft Edge 38, Firefox 52, Safari 11, Opera 43, and Google Chrome 57. More recent versions may have come out since the publication of this book. Students should go to the Web browser home page to download the most current version. All browsers interpret HTML5 and CSS3 code in slightly different ways. It is highly recommended that students have several different browsers installed on their systems for comparison and, if possible, access to a mobile browser or a mobile emulator. Students might also want to run older versions of these browsers to highlight compatibility issues. The screen-shots in this book were produced using Google Chrome 57 running on Windows 10 (64-bit), unless otherwise noted. If students are using different devices, browsers, or operating systems, their screens might vary from those shown in the book; this should not present any problems in completing the tutorials.

The New Perspectives Approach

"New Perspectives texts provide up-to-date, real-world application of content, making book selection easy. The step-by-step, hands-on approach teaches students concepts they can apply immediately."
—John Taylor
Southeastern Technical College

VISUAL OVERVIEW

PROSKILLS

KEY STEP

INSIGHT

TIP

REVIEW
APPLY
CHALLENGE
CREATE

REFERENCE

GLOSSARY/INDEX

Context
Each tutorial begins with a problem presented in a "real-world" case that is meaningful to students. The case sets the scene to help students understand what they will do in the tutorial.

Hands-on Approach
Each tutorial is divided into manageable sessions that combine reading and hands-on, step-by-step work. Colorful screenshots help guide students through the steps. **Trouble?** tips, which anticipate common mistakes or problems, help students stay on track and continue with the tutorial.

Visual Overviews
Each session begins with a Visual Overview, a two-page spread that includes colorful, enlarged figures with numerous callouts and key term definitions, giving students a comprehensive preview of the topics covered in the session, as well as a handy study guide.

ProSkills Boxes
ProSkills boxes provide guidance for applying concepts to real-world, professional situations, involving one or more of the following soft skills: decision making, problem solving, teamwork, verbal communication, and written communication.

Key Steps
Important steps are highlighted in yellow with attached margin notes to help students pay close attention to completing the steps correctly and avoid time-consuming rework.

InSight Boxes
InSight boxes offer expert advice and best practices to help students achieve a deeper understanding of the concepts behind the software features and skills.

Margin Tips
Margin Tips provide helpful hints and shortcuts for more efficient use of the software. The Tips appear in the margin at key points throughout each tutorial, giving students extra information when and where they need it.

Assessment
Retention is a key component to learning. At the end of each session, a series of Quick Check questions helps students test their understanding of the material before moving on. Engaging end-of-tutorial Review Assignments and Case Problems have always been a hallmark feature of the New Perspectives Series. Colorful bars and brief descriptions accompany the exercises, making it easy to understand both the goal and level of challenge a particular assignment holds.

Reference
Within each tutorial, Reference boxes appear before a set of steps to provide a succinct summary or preview of how to perform a task. In addition, each book includes a combination Glossary/Index to promote easy reference of material.

Our Complete System of Instruction

Coverage To Meet Your Needs

Whether you're looking for just a small amount of coverage or enough to fill a semester-long class, we can provide you with a textbook that meets your needs.

- Introductory books contain an average of 5 to 8 tutorials and include essential skills on the books concepts.
- Comprehensive books, which cover additional concepts and skills in depth, are great for a full-semester class, and contain 9 to 12+ tutorials.

So, if you are looking for just the essential skills or more complete in-depth coverage of a topic, we have an offering available to meet your needs. Go to our website or contact your Cengage Learning sales representative to find out what else we offer.

MindTap

MindTap is a personalized learning experience with relevant assignments that guide students to analyze, apply, and improve thinking, allowing you to measure skills and outcomes with ease.

For instructors: personalized teaching becomes yours with a Learning Path that is built with key student objectives. Control what students see and when they see it. Use as-is, or match to your syllabus exactly: hide, rearrange, add, or create your own content.

For students: a unique Learning Path of relevant readings, multimedia, and activities that guide you through basic knowledge and comprehension to analysis and application.

Better outcomes: empower instructors and motivate students with analytics and reports that provide a snapshot of class progress, time in course, engagement, and completion rates.

The MindTap for HTML5, CSS3, and JavaScript includes coding labs, study tools, and interactive quizzing, all integrated into an eReader that includes the full content of the printed text.

Instructor Resources

We offer more than just a book. We have all the tools you need to enhance your lectures, check students' work, and generate exams in a new, easier-to-use and completely revised package. This book's Instructor's Manual, Cognero testbank, PowerPoint presentations, data files, solution files, figure files, and a sample syllabus are all available at sso.cengage.com.

Acknowledgments

I would like to thank the people who worked so hard to make this book possible. Special thanks to my developmental editor, Pam Conrad, for her hard work, attention to detail, and valuable insights, and to Associate Content Developer, Maria Garguilo, who has worked tirelessly in overseeing this project and made my task so much easier with enthusiasm and good humor. Other people at Cengage who deserve credit are Kathleen McMahon, Sr. Product Manager; Kate Mason, Associate Product Manager; Jake Toth, Product Assistant; Jen Feltri-George, Senior Content Project Manager; Diana Graham, Art Director; Fola Orekoya, Manufacturing Planner; GEX Publishing Services, Compositor, as well as the MQA tester Danielle Shaw.

Feedback is an important part of writing any book, and thanks go to the following reviewers for their helpful ideas and comments: Alison Consol, Wake Technical Community College; Dana Hooper, The University of Alabama; Kenneth Kleiner, Fayetteville Technical Community College; and Laurie Crawford, Franklin University.

I want to thank my wife Joan and my six children for their love, encouragement, and patience in putting up with a sometimes distracted husband and father. This book is dedicated to my grandchildren: Benedict, David, Elanor, and Nicholas.
– Patrick Carey

BRIEF CONTENTS

HTML

TABLE OF CONTENTS

HTML

Getting Started with HTML5

Creating a Website for a Food Vendor

OBJECTIVES

Session 1.1
- Explore the history of the web
- Create the structure of an HTML document
- Insert HTML elements and attributes
- Insert metadata into a document
- Define a page title

Session 1.2
- Mark page structures with sectioning elements
- Organize page content with grouping elements
- Mark content with text-level elements
- Insert inline images
- Insert symbols based on character codes

Session 1.3
- Mark content using lists
- Create a navigation list
- Link to files within a website with hypertext links
- Link to e-mail addresses and telephone numbers

Case | *Curbside Thai*

Sajja Adulet is the owner and master chef of Curbside Thai, a restaurant owner and now food truck vendor in Charlotte, North Carolina that specializes in Thai dishes. Sajja has hired you to develop the company's website. The website will display information about Curbside Thai including the truck's daily locations, menu, catering opportunities, and contact information. Sajja wants the pages to convey the message that customers will get the same great food and service whether they order in the restaurant or from the food truck. Some of the materials for these pages have already been completed by a former employee and Sajja needs you to finish the job by converting that work into a collection of web page documents. To complete this task, you'll learn how to write and edit HTML5 code and how to get your HTML files ready for display on the World Wide Web.

STARTING DATA FILES

html01 →

tutorial
ct_catering_txt.html
ct_contact_txt.html
ct_locations_txt.html
ct_menu_txt.html
ct_reviews._txt.html
+ 16 files

review
mp_catering_txt.html
mp_events_txt.html
mp_index_txt.html
mp_menu_txt.html
+ 5 files

case1
jtc_index_txt.html
jtc_services_txt.html
+ 6 files

case2
ms_euler_txt.html
+ 5 files

case3
dr_faq_txt.html
dr_index_txt.html
dr_info_txt.html
+ 9 files

case4
hg_ alliance _txt.html
hg_index_txt.html
hg_ towers_txt.html
+ 4 files

demo
demo_characters.html
demo_html.html
+ 4 files

Session 1.1 Visual Overview:

The **document type declaration** is a processing instruction indicating the markup language used in the document.

The **<html>** tag marks the beginning of the HTML document.

The **<head>** tag marks the **document head** containing information about the document.

The **<meta>** tag marks metadata containing information about the document.

An **HTML comment** is a descriptive note added to the HTML file.

The **<title>** tag marks the page title that appears on the browser title bar or browser tab.

The **<body>** tag marks the **document body** containing all of the content that will appear in the page.

An **opening tag** marks the start of the element content; this tag marks the start of page footer.

A **closing tag** marks the end of the element content; this tag marks the end of the page footer.

```
<!DOCTYPE html>
<html>

<head>
    <!-- Curbside Thai Starting Page -->

    <meta charset="utf-8" />
    <link href="ct_base.css" rel="stylesheet" />
    <link href="ct_layout1.css" rel="stylesheet" />
    <title>Curbside Thai</title>
</head>

<body>
    <header>
        <img src="ct_logo.png" alt="Curbside Thai" />
    </header>
    <nav>
        <a href="ct_about.html"><img src="ct_about.png" alt="About Us" /></a>
        <a href="ct_locations.html"><img src="ct_locations.png" alt="Locations" /></a>
        <a href="ct_menu.html"><img src="ct_menu.png" alt="Menu" /></a>
        <a href="ct_reviews.html"><img src="ct_reviews.png" alt="Reviews" /></a>
        <a href="ct_catering.html"><img src="ct_catering.png" alt="Catering" /></a>
        <a href="ct_contact.html"><img src="ct_contact.png" alt="Contact Us" /></a>
    </nav>
    <footer>
        Curbside Thai &#8226; 411 Belde Drive, Charlotte NC 28201 &#8226; 704-555-1151
    </footer>
</body>

</html>
```

The Structure of an HTML Document

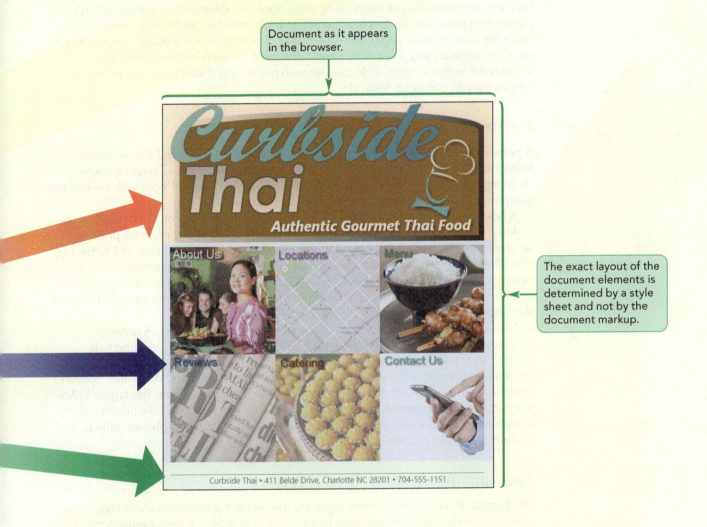

Document as it appears in the browser.

The exact layout of the document elements is determined by a style sheet and not by the document markup.

Curbside Thai • 411 Belde Drive, Charlotte NC 28201 • 704-555-1151

Exploring the World Wide Web

It is no exaggeration to say that the World Wide Web has had as profound an effect on human communication as the printing press. One key difference is that operation of the printing press was limited to a few select tradesmen but on the web everyone has his or her own printing press; everyone can be a publisher of a website. Before creating your first website, you'll examine a short history of the web because that history impacts the way you write code for your web pages. You'll start by exploring the basic terminology of computer networks.

Networks

A **network** is a structure in which information and services are shared among devices known as **nodes** or **hosts**. A host can be any device that is capable of sending and/or receiving data electronically. The most common hosts that you will work with are desktop computers, laptops, tablets, mobile phones, and printers.

A host that provides information or a service to other devices on the network is called a **server**. For example, a print server is a network host that provides printing services and a file server is a host that provides storage space for saving and retrieving files. The device that receives these services is called a **client**. A common network design is the **client-server network**, in which the clients access information provided by one or more servers. You might be using such a network to access your data files for this tutorial.

Networks are classified based on the range of devices they cover. A network confined to a small geographic area, such as within a building or department, is referred to as a **local area network** or **LAN**. A network that covers a wider area, such as several buildings or cities, is called a **wide area network** or **WAN**. Wide area networks typically consist of two or more interconnected local area networks. The largest WAN in existence is the **Internet**, which incorporates an almost uncountable number of networks and hosts involving computers, mobile devices (such as phones, tablets, and so forth), MP3 players, and gaming systems.

Locating Information on a Network

The biggest obstacle to effectively using the Internet is the network's sheer scope and size. Most of the early Internet tools required users to master a bewildering array of terms, acronyms, and commands. Because network users had to be well versed in computers and network technology, Internet use was largely limited to programmers and computer specialists working for universities, large businesses, and the government.

The solution to this problem was developed in 1989 by Timothy Berners-Lee and other researchers at the CERN nuclear research facility near Geneva, Switzerland. They needed an information system that would make it easy for their researchers to locate and share data on the CERN network. To meet this need, they developed a system of hypertext documents. **Hypertext** is a method of organization in which data sources are interconnected through a series of links or **hyperlinks** that users activate to jump from one data source to another. Hypertext is ideally suited for the Internet because end users don't need to know where a particular document, information source, or service is located—they only need to know how to activate the link. The effectiveness of this technique quickly spread beyond Geneva and was adopted with other networks across the Internet. The totality of these interconnected hypertext documents became known as the **World Wide Web**. The fact that the Internet and the World Wide Web are synonymous in many users' minds is a testament to the success of the hypertext approach.

Web Pages and Web Servers

Documents on the web are stored on **web servers** in the form of **web pages** and accessed through a software program called a **web browser**. The browser retrieves the document from the web server and renders it locally in a form that is readable on a client device. However, because there is a wide selection of client devices ranging from desktop computers to mobile phones to screen readers that relay data aurally, each web page must be written in code that is compatible with every device. How does the same document work with so many different devices? To understand, you need to look at how web pages are created.

Introducing HTML

A web page is a simple text file written in **HTML** (**Hypertext Markup Language**). You've already read about hypertext, but what is a markup language? A **markup language** is a language that describes the content and structure of a document by "marking up" or tagging, different document elements. For example, this tutorial contains several document elements such as the tutorial title, main headings, subheadings, paragraphs, figures, figure captions, and so forth. Using a markup language, each of these elements could be tagged as a distinct item within the "tutorial document." Thus, a Hypertext Markup Language is a language that supports both the tagging of distinct document elements and connecting documents through hypertext links.

The History of HTML

In the early years, no single organization defined the rules or **syntax** of HTML. Browser developers were free to define and modify the language in different ways which, of course, led to problems as different browsers supported different "flavors" of HTML and a web page that was written based on one browser's standard might appear totally different when rendered by another browser. Ultimately, a group of web designers and programmers called the **World Wide Web Consortium**, or the **W3C**, settled on a set of standards or specifications for all browser manufacturers to follow. The W3C has no enforcement power, but, because using a uniform language is in everyone's best interest, the W3C's recommendations are usually followed, though not always immediately. Each new version of HTML goes through years of discussion and testing before it is formally adopted as the accepted standard. For more information on the W3C and its services, see its website at *www.w3.org*.

By 1999, HTML had progressed to the fourth version of the language, **HTML 4.01**, which provided support for multimedia, online commerce, and interactive scripts running within the web page. However, there were still many incompatibilities in how HTML was implemented across different browsers and how HTML code was written by web developers. The W3C sought to take control of what had been a haphazard process and enforce a stricter set of standards in a different version of the language called **XHTML** (**Extensible Hypertext Markup Language**). By 2002, the W3C had released the specifications for XHTML 1.1. But XHTML 1.1 was intended to be only a minor upgrade on the way to XHTML 2.0, which would correct many of the deficiencies found in HTML 4.01 and become the future language of the web. One problem was that XHTML 2.0 would not be backward compatible with HTML and, as a result, older websites could not be easily brought into the new standard.

Web designers rebelled at this development and, in response, the **Web Hypertext Application Technology Working Group** (**WHATWG**) was formed in 2004 with the mission to develop a rival version to XHTML 2.0, called **HTML5**. Unlike XHTML 2.0, HTML5 would be compatible with earlier versions of HTML and would not apply the same strict standards that XHTML demanded. For several years, it was unclear which specification would win out; but by 2006, work on XHTML 2.0 had completely stalled and the W3C issued a new charter for WHATWG to develop HTML5 as the de facto standard for the next generation of HTML. Thus today, HTML5 is the current version of the HTML language and it is supported by all current browsers and devices. You can learn more about WHATWG and its current projects at *www.whatwg.org*.

As HTML has evolved, features and code found in earlier versions of the language are often **deprecated**, or phased out, and while deprecated features might not be part of HTML5, that doesn't mean that you won't encounter them in your work—indeed, if you are maintaining older websites, you will often need to interpret code from earlier versions of HTML. Moreover, there are still many older browsers and devices in active use that do not support HTML5. Thus, a major challenge for website designers is writing code that takes advantage of HTML5 but is still accessible to older technology.

Figure 1-1 summarizes some of the different versions of HTML that have been implemented over the years. You can read detailed specifications for these versions at the W3C website.

Figure 1-1	**HTML version history**

Version	Date	Description
HTML 1.0	1989	The first public version of HTML
HTML 2.0	1995	HTML version that added interactive elements including web forms
HTML 3.2	1997	HTML version that provided additional support for web tables and expanded the options for interactive form elements and a scripting language
HTML 4.01	1999	HTML version that added support for style sheets to give web designers greater control over page layout and appearance, and provided support for multimedia elements such as audio and video
XHTML 1.0	2001	A reformulation of HTML 4.01 using the XML markup language in order to provide enforceable standards for HTML content and to allow HTML to interact with other XML languages
XHTML 2.0	discontinued in 2009	The follow-up version to XHTML 1.1 designed to fix some of the problems inherent in HTML 4.01 syntax
HTML 5.0	2012	The current HTML version providing support for mobile design, semantic page elements, column layout, form validation, offline storage, and enhanced multimedia

© 2016 Cengage Learning

This book focuses on HTML5, but you will also review some of the specifications for HTML 4.01 and XHTML 1.1. Note that in the figures that follow, code that was introduced starting with HTML5 will be identified with the label [*HTML5*].

Tools for Working with HTML

Because HTML documents are simple text files, the first tool you will need is a text editor. You can use a basic text editor such as Windows Notepad or TextEdit for the Macintosh, but it is highly recommended that you use one of the many inexpensive editors that provide built-in support for HTML. Some of the more popular HTML editors are Notepad++ (*notepad-plus-plus.org*), UltraEdit (*www.ultraedit.com*), CoffeeCup (*www.coffeecup.com*), BBEdit (*www.barebones.com*) and ConTEXT (*www.contexteditor.org*). These editors include such features as syntax checking to weed out errors, automatic insertion of HTML code, and predesigned templates with the initial code already prepared for you.

These enhanced editors are a good way to start learning HTML and they will be all you need for most basic projects, but professional web developers working on large websites will quickly gravitate toward using a web **IDE (Integrated Development Environment)**, which is a software package providing comprehensive coverage of all phases of the development process from writing HTML code to creating scripts for programs running on web servers. Some of the popular IDEs for web development include Adobe Dreamweaver (*www.adobe.com*), Aptana Studio (*www.aptana.com*), NetBeans IDE (*netbeans.org*) and Komodo IDE (*komodoide.com*). Web IDEs can be very expensive, but most software companies will provide a free evaluation period for you to test their product to see if it meets your needs.

Testing your Code

Once you've written your code, you can test whether your HTML code employs proper syntax and structure by validating it at the W3C validation website (*validator.w3.org*). **Validators**, like the one available through the W3C website, are programs that test code to ensure that it contains no syntax errors. The W3C validator will highlight all of the syntax errors in your document with suggestions about how to fix those errors.

Finally, you'll need to test it to ensure that your content is rendered correctly. You should test your code under a variety of screen resolutions, on several different browsers and, if possible, on different versions of the same browser because users are not always quick to upgrade their browsers. What may look good on a widescreen monitor might look horrible on a mobile phone. At a minimum you should test your website using the following popular browsers: Google Chrome, Internet Explorer, Apple Safari, Mozilla Firefox, and Opera.

It is not always possible to load multiple versions of the same browser on one computer, so, in order to test a website against multiple browser versions, professional designers will upload their code to online testing services that report on the website's compatibility across a wide range of browsers, screen resolutions, and devices, including both desktop and mobile devices. Among the popular testing services are BrowserStack (*www.browserstack.com*), CrossBrowserTesting (*www.crossbrowsertesting.com*), and Browsera (*www.browsera.com*). Most of these sites charge a monthly connection fee with a limited number of testing minutes, so you should not upload your code until you are past the initial stages of development.

Supporting the Mobile Web

Currently, the most important factor impacting website design is the increased use of mobile devices to access the Internet. By the end of 2014, the number of mobile Internet users exceeded the number of users accessing the web through laptop or desktop devices. The increased reliance on mobile devices means that web designers must be careful to tailor their websites to accommodate both the desktop and mobile experience. You'll explore the challenge of designing for the mobile web in more detail in Tutorial 5.

Exploring an HTML Document

Now that you have reviewed the history of the web and some of the challenges in developing your own website, you will look at the code of an actual HTML file. To get you started, Sajja Adulet has provided you with the ct_start.html file containing the code for the initial page users see when they access the Curbside Thai website. Open Sajja's file now.

To open the ct_start.html file:

1. Use the editor of your choice to open the **ct_start.html** file from the html01 ► tutorial folder.

   Figure 1-2 shows the complete contents of the file as viewed in the Notepad++ editor.

Figure 1-2   **Elements and attributes from an HTML document**

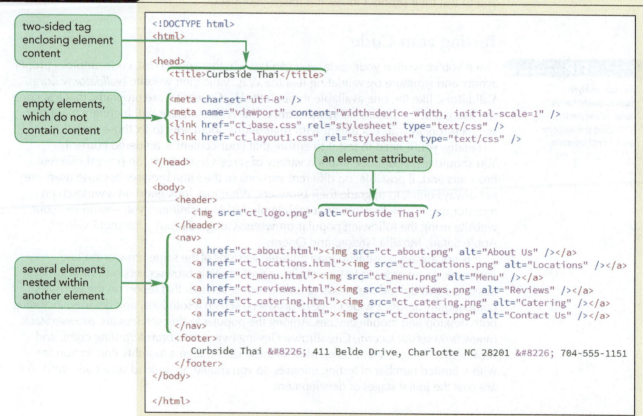

two-sided tag enclosing element content

empty elements, which do not contain content

an element attribute

several elements nested within another element

```
<!DOCTYPE html>
<html>

<head>
     <title>Curbside Thai</title>

<meta charset="utf-8" />
<meta name="viewport" content="width=device-width, initial-scale=1" />
<link href="ct_base.css" rel="stylesheet" type="text/css" />
<link href="ct_layout1.css" rel="stylesheet" type="text/css" />

</head>

<body>
     <header>
          <img src="ct_logo.png" alt="Curbside Thai" />
     </header>
     <nav>
          <a href="ct_about.html"><img src="ct_about.png" alt="About Us" /></a>
          <a href="ct_locations.html"><img src="ct_locations.png" alt="Locations" /></a>
          <a href="ct_menu.html"><img src="ct_menu.png" alt="Menu" /></a>
          <a href="ct_reviews.html"><img src="ct_reviews.png" alt="Reviews" /></a>
          <a href="ct_catering.html"><img src="ct_catering.png" alt="Catering" /></a>
          <a href="ct_contact.html"><img src="ct_contact.png" alt="Contact Us" /></a>
     </nav>
     <footer>
          Curbside Thai &#8226; 411 Belde Drive, Charlotte NC 28201 &#8226; 704-555-1151
     </footer>
</body>

</html>
```

Trouble? Depending on your editor and its configuration, the text style applied to your code might not match that shown in Figure 1-2. This is not a problem. Because HTML documents are simple text files, any text styles are a feature of the editor and have no impact on how the document is rendered by the browser.

2. Scroll through the document to become familiar with its content but do not make any changes to the text.

The Document Type Declaration

The first line in an HTML file is the document type declaration or doctype, which is a processing instruction indicating the markup language used in the document. The browser uses the document type declaration to know which standard to use to display the content. For HTML5, the doctype is entered as

```
<!DOCTYPE html>
```

You might also see the doctype entered in lowercase letters as

```
<!doctype html>
```

Both are accepted by all browsers. Older versions of HTML had more complicated doctypes. For example, the doctype for HTML 4.01 is the rather foreboding

```
<!DOCTYPE HTML PUBLIC "-//W3C//DTD HTML 4.01//EN"
  "http://www.w3.org/TR/html4/strict.dtd">
```

You might even come across older HTML files that do not have a doctype. Because early versions of HTML did not require a doctype, many browsers interpret the absence of the doctype as a signal that the page should be rendered in **quirks mode**, based on styles and practices from the 1990s and early 2000s. When the doctype is present, browsers will render the page in **standards mode**, employing the most current specifications of HTML. The difference between quirks mode and standards mode can mean the difference between a nicely laid-out page and a confusing mess, so, as a result, you should always put your HTML5 file in standards mode by including the doctype.

Introducing Element Tags

The fundamental building block in every HTML document is the **element tag**, which marks an element in the document. A **starting tag** indicates the beginning of that element, while an **ending tag** indicates the ending. The general syntax of a two-sided element tag is

```
<element>content</element>
```

where *element* is the name of the element, *content* is the element's content, *<element>* is the starting tag, and *</element>* is the ending tag. For example, the following code marks a paragraph element:

```
<p>Welcome to Curbside Thai.</p>
```

Here the `<p></p>` tags are the starting and ending HTML tags that indicate the presence of a paragraph and the text *Welcome to Curbside Thai.* comprises the paragraph text.

Not every element tag encloses document content. **Empty elements** are elements that are either nontextual (such as images) or contain directives to the browser about how the page should be treated. An empty element is entered using one of the following forms of the **one-sided element tag**:

```
<element />
```

or

```
<element>
```

For example, the following `br` element, which is used to indicate the presence of a line break in the text, is entered with the one-sided tag:

```
<br />
```

Note that, while this code could also be entered as `<br>`, the ending slash `/>` form is the required form in XHTML documents as well as other markup languages. While HTML5 allows for either form, it's a good idea to get accustomed to using the ending slash `/>` form if you intend to work with other markup languages in the future. We'll follow the `/>` convention in the code in this book.

Elements can contain other elements, which are called **nested elements**. For example, in the following code, the `em` element (used to mark emphasized text) is nested within the paragraph element by placing the `em` markup tag completely within the `p` markup tag.

Proper syntax:

```
<p>Welcome to <em>Curbside Thai</em>.</p>
```

Note that when nesting one element inside of another, the entire code of the inner element must be contained within the outer element, including opening and closing tags. Thus, it would not be correct syntax to place the closing tag for the em element outside of the p element as in the following code:

Improper syntax:

```
<p>Welcome to <em>Curbside Thai</p>.</em>
```

Now that you've examined the basics of tags, you'll look at how they're used within an HTML file.

The Element Hierarchy

The entire structure of an HTML document can be thought of as a set of nested elements in a hierarchical tree. At the top of the tree is the html element, which marks the entire document. Within the html element is the head element used to mark information about the document itself and the body element used to mark the content that will appear in the web page. Thus, the general structure of an HTML file, like the one shown in Figure 1-2, is

```
<!DOCTYPE html>
<html>
<head>
    head content
</head>

<body>
    body content
</body>
</html>
```

where *head content* and *body content* are nested elements that mark the content of the document head and body. Note that the body element is always placed after the head element.

Creating the Basic Structure of an HTML File

- To create the basic structure of an HTML file, enter the tags

```
<!DOCTYPE html>
<html>
<head>
    head content
</head>

<body>
    body content
</body>
</html>
```

where *head*, *content*, and *body content* contain nested elements that mark the content of the head and body sections.

Introducing Element Attributes

Elements will often contain one or more **element attributes**. Each attribute provides additional information to the browser about the purpose of the element or how the element should be handled by the browser. The general syntax of an element attribute within a two-sided tag is

```
<element attr1="value1" attr2="value2" …>
   content
</element>
```

Or, for a one-sided tag

```
<element attr1="value1" attr2="value2" … />
```

where `attr1`, `attr2`, and so forth are attributes associated with `element` and `value1`, `value2`, and so forth are the corresponding attribute values. For example, the following code adds the `id` attribute with the value "intro" to the `<p>` tag in order to identify the paragraph as an introductory paragraph.

```
<p id="intro">Welcome to Curbside Thai.</p>
```

HTML editors will often color-code attributes and their values. The attributes in Figure 1-2 are rendered in a blue font while the corresponding attribute values are rendered in magenta.

Each element has its own set of attributes but, in addition to these element-specific attributes, there is a core set of attributes that can be applied to almost every HTML element. Figure 1-3 lists some of the most commonly used core attributes; others are listed in Appendix B.

Figure 1-3   Commonly used core HTML attributes

Attribute	Description
`class="text"`	Defines the general classification of the element
`dir="ltr|rtl|auto"`	Defines the text direction of the element content as left-to-right, right-to-left, or determined by the browser
`hidden`	Indicates that the element should be hidden or is no longer relevant [**HTML5**]
`id="text"`	Provides a unique identifier for the element
`lang="text"`	Specifies the language of the element content
`style="definition"`	Defines the style or appearance of the element content
`tabindex="integer"`	Specifies the tab order of the element (when the tab button is used to navigate the page)
`title="text"`	Assigns a title to the element content

© 2016 Cengage Learning

Some attributes do not require a value, so, as a result, HTML supports **attribute minimization** in which no value is shown in the document. For example, the `hidden` attribute used in the following code does not require a value, its mere presence indicates that the marked paragraph should be hidden in the rendered page.

```
<p hidden>Placeholder Text</p>
```

Attribute minimization is another example of how HTML5 differs from other markup languages such as XHTML in which minimization is not allowed and all attributes must have attribute values.

Adding an Attribute to an Element

- To add an attribute to an element, enter

```
<element attr1="value1" attr2="value2" …>
   content
</element>
```

where *attr1*, *attr2*, and so forth are HTML attributes associated with *element* and *value1*, *value2*, and so forth are the corresponding attribute values.

Handling White Space

Because an HTML file is a text file, it is composed only of text characters and white-space characters. A **white-space character** is any empty or blank character such as a space, tab, or line break. When the browser reads an HTML file, it ignores the presence of white-space characters between element tags and makes no distinction between spaces, tabs, or line breaks. Thus, a browser will treat the following two pieces of code in exactly the same way:

```
<p>Welcome to <em>Curbside Thai</em>.</p>
```

and

```
<p>
     Welcome to <em>Curbside Thai</em>.
</p>
```

The browser will also collapse consecutive occurrences of white-space characters into a single occurrence. This means that the text of the paragraph in the following code is still treated as "Welcome to Curbside Thai" because the extra white spaces between "Curbside" and "Thai" are ignored by the browser.

```
<p>
     Welcome to <em>Curbside          Thai</em>.
</p>
```

The bottom line is that it doesn't matter how you lay out your HTML code because the browser is only interested in the text content and not how that text is entered. This means you can make your file easier to read by indenting lines and by adding extra white-space characters to separate one code block from another. However, this also means that any formatting you do for the page text to make the code more readable, such as tabs or extra white spaces, is *not* transferred to the web page.

Viewing an HTML File in a Browser

The structure of the HTML file shown in Figure 1-2 should now be a little clearer, even if you don't yet know how to interpret the meaning and purpose of each of element and attribute. To see what this page looks like, open it within a web browser.

To open the ct_start.html file in a web browser:

1. Open your web browser. You do not need to be connected to the Internet to view local files stored on your computer.

2. After your browser loads its home page, open the ct_start.html file from the html01 ▸ tutorial folder. Figure 1-4 shows the page as it appears on a mobile phone and on a tablet device. The two devices have different screen widths, which affects how the page is rendered.

Figure 1-4   **The Curbside Thai starting page as rendered by a mobile and tablet device**

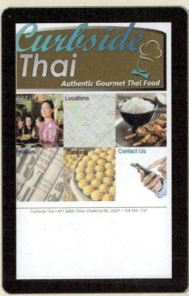

© 2016 Cengage Learning; © Kzenon/Shutterstock.com; © martiapunts/Shutterstock.com; © Brian A Jackson/Shutterstock.com; © sayhmog/Shutterstock.com; © rangizzz/Shutterstock.com; BenBois/openclipart; Jmlevick/openclipart

mobile device   tablet device

Trouble? If you're not sure how to open a local file with your browser, check for an Open or Open File command under the browser's File menu. You can also open a file by double-clicking the file name from within Windows Explorer or Apple Finder.

3. Reduce the width of your browser window and note that when the width falls below a certain value (in this case 480 pixels), the layout automatically changes to a stacked row of images (as shown in the mobile device image in Figure 1-4) that are better suited to the narrower layout.

4. Increase the width of the browser window and confirm that the layout changes to a 2×3 grid of images (as shown in the tablet device image in Figure 1-4), which is a design more appropriate for the wider window.

Figure 1-4 illustrates an important principle: *HTML does not describe the document's appearance, it only describes the document's content and structure.* The same HTML document can be rendered completely differently between one device and another or between one screen size and another. The actual appearance of the document is determined by style sheets—a topic you'll explore later in this tutorial.

Creating an HTML File

Now that you've studied the structure of an HTML file, you'll start creating your own documents for the Curbside Thai website. Sajja wants you to create a web page containing information about the restaurant. Start by inserting the doctype and the markup tags for the `html`, `head`, and `body` elements.

TIP

HTML filenames should be entered in lowercase letters and have *no* blank spaces.

To begin writing the HTML file:

1. Using the editor of your choice, create a new blank HTML file in the html01 ▸ tutorial folder, saving the file as **ct_about.html**.

2. Enter the following code into the file:

```
<!DOCTYPE html>
<html>

<head>
</head>

<body>
</body>

</html>
```

Figure 1-5 shows the initial elements in the document.

Figure 1-5	Initial structure of the ct_about.html file

document type declaration identifies the markup language as html

opening <html> tag marks the start of the document

head element will contain information about the document

body element will contain the content displayed by the browser

closing </html> tag marks the end of the document

```
<!DOCTYPE html>
<html>

<head>
</head>

<body>
</body>

</html>
```

3. Save your changes to the file.

Next, you'll add elements to the document head.

Written Communication: Writing Effective HTML Code

Part of writing good HTML code is being aware of the requirements of various browsers and devices, as well as understanding the different versions of the language. Here are a few guidelines for writing good HTML code:

- Become well versed in the history of HTML and the various versions of HTML and XHTML. Unlike other languages, HTML's history does impact how you write your code.
- Know your market. Do you have to support older browsers, or have your clients standardized on one particular browser or browser version? Will your web pages be viewed on a single device such as a computer, or do you have to support a variety of devices?
- Test your code on several different browsers and browser versions. Don't assume that if your page works in one browser, it will work in other browsers or even in earlier versions of the same browser. Also check on the speed of the connection. A large file that performs well with a high-speed connection might be unusable with a slower connection.
- Read the documentation on the different versions of HTML and XHTML at the W3C website and keep up to date with the latest developments in the language.

To effectively communicate with customers and users, you need to make sure your website content is always readable. Writing good HTML code is a great place to start.

Creating the Document Head

The document head contains **metadata**, which is content that describes the document or provides information about how the document should be processed by the browser. Figure 1-6 describes the different metadata elements found in the document head.

Figure 1-6   **HTML metadata elements**

Element	Description
head	Contains a collection of metadata elements that describe the document or provide instructions to the browser
base	Specifies the document's location for use with resolving relative hypertext links
link	Specifies an external resource that the document is connected to
meta	Provides a generic list of metadata values such as search keywords, viewport properties, and the file's character encoding
script	Provides programming code for programs to be run within the document
style	Defines the display styles used to render the document content
title	Stores the document's title or name, usually displayed in the browser title bar or on a browser tab

© 2016 Cengage Learning

The first metadata you'll add to the About Curbside Thai web page is the `title` element.

Setting the Page Title

The `title` element is part of the document head because it's not actually displayed as part of the web page, but rather appears externally within the browser title bar or browser tab. Page titles are defined using the following `title` element

```
<title>document title</title>
```

where `document title` is the text of the title. Add a page title to the Curbside Thai page now.

REFERENCE

Adding a Document Title

- To define the document title, enter the following tag into the document head:

  `<title>document title</title>`

  where *document title* is the text that will appear on the browser title bar or a browser tab.

To insert the document title:

TIP

Document titles should be no more than 64 characters in length to ensure that the text fits on the browser title bar or a browser tab.

1. Directly after the opening `<head>` tag, insert the following `title` element, indented to make the code easier to read.

   `<title>About Curbside Thai</title>`

   Figure 1-7 highlights the code for the page title.

Figure 1-7 | **Entering the document title**

title text that appears in the browser title bar or on a browser tab

```
<!DOCTYPE html>
<html>

<head>
    <title>About Curbside Thai</title>
</head>
```

2. Save your changes to the file.

Adding Metadata to the Document

Another metadata is the `meta` element, which is used for general lists of metadata values. The `meta` element structure is

   `<meta attributes />`

where *attributes* define the type of metadata that is to be added to a document. Figure 1-8 lists the attributes of the `meta` element.

Figure 1-8 | **Attributes of the meta element**

Attribute	Description
`charset="encoding"`	Specifies the character encoding used in the HTML document [**HTML5**]
`content="text"`	Provides the value associated with the `http-equiv` or `name` attributes
`http-equiv="content-type|default-style|refresh"`	Provides an HTTP header for the document's content, default style, or refresh interval (in seconds)
`name="text"`	Sets the name associated with the metadata

For example, you can use the following `meta` element to provide a collection of keywords for the Curbside Thai website that would aid web search engines, such as Google or Bing search tools, to locate the page for potential customers:

```
<meta name="keywords" content="Thai, restaurant, Charlotte,
food" />
```

In this tag, the `name` attribute defines the type of metadata and the `content` attribute provides the data values. HTML does not specify a set of values for the `name` attribute, but commonly used names include `keywords`, `description`, `author`, and `viewport`.

Another use of the `meta` element is to define the character encoding used in the HTML file. **Character encoding** is the process by which the computer converts text into a sequence of bytes when it stores the text and then converts those bytes back into characters when the text is read. The most common character encoding in use is **UTF-8**, which supports almost all of the characters you will need. To indicate that the document is written using UTF-8, you add the following `meta` element to the document head:

```
<meta charset="utf-8" />
```

The `charset` attribute was introduced in HTML5 and replaces the following more complicated expression used in earlier versions of HTML:

```
<meta http-equiv="Content-Type" content="text/html;
charset=UTF-8" />
```

TIP

The `title` element and the `charset` meta element are both required in a valid HTML5 document.

REFERENCE

Adding Metadata to the Document

- To define the character encoding used in the document, enter

  ```
  <meta charset="encoding" />
  ```

  where *encoding* is the character encoding used in the document.
- To define search keywords associated with the document, enter

  ```
  <meta name="keywords" content="terms" />
  ```

  where *terms* is a comma-separated list of keyword terms.

Add `meta` elements to the document head now, providing the character set and a list of keywords describing the page.

To insert metadata:

TIP

The `<meta>` tag that defines the character encoding should always be the first `meta` element in the document head.

1. Directly after the opening `<head>` tag, insert the following `meta` elements, indented to make the code easier to read:

   ```
   <meta charset="utf-8" />
   <meta name="keywords"
    content="Thai, restaurant, Charlotte, food" />
   ```

   Figure 1-9 highlights the newly added `meta` elements used in the document head.

Figure 1-9 **Adding metadata to a document**

> character encoding used in the document

> keywords used for search engines

```
<head>
   <meta charset="utf-8" />
   <meta name="keywords" content="Thai, restaurant, Charlotte, food" />
   <title>About Curbside Thai</title>
</head>
```

2. Save your changes to the file.

3. Open the **ct_about.html** file in your browser. Confirm that the browser tab or browser title bar contains the text "About Curbside Thai". There should be no text displayed in the browser window because you have not added any content to the page body yet.

Before continuing with your edits to the ct_about.html file, you should document your work. You can do this with a comment.

Adding Comments to your Document

A comment is descriptive text that is added to the HTML file but that does not appear in the browser window when the page is displayed. Comments can include the name of the document's author, the date the document was created, and the purpose for which the document was created. Comments are added with the following markup:

```
<!-- comment -->
```

where *comment* is the text of the comment or note. For example, the following code inserts a comment describing the page you're creating for Curbside Thai:

```
<!-- General Information about Curbside Thai -->
```

A comment can be spread across several lines as long as the comment text begins with <!-- and ends with -->. Because comments are ignored by the browser, they can be added anywhere within a document, though it's good practice to always include a comment in the document head in order to describe the document content that follows.

REFERENCE

Adding a Comment to an HTML Document

• To insert a comment anywhere within your HTML document, enter

```
<!-- comment -->
```

where *comment* is the text of the HTML comment.

Add comments to the ct_about.html file indicating the document's author, date of creation, and purpose.

To add a comment to the document:

1. Return to the **ct_about.html** file in your HTML editor.

2. Directly after the opening `<head>` tag, insert the following comment text, indented to make the code easier to read:

HTML comments must be closed with the `-->` characters.

```
<!--
New Perspectives on HTML5 and CSS3, 7th Edition
Tutorial 1
Tutorial Case
General Information about Curbside Thai
Author: your name
Date:   the date

Filename: ct_about.html
-->
```

where **your name** is your name and **the date** is the current date. Figure 1-10 highlights the newly added comment in the file.

| Figure 1-10 | Adding a comment to the document |

```
<head>
   <!--
   New Perspectives on HTML5 and CSS3, 7th Edition
   Tutorial 1
   Tutorial Case
   General Information about Curbside Thai
   Author: your name
   Date:   the date

   Filename: ct_about.html
   -->
   <meta charset="utf-8" />
   <meta name="keywords" content="Thai, restaurant, Charlotte, food" />
   <title>About Curbside Thai</title>
</head>
```

Comment added to the document

3. Save your changes to the file.

Conditional Comments and Internet Explorer

Another type of comment you will encounter in many HTML files is a **conditional comment**, which encloses content that should only be run by particular versions of the Internet Explorer browser. The general form of the conditional comment is

```
<!--[if operator IE version]>
   content
<![endif]-->
```

where *operator* is a logical operator (such as less than or greater than), *version* is the version number of an Internet Explorer browser, and *content* is the HTML code that will be run only if the conditional expression is true. The following code uses the lt (less than) logical operator to warn users that they need to upgrade their browser if they are running Internet Explorer prior to version 8.

```
<!--[if lt IE 8]>
   <p>Upgrade your browser to view this page.</p>
<![endif]-->
```

Other logical operators include lte (less than or equal to), gt (greater than), gte (greater than or equal to) and ! (not). For example, the following code uses the logical operator ! to display the paragraph text only when the browser is *not* Internet Explorer:

```
<!--[if !IE]>
   <p>You are not running Internet Explorer.</p>
<![endif]-->
```

Note that if you omit the version number, the conditional comment is applied to all Internet Explorer versions.

The need for conditional comments arose because Internet Explorer significantly differed from other browsers in how it implemented HTML and there was a need to separate the code meant for the IE browser from code meant for other browsers. This is not as much of a problem with recent versions of Internet Explorer, but you may still need to use conditional comments if you are writing code that will be compatible with versions of Internet Explorer earlier than IE 8.

In the next session, you'll continue your work on the ct_about.html file by adding content to the page body.

REVIEW

Session 1.1 Quick Check

1. What is a markup language?

2. What is XHTML? How does XHTML differ from HTML?

3. What is the W3C? What is the WHATWG?

4. What is a doctype? What is the doctype for an HTML5 document?

5. What is incorrect about the following code? Suggest a possible revision of the code to correct the error.

   ```
   <p><strong>Curbside Thai now delivers!</p></strong>
   ```

6. Provide code to mark *Curbside Thai Employment Opportunities* as the document title.

7. Provide code to create metadata adding the keywords *food truck*, *North Carolina*, and *dining* to the document.

8. Provide code to tell the browser that the character encoding UTF-16 is used in the document.

9. Provide code to add the comment *Created by Sajja Adulet* to the document.

Session 1.2 Visual Overview:

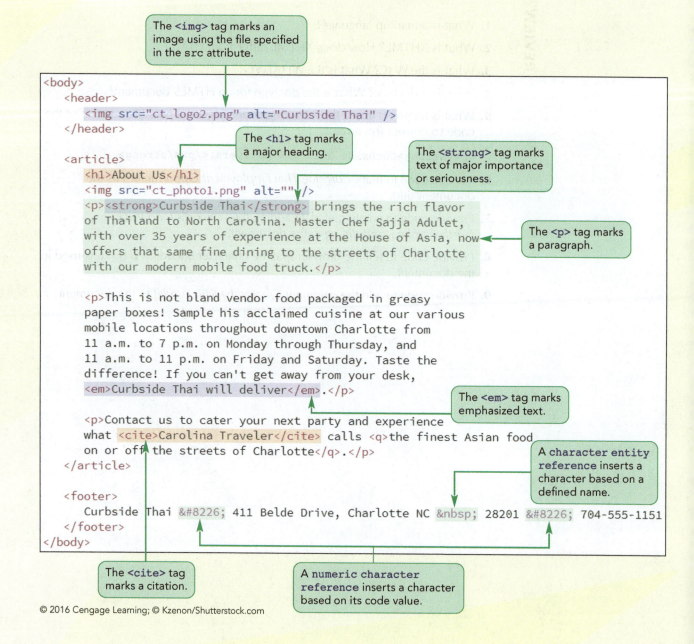

The `<img>` tag marks an image using the file specified in the src attribute.

The `<h1>` tag marks a major heading.

The `<strong>` tag marks text of major importance or seriousness.

The `<p>` tag marks a paragraph.

The `<em>` tag marks emphasized text.

A **character entity reference** inserts a character based on a defined name.

The `<cite>` tag marks a citation.

A **numeric character reference** inserts a character based on its code value.

```
<body>
   <header>
      <img src="ct_logo2.png" alt="Curbside Thai" />
   </header>

   <article>
      <h1>About Us</h1>
      <img src="ct_photo1.png" alt="" />
      <p><strong>Curbside Thai</strong> brings the rich flavor
      of Thailand to North Carolina. Master Chef Sajja Adulet,
      with over 35 years of experience at the House of Asia, now
      offers that same fine dining to the streets of Charlotte
      with our modern mobile food truck.</p>

      <p>This is not bland vendor food packaged in greasy
      paper boxes! Sample his acclaimed cuisine at our various
      mobile locations throughout downtown Charlotte from
      11 a.m. to 7 p.m. on Monday through Thursday, and
      11 a.m. to 11 p.m. on Friday and Saturday. Taste the
      difference! If you can't get away from your desk,
      <em>Curbside Thai will deliver</em>.</p>

      <p>Contact us to cater your next party and experience
      what <cite>Carolina Traveler</cite> calls <q>the finest Asian food
      on or off the streets of Charlotte</q>.</p>
   </article>

   <footer>
      Curbside Thai &#8226; 411 Belde Drive, Charlotte NC   28201 &#8226; 704-555-1151
   </footer>
</body>
```

HTML Page Elements

The opening paragraph of the article is marked with the <p> tag.

Images are added to the web page.

About Us

The restaurant name marked with the <strong> tag to indicate its importance.

The main heading of the article is marked with the <h1> tag.

Curbside Thai brings the rich flavor of Thailand to North Carolina. Owner and chef Sajja Adulet, with over 35 years of experience as the award-winning master chef at the House of Asia, now offers that same fine dining to the streets of Charlotte through our modern mobile food truck.

This is not bland vendor food packaged in greasy paper boxes! Sample our acclaimed cuisine at our various mobile locations throughout downtown Charlotte from 11 a.m. to 7 p.m. (M-R) and 11 a.m. to 11 p.m. on Friday and Saturday. Taste the difference! If you can't get away from your desk, *Curbside Thai will deliver.*

Nonbreaking space is inserted with the   character entity reference.

Contact us to cater your next party and experience what *Carolina Traveler* calls "the finest Asian food on or off the streets of Charlotte."

A citation to a magazine is marked with the <cite> tag.

Curbside Thai • 411 Belde Drive, Charlotte NC 28201 • 704-555-1151

An example of emphasized text is marked with the <em> tag.

Bullet characters are inserted with the • numeric character reference.

Writing the Page Body

Now that you have created the document head of the About Curbside Thai web page, you'll begin writing the document body. You will start with general markup tags that identify the major sections of the page body and then work inward to more specific content within those sections.

Using Sectioning Elements

The first task in designing the page body is to identify the page's major topics. A page typically has a header, one or more articles that are the chief focus of the page, and a footer that provides contact information for the author or company. HTML marks these major topical areas using the **sectioning elements** described in Figure 1-11.

Figure 1-11	HTML sectioning elements

Element	Description
address	Marks contact information for an individual or group
article	Marks a self-contained composition in the document such as a newspaper story [**HTML5**]
aside	Marks content that is related to a main article [**HTML5**]
body	Contains the entire content of the document
footer	Contains closing content that concludes an article or section [**HTML5**]
h1, h2, h3, h4, h5, h6	Marks major headings with h1 representing the heading with the highest rank, h2 representing next highest-ranked heading, and so forth
header	Contains opening content that introduces an article or section [**HTML5**]
nav	Marks a list of hypertext or navigation links [**HTML5**]
section	Marks content that shares a common theme or purpose on the page [**HTML5**]

© 2016 Cengage Learning

For example, a news blog page might contain several major topics. To identify these areas, the HTML code for the blog might include the following elements to mark off the page's header, navigation list, article, aside, and footer.

```
<body>
   <header>
   </header>
   <nav>
   </nav>
   <article>
   </article>
   <aside>
   </aside>
   <footer>
   </footer>
</body>
```

TIP

Sectioning elements can be nested within each other; for example, an article might contain its own header, footer, and collection of navigation links.

These sectioning elements are also referred to as **semantic elements** because the tag name describes the purpose of the element and the type of content it contains. Even without knowing much about HTML, the page structure defined in the above code is easily understood because of the tag names.

REFERENCE

Defining Page Sections

- To mark the page header, use the `header` element.
- To mark self-contained content, use the `article` element.
- To mark a navigation list of hypertext links, use the `nav` element.
- To mark a sidebar, use the `aside` element.
- To mark the page footer, use the `footer` element.
- To group general content, use the `section` element.

The About Curbside Thai page will have a simple structure containing a header, a single article, and a footer. Within the header, there will be an `h1` element providing the page title (not to be confused with the document title, which is displayed on the browser title bar or a browser tab). Add this structure to the document body.

To define the sections in the page body:

1. If you took a break after the previous session, return to the **ct_about.html** file in your HTML editor.

2. Directly after the opening `<body>` tag, insert the following HTML code, indented to make the code easier to read:

```
<header>
   <h1>Curbside Thai</h1>
</header>
<article>
   <h1>About Us</h1>
</article>
<footer>
   Curbside Thai 411 Belde Drive, Charlotte NC 28201 704-555-1151
</footer>
```

Figure 1-12 highlights the sectioning elements used in the page body.

Figure 1-12   Adding sectioning elements to the page body

```
<body>
   <header>
      <h1>Curbside Thai</h1>          page heading
   </header>
   <article>
      <h1>About Us</h1>              article heading
   </article>
   <footer>
      Curbside Thai 411 Belde Drive, Charlotte NC 28201 704-555-1151
   </footer>
</body>

</html>
```

document header → `<header>`
main article in the document → `<article>`
document footer → `<footer>`

3. Save your changes to the file.

Comparing Sections in HTML4 and HTML5

Many of the sectioning elements described in Figure 1-11 were introduced in HTML5. Prior to HTML5, sections were defined as divisions created using the following `div` element:

```
<div id="id">
    content
</div>
```

where *id* is a name that uniquely identifies the division. Figure 1-13 shows how the same page layout marked up using sectioning elements in HTML5 would have been defined in HTML 4.01 using `div` elements.

Figure 1-13 **Sections in HTML 5.0 vs. divisions in HTML 4.01**

© 2016 Cengage Learning

One problem with `div` elements is that there are no rules for the ids. One web designer might identify the page heading with the id *header* while another designer might use *heading* or *top*. The lack of consistency makes it harder for search engines to identify the page's main topics. The advantage of the HTML5 sectioning elements is that their tag name indicates their purpose in the document, leading to greater uniformity in how pages are designed and interpreted.

Using Grouping Elements

Within sectioning elements are **grouping elements**. Each grouping element organizes similar content into a distinct group, much like a paragraph groups sentences that share a common theme. Figure 1-14 describes all the HTML grouping elements.

Figure 1-14	HTML grouping elements

Element	Description
blockquote	Contains content that is quoted from another source, often with a citation and often indented on the page
div	Contains a generic grouping of elements within the document
dl	Marks a description list containing one or more dt elements with each followed by one or more dd elements
dt	Contains a single term from a description list
dd	Contains the description or definition associated with a term from a description list
figure	Contains an illustration, photo, diagram, or similar object that is cross-referenced elsewhere in the document [**HTML5**]
figcaption	Contains the caption associated with a figure [**HTML5**]
hr	Marks a thematic break such as a scene change or a transition to a new topic (often displayed as a horizontal rule)
main	Marks the main content of the document or application; only one main element should be used in the document [**HTML5**]
ol	Contains an ordered list of items
ul	Contains an unordered list of items
li	Contains a single item from an ordered or unordered list
p	Contains the text of a paragraph
pre	Contains a block of preformatted text in which line breaks and extra spaces in the code are retained (often displayed in a monospace font)

© 2016 Cengage Learning

For example, the following code shows three paragraphs nested within a page article with each paragraph representing a group of similar content:

```
<article>
    <p>Content of 1st paragraph.</p>
    <p>Content of 2nd paragraph.</p>
    <p>Content of 3rd paragraph.</p>
</article>
```

When a browser encounters a sectioning element or a grouping element, the default style is to start the enclosed content on a new line, separating it from any content that appears before it. Thus, each of these paragraphs will be started on a new line as will the article itself. Note that the exact appearance of the paragraphs and the space between them depends on the styles applied by the browser to those elements. You'll learn more about styles later in this tutorial.

REFERENCE

Defining Page Groups

- To mark a paragraph, use the p element.
- To mark an extended quote, use the blockquote element.
- To mark the main content of a page or section, use the main element.
- To mark a figure box, use the figure element.
- To mark a generic division of page content, use the div element.

Sajja has written up the article describing Curbside Thai in a text file. Enter his text into the `article` element in the About Curbside Thai web page and use p elements to mark the paragraphs in the article.

To group the page text into paragraphs:

1. Use a text editor to open the **ct_pages.txt** file from the html01 ▸ tutorial folder.

2. Select and copy the three paragraphs of text directly after the About Us title.

3. Close the file, but do not save any changes you may have inadvertently made to the document.

4. Return to the **ct_about.html** file in your HTML editor.

5. Directly after the `<h1>About Us</h1>` line within the page article, insert a new blank line and paste the text you copied.

6. Enclose each of the three paragraphs of pasted content between an opening `<p>` tag and a closing `</p>` tag. Indent the code within the `article` element to make the code easier to read.

Figure 1-15 highlights the newly added code for the three paragraphs of article text

Figure 1-15	Grouping article content by paragraphs

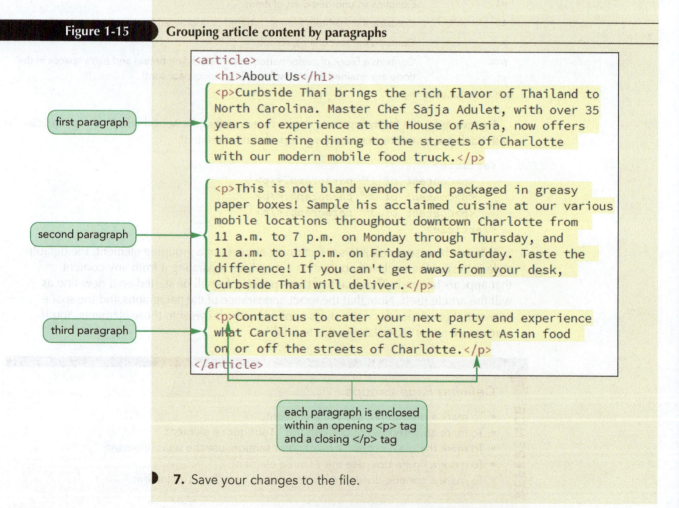

7. Save your changes to the file.

Using Text-Level Elements

Within each grouping element are **text-level elements**, which act like phrases or characters within a paragraph. Unlike sectioning or grouping elements that start content on a new line and mark a self-contained block of content, text-level elements appear in line with the surrounding content and are known as **inline elements**. For example, the *italicized* or **boldface** text in this paragraph is considered inline content because it appears alongside the surrounding text. Figure 1-16 describes some of the many text-level elements in HTML.

Figure 1-16	HTML text-level elements

Element	Description
a	Marks content that acts as a hypertext link
abbr	Marks an abbreviation or acronym
b	Indicates a span of text to which attention should be drawn (text usually appears in bold)
br	Represents a line break within the grouping element
cite	Marks a citation to a title or author of a creative work (text usually appears in italics)
code	Marks content that represents computer code (text usually appears in a monospace font)
data	Associates a data value with the marked text with the value attribute providing the value [**HTML5**]
dfn	Marks a defined term for which a definition is given elsewhere in the document
em	Indicates content that is emphasized or stressed (text usually appears in italics)
i	Indicates a span of text that expresses an alternate voice or mood (text usually appears in italics)
kbd	Marks text that represents user input, typically from a computer keyboard or a voice command
marks	Contains a row of text that is marked or highlighted for reference purposes [**HTML5**]
q	Marks content that is quoted from another source
s	Marks content that is no longer accurate or relevant (text is usually struck through)
samp	Marks text that represents the sample output from a computer program or application
small	Marks side comments (text usually in small print)
span	Contains a generic run of text within the document
strong	Indicates content of strong importance or seriousness (text usually appears in bold)
sub	Marks text that should be treated as a text subscript
sup	Marks text that should be treated as a text superscript
time	Marks a time value or text string [**HTML5**]
u	Indicates text that appears stylistically different from normal text (text usually appears underlined)
var	Marks text that is treated as a variable in a mathematical expression or computer program
wbr	Represents where a line break should occur, if needed, for a long text string [**HTML5**]

© 2016 Cengage Learning

The following HTML code demonstrates how to employ text-level elements to mark select phrases or characters within a paragraph.

```
<p>
    Contact us to cater your next party and experience what
    <cite>Carolina Traveler</cite> calls <q>the finest
    Asian food on or off the streets of Charlotte.</q>
</p>
```

Two text-level elements are used in this paragraph: the `cite` element to mark the citation to the *Carolina Traveler* magazine and the `q` element to mark the direct quote from the magazine's review of Curbside Thai. Both the citation and the quoted material will appear specially formatted within the paragraph alongside the other, unmarked, text.

REFERENCE

Defining Text-Level Content

- To mark emphasized text, use the `em` element.
- To mark text of great importance, use the `strong` element.
- To mark a citation, use the `cite` element.
- To mark a selection of quoted material, use the `q` element.
- To mark a subscript, use the `sub` element; to mark a superscript, use the `sup` element.
- To mark a generic selection of text-level content, use the `span` element.

Use text-level elements in the About Curbside Thai web page to mark examples of emphasized text, strongly important text, citations, and quoted material.

To apply text-level elements to a page:

1. Go to the first paragraph within the page article and enclose the opening words *Curbside Thai* within a set of opening and closing **<strong>** tags. You use the **<strong>** tags when you want to strongly reinforce the importance of the text, such as the restaurant name, for the reader.

2. In the second paragraph, enclose the phrase, *Curbside Thai will deliver* within a set of opening and closing **<em>** tags to emphasize this text.

3. Go the third paragraph and mark *Carolina Traveler* using the `cite` element and then mark the extended quote, *the finest Asian food on or off the streets of Charlotte*, using the q element.

   Figure 1-17 highlights the application of the four text-level elements to the paragraph text.

Figure 1-17   **Marking text-level content**

```
<article>
   <h1>About Us</h1>
   <p><strong>Curbside Thai</strong> brings the rich flavor of Thailand to
   North Carolina. Master Chef Sajja Adulet, with over 35
   years of experience at the House of Asia, now offers
   that same fine dining to the streets of Charlotte
   with our modern mobile food truck.</p>

   <p>This is not bland vendor food packaged in greasy
   paper boxes! Sample his acclaimed cuisine at our various
   mobile locations throughout downtown Charlotte from
   11 a.m. to 7 p.m. on Monday through Thursday, and
   11 a.m. to 11 p.m. on Friday and Saturday. Taste the
   difference! If you can't get away from your desk,
   <em>Curbside Thai will deliver</em>.</p>

   <p>Contact us to cater your next party and experience
   what <cite>Carolina Traveler</cite> calls <q>the finest Asian food
   on or off the streets of Charlotte</q>.</p>
</article>
```

strong and important text marked with the <strong> tag

emphasized text marked with the <em> tag

citation marked with the <cite> tag

quoted material marked with the <q> tag

4. Save your changes to the file.

5. Open the **ct_about.html** file in your browser to view how your browser renders the page content.

Figure 1-18 shows the current appearance of the page.

| **Figure 1-18** | **The About Curbside Thai page as rendered by the browser** |

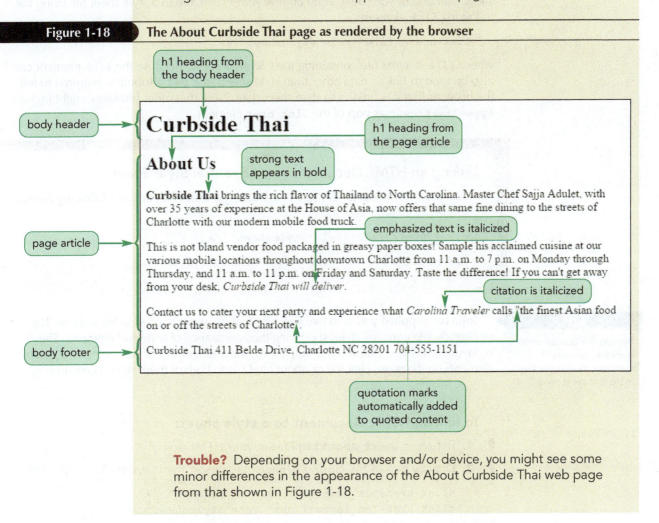

Trouble? Depending on your browser and/or device, you might see some minor differences in the appearance of the About Curbside Thai web page from that shown in Figure 1-18.

In rendering the page, the browser made the following stylistic choices for the different page elements:

- The h1 heading from the body header is assigned the largest font and is displayed in bold to emphasize its importance. The h1 heading from the page article is given a slightly smaller font but is still displayed in bold.
- Strong text is displayed in bold while emphasized text is displayed in italics.
- Citations are displayed in italic while quoted material is automatically surrounded by quotation marks.

It needs to be emphasized again that all of these stylistic choices are not determined by the markup tags; they are default styles used by the browser. Different browsers and different devices might render these page elements differently. To exert more control over your page's appearance, you can apply a style sheet to document contents.

Linking an HTML Document to a Style Sheet

A **style sheet** is a set of rules specifying how page elements are displayed. Style sheets are written in the **Cascading Style Sheets** (**CSS**) language. Like HTML, the CSS language was developed and enhanced as the web grew and changed and, like HTML, CSS specifications are managed by the W3C. To replace the browser's internal style sheet with one of your own, you can link your HTML file to a style sheet file using the following `link` element:

```
<link href="file" rel="stylesheet" />
```

where *file* is a text file containing the CSS style sheet. Because the `link` element can also be used to link to data other than style sheets, the `rel` attribute is required to tell the browser that it is linking to style sheet data. Note that older browsers might include `type="text/css"` as part of the `link href` element.

Linking an HTML Document to an External Style Sheet

- To link an HTML document to an external style sheet file, add the following element to the document head:

```
<link href="file" rel="stylesheet" />
```

where *file* is a text file containing the CSS style rules.

TIP

Because the `link` element is another example of metadata, it's always added to the document head.

Sajja has supplied you with two CSS files that he wants applied to his website. The ct_base.css file contains styles specifying the appearance of text-level elements. The ct_layout2.css file contains styles that govern the arrangement of sectioning and grouping elements on the page. Link the ct_about.html file to both of these style sheets now.

To link an HTML document to a style sheet:

1. Return to the **ct_about.html** file in your HTML editor.

2. Directly before the closing `</head>` tag, insert the following `link` elements:

```
<link href="ct_base.css" rel="stylesheet" />
<link href="ct_layout2.css" rel="stylesheet" />
```

Figure 1-19 highlights the two style sheet links added to the document.

Figure 1-19 Linking to style sheets

filename of the CSS style sheet

rel attribute indicates the type of link relationship

```
<meta charset="utf-8" />
<meta name="keywords" content="Thai, restaurant, Charlotte, food" />
<title>About Curbside Thai</title>
<link href="ct_base.css" rel="stylesheet" />
<link href="ct_layout2.css" rel="stylesheet" />
</head>
```

link elements link the web page to a style sheet file

3. Save your changes to the file and then reload the ct_about.html file in your browser. Figure 1-20 shows the new appearance of the page using the style sheets provided by Sajja.

| Figure 1-20 | The About Curbside Thai page rendered under a new style sheet |

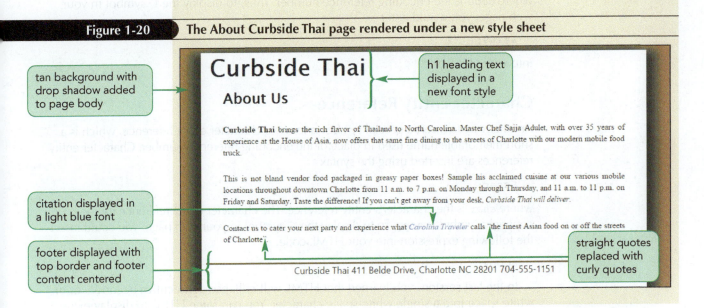

tan background with drop shadow added to page body

Curbside Thai

h1 heading text displayed in a new font style

About Us

Curbside Thai brings the rich flavor of Thailand to North Carolina. Master Chef Sajja Adulet, with over 35 years of experience at the House of Asia, now offers that same fine dining to the streets of Charlotte with our modern mobile food truck.

This is not bland vendor food packaged in greasy paper boxes! Sample his acclaimed cuisine at our various mobile locations throughout downtown Charlotte from 11 a.m. to 7 p.m. on Monday through Thursday, and 11 a.m. to 11 p.m. on Friday and Saturday. Taste the difference! If you can't get away from your desk, *Curbside Thai will deliver*.

citation displayed in a light blue font

Contact us to cater your next party and experience what *Carolina Traveler* calls "the finest Asian food on or off the streets of Charlotte".

footer displayed with top border and footer content centered

straight quotes replaced with curly quotes

Curbside Thai 411 Belde Drive, Charlotte NC 28201 704-555-1151

Applying these style sheets to the HTML code causes the page body to be displayed on a tan background with a drop shadow, the font used in the two h1 headings has changed, a top border has been added to the footer to set it off from the preceding content, and the citation to the *Carolina Traveler* magazine is displayed in a light blue font. The effect makes the page content easier to read and more pleasing to the eye.

Sajja is concerned that the contact information in the page footer is difficult to read. He wants you to add bullet characters (•) separating the name of the restaurant, the street address, and the restaurant phone number. However, this character is not represented by any keys on your keyboard. How then, do you insert this symbol into the web page?

Working with Character Sets and Special Characters

Every character that your browser is capable of rendering belongs to a collection of characters and symbols called a **character set**. The character set used for the English alphabet is the **American Standard Code for Information Interchange** more simply known as **ASCII**. A more extended character set, called **Latin-1** or the **ISO 8859-1** character set, supports 255 characters and can be used by most languages that employ the Latin alphabet, including English, French, Spanish, and Italian. **Unicode**, the most extended character set, supports up to 65,536 symbols and can be used with any of the world's languages.

Character Encoding

Each character from a character set is associated with an encoding value that can then be stored and read by a computer program. For example, the copyright symbol © from the Unicode character set is encoded with the number 169. If you know the encoding value, you can insert the corresponding character directly into your web page using the following character encoding reference:

```
&#code;
```

where *code* is the encoding reference number. Thus, to display the © symbol in your web page, you would enter

```
&#169;
```

into your HTML file.

Character Entity References

Another way to insert a special symbol is to use a character entity reference, which is a short memorable name used in place of the encoding reference number. Character entity references are inserted using the syntax

```
&char;
```

where *char* is the character's entity reference. The character entity reference for the copyright symbol is copy, so to display the © symbol in your web page, you could insert the following expression into your HTML code:

```
&copy;
```

In the last session, you learned that HTML will collapse consecutive occurrences of white space into a single white-space character. You can force HTML to display extra white space by using the following character entity reference

```
 
```

where nbsp stands for *nonbreaking space*. When you want to display extra white space, you need to insert the nonbreaking space character reference in the HTML code for each space you want to display.

REFERENCE

Inserting Symbols from a Character Set

- To insert a symbol based on the character encoding reference number, enter

  ```
  &#code;
  ```

  where *code* is the character encoding reference number.
- To insert a symbol based on a character entity reference, enter

  ```
  &char;
  ```

  where *char* is the name assigned to the character.
- To insert a white-space character, use

  ```
   
  ```

For the footer in the About Curbside Thai page, use the bullet symbol (•), which has the encoding value 8226, to separate the restaurant name, address, and phone number. Use the   character reference to insert an extra blank space prior to the postal code in the restaurant address.

To insert a character encoding reference number and an entity reference:

1. Return to the **ct_about.html** file in your HTML editor.

2. Go to the `footer` element and insert the character encoding number `&#8226;` directly after the word *Thai* and after the postal code *28201*. Insert the character reference ` ` directly before the postal code.

   Figure 1-21 highlights the character codes and references added to the footer.

Figure 1-21	Inserting special characters

character encoding reference for a bullet character (•)

```
<footer>
   Curbside Thai &#8226; 411 Belde Drive, Charlotte NC   28201 &#8226; 704-555-1151
</footer>
</body>
```

character entity reference for a nonbreaking space

3. Save your changes to the file and then reload the ct_about.html file in your browser. Confirm that the footer now shows the characters displayed in Figure 1-22.

Figure 1-22	Revised page footer

Contact us to cater your next party and experience what *Carolina Traveler* calls "the finest Asian food on or off the streets of Charlotte".

Curbside Thai • 411 Belde Drive, Charlotte NC 28201 • 704-555-1151

bullet characters

extra nonbreaking space

Presentational Attributes

Early versions of HTML supported **presentational elements** and **presentational attributes** designed to describe how each element should be rendered by web browsers. For example, to align text on a page, web authors would use the following align attribute

```
<element align="alignment">content</element>
```

where *alignment* is either left, right, center, or justify. Thus, to center an h1 heading on a page, they would use the following code:

```
<h1 align="center">Curbside Thai</h1>
```

Almost all presentational elements and attributes are now deprecated in favor of style sheets, but you may still see them in the code from older websites. Using a deprecated attribute like align would probably not cause your web page to fail, however, it's still best practice to adhere to a standard in which HTML is used only to describe the content and structure of the document and style sheets are used to format its appearance.

So far your work on the Curbside Thai page has been limited to textual content. Next, you'll explore how to add graphical content to your web page.

Working with Inline Images

Most web pages include **embedded content**, which is content imported from another resource, often nontextual, such as graphic images, audio soundtracks, video clips, or interactive games. To support this type of content, HTML provides the **embedded elements** listed in Figure 1-23.

Figure 1-23	HTML embedded elements

Element	Description
audio	Represents a sound clip or audio stream [**HTML5**]
canvas	Contains programming scripts used to construct bitmap images and graphics [**HTML5**]
embed	Contains general embedded content including application or interactive content
iframe	Contains the contents of an external web page or Internet resource
img	Contains a graphic image retrieved from an image file
object	Contains general embedded content including application or interactive content
video	Represents a video clip or video stream with captions [**HTML5**]

© 2016 Cengage Learning

TIP

Always include the alt attribute; it is required in XHTML code and is highly recommended as a way of accommodating users running nonvisual web browsers.

These elements are also known as **interactive elements** because they allow for interaction between the user and the embedded object. For example, embedded audio or video content usually contains player buttons to control the playback.

Images are inserted into a web page using the following img element

```
<img src="file" alt="text" />
```

where *file* is the name of the image file. If the browser cannot display images, the text in the alt attribute is used in place of the image. As with other one-sided tags, the img element can be entered without the closing slash as

```
<img src="file" alt="text">
```

Images are also known as **inline images** because they are placed, like text-level elements, in line with surrounding content.

By default, the image size matches the size of the image in the file but you can specify a different size by adding the following `width` and `height` attributes to the `img` element

```
width="value" height="value"
```

where the `width` and `height` values are expressed in pixels. If you specify only the width, browsers automatically set the height to maintain the proportions of the image; similarly, if you define the height, browsers automatically set the width to maintain the image proportions. Image sizes can also be set within the document's style sheet.

REFERENCE

Embedding an Inline Image

- To embed an inline image into the document, use

  ```
  <img src="file" alt="text" />
  ```

  where `file` is the name of the graphic image file and `text` is text displayed by browsers in place of the graphic image.

Sajja has provided you with two images. The image from the ct_logo2.png file displays the restaurant logo, while the ct_photo1.png image provides an image of customers being served by an employee at his brick-and-mortar restaurant. Sajja included this image to emphasize that the food from his food truck is the same quality and great taste as the food at his award winning restaurant. Add both of these images to the ct_about.html file.

To insert inline images into a document:

1. Return to the **ct_about.html** file in your HTML editor.

2. Go to the `header` element and replace the `h1` element with the tag

   ```
   <img src="ct_logo2.png" alt="Curbside Thai" />
   ```

3. Go to the `article` element and, directly after the `h1` element, insert the tag

   ```
   <img src="ct_photo1.png" alt="" />
   ```

   Figure 1-24 highlights the newly added `img` elements in the document.

TIP

Include the alt attribute as a blank text string if the image file does not convey any text message to the user.

Figure 1-24   Inserting inline images

```
<header>
    <img src="ct_logo2.png" alt="Curbside Thai" />
</header>
<article>
    <h1>About Us</h1>
    <img src="ct_photo1.png" alt="" />
    <p><strong>Curbside Thai</strong> brings the rich flavor of Thailand to
    North Carolina. Master Chef Sajja Adulet, with over 35
    years of experience at the House of Asia, now offers
    that same fine dining to the streets of Charlotte
    with our modern mobile food truck.</p>
```

image added to the About Us article

h1 heading replaced with an inline image

4. Save your changes to the file and then reload the ct_about.html file in your browser. Figure 1-25 displays the newly added graphic images in the web page.

Figure 1-25   Images on the About Curbside Thai page

restaurant logo used for the page header

About Us

Curbside Thai brings the rich flavor of Thailand to North Carolina. Master Chef Sajja Adulet, with over 35 years of experience at the House of Asia, now offers that same fine dining to the streets of Charlotte with our modern mobile food truck.

This is not bland vendor food packaged in greasy paper boxes! Sample his acclaimed cuisine at our various mobile locations throughout downtown Charlotte from 11 a.m. to 7 p.m. on Monday through Thursday, and 11 a.m. to 11 p.m. on Friday and Saturday. Taste the difference! If you can't get away from your desk, *Curbside Thai will deliver.*

© 2016 Cengage Learning; © Kzenon/Shutterstock.com

photo floated on the right margin of the article

Trouble? The exact appearance of the text as it flows around the image will vary depending on the width of your browser window.

Note that the photo of the Curbside Thai customers is floated alongside the right margin of the article, with the surrounding paragraphs flowing around the image. This is the result of code in the style sheets. You'll learn about styles used to float images in Tutorial 3.

Line Breaks and Other Empty Elements

The `img` element is inserted using the empty element tag because it does not enclose any page content, but instead links to an external image file. Another important empty element is the following `br` element, which creates a line break

```
<br />
```

Line breaks are placed within grouping elements, such a paragraphs or headings, to force page content to start on a new line within the group. While useful for controlling the flow of text within a group, the `br` element should not be used as a formatting tool. For example, it would not make semantic sense to insert two or more `br` elements in a row if the only reason to do so is to increase the spacing between lines of text. Instead, all such formatting choices belong in a style sheet.

If the text of a line cannot fit within the width of the viewing window, the browser will wrap the text automatically at the point the browser identifies as the most appropriate. To recommend a different line break point, use the `wbr` (word break) element to indicate where a line break should occur if needed. For example, the following HTML code uses the `wbr` element to break a long web address between ".com/" and "general", but this break happens only if the address will not fit on one line.

```
www.curbsidethai.com/<wbr />general/docs/ct_about.html
```

Finally, another oft-used empty element is the following `hr` or horizontal rule element

```
<hr />
```

Today, the purpose of this element is to denote a major topic change within a section. Originally, the `hr` element was used to insert horizontal lines into the page and, although that task is better left to style sheets, you will still see the `hr` element used in that capacity in older web pages.

Working with Block Quotes and Other Elements

Now that you've written the code for the ct_about.html file, you'll work on other pages in the Curbside Thai website. The ct_reviews.html file provides excerpts of reviews from food critics and magazines. Because these excerpts contain extended quotes, you'll place each review in the following `blockquote` element

```
<blockquote>
   content
</blockquote>
```

where *content* is the text of the quote. By default, most browsers render block quotes by indenting the quoted material to separate from it from the website author's words, however, you can substitute your own style with a custom style sheet.

Sajja has created much of the code required for the reviews page. The code is contained in the two style sheets that are already linked to the reviews page. Complete the page by adding the excerpts of the reviews marked as block quotes.

To create the reviews page:

▶ **1.** Open the **ct_reviews_txt.html** file from the html01 ▶ tutorial folder in your HTML editor. Enter **your name** and **the date** in the comment section and save the file as **ct_reviews.html**.

▶ **2.** Go to the **ct_pages.txt** file in your text editor.

▶ **3.** Locate the section containing the restaurant reviews and copy the text of the four reviews and awards.

4. Return to the **ct_reviews.html** file in your HTML editor and paste the text of the four reviews directly after the `<h1>Reviews</h1>` line.

5. Enclose each review within a set of `<blockquote>` tags. Enclose each paragraph within each review with a set of `<p>` tags. Align and indent your code to make it easier to read.

Figure 1-26 highlights the newly added code in the document.

Figure 1-26	Marking extended text as block quotes

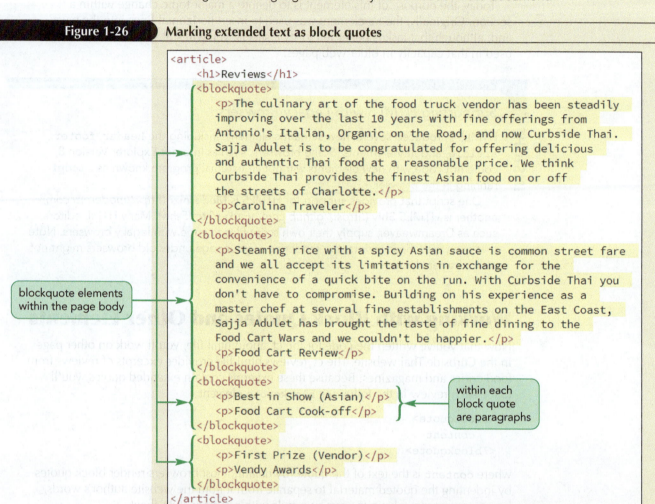

blockquote elements within the page body

within each block quote are paragraphs

6. Save your changes to the file and then open the **ct_reviews.html** file in your browser. Figure 1-27 shows the appearance of the restaurant review quotes using Sajja's style sheet.

Figure 1-27   **Block quotes of restaurant reviews**

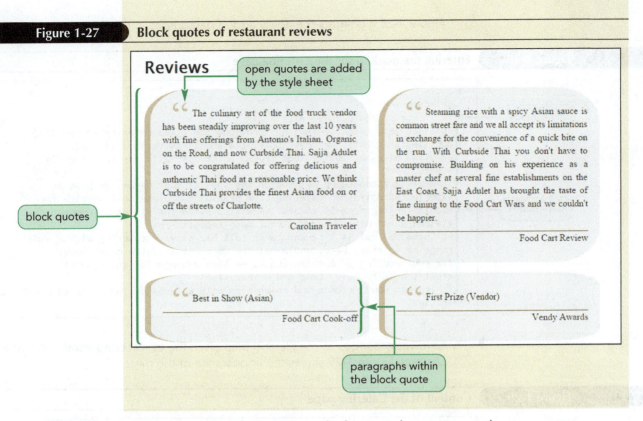

Because of the styles in Sajja's style sheets, each `blockquote` element appears within its own formatted box with an opening quote character added to reinforce the fact that this is quoted material.

The next page you'll create contains information about catering from Curbside Thai. The structure of this page is identical to the structure of the About Curbside Thai page. Sajja has linked the catering page to two style sheets containing the style rules that dictate how the page will look when the page is rendered in a browser.

To create the Catering page:

1. Open the **ct_catering_txt.html** file from the html01 ▸ tutorial folder in your HTML editor. Enter *your name* and *the date* in the comment section and save the file as **ct_catering.html**.

2. Return to the **ct_pages.txt** file in your text editor.

3. Locate the section containing information about Curbside Thai's catering service and copy the four paragraphs of information.

4. Return to the **ct_catering.html** file in your HTML editor and paste the copied text directly after the `<h1>Catering</h1>` line.

5. Mark each paragraph in the article using the p element. Align and indent your code to make it easier to read.

6. Directly after the `<h1>Catering</h1>` tag, insert an inline image using **ct_photo2.png** as the source and an empty text string for the `alt` attribute.

Figure 1-28 highlights the newly added paragraphs in the document.

Figure 1-28 Entering the markup for the Catering page

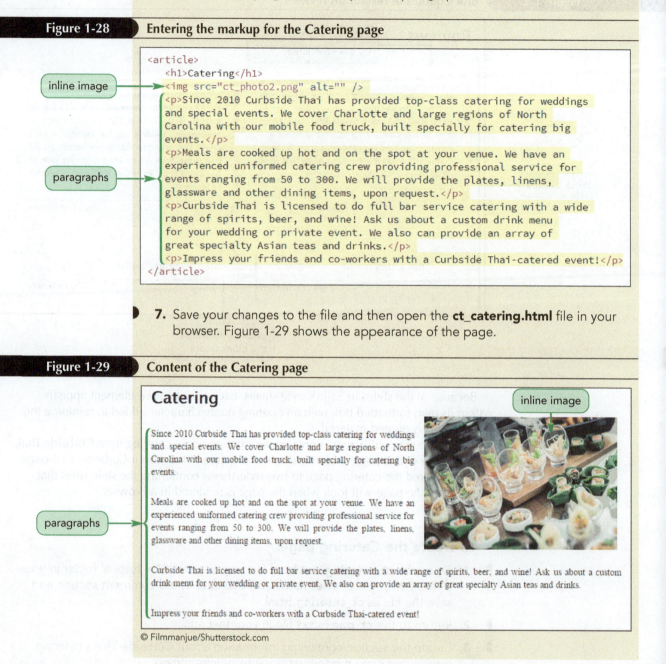

7. Save your changes to the file and then open the **ct_catering.html** file in your browser. Figure 1-29 shows the appearance of the page.

Figure 1-29 Content of the Catering page

© Filmmanjue/Shutterstock.com

The final page you'll create in this session will contain contact information for Curbside Thai. Mark the content using paragraphs within the main page article.

To create the Contact Us page:

1. Open the **ct_contact_txt.html** file from the html01 ▸ tutorial folder in your HTML editor. Enter **your name** and ***the date*** in the comment section and save the file as **ct_contact.html**. Note that this page is linked to two style sheets that Sajja created.

2. Go to the **ct_pages.txt** file in your text editor.

3. Copy the Contact Us section in the text file (excluding the title).

4. Return to the **ct_contact.html** file in your HTML editor and paste the copied text directly after the `<h1>Contact Us</h1>` tag.

5. Enclose the introductory paragraph within a set of opening and closing `<p>` tags to mark it as a paragraph.

6. Enclose the three lines containing the street address within a set of opening and closing `<address>` tags to mark that content as an address. Insert the `<br />` tag at the end of the first two lines to create a line break between the name of the restaurant and the street address.

7. Mark the last two lines as paragraphs using the p element.

   Figure 1-30 highlights the marked up code for Curbside Thai's contact information.

| Figure 1-30 | Entering the markup for the Contact Us page |

```
<article>
    <h1>Contact Us</h1>
    <p>Contact Curbside Thai for your next event or just to find
       out when our mobile truck will next be in your area.
       Employment opportunities available now!</p>

    <address>Curbside Thai<br />
    411 Belde Drive<br />
    Charlotte NC 28201
    </address>

    <p>Call: (704) 555-1151</p>
    <p>Email: curbside.thai@example.com</p>
</article>
```

address element to mark up a mailing address

line breaks to start the next part of the address on a new line

8. Save your changes to the file and then open the **ct_contact.html** file in your browser as shown in Figure 1-31.

Figure 1-31	Content of the Contact Us page

Contact Us

Contact Curbside Thai for your next event or just to find out when our mobile truck will next be in your area. Employment opportunities available now!

street address

Curbside Thai
411 Belde Drive
Charlotte NC 28201

Call: (704) 555-1151

Email: curbside.thai@example.com

The Contact Us page only provides the text of the contact information but that text is static. In the next session, you'll learn how to make this content interactive by turning the contact information into hypertext.

PROSKILLS

Problem Solving: Making your Page Accessible with ARIA

The web is for everyone and that presents a special challenge when writing code for the visually impaired who will be accessing your website with a screen reader. One standard to assist screen readers is **Accessible Rich Internet Applications** (**ARIA**), which supplements HTML elements with additional attributes that provide clues as to the element's purpose as well as provide information on the current status of every page element.

One of the cornerstones of ARIA is the `role` attribute, which specifies the purpose of a given element. For example, the following `role` attribute indicates that the `header` element contains a banner, such as a logo that introduces the web page

```
<header role="banner">
    content
</header>
```

ARIA supports a list of approved role names including the following:
- alert   Content with important and usually time-sensitive information
- application   A web application, as opposed to a web document
- definition   A definition term or concept
- dialog   An application window that will require user input
- log   A region of data that is constantly modified and updated
- progress bar   Content that displays the progress status for ongoing tasks
- search   Content that provides search capability to the user
- separator   A divider that separates one region of content from another
- timer   A region that contains a numerical counter reporting on elapsed time

You can view the complete list of role attribute values and how to apply them at *www.w3.org/TR/wai-aria/roles*.

ARIA is a useful tool for enhancing the accessibility of your web page and making the rich resource that is the World Wide Web open to all. A side benefit is that accessibility and usability go hand-in-hand. A website that is highly accessible is also highly usable and that is of value to all users.

In the next session, you'll continue to work on the Curbside Thai website by adding pages describing the restaurant menu and listing the time and locations where the mobile food truck is parked.

REVIEW

Session 1.2 Quick Check

1. Provide code to mark the text *Gourmet Thai Cooking* as a heading with the second level of importance.

2. What element should you use to mark page content as a sidebar?

3. What is the `div` element and why will you often encounter it in pre-HTML5 code?

4. What element would you use to indicate a change of topic within a section?

5. Provide the code to mark the text *Daily Special* as emphasized text.

6. Provide the code to mark the text H_2SO_4 with subscripts.

7. Provide the code to link the web page to the CSS file mystyles.css.

8. Provide the expression to insert an em dash into a web page using the character code 8212.

9. Provide the code to insert an inline image using the source file awlogo.png and the alternate text *Art World*.

Session 1.3 Visual Overview:

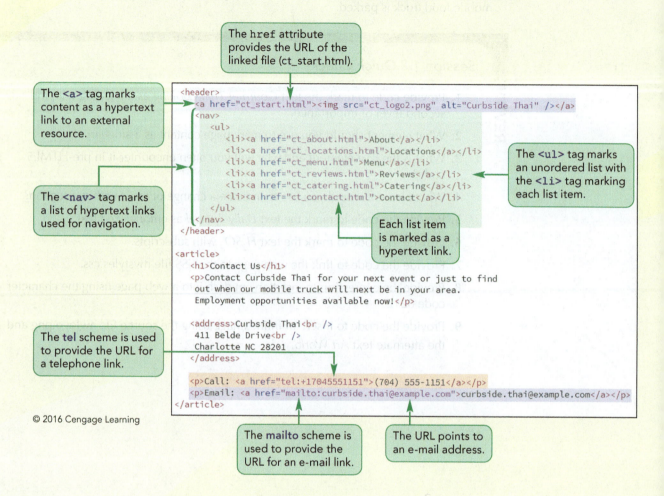

The `href` attribute provides the URL of the linked file (ct_start.html).

The `<a>` tag marks content as a hypertext link to an external resource.

The `<nav>` tag marks a list of hypertext links used for navigation.

The `<ul>` tag marks an unordered list with the `<li>` tag marking each list item.

Each list item is marked as a hypertext link.

The **tel** scheme is used to provide the URL for a telephone link.

```
<header>
<a href="ct_start.html"><img src="ct_logo2.png" alt="Curbside Thai" /></a>
<nav>
    <ul>
        <li><a href="ct_about.html">About</a></li>
        <li><a href="ct_locations.html">Locations</a></li>
        <li><a href="ct_menu.html">Menu</a></li>
        <li><a href="ct_reviews.html">Reviews</a></li>
        <li><a href="ct_catering.html">Catering</a></li>
        <li><a href="ct_contact.html">Contact</a></li>
    </ul>
</nav>
</header>

<article>
    <h1>Contact Us</h1>
    <p>Contact Curbside Thai for your next event or just to find
    out when our mobile truck will next be in your area.
    Employment opportunities available now!</p>

    <address>Curbside Thai<br />
    411 Belde Drive<br />
    Charlotte NC 28201
    </address>

    <p>Call: <a href="tel:+17045551151">(704) 555-1151</a></p>
    <p>Email: <a href="mailto:curbside.thai@example.com">curbside.thai@example.com</a></p>
</article>
```

The **mailto** scheme is used to provide the URL for an e-mail link.

The URL points to an e-mail address.

Lists and Hypertext Links

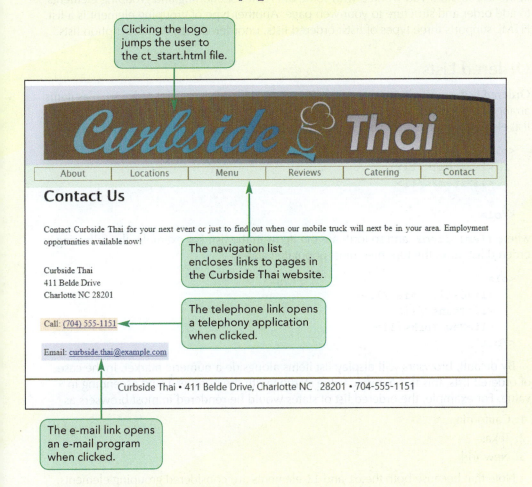

Clicking the logo jumps the user to the ct_start.html file.

The navigation list encloses links to pages in the Curbside Thai website.

The telephone link opens a telephony application when clicked.

The e-mail link opens an e-mail program when clicked.

Contact Us

Contact Curbside Thai for your next event or just to find out when our mobile truck will next be in your area. Employment opportunities available now!

Curbside Thai
411 Belde Drive
Charlotte NC 28201

Call: (704) 555-1151

Email: curbside.thai@example.com

Curbside Thai • 411 Belde Drive, Charlotte NC 28201 • 704-555-1151

Working with Lists

In the last session, you worked with some of HTML's sectioning and grouping elements to add order and structure to your web page. Another type of grouping element is a list. HTML supports three types of lists: ordered lists, unordered lists, and description lists.

Ordered Lists

Ordered lists are used for items that follow some defined sequential order, such as items arranged alphabetically or numerically. An ordered list is marked using the `ol` (ordered list) element with each list item marked using the `li` element. The general structure is

```
<ol>
    <li>item1</li>
    <li>item2</li>
    ...
</ol>
```

where *item1*, *item2*, and so forth are the items in the list. For example, the following ordered list ranks the top-three most populated states:

```
<ol>
    <li>California</li>
    <li>Texas</li>
    <li>New York</li>
</ol>
```

By default, browsers will display list items alongside a numeric marker. In the case of ordered lists, this is a numeric value starting with the number 1 and ascending in value. For example, the ordered list of states would be rendered in most browsers as

1. California
2. Texas
3. New York

Note that because both the `ol` and `li` elements are considered grouping elements, each list item will appear, by default, on a new line in the document unless a different style is applied to those elements.

To display different numbering, you use the `start` and `reversed` attributes of the `ol` element. The `start` attribute provides the numeric value for the first item in the list, while the `reversed` attribute specifies that the list numbers should be displayed in descending order. Thus, the following HTML code that lists the most populated states

```
<ol reversed start="50">
    <li>California</li>
    <li>Texas</li>
    <li>New York</li>
</ol>
```

would be rendered as a list in descending order starting from 50

50. California
49. Texas
48. New York

You can explicitly define the item value by adding the `value` attribute to each list item. The list shown previously could also have been generated with the following code:

```
<ol>
   <li value="50">California</li>
   <li value="49">Texas</li>
   <li value="48">New York</li>
</ol>
```

You can use style sheets to display lists using alphabetical markers (A, B, C, …) or Roman Numerals (I, II, III, …) in place of numeric values. You'll explore this technique in Tutorial 2.

Unordered Lists

Unordered lists are used for lists in which the items have no sequential order. The structure for an unordered list is similar to that used with ordered lists except that the list items are grouped within the following ul (unordered list) element:

```
<ul>
   <li>item1</li>
   <li>item2</li>
   …
</ul>
```

For example, the following HTML code creates an ordered list of all of the states along the Pacific coast:

```
<ul>
   <li>California</li>
   <li>Oregon</li>
   <li>Washington</li>
</ul>
```

By default, browsers will display items from an unordered list alongside a marker such as a bullet point. Thus, an unordered list of Pacific coast states might be rendered as

- California
- Oregon
- Washington

Once again, the exact appearance of an unordered list will depend on the style sheet that is applied to the element.

Creating a Nested List

Because the `li` element is itself a grouping element, it can be used to group other lists, which in turn creates a series of **nested lists**. The general structure for a nested collection of unordered list is

```
<ul>
    <li>Item 1</li>
    <li>Item 2
        <ul>
            <li>Sub Item 1</li>
            <li>Sub Item 2</li>
        </ul>
    </li>
</ul>
```

where *Sub Item 1*, *Sub Item 2*, and so forth are items contained within the *Item 2* list. For example, an unordered list of states and cities within those states could be marked up as

```
<ul>
    <li>California</li>
    <li>Oregon
        <ul>
            <li>Portland</li>
            <li>Salem</li>
        </ul>
    </li>
    <li>Washington</li>
</ul>
```

Most browsers will differentiate the various levels by increasing the indentation and using a different list symbol at each level of nested lists, for example, rendering the HTML code above as

- California
- Oregon
  - Portland
  - Salem
- Washington

The markers used at each level and the amount of indentation applied to each nested list is determined by style sheets, either those built into the browser or those supplied by the page designer. You'll explore this technique in Tutorial 2.

Description Lists

A third type of list is the **description list** containing a list of terms and matching descriptions. The description list is grouped by the dl (description list) element, the terms are marked with the dt (description term) element, and the description(s) associated with each term is marked by the dd element. The general structure is

```
<dl>
    <dt>term1</dt>
    <dd>description1</dd>
    <dt>term2</dt>
    <dd>description2a</dd>
    <dd>description2b</dd>
    ...
</dl>
```

where *term1*, *term2*, and so forth are the terms in the list and *description1*, *description2a*, *description2b*, and so forth are the descriptions associated with the terms. Note that descriptions must always directly follow the term they describe and that more than one description may be provided with each term.

By default, most browsers will indent the descriptions associated with each term. Markers are rarely displayed alongside either the description term or the description.

Sajja wants to use a description list in a page that displays some of the menu items sold by Curbside Thai. He's already started work on the HTML code but needs you to complete it by adding the markup for the description list.

To Complete the Menu Page:

1. Open the **ct_menu_txt.html** file from the html01 ▸ tutorial folder in your HTML editor. Enter *your name* and *the date* in the comment section and save the file as **ct_menu.html**.

2. Open the **ct_pages.txt** file in your text editor if it is not already open and copy the five menu items listed in the Mobile Menu section.

3. Return to the **ct_menu.html** file in your HTML editor and paste the copied text directly after the <h1>Mobile Menu</h1> tag.

4. Enclose the entire menu within an opening and closing **<dl>** tag.

5. Mark the name of each menu item using the **dt** element. Mark the corresponding description using the **dd** element. Indent your code to make it easier to read and interpret.

   Figure 1-32 shows the completed code for the description list of the mobile menu.

Figure 1-32 | **Marking the restaurant menu as a description list**

the name of each menu item is
marked as a description term;
information about the item is
marked as a description

description list →

```
<article>
  <h1>Mobile Menu</h1>
  <dl>
    <dt>Basil Beef Sesame Salad</dt>
    <dd>Spicy Angus beef and sweet basil on top of fresh spring mix,
        red cabbage, carrot, cucumber and tomatoes; served with
        sesame vinaigrette ($9.95)</dd>
    <dt>Curbside Rice</dt>
    <dd>Stir-fried rice with onions, red bell peppers, peas and
        carrots, garnished with red cabbage, cucumbers, scallions,
        and fried garlic ($6.50); add chicken ($8.50)
        or shrimp ($9.50)</dd>
    <dt>Garlic Pepper Pork</dt>
    <dd>Marinated pork stir-fried with fresh garlic and pepper;
        served with steamed Jasmine rice, red cabbage, carrot,
        cucumbers, scallions, and fried garlic ($8.50)</dd>
    <dt>Pad Thai</dt>
    <dd>Stir-fried rice noodles with bean sprouts and chives,
        garnished with red cabbage, carrot,
        scallions, lime, and crushed peanuts ($7.50);
        add chicken ($8.50) or shrimp ($9.50)</dd>
    <dt>Thai Red Curry</dt>
    <dd>Traditional red curry sauce cooked in coconut milk with
        bamboo shoots, fresh basil, lime, and Thai chili and
        served on a bed of steamed Jasmine rice ($7.50); add
        chicken ($8.50) or shrimp ($9.50)</dd>
  </dl>
</article>
```

6. Save your changes to the file and then open the **ct_menu.html** file in your browser. Figure 1-33 shows the completed menu for Curbside Thai.

Figure 1-33	Curbside Thai menu as a description list

Note that the style sheet that Sajja uses for his website inserts a dividing line between each term and description in the list.

Description lists can also be used with any general list that pairs one list of items with another list that provides additional information about the items in the first list. For example, Sajja has a page that lists the times and locations at which the Curbside Thai will make an appearance. Complete this page by enclosing the content within a description list, marking the times as the list "terms" and the locations as the list "descriptions".

To Create a Page of Times and Locations:

1. Open the **ct_locations_txt.html** file from the html01 ▸ tutorial folder in your HTML editor. Enter **your name** and **the date** in the comment section and save the file as **ct_locations.html**.

2. Return to **the ct_pages.txt** file in your text editor and copy the four locations from the Today's Locations section.

3. Return to the **ct_locations.html** file in your HTML editor and paste the copied text directly after the `<h1>Today's Locations</h1>` tag.

4. Mark the entire list of times and locations using the **dl** element. Mark each time using the **dt** element and each location using the **dd** element. Indent your code to make it easier to read and interpret.

5. In order to distinguish this description list from other description lists in the website, add the attribute **id="ct_locations"** to the opening `<dl>` tag.

6. Sajja has a map that he wants displayed alongside the list of times and locations. Directly after the **h1** element within the **article** element, insert the following inline image:

```
<img src="ct_map.png" alt="" />
```

Figure 1-34 highlights the newly added code for the Today's Locations page.

Figure 1-34 **Creating a description list**

7. Save your changes to the file and then open the **ct_locations.html** file in your browser. Figure 1-35 shows the appearance of the page. Remember, the placement of items on the screen is a result of the style sheets.

Figure 1-35 **Locations of the Curbside Thai food truck**

© 2016 Cengage Learning

From this page, Curbside Thai customers can quickly find the mobile truck. A page like this will have to be updated, probably daily, as the truck moves around. This is often better accomplished using database programs on the web server that will generate both the HTML and the inline image file.

INSIGHT

Marking Dates and Times

The adage that nothing ever quite disappears on the Internet also means that the web is populated with old articles, documents, and news stories that are no longer relevant or perhaps, even accurate. Any content you publish to the web should be time-stamped to document its history. One way of marking a date-time value is with the following `time` element

```
<time datetime="value">content</time>
```

where `value` is the date and time associated with the enclosed content. Dates should be entered in the *yyyy-mm-dd* format where *yyyy* is the four-digit year value, *mm* is the two-digit month value, and *dd* is the two-digit day value. Times should be entered in the *hh:mm* format for the two-digit hour and minute values entered in 24-hour time. To combine both dates and times, enter the date and time values separated by a space or the letter T as in the following code:

```
<footer>Last updated at:
   <time datetime="2017-03-01T14:52">March 1 2017 at 2:52
p.m.</time>
</footer>
```

For international applications, you can base your time values on the common standard of Greenwich Mean Time. For example, the following code includes the information that the time is based on the Eastern time zone, which is 5 hours behind Greenwich Mean Time:

```
<p>Webinar starts at:
   <time datetime="2017-03-10T20:30-05:00">3:30 p.m.
(EST)</time>
</p>
```

While the value of the `datetime` attribute is not visible to users, it is readable by machines such as search engines, which can include the date and time in reporting search results. You can read more about the `time` element on the W3C website, including information on marking a time duration between two events.

You've now created six web pages for the Curbside Thai website. Next, you'll link these pages together so that users can easily navigate between the pages in the website. You'll start by creating a navigation list.

Navigation Lists

A **navigation list** is an unordered list of hypertext links placed within the `nav` element. The general structure is

```
<nav>
   <ul>
      <li>link1</li>
      <li>link2</li>
...
   </ul>
</nav>
```

where *link1*, *link2*, and so forth are hypertext links. While hypertext links can be placed anywhere within the page, having a central list of links makes the website easier to work with and navigate.

Add this structure to the About Curbside Thai web page, creating entries for each of the six web pages you created in this tutorial.

To Create a Navigation List:

1. Open the **ct_about.html** file in your HTML editor if it is not already open.

2. Go to the body header and, directly below the inline image for the Curbside Thai logo, insert the following navigation list:

```
<nav>
    <ul>
        <li>About</li>
        <li>Locations</li>
        <li>Menu</li>
        <li>Reviews</li>
        <li>Catering</li>
        <li>Contact</li>
    </ul>
</nav>
```

Figure 1-36 highlights the structure of the navigation list.

Figure 1-36   **Creating a navigation list**

```
<body>
    <header>
        <img src="ct_logo2.png" alt="Curbside Thai" />
        <nav>
            <ul>
                <li>About</li>
                <li>Locations</li>
                <li>Menu</li>
                <li>Reviews</li>
                <li>Catering</li>
                <li>Contact</li>
            </ul>
        </nav>
    </header>
```

navigation list section created with the nav element

unordered list within the nav section

3. Save your changes to the file and then reopen the **ct_about.html** file in your browser.

Figure 1-37 shows appearance of the navigation list.

Navigation list for the Curbside Thai website

layout of the navigation list based on Sajja's style sheet

items within the navigation list

© 2016 Cengage Learning; © Kzenon/Shutterstock.com

Note that the appearance of the navigation list in the ct_about.html file is based on styles in Sajja's style sheets. Navigation lists can be displayed in a wide variety of ways depending on the styles being employed and the same navigation list might be arranged one way for desktop devices and another way for mobile devices. You'll learn more about this in Tutorial 5.

Now that you've created the structure of the navigation list, you can mark the items within the list as hypertext links.

Working with Hypertext Links

Hypertext is created by enclosing content within a set of opening and closing <a> tags in the following structure

```
<a href="url">content</a>
```

where `url` is the **Uniform Resource Locator** (**URL**), which is a standard address format used to link to a variety of resources including documents, e-mail addresses, telephone numbers, and text messaging services, and `content` is the document content marked as a link. When linking to another HTML file in the same folder, the URL is simply the name of the file. For example, a hypertext link to the ct_menu.html file would be marked as

```
<a href="ct_menu.html">Menu</a>
```

When the user clicks or touches the word *Menu*, the browser will load the ct_menu.html file in the browser. Note that filenames are case sensitive on some web servers, which means those servers differentiate between files named ct_menu.html and CT_Menu.html. The standard for all web filenames is to always use lowercase letters and to avoid using special characters and blank spaces.

The default style is to underline hypertext links and to display a hypertext link in a different text color if the user has previously visited the page. However, page designers can substitute different hypertext link styles from their own style sheets. We'll explore this technique in Tutorial 2.

Marking a Hypertext Link

• To mark content as a hypertext link, use

```
<a href="url">content</a>
```

where *url* is the address of the linked document and *content* is the document content that is being marked as a link.

Mark the six entries in the navigation list, pointing each entry to the corresponding Curbside Thai page.

To create hypertext links:

1. Return to the **ct_about.html** file in your HTML editor.

2. Mark the first entry as a hypertext link pointing to ct_about.html file by changing the list item to

   ```
   <a href="ct_about.html">About</a>
   ```

3. Change the code of the second list item to

   ```
   <a href="ct_locations.html">Locations</a>
   ```

4. Continuing in the same fashion, change the Menu entry to a link pointing to the **ct_menu.html** file, the Reviews entry to a link pointing to the **ct_reviews.html** file, the Catering entry to a link pointing to the **ct_catering.html** file, and the Contact entry to a link pointing to the **ct_contact.html** file.

   Figure 1-38 highlights the newly added code that changes all of the items in the navigation list to hypertext links.

Figure 1-38   **Marking hypertext links**

each item in the navigation list is marked as a hypertext link

```
<nav>
   <ul>
      <li><a href="ct_about.html">About</a></li>
      <li><a href="ct_locations.html">Locations</a></li>
      <li><a href="ct_menu.html">Menu</a></li>
      <li><a href="ct_reviews.html">Reviews</a></li>
      <li><a href="ct_catering.html">Catering</a></li>
      <li><a href="ct_contact.html">Contact</a></li>
   </ul>
</nav>
```

linked file   hypertext

5. Save your changes to the file and then reopen the **ct_about.html** file in your browser.

6. Click each of the six navigation list entries and verify that the browser loads the corresponding web page. Use the Back button on your browser to return to the About Curbside Thai page after you view each document.

Trouble? If the links do not work, be sure your code matches Figure 1-38. For example, check the spelling of each filename in the `href` attribute of each `<a>` tag to ensure it matches the filename of the corresponding Curbside Thai web page and check to be sure you have all needed opening and closing tags.

You may have noticed that when your mouse pointer moved over a hypertext link in the navigation list, the appearance of the link changed to white text on a black background. This is an example of a **rollover effect**, which is used to provide visual clues that the text is hypertext rather than normal text. You'll learn how to create rollover effects in Tutorial 2.

Turning an Inline Image into a Link

Inline images can also be turned into links by enclosing the image within opening and closing `<a>` tags. Turn the Curbside Thai logo into a hyperlink that points to the Startup page you opened in the first session.

To mark an image as a hypertext link:

▶ **1.** Return to the **ct_about.html** file in your HTML editor.

▶ **2.** Mark the image in the body header as a hyperlink by changing the HTML code to

```
<a href="ct_start.html"><img src="ct_logo2.png"
alt="Curbside Thai" /></a>
```

Figure 1-39 highlights the code to change the logo image to a hypertext link.

Figure 1-39   **Marking an inline image as a hypertext link**

reference to the hypertext link

```
<body>
    <header>
        <a href="ct_start.html"><img src="ct_logo2.png" alt="Curbside Thai" /></a>
        <nav>
            <ul>
```

▶ **3.** Save your changes to the file and then reopen the **ct_about.html** file in your browser.

▶ **4.** Click the Curbside Thai logo and verify that the browser opens the Curbside Thai Startup page. Click the Back button to return to the About Curbside Thai page.

Sajja wants to be able to jump to any document in the Curbside Thai website from any page. He asks you to copy the hypertext links, including the image hyperlink, you just created in the ct_about.html file to the other documents in the website.

To copy and paste the hypertext links:

▶ **1.** Return to the **ct_about.html** file in your HTML editor.

▶ **2.** Copy the entire content of the page header from the opening `<header>` tag through to the closing `</header>` tag, including the revised code for the company logo and navigation list.

3. Go to the **ct_locations.html** file in your HTML editor. Paste the copied HTML code, replacing the previous page header in this document. Save your changes to the file.

4. Repeat the previous step for the **ct_menu.html**, **ct_reviews.html**, **ct_catering.html**, and **ct_contact.html** files, replacing the body header in each of those documents with the revised header from ct_about.html. Save your changes to each file.

5. Reopen the **ct_locations.html** file in your browser and verify that you can jump from one page to another by clicking items in the navigation list at the top of each page. Also verify that you can jump to the Startup page at any time by clicking the Curbside Thai logo.

Specifying the Folder Path

In the links you created, the browser assumed that the linked files were in the same folder as the current page. However, large websites containing hundreds of documents often place documents in separate folders to make them easier to manage.

Figure 1-40 shows a preview of how Sajja might organize his files as the Curbside Thai website increases in size and complexity. In this structure, all folders start from a **root folder** named *thai* that contains the site's home page, which Sajja has stored in the index.html file. Sajja has moved all of his images and CSS style sheet files into their own folders. He has divided the rest of the web pages among three subfolders: the general folder for pages containing general information about the restaurant, the mobile folder for pages with content specifically about the mobile food service, and the catering folder for pages describing Curbside Thai's catering opportunities.

Figure 1-40   A sample folder structure

© 2016 Cengage Learning

To create links between files in separate folders, you must provide a path to the linked file. HTML supports two kinds of paths: absolute and relative.

Absolute Paths

An **absolute path** is a path that starts from the root folder and processes down the entire folder structure described with the expression

`/folder1/folder2/folder3/file`

where `folder1` is the root folder, followed by the subfolders `folder2`, `folder3`, and so forth, down to the linked file. For example, based on the structure shown previously in Figure 1-40, an absolute path pointing to the ct_catering.html file would have the expression

`/thai/docs/catering/ct_catering.html`

If files are located on different drives as well as in different folders, you must include the drive letter in the path with the expression

`/drive|/folder1/folder2/folder3/file`

where `drive` is the letter assigned to the drive. Note that the drive letter must be followed by the | character. Thus, if the ct_catering.html file were located on drive E, the absolute path that includes the drive would have the expression

`/E|/thai/docs/catering/ct_catering.html`

Note that you don't have to include a drive letter if the linked document is located on the same drive as the current file.

Relative Paths

When many folders and subfolders are involved, absolute path expression can quickly become long and cumbersome to work with. For this reason, most web designers prefer **relative paths** in which the path is expressed relative to the location of the current document. If the current document and linked file are in the same folder, there is no path and you need only include the filename. If the linked file is in a subfolder of the current document, the path includes all of the subfolder names starting from the location of the current page using the expression

`folder1/folder2/folder3/file`

where `folder1`, `folder2`, `folder3`, and so forth are subfolders of the current document. For example, the relative path to the ct_about.html file starting from the index.html file is

`docs/general/ct_about.html`

Note that relative paths are often expressed in terms of familial relationships such as parent, child, descendant, sibling, and so forth in order to indicate the hierarchical nature of the folder structure. Relative paths can also go up the hierarchy to parent folders by including the symbol (`..`), which means "go up one level." Thus, to go from ct_about.html in the general folder up two levels to the index.html file, you would enter the expression

`../../index.html`

TIP

You can reference the current folder using a single period (.) character.

Finally, to go sideways in the folder structure by going to a file in a different folder but on the same level, you go up to the parent folder and then back down to a different child folder. For example, to go from the ct_about.html file in the general folder to the ct_locations.html file in the mobile folder, you would use the relative path expression

`../mobile/ct_locations.html`

In this expression, the link goes up to the parent folder docs through the use of the `..` reference and then back down through the mobile folder to ct_locations.html.

You should almost always use relative paths in your links. If you have to move your files to a different computer or server, you can move the entire folder structure without having to edit the relative paths you've created. If you use absolute paths, you will have to revise each link to reflect the new location of the folder tree on the new device.

Setting the Base Path

As you've just seen, a browser resolves relative paths based on the location of the current document. You define a different starting point for relative paths by adding the following `base` element to the document head

```
<base href="url" />
```

where `url` is the location that you want the browser to use when resolving relative paths in the current document. The `base` element is useful when a single document from the website is moved to a new folder. Rather than rewriting all of the relative paths to reflect the document's new location, the `base` element can point to the document's old location allowing relative paths to work as before.

Decision Making: Managing Your Website

Websites can quickly grow to dozens or hundreds of pages. As the size of a site increases, it becomes more difficult to get a clear picture of the site's structure and content. Imagine deleting or moving a file in a website that contains dozens of folders and hundreds of files. Could you easily project the effect of this change? Would all of your hypertext links still work after you moved or deleted the file?

To effectively manage a website, you should implement clear decision making skills by following a few important rules. The first is to be consistent in how you structure the site. If you decide to collect all image files in one folder, you should continue that practice as you add more pages and images. Websites are more likely to break down if files and folders are scattered throughout the server without a consistent rule or pattern. Decide on a structure early and stick with it.

A second rule is to decide on and then create a folder structure that matches the structure of the website itself. If the pages can be easily categorized into different groups, those groupings should also be reflected in the groupings of the subfolders. The names you assign to your files and folders should also reflect their uses on the website. This makes it easier for you to predict how modifying a file or folder might impact other pages on the website.

Finally, you should document your work by adding comments to each new web page. Comments are useful not only for colleagues who may be working on the site but also for the author who must revisit those files months or even years after creating them. The comments should include

- The page's filename and location
- The page's author and the date the page was initially created
- A list of any supporting files used in the document, such as image and audio files
- A list of the files that link to the page and their locations
- A list of the files that the page links to and their locations

By following these rules, you can reduce a lot of the headaches associated with maintaining a large and complex website.

Linking to a Location within a Document

Hypertext can point to locations within a document. For example, you could link to a specific definition within a long glossary page to save users the trouble of scrolling through the document. Websites containing the text of novels or plays can contain links to key passages or phrases within those works. When a link is established to a location within a document, the browser will jump to that location automatically scrolling the page to the linked location.

Marking Locations with the `id` Attribute

In order to enable users to jump to a specific location within a document, you need to identify that location by adding the following `id` attribute to an element tag at that location

```
id="text"
```

where `text` is the name assigned to the ID. Imagine that Sajja writes a long page describing the full menu offered by Curbside Thai. He could mark the location in the page where the lunch menu is displayed by adding the following `id` attribute to the h2 heading that marks the start of the Lunch Menu section.

```
<h2 id="lunch">Lunch Menu</h2>
```

Note that IDs must be unique. If you assign the same ID to more than one element, the browser will jump to the first occurrence of that ID value.

Linking to an `id`

Once you've marked the location with an ID, you link to that element using the following hypertext link:

```
<a href="file#id">content</a>
```

where `file` points to the location and filename of the linked document and `id` is the value of an `id` attribute within that document. For example the following hypertext link points to the element with the ID "lunch" within the ct_fullmenus.html file.

```
<a href="ct_fullmenus.html#lunch">View our Lunch Menu</a>
```

To link to a location within the current page, include only the ID value along with the # symbol. Thus, the following hypertext link points to the lunch ID within the current web page:

```
<a href="#lunch">View our Lunch Menu</a>
```

In both cases, clicking or touching the link will cause the browser to automatically scroll to the location within the page.

Anchors and the `name` Attribute

Early web pages did not support the use of the `id` attribute as a way of marking locations within a document. Instead, they used the `<a>` tag as an anchor to mark that page location (hence the "a" in `<a>` tag). The general form of the anchor was

```
<a name="anchor">content</a>
```

where `anchor` is the name given to the anchored text. Inserting content within the `<a>` tag was optional because the primary purpose of the tag was to mark a document location, not to mark up content. For example, the following code would establish an anchor at the start of the lunch section in the Curbside Thai full menu:

```
<h2><a name="lunch"></a>Lunch Menu</h2>
```

Once an anchor had been set, you would link to the anchor using the same syntax you would use with the `id` attribute. The use of anchors is a deprecated feature of HTML and is not supported in strict applications of XHTML, but you will still see anchors used in older code.

Linking to a Location Within a Document

- To mark a location, add a unique ID to an element at that document location using the following `id` attribute

  ```
  id="text"
  ```

  where *text* is the value of the ID.
- To link to that location from a different document, use the hypertext reference

  ```
  <a href="file#text">content</a>
  ```

  where *file* is the name and path location (if necessary) of the external file and *text* is the value of the ID.
- To link to that location from within the same document, use the hypertext reference

  ```
  <a href="#text">content</a>
  ```

Linking to the Internet and Other Resources

The type of resource that a hypertext link points to is indicated by the link's URL. All URLs share the general structure

```
scheme:location
```

where *scheme* indicates the resource type and *location* provides the resource location. The name of the scheme is taken from the network protocol used to access the resource where a **protocol** is a set of rules defining how information is passed between two devices. Pages on the web use the **Hypertext Transfer Protocol** (**HTTP**) protocol and therefore the URL for many web pages start with the `http` scheme. Other schemes that can be included within a URL are described in Figure 1-41.

Figure 1-41	Commonly used URL schemes

Scheme	Description
`fax`	A FAX phone number
`file`	A document stored locally on a user's computer
`ftp`	A document stored on an FTP server
`geo`	A geophysical coordinate
`http`	A resource on the World Wide Web
`https`	A resource on the World Wide Web accessed over a secure encrypted connection
`mailto`	An e-mail address
`tel`	A telephone number
`sms`	A mobile text message sent via the Short Message Service

© 2016 Cengage Learning

Linking to a Web Resource

If you have ever accessed the web, you should be very familiar with website URLs, which have the general structure

```
http://server/path/filename#id
```

or for secure connections

```
https://server/path/filename#id
```

where *server* is the name of the web server hosting the resource, *path* is the path to the file on that server, *filename* is the name of the file, and if necessary, *id* is the name of an id or anchor within the file. For example, the following URL uses the HTTP protocol to access the web server at *www.curbsidethai.com*, linking to the document location named *lunch* within the ct_menus.html file in the /thai/docs folder:

```
http://www.curbsidethai.com/thai/docs/ct_menus.html#lunch
```

URLs are often entered in a more abbreviated form, *http://www.curbsidethai.com* for example, with no path or filename. Those URLs point to the default home page located in the top folder in the server's folder tree. Many servers use index.html as the filename for the default home page, so the URL *http://www.curbsidethai.com* would be equivalent to *http://www.curbsidethai.com/index.html*.

Understanding Domain Names

The server name portion of a URL is also called the **domain name**. By studying a domain name, you learn about the server hosting the website. Each domain name contains a hierarchy of names separated by periods (.), with the top level appearing at the far right end. The top level, called an **extension**, indicates the general audience supported by the web server. For example, *.edu* is the extension reserved for educational institutions, *.gov* is used for agencies of the United States government, and *.com* is used for commercial sites or general-use sites.

The next lower level appearing to the immediate left of the extension displays the name of the individual or organization hosting the site. The domain name *curbsidethai.com* indicates a commercial or general-use site owned by Curbside Thai. To avoid duplicating domain names, the top two levels of the domain must be registered with the **Internet Assigned Numbers Authority (IANA)** before they can be used. You can usually register your domain name through your web hosting company. Note: You must pay an annual fee to keep a domain name.

The lowest levels of the domain, which appear farthest to the left in the domain name, are assigned by the individual or company hosting the site. Large websites involving hundreds of pages typically divide their domain names into several levels. For example, a large company like Microsoft might have one domain name for file downloads—*downloads.microsoft.com*—and another domain name for customer service—*service.microsoft.com*. Finally, the first part of the domain name displays the name of the hard drive or resource storing the website files. Many companies have standardized on www as the initial part of their domain names.

Linking to an E-Mail Address

Many websites use e-mail to allow users to communicate with a site's owner, sales representative, or technical support staff. You can turn an e-mail address into a hypertext link using the URL:

```
mailto:address
```

where *address* is the e-mail address. Activating the link opens the user's e-mail program with the e-mail address automatically inserted into the To field of a new outgoing message. To create a hypertext link to the e-mail address *s.adulet@example.com*, you could use the following URL:

```
mailto:s.adulet@example.com
```

The mailto protocol also allows you to insert additional fields into the e-mail message using the URL:

```
mailto:address?field1=value1&field2=value2&...
```

where *field1*, *field2*, and so forth are different e-mail fields and *value1*, *value2*, and so forth are the field values. Fields include `subject` for the subject line of the e-mail message and `body` for the message body. To create a link to an e-mail message with the following content

```
TO: s.adulet@example.com
SUBJECT: Test
BODY: Test Message
```

you would use the URL

```
mailto:s.adulet@example.com?subject=Test&body=Test%20Message
```

Notice that the body text uses `%20` character code to represent a blank space since URLs cannot contain blank spaces.

On the Contact Us page, Sajja has inserted the Curbside Thai's e-mail address. Convert this e-mail address into a hypertext link.

To link to an e-mail address:

1. Go to the **ct_contact.html** file in your HTML editor.

A mailto hypertext link to an external resource must include the mailto scheme name in order to be recognized by the browser.

2. Change the Curbside Thai e-mail address into the following mailto hypertext link:

```
<a href="mailto:curbside.thai@example.com">
    curbside.thai@example.com
</a>
```

Note that this is a fictional e-mail address. If you want to test this link, change the URL to a link pointing to your own e-mail address. Figure 1-42 highlights the hypertext code to the linked e-mail address.

Figure 1-42 Linking to an e-mail address

e-mail address

e-mail address marked as a hyperlink

mailto scheme indicates that this is an e-mail link

```
<p>Call: (704) 555-1151</p>
<p>Email: <a href="mailto:curbside.thai@example.com">curbside.thai@example.com</a></p>
</article>
```

3. Save your changes to the file and then reopen the **ct_contact.html** file in your browser.

4. Click the e-mail address link and verify that your device opens your e-mail program with the Curbside Thai address already entered. Close the e-mail program without sending a message.

Trouble? Depending on your device, you may have to set up your e-mail program to accept hypertext links.

E-Mail Links and Spam

Use caution when adding e-mail links to your website. While it may make it more convenient for users to contact you, it also might make you more vulnerable to spam. **Spam** is unsolicited e-mail sent to large numbers of people, promoting products, services, and in some cases inappropriate websites. Spammers create their e-mail lists by scanning discussion groups, stealing Internet mailing lists, and using programs called **e-mail harvesters** to scan HTML code for the e-mail addresses contained in mailto URLs. Many developers have removed e-mail links from their websites in order to foil these harvesters, replacing the links with web forms that submit e-mail requests to a secure server.

There is no quick and easy solution to this problem. Fighting spammers is an ongoing battle, and they have proved very resourceful in overcoming some of the defenses people have created. As you develop your website, you should carefully consider how to handle e-mail addresses and review the most current methods for safeguarding that information.

Linking to a Phone Number

With the increased use of mobile phones to access the web, many developers now include links to phone numbers for their company's customer service or help line. Activating the link brings up the user's phone app with the number already entered, making it easier and more convenient to call the business or organization. The URL for a phone link is

```
tel:phone
```

where *phone* are the digits of the linked number. For example, the following code creates a telephone link to the Curbside Thai number:

```
Call: <a href="tel:+17045551151">(704) 555-1151</a>
```

Because websites are international, any telephone link should include the international dialing prefix (+1 for the United States) and the area code. Spaces or dashes between digits are optional with the exception of the + symbol before the international calling code. However, you can insert pauses in the phone number (used when accessing an extension) by inserting the `p` symbol, as in the following telephone link:

```
<a href="tel:+17045551151p22">Call: 555-1151 ext. 22</a>
```

Sajja asks you to change the telephone number from the Contact Us page into a telephone link.

To link to a phone number:

1. Return to the **ct_contact.html** file in your HTML editor.

2. Change the Curbside Thai phone number into the following hypertext link:

   ```
   <a href="tel:+17045551151">
      (704) 555-1151
   </a>
   ```

   Once again this number is fictional; you can change the URL to a link pointing to your own phone number if you want to test the link on a mobile device. Figure 1-43 highlights the hypertext code of the telephone link.

Figure 1-43	Marking a telephone link

telephone number including international dialing code and area code

telephone number marked as a hyperlink

tel scheme indicates that this is a telephone link

```
    <p>Call: <a href="tel:+17045551151">(704) 555-1151</a></p>
    <p>Email: <a href="mailto:curbside.thai@example.com">curbside.thai@example.com</a></p>
</article>
```

3. Save your changes to the file.

HTML supports links to other types of telephony devices. For example, you can create a link to a fax machine using the `fax:` scheme and a link to your text messaging app by using the `sms:` scheme.

Working with Hypertext Attributes

HTML provides several attributes to the a element that control the behavior and appearance of hypertext links. Figure 1-44 describes these attributes.

Figure 1-44	Attributes of the a element

Attribute	Description
href="*url*"	Provides the *url* of the hypertext link
target=(_blank|_parent|_self|_top)	Specifies where to open the linked document
download="*filename*"	Indicates that the link should be downloaded as a file, where *filename* is the name given to the downloaded file [**HTML5**]
rel="*type*"	Provides the relationship between the linked document and the current page
hreflang="*lang*"	Indicates the language of the linked document
type="*mime-type*"	Indicates the media type of the linked document

© 2016 Cengage Learning

Using the `target` attribute, you can control how a page is opened. By default the target of a link replaces the contents of the current page in the browser window. In some websites, you will want to open a link in a new browser window or tab so that you can keep the current page and the linked page in view. To force a document to appear in a new window or tab, add the following `target` attribute to the `<a>` tag:

```
<a href="url" target="window">content</a>
```

where `window` is a name assigned to the browser window or browser tab in which the linked page will appear. You can choose any name you wish for the browser window or you can use one of the following target names:

- `_self` opens the page in the current window or tab (the default)
- `_blank` opens the page in a new unnamed window or tab, depending on how the browser is configured
- `_parent` opens the page in the parent of the current frame (for framed websites)
- `_top` opens the page in the top frame (for framed websites)

You should use the `target` attribute sparingly in your website. Creating secondary windows can clutter up a user's desktop. Also, because the page is placed in a new window, users cannot use the Back button to return to the previous page in that window; they must click the browser's program button or the tab for the original website. This confuses some users and annoys others. Many designers now advocate not using the `target` attribute at all, but instead provide the user with the choice of opening a link in a new tab or window.

PROSKILLS

Written Communication: Creating Effective Hypertext Links

To make it easier for users to navigate your website, the text of your hypertext links should tell readers exactly what type of document the link points to. For example, the link text

Click <u>here</u> for more information.

doesn't tell the user what type of document will appear when <u>here</u> is clicked. In place of phrases like "click here", you should use descriptive link text such as

For more information, view our list of <u>frequently asked questions</u>.

If the link points to a non-HTML file, such as a PDF document, include that information in the link text. If the linked document is extremely large and will take a while to download to the user's computer, include that information in your link text so that users can decide whether or not to initiate the transfer. For example, the following link text informs users of both the type of document and its size so users have this information before they initiate the link:

Download our <u>complete manual (PDF 2 MB)</u>.

Finally, when designing the style of your website, make your links easy to recognize. Users should never be confused about a link. Also, if you apply a color to your text, do not choose colors that make your hyperlinks harder to pick out against the web page background.

You've completed your work on the Curbside Thai website. Sajja will study your work and get back to you with future projects for his restaurant. For now, you can close any open files or applications.

Session 1.3 Quick Check

1. Provide the code to mark the unordered list containing the items: Packers, Vikings, Bears, Lions.

2. Provide the code to mark the following list of the top-five most popular movies ranked in descending order according to IMDB:

   5. Pulp Fiction
   4. The Dark Knight
   3. The Godfather: Part II
   2. The Godfather
   1. The Shawshank Redemption

3. Describe the three HTML elements used in a description list.

4. Provide the code to create a navigation list for the following list items: Home, FAQ, Contact Us and pointing to the index.html, faq.html, and contacts.html files respectively.

5. Using the folder structure shown in Figure 1-40, provide the relative path going from the ct_about.html file to the ct_catering.html file.

6. Provide the URL pointing to the element in the glossary.html file with the ID *c_terms*. Assume that the glossary.html file is in the same folder as the current page.

7. Provide the URL to access the website at the address *www.example.com/curbside* over a secure connection.

8. Provide the URL for an e-mail link to the address *sajja@curbside.com* with the subject line *FYI*.

9. Provide the URL for a telephone link to the U.S. phone number 970-555-0002.

Review Assignments

Data Files needed for the Review Assignments: mp_index_txt.html, mp_menu_txt.html, mp_events_txt.html, mp_catering_txt.html, 2 CSS files, 2 PNG files, 1 TXT file

Curbside Thai has partnered with another food truck vendor Mobile Panini. Sajja asks you to create a website for the company similar to what you did for his restaurant. The site will have a home page, an online menu, a description of catering opportunities, and a calendar of upcoming events that Mobile Panini will host. A preview of the home page is shown in Figure 1-45.

Figure 1-45   Mobile Panini home page

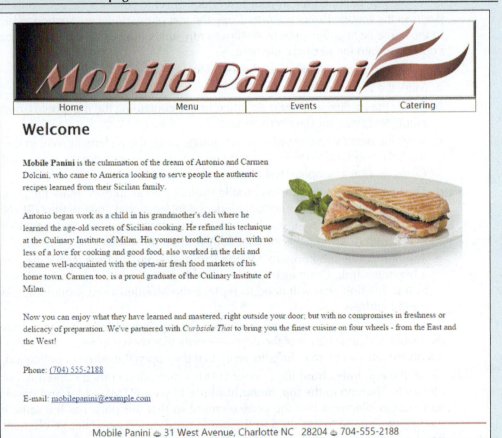

© 2016 Cengage Learning; © Glenn Price/Shuttertock.com

The page text has already been written for you and style sheets and graphic files have been created. Your job will be to complete this project by writing the HTML markup.

Complete the following:

1. Use your HTML editor to open the **mp_index_txt.html**, **mp_menu.txt.html**, **mp_events_txt.html**, and **mp_catering_txt.html** files from the html01 ► review folder. Enter *your name* and *the date* in the comment section of each file, and save them as **mp_index.html**, **mp_menu.html**, **mp_events.html**, and **mp_catering.html** respectively.

2. Go to the **mp_index.html** file in your HTML editor. Within the document head, do the following:

    a. Use the meta element to set the character encoding of the file to **utf-8**.

    b. Add the following search keywords to the document: **Italian**, **Mobile**, **food**, and **Charlotte**.

    c. Set the title of the document to **Mobile Panini**.

    d. Link the document to the mp_base.css and mp_layout.css style sheet files.

3. Go to the document body and insert a `header` element containing the following:

   a. An inline image from the mp_logo.png file with the alternate text **Mobile Panini**. Mark the image as a hypertext link pointing to the mp_index.html file.

   b. A navigation list containing an unordered list with the following list items: **Home**, **Menu**, **Events**, and **Catering**. Link the items to the mp_index.html, mp_menu.html, mp_events.html, and mp_catering.html files respectively.

4. Below the `header` element insert an `article` element. Below the `article` element, insert a `footer` element containing the following text:

   Mobile Panini ♨ 31 West Avenue, Charlotte NC 28204 ♨ 704-555-2188

   where ♨ is inserted using the **9832** character code and an extra space is added between NC and **28204** using the `nbsp` character name.

5. Go to the **mp_pages.txt** file in your text editor. This file contains the text content of the four pages in the Mobile Panini website. Copy the text of the Welcome section, which will be used in the home page of the website. Return to **mp_index.html** in your HTML editor and paste the copied text into the `article` element.

6. Within the `article` element, do the following:

   a. Mark the Welcome line as an h1 heading.

   b. Below the `h1` element, insert an inline image containing the mp_photo1.png file with an empty text string for the alternate text.

   c. Mark the next five paragraphs as paragraphs using the p element. Within the first paragraph, mark the text *Mobile Panini* as strong text. Within the third paragraph mark the text *Curbside Thai* as emphasized text.

   d. The fourth paragraph contains Mobile Panini's phone number. Mark the phone number as a telephone link and be sure to include the international code in the URL. Note that this number is fictional, so, if you have access to a mobile browser and want to test the link, you might want to replace this number with your phone number.

   e. The fifth paragraph contains Mobile Panini's e-mail address. Mark the e-mail address as a hypertext link. Once again, note that this e-mail address is fictional, so, if you want to test this link, you will need to replace the Mobile Panini e-mail address with your e-mail address.

7. Save your changes to the file and then open the **mp_index.html** file in your browser. Verify that the layout and appearance of the page resemble that shown in Figure 1-45. If possible, test the telephone links and e-mail links to verify that they open the correct application.

8. Go to the **mp_index.html** file in your HTML editor, and copy the `header` and `footer` elements. Then go to the **mp_menu.html** file in your HTML editor and paste the `header` and `footer` elements into the `body` element so that this page has the same logo and navigation list and footer used in the home page. Insert an `article` element between the header and footer.

9. Return to the **mp_pages.txt** file in your text editor and copy the contents of the Mobile Panini menu. Then, go to the **mp_menu.html** file in your HTML editor and paste the copied text into the `article` element.

10. Within the article element of the mp_menu.htm file, do the following:

    a. Mark the text title *Our Menu* as an h1 heading.

    b. Enclose the menu items in a description list with the name of each menu item marked with the `dt` element and each menu description marked with the `dd` element.

11. Save your changes to mp_menu.html file. Open the page in your browser and verify that each menu item name appears in a bold font and is separated from the indented item description by a horizontal line.

12. Go to the **mp_index.html** file in your HTML editor and copy the `header` and `footer` elements. Then, go to the **mp_events.html** file in your HTML editor and paste the `header` and `footer` elements into the `body` element. Insert an `article` element between the header and footer.

13. Return to the **mp_pages.txt** file in your text editor and copy the list of upcoming events under the Calendar section heading. Then, go to the **mp_events.html** file in your HTML editor and paste the copied text into the `article` element.

14. Within the `article` element, do the following:
    a. Mark the text *Where Are We This Week*? as an h1 heading.
    b. Enclose each day's worth of events within a separate `div` (or division) element.
    c. Within each of the seven day divisions, enclose the day and date as an h1 heading. Enclose the location within a paragraph element. Insert a line break element, `<br />`, directly before the time of the event so that each time interval is displayed on a new line within the paragraph.

15. Save your changes to mp_events.html file. Open the page in your browser and verify that each calendar event appears in its own box with the day and date rendered as a heading.

16. Go to the **mp_index.html** file in your HTML editor and copy the `header` and `footer` elements. Then, go to the **mp_catering.html** file in your HTML editor and paste the `header` and `footer` elements into the `body` element. Insert an `article` element between the header and footer and then insert an `aside` element within the article.

17. Directly after the opening `<article>` tag, insert an `h1` element containing the text **Catering**.

18. Return to the **mp_pages.txt** file in your text editor and copy the text about the mobile kitchen, including the heading. Then, go to the **mp_catering.html** file in your HTML editor and paste the copied text into the `aside` element.

19. Within the `article` element, do the following:
    a. Mark the text *About the Mobile Kitchen* as an h1 heading.
    b. Mark the next two paragraphs as paragraphs.

20. Return to the **mp_pages.txt** file in your text editor and copy the text describing Mobile Panini's catering opportunities; do not copy the Catering head. Then, go to the **mp_catering.html** file in your HTML editor and paste the copied text directly after the `aside` element.

21. Make the following edits to the pasted text:
    a. Mark the first two paragraphs as paragraphs.
    b. Enclose the list of the six catering possibilities within an unordered list with each item marked as a list item.
    c. Mark the concluding paragraph as a paragraph.

22. Save your changes to mp_catering.html file. Open the page in your browser and verify that the information about the mobile kitchen appears as a sidebar on the right edge of the article.

23. Return to the **mp_index.html** file in your browser and verify that you can jump from one page to another by clicking the entries in the navigation list at the top of each page.

Case Problem 1

Data Files needed for this Case Problem: jtc_index_txt.html, jtc_services_txt.html, 2 CSS files, 3 PNG files, 1 TXT file

Jedds Tree Care Carol Jedds is the owner and operator of Jedds Tree Care and tree removal and land-scaping company in Lansing, Michigan. She has asked for your help in developing her company's website. She has already written some of the text for a few sample pages and wants you to write the HTML code. Figure 1-46 shows a preview of the company's home page that you'll create.

Figure 1-46   **Jedds Tree Care home page**

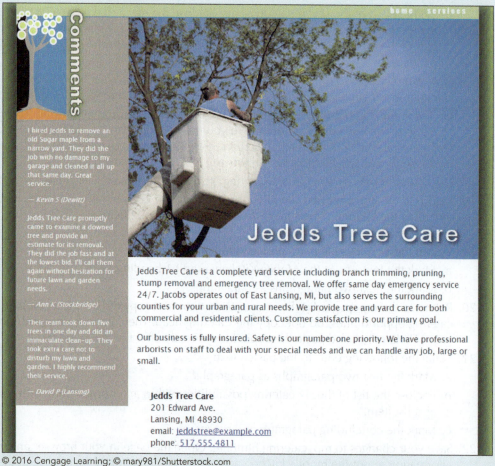

© 2016 Cengage Learning; © mary981/Shutterstock.com

The style sheets and graphic files have already been created for you. Your job is to write the HTML markup.

Complete the following:

1. Using your editor, open the **jtc_index_txt.html** and **jtc_services_txt.html** files from the html01 ▶ case1 folder. Enter ***your name*** and ***the date*** in the comment section of each file, and save them as **jtc_index.html** and **jtc_services.html** respectively.

2. Go to the **jtc_index.html** file in your HTML editor. Within the document head, do the following:

   a. Use the `meta` element to set the character encoding of the file to **utf-8**.

   b. Set the document title to **Jedds Tree Care**.

   c. Link the document to the jtc_base.css and jtc_layout.css style sheet files.

3. Within the document body, insert a `header` element, an `aside` element, and an `article` element.

4. Within the `header` element, insert a navigation list with links to jtc_index.html and jtc_services.html file. The text of the links should be **home** and **services** respectively.

5. Go to the **jtc_pages.txt** file in your text editor. The first section in the file contains comments made by Jedds Tree Care customers. Copy the text of the three reviews including the reviewer names. Then, go to the **jtc_index.html** file in your HTML editor and paste the copied text within the `aside` element.

6. Within the `aside` element, add the following content and markup:
   a. Directly after the opening `<aside>` tag, insert an inline image for the jtc_comments.png file. Specify **Comments** as the alternate text.
   b. Enclose each of the three reviewer comments within a `blockquote` element, including both the text of the quote and the name of the review.
   c. Within each of the three `blockquote` elements,
      i. mark the review as a paragraph.
      ii. mark the line containing the reviewer name as a `cite` element.
      iii. replace the "---" text with the em dash character (–) using the character reference name `mdash`.

7. Go to the `article` element and insert a `header` element containing the inline image file jtc_photo1.png with the alternate text *Jedds Tree Care*.

8. Return to the **jtc_pages.txt** file in your text editor and copy the second section of text containing the description of the company and its contact information. Then, go to the **jtc_index.html** file in your HTML editor and paste the copied text in the `article` element, directly below the article header.

9. Mark up the content of the page article as follows:
   a. Mark the first two paragraphs using the `<p>` tag.
   b. Enclose the five lines of the contact information within an `address` element. Insert a line break element at the end of the first four lines so that each part of the address appears on a new line in the rendered page.
   c. Mark the text *Jedds Tree Care* in the first line of the address as a `strong` element.
   d. Mark the e-mail address as a hypertext link. Make the telephone number a telephone link, including the international access code.

10. Save your changes to the jtc_index.html file. Open the page in your browser and verify that the layout and contents of the page resemble that shown in Figure 1-46. Note that under the smaller screen widths associated with mobile devices, the text of the reviewer comments is not displayed.

11. Go to the **jtc_services.html** file in your HTML editor. Insert the same metadata in the document head to match what you did for the jtc_index.html file *except* name the page title **Jedds Tree Care Services**.

12. Go to the **jtc_index.html** file in your HTML editor and copy the body header. Then, go to the **jtc_services.html** file and paste the copied header into the document body so that both files share a common header design.

13. Return to the **jtc_pages.txt** file in your text editor and copy the content of the third section, which contains information on the services offered by Jedds Tree Care. Be sure to copy the heading as well. Then, go to the **jtc_services.html** file in your HTML editor and paste the copied text directly after the header.

14. Mark the content describing Jedds Tree Care services as follows:
   a. Mark the heading *Jedds Tree Care Services* as an h1 heading.
   b. Directly after the `h1` element, insert an inline image file for the **jtc_photo2.png** with the alternate text set to empty.
   c. Mark each of the headings associated with individual services as h2 headings.
   d. Mark each service description as a paragraph.

15. Directly after the text of the last service, insert a `footer` element containing the following text:
    Jedds Tree Care ◆ 201 Edward Ave. ◆ Lansing, MI 48930
    where the ◆ symbol is inserted using the character code **9830**.

16. Save your changes to the file and open the **jtc_services.html** file in your browser. Verify that the page title is displayed as a major heading and the name of each service is displayed as a second level heading.

Case Problem 2

Data Files needed for this Case Problem: ms_euler_txt.html, 2 CSS files, 2 PNG files, 1 TXT file

Math Strings Professor Lauren Coe of the Mathematics Department of Coastal University in Anderson, South Carolina, is one of the founders of *Math Strings*, a website containing articles and course materials for high school and college math instructors. She has written a series of biographies of famous mathematicians for the website and would like you to use that content in a web page. You'll create the first one in this exercise. Figure 1-47 shows a preview of the page you'll create, which profiles the mathematician Leonhard Euler.

Figure 1-47   Math Strings Leonhard Euler page

Leonhard Euler (1707-1783)

The greatest mathematician of the eighteenth century, **Leonhard Euler** was born in Basel, Switzerland. There, he studied under another giant of mathematics, **Jean Bernoulli**. In 1731 Euler became a professor of physics and mathematics at St. Petersburg Academy of Sciences. Euler was the most prolific mathematician of all time, publishing over *800 different books and papers*. His influence was felt in physics and astronomy as well.

He is perhaps best known for his research into mathematical analysis. Euler's work, *Introductio in analysin infinitorum (1748)*, remained a standard textbook in the field for well over a century. For the princess of Anhalt-Dessau, he wrote *Lettres à une princesse d'Allemagne (1768-1772)*, giving a clear non-technical outline of the main physical theories of the time.

One can hardly write a mathematical equation without copying Euler. Notations still in use today, such as e and π, were introduced in Euler's writings. Leonhard Euler died in 1783, leaving behind a legacy perhaps unmatched, and certainly unsurpassed, in the annals of mathematics.

The Most Beautiful Equation in Math?

Perhaps the most elegant equation in the history of math is:

$$\cos(x) + i\sin(x) = e^{xi}$$

which demonstrates the relationship between algebra, complex analysis, and trigonometry. From this equation, it's easy to derive the identity:

$$e^{\pi i} + 1 = 0$$

which relates the fundamental constants: 0, 1, π, e, and i in a single beautiful and elegant statement. A poll of readers conducted by *The Mathematical Intelligencer* magazine named Euler's Identity as the most beautiful theorem in the history of mathematics.

Learn more about Euler

Euler at Wikipedia

The Euler Archive

Euler at Biography.com

Euler at Famous Scientists

Math Strings: A Site for Educators and Researchers

The style sheet and graphics are provided for you. Your job is to write the HTML markup.

Complete the following:

1. Using your editor, open the **ms_euler_txt.html** file from the html01 ▸ case2 folder. Enter *your name* and *the date* in the comment section of the file, and save it as **ms_euler.html**.

2. Add the following to the document head:
   a. Set the character encoding of the file to **utf-8**.
   b. Add the following search keywords: **math**, **Euler**, **pi**, and **geometry**.
   c. Set the title of the document to **Leonhard Euler (1707-1783)**.
   d. Link the document to the ms_base.css and ms_layout.css style sheet files.

3. Add a `header`, `article`, `aside`, `nav`, and `footer` element to the document body.

4. Within the body header, insert an inline image for the ms_logo.png file with the alternate text **Math Strings**.

5. Go to the **ms_pages.txt** file in your text editor and copy the text of the main article (located in the first section of the file), including the title. Then, go to the **ms_euler.html** file in your HTML editor and paste the copied text into the `article` element.

6. Within the `article` element, make the following markup changes:
   a. Mark the text *Leonhard Euler (1707-1783)* as an h1 heading.
   b. Mark the three paragraphs of the article content using the p element.
   c. In the first paragraph, mark the names *Leonhard Euler* and *Jean Bernoulli* as strong text. Mark the phrase *800 different books and papers* as emphasized text.
   d. In the second paragraph mark the works *Introductio in analysin infinitorum (1748)* and *Lettres à une princesse d'Allemagne (1768-1772)* as citations. Insert the à character using the character reference `&agrave;`.
   e. In the third paragraph, mark the mathematical symbols *e* and π using the `var` (variable) element. Insert the π character by replacing [pi] with the `&pi;` character reference.

7. Return to the **ms_pages.txt** in your text editor and copy the text of the second section containing information about Euler's Equation, the most beautiful equation in math. Then, go to the ms_euler.html file in your HTML editor and paste the copied text into the `aside` element.

8. Within the `aside` element, add the following markup:
   a. Mark the title *The Most Beautiful Equation in Math?* as an h1 heading.
   b. Mark the two equations in the pasted text using the `code` element. Mark the three other text groups as paragraphs.
   c. Throughout the text of the `aside` element, mark *x*, *i*, *e*, *xi*, and *pi* using the `var` element, replacing [pi] from the pasted text with the character reference `&pi;`.
   d. Use the `sup` element in the following equations to mark *xi* and π*i* as superscripts:
      $\cos(x) + i\sin(x) = e^{xi}$
      $e^{\pi i} + 1 = 0$
   e. Mark the text *The Mathematical Intelligencer* as a citation.

9. Return to the **ms_pages.txt** file in your text editor and copy the text of the third section listing more ways to learn about Euler. Then, go to the **ms_euler.html** file in your HTML editor and paste the copied text into the `nav` element.

10. Within the `nav` element, add the following markup:
    a. Mark the title *Learn more about Euler* as an h1 heading.
    b. Mark the four Euler websites as an unordered list.
    c. Change the text of the Euler websites to hypertext links pointing to the following URLs:
       Euler at Wikipedia linked to *http://en.wikipedia.org/wiki/Leonhard_Euler*
       The Euler Archive linked to *http://eulerarchive.maa.org/*
       Euler at Biography.com linked to *http://www.biography.com/people/leonhard-euler-21342391*
       Euler at Famous Scientists linked to *http://www.famousscientists.org/leonhard-euler*

11. Within the footer element, insert the text **Math Strings: A Site for Educators and Researchers**.

12. Save your changes to the file and open the **ms_euler.html file** in your browser. Verify that the equations in the sidebar match the ones shown in Figure 1-47 and that all occurrences of the [pi] character have been replaced with π. Click the four links in the navigation list and verify that your browser opens the websites.

CHALLENGE

Case Problem 3

Data Files needed for this Case Problem: dr_index_txt.html, dr_info_txt.htm, dr_faq_txt.html, 4 CSS files, 2 PNG files, 3 TXT files

Diane's Run *Diane's Run* is a charity run to raise money for breast cancer awareness and research funding. Peter Wheaton is the charity run's organizer and he has asked you to help modify the run's website. He has revised text that he wants added to the current site. A preview of the page you'll create is shown in Figure 1-48.

Figure 1-48   **Diane's Run home page**

FAQ   Race Info   Home

What Your Support Does

Every 10 minutes a woman is diagnosed with breast cancer. Her first reaction is fear and confusion. Support is just a phone call or mouse click away. Our free services offer a friendly ear and expert guidance to anyone dealing with this life-threatening illness.

By running or walking with us, you can ensure that we are there when people need us. Here is how your contribution can help:

- **$15** pays for a headscarf set, boosting the confidence of women who have lost their hair from her breast cancer treatment.

- **$50** trains a member of our support network for a year to help improve the care of women with breast cancer.

- **$125** covers the cost of counselling sessions to help women cope with the distress of their cancer treatment.

- **$250** funds a hospital information station for a year so that people affected by breast cancer have easy access to the latest resources and help.

Diane's Run - September 9, 2017

Join over 2000 athletes in Cheyenne, Wyoming, for **Diane's Run** to raise money for breast cancer awareness and research. The 5K and 10K races are challenging, yet attainable. You can aim for a personal best while taking part to raise money for this important charity. If you can't run, consider walking; joining young and old in the fight by participating in the 1-Mile Walk for Hope.

How to Join

You can guarantee a spot by filling out the entry form and mailing it to dianesrun@example.com. The $35 entry fee is tax deductible and goes directly to important research and women in need. We keep our overhead very low so every dollar counts. More than 75% of the net proceeds fund screening and treatment programs in your communities. We welcome out-of-town visitors. We will help you find accommodations during your visit.

History

Since its inception in 2004, Diane's Run has grown from a purely local event involving 100 runners to a signature Wyoming event with more than 2000 participants annually. The event is enormously effective in spreading the message that breast cancer need not be fatal if caught early enough with mammography and breast self-exam. As well as a top-flight athletic event, Diane's Run is an emotionally moving event attracting many first timers and recreational runners. This event provides all of us with the opportunity to spread a hopeful message about breast cancer to our families and our communities.

Remembering Diane

Diane's Run is named in remembrance of Diane Wheaton, mother of 2 and wife of Peter, who passed away in May, 2003. Diane was an outspoken advocate of physical fitness and healthy living. She was an inspiration to all who knew her and continues to be an inspiration to the thousands of runners who have participated in this event.

We hope you can join us this year and become part of the Diane's Run family.

Diane's Run ♥ 45 Mountain Drive ♥ Cheyenne, WY 82001

Peter has supplied you with the text content, the graphic images, and style sheets you need for the project. Your job will be to write HTML code for three pages: the site's home page, a page containing race information, and finally a page containing a list of frequently asked questions (FAQ's).

Complete the following:

1. Using your editor, open the **dr_index_txt.html**, **dr_info_txt.html**, and **dr_faq_txt.html** files from the html01 ► case3 folder. Enter *your name* and *the date* in the comment section of each file, and save them as **dr_index.html**, **dr_info.html**, and **dr_faq.html** respectively.

2. Go to the **dr_index.html** file in your HTML editor. Within the document head, add the following metadata:

   a. Set the character encoding of the file to **utf-8**.

   b. Insert the search keywords: **breast cancer**, **run**, **race**, and **charity**.

   c. Set the title of the document to **Diane's Run**.

   d. Link the document to the dr_base.css and dr_layout.css style sheet files.

3. Within the document body, insert a `header` element, two `section` elements, and a `footer` element.

4. In the `header` element, insert a navigation list containing an unordered list with the items: **Home**, **Race Info**, and **FAQ**. Link the items to the dr_index.html, dr_info.html, and dr_faq.html files respectively.

5. The file dr_index.txt contains the text to be inserted into the Diane's Run home page. Go to the **dr_index.txt** file in your text editor and copy the text from the first section of the file. Then, go to the **dr_index.html** file in your HTML editor and paste it into the first `section` element.

6. Add the following markup to the content of the first `section` element:

   a. Mark the line *What Your Support Does* as an h1 heading.

   b. Mark the next two paragraphs as paragraphs using the `p` element.

   c. Mark the four ways a contribution can help as an unordered list. Mark the dollar amounts of each list item using the `strong` element.

7. Return to the **dr_index.txt** file in your text editor, copy the text from the second section, then close the dr_index.txt file. Go to the **dr_index.html** file in your HTML editor and paste the copied text within the second `section` element.

8. Within the second `section` element in the dr_index.html file, add the following:

   a. Enclose the opening heading *Diane's Run - September 9, 2017* within a `header` element and marked as an h1 heading. Directly above this heading, insert the inline image file dr_photo1.png with **Diane's Run** as the alternate text of the image.

   b. Mark the first paragraph after the header as a paragraph. Mark the text *Diane's Run* in this opening paragraph using the `strong` element.

   c. Mark the minor headings *How to Join*, *History*, and *Remembering Diane* as h2 headings. Mark the other blocks of text as paragraphs.

9. Within the `footer` element, insert the following text:

   Diane's Run ♥ 45 Mountain Drive ♥ Cheyenne, WY 82001

   where the ♥ character is inserted using the character code **9829**.

10. Save your changes to the file and then open **dr_index.html** in your browser. Verify that the content and the layout of the page resemble that shown in Figure 1-48.

11. Go to the **dr_info.html** file in your HTML editor. Within the document head, link the page to the dr_base.css and dr_layout2.css style sheets.

12. Go to the **dr_index.html** file in your HTML editor and copy the body header content. Then, go to the **dr_info.html** file in your HTML editor and paste the copied content into the document body. Repeat for the body footer so that the Racing Information page has the same navigation list and footer as the home page. Between the `header` and `footer` element, insert a `section` element.

⊕ **Explore** 13. Within the `section` element, insert a `header` element with the following content:

    a. Insert a paragraph with the text **Page last updated: Tuesday, August 29, 2017.** Mark the date using the `time` element with the `datetime` attribute equal to **2017-08-29.**

    b. Add the text **Race Information** as an h1 heading.

    c. Insert the inline image file dr_logo.png with **Diane's Run** as the alternate text.

14. Go to the **dr_info.txt** file in your text editor. This file contains the text describing the race. Copy the content describing the race from the file, then close the dr_info.txt file. Go to the dr_info.html file in your HTML editor and paste the copied text into the `section` element, directly after the section header.

15. Mark the content of the `section` element as follows:

    a. Mark the opening block of text directly after the section header as a paragraph.

    b. Mark the headings *Race Times*, *Goodies and Stuff*, and *Notes* as h2 headings.

    c. Below each of the `h2` elements, mark the list of items that follows as an unordered list.

16. Save your changes to the file and then load **dr_info.html** in your browser to verify that the layout and content are readable.

17. Go to the **dr_faq.html** file in your HTML editor. Within the document head, link the page to the dr_base.css and dr_layout3.css style sheets.

18. Go to the **dr_index.html** file in your HTML editor and copy the body header content. Then, go to the **dr_faq.html** file in your HTML editor and paste the copied content into the document body. Repeat with the body footer so that the FAQ page has the same navigation list and footer as was used in the home page. Between the `header` and `footer` element, insert a `section` element.

19. Within the `section` element, insert a `header` element with the `id` attribute **pagetop**. Within the header, insert the inline image file dr_logo.png with the alternate text **Diane's Run** followed by the `h1` element with the text **Frequently Asked Questions**.

20. Go to the **dr_faq.txt** file in your text editor. This file contains a list of frequently asked questions followed by the question answers. Copy the text and then close the dr_faq.txt file. Then, go to the dr_faq.html file in your HTML editor and paste the copied text into the `section` element, directly after the section header.

⊕ **Explore** 21. Next, you'll create a series of hypertext links between the list of questions and their answers within the same document. Make the following changes to the `section` element in the dr_faq.html file:

    a. Mark the 13 questions at the top of the section as an ordered list.

    b. Notice that below the ordered list you just created, the questions are repeated and each question is followed by its answer. Mark the text of those questions as an h2 heading and the answer as a paragraph. Add an `id` attribute to each of the 13 h2 headings with the first heading given the id **faq1**, the second heading **faq2**, and so forth down to **faq13** for the last h2 heading.

    c. After the last answer, insert a paragraph with the text **Return to the Top** and mark the text as a hypertext link pointing to the `header` element with the id **pagetop**.

    d. Return to the ordered list at the top of the section that you created in Step a. Change each item in the ordered list to a hypertext link pointing to the h2 heading containing the question's answer that you created in Step b. For example, the first question *How do I sign up?* should be linked to the h2 heading with the faq1 id.

22. Save your changes to the file and then open **dr_faq.html** in your browser. Verify that by clicking a question within the ordered list, the browser jumps to that question's answer. Further, verify that clicking the Return to the Top link at the bottom of the page causes the browser to return to the top of the page.

⊕ **Explore** 23. Return to the **dr_index.html** file in your HTML editor. Add the following two hypertext links to the *How to Join* paragraph in the second `section` element:

   a. Change the e-mail address *dianesrun@example.com* to an e-mail link with the subject heading Entry Form.

   b. Change the word *accommodations* to a hypertext link pointing to the element with the id faq13 in the dr_faq.html file.

24. Save your changes to the file and reload dr_index.html in your browser. Verify that clicking the e-mail link brings up your e-mail program with the e-mail address and the subject heading already filled in.

25. Click the accommodations hypertext link and verify that the browser goes to the last answer on the FAQ page.

26. Verify that you can jump between all three pages by clicking the navigation links at the top of the page.

CREATE

Case Problem 4

Data Files needed for this Case Problem: hg_index_txt.html, hg_towers_txt.html, hg_alliance_txt.html, 3 PNG files, 1 TXT file

Harpe Gaming Sean Greer is the owner of *Harpe Gaming*, a small board game store in Morgantown, West Virginia. You've been asked to work on the store's new website. Sean wants you to write the HTML code for the store's home page. Sean also publishes reviews of new games as a service to his loyal customers. He would also like you to write the HTML code for two new reviews that Sean has written for the *Towers and Temples* game and the *Alliance* game. Sean has already written all of the content for the three pages and only requires your help to turn them into HTML documents.

Complete the following:

1. Using your editor, open the **hg_index_txt.html**, **hg_towers_txt.html**, and **hg_alliance_txt.html** files from the html01 ▸ case4 folder. Save them as **hg_index.html**, **hg_towers.html**, and **hg_alliance.html** respectively.

2. Content for each of the three pages is contained in the hg_text.txt file. Take some time to review the content of this file. The Harpe Gaming home page will have a short introduction to the store and its philosophy and includes contact information for the interested customer. The Towers and Temples page and the Alliance page have an overview of each game with the Harpe Gaming's rating and reviews from popular gaming magazines and websites. Sean has also supplied you with the hg_logo.png, hg_towers.png, and hg_alliance.png files as images to be used in the files. You are free to supplement Sean's material with appropriate material of your own.

3. Once you are familiar with the content that needs to be inserted into the web pages, start creating the HTML code for each page. For each file, insert the structure of an HTML document including the opening doctype, `html` element, document head, and document body.

4. For the document head of each file, do the following (there are no style sheets for this project, so you do *not* have to include links to any style sheet files):

   a. Insert a comment that includes **your name** and **the date** and the purpose of the page.

   b. Insert metadata that sets the character encoding used in the file.

   c. Insert metadata that specifies the page title.

   d. Insert a list of search keywords appropriate to the content of each file.

5. Within the document body, insert a navigation list within a body header that has hypertext links to all three pages in this sample website.

6. Use the content from the hg_text.txt file to populate the content of the three pages. The markup used in the three pages is up to you. In your website there should be at least one example of the following:

   a. Sectioning elements, including the `header`, `article`, `aside`, `section`, and `footer` elements

   b. Grouping elements, including paragraphs, block quotes, and lists

   c. Text-level elements used to mark single words or phrases from within a grouping element. Include at least one example of the `strong` element and the `em` element.

   d. An inline image, including appropriate alternate text for the image

   e. A character symbol inserted using its character name or encoding number

   f. A hypertext link to an individual's e-mail address

   g. A hypertext link to a phone number

   h. A hypertext link to a website URL

7. Save your changes to the files and then open them in your browser. Verify that the links work as expected when moving between the pages in the website, when accessing your e-mail program, and when accessing external links on the web. If you have a telephony application on your computer, test that clicking the phone link opens that application.

TUTORIAL 2

Getting Started with CSS

Designing a Website for a Fitness Club

OBJECTIVES

Session 2.1
- Explore the history of CSS
- Study different types of style sheets
- Explore style precedence and inheritance
- Apply colors in CSS

Session 2.2
- Use contextual selectors
- Work with attribute selectors
- Apply text and font styles
- Use a web font

Session 2.3
- Define list styles
- Work with margins and padding space
- Use pseudo-classes and pseudo-elements
- Insert page content with CSS

Case | *Tri and Succeed Sports*

Alison Palmer runs Tri and Succeed Sports, an athletic club in Austin, Texas that specializes in coaching men and women aspiring to compete in triathlons and other endurance sports. The center provides year-round instruction in running, swimming, cycling, and general fitness with one-on-one and group training classes. Alison has asked you to work on the company's new website.

Alison designed the original Tri and Succeed Sports website several years ago but she now feels that the site needs a makeover. She wants a new design that uses color and interesting typography to create visual interest and impact. She wants you to use CSS to help give the website a new look.

STARTING DATA FILES

html02 → **tutorial**
tss_bike_txt.html
tss_home_txt.html
tss_run_txt.html
tss_swim_txt.html
tss_styles_txt.css
+ 8 files

review
tss_coach_txt.html
coach_styles_txt.css
+ 8 files

case1
ph_plays_txt.html
ph_styles_txt.css
+ 8 files

case2
mw_tour_txt.html
mw_styles_txt.css
+ 2 files

case3
cw_class_txt.html
cw_styles_txt.css
+ 3 files

case4
lake_home_txt.html
lake_styles_txt.css
+ 7 files

demo
demo_css.html
demo_color_names.html
+ 3 files

Session 2.1 Visual Overview:

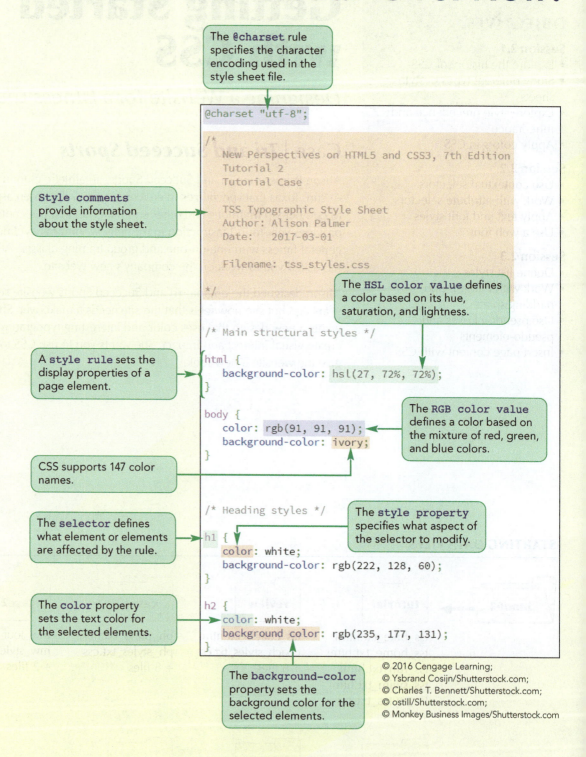

The **@charset** rule specifies the character encoding used in the style sheet file.

Style comments provide information about the style sheet.

The **HSL color value** defines a color based on its hue, saturation, and lightness.

A **style rule** sets the display properties of a page element.

The **RGB color value** defines a color based on the mixture of red, green, and blue colors.

CSS supports 147 color names.

The **selector** defines what element or elements are affected by the rule.

The **style property** specifies what aspect of the selector to modify.

The **color** property sets the text color for the selected elements.

The **background-color** property sets the background color for the selected elements.

```
@charset "utf-8";

/*
    New Perspectives on HTML5 and CSS3, 7th Edition
    Tutorial 2
    Tutorial Case

    TSS Typographic Style Sheet
    Author: Alison Palmer
    Date:   2017-03-01

    Filename: tss_styles.css

*/

/* Main structural styles */

html {
    background-color: hsl(27, 72%, 72%);
}

body {
    color: rgb(91, 91, 91);
    background-color: ivory;
}

/* Heading styles */

h1 {
    color: white;
    background-color: rgb(222, 128, 60);
}

h2 {
    color: white;
    background color: rgb(235, 177, 131);
}
```

CSS Styles and Colors

The browser window background color is set to the color value hsl(27, 73%, 72%) using the html style rule.

The h1 headings appear in white on a dark orange background as specified by the h1 style rule.

and Succeed Sports

Links

- Home
- Running
- Cycling
- Swimming
- Active.com
- Runner's World
- endomondo.com
- Strava
- Bicycling Magazine
- VeloNews
- Bicycle Tutor
- Swim Smooth
- Swimming World
- USA Swimming
- triathlon.org
- usatriathlon.org
- Texas Triathlons
- CapTex Triathlon
- Triathlon Calendar
- Triathlete.com
- Trifuel.com

The h2 headings appear in white on a light orange background as specified by the h2 style rule.

About TSS

Since 2002, **Tri and Succeed Sports** has provided Austin with a first class training center for athletes of all abilities and goals. We specialize in helping you reach your full potential. You tell us what you want to do; we work to fulfill your needs.

Want to swim? Great! Interested in improving your cycling? Fantastic! Want to tackle a triathlon? We're there for you: before, during, and after the race. Or do you just want to get more fit? We are on it. We customize our instruction to match your goals. And you will finish what you start.

Classes

Winter instruction starts soon. Get a jump on your summer goals by joining us for individual or group instruction in:

- **Running**: We start with the basics to help you run faster and farther than you ever thought possible without aches and pains.
- **Cycling**: The indoor bike trainers at TSS include everything you need to refine your technique, stamina, and power for improved results on the road.
- **Swimming**: The open water swim can be one of the most frightening sports to master. Our classes begin with basic techniques so that your swim can be very enjoyable, and not a chore.

Contact us to set up individual instruction and assessment.

Our Philosophy

Athletes are the foundation of every successful training program. The best coach is an experienced guide who begins with each athlete's hopes, dreams and desires and then tailors a training plan based on that individuals's current fitness and lifestyle. Since 2002, TSS has helped hundreds of individuals achieve success in many fitness areas. The winner is not the one who finishes first but anyone who starts the race and perseveres. Join us and begin exploring the possible.

Comments

Thank you for all that you have done. I am amazed at my progress. I realize that I have l lofty goals but you have me well on my way.

Alison kept me focused working toward my dreams. She fosters a supportive and caring environment for growth as an athlete and as a person. Thank you!

You do it right! Your track record proves it. Proud to be a TSS athlete and I'm honored to have you all as my coaches and support team.

The coaches at TSS treat you with the highest respect: whether you're an individual getting off the couch for the first time or an elite athlete training for the Iron Man. They know their stuff.

Page body background color is set to ivory using the body style rule.

Page text is set to the color value rgb(91, 91, 91).

Introducing CSS

One of the important principles discussed in the previous tutorial was that HTML does not define how a document should be displayed; it only defines the document's structure and content. The appearance of the page is determined by one or more style sheets written in the Cascading Style Sheets (CSS) language. Starting with this tutorial, you'll learn how to write your own CSS style sheets.

The CSS specifications are maintained by the same World Wide Web Consortium (W3C) that defines the standards for HTML. As with HTML, the CSS language has gone through several versions, the latest of which is CSS Version 3, more commonly known as **CSS3**. CSS3 is not based on a single specification but rather is built upon several **modules**, where each module is focused on a separate design topic. At the time of this writing, there were over 50 CSS3 modules with each module experiencing a different level of browser support. The W3C continues to expand the scope of the language, which means that many new design features are still at the stage where few, if any, browsers support them.

In these tutorials, you'll focus mostly on CSS features that have near-universal support among current browsers. However, you'll also examine workarounds to support older browsers and study ways to accommodate the difference between browsers in how they implement CSS designs.

TIP

You can research the support for CSS by browser version at www.caniuse.com.

Types of Style Sheets

A website's design is usually not the product of a single style sheet; rather, it is a combination of styles starting from the browser style sheet and then superseded by the user-defined style sheet, external style sheets, embedded style sheets, and concluding with inline styles (see Figure 2-1.) Let's examine each of these style sources in more detail.

Figure 2-1   **Hierarchy of styles**

inline styles

embedded styles

external styles

user-defined styles

browser styles

© 2016 Cengage Learning

The first styles to be processed are the **browser styles** or **user agent styles**, which are the styles built into the browser itself. In the absence of competing styles from other style sheets, a browser style is the one applied to the web page.

The next styles to be processed are the **user-defined styles**, which are styles defined by the user based on the settings he or she makes in configuring the browser. For example, a user with a visual impairment could alter the browser's default settings to display text with highly contrasting colors and a large font size for improved readability. Any user-defined style has precedence over its browser style counterpart.

User-defined styles can be superseded by **external styles**, which are the styles that the website author creates and places within a CSS file and links to the page. You used external style sheets in the last tutorial when you linked the Curbside Thai website to a collection of CSS files. As you saw in that tutorial, multiple documents can access the same style sheet, which makes it easy to apply a common design to an entire website.

Above the external styles in the hierarchy of style sheets are **embedded styles**, which are the styles added to the head of an HTML document. Embedded styles only apply to the HTML document in which they are created and they are not accessible to other documents in the website, but they do override any styles in an external style sheet.

Finally, at the highest order of precedence are **inline styles**, which are added as element attributes within an HTML document and thus apply to that element alone. Embedded styles and inline styles are not considered best practice and their use should be avoided because they violate the basic tenets of HTML, which is that HTML should only describe the content and structure of the document and that design styles should be placed outside of the HTML code.

The overall design of a web page is based on a combination of the styles from these different sources. Some of the styles might originate from the browser style sheet while others will be defined in an external style sheet or an embedded style sheet. Part of the challenge of CSS is determining how styles from these different style sheets interact to determine the page's final appearance.

Viewing a Page Using Different Style Sheets

You'll start your work on the Tri and Succeed Sports website by viewing how the home page appears when it is rendered in the default styles of the style sheet built into your browser.

To view the Tri and Succeed Sports home page:

▶ 1. Use your editor to open the **tss_home_txt.html** file from the html02 ▶ tutorial folder. Enter *your name* and *the date* in the comment section of the file and save the document as **tss_home.html**.

▶ 2. Take some time to scroll through the document to become familiar with its content and structure.

▶ 3. Open the **tss_home.html** page in your browser. Part of the appearance of the page is shown in Figure 2-2.

Figure 2-2   **The TSS home page rendered using only the browser style sheet**

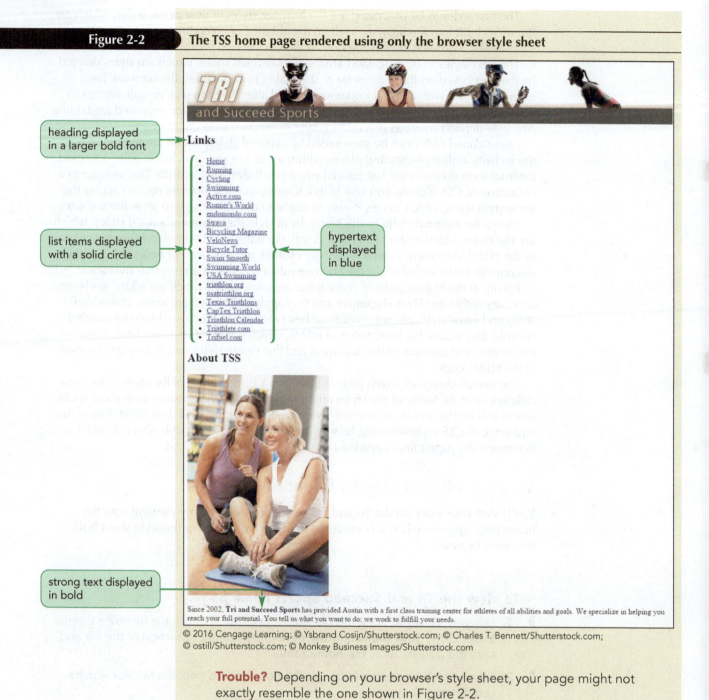

heading displayed in a larger bold font

list items displayed with a solid circle

hypertext displayed in blue

strong text displayed in bold

© 2016 Cengage Learning; © Ysbrand Cosijn/Shutterstock.com; © Charles T. Bennett/Shutterstock.com; © ostill/Shutterstock.com; © Monkey Business Images/Shutterstock.com

Trouble? Depending on your browser's style sheet, your page might not exactly resemble the one shown in Figure 2-2.

The browser style sheet applies a few specific styles to the page, including adding solid circles to the navigation list items, as well as displaying hypertext in blue, headings in a large bold font, and strong text in a bold font.

However the page layout is difficult to read. Alison has an external style sheet containing styles that will present this page in a more pleasing three-column layout. Link this page now to her style sheet file and then reload the document in your browser to view the impact on the page's appearance.

To change the layout of the TSS home page:

1. Return to the **tss_home.html** file in your HTML editor and add the following `link` element to the head section directly after the `title` element:

   ```
   <link href="tss_layout.css" rel="stylesheet" />
   ```

   Figure 2-3 highlights the newly added code in the document.

Figure 2-3	Linking to the tss_layout.css file

```
<meta charset="utf-8" />
<meta name="keywords" content="triathlon, running, swimming, cycling" />
<title>Tri and Succeed Sports</title>
<link href="tss_layout.css" rel="stylesheet" />
</head>
```

rel attribute indicates that the file is a style sheet

filename of style sheet

2. Save your changes to the file and then reopen the **tss_home.html** file in your browser. Figure 2-4 shows the appearance of the page using the layout styles defined in the tss_layout.css file.

Figure 2-4	The TSS home page using the tss_layout.css style sheet

© 2016 Cengage Learning; © Ysbrand Cosijn/Shutterstock.com; © Charles T. Bennett/Shutterstock.com; © ostill/Shutterstock.com; © Monkey Business Images/Shutterstock.com

The tss_layout.css file controls the placement of the page elements but not their appearance. The colors, fonts, and other design styles are still based on the browser style sheet.

Exploring Style Rules

If the element tag is the building block of the HTML file, then the **style rule**, which defines the styles applied to an element or group of elements, is the building block of the CSS style sheet. Style rules have the general form

```
selector {
    property1: value1;
    property2: value2;
    ...
}
```

where *selector* identifies an element or a group of elements within the document and the *property: value* pairs specify the style properties and their values applied to that element or elements. For example, the following style rule has a selector of h1 to match all h1 elements in the document and it has *property: value* pairs of color: red and text-align: center that tell the browser to display all h1 headings in red and centered on the page:

```
h1 {
    color: red;
    text-align: center;
}
```

Selectors can also be entered as comma-separated lists as in the following style rule that displays both h1 and h2 headings in red:

```
h1, h2 {
    color: red;
}
```

Like HTML, CSS ignores the use of white space, so you can also enter this style more compactly as follows:

```
h1, h2 {color: red;}
```

Writing a style rule on a single line saves space, but entering each style property on a separate line often makes your code easier to read and edit. You will see both approaches used in the CSS files you encounter on the web.

Browser Extensions

In addition to the W3C-supported style properties, most browsers supply their own extended library of style properties, known as **browser extensions**. Many of the styles that become part of the W3C specifications start as browser extensions and for older browser versions, sometimes the only way to support a particular CSS feature is through a browser extension tailored to a particular browser.

Browser extensions are identified through the use of a **vendor prefix**, which indicates the browser vendor that created and supports the property. Figure 2-5 lists the browser extensions you'll encounter in your work on web design.

Figure 2-5 **Vendor prefixes for browser extensions**

Vendor Prefix	Rendering Engine	Browsers
-khtml-	KHTML	Konqueror
-moz-	Mozilla	Firefox, Camino
-ms-	Trident	Internet Explorer
-o-	Presto	Opera, Nintendo Wii browser
-webkit-	WebKit	Android browser, Chrome, Safari

For example, one of the more recent style features added to CSS3 is the layout style to display content in separate columns. The number of columns is indicated using the `column-count` property. To apply this style in a way that supports both older and current browsers, you would include the browser extensions first followed by the most current CSS specification:

```
article {
    -webkit-column-count: 3;
    -moz-column-count: 3;
    column-count: 3;
}
```

In general, browsers process style properties in the order they're listed, ignoring those properties they don't recognize or support, so you always want the most current specifications listed last.

Embedded Style Sheets

The style rule structure is also used in embedded style sheets and inline styles. Embedded styles are inserted directly into the HTML file as metadata by adding the following `style` element to the document head

```
<style>
    style rules
</style>
```

where *style rules* are the different rules you want to embed in the HTML page. For example, the following embedded style applies the same style rules described previously to make all h1 headings in the current document appear in red and centered:

```
<style>
    h1 {
        color: red;
        text-align: center;
    }
</style>
```

Remember that, when all else is equal, the style that is loaded last has precedence over styles defined earlier. In the following code, the browser will load the embedded style sheet last, giving it precedence over the style rules in the tss_styles.css file.

```
<link href="tss_styles.css" rel="stylesheet" />
<style>
    style rules
</style>
```

TIP

To avoid confusion, always place your embedded styles after any links to external style sheet files so that the embedded styles always have precedence.

If the order of the `link` and `style` elements is reversed, the styles from the tss_styles.css file are loaded last and given precedence.

Inline Styles

The very last styles to be interpreted by the browser are inline styles, which are styles applied directly to specific elements using the following `style` attribute

```
<element style="property1: value1;property2: value2; …">
   content
</element>
```

where the `property: value` pairs define the styles, which are applied directly to that element. Thus, the following inline style sets the appearance of the h1 heading to red text centered on the page:

```
<h1 style="color: red; text-align: center;">
   Tri and Succeed Sports
</h1>
```

This style applies only to this particular h1 heading and not to any other h1 heading on the page or in the website. The advantage of inline styles is that it is clear exactly what page element is being formatted; however, inline styles are not recommended in most cases because they make changing designs tedious and inefficient. For example, if you used inline styles to format all of your headings, you would have to locate all of the h1 through h6 elements in all of the pages within the entire website and add `style` attributes to each tag. This would be no small task on a large website containing hundreds of headings spread out among dozens of pages. Likewise, it would be a nightmare if you had to modify the design of those headings at a later date. Thus, the recommended practice is to always use external style sheets that can be applied across pages and page elements.

Style Specificity and Precedence

With so many different style rules to be applied to the same document, there has to be an orderly method by which conflicts between those different rules are resolved. You've already learned that the style that is defined last has precedence, but that is not the whole story. Another important principle is that *the more specific style rule has precedence over the more general style rule*. Thus, a rule applied to a specific paragraph takes precedence over a rule applied to the entire page, and a rule applied to a section of text within that paragraph takes precedence over the rule for the paragraph. For example, in the following style rules, the color of the text in all paragraphs is set to red, taking precedence over the color black applied to the rest of the text in the page:

```
p {color: red;}
body {color: black;}
```

Note that specificity is only an issue when two or more styles conflict, as in the example above. When the style rules involve different properties (such as color and size), there is no conflict and both rules are applied. If two rules have equal specificity and thus, equal importance, then the one that is defined last has precedence.

Style Inheritance

An additional factor in how an element is rendered is that properties are passed from a parent element to its children in a process known as **style inheritance**. Thus, the following style rule sets the color of article text to blue and that rule is passed to any paragraph, header, footer, or other element nested within that article. In addition, the text in a paragraph within that article is centered:

```
article {color: blue;}
p {text-align: center;}
```

Thus, the final rendering of any page element is the result of styles drawn from rules across multiple style sheets and from properties passed down from one element to another within the hierarchy of page elements. These style sheets and style rules form the "cascade" of styles in Cascading Style Sheets.

Browser Developer Tools

If the idea of multiple style sheets and multiple style rules is intimidating, there are tools available to help you manage your styles. Most browsers include developer tools allowing the designer to view HTML code, CSS styles, and other parts of the web page. These developer tools make it easier for the designer to locate the source of a style that has been applied to a specific page element.

Each browser's developer tools are different and are constantly being updated and improved with every new browser version. However, to give you the flavor of the tools you have at your disposal, you'll examine both the HTML code and the CSS style sheet under the developer tools built into your desktop browser. Note that the figures in the steps that follow use the desktop version of the Google Chrome browser.

Accessing the Browser Developer Tools:

1. Return to the **tss_home.html** file in your browser.

2. Press **F12** to open the developer tools window.

   Trouble? If pressing F12 doesn't open the developer tools, your browser might need a different keyboard combination. In Safari for the Macintosh, you can view the developer tools by pressing ctrl+shift+I or command+option+I.

3. From the hierarchical list of elements in the web page, click the `<body>` tag if it is not already selected.

   Figure 2-6 shows the layout of panes using the developer tools under Google Chrome for the desktop.

Figure 2-6 **Developer tools in Google Chrome**

hierarchical list of elements on the web page

styles applied to the body element from tss_layout.css style sheet

the margin style in the browser style sheet has been superseded by the margin style in the tss_layout.css style sheet

diagram of the layout of the body element

styles applied to the body element from the browser style sheet

layout styles applied to the body element

© 2016 Cengage Learning; © Ysbrand Cosijn/Shutterstock.com; © Charles T. Bennett/Shutterstock.com;
© ostill/Shutterstock.com; © Monkey Business Images/Shutterstock.com

As shown in Figure 2-6, the styles pane lists the styles that have been applied to the body element. Note that the margin property from the browser style sheet has been crossed out, indicating that this browser style has been superseded by a style defined in the external style sheet.

Trouble? Every browser has a different set of developer tools and configurations. Your tools might not resemble those shown in Figure 2-6.

4. Take some time to explore the content and styles used in the other page elements by selecting the elements tags from the hierarchical list of elements.

5. Press **F12** again to close the developer tools window.

Trouble? In Safari, you can close the developer tools by pressing ctrl+shift+I or by command+option+I.

In this and future tutorials, you may find that your browser's developer tools are a great aid to working through your website designs. Most developer tools allow the user to insert new style rules in order to view their immediate impact on the page's appearance; however, these modifications are only applied during the current session and are not saved permanently. So, once you find a setting that you want to use, you must enter it in the appropriate style sheet for it to take effect permanently.

INSIGHT

Defining an !important Style

You can override the style cascade by marking a particular property with the following `!important` keyword:

```
property: value !important;
```

The following style rule sets the color of all h1 headings to orange; and because this property is marked as important, it takes precedence over any conflicting styles found in other style sheets.

```
h1 {color: orange !important;}
```

The `!important` keyword is most often used in user-defined style sheets in which the user needs to substitute his or her own styles in place of the designer's. For example, a visually impaired user might need to have text displayed in a large font with highly contrasting colors. In general, designers should not use the `!important` keyword because it interferes with the cascade order built into the CSS language.

Creating a Style Sheet

Now that you've reviewed some history and concepts behind style sheets, you'll start creating your own. You should usually begin your style sheets with comments that document the purpose of the style sheet and provide information about who created the document and when.

Writing Style Comments

Style sheet comments are entered as

```
/*
 comment
*/
```

where *comment* is the text of the comment. Because CSS ignores the presence of white space, you can insert your comments on a single line to save space as:

```
/* comment */
```

Create a style sheet file now, placing a comment with your name and the current date at the top of the file.

Writing a Style Comment:

1. Use your editor to open the **tss_styles_txt.css** file from the html02 ▸ tutorial folder.

2. Within the comment section at the top of the file, enter **your name** following the Author: comment and **the date** following the Date: comment.

3. Save the file as **tss_styles.css**.

4. Return to the **tss_home.html** file in your HTML editor and add the following `link` element directly before the closing `</head>` tag.

   ```
   <link href="tss_styles.css" rel="stylesheet" />
   ```

5. Close the tss_home.html file, saving your changes.

Defining the Character Encoding

As with HTML files, it is a good idea in every CSS document to define the character encoding used in the file. In CSS, you accomplish this using the following @charset rule

```
@charset "encoding";
```

where *encoding* defines the character encoding used in the file. Add the @charset rule to the tss_styles.css style sheet file now, specifying that the UTF-8 character set is used in the CSS code.

To indicate the character encoding:

1. Return to the **tss_styles.css** file in your editor.

2. Directly above the initial comment section, insert the line: `@charset "utf-8";`.

   Figure 2-7 highlights the new code in the style sheet.

Figure 2-7 Adding the @charset rule and style comments

the charset rule defines the character encoding used in the style sheet

```
@charset "utf-8";
/*
        New Perspectives on HTML5 and CSS3, 7th Edition
        Tutorial 2
        Tutorial Case

        TSS Typographic Style Sheet
        Author: Alison Palmer
        Date:   2017-03-01

        Filename: tss_styles.css
*/
```

CSS comments provide information about the style sheet

author name and current date

Note that only one @charset rule should appear in a style sheet and it should always precede any other characters, including comments.

3. Save your changes to the file.

Importing Style Sheets

TIP

The @import statement must always come before any other style rules in the style sheet.

The @charset rule is an example of a **CSS at-rule**, which is a rule used to send directives to the browser indicating how the contents of the CSS file should be interpreted and parsed. Another at-rule is the following @import used to import the contents of a style sheet file

```
@import url(url);
```

where *url* is the URL of an external style sheet file.

The @import is used to combine style rules from several style sheets into a single file. For example, an online store might have one style sheet named basic.css containing all of the basic styles used in every web page and another style sheet named sales.css containing styles used with merchandise-related pages. The following code imports styles from both files:

```
@import url(company.css);
@import url(support.css);
```

Using multiple `@import` rules in a CSS file has the same impact as adding multiple `link` elements to the HTML file. One advantage of the `@import` rule is that it simplifies your HTML code by placing the decision about which style sheets to include and exclude in the CSS file rather than in the HTML file.

Working with Color in CSS

The first part of your style sheet for the Tri and Succeed Sports website will focus on color. If you've worked with graphics software, you've probably made your color selections using a graphical interface where you can see your color options. Specifying color with CSS is somewhat less intuitive because CSS is a text-based language and requires colors to be defined in textual terms. This is done through either a color name or a color value.

Color Names

TIP

You can view the complete list of CSS color names by opening the demo_color_names.html file in the html02 ▶ demo folder.

You've already seen from previous code examples that you can set the color of page text using the `color` property along with a color name such as red, blue, or black. CSS supports 147 color names covering common names such as red, green, and yellow to more exotic colors such as ivory, orange, crimson, khaki, and brown.

PROSKILLS

Written Communication: Communicating in Color

Humans are born to respond to color. Studies have shown that infants as young as two months prefer bright colors with strong contrast to drab colors with little contrast, and market research for clothing often focuses on what colors are "in" and what colors are passé.

Your color choices can impact the way your website is received so you want to choose a color scheme that is tailored to the personality and interests of your target audience. Color can evoke an emotional response and is associated with particular feelings or concepts, such as

- *red*—assertive, powerful, sexy, dangerous
- *pink*—innocent, romantic, feminine
- *black*—strong, classic, stylish
- *gray*—business-like, detached
- *yellow*—warm, cheerful, optimistic
- *blue*—consoling, serene, quiet
- *orange*—friendly, vigorous, inviting
- *white*—clean, pure, straightforward, innocent

If your website will be used internationally, you need to be aware of how cultural differences can affect your audience's response to color. For instance, white, which is associated with innocence in Western cultures, is the color of mourning in China; yellow, which is considered a bright, cheerful color in the West, represents spirituality in Buddhist countries.

RGB Color Values

Because a palette of 147 color names is extremely limited for graphic design and color names can be constricting (how do you name a color that is slightly redder than ivory with a tinge of blue?), CSS also supports **color values**, in which the color is given by an exact numeric representation. CSS3 supports two types of color values: RGB values and HSL values.

RGB color values are based on classical color theory in which all colors are determined by adding three primary colors—red, green, and blue—at different levels of intensity. For example, adding all three primary colors at maximum intensity produces the color white, while adding any two of the three primary colors at maximum intensity produces the trio of complementary colors—yellow, magenta, and cyan (see Figure 2-8).

Figure 2-8	Color addition in the RGB color model

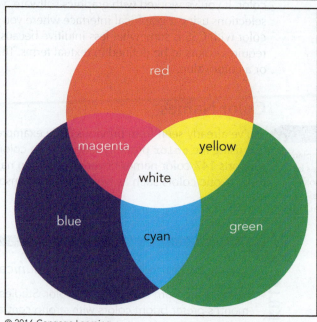

© 2016 Cengage Learning

Varying the intensity of the three primary colors extends the palette to other colors. Orange, for example, is created from a high intensity of red, a moderate intensity of green, and a total absence of blue. CSS represents these intensities mathematically as a set of numbers called an **RGB triplet**, which has the format

    rgb(red, green, blue)

where *red*, *green*, and *blue* are the intensities of the red, green, and blue components of the color. Intensities range from 0 (absence of color) to 255 (maximum intensity); thus, the color white has the value rgb(255, 255, 255), indicating that red, green, and blue are mixed equally at the highest intensity, and orange is represented by rgb(255, 165, 0). RGB triplets can describe 256^3 (16.7 million) possible colors, which is a greater number of colors than the human eye can distinguish.

RGB values are sometimes expressed as hexadecimal numbers where a **hexadecimal number** is a number expressed in the base 16 numbering system rather than in the commonly used base 10 system. In base 10 counting, numeric values are expressed using combinations of 10 characters (0 through 9). Hexadecimal numbering includes these ten numeric characters and six extra characters: A (for 10), B (for 11), C (for 12), D (for 13), E (for 14), and F (for 15). For values above 15, you use a combination of those 16 characters. For example, the number 16 has a hexadecimal representation of 10, and a value of 255 has a hexadecimal representation of FF. The style value for color represented as a hexadecimal number has the form

    #redgreenblue

where *red*, *green*, and *blue* are the hexadecimal values of the red, green, and blue components. Therefore, the color yellow could be represented either by the RGB triplet

    rgb(255,255,0)

or more compactly as the hexadecimal

    #FFFF00

Most HTML editors and graphic programs provide color picking tools that allow the user to choose a color and then copy and paste the RGB or hexadecimal color value. Hexadecimal color values have the advantage of creating smaller style sheets, which can be loaded faster—an important consideration for mobile devices. However, for others viewing and studying your style sheet code, they are more difficult to interpret than RGB values.

Finally you can enter each component value as a percentage, with 100% representing the highest intensity. In this form, you would specify the color orange with the following values

    rgb(100%, 65%, 0%)

which is equivalent to the rgb(255, 165, 0) value described above.

HSL Color Values

HSL color values were introduced in CSS3 and are based on a color model in which each color is determined by its hue, saturation, and lightness. **Hue** is the tint of the color and is usually represented by a direction on a color wheel. Hue values range from 0° up to 360°, where 0° matches the location of red on the color wheel, 120° matches green, and 240° matches blue. **Saturation** measures the intensity of the chosen color and ranges from 0% (no color) up to 100% (full color). Finally, **lightness** measures the brightness of the color and ranges from 0% (black) up to 100% (white). Figure 2-9 shows how setting the hue to 38°, the saturation to 90%, and the lightness to 60% results in a medium shade of orange.

Figure 2-9   Defining the color orange under the HSL color model

© 2016 Cengage Learning

Color values using the HSL model are described in CSS3 using

`hsl(hue, saturation, lightness)`

where *hue* is the tint of the color in degrees, *saturation* is the intensity in percent, and *lightness* is the brightness in percent of the color. Thus, a medium orange color would be represented as

`hsl(38, 90%, 60%)`

Graphic designers consider HSL easier to use because it allows them to set the initial color based on hue and then fine-tune the saturation and lightness values. This is more difficult in the RGB model because you have to balance three completely different colors to achieve the right mix. For example, the RGB equivalent to the color orange in Figure 2-9 would be the color value rgb(245, 177, 61); however, it's not immediately apparent why that mixture of red, green, and blue would result in that particular shade of orange.

Defining Semi-Opaque Colors

CSS3 introduced opacity to the CSS color models where **opacity** defines how solid the color appears. The color's opacity can be specified using either of the following `rgba` and `hsla` properties

`rgba(red, green, blue, opacity)`
`hsla(hue, saturation, lightness, opacity)`

where *opacity* sets the opacity of the color ranging from 0 (completely transparent) up to 1.0 (completely opaque). For example, the following style property uses the HSL color model to define a medium orange color with an opacity of 0.7:

`hsla(38, 90%, 60%, 0.7)`

The final appearance of a semi-opaque color is influenced by the background color. Displayed against a white background, a medium orange color would appear in a lighter shade of orange because the orange will appear mixed with the background white.

On the other hand, the same orange color displayed on a black background would appear as a darker shade of orange. The advantage of using semi-transparent colors is that it makes it easier to create a color theme in which similarly tinted colors are blended with other colors on the page.

Setting Text and Background Colors

Now that you've studied how CSS works with colors, you can start applying color to some of the elements displayed on the Tri and Succeed Sports website. CSS supports the following styles to define both the text and background color for each element on your page

```
color: color;
background-color: color;
```

where *color* is either a color value or a color name.

Alison wants to use an HSL color value (27, 72%, 72%) to set the background of the document to orange and she would like the text of the home page to appear in a medium gray color on an ivory background. The style rules to modify the appearance of these document elements are

```
html {
    background-color: hsl(27, 72%, 72%);
}
body {
    color: rgb(91, 91, 91);
    background-color: ivory;
}
```

The `html` selector in this code selects the entire HTML document so that any part of the browser window background that is not within the page body will be displayed using the HSL color (27, 72%, 72%).

Within the page body, Alison wants the h1 and h2 headings to be displayed in white text on dark and lighter orange colors using the RGB color values (222, 128, 60) and (235, 177, 131) respectively. The style rules are

```
h1 {
    color: white;
    background-color: rgb(222, 128, 60);
}

h2 {
    color: white;
    background-color: rgb(235, 177, 131);
}
```

REFERENCE

Setting Text and Background Color

- To set the text color of an element, use the following property

  ```
  color: color;
  ```

- To set the background color of an element, use the following property

  ```
  background-color: color;
  ```

  where *color* is a color name or a color value.

Next, add style rules for text and background colors to the tss_styles.css file.

To define background and text colors:

1. Add the following code within the HTML and Body Styles section:

```
html {
    background-color: hsl(27, 72%, 72%);
}

body {
    color: rgb(91, 91, 91);
    background-color: ivory;
}
```

Saturation and lightness values in an hsl color value must be expressed as percentages.

2. Add the following style rules within the Heading Styles section:

```
h1 {
    color: white;
    background-color: rgb(222, 128, 60);
}

h2 {
    color: white;
    background-color: rgb(235, 177, 131);
}
```

TIP

Almost 8% of all men and 0.5% of all women have some sort of color blindness. Because red-green color blindness is the most common type of color impairment, you should avoid using red text on a green background and vice-versa.

Figure 2-10 highlights the new style rules.

Figure 2-10 **Adding text and background colors**

```
/* HTML and Body Styles */        selects the HTML
                                   element
html {
    background-color: hsl(27, 72%, 72%);
}
                                   selects the body
                                   element
body {
    color: rgb(91, 91, 91);
    background-color: ivory;
}


/* Heading Styles */              selects all h1 headings

h1 {
    color: white;
    background-color: rgb(222, 128, 60);
}
                                  selects all h2 headings

h2 {
    color: white;
    background-color: rgb(235, 177, 131);
}
```

sets the document background to a medium orange color

displays page body text in gray on an ivory background

displays h1 heading text in white on a dark orange background

displays h2 heading text in white on a medium orange background

3. Save your changes to the file and then reload the **tss_home.html** file in your browser. Figure 2-11 shows the appearance of the page under the new styles.

Figure 2-11   **Text and background colors in the web page**

white h1 heading text on a dark orange background

browser window background is medium orange

white h2 heading text on a light orange background

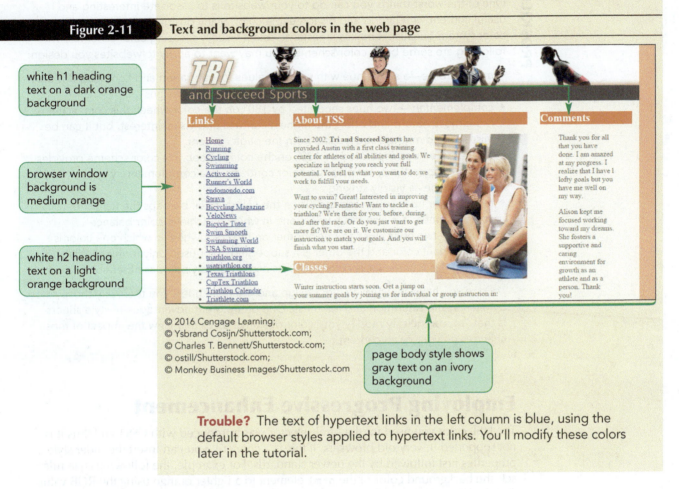

© 2016 Cengage Learning;
© Ysbrand Cosijn/Shutterstock.com;
© Charles T. Bennett/Shutterstock.com;
© ostill/Shutterstock.com;
© Monkey Business Images/Shutterstock.com

page body style shows gray text on an ivory background

Trouble? The text of hypertext links in the left column is blue, using the default browser styles applied to hypertext links. You'll modify these colors later in the tutorial.

Problem Solving: Choosing a Color Scheme

One of the worst things you can do to your website is to associate interesting and useful content with jarring and disagreeable color. Many designers prefer the HSL color system because it makes it easier to select visually pleasing color schemes. The following are some basic color schemes you may want to apply to websites you design:

- *monochrome*—a single hue with varying values for saturation and lightness; this color scheme is easy to manage but is not as vibrant as other designs
- *complementary*—two hues separated by 180° on the color wheel; this color scheme is the most vibrant and offers the highest contrast and visual interest, but it can be misused and might distract users from the page content
- *triad*—three hues separated by 120° on the color wheel; this color scheme provides the same opportunity for pleasing color contrasts as a complementary design, but it might not be as visibly striking
- *tetrad*—four hues separated by 90° on the color wheel; perhaps the richest of all color schemes, it is also the hardest one in which to achieve color balance
- *analogic*—two hues close to one another on the color wheel in which one color is the dominant color and the other is a supporting color used only for highlights and nuance; this scheme lacks color contrasts and is not as vibrant as other color schemes

Once you have selected a color design and the main hues, you then vary those colors by altering the saturation and lightness. One of the great advantages of style sheets is that you can quickly modify your color design choices and view the impact of those changes on your page content.

Employing Progressive Enhancement

The HSL color you used for the html selector was introduced with CSS3 and thus it is not supported in very old browsers. If this is a concern, you can insert the older style properties first followed by the newer standards. For example, the following style rule sets the background color of the `html` element to a lighter orange using the RGB value first, and then the equivalent HSL value.

```
html {
    background-color: rgb(235, 177, 131);
    background-color: hsl(27, 72%, 72%);
}
```

Old browsers that don't recognize the HSL color value will ignore it and use the RGB value, while browsers that recognize both values will use the one that is defined last, which in this case is the HSL value. This is an example of a technique known as **progressive enhancement**, which places code conforming to older standards before newer properties, providing support for old browsers but still allowing newer standards and techniques to be used by the browsers that support them.

You show Alison the work you've done on colors. She's pleased with the ease of using CSS to modify the design and appearance of elements on the Tri and Succeed Sports website. In the next session, you'll continue to explore CSS styles, focusing on text styles.

REVIEW

Session 2.1 Quick Check

1. What are inline styles, embedded styles, and external style sheets? Which would you use to define a design for an entire web site?
2. What keyword do you add to a style property to override style precedence and style inheritance?
3. Provide the code to enter the style comment "Tri and Succeed Sports Color Styles".
4. Provide the style rule to display block quote text in red using an RGB triplet.
5. The color chartreuse is located at 90° on the color wheel with 100% saturation and 50% lightness. Provide a style rule to display address text in black with chartreuse as the background color.
6. What is progressive enhancement?
7. Based on the following style rule for paragraph text, which style property will be used by an older browser that supports only CSS2?

```
p {
    color: rgb(232, 121, 50);
    color: hsla(23, 80%, 55%, 0.75);
}
```

8. Provide a style rule to display h1 and h2 headings with a background color of yellow (an equal mixture of red and green at highest intensity with no blue) at 70% opacity.

Session 2.2 Visual Overview:

The `@font-face` rule imports a web font into the style sheet.

```css
@font-face {
    font-family: Quicksand;
    src: url('Quicksand-Regular.woff') format('woff'),
         url('Quicksand-Regular.ttf') format('truetype');
}

body {
    color: rgb(91, 91, 91);
    background-color: ivory;
    font-family: Verdana, Geneva, sans-serif;
}

h1 {font-size: 2.2em;}
h2 {font-size: 1.5em;}

h1, h2 {
    font-family: Quicksand, Verdana, Geneva, sans-serif;
    letter-spacing: 0.1em;
}

aside blockquote {
    color: rgb(232, 165, 116);
}

nav > ul {
    line-height: 2em;
}

body > footer address {
    background-color: rgb(222,128,60);
    color: rgba(255, 255, 255, 0.7);
    font: normal small-caps bold 0.9em/3em
          Quicksand, Verdana, Geneva, sans-serif;
    text-align: center;
}
```

The `font-family` property lists the possible fonts used for the element text.

The `font-size` property sets the text size in absolute or relative units.

The `em unit` is a relative unit of length that expresses a size relative to the font size of the containing element.

The `letter-spacing` property sets the **kerning** or space between letters.

The aside blockquote selector selects blockquote elements that are descendants of the aside element.

The nav > ul selector selects ul elements that are direct children of the nav element.

The `line-height` property sets the height of the lines of text in the element.

The `text-align` property sets the horizontal alignment of the text.

CSS Typography

The h1 heading is displayed in the Quicksand font with a font size of 2.2em and letter spacing of 0.1em.

Links

- Home
- Running
- Cycling
- Swimming
- Active.com
- Runner's World
- endomondo.com
- Strava
- Bicycling Magazine
- VeloNews
- Bicycle Tutor
- Swim Smooth
- Swimming World
- USA Swimming
- triathlon.org
- usatriathlon.org
- Texas Triathlons
- CapTex Triathlon
- Triathlon Calendar
- Triathlete.com
- Trifuel.com

Navigation list is double-spaced with a line height of 2em.

About TSS

Since 2002, **Tri and Succeed Sports** has provided Austin with a first class training center for athletes of all abilities and goals. We specialize in helping you reach your full potential. You tell us what you want to do; we work to fulfill your needs.

Want to swim? Great! Interested in improving your cycling? Fantastic! Want to tackle a triathlon? We're there for you: before, during, and after the race. Or do you just want to get more fit? We are on it. We customize our instruction to match your goals. And you will finish what you start.

Body text is displayed in a Verdana font.

Classes

Winter instruction starts soon. Get a jump on your summer goals by joining us for individual or group instruction in:

- **Running**: We start with the basics to help you run faster and farther than you ever thought possible without aches and pains.
- **Cycling**: The indoor bike trainers at TSS include everything you need to refine your technique, stamina, and power for improved results on the road.
- **Swimming**: The open water swim can be one of the most frightening sports to master. Our classes begin with basic techniques so that your swim can be very enjoyable, and not a chore.

Contact us to set up individual instruction and assessment.

Our Philosophy

Athletes are the foundation of every successful training program. The best coach is an experienced guide who begins with each athlete's hopes, dreams and desires and then tailors a training plan based on that individuals's current fitness and lifestyle. Since 2002, TSS has helped hundreds of individuals achieve success in many fitness areas. The winner is not the one who finishes first but anyone who starts the race and perseveres. Join us and begin exploring the possible.

Comments

Thank you for all that you have done. I am amazed at my progress. I realize that I have l lofty goals but you have me well on my way.

Alison kept me focused working toward my dreams. She fosters a supportive and caring environment for growth as an athlete and as a person. Thank you!

You do it right! Your track record proves it. Proud to be a TSS athlete and I'm honored to have you all as my coaches and support team.

The coaches at TSS treat you with the highest respect: whether you're an individual getting off the couch for the first time or an elite athlete training for the Iron Man. They know their stuff.

I just completed my first marathon, following your fitness schedule to the letter. Never once did I come close to bonking and two days later I felt ready for another race!

TRI AND SUCCEED SPORTS • 41 VENTURE DR. • AUSTIN, TX 78711 • 512.555.9917

Page footer is centered and displayed in small caps as specified by the body > footer address style rule.

The h2 headings are displayed in the Quicksand font with a font size of 1.5em and letter spacing of 0.1em.

Exploring Selector Patterns

The following style rule matches every h1 element in the HTML document, regardless of the location of the h1 heading:

```
h1 {
    color: red;
}
```

This style rule will match an h1 heading located within a page article in the same way it matches an h1 heading nested within an aside element or the body header or the body footer. Often, however, you will want your style rules to apply to specific elements, such as h1 headings found within articles but not anywhere else. To direct a style rule to specific elements, you'll use **selector patterns** to match only those page elements that correspond to a specified pattern.

Contextual Selectors

The first selector pattern you'll examine is a **contextual selector**, which specifies the context under which a particular page element is matched. Context is based on the hierarchical structure of the document, which involves the relationships between a **parent element** containing one or more **child elements** and within those child elements several levels of **descendant elements**. A contextual selector relating a parent element to its descendants has the following pattern

```
parent descendant { styles }
```

where *parent* is a parent element, *descendant* is a descendant of that parent and *styles* are styles applied to the descendant element. For example, the following style rule sets the text color of h1 headings to red but only when those headings are nested within the header element:

```
header h1 {
    color: red;
}
```

As shown in the code that follows, the descendant element does not have to be a direct child of the parent; in fact, it can appear several levels below the parent in the hierarchy. This means that the above style rule matches the h1 element in the following HTML code:

```
<header>
    <div>
        <h1>Tri and Succeed Sports</h1>
    </div>
</header>
```

In this example, the h1 element is a direct child of the div element; but, because it is still a descendant of the header element, the style rule still applies.

Contextual selectors follow the general rule discussed in the last session; that is, the more specific style is applied in preference to the more general rule. For instance, the following style rules would result in h1 headings within the section element being displayed in red while all other h1 headings would appear in blue:

```
section h1 {color: red;}
h1          {color: blue;}
```

Figure 2-12 describes some of the other contextual selectors supported by CSS.

Figure 2-12   **Contextual selectors**

Selector	Description
*	Matches any element
elem	Matches the element elem located anywhere in the document
elem1, elem2, …	Matches any of the elements elem1, elem2, etc.
parent descendant	Matches the descendant element that is nested within the parent element at some level
parent > child	Matches the child element that is a child of the parent element
elem1 + elem2	Matches elem2 that is immediately preceded by the sibling element elem1
elem1 ~ elem2	Matches elem2 that follows the sibling element elem1

To match any element, use the **wildcard selector** with the * character. For example, the following style rule matches every child of the article element, setting the text color to blue:

```
article > * {color: blue;}
```

Sibling selectors are used to select elements based on elements that are adjacent to them in the document hierarchy. The following style rule uses the + symbol to select the h2 element, but only if it is immediately preceded by an h1 element:

```
h1+h2 {color: blue;}
```

On the other hand, the following style rule uses the ~ symbol to select any h2 element that is preceded (but, not necessarily immediately) by an h1 element:

```
h1 ~ h2 {color: blue;}
```

Figure 2-13 provides additional examples of selectors and highlights in red those elements in the document that would be selected by the specified selector.

Figure 2-13   **Contextual selector patterns**

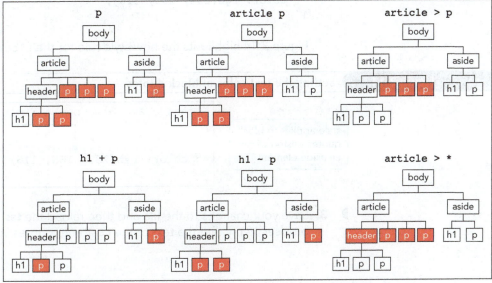

Remember that, because of style inheritance, any style applied to an element is passed down the document tree. Thus, a style applied to a `header` element is automatically passed down to elements contained within that header unless that style conflicts with a more specific style.

REFERENCE

Using Contextual Selectors

- To select all elements, use the * selector.
- To select a single element, use the `elem` selector, where `elem` is the name of the element.
- To select a descendant element, use the `parent descendant` selector where `parent` is a parent element and `descendant` is an element nested within the parent at some lower level.
- To select a child element, use the `parent > child` selector.
- To select a sibling element, `elem2`, that directly follows `elem1`, use the `elem1 + elem2` selector.
- To select a sibling element, `elem2`, that follows, but not necessarily directly `elem1`, use the `elem1 ~ elem2` selector.

Now, you'll create a style rule to change the text color of the customer testimonials on the Tri and Succeed Sports home page to a dark orange using the RGB color value rgb(232, 165, 116). You'll use a contextual selector to apply the style rule only to block quotes that are descendants of the `aside` element.

To create style rule with a contextual selector:

1. If you took a break after the previous session, make sure the **tss_styles.css** file is open in your editor.

2. Within the Aside and Blockquote Styles section, insert the following style rule:

```
aside blockquote {
    color: rgb(232, 165, 116);
}
```

Figure 2-14 highlights the new style rule for the `blockquote` element.

Figure 2-14   **Setting the text color of block quotes**

```
/* Aside and Blockquote Styles */

aside blockquote {
    color: rgb(232, 165, 116);
}
```

style applies to block quotes nested within an aside element

sets the text color to dark orange

3. Save your changes to the file and then reload the **tss_home.html** file in your browser. Verify that the text of the customer quotes appears in orange.

Attribute Selectors

Selectors also can be defined based on attributes and attribute values within elements. Two attributes, id and class, are often key in targeting styles to specific elements. Recall that the id attribute is used to identify specific elements within the document. To apply a style to an element based on its id, you use either the selector

```
#id
```

or the selector

```
elem#id
```

where id is the value of the id attribute and elem is the name of the element. Because ids are supposed to be unique, either form is acceptable but including the element name removes any confusion about the location of the selector. For example, the selector for the following h1 heading from the HTML file

```
<h1 id="title">Tri and Succeed Sports</h1>
```

can be entered as either #title or h1#title in your CSS style sheet.

Because no two elements can share the same ID, HTML uses the class attribute to identify groups of elements that share a similar characteristic or property. For example, the following h1 element and paragraph element both belong to the intro class of elements:

```
<h1 class="intro">Tri and Succeed Sports</h1>
<p class="intro"> … </p>
```

To select an element based on its class value, use the selector

```
elem.class
```

where class is the value of the class attribute. Thus the following style rule displays the text of h1 headings from the intro class in blue:

```
h1.intro {color: blue;}
```

TIP

An element can belong to several classes by including the class names in a space-separated list in the class attribute.

To apply the same style rule to all elements of a particular class, omit the element name. The following style rule displays the text of all elements from the intro class in blue:

```
.intro {color: blue;}
```

While id and class are the most common attributes to use with selectors, any attribute or attribute value can be the basis for a selector. Figure 2-15 lists all of the CSS attribute selector patterns based on attributes and attribute values.

Figure 2-15 Attribute selectors

Selector	Selects	Example	Selects
elem#id	Element *elem* with the ID value *id*	h1#intro	The h1 heading with the id *intro*
#id	Any element with the ID value *id*	#intro	Any element with the id *intro*
elem.class	All *elem* elements with the class attribute value *class*	p.main	All paragraphs belonging to the *main* class
.class	All elements with the class value *class*	.main	All elements belonging to the *main* class
elem[att]	All *elem* elements containing the *att* attribute	a[href]	All hypertext elements containing the href attribute
elem[att="text"]	All *elem* elements whose *att* attribute equals *text*	a[href="top.html"]	All hypertext elements whose href attribute equals *top.html*
elem[att~="text"]	All *elem* elements whose *att* attribute contains the word *text*	a[rel~="glossary"]	All hypertext elements whose rel attribute contains the word *glossary*
elem[att|="text"]	All *elem* elements whose *att* attribute value is a hyphen-separated list of words beginning with *text*	p[id|="first"]	All paragraphs whose id attribute starts with the word *first* in a hyphen-separated list of words
elem[att^="text"]	All *elem* elements whose *att* attribute begins with *text* [**CSS3**]	a[rel^="prev"]	All hypertext elements whose rel attribute begins with *prev*
elem[att$="text"]	All *elem* elements whose *att* attribute ends with *text* [**CSS3**]	a[href$="org"]	All hypertext elements whose href attribute ends with *org*
elem[att*="text"]	All *elem* elements whose *att* attribute contains the value *text* [**CSS3**]	a[href*="faq"]	All hypertext elements whose href attribute contains the text string *faq*

Note that some of the attribute selectors listed in Figure 2-15 were first introduced in CSS3 and, thus, might not be supported in older browsers.

Using Attribute Selectors

- To select an element based on its ID, use the *elem#id* or *#id* selector, where *elem* is the name of the element and *id* is the value of the id attribute.
- To select an element based on its class value, use the *.class* or the *elem.class* selectors, where *class* is the value of the class attribute.
- To select an element that contains an *att* attribute, use *elem[att]*.
- To select an element based on whether its attribute value equals a specified value, *val*, use *elem[att="val"]*.

In the Tri and Succeed Sports home page, the main content is enclosed within an `article` element with the ID *about_tss*. Alison wants the h1 and h2 heading styles you entered in the last session to be applied only to `h1` and `h2` elements within articles that have this particular ID. Revise the style sheet now.

To apply an id selector:

1. Return to the **tss_styles.css** file in your editor.

2. Change the selectors for the `h1` and `h2` elements in the Heading Styles section to `article#about_tss h1` and `article#about_tss h2` respectively.

   Figure 2-16 highlights the revised selectors in the style sheet.

Figure 2-16   Using an id selector

selects h1 headings within an article element with the about_tss id

selects h2 headings within an article element with the about_tss id

```
/* Heading Styles */

article#about_tss h1 {
    color: white;
    background-color: rgb(222, 128, 60);
}

article#about_tss h2 {
    color: white;
    background-color: rgb(235, 177, 131);
}
```

3. Save your changes to the file and then reload the **tss_home.html** file in your browser. Verify that the design of the h1 and h2 headings is only applied to the headings in the about_tss article but not to the other headings on the page.

The `article` element will be used in other pages in the Tri and Succeed Sports website. Alison has provided you with three additional HTML files containing descriptions of the instruction her company offers for runners, cyclists, and swimmers. On those pages the `article` elements have the `class` attribute with the value *syllabus*. Create style rules for the `h1` and `h2` elements within the articles on those pages.

To apply a class selector:

1. Use your editor to open the **tss_run_txt.html**, **tss_bike_txt.html**, and **tss_swim_txt.html** files from the html02 ▸ tutorial folder. Enter *your name* and *the date* in the comment section of each file and save them as **tss_run.html**, **tss_bike.html**, and **tss_swim.html** respectively.

2. Within each of the three files insert the following `link` elements before the closing `</head>` tag to link these files to the tss_layout.css and tss_styles.css files, respectively:

```
<link href="tss_layout.css" rel="stylesheet" />
<link href="tss_styles.css" rel="stylesheet" />
```

3. Take some time to study the content and structure of the files. Note that the `article` element has the `class` attribute with the value *syllabus*. Save your changes to the files.

4. Return to the **tss_style.css** file in your editor.

5. Within the Heading Styles section, add the following style rule to display the text of h1 and h2 headings in medium gray on a light purple background:

```
article.syllabus h1, article.syllabus h2 {
   background-color: rgb(255, 185, 255);
   color: rgb(101, 101, 101);
}
```

Figure 2-17 highlights the new style rule in the file.

Figure 2-17   Using a class selector

selects h1 and h2 headings within article elements of the syllabus class

displays the content in medium gray text on a light purple background

```
article.syllabus h1, article.syllabus h2 {
   background-color: rgb(255, 185, 255);
   color: rgb(101, 101, 101);
}

/* Aside and Blockquote Styles */
```

6. Save your changes to the style sheet and then open the **tss_run.html** file in your browser. Figure 2-18 shows the appearance of the h1 and h2 headings on this page.

Figure 2-18   Headings on the running class page

h1 heading text shows medium gray on a light purple background

Guided Running and Racing

The TSS running program is designed is to guide and motivate runners to a personal best in their run training and racing. The training program is heavily coached and has a moderately aggressive approach to achieving your personal best. We will educate you on proper running form, biomechanics, training, nutrition and mental toughness

You will work with a TSS coach twice weekly to help you accomplish your goals and you'll have the companionship of others reaching for similar goals. At times, we'll have assistant coaches to decrease the coach to athlete ratio for a higher quality experience. Spend your workouts completing track workouts, hills repeats tempo runs, strength/power running, endurance strength training, and more. Each week will challenge you, and be tailored towards your goals from sprint races, 5K runs, or full-distance marathons.

The course meets for 90 minutes twice a week. You have the choice among the following morning and evening sessions:

- 11:30 AM - 1:00 PM (MW)
- 5:00 PM - 6:30 PM (TR)

h2 heading text shows medium gray on a light purple background

Course Outline

The running class will meet at the Falk Running Center and when weather permits we'll be outside at the Falk Running Track.

7. Use the navigation links on the page to view the content and design of the cycling and the swimming pages, and then confirm that the h1 and h2 headings on these pages have similar formats.

INSIGHT

Calculating Selector Specificity

The general rule in CSS is that the more specific selector takes precedence over the more general selector, but the application of this rule is not always clear. For example, which of the following selectors is the more specific?

```
header h1.top
```

vs.

```
#main h1
```

To answer that question, CSS assigns a numeric value to the specificity of the selector using the formula

```
(inline, ids, classes, elements)
```

where *inline* is 1 for an inline style and 0 otherwise, *ids* is 1 for every id in the selector, *classes* is 1 for every class or attribute in the selector, and *elements* is 1 for every element in the selector. For example, the selector `ul#links li.first` would have a value of (0, 1, 1, 2) because it references one id value (`#links`), 1 class value (`.first`) and two elements (`ul` and `li`). Specificity values are read from left to right with a larger number considered more specific than a smaller number.

To answer our earlier question: the selector `header h1.top` has a value of (0, 0, 1, 2) but `#main h1` has a value of (0, 1, 0, 1) and, thus, is considered more specific because 0101 is larger than 0012.

By the way, every inline style has the value (1, 0, 0, 0) and thus will always be more specific than any style set in an embedded or external style sheet.

Working with Fonts

Typography is the art of designing the appearance of characters and letters on a page. So far, the only typographic style you've used is the `color` property to set the text color. For the rest of this session, you'll explore other properties in the CSS family of typographical styles, starting with choosing the text font.

Choosing a Font

Text characters are based on **fonts** that define the style and appearance of each character in the alphabet. The default font used by most browsers for displaying text is Times New Roman, but you can specify a different font for any page element using the following `font-family` property

```
font-family: fonts;
```

where *fonts* is a comma-separated list, also known as a **font stack**, of specific or generic font names. A **specific font** is a font that is identified by name, such as Times New Roman or Helvetica, and based on a font definition file that is stored on the user's computer or accessible on the web. A **generic font** describes the general appearance of the characters in the text but does not specify any particular font definition file. Instead, the font definition file is selected by the browser to match the general characteristics of the generic font. CSS supports the following generic font groups:

- **serif**—a typeface in which a small ornamentation appears at the tail end of each character
- **sans-serif**—a typeface without any serif ornamentation
- **monospace**—a typeface in which each character has the same width; often used to display programming code
- **cursive**—a typeface that mimics handwriting with highly stylized elements and flourishes; best used in small doses for decorative page elements
- **fantasy**—a highly ornamental typeface used for page decoration; should never be used as body text

Because you have no control over which font definition file the browser will choose for a generic font, the common practice is to list specific fonts first, in order of preference, and end the font stack with a generic font. If the browser cannot find any of the specific fonts listed, it uses a generic font of its own choosing. For example, the style

```
font-family: 'Arial Black', Gadget, sans-serif;
```

tells a browser to use the Arial Black font if available; if not, to look for the Gadget font; and if neither of those fonts are available, to use its generic sans-serif font. Note that font names containing one or more blank spaces (such as Arial Black) must be enclosed within single or double quotes.

Because the available fonts vary by operating system and device, the challenge is to choose a font stack limited to **web safe fonts**, which are fonts that will be displayed in mostly the same way in all operating systems and on all devices. Figure 2-19 lists several commonly used web safe font stacks.

| Figure 2-19 | Web safe font stacks |

Arial
abcdefghijklmnopqrstuvwxyz/1234567890
font-family: Arial, Helvetica, sans-serif;

Arial Black
abcdefghijklmnopqrstuvwxyz/1234567890
font-family: 'Arial Black', Gadget, sans-serif;

Century Gothic
abcdefghijklmnopqrstuvwxyz/1234567890
font-family: 'Century Gothic', sans-serif;

Comic Sans MS
abcdefghijklmnopqrstuvwxyz/1234567890
font-family: 'Comic Sans MS', cursive;

Courier New
abcdefghijklmnopqrstuvwxyz/1234567890
font-family: 'Courier New', Courier, monospace;

Georgia
abcdefghijklmnopqrstuvwxyz/1234567890
font-family: Georgia, serif;

Impact
abcdefghijklmnopqrstuvwxyz/1234567890
font-family: Impact, Charcoal, sans-serif;

Lucida Console
abcdefghijklmnopqrstuvwxyz/1234567890
font-family: 'Lucida Console', Monaco, monospace;

Lucida Sans Unicode
abcdefghijklmnopqrstuvwxyz/1234567890
font-family: 'Lucida Sans Unicode', 'Lucida Grande', sans-serif;

Palatino Linotype
abcdefghijklmnopqrstuvwxyz/1234567890
font-family: 'Palatino Linotype', 'Book Antiqua', Palatino, serif;

Tahoma
abcdefghijklmnopqrstuvwxyz/1234567890
font-family: Tahoma, Geneva, sans-serif;

Times New Roman
abcdefghijklmnopqrstuvwxyz/1234567890
font-family: 'Times New Roman', Times, serif;

Trebuchet MS
abcdefghijklmnopqrstuvwxyz/1234567890
font-family: 'Trebuchet MS', Helvetica, sans-serif;

Verdana
abcdefghijklmnopqrstuvwxyz/1234567890
font-family: Verdana, Geneva, sans-serif;

TIP

Including too many fonts can make your page difficult to read. Don't use more than two or three typefaces within a single page.

A general rule for printing is to use sans-serif fonts for headlines and serif fonts for body text. For computer monitors, which have lower resolutions than printed material, the general rule is to use sans-serif fonts for headlines and body text, leaving serif fonts for special effects and large text.

Currently, the body text for the Tri and Succeed Sports website is based on a serif font applied by the browser. You'll add the following font stack for sans-serif fonts, which will take precedence over the browser font style rule:

```
font-family: Verdana, Geneva, sans-serif;
```

As a result of this style rule, the browser will first try to load the Verdana font, followed by the Geneva font. If both of these fonts are unavailable, the browser will load a generic sans-serif font of its own choosing. Add this font family to the style rule for the page body.

To specify a font family for the page body:

1. Return to the **tss_styles.css** file in your editor.

2. Add the following style to the style rule for the body element:

   `font-family: Verdana, Geneva, sans-serif;`

   Figure 2-20 highlights the new style for the body element.

Font stacks should be listed in a comma-separated list with the most desired fonts listed first.

Figure 2-20	Specifying a font stack

browser attempts to use the Verdana font first, followed by Geneva, and finally any generic sans-serif font

```
body {
    color: rgb(91, 91, 91);
    background-color: ivory;
    font-family: Verdana, Geneva, sans-serif;
}
```

3. Save your changes to the file and then reload the **tss_home.html** file in your browser. Figure 2-21 shows the revised appearance of the body text using the sans-serif font.

Figure 2-21	Sans-serif font applied to the home page

Links

- Home
- Running
- Cycling
- Swimming
- Active.com
- Runner's World
- endomondo.com
- Strava
- Bicycling Magazine
- VeloNews
- Bicycle Tutor
- Swim Smooth
- Swimming World
- USA Swimming
- triathlon.org
- usatriathlon.org
- Texas Triathlons
- CapTex Triathlon
- Triathlon Calendar
- Triathlete.com
- Trifuel.com

About TSS

Since 2002, **Tri and Succeed Sports** has provided Austin with a first class training center for athletes of all abilities and goals. We specialize in helping you reach your full potential. You tell us what you want to do; we work to fulfill your needs.

Want to swim? Great! Interested in improving your cycling? Fantastic! Want to tackle a triathlon? We're there for you: before, during, and after the race. Or do you just want to get more fit? We are on it. We customize our instruction to match your goals. And you will finish what you start.

Classes

Winter instruction starts soon. Get a jump on your summer goals by joining us for individual or group instruction in:

Comments

Thank you for all that you have done. I am amazed at my progress. I realize that I have I lofty goals but you have me well on my way.

Alison kept me focused working toward my dreams. She fosters a supportive and caring environment for growth as an athlete and as a person. Thank you!

4. View the other three pages in the website to verify that the sans-serif font is also applied to the body text on those pages.

Exploring Web Fonts

Because web safe fonts limit your choices to a select number of fonts that have universal support, another approach is to supply a **web font** in which the definition font is supplied to the browser in an external file. Figure 2-22 describes the different web font file formats and their current levels of browser support. The format most universally accepted in almost all current browsers and on almost all devices is the Web Open Font Format (WOFF).

Figure 2-22　　**Web font formats**

Format	Description	Browser
Embedded OpenType (EOT)	A compact form of OpenType fonts designed for use as embedded fonts in style sheets	IE
TrueType (TTF)	Font standard used on the Mac OS and Microsoft Windows operating systems	IE, Firefox, Chrome, Safari, Opera
OpenType (OTF)	Font format built on the TrueType format developed by Microsoft	IE, Firefox, Chrome, Safari, Opera
Scalable Vector Graphics (SVG)	Font format based on an XML vocabulary designed to describe resizable graphics and vector images	Chrome, Safari
Web Open Font Format (WOFF)	The W3C recommendation font format based on OpenType and TrueType with compression and additional metadata	IE, Firefox, Chrome, Safari, Opera

Web font files can be downloaded from several sites on the Internet. In many cases, you must pay for their use; in some cases, the fonts are free but are licensed only for non-commercial use. You should always check the EULA (End User License Agreement) before downloading and using a web font to make sure you are in compliance with the license. Finally, many web fonts are available through Web Font Service Bureaus that supply web fonts on their servers, which page designers can link to for a fee.

The great advantage of a web font is that it gives the author more control over the fonts used in the document; the disadvantage is that it becomes another file for the browser to download, adding to the time required to render the page. This can be a huge issue with mobile devices in which you want to limit the number and size of files downloaded by the browser.

The @font-face Rule

To access and load a web font, you add the following @font-face rule to the style sheet

```
@font-face {
    font-family: name;
    src: url('url1') format('text1'),
         url('url2') format('text2'),
    …;
    descriptor1: value1;
    descriptor2: value2;
    …
}
```

where *name* is the name of the font, *url* is the location of the font definition file, *text* is an optional text description of the font format, and the *descriptor: value* pairs are optional style properties that describe when the font should be used. Note several font definition files can be placed in a comma-separated list, allowing the browser to pick the file format it supports. For example, the following `@font-face` rule defines a font named Gentium installed from either the Gentium.woff file or if that fails, the Gentium.ttf file:

```
@font-face {
    font-family: Gentium;
    src: url('Gentium.woff') format('woff'),
        url('Gentium.ttf') format('truetype');
}
```

If the style sheet includes instructions to display a web font in italics, boldface, or other variants, the browser will modify the font, which sometimes results in poorly rendered text. However if the manufacturer has supplied its own version of the font variant, you can direct the browser to use that font file. For example the following `@font-face` rule directs the browser to use the GentiumBold.woff or GentiumBold.ttf file when it needs to display Gentium in bold.

```
@font-face {
    font-family: Gentium;
    src: url('GentiumBold.woff') format('woff'),
        url('GentiumBold.ttf') format('truetype');
    font-weight: bold;
}
```

Note that the web font is given the same font-family name Gentium, which is the font name you use in a font stack. The added *descriptor: value* pair and `font-weight: bold` declarations tell the browser that these font files should be used with boldface Gentium.

Once you've defined a web font using the `@font-face` rule, you can include it in a font stack. For example, the following style will attempt to load the Gentium font first, followed by Arial Black, Gadget, and then a sans-serif font of the browser's choosing:

```
font-family: Gentium, 'Arial Black', Gadget, sans-serif;
```

Alison decides that the rendering of the Verdana font in the h1 and h2 heading text is too thick and heavy. She has located a web font named Quicksand that she is free to use under the End User License Agreement and she thinks it would work better for the page headings. She asks you to add this font to the style sheet and apply it to all `h1` and `h2` elements.

To install and use a web font:

1. Return to the **tss_styles.css** file in your editor.

2. Directly after the `@charset` rule at the top of the file, insert the following `@font-face` rule:

```
@font-face {
    font-family: Quicksand;
    src: url('Quicksand-Regular.woff') format('woff'),
        url('Quicksand-Regular.ttf') format('truetype');
}
```

3. At the top of the section for Heading Styles, insert the style rule:

```
h1, h2 {
    font-family: Quicksand, Verdana, Geneva, sans-serif;
}
```

Figure 2-23 highlights the code to create and use the Quicksand web font.

Figure 2-23   Accessing a web font

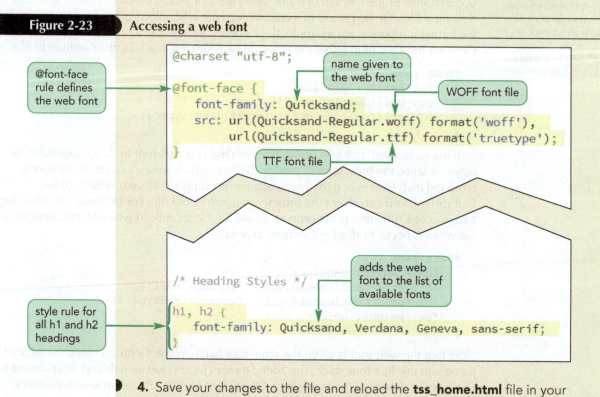

4. Save your changes to the file and reload the **tss_home.html** file in your browser. Figure 2-24 shows the revised appearance of the h1 and h2 headings using the Quicksand web font.

Figure 2-24   Quicksand font used for all h1 and h2 headings

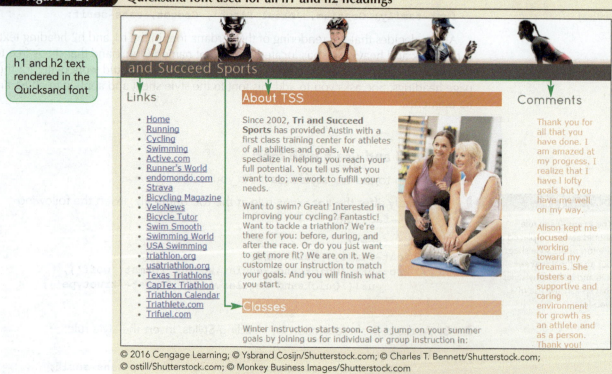

© 2016 Cengage Learning; © Ysbrand Cosijn/Shutterstock.com; © Charles T. Bennett/Shutterstock.com; © ostill/Shutterstock.com; © Monkey Business Images/Shutterstock.com

Using Google Fonts

Google Fonts (*google.com/fonts*) hosts a library of free web fonts. Once you have selected fonts from the Google Font catalog, you will receive the code for the `link` element to access the font files. For example, the following `link` element accesses a style sheet for a Google font named Monoton:

```
<link href="http://fonts.googleapis.com/css?family=Monoton"
 rel="stylesheet" />
```

To use the Monoton font, include the following `font-family` property in the CSS style sheet:

```
font-family: Monoton, fantasy;
```

Google fonts, like all web fonts, need to be used in moderation because they can greatly increase the load times for your website. To help you know when you have exceeded a reasonable limit, the Google Fonts page shows a timer estimating the load times for all of the fonts you have selected. You can also limit the size of the font file by using the `&text` parameter to specify only those characters you want to download. For example, the following `link` element limits the Monoton font file to only the characters found in "TSS Sports":

```
<link href="http://fonts.googleapis.com/css?family=Monoton
 &text=TSS%20Sports" rel="stylesheet" />
```

Note that blank spaces are indicated using the `%20` character. If you have a longer text string, you can shorten the value of the `href` attribute by removing duplicate characters, as the order of characters doesn't matter.

Setting the Font Size

Another important consideration in typography is the text size, which is defined using the following `font-size` property

```
font-size: size;
```

where *size* is a length in a CSS unit of measurement. Size values for any of these measurements can be whole numbers (0, 1, 2 ...) or decimals (0.5, 1.6, 3.9 ...). Lengths (and widths) in CSS are expressed in either absolute units or relative units.

Absolute Units

Absolute units are units that are fixed in size regardless of the output device and are usually used only with printed media. They are specified in one of five standard units of measurement: `mm` (millimeters), `cm` (centimeters), `in` (inches), `pt` (points), and `pc` (picas). For example, to set the font size of your page body text to a 12pt font, you would apply the following style rule:

```
body {font-size: 12pt;}
```

Note that you should not insert a space between the size value and the unit abbreviation.

Relative Units

Absolute units are of limited use because, in most cases, the page designer does not know the exact properties of the device rendering the page. In place of absolute units, designers use **relative units**, which are expressed relative to the size of other objects within the web page or relative to the display properties of the device itself.

The basic unit for most devices is the **pixel (px)**, which represents a single dot on the output device. A pixel is a relative unit because the actual pixel size depends on the resolution and density of the output device. A desktop monitor might have a pixel density of about 96ppi (pixels per inch), laptops are about 100 to 135ppi, while mobile phones have dense displays at 200 to 300ppi or more. Typically, most browsers will apply a base font size of 16px to body text with slightly larger font sizes applied to h1, h2, and h3 headings. You can override these default sizes with your own style sheet. For example, the following style rules set the font size of the text on the page body to 10px and the font size of all h1 headings text to 14px:

```
body {font-size: 10px;}
h1 {font-size: 14px;}
```

TIP

You explore typography styles using the demo_css.html file from the html02 ▶ demo folder.

The exact appearance of the text depends greatly on the device's pixel density. While a 10px font might be fine on a desktop monitor, that same font size could be unreadable on a mobile device.

Scaling Fonts with ems and rems

Because the page designer doesn't know the exact properties of the user's device, the common practice is to make the text **scalable** with all font sizes expressed relative to a default font size. There are three relative measurements used to provide scalability: percentages, ems, and rems.

A percentage sets the font size as a percent of the font size used by the containing element. For example, the following style rule sets the font size of an h1 heading to 200% or twice the font size of the h1 heading's parent element:

```
h1 {font-size: 200%;}
```

The em unit acts the same way as a percentage, expressing the font size relative to the font size of the parent element. Thus, to set the font size of h1 headings to twice the font size used in their parent elements, you can also use the style rule:

```
h1 {font-size: 2em;}
```

The em unit is the preferred style unit for web page text because it makes it easy to develop pages in which different page elements have consistent relative font sizes under any device.

Context is very important with relative units. For example, if this h1 element is placed within a body element where the font size is 16px, the h1 heading will have a font size twice that size or 32px. On the other hand, an h1 heading nested within an article element where the font size is 9px will have a font size of 18px. In general, you can think of font sizes based on percentages and em units as relative to the size of immediately adjacent text.

The fact that relative units cascade through the style sheet can lead to confusing outcomes. For example, consider the following set of style rules for an h1 element nested within an article element in the page body:

```
body {font-size: 16px;}
body > article {font-size: 0.75em;}
body > article > h1 {font-size: 1em;}
```

Glancing at the style rules, you might conclude that the font size of the h1 element is larger than the font size used in the article element (since 1em > 0.75em). However, this is not the case: both font sizes are the same. Remember, em unit expresses the text size relative to font size used in the parent element and since the h1 heading is contained within the article element its font size of 1em indicates that it will have the same size used in the article element. In this case, the font size in the article element is 75% of 16px or 12 pixels as is the size of h1 headings in the article.

Because of this confusion, some designers advocate using the **rem** or **root em unit** in which all font sizes are always expressed relative to the font size used in the html element. Using rems, the following style rule sets the font size of article text to 75% of 16 pixels or 12 pixels while the h1 heading size is set to 16 pixels:

```
html {font-size: 16px;}
article {font-size: 0.75rem;}
article > h1 {font-size: 1rem;}
```

The rem unit has become increasingly popular with designers as browser support grows and its use might possibly replace the use of the em unit as the font size unit of choice in upcoming years.

Using Viewport Units

Another relative unit is the **viewport unit** in which lengths are expressed as a percentage of the width or height of the browser window. As the browser window is resized, the size of text based on a viewport unit changes to match. CSS3 introduced four viewport units: vw, vh, vmin, and vmax where

- 1vw = 1% of the browser window width
- 1vh = 1% of the browser window height
- 1vmin = 1vw or 1vh (whichever is smaller)
- 1vmax = 1vw or 1vh (whichever is larger)

For example, if the browser window is 1366 pixels wide, a length of 1vw would be equal to 13.66px. If the width of the window is reduced to 780 pixels, 1vw is automatically rescaled to 7.8 pixels. Auto-rescaling has the advantage that font sizes set with a viewport unit will be sized to match the browser window, maintaining a consistent page layout. The disadvantage is that page text can quickly become unreadable if the browser window becomes too small.

Sizing Keywords

Finally, you also can express font sizes using the following keywords: xx-small, x-small, small, medium, large, x-large, xx-large, larger, or smaller. The font size corresponding to each of these keywords is determined by the browser. Note that the larger and smaller keywords are relative sizes, making the font size of the element one size larger or smaller than the font size of the container element. For example, the following style rules set the sidebar to be displayed in a small font, while an h1 element nested within that aside element is displayed in a font one size larger (medium):

```
aside {font-size: small;}
aside > h1 {font-size: larger;}
```

Use em units now to set the font size for the h1 and h2 headings, as well as the text within the navigation list and the aside element.

To set font sizes of the page elements:

▶ 1. Return to the **tss_styles.css** file in your editor.

▶ 2. Add the following style rules directly below the Heading Styles comment to define the font sizes for h1 and h2 headings throughout the website:

```
h1 {
    font-size: 2.2em;
}

h2 {
    font-size: 1.5em;
}
```

3. Go to the Aside and Blockquote Styles section and add the following style rule to set the default font size of text in the aside element to 0.8em:

```
aside {
    font-size: 0.8em;
}
```

4. Go to the Navigation Styles section and add the following style rule to set the default font size of text in the navigation list to 0.8em:

```
nav {
    font-size: 0.8em;
}
```

Figure 2-25 highlights the new font sizes for the website.

Figure 2-25 **Setting font sizes for the website**

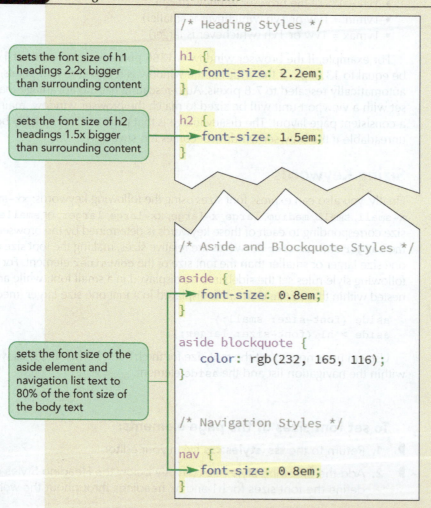

sets the font size of h1 headings 2.2x bigger than surrounding content

sets the font size of h2 headings 1.5x bigger than surrounding content

sets the font size of the aside element and navigation list text to 80% of the font size of the body text

```
/* Heading Styles */

h1 {
    font-size: 2.2em;
}

h2 {
    font-size: 1.5em;
}
```

```
/* Aside and Blockquote Styles */

aside {
    font-size: 0.8em;
}

aside blockquote {
    color: rgb(232, 165, 116);
}


/* Navigation Styles */

nav {
    font-size: 0.8em;
}
```

5. Save your changes to the file and then reload the **tss_home.html** file in your browser. Figure 2-26 shows the revised font sizes of the headings, navigation list, and aside element.

Figure 2-26   Revised font sizes in the About TSS page

© 2016 Cengage Learning; © Monkey Business Images/Shutterstock.com

Note that the text of the h1 heading in the page article is larger than the text in the h1 headings from the navigation list and the aside element even though all headings have a font size of 2.2em. This is because you reduced the default font size of the text in the navigation list and aside elements by 80% and thus the h1 headings in those elements are also reduced by the same proportion.

Controlling Spacing and Indentation

CSS supports styles to control some basic typographic attributes, such as kerning, tracking, and leading. Kerning measures the amount of space between characters, while **tracking** measures the amount of space between words. The properties to control an element's kerning and tracking are

```
letter-spacing: value;
word-spacing:   value;
```

where *value* is the size of space between individual letters or words. You specify these sizes with the same units that you use for font sizing. The default value for both kerning and tracking is 0 pixels. A positive value increases the letter and word spacing, while a negative value reduces the space between letters and words. If you choose to make your text scalable under a variety of devices and resolutions, you can express kerning and tracking values as percentages or em units.

Leading measures the amount of space between lines of text and is set using the following line-height property

```
line-height: size;
```

TIP

You can give multi-line titles more impact by tightening the space between the lines using a large font-size along with a small line-height.

where *size* is a value or a percentage of the font size of the text on the affected lines. If no unit is specified, the size value represents the ratio of the line height to the font size. The default value is 1.2 or 1.2em so that the line height is 20% larger than the font size. By contrast, the following style sets the line height to twice the font size, making the text appear double-spaced:

```
line-height: 2em;
```

An additional way to control text spacing is to set the indentation for the first line of a text block by using the following `text-indent` property

```
text-indent: size;
```

where *size* is expressed in absolute or relative units, or as a percentage of the width of the text block. For example, an indentation value of 5% indents the first line by 5% of the width of the block. The indentation value also can be negative, extending the first line to the left of the text block to create a **hanging indent**.

Alison suggests you increase the kerning used in the h1 and h2 headings to 0.1em so that the letters don't crowd each other on the page. She also asks that you increase the line height of the text of the navigation list to 2em so that the list of links on the home page is double-spaced.

To set font sizes of the page elements:

▶ 1. Return to the **tss_styles.css** file in your editor.

▶ 2. In the Heading Styles section, insert the following style as part of the style rule for the h1, h2 selector:

```
letter-spacing: 0.1em;
```

▶ 3. Scroll down to the Navigation Styles section near the bottom of the file and insert the following style rule for the text of ul elements nested within the nav element:

```
nav > ul {
    line-height: 2em;
}
```

Figure 2-27 highlights the letter-spacing and line-height styles for the website.

Figure 2-27   **Controlling letter spacing and line height**

```
h1, h2 {
    font-family: Quicksand, Verdana, Geneva, sans-serif;
    letter-spacing: 0.1em;
}
```

sets the space between letters to 0.1em

```
/* Navigation Styles */

nav {
    font-size: 0.8em;
}

nav > ul {
    line-height: 2em;
}
```

double spaces the list of hypertext links

> **4.** Save your changes to the file and then reload the **tss_home.html** file in your browser. Verify that the space between letters in the h1 and h2 headings has been increased and the list of links is now double-spaced.

By increasing the kerning in the headings, you've made the text appear less crowded, making it easier to read.

Working with Font Styles

The style sheet built into your browser applies specific styles to key page elements; for instance, `address` elements are often displayed in italic, headings are often displayed in boldface. You can specify a different font style using the following `font-style` property

```
font-style: type;
```

where `type` is `normal`, `italic`, or `oblique`. The italic and oblique styles are similar in appearance, but might differ subtly depending on the font in use.

To change the weight of the text, use the following `font-weight` property

```
font-weight: weight;
```

where `weight` is the level of bold formatting applied to the text. CSS uses the keyword `bold` for boldfaced text and `normal` for non-boldfaced text. You also can use the keywords `bolder` or `lighter` to express the weight of the text relative to its surrounding content. Finally for precise weights, CSS supports weight values ranging from 100 (extremely light) up to 900 (extremely heavy) in increments of 100. In practice, however, it's difficult to distinguish font weights at that level of precision.

You can apply decorative features to text through the following `text-decoration` property

```
text-decoration: type;
```

where `type` equals `none` (for no decoration), `underline`, `overline`, or `line-through`. The `text-decoration` property supports multiple types so that the following style places a line under and over the element text:

```
text-decoration: underline overline;
```

Note that the `text-decoration` style has no effect on non-textual elements, such as inline images.

To control the case of the text within an element, use the following `text-transform` property

```
text-transform: type;
```

where `type` is `capitalize`, `uppercase`, `lowercase`, or `none` (to make no changes to the text case). For example, to capitalize the first letter of each word in an element, apply the style:

```
text-transform: capitalize;
```

Finally, CSS supports variations of the text using the `font-variant` property

```
font-variant: type;
```

where `type` is `normal` (for no variation) or `small-caps` (small capital letters). Small caps are often used in legal documents, such as software agreements, in which the capital letters indicate the importance of a phrase or point, but the text is made small so as not to detract from other elements in the document.

Aligning Text Horizontally and Vertically

Text can be aligned horizontally or vertically within an element. To align the text horizontally, use the following `text-align` property

```
text-align: alignment;
```

where `alignment` is `left`, `right`, `center`, or `justify` (align the text with both the left and the right margins).

To vertically align the text within each line, use the `vertical-align` property

```
vertical-align: alignment;
```

where `alignment` is one of the keywords described in Figure 2-28.

| Figure 2-28 | Values of the vertical-align property |

Value	Description
baseline	Aligns the baseline of the element with the baseline of the parent element
bottom	Aligns the bottom of the element with the bottom of the lowest element in the line
middle	Aligns the middle of the element with the middle of the surrounding content in the line
sub	Subscripts the element
super	Superscripts the element
text-bottom	Aligns the bottom of the element with the bottom of the text in the line
text-top	Aligns the top of the element with the top of the text in the line
top	Aligns the top of the element with the top of the tallest object in the line

TIP

The subscript and superscript styles lower or raise text vertically, but do not resize it. To create true subscripts and superscripts, you also must reduce the font size.

Instead of using keywords, you can specify a length or a percentage for an element to be vertically aligned relative to the surrounding content. A positive value moves the element up as in the following style that raises the element by half the line height of the surrounding content:

```
vertical-align: 50%;
```

A negative value drops the content. For example the following style drops the element an entire line height below the baseline of the current line:

```
vertical-align: -100%;
```

Combining All Text Formatting in a Single Style

You can combine most of the text and font style properties into the following shorthand `font` property

```
font: style variant weight size/height family;
```

where `style` is the font's style, `variant` is the font variant, `weight` is the font weight, `size` is the font size, `height` is the height of each line, and `family` is the font stack. For example, the following style rule displays the element text in italic, bold, and small capital letters using Arial or another sans-serif font, with a font size of 1.5em and a line height of 2em:

```
font: italic small-caps bold 1.5em/2em Arial, sans-serif;
```

You do not have to include all of the values in the shorthand `font` property; the only required values are the *size* and *family* values. A browser assumes the default value for any omitted property; however, you must place any properties that you do include in the order indicated above.

At the bottom of each page in the Tri and Succeed Sports website, Alison has nested an `address` element within the body footer. The default browser style sheet displays address text in italics. Alison suggests that you display the text in a semi-transparent bold white font on a dark orange background and centered on the page. She also suggests that you use the small-cap font variant to add visual interest, and she wants you to increase the height of the address line to 3em. To make your CSS code more compact, you'll set all of the font values using the shorthand `font` property.

To apply the font property:

▶ 1. Return to the **tss_styles.css** file in your editor.

▶ 2. Go down to the Footer Styles section and add the following style rule:

```
body > footer address {
    background-color: rgb(222,128,60);
    color: white;
    color: rgba(255, 255, 255, 0.7);
    font: normal small-caps bold 0.9em/3em
            Quicksand, Verdana, Geneva, sans-serif;
    text-align: center;
}
```

Note that this style rule uses progressive enhancement by placing each color rule on its own line so that browsers that do not support semi-transparent colors will display the address text in white. Figure 2-29 highlights the style rule for the footer.

Figure 2-29 ▶ **Style rule for the body footer**

▶ 3. Save your changes to the file and then reload the **tss_home.html** file in your browser. Figure 2-30 shows the revised appearance of the body footer.

Figure 2-30   **Formatted body footer**

Athletes are the foundation of every successful training program. The best coach is an experienced guide who begins with each athlete's hopes, dreams and desires and then tailors a training plan based on that individuals's current fitness and lifestyle. Since 2002, TSS has helped hundreds of individuals achieve success in many fitness areas. The winner is not the one who finishes first but anyone who starts the race and perseveres. Join us and begin exploring the possible.

Our Philosophy

I just completed my first marathon, following your fitness schedule to the letter. Never once did I come close to bonking and two days later I felt ready for another race!

body footer

Tri and Succeed Sports • 41 Venture Dr. • Austin, TX 78711 • 512.555.9917

PROSKILLS

Decision Making: Selecting a Font

HTML and CSS provide a lot of typographic design options. Your main goal, however, is always to make your text easily readable. When designing your page, keep in mind the following principles:

- *Keep it plain*—Avoid large blocks of italicized text and boldfaced text. Those styles are designed for emphasis, not readability.
- *Sans-serif vs. serif*—Sans-serif fonts are more readable on a computer monitor and should be used for body text. Reserve the use of serif, cursive, and fantasy fonts for page headings and special decorative elements.
- *Relative vs. absolute*—Font sizes can be expressed in relative or absolute units. A relative unit like the em unit is more flexible and will be sized to match the screen resolution of the user's device, but you have more control over your page's appearance with an absolute unit. Generally, you want to use an absolute unit only when you know the configuration of the device the reader is using to view your page.
- *Size matters*—Almost all fonts are readable at a size of 14 pixels or greater; however, for smaller sizes, you should choose fonts that were designed for screen display, such as Verdana and Georgia. If you have to go really small (at a size of only a few pixels), you should either use a web font that is specially designed for that purpose or replace the text with an inline image.
- *Avoid long lines*—In general, try to keep the length of your lines to 60 characters or fewer. Anything longer is difficult to read.

When choosing any typeface and font style, the key is to test your selection on a variety of browsers, devices, screen resolutions, and densities. Don't assume that text that is readable and pleasing to the eye on your computer screen will work as well on another device.

Alison likes the typographic changes you made to her website. In the next session, you'll explore how to design styles for hypertext links and lists, and you'll learn how to use CSS to add special visual effects to your web pages.

REVIEW

Session 2.2 Quick Check

1. Provide a selector to match all `address` elements that are direct children of the `footer` element.

2. The initial h1 heading in a document has the ID *top*. Provide a style rule to display the text of this h1 heading in Century Gothic, Helvetica, or a sans-serif font.

3. For the following style rules, what is the font size of the h1 heading in pixels?

```
body {font-size: 16px;}
body > article {font-size: 0.75em;}
body > article > h1 {font-size: 1.5em;}
```

4. Provide a style rule to set the size of body text to 2% of the viewport width.

5. Provide a style rule to remove underlining from the hypertext links marked with the <a> tag and nested within a navigation list.

6. Provide the `@font-face` rule to create a web font named Cantarell based on the font files cantarell.woff and cantarell.ttf.

7. Provide a style rule to display all `blockquote` elements belonging to the Reviews class in italic and indented 3em.

8. Provide a style rule to horizontally center all h1 through h6 headings and to display their text with normal weight.

Session 2.3 Visual Overview:

The `list-style-type` property defines the appearance of the list marker.

The `visited` pseudo-class selects previously-visited links; the `link` pseudo-class selects unvisited links.

The `margin-top` property sets the margin space above the element.

The `hover` pseudo-class selects links that are hovered over; the `active` pseudo-class selects actively-clicked links.

The `first-of-type` pseudo-class selects the first element type of the parent element.

The `list-style-image` property is used to insert an image for the list marker.

The `quotes` property defines characters for quotation marks.

The `content` property is used to insert content into a page element.

The `nth-of-type` pseudo-class selects the nth element type of the parent.

The `last-of-type` pseudo-class selects the last element type of the parent element.

The `before` and `after` pseudo-elements are used to select page space before and after a page element.

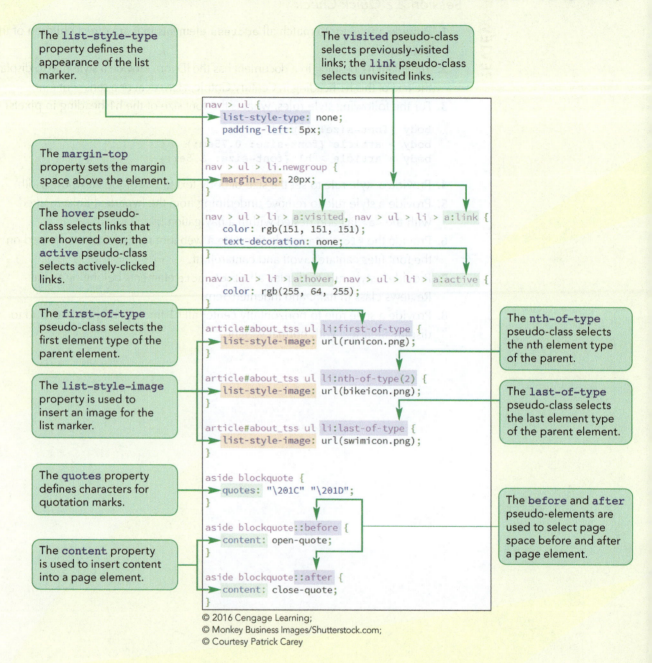

```
nav > ul {
    list-style-type: none;
    padding-left: 5px;
}

nav > ul > li.newgroup {
    margin-top: 20px;
}

nav > ul > li > a:visited, nav > ul > li > a:link {
    color: rgb(151, 151, 151);
    text-decoration: none;
}

nav > ul > li > a:hover, nav > ul > li > a:active {
    color: rgb(255, 64, 255);
}

article#about_tss ul li:first-of-type {
    list-style-image: url(runicon.png);
}

article#about_tss ul li:nth-of-type(2) {
    list-style-image: url(bikeicon.png);
}

article#about_tss ul li:last-of-type {
    list-style-image: url(swimicon.png);
}

aside blockquote {
    quotes: "\201C" "\201D";
}

aside blockquote::before {
    content: open-quote;
}

aside blockquote::after {
    content: close-quote;
}
```

© 2016 Cengage Learning;
© Monkey Business Images/Shutterstock.com;
© Courtesy Patrick Carey

Pseudo Elements and Classes

Style of the link changes when the mouse pointer hovers over it.

Open quote character is inserted using the content property.

Close quote character is inserted using the content property.

Links

Home
Running
Cycling
Swimming
Active.com
Runner's World
endomondo.com
Strava
Bicycling Magazine
VeloNews
Bicycle Tutor
Swim Smooth
Swimming World
USA Swimming

triathlon.org
usatriathlon.org
Texas Triathlons
CapTex Triathlon
Triathlon Calendar
Triathlete.com
Trifuel.com

Top margins at each newgroup class are set to 20 pixels.

An image is used to mark each of the three list markers.

About TSS

Since 2002, **Tri and Succeed Sports** has provided Austin with a first class training center for athletes of all abilities and goals. We specialize in helping you reach your full potential. You tell us what you want to do; we work to fulfill your needs.

Want to swim? Great! Interested in improving your cycling? Fantastic! Want to tackle a triathlon? We're there for you: before, during, and after the race. Or do you just want to get more fit? We are on it. We customize our instruction to match your goals. And you will finish what you start.

Classes

Winter instruction starts soon. Get a jump on your summer goals by joining us for individual or group instruction in:

- **Running**: We start with the basics to help you run faster and farther than you ever thought possible without aches and pains.

- **Cycling**: The indoor bike trainers at TSS include everything you need to refine your technique, stamina, and power for improved results on the road.

- **Swimming**: The open water swim can be one of the most frightening sports to master. Our classes begin with basic techniques so that your swim can be very enjoyable, and not a chore.

This is the first li element.

This is the last li element.

This is the second li element.

Comments

" Thank you for all that you have done. I am amazed at my progress. I realize that I have I lofty goals but you have me well on my way."

" Alison kept me focused working toward my dreams. She fosters a supportive and caring environment for growth as an athlete and as a person. Thank you!"

" You do it right! Your track record proves it. Proud to be a TSS athlete and I'm honored to have you all as my coaches and support team."

" The coaches at TSS treat you with the highest respect: whether you're an individual getting off the couch for the first time or an elite athlete training for the Iron Man. They know their stuff."

" I just completed my first marathon, following your fitness schedule to the letter. Never once did I come close to bonking and two days later I felt ready for another race!"

Formatting Lists

In this session, you'll explore how to use CSS to create styles for different types of lists that you learned about in Tutorial 1. You'll start by examining how to create styles for the list marker.

Choosing a List Style Type

The default browser style for unordered and ordered lists is to display each list item alongside a symbol known as a **list marker**. By default, unordered lists are displayed with a solid disc while ordered lists are displayed with numerals. To change the type of list marker or to prevent any display of a list marker, apply the following list-style-type property

```
list-style-type: type;
```

where `type` is one of the markers described in Figure 2-31.

Figure 2-31	Values of the list-style-type property

list-style-type	Marker(s)
disc	●
circle	○
square	■
decimal	1, 2, 3, 4, ...
decimal-leading-zero	01, 02, 03, 04, ...
lower-roman	i, ii, iii, iv, ...
upper-roman	I, II, III, IV, ...
lower-alpha	a, b, c, d, ...
upper-alpha	A, B, C, D, ...
lower-greek	α, β, γ, δ, ...
upper-greek	A, B, Γ, Δ, ...
none	no marker displayed

TIP

List style properties can be applied to individual items in a list, through the li element.

For example, the following style rule marks each item from an ordered list with an uppercase Roman numeral:

```
ol {list-style-type: upper-roman;}
```

Creating an Outline Style

Nested lists can be displayed in an outline style through the use of contextual selectors. For example, the following style rules create an outline style for a nested ordered list:

```
ol {list-style-type: upper-roman;}
ol ol {list-style-type: upper-alpha;}
ol ol ol {list-style-type: decimal;}
```

In this style, the `ol` selector selects the top level of the list, displaying the list items with a Roman numeral. The `ol ol` selector selects the second level, marking the items with capital letters. The third level indicated by the `ol ol ol` selector is marked with decimal values.

To see how these style rules are rendered on a page, you'll apply them to the three pages that Alison has set up describing the running, cycling, and swimming programs offered by Tri and Succeed sports. Each page contains a syllabus outlining the course of study for the next several weeks.

To apply an outline style:

1. If you took a break after the previous session, make sure the **tss_styles.css** file is open in your editor.

2. Scroll down to the List Styles section and insert the following style rules to format nested ordered lists within the syllabus article:

```
article.syllabus ol {
    list-style-type: upper-roman;
}

article.syllabus ol ol {
    list-style-type: upper-alpha;
}

article.syllabus ol ol ol {
    list-style-type: decimal;

}
```

Figure 2-32 highlights the style rule for the nested lists.

Figure 2-32   **Creating an outline style for a nested list**

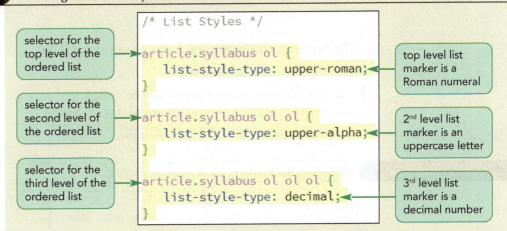

3. Save your changes to the file and then open the **tss_run.html** file in your browser. As shown in Figure 2-33, the syllabus for the class should now be displayed in an outline style.

Figure 2-33 Class outline

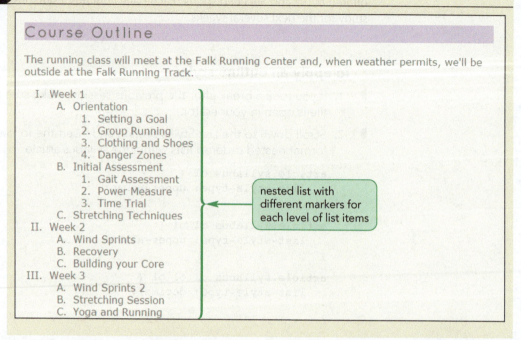

Course Outline

The running class will meet at the Falk Running Center and, when weather permits, we'll be outside at the Falk Running Track.

I. Week 1
  A. Orientation
    1. Setting a Goal
    2. Group Running
    3. Clothing and Shoes
    4. Danger Zones
  B. Initial Assessment
    1. Gait Assessment
    2. Power Measure
    3. Time Trial
  C. Stretching Techniques
II. Week 2
  A. Wind Sprints
  B. Recovery
  C. Building your Core
III. Week 3
  A. Wind Sprints 2
  B. Stretching Session
  C. Yoga and Running

nested list with different markers for each level of list items

Alison points out that the hypertext links from the navigation list are displayed with a disc marker. She asks you to remove the markers from the navigation list by setting the `list-style-type` property to `none`.

To remove the markers from navigation lists:

1. Return to the **tss_styles.css** file in your editor.

2. Go to the Navigation Styles section and, within the style rule for the `nav > ul` selector, add the style `list-style-type: none;`

   Figure 2-34 highlights the new style.

Figure 2-34 Removing list markers from navigation lists

```
nav > ul {
    line-height: 2em;
    list-style-type: none;
}
```

displays no markers for unordered lists within the nav element

3. Save your changes to the file and then open the **tss_home.html** file in your browser. Verify that there are no markers next to the navigation list items in the left column.

4. Go to the other three pages in the website and verify that navigation lists in these pages also do not have list markers.

Designing a List

- To define the appearance of the list marker, use the property

  ```
  list-style-type: type;
  ```

  where *type* is disc, circle, square, decimal, decimal-leading-zero, lower-roman, upper-roman, lower-alpha, upper-alpha, lower-greek, upper-greek, or none.
- To insert a graphic image as a list marker, use the property

  ```
  list-style-image: url(url);
  ```

  where *url* is the URL of the graphic image file.
- To set the position of list markers, use the property

  ```
  list-style-position: position;
  ```

  where *position* is inside or outside.
- To define all of the list style properties in a single style, use the property

  ```
  list-style: type url(url) position;
  ```

Using Images for List Markers

You can supply your own graphic image for the list marker using the following `list-style-image` property

```
list-style-image: url(url);
```

where *url* is the URL of a graphic file containing the marker image. Marker images are only used with unordered lists in which the list marker is the same for every list item. For example, the following style rule displays items from unordered lists marked with the graphic image in the redball.png file:

```
ul {list-style-image: url(redball.png);}
```

Alison has an icon image in a file named runicon.png that she wants to use for the classes listed on the Tri and Succeed Sports home page in the About TSS article. Apply her image file to the list now.

To use an image for a list marker:

1. Return to the **tss_styles.css** file in your editor.

2. At the top of the List Styles section, insert the following style rule:

   ```
   article#about_tss ul {
       list-style-image: url(runicon.png);
   }
   ```

   Figure 2-35 highlights the style rule to use the runicon.png file as the list marker image.

Figure 2-35

Figure 2-35 **Displaying an image in place of a list marker**

style rule applied to the unordered list within the about_tss article

```
/* List Styles */

article#about_tss ul {
    list-style-image: url(runicon.png);
}
```

displays the runicon.png file as the list marker

3. Save your changes to the file and then open the **tss_home.html** file in your browser. As shown in Figure 2-36 the items in the unordered list now use the runicon.png image file as their list marker.

Figure 2-36 **Unordered list with the runicon.png image marker**

Classes

Winter instruction starts soon. Get a jump on your summer goals by joining us for individual or group instruction in:

Running: We start with the basics to help you run faster and farther than you ever thought possible without aches and pains.

Cycling: The indoor bike trainers at TSS include everything you need to refine your technique, stamina, and power for improved results on the road.

Swimming: The open water swim can be one of the most frightening sports to master. Our classes begin with basic techniques so that your swim can be very enjoyable, and not a chore.

runicon.png image file

© Courtesy Patrick Carey

Notice that the list marker is aligned with the baseline of the first line in each list item. This is the default placement for list marker images.

Setting the List Marker Position

CSS treats each list item as a block-level element, placed within a virtual box in which the list marker is placed outside of the list text. You can change this default behavior using the following `list-style-position` property

```
list-style-position: position;
```

where *position* is either `outside` (the default) or `inside`. Placing the marker inside the virtual box causes the list text to flow around the marker. Figure 2-37 shows how the `list-style-position` property affects the flow of the text around the bullet marker.

Figure 2-37   Values of the list-style-position property

All three of the list styles just discussed can be combined within the following shorthand `list-style` property

```
list-style: type image position;
```

where `type` is the marker type, `image` is an image to be displayed in place of the marker, and `position` is the location of the marker. For example, the following style rule displays unordered lists using the marker found in the bullet.png image placed inside the containing block:

```
ul {list-style: circle url(bullet.png) inside;}
```

If a browser is unable to display the bullet.png image, it uses a default circle marker instead. You do not need to include all three style properties with the list style. Browsers will set any property you omit to the default value.

Allison notes that there is a lot of unused space to the left of the items in the navigation list now that the list markers have been removed. She wants you to move the navigation list into that empty space. To do this, you'll work with the CSS styles for margin and padding space.

Working with Margins and Padding

Block-level elements like paragraphs or headings or lists follow the structure of the **box model** in which the content is enclosed within the following series of concentric boxes:

- the content of the element itself
- the **padding space**, which extends from the element's content to a border
- the **border** surrounding the padding space
- the **margin space** comprised of the space beyond the border up to the next page element

Figure 2-38 shows a schematic diagram of the box model for a sample paragraph discussing athletes at Tri and Succeed Sports.

Figure 2-38 The CSS box model

© 2016 Cengage Learning

The browser's internal style sheet sets the size of the padding, border, and margin spaces but you can specify different sizes in your style sheet.

Setting the Padding Space

To set the width of the padding space, use the following `padding` property

    padding: size;

where `size` is expressed in one of the CSS units of length or the keyword `auto` to let the browser automatically choose the padding. For example, the following style rule sets the padding space around every paragraph to 20 pixels:

    p {padding: 20px;}

The padding space can also be defined for each of the four sides of the virtual box by writing the padding property as follows

    padding: top right bottom left;

where `top` is the size of the padding space along the top edge of the content, `right` is padding along the right edge, `bottom` is the size of the bottom padding, and `left` is the size of the padding along the left edge. Thus, the following style rule creates a padding space that is 10 pixels on top, 0 pixels to the right, 15 pixels on the bottom and 5 pixels to the left:

    p {padding: 10px 0px 15px 5px;}

To help remember this order, think of moving clockwise around the box, starting with the top edge. While you don't have to supply values for all of the edges, the values you supply are interpreted based on how many values you supply. So, if you specify a single value, it's applied to all four sides equally. Likewise, two values set the padding spaces for the top/bottom edges and then the right/left edges. For example, the following style rule sets the top and bottom padding spaces at 10 pixels and the right and left padding spaces at 5 pixels:

    p {padding: 10px 5px;}

If you insert three values, the padding spaces are set for the top, right/left, and bottom edges. Thus, the following rule sets the size of the top padding space to 10 pixels, the left/right spaces to 5 pixels, and the bottom space to 0 pixels:

    p {padding: 10px 5px 0px;}

If you want to define the padding space for one edge but not for the others, you can apply the following style properties:

```
padding-top: size;
padding-right: size;
padding-bottom: size;
padding-left: size;
```

The following style rule sets the top padding of every paragraph to 10 pixels but it does not specify a padding size for any of the other three remaining edges:

```
p {padding-top: 10px;}
```

With ordered and unordered lists, the default style used by most browsers is to set the left padding space to 40 pixels in order to provide the extra space needed for the list markers. Removing the list markers doesn't remove this padding space. Allison suggests you recover this unused space by reducing the size of the left padding space in the navigation list to 5 pixels.

To change the left padding used in the navigation list:

1. Return to the **tss_styles.css** file in your editor.

2. Locate the `nav > ul` style rule in the Navigation Styles section and insert the style **padding-left: 5px;**.

   Figure 2-39 highlights the new style for all navigation lists.

> Include the unit in any style involving padding or margin spaces.

Figure 2-39	Setting the size of the left padding space

selects unordered lists within the nav element

```
nav > ul {
    line-height: 2em;
    list-style-type: none;
    padding-left: 5px;
}
```

sets the padding on the left edge to 5 pixels

3. Save your changes to the file and then reload the **tss_home.html** file in your browser. Verify that the entries in the navigation list in the left column have been shifted to the left, which is the result of changing the left padding setting to 5 pixels.

Now that you've worked with the padding space, you'll examine how to work with margins.

Setting Padding and Margin Space

- To set the padding space around all sides of the element, use

  padding: *size*;

  where *size* is the size of the padding using one of the CSS units of length.
- To set the margin space around all sides of the element, use

  margin: *size*;

- To set padding or margin on only one side (top, right, bottom, or left) include the name of the side in the property as

  padding-*side*: *size*;
  margin-*side*: *size*;

  where *side* is top, right, bottom, or left.
- To set different padding or margins on each side of the element, enter the sides as

  padding: *top right bottom left*;
  margin: *top right bottom left*;

  where *top*, *right*, *bottom*, and *left* are individual sizes for the associated side.

Setting the Margin and the Border Spaces

Styles to set the margin space have the same form as styles to set the padding space. To set the size of the margin around your block-level elements, use either of the following properties:

    margin: *size*;

or

    margin: *top right bottom left*;

The margins of individual sides are set using the style properties

    margin-top: *size*;
    margin-right: *size*;
    margin-bottom: *size*;
    margin-left: *size*;

where once again *size* is expressed in one of the CSS units of length or using the keyword auto to have the browser automatically set the margin.

The size of the border space is set using the following border-width property

    border-width: *size*;

or

    border-width: *top right bottom left*;

or with the properties border-top-width, border-right-width, border-bottom-width, and border-left-width used to specify the size of individual borders. You'll explore borders in more detail in Tutorial 4.

The navigation list that Alison created for the home page groups the list into those links for pages within the Tri and Succeed Sports website and those links to external websites. The list item at the start of each group is marked with the class value *newgroup*. Alison suggests you increase the top margin above each group of links to 20 pixels in order to offset it from the preceding group. The groups will be easier to recognize after the top margin for each group has been increased.

To increase the top margin:

1. Return to the **tss_styles.css** file in your editor.

2. Directly below the style rule for the `nav > ul` selector in the Navigation Styles section, insert the following rule:

```
nav > ul > li.newgroup {
    margin-top: 20px;
}
```

Figure 2-40 highlights the style rule setting the top margin value.

Figure 2-40   **Setting the size of the top margin**

```
nav > ul {
    line-height: 2em;
    list-style-type: none;
    padding-left: 5px;
}

nav > ul > li.newgroup {
    margin-top: 20px;
}
```

selects the list items belonging to the newgroup class found within the unordered navigation list

sets the margin space on the top edge to 20 pixels

3. Save your changes to the file and then reload the **tss_home.html** file in your browser. Verify that the entries in the navigation list are now split into three groups: the first group containing the links from the Tri and Succeed Sports website; the second group containing links to websites on running, cycling, and swimming; and the third group containing links to triathlon websites.

Alison has also noticed that the block quotes in the right column of the home page have unused space to the left, leaving less space for the customer quotes. The default browser style for the `blockquote` element offsets block quotes from the surrounding text by setting the left and right margins to 40 pixels. To adjust this spacing and to make the block quotes more readable, you'll reduce the left/right margins to 5 pixels. You'll also increase the top/bottom margins to 20 pixels to better separate one customer quote from another.

To change the margin space around block quotes:

1. Return to the **tss_styles.css** file in your editor.

2. Locate the style rule for the `aside blockquote` selector in the Aside and Blockquote Styles section and insert the **margin: 20px 5px;** style into the style rule.

Figure 2-41 displays the style to change the margin space around the `blockquote` element.

Figure 2-41 **Setting the margin size for block quotes**

selects block quotes within the aside element →

```
aside blockquote {
    color: rgb(232, 165, 116);
    margin: 20px 5px;
}
```

sets the size of the top and bottom margins to 20 pixels

sets the size of the left and right margins to 5 pixels

3. Save your changes to the file and then reload the **tss_home.html** file in your browser. Figure 2-42 displays the revised appearance of the page with the new padding and margin sizes applied to the navigation list and the block quotes.

Figure 2-42 **Home page with new margins and padding**

each block quote surrounded by a 20 pixel top/bottom margin and a 5 pixel left/right margin

left padding set to 5 pixels

each new group offset by a 20 pixel top margin

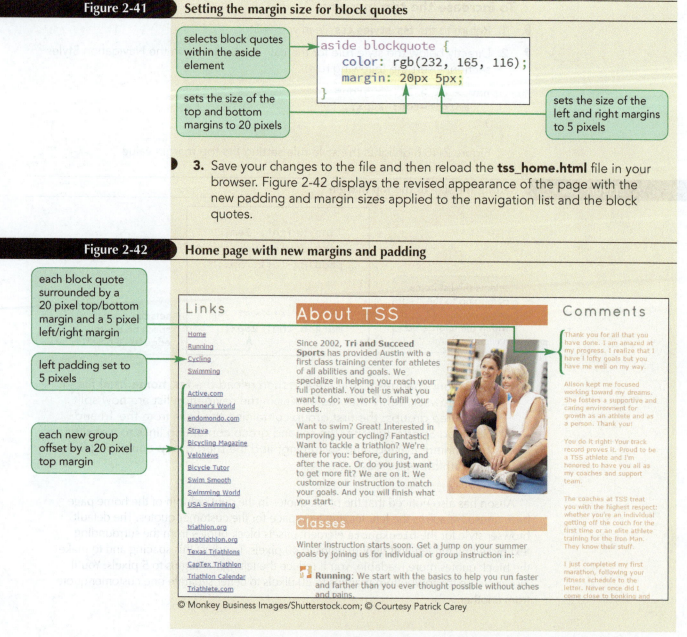

© Monkey Business Images/Shutterstock.com; © Courtesy Patrick Carey

Alison thinks the revised appearance of the navigation list and the customer quotes is a big improvement. However, she doesn't like the underlining in the navigation list. She would like the underlining to appear only when the user hovers the mouse pointer over the link. She would also like a different list marker to appear next to each list item in the classes section. You can make these changes using pseudo-classes and pseudo-elements.

Using Pseudo-Classes and Pseudo-Elements

Not everything that appears in the rendered page is marked up in the HTML file. For example, a paragraph has a first letter or a first line but those are not marked up as distinct elements. Similarly, an element can be classified based on a particular property without having a `class` attribute. The initial entry from an ordered list has the property of being the first item, but no `class` attribute in the HTML file identifies it as such. These elements and `class` attributes that exist only within the rendered page but not within the HTML document are known as pseudo-elements and pseudo-classes. Despite not being part of the HTML document, you can still write style rules for them.

Pseudo-Classes

A **pseudo-class** is a classification of an element based on its current status, position, or use in the document. The style rule for a pseudo-class is entered using the selector

    element:pseudo-class

where *element* is an element from the document and *pseudo-class* is the name of a CSS pseudo-class. Pseudo-classes are organized into structural and dynamic classes. A **structural pseudo-class** classifies an element based on its location within the structure of the HTML document. Figure 2-43 lists the structural pseudo-classes supported in CSS.

Figure 2-43   **Structural pseudo-classes**

Pseudo-Class	Matches
`:root`	The top element in the document hierarchy (the `html` element)
`:empty`	An element with no content
`:only-child`	An element with no siblings
`:first-child`	The first child of the parent element
`:last-child`	The last child of the parent element
`:first-of-type`	The first descendant of the parent that matches the specified type
`:last-of-type`	The last descendant of the parent that matches the specified type
`:nth-of-type(n)`	The nth element of the parent of the specified type
`:nth-last-of-type(n)`	The nth from the last element of the parent of the specified type
`:only-of-type`	An element that has no siblings of the same type
`:lang(code)`	The element that has the specified language indicated by *code*
`:not(selector)`	An element not matching the specified *selector*

For example, the `first-of-type` pseudo-class identifies the first element of a particular type. The following selector uses this `first-of-type` pseudo-class to select the first list item found within an unordered list:

    ul > li:first-of-type

This selector will not select any other list item and it will not select the first list item if it is not part of an unordered list.

Alison would like to modify the marker images used with the list of classes on the home page. Currently the runicon.png image file is used as the marker for all three list items. Instead, she would like to use the runicon.png image only for the first item, the bikeicon.png image as the marker for the second list item, and the swimicon.png as the third and last item's maker. You can use the `first-of-type`, `nth-of-type`, and `last-of-type` pseudo-classes to match the appropriate png file with each item.

To apply pseudo-classes to an unordered list:

1. Return to the **tss_styles.css** file in your editor.

2. Go to the List Styles section at the bottom of the style sheet, delete the `article#about_tss ul` style rule that sets the list style image marker and replace it with the following three style rules:

```css
article#about_tss ul li:first-of-type {
    list-style-image: url(runicon.png);
}

article#about_tss ul li:nth-of-type(2) {
    list-style-image: url(bikeicon.png);
}

article#about_tss ul li:last-of-type {
    list-style-image: url(swimicon.png);
}
```

Figure 2-44 highlights the three selectors and their associated style rules using pseudo-classes with the unordered list items.

Figure 2-44   Applying pseudo-classes to list items

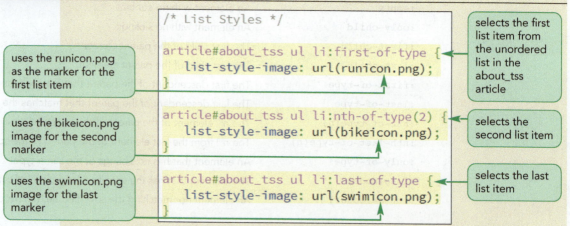

uses the runicon.png as the marker for the first list item

uses the bikeicon.png image for the second marker

uses the swimicon.png image for the last marker

selects the first list item from the unordered list in the about_tss article

selects the second list item

selects the last list item

3. Save your changes to the file and then reload the **tss_home.html** file in your browser. Figure 2-45 shows the new format of the unordered list with different image markers used with each of the list items.

Figure 2-45   **List marker images for each item**

runicon.png image

bikeicon.png image

swimicon.png image

Classes

Winter instruction starts soon. Get a jump on your summer goals by joining us for individual or group instruction in:

Running: We start with the basics to help you run faster and farther than you ever thought possible without aches and pains.

Cycling: The indoor bike trainers at TSS include everything you need to refine your technique, stamina, and power for improved results on the road.

Swimming: The open water swim can be one of the most frightening sports to master. Our classes begin with basic techniques so that your swim can be very enjoyable, and not a chore.

© Courtesy Patrick Carey

INSIGHT

Exploring the nth-of-type Pseudo-class

The `nth-of-type` pseudo-class is a powerful tool for formatting groups of elements in cyclical order. Cycles are created using the selector

```
nth-of-type(an+b)
```

where *a* is the length of the cycle, *b* is an offset from the start of the cycle, and n is a counter, which starts at 0 and increases by 1 through each iteration of the cycle. For example, the following style rules create a cycle of length 3 with the first list item displayed in red, the second displayed in blue, and the third displayed in green, after which the cycle repeats red-blue-green until the last item is reached:

```
li:nth-of-type(3n+1) {color: red;}
li:nth-of-type(3n+2) {color: blue;}
li:nth-of-type(3n+3) {color: green;}
```

When the cycle length is 1, the `nth-of-type` selector selects elements after the specified offset has passed. The following style rule sets the text color to blue for all list items starting from the 5th item

```
li:nth-of-type(n+5) {color: blue;}
```

CSS also supports the keywords **even** and **odd** so that two-length cycles can be more compactly entered as

```
li:nth-of-type(even) {color: red;}
li:nth-of-type(odd) {color: blue;}
```

with a red font applied to the even-numbered list items and a blue font applied to the odd-numbered items.

The same cyclical methods described above can be applied to the `nth-child` selector with the important difference that the `nth-child` selector selects any child element of the parent while the `nth-of-type` selector only selects elements of a specified type.

Pseudo-classes for Hypertext

Another type of pseudo-class is a **dynamic pseudo-class** in which the class can change state based on the actions of the user. Dynamic pseudo-classes are used with hypertext links such as the `visited` class, which indicates whether the target of the link has already been visited by the user. Figure 2-46 describes the dynamic pseudo-classes.

| Figure 2-46 | Dynamic pseudo-classes |

Pseudo-Class	Description
:link	The link has not yet been visited by the user.
:visited	The link has been visited by the user.
:active	The element is in the process of being activated or clicked by the user.
:hover	The mouse pointer is hovering over the element.
:focus	The element is receiving the focus of the keyboard or mouse pointer.

For example, to display all previously visited links in a red font, you could apply the following style rule to the a element:

```
a:visited {color: red;}
```

To change the text color to blue when the mouse pointer is hovered over the link, apply the following rule:

```
a:hover {color: blue;}
```

TIP

The hover, active, and focus pseudo-classes also can be applied to non-hypertext elements to create dynamic page elements that change their appearance in response to user actions.

In some cases, two or more pseudo-classes can apply to the same element. For example, a hypertext link can be both visited previously and hovered over. In such situations, the standard cascading rules apply with the pseudo-class listed last applied to the element. As a result, you should enter the hypertext pseudo-classes in the following order—link, visited, hover, and active. The link pseudo-class comes first because it represents a hypertext link that has not been visited yet. The visited pseudo-class comes next, for links that have been previously visited. The hover pseudo-class follows, for the situation in which a user has moved the mouse pointer over a hypertext link prior to clicking the link. The active pseudo-class is last, representing the exact instant in which a link is activated.

Users with disabilities might interact with hypertext links through their keyboard rather than through a mouse pointer. Most browsers allow users to press the Tab key to navigate through the list of hypertext links on the page and to activate those links by pressing the Enter key. A link reached through the keyboard has the focus of the page and most browsers will indicate this focus by displaying an outline around the linked text. You can substitute your own style by using the focus pseudo-class in the same way that you used the hover pseudo-class.

REFERENCE

Using Dynamic Pseudo-Class to Create Hypertext

- To create a rollover for a hypertext link, use the pseudo-classes

  ```
  a:link
  a:visited
  a:hover
  a:active
  ```

  where the link pseudo-element matches unvisited link, visited matches previously visited links, hover matches links that have the mouse pointer hovering over them, and active matches links that are in the action of being clicked.

The default browser style is to underline all hypertext links; displaying the links in a blue font with previously visited links in purple. Alison wants the links in the navigation list to appear in a medium gray font with no distinction between unvisited and previously visited links. She does not want the hypertext underlined in the navigation list except when the link is hovered over or active. She also wants hovered or active links to appear in purple. Add these style rules to the style sheet now.

To apply pseudo-classes to a hypertext links:

▸ 1. Return to the **tss_styles.css** file in your editor.

▸ 2. Go to the Navigation Styles section and insert the following style rules for hypertext links that have been visited or not visited.

```
nav > ul > li > a:link, nav > ul > li > a:visited {
    color: rgb(151, 151, 151);
    text-decoration: none;
}
```

▸ 3. Add the following new style rules for links that are being hovered over or are active:

```
nav > ul > li > a:hover, nav > ul > li > a:active {
    color: rgb(255, 64, 255);
    text-decoration: underline;
}
```

Figure 2-47 highlights the style rules for hypertext links in the navigation list.

Figure 2-47   **Using pseudo-classes with hypertext links**

selects links in the navigation list that either have been visited (a:visited) or haven't been visited (a:link)

selects links that the user is hovering over (a:hover) or that are currently being activated (a:active)

adds underlining to the hypertext link

```
nav > ul > li.newgroup {
    margin-top: 20px;
}

nav > ul > li > a:link, nav > ul > li > a:visited {
    color: rgb(151, 151, 151);
    text-decoration: none;
}

nav > ul > li > a:hover, nav > ul > li > a:active {
    color: rgb(255, 64, 255);
    text-decoration: underline;
}
```

sets the text color to medium gray

removes underlining from the hypertext link

sets the text color to medium purple

▸ 4. Save your changes to the file and then reload the **tss_home.html** file in your browser and hover your mouse pointer over the links in the navigation list. Figure 2-48 shows the hover effect applied to the link to the TSS swimming class.

Figure 2-48   **Style applied to a hovered link**

link color changed to medium gray and underlining is removed

link changes color and decoration in response to the hover event

© 2016 Cengage Learning; © Monkey Business Images/Shutterstock.com

PROSKILLS

Problem Solving: Hover with Touch Devices

The hover pseudo-class was written to apply only to user interfaces that support mice or similar pointing devices. Technically, there is no hover event with touch devices, such as mobile phones and tablets. However, most mobile devices will still respond to a hover style by briefly applying the style when the user initially touches a hypertext link.

Many mobile devices also apply a "double tap" response so that initially touching a page element invokes the hover style and then immediately tapping the page element a second time invokes the click event. This technique is most often used for web pages that use the hover event to reveal hidden menus and page objects. You'll explore how to work with this technique to create hidden menus on mobile devices in Tutorial 5.

With the increasing importance of touch devices, a good guiding principle is that you should avoid making support for the hover style a necessary condition for the end-user. Hover effects should be limited to enhancing the user experience but they should not be a critical component of that experience.

Pseudo-Elements

Another type of pseudo selector is a **pseudo-element**, which is an object that exists only in the rendered page. For example, a paragraph is an element that is marked in the HTML file, but the first line of that paragraph is not. Similarly, the first letter of that paragraph is also not a document element, but it certainly can be identified as an object in the web page. Pseudo-elements can be selected using the following CSS selector

```
element::pseudo-element
```

where *element* is an element from the HTML file and *pseudo-element* is the name of a CSS pseudo-element. Figure 2-49 describes the pseudo-elements supported in CSS.

Figure 2-49	Pseudo-elements

Pseudo-Element	Description
::first-letter	The first letter of the element text
::first-line	The first line of the element text
::before	Content inserted directly before the element
::after	Content inserted directly after the element

For example, the following style rule matches the first displayed line of every paragraph in the rendered web page and transforms the text of that line to uppercase letters:

```
p::first-line {text-transform: uppercase;}
```

The following style rule matches the first letter of every paragraph within a block quote and displays the character in a Times New Roman font that is 250% larger than the surrounding text:

```
blockquote p::first-letter {
    font-family: 'Times New Roman', Times, serif;
    font-size: 250%;
}
```

Note that the double colon separator "::" was introduced in CSS3 to differentiate pseudo-elements from pseudo-classes. Older browsers use the singe colon ":" for both pseudo-elements and pseudo-classes.

Generating Content with CSS

Another type of pseudo-element is used to generate content for the web page. New content can be added either before or after an element using the following before and after pseudo-elements

```
element::before {content: text;}
element::after {content: text;}
```

where text is the content to be inserted into the rendered web page. The content property supports several types of text content as described in Figure 2-50.

Figure 2-50	Values of the content property

Value	Description
none	Sets the content to an empty text string
counter	Displays a counter value
attr(attribute)	Displays the value of the selector's attribute
text	Displays the specified text
open-quote	Displays an opening quotation mark
close-quote	Displays a closing quotation mark
no-open-quote	Removes an opening quotation mark, if previously specified
no-close-quote	Removes a closing quotation mark, if previously specified
url(url)	Displays the content of the media (image, video, etc.) from the file located at url

For example, the following style rules combine the `before` and `after` pseudo-elements with the `hover` pseudo-class to insert the "<" and ">" characters around every hypertext link in a navigation list:

```
nav a:hover::before {content: "<";}
nav a:hover::after {content: ">";}
```

Note that these style rules use both the `hover` pseudo-class and the `before`/`after` pseudo-elements so that the content is only inserted in response to the hover event.

If you want to insert a special symbol, you have to insert the code number for that symbol using text string `"\code"` where *code* is the code number. For example, if instead of single angled brackets as indicated above, you wanted to show double angled brackets, « and », you would need to use the Unicode character code for these characters, `00ab` and `00bb` respectively. To insert these characters before and after a navigation list hypertext link, you would apply the following style rules:

```
nav a:hover::before {content: "\00ab";}
nav a:hover::after {content: "\00bb";}
```

In addition to adding content to an element as just discussed, you can also insert content that is a media file, such as an image or video clip, by using the following `content` property

```
content: url(url);
```

where *url* is the location of the media file. For example, the following style rule appends the image file uparrow.png to any hypertext link in the document when it is hovered over:

```
a:hover::after {content: url(uparrow.png);}
```

An image file or any content generated by the style sheet should not consist of material that is crucial to understanding your page. Instead, generated content should only consist of material that supplements the page for artistic or design-related reasons. If the generated content is crucial to interpreting the page, it should be placed in the HTML file in the first place.

Displaying Attribute Values

The content property can also be used to insert an attribute value into the rendered web page through the use of the following `attr()` function

```
content: attr(attribute);
```

where *attribute* is an attribute of the selected element. One application of the `attr()` function is to add the URL of any hypertext link to the link text. In the following code, the value of the `href` attribute is appended to every occurrence of text marked with the a element:

```
a::after {
    content: "( " attr(href) ")";
}
```

Notice that URL is enclosed within opening and closing parentheses. Thus, a hypertext link in an HTML document, such as

```
<a href="http://www.triathlon.org">Triathlons</a>
```

will be displayed in the rendered web page as:

Triathlons (http://www.triathlon.org)

This technique is particularly useful for printed output in which the author wants to have the URLs of all links displayed on the printed page for users to read and have as references. You'll explore this issue further in Tutorial 5.

Inserting Content using CSS

- To insert content directly before a page element, use the style rule

  ```
  element::before {content: text;}
  ```

  where *element* is the page element and *text* is the content to be inserted before the element.
- To insert content directly after a page element, use the style rule

  ```
  element::after {content: text;}
  ```

Inserting Quotation Marks

The `blockquote` and `q` elements are used for quoted material. The content of these elements is usually placed in quotation marks and, while you can insert these quotation marks within the HTML file, you can also insert decorative opening and closing quotation marks using the `content` property with the following values:

```
content: open-quote;
content: close-quote;
```

The actual characters used for the open and closing quotation marks are defined for the selector with the following `quotes` property

```
quotes: "open1" "close1" "open2" "close2" …;
```

where *open1* is the character used for the opening quotation mark and *close1* is character used for the closing quotation mark. The text strings *open2*, *close2*, and so on are used for nested quotation marks. In the example that follows, character codes are used to define the curly quotes for opening and closing quotation marks

```
quotes: "\201C" "\201D" "\2018" "\2019";
```

where the character code 201C returns the opening curly double quote ", the code 201D returns the closing curly double quote ", the code 2018 returns the nested opening single quote ', and 2019 provides the closing single quote '.

Alison suggests that you use decorative quotes for the customer comments on the Tri and Succeed Sports home page. You display curly quotes in a bold Times New Roman font with a font size of 1.6em (which is slightly bigger than the font size of the block quote text.)

To insert quotes into block quotes:

1. Return to the **tss_styles.css** file in your editor.

2. Go to the Aside and Blockquote Styles section and, within the style rule for the `aside blockquote` selector, insert the following `quotes` property to use curly quotes for the quotation marks:

   ```
   quotes: "\201C" "\201D";
   ```

3. Add the following style rules to insert quotation marks before and after each block quote in the `aside` element:

   ```
   aside blockquote::before {
       content: open-quote;
       font-family: 'Times New Roman', Times, serif;
       font-size: 1.6em;
       font-weight: bold;
   }
   ```

```
aside blockquote::after {
    content: close-quote;
    font-family: 'Times New Roman', Times, serif;
    font-size: 1.6em;
    font-weight: bold;
}
```

Figure 2-51 highlights the styles to add curly quotes before and after each block quote.

Figure 2-51   Adding quotation marks to block quotes

character codes for the
" and " curly quotes

```
aside blockquote {
    color: rgb(232, 165, 116);
    margin: 20px 5px;
    quotes: "\201C" "\201D";
}
```

displays the open quote character before each block quote

before pseudo-element

```
aside blockquote::before {
    content: open-quote;
    font-family: 'Times New Roman', Times, serif;
    font-size: 1.6em;
    font-weight: bold;
}
```

displays the close quote character after each block quote

format applied to the opening and closing quotation marks

after pseudo-element

```
aside blockquote::after {
    content: close-quote;
    font-family: 'Times New Roman', Times, serif;
    font-size: 1.6em;
    font-weight: bold;
}
```

4. Save your changes to the file and then reload the **tss_home.html** file in your browser. As shown in Figure 2-52, bold quotation marks have been added before and after each customer comment.

Figure 2-52   Quotation marks added to reviewer comments

opening and closing quotes enclose each comment

About TSS

Since 2002, **Tri and Succeed Sports** has provided Austin with a first class training center for athletes of all abilities and goals. We specialize in helping you reach your full potential. You tell us what you want to do; we work to fulfill your needs.

Want to swim? Great! Interested in improving your cycling? Fantastic!

Comments

" Thank you for all that you have done. I am amazed at my progress. I realize that I have l lofty goals but you have me well on my way."

" Alison kept me focused working toward my dreams. She fosters a supportive and caring environment for growth as an athlete and as a person. Thank you!"

© 2016 Cengage Learning; © Monkey Business Images/Shutterstock.com

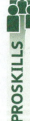

Teamwork: Managing a Style Sheet

Your style sheets often will be as long and as complex as your website content. As the size of a style sheet increases, you might find yourself overwhelmed by multiple style rules and definitions. This can be an especially critical problem in a workplace where several people need to interpret and sometimes edit the same style sheet. Good management skills are as crucial to good design as a well-chosen color or typeface are. As you create your own style sheets, here are some techniques to help you manage your creations:

- Use style comments throughout, especially at the top of the file. Clearly describe the purpose of the style sheet, where it's used, who created it, and when it was created.
- Because color values are not always immediately obvious, include comments that describe your colors. For example, annotate a color value with a comment such as "body text is tan".
- Divide your style sheet into sections, with comments marking the section headings.
- Choose an organizing scheme and stick with it. You may want to organize style rules by the order in which they appear in your documents, or you may want to insert them alphabetically. Whichever you choose, be consistent and document the organizing scheme in your style comments.
- Keep your style sheets as small as possible, and break them into separate files if necessary. Use one style sheet for layout, another for text design, and perhaps another for color and graphics. Combine the style sheets using the @import rule, or combine them using the link element within each page. Also, consider creating one style sheet for basic pages on your website, and another for pages that deal with special content. For example, an online store could use one style sheet (or set of sheets) for product information and another for customer information.

By following some of these basic techniques, you'll find your style sheets easier to manage and develop, and it will be easier for your colleagues to collaborate with you to create an eye-catching website.

Alison is pleased with the work you've done on the typography and design of the Tri and Succeed Sports website. Alison will continue to develop the new version of the website and will get back to you with future changes and design ideas.

Session 2.3 Quick Check

1. Provide a style rule to display all unordered lists with lowercase letters as the list marker.

2. Provide a style rule to display all unordered lists using the star.png image file, placed inside the virtual box.

3. Provide a style rule to display the text of all previously visited hypertext links in gray.

4. Provide the style rule to set the padding around every h1 heading in a `section` element to 1em on top, 0.5em on the left and right, and 2em on the bottom.

5. Provide the style rule to change the left margin of the `figure` element to 20 pixels.

6. Describe the item selected by the following selector:

   `#top > p:first-of-type:first-line`

7. Describe the items selected by the following selector:

   `div.Links img[usemap]`

8. Provide a style rule to insert the text string "***" before every paragraph belonging to the Review class.

9. Provide the style property to set the opening quotation mark and closing quotation marks to curly quotes with Unicode values of 2018 and 2019 respectively.

PRACTICE

Review Assignments

Data Files needed for the Review Assignments: coach_styles_txt.css, tss_coach_txt.html, 1 CSS file, 5 PNG files, 1 TTF file, 1 WOFF file

Alison has created another page for the Tri and Succeed Sports website providing biographies of the coaches at the club. She has already written the page content, acquired image files, and created a style sheet for the page layout. She wants you to finish the design of the page by developing a style sheet for the page's color scheme and typography. A preview of the page you'll design is shown in Figure 2-53.

Figure 2-53   **TSS coaches profile page**

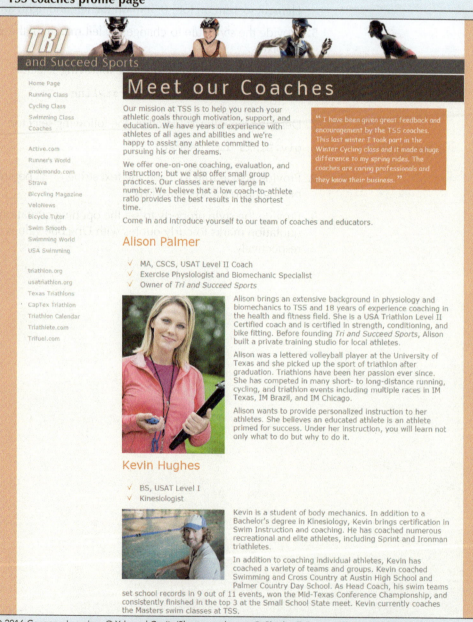

© 2016 Cengage Learning; © Ysbrand Cosijn/Shutterstock.com; © Charles T. Bennett/Shutterstock.com;
© ostill/Shutterstock.com; © eurobanks/Shutterstock.com; © wavebreakmediaShutterstock.com

Complete the following:

1. Use your HTML editor to open the **tss_coach_txt.html** and **coach_styles_txt.css** files from the html02 ▸ review folder. Enter *your name* and *the date* in the comment section of each file, and save them as **tss_coach.html** and **coach_styles.css** respectively.

2. Go to the **tss_coach.html** file in your editor and then within the document head, create links to the **coach_layout.css** and **coach_styles.css** style sheets.

3. Take some time to study the content and structure of the file and then close the document, saving your changes.

4. Go to the **coach_styles.css** file in your editor. At the top of the file and before the comment section do the following:
   a. Insert an `@charset` rule to set the character encoding for the file to utf-8.
   b. Use the `@font-face` rule to define a web font named Nobile, which is based on the nobile-webfont.woff file and, if that format is not supported, on the nobile-webfont.ttf file.

5. Go to the Main Structural Styles section and do the following:
   a. Change the background color of the browser window by creating a style rule for the `html` element that sets the background color to the value hsl(27, 72%, 72%).
   b. For the `body` element, create a style rule to set the text color to the value rgb(91, 91, 91), the background color to ivory, and body text to the font stack: Verdana, Geneva, sans-serif.

6. Create a style rule for the `body > footer address` selector containing the following styles:
   a. The background color set to the value rgb(222, 128, 60)
   b. The font color to white and then to the semitransparent value rgba(255, 255, 255, 0.6)
   c. The font style to normal displayed in bold small capital letters with a font size of 0.9em and a line height of 3em using the font stack Nobile, Verdana, Geneva, sans-serif
   d. The text horizontally centered on the page

7. Go to the Heading Styles section and create a style rule for every h1 heading that displays the text with a normal font weight from the font stack: Nobile, Verdana, Geneva, sans-serif. Set the letter spacing to 0.2em and the margin to 0 pixels.

8. Alison wants you to format the main h1 heading at the top of the page. Create a style rule for the `section#tss_coaches h1` selector that sets the font size to 2.5em with a color value of hsl(27, 82%, 85%) and background color of hsl(27, 6%, 21%). Set the left padding space to 10 pixels.

9. Alison also wants you to format the h2 headings for each coach. Create a style rule for the `article.coach_bio h2` selector that sets the font size to 1.6em with normal weight and the font color to rgb(240, 125, 0).

10. Alison has inserted a comment from an athlete about the coaches. Format this comment by going to the Blockquote Styles section and creating a style rule for the `aside blockquote` selector to do the following:
    a. Set the font size to 0.95em using the font stack 'Comic Sans MS', cursive.
    b. Set the font color to rgba(255, 255, 255, 0.75) and use a semi-transparent background color with the value rgb(222, 128, 60).
    c. Set the padding space to 10 pixels.
    d. Define opening and closing quotes for the element using the Unicode character 201C and 201D respectively.

11. Format the appearance of the opening quotes by creating a style rule for the `aside blockquote::before` selector to write a boldfaced open quote before the block quote with the font size set to 1.6em from the font stack 'Times New Roman', Times, serif.

12. Format the appearance of the closing quotes by creating a style rule for the `aside blockquote::after` selector to write a boldfaced open quote after the block quote with the font size once again set to 1.6em from the font stack 'Times New Roman', Times, serif.

13. Next, you'll format the appearance of the navigation list by going to the Navigation Styles section and creating a style rule for `body > nav` selector that sets the text of the navigation list in a 0.8em font size with a line height of 2em.

14. Create a style rule for the `nav > ul` selector that removes the list marker and sets the left padding to 5 pixels.

15. Alison wants to break up the long list of links in the navigation list. Create style rules for the 6th and 16th `li` elements within the `nav > ul` selector that sets the size of the top margin of those items to 20 pixels.

16. For every previously visited or unvisited hypertext link within the `nav > ul > li` selector, set the text to the RGB color value rgb(151, 151, 151) and remove the underlining from the text link.

17. For every hovered or active hypertext link within the `nav > ul > li` selector, set the text color to RGB value rgb(222, 128, 60) and underline the hypertext link.

18. Go to the Paragraph Styles section and insert a style rule that sets the top margin and bottom margin to 10 pixels, the right margin to 30 pixels, and the left margin to 0 pixels for every paragraph in the document.

19. Every coach has a list of accomplishments. Go to the List Styles section and insert a style rule for the `article.coach_bio > header > ul` selector that displays the check.png file as the list marker and sets the margin space to 0 pixels, except for the bottom margin, which should be set to 10 pixels.

20. Save your changes to the style sheet and then open the **tss_coach.html** file in your browser. Verify that the color and typography match that shown in Figure 2-53. Verify that when you hover the mouse pointer over the links in the navigation list the text is displayed in an underlined orange font.

Case Problem 1

APPLY

Data Files needed for this Case Problem: ph_plays_txt.html, ph_styles_txt.css, 1 CSS file, 1 PNG file, 3 TTF files, 3 WOFF files

Philip Henslowe Classic Theatre   Randall Chen is the media director for the *Philip Henslowe Classic Theatre*, a regional classical theatre in Coeur d'Alene, Idaho. You've been asked to work on the website design for the company. The first page you'll manage lists the plays for next summer's repertoire. A preview of the page is shown in Figure 2-54.

Figure 2-54   List of Plays at the Philip Henslowe Classic Theatre

© 2016 Cengage Learning; © Christian Bertrand/Shutterstock.com

The content and layout of the page has already been created for you. Your job will be to create a style sheet for the typography of the page.

Complete the following:

1. Using your editor, open the **ph_plays_txt.html** and **ph_styles_txt.css** files from the html02 ▶ case1 folder. Enter *your name* and *the date* in the comment section of each file, and save them as **ph_plays.html** and **ph_styles.css** respectively.

2. Go to the **ph_plays.html** file in your HTML editor, and within the document head create links to the **ph_layout.css** and **ph_styles.css** style sheet files. Take some time to study the content and structure of the document and then close the file, saving your changes.

3. Go to the **ph_styles.css** file in your editor, and at the top of the file before the comment section, define the character encoding used in the document as utf-8.

4. Randall has several web fonts that he wants used for the titles of the plays produced by the company. Add the following web fonts to the style sheet, using `@font-face` rules before the comment section:

   a. The Champagne font using the cac_champagne.woff and cac_champagne.ttf files

   b. The Grunge font using the 1942.woff and 1942.ttf files

   c. The Dobkin font using the DobkinPlain.woff and DobkinPlain.ttf files

5. Go to the Structural Styles section, creating a style rule that sets the background color of the `html` element to the value hsl(91, 8%, 56%).

6. Add a style rule for the `body` element to set the background color to the value hsl(58, 31%, 84%) and the font of the body text to the font stack: 'Palatino Linotype', 'Book Antiqua', Palatino, serif.

7. Create a style rule for the `header` element that sets the background color to black.

8. Create a style rule for every paragraph that sets the margin space to 0 pixels and the padding space to 5 pixels on top and 25 pixels on the right, bottom, and left.

9. For paragraphs that are direct children of the body element, create a style rule that sets the font size to 1.1em and horizontally centers the paragraph text.

10. Create a style rule for the address element that sets the font style to normal with a font size of 0.9em, horizontally centered on the page. Set the top and bottom padding to 10 pixels.

11. Next, you'll format the appearance of navigation lists on the page. Go to the Navigation Styles section and create a style rule for the `nav a` selector that displays the hypertext links using the font stack 'Trebuchet MS', Helvetica, sans-serif, and sets the top and bottom padding to 10 pixels.

12. For every unvisited and previously visited hypertext link within a `nav` element, set the text color to white, remove underlining from the link text, and set the background color to the semi-transparent value hsla(0, 0%, 42%, 0.4).

13. For every active or hovered link in a `nav` element, set the text color to the semi-transparent value hsla(0, 0%, 100%, 0.7) and set the background color to the semi-transparent value hsl(0, 0%, 42%, 0.7).

14. Go to the Section Styles section of the style sheet. In this section, you'll define the appearance of the four playbills. You'll start with the h1 headings from the sections. Create a style rule for the `section.playbill h1` selector that sets the font size to 3em and the font weight to normal. Set the margin space around the h1 headings to 0 pixels. Set the padding space to 20 pixels on top, 0 pixels on the right, 10 pixels on the bottom, and 20 pixels on the left.

15. Each playbill section is identified by a different ID value ranging from play1 to play4. Create style rules that set a different background color for each playbill using the following background colors:

   ID: play1 set to hsl(240, 100%, 88%)

   ID: play2 set to hsl(25, 88%, 73%)

   ID: play3 set to hsl(0, 100%, 75%)

   ID: play4 set to hsl(296, 86%, 86%)

16. Each playbill section heading will also have a different font. For the h1 headings within the four different playbills, create style rules to apply the following font stacks:

   ID: play1 set to Champagne, cursive

   ID: play2 set to Grunge, 'Times New Roman', Times, serif

   ID: play3 set to Impact, Charcoal, sans-serif

   ID: play4 set to Dobkin, cursive

17. Randall has put the author and the director of each play within a definition list. Format these definition lists now by going to the Definition List Styles section and creating a style rule for the dt element that sets the font size to 1.3em, the font weight to bold, and the font color to the semi-transparent value hsla(0, 0%, 0%, 0.4).

18. Create a style rule for every dd element to set the font size to 1.3em, the left margin space to 0 pixels, and the bottom margin space to 10 pixels.

19. Save your changes to the file and then open the **ph_plays.html** file in your browser. Verify that the typography and colors used in the document match those shown in Figure 2-54. Also, verify that, when you hover the mouse pointer over an item in the navigation lists for the entire page and for each play, the background color of the link becomes more opaque.

CHALLENGE

Case Problem 2

Data Files needed for this Case Problem: mw_styles_txt.css, mw_tour_txt.html, 1 CSS file, 1 PNG file

Mountain Wheels   Adriana and Ivan Turchenko are the co-owners of Mountain Wheels, a bike shop and touring company in Littleton, Colorado. One of their most popular tours is the Bike the Mountains Tour, a six-day excursion over some of the highest roads in Colorado. Adriana wants to update the company's website to provide more information about the tour. She already has had a colleague design a three-column layout with a list of links in the first column and descriptive text in the second and third columns. She has asked for your help in completing the design by formatting the text and colors in the page. Figure 2-55 shows a preview of the design used in the final page.

Figure 2-55   **Description of the Bike the Mountains tour**

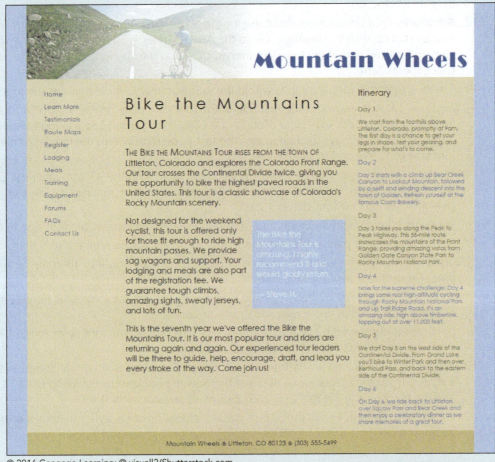

© 2016 Cengage Learning; © visuall2/Shutterstock.com

Complete the following:

1. Using your editor, open the **mw_tour_txt.html** and **mw_styles_txt.css** files from the html02 ▶ case2 folder. Enter *your name* and *the date* in the comment section of each file, and save them as **mw_tour.html** and **mw_styles.css** respectively.

2. Go to the **mw_tour.html** file in your HTML editor. Within the document head, create links to the **mw_layout.css** and **mw_styles.css** style sheet files. Study the content and structure of the document and then close the file, saving your changes.

3. Go to the **mw_styles.css** file in your editor. At the top of the file, insert the `@charset` rule to set the encoding for this style sheet to utf-8.

4. Go to the Structural Styles section and create a style rule that sets the background color of the browser window to rgb(173, 189, 227).

5. Create a style rule for the `body` element that sets the background color to rgb(227, 210, 173) and sets the body font to the font stack: 'Century Gothic', sans-serif.

6. Create a style rule to display the body footer with a background color of rgb(208, 184, 109) and set the top and bottom padding space to 5 pixels.

7. Create a style rule for the `address` element to display the text in a normal font with a font size of 0.9em, horizontally center the text, and set the top and bottom padding to 10 pixels.

8. Go to the Heading Styles section and create a style rule to set the font weight of all h1 and h2 headings to normal.

9. Go to the Navigation Styles section and create a style rule for the `nav > ul` selector that removes all list markers, sets the line height to 2em, and sets the font size to 0.9em.

10. For every previously visited or unvisited hypertext link within the navigation list, create a style rule to remove the underlining from the hypertext link and to set the text color to rgb(43, 59, 125).

11. For every hovered or active link within the navigation list, create a style rule to set the text color to rgb(212, 35, 35).

12. Adriana has put information about the tour in an article with the ID "tour_summary". Format this article, starting with the heading. Go to the Article Styles section and create a style rule for `h1` elements nested within the tour_summary article that sets the font size to 2.2em and the letter spacing to 0.2em.

13. Create a style rule for paragraphs within the tour_summary article that sets the font size to 1.1em.

✦ **Explore** 14. Adriana wants the first line in the tour_summary article to appear in small capital letters. Use the `first-of-type` pseudo-class and the `first-line` pseudo-element to create a style rule that displays the first line of the first paragraph within the tour_summary article at a font size of 1.2em and in small caps.

15. The tour itinerary is displayed within an `aside` element with the ID *tour_itinerary*. Go to the Aside Styles section and for every `h1` element nested within the tour_itinerary `aside` element, create a style rule that sets the font size to 1.2em.

16. For every h2 element within the tour_itinerary `aside` element, set the font size to 0.9em.

17. Set the font size of paragraphs within the tour_itinerary `aside` element to 0.8em.

✦ **Explore** 18. Adriana wants the text color of each day's schedule to alternate between gray and blue. Create the following style rules:

   a. For odd-numbered h2 headings and paragraphs that set the font color to rgb(79, 91, 40). (*Hint*: Use the `nth-of-type(odd)` pseudo-class.)

   b. For even-numbered h2 headings and paragraphs that set the font color to rgb(81, 95, 175). (*Hint*: Use the `nth-of-type(even)` pseudo-class.)

19. The page contains a review within a block quote. Go to the Blockquote Styles section and create a style rule for the `blockquote` element that sets the background color to rgb(173, 189, 227) and the text color to the rgb(255, 255, 255) with an opacity of 0.65.

20. For every paragraph within the `blockquote` element create a style rule that sets the top/bottom padding space to 2.5 pixels and the left/right padding space to 10 pixels.

21. Save your changes to the file and then open the **mw_tour.html** file in your browser. Verify that your design matches that shown in Figure 2-55 including the format applied to the first paragraph of the tour_itinerary article and the alternating colors used in the listing of the itinerary days.

Case Problem 3

Data Files needed for this Case Problem: cw_class_txt.html, cw_styles_txt.css, 1 CSS file, 2PNG files

The Civil War and Reconstruction   Peter Craft is a professor of military history at Mountain Crossing University. The university is offering a series of online courses, one of which is "The Civil War and Reconstruction" taught by Professor Craft. He has developed the online content and has had a colleague help with the page layout. You've been asked to complete the project by creating text and color styles. A preview of the sample page is shown in Figure 2-56.

CHALLENGE

Figure 2-56   Civil War History home page

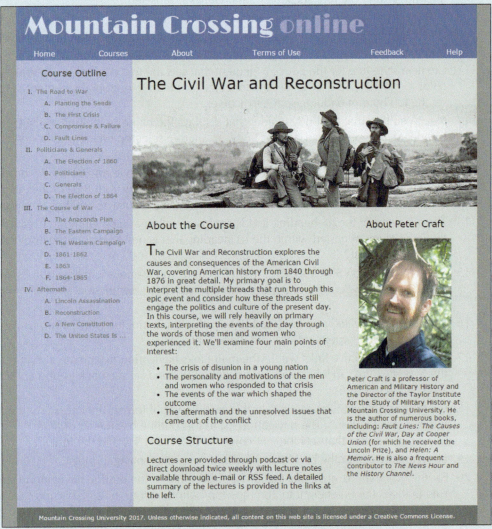

Complete the following:

1. Using your editor, open the **cw_class_txt.html** and **cw_styles_txt.css** files from the html02 ▸ case3 folder. Enter *your name* and *the date* in the comment section of each file, and save them as **cw_class.html** and **cw_styles.css** respectively.

2. Go to the **cw_class.html** file in your HTML editor. Within the document head, create a link to the **cw_styles.css** style sheet file.

✪ **Explore** 3. Using the Google Fonts website, locate the Limelight font. Copy the code for the `link` element to use this font and paste the copied code to the document head in the cw_class.html file.

4. Study the content and structure of the cw_class.html file and then close the file, saving your changes.

5. Go to the **cw_styles.css** file in your editor. At the top of the file, define the character encoding as utf-8.

✪ **Explore** 6. On the next line, use the `@import` rule to import the contents of the cw_layout.css file into the style sheet.

7. Go to the Structural Styles section. Within that section create a style rule to set the background color of the browser window to rgb(151, 151, 151).

8. Create a style rule to set the background color of the page body to rgb(180, 180, 223) and set the body text to the font stack: Verdana, Geneva, sans-serif.

9. Display all h1 and h2 headings with normal weight.

10. Create a style rule for every hypertext link nested within a navigation list that removes underlining from the text.

11. Create a style rule for the `footer` element that sets the text color to white and the background color to rgb(101, 101, 101). Set the font size to 0.8em. Horizontally center the footer text, and set the top/bottom padding space to 1 pixel.

12. Next, you'll format the body header that displays the name of the university. Go to the Body Header Styles section and, for the `body > header` selector, create a style rule that sets the background color to rgb(97, 97, 211).

13. The university name is stored in an h1 heading. Create a style rule for the h1 heading that is a direct child of the body header that sets the font size to 4vw with the color value rgba(255, 255, 255, 0.8). Display the text with the font stack: Limelight, cursive. Set the margin space to 0 pixels.

14. The last word of the h1 heading text is enclosed within a `span` element. Create a style rule for the `span` element nested within the h1 heading that is nested within the body header, setting the text color to rgba(255, 255, 255, 0.4).

15. Go the Navigation Styles section. In this section, you format the navigation list that has the ID *mainLinks*. For hypertext links within this navigation list, set the top and bottom padding space to 5 pixels.

16. For previously visited and unvisited links within the mainLinks navigation list, create a style rule that displays the hypertext links in a white font.

17. For hovered or active links within the mainLinks navigation list, create a style rule that displays the hypertext links in white with an opacity of 0.8 and set the background color to the value rgba(51; 51, 51, 0.5).

18. Go to the Outline Styles section. In this section, you'll format the course outline that appears on the page's left column. The navigation list in this outline has the ID *outline*. Create a style rule for this navigation list that sets the text color to rgb(51, 51, 51) and the font size to 0.8em.

19. Horizontally center the h1 headings within the outline navigation list.

20. For the first level ol elements that are a direct child of the outline navigation list, create a style rule that sets the line height to 2em, the top/bottom margin to 0 pixels and the left/right margin to 5 pixels. Display the list marker as an upper-case Roman numeral.

21. Display the second level of ol elements nested within the outline navigation list with an upper-case letter as the list marker.

22. Display all previously visited and unvisited links in the outline navigation list using the color value rgb(101, 101, 101).

23. Display hovered and active links in the outline navigation list using the color value rgb(97, 97, 211) with the text underlined.

24. Go to the Section Styles section. In this section, format the description of the course. Create a style rule that sets the background color of the `section` element to rgb(220, 220, 220).

25. Format the heading of this section by creating a style rule for the `section header h1` selector that sets the font size of 2.2em and the left padding space to 10 pixels.

26. Go to the Article Styles section and create a style rule for h2 headings within the `article` element that sets the font size to 1.4em.

⊕ **Explore** 27. Display the first letter of the first paragraph within the `article` element with a font size of 2em and vertically aligned with the baseline of the surrounding text. (*Hint*: Use the `first-of-type` pseudo-class and the `first-letter` pseudo-element.)

28. Information about Peter Craft has been placed in an `aside` element. Go to the Aside Styles section and create a style rule that sets the font size of text in the `aside` element to 0.9em.

29. For h1 headings nested within the `aside` element, create a style rule that sets the font size to 1.4em and horizontally centers the text.

30. Save your changes to the file and then open the `cw_class.html` file in your browser. Verify that the appearance of the page resembles that shown in Figure 2-56. Confirm that when you change the width of the browser window, the size of the page heading text changes in response to setting the heading text using the vw unit.

Case Problem 4

Data Files needed for this Case Problem: lake_home_txt.html, lake_styles_txt.css, 1 CSS file, 2 PNG files, 2 TTF files, 2 WOFF files

The Great Lakescape Lodge Ron Nelson is the owner of The Great Lakescape Lodge in Baileys Harbor, Wisconsin. He has hired you to work on the redesign of the lodge's website. You'll start by working on the site's home page. Ron has already written the text of the page, gathered all of the graphic files, and had a colleague design the page layout. He wants you to work on the page's color scheme and typography. A possible solution is shown in Figure 2-57.

CREATE

Figure 2-57   Home page of the Great Lakescape Lodge

© 2016 Cengage Learning; © Courtesy Patrick Carey; © Dmitry Kalinovsky/Shutterstock.com

Complete the following:

1. Using your editor, open the **lake_home_txt.html** and **lake_styles_txt.css** files from the html02 ▶ case4 folder. Save them as **lake_home.html** and **lake_styles.css** respectively.

2. Go to the **lake_home.html** file in your editor and link it to the **lake_layout.css** and **lake_styles.css** style sheet file. Take some time to study the content and structure of the document and then save your changes to the file.

3. Go to the **lake_styles.css** file in your editor and begin creating the color scheme and typographic styles for the lodge's home page. The final design is up to you but it should include the following features:

   - Definition of the character encoding used in the style sheet file
   - Application of a web font (Two fonts are supplied for you in the html02 ▶ case4 folder.)
   - Setting background and text colors using both color values and color names
   - An application of a semi-transparent color
   - Selectors showing style rules applied to nested elements, child elements, and elements based on the `id` attribute
   - Styles that modify the appearance of list and list markers
   - Use of pseudo-elements and pseudo-classes as selectors
   - Styles that modify the padding space and margin space around an element
   - A style rule to generate content in the rendered page

4. Include informative style comments throughout the style sheet.

5. Save your completed style sheet.

TUTORIAL **3**

Designing a Page Layout

Creating a Website for a Chocolatier

Case | *Pandaisia Chocolates*

Anne Ambrose is the owner and head chocolatier of *Pandaisia Chocolates*, a chocolate shop located in Essex, Vermont. You have been asked to assist on the redesign of the company's website. Anne has provided you with three pages from the website to start your work. She has written all of the content, compiled the necessary images and graphics, and written some of the text and color styles. She needs you to complete the project by designing the page layout using the CSS layout properties.

STARTING DATA FILES

html03 → **tutorial**

pc_about_txt.html
pc_home_txt.html
pc_info_txt.html
pc_grids_txt.css
pc_home_txt.css
pc_info_txt.css
pc_reset_txt.css
+ 22 files

review

pc_specials_txt.html
pc_specials_txt.css
pc_reset2.css
+ 11 files

case1

sp_home_txt.html
sp_layout_txt.css
+ 13 files

case2

ce_front_txt.html
ce_grids_txt.css
ce_styles_txt.css
+ 21 files

case3

ss_dday_txt.html
ss_styles_txt.css
+ 4 files

case4

pcg_front_txt.html
pcg_paper_txt.css
+ 9 files

demo

demo_positioning.html
+ 5 files

Session 3.1 Visual Overview:

To horizontally center a block element, set the left and right margins to auto.

The **width** property defines the width of an element, the **max-width** property sets its maximum possible width, the **min-width** property sets its minimum width.

The **display** property defines how an element should be laid out.

The **clear** property displays the element only when the left, right, or both floated objects have been cleared.

The vertical navigation list and Contact Info section are floated as separate columns.

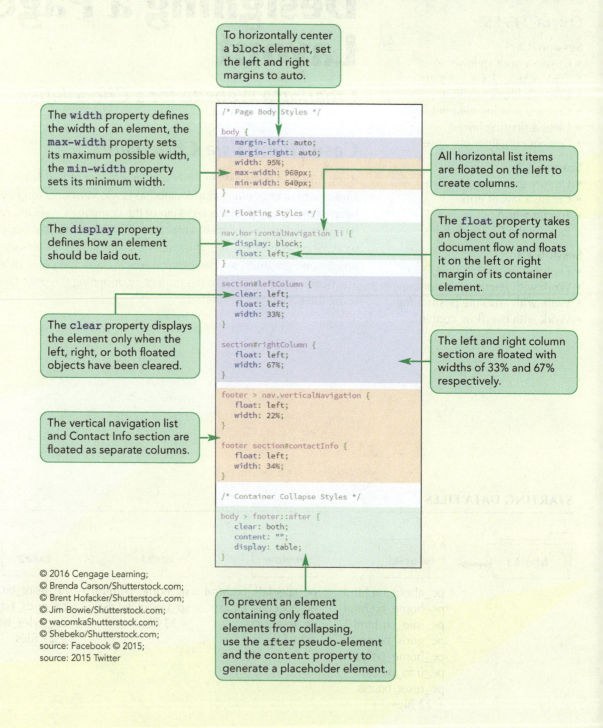

```
/* Page Body Styles */

body {
    margin-left: auto;
    margin-right: auto;
    width: 95%;
    max-width: 960px;
    min-width: 640px;
}

/* Floating Styles */

nav.horizontalNavigation li {
    display: block;
    float: left;
}

section#leftColumn {
    clear: left;
    float: left;
    width: 33%;
}

section#rightColumn {
    float: left;
    width: 67%;
}

footer > nav.verticalNavigation {
    float: left;
    width: 22%;
}

footer section#contactInfo {
    float: left;
    width: 34%;
}

/* Container Collapse Styles */

body > footer::after {
    clear: both;
    content: "";
    display: table;
}
```

All horizontal list items are floated on the left to create columns.

The **float** property takes an object out of normal document flow and floats it on the left or right margin of its container element.

The left and right column section are floated with widths of 33% and 67% respectively.

To prevent an element containing only floated elements from collapsing, use the **after** pseudo-element and the **content** property to generate a placeholder element.

Page Layout with Floating Elements

Page body is horizontally centered within the browser window.

Horizontal list items are floated into separate columns.

Left and right sections are floated into separate columns.

The contents of the page footer are floated into separate columns.

Introducing the `display` Style

The study of page layout starts with defining how an individual element is presented on the page. In the first tutorial, you learned that HTML elements are classified into block elements such as paragraphs or headings, or into inline elements, such as emphasized text or inline images. However, whether an element is displayed as a block or as inline depends on the style sheet. You can define the display style for any page element with the following `display` property

```
display: type;
```

where `type` defines the display type. A few of the many `type` values are shown in Figure 3-1.

Figure 3-1	Some values of the display property

Display Value	Appearance
block	Displayed as a block
table	Displayed as a web table
inline	Displayed in-line within a block
inline-block	Treated as a block placed in-line within another block
run-in	Displayed as a block unless its next sibling is also a block, in which case, it is displayed in-line, essentially combining the two blocks into one
inherit	Inherits the display property of the parent element
list-item	Displayed as a list item along with a bullet marker
none	Prevented from displaying, removing it from the rendered page

© 2016 Cengage Learning

For example, to supersede the usual browser style that displays images inline, you can apply the following style rule to display all of your images as blocks:

```
img {display: block;}
```

If you want to display all block quotes as list items, complete with list markers, you can add the following style rule to your style sheet:

```
blockquote {display: list-item;}
```

You can even prevent browsers from displaying an element by setting its `display` property to `none`. In that case, the element is still part of the document structure but it is not shown to users and does not occupy space in the displayed page. This is useful for elements that include content that users shouldn't see or have no need to see.

You'll use the `display` property in creating a reset style sheet.

Creating a Reset Style Sheet

You learned in the last tutorial that your browser applies its own styles to your page elements unless those styles are superseded by your own style sheet. Many designers prefer to work with a "clean slate" and not have any browser style rules creep into the final design of their website. This can be accomplished with a **reset style sheet** that supersedes the browser's default styles and provides a consistent starting point for page design.

You'll create a reset style sheet for the Pandaisia Chocolates website. The first style rules in your sheet will use the `display` property to display all of the HTML5 structural elements in your web page as blocks. While current browsers already do this, there are some older browsers that do not recognize or have predefined display styles for elements as such `header`, `article`, or `footer`. By including the `display` property in a reset style sheet, you add a little insurance that these structural elements will be rendered correctly.

To create a reset style sheet:

1. Use the text editor or HTML editor of your choice to open the **pc_reset_txt.css** file from the html03 ▸ tutorial folder. Enter **your name** and **the date** in the comment section of the file and save the document as **pc_reset.css**.

2. Within the Structural Styles section, insert the following style rule to define the display properties of several HTML5 structural elements.

```
article, aside, figcaption, figure,
footer, header, main, nav, section {
   display: block;
}
```

Figure 3-2 highlights the new style rule in the document.

Figure 3-2 ▸ **Displaying HTML5 structural elements as blocks**

```
/* Structural Styles */

article, aside, figcaption, figure,
footer, header, main, nav, section {
   display: block;
}
```

You will complete the reset style sheet by adding other style rules that set default padding and margins around commonly used page elements, define some basic typographic properties, and remove underlining from hypertext links found within navigation lists.

To complete the reset style sheet:

1. Within the Typographic Styles section, insert the following style rule to define the typographic styles for several page elements:

```
address, article, aside, blockquote, body, cite,
div, dl, dt, dd, em, figcaption, figure, footer,
h1, h2, h3, h4, h5, h6, header, html, img,
li, main, nav, ol, p, section, span, ul {

   background: transparent;
   font-size: 100%;
   margin: 0;
   padding: 0;
   vertical-align: baseline;
}
```

2. Add the following style rules to remove list markers from list items found within navigation lists:

```
nav ul {
    list-style: none;
    list-style-image: none;
}


nav a {
    text-decoration: none;
}
```

3. Set the default line height to 1 (single-spaced) by applying the following style rule to the page body:

```
body {
    line-height: 1;
}
```

Figure 3-3 describes the new style rules in the document.

Figure 3-3 **Completing the reset style sheet**

```
/* Typographic Styles */

address, article, aside, blockquote, body, cite,
div, dl, dt, dd, em, figcaption, figure, footer,
h1, h2, h3, h4, h5, h6, header, html, img,
li, main, nav, ol, p, section, span, ul {
    background: transparent;
    font-size: 100%;
    margin: 0;
    padding: 0;
    vertical-align: baseline;
}

nav ul {
    list-style: none;
    list-style-image: none;
}

nav a {
    text-decoration: none;
}

body {
    line-height: 1;
}
```

makes the background color transparent

removes all margin and padding spaces

aligns all content with the baseline

sets the font size equal to the font size of the parent

does not display markers for unordered lists within navigation lists

does not underline hypertext links within navigation lists

single spaces all body text

4. Save your changes to the file.

This is a very basic reset style sheet. There are premade reset style sheets freely available on the web that contain more style rules used to reconcile the various differences between browsers and devices. Before using any of these reset style sheets, you should study the CSS code and make sure that it meets the needs of your website. Be aware that some reset style sheets may contain more style rules than you actually need and you can speed up your website by paring down the reset sheet to use only the elements you need for your website.

The first page you will work on for Pandaisia Chocolates is the site's home page. Anne has already created a typographical style sheet in the pc_styles1.css file. Link to the style sheet file now as well as the pc_reset.css style sheet you just created and the pc_home.css style sheet that you will work on for the remainder of this session to design the page layout.

To get started on the Pandaisia Chocolates home page:

1. Use your editor to open the **pc_home_txt.css** file from the html03 ▸ tutorial folder. Enter *your name* and *the date* in the comment section of the file and save the document as **pc_home.css**.

2. Use your editor to open the **pc_home_txt.html** file from the same folder. Enter *your name* and *the date* in the comment section and save the file as **pc_home.html**.

3. Within the document head, directly after the `title` element, insert the following `link` elements to link the home page to the pc_reset.css, pc_styles1.css, and pc_home.css style sheets.

   ```
   <link href="pc_reset.css" rel="stylesheet" />
   <link href="pc_styles1.css" rel="stylesheet" />
   <link href="pc_home.css" rel="stylesheet" />
   ```

4. Take some time to study the content and structure of the pc_home.html document. Pay particular attention to the use of ID and class names throughout the document.

5. Save your changes to the file. You might want to keep this file open as you work with the pc_home.css style sheet so that you can refer to its content and structure.

TIP

The reset style sheet should *always* be the first style sheet listed before any other style sheets to ensure that your default styles are applied first.

Anne has sketched the general layout she wants for the home page, shown in Figure 3-4. Compare the pc_home.html file content to the sketch shown in Figure 3-4 to get a better understanding of how the page content relates to Anne's proposed layout.

Figure 3-4   Proposed home page layout

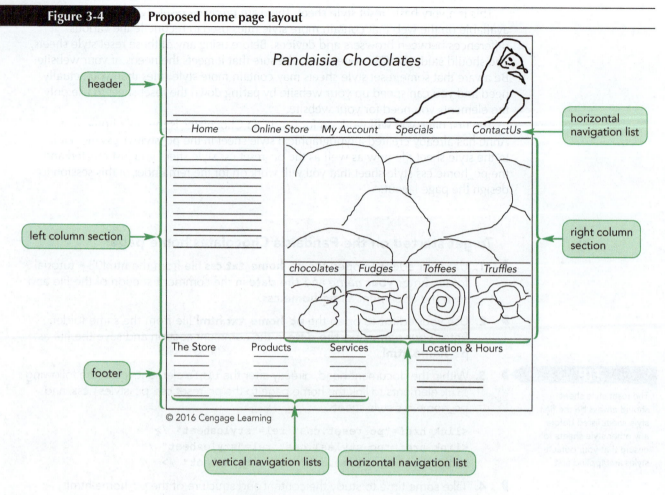

© 2016 Cengage Learning

Before creating the page layout that Anne has sketched out for you, you'll examine different types of layout designs.

Exploring Page Layout Designs

One challenge of layout is that your document will be viewed on many different devices with different screen resolutions. When designing for the web, you're usually more concerned about the available screen width than screen height because users can scroll vertically down the length of the page, but it is considered bad design to make them scroll horizontally.

A page designer needs to cope with a wide range of possible screen widths ranging from wide screen monitors with widths of 1680 pixels or more, down to mobile devices with screen widths of 320 pixels and even less. Complicating matters even more is that a screen width represents the maximum space available to the user, but some space is always taken up by toolbars, sidebar panes and other browser features. In addition, the user might not even have the browser window maximized to fill the entire screen. Thus, you need a layout plan that will accommodate a myriad of screen resolutions and browser configurations.

Fixed, Fluid, and Elastic Layouts

Web page layouts fall into three general categories: fixed, fluid, and elastic. A **fixed layout** is one in which the size of the page and the size of the page elements are fixed, usually using pixels as the unit of measure. The page width might be set at 960 pixels and the width of the company logo set to 780 pixels. These widths are set regardless of the screen resolution of the user's device and this can result in the page not fitting into the browser window if the device's screen is not wide enough.

By contrast, a **fluid layout** sets the width of page elements as a percent of the available screen width. For example, the width of the page body might be set to fill 90% of the screen and the width of the company logo might be set to fill 80% of that page body. Under a fluid layout, the page resizes automatically to match the screen resolution of the user's device. Figure 3-5 shows how a three-column layout might appear in both a fixed and a fluid design.

| Figure 3-5 | Fixed layouts vs. fluid layouts |

© 2016 Cengage Learning

With different devices accessing your website, it's usually best to work with a fluid layout that is more adaptable to a range of screen resolutions. Fixed layouts should only be used when you have more control over the devices that will display your page, such as a web page created specifically for a digital kiosk at a conference.

Another layout design is an **elastic layout** in which all measurements are expressed in em units and based on the default font size used in the page. If a user or the designer increases the font size, then the width, height, and location of all of the other page elements, including images, change to match. Thus, images and text are always sized in proportion to each other and the layout never changes with different font sizes. The disadvantage to this approach is that, because sizing is based on the font size and not on the screen resolution, there is a danger that if a user sets the default font size large enough, the page will extend beyond the boundaries of the browser window.

Finally, the web is moving quickly toward the principles of **responsive design** in which the layout and design of the page changes in response to the device that is rendering it. The page will have one set of styles for mobile devices, another for tablets, and yet another for laptops or desktop computers. You'll explore how to implement responsive design in Tutorial 5.

Because width is such an integral part of layout, you will start designing the Pandaisia Chocolates home page by defining the width of the page body and elements within the page.

Working with Width and Height

The width and height of an element are set using the following width and height properties

```
width: value;
height: value;
```

where *value* is the width or height using one of the CSS units of measurement or as a percentage of the width or height of the parent element. For example, the following style rule sets the width of the page body to 95% of the width of its parent element (the browser window):

```
body {width: 95%;}
```

Usually, you do not set the height value because browsers automatically increase the height of an element to match its content. Note that all block elements, like the body element, have a default width of 100%. Thus, this style rule makes the body element width slightly smaller than it would be by default.

Setting Maximum and Minimum Dimensions

You can set limits on the width or height of a block element by applying the following properties

```
min-width: value;
min-height: value;
max-width: value;
max-height: value;
```

where *value* is once again a length expressed in one of the CSS units of measure (usually pixels to match the measurement unit of the display device). For example, the following style rule sets the width of the page body to 95% of the browser window width but confined within a range of 640 to 1680 pixels:

```
body {
    width: 95%;
    min-width: 640px;
    max-width: 1680px;
}
```

Maximum and minimum widths are often used to make page text easier to read. Studies have shown that lines of text that are too wide are difficult to read because the eye has to scan across a long section of content and that lines of text that are too narrow with too many line returns, break the flow of the material.

Setting Widths and Heights

REFERENCE

- To set the width and height of an element, use the styles

```
width: value;
height: value;
```

where *value* is the width or height in one of the CSS units of measurement or a percentage of the width or height of the parent element.

- To set the minimum possible width or height, use the styles

```
min-width: value;
min-height: value;
```

- To set the maximum possible width or height, use the styles

```
max-width: value;
max-height: value;
```

Set the width of the page body for the Pandaisia Chocolates home page to 95% of the browser window ranging from 640 pixels to 960 pixels. Also display the company logo image as a block with its width set to 100% so that it extends across the page body. You do not have to set the height of the logo because the browser will automatically scale the height to keep the original proportions of the image.

To set the initial dimensions of the page:

1. Return to the **pc_home.css** file in your editor and add the following style rule to the Body Styles section:

```
body {
    max-width: 960px;
    min-width: 640px;
    width: 95%;
}
```

2. Within the Body Header Styles section insert the following style rule to set the display type and width of the logo image:

```
body > header > img {
    display: block;
    width: 100%;
}
```

Figure 3-6 highlights the newly added style rules in the style sheet.

Figure 3-6   Setting the width of the page body and logo

web page width is 95% of the browser window ranging from 640 pixels to 960 pixels

displays the logo image as a block element

sets the width of the logo to 100% of the page body

```
/* Body Styles */

body {
    max-width: 960px;
    min-width: 640px;
    width: 95%;
}

/* Body Header Styles */

body > header > img {
    display: block;
    width: 100%;
}
```

3. Save your changes to the file and then open the **pc_home.html** file in your browser. Figure 3-7 shows the current layout of the page body and logo.

Figure 3-7   Initial view of the body header

page body width is 95% of the browser window

browser window background

Pandaisia Chocolates

414 Tree Lane • Essex, VT 05452

Home

Online Store

© 2016 Cengage Learning

logo is 100% of the body width

body background

4. Change the width of your browser window and verify that the size of the page body and the size of the logo resize as needed within the range of 640 to 960 pixels.

The page body is currently placed on the left margin of the browser window. Anne would like it centered horizontally within the browser window.

Centering a Block Element

Block elements can be centered horizontally within their parent element by setting both the left and right margins to auto. Thus, you can center the page body within the browser window using the style rule:

```
body {
    margin-left: auto;
    margin-right: auto;
}
```

Modify the style rule for the page body to center the Pandaisia Chocolates home page horizontally by setting the left and right margins to auto.

To center the page body horizontally:

1. Return to the **pc_home.css** file in your editor and, within the style rule for the body selector, insert the properties:

   ```
   margin-left: auto;
   margin-right: auto;
   ```

   Figure 3-8 highlights the newly added styles.

Figure 3-8   **Centering the page body**

```
body {
    margin-left: auto;
    margin-right: auto;
    max-width: 960px;
    min-width: 640px;
    width: 95%;
}
```

setting the left and right margins to auto forces block elements to be horizontally centered within their parent

2. Save your changes to the file and then reload the **pc_home.html** file in your browser. Verify that the page body is now centered within the browser window.

INSIGHT

Working with Element Heights

The fact that an element's height is based on its content can cause some confusion. For example, the following style rule appears to set the height of the header to 50% of the height of the page body:

```
body > header {height: 50%;}
```

However, because the total height of the page body depends on the height of its individual elements, including the body header, there is circular reasoning in this style rule. You can't set the page body height without knowing the height of the body header and you can't set the body header height unless you know the height of the page body. Most browsers deal with this circularity by leaving the body header height undefined, resulting in no change in the layout.

Heights need to be based on known values, as in the following style rules where the body height is set to 1200 pixels and thus the body header is set to half of that or 600 pixels.

```
body {height: 1200px;}
body > header {height: 50%;}
```

It is common in page layout design to extend the page body to the height of the browser window. To accomplish this, you set the height of the `html` element to 100% so that it matches the browser window height (a known value defined by the physical properties of the screen) and then you set the minimum height of the page body to 100% as in the following style rules:

```
html {height: 100%;}
body {min-height: 100%;}
```

The result is that the height of the page body will always be at least equal to the height of the browser window, but it will extend beyond that if necessary to accommodate extra page content.

Vertical Centering

Centering an element vertically within its parent element is not easily accomplished because the height of the parent element is usually determined by its content, which might not be a defined value. One solution is to display the parent element as a table cell with a defined height and then set the `vertical-align` property set to `middle`. For example, to vertically center the following h1 heading within the `div` element

```
<div>
   <h1>Pandaisia Chocolates</h1>
</div>
```

you would apply the style rule:

```
div {
   height: 40px;
   display: table-cell;
   vertical-align: middle;
}
```

Using this style rule, the h1 heading will be vertically centered.

To vertically center a single line of text within its parent element, set the line height of the text larger than the text's font size. The following style rule will result in an h1 heading with vertically centered heading text.

```
h1 {
    font-size: 1.4em;
    line-height: 2em;
}
```

Note that this approach will only work for a single line of text. If the text wraps to a second line, it will no longer be vertically centered. Vertical centering is a common design challenge and there are several other workarounds that have been devised over the years. You can do a search on the web for other solutions to vertical centering.

Next, you will lay out the links in the navigation list. Anne wants the links displayed horizontally rather than vertically. You can accomplish this using CSS floats.

Floating Page Content

By default, content is displayed in the page in the order it appears within the HTML file as part of the normal document flow. **Floating** an element takes it out of position and places it along the left or right edge of its parent element. Subsequent content that is not floated occupies the space previously taken up by the floated element. Figure 3-9 shows a diagram of an element that is floated along the right margin of its container and its effect on the placement of subsequent content.

Figure 3-9   Floating an element

original layout   element is floated on the right margin
                               and the subsequent page content
                               wraps around it

© 2016 Cengage Learning

To float an element, apply the following `float` property

```
float: position;
```

where `position` is `none` (the default), `left` to float the object on the left margin, or `right` to float the object on the right margin. If sibling elements are floated along the same margin, they are placed alongside each other within a row as shown in Figure 3-10.

Figure 3-10 Floating multiple elements in a row

original layout

float: left   float: left   float: left

when several elements are floated on the
same margin, they are aligned within a row

© 2016 Cengage Learning

Note that for the elements to be placed within a single row, the combined width of the elements cannot exceed the total width of their parent element, otherwise any excess content will automatically wrap to a new row.

Floating an Element

- To float an element within its container, apply the style

  `float: position;`

  where *position* is none (the default), `left`, or `right`.

Anne wants you display the content of navigation lists belonging to the horizontalNavigation class within a single row. You will accomplish this by floating each item in those navigation lists on the left margin using the `float` property. Create this style rule now.

> To be confined to a single row, the total width of floated elements cannot exceed the width of the container.

To lay out horizontal navigation list items:

1. Return to the **pc_home.css** file in your editor and go to the Body Header Styles section.

2. Because there are five links in the navigation list, you'll make each list item 20% of the width of the navigation list by adding the following style rule:

```
body > header > nav.horizontalNavigation li {
    width: 20%;
}
```

3. Insert the following style rule within the Horizontal Navigation Styles section to display every list item within a horizontal navigation list as a block floated on the left.

```
nav.horizontalNavigation li {
   display: block;
   float: left;
}
```

Figure 3-11 highlights the styles used with list items.

| Figure 3-11 | Floating items in the navigation list |

```
/* Body Header Styles */

body > header > img {
   display: block;
   width: 100%;
}

body > header > nav.horizontalNavigation li {
   width: 20%;
}


/* Horizontal Navigation Styles */

nav.horizontalNavigation li {
   display: block;
   float: left;
}
```

sets the width of the list item to 20% of the width of the navigation list

floats the list item within every horizontal navigation list as a block on the left

4. Save your changes to the file and then reload the **pc_home.html** file in your browser. Figure 3-12 shows the revised layout of the navigation list in the page header.

| Figure 3-12 | Floating items in a horizontal navigation list |

the width of each list item set to 20% and floated on the left margin

Anne doesn't like the appearance of the hypertext links in the navigation list. Because the links are inline elements, the background color extends only as far as the link text. She suggests you change the links to block elements and center the link text within each block.

To change the display of the hypertext links:

1. Return to the **pc_home.css** file in your editor.

2. Within the Horizontal Navigation Styles section, insert the following style rule to format the appearance of the hypertext links within the horizontal navigation lists.

```
nav.horizontalNavigation a {
    display: block;
    text-align: center;
}
```

Figure 3-13 highlights the style rule for the hypertext links.

Figure 3-13   Formatting hyperlinks in horizontal navigation lists

```
/* Horizontal Navigation Styles */

nav.horizontalNavigation li {
    display: block;
    float: left;                    displays the
}                                   link as a block

nav.horizontalNavigation a {
    display: block;
    text-align: center;
}
```

centers the link text within the block

3. Save your changes to the file and then reload the **pc_home.html** file in your browser.

4. Hover your mouse pointer over the links in the navigation list. Note that the link text is centered within its block and the background color extends fully across the block rather than confined to the link text. See Figure 3-14.

Figure 3-14   Links in the body header

each hypertext link displayed as a block with the link text centered within the block

© 2016 Cengage Learning

Trouble? Don't worry about the jumble of elements displayed after the body header. You'll straighten out those objects next.

You have completed the design of the body header. Next, you will lay out the middle section of the home page.

Clearing a Float

In some layouts, you will want an element to be displayed on a new row, clear of previously floated objects. To ensure that an element is always displayed below your floated elements, apply the following `clear` property:

    clear: position;

where *position* is `left`, `right`, `both`, or `none`. A value of `left` displays the element only when the left margin is clear of floating objects. A value of `right` displays the element only when the right margin is clear. A value of `both` displays the element only when both margins are clear of floats. The default clear value is `none`, which allows the element to be displayed alongside any floated objects.

Figure 3-15 shows how use of the `clear` property prevents an element from being displayed until the right margin is clear of floats. The effect on the page layout is that the element is shifted down and is free to use the entire page width since it is no longer displayed alongside a floating object.

| **Figure 3-15** | **Clearing a float** |

original layout

floating an element on the right margin

last element is displayed once the right margin is clear of floated objects

© 2016 Cengage Learning

The next part of the Pandaisia Chocolates home page contains two `section` elements named "leftColumn" and "rightColumn". Set the width of the left column to 33% of the body width and set the width of the right column to 67%. Float the sections side-by-side on the left margin, but only when the left margin is clear of all previously floated objects.

To float the left and right column sections:

1. Return to the **pc_home.css** file in your editor. Go to the Left Column Styles section and insert the style rule:

```
section#leftColumn {
    clear: left;
    float: left;
    width: 33%;
}
```

2. Within the Right Column Styles section, insert:

```
section#rightColumn {
    float: left;
    width: 67%;
}
```

Note that you do not apply the `clear` property to the right column because you want it to be displayed in the same row alongside the left column. Figure 3-16 highlights the style rules for the left and right columns.

Figure 3-16 Float the left and right column sections

```
/* Left Column Styles */

section#leftColumn {
    clear: left;
    float: left;
    width: 33%;
}

/* Right Column Styles */

section#rightColumn {
    float: left;
    width: 67%;
}
```

displays the left column once the left margin is clear of previously floated elements

floats the left column on the left margin with a width of 33% of the page body

floats the right column alongside the left column with a width of 67%

The right column contains a horizontal navigation list containing four items, each consisting of an image and a label above the image. Anne wants the four items placed side-by-side with their widths set to 25% of the width of the navigation list. Anne also wants the images in the right column displayed as blocks with their widths set to 100% of their parent element.

To complete the right column section:

1. Within the Right Column Styles section, insert the following style rules to format the inline images and list items:

```
section#rightColumn img {
   display: block;
   width: 100%;
}
```

```
section#rightColumn > nav.horizontalNavigation li {
   width: 25%;
}
```

Note that you do not have to include a style rule to float the items in the horizontal navigation list because you have already created that style rule in Figure 3-11. Figure 3-17 describes the new style rules in the style sheet.

Figure 3-17   **Formatting the right column section**

```
/* Right Column Styles */

section#rightColumn {
   float: left;
   width: 67%;
}

section#rightColumn img {
   display: block;
   width: 100%;
}

section#rightColumn > nav.horizontalNavigation li {
   width: 25%;
}
```

displays every image in the right column as a block with a width equal to the width of its parent element

sets the width of each list item to 25% of the width of the navigation list

2. Save your changes to the file and then reload the **pc_home.html** file in your browser. Figure 3-18 shows the layout of the left and right column sections.

Figure 3-18   Layout of the left and right columns

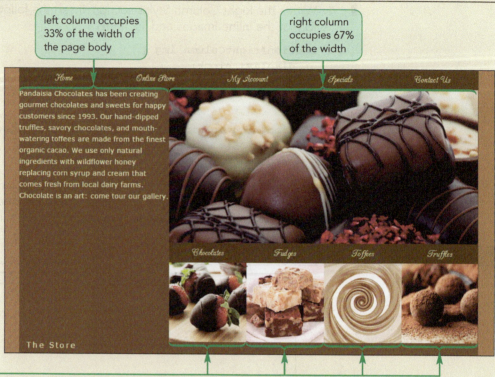

left column occupies 33% of the width of the page body

right column occupies 67% of the width

horizontal navigation list with each image and label set to 25% of the list width

© Brenda Carson/Shutterstock.com; © Brent Hofacker/Shutterstock.com; © Jim Bowie/Shutterstock.com; © wacomkaShutterstock.com; © Shebeko/Shutterstock.com

Anne doesn't like that the text in the left column crowds the right column and page boundary. She suggests that you provide more interior space by increasing the padding in the left column.

To increase the left column padding:

1. Return to the **pc_home.css** file in your editor and go to the Left Column Styles section.

2. Insert the property **padding: 1.5em;** into the section#leftColumn style rule as shown in Figure 3-19.

Figure 3-19   Increasing the padding of the left column

```
/* Left Column Styles */

section#leftColumn {
    clear: left;
    float: left;
    padding: 1.5em;
    width: 33%;
}
```

increases the interior padding to 1.5em

3. Save your changes to the style sheet and then reload the **pc_home.html** file in your browser. Figure 3-20 shows the result of your change.

| Figure 3-20 | Page layout crashes with increased padding |

increased padding increases the width of the left column, making it bigger than 33% of the page body width

the right column is forced to wrap to a new row, ruining the page layout

© Brenda Carson/Shutterstock.com; source: Facebook © 2015; source: 2015 Twitter

This simple change has caused the layout to crash. What went wrong?

Refining a Floated Layout

When the total width of floated objects exceeds the width of their parent, excess content is automatically wrapped to a new row. The reason the layout for the Pandaisia Chocolates home page crashed is that increasing the padding in the left column, increased the column's width beyond its set value of 33%. Even this small increase caused the total width of the two columns to exceed 100% and, as a result, the right column moved to a new row.

To keep floats within the same row, you have to understand how CSS handles widths. Recall that block elements are laid out according to the box model, as illustrated previously in Figure 2-38, in which the content is surrounded by the padding space, the border space, and finally the margin space. By default, browsers measure widths using the **content box model** in which the width property only refers to the width of the element content and any padding or borders constitute added space.

CSS also supports the **border box model**, in which the width property is based on the sum of the content, padding, and border spaces and any space taken up by the padding and border is subtracted from space given to the content. Figure 3-21 shows how the two different models interpret the same width, padding, and border values.

Figure 3-21 Comparing the Content Box and Border Box models

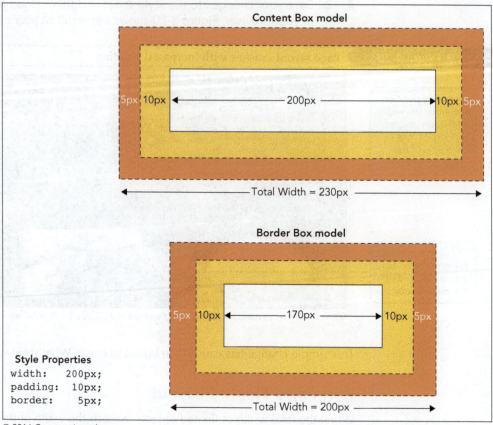

Content Box model

5px 10px ←—— 200px ——→ 10px 5px

←———— Total Width = 230px ————→

Border Box model

5px 10px ←— 170px —→ 10px 5px

Style Properties
```
width:    200px;
padding:  10px;
border:     5px;
```

←———— Total Width = 200px ————→

© 2016 Cengage Learning

You can choose the layout model using the following `box-sizing` property

```
box-sizing: type;
```

where *type* is `content-box` (the default), `border-box`, or `inherit` (to inherit the property defined for the element's container). This CSS3 `box-sizing` property was initially introduced as a browser extension, so, in order to support older browsers, it is commonly entered using progressive enhancement with the following extensions

```
-webkit-box-sizing: type;
-moz-box-sizing: type;
box-sizing: type;
```

where *type* has the same values as before. Many designers prefer to use the border box model in page layout so that there is no confusion about the total width of each element.

REFERENCE

Defining How Widths Are Interpreted

• To define what the `width` property measures, use the style:

```
box-sizing: type;
```

where *type* is `content-box` (the default), `border-box`, or `inherit` (to inherit the property defined for the element's container).

Add the `box-sizing` property to the reset style sheet and apply it to all block elements.

To set the block layout model:

1. Return to the **pc_reset.css** file in your editor.

2. Add the following style properties to the style rule for the list of block elements

   ```
   -webkit-box-sizing: border-box;
   -moz-box-sizing: border-box;
   box-sizing: border-box;
   ```

   Figure 3-22 highlights the revised style rule.

Figure 3-22   **Adding the border-box style to the reset style sheet**

```
address, article, aside, blockquote, body, cite,
div, dl, dt, dd, em, figcaption, figure, footer,
h1, h2, h3, h4, h5, h6, header, html, img,
li, main, nav, ol, p, section, span, ul {
    background: transparent;
    font-size: 100%;
    margin: 0;
    padding: 0;
    vertical-align: baseline;
    -webkit-box-sizing: border-box;
    -moz-box-sizing: border-box;
    box-sizing: border-box;
}
```

applies border box sizing to all of the listed block elements

3. Save your changes to the style sheet and then reload the **pc_home.html** file in your browser. Verify that the layout of the left and right columns has been restored and additional padding has been added within the left column.

The final part of the Pandaisia Chocolates home page is the footer, which contains three vertical navigation lists and a `section` element with contact information for the store. Once the left margin is clear of previously floated objects, float these four elements on the left margin with the widths of the three navigation lists each set to 22% of the body width and the `section` element occupying the remaining 34%.

To lay out the page footer:

1. Return to the **pc_home.css** file in your editor and scroll down to the Footer Styles section.

2. Insert the following style rules:

   ```
   footer {
       clear: left;
   }


   footer > nav.verticalNavigation {
       float: left;
       width: 22%;
   }
   ```

```
footer > section#contactInfo {
    float: left;
    width: 34%;
}
```

Figure 3-23 highlights the layout style rules for the page footer.

Figure 3-23 **Setting the layout of the page footer**

```
/* Footer Styles */

footer {
    clear: left;
}

footer > nav.verticalNavigation {
    float: left;
    width: 22%;
}

footer > section#contactInfo {
    float: left;
    width: 34%;
}
```

displays the footer once the left margin is clear of floated objects

sets the width of the vertical navigation lists to 22% and floats them on the left

sets the width of the contactInfo section to 34% and floats it on the left

3. Save your changes to the style sheet and then reload **pc_home.html** in your browser. Figure 3-24 shows the new layout of the footer.

Figure 3-24 **Page footer layout**

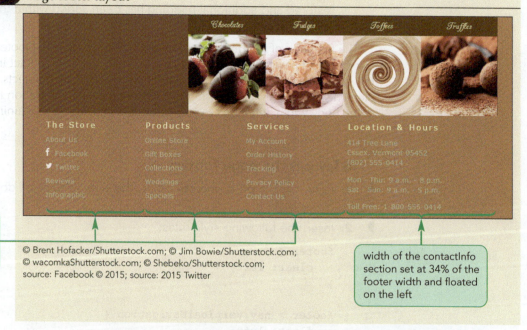

each vertical navigation list set at 22% of the footer width and floated on the left

© Brent Hofacker/Shutterstock.com; © Jim Bowie/Shutterstock.com;
© wacomkaShutterstock.com; © Shebeko/Shutterstock.com;
source: Facebook © 2015; source: 2015 Twitter

width of the contactInfo section set at 34% of the footer width and floated on the left

Anne asks you to change the background color of the footer to a dark brown to better show the text content.

To set the footer background color:

1. Return to the **pc_home.css** file in your editor and go to the Footer Styles section.

2. Insert the following property for the `footer` selector:

   `background-color: rgb(71, 52, 29);`

   Figure 3-25 highlights the footer background color style.

Figure 3-25 ▸ Setting the footer background color

```
footer {
    background-color: rgb(71, 52, 29);
    clear: left;
}
```

footer background set to a dark brown →

---

3. Save your changes to the style sheet and then reload **pc_home.html** in your browser. Note that the background color is *not changed*.

Why didn't the change to the background color take effect? To help you understand why, you'll look once again at the nature of floated elements.

Working with Container Collapse

Recall that a floated element is taken out of the document flow so that it is no longer "part" of the element that contains it. Literally it is floating free of its container. When every element in a container is floated, there is no content left. As far as the browser is concerned, the container is empty and thus has no height and no background to color, a situation known as **container collapse**. Figure 3-26 demonstrates container collapse for a container that has three floating objects that exceed the boundaries of their container.

Figure 3-26 ▸ Container collapse

container doesn't enclose floated content

container expanded to enclose floated content

© 2016 Cengage Learning

What you usually want in your layout is to have the container expand to surround all of its floating content. One way this can occur is if the container is followed by another element that is displayed only when the margins are clear of floats. In that situation, the container's height will expand up to that trailing element and in the process surround its floating content.

The problem with the footer in the Pandaisia home page is that there is no trailing element—the footer is the last element in the page body. One way to fix that problem is to use the `after` pseudo-element to add a placeholder element after the footer. The general style rule is

```
container::after {
    clear: both;
    content: "";
    display: table;
}
```

TIP

To find other ways to prevent container collapse, search the web using the keywords *CSS clearfix*.

where *container* is the selector for the element containing floating objects. The `clear` property keeps this placeholder element from being inserted until both margins are clear of floats. The element itself is a web table but contains only an empty text string so that no actual content is written to the web page. That's okay because the mere presence of this placeholder element is enough to keep the container from collapsing.

Add a style rule now to create a placeholder element that keeps the footer from collapsing around its floating content.

To keep the footer from collapsing:

1. Return to Footer Styles section in the **pc_home.css** file and, after the style rule for the footer element, insert the following rule:

```
footer::after {
    clear: both;
    content: "";
    display: table;
}
```

Figure 3-27 highlights the new rule in the style sheet.

Figure 3-27 Preventing the footer from collapsing

```
footer {
    background-color: rgb(71, 52, 29);
    clear: left;
}
```
creates an element after the footer

```
footer::after {
    clear: both;
    content: "";
    display: table;
}
```
places the element after both the margins are clear

the element consists of an empty web table

2. Save your changes to the style sheet and then reload **pc_home.html** in your browser. Figure 3-28 shows the completed layout of the Pandaisia Chocolates home page.

Figure 3-28   Final layout of the Pandaisia Chocolates home page

footer has expanded to contain all floated content

© 2016 Cengage Learning; © Brenda Carson/Shutterstock.com; © Brent Hofacker/Shutterstock.com; © Jim Bowie/
Shutterstock.com; © wacomkaShutterstock.com; © Shebeko/Shutterstock.com; source: Facebook © 2015; source: 2015 Twitter

Note that the footer now has a dark brown background because it has expanded in height to contain all of its floated content.

3. Close any of the documents you opened for this session.

Keeping a Container from Collapsing

• To prevent a container from collapsing around its floating content, add the following style rule to the container

```
container::after {
   clear: both;
   content: "";
   display: table;
}
```

where *container* is the selector for the element containing the floating content.

Problem Solving: The Virtue of Being Negative

It's common to think of layout in terms of placing content, but good layout also must be concerned with placing emptiness. In art and page design, this is known as working with positive and negative space. Positive space is the part of the page occupied by text, graphics, borders, icons, and other page elements. Negative space, or white space, is the unoccupied area, and provides balance and contrast to elements contained in positive space.

A page that is packed with content leaves the eye with no place to rest; which also means that the eye has no place to focus and maybe even no clear indication about where to start reading. Negative space is used to direct users to resting stops before moving on to the next piece of page content. This can be done by providing a generous margin between page elements and by increasing the padding within an element. Even increasing the spacing between letters within an article heading can alleviate eye strain and make the text easier to read.

White space also has an emotional aspect. In the early days of print advertising, white space was seen as wasted space, and thus, smaller magazines and direct mail advertisements would tend to crowd content together in order to reduce waste. By contrast, upscale magazines and papers could distinguish themselves from those publications with an excess of empty space. This difference carries over to the web, where a page with less content and more white space often feels more classy and polished, while a page crammed with a lot of content feels more commercial. Both can be effective; you should decide which approach to use based on your customer profile.

You've completed your work on the Pandaisia Chocolates home page. In the next session, you'll work on page layout using the technique of grids.

REVIEW

Session 3.1 Quick Check

1. Provide the style rule to display all hypertext links within a navigation list as block elements with a gray background.

2. Briefly describe the three types of page layouts.

3. Provide a style rule to set the width of the page body to 90% of the browser window ranging from 320 pixels up to 960 pixels.

4. Provide a style rule to horizontally center the `header` element within the `body` element. Assume that the header is a direct child of the page body.

5. Provide a style rule to set the width of the `aside` element to 240 pixels and to float on the right margin of its container.

6. Provide a style rule to display the `footer` element only after all floated elements have cleared.

7. Your layout has four floated elements in a row but unfortunately the last element has wrapped to a new line. What is the source of the layout mistake?

8. Provide a style rule to change the `width` property for the `header` element so that it measures the total width of the header content, padding, and border spaces. Include web extensions for older browsers.

9. Provide a style rule to prevent the `header` element from collapsing around its floating content.

Session 3.2 Visual Overview:

The col-2-3 class indicates a column that is 2/3 of the width of its row. The col-1-2 class indicates a column that is half the width of its row.

In a grid layout, rows and columns are marked using the div element.

```
<div class="col-2-3">
  <h2>Our Company</h2>
  <img src="pc_photo6.png" alt="" />
  <p>We are a company located in Essex, Vermont, dedicated to
     making delicious chocolate and other treats. For our founder,
     chocolatier Anne Ambrose, this means using only the finest
     organic ingredients, incorporating a harmonious blend of rich
     flavors and smooth textures.</p>
  <div class="row">
    <h2>About Chocolate</h2>
    <div class="col-1-2">
      <h3>Enjoying Chocolate</h3>
      <p>The best chocolate is fresh chocolate.
         Preservatives change the flavor and texture of chocolate.
         For the best results, our chocolates should be consumed
         within a few days of purchase. Store them in a
         cool, dark place at a temperature of 60&deg; to 70&deg; and
         then enjoy!</p>
    </div>
    <div class="col-1-2">
      <h3>Healthy Chocolate</h3>
      <p>Chocolate has a bad reput
         quality of mass-produced
         sugar, and butter &mdash;
         healthy. We keep the proc
         produce dark chocolate th
    </div>
  </div>
</div>
```

Pseudo content is added after a grid row to keep it from collapsing around the columns.

All grid columns are floated within their rows.

The class name provides a hint as to the width of the grid columns.

```
div.row {clear: both;}

div.row::after {
    content: "";
    display: table;
    clear: both;
}

div[class^='col-'] {float: left;}

div.col-1-2 {width: 50%;}
div.col-1-3 {width: 33.33%;}
div.col-2-3 {width: 66.67%;}

div {
    outline: 1px solid red;
}
```

Grid rows are only displayed after the floating columns are cleared.

The outline property draws a line around the selected element(s).

© 2016 Cengage Learning; © Twin Design/Shutterstock.com

Figure 3-30   Layout based on a grid

© 2016 Cengage Learning

It should be stressed that the grid is not part of the web page content. Instead, it's a systematic approach to visualizing how to best fit content onto the page. Working from a grid has several aesthetic and practical advantages, including

- Grids add order to the presentation of page content, adding visual rhythm, which is pleasing to the eye.
- A consistent logical design gives readers the confidence to find the information they seek.
- New content can be easily placed within a grid in a way that is consistent with previously entered information.
- A well designed grid is more easily accessible for users with disabilities and special needs.
- Grids speed up the development process by establishing a systematic framework for the page layout.

There are two basic types of grid layouts: fixed grids and fluid grids.

Fixed and Fluid Grids

In a **fixed grid**, the widths of the columns and margins are specified in pixels, where every column has a fixed position. Many fixed grid layouts are based on a page width of 960 pixels because most desktop screen widths are at 1024 pixels (or higher) and a 960-pixel width leaves room for browser scrollbars and other features. The 960-pixel width is also easily divisible into halves, thirds, quarters, and so forth, making it easier to create evenly spaced columns.

The problem of course with a fixed grid layout is that it does not account for other screen sizes and thus, a **fluid grid**, in which column widths are expressed in percentages rather than pixels, is often used to provide more support across different devices. In the examples to follow, you'll base your layouts on a fluid grid system.

Grids are often used with responsive design in which one grid layout is used with mobile devices, another grid layout is used with tablets, and yet another layout is used with desktop computers. A layout for a mobile device is typically based on a 1-column grid, tablet layouts are based on grids of 4 to 12 columns, and desktop layouts are often based on layouts with 12 or more columns.

CSS Frameworks

Designing your own grids can be time-consuming. To simplify the process, you can choose from the many CSS frameworks available on the web. A **framework** is a software package that provides a library of tools to design your website, including style sheets for grid layouts and built-in scripts to provide support for a variety of browsers and devices. Most frameworks include support for responsive design so that you can easily scale your website for devices ranging from mobile phones to desktop computers.

Some popular CSS frameworks include

- **Bootstrap** (*getbootstrap.com*)
- **YAML4** (*www.yaml.de*)
- **960 Grid System** (*960.gs*)
- **Foundation 3** (*foundation.zurb.com*)
- **HTML5 Boilerplate** (*html5boilerplate.com*)
- **Skeleton** (*getskeleton.com*)

While a framework does a lot of the work in building the grid, you still need to understand how to interact with the underlying code, including the style sheets used to create a grid layout. In this session, you'll create your own style sheet based on a simple grid, which will help you get started if you choose to work with commercial CSS frameworks.

Setting up a Grid

A grid layout is based on rows of floating elements, much as you did in the layout of the Pandaisia home page in the last session. Each floating element constitutes a column. The set of elements floating side-by-side establishes a row. To give a consistent structure to these floating objects, many grid layouts use the `div` (or division) element to mark distinct rows and columns of the grid. Let's examine the following simple example of a grid consisting of a single row with two columns:

```
<div class="row">
    <div class="column1"></div>
    <div class="column2"></div>
</div>
```

Within these `div` elements, you place your page content, but you don't need to worry about that yet. For more elaborate layouts, a column can contain its own grid of rows and columns. The following code expands the previous grid layout by placing a grid of two rows and two columns within each row `div` within the column1 `div` element:

```
<div class="row">
    <div class="column1">
        <div class="row">
            <div class="column1a"></div>
            <div class="column1b"></div>
        </div>
        <div class="row">
            <div class="column1c"></div>
            <div class="column1d"></div>
        </div>
    </div>
    <div class="column2"></div>
</div>
```

It's common in grid layouts to give the columns class names indicating their width. For example, use a class name of "col-1-4" to indicate a column with a width of 1/4 or 25% or use a class name of "col-2-3" to indicate a column with a width of 2/3 or 67%. Using this class name system, the following HTML markup

```
<div class="row">
  <div class="col-2-3">
    <div class="row">
      <div class="col-1-4"></div>
      <div class="col-1-4"></div>
      <div class="col-1-2"></div>
    </div>
    <div class="row">
      <div class="col-1-1"></div>
    </div>
  </div>
  <div class="col-1-3"></div>
</div>
```

results in the grid layout shown in Figure 3-31. Note that this layout consists of a single row with two columns with the first column itself containing three columns arranged across two rows. Remember though that the actual column widths are not set by the class names, instead they are defined in the style sheet. The class names are just aids for us to interpret the grid layout in the HTML file.

Figure 3-31	Sample grid layout

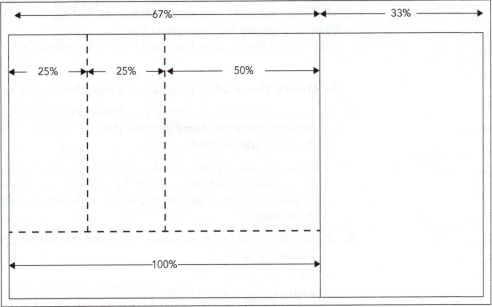

© 2016 Cengage Learning

Now that you've seen the general structure for the HTML code in a layout grid, you'll create one for a new page in the Pandaisia Chocolates website that provides information about chocolate and the company. Anne has laid out a grid for the page's content shown in Figure 3-32.

Figure 3-32   Proposed grid layout for the About Pandaisia Chocolates page

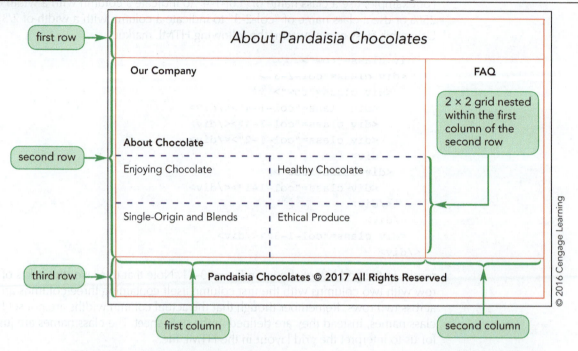

Anne's layout consists of three main rows. The first row contains the page title and the third row contains the page footer. The second row consists of two columns: the first column displaying information about the company and the second column displaying a list of frequently asked questions. Within the first row is a nested 2 × 2 grid containing short articles about chocolate.

Add the `div` elements for this grid layout to the About Pandaisia Chocolates page.

To create the About Pandaisia Chocolates page:

1. Use your editor to open the **pc_about_txt.html** file from the html03 ▸ tutorial folder. Enter *your name* and *the date* in the comment section and save the file as **pc_about.html**.

   Anne has already added the same header used for the Pandaisia Chocolates home page to this page. Using the same header tags keeps a consistent header for each page and, therefore, a consistent look and feel across pages in the website.

2. Below the closing `</header>` tag, insert the following `div` elements for the first row in the grid.

   ```
   <div class="row">
   </div>
   ```

3. Next, insert the following `div` elements for the second row containing two columns within the nested 2 × 2 grid in the first column.

   ```
   <div class="row">
       <div class="col-2-3">
           <div class="row">
               <div class="col-1-2">
               </div>
               <div class="col-1-2">
               </div>
           </div>
   ```

```
        <div class="row">
           <div class="col-1-2">
           </div>
           <div class="col-1-2">
           </div>
        </div>
     </div>
     <div class="col-1-3">
     </div>
  </div>
```

4. Finally, insert the following `div` elements for the third row of the grid:

```
<div class="row">
</div>
```

Figure 3-33 highlights the complete code for the grid you've created.

Figure 3-33	div elements in the About Pandaisia Chocolates page

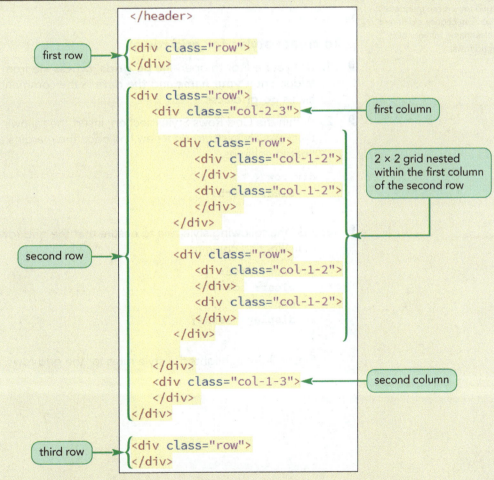

5. Take some time to review your code, making sure that it matches the structure and class names shown in Figure 3-33.

6. Save your changes to the file but do not close it.

Now that you've established the grid for the page content, you'll set up the styles for the grid, starting with the grid row.

Designing the Grid Rows

Grid rows contain floating columns. Since a grid row starts a new line within the page, it should only be displayed when both margins are clear of previously floated columns. Since it contains its own set of floating columns, it has to be able to expand in height to cover those objects (or else the floating columns run the risk of bleeding into the next row.) As with the page footer from the last session, you can establish these rules for grid rows using the following style rule:

```
div.row::after {
    clear: both;
    content: "";
    display: table;
}
```

Add this style rule to a new style sheet, pc_grids.css, that you will use to format the grid layout used in the pc_about.html file.

To create styles for grid rows:

1. Use your editor to open the **pc_grids_txt.css** file from the html03 ► tutorial folder. Enter **your name** and **the date** in the comment section and save the file as **pc_grids.css**.

2. Within the Grid Rows Styles section, insert the following style rules to ensure that rows always start on a new line once the margins are clear of previously floated columns.

   ```
   div.row {
       clear: both;
   }
   ```

3. Add the following style rule to ensure that the grid row expands to cover all of its floating columns:

   ```
   div.row::after {
       clear: both;
       content: "";
       display: table;
   }
   ```

   Figure 3-34 highlights the style rules for the grid rows.

Figure 3-34   **Styles for row div elements**

```
/* Grid Rows Styles */

div.row {
    clear: both;
}

div.row::after {
    clear: both;
    content: "";
    display: table;
}
```

displays the row only when both margins are clear of previously-floated columns

automatically expands the row to cover floating columns

Next, you'll create style rules for the grid columns.

Designing the Grid Columns

Every grid column needs to be floated within its row. In the grid you set up for the About Pandaisia Chocolates page, grid columns are placed within a `div` element having the general class name

```
class="col-numerator-denominator"
```

TIP

For a review of attribute selectors, and specifically `elem[att^="text"]`, refer to Figure 2-15 in Tutorial 2.

where *numerator-denominator* provides the fractional width of the column. For example, the col-1-3 class indicates that the column is one-third the total row width. To float all grid columns, you can use the following attribute selector, which matches all `div` elements whose `class` attribute begins with the text string "col-":

```
div[class^="col-"] {
    float: left;
}
```

Add this style rule to the pc_grids.css style sheet file now.

To float the grid columns:

1. Within the Grid Columns Styles section, insert the following style rule:

```
div[class^="col-"] {
    float: left;
}
```

Figure 3-35 highlights the style rule for the grid columns.

Figure 3-35   **Style for column div elements**

matches all div elements whose class attribute starts with "col-"

```
/* Grid Columns Styles */

div[class^="col-"] {
    float: left;
}
```

floats every column on the left

2. Save your changes to the file.

Finally, you have to establish the width of each column based on its class name. For example div elements with the class name col-1-3 will use the following style rule to set their width to 1/3 or 33.33% of the width of the parent element—the grid row.

```
div.col-1-3 {width: 33.33%;}
```

Add style rules for column widths ranging from 25% up to 100%.

To set the width of the grid columns:

The class name associated with each column provides a clue to the column's width.

1. Within the Grid Columns Styles section, add the following style rules:

```
div.col-1-1 {width: 100%;}
div.col-1-2 {width: 50%;}
div.col-1-3 {width: 33.33%;}
div.col-2-3 {width: 66.67%;}
div.col-1-4 {width: 25%;}
div.col-3-4 {width: 75%;}
```

Figure 3-36 highlights the width values assigned to div elements of different classes.

Figure 3-36   Setting the column widths

```
div[class^="col-"] {
    float: left;
}

div.col-1-1 {width: 100%;}
div.col-1-2 {width: 50%;}
div.col-1-3 {width: 33.33%;}
div.col-2-3 {width: 66.67%;}
div.col-1-4 {width: 25%;}
div.col-3-4 {width: 75%;}
```

full width column

half width column

one-third and two-thirds width columns

one-fourth and three-fourths width columns

2. Save your changes to the file.

Continuing in this same fashion, you could have included styles for other column widths based on percentages. For example, a one-sixth column would have a width of 16.66%, a one-twelfth column would have a width of 8.33%, and so forth.

Adding the Page Content

TIP

Choose percent values for the column widths so that the total width of all of the columns in the row does not exceed 100%.

Now that you have established the basic framework for your grid you can add the page content to each of its rows and columns. To save you from typing the content, Anne has prepared a file containing the text of the articles to appear in the About Pandaisia Chocolates page. Insert this content now starting with the text of the first row in the grid.

To insert page content into the grid:

1. Return to the **pc_about.html** file in your editor.

2. Directly after the opening `<div class="row">` tag, insert the following h1 heading:

   ```
   <h1>About Pandaisia Chocolates</h1>
   ```

   Figure 3-37 shows the placement of the h1 heading in the first grid row.

Figure 3-37   **Adding the heading to the first row of the grid**

```
</header>

<div class="row">
    <h1>About Pandaisia Chocolates</h1>
</div>
```

Next, you'll insert the text for the left column of the second row of the grid.

3. Open the **pc_text.txt** file using your text editor and copy the HTML code from the About the Company section, which includes the h2 heading, an `img` element, and two paragraphs.

4. Paste the copied code directly after the first `<div class="col-2-3">` tag near the top of the grid.

   Figure 3-38 shows the placement of the left column text.

Figure 3-38   **Adding information about the company**

```
<div class="row">
    <h1>About Pandaisia Chocolates</h1>
</div>

<div class="row">
    <div class="col-2-3">
        <h2>Our Company</h2>
        <img src="pc_photo6.png" alt="" />
        <p>We are a company located in Essex, Vermont, dedicated to
            making delicious chocolate and other treats. For our founder,
            chocolatier Anne Ambrose, this means using only the finest
            organic ingredients, incorporating a harmonious blend of rich
            flavors and smooth textures.</p>
        <p>Anne learned her trade as part of a three-year apprenticeship
            program in Switzerland. Her introduction into the world of
            confectioneries was a springboard to working with leaders in
            the field. Early in 1993 she brought that expertise back to
            Vermont and Pandaisia Chocolates was born.</p>
        <div class="row">
```

content pasted into the left column

Within the left column are two nested rows containing short articles about chocolate. You will add this content to the grid now.

5. Directly after the nested `<div class="row">` tag, insert the heading tag `<h2>About Chocolate</h2>`

6. Return to the **pc_text.txt** file in your editor and copy the HTML code from the first of four Enjoying Chocolates sections, which includes the h3 heading and a paragraph. Paste the copied text into the first of the four nested half-width columns, as shown in Figure 3-39.

Figure 3-39   Adding content about chocolate

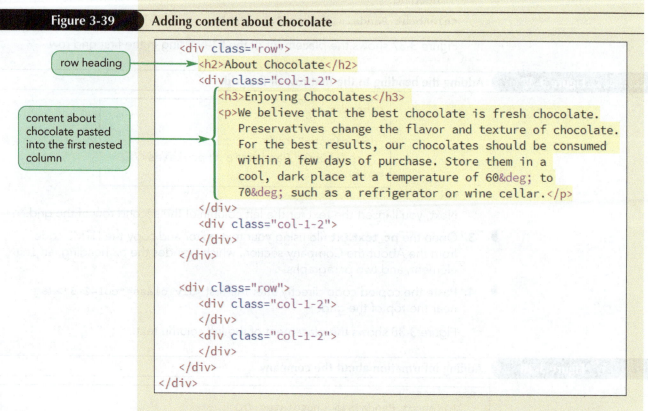

row heading

content about chocolate pasted into the first nested column

```
<div class="row">
  <h2>About Chocolate</h2>
  <div class="col-1-2">
    <h3>Enjoying Chocolates</h3>
    <p>We believe that the best chocolate is fresh chocolate.
      Preservatives change the flavor and texture of chocolate.
      For the best results, our chocolates should be consumed
      within a few days of purchase. Store them in a
      cool, dark place at a temperature of 60&deg; to
      70&deg; such as a refrigerator or wine cellar.</p>
  </div>
  <div class="col-1-2">
  </div>
</div>

<div class="row">
  <div class="col-1-2">
  </div>
  <div class="col-1-2">
  </div>
</div>
```

7. Add the content for the remaining three half-width nested columns by returning to the **pc_text.txt** file in your editor and copying the HTML code from the last three Enjoying Chocolate sections: Healthy Chocolate, Single-Origin and Blends, and Ethical Produce. Each section includes an h3 heading and a paragraph. Paste the copied code from each section into one of the three remaining nested half-width columns. Figure 3-40 shows the placement of the copied HTML code for the last three half-width nested columns.

| Figure 3-40 | Adding content to the rest of the nested columns |

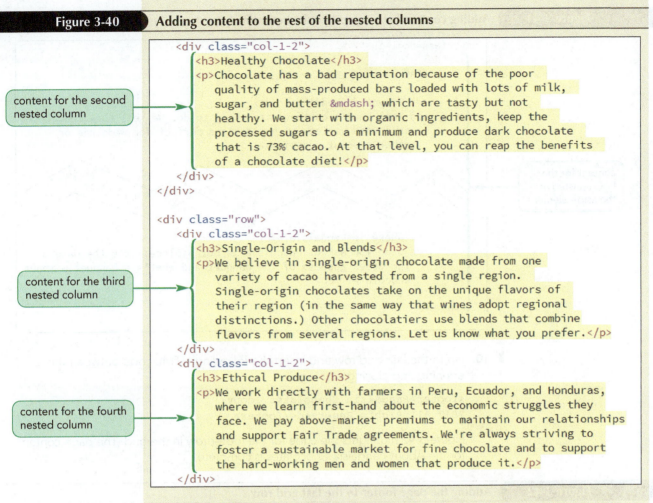

content for the second nested column

content for the third nested column

content for the fourth nested column

```
<div class="col-1-2">
    <h3>Healthy Chocolate</h3>
    <p>Chocolate has a bad reputation because of the poor
        quality of mass-produced bars loaded with lots of milk,
        sugar, and butter &mdash; which are tasty but not
        healthy. We start with organic ingredients, keep the
        processed sugars to a minimum and produce dark chocolate
        that is 73% cacao. At that level, you can reap the benefits
        of a chocolate diet!</p>
</div>
</div>

<div class="row">
    <div class="col-1-2">
        <h3>Single-Origin and Blends</h3>
        <p>We believe in single-origin chocolate made from one
            variety of cacao harvested from a single region.
            Single-origin chocolates take on the unique flavors of
            their region (in the same way that wines adopt regional
            distinctions.) Other chocolatiers use blends that combine
            flavors from several regions. Let us know what you prefer.</p>
    </div>
    <div class="col-1-2">
        <h3>Ethical Produce</h3>
        <p>We work directly with farmers in Peru, Ecuador, and Honduras,
            where we learn first-hand about the economic struggles they
            face. We pay above-market premiums to maintain our relationships
            and support Fair Trade agreements. We're always striving to
            foster a sustainable market for fine chocolate and to support
            the hard-working men and women that produce it.</p>
    </div>
</div>
```

8. The right column of the second grid row contains a list of frequently asked questions. Return to the **pc_text.txt** file in your editor and copy the aside element and its contents from the Frequently Asked Questions section.

9. Return to the **pc_about.html** file in your editor and paste the copied code within the right column, as shown in Figure 3-41.

Figure 3-41   **Adding content for frequently asked questions**

```html
<div class="col-1-3">
    <aside>
        <h2>FAQ</h2>
        <dl>
            <dt>Do you do weddings?</dt>
            <dd>Yes! That's our favorite thing to do. We sell bulk chocolates
                in a wide variety of box designs perfect for weddings or
                other special occasions.</dd>

            <dt>Where is Pandaisia?</dt>
            <dd>Glad you asked. Pandaisia is not a place; it's the name of
                the Greek goddess of the banquet and what's a banquet without
                chocolate?</dd>
        </dl>
    </aside>
</div>
```

content for the FAQs pasted into the aside element

10. Go to the last grid row and insert the following HTML code between the opening and closing div tags:

```html
<footer>Pandaisia Chocolates &copy;
2017 All Rights Reserved</footer>
```

Figure 3-42 highlights the code for the footer row in the grid. The page content for the About Pandaisia Chocolates is complete.

Figure 3-42   **Adding the page footer to the last grid row**

```html
<div class="row">
    <footer>Pandaisia Chocolates&copy; 2017 All Rights Reserved</footer>
</div>

</body>
```

last row in the grid

11. Save your changes to the file.

Anne has already created style sheets containing the typographic and color styles for the content of this page. Link the pc_about.html file to the pc_reset.css, pc_grids.css and pc_styles2.css style sheet files.

To link to the style sheets:

1. Scroll to the top of the document and insert the following link elements directly after the title element:

```html
<link href="pc_reset.css" rel="stylesheet" />
<link href="pc_grids.css" rel="stylesheet" />
<link href="pc_styles2.css" rel="stylesheet" />
```

2. Save your changes to the file and then reload the **pc_about.html** file in your browser. Figure 3-43 shows the final layout of the page content.

| Figure 3-43 | Format of the content in the About Pandaisia Chocolates page |

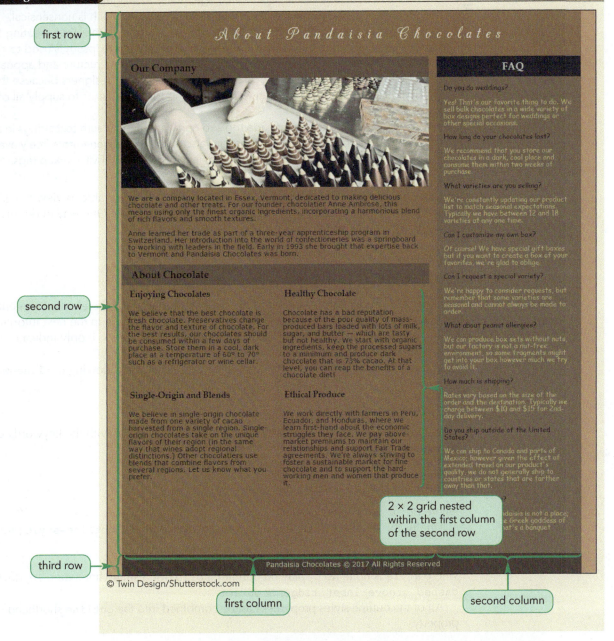

first row

second row

third row

2 × 2 grid nested within the first column of the second row

first column

second column

© Twin Design/Shutterstock.com

Compare the appearance of the page content with the schematic diagram shown earlier in Figure 3-32 to see how using a grid provided a unified layout for the page. As you become more experienced with setting up and applying grids, you can move to more intricate and interesting page layouts.

Generating Content with Lorem Ipsum

Lorem ipsum dolor sit amet, consectetur adipiscing elit. Integer nec odio. Praesent libero. Sed cursus ante dapibus diam. Sed nisi. Nulla quis sem at nibh elementum imperdiet. Duis sagittis ipsum. Vestibulum lacinia arcu eget nulla. Sed dignissim lacinia nunc.

That previous paragraph is an example of **lorem ipsum**, which is nonsensical, improper Latin commonly used in page design as filler text. Rather than creating large portions of sample text before you can view your layout, lorem ipsum is used to quickly generate sentences, lines, and paragraphs that resemble the structure and appearance of real text. Lorem ipsum is a particularly useful tool for web designers because they can begin working on page design without waiting for their clients to supply all of the page content.

Many popular web editors include tools to generate lorem ipsum text strings in a wide variety of formats and styles. There are also lorem ipsum generators freely available on the web, which will supplement the lorem ipsum text with HTML markup tags.

Once you've established a grid layout, you might want to be able to view the grid structure to confirm that the content has been placed properly. One way to do this is by using the outline style.

Outlining a Grid

Outlines are simply lines drawn around an element, enclosing the element content, padding, and border spaces. Unlike borders, which you'll study in the next tutorial, an outline doesn't add anything to the width or height of the object, it only indicates the extent of the element on the rendered page.

The width of the line used in the outline is defined by the following `outline-width` property

```
outline-width: value;
```

where `value` is expressed in one of the CSS units of length, or with the keywords `thin`, `medium`, or `thick`.

The line color is set using the `outline-color` property

```
outline-color: color;
```

where `color` is a CSS color name or value.

Finally, the design of the line can be set using the following `outline-style` property

```
outline-style: style;
```

where `style` is none (to display no outline), `solid` (for a single line), `double`, `dotted`, `dashed`, `groove`, `inset`, `ridge`, or `outset`.

All of the outline styles properties can be combined into the `outline` shorthand property

```
outline: width style color;
```

where `width`, `style`, and `color` are the values for the line's width, design, and color. For example, the following style rule uses the wildcard selector along with the `outline` shorthand property to draw a 1px dotted green line around every element on the web page:

```
* {
    outline: 1px dotted green;
}
```

TIP

Outlines can also be applied to inline elements such as inline images, citations, quotations, and italicized text.

Note that there are no separate outline styles for the left, right, top, or bottom edge of the object. The outline always surrounds an entire element.

REFERENCE

Adding an Outline

- To add an outline around an element, use the property

  ```
  outline: width style color;
  ```

  where *width*, *style*, and *color* are the outline width, outline design, and outline color respectively. These attributes can be listed in any order.

Use the `outline` property now to outline every `div` element in your grid so that you can see how the page content is related to the grid you created.

To outline the grid:

1. Return to the **pc_grids.css** file in your editor.

2. Go to the Grid Outline Styles section and insert the following style rule:

   ```
   div {
       outline: 1px solid red;
   }
   ```

   Figure 3-44 describes the use of the `outline` shorthand property.

Figure 3-44   **Add outlines to grid rows and columns**

3. Save your changes to the style sheet.

4. Reload the **pc_about.html** file in your browser. Figure 3-45 shows the appearance of the part of the page with the grid lines superimposed on the page layout.

Figure 3-45 **Outlines added to every div element**

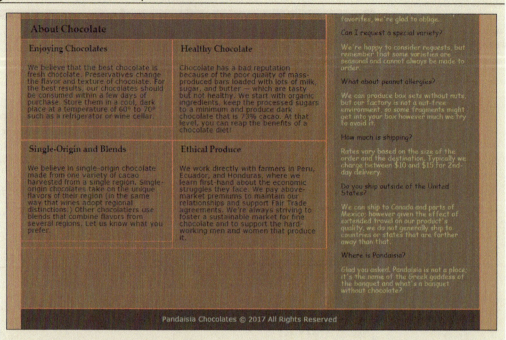

Enjoying Chocolates

We believe that the best chocolate is fresh chocolate. Preservatives change the flavor and texture of chocolate. For the best results, our chocolates should be consumed within a few days of purchase. Store them in a cool, dark place at a temperature of 60° to 70° such as a refrigerator or wine cellar.

Single-Origin and Blends

We believe in single-origin chocolate made from one variety of cacao harvested from a single region. Single-origin chocolates take on the unique flavors of their region (in the same way that wines adopt regional distinctions.) Other chocolatiers use blends that combine flavors from several regions. Let us know what you prefer.

Healthy Chocolate

Chocolate has a bad reputation because of the poor quality of mass-produced bars loaded with lots of milk, sugar, and butter — which are tasty but not healthy. We start with organic ingredients, keep the processed sugars to a minimum and produce dark chocolate that is 73% cacao. At that level, you can reap the benefits of a chocolate diet!

Ethical Produce

We work directly with farmers in Peru, Ecuador, and Honduras, where we learn first-hand about the economic struggles they face. We pay above-market premiums to maintain our relationships and support Fair Trade agreements. We're always striving to foster a sustainable market for fine chocolate and to support the hard-working men and women that produce it.

favorites, we're glad to oblige.

Can I request a special variety?

We're happy to consider requests, but remember that some varieties are seasonal and cannot always be made to order.

What about peanut allergies?

We can produce box sets without nuts, but our factory is not a nut-free environment, so some fragments might get into your box however much we try to avoid it.

How much is shipping?

Rates vary based on the size of the order and the destination. Typically we charge between $10 and $15 for 2nd-day delivery.

Do you ship outside of the United States?

We can ship to Canada and parts of Mexico; however given the effect of extended travel on our product's quality, we do not generally ship to countries or states that are farther away than that.

Where is Pandaisia?

Glad you asked. Pandaisia is not a place; it's the name of the Greek goddess of the banquet and what's a banquet without chocolate?

5. Close any of your open files now.

Anne appreciates the work you've done on the About Pandaisia Chocolates page. She thinks that the outlines around the grid rows and columns make it easier to view the layout style, which will make it easier to make modifications in future pages. For now, you'll leave the outlines in place to aid her in future work on the page design.

Creating Drop Caps with CSS

A popular design element is the **drop cap**, which consists of an enlarged initial letter in a body of text that drops down into the text body. To create a drop cap, you increase the font size of an element's first letter and float it on the left margin. Drop caps also generally look better if you decrease the line height of the first letter, enabling the surrounding content to better wrap around the letter. Finding the best combination of font size and line height is a matter of trial and error; and unfortunately, what looks best in one browser might not look as good in another. The following style rule works well in applying a drop cap to the first paragraph element:

```
p:first-of-type::first-letter {
    font-size: 4em;
    float: left;
    line-height: 0.8;
}
```

For additional design effects, you can change the font face of the drop cap to a cursive or decorative font.

Introducing CSS Grids

Grids are a fast and flexible way of creating a layout, but they are not without their problems. The most obvious problem is that setting up the grid increases the size and complexity of the HTML code by adding another level of markup. Another equally serious problem is that grids undermine the fundamental rule that the HTML file should consist solely of informational content while all instructions regarding presentation should be placed within an external style sheet. However, under the HTML grid system, the `div` elements have no purpose other than for defining how the page should be rendered. And if the designer wants to change the layout, the HTML file and the style sheet will both have to be modified, adding another layer of complexity to the site design.

Defining a CSS Grid

Since grids are an important and useful design tool, the W3C is working toward adding grid styles to CSS. To create a grid display without the use of `div` elements, CSS is now adding the following grid-based properties:

```
selector {
   display: grid;
   grid-template-rows: track-list;
   grid-template-columns: track-list;
}
```

The `grid` keyword for the `display` property establishes that the selected element(s) will be displayed as a grid. The number of rows and columns in the grid are set by the `grid-template-rows` and `grid-template-columns` properties where `track-list` is a space-separated list of row heights or column widths. Heights and widths can be expressed in any of the CSS units of measurement, including the keyword `auto` where the row or column will be automatically sized according to its content.

For example, the following style rule establishes a grid for the section element. The grid consists of three rows with the height of the first and last rows set to 100 pixels and the middle row automatically sized to match its content The grid also consists of three columns with the first and last column widths set to 25% and the middle column occupying half of each grid row.

```
section {
   display: grid;
   grid-template-rows: 100px auto 100px;
   grid-template-columns: 25% 50% 25%;
}
```

The CSS grid styles also introduce the **fr unit**, which represents the fraction of available space left on the grid after all other rows or columns have attained their maximum allowable size. For example, the following style creates four columns: two columns that are 200 and 250 pixels wide respectively and then two columns that are 1fr and 2fr respectively:

```
grid-template-columns: 200px 250px 1fr 2fr;
```

The `fr` unit can be thought of as a "share" of the available space so that, in this example, after 450 pixels have been given to the first two columns, whatever space remains is divided between the last two columns with 1fr or one-third allotted to the third column and 2fr or two-thirds to the fourth column.

Assigning Content to Grid Cells

Once you've established a CSS grid, you place a specific element within a **grid cell** at the intersection of a specified row and column. By default, all of the specified elements are placed in the grid cell located at the intersection of the first row and first column. To place the element in a different cell, use the following properties

```
grid-row-start: integer;
grid-row-end: integer;
grid-column-start: integer;
grid-column-end: integer;
```

where *integer* defines the starting and ending row or column that contains the content. For example, the following style rule places the `aside` element to cover the second and third rows and the first and second columns of the grid.

```
aside {
    grid-row-start: 2;
    grid-row-end: 3;
    grid-column-start: 1;
    grid-column-end: 2;
}
```

These coordinates can also be written in a more compact form as

```
grid-row: start/end;
grid-column: start/end;
```

where *start* and *end* are the starting and ending coordinates of the row and columns containing the element. Thus, you can place the `aside` element in the same location described above using the equivalent style rule, which follows:

```
aside {
    grid-row: 2/3;
    grid-column: 1/2;
}
```

If you specify a single number, the content is placed within a single grid cell. The following style rule places the `aside` element in the second row and first column of the grid:

```
aside {
    grid-row: 2;
    grid-column: 1;
}
```

REFERENCE

Defining Grids with CSS

- To assign a CSS grid to an element, use the property

  ```
  display: grid;
  ```

- To define the number of rows and columns within the grid, use the properties

  ```
  grid-template-rows: track-list;
  grid-template-columns: track-list;
  ```

  where *track-list* is a space-separated list of row heights or column widths.

- To place an element within a specific intersection of grid rows and columns, use the properties

  ```
  grid-row-start: integer;
  grid-row-end: integer;
  grid-column-start: integer;
  grid-column-end: integer;
  ```

  where *integer* defines the starting and ending row or column that contains the content.

- To more compactly set the location of the element within the grid, use the properties

  ```
  grid-row: start/end;
  grid-column: start/end;
  ```

  where *start* and *end* are the starting and ending coordinates of the row and columns containing the element.

You have only just scratched the surface of the future of grid design using CSS. Other properties in the current draft include styles for creating nested grids, collapsing and expanding rows and columns, and creating named grid areas. You can view the most current draft specifications at the W3C website. The CSS grid styles are not well-supported by current browsers at the time of this writing. Internet Explorer supports grid styles using the `-ms-` browser prefix. Other browsers are starting to provide support through experimental extensions. Eventually, CSS-based grids will supplant grid designs created via `div` elements, once again separating layout from content. Until that time, you should continue to either create your own grids using the techniques described in this session or use one of the many CSS frameworks available on the web.

Written Communication: Getting to the Point with Layout

Page layout is one of the most important aspects of web design. A well-constructed page layout naturally guides a reader's eyes to the most important information in the page. You should use the following principles to help your readers quickly get to the point:

- *Guide the eye.* Usability studies have shown that a reader's eye first lands in the top center of the page, then scans to the left, and then to the right and down. Arrange your page content so that the most important items are the first items a user sees.

- *Avoid clutter.* If a graphic or an icon is not conveying information or making the content easier to read, remove it.

- *Avoid overcrowding.* Focus on a few key items that will be easy for readers to locate while scanning the page, and separate these key areas from one another with ample white space. Don't be afraid to move a topic to a different page if it makes the current page easier to scan.

- *Make your information manageable.* It's easier for the brain to process information when it's presented in smaller chunks. Break up long extended paragraphs into smaller paragraphs or bulleted lists.

- *Use a grid.* Users find it easier to scan content when page elements are aligned vertically and horizontally. Use a grid to help you line up your elements in a clear and consistent way.

- *Cut down on the noise.* If you're thinking about using blinking text or a cute animated icon, don't. The novelty of such features wears off very quickly and distracts users from the valuable content in your page.

Always remember that your goal is to convey information to readers, and that an important tool in achieving that is to make it as easy as possible for readers to find that information. A thoughtfully constructed layout is a great aid to effective communication.

In the next session, you'll explore how to create page layouts that are not based on grids but instead allow objects to be placed anywhere within the rendered page.

Session 3.2 Quick Check

1. What is the difference between a fixed grid and a fluid grid?

2. What is a CSS framework?

3. In a proposed grid, all of the grid rows have the class name *container*. Create a style rule to expand those grid rows around their floating columns.

4. In a proposed grid, the columns all have the class names "span-*integer*" where *integer* indicates the size of the column. Create a style rule to float every grid column on the left margin.

5. Create a style rule to set the width of columns belonging to the span-4 class to 25% of the row width.

6. What is lorem ipsum?

7. Create a style rule for the grid rows described in question 3 above so that their sizes are measured using the Border Box model.

8. Create a style that adds a 2 pixel green dotted outline around all block quotes in the document.

9. Using the proposed specifications for CSS-based grids, create a grid for the body element that has three rows with heights automatically defined by the page content and five columns with widths of 25%, 2.5%, 50%, 2.5%, and 20%. Place the nav element in the first column, the article element in the third column, and the aside element in the fifth column.

Session 3.3 Visual Overview:

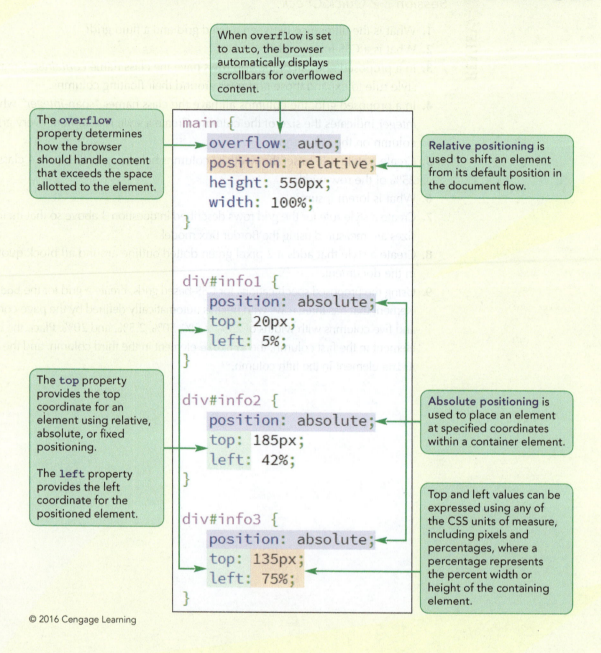

When overflow is set to auto, the browser automatically displays scrollbars for overflowed content.

The overflow property determines how the browser should handle content that exceeds the space allotted to the element.

Relative positioning is used to shift an element from its default position in the document flow.

```
main {
    overflow: auto;
    position: relative;
    height: 550px;
    width: 100%;
}
```

```
div#info1 {
    position: absolute;
    top: 20px;
    left: 5%;
}
```

The top property provides the top coordinate for an element using relative, absolute, or fixed positioning.

The left property provides the left coordinate for the positioned element.

```
div#info2 {
    position: absolute;
    top: 185px;
    left: 42%;
}
```

Absolute positioning is used to place an element at specified coordinates within a container element.

```
div#info3 {
    position: absolute;
    top: 135px;
    left: 75%;
}
```

Top and left values can be expressed using any of the CSS units of measure, including pixels and percentages, where a percentage represents the percent width or height of the containing element.

Layout with Positioning Styles

info1 is placed 20 pixels from the top of the main element and 5% from the left edge.

info2 is placed 185 pixels from the top and 42% from the left edge of the main element.

Vertical scrollbar is automatically added to view the overflowed content.

info3 is placed 135 pixels from the top and 75% from the left edge.

414 Tree Lane • Essex, VT 05452

Home   Online Store   My Account   Specials   Contact Us

All About Chocolate

The first box of Valentine's Day chocolates was created by British chocolatier Richard Cadbury in 1868.

A single cocoa tree produces about 800 bars of milk chocolate or 400 bars of dark chocolate every year.

The Ivory Coast accounts for 40% of worldwide cocoa production.

The word *chocolate* comes

Pandaisia Chocolate © 2017 All Rights Reserved

20px
185px
135px
5%
42%
75%

Positioning Objects

In the last session, you developed a layout in which page objects were strictly aligned according to the rows and columns of a grid. While a grid layout gives a page a feeling of uniformity and structure, it does limit your freedom to place objects at different locations within the page. In this session, you'll explore how to "break out" of the grid using the CSS positioning styles.

The CSS Positioning Styles

CSS supports several properties to place objects at specific coordinates within the page or within their container. To place an element at a specific position within its container, you use the following style properties

```
position: type;
top: value;
right: value;
bottom: value;
left: value;
```

where `type` indicates the kind of positioning applied to the element, and the `top`, `right`, `bottom`, and `left` properties indicate the coordinates of the top, right, bottom, and left edges of the element, respectively. The coordinates can be expressed in any of the CSS measuring units or as a percentage of the container's width or height.

CSS supports five kinds of positioning: `static` (the default), `relative`, `absolute`, `fixed`, and `inherit`. In **static positioning**, the element is placed where it would have fallen naturally within the flow of the document. This is essentially the same as not using any CSS positioning at all. Browsers ignore any values specified for the `top`, `left`, `bottom`, or `right` properties under static positioning.

Relative Positioning

Relative positioning is used to nudge an element out of its normal position in the document flow. Under relative positioning, the `top`, `right`, `bottom`, and `left` properties indicate the extra space that is placed alongside the element as it is shifted into a new position. For example, the following style rule adds 250 pixels of space to the top of the element and 450 pixels to the left of the element, resulting in the element being shifted down and to the right (see Figure 3-46):

```
div {
    position: relative;
    top: 250px;
    left: 450px;
}
```

Figure 3-46   **Moving an object using relative positioning**

original layout   layout under relative positioning

© 2016 Cengage Learning

Note that the layout of the other page elements are not affected by relative positioning; they will still occupy their original positions on the rendered page, just as if the object had never been moved at all.

Relative positioning is sometimes used when the designer wants to "tweak" the page layout by slightly moving an object from its default location to a new location that fits the overall page design better. If no top, right, bottom, or left values are specified with relative positioning, their assumed values are 0 and the element will not be shifted at all.

Absolute Positioning

Absolute positioning places an element at specific coordinates within a container where the `top` property indicates the position of the element's top edge, the `right` property sets the position of the right edge, the `bottom` property sets the bottom edge position, and the `left` property sets the position of the left edge.

For example, the following style rule places the `header` element 620 pixels from the top edge of its container and 30 pixels from the left edge (see Figure 3-47).

```
header {
    position: absolute;
    top: 620px;
    left: 30px;
}
```

TIP

To place an element at the bottom right corner of its container, use absolute positioning with the right and bottom values set to 0 pixels.

Figure 3-47   **Moving an object using absolute positioning**

other page elements move into the space previously occupied by the now absolutely positioned object

top-left corner of object placed 620 pixels down and 30 pixels to the right of the top-left edge of the web page

620px

30px

```
position:
absolute;
top: 620px;
left: 30px;
```

original layout

layout under absolute positioning

© 2016 Cengage Learning

To place an object with absolute positioning, you use either the top/left coordinates or the bottom/right coordinates, but you don't use all four coordinates at the same time because that would confuse the browser. For example an object cannot be positioned along both the left and right edge of its container simultaneously.

As with floating an element, absolute positioning takes an element out of normal document flow with subsequent elements moving into the space previously occupied by the element. This can result in an absolutely positioned object overlapping other page elements.

The interpretation of the coordinates of an absolutely positioned object are all based on the edges of the element's container. Thus the browser needs to "know" where the object's container is before it can absolutely position objects within it. If the container has been placed using a `position` property set to `relative` or `absolute`, the container's location is known and the coordinate values are based on the edges of the container. For example the following style rules place the `article` element at a coordinate that is 50 pixels from the top edge of the section element and 20 pixels from the left edge.

```
section {
    position: relative;
}
section > article {
    position: absolute;
    top: 50px;
    left: 20px;
}
```

Note that you don't have to define coordinates for the `section` element as long as you've set its position to relative.

The difficulty starts when the container has not been set using relative or absolute positioning. In that case, the browser has no context for placing an object within the container using absolute positioning. As a result, the browser must go up a level in the hierarchy of page elements, that is, to the container's container. If that container has been placed with absolute or relative positioning, then any object nested within it can be placed with absolute positioning. For example, in the following style rule, the position of the `article` element is measured from the edges of the `body` element, not the `section` element:

```
body {position: absolute;}

body > section {position: static;}

body > section > article {
    position: absolute;
    top: 50px;
    left: 20px;
}
```

TIP

If all of the objects within a container are placed using absolute positioning, the container will have no content and will collapse.

Proceeding in this fashion the browser will continue to go up the hierarchy of elements until it finds a container that has been placed with absolute or relative positioning or it reaches the root `html` element. If it reaches the `html` element, the coordinates of any absolutely positioned object are measured from the edges of the browser window itself. Figure 3-48 shows how the placement of the same object can differ based on which container supplies the context for the top and left values.

Figure 3-48	Context of the top and left coordinates

because the inner container has not been placed using relative or absolute positioning, the context shifts up the hierarchy to the outer container

© 2016 Cengage Learning

Coordinates can be expressed in percentages as well as pixels. Percentages are used for flexible layouts in which the object should be positioned in relation to the width or height of its container. Thus, the following style rule places the `article` element halfway down and 30% to the right of the top-left corner of its container.

```
article {
    position: absolute;
    top: 50%;
    left: 30%;
}
```

As the container of the article changes in width or height, the article's position will automatically change to match.

Fixed and Inherited Positioning

When you scroll through a document in the browser window, the page content scrolls along. If you want to fix an object within the browser window so that it doesn't scroll, you can set its `position` property to **fixed**. For example, the following style rule keeps the `footer` element at a fixed location, 10 pixels up from the bottom of the browser window:

```
footer {
    position: fixed;
    bottom: 10px;
}
```

Note that a fixed object might cover up other page content, so you should use it with care in your page design.

Finally, you can set the `position` property to **inherit** so that an element inherits the position value of its parent element.

REFERENCE

Positioning Objects with CSS

- To shift an object from its default position, use the properties

```
position: relative;
top: value;
left: value;
bottom: value;
right: value;
```

where *value* is the distance in one of the CSS units of measure that the object should be shifted from the corresponding edge of its container.
- To place an object at a specified coordinate within its container, use the properties

```
position: absolute;
top: value;
left: value;
bottom: value;
right: value;
```

where *value* is a distance in one of the CSS units of measure or a percentage of the container's width or height.
- To fix an object within the browser window so that it does not scroll with the rest of the document content, use the property

```
position: fixed;
```

Using the Positioning Styles

Anne wants you to work on the layout for a page that contains an infographic on chocolate. She sketched the layout of the infographic page, as shown in Figure 3-49.

Figure 3-49   Proposed layout of the chocolate infographic

The first box of Valentine's Day chocolates was created by British chocolatier Richard Cadbury in 1868.

The Ivory Coast accounts for 40% of the worldwide cocoa production.

A single cocoa tree produces about 800 bars of milk chocolate or 400 bars of dark chocolate every year.

The word *chocolate* comes from the Azetc word, *xocalatl*, which means *bitter water*.

White 9%

Dark 36%

Milk 55%

Top Chocolate-Loving Nations (per capita)

Favorite Box Chocolates

Dark chocolate is one of the most potent sources of antioxidants, having up to 5 times more antioxidant power than so-called "super berries."

Eating 40 grams of good quality organic dark chocolate every day significantly reduces your levels of stress hormones and improvesyour overall health.

22% of all chocolate consumption takes place between 8 p.m. and midnight.

Because the placement of the text and figures do not line up nicely within a grid, you'll position each graphic and text box using the CSS positioning styles. Anne has already created the content for this page and written the style sheets to format the appearance of the infographic. You will write the style sheet to layout the infographic contents using the CSS positioning styles.

To open the infographic file:

1. Use your editor to open the **pc_info_txt.html** file from the html03 ▶ tutorial folder. Enter *your name* and *the date* in the comment section of the file and save the document as **pc_info.html**.

2. Directly after the `title` element, insert the following `link` elements to attach the file to the pc_reset.css, pc_styles3.css, and pc_info.css style sheets.

   ```
   <link href="pc_reset.css" rel="stylesheet" />
   <link href="pc_styles3.css" rel="stylesheet" />
   <link href="pc_info.css" rel="stylesheet" />
   ```

3. Take some time to study the structure and content of the pc_info.html document. Note that Anne has placed eight information graphics, each within a separate `div` element with a class name of infobox and an id name ranging from info1 to info8.

4. Close the file, saving your changes.

Next, you'll start working on the pc_info.css file, which will contain the positioning and other design styles for the objects in the infographic. You will begin by formatting the `main` element, which contains the infographics. Because you'll want the position of each infographic to be measured from the top-left corner of this container, you will place the `main` element with relative positioning and extend the height of the container to 1400 pixels so that it can contain all eight of the graphic elements.

To format the main element:

1. Use your editor to open the **pc_info_txt.css** file from the html03 ▶ tutorial folder. Enter *your name* and *the date* in the comment section of the file and save the document as **pc_info.css**.

2. Go to the Main Styles section and insert the following style rule to format the appearance of the `main` element:

   ```
   main {
       position: relative;
       height: 1400px;
       width: 100%;
   }
   ```

   It will be easier to see the effect of placing the different `div` elements if they are not displayed until you are ready to position them. Add a rule to hide the `div` elements, then as you position each element, you can add a style rule to redisplay it.

3. Directly before the Main Styles section, insert the following style rule to hide all of the infoboxes:

   ```
   div.infobox {display:none;}
   ```

   Figure 3-50 highlights the newly added code in the style sheet.

> When you want to position objects in an exact or absolute position within a container, set the `position` property of the container to `relative`.

Figure 3-50	Setting the display styles of the main element

hides the div elements of
the infobox class

```
div.infobox {display: none;}

/* Main Styles */

main {
    position: relative;
    height: 1400px;
    width: 100%;
}
```

places the main
element using
relative positioning

sets the height of the main
element to 1400 pixels
and makes it the width of
the page body

4. Save your changes to the file and then open the **pc_info.html** file in your browser. Verify that the browser shows an empty box, about 1400 pixels high, where the infographic will be placed.

Next, you will add a style rule for all of the information boxes so that they are placed within the main element using absolute positioning.

To position the information boxes:

1. Return to the **pc_info.css** file in your editor and scroll down to the Infographic Styles section.

2. Add the following style rule to set the position type of all of the information boxes.

```
div.infobox {
    position: absolute;
}
```

3. Position the first information box 20 pixels from the top edge of its container and 5% from the left edge.

```
div#info1 {
    display: block;
    top: 20px;
    left: 5%;
}
```

Note that we set the `display` property to `block` so that the first information box is no longer hidden on the page. Figure 3-51 highlights the style rules for all of the information boxes and the placement of the first information box.

Figure 3-51 **Placing the first information box**

```
/* Infographic Styles */

div.infobox {
    position: absolute;
}

/* First Infographic */

div#info1 {
    display: block;
    top: 20px;
    left: 5%;
}
```

places every information box using absolute positioning

places the first box 20 pixels from the top edge of the main element and 5% from the left

4. Save your changes to the file and then reload the **pc_info.html** file in your browser. Figure 3-52 shows the placement of the first information box.

Figure 3-52 **Appearance of the first information box**

placement of the first information box

Now place the second and third information boxes.

To place the next two boxes:

1. Return to the **pc_info.css** file in your editor and go to the Second Infographic section.

2. Add the following style rule to place the second box 185 pixels down from the top of the container and 42% from the left edge.

```
div#info2 {
    display: block;
    top: 185px;
    left: 42%;
}
```

3. Within the Third Infographic section insert the following style rule to place the third box 135 pixels from the top edge and 75% of the width of its container from the left edge.

```
div#info3 {
    display: block;
    top: 135px;
    left: 75%;
}
```

Figure 3-53 highlights the style rules to position the second and third information boxes.

Figure 3-53	Positions of the second and third boxes

```
/* Second Infographic */

div#info2 {
    display: block;
    top: 185px;
    left: 42%;
}

/* Third Infographic */

div#info3 {
    display: block;
    top: 135px;
    left: 75%;
}
```

places the second box 185 pixels from the top and 42% from the left

places the third box 135 pixels from the top and 75% from the left

4. Save your changes to the file and reload **pc_info.html** in your browser. Figure 3-54 shows the placement of the first three information boxes.

Figure 3-54	Placement of the first three boxes

second information box

The first box of Valentine's Day chocolates was created by British chocolatier Richard Cadbury in 1868.

A single cocoa tree produces about 800 bars of milk chocolate or 400 bars of dark chocolate every year.

The Ivory Coast accounts for 40% of worldwide cocoa production.

third information box

Place the next three information boxes.

To place the next three boxes:

1. Return to the **pc_info.css** file in your editor, go to the Fourth Infographic section and place the fourth box 510 pixels from the top edge and 8% from the left edge.

```
div#info4 {
    display: block;
    top: 510px;
    left: 8%;
}
```

2. Add the following style rule to the Fifth Infographic section to position the fifth box:

```
div#info5 {
    display: block;
    top: 800px;
    left: 3%;
}
```

3. Add the following style rule to the Sixth Infographic section to position the sixth box:

```
div#info6 {
    display: block;
    top: 600px;
    left: 48%;
}
```

Figure 3-55 highlights the positioning styles for the fourth, fifth, and sixth information boxes.

Figure 3-55   **Positions of the fourth, fifth, and sixth boxes**

```
/* Fourth Infographic */

div#info4 {
    display: block;
    top: 510px;
    left: 8%;
}

/* Fifth Infographic */

div#info5 {
    display: block;
    top: 800px;
    left: 3%;
}

/* Sixth Infographic */

div#info6 {
    display: block;
    top: 600px;
    left: 48%;
}
```

> places the fourth box 510 pixels from the top and 8% from the left

> places the fifth box 800 pixels from the top and 3% from the left

> places the sixth box 600 pixels from the top and 48% from the left

4. Save your changes to the file and reload **pc_info.html** in your browser. Figure 3-56 shows the revised layout of the infographic.

Figure 3-56   **Placement of the next three boxes**

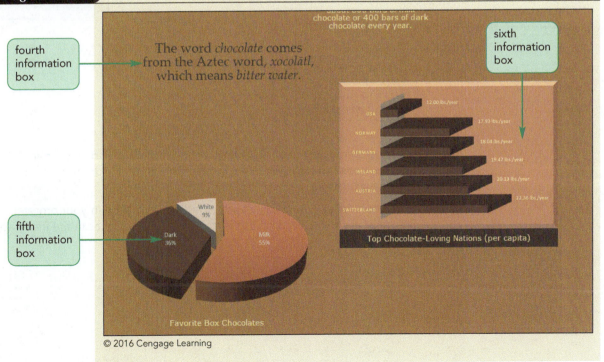

> fourth information box

> fifth information box

> sixth information box

© 2016 Cengage Learning

Complete the layout of the infographic by placing the final two boxes on the page.

To place the last two boxes:

1. Return to the **pc_info.css** file in your editor, go to the Seventh Infographic section and insert the following style rules:

```
div#info7 {
    display: block;
    top: 1000px;
    left: 68%;
}
```

2. Add the following style rules to the Eighth Infographic section:

```
div#info8 {
    display: block;
    top: 1100px;
    left: 12%;
}
```

Figure 3-57 highlights the style rules for the seventh and eighth information boxes.

Figure 3-57   **Positioning the seventh and eighth boxes**

```
/* Seventh Infographic */

div#info7 {
    display: block;
    top: 1000px;
    left: 68%;
}

/* Eighth Infographic */

div#info8 {
    display: block;
    top: 1100px;
    left: 12%;
}
```

places the seventh box 1000 pixels from the top and 68% from the left

places the eighth box 1100 pixels from the top and 12% from the left

3. Scroll up to before the Main Styles section and delete the style rule `div.infobox {display: none;}` because you no longer need to hide any information boxes.

4. Save your changes to the file and reload **pc_info.html** in your browser. Figure 3-58 show the complete layout of the eight boxes in the infographic.

Figure 3-58   **Final layout of the infographic**

Anne likes the appearance of the infographic, but she is concerned about its length. She would like you to reduce the height of the infographic so that it appears within the boundaries of the browser window. This change will create overflow because the content is longer than the new height. You will read more about overflow and how to handle it now.

Creating an Irregular Line Wrap

Many desktop publishing and word-processing programs allow designers to create irregular line wraps in which the text appears to flow tightly around an image. This is not easily done in a web page layout because all images appear as rectangles rather than as irregularly shaped objects. However, with the aid of a graphics package, you can simulate an irregularly shaped image.

The trick is to use your graphics package to slice the image horizontally into several pieces and then crop the individual slices to match the edge of the image you want to display. Once you've edited all of the slices, you can use CSS to stack the separate slices by floating them on the left or right margin, displaying each slice only after the previous slice has been cleared. For example, the following style rule stacks all inline images that belong to the "slice" class on the right margin:

```
img.slice {
    clear: right;
    float: right;
    margin-top: 0px;
    margin-bottom: 0px;
}
```

Now any text surrounding the stack of images will tightly match the image's boundary, creating the illusion of an irregular line wrap. Note that you should always set the top and bottom margins to 0 pixels so that the slices join together seamlessly.

Handling Overflow

The infographic is long because it displays several information boxes. If you reduce the height of the infographic you run the risk of cutting off several of the boxes that will no longer fit within the reduced infographic. However you can control how your browser handles this excess content using the following `overflow` property

```
overflow: type;
```

where `type` is `visible` (the default), `hidden`, `scroll`, or `auto`. A value of `visible` instructs browsers to increase the height of an element to fit the overflow content. The `hidden` value keeps the element at the specified height and width, but cuts off excess content. The `scroll` value keeps the element at the specified dimensions, but adds horizontal and vertical scroll bars to allow users to scroll through the overflowed content. Finally, the `auto` value keeps the element at the specified size, adding scroll bars only as they are needed. Figure 3-59 shows examples of the effects of each overflow value on content that is too large for its space.

| Figure 3-59 | Values of the overflow property |

overflow: visible;	overflow: hidden;	overflow: scroll;	overflow: auto;
We are a company located in Essex, Vermont, dedicated to making delicious chocolate and other treats. For our founder, chocolatier Anne Ambrose, this means using only the finest organic ingredients, incorporating a harmonious blend of rich flavors and smooth textures. Anne learned her trade as part of a three-year apprenticeship program in Switzerland. Her introduction into the world of confectioneries was a springboard to working with leaders in the field. Early in 1993 she brought that expertise back to Vermont and Pandaisia Chocolates was born.	We are a company located in Essex, Vermont, dedicated to making delicious chocolate and other treats. For our founder, chocolatier Anne Ambrose, this means using only the finest organic ingredients, incorporating a harmonious blend of rich flavors and smooth textures. Anne learned her trade as part of a three-year apprenticeship program in Switzerland. Her introduction into the world of confectioneries was a springboard to working with leaders in the field. Early in 1993 she brought that expertise back to	We are a company located in Essex, Vermont, dedicated to making delicious chocolate and other treats. For our founder, chocolatier Anne Ambrose, this means using only the finest organic ingredients, incorporating a harmonious blend of rich flavors and smooth textures. Anne learned her trade as part of a three-year apprenticeship program in Switzerland. Her introduction into the world of confectioneries was a	We are a company located in Essex, Vermont, dedicated to making delicious chocolate and other treats. For our founder, chocolatier Anne Ambrose, this means using only the finest organic ingredients, incorporating a harmonious blend of rich flavors and smooth textures. Anne learned her trade as part of a three-year apprenticeship program in Switzerland. Her introduction into the world of confectioneries was a springboard to working with
box extends to make all of the content visible	overflowed content is hidden from the reader	horizontal and vertical scrollbars are added to the box	scrollbars are added only where needed

CSS3 also provides the `overflow-x` and `overflow-y` properties to handle overflow specifically in the horizontal and vertical directions.

Working with Overflow

- To specify how the browser should handle content that overflows the element's boundaries, use the property

  overflow: *type*;

  where *type* is visible (the default), hidden, scroll, or auto.

You decide to limit the height of the infographic to 450 pixels and to set the `overflow` property to `auto` so that browsers displays scroll bars as needed for the excess content.

To apply the overflow property:

1. Return to the **pc_info.css** file in your editor and go to the Main Styles section.

2. Within the style rule for the main selector, insert the property **overflow: auto;**.

3. Reduce the height of the element from 1400px to **450px**.

   Figure 3-60 highlights the revised code in the style rule.

Figure 3-60 Setting the overflow property

```
/* Main Styles */

main {
    overflow: auto;
    position: relative;
    height: 450px;
    width: 100%;
}
```

displays scrollbars if the content overflows the allotted height

sets the height of the infographic to 450 pixels

4. Close the file, saving your changes.

5. Reload the **pc_info.html** file in your browser. As shown in Figure 3-61, the height of the infographic has been reduced to 450 pixels and scrollbars have been added that you can use to view the entire infographic.

Figure 3-61 Final layout of the infographic page

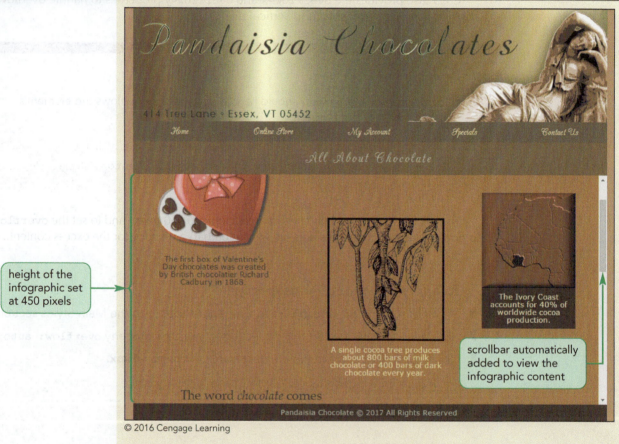

height of the infographic set at 450 pixels

scrollbar automatically added to view the infographic content

© 2016 Cengage Learning

6. Close any open files now.

Managing White Space with CSS

Scroll bars for overflow content are usually placed vertically so that you scroll down to view the extra content. In some page layouts, however, you may want to view content in a horizontal rather than a vertical direction. You can accomplish this by adding the following style properties to the element:

```
overflow: auto;
white-space: nowrap;
```

The white-space property defines how browsers should handle white space in the rendered document. The default is to collapse consecutive occurrences of white space into a single blank space and to automatically wrap text to a new line if it extends beyond the width of the container. However, you can set the white-space property of the element to nowrap to keep inline content on a single line, preventing line wrapping. With the content thus confined to a single line, browsers will display only horizontal scroll bars for the overflow content. Other values of the white-space property include normal (for default handling of white space), pre (to preserve all white space from the HTML file), and pre-wrap (to preserve white space but to wrap excess content to a new line).

Clipping an Element

Closely related to the overflow property is the clip property, which defines a rectangular region through which an element's content can be viewed. Anything that lies outside the boundary of the rectangle is hidden. The syntax of the clip property is

```
clip: rect(top, right, bottom, left);
```

where top, right, bottom, and left define the coordinates of the clipping rectangle. For example, a clip value of rect(100px, 270px, 260px, 65px) defines a clip region whose top and bottom boundaries are 100 and 260 pixels from the top edge of the element, and whose right and left boundaries are 270 and 65 pixels from the element's left edge. See Figure 3-62.

Figure 3-62   **Clipping an image**

clip: rect(100px, 270px, 260px, 65px)   clipped image

© Brent Hofacker/Shutterstock.com

The top, right, bottom, and left values also can be set to `auto`, which matches the specified edge of the clipping region to the edge of the parent element. A clip value of rect(10, auto, 125, 75) creates a clipping rectangle whose right edge matches the right edge of the parent element. To remove clipping completely, apply the style `clip: auto`. Clipping can only be applied when the object is placed using absolute positioning.

Stacking Elements

Positioning elements can sometimes lead to objects that overlap each other. By default, elements that are loaded later by the browser are displayed on top of elements that are loaded earlier. In addition, elements placed using CSS positioning are stacked on top of elements that are not. To specify a different stacking order, use the following `z-index` property:

`z-index:` *`value`*`;`

where *`value`* is a positive or negative integer, or the keyword `auto`. As shown in Figure 3-63, objects with the highest z-index values are placed on top of other page objects. A value of `auto` stacks the object using the default rules.

Figure 3-63 **Using the z-index property to stack elements**

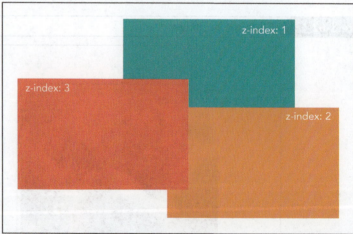

© 2016 Cengage Learning

The `z-index` property works only for elements that are placed with absolute positioning. Also, an element's z-index value determines its position relative only to other elements that share a common parent; the style has no impact when applied to elements with different parents. Figure 3-64 shows a layout in which the object with a high z-index value of 4 is still covered because it is nested within another object that has a low z-index value of 1.

Figure 3-64   **Stacking nested objects**

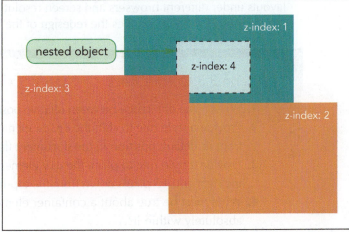

© 2016 Cengage Learning

You do not need to include the `z-index` property in your style sheet because none of the elements in the infographic page are stacked upon another.

Problem Solving: Principles of Design

Good web page design is based on the same common principles found in other areas of art, which include balance, unity, contrast, rhythm, and emphasis. A pleasing layout involves the application of most, if not all, of these principles, which are detailed below:

- **Balance** involves the distribution of elements. It's common to think of balance in terms of **symmetrical balance**, in which similar objects offset each other like items on a balance scale; but you often can achieve more interesting layouts through asymmetrical balance, in which one large page object is balanced against two or more smaller objects.
- **Unity** is the ability to combine different design elements into a cohesive whole. This is accomplished by having different elements share common colors, font styles, and sizes. One way to achieve unity in a layout is to place different objects close to each other, forcing your viewers' eyes to see these items as belonging to a single unified object.
- **Contrast** consists of the differences among all of the page elements. To create an effective design, you need to vary the placement, size, color, and general appearance of the objects in the page so that your viewers' eyes aren't bored by the constant repetition of a single theme.
- **Rhythm** is the repetition or alteration of a design element in order to provide a sense of movement, flow, and progress. You can create rhythm by tiling the same image horizontally or vertically across the page, by repeating a series of elements that progressively increase or decrease in size or spacing, or by using elements with background colors of the same hue but that gradually vary in saturation or lightness.
- **Emphasis** involves working with the focal point of a design. Your readers need a few key areas to focus on. It's a common design mistake to assign equal emphasis to all page elements. Without a focal point, there is nothing for your viewers' eyes to latch onto. You can give a page element emphasis by increasing its size, by giving it a contrasting color, or by assigning it a prominent position in the page.

Designers usually have an intuitive sense of what works and what doesn't in page design, though often they can't say why. These design principles are important because they provide a context in which to discuss and compare designs. If your page design doesn't feel like it's working, evaluate it in light of these principles to identify where it might be lacking.

Anne is pleased with the final design of the infographic page and all of the other pages you've worked on. She'll continue to develop the website and test her page layouts under different browsers and screen resolutions. She'll get back to you with future projects as she continues the redesign of the Pandaisia Chocolates website.

REVIEW

Session 3.3 Quick Check

1. What is the difference between relative positioning and absolute positioning?
2. Provide a style rule to shift the `aside` element 5% to the right and 10% down from its default position in the document flow.
3. Provide a style rule to place the `div` element with the id *graph1* 50 pixels to the right and 15 pixels down from the top-left corner of its container element.
4. What must be true about a container element to have objects positioned absolutely within it?
5. Provide a style rule to set the height of a navigation list with the id *nav1* to 300 pixels but to be displayed with a scrollbar if there are too many entries to fit within the navigation list's boundaries.
6. An inline image with the id *logo_img* is 400 pixels wide by 300 pixels high. Provide a style rule to clip this image by 10 pixels on each edge.
7. One element has a `z-index` value of 1; a second element has a `z-index` value of 5. Will the second element always be displayed on top of the first? Explain why or why not.

Review Assignments

Data Files needed for the Review Assignments: pc_specials_txt.html, pc_specials_txt.css, 2 CSS files, 8 PNG files, 1 TTF file, 1 WOFF file

Anne wants you to work on another page for the Pandaisia Chocolates website. This page will contain information on some of the specials offered by the company in March; it will also display a list of some awards that the company has won. As you work on the page, you will use clip art images as placeholders until photographs of the awards are available. A preview of the completed page is shown in Figure 3-65.

Figure 3-65   **March Specials web page**

© 2016 Cengage Learning; © Arina P Habich/Shutterstock.com;
© Brenda Carson/Shutterstock.com; © dotshock/Shutterstock.com

Anne has already created the page content and some of the design styles to be used in the page. Your job will be to come up with the CSS style sheet to set the page layout.

Complete the following:

1. Use your editor to open the **pc_specials_txt.html** and **pc_specials_txt.css** files from the html03 ▶ review folder. Enter *your name* and *the date* in the comment section of each file, and save them as **pc_specials.html** and **pc_specials.css** respectively.

2. Go to the **pc_specials.html** file in your editor. Within the document head, create links to the pc_reset2.css, pc_styles4.css, and pc_specials.css style sheets.

3. Take some time to study the content and structure of the document, paying careful attention to the use of ids and class names in the file. Save your changes to the file.

4. Go to the **pc_specials.css** file in your editor. Within the Page Body Styles section, add a style rule for the `body` element that sets the width of the page body to 95% of the browser window width within the range 640 pixels to 960 pixels. Horizontally center the page body within the window by setting the left and right margins to `auto`.

5. Go to the Image Styles section and create a style rule that displays all `img` elements as blocks with a width of 100%.

6. Anne wants the navigation list to be displayed horizontally on the page. Go to the Horizontal Navigation Styles section and create a style rule for every list item within a horizontal navigation list that displays the list item as a block floated on the left margin with a width of 16.66%.

7. Display every hypertext link nested within a navigation list item as a block.

8. Next, you'll create the style rules for the grid section of the March Specials page. Go to the Row Styles section. For every `div` element of the newRow class, create a style rule that displays the element with a width of 100% and only when all floated elements have been cleared. Using the technique from this tutorial, add another style rule that uses the `after` pseudo-element to expand each newRow class of the `div` element around its floating columns.

9. Next, you'll format the grid columns. Go to the Column Styles section. Create a style rule to float all `div` elements whose class value starts with "col-" on the left margin. Set the padding around all such elements to 2%. Finally, apply the Border Box Sizing model to the content of those elements. (*Note*: Remember to use web extensions to provide support for older browsers.)

10. In the same section, create style rules for `div` elements with class names col-1-1, col-1-2, col-1-3, col-2-3, col-1-4, and col-3-4 to set their widths to 100%, 50%, 33.33%, 66.67%, 25%, and 75% respectively.

11. Go to the Specials Styles section. In this section, you will create styles for the monthly specials advertised by the company. Create a style rule for all `div` elements of the specials class that sets the minimum height to 400 pixels and adds a 1 pixel dashed outline around the element with a color value of rgb(71, 52, 29).

12. Go to the Award Styles section. In this section, you will create styles for the list of awards won by Pandaisia Chocolates. Information boxes for the awards are placed within the `div` element with id *awardList*. Create a style rule for this element that places it using relative positioning, sets its height to 650 pixels, and automatically displays scrollbars for any overflow content.

13. Every information box in the awardList element is stored in a `div` element belonging to the awards class. Create a style rule that places these elements with absolute positioning and sets their width to 30%.

14. Position the individual awards within the awardList box by creating style rules for the `div` elements with id values ranging from award1 to award5 at the following (*top*, *left*) coordinates: award1 (80px, 5%), award2 (280px, 60%), award3 (400px, 20%), award4 (630px, 45%), and award5 (750px, 5%). (Hint: In the pc_specials.html file, the five awards have been placed in a `div` element belonging to the awards class with id values ranging from award1 to award5.)

15. Go to the Footer Styles section and create a style rule for the body footer that displays the footer once both margins are clear of previously floated elements.

16. Save your changes to the style sheet and then open the **pc_specials.html** file in your browser. Verify that the layout and design styles resemble the page shown in Figure 3-65.

Case Problem 1

Data Files needed for this Case Problem: sp_home_txt.html, sp_layout_txt.css, 2 CSS files, 11 PNG files

Slate & Pencil Tutoring   Karen Cooke manages the website for *Slate & Pencil Tutoring*, an online tutoring service for high school and college students. Karen is overseeing the redesign of the website and has hired you to work on the layout of the site's home page. Figure 3-66 shows a preview of the page you'll create for Karen.

Figure 3-66	Slate & Pencil Tutoring home page

© 2016 Cengage Learning; © Monkey Business Images/Shutterstock.com;
© Courtesy Patrick Carey

Karen has supplied you with the HTML file and the graphic files. She has also given you a base style sheet to initiate your web design and a style sheet containing several typographic styles. Your job will be to write up a layout style sheet according to Karen's specifications.

Complete the following:

1. Using your editor, open the **sp_home_txt.html** and **sp_layout_txt.css** files from the html03 ▶ case1 folder. Enter *your name* and *the date* in the comment section of each file, and save them as **sp_home.html** and **sp_layout.css** respectively.

2. Go to the **sp_home.html** file in your editor. Within the document head, create links to the **sp_base.css**, **sp_styles.css**, and **sp_layout.css** style sheet files. Study the content and structure of the file and then save your changes to the document.

3. Go to the **sp_layout.css** file in your editor. Go to the Window and Body Styles section. Create a style rule for the `html` element that sets the height of the browser window at 100%.

4. Create a style rule for the page body that sets the width to 95% of the browser window ranging from 640 pixels up to 960 pixels. Horizontally center the page body within the browser window. Finally, Karen wants to ensure that the height of the page body is always at least as high as the browser window itself. Set the minimum height of the browser window to 100%.

5. Create a style rule to apply the Border Box model to all `header`, `ul`, `nav`, `li`, and `a` elements in the document.

6. Go to the Row Styles section. Karen has placed all elements that should be treated as grid rows in the row class. For every element of the row class, create a style rule that expands the element to cover any floating content within the element. (Hint: Use the technique shown in the tutorial that employs the `after` pseudo-element.)

7. Go to the Page Header Styles section. In this section, you will create styles for the content of the body header. Create a style rule for the logo image within the body header that displays the image as a block with a width of 70% of the header, floated on the left margin.

8. The header also contains a navigation list that Karen wants to display vertically. Create a style rule for the `nav` element within the body header that: a) floats the navigation list on the left, b) sets the size of the left and right padding to 2%, and c) sets the width of the navigation list to 30% of the width of the header.

9. The hypertext links in the navigation list should be displayed as blocks. Create a style rule for every `a` element in the header navigation list that displays the element as a block with a width of 100%.

10. Go to the Horizontal Navigation List Styles section. Karen has added a second navigation list that she wants to display horizontally. For all list items within the horizontal navigation list, create a style rule that displays the items as blocks with a width of 12.5% floated on the left margin.

11. Go to the Topics Styles section. This section sets the styles for a list of four topics describing what the company is offering. Karen wants this list to also be displayed horizontally on the page. For list items within the `ul` element with the id *topics*, create a style rule to: a) display the items as blocks with a width of 20%, b) float the items on the left margin, and c) set the size of the left margin space to 0% and the right margin space to 1.5%.

12. Karen wants the topics list to be well away from the left and right edges of the page body. In the same section, create a rule that sets the size of the left margin of the first item in the topics list to 7.75% and sets the right margin of the last item to 7.75%.

13. In the same section, create a rule that displays the image within each list item in the topics list as a block with a width of 50% and centered within the list item block. (Hint: Set the left and right margins to auto.)

14. Go to the HR Styles section. The `hr` element is used to display a horizontal divider between sections of the page. Add a style rule that sets the width of the `hr` element to 50%.

15. Go to the Customer Comment Styles section. In this section, you will create style rules for the customer comments displayed near the bottom of the page. For the `ul` element with the id *comments*, create a style rule that sets the width to 75% and centers the element by setting the top/bottom margin to 40 pixels and the left/right margin to auto.

16. Karen wants the list items to appear in two columns on the page. In the same section, create a style rule for every list item in the comments list that: a) displays the item as a block with a width of 50% floated on the left and b) sets the size of the bottom margin to 30 pixels.

17. Every customer comment is accompanied by an image of the student. Karen wants these images displayed to the left of the comment. Create a style rule to display the image within each comment list item as a block with a width of 20%, floated on the left, and with a left/right margin of 5%.

18. Create a style rule for every paragraph nested within a customer list item that floats the paragraph on the left margin with a width of 70%.

19. Go to the Footer Styles section and create a style rule that displays the footer only when both margins are clear of floating objects.

20. Save your changes to the file and then open the **sp_home.html** file in your browser. Verify that the layout and appearance of the page elements resemble that shown in Figure 3-66.

Case Problem 2

Data Files needed for this Case Problem: ce_front_txt.html, ce_grids_txt.css, ce_styles_txt.css, 21 PNG files

Costume Expressions   Richard Privette is the owner of *Costume Expressions*, a small but growing costume and party business located in Rockville, Maryland. He has asked you to work on the website for the company. Richard envisions a front page that resembles the jumbled advertising pages often found in the back pages of the comic books from his youth. Figure 3-67 shows a preview of the grid-based layout he has in mind.

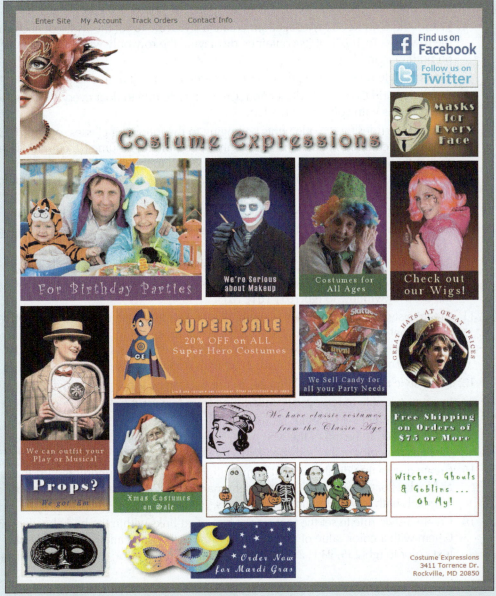

Richard has supplied you with the HTML code and all of the image files required for this page. You'll supply him with style sheets based on a grid layout that he can use to render his page's content.

Complete the following:

1. Using your editor, open the **ce_front_txt.html**, **ce_styles_txt.css**, and **ce_grids_txt.css** files from the html03 ▸ case2 folder. Enter *your name* and *the date* in the comment section of each file, and save them as **ce_front.html**, **ce_styles.css**, and **ce_grids.css** respectively.

2. Go to the **ce_front.html** file in your editor. Within the document head, create links to the **ce_styles.css** and **ce_grids.css** style sheet files. Take some time to study the structure of the document. Note that Richard has placed much of the document content within a `div` element with the name container and that grid rows are marked with the row class and grid columns are marked with the column *size* class where *size* indicates the width of the column. The content of the page consists almost entirely of images that Richard will link to pages in the Costume Expressions website later.

3. Save your changes to the file and then go to the **ce_grids.css** file in your editor.

4. Within the Grid Rows Styles section, create a style rule to set the width of each `div` element of the row class to 100% of its container, displaying the row only when it's clear of floated content on both margins.

5. Create a style rule to allow grid rows to expand around all of their floated content.

6. Go to the Grid Columns Style section. Create a style rule to float every `div` element whose class name begins with *column* on the left.

7. Create style rules for `div` elements belonging to the following classes: column100, column50, column33, column67, column25, column75, column20, column40, column60, and column80 so that the width of each column is a percent equal to the size value. For example, `div` elements belonging to the column100 class should have widths of 100%, column50 should have widths of 50%, and so forth.

8. Go to the Grid Spacing Styles section. Create a style rule to apply the Border Box model to the `div` elements belonging to the following classes: container, row, classes that begin with *column*, cell, and `a` elements nested within `div` elements belonging to the cell class.

9. Save your changes to the **ce_grids.css** file and then go to the **ce_styles.css** file in your editor.

10. Go to the Window and Body Styles section and create a style rule to set the background color of the browser window to rgb(101, 101, 101).

11. Create a style rule for the `body` element that: a) sets the background color to white, b) sets the default font to the stack: Verdana, Geneva, Arial, sans-serif, c) centers the page by setting the top/bottom margins to 20 pixels and the left/right margins to auto, and d) sets the width of the page body to 95% ranging from 320 pixels up to 960 pixels.

12. Insert style rules to display all images in the document as blocks with widths of 100%.

13. Insert a style rule to remove all underlining from hypertext links within navigation lists.

14. Go to the Body Header Styles section. Richard wants you to format the links that are displayed in the header at the top of the web page. To format the links, create a style rule that sets the background color of the body header to rgb(191, 68, 70) and sets the height to 40 pixels.

15. Create a style that displays all list items within the navigation unordered list in the body header as blocks, floated on the left, with a right margin of 20 pixels and top/bottom padding of 10 pixels with left/right padding of 0 pixels.

16. Create a style rule to set the font size of hypertext links within the body header navigation list to 0.9em with a color value of rgb(51, 51, 51) for both visited and non-visited links. Change the text color to rgb(255, 211, 211) when the user hovers over or activates those links.

17. Go to the DIV Container Styles section. Richard wants you to add some additional spacing between the images and the edge of the page body. To add this spacing, create a style rule that sets the right and bottom padding of the div element with the id *container* to 8 pixels.

18. For every a element within a div element belonging to the cell class, create a style rule to: a) display the hypertext link as a block with a width of 100% and b) set the left and top padding to 8 pixels.

19. Richard wants the page footer to be displayed in the bottom right corner of the web page. To place the footer in this position, go to the Windows and Body Styles section and set the `position` property of the `body` element to relative, then go to the Footer Styles section and create a style rule for the `footer` element to do the following: a) set the `position` property of the footer to absolute with a right coordinate and bottom coordinate of 8 pixels, b) set the text of the footer to rgb(143, 33, 36), c) right-align the footer text, and d) set the font size to 2vmin so that the text resizes automatically with the width and/or height of the browser window.

20. Save your changes to the **ce_styles.css** file and then open the **ce_front.html** file in your browser. Verify that the layout resembles that shown in Figure 3-67.

CHALLENGE

Case Problem 3

Data Files needed for this Case Problem: ss_dday_txt.html, ss_layout_txt.css, 1 CSS file, 3 PNG files

A Soldier's Scrapbook   Jakob Bauer is a curator at the Veteran's Museum in Raleigh, North Carolina. Currently he is working on an exhibit called *A Soldier's Scrapbook* containing mementos, artifacts, journals, and other historic items from the Second World War. You've been asked to work on a page for an interactive kiosk used by visitors to the exhibit. Jakob has already supplied much of the text and graphics for the kiosk pages but he wants you to complete the job by working on the page layout.

The page you will work on provides an overview of the Normandy beach landings on June 6th, 1944. Since this page will be displayed only on the kiosk monitor, whose screen dimensions are known, you'll employ a fixed layout based on a screen width of 1152 pixels.

Jakob also wants you to include an interactive map of the Normandy coast where the user can hover a mouse pointer over location markers to view information associated with each map point. To create this effect, you'll mark each map point as a hypertext link so that you can apply the `hover` pseudo-class to the location. In addition to the interactive map, Jakob wants you to create a drop cap for the first letter of the first paragraph in the article describing the Normandy invasion. Figure 3-68 shows a preview of the page you'll create.

Figure 3-68   Normandy Invasion kiosk page

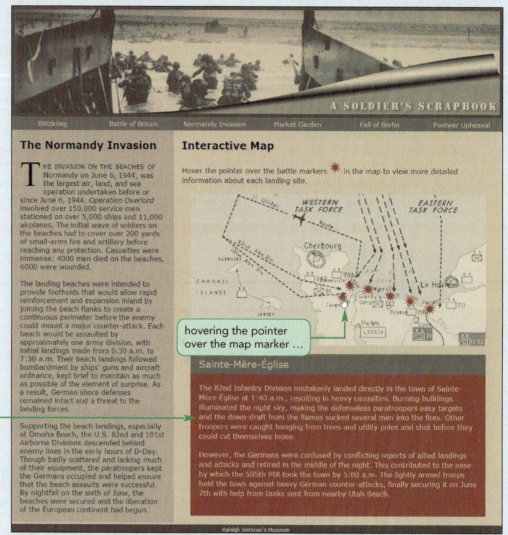

© 2016 Cengage Learning; source: Chief Photographer's Mate (CPHOM) Robert F. Sargent, U.S. Coast Guard; source: U.S Department of Defense; © Patrick Carey

Complete the following:

1. Using your editor, open the **ss_dday_txt.html** and **ss_layout_txt.css** files from the html03 ▶ case3 folder. Enter *your name* and *the date* in the comment section of each file, and save them as **ss_dday.html** and **ss_layout.css** respectively.

2. Go to the **ss_dday.html** file in your editor. Within the document head, create links to the **ss_styles.css** and **ss_layout.css** style sheet files. Study the content and structure of the document. Note that within the `aside` element is an image for the battle map with the id *mapImage*. Also note that there are six marker images enclosed within hypertext links with ids ranging from marker1 to maker6. After each marker image are `div` elements of the mapInfo class with IDs ranging from info1 to info6. Part of your style sheet will include style rules to display these `div` elements in response to the mouse pointer hovering over each of the six marker images.

3. Save your changes to the file and then go to the **ss_layout.css** file in your editor.

4. Go to the Article Styles section. Within this section, you'll lay out the article describing the Normandy Invasion. Create a style rule to float the `article` element on the left margin and set its width to 384 pixels.

✪ **Explore** 5. Jakob wants the first line from the article to be displayed in small capital letters. Go to the First Line and Drop Cap Styles section and create a style rule for the first paragraph of the article element and the first line of that paragraph, setting the font size to 1.25em and the font variant to small-caps. (Hint: Use the `first-of-type` pseudo-class for the paragraph and the `first-line` pseudo-element for the first line of that paragraph.)

✪ **Explore** 6. Jakob also wants the first letter of the first line in the article's opening paragraph to be displayed as a drop cap. Create a style rule for the article's first paragraph and first letter that applies the following styles: a) sets the size of the first letter to 4em in a serif font and floats it on the left, b) sets the line height to 0.8em, and c) sets the right and bottom margins to 5 pixels. (Hint: Use the `first-letter` pseudo-element for the first letter of that paragraph.)

7. The interactive map is placed within an `aside` element that Jakob wants displayed alongside the Normandy Invasion article. Go the Aside Styles section and create a style rule that sets the width of the aside element to 768 pixels and floats it on the left margin.

8. Next, you will lay out the interactive map. The interactive map is placed within a `div` element with the ID *battleMap*. Go to the Map Styles section and create a style rule for this element that sets its width to 688 pixels. Center the map by setting its top/bottom margins to 20 pixels and its left/right margins to `auto`. Place the map using relative positioning.

9. The actual map image is placed within an `img` element with the ID *mapImage*. Create a style rule for this element that displays it as a block with a width of 100%.

10. Go to the Interactive Map Styles section. Within this section, you'll create style rules that position each of the six map markers onto the battle map. The markers are placed within hypertext links. Create a style rule for every `a` element of the battleMarkers class that places the hypertext link using absolute positioning.

11. Create style rules for the six `a` elements with IDs ranging from marker1 to marker6, placing them at the following (*top*, *left*) coordinates:

marker1   (220, 340)
marker2   (194, 358)
marker3   (202, 400)
marker4   (217, 452)
marker5   (229, 498)
marker6   (246, 544)

12. The information associated with each map marker has been placed in `div` elements belonging to the mapInfo class. Go to the Map Information Styles section and create a style rule that hides this class of elements so that this information is not initially visible on the page.

✪ **Explore** 13. To display the information associated with each map maker, you need to create a style rule that changes the map information's `display` property in response to the mouse pointer hovering over the corresponding map marker. Since the map information follows the map marker in the HTML file, use the following selector (see Figure 2-12) to select the map information corresponding to the hovered map marker: `a.battleMarkers:hover + div.mapInfo`. Write a style rule for this selector that sets its `display` property to `block`.

14. Save your changes to the style sheet and then load **ss_dday.html** in your browser. Verify that a drop cap appears for the first letter of the Normandy Invasion article and the first line of the first paragraph is displayed in small caps. Test the interactive map by first verifying that none of the information about the six battle locations appears on the page unless you hover your mouse pointer over the marker on the battle map. Further verify that when you are not hovering over the battle marker, the information is once again not visible on the page.

CREATE

Case Problem 4

Data Files needed for this Case Problem: pcg_front_txt.html, pcg_paper_txt.css, 2 JPG files, 7 TXT files

The Park City Gazette Estes Park, Colorado, is a rural mountain community next to Rocky Mountain National Park. Kevin Webber is the editor of the weekly *Park City Gazette*. The paper recently redesigned its printed layout, and Kevin wants you to do the same thing for the online version. He's prepared several files containing sample text from recent articles and a few lists of links that usually appear in the front page of the newspaper's website. He's also provided you with image files that can be used for the paper's logo and background. Your job will be to use all of these pieces to create a sample web page for him to evaluate.

Complete the following:

1. Using your editor, open the **pcg_front_txt.html** and **pcg_paper_txt.css** files from the html03 ▶ case4 folder. Save them as **pcg_front.html** and **pcg_paper.css** respectively.

2. Using the content of the address, two links, and four story text files, create the content and structure of the pcg_front.html file. You are free to supplement the material in these text files with additional content of your own if appropriate. Use the # symbol for the value of the href attribute in your hypertext links because you will be linking to pages that don't actually exist.

3. Link the pcg_front.html file to the pcg_paper.css style sheet file and then save your changes.

4. Go to the **pcg_paper.css** style sheet file in your editor and create a layout for your Park City Gazette sample page. The layout should be based on a fluid design ranging from 640 pixels up to 960 pixels.

5. The specifics of the page design are up to your imagination and skill but must include the following features:
   - Use of the display property
   - Application of width and height style properties
   - Floated elements and cleared elements
   - A container element with a style rule so that it expands around its floated content
   - Defined margin and padding spaces as well as maximum and minimum widths
   - An example of relative or absolute positioning

6. Test your layout and design on a variety of devices, browsers, and screen resolutions to ensure that your sample page is readable under different conditions.

TUTORIAL **4**

Graphic Design with CSS

Creating a Graphic Design for a Genealogy Website

OBJECTIVES

Session 4.1
- Create a figure box
- Add a background image
- Add a border to an element
- Create rounded borders
- Create a graphic border

Session 4.2
- Create a text shadow
- Create a box shadow
- Create linear and radial gradients
- Set the opacity of an element

Session 4.3
- Apply a 2D and 3D transformation
- Apply a CSS filter
- Create an image map

Case | *Tree and Book*

Kevin Whitmore is the founder of *Tree and Book*, a social networking website for people interested in documenting their family histories, creating online photo albums, and posting stories and information about members of their extended families. He has come to you for help in upgrading the site's design. Kevin wants to take advantage of some of the CSS styles that can be used to add interesting visual effects to his site in order to give his website more impact and visual interest.

STARTING DATA FILES

html04

tutorial
tb_genta_txt.html
tb_komatsu_txt.html
tb_visual1_txt.css
tb_visual2_txt.css
+ 21 files

review
tb_ferris_txt.html
tb_kathleen_txt.html
tb_visual3_txt.css
tb_visual4_txt.css
+ 16 files

case1
sd_messier_txt.html
sd_effects_txt.css
+ 11 files

case2
sf_torte_txt.html
sf_effects_txt.css
+ 11 files

case3
cf_home_txt.html
cf_effects_txt.css
+ 9 files

case4
br_listing2048_txt.html
br_styles_txt.css
+ 13 files

demo
demo_box_shadows.html
demo_filters.html
demo_linear_gradients.html
demo_radial_gradients.html
demo_repeat_linear_gradients.html
demo_repeat_radial_gradients.html
demo_text_shadows.html
demo_transformations.html
demo_transformations3d.html
+ 4 files

Session 4.1 Visual Overview:

The **background-image** property applies an image file to the element background.

The **background** property defines all background options, including the use of multiple backgrounds.

The **cover** keyword specifies that the background image should completely cover the background.

The **border-left** and **border-right** properties add borders to the left and right edge of the element.

The **border-radius** property creates rounded corners with the specified radius.

```
/* Background Styles */

html {
    background-image: url(tb_back1.png);
}

article {
    background: url(tb_back2.png) bottom right / 15% no-repeat content-box,
                url(tb_back3.png) bottom left / 15% no-repeat content-box,
                url(tb_back4.png)  100%/cover no-repeat padding-box;
}

/* Border Styles */

body {
    border-left: 1px solid rgb(51, 51, 51);
    border-right: 1px solid rgb(51, 51, 51);
}

aside {
    border: 4px double rgb(45, 93, 62);
    border-radius: 30px;
}

body > article > header > figure {
    border-width: 25px;
    border-style: solid;
    border-image: url(tb_border.png) 50 repeat;
}
```

The **content-box** keyword specifies that the background extends only over the element content.

The **no-repeat** keyword specifies that no tiling is done with the background image.

Every border is defined by its width, style, and color.

The **border** property adds a border around all sides of the element.

The **border-image** property defines an image file used to create a graphic border.

The border images are based on an image file, the size of the slice from the image, and how slices are displayed along the element edge.

The **padding-box** keyword specifies that the background extends through the padding space.

Backgrounds and Borders

The tb_back1.png image is tiled to fill the element background.

The background image tb_back4.png covers the entire article's padding space.

The border image is based on the tb_border.png file.

The background image tb_back3.png is placed at the lower-left corner of the article.

The aside element has a rounded corner with a radius of 30 pixels.

The aside element has a 4-pixel wide double border.

The background image tb_back2.png is placed at the right corner of the article.

Creating Figure Boxes

So far your work with CSS visual design styles has been limited to typographical styles and styles that modify the page's color scheme. In this tutorial, you'll explore other CSS styles that allow you to add figure boxes, background textures, background images, and three dimensional effects to your web pages.

You'll start by examining how to work with figure boxes. In books and magazines, figures and figure captions are often placed within a separate box that stands apart from the main content of the article. HTML5 introduced a similar structural element with the following `figure` and `figcaption` elements:

```
<figure>
   content
   <figcaption>caption text</figcaption>
</figure>
```

where *content* is the content that will appear within the figure box and *caption text* is the description text that accompanies the figure. The `figcaption` element is optional and can be placed either directly before or directly after the figure box content. For example, the following code marks a figure box containing the tb_komatsu.png image file with the caption *(L-R): Ikko, Mika, Hiroji, Genta, Suzuko*.

```
<figure>
   <img src="tb_komatsu.png" alt="family portrait" />
   <figcaption>(L-R): Ikko, Mika, Hiroji, Genta, Suzuko</figcaption>
</figure>
```

TIP

The semantic difference between the `figure` and `aside` elements is that the `figure` element should be used for content that is directly referenced from within an article while the `aside` element is used for extraneous content.

While the `figure` element is used to contain an image file, it can also be used to mark any page content that you want to stand apart from the main content of an article. For instance, the `figure` element could contain a text excerpt, as the following code demonstrates:

```
<figure>
   <p>'Twas brillig, and the slithy toves<br />
      Did gyre and gimble in the wabe;<br />
      All mimsy were the borogoves,<br />
      And the mome raths outgrabe.</p>
   <figcaption>
      <cite>Jabberwocky, Lewis Carroll, 1832-98</cite>
   </figcaption>
</figure>
```

Kevin plans on using figure boxes throughout the Tree and Book website to mark up family and individual photos along with descriptive captions. He's created a set of sample pages for the Komatsu family that you will work on to learn about HTML and CSS visual elements and styles. Open the family's home page and create a figure box displaying the family portrait along with a descriptive caption.

To create a figure box:

1. Use your editor to open the **tb_komatsu_txt.html** file from the html04 ▶ tutorial folder. Enter *your name* and *the date* in the comment section of the file and save it as **tb_komatsu.html**.

   For this web page, you'll work with a new style sheet named tb_visual1.css. Kevin has already created a reset style sheet and a typographical style sheet in the tb_reset.css and tb_styles1.css files respectively.

2. Within the document head, insert the following `link` elements to link the page to the tb_reset.css, tb_styles1.css, and tb_visual1.css style sheet files.

```
<link href="tb_reset.css" rel="stylesheet" />
<link href="tb_styles1.css" rel="stylesheet" />
<link href="tb_visual1.css" rel="stylesheet" />
```

3. Scroll down to the `article` element and, directly after the `h1` element, insert the following code for the figure box displaying the Komatsu family portrait.

```
<figure>
    <img src="tb_komatsu.png" alt="family portrait" />
    <figcaption>(L-R): Ikko, Mika, Hiroji,
                  Genta, Suzuko
    </figcaption>
</figure>
```

Figure 4-1 highlights the code for the family portrait figure box.

Figure 4-1	Inserting a figure box

```
<article>
    <header>
        <h1>The Komatsu Family</h1>
        <figure>
            <img src="tb_komatsu.png" alt="family portrait" />
            <figcaption>(L-R): Ikko, Mika, Hiroji, Genta, Suzuko</figcaption>
        </figure>
    </header>
```

image within the figure box

caption associated with the image

4. Take some time to review the content and structure of the rest of the document and then save your changes to the file.

Format the appearance of the figure box by adding new style rules to the tb_visual1.css style sheet file.

To format and view the figure box:

1. Use your editor to open the **tb_visual1_txt.css** files from the html04 ▸ tutorial folder. Enter **your name** and **the date** in the comment section of the file and save it as **tb_visual1.css**.

2. Scroll down to the Figure Box Styles section at the bottom the document and insert the following style rule for the `figure` element:

```
figure {
    margin: 20px auto 0px;
    width: 80%;
}
```

3. Add the following style to format the appearance of the image within the figure box:

```
figure img {
    display: block;
    width: 100%;
}
```

4. Finally, insert the following rule for the figure caption:

```
figure figcaption {
    background-color: white;
    font-family: 'Palatino Linotype', Palatino,
                 'Times New Roman', serif;
    font-style: italic;
    padding: 10px 0;
    text-align: center;
}
```

Figure 4-2 highlights the style rules for the figure box, image, and caption.

Figure 4-2   **Formatting the figure box and caption**

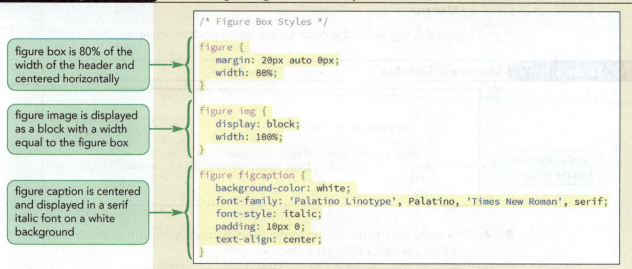

figure box is 80% of the width of the header and centered horizontally

figure image is displayed as a block with a width equal to the figure box

figure caption is centered and displayed in a serif italic font on a white background

```
/* Figure Box Styles */

figure {
    margin: 20px auto 0px;
    width: 80%;
}

figure img {
    display: block;
    width: 100%;
}

figure figcaption {
    background-color: white;
    font-family: 'Palatino Linotype', Palatino, 'Times New Roman', serif;
    font-style: italic;
    padding: 10px 0;
    text-align: center;
}
```

5. Save your changes to the file and then open the **tb_komatsu.html** file in your browser. Figure 4-3 shows the initial appearance of the page.

Figure 4-3   Initial design of the Komatsu family page

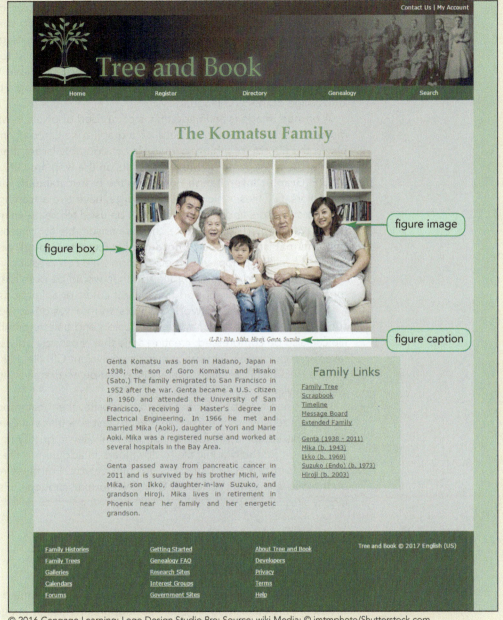

With all of the content for the Komatsu Family page now added, you will start working on enhancing the page's appearance, starting with the CSS background styles.

INSIGHT

Choosing your Graphic File Format

Graphic files on the web fall into two basic categories: vector images and bitmap images. A **vector image** is an image comprised of lines and curves that are based on mathematical functions. The great advantage of vector images is that they can be easily resized without losing their clarity and vector files tend to be compact in size. The most common vector format for the web is **SVG (Scalable Vector Graphics)**, which is an XML markup language that can be created using a basic text editor and knowledge of the SVG language.

A **bitmap image** is an image that is comprised of pixels in which every pixel is marked with a different color. Because a graphic file can be comprised of thousands of pixels, the file size of a bitmap image is considerably larger than the file size of a vector image. The most common bitmap formats on the web are GIF, JPEG, and PNG.

GIF (Graphic Interchange Format) is the oldest standard with a palette limited to 256 colors. GIF files, which tend to be large, have two advantages: first, GIFs support transparent colors and second, GIFs can be used to create animated images. Because GIFs have a limited color palette, they are unsuitable for photos. The most popular photo format is **JPEG (Joint Photographic Experts Group)**, which supports a palette of over 16 million colors. JPEGs also support file compression, allowing a bitmap image to be stored at a smaller file size than would be possible with other bitmap formats. JPEGs do not support transparent colors or animations.

The **PNG (Portable Network Graphics)** format was designed to replace GIFs with its support for several levels of transparent colors and palette of millions of colors. A PNG file can also be compressed, creating a file that is considerably smaller and, therefore, takes up considerably less space than its equivalent GIF file. PNG files also contain color correction information so that PNGs can be accurately rendered across a variety of display devices.

In choosing a graphic format for your website, the most important consideration is often file size; you want to choose the smallest size that still gives you an acceptable image. This combination means that users will view a quality image but they will not have to wait for the graphic file to download. In addition to file size, you want to choose a format that supports a large color palette. For these reasons, most graphics on the web are now in either JPEG or PNG format, though GIFs are still often found on legacy sites.

Exploring Background Styles

Thus far, your design choices for backgrounds have been limited to color using either the RGB or HSL color models. CSS also supports the use of images for backgrounds through the following `background-image` style:

```
background-image: url(url);
```

where *url* specifies the name and location of the background image. For example, the following style rule uses the trees.png file as the background of the page body.

```
body {
    background-image: url(trees.png);
}
```

This code assumes that the trees.png file is in the same folder as the style sheet; if the figure is not in the same folder, then you will have to include path information pointing to the folder location in which the image file resides.

Tiling a Background Image

The default browser behavior is to place the background image at the top-left corner of the element and repeat the image in both the vertical and horizontal direction until the background is filled. This process is known as **tiling** because of its similarity to the process of filling up a floor or other surface with tiles.

You can specify the type of tiling to be applied to the background image, or even turn off tiling, by applying the following background-repeat style:

```
background-repeat: type;
```

where `type` is `repeat` (the default), `repeat-x`, `repeat-y`, `no-repeat`, `round`, or `space`. Figure 4-4 displays the effect of each `background-repeat` type.

Figure 4-4	Examples of background-repeat types

background-repeat: repeat;

image is tiled both horizontally and vertically

background-repeat: repeat-x;

image is tiled horizontally

background-repeat: repeat-y;

image is tiled vertically

background-repeat: no-repeat;

image is not tiled

background-repeat: round;

background image is tiled and resized to fit in the container a whole number of times

background-repeat: space;

background image is tiled and spaces added to fit in the container a whole number of times

© 2016 Cengage Learning

Adding a Background Image

- To add an image to the background, use the CSS style

  ```
  background-image: url(url);
  ```

  where `url` specifies the name and location of the background image.
- To specify how the image should be tiled, use

  ```
  background-repeat: type;
  ```

  where `type` is repeat (the default), repeat-x, repeat-y, no-repeat, round, or space.

Kevin has supplied you with an image file, tb_back1.png to fill the background of the browser window. Use the default option for tiling so that the image is displayed starting from the top-left corner of the window and repeating until the entire window is filled.

To add a background image to the browser window:

1. Return to the **tb_visual1.css** file in your editor.

2. Go to the HTML Styles section and add the following style rule to change the background of the browser window:

   ```
   html {
       background-image: url(tb_back1.png);
   }
   ```

   Note that because you are using the default setting for tiling the background image, you do not need to include the `background-repeat` style rule. Figure 4-5 highlights the new style rule.

Figure 4-5   Defining a background image

tiles the tb_back1.png
image file across the
browser window
background

```
/* HTML Styles */

html {
    background-image: url(tb_back1.png);
}
```

3. Save your changes to the file and then reload tb_komatsu.html in your browser. Figure 4-6 shows the tiled background in the browser window.

Figure 4-6   **Tiled background image in the browser window**

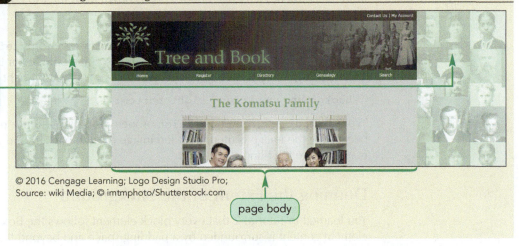

tiled image in browser window background

page body

© 2016 Cengage Learning; Logo Design Studio Pro;
Source: wiki Media; © imtmphoto/Shutterstock.com

Note that the page body covers part of the tiled images in the browser window. However, even though the background images are hidden, the tiling still continues behind the page body.

Attaching the Background Image

A background image is attached to its element so that as you scroll through the element content, the background image scrolls with it. You can change the attachment using the following `background-attachment` property

```
background-attachment: type;
```

where `type` is `scroll` (the default), `fixed`, or `local`. The `scroll` type sets the background to scroll with the element content. The `fixed` type creates a background that stays in place even as the element content is scrolled horizontally or vertically. Fixed backgrounds are sometimes used to create **watermarks**, which are translucent graphics displayed behind the content with a message that the content material is copyrighted or in draft form or some other message directed to the reader. The `local` type is similar to `scroll` except that it is used for elements, such as scroll boxes, to allow the element background to scroll along with the content within the box.

Setting the Background Image Position

By default, browsers place the background image in the element's top-left corner. You can place the background image at a different position using the following `background-position` property:

```
background-position: horizontal vertical;
```

where `horizontal` and `vertical` provide the coordinates of the image within the element background expressed using one of the CSS units of measure or as a percentage of the element's width and height. For example, the following style places the image 10% of the width of the element from the left edge of the background and 20% of the element's height from the background's top edge.

```
background-position: 10% 20%;
```

If you specify a single value, the browser applies that value to both the horizontal and vertical position. Thus, the following style places the background image 30 pixels from the element's left edge and 30 pixels down from the top edge.

```
background-position: 30px;
```

You can also place the background image using the keywords `left`, `center`, and `right` for the horizontal position and `top`, `center`, and `bottom` for the vertical position. The following style places the background image in the bottom-right corner of the element.

```
background-position: right bottom;
```

Typically, the `background-position` property is only useful for non-tiled images because, if the image is tiled, the tiled image fills the background and it usually doesn't matter where the tiling starts.

Defining the Extent of the Background

You learned in Tutorial 2 that every block element follows the Box Model in which the element content is surrounded by a padding space and beyond that a border space (see Figure 2-38). However, the element's background is defined, by default, to extend only through the padding space and not to include the border space. You can change this definition using the following `background-clip` property:

```
background-clip: type;
```

where *type* is `content-box` (to extend the background only through the element content), `padding-box` (to extend the background through the padding space), or `border-box` (to extend the background through the border space). For example, the following style rule defines the background for the page body to extend only as far as the page content. The padding and border spaces would not be considered part of the background and thus would not show any background image.

```
body {
    background-clip: content-box;
}
```

Because the background extends through the padding space by default, all coordinates for the background image position are measured from the top-left corner of that padding space. You can choose a different context by applying the following `background-origin` property:

```
background-origin: type;
```

where *type* is once again `content-box`, `padding-box`, or `border-box`. Thus, the following style rule places the background image at the bottom-left corner of the page body content and not the bottom-left corner of the padding space (which would be the default).

```
body {
    background-position: left bottom;
    background-origin: content-box;
}
```

Based on this style rule, the padding space of page body would not have any background image or color, other than what would be defined for the browser window itself.

Sizing and Clipping an Image

The size of the background image is equal to the size stored in the image file. To specify a different size, apply the following `background-size` property:

```
background-size: width height;
```

where `width` and `height` are the width and height of the image in one of the CSS units of length or as a percentage of the element's width and height. The following style sets the size of the background image to 300 pixels wide by 200 pixels high.

```
background-size: 300px 200px;
```

CSS also supports the sizing keywords `auto`, `cover`, and `contain`. The `auto` keyword tells the browser to automatically set the width or height value based on the dimensions of the original image. The following style sets the height of the image to 200 pixels and automatically scales the width to keep the original proportions of the image:

```
background-size: auto 200px;
```

The `cover` keyword tells the browser to resize the image to cover all of the element background while still retaining the image proportions. Depending on the size of the element, this could result in some of the background image being cropped. The `contain` keyword scales the image so that it's completely contained within the element, even if that means that not all of the element background is covered. Figure 4-7 displays examples of a background set to a specific size, as well as resized to either cover the background or to have the image completely contained within the background.

Figure 4-7	Examples of background-size types

```
background-size: 200px 300px;   background-size: cover;   background-size: contain;
```

300px

200px

image is scaled at the specified dimensions

image is resized to fill the background, but part of the image is cropped

image is resized so that it is contained within the element, but part of the background is left uncovered

© 2016 Cengage Learning; Source: wiki Media

Setting Background Image Options

- To specify how the image is attached to the background, use

  ```
  background-attachment: type;
  ```

  where *type* is scroll (the default), fixed, or local.
- To set the position of the background image, use

  ```
  background-position: horizontal vertical;
  ```

  where *horizontal* and *vertical* provide the coordinates of the image within the element background.
- To define the extent of the background, use

  ```
  background-clip: type;
  ```

  where *type* is content-box, padding-box (the default), or border-box.
- To define how position coordinates are measured, use

  ```
  background-origin: type;
  ```

  where *type* is content-box, padding-box (the default), or border-box.

The background Property

All of these different background options can be organized in the following background property:

```
background: color url(url) position / size repeat attachment
origin clip;
```

where *color* is the background color, *url* is the source of the background image, *position* is the image's position, *size* sets the image size, *repeat* sets the tiling of the image, *attachment* specifies whether the image scrolls with the content or is fixed, *origin* defines how positions are measured on the background, and *clip* specifies the extent over which the background is spread. For example, the following style rule sets the background color to ivory and then uses the draft.png file as the background image fixed at the horizontal and vertical center of the page body and sized at 10% of the body's width and height:

```
body {
    background: ivory url(draft.png)
                center center / 10% 10%
                no-repeat fixed content-box content-box;
}
```

The rest of the property sets the image not to repeat and to use the content box for defining the background origin and clipping. Note that the page body will have an ivory background color at any location where the draft.png image is not displayed. If you don't specify all of the option values, the browser will assume the default values for the missing options. Thus, the following style rule places the draft.png at the horizontal and vertical center of the page body without tiling:

```
body {
    background: ivory url(draft.png) center center no-repeat;
}
```

TIP

The background property includes the "/" character only when you need to separate the image position value from the image size value.

Since no *size*, *attachment*, *origin*, and *clip* values are specified, the size of the image will be based on the dimensions from the image file, the image will scroll with the body content, and the background origin and clipping will extend through the page body's padding space.

Kevin wants you to include a semi-transparent image of the family patriarch, Genta Komatsu, as a background image placed in the lower-right corner of the article on the Komatsu family. Add a style rule to the tb_visual1.css file to display the tb_back2.png image within that element without tiling.

To add a background image to the page article:

1. Return to the **tb_visual1.css** file in your editor and scroll down to the Article Styles section.

2. Add the following style rule:

```
article {
    background: url(tb_back2.png) bottom right / 15%
                no-repeat content-box;
}
```

Figure 4-8 highlights the style rule applied to the page article.

Figure 4-8	Adding a background to the page article

places the image at the lower-right corner

does not tile the image

```
/* Article Styles */

article {
    background: url(tb_back2.png) bottom right / 15% no-repeat content-box;
}
```

image file

sets the width of the image to 15% of the article width

positions the image with respect to the article content

3. Save your changes and then reload tb_komatsu.html in your browser. Figure 4-9 shows the placement of the background image.

Figure 4-9	Placement of the background image

background image placed in lower-right corner of the article content with no tiling

Kevin likes the addition of the image of Genta Komatsu and would like you to add another background image showing the family matriarch, Mika Komatsu, and a third image giving the article a paper-textured background.

Adding Multiple Backgrounds

To add multiple backgrounds to the same element, you list the backgrounds in the following comma-separated list:

```
background: background1, background2, ...;
```

where *background1*, *background2*, and so on are the properties for each background. For example the following style rule applies three different backgrounds to the `header` element:

```
header {
    background: url(back2.png) top left no-repeat,
                url(back1.png) bottom right no-repeat,
                rgb(191, 191, 191);
}
```

TIP

Always list the background color last so that it provides the foundation for your background images.

Backgrounds are added in the reverse order in which they're listed in the style rule. In this style rule, the background color is applied first, the back1.png background image is placed on top of that, and finally the back2.png background image is placed on top of those two backgrounds.

Individual background properties can also contain multiple options placed in a comma-separated list. The following style rule creates the same multiple backgrounds for the `header` element without using the `background` property:

```
header {
    background-image: url(back2.png), url(back1.png);
    background-position: top left, bottom right;
    background-repeat: no-repeat;
    background-color: rgb(191, 191, 191);
}
```

Note that if a background style is listed once, it is applied across all of the backgrounds. Thus the `background-color` and the `background-repeat` properties are used in all the backgrounds.

Revise the style rule for the `article` element to add two more backgrounds.

To add a background image to the page article:

1. Return to the **tb_visual1.css** file in your editor and return to the Article Styles section.

The properties for multiple backgrounds need to be separated by commas.

2. Type a comma after the first background listed for the `article` element and before the semicolon (;), then press **Enter**.

3. Be sure the insertion point is before the semicolon (;), then add the following code to display two more background images followed by a background color:

```
url(tb_back3.png) bottom left / 15% no-repeat content-box,
url(tb_back4.png) 100%/cover no-repeat,
rgb(211, 211, 211)
```

The background color acts as a fallback design element and will not be displayed except for browsers that are incapable of displaying background images. Figure 4-10 displays the code for the multiple backgrounds applied to the page article.

Figure 4-10	Adding multiple background images

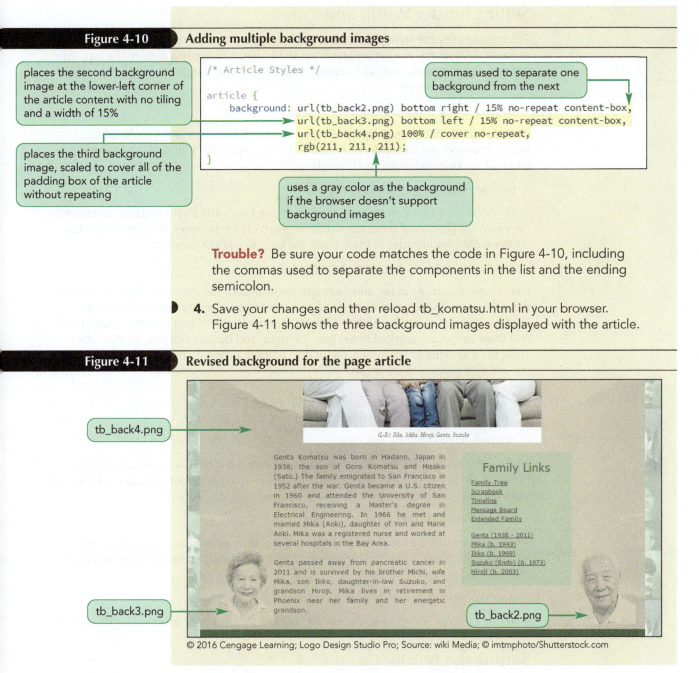

places the second background image at the lower-left corner of the article content with no tiling and a width of 15%

places the third background image, scaled to cover all of the padding box of the article without repeating

commas used to separate one background from the next

uses a gray color as the background if the browser doesn't support background images

```
/* Article Styles */

article {
    background: url(tb_back2.png) bottom right / 15% no-repeat content-box,
                url(tb_back3.png) bottom left / 15% no-repeat content-box,
                url(tb_back4.png) 100% / cover no-repeat,
                rgb(211, 211, 211);
}
```

Trouble? Be sure your code matches the code in Figure 4-10, including the commas used to separate the components in the list and the ending semicolon.

4. Save your changes and then reload tb_komatsu.html in your browser. Figure 4-11 shows the three background images displayed with the article.

Figure 4-11	Revised background for the page article

tb_back4.png

tb_back3.png

tb_back2.png

(L-R): Ikko, Mika, Hiroji, Genta, Suzuko

Genta Komatsu was born in Hadano, Japan in 1938; the son of Goro Komatsu and Hisako (Sato.) The family emigrated to San Francisco in 1952 after the war. Genta became a U.S. citizen in 1960 and attended the University of San Francisco, receiving a Master's degree in Electrical Engineering. In 1966 he met and married Mika (Aoki), daughter of Yori and Marie Aoki. Mika was a registered nurse and worked at several hospitals in the Bay Area.

Genta passed away from pancreatic cancer in 2011 and is survived by his brother Michi, wife Mika, son Ikko, daughter-in-law Suzuko, and grandson Hiroji. Mika lives in retirement in Phoenix near her family and her energetic grandson.

Family Links

Family Tree
Scrapbook
Timeline
Message Board
Extended Family

Genta (1938 - 2011)
Mika (b. 1943)
Ikko (b. 1969)
Suzuko (Endo) (b. 1973)
Hiroji (b. 2003)

© 2016 Cengage Learning; Logo Design Studio Pro; Source: wiki Media; © imtmphoto/Shutterstock.com

Kevin is pleased with the revised backgrounds for the browser window and the page article. Next, you will explore how to work with CSS border properties.

Working with Borders

So far, you have only worked with the content, padding, and margin spaces from the CSS Box model. Now, you will examine the border space that separates the element's content and padding from its margins and essentially marks the extent of the element as it is rendered on the page.

Setting Border Width and Color

CSS supports several style properties that are used to format the border around each element. As with the margin and padding styles, you can apply a style to the top, right, bottom, or left border, or to all borders at once. To define the thickness of a specific border, use the property

```
border-side-width: width;
```

where `side` is either `top`, `right`, `bottom`, or `left` and `width` is the width of the border in one of the CSS units of measure. For example, the following style sets the width of the bottom border to 10 pixels.

```
border-bottom-width: 10px;
```

Border widths also can be expressed using the keywords `thin`, `medium`, or `thick`; the exact application of these keywords depends on the browser. You can define the border widths for all sides at once using the `border-width` property

```
border-width: top right bottom left;
```

where `top`, `right`, `bottom`, and `left` are the widths of the matching border. As with the `margin` and `padding` properties, if you enter one value, it's applied to all four borders; two values set the width of the top/bottom and left/right borders, respectively; and three values are applied to the top, left/right, and bottom borders, in that order. Thus, the following property sets the widths of the top/bottom borders to 10 pixels and the left/right borders to 20 pixels:

```
border-width: 10px 20px;
```

The color of each individual border is set using the property

```
border-side-color: color;
```

where `side` once again specifies the border side and `color` is a color name, color value, or the keyword `transparent` to create an invisible border. The color of the four sides can be specified using the following `border-color` property

```
border-color: top right bottom left;
```

where `top right bottom left` specifies the side to which the color should be applied. Thus, the following style uses gray for the top and left borders and black for the right and bottom borders:

```
border-color: gray black black gray;
```

If no border color is specified, the border will use the text color assigned to the element.

Setting the Border Design

CSS allows you to further define the appearance of borders using the following border styles:

```
border-side-style: style;
```

where `side` once again indicates the border side and `style` specifies one of the nine border styles displayed in Figure 4-12.

Figure 4-12   **Examples of border styles**

© 2016 Cengage Learning

Or to specify styles for all four borders use the property:

```
border-style: top right bottom left;
```

As with the other border rules, you can modify the style of all borders or combinations of the borders. For example, the following style uses a double line for the top/bottom borders and a single solid line for the left/right borders.

```
border-style: double solid;
```

All of the border styles discussed above can be combined into the following property that formats the width, style, and color of all of the borders

```
border: width style color;
```

where *width* is the thickness of the border, *style* is the style of the border, and *color* is the border color. The following style rule inserts a 2-pixel-wide solid blue border around every side of each h1 heading in the document:

```
h1 {border: 2px solid blue;}
```

To modify the width, style, and color of a single border, use the property

```
border-side: width style color;
```

where *side* is either top, right, bottom, or left.

REFERENCE

Adding a Border

- To add a border around every side of an element, use the CSS property

  border: *width style color*;

  where *width* is the width of the border, *style* is the design style, and *color* is the border color.
- To apply a border to a specific side, use

  border-*side*: *width style color*;

  where *side* is top, right, bottom, or left for the top, right, bottom, and left borders.
- To set the width, style, or color of a specific side, use the properties

  border-*side*-width: *width*;
  border-*side*-style: *style*;
  border-*side*-color: *color*;

Kevin wants the page body to stand out better against the tiled images used as the background for the browser window. He suggests you add solid borders to the left and right edges of the page body and that you add a double border around the aside element containing links to other Komatsu family pages.

To add borders to the page elements:

1. Return to the **tb_visual1.css** file in your editor and go to the Page Body Styles section.

2. Add the following style rule for the page body:

   ```
   body {
      border-left: 1px solid rgb(51, 51, 51);
      border-right: 1px solid rgb(51, 51, 51);
   }
   ```

3. Go to the Aside Styles section and add the following style rule for the aside element:

   ```
   aside {
      border: 4px double rgb(45, 93, 62);
   }
   ```

   Figure 4-13 highlights the style rules that create borders for the page body and aside element.

Figure 4-13	Adding borders to the page body and aside element

adds a 1-pixel solid gray border to the left and right edges of the page body

adds a 4-pixel double medium green border to the aside element

```
/* Page Body Styles */

body {
    border-left: 1px solid rgb(51, 51, 51);
    border-right: 1px solid rgb(51, 51, 51);
}


/* Aside Styles */

aside {
    border: 4px double rgb(45, 93, 62);
}
```

4. Save your changes to the file and then reload tb_komatsu.html in your browser. Figure 4-14 shows the appearance of the page with the newly added borders. Note that the background color and other styles associated with the aside element are in the tb_styles1.css file.

Figure 4-14	Page design with borders

left page border

right page border

double border around the aside element

© 2016 Cengage Learning; Logo Design Studio Pro; Source: wiki Media; © imtmphoto/Shutterstock.com

Kevin is concerned that the design of the page is too boxy and he wants you to soften the design by adding curves to some of the page elements. You can create this effect using rounded corners.

Creating Rounded Corners

To round off any of the four corners of a border, apply the following border-radius property:

    border-radius: *top-left top-right bottom-right bottom-left*;

where *top-left*, *top-right*, *bottom-right*, and *bottom-left* are the radii of the individual corners. The radii are equal to the radii of hypothetical circles placed at the corners of the box with the arcs of the circles defining the rounded corners (see Figure 4-15).

Figure 4-15 **Setting rounded corners based on corner radii**

border-radius: 20px 60px 100px 140px;

© 2016 Cengage Learning

If you enter only one radius value, it is applied to all four corners; if you enter two values, the first is applied to the top-left and bottom-right corners, and the second is applied to the top-right and bottom-left corners. If you specify three radii, they are applied to the top-left, top-right/bottom-left, and bottom-right corners, in that order. For example, the following style rule creates rounded corners for the `aside` element in which the radii of the top-left and bottom-right corners is 50 pixels and the radii of the top-right and bottom-left corners is 20 pixels.

```
aside {border-radius: 50px 20px;}
```

To set the curvature for only one corner, use the property:

```
border-corner-radius: radius;
```

where *corner* is either `top-left`, `top-right`, `bottom-right`, or `bottom-left`.

The corners do not need to be circular. Elongated or elliptical corners are created by specifying the ratio of the horizontal radius to the vertical radius using the style:

```
border-radius: horizontal/vertical;
```

where *horizontal* is the horizontal radius of the corner and *vertical* is the vertical radius of the same corner (see Figure 4-16).

Figure 4-16   **Creating an elongated corner**

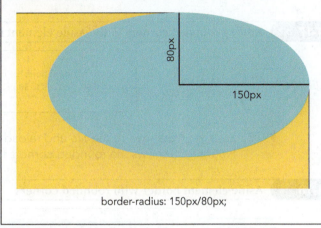

80px

150px

border-radius: 150px/80px;

© 2016 Cengage Learning

Thus, the following style rule creates elongated corners in which the ratio of the horizontal to vertical radius is 50 pixels to 20 pixels.

```
border-radius: 50px/20px;
```

Note that using percentages for the radius value can result in elongated corners if the element is not perfectly square. The following style rule sets the horizontal radius to 15% of element width and 15% of the element height. If the element is twice as wide as it is high for example, the corners will not be rounded but elongated.

```
border-radius: 15%;
```

When applied to a single corner, the format to create an elongated corner is slightly different. You remove the slash between the horizontal and vertical values and use the following syntax:

```
border-corner-radius: horizontal vertical;
```

For example, the following style creates an elongated bottom-left corner with a horizontal radius of 50 pixels and a vertical radius of 20 pixels.

```
border-bottom-left-radius: 50px 20px;
```

Rounded and elongated corners do not clip element content. If the content of the element extends into the corner, it will still be displayed as part of the background. Because this is often unsightly, you should avoid heavily rounded or elongated corners unless you can be sure they will not obscure or distract from the element content.

Add rounded corners with a radius of 30 pixels to the `aside` element.

To add rounded corners to an element:

1. Return to the **tb_visual1.css** file in your editor and go to the Aside Styles section.

2. Add the following style to the style rule for the `aside` element:

   ```
   border-radius: 30px;
   ```

   Figure 4-17 highlights the style to create the rounded corners for the aside border.

Adding rounded corners to the aside element border

sets the radius at each
border corner to 30 pixels →

```
aside {
    border: 4px double rgb(45, 93, 62);
    border-radius: 30px;
}
```

3. Save your changes to the file and reload tb_komatsu.html in your browser. Figure 4-18 shows the rounded corners for the `aside` element border.

Aside element border with rounded corners

rounded corner →

© imtmphoto/Shutterstock.com

Kevin likes the revision to the border for the `aside` element. He also wants you to add a border to the family portrait on the Komatsu Family page. However, rather than using one of the styles shown in Figure 4-12, Kevin wants you to use a graphic border that makes it appear as if the figure box came from a torn piece of paper. You can create this effect using border images.

Applying a Border Image

A border image is a border that it is based on a graphic image. The graphic image is sliced into nine sections representing the four corners, the four sides, and the interior piece. The interior piece is discarded because that is where the content of the object will appear; the four corners become the corners of the border and the four sides are either stretched or tiled to fill in the border's top, right, bottom, and left sides. Figure 4-19 shows an example of an image file, frame.png, sliced into nine sections to create a border image.

Figure 4-19	Slicing a graphic image to create a border

border-image: url(frame.png) 20 stretch;

slices are stretched to match the image border

border slices

© 2016 Cengage Learning; © imtmphoto/Shutterstock.com

To apply a border image, use the following property

```
border-image: url(url) slice repeat;
```

where *url* is the source of the graphic image, *slice* is the width or height of the slices used to create the sides and corners, and *repeat* indicates whether the side slices should be stretched or tiled to cover the border's four sides. The *repeat* option supports the following values:

- `stretch:` The slices are stretched to fill each side.
- `repeat:` The slices are tiled to fill each side.
- `round:` The slices are tiled to fill each side; if they don't fill the sides with an integer number of tiles, the slices are rescaled until they do.
- `space:` The slices are tiled to fill each side; if they don't fill the sides with an integer number of tiles, extra space is distributed around the tiles.

For example, the following style cuts 10-pixel-wide slices from the frame.png image file with the four side slices stretched to cover the length of the four sides of the object's border:

```
border-image: url(frame.png) 10 stretch;
```

The size of the slices is measured either in pixels or as a percentage of the image file width and height. A quirk of this property is that you should *not* specify the pixel unit if you want the slices measured in pixels but you must include the % symbol when slices are measured in percentages.

You can create slices of different widths or heights by entering the size values in a space-separated list. For instance, the following style slices the graphic image 5 pixels on the top, 10 pixels on the right, 15 pixels on the bottom, and 25 pixels on the left:

```
border-image: url(frame.png) 5 10 15 25 stretch;
```

The slice sizes follow the same top/right/bottom/left syntax used with all of the CSS border styles. Thus, the following style slices 5% from the top and bottom sides of the graphic image, and 10% from the left and right sides:

```
border-image: url(frame.png) 5% 10% stretch;
```

You can also apply different repeat values to different sides of the border. For example, the following style stretches the border slices on the top and bottom but tiles the left and right slices:

```
border-image: url(frame.png) 10 stretch repeat;
```

REFERENCE

Creating a Graphic Border

• To create a border based on a graphic image, use

```
border-image: url(url) slice repeat;
```

where *url* is the source of the border image file, *slice* is the size of the border image cut off to create the borders, and *repeat* indicates whether the side borders should be either stretched or tiled to cover the object's four sides.

The torn paper image that Kevin wants to use is based on the graphic image file tp_border.png file. Use the `border-image` property to add a border image around the figure box on the Komatsu Family page, tiling the border slices to fill the sides. Note that in order for the border image to appear you must include values for the `border-width` and `border-style` properties.

To create a graphic border:

1. Return to the **tb_visual1.css** file in your editor and scroll to the Figure Box Styles at the top of the file.

2. Add the following style to the style rule for the figure box:

```
border-style: solid;
border-width: 25px;
border-image: url(tb_border.png) 50 repeat;
```

Figure 4-20 displays the styles used to create the graphic border.

Figure 4-20   **Adding a border image**

border width and style values are required for the border image

```
figure {
    border-style: solid;
    border-width: 25px;
    border-image: url(tb_border.png) 50 repeat;
    margin: 20px auto 0px;
    width: 80%;
}
```

uses the tb_border.png file for the graphical border

slices 50 pixels from each side of the border image

tiles the side slices to fill the border sides

3. Save your changes and reload tb_komatsu.html in your browser. Figure 4-21 shows the appearance of the border image.

Figure 4-21   **Figure box with border image**

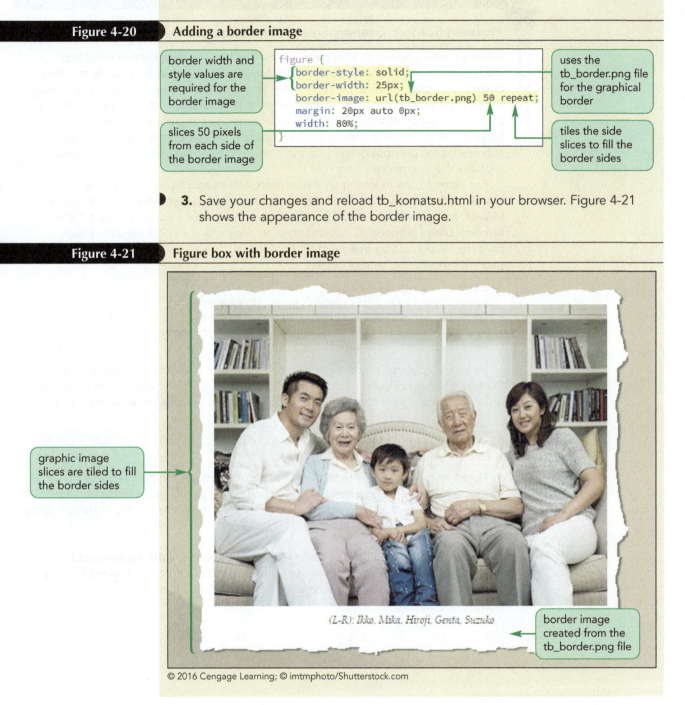

graphic image slices are tiled to fill the border sides

(L-R): Ikko, Mika, Hiroji, Genta, Suzuko

border image created from the tb_border.png file

Kevin appreciates the effect you created, making it appear as if the family portrait was torn from an album and laid on top of the web page.

Problem Solving: Graphic Design and Legacy Browsers

Adding snazzy graphics to your page can be fun, but you must keep in mind that the fundamental test of your design is not how cool it looks but how usable it is. Any design you create needs to be compatible across several browser versions if you want to reach the widest user base. To support older browsers, your style sheet should use progressive enhancement in which the older properties are listed first, followed by browser extensions, and then by the most current CSS properties. As each property supersedes the previous properties, the browser will end up using the most current property that it supports.

For example, the following style rule starts with a basic 5-pixel blue border that will be recognized by every browser. It is followed by browser extensions for Opera, Mozilla, and WebKit to support older browsers that predate adoption of the CSS3 `border-image` property. Finally, the style list ends with the CSS3 `border-image` property, recognized by every current browser. In this way, every browser that opens the page will show some type of border.

```
border: 5px solid blue;
-o-border-image: url(paper.png) 30 repeat;
-moz-border-image: url(paper.png) 30 repeat;
-webkit-border-image: url(paper.png) 30 repeat;
border-image: url(paper.png) 30 repeat;
```

Be aware, however, that the syntax for an extension may not match the syntax for the final CSS3 specification. For example, the following list of styles creates a rounded top-right corner that is compatible across a wide range of browser versions:

```
-moz-border-radius-top-right: 15px;
-webkit-border-top-right-radius: 15px;
border-top-right-radius: 15px;
```

Note that the syntax for the Mozilla extension does not match the syntax for the WebKit extension or for the final CSS3 specification. As always, you need to do your homework to learn exactly how different browser versions handle these CSS design styles.

In the next session, you'll continue to work with the CSS graphic styles to add three-dimensional effects through the use of drop shadows and color gradients. If you want to take a break, you can close your open files and documents now.

REVIEW

Session 4.1 Quick Check

1. Provide code to create a figure box containing the logo.png image file, no alt text, and a caption with the text *Tree and Book*.

2. What is the difference between a vector image and a bitmap image?

3. Provide the code to use the sidebar.png file as the background image for the page body. Have the image placed in the top-left corner of the page and tiled only in the horizontal direction.

4. Create a style rule for the `header` element that fills the header background with tiled images of the back.png, but only over the element content.

5. Provide a style rule to display the logo.png and side.png image files in the top-left corner of the page body's background. Do not tile the logo.png image, but tile the side.png image vertically. Design your style rule so that logo.png appears on top of the side.png. For the rest of the page body, set the background color to ivory.

6. Provide a style rule to add a 5-pixel dotted brown border around the `aside` element.

7. Provide a style rule to add a 3-pixel solid blue border around the `header` element with rounded corners of 15 pixels.

8. Provide a style rule to add elongated corners with a 5-pixel gray inset border around the `aside` element and with a horizontal radius of 10 pixels and vertical radius of 5 pixels.

9. Provide a style rule to use the graphic image file border.png as a solid border for the `article` element. Set the size of the image slice to 30 pixels and stretch the sides to match the sides of the element. Assume a border width of 10 pixels.

Session 4.2 Visual Overview:

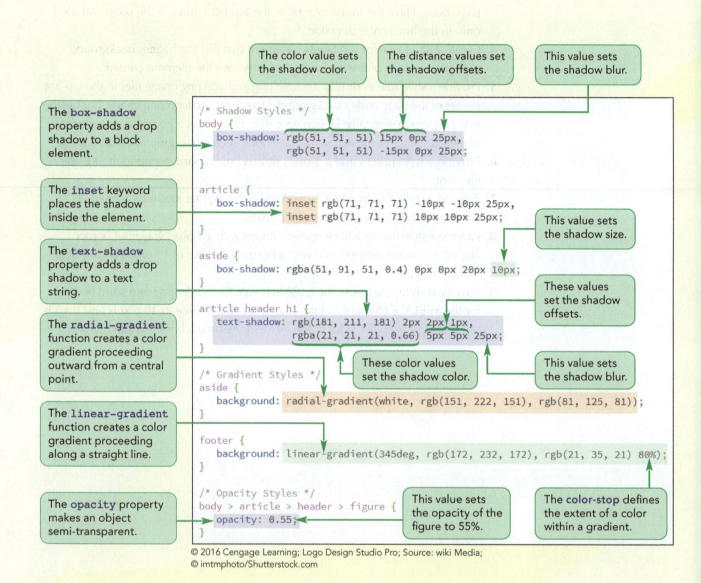

The color value sets the shadow color.

The distance values set the shadow offsets.

This value sets the shadow blur.

The **box-shadow** property adds a drop shadow to a block element.

```
/* Shadow Styles */
body {
    box-shadow: rgb(51, 51, 51) 15px 0px 25px,
                rgb(51, 51, 51) -15px 0px 25px;
}
```

The **inset** keyword places the shadow inside the element.

```
article {
    box-shadow: inset rgb(71, 71, 71) -10px -10px 25px,
                inset rgb(71, 71, 71) 10px 10px 25px;
}
```

This value sets the shadow size.

The **text-shadow** property adds a drop shadow to a text string.

```
aside {
    box-shadow: rgba(51, 91, 51, 0.4) 0px 0px 20px 10px;
}
```

These values set the shadow offsets.

```
article header h1 {
    text-shadow: rgb(181, 211, 181) 2px 2px 1px,
                 rgba(21, 21, 21, 0.66) 5px 5px 25px;
}
```

The **radial-gradient** function creates a color gradient proceeding outward from a central point.

These color values set the shadow color.

This value sets the shadow blur.

```
/* Gradient Styles */
aside {
    background: radial-gradient(white, rgb(151, 222, 151), rgb(81, 125, 81));
}
```

The **linear-gradient** function creates a color gradient proceeding along a straight line.

```
footer {
    background: linear-gradient(345deg, rgb(172, 232, 172), rgb(21, 35, 21) 80%);
}
```

The **opacity** property makes an object semi-transparent.

```
/* Opacity Styles */
body > article > header > figure {
    opacity: 0.55;
}
```

This value sets the opacity of the figure to 55%.

The **color-stop** defines the extent of a color within a gradient.

Shadows and Gradients

This shows a box shadow on the left edge of the page body.

This shows a box shadow inside the page article.

This shows the figure box is displayed as 55% opaque.

There is a box shadow on the right edge of the page body.

The heading text has a text shadow.

The box shadow creates a halo around the aside element.

The radial gradient proceeds from white in the center to medium green on the edges.

The linear gradient proceeds at an angle of 15° counter-clockwise from light green to dark green.

Creating Drop Shadows

In this session, you will examine some design styles that create 3D effects, making the page content appear to jump out of the browser window. The first styles you'll explore are used to create drop shadows around text strings and element boxes.

Creating a Text Shadow

To give the text on your page visual impact, you can use CSS to add a shadow using the following `text-shadow` property

```
text-shadow: color offsetX offsetY blur;
```

where `color` is the shadow color, `offsetX` and `offsetY` are the distances of the shadow from the text in the horizontal and vertical directions, and `blur` defines the amount by which the shadow spreads out, creating a blurred effect. The shadow offset values are expressed so that positive values push the shadow to the right and down while negative values move the shadow to the left and up. The default `blur` value is 0, creating a shadow with distinct hard edges; as the blur value increases, the edge of the shadow becomes less distinct and blends more in the text background.

The following style creates a red text shadow that is 10 pixels to the right and 5 pixels down from the text with blur of 8 pixels:

```
text-shadow: red 10px 5px 8px;
```

Multiple shadows can be added to text by including each shadow definition in the following comma-separated list.

```
text-shadow: shadow1, shadow2, shadow3, …;
```

where `shadow1`, `shadow2`, `shadow3`, and so on are shadows applied to the text with the first shadow listed displayed on top of subsequent shadows when they overlap. The following style rule creates two shadows with the first red shadow placed 10 pixels to the left and 5 pixels up from the text and the second gray shadow is placed 3 pixels to the right and 4 pixels down from the text. Both shadows have a blur of 6 pixels:

```
text-shadow: red -10px -5px 6px,
             gray 3px 4px 6px;
```

TIP

You can explore more text shadows using the demo_text_shadows.html file from the demo folder.

Figure 4-22 shows examples of how the `text-shadow` style can be used to achieve a variety of text designs involving single and multiple shadows.

Figure 4-22   **Examples of text shadows**

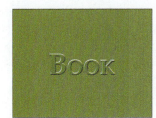

text-shadow: gray 4px 6px 5px;

color: rgb(150, 187, 60);
text-shadow: black -4px -3px 5px;

color: white;
text-shadow: black 0px 0px 1px;

color: white;
text-shadow: green 0px 0px 25px;

color: white;
text-shadow: black 0px 0px 3px,
                   green 4px 4px 4px,
                   blue 0px 0px 55px;

background-color:
rgb(110, 137, 20);
color: rgb(90, 127, 0);
text-shadow: black 1px 1px 1px,
                   white 0px -2px 0px;

REFERENCE

Creating a Text Shadow

- To add a shadow to a text string, use the property

  ```
  text-shadow: color offsetX offsetY blur;
  ```

  where *color* is the shadow color, *offsetX* and *offsetY* are the distances of the shadow from the text in the horizontal and vertical directions, and *blur* defines the amount by which the shadow is stretched.

Kevin wants you to add two text shadows to the h1 heading *The Komatsu Family*. The first text shadow will be a light-green highlight with hard edges and the second shadow will be semi-transparent gray and blurred.

To add a text shadow:

1. If you took a break after the previous session, reopen or return to the **tb_visual1.css** file in your editor and scroll to the Article Styles section.

2. Add the following style for the h1 heading in the article header:

   ```
   article header h1 {
       text-shadow: rgb(181, 211, 181) 2px 2px 1px,
                    rgba(21, 21, 21, 0.66) 5px 5px 25px;
   }
   ```

   Figure 4-23 highlights the style to add text shadows to the h1 heading.

Figure 4-23 **Adding text shadows**

```
article {
    background: url(tb_back2.png) bottom right / 15% no-repeat content-box,
               url(tb_back3.png) bottom left / 15% no-repeat content-box,
               url(tb_back4.png) 100% / cover no-repeat,
               rgb(211, 211, 211);
}

article header h1 {
    text-shadow: rgb(181, 211, 181) 2px 2px 1px,
                 rgba(21, 21, 21, 0.66) 5px 5px 25px;
}
```

light green text shadow with hard edges

semi-transparent gray shadow with soft edges

shadow color

horizontal offset

vertical offset

blur size

3. Save your changes and reload tb_komatsu.html in your browser. Figure 4-24 shows the shadow effect added to the h1 heading.

Figure 4-24 **Article heading with text shadows**

soft gray background shadow

light green highlight shadow

© 2016 Cengage Learning; © imtmphoto/Shutterstock.com

Kevin likes the shadow effect and the use of the light green shadow, which appears to give a highlight to the heading text. Next, he wants you to add shadows to other page objects.

Creating a Box Shadow

Shadows can be added to any block element in the web page by using the box-shadow property

```
box-shadow: color offsetX offsetY blur;
```

TIP

If no shadow color is provided, the browser uses black as the default color.

where *color*, *offsetX*, *offsetY*, and *blur* have the same meanings for box shadows as they do for text shadows. As with text shadows, you can add multiple shadows by including them in the following comma-separated list

```
box-shadow: shadow1, shadow2 …;
```

where once again the first shadow listed is displayed on top of subsequent shadows.

In the last session, you used left and right borders to set off the page body from the browser window background. Kevin would like you to increase this visual distinction by adding drop shadows to the left and right sides of the page body.

To add a box shadow:

▶ **1.** Return to the **tb_visual1.css** file in your editor and go to the Page Body Styles section.

▶ **2.** Within the style rule for the body element, insert the following styles:

```
box-shadow: rgb(51, 51, 51) 15px 0px 25px,
            rgb(51, 51, 51) -15px 0px 25px;
```

Figure 4-25 highlights the style to add box shadows to the page body.

Figure 4-25	Adding box shadows

drop shadow on the page body's right edge

drop shadow on the page body's left edge

```
body {
    border-left: 1px solid rgb(51, 51, 51);
    border-right: 1px solid rgb(51, 51, 51);
    box-shadow: rgb(51, 51, 51) 15px 0px 25px,
        rgb(51, 51, 51) -15px 0px 25px;
}
```

gray shadow color

▶ **3.** Save your changes and reload tb_komatsu.html in your browser. Figure 4-26 shows the drop shadows added to the page body.

Figure 4-26	Page body with drop shadows

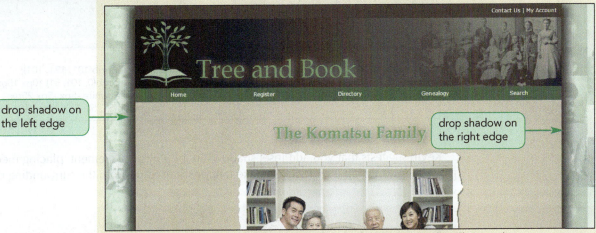

drop shadow on the left edge

drop shadow on the right edge

© 2016 Cengage Learning; Logo Design Studio Pro; Source: wiki Media; © imtmphoto/Shutterstock.com

Box shadows can be placed inside the element as well as outside. By adding an interior shadow you can create the illusion of a beveled edge in which the object appears to rise out of its background. To create an interior shadow, add the `inset` keyword to the `box-shadow` property

```
box-shadow: inset color offsetX offsetY blur;
```

TIP

You can learn more about box shadows using the demo_box_shadows.html file from the demo folder.

where the meanings of the *offsetX* and *offsetY* values are switched when applied to interior shadowing so that positive *offsetX* and *offsetY* values move the shadow to the left and up within the box, while negative *offsetX* and *offsetY* values move the shadow to the right and down.

An object can contain a mixture of exterior and interior shadows. Figure 4-27 shows examples of box shadows, including one example that mixes both interior and exterior shadows.

Figure 4-27   **Examples of box shadows**

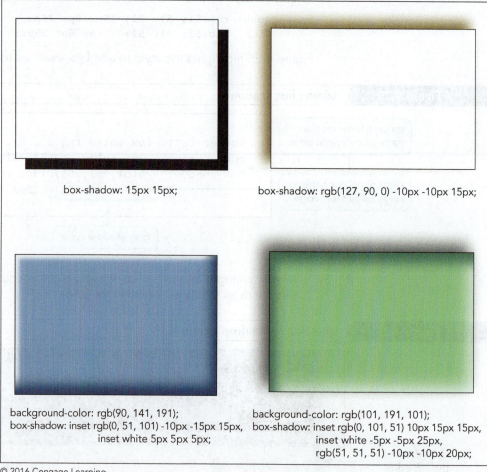

box-shadow: 15px 15px;

box-shadow: rgb(127, 90, 0) -10px -10px 15px;

background-color: rgb(90, 141, 191);
box-shadow: inset rgb(0, 51, 101) -10px -15px 15px,
            inset white 5px 5px 5px;

background-color: rgb(101, 191, 101);
box-shadow: inset rgb(0, 101, 51) 10px 15px 15px,
            inset white -5px -5px 25px,
            rgb(51, 51, 51) -10px -10px 20px;

© 2016 Cengage Learning

Kevin suggests that you add inset shadows to the `article` element, placing medium gray shadows within the article to make it appear raised up from the surrounding page content.

Positive and negative offset values for interior shadows have the opposite meaning from positive and negative offset values for exterior shadows.

To add inset shadows:

1. Return to the **tb_visual1.css** file in your editor and go to the Article Styles section.

2. Within the style rule for the `article` element, insert the following `box-shadow` style:

```
box-shadow: inset rgb(71, 71, 71) -10px -10px 25px,
            inset rgb(71, 71, 71) 10px 10px 25px;
```

Figure 4-28 highlights the newly added code for the inset box shadow.

Figure 4-28	Adding an inset shadow

places a medium-gray shadow in the lower-right interior corner

inset keyword places shadow inside the object

```
article {
    background: url(tb_back2.png) bottom right / 15% no-repeat content-box,
               url(tb_back3.png) bottom left / 15% no-repeat content-box,
               url(tb_back4.png) 100% / cover no-repeat,
               rgb(211, 211, 211);
    box-shadow: inset rgb(71, 71, 71) -10px -10px 25px,
                inset rgb(71, 71, 71) 10px 10px 25px;
}
```

places a medium-gray shadow in the upper-left interior corner

3. Save your changes and reload tb_komatsu.html in your browser. The inset shadow for the page body element is shown in Figure 4-29.

Figure 4-29	Page article with interior shadowing

interior shadow placed on the left and up based on positive offset values

interior shadow placed on the right and down based on negative offset values

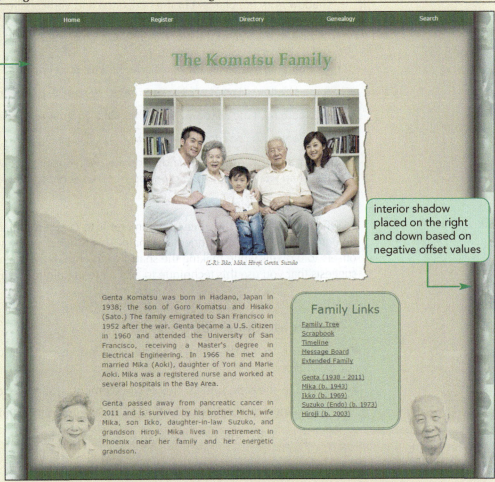

© 2016 Cengage Learning; Logo Design Studio Pro; Source: wiki Media; © imtmphoto/Shutterstock.com

By default, a box shadow has the same size and dimensions as its page object offset in the horizontal and vertical direction. To change the shadow size, add the *spread* parameter to the box-shadow property, specifying the size of the shadow relative to the size of the page object. A positive value increases the size of the shadow, while a negative value decreases it. For example, the following style creates a gray shadow that is offset from the page object by 5 pixels in both the vertical and horizontal direction with no blurring but with a shadow that is 15 pixels larger in the horizontal and vertical directions than the object:

```
box-shadow: gray 5px 5px 0px 15px;
```

On the other hand, the following style creates a shadow that is 15 pixels smaller than the page object:

```
box-shadow: gray 5px 5px 0px -15px;
```

Creating a Box Shadow

- To add a shadow to a block element, use

  ```
  box-shadow: color offsetX offsetY blur spread;
  ```

  where *color* is the shadow color, *offsetX* and *offsetY* are the distances of the shadow from the element in the horizontal and vertical directions, *blur* defines the amount by which the shadow is stretched and *spread* sets the size of the shadow relative to the size of the block element. If no *spread* is specified, the shadow has the same size as the block element.
- To create an interior shadow, include the `inset` keyword

  ```
  box-shadow: inset color offsetX offsetY blur spread;
  ```

- To create multiple shadows place them in a comma-separated list:

  ```
  box-shadow: shadow1, shadow2, …;
  ```

  where *shadow1*, *shadow2*, and so on are definitions for individual shadows with the first shadows listed displayed on top of subsequent shadows.

One application of the *spread* parameter is to create a visual effect in which the object appears to be surrounded by a halo. This is achieved by setting the shadow offsets to 0 pixels while making the shadow larger than the page object itself. Kevin suggests that you use this technique to add a green halo to the `aside` element.

To increase the shadow size:

1. Return to the **tb_visual1.css** file in your editor and go to the Asides Styles section.

2. Within the style rule for the `aside` element, insert the following style:

   ```
   box-shadow: rgba(51, 91, 51, 0.4) 0px 0px 20px 10px;
   ```

   Figure 4-30 highlights the style to add a halo to the `aside` element.

Figure 4-30   Creating a spreading shadow

```
aside {
    border: 4px double rgb(45, 93, 62);
    border-radius: 30px;
    box-shadow: rgba(51, 91, 51, 0.4) 0px 0px 20px 10px;
}
```

20-pixel blur

semi-transparent green shadow

zero shadow offset in the horizontal and vertical direction

shadow is 10 pixels wider and taller than the object

3. Save your changes and reload tb_komatsu.html in your browser. Figure 4-31 shows the revised appearance of the aside element with the glowing green shadow.

Figure 4-31   Aside element with glowing effect

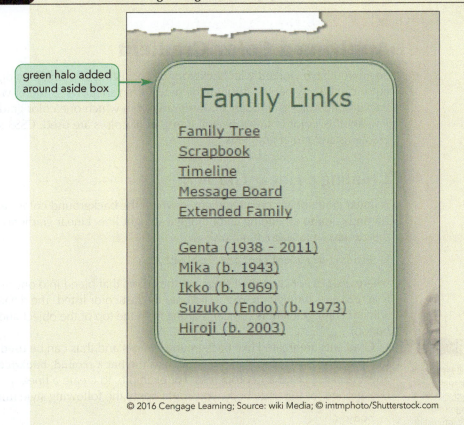

green halo added around aside box

Family Links

Family Tree
Scrapbook
Timeline
Message Board
Extended Family

Genta (1938 - 2011)
Mika (b. 1943)
Ikko (b. 1969)
Suzuko (Endo) (b. 1973)
Hiroji (b. 2003)

© 2016 Cengage Learning; Source: wiki Media; © imtmphoto/Shutterstock.com

Creating a Reflection

WebKit, the rendering engine for Safari and Google Chrome, includes support for adding reflections to page objects through the following property

```
-webkit-box-reflect: direction offset mask-box-image;
```

where *direction* is the placement of the reflection using the keywords `above`, `below`, `left`, or `right`; *offset* is the distance of the reflection from the edge of the element box, and *mask-box-image* is an image that can be used to overlay the reflection. For example, the following style rule creates a reflection that is 10 pixels below the inline image:

```
img {
    -webkit-box-reflect: below 10px;
}
```

There is no equivalent `reflect` property in the official W3C CSS3 specifications. Before using the `reflect` property, you should view the current browser support for the `-webkit-box-reflect` property at *caniuse.com*.

Applying a Color Gradient

So far you have worked with backgrounds consisting of a single color, though that color can be augmented through the use of drop shadows. Another way to modify the background color is through a **color gradient** in which one color gradually blends into another color or fades away if transparent colors are used. CSS3 supports linear gradients and radial gradients.

Creating a Linear Gradient

A linear gradient is a color gradient in which the background color transitions from a starting color to an ending color along a straight line. Linear gradients are created using the `linear-gradient` function

```
linear-gradient(color1, color2, …)
```

where *color1*, *color2*, and so on are the colors that blend into one another starting from *color1*, through *color2*, and onto the last color listed. The default direction for a linear color gradient is vertical, starting from the top of the object and moving to the bottom.

Gradients are treated like background images and thus can be used with any CSS property that accepts an image such as the `background`, `background-image`, and `list-style-image` properties. For example, to create a linear gradient as a background for the page body, you could apply the following style rule:

```
body {
    background: linear-gradient(red, yellow, blue);
}
```

Figure 4-32 shows the appearance of this vertical gradient as the background color transitions gradually from red down to yellow and then from yellow down to blue.

Figure 4-32	Linear gradient with three colors

linear-gradient(red, yellow, blue)

© 2016 Cengage Learning

To change from the default vertical direction, you add a *direction* value to the `linear-gradient` function

```
linear-gradient(direction, color1, color2, …)
```

where *direction* is the direction of the gradient using keywords or angles. Direction keywords are written in the form `to` *position* where *position* is either a side of the object or a corner. For example the following linear gradient moves in a straight line to the left edge of the object blending from red to yellow to blue:

```
background: linear-gradient(to left, red, yellow, blue);
```

To move toward the corner, include both corner edges. The following style moves the gradient in the direction of the object's bottom right corner:

```
background: linear-gradient(to bottom right, red, yellow, blue);
```

TIP

For square objects, a direction of 45deg is equivalent to a direction of to right top.

To move in a direction other than a side or corner, you can express the direction using an angle value. Angles are measured in degrees with 0deg equal to `to` `top`, 90deg equal to `to` `right`, 180deg equal to `to` `bottom`, and 270deg equal to `to` `left` (see Figure 4-33.)

Figure 4-33 **Linear gradient directions**

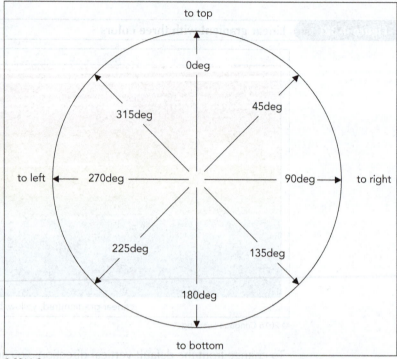

© 2016 Cengage Learning

For example, the following gradient points at a 60 degree angle:

```
background: linear-gradient(60deg, red, yellow, blue);
```

Figure 4-34 shows other examples of linear gradients moving in different directions using both syntaxes.

INSIGHT

Transparency and Gradients

Interesting gradient effects can be achieved using transparent colors so that the background color gradually fades away as it moves in the direction of the gradient. For example, the following style creates a linear gradient that gradually fades away from its initial solid red color:

```
linear-gradient(rgba(255, 0, 0, 1), rgba(255, 0, 0, 0))
```

Note that since the final color is completely transparent it will adopt the background color of the parent element.

You can also use gradients to create background images that appear to fade by using multiple backgrounds in which the gradient appears on top of an image. For example, the following background style creates a fading background using the back.png image file:

```
background: linear-gradient(rgb(255, 255, 255, 0), rgb(255,
255, 255, 1)),url(back.png));
```

When rendered by the browser, the background image will start as solid but gradually fade to white as the linear gradient proceeds through the element background.

| Figure 4-34 | **Directions of linear gradients** |

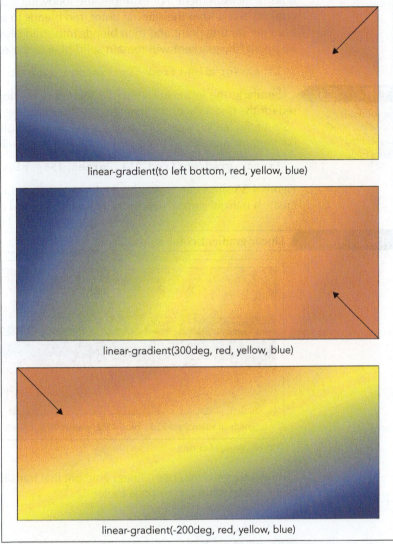

linear-gradient(to left bottom, red, yellow, blue)

linear-gradient(300deg, red, yellow, blue)

linear-gradient(-200deg, red, yellow, blue)

© 2016 Cengage Learning

Note that the degree values can be negative in which case the direction is pointed counter-clockwise around the circle shown in Figure 4-33. A negative angle of –45deg for example would be equivalent to a positive angle of 315deg, an angle of –200deg would be equal to 160deg, and so forth.

Gradients and Color Stops

The colors specified in a gradient are evenly distributed so that the following gradient starts with a solid red, solid green appears halfway through the gradient, and finishes with solid blue:

```
background: linear-gradient(red, green, blue);
```

To change how the colors are distributed, you define color stops, which represent the point at which the specified color stops and the transition to the next color begins. The `linear-gradient` function using color stops has the general form

```
linear-gradient(direction, color-stop1, color-stop2, …)
```

where *color-stop1*, *color-stop2*, and so on are the colors and their stopping positions within the gradient. Stopping positions can be entered using any of the CSS units of measurement. For example, the following gradient starts with solid red up until 50 pixels from the starting point, red blends to solid green stopping at 60 pixels from the starting point and then blends into solid blue 80 pixels from the start. After 80 pixels, the gradient will remain solid blue to the end of the background.

```
linear-gradient(red 50px, green 60px, blue 80px)
```

Similarly, the following style rule sets the color stops using percentages with solid red for the first 25% of the background, transitioning to solid green from 25% to 75% of the background, and then transitioning to solid blue from 75% to 95% of the background size. From that point to the end, the background remains solid blue.

```
linear-gradient(red 25%, green 75%, blue 95%)
```

Figure 4-35 shows an example of a linear gradient in which color stops are used to create a narrow strip of yellow within a background of red blended into blue.

Figure 4-35	Linear gradient color stops

solid red (start to 25%)

red to blue (25% to 45%)

blue to yellow to blue (45% to 49% to 51%)

blue to red (51% to 75%)

solid red (75% to end)

linear-gradient(red 25%, blue 45%, yellow 49%, blue 51%, red 75%)

© 2016 Cengage Learning

Kevin suggests you use a linear gradient that transitions from light green to dark green as the background for the page footer.

To apply a linear gradient:

1. Return to the **tb_visual1.css** file in your editor and go to the Footer Styles section.

2. Insert the following style rule for the `footer` element:

```
footer {
    background: linear-gradient(345deg, rgb(172, 232, 172),
                                rgb(21, 35, 21) 80%);
}
```

Figure 4-36 highlights the style to create the linear gradient.

Figure 4-36   **Applying a linear gradient**

```
/* Footer Styles */

footer {
    background: linear-gradient(345deg, rgb(172, 232, 172),
                               rgb(21, 35, 21) 80%);
}
```

gradient is pointed at a 345° angle

initial color is light green

final color is dark green

background is dark green from 80% to the end

3. Save your changes and reload tb_komatsu.html in your browser. Figure 4-37 shows the revised appearance of the page footer with a linear gradient.

Figure 4-37   **Page footer with linear gradient background**

end of gradient

Family Histories	Getting Started	About Tree and Book	Tree and Book © 2017 English (US)
Family Trees	Genealogy FAQ	Developers	
Galleries	Research Sites	Privacy	
Calendars	Interest Groups	Terms	
Forums	Government Sites	Help	

start of gradient

The other color gradient supported in CSS3 is a radial gradient. You will explore how to create radial gradients now.

Creating a Radial Gradient

A **radial gradient** is a color gradient that starts from a central point and proceeds outward in a series of concentric circles or ellipses. Figure 4-38 shows an example of a radial gradient consisting of a series of concentric ellipses radiating from a central red color to an ending blue color.

Figure 4-38   **A radial gradient of three colors**

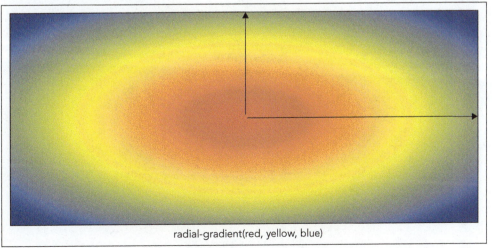

radial-gradient(red, yellow, blue)

Radial gradients are created using the following `radial-gradient` function.

```
radial-gradient(shape size at position, color-stop1,
color-stop2, …)
```

The *shape* value defines the shape of the gradient and is either `ellipse` (the default) or `circle`. The *size* value defines the extent of the gradient as it radiates outward and can be expressed with a CSS unit of measure, a percentage of the background's width and height, or with one of the following keywords:

- `farthest-corner` (the default) Gradient extends to the background corner farthest from the gradient's center.
- `farthest-side` Gradient extends to background side farthest from the gradient's center.
- `closest-corner` Gradient extends to the nearest background corner.
- `closest-side` Gradient extends to the background side closest to the gradient's center.

The `position` defines where the gradient radiates from and can be expressed in coordinates using pixels, percentages of the element's width and height, or with the keywords: `left`, `center`, `right`, `top`, and `bottom`. The default is to place the gradient within the center of the background.

Finally the *color-stop1*, *color-stop2* … values are the colors and their stopping positions within the gradient and have the same interpretation used for linear gradients except they mark stopping points as the gradient radiates outward. Note that the color stops are optional, just as they are in linear gradients. For example the following function defines a circular gradient radiating from the horizontal and vertical center of the background through the colors red, yellow, and blue:

```
radial-gradient(circle closest-corner at center center,
                red, yellow, blue)
```

The gradient ends when it reaches the closest background corner. Anything outside of the gradient will be a solid blue.

Figure 4-39 shows other examples of the different effects that can be accomplished using the `radial-gradient` function. Note that when parameters of the radial-gradient function are omitted they take their default values.

TIP

You can explore how to work with the parameters of the `radial-gradient` function using the demo_radial_gradients.html file from the demo folder.

Figure 4-39   **Examples of radial gradients**

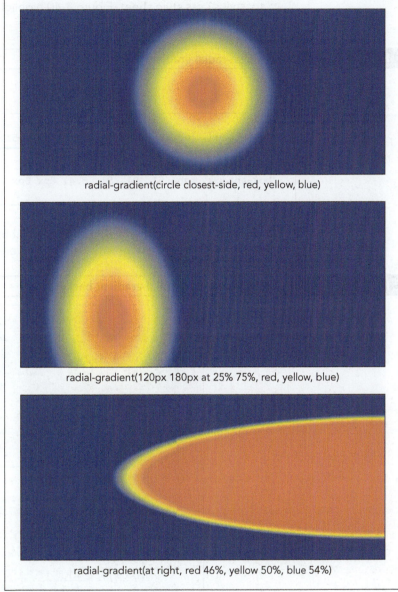

radial-gradient(circle closest-side, red, yellow, blue)

radial-gradient(120px 180px at 25% 75%, red, yellow, blue)

radial-gradient(at right, red 46%, yellow 50%, blue 54%)

© 2016 Cengage Learning

Kevin would like you to apply a radial gradient to the background of the `aside` element. The gradient will start from a white center blending into to a medium green and then into a darker shade of green.

To apply a radial gradient:

1. Return to the **tb_visual1.css** file in your editor and go to the Aside Styles section.

2. Add the following style to the style rule for the `aside` element:

```
background:
radial-gradient(white, rgb(151, 222, 151),
          rgb(81, 125, 81));
```

Note that this style supersedes the previous background style created in the tb_styles1.css style sheet. Figure 4-40 highlights the code to create the radial gradient.

Figure 4-40   **Applying a radial gradient**

color at the center

outside color

```
aside {
    background: radial-gradient(white, rgb(151, 222, 151), rgb(81, 125, 81));
    border: 4px double rgb(45, 93, 62);
    border-radius: 30px;
    box-shadow: rgba(51, 91, 51, 0.4) 0px 0px 20px 10px;
}
```

color in the middle

3. Save your changes and reload tb_komatsu.html in your browser. Figure 4-41 shows the radial gradient within the aside element.

Figure 4-41   **Aside element with radial gradient background**

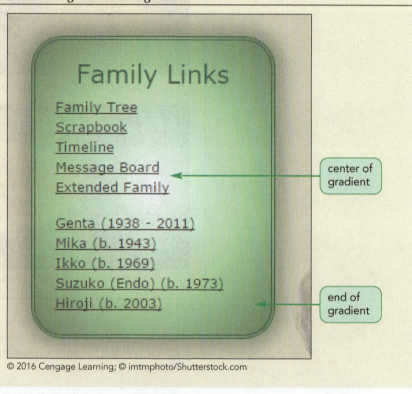

center of gradient

end of gradient

© 2016 Cengage Learning; © imtmphoto/Shutterstock.com

Kevin likes the effect of the radial gradient on the aside element and feels that it works well with the glowing effect you added earlier.

Gradients and Browser Extensions

The gradient functions were heavily revised as they went from being browser-specific properties to the final syntax approved by the W3C. If you work with older browsers, you may need to accommodate their versions of these gradient functions. For example, the following linear gradient that blends red to blue going in the direction to the right edge of the background

```
linear-gradient(to right, red, blue)
```

would be expressed using the old WebKit gradient function as:

```
-webkit-gradient(linear, left, right, from(red), to(blue))
```

Other older versions of browsers such as Mozilla, Internet Explorer, and Opera have their own gradient functions with different syntax. You can study these functions using the online support at the browser websites or doing a search on the Web for CSS gradient functions.

Note that not all browser extensions support the same types of gradients, which means that it is difficult and sometimes impossible to duplicate a particular gradient background for every browser. Thus, you should not make gradients an essential feature of your design if you want to be compatible with older browsers.

Repeating a Gradient

As you add more color stops, the gradient function can become unwieldy and overly complicated. One alternative is to repeat the gradient design. You can repeat linear and radial gradients using the functions

```
repeating-linear-gradient(params)
repeating-radial-gradient(params)
```

where *params* are the parameters of the linear-gradient or the radial-gradient functions already discussed. The only requirement for a repeating gradient is that a stopping position is required for the last color in the list that is less than the size of the object background. Once the last color in the color list is reached, the gradient starts over again. For example, the following function repeats a vertical gradient starting with white transitioning to black, transitioning back to white at 10% of the height of the object, and then repeating that pattern each time it reaches the next 10% of the height of the object:

```
repeating-linear-gradient(white, black 10%)
```

Figure 4-42 shows some other examples of repeating linear and radial gradients.

Figure 4-42 **Repeating a gradient**

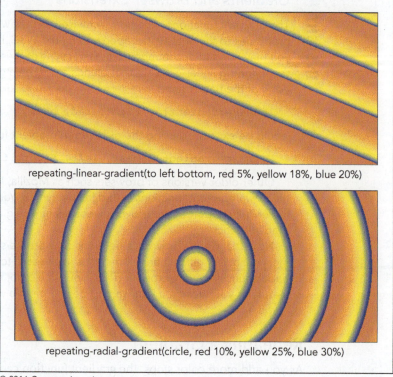

repeating-linear-gradient(to left bottom, red 5%, yellow 18%, blue 20%)

repeating-radial-gradient(circle, red 10%, yellow 25%, blue 30%)

© 2016 Cengage Learning

Creating a Gradient

- To create a linear gradient, use the function

  `linear-gradient(`*direction*`, `*color-stop1*`, `*color-stop2*`, …)`

  where *direction* is the direction of the gradient and *color-stop1*, *color-stop2*, and so on are the colors and their stopping positions within the gradient.
- To create a radial gradient, use the function

  `radial-gradient(`*shape size* `at `*position*`, `*color-stop1*`, `*color-stop2*`, …)`

  where *shape* defines the shape of the gradient, *size* sets the gradient size, *position* places the center of the gradient, and *color-stop1*, *color-stop2*, and so on are the colors and their stopping positions within the gradient.
- To repeat a gradient, use the functions

  `repeating-linear-gradient(`*params*`)`
  `repeating-radial-gradient(`*params*`)`

  where *params* are the parameters of the `linear-gradient` or the `radial-gradient` functions.

The last visual effect that Kevin wants you to add to the Komatsu Family page is to make the figure box semi-transparent so that it blends in better with its background.

Creating Semi-Transparent Objects

In Tutorial 2, you learned that you could create semi-transparent colors that blend with the background color. You can also create whole page objects that are semi-transparent using the following opacity property:

```
opacity: value;
```

where *value* ranges from 0 (completely transparent) up to 1 (completely opaque.) For example, the following style rule makes the page body 70% opaque, allowing a bit of the browser window background to filter through

```
body {
    opacity: 0.7;
}
```

Making a Semi-transparent Object

- To make a page object semi-transparent, use the property

  ```
  opacity: value;
  ```

  where *value* ranges from 0 (completely transparent) up to 1 (completely opaque).

Kevin suggests that you set the opacity of the figure box to 55% in order to blend the figure box with the paper texture background you added to the article element.

To create a semi-transparent object:

1. Return to the **tb_visual1.css** file in your editor and scroll up to the Figure Box Styles section.

2. Within the style rule for the figure element, insert the following style:

   ```
   opacity: 0.55;
   ```

   Figure 4-43 highlights the code to make the figure box semi-transparent.

| Figure 4-43 | Creating a semi-transparent object |

```
figure {
    border-style: solid;
    border-width: 25px;
    border-image: url(tb_border.png) 50 repeat;
    margin: 20px auto 0px;
    opacity: 0.55;
    width: 80%;
}
```

sets the opacity of the figure box to 55%

3. Save your changes and reload tb_komatsu.html in your browser. Figure 4-44 displays the semi-transparent figure box with part of the background paper texture showing through.

Figure 4-44 Changing the opacity of the figure box

part of the background page texture shows through in the figure box

© 2016 Cengage Learning; © imtmphoto/Shutterstock.com

PROSKILLS

Written Communication: How to Use Visual Effects

The CSS visual styles can add striking effects to your website, but they might not be supported by older browsers. This leaves you with the dilemma of when and how to use these styles. Here are some tips to keep in mind when applying visual effects to your website:

- Because not every user will be able to see a particular visual effect, design your page so that it is still readable to users with or without the effect.
- Be aware that some visual effects that flicker or produce strobe-like effects can cause discomfort and even photo-epileptic seizures in susceptible individuals. Avoid clashing color combinations and optical illusions that can cause these conditions.
- If you need to create a cross-browser solution, use browser extensions and be aware that the browser extension syntax might not match the syntax of the CSS3 standard.
- Consider using graphic images to create your visual effects. For example, rather than using the CSS gradient functions, create a background image file containing the gradient effect of your choice.

No matter how you employ visual effects on your website, remember that the most important part of your site is its content. Do not let visual effects distract from your content and message.

At this point you've completed your work on the design of the Komatsu Family page. In the next session, you will learn how to use CSS to apply transformations and filters. You will also learn how to work with image maps to create linkable images. Close any open files now.

REVIEW

Session 4.2 Quick Check

1. Provide code to add a red text shadow to all h1 headings; the shadow should be offset 5 pixels to the left and 10 pixels down with a blur of 7 pixels.

2. Add a gray box shadow to all `aside` elements; the shadow should be placed 2 pixels to the left and 5 pixels above the element with a blur of 10 pixels.

3. Add an inset gray shadow to all footers; the shadow should be offset by 10 pixels to the left and 15 pixels down with a blur of 5 pixels.

4. Create a red halo effect around the `main` element with no shadow offset, a blur of 15 pixels and a shadow size that is 10 pixels larger than the element.

5. Provide code for a linear gradient that moves in the direction of the lower-left corner of the element through the colors: orange, yellow, and green.

6. Create a linear gradient that moves at a 15 degree angle with the color orange stopping at 10% of the background, yellow stopping at 50%, and green stopping at 55%.

7. Create a radial gradient that extends to the farthest background corner, going through the colors orange, yellow, and green.

8. Create a repeating circular gradient of orange, yellow, and green bands centered at the right edge of the element with the colors stopped at 10%, 20%, and 30% respectively.

9. Create a style rule to set the opacity of all inline images to 75%.

Session 4.3 Visual Overview:

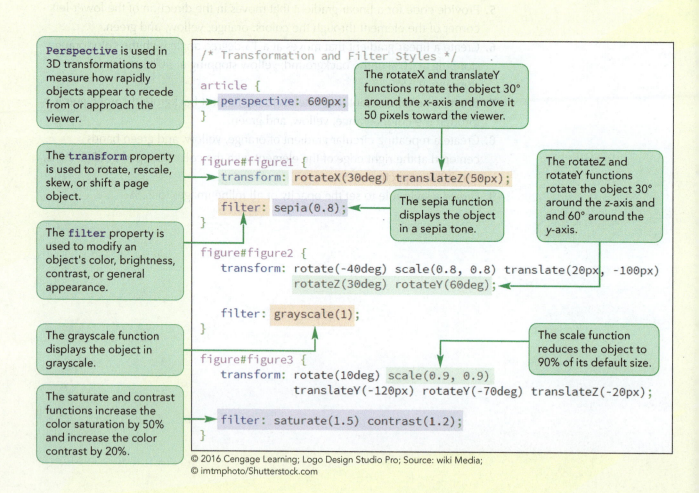

Perspective is used in 3D transformations to measure how rapidly objects appear to recede from or approach the viewer.

The **transform** property is used to rotate, rescale, skew, or shift a page object.

The **filter** property is used to modify an object's color, brightness, contrast, or general appearance.

The grayscale function displays the object in grayscale.

The saturate and contrast functions increase the color saturation by 50% and increase the color contrast by 20%.

The rotateX and translateY functions rotate the object 30° around the x-axis and move it 50 pixels toward the viewer.

The sepia function displays the object in a sepia tone.

The rotateZ and rotateY functions rotate the object 30° around the z-axis and and 60° around the y-axis.

The scale function reduces the object to 90% of its default size.

```css
/* Transformation and Filter Styles */

article {
    perspective: 600px;
}

figure#figure1 {
    transform: rotateX(30deg) translateZ(50px);

    filter: sepia(0.8);
}

figure#figure2 {
    transform: rotate(-40deg) scale(0.8, 0.8) translate(20px, -100px)
               rotateZ(30deg) rotateY(60deg);

    filter: grayscale(1);
}

figure#figure3 {
    transform: rotate(10deg) scale(0.9, 0.9)
               translateY(-120px) rotateY(-70deg) translateZ(-20px);

    filter: saturate(1.5) contrast(1.2);
}
```

Transformations and Filters

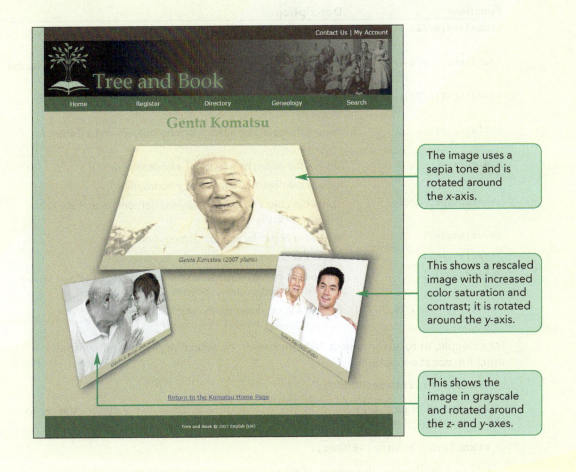

The image uses a sepia tone and is rotated around the *x*-axis.

This shows a rescaled image with increased color saturation and contrast; it is rotated around the *y*-axis.

This shows the image in grayscale and rotated around the *z*- and *y*-axes.

Transforming Page Objects

In this session, you will examine some CSS3 styles that can be used to transform the appearance of page objects through rotation, rescaling, and translation in space. To accomplish these transformations, you'll use the following transform property:

```
transform: effect(params);
```

where *effect* is a transformation function that will be applied to the page object and *params* are any parameters required by the function. Figure 4-45 describes some of the CSS3 transformation functions.

Figure 4-45 **CSS3 2D transformation functions**

Function	Description
translate(*offX*, *offY*)	Moves the object *offX* pixels to the right and *offY* pixels down; negative values move the object to the left and up
translateX(*offX*)	Moves the object *offX* pixels to the right; negative values move the object to the left
translateY(*offY*)	Moves the object *offY* pixels down; negative values move the object up
scale(*x*, *y*)	Resizes the object by a factor of *x* horizontally and a factor of *y* vertically
scaleX(*x*)	Resizes the object by a factor of *x* horizontally
scaleY(*y*)	Resizes the object by a factor of *y* horizontally
skew(*angleX*, *angleY*)	Skews the object by *angleX* degrees horizontally and *angleY* degrees vertically
skewX(*angleX*)	Skews the object by *angleX* degrees horizontally
skewY(*angleY*)	Skews the object by *angleY* degrees vertically
rotate(*angle*)	Rotates the object by *angle* degrees clockwise; negative values rotate the object counter-clockwise
matrix(*n*, *n*, *n*, *n*, *n*, *n*)	Applies a 2D transformation based on a matrix of six values

For example, to rotate an object 30° clockwise, you would apply the following style using the rotate function:

```
transform: rotate(30deg);
```

To rotate an object counter-clockwise, you would use a negative value for the angle of rotation. Thus, the following style rotates an object 60° counter-clockwise:

```
transform: rotate(-60deg);
```

Figure 4-46 displays the effects of other transformation functions on a sample page image.

Figure 4-46   **Examples of CSS3 Transformations**

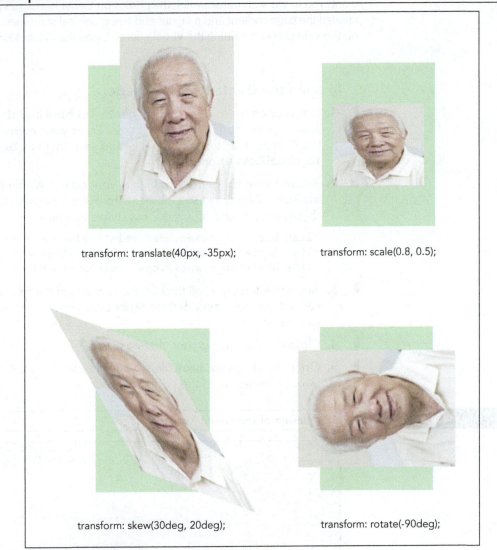

transform: translate(40px, -35px);   transform: scale(0.8, 0.5);

transform: skew(30deg, 20deg);   transform: rotate(-90deg);

© imtmphoto/Shutterstock.com

Transforming an object has no impact on the page layout. All of the other page objects will retain their original positions.

You can apply multiple transformations by placing the effect functions in a space-separated list. In this situation, transformations are applied in the order listed. For example, the following style first rotates the object 30° clockwise and then shifts it 20 pixels to the right.

```
transform: rotate(30deg) translateX(20px);
```

REFERENCE

Applying a CSS Transformation

- To apply a transformation to a page object, use the property

```
transform: effect(params);
```

where *effect* is a transformation function that will be applied to the page object and *params* are any parameters required by the function.

The website has pages with photos for each individual in the Komatsu family. Kevin wants you to work on transforming the photos on Genta Komatsu's page. Kevin has already created the page content and a layout and typographical style sheet but wants you to work on the style sheet containing the visual effects. Open the Genta Komatsu page now.

To open the Genta Komatsu page:

1. Use your editor to open the **tb_genta_txt.html** and **tb_visual2_txt.css** files from the html04 ▸ tutorial folder. Enter *your name* and *the date* in the comment section of both files and save them as **tb_genta.html** and **tb_visual2.css** respectively.

2. Return to the **tb_genta.html** file in your editor. Within the document head, insert the following `link` elements to link the page to the tb_reset.css, tb_styles2.css, and tb_visual2.css style sheet files.

   ```
   <link href="tb_reset.css" rel="stylesheet" />
   <link href="tb_styles2.css" rel="stylesheet" />
   <link href="tb_visual2.css" rel="stylesheet" />
   ```

3. Take some time to scroll through the contents of the file. Note that the document content consists mainly of three figure boxes each containing a different photo of Genta Komatsu.

4. Close the file, saving your changes.

5. Open the **tb_genta.html** file in your browser. Figure 4-47 shows the initial layout and design of the page content.

Figure 4-47	Initial design of the Genta Komatsu page

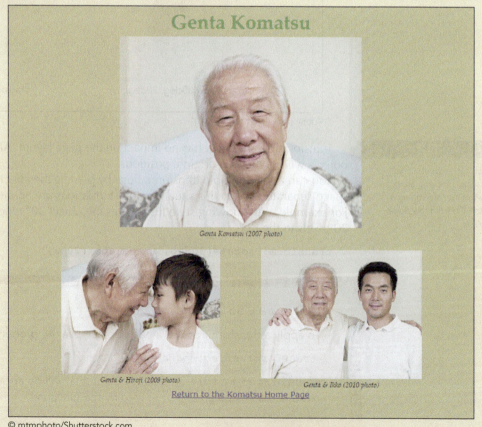

Genta Komatsu (2007 photo)

Genta & Hiroji (2009 photo)

Genta & Ikko (2010 photo)

Return to the Komatsu Home Page

© mtmphoto/Shutterstock.com

Kevin feels that the page lacks visual interest. He suggests you transform the bottom row of photos by rotating them and shifting them upward to partially cover the main photo, creating a collage-style layout. Apply the transform property now to make these changes.

To apply the transform style:

1. Go to the **tb_visual2.css** file in your editor and scroll as needed to the Transformation Styles section.

2. Insert the following style rule to rotate the figure2 figure box 40° counter-clockwise, reduce it to 80% of its former size, and shift it 20 pixels to the right and 100 pixels up. Also, add a style to create a drop shadow using the code that follows:

```
figure#figure2 {
    transform: rotate(-40deg) scale(0.8, 0.8)
               translate(20px, -100px);
    box-shadow: rgb(101, 101, 101) 10px 10px 25px;
}
```

3. Add the following style rule to rotate the figure3 figure box 10° clockwise, resize it to 90% of its current size, and shift it 120 pixels upward. Also add a drop shadow to the figure box using the following style rule:

```
figure#figure3 {
    transform: rotate(10deg) scale(0.9, 0.9)
               translateY(-120px);
    box-shadow: rgb(101, 101, 101) 10px -10px 25px;
}
```

Figure 4-48 describes the newly added style rules.

Figure 4-48   **Transforming the figure boxes**

rotates the box 40° counter-clockwise

reduces the box size to 80% of its original size

```
/* Transformation Styles */

figure#figure2 {
    transform: rotate(-40deg) scale(0.8, 0.8) translate(20px, -100px);
    box-shadow: rgb(101, 101, 101) 10px 10px 25px;
}

figure#figure3 {
    transform: rotate(10deg) scale(0.9, 0.9) translateY(-120px);
    box-shadow: rgb(101, 101, 101) 10px -10px 25px;
}
```

moves the box 20 pixels to the right and 100 pixels up

rotates the box 10° clockwise

reduces the box size to 90% of its original size

moves the box 120 pixels up

4. Save your changes to the file and then reload tb_genta.html in your browser. Figure 4-49 shows the revised design of the page's content.

Figure 4-49 **Viewing the transformed figure boxes**

box rotated 40° counter-clockwise, rescaled and shifted up and to the right

box rotated 10° clockwise, rescaled and shifted up

©imtmphoto/Shutterstock.com

The transformations you applied rotated the figure boxes along a two-dimensional or 2D space that consisted of a horizontal and vertical axis. CSS also supports transformations that operate in a three-dimensional or 3D space.

Transformations in Three Dimensions

A **3D transformation** is a change that involves three spatial axes: an *x*-axis that runs horizontally across the page, a *y*-axis that runs vertically, and a *z*-axis that comes straight out of the page toward and away from the viewer. Positive values along the axes are to the right, down, and toward the reader; negative values are to the left, up, and away from the reader (see Figure 4-50.)

Figure 4-50 **A page object viewed in 3D**

© 2016 Cengage Learning; © imtmphoto/Shutterstock.com

With the addition of a third spatial axis, you can create effects in which an object appears to zoom toward and away from users, or to rotate in three dimensional space. Figure 4-51 describes the 3D transformations supported by CSS.

Figure 4-51	CSS3 3D transformation functions

Function	Description
translate3d(offX, offY, offZ)	Shifts the object offX pixels horizontally, offY pixels vertically, and offZ pixels along the z-axis
translateX(offX) translateY(offY) translateZ(offZ)	Shifts the object offX, offY, or offZ pixels along the specified axis
rotate3d(x, y, z, angle)	Rotates the object around the three-dimensional vector (x, y, z) at a direction of angle
rotateX(angle) rotateY(angle) rotateZ(angle)	Rotates the object around the specified axis at a direction of angle
scale3d(x, y, z)	Resizes the object by a factor of x horizontally, a factor of y vertically, and a factor of z along the z-axis
scaleX(x) scaleY(y) scaleZ(z)	Resizes the object by a factor of x, y, or z along the specified axis
perspective(p)	Sets the size of the perspective effect to p
matrix3d(n, n, …, n)	Applies a 3D transformation based on a matrix of 16 values

For example the following style rotates the object 60° around the x-axis, making it appear as if the top of the object is farther from the viewer and the bottom is closer to the viewer.

```
transform: rotateX(60deg);
```

To truly create the illusion of 3D space however, you also need to set the perspective of that space.

Understanding Perspective

Perspective is a measure of how rapidly objects appear to recede from the viewer in a 3D space. You can think of perspective in terms of a pair of railroad tracks that appear to converge at a point, known as the **vanishing point**. A smaller perspective value causes the tracks to converge over an apparently shorter distance while a larger perspective value causes the tracks to appear to go farther before converging.

You define the perspective of a 3D space using the `perspective` property

```
perspective: value;
```

where `value` is a positive value that measures the strength of the perspective effect with lower values resulting in more extreme distortion. For example, the following style rule sets the perspective of the space within the `div` element to 400 pixels.

```
div {
    perspective: 400px;
}
```

Any 3D transformations applied to children of that `div` element will assume a perspective value of 400 pixels. Perspective can also be set for individual transformations using the following `perspective` function:

```
transform: perspective(value);
```

Thus, the following style rule sets the perspective only for the figure1 figure box within the `div` element as the figure box is rotated 60° around the x-axis.

```
div figure#figure1 {
    transform: perspective(400px) rotateX(60deg);
}
```

You use the `perspective` property when you have several transformed objects within a container that all need to appear within the same 3D space with a common perspective. You use the `perspective` function when you have only one object that needs to be transformed in the 3D space. Figure 4-52 compares two different perspective values for an object rotated 60° around the *x*-axis in 3D space.

Figure 4-52   **Transformations in three dimensions**

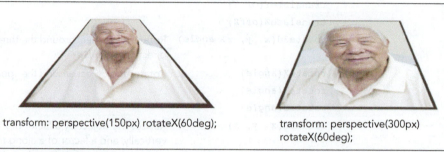

transform: perspective(150px) rotateX(60deg);   transform: perspective(300px) rotateX(60deg);

© imtmphoto/Shutterstock.com

Note that the smaller perspective value results in a more extreme distortion as the top of the object appears to more quickly recede from the viewer while the bottom appears to approach the viewer more rapidly.

REFERENCE

Setting Perspective in 3D

- To set the perspective for a container and the objects it contains, use the property

  `perspective: value;`

  where `value` is a positive value that measures the strength of the perspective effect with lower values resulting in more extreme distortion.
- To set the perspective of a single object or to set the perspective individually of objects within a group of objects, use the `perspective` function

  `transform: perspective(value);`

Add a 3D transformation to each of the three figure boxes in the Genta Komatsu page, making it appear that they have been rotated in three dimensional space along the *x*-, *y*-, and *z*-axes, setting the perspective value to 600 pixels for all of the objects in the page article.

To apply the 3D transformations:

1. Return to the **tb_visual2.css** file in your editor.

2. Directly after the Transformation Styles comment, insert the following style rule to set the perspective of the 3D space of the `article` element.

```
article {
    perspective: 600px;
}
```

3. Next, insert the following style rule for the figure1 figure box to rotate it 30° around the x-axis, shift it 50 pixels along the z-axis, and add a drop shadow.

```
figure#figure1 {
    transform: rotateX(30deg) translateZ(50px);
    box-shadow: rgb(51, 51, 51) 0px 10px 25px;
}
```

4. Add the following functions to the transform property for the figure2 figure box to rotate the box 30° around the z-axis and 60° around the y-axis:

```
rotateZ(30deg) rotateY(60deg)
```

5. Add the following functions to the transform property for the figure3 figure box to rotate the box counter-clockwise 70° around the y-axis and shift it 20 pixels away from the user along the z-axis:

```
rotateY(-70deg) translateZ(-20px)
```

Figure 4-53 highlights the 3D transformations styles in the style sheet.

Figure 4-53	Applying 3D transformations

```
/* Transformation Styles */

article {
    perspective: 600px;
}

figure#figure1 {
    transform: rotateX(30deg) translateZ(50px);
    box-shadow: rgb(51, 51, 51) 0px 10px 25px;
}

figure#figure2 {
    transform: rotate(-40deg) scale(0.8, 0.8)
               translate(20px, -100px)
               rotateZ(30deg) rotateY(60deg);
    box-shadow: rgb(101, 101, 101) 10px 10px 25px;
}

figure#figure3 {
    transform: rotate(10deg) scale(0.9, 0.9)
               translateY(-120px)
               rotateY(-70deg) translateZ(-20px);
    box-shadow: rgb(101, 101, 101) 10px -10px 25px;
}
```

sets the perspective of the article space to 600 pixels

rotates the box 30° around the x-axis and shifts it forward 50 pixels along the z-axis

adds a box shadow on the box's bottom border

rotates the box 30° around the z-axis and 60° around the y-axis

rotates the box 70° counter-clockwise around the y-axis and shifts it backward 20 pixels along the z-axis

6. Save your changes to the file and then reload tb_genta.html in your browser. Figure 4-54 shows the result of applying 3D transformations to each of the figure boxes on the page.

Figure 4-54   **Figure boxes in 3D space**

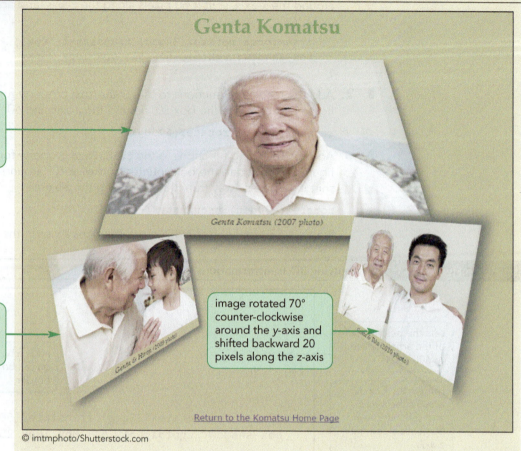

image rotated 30° around the x-axis and moved forward 50 pixels along the z-axis

image rotated 30° around the z-axis and 60° around the y-axis

image rotated 70° counter-clockwise around the y-axis and shifted backward 20 pixels along the z-axis

© imtmphoto/Shutterstock.com

You have only scratched the surface of what can be done using transformations. For example you can create a mirror image of an object by rotating it 180° around the y-axis. You can create virtual 3D objects like cubes that can be viewed from any angle or spun. You are only limited by your imagination.

Exploring CSS Filters

A final way to alter an object is through a CSS filter. Filters adjust how the browser renders an image, a background, or a border by modifying the object's color, brightness, contrast, or general appearance. For example, a filter can be used to change a color image to grayscale, increase the image's color saturation, or add a blurring effect. Filters are applied using the `filter` property

```
filter: effect(params);
```

where *effect* is a filter function and *params* are the parameters of the function. Filters were originally introduced as a WebKit browser extension; it is still the best practice to include the following browser extension whenever filters are used:

```
-webkit-filter: effect(params);
filter: effect(params);
```

Figure 4-55 describes the different filter functions supported by WebKit and most current browsers.

| **Figure 4-55** | **CSS3 filter functions** |

Function	Description
blur(*length*)	Applies a blur to the image where *length* defines the size of blur in pixels
brightness(*value*)	Adjusts the brightness where values from 0 to 1 decrease the brightness and values greater than 1 increase the brightness
contrast(*value*)	Adjusts the contrast where values from 0 to 1 decrease the contrast and values greater than 1 increase the contrast
drop-shadow(*offsetX offsetY blur color*)	Adds a drop shadow to the image where *offsetX* and *offsetY* are horizontal and vertical distances of the shadow, *blur* is the shadow blurring, and *color* is the shadow color
grayscale(*value*)	Displays the image in grayscale from 0, leaving the image unchanged, up to 1, displaying the image in complete grayscale
hue-rotate(*angle*)	Adjusts the hue by *angle* in the color wheel where 0deg leaves the hue unchanged, 180deg displays the complimentary colors and 360deg again leaves the hue unchanged
invert(*value*)	Inverts the color from 0 (leaving the image unchanged), up to 1 (completely inverting the colors)
opacity(*value*)	Applies transparency to the image from 0 (making the image transparent), up to 1 (leaving the image opaque)
saturate(*value*)	Adjusts the color saturation where values from 0 to 1 decrease the saturation and values greater than 1 increase the saturation
sepia(*value*)	Displays the color in a sepia tone from 0 (leaving the image unchanged), up to 1 (image completely in sepia)
url(*url*)	Loads an SVG filter file from *url*

Figure 4-56 shows the impact of some of the filter functions on a sample image.

| **Figure 4-56** | **CSS filter examples** |

filter: none;   filter: sepia(0.8);   filter: saturate(2.5);

filter: blur(3px);   filter: hue-rotate(60deg);   filter: invert(0.9);

Filter functions can be combined in a space-separated list to create new effects. For example, the following style reduces the object's color contrast and applies a sepia tone.

```
filter: contrast(75%) sepia(100%);
```

With multiple filter effects, the effects are applied in the order they are listed. Thus, a style in which the sepia effect is applied first followed by the contrast effect will result in a different image than if the order is reversed.

REFERENCE

Applying a CSS Filter

- To apply a CSS filter to a page object, use the property

  ```
  filter: effect(params);
  ```

  where *effect* is a filter function and *params* are the parameters of the function.

Kevin wants you to apply filters to the photos in the Genta Komatsu page. He wants a sepia tone applied to the first photo, a grayscale filter applied to the second photo, and a color enhancement applied to the third photo.

To apply the CSS filters:

To provide the most cross-browser support, use browser extensions with progressive enhancement.

1. Return the **tb_visual2.css** file in your editor and go down to the Filter Styles section.

2. Change the figure1 figure box to a sepia tone by adding the following style rule:

   ```
   figure#figure1 {
       -webkit-filter: sepia(0.8);
       filter: sepia(0.8);
   }
   ```

3. Change the figure2 figure box to grayscale by adding the style rule:

   ```
   figure#figure2 {
       -webkit-filter: grayscale(1);
       filter: grayscale(1);
   }
   ```

4. Increase the saturation and contrast for the figure3 figure box with the style rule:

   ```
   figure#figure3 {
       -webkit-filter: saturate(1.5) contrast(1.2);
       filter: saturate(1.5) contrast(1.2);
   }
   ```

   Figure 4-57 highlights the CSS filters added to the style sheet.

Figure 4-57	Applying the filter property

```
/* Filter Styles */

figure#figure1 {
    -webkit-filter: sepia(0.8);
    filter: sepia(0.8);
}

figure#figure2 {
    -webkit-filter: grayscale(1);
    filter: grayscale(1);
}

figure#figure3 {
    -webkit-filter: saturate(1.5) contrast(1.2);
    filter: saturate(1.5) contrast(1.2);
}
```

provides more cross-browser support by adding the WebKit browser extension

displays the figure1 figure box in sepia

displays the figure2 figure box in grayscale

increases the color saturation and contrast in the figure3 figure box

5. Save your changes to the file and then reload tb_genta.html in your browser. Figure 4-58 shows the final design of the Genta Komatsu page.

Figure 4-58	Filters applied to the web page photos

sepia tone

grayscale

color saturation and contrast increased

© imtmphoto/Shutterstock.com

Trouble? CSS filters are not supported by all browsers. Depending on your browser, you might not see any effect from the filters. In particular, Internet Explorer does not support these filter styles at the time of this writing.

Box Shadows and Drop Shadows

You may wonder why you need a `drop-shadow` filter if you already have the `box-shadow` property. While they both can be used to add shadowing to a page object, one important difference is that the `drop-shadow` filter creates a shadow that traces the shape of the object, while the `box-shadow` property always applies a rectangular shadow. Another important difference is that you can only change the size of a shadow using the `box-shadow` property. Thus, if you want to apply a drop shadow around objects such as text or a circular shape, use the `drop-shadow` filter. However, if you need to create an internal shadow or change the size of the drop shadow shadow, use the `box-shadow` property.

You've completed your redesign of the Genta Komatsu page by adding transformation and filter effects to make a more visually striking page. Kevin now wants to return to the page for the Komatsu family. He wants you to edit the family portrait on the page so that individual pages like the Genta Komatsu page can be accessed by clicking the person's face on the family portrait. You can create this effect using an image map.

Working with Image Maps

When you mark an inline image as a hyperlink, the entire image is linked to the same file; however, HTML also allows you to divide an image into different zones, or **hotspots**, which can then be linked to different URLs through information provided in an **image map**. HTML supports two kinds of image maps: client-side image maps and server-side image maps. A **client-side image map** is an image map that is defined within the web page and handled entirely by the web browser, while a **server-side image map** relies on a program running on the web server to create and administer the map. Generally client-side maps are easier to create and do not rely on a connection to the server in order to run.

Defining a Client-Side Image Map

Client-side image maps are defined with the following `map` element

```
<map name="text">
   hotspots
</map>
```

where `text` is the name of the image map and `hotspots` are defined regions within an image that are linked to different URLs. Client-side image maps can be placed anywhere within the body of a web page because they are not actually displayed by browsers but are simply used as references for mapping the locations of the hotspots within the image. The most common practice is to place a `map` element below the corresponding inline image.

Each hotspot within the `map` element is defined using the following `area` element:

```
<area shape="shape" coords="coordinates"
      href="url" alt="text" />
```

where `shape` is the shape of the hotspot region, `coordinates` are the list of points that define the boundaries of that region, `url` is the URL of the hypertext link, and `text` is alternate text displayed for non-graphical browsers.

Hotspots can be created as rectangles, circles, or polygons (multisided figures) using *shape* values of `rect`, `circle`, and `poly` respectively. A fourth possible *shape* value, `default`, represents the remaining area of the inline image not covered by any hotspots. There is no limit to the number of hotspots you can add to an image map.

For rectangular hotspots, the `shape` and `coords` attributes have the general form:

`shape="rect" coords="`*left,top,right,bottom*`"`

where *left*, *top* are the coordinates of the top-left corner of the rectangle and *right*, *bottom* are the coordinates of the bottom-right corner. Coordinates for hotspot shapes are measured in pixels and thus, the following attributes define a rectangular hotspot with the left-top corner at the coordinates (100, 20) and the right-bottom corner at (230, 220):

`shape="rect" coords="100,20,230,220"`

To determine the coordinates of a hotspot, you can use either a graphics program such as Adobe Photoshop or image map software that automatically generates the HTML code for the hotspots you define. Note that coordinates are always expressed relative to the top-left corner of the image, regardless of the position of the image on the page. For example, in Figure 4-59, the top-left corner of this rectangular hotspot is 100 pixels right of the image's left border and 20 pixels down from the top border.

Figure 4-59   **Defining a rectangular hotspot**

`shape="rect" coords="100,20,230,220"`

©imtmphoto/Shutterstock.com

Circular hotspots are defined using the attributes

`shape="circle" coords="`*x,y,radius*`"`

where *x* and *y* are the coordinates of the center of the circle and *radius* is the circle's radius. Figure 4-60 shows the coordinates for a circular hotspot where the center of the circle is located at the coordinates (160, 130) with a radius of 105 pixels.

Figure 4-60   **Defining a circular hotspot**

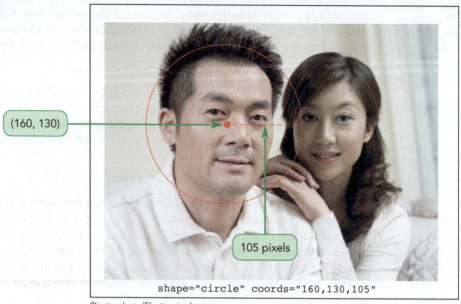

©imtmphoto/Shutterstock.com

Polygonal hotspots have the attributes

```
shape="poly" coords="x1,y1,x2,y2,…"
```

where (*x1*, *y1*), (*x2*, *y2*), … set the coordinates of each vertex in the shape. Figure 4-61 shows the coordinates for a 5-sided polygon.

Figure 4-61   **Defining a polygonal hotspot**

© imtmphoto/Shutterstock.com

TIP

Default hotspots should always be listed last.

To define the default hotspot for an image, create the following hotspot:

```
shape="default" coords="0,0,width,height"
```

where *width* is the width of the image in pixels and *height* is the image's height. Any region in the image that is not covered by another hotspot activates the default hotspot link.

REFERENCE

Creating an Image Map

- To create an image map, use

```
<map name="text">
   hotspots
</map>
```

where *text* is the name of the image map and *hotspots* are the hotspots within the image.

- To define each hotspot, use

```
<area shape="shape" coords="coordinates" href="url" alt="text" />
```

where *shape* is the shape of the hotspot region, *coordinates* list the points defining the boundaries of the region, *url* is the URL of the hypertext link, and *text* is alternate text that is displayed for non-graphical browsers.

- To define a rectangular hotspot, use the shape and attribute values

```
shape="rect" coords="left,top,right,bottom"
```

where *left*, *top* are the coordinates of the top-left corner of the rectangle and *right*, *bottom* are the coordinates of the bottom-right corner.

- To define a circular hotspot, use

```
shape="circle" coords="x,y,radius"
```

where *x* and *y* are the coordinates of the center of the circle and *radius* is the circle's radius.

- To define a polygonal hotspot, use

```
shape="poly" coords="x1,y1,x2,y2,…"
```

where (*x1*, *y1*), (*x2*, *y2*), and so on provide the coordinates of each vertex in the multisided shape.

- To define the default hotspot link, use

```
shape="default" coords="0,0,width,height"
```

where *width* and *height* is the width and height of the image.

Kevin has provided you with the coordinates for five rectangular hotspots to cover the five faces on the Komatsu family portrait. Add an image map named "family_map" to the tb_komatsu.html page with rectangular hotspots for each of the faces in the family portrait.

To create an image map:

1. Open or return to the **tb_komatsu.html** file in your editor.

2. Directly below the figure box, insert the following HTML code:

```
<map name="family_map">
   <area shape="rect" coords="74,74,123,141"
    href="tb_ikko.html" alt="Ikko Komatsu" />
   <area shape="rect" coords="126,109,177,172"
    href="tb_mika.html" alt="Mika Komatsu" />
   <area shape="rect" coords="180,157,230,214"
    href="tb_hiroji.html" alt="Hiroji Komatsu" />
```

```
       <area shape="rect" coords="258,96,312,165"
        href="tb_genta.html" alt="Genta Komatsu" />
       <area shape="rect" coords="342,86,398,162"
        href="tb_suzuko.html" alt="Suzuko Komatsu" />
    </map>
```

Figure 4-62 highlights the HTML code for the image map and hotspots.

Figure 4-62   **Inserting an image map**

```
<figure>
   <img src="tb_komatsu.png" alt="family portrait" />
   <figcaption>(L-R): Ikko, Mika, Hiroji, Genta, Suzuko</figcaption>      name of the
</figure>                                                                  image map
<map name="family_map">
   <area shape="rect" coords="74,74,123,141" href="tb_ikko.html" alt="Ikko Komatsu" />
   <area shape="rect" coords="126,109,177,172" href="tb_mika.html" alt="Mika Komatsu" />
   <area shape="rect" coords="180,157,230,214" href="tb_hiroji.html" alt="Hiroji Komatsu" />
   <area shape="rect" coords="258,96,312,165" href="tb_genta.html" alt="Genta Komatsu" />
   <area shape="rect" coords="342,86,398,162" href="tb_suzuko.html" alt="Suzuko Komatsu" />
</map>
```

shape of the hotspot | coordinates of the rectangular hotspot | URL of the hotspot link | alternate text for the hotspot

3. Save your changes to the file.

With the image map defined, your next task is to apply that map to the image in the figure box.

Applying an Image Map

To apply an image map to an image, you add the following usemap attribute to the img element

```
<img src="url" alt="text" usemap="#map" />
```

where *map* is the name assigned to the image map within the current HTML file.

REFERENCE

Applying an Image Map

• To apply an image map to an image, add the usemap attribute to the img element

```
<img src="url" alt="text" usemap="#map" />
```

where *map* is the name assigned to the image map.

Apply the family_map image map to the figure box and then test it in your web browser.

To apply an image map:

1. Add the attribute `usemap="#family_map"` to the `img` element for the family portrait.

   Figure 4-63 highlights the code to apply the image map.

Figure 4-63 ▶ **Applying an image map**

> Applies the family_map image map to the image

```
<figure>
   <img src="tb_komatsu.png" alt="family portrait" usemap="#family_map" />
   <figcaption>(L-R): Ikko, Mika, Hiroji, Genta, Suzuko</figcaption>
</figure>
```

2. Save your changes to the file and then reload tb_komatsu.html in your browser.

3. Click the five faces in the family portrait and verify each face is linked to a separate HTML file devoted to that individual. Use the link under the image of each individual to return to the home page.

Kevin likes the addition of the image map and plans to use it on other photos in the website.

PROSKILLS

Problem Solving: Image Maps with Flexible Layouts

Image maps are not easily applied to flexible layouts in which the size of the image can change based on the size of the browser window. The problem is that, because hotspot coordinates are expressed in pixels, they don't resize and will not point to the correct region of the image if the image is resized.

One way to deal with flexible layouts is to create hotspots using hypertext links that are sized and positioned using relative units. The image and the hypertext links would then be nested within a `figure` element as follows:

```
<figure class="map">
   <img src="image" alt="" />
   <a href="url" id="hotspot1"></a>
   <a href="url" id="hotspot2"></a>
   …
</figure>
```

The figure box itself needs to be placed using relative or absolute positioning and the image should occupy the entire figure box. Each hypertext link should be displayed as a block with width and height defined using percentages instead of pixels and positioned absolutely within the figure box, also using percentages for the coordinates. As the figure box is resized under the flexible layout, the hotspots marked with the hypertext links will automatically be resized and moved to match. The opacity of the hotspot links should be set to 0 so that the links do not obscure the underlying image file. Even though the hotspots will be transparent to the user, they will still act as hypertext links.

This approach is limited to rectangular hotspots. To create a flexible layout for other shapes, you need to use a third-party add-in that automatically resizes the shape based on the current size of the image.

You've completed your work on the Komatsu Family pages for *Tree and Book*. Kevin will incorporate your work and ideas with other family pages as he continues on the site redesign. He'll get back to you with more projects in the future. For now you can close any open files or applications.

REVIEW

Session 4.3 Quick Check

1. Provide the transformation to shift a page object 5 pixels to the right and 10 pixels up.

2. Provide the transformation to reduce the horizontal and vertical size of an object by 50%.

3. Provide the transformation to rotate an object 30° counter-clockwise around the x-axis.

4. What is the difference between using the `perspective` property and using the `perspective` function?

5. Provide the filter to increase the brightness of an object by 20%.

6. Provide the filter to decrease the contrast of an object to 70% of its default value and to change the hue by 180°.

7. Provide code to create a circular hotspot centered at the coordinates (150, 220) with a radius of 60 pixels, linked to the help.html file.

8. Provide the code to create a triangular hotspot with vertices at (200, 5), (300, 125), and (100, 125), linked to the info.html file.

9. Revise the following `img` element to attach it to the mapsites image map:

```
<img src="logo.png" alt="" />
```

Review Assignments

Data Files needed for the Review Assignments: tb_ferris_txt.html, tb_kathleen_txt.html, tb_visual3_txt.css, tb_visual4_txt.css, 3 CSS files, 1 HTML file, 10 PNG files, 1 TTF file, 1 WOFF file

Kevin wants you to work on another family page for the Tree and Book website. The page was created for the Ferris family with content provided by Linda Ferris-White. Kevin is examining a new color scheme and design style for the page. A preview of the design you'll create is shown in Figure 4-64.

Figure 4-64   **Ferris Family page**

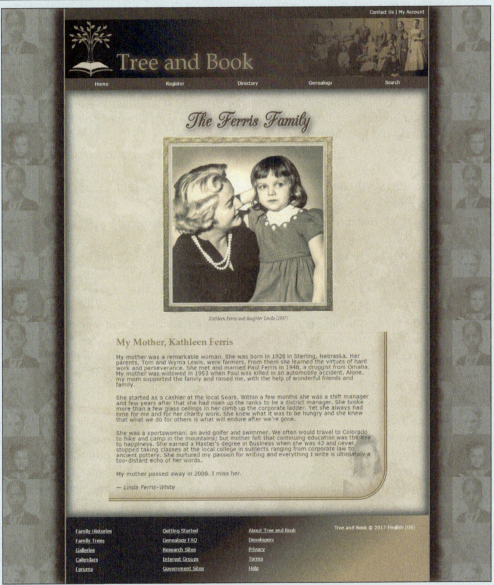

All of the HTML content and the typographical and layout styles have already been created for you. Your task will be to complete the work by writing the visual style sheet to incorporate Kevin's suggestions.

Complete the following:

1. Use your HTML editor to open the **tb_visual3_txt.css**, **tb_visual4_txt.css**, **tb_ferris_txt.html** and **tb_kathleen_txt.html** files from the html04 ▶ review folder. Enter *your name* and *the date* in the comment section of each file, and save them as **tb_visual3.css**, **tb_visual4.css**, **tb_ferris.html**, and **tb_kathleen.html** respectively.

2. Go to the **tb_ferris.html** file in your editor. Add links to the tb_base.css, tb_styles3.css, and tb_visual3.css style sheets in the order listed.

3. Scroll down and, within the `main` element header and after the h1 heading, insert a figure box containing: a) the tb_ferris.png inline image with the alternate text *Ferris Family* using the image map named *portrait_map* and b) a figure caption with the text *Kathleen Ferris and daughter Linda (1957)*.

4. Directly below the figure box, create the portrait_map image map containing the following hotspots: a) a rectangular hotspot pointing to the tb_kathleen.html file with the left-top coordinate (10, 50) and the right-bottom coordinate (192, 223) and alternate text, "Kathleen Ferris" and b) a circular hotspot pointing to the tb_linda.html file with a center point at (264, 108) and a radius of 80 pixels and the alternate text, *Linda Ferris-White*.

5. Take some time to study the rest of the page content and structure and then save your changes to the file.

6. Go to the **tb_visual3.css** file in your editor. In this file, you'll create the graphic design styles for the page.

7. Go to the HTML Styles section and create a style rule for the `html` element to use the image file tb_back5.png as the background.

8. Go to the Page Body Styles section and create a style rule for the `body` element that: a) adds a left and right 3-pixel solid border with color value rgb(169, 130, 88), b) adds a box shadow to the right border with a horizontal offset of 25 pixels, a vertical offset of 0 pixels and a 35-pixel blur and a color value of rgb(53, 21, 0), and then adds the mirror images of this shadow to the left border.

9. Go to the Main Styles section. Create a style rule for the `main` element that: a) applies the tb_back7.png file as a background image with a size of 100% covering the entire background with no tiling and positioned with respect to the padding box and b) adds two inset box shadows, each with a 25-pixel blur and a color value of rgb(71, 71, 71), and then one with offsets of –10 pixels in the horizontal and vertical direction and the other with horizontal and vertical offsets of 10 pixels.

10. Create a style rule for the h1 heading within the main header that adds the following two text shadows: a) a shadow with the color value rgb(221, 221, 221) and offsets of 1 pixels and no blurring and b) a shadow with the color value rgba(41, 41, 41, 0.9) and offsets of 5 pixels and a 20-pixel blur.

11. Go to the Figure Box Styles section. Create a style rule for the figure element that sets the top/bottom margin to 10 pixels and the left/right margin to `auto`. Set the width of the element to 70%.

12. Next, you'll modify the appearance of the figure box image. Create a style rule for the image within the figure box that: a) sets the border width to 25 pixels, b) sets the border style to solid, c) applies the tb_frame.png file as a border image with a slice size of 60 pixels stretched across the sides, d) displays the image as a block with a width of 100%, and e) applies a sepia tone to the image with a value of 80% (include the WebKit browser extension in your style sheet).

13. Create a style rule for the figure caption that: a) displays the text using the font stack 'Palatino Linotype', Palatino, 'Times New Roman', serif, b) sets the style to italic, c) sets the top/bottom padding to 10 pixels and the left/right padding to 0 pixels, and d) centers the text.

14. Go to the Article Styles section. Here you'll create borders and backgrounds for the article that Linda Ferris-White wrote about her mother. Create a style rule for the `article` element that: a) displays the background image file tb_back6.png placed at the bottom-right corner of the element with a size of 15% and no tiling, b) adds an 8-pixel double border with color value rgb(147, 116, 68) to

the right and bottom sides of the `article` element, c) creates a curved bottom-right corner with a radius of 80 pixels, and d) adds an interior shadow with horizontal and vertical offsets of –10 pixels, a 25-pixel blur, and a color value of rgba(184, 154, 112, 0.7).

15. Kevin wants a gradient background for the page footer. Go to the Footer Styles section and create a style rule for the footer that adds a linear gradient background with an angle of 325°, going from the color value rgb(180, 148, 104) with a color stop at 20% of the gradient length to the value rgb(40, 33, 23) with a color stop at 60%.

16. Save your changes to the style sheet and then open **tb_ferris.html** in your browser. Verify that the colors and designs resemble that shown in Figure 4-64.

Next, you will create the design styles for individual pages about Kathleen Ferris and Linda Ferris-White. A preview of the content of the Kathleen Ferris page is shown in Figure 4-65.

Figure 4-65   **Kathleen Ferris page**

Kathleen Ferris

High School Photo (1945)

Before her Beloved Piano (1973)

Still Swimming (2001)

Return to the Ferris Family page

© Elzbieta Sekowska/Shutterstock.com

17. Go to the **tb_kathleen.html** file in your editor and create links to the tb_base.css, tb_styles4.css, and tb_visual4.css files. Study the contents of the file and then close it, saving your changes.

18. Go to the **tb_visual4.css** file in your editor. Scroll down to the Transformation Styles section and add a style rule for the `article` element to set the size of the perspective space to 800 pixels.

19. Create a style rule for the figure1 figure box to translate it –120 pixels along the z-axis.

20. Create a style rule for the figure2 figure box to translate it –20 pixels along the y-axis and rotate it 50° around the y-axis.

21. Create a style rule for the figure3 figure box to translate it –30 pixels along the y-axis and rotate it –50° around the y-axis.

22. Go to the Filter Styles section to apply CSS filters to the page elements. Make sure that you include the WebKit browser extension in your style. Create a style rule for the figure1 figure box that applies a saturation filter with a value of 1.3.

23. Create a style rule for the figure2 figure box that sets the brightness to 0.8 and the contrast to 1.5.

24. Create a style rule for the figure3 figure box that sets the hue rotation to 170°, the saturation to 3, and the brightness to 1.5.

25. Save your changes to the file and then return to the **tb_ferris.html** file in your browser. Verify that you can display the individual pages for Kathleen Ferris and Linda Ferris-White by clicking on their faces in the family portrait. Further verify that the appearance of the Kathleen Ferris page resembles that shown in Figure 4-65. (Note: Use the link under the pictures to return to the home page.)

APPLY

Case Problem 1

Data Files needed for this Case Problem: sd_messier_txt.html, sd_effects_txt.css, 2 CSS files, 9 PNG files

Sky Dust Stories   Dr. Andrew Weiss of Thomson & Lee College maintains an astronomy site called *Sky Dust Stories* for the students in his class. On his website, he discusses many aspects of astronomy and star-gazing and shares interesting stories from the history of stargazing. He wants your help with one page that involves the Messier catalog, which lists the deep sky objects of particular interest to professional and amateur astronomers.

Dr. Weiss has already created the page content and layout but wants you to add some CSS graphic design styles to complete the page. A preview of the page you'll create is shown in Figure 4-66.

Figure 4-66   **The Messier Objects web page**

© 2016 Cengage Learning; Source: WikiImages; Source: Étienne Léopold Trouvelot; Source: Fryns; Source: public domain images/Summer woods; Source:PublicDomainArchive; Source: Ansiaume (1729—1786)

Complete the following:

1. Using your editor, open the **sd_messier_txt.html** and **sd_effects_txt.css** files from the html04 ▸ case1 folder. Enter *your name* and *the date* in the comment section of each file, and save them as **sd_messier.html** and **sd_effects.css** respectively.

2. Go to the **sd_messier.html** file in your HTML editor. Within the document head, create links to the sd_base.css, sd_layout.css, and sd_effects.css style sheet files in the order listed. Study the content and structure of the web page and then save your changes to the document.

3. Go to the **sd_effects.css** file in your editor. Andrew wants you to create a fixed background for the browser window. Within the HTML Styles section, insert a style rule for the `html` element to display the sd_back1.png file as the background image with a width of 100% covering the entire browser window. Have the background image fixed so that it does not scroll with the browser window.

4. Andrew wants the web page body background to combine several images and effects. Go to the Body Styles section and create a style rule for the `body` element that adds the following backgrounds in the order listed:

   a. A background containing the night sky image, sd_back2.png

   b. A radial gradient circle with a size extending to the closest corner and placed at the coordinates (40%, 70%) containing the color white stopping at 15% of the gradient and the color value rgba(151, 151, 151, 0.5) stopping at 50%

   c. A radial gradient circle also extending to the closest corner and placed at (80%, 40%) containing the color white stopping at 15% and followed by the color rgba(0, 0, 0, 0) at 30%

   d. A radial gradient extending to the closest side and placed at (10%, 20%) containing the color white stopping at 20% and followed by the color rgba(0, 0, 0, 0) stopping at 45%

   e. A radial gradient with a size of 5% in the horizontal and vertical directions placed at (90%, 10%) with the color white stopping at 15% and followed by the color rgba(0, 0, 0, 0) stopping at 40%

   f. The background color rgb(151, 151, 151) set as a base for the preceding background image and radial gradients

5. Within the style rule for the page body, add styles to place box shadows on the left and right borders. Set the color of the first shadow to rgb(31, 31, 31) with horizontal and vertical offsets of 30 pixels and 0 pixels and a blur of 45 pixels. Set the second shadow equal to the first except that the horizontal offset should be –30 pixels.

6. Go to the Navigation List Styles section. Format the hypertext links in the body header by adding a style rule for the `body > header a` that adds a 5-pixel outset border with color value rgb(211, 211, 255).

7. Next, format the appearance of the article title. Go to the Section Left Styles section and create a style rule for the h1 heading in the left section article that changes the text color to rgb(211, 211, 211) and adds a black text shadow with 0-pixel offsets and a blur size of 5 pixels.

8. Andrew has included an image of Charles Messier, the originator of the Messier catalog of stellar objects. The image is marked with the id "mportrait". In the Section Left Styles section, create a style rule for this object that modifies the appearance of this image by applying the following filters: a) the drop-shadow filter with a horizontal offset of –15 pixels, a blur of 5 pixels, and a color of rgba(51, 51, 51, 0.9); b) a grayscale filter with a value of 0.7; and c) an opacity filter with a value of 0.6.

9. Andrew wants the Charles Messier image flipped horizontally. Add a style to transform the image by rotating it 180° around the *y*-axis.

10. Go to the Footer Styles section and create a style rule for the `footer` element that adds a 2-pixel solid border to the top edge of the footer with a color value of rgb(171, 171, 171).

11. Save your changes to the style sheet file and then open **sd_messier.html** in your browser. Verify that the design of the page resembles that shown in Figure 4-66. Verify that when you scroll through the web page, the browser window background stays fixed. (Note: Some versions of Internet Explorer do not support the `filter` style, which means that you will not see modifications to the Charles Messier image.)

Case Problem 2

Data Files needed for this Case Problem: sf_torte_txt.html, sf_effects_txt.css, 2 CSS files, 9 PNG files

Save your Fork   Amy Wu has asked for your help in redesigning her website, *Save your Fork*, a baking site for people who want to share dessert recipes and learn about baking in general. She has prepared a page containing a sample dessert recipe and links to other pages on the website. A preview of the page you'll create is shown in Figure 4-67.

Figure 4-67   **Save your Fork sample recipe page**

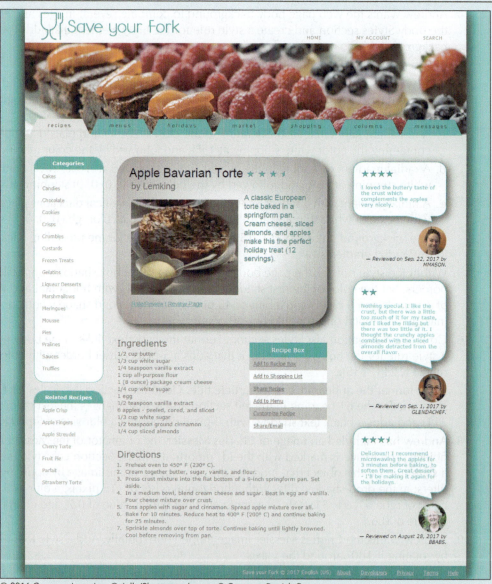

© 2016 Cengage Learning; © Jelly/Shutterstock.com; © Courtesy Patrick Carey

Amy has already created a style sheet for the page layout and typography, so your work will be focused on enhancing the page with graphic design styles.

Complete the following:

1. Using your editor, open the **sf_torte_txt.html** and **sf_effects_txt.css** files from the html04 ▸ case2 folder. Enter *your name* and *the date* in the comment section of each file, and save them as **sf_torte.html** and **sf_effects.css** respectively.

2. Go to the **sf_torte.html** file in your editor. Within the document head create links to the sf_base.css, sf_layout.css, and sf_effects.css style sheet files in that order. Take some time to study the structure of the document and then close the document, saving your changes.

3. Go to the **sf_effects.css** file in your editor. Within the Body Header Styles section, create a style rule for the `body` element to add drop shadows to the left and right border of the page body with an offset of 10 pixels, a blur of 50 pixels, and the color rgb(51, 51, 51). Note that the right border is a mirror image of the left border.

4. Go to the Navigation Tabs List Styles section. Amy has created a navigation list with the class name `tabs` that appears at the top of the page with the body header. Create a style rule for the `body > header nav.tabs` selector that changes the background to the image file sf_back1.png with no tiling, centered horizontally and vertically within the element and sized to cover the entire navigation list.

5. Amy wants the individual list items in the tabs navigation list to appear as tabs in a recipe box. She wants each of these "tabs" to be trapezoidal in shape. To create this effect, you'll create a style rule for the `body > header nav.tabs li` selector that transforms the list item by setting the perspective of its 3D space to 50 pixels and rotating it 20° around the x-axis.

6. As users hover the mouse pointer over the navigation tabs, Amy wants a rollover effect in which the tabs appear to come to the front. Create a style rule for the `body > header nav.tabs li` selector that uses the pseudo-element `hover` that changes the background color to rgb(231, 231, 231).

7. Go to the Left Section Styles section. Referring to Figure 4-67, notice that in the left section of the page, Amy has placed two vertical navigation lists. She wants these navigation lists to have rounded borders. For the vertical navigation lists in the left section, create a style rule for the `section#left nav.vertical` selector that adds a 1-pixel solid border with color value rgb(20, 167, 170) and has a radius of 25 pixels at each corner.

8. The rounded corner also has to apply to the h1 heading within each navigation list. Create a style rule for `h1` elements nested within the left section vertical navigation list that sets the top-left and top-right corner radii to 25 pixels.

9. Go to the Center Article Styles section. The `article` element contains an image and brief description of the Apple Bavarian Torte, which is the subject of this sample page. Create a style rule for the `section#center article` selector that adds the following: a) a radial gradient to the background with a white center with a color stop of 30% transitioning to rgb(151, 151, 151), b) a 1-pixel solid border with color value rgb(151, 151, 151) and a radius of 50 pixels, and c) a box shadow with horizontal and vertical offsets of 10 pixels with a 20-pixel blur and a color of rgb(51, 51, 51).

10. Go to the Blockquote Styles section. Amy has included three sample reviews from users of the Save your Fork website. Amy wants the text of these reviews to appear within the image of a speech bubble. For every `blockquote` element, create a style rule that does the following: a) sets the background image to the sf_speech.png with no tiling and a horizontal and vertical size of 100% to cover the entire block quote, and b) uses the `drop-shadow` filter to add a drop shadow around the speech bubble with horizontal and vertical offsets of 5 pixels, a blur of 10 pixels and the color rgb(51, 51, 51).

11. Amy has included the photo of each reviewer registered on the site within the citation for each review. She wants these images to appear as circles rather than squares. To do this, create a style rule for the selector `cite img` that sets the border radius to 50%.

12. Save your changes to the style sheet file and then open **sf_torte.html** in your browser. Verify that the design of your page matches that shown in Figure 4-67. Confirm that when you hover the mouse over the navigation tabs the background color changes to match the page color. (Note: Some versions of Internet Explorer do not support the `filter` style, which means that you will not see drop shadows around the speech bubbles.)

Case Problem 3

Data Files needed for this Case Problem: cf_home_txt.html, cf_effects_txt.css, 2 CSS files, 7 PNG files

Chupacabra Music Festival   Debra Kelly is the director of the website for the *Chupacabra Music Festival*, which takes place every summer in San Antonio, Texas. Work is already underway on the website design for the 15th annual festival and Debra has approached you to work on the design of the home page.

Debra envisions a page that uses semi-transparent colors and 3D transformations to make an attractive and eye-catching page. A preview of her completed design proposal is shown in Figure 4-68.

Figure 4-68   Chupacabra 15 home page

© 2016 Cengage Learning; © Memo Angeles/Shutterstock.com; © Ivan Galashchuk/Shutterstock.com;
© Andrey Armyagov/Shutterstock.com; © Away/Shutterstock.com

Debra has provided you with the HTML code and the layout and reset style sheets. Your job will be to finish her work by inserting the graphic design styles.

Complete the following:

1. Using your editor, open the **cf_home_txt.html** and **cf_effects_txt.css** files from the html04 ▸ case3 folder. Enter *your name* and *the date* in the comment section of each file, and save them as **cf_home.html** and **cf_effects.css** respectively.

2. Go to the **cf_home.html** file in your HTML editor. Within the document head, create a link to the cf_reset.css, cf_layout.css, and cf_effects.css style sheets. Take some time to study the content and structure of the document. Pay special note to the nested `div` elements in the center section of the page; you will use these to create a 3D cube design. Close the file, saving your changes.

3. Return to the **cf_effects.css** file in your editor and go to the HTML Styles section. Debra wants a background displaying a scene from last year's festival. Add a style rule for the `html` element that displays the cf_back1.png as a fixed background, centered horizontally and vertically in the browser window and covering the entire window.

4. Go to the Body Styles section and set the background color of the page body to rgba(255, 255, 255, 0.3).

5. Go to the Body Header Styles section and change the background color of the body header to rgba(51, 51, 51, 0.5).

6. Debra has placed useful information for the festival in `aside` elements placed within the left and right `section` elements. Go to the Aside Styles section and create a style rule for the `section aside` selector that adds a 10-pixel double border with color rgba(92, 42, 8, 0.3) and a border radius of 30 pixels.

7. Debra wants a curved border for every h1 heading within an `aside` element. For the selector `section aside h1`, create a style rule that sets the border radius of the top-left and top-right corners to 30 pixels.

8. Define the perspective of the 3D space for the left and right sections by creating a style rule for those two sections that sets their perspective value to 450 pixels.

9. Create a style rule that rotates the `aside` elements within the left section 25° around the y-axis. Create another style rule that rotates the `aside` elements within the right section –25° around the y-axis.

⊕ **Explore** 10. Go to the Cube Styles section. Here you'll create the receding cube effect that appears in the center of the page. The cube has been constructed by creating a `div` element with the id `cube` containing five `div` elements belonging to the `cube_face` class with the ids `cube_bottom`, `cube_top`, `cube_left`, `cube_right`, and `cube_front`. (There will be no back face for this cube.) Currently the five faces are superimposed upon each other. To create the cube you have to shift and rotate each face in 3D space so that they form the five faces of the cube. First, position the cube on the page by creating a style rule for the `div#cube` selector containing the following styles:

  a. Place the element using relative positioning.

  b. Set the top margin to 180 pixels, the bottom margin to 150 pixels, and the left/right margins to `auto`.

  c. Set the width and height to 400 pixels.

  d. Set the perspective of the space to 450 pixels.

11. For each `div` element of the `cube_face` class, create a style rule that places the faces with absolute positioning and sets their width and height to 400 pixels.

⊕ **Explore** 12. Finally, you'll construct the cube by positioning each of the five faces in 3D space so that they form the shape of a cube. Add the following style rules for each of the five faces to transform their appearance.

  a. Translate the cube_front `div` element –50 pixels along the z-axis.

  b. Translate the cube_left `div` element –200 pixels along the x-axis and rotate it 90° around the y-axis.

  c. Translate the cube_right `div` element 200 pixels along the x-axis and rotate it 90° counter-clockwise around the y-axis.

  d. Translate the cube_top `div` element –200 pixels along the y-axis and rotate it 90° counter-clockwise around the x-axis.

  e. Translate the cube_bottom `div` element 200 pixels along the y-axis and rotate it 90° around the x-axis.

13. Save your changes to style sheet file and open **cf_home.html** in your browser. Verify that the layout of your page matches Figure 4-68 including the center cube with the five faces of photos and text.

Case Problem 4

Data Files needed for this Case Problem: br_listing2048_txt.html, br_styles_txt.css, 1 CSS file, 11 PNG files, 1 TXT file

CREATE

Browyer Realty   Linda Browyer is the owner of *Browyer Realty*, a real estate company operating in Owatonna, Minnesota. She's asked you to help create a style design for the pages on her site that describe residential listings. Linda has already written up sample content for a listing and collected images of the property. She needs you to create the HTML file and write up the style sheets.

Complete the following:

1. Using your editor, open the **br_listing2048_txt.html** and **br_styles_txt.css** files from the html04 ► case4 folder. Enter *your name* and *the date* in the comment section of each file and save them as **br_listing2048.html** and **br_styles.css** respectively.

2. Using the content of the br_listing2048.txt file, create the content and structure of the br_listing2048.html page. You are free to supplement the material in these text files with additional content of your own if appropriate. Use the # symbol for the value of the href attribute in your hypertext links because you will be linking to pages that don't actually exist.

3. Link your home page to the br_reset.css and br_styles.css style sheets. Save your changes to the file.

4. Go to the **br_styles.css** file in your editor and create the layout and design styles to be used in your page. The page design is up to you, but must include at least one example of the following graphic design features:

   • A background image
   • A border around a page element, including an example of a curved border
   • A box shadow around a page element
   • A text shadow around a section of element text
   • A background featuring a linear gradient and a radial gradient
   • Changing the appearance of an element using the transform property
   • Changing the appearance of an element using the filter property

5. Include comments in your style sheet to make it easy for other users to interpret.

6. Test your layout and design on a variety of devices, browsers, and screen resolutions to ensure that your sample page is readable under different conditions.

TUTORIAL 5

OBJECTIVES

Session 5.1
- Create a media query
- Work with the browser viewport
- Apply a responsive design
- Create a pulldown menu with CSS

Session 5.2
- Create a flexbox
- Work with flex sizes
- Explore flexbox layouts

Session 5.3
- Create a print style sheet
- Work with page sizes
- Add and remove page breaks

Designing for the Mobile Web

Creating a Mobile Website for a Daycare Center

Case | *Trusted Friends Daycare*

Marjorie Kostas is the owner of *Trusted Friends Daycare*, an early childhood education and care center located in Carmel, Indiana. You've been hired to help work on the redesign of the company's website. Because many of her clients access the website from their mobile phones, Marjorie is interested in improving the site's appearance on mobile devices. However, your design still has to be compatible with tablet devices and desktop computers. Finally, the site contains several pages that her clients will want to print, so your design needs to meet the needs of printed media.

STARTING DATA FILES

html05 → **tutorial**

tf_articles_txt.html
tf_home_txt.html
tf_prek_txt.html
tf_flex_txt.css
tf_navicon_txt.css
tf_print_txt.css
tf_styles1_txt.css
+ 9 files

review

tf_tips_txt.html
tf_print2_txt.css
tf_styles4_txt.css
+ 6 files

case1

gp_cover_txt.html
gp_page1_txt.html
gp_page2_txt.html
gp_page3_txt.html
gp_layout_txt.css
gp_print_txt.css
+ 23 files

case2

wc_styles_txt.css
+ 40 files

case3

cw_home_txt.html
cw_styles_txt.css
+ 12 files

case4

jb_home_txt.html
jb_styles_txt.css
+ 11 files

Session 5.1 Visual Overview:

The `viewport meta` tag is used to set the properties of the layout viewport.

This sets the width of the layout viewport equal to the width of the visual viewport.

This sets the initial scale of the viewport to 1.0.

```
<meta name="viewport" content="width=device-width, initial-scale=1" />
```

Responsive designs should start with base styles that apply to all devices, followed by mobile styles, tablet styles, and then desktop styles.

```
/* =================================
      Base Styles
   =================================
*/

style rules
```

```
/* =================================
      Mobile Styles: 0 to 480 pixels
   =================================
*/

@media only screen and (max-width: 480px) {

    style rules

}
```

A **media query** is used to apply specified style rules to a device based on the device type and the device features.

This media query matches screens with a maximum width of 480 pixels.

Within a media query are style rules that are only applied to devices that match the query.

```
/* =================================
      Tablet Styles: 481px and greater
   =================================
*/

@media only screen and (min-width: 481px) {

    style rules

}
```

This media query matches screens with a minimum width of 481 pixels.

```
/* =================================
      Desktop Styles: 769px and greater
   =================================
*/

@media only screen and (min-width: 769px) {

    style rules

}
```

This media query matches screens with a minimum width of 769 pixels.

Media Queries

Mobile styles are applied when the screen width is 0 to 480 pixels.

Tablet styles are applied once the screen width exceeds 480 pixels.

Desktop styles are applied once the screen width is 769 pixels and greater.

Introducing Responsive Design

In the first four tutorials, you created a single set of layout and design styles for your websites without considering what type of device would be rendering the site. However, this is not always a practical approach and with many users increasingly accessing the web through mobile devices, a web designer must take into consideration the needs of those devices. Figure 5-1 presents some of the important ways in which designing for the mobile experience differs from designing for the desktop experience.

Figure 5-1   Designing for mobile and desktop devices

User Experience	Mobile	Desktop
Page Content	Content should be short and to the point.	Content can be extensive, giving readers the opportunity to explore all facets of the topic.
Page Layout	Content should be laid out within a single column with no horizontal scrolling.	With a wider screen size, content can be more easily laid out in multiple columns.
Hypertext Links	Links need to be easily accessed via a touch interface.	Links can be activated more precisely using a cursor or mouse pointer.
Network Bandwidth	Sites tend to take longer to load over cellular networks and thus overall file size should be kept small.	Sites are quickly accessed over high-speed networks, which can more easily handle large file sizes.
Lighting	Pages need to be easily visible in outdoor lighting through the use of contrasting colors.	Pages are typically viewed in an office setting, allowing a broader color palette.
Device Tools	Mobile sites often need access to devices such as phone dialing, messaging, mapping, and built-in cameras and video.	Sites rarely have need to access desktop devices.

© 2016 Cengage Learning

Viewing a web page on a mobile device is a fundamentally different experience than viewing the same web page on a desktop computer. As a result, these differences need to be taken into account when designing a website. Figure 5-2 shows the current home page of the Trusted Friends website as it appears on a mobile device.

Figure 5-2   Trusted Friends home page displayed on a mobile device

the small text in the links are difficult to activate using touch

small article text is difficult to read

double column layout reduces the size of the page text within the columns

empty space indicates poor use of the available screen

© 2016 Cengage Learning; © Robert Kneschke/Shutterstock.com; BenBois/openclipart

Notice that the mobile device has automatically zoomed out to display the complete page width resulting in text that is difficult to read and small hypertext links that are practically unusable with a touch interface. While the design might be fine for a desktop monitor in landscape orientation, it's clear that it is ill-suited to a mobile device.

What this website requires is a design that is not only specifically tailored to the needs of her mobile users but also is easily revised for tablet and desktop devices. This can be accomplished with responsive design in which the design of the document changes in response to the device rendering the page. An important leader in the development of responsive design is Ethan Marcotte, who identified three primary components of responsive design theory:

TIP

For more information on the development of responsive design, refer to *Responsive Web Design* by Ethan Marcotte (http://alistapart.com/article/responsive-web-design).

- **flexible layout** so that the page layout automatically adjusts to screens of different widths
- **responsive images** that rescale based on the size of the viewing device
- **media queries** that determine the properties of the device rendering the page so that appropriate designs can be delivered to specific devices

In the preceding tutorials, you've seen how to create grid-based fluid layouts and you've used images that scaled based on the width of the browser window and web page. In this session, you'll learn how to work with media queries in order to create a truly responsive website design.

Introducing Media Queries

Media queries are used to associate a style sheet or style rule with a specific device or list of device features. To create a media query within an HTML file, add the following `media` attribute to either the `link` or `style` element in the document head

```
media="devices"
```

where *devices* is a comma-separated list of supported media types associated with a specified style sheet. For example, the following `link` element accesses the output.css style sheet file, but only when the device is a printer or projection device:

```
<link href="output.css" media="print, projection" />
```

If any other device accesses this web page, it will not load the output.css style sheet file. Figure 5-3 lists other possible media type values for the `media` attribute.

Figure 5-3   **Media types**

Media Type	Used For
`all`	All output devices (the default)
`braille`	Braille tactile feedback devices
`embossed`	Paged Braille printers
`handheld`	Mobile devices with small screens and limited bandwidth
`print`	Printers
`projection`	Projectors
`screen`	Computer screens
`speech`	Speech and sound synthesizers, and aural browsers
`tty`	Fixed-width devices such as teletype machines and terminals
`tv`	Television-type devices with low resolution, color, and limited scrollability

© 2016 Cengage Learning

When no `media` attribute is used, the style sheet is assumed to apply to all devices accessing the web page.

The @media Rule

Media queries can also be used to associate specific style rules with specific devices by including the following `@media` rule in a CSS style sheet file

```
@media devices {
    style rules
}
```

where *devices* are supported media types and *style rules* are the style rules associated with those devices. For example, the following style sheet is broken into three sections: an initial style rule that sets the font color of all h1 headings regardless of device, a second section that sets the font size for h1 headings on screen or television devices, and a third section that sets the font size for h1 headings that are printed:

```
h1 {
    color: red;
}

@media screen, tv {
    h1 {font-size: 2em;}
}

@media print {
    h1 {font-size: 16pt;}
}
```

Note that in this style sheet, the font size for screen and television devices is expressed using the relative em unit but the font size for print devices is expressed using points, which is a more appropriate sizing unit for that medium.

Finally, you can specify media devices when importing one style sheet into another by adding the media type to the `@import` rule. Thus, the following CSS rule imports the screen.css file only when a screen or projection device is being used:

```
@import url("screen.css") screen, projection;
```

The initial hope was that media queries could target mobile devices using the `handheld` device type; however, as screen resolutions improved to the point where the cutoff between mobile, tablet, laptop, and desktop was no longer clear, media queries began to be based on what features a device supported and not on what the device was called.

Media Queries and Device Features

To target a device based on its features, you add the feature and its value to the `media` attribute using the syntax:

```
media="devices and|or (feature:value)"
```

where *feature* is the name of a media feature and *value* is the feature's value. The and and or keywords are used to create media queries that involve different devices or different features, or combinations of both.

The `@media` and `@import` rules employ similar syntax:

```
@media devices and|or (feature:value) {
    style rules
}
```

and

```
@import url(url) devices and|or (feature:value);
```

For example, the following media query applies the style rules only for screen devices with a width of 320 pixels.

```
@media screen and (device-width: 320px) {
    style rules
}
```

Figure 5-4 provides a list of the device features supported by HTML and CSS.

Figure 5-4   **Media features**

Feature	Description
aspect-ratio	The ratio of the width of the display area to its height
color	The number of bits per color component of the output device; if the device does not support color, the value is 0
color-index	The number of colors supported by the output device
device-aspect-ratio	The ratio of the device-width value to the device-height value
device-height	The height of the rendering surface of the output device
device-width	The width of the rendering surface of the output device
height	The height of the display area of the output device
monochrome	The number of bits per pixel in the device's monochrome frame buffer
orientation	The general description of the aspect ratio: equal to portrait when the height of the display area is greater than the width; equal to landscape otherwise
resolution	The resolution of the output device in pixels, expressed in either dpi (dots per inch) or dpcm (dots per centimeter)
width	The width of the display area of the output device

© 2016 Cengage Learning

All of the media features in Figure 5-4, with the exception of `orientation`, also accept min- and max- prefixes, where `min-` provides a minimum value for the specified feature, and `max-` provides the feature's maximum value. Thus, the following media query applies style rules only for screen devices whose width is at most 700 pixels:

```
@media screen and (max-width: 700px) {
    style rules
}
```

Similarly, the following media query applies style rules only to screens that are at least 400 pixels wide:

```
@media screen and (min-width: 400px) {
    style rules
}
```

You can combine multiple media features using logical operators such as and, not, and or. The following query applies the enclosed styles to all media types but only when the width of the output devices is between 320 and 480 pixels (inclusive):

```
@media all and (min-width: 320px and max-width: 480px) {
    style rules
}
```

Some media features are directed toward devices that do not have a particular property or characteristic. This is done by applying the `not` operator, which negates any features found in the expression. For example, the following query applies only to media devices that are not screen or do not have a maximum width of 480 pixels:

```
@media not screen and (max-width: 480px) {
    style rules
}
```

TIP

If you specify a feature without specifying a device, the media query will apply to all devices.

For some features, you do not have to specify a value but merely indicate the existence of the feature. The following query matches any screen device that also supports color:

```
@media screen and (color) {
    style rules
}
```

Finally, for older browsers that do not support media queries, CSS3 provides the `only` keyword to hide style sheets from those browsers. In the following code, older browsers will interpret `only` as an unsupported device name and so will not apply the enclosed style rules, while newer browsers will recognize the keyword and continue to apply the style rules.

```
@media only screen and (color) {
    style rules
}
```

All current browsers support media queries, but you will still see the `only` keyword used in many website style sheets.

REFERENCE

Creating a Media Query

- To create a media query that matches a device in a `link` or `style` element within an HTML file, use the following `media` attribute

  media="*devices* and|or (*feature*:*value*)"

  where *devices* is a comma-separated list of media types, *feature* is the name of a media feature, and *value* is the feature's value
- To create a media query, create the following `@media` rule within a CSS style sheet

  ```
  @media devices and|or (feature:value) {
      style rules
  }
  ```

  where *style rules* are the style rules applied for the specified device and feature.
- To import a style sheet based on a media query, apply the following `@import` rule within a CSS style sheet

  @import url(*url*) *devices* and|or (*feature*:*value*);

Applying Media Queries to a Style Sheet

You meet with Marjorie to discuss her plans for the home page redesign. She envisions three designs: one for mobile devices, a different design for tablets, and finally a design for desktop devices based on the current appearance of the site's home page (see Figure 5-5).

| Figure 5-5 | **Trusted Friends home page for different screen widths** |

© 2016 Cengage Learning; © Robert Kneschke/Shutterstock.com; © dotshock/Shutterstock.com; BenBois/openclipart; JMLevick/openclipart; Molumen/openclipart

The mobile design will be used for screen widths up to 480 pixels, the tablet design will be used for widths ranging from 481 pixels to 768 pixels, and the desktop design will be used for screen widths exceeding 768 pixels. To apply this approach, you'll create a style sheet having the following structure:

```
/* Base Styles */
   style rules

/* Mobile Styles */
@media only screen and (max-width: 480px) {
   style rules
}

/* Tablet Styles */
@media only screen and (min-width: 481px) {
   style rules
}

/* Desktop Styles */
@media only screen and (min-width: 769px) {
   style rules
}
```

Note that this style sheet applies the principle **mobile first** in which the overall page design starts with base styles that apply to all devices followed by style rules specific to mobile devices. Tablet styles are applied when the screen width is 481 pixels or greater and desktop styles build upon the tablet styles when the screen width exceeds 768 pixels. Thus, as your screen width increases, you add on more features or replace features found in smaller devices. In general, with responsive design, it is easier to add new styles through progressive enhancement than to replace styles.

Marjorie has supplied you with the HTML code and initial styles for her website's home page. Open her HTML file now.

To open the site's home page:

1. Use your editor to open the **tf_home_txt.html** and **tf_styles1_txt.css** files from the html05 ▸ tutorial folder. Enter **your name** and **the date** in the comment section of each file and save them as **tf_home.html** and **tf_styles1.css** respectively.

2. Return to the **tf_home.html** file in your editor and, within the document head, create links to the **tf_reset.css** and **tf_styles1.css** style sheet files.

3. Take some time to scroll through the contents of the document to become familiar with its contents and structure and then save your changes to the file, but do not close it.

Next, you'll insert the structure for the responsive design styles in the tf_styles1.css style sheet, adding sections for mobile, tablet, and desktop devices.

To add media queries to a style sheet:

1. Return to the **tf_styles1.css** file in your editor.

2. Marjorie has already inserted the base styles that will apply to all devices at the top of the style sheet file. Take time to review those styles.

3. Scroll to the bottom of the document and add the following code and comments after the New Styles Added Below comment.

```
/* ===============================
   Mobile Styles: 0px to 480px
   ===============================
*/
@media only screen and (max-width: 480px) {

}

/* ===============================
   Tablet Styles: 481px and greater
   ===============================
*/
@media only screen and (min-width: 481px) {

}

/* ===============================
   Desktop Styles: 769px and greater
   ===============================
*/
@media only screen and (min-width: 769px) {

}
```

Figure 5-6 highlights the media queries in the style sheet file.

Figure 5-6	Creating media queries for different screen widths

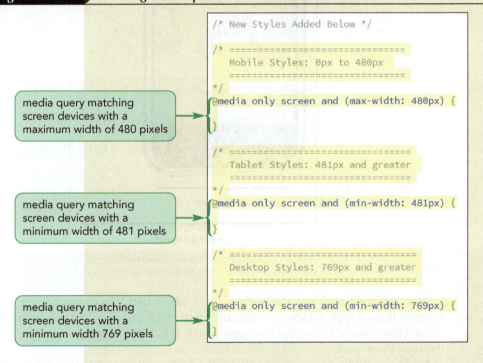

media query matching screen devices with a maximum width of 480 pixels

media query matching screen devices with a minimum width of 481 pixels

media query matching screen devices with a minimum width 769 pixels

4. Save your changes to the file.

The media queries you've written are based on the screen width. However, before you can begin writing styles for each media query, you have to understand how those width values are interpreted by your browser.

Exploring Viewports and Device Width

Web pages are viewed within a window called the viewport. For desktop computers, the viewport is the same as the browser window; however, this is not the case with mobile devices. Mobile devices have two types of viewports: a **visual viewport** displaying the web page content that fits within a mobile screen and a **layout viewport** containing the entire content of the page, some of which may be hidden from the user.

The two viewports exist in order to accommodate websites that have been written with desktop computers in mind. A mobile device will automatically zoom out of a page in order to give users the complete view of the page's contents, but as shown earlier in Figure 5-2, this often results in a view that is too small to be usable. While the user can manually zoom into a page to make it readable within the visual viewport, this is done at the expense of hiding content, as shown in Figure 5-7.

Figure 5-7	Comparing the visual and layout viewports

© 2016 Cengage Learning; © Robert Kneschke/Shutterstock.com;
© dotshock/Shutterstock.com; BenBois/openclipart

Notice in the figure how the home page of the Trusted Friends website has been zoomed in on a mobile device so that only part of the page is displayed within the visual viewport and the rest of the page, which is hidden from the user, extends into the layout viewport.

Widths in media queries are based on the width of the layout viewport, not the visual viewport. Thus, depending on how the page is scaled, a width of 980 pixels might match the physical width of the device as shown in Figure 5-2 or it might extend beyond it as shown in Figure 5-7. In order to correctly base a media query on the physical width of the device, you have to tell the browser that you want the width of the layout viewport matched to the device width by adding the following `meta` element to the HTML file:

```
<meta name="viewport" content="properties" />
```

where *properties* is a comma-separated list of viewport properties and their values, as seen in the example that follows:

```
<meta name="viewport"
  content="width=device-width, initial-scale=1" />
```

In this `meta` element, the `device-width` keyword is used to set the width of the layout viewport to the physical width of the device's screen. For a mobile device, this command sets the width of the layout viewport to the width of the device. The line `initial-scale=1` is added so that the browser doesn't automatically zoom out of the web page to fit the page content within the width of the screen. We want the viewport to match the device width, which is what the above meta element tells the browser to do.

Configuring the Layout Viewport

- To configure the properties of the layout viewport for use with media queries, add the following `meta` element to the HTML file

  ```
  <meta name="viewport" content="properties" />
  ```

  where *properties* is a comma-separated list of viewport properties and their values.
- To size the layout viewport so that it matches the width of the device without rescaling, use the following viewport `meta` element

  ```
  <meta name="viewport"
    content="width=device-width, initial-scale=1" />
  ```

Add the viewport `meta` element to the tf_home.html file now, setting the width of the layout viewport to match the device width and the initial scale to 1.

To define the visual viewport:

1. Return to the **tf_home.html** file in your editor.

2. Below the `meta` element that defines the character set, insert the following HTML tag:

   ```
   <meta name="viewport"
     content="width=device-width, initial-scale=1" />
   ```

   Figure 5-8 highlights the code for the viewport `meta` element.

Figure 5-8	Setting the properties of the viewport

sets the width of the layout viewport to the width of the device

page does not automatically zoom out when the page is initially opened by the browser

```
<title>Trusted Friends Daycare</title>
<meta charset="utf-8" />
<meta name="viewport" content="width=device-width, initial-scale=1" />
<link href="tf_reset.css" rel="stylesheet" />
<link href="tf_styles1.css" rel="stylesheet" />
</head>
```

3. Save your changes to the file.

4. Open the **tf_home.html** file in your browser. Figure 5-9 shows the initial design of the page.

Figure 5-9	Mobile layout of the Trusted Friends home page

company logo

submenu title

submenu

navigation menu

main article

aside comments

footer

© 2016 Cengage Learning; © Robert Kneschke/Shutterstock.com

Now that you've set up the media queries and configured the viewport, you can work on the design of the home page. You'll start by designing for mobile devices.

Not All Pixels Are Equal

While pixels are a basic unit of measurement in web design, there are actually two types of pixels to consider as you design a website. One is a **device pixel**, which refers to the actual physical pixel on a screen. The other is a **CSS pixel**, which is the fundamental unit in CSS measurements. The difference between device pixels and CSS pixels is easiest to understand when you zoom into and out of a web page. For example, the following style creates an `aside` element that is 300 CSS pixels wide:

```
aside: {width: 300px;}
```

However, the element is not necessarily 300 device pixels. If the user zooms into the web page, the apparent size of the article increases as measured by device pixels but remains 300 CSS pixels wide, resulting in 1 CSS pixel being represented by several device pixels.

The number of device pixels matched to a single CSS pixel is known as the **device-pixel ratio**. When a page is zoomed at a factor of 2x, the device-pixel ratio is 2, with a single CSS pixel represented by a 2×2 square of device pixels.

One area where the difference between device pixels and CSS pixels becomes important is in the development of websites optimized for displays with high device-pixel ratios. Some mobile devices are capable of displaying images with a device pixel ratio of 3, resulting in free crisp and clear images. Designers can optimize their websites for these devices by creating one set of style sheets for low-resolution displays and another for high-resolution displays. The high-resolution style sheet would load extremely detailed, high-resolution images, while the low-resolution style sheet would load lower resolution images better suited to devices that are limited to smaller device-pixel ratios. For example, the following media query

```
<link href="retina.css" rel="stylesheet"
  media="only screen and (-webkit-min-device-pixel-ratio: 2) " />
```

loads the retina.css style sheet file for high-resolution screen devices that have device-pixel ratios of at least 2. Note that currently the `device-pixel-ratio` feature is a browser-specific extension supported only by WebKit.

Creating a Mobile Design

A mobile website design should reflect how users interact with their mobile devices. Because your users will be working with a small handheld touchscreen device, one key component in your design is to have the most important information up-front and easily accessible, which means your home page on a mobile device needs to be free of unnecessary clutter. Another important principle of designing for mobile devices is that you should limit the choices you offer to your users. Ideally, there should only be a few navigation links on the screen at any one time.

With these principles in mind, consider the current layout of the Trusted Friends home page shown in Figure 5-9. The content is arranged within a single column providing the maximum width for the text and images, but an area of concern for Marjorie is the long list of hypertext links, which forces the user to scroll vertically down the page to view information about the center. Most mobile websites deal with this issue by hiding extensive lists of links in pulldown menus, appearing only in response to a tap of a major heading in the navigation list. You'll use this technique for the Trusted Friends home page.

Creating a Pulldown Menu with CSS

Marjorie has already laid the foundation for creating a pulldown menu in her HTML code. Figure 5-10 shows the code used to mark the contents of the navigation list in the body header.

Figure 5-10   **Submenus in the navigation list**

```
<nav class="horizontal">
  <ul class="mainmenu">
    <li><a href="tf_home.html">Home</a></li>
    <li><a href="#" class="submenuTitle">Classes &#9654;</a>
    <ul class="submenu">
      <li><a href="#">Infants</a></li>
      <li><a href="#">Toddlers</a></li>
      <li><a href="tf_prek.html">Pre-K</a></li>
      <li><a href="#">After School</a></li>
    </ul>
    </li>
    <li><a href="#" class="submenuTitle">Parents &#9654;</a>
    <ul class="submenu">
      <li><a href="tf_articles.html">Articles</a></li>
      <li><a href="#">Blog</a></li>
      <li><a href="#">Forms</a></li>
      <li><a href="#">Legal</a></li>
    </ul>
    </li>
    <li><a href="#" class="submenuTitle">About Us &#9654;</a>
    <ul class="submenu">
      <li><a href="#">History</a></li>
      <li><a href="#">Accreditation</a></li>
      <li><a href="#">Reviews</a></li>
    </ul>
    </li>
    <li><a href="#">Contact Us</a> </li>
  </ul>
</nav>
```

submenu titles

nested submenu lists associated with submenu titles

Marjorie has created a navigation bar that includes topical areas named Classes, Parents, and About Us. Within each of these topical areas are nested lists containing links to specific pages on the Trusted Friends website. Marjorie has put each of these nested lists within a class named *submenu*. So, first you'll hide each of these submenus to reduce the length of the navigation list as it is rendered within the user's browser. You'll place this style rule in the section for Base Styles because it will be used by both mobile and tablet devices (but not by desktop devices as you'll see later).

To hide a submenu:

1. Return to the **tf_styles1.css** file in your editor.

2. Scroll to the Pulldown Menu Styles section and add the following style rule:

```
ul.submenu {
    display: none;
}
```

Figure 5-11 highlights the styles to hide the navigation list submenus.

Figure 5-11   Hiding the navigation list submenus

prevents the submenu unordered lists from being displayed

```
/* Pulldown Menu Styles */

ul.submenu {
    display: none;
}
```

3. Save your changes to the file and then reload the tf_home.html file in your browser. Verify that the navigation list no longer shows the contents of the submenus but only the Home, Classes, Parents, About Us, and Contact Us links. See Figure 5-12.

Figure 5-12   Navigation list with hidden submenus

submenu lists are hidden

HOME
CLASSES ▶
PARENTS ▶
ABOUT US ▶
CONTACT US

Trusted Friends Daycare provides childhood education and daycare, conveniently located for you and your child. We treat each child based on his or her own

© Robert Kneschke/Shutterstock.com

Next, you want to display a nested submenu only when the user hovers the mouse pointer over its associated submenu title, which for this page are the Classes, Parents, and About Us titles. Because the submenu follows the submenu title in the HTML file (see Figure 5-10), you can use the following selector to select the submenu that is immediately preceded by a hovered submenu title:

```
a.submenuTitle:hover+ul.submenu
```

However, this selector is not enough because you want the submenu to remain visible as the pointer moves away from the title and hovers over the now-visible submenu. So, you need to add `ul.submenu:hover` to the selector:

```
a.submenuTitle:hover+ul.submenu, ul.submenu:hover
```

To make the submenu visible, you change its display property back to `block`, resulting in the following style rule:

```
a.submenuTitle:hover+ul.submenu, ul.submenu:hover {
        display: block;
}
```

You may wonder why you don't use only the `ul.submenu:hover` selector. The reason is that you can't hover over the submenu until it's visible and it won't be visible until you first hover over the submenu title. Add this rule now to the tf_styles1.css style sheet and test it.

To redisplay the navigation submenus:

1. Return to the **tf_styles1.css** file in your editor.

2. Add the following style rule to the Pulldown Menu Styles section:

   ```
   a.submenuTitle:hover+ul.submenu, ul.submenu:hover {
       display: block;
   }
   ```

   Figure 5-13 highlights the styles to display the navigation list submenus.

Figure 5-13   Displaying the hidden submenus

```
/* Pulldown Menu Styles */

ul.submenu {
    display: none;
}

a.submenuTitle:hover+ul.submenu, ul.submenu:hover {
    display: block;
}
```

selects the submenu that is preceded by a hovered-over submenu title

makes the submenu visible by changing the display property to block

selects the now-visible submenu as it's being hovered over

3. Save your changes to the file and then reload the tf_home.html file in your browser. Hover your mouse pointer over each of the submenu titles and verify that the corresponding submenu becomes visible and remains visible as you move the mouse pointer over its contents.

   Figure 5-14 shows the revised appearance of the navigation list using the pulldown menus.

Figure 5-14   **Displaying the contents of a pulldown menu**

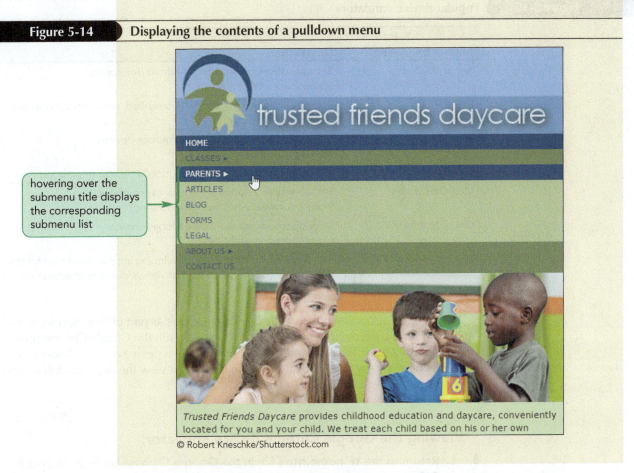

hovering over the submenu title displays the corresponding submenu list

Trusted Friends Daycare provides childhood education and daycare, conveniently located for you and your child. We treat each child based on his or her own

© Robert Kneschke/Shutterstock.com

The hover event is used with mouse pointers on desktop computers but it has a different interpretation when applied to mobile devices. Because almost all mobile devices operate via a touch interface, there is no hovering. A mobile browser will interpret a hover event as a tap event in which the user taps the page object. When the hover event is used to hide an object or display it (as we did with the submenus), mobile browsers employ a double-tap event in which the first tap displays the page object and a second tap, immediately after the first, activates any hypertext links associated with the object. To display the Trusted Friends submenus, the user would tap the submenu title and to hide the submenus the user would tap elsewhere on the page.

To test the hover action, you need to view the Trusted Friends page on a mobile device or a mobile emulator.

Testing your Mobile Website

The best way to test a mobile interface is to view it directly on a mobile device. However, given the large number of mobile devices and device versions, it's usually not practical to do direct testing on all devices. An alternative to having the physical device is to emulate it through a software program or an online testing service. Almost every mobile phone company provides a software development kit or SDK that developers can use to test their programs and websites. Figure 5-15 lists some of the many **mobile device emulators** available on the web at the time of this writing.

Figure 5-15 Popular device emulators

Mobile Emulators	Description
Android SDK	Software development kit for Android developers (*developer.android.com/sdk*)
iOS SDK	Software development kit for iPhone, iPad, and other iOS devices (*developer.apple.com*)
Mobile Phone Emulator	Online emulation for a variety of mobile devices (*www.mobilephoneemulator.com*)
Mobile Test Me	Online emulation for a variety of mobile devices (*mobiletest.me*)
MobiOne Studio	Mobile emulator software for a variety of devices (*https://www.genuitec.com/products/mobile/*)
Opera Mobile SDK	Developer tools for the Opera Mobile browser (*www.opera.com/developer*)
Windows Phone SDK	Software development kit for developing apps and websites for the Windows Phone (*dev.windows.com/en-us/develop/download-phone-sdk*)

© 2016 Cengage Learning

Browsers are also starting to include device emulators as part of their developer tools. You will examine the device emulator that is supplied with the Google Chrome browser and use it to view the Trusted Friends home page under a device of your choosing. If you don't have access to the Google Chrome browser, review the steps that follow and apply them to the emulator of your choice.

Viewing the Google Chrome device emulator:

1. Return to the **tf_home.html** file in the Google Chrome browser and press **F12** to open the developer tools pane.

2. Click the **device** icon located at the top of the developer pane to display a list of devices in the developer window.

3. Select a device of your choosing from the list of mobile devices in the top-left corner in the developer window. Note that the device's width and height (for example, 400 × 640) are displayed below the device name.

4. Refresh or reload the web page to ensure that the display parameters of your selected device are applied to the rendered page.

   The emulator also allows you to view the effect of changing the orientation of the phone from portrait to landscape.

5. Click the **swap dimensions** button located below the name of the mobile device to switch to landscape orientation. Click the **swap dimensions** button again to switch back to portrait mode.

   Google Chrome's device emulator can also emulate the touch action. The touch point is represented by a semi-transparent circle ●.

6. Move the touch point over Classes, Parents, or About Us and verify that when you click (tap) the touch point on a submenu title the nested submenu contents are displayed.

7. Verify that you when you click elsewhere in the page the submenu contents are hidden.

   Figure 5-16 shows the effect of opening a submenu with the touch emulator.

Figure 5-16	Using the Google Chrome device emulator tool

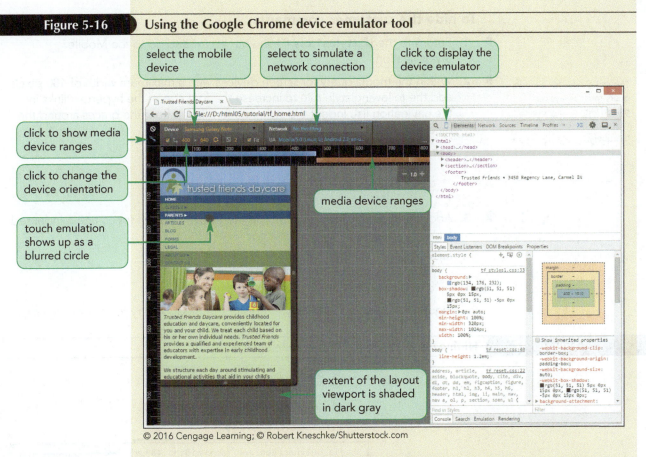

© 2016 Cengage Learning; © Robert Kneschke/Shutterstock.com

> **8.** Continue to explore Google Chrome's device emulators, trying out different combinations of devices and screen orientations. Press **F12** again to close the developer window.

An important aspect of mobile design is optimizing your site's performance under varying network conditions. Thus, in addition to emulating the properties of the mobile device, Google Chrome's device emulator can also emulate network connectivity. You can test the performance of your mobile site under a variety of simulated network connections including WiFi, DSL, 2G, 3G, and 4G mobile connections, as well as offline connections.

Marjorie wants to increase the font size of the links in the navigation list to make them easier to access using touch. She also wants to hide the customer comments that have been placed in the `aside` element (because she doesn't feel this will be of interest to mobile users). Because these changes only apply to the mobile device version of the page, you'll add the style rules within the media query for mobile devices.

To hide the customer comments:

1. Return to the **tf_styles1.css** file in your editor and go to the Mobile Styles section.

2. Within the media query for screen devices with a maximum width of 480 pixels, add the following style rule to increase the font size of the hypertext links in the navigation list. Indent the style rule to offset it from the braces around the media query.

```
nav.horizontal a {
   font-size: 1.5em;
   line-height: 2.2em;
}
```

3. Add the following style rule to hide the `aside` element (once again indented from the surrounding media query):

```
aside {
   display: none;
}
```

Figure 5-17 highlights the style rules in the media query for mobile devices.

> The styles rules for a media query must always be placed within curly braces to define the extent of the query.

Figure 5-17   **Hiding the aside element for mobile devices**

applies the style rules only for screen devices with a maximum width of 480 pixels

```
@media only screen and (max-width: 480px) {
   nav.horizontal a {
      font-size: 1.5em;
      line-height: 2.2em;
   }
   aside {
      display: none;
   }
}
```

opening curly brace for the media query

increases the size of the navigation links

hides the aside element

closing curly brace for the media query

4. Save your changes to the file and then reload the tf_home.html file in your browser. Reduce the width of the browser window to 480 pixels or below (or view the page in your mobile emulator). Verify that the customer comments are no longer displayed on the web page and that the size of the navigation links has been increased.

Figure 5-18 shows the final design of the mobile version.

Figure 5-18   **Final design of the mobile version of the home page**

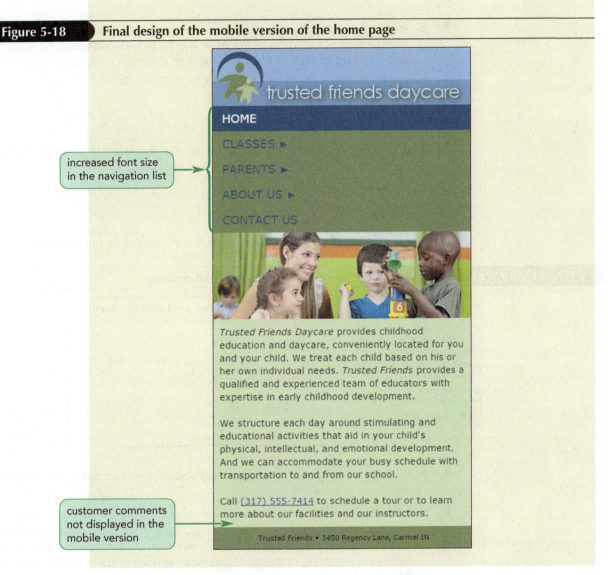

increased font size
in the navigation list

customer comments
not displayed in the
mobile version

Now that you've completed the mobile design of the page, you'll start to work on the design for tablet devices.

Creating a Tablet Design

Under the media query you've set up, your design for tablet devices will be applied for screen widths greater than 480 pixels. The pulldown menu you created was part of the base styles, so it is already part of the tablet design; however, with the wider screen, Marjorie would like the submenus displayed horizontally rather than vertically. You can accomplish this by adding a style rule to the tablet media query to float the submenus side-by-side.

To begin writing the tablet design:

▶ **1.** Return to the **tf_styles1.css** file in your editor and scroll down to the media query for the tablet styles.

2. Within the media query, add the following style to float the five list items, which are direct children of the main menu, side-by-side. Set the width of each list item to 20% of the total width of the main menu.

```
ul.mainmenu > li {
    float: left;
    width: 20%;
}
```

3. Double the widths of the submenus so that they stand out better from the main menu titles by adding the following style rule.

```
ul.submenu {
    width: 200%;
}
```

Figure 5-19 highlights the style rule within the media query for tablet devices.

Figure 5-19   **Formatting the navigation menus for tablet devices**

```
@media only screen and (min-width: 481px) {

    ul.mainmenu > li {
        float: left;
        width: 20%;
    }

    ul.submenu {
        width: 200%;
    }
}
```

floats the menu list items horizontally with a width of 20% of the main menu

doubles the width of each submenu

4. Save your changes to the style sheet and then reload the tf_home.html file in your web browser.

5. Increase the width of the browser window beyond 480 pixels to switch from the mobile design to the tablet design. Verify that the submenu titles are now laid out horizontally and that if you hover your mouse pointer over the submenu titles, the contents of the submenu are made visible on the screen. See Figure 5-20.

Figure 5-20   **Pulldown menus for the tablet layout**

pulldown menu appears when the user hovers the mouse pointer over the submenu title

menu items floated side-by-side

opening the submenu pushes the subsequent page content down

width of the submenu is double the width of the submenu title

Trusted Friends Daycare provides childhood education and daycare, conveniently located for you and your child. We treat each child based on

© 2016 Cengage Learning; © Robert Kneschke/Shutterstock.com;

6. Scroll down as needed and note that the customer comments now appear at the bottom of the page because they were only hidden for the mobile version of this document.

Marjorie notices that opening the submenus pushes the subsequent page content down to make room for the submenu. She prefers the submenus to overlay the page content. You can accomplish this by placing the submenus with absolute positioning. Remember that objects placed with absolute positioning are removed from the document flow and thus, will overlay subsequent page content. To keep the submenus in their current position on the page, you'll make each main list item a container for its submenu by setting its `position` property to `relative`. Thus, each submenu will be placed using absolute positioning with its main list item. You will not need to set the `top` and `left` coordinates for these items because you'll use the default value of 0 for both. Because the submenus will overlay page content, Marjorie suggests you add a drop shadow so, when a submenu is opened, it will stand out more from the page content.

To position the navigation submenus:

1. Return to the **tf_styles1.css** style sheet in your editor.

2. Locate the style rule for the `ul.mainmenu > li` selector in the Tablet Styles section and add the following style:

`position: relative;`

3. Add the following style to the `ul.submenu` selector in the Tablet Styles section:

```
box-shadow: rgb(51, 51, 51) 5px 5px 15px;
position: absolute;
```

Figure 5-21 highlights the new styles.

Figure 5-21   Placing the pulldown menus with absolute positioning

applies the style rules only for screen devices with a minimum width of 481 pixels

```
@media only screen and (min-width: 481px) {

    ul.mainmenu > li {
        float: left;
        position: relative;
        width: 20%;
    }

    ul.submenu {
        box-shadow: rgb(51, 51, 51) 5px 5px 15px;
        position: absolute;
        width: 200%;
    }
}
```

places the menu list items using relative positioning

adds a drop shadow to each submenu

absolutely positions the submenus within each menu list item

4. Save your changes to the style sheet and then reload the tf_home.html file in your web browser.

5. Verify that when you open the pulldown menus, the subsequent page content is not shifted downward. Figure 5-22 highlights the final design for the tablet version of the home page.

Figure 5-22   Revised design of the pulldown menus

page content does not shift when the pulldown menu is opened

Trusted Friends Daycare provides childhood education and daycare, conveniently located for you and your child. We treat each child based on his

© Robert Kneschke/Shutterstock.com

You'll complete your work on the home page by creating the desktop version of the page design.

Creating a Desktop Design

Some of the designs that will be used in the desktop version of the page have already been placed in the Base Styles section of the tf_styles1.css style sheet. For example, the maximum width of the web page has been set to 1024 pixels. For browser windows that exceed that width, the web page will be displayed on a fixed background image of children playing. Other styles are inherited from the style rules for tablet devices. For example, desktop devices will inherit the style rule that floats the navigation submenus alongside each other within a single row. All of which illustrates an important principle in designing for multiple devices: *don't reinvent the wheel.* As much as possible allow your styles to build upon each other as you move to wider and wider screens.

However, there are some styles that you will have to implement only for desktop devices. With the wider screen desktop screens, you don't need to hide the submenus in a pulldown menu system. Instead you can display all of the links from the navigation list. You'll change the submenu background color to transparent so that it blends in with the navigation list and you'll remove the drop shadows you created for the tablet design. The submenus will always be visible, so you'll change their `display` property from none to `block`. Finally, you'll change their position to relative because you no longer want to take the submenus out of the document flow and you'll change their width to 100%. Apply the styles now to modify the appearance of the submenus.

To start working on the desktop design:

1. Return to the **tf_styles1.css** style sheet in your editor and within the media query for devices with screen widths 769 pixels or greater insert the following style rule to format the appearance of the navigation submenus.

```
ul.submenu {
    background: transparent;
    box-shadow: none;
    display: block;
    position: relative;
    width: 100%;
}
```

2. The navigation list itself needs to expand so that it contains all of its floated content. Add the following style rule to the media query for desktop devices:

```
nav.horizontal::after {
    clear: both;
    content: "";
    display: table;
}
```

3. Finally with no hidden submenus, there is no reason to have a submenu title. Add the following style rule to remove the submenu titles:

```
nav.horizontal a.submenuTitle {
    display: none;
}
```

Figure 5-23 highlights the new style rules in the desktop media query.

Figure 5-23 Adding design styles for the browser background and page body

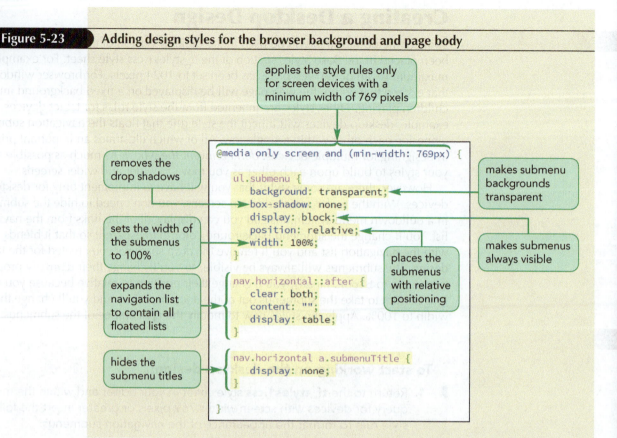

With a wider screen, you want to order to avoid long lines of text, which are difficult to read. Modify the layout of the desktop design so that the main article and the customer comments are floated side-by-side within the same row.

To change the layout of the article and aside elements:

1. Within the media query for desktop devices, add the following style rules to float the `article` and `aside` elements:

```
article {
    float: left;
    margin-right: 5%;
    width: 55%;
}
aside {
    float: left;
    width: 40%;
}
```

Figure 5-24 highlights the final style rules in the desktop media query.

Figure 5-24   **Styles for the article and aside elements**

```
nav.horizontal a.submenuTitle {
    display: none;
}

article {
    float: left;
    margin-right: 5%;
    width: 55%;
}

aside {
    float: left;
    width: 40%;
}
```

floats the main article with a width of 55% and a right margin of 5%

floats the aside element with a width of 40%

2. Save your changes to the style sheet and then reload tf_home.html in your browser.

Figure 5-25 shows the final appearance of the desktop design.

Figure 5-25   **Final desktop design for the Trusted Friends home page**

submenus are laid out horizontally and are always visible

article and aside elements are arranged in two columns

navigation list expands to contain floated content

© 2016 Cengage Learning; © Robert Kneschke/Shutterstock.com; © dotshock/Shutterstock.com; Shutterstock.com

3. Resize your web browser and verify that as you change the browser window width, the layout changes from the mobile to the tablet to the desktop design.

You show the final design of the home page to Marjorie. She is pleased by the changes you've made and likes that the page's content and layout will automatically adapt to different screen widths.

Problem Solving: Optimizing Your Site for the Mobile Web

The mobile browser market is a rapidly evolving and growing field with more new devices and apps introduced each month. Adapting your website for the mobile web is not a luxury, but a necessity.

A good mobile design matches the needs of consumers. Mobile users need quick access to main sources of information without a lot of the extra material often found in the desktop versions of their favorite sites. Here are some things to keep in mind as you create your mobile designs:

- *Keep it simple.* To accommodate the smaller screen sizes and slower connection speeds, scale down each page to a few key items and articles. Users are looking for quick and obvious information from their mobile sites.
- *Resize your images.* Downloading several images can bring a mobile device to a crawl. Reduce the number of images in your mobile design, and use a graphics package to resize the images so they are optimized in quality and sized for a smaller screen.
- *Scroll vertically.* Readers can more easily read your page when they only have to scroll vertically. Limit yourself to one column of information in portrait orientation and two columns in landscape.
- *Make your links accessible.* Clicking a small hypertext link is extremely difficult to do on a mobile device with a touch screen interface. Create hypertext links that are easy to locate and activate.

Above all, test your site on a variety of devices and under different conditions. Mobile devices vary greatly in size, shape, and capability. What works on one device might fail utterly on another. Testing your code on a desktop computer is only the first step; you may also need access to the devices themselves. Even emulators cannot always capture the nuances involved in the performance of an actual mobile device.

You've completed your work on the design of the Trusted Friends home page with a style sheet that seamlessly transitions between mobile, tablet, and desktop devices. In the next session, you'll explore how to use flexible boxes to achieve a responsive design.

REVIEW

Session 5.1 Quick Check

1. What is responsive design?
2. What are the three primary parts of responsive design theory?
3. Provide the code to create a `link` element that loads the talk.css style sheet for aural browsers.
4. Provide the general syntax of a CSS rule that loads style rules for braille devices.
5. Provide the general syntax of a CSS rule that loads style rules for screen devices up to a maximum width of 780 pixels.
6. Provide the code for a `link` element that loads the tablet.css style sheet for screen devices whose width ranges from 480 pixels up to 780 pixels (inclusive).
7. How should you arrange the media queries in your style sheet if you want to support mobile, tablet, and desktop devices?
8. What is the difference between the visual viewport and the layout viewport?
9. Provide the code that sets the width of the layout viewport equal to the width of the device with an initial scale factor of 1.

Session 5.2 Visual Overview:

A **flexbox** contains items whose size automatically expands or contracts to match the dimensions of the box.

To create a flexbox, set the `display` property to flex (or –webkit-flex for older browsers).

To define the orientation of the flexbox and whether items can wrap to a new line, apply the `flex-flow` property.

Use the `flex` property to define the size of the flex items and how they will grow or shrink in response to the changing size of the flexbox.

The **flex-basis** value provides the basis or initial size of the item prior to flexing.

The **flex-grow** value specifies how fast the item grows above its basis size relative to other items in the flexbox.

The **flex-shrink** value specifies how fast the item shrinks below its basis size relative to other items in the flexbox.

```css
body {
    display: -webkit-flex;
    display: flex;
    -webkit-flex-flow: row wrap;
    flex-flow: row wrap;
}

header, footer {
    width: 100%;
}

aside {
    -webkit-flex: 1 1 120px;
    flex: 1 1 120px;
}

section#main {
    -webkit-flex: 3 1 361px;
    flex: 3 1 361px;
}

section#topics {
    display: -webkit-flex;
    display: flex;
    -webkit-flex-flow: row wrap;
    flex-flow: row wrap;
}

section#topics article {
    -webkit-flex: 1 1 200px;
    flex: 1 1 200px;
}
```

© 2016 Cengage Learning; © dotshock/Shutterstock.com; BenBois/openclipart; JMLevick/openclipart

Flexbox Layouts

With narrower screens, a flexbox layout automatically places items within a single column.

With wider screens, the items are free to expand, automatically placing themselves into multiple columns.

Introducing Flexible Boxes

So far our layouts have been limited to a grid system involving floating elements contained within a fixed or fluid grid of rows and columns. One of the challenges of this approach under responsive design is that you need to establish a different grid layout for each class of screen size. It would be much easier to have a single specification that automatically adapts itself to the screen width without requiring a new layout design. One way of achieving this is with flexible boxes.

Defining a Flexible Box

A flexible box or flexbox is a box containing items whose sizes can shrink or grow to match the boundaries of the box. Thus, unlike a grid system in which each item has a defined size, flexbox items adapt themselves automatically to the size of their container. This makes flexboxes a useful tool for designing layouts that can adapt to different page sizes.

Items within a flexbox are laid out along a **main axis**, which can point in either the horizontal or vertical direction. Perpendicular to the main axis is the **cross axis**, which is used to define the height or width of each item. Figure 5-26 displays a diagram of two flexboxes with items arranged either horizontally or vertically along the main axis.

Figure 5-26   **Horizontal and vertical flexboxes**

© 2016 Cengage Learning

To define an element as a flexbox, apply either of the following `display` styles

    display: flex;

or

    display: inline-flex;

where a value of `flex` starts the flexbox on a new line (much as a block element starts on a new line) and a value of `inline-flex` keeps the flexbox in-line with its surrounding content.

Cross-Browser Flexboxes

The syntax for flexboxes has gone through major revisions as it has developed from the earliest drafts to the latest specifications. Many older browsers employ a different flexbox syntax, in some cases replacing the word *flex* with *box* or *flexbox*. The complete list of browser extensions that define a flexbox would be entered as:

```
display: -webkit-box;
display: -moz-box;
display: -ms-flexbox;
display: -webkit-flex:
display: flex;
```

To simplify the code in the examples that follow, you will limit your code to the latest WebKit browser extension and the current W3C specification. This will cover the current browsers at the time of this writing. However, if you need to support older browsers, you may have to include a long list of browser extensions for each flex property.

Setting the Flexbox Flow

By default, flexbox items are arranged horizontally starting from the left and moving to the right. To change the orientation of the flexbox, apply the following `flex-direction` property

```
flex-direction: direction;
```

where *direction* is row (the default), `column`, `row-reverse`, or `column-reverse`. The `row` option lays out the flex items from left to right, `column` creates a vertical layout starting from the top and moving downward, and the `row-reverse` and `column-reverse` options lay out the items bottom-to-top and right-to-left respectively.

Flex items will all try to fit within a single line, either horizontally or vertically. But if they can't, those items can wrap to a new line as needed by applying the following `flex-wrap` property to the flexbox

```
flex-wrap: type;
```

where *type* is either `nowrap` (the default), `wrap` to wrap the flex items to a new line, or `wrap-reverse` to wrap flex items to a new line starting in the opposite direction from the current line. For example, the following style rules create a flexbox in which the items are arranged in a column starting from the top and going down with any flex items that wrap to the second column starting from the bottom and moving up.

```
display: flex;
flex-direction: column;
flex-wrap: wrap-reverse;
```

Additional items in this flexbox will continue to follow a snake-like curve with the third column starting at the top, moving down, and so forth.

Both the `flex-direction` and `flex-wrap` properties can be combined into the following `flex-flow` style

```
flex-flow: direction wrap;
```

where *direction* is the direction of the flex items and *wrap* defines whether the items will be wrapped to a new line when needed. Figure 5-27 shows an example of flexboxes laid out in rows and columns in which the flex items are forced to wrap to a new line. Note that the column-oriented flexbox uses wrap-reverse to start the new column on the bottom rather than the top.

TIP

Some older browsers do not support the `flex-flow` property, so for full cross-browser support, you might use the `flex-direction` and `flex-wrap` properties instead.

Figure 5-27 Flexbox layouts

© 2016 Cengage Learning

Defining a Flexbox

- To display an element as a flexbox, apply the display style

  display: flex;

- To set the orientation of the flexbox, apply the style

  flex-direction: *direction*;

  where *direction* is row (the default), column, row-reverse, or column-reverse.
- To define whether or not flex items wrap to a new line, apply the style

  flex-wrap: *type*;

  where *type* is either nowrap (the default), wrap to wrap flex items to a new line, or wrap-reverse to wrap flex items to a new line starting in the opposite direction from the current line.
- To define the flow of items within a flexbox, apply the style

  flex-flow: *direction wrap*;

  where *direction* is the direction of the flex items and *wrap* defines whether the items will be wrapped to a new line when needed.

Marjorie wants you to use flexboxes to design a page she's created describing the pre-k classes offered by Trusted Friends. She has already created the content of the page and several style sheets to format the appearance of the page elements. You'll create a style sheet that lays out the page content drawing from a library of flexbox styles.

To open the pre-k page and style sheet:

1. Use your editor to open the **tf_prek_txt.html** and **tf_flex_txt.css** files from the html05 ▸ tutorial folder. Enter **your name** and **the date** in the comment section of each file and save them as **tf_prek.html** and **tf_flex.css** respectively.

2. Return to the **tf_prek.html** file in your editor and, within the document head, create links to the **tf_reset.css**, **tf_styles2.css**, and **tf_flex.css** style sheets in that order.

3. Take some time to scroll through the contents of the document to become familiar with its contents and structure and then save your changes to the file, leaving it open.

4. Go to the **tf_flex.css** file in your editor.

5. Go to the Base Flex Styles section and insert the following style rules to display the entire page body as a flexbox oriented horizontally with overflow flex items wrapped to a new row as needed:

```
body {
    display: -webkit-flex;
    display: flex;

    -webkit-flex-flow: row wrap;
    flex-flow: row wrap;
}
```

Figure 5-28 highlights the new flexbox styles in the style sheet.

Include at least the WebKit browser extension for your flexbox style to ensure compatibility across browsers.

Figure 5-28   Setting the flex display style

```
/* =================
   Base Flex Styles
   =================
*/

body {
   display: -webkit-flex;
   display: flex;

   -webkit-flex-flow: row wrap;
   flex-flow: row wrap;
}
```

displays the page body as a flexbox

orients the flexbox by rows, wrapping to a new line as needed

WebKit browser extension

6. Save your changes to the file.

Now that you've defined the page body as a flexbox, you'll work with styles that define how items within a flexbox expand and contract to match the flexbox container.

Working with Flex Items

Flex items behave a lot like floated objects though with several advantages, including that you can float them in either the horizontal or vertical direction and that you can change the order in which they are displayed. While the size of a flex item can be fixed using the CSS `width` and `height` properties, they don't have to be. They can also be "flexed" — automatically adapting their size to fill the flexbox. A flex layout is fundamentally different from a grid layout and requires you to think about sizes and layout in a new way.

TIP

Because flexboxes can be aligned horizontally or vertically, the flex-basis property sets either the initial width or the initial height of the flex item depending on the orientation of the flexbox.

Setting the Flex Basis

When items are allowed to "flex" their rendered size is determined by three properties: the basis size, the growth value, and the shrink value. The basis size defines the initial size of the item before the browser attempts to fit it to the flexbox and is set using the following `flex-basis` property

```
flex-basis: size;
```

where *size* is one of the CSS units of measurement, a percentage of the size of the flexbox, or the keyword `auto` (the default), which sets the initial size of the flex item based on its content or the value of its `width` or `height` property. For example, the following style rule sets the initial size of the `aside` element to 200 pixels:

```
aside {
    flex-basis: 200px;
}
```

The `flex-basis` property should not be equated with the `width` and `height` properties used with grid layouts; rather, it serves only as a starting point. The actual rendered size of the `aside` element in this example is not necessarily 200 pixels but will be based on the size of the flexbox, as well as the size of the other items within the flexbox.

Defining the Flex Growth

Once the basis size of the item has been defined, the browser will attempt to expand the item into its flexbox. The rate at which a flex item grows from its basis size is determined by the following `flex-grow` property

```
flex-grow: value;
```

where *value* is a non-negative value that expresses the growth of the flex item relative to the growth of the other items in the flexbox. The default `flex-grow` value is 0, which is equivalent to not allowing the flex item to grow but to remain at its basis size. Different items within a flexbox can have different growth rates and the growth rate largely determines how much of the flexbox is ultimately occupied by each item.

Figure 5-29 shows an example of how changing the size of a flexbox alters the size of the individual flexbox items.

Figure 5-29 **Growing flex items beyond their basis size**

both flex items have the same basis size

second item grows at 3x the rate of the first as the flexbox expands

In the figure, the basis sizes of the two items are 100 pixels each with the growth of the first item set to 1 and the growth of the second item set to 3. The growth values indicate that as the flex items expand to fill the flexbox, item1 will increase 1 pixel for every 3 pixels that item2 increases. Thus, to fill up the remaining 200 pixels of a 400-pixel wide flexbox, 50 pixels will be allotted to the first item and 150 pixels will be allotted to the second item, resulting in final sizes of 150 pixels and 250 pixels respectively. If the width of the flexbox were to increase to 600 pixels, item1 and item2 will divide the extra 400 pixels once again in a ratio of 1 to 3. Item1 will have a total size of 200 pixels (100px + 100px) and item2 will expand to a size of 400 pixels (100px + 300px).

TIP

If all items have flex-grow set to 1 and an equal flex basis, they will always have an equal size within the flexbox.

Notice that unlike a grid layout, the relative proportions of the items under a flex layout need not be constant. For the layout shown in Figure 5-29, the two items share the space equally when the flexbox is 200 pixels wide, but at 400 pixels the first item occupies 37.5% of the box while the second item occupies the remaining 62.5%.

To keep a constant ratio between the sizes of the flex items, set their basis sizes to 0 pixels. For example, the following style rules will result in a flexbox in which the first item is always half the size of the second item no matter how wide or tall the flexbox becomes.

```
div#item1 {
    flex-basis: 0px;
    flex-grow: 1;
}
div#item2 {
    flex-basis: 0px;
    flex-grow: 2;
}
```

One of the great advantages of the flexible box layout is that you don't need to know how many items are in the flexbox to keep their relative proportions the same. The following style rule creates a layout for a navigation list in which each list item is assigned an equal size and grows at the same rate.

```
nav  ul {
    display: flex;
}

nav  ul  li {
    flex-basis: 0px;
    flex-grow: 1;
}
```

If there are four items in this navigation list, each will be 25% of the total list size and if at a later date a fifth item is added, those items will then be allotted 20% of the total size. Thus, unlike a grid layout, there is no need to revise the percentages to accommodate new entries in the navigation list; a flexible box layout handles that task automatically.

Note that if the flex-grow value is set to 0, the flex item will not expand beyond its basis size, making that basis value the maximum width or height of the item.

Defining the Shrink Rate

What happens when the flexbox size falls below the total space allotted to its flex items? There are two possibilities depending on whether the flexbox is defined to wrap its contents to a new line. If the flexbox-wrap property is set to wrap, one or more of the flex items will be shifted to a new line and expanded to fill in the available space on that line. Figure 5-30 shows a flexbox layout in which three items each have a basis size of 200 pixels with the same growth value of 1.

Figure 5-30   **Shrinking flex items smaller than their basis size**

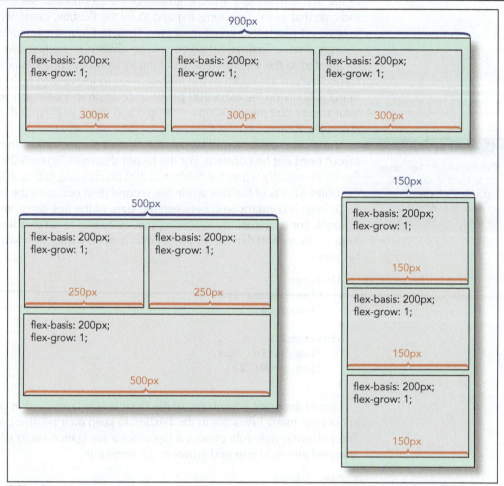

© 2016 Cengage Learning

As shown in the figure, as long as the flexbox is at least 600 pixels wide, the items will equally share a single row. However, once the flexbox size falls below 600 pixels, the three items can no longer share that row and the last item is wrapped to a new row. Once on that new row, it's free to fill up the available space while the first two items equally share the space on the first row. As the flexbox continues to contract, falling below 400 pixels, the first two items can no longer share a row and the second item now wraps to its own row. At this point the three items fill separate rows and as the flexbox continues to shrink, their sizes also shrink.

If the flexbox doesn't wrap to a new line as it is resized, then the flex items will continue to shrink, still sharing the same row or column. The rate at which they shrink below their basis size is given by the following `flex-shrink` property

```
flex-shrink: value;
```

where `value` is a non-negative value that expresses the shrink rate of the flex item relative to the shrinkage of the other items in the flexbox. The default `flex-shrink` value is 1. For example, in the following style rules, item1 and item2 will share the flexbox equally as long as the width of the flexbox is 400 pixels or greater.

```
div {
    display: flex;
    flex-wrap: nowrap;
}
```

```
div #item1 {
   flex-basis: 200px;
   flex-grow: 1;
   flex-shrink: 3;
}
div #item2 {
   flex-basis: 200px;
   flex-grow: 1;
   flex-shrink: 1;
}
```

However, once the flexbox falls below 400 pixels, the two items begin to shrink with item1 losing 3 pixels for every 1 pixel lost by item2. Note that if the `flex-shrink` value is set to 0, then the flex item will not shrink below its basis value, making that basis value the minimum width or height of the item.

The flex Property

All of the size values described above are usually combined into the following `flex` property

```
flex: grow shrink basis;
```

where *grow* defines the growth of the flex item, *shrink* provides its shrink rate, and *basis* sets the item's initial size. The default `flex` value is

```
flex: 0 1 auto;
```

which automatically sets the size of the flex item to match its content or the value of its `width` and `height` property. The flex item will not grow beyond that size but, if necessary, it will shrink as the flexbox contracts.

The `flex` property supports the following keywords:

- `auto`   Use to automatically resize the item from its default size (equivalent to `flex: 1 1 auto;`)
- `initial` The default value (equivalent to `flex: 0 1 auto;`)
- `none`   Use to create an inflexible item that will not grow or shrink (equivalent to `flex: 0 0 auto;`)
- `inherit` Use to inherit the flex values of its parent element

As with other parts of the flex layout model, the `flex` property has gone through several syntax changes on its way to its final specification. To support older browsers, use the browser extensions: `-webkit-box`, `-moz-box`, `-ms-flexbox`, `-webkit-flex`, and `flex` in that order.

REFERENCE

Sizing Flex Items

- To set the initial size of a flex item, apply the style

  `flex-basis: size;`

  where *size* is measured in one of the CSS units of measurement or as a percentage of the size of the flexbox or the keyword `auto` (the default).
- To define the rate at which a flex item grows from its basis size, apply the style

  `flex-grow: value;`

  where *value* is a non-negative value that expresses the growth of the flex item relative to the growth of the other items in the flexbox (the default is 0).
- To define the rate at which a flex item shrinks below its basis value, apply

  `flex-shrink: value;`

  where *value* is a non-negative value that expresses the shrink rate of the flex item relative to other items in the flexbox (the default is 0).
- To define the overall resizing of a flex item, apply

  `flex: grow shrink basis;`

  where *grow* defines the growth of the flex item, *shrink* provides its shrink rate, and *basis* sets the item's initial size.

Applying a Flexbox Layout

Now that you've seen how to size items within a flexbox, you can return to the layout for the Pre-K Classes page at Trusted Friends daycare. The `body` element, which you already set up as a flexbox, has four child elements: the page header, an `aside` element describing the daily class schedule, a `section` element describing the classes, and the page footer. Marjorie wants the header and the footer to always occupy a single row at 100% of the width of the page body. For wide screens, she wants the `aside` and `section` elements displayed side-by-side with one-fourth of the width assigned to the `aside` element and three-fourths to the `section` element. For narrow screens she wants the `aside` and `section` elements displayed within a single column. Figure 5-31 displays the flex layout that Marjorie wants you to apply.

Figure 5-31	Proposed flex layout for the Pre-K page

© 2016 Cengage Learning

Using the techniques of the first session, this would require media queries with one grid layout for narrow screens and a second grid layout for wide screens. However, you can accomplish the same effect with a single flex layout. First, you set the width of the body header and footer to 100% because they will always occupy their own row:

```
header, footer {
    width: 100%;
}
```

Then, you set the basis size of the `aside` and `section` elements to 120 and 361 pixels respectively. As long as the screen width is 481 pixels or greater, these two elements will be displayed side-by-side; however, once the screen width drops below 481 pixels, the elements will wrap to separate rows as illustrated in the narrow screen image in Figure 5-31. Because you want the main `section` element to grow at a rate three times faster than the `aside` element (in order to maintain the 3:1 ratio in their sizes), you set the `flex-growth` values to 1 and 3 respectively. The flex style rules are

```
aside {
    flex: 1 1 120px;
}
```

```
section#main {
    flex: 3 1 361px;
}
```

Note that you choose 481 pixels as the total initial size of the two elements to match the cutoff point in the media query between mobile and tablet/desktop devices. Generally, you want your flex items to follow the media query cutoffs whenever possible. Add these style rules to the tf_flex.css style sheet now.

To define the flex layout:

▸ **1.** Within the tf_flex.css file in your editor, add the following style rules to the Base Flex Styles section:

```
header, footer {
   width: 100%;
}

aside {
   -webkit-flex: 1 1 120px;
   flex: 1 1 120px;
}

section#main {
   -webkit-flex: 3 1 361px;
   flex: 3 1 361px;
}
```

Figure 5-32 highlights the newly added style rules to define the flex item sizes.

Figure 5-32   **Set the flex properties of the flex items in the page body**

```
body {
   display: -webkit-flex;
   display: flex;

   -webkit-flex-flow: row wrap;
   flex-flow: row wrap;
}

header, footer {
   width: 100%;
}

aside {
   -webkit-flex: 1 1 120px;
   flex: 1 1 120px;
}

section#main {
   -webkit-flex: 3 1 361px;
   flex: 3 1 361px;
}
```

displays the header and footer at a width of 100%, occupying an entire row

sets the initial size of the aside element to 120 pixels and sets the growth and shrink factors to 1

sets the initial size of the main section to 361 pixels and has it grow and shrink at a 3:1 ratio compared to the aside element

▸ **2.** Save your changes to the file and then open the tf_prek.html file in your web browser.

▸ **3.** Change the size of the browser window or use the device emulator tools in your browser to view the page under different screen widths. As shown in Figure 5-33, the layout of the page changes as the screen narrows and widens.

Figure 5-33   Flex layout under different screen widths

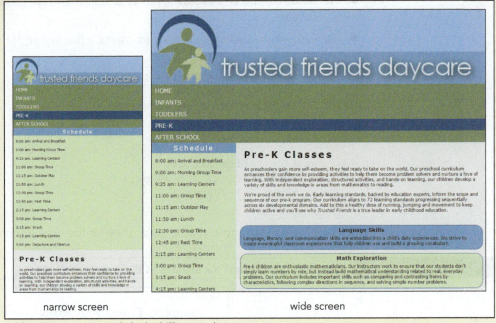

narrow screen   wide screen

© 2016 Cengage Learning; © dotshock/Shutterstock.com

Flexboxes can be nested within one another and a flex item can itself be a flexbox for its child elements. Within the topics section, Marjorie has created six articles describing different features of the center's pre-k curriculum. She wants these articles to share equal space within a row-oriented flexbox, with each article given a basis size of 200 pixels. The style rules are:

```
section#topics {
   display: flex;
   flex-flow: row wrap;
}

section#topics article {
   flex: 1 1 200px;
}
```

Marjorie also wants the items in the navigation list to appear in a row-oriented flexbox for tablet and desktop devices by adding the following style rules to the media query for screen devices whose width exceeds 480 pixels:

```
nav.horizontal ul {
   display: flex;
   flex-flow: row nowrap;
}

nav.horizontal li {
   flex: 1 1 auto;
}
```

The navigation list items will appear in a single row with no wrapping and the width of each item will be determined by the item's content so that longer entries are given more horizontal space. With the growth and shrink values set to 1, each list item will grow and shrink at the same rate, keeping the layout consistent across different screen widths.

Add these style rules now.

To lay out the topic articles and navigation list:

1. Return to the **tf_flex.css** file in your editor and go to the Base Flex Styles section.

2. Add the following style rules to create a flex layout for the page articles.

```css
section#topics {
    display: -webkit-flex;
    display: flex;
    -webkit-flex-flow: row wrap;
    flex-flow: row wrap;
}

section#topics article {
    -webkit-flex: 1 1 200px;
    flex: 1 1 200px;
}
```

Figure 5-34 highlights the style rules for the article topics layout.

Figure 5-34	Creating a flex layout for articles in the topics section

```css
section#main {
    -webkit-flex: 3 1 361px;
    flex: 3 1 361px;
}

section#topics {
    display: -webkit-flex;
    display: flex;
    -webkit-flex-flow: row wrap;
    flex-flow: row wrap;
}

section#topics article {
    -webkit-flex: 1 1 200px;
    flex: 1 1 200px;
}
```

displays the topics section as a flexbox

orients the flexbox as a row and wraps items to a new line as needed

sets the basis size of each article to 200 pixels, growing and shrinking at the same rate

3. Scroll down to the media query for tablet and desktop devices and add the following style rule to create a flex layout for the navigation list. (Indent your code to set it off from the media query braces.)

```css
nav.horizontal ul {
    display: -webkit-flex;
    display: flex;
    -webkit-flex-flow: row nowrap;
    flex-flow: row nowrap;
}

nav.horizontal li {
    -webkit-flex: 1 1 auto;
    flex: 1 1 auto;
}
```

Figure 5-35 highlights the style rules for the navigation list and list items.

Figure 5-35	Creating a flex layout for the navigation list

```
/*  ===========================================
     Tablet and Desktop Styles: 481px and greater
     ===========================================
*/

@media only screen and (min-width: 481px) {

   nav.horizontal ul {
      display: -webkit-flex;
      display: flex;
      -webkit-flex-flow: row nowrap;
      flex-flow: row nowrap;
   }

   nav.horizontal li {
      -webkit-flex: 1 1 auto;
      flex: 1 1 auto;
   }

}
```

displays the unordered list as a flexbox

orients the flex in the row direction with no wrapping

bases the size of each item on its content and has them grow and shrink at the same rate

4. Save your changes to the file and reload the **tf_prek.html** file in your web browser.

5. View the page under different screen widths and verify that, for tablet and desktop screen widths, the navigation list entries appear in a single row. Also, verify that the articles in the topics section flex from a single column layout to two or more rows of content. See Figure 5-36.

navigation list appears in a single row for tablet and desktop devices

articles flex in layout from a single column to a 2 × 3 grid, depending on the screen width

© 2016 Cengage Learning

Marjorie likes how using flexboxes has made it easy to create layouts that match a wide variety of screen sizes. However, she is concerned that under the single column layout used for mobile devices the daily schedule appears first before any description of the classes. She would like the daily schedule to appear at the bottom of the page. She asks if you can modify the layout to achieve this.

Reordering Page Content with Flexboxes

One of the principles of web page design is to, as much as possible, separate the page content from page design. However, a basic feature of any design is the order in which the content is displayed. Short of editing the content of the HTML file, there is not an easy way to change that order.

That at least was true before flexboxes. Under the flexbox model you can place the flex items in any order you choose using the following order property

```
order: value;
```

where value is an integer where items with smaller order values are placed before items with larger order values. For example, the following style arranges the div elements starting first with item2, followed by item3, and ending with item1. This is true regardless of how those div elements have been placed in the HTML document.

```
div#item1 {order: 100;}
div#item2 {order: -1;}
div#item3 {order: 5;}
```

TIP

If flex items have the same order value, they are arranged in document order.

Note that order values can be negative. The default order value is 0.

For complete cross-browser support, you can apply the following browser extensions with flex item ordering:

```
-webkit-box-ordinal-group: value;
-moz-box-ordinal-group: value;
-ms-flex-order: value;
-webkit-order: value;
order: value;
```

Most current browsers support the CSS specifications or the latest WebKit browser extension, so you will limit your code to those properties.

REFERENCE

Reordering a Flex Item

- To reorder a flex item, apply the style

  order: value;

  where value is an integer where items with smaller order values are placed before items with larger order values.

For mobile devices, Marjorie wants the page header displayed first, followed by the main section, the aside element, and ending with the page footer. Add style rules now to the mobile device media query in the tf_flex.css style sheet to reorder the flex items.

To lay out the topic articles and navigation list:

1. Return to the **tf_flex.css** file in your editor and go to the Mobile Devices media query.

2. Add the following style rules, indented to offset them from the braces in the media query:

```
aside {
    -webkit-order: 99;
    order: 99;
}

footer {
    -webkit-order: 100;
    order: 100;
}
```

Note that the other flex items will have a default order value of 0 and thus will be displayed in document order before the aside and footer elements.

Figure 5-37 highlights the style rules to set the order of the aside and footer elements.

Figure 5-37   **Setting the order of a flex item**

```
/*  ==========================
    Mobile Styles: 0 to 480px
    ==========================
*/

@media only screen and (max-width: 480px) {

    aside {
        -webkit-order: 99;
        order: 99;
    }

    footer {
        -webkit-order: 100;
        order: 100;
    }

}
```

places the aside element before the body footer

places the body footer at the end of the flexbox

3. Save your changes to the file and then reload the tf_prek.html file in your web browser.

4. Reduce the width of the browser window below 480 pixels to show the mobile layout. Verify that the class schedule now appears at the bottom of the file directly before the body footer.

You've completed the ordering and flex layout of the Pre-K Classes page. You'll conclude your review of flexboxes by examining how flex items can be arranged within the flexbox container.

Exploring Flexbox Layouts

You can control how flex items are laid out using the justify-content, align-items, and align-content properties. You examine each property to see how flexboxes can be used to solve layout problems that have plagued web designers for many years.

Aligning Items along the Main Axis

Recall from Figure 5-26 that flexboxes have two axes: the main axis along which the flex items flow and the cross axis, which is perpendicular to the main axis. By default, flex items are laid down at the start of the main axis. To specify a different placement, apply the following justify-content property

    justify-content: placement;

where placement is one of the following keywords:

- flex-start   Items are positioned at the start of the main axis (the default).
- flex-end   Items are positioned at the end of the main axis.
- center   Items are centered along the main axis.

- `space-between`   Items are distributed evenly with the first and last items aligned with the start and end of the main axis.
- `space-around`   Items are distributed evenly along the main axis with equal space between them and the ends of the flexbox.

Figure 5-38 shows the impact of different `justify-content` values on a flexbox oriented horizontally.

Figure 5-38   **Values of the justify-content property**

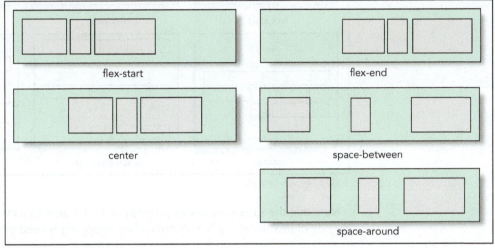

© 2016 Cengage Learning

Remember that, because items can flow in any direction within a flexbox, these diagrams will look different for flexboxes under column orientation or when the content flows from the right to the left. Note that the `justify-content` property has no impact when the items are flexed to fill the entire space. It is only impactful for flex items with fixed sizes that do not fill in the entire flexbox.

Aligning Flex Lines

The `align-content` property is similar to the `justify-content` property except that it arranges multiple lines of content along the flexbox's cross axis. The syntax of the `align-content` property is:

```
align-content: value;
```

where `value` is one of the following keywords:

- `flex-start`   Lines are positioned at the start of the cross axis.
- `flex-end`   Lines are positioned at the end of the cross axis.
- `stretch`   Lines are stretched to fill up the cross axis (the default).
- `center`   Lines are centered along the cross axis.
- `space-between`   Lines are distributed evenly with the first and last lines aligned with the start and end of the cross axis.
- `space-around`   Lines are distributed evenly along the cross axis with equal space between them and the ends of the cross axis.

Figure 5-39 displays the effect of the `align-content` values on three lines of flex items arranged within a flexbox.

Figure 5-39   **Values of the align-content property**

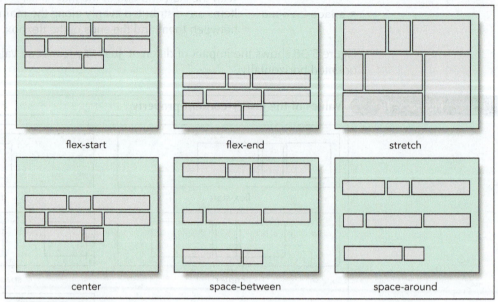

flex-start   flex-end   stretch

center   space-between   space-around

© 2016 Cengage Learning

Note that the `align-content` property only has an impact when there is more than one line of flex items, such as occurs when wrapping is used with the flexbox.

Aligning Items along the Cross Axis

Finally, the `align-items` property aligns each flex item about the cross axis, having the syntax

    align-items: value;

where *value* is one of the following keywords:

- `flex-start`   Items are positioned at the start of the cross axis.
- `flex-end`   Items are positioned at the end of the cross axis.
- `center`   Items are centered along the cross axis.
- `stretch`   Items are stretched to fill up the cross axis (the default).
- `baseline`   Items are positioned so that the baselines of their content align.

Figure 5-40 displays the effect of the `align-items` values on three flex items placed within a single line.

Figure 5-40   **Values of the align-items property**

© 2016 Cengage Learning

Note that the `align-items` property is only impactful when there is a single line of flex items. With multiple lines, you use the `align-content` property to layout the flexbox content. To align a single item out of a line of flex items, use the following `align-self` property

```
align-self: value;
```

where `value` is one of the alignment choices supported by the `align-items` property. For example, the following style rule places the footer at the end of the flexbox cross axis, regardless of the placement of the other flex items.

```
footer {
    align-self: flex-end;
}
```

Both the `align-content` and `align-items` properties have a default value of `stretch` so that the flex items are stretched to fill the space along the cross-axis. The effect is that all flex items within a row will share a common height. This can be observed earlier in Figure 5-36 in which all of the article boxes have the same height, regardless of their content. It's difficult to achieve this simple effect in a grid layout unless the height of each item is explicitly defined, but flexboxes do it automatically.

INSIGHT

Solving the Centering Problem with Flexboxes

One of the difficult layout challenges in web design is vertically centering an element within its container. While there are many different fixes and "hacks" to create vertical centering, it has not been easily achieved until flexboxes. By using the `justify-content` and `align-items` properties, you can center an object or group of objects within a flexbox container. For example, the following style rule centers the child elements of the `div` element both horizontally and vertically:

```
div {
    display: flex;
    justify-content: center;
    align-content: center;
}
```

For a single object or a group of items on a single line within a container, use the `align-items` property as follows:

```
div {
    display: flex;
    justify-content: center;
    align-items: center;
}
```

You can also use the `align-self` property to center one of the items in the flexbox, leaving the other items to be placed where you wish.

Creating a Navicon Menu

A common technique for mobile websites is to hide navigation menus but to indicate their presence with a **navicon**, which is a symbol usually represented as three horizontal lines ≡. When the user hovers or touches the icon, the navigation menu is revealed.

Marjorie has supplied you with a navicon image that she wants you to use with the mobile layout of the Pre-K Classes page. Add this image to the Pre-K Classes web page within the navigation list in the body header.

To insert the navicon image:

1. Return to the **tf_prek.html** file in your editor.

2. Directly after the opening `<nav>` tag in the body header, insert the following hypertext link and inline image.

   ```
   <a id="navicon" href="#">
     <img src="tf_navicon.png" alt="" />
   </a>
   ```

   Figure 5-41 highlights the code to create the navicon.

Figure 5-41   **Inserting the navicon**

```html
<nav class="horizontal">
   <a id="navicon" href="#"><img src="tf_navicon.png" alt="" /></a>
   <ul>
      <li><a href="tf_home.html">Home</a></li>
      <li><a href="#">Infants</a></li>
      <li><a href="#">Toddlers</a></li>
      <li><a href="#" id="currentPage">Pre-K</a></li>
      <li><a href="#">After School</a></li>
   </ul>
</nav>
```

navicon image

Next, you'll insert the styles to hide and display the contents of the navigation list in a style sheet named tf_navicon.css. You'll apply the same styles for navicon that you used in the last session to hide and display the navigation submenus in the Trusted Friends home page. As with those menus, you'll use the hover pseudo-class to display the navigation list links whenever the user hovers over the navicon, or in the case of mobile devices, touches the navicon. Add these styles now.

To add styles for the navicon image:

1. Within the document head of the **tf_prek.html** file, add a link to the **tf_navicon.css** style sheet file after the link for the tf_flex.css file. Save your changes to the file.

2. Use your editor to open the **tf_navicon_txt.css** files from the html05 ▶ tutorial folder. Enter *your name* and *the date* in the comment section of the file and save it as **tf_navicon.css**.

3. By default, the navicon will be hidden from the user. Go to the Base Styles section and add the following style rule:

   ```css
   a#navicon {
       display: none;
   }
   ```

4. The navicon will be displayed only for mobile devices. Go to the media query for mobile devices and add the following style rule to display the navicon.

   ```css
   a#navicon {
       display: block;
   }
   ```

5. When the navicon is displayed, you want the contents of the navigation list to be hidden. Add the following style rule within the mobile device media query:

   ```css
   nav.horizontal ul {
       display: none;
   }
   ```

6. Finally, add the following style rule to the mobile device query that displays the contents of the navigation list when the user hovers over the navicon or the contents of the navigation list.

   ```css
   a#navicon:hover+ul, nav.horizontal ul:hover {
       display: block;
   }
   ```

Figure 5-42 highlights the style rules for the navicon hypertext link.

Figure 5-42 Style rules for the navicon image

do not display the navicon for most devices →

```
a#navicon {
    display: none;
}

/* ===================================
    Mobile Devices: 0 to 480px
   ===================================
*/

@media only screen and (max-width: 480px) {
```

displays the navicon for mobile devices →

```
    a#navicon {
        display: block;
    }
```

hides the navigation list for mobile devices →

```
    nav.horizontal ul {
        display: none;
    }
```

displays the navigation list when the user hovers over the navicon or moves the mouse pointer over the navigation list →

```
    a#navicon:hover+ul, nav.horizontal ul:hover {
        display: block;
    }
}
```

▶ **7.** Save your changes to the file and then reload the tf_prek.html file in your browser or mobile devices. Resize the viewport as needed to display the mobile layout.

▶ **8.** Verify that as you hover over or touch the navicon, the navigation list appears, as shown in Figure 5-43.

Figure 5-43   **Action of the navicon for mobile devices**

© 2016 Cengage Learning; BenBois/openclipart

9. Verify that hovering over or touching other parts of the page hides the navigation list.

The methods you used in this tutorial to create pulldown menus and navicon menus represent what you can accomplish when limited to CSS3 and the `hover` pseudo-class. As you increase your skill and knowledge of HTML, you'll learn other, more efficient ways of creating mobile navigation menus using program scripts and web frameworks. If you want to explore how to take advantage of these tools, search the web for navicon libraries of pre-written code that can be inserted into your website.

Written Communication: Speeding up your Website by Minifying and Compressing

Once your website is working and you are ready to distribute it to the web, you have one task remaining: minifying your code. **Minifying** refers to the process of removing unnecessary characters that are not required for your site to execute properly. For example, the following text in a CSS file contains comments and line returns and blank spaces, which makes the text easy to read but these features are not required and have no impact on how the browser renders the page:

```
/* Tablet Styles */

nav.horizontal > ul > li {
    display: block;
}
```

A minified version of this code removes the comment and the extraneous white-space characters leaving the following compact version:

```
nav.horizontal>ul>li{display:block;}
```

Minifying has several important advantages:

- Minifying reduces the amount of bandwidth required to retrieve the website because the files are smaller.
- The smaller minified files load faster and are faster to process because extraneous code does not need to be parsed by the browser.
- A faster site provides a better user experience.
- Smaller files means less server space required to host the website.
- Search engines, such as Google, evaluate your website based on page load speed and will downgrade sites with bloated code that take too long to load.

There are several free tools available on the web to automate the minification process including CSS Minifier, Compress HTML, HTML Minifier, and CSS Compressor. Also, many HTML editors include built-in minifying tools. Remember, a minified file is still a text file and can be read (though with difficulty) in a text editor.

To further reduce your file sizes, consider compressing your files using utilities like Gzip. A compressed file is no longer in text format and must be uncompressed before it is readable. All modern browsers support Gzip compression for files retrieved from a server. Make sure you know how to properly configure your web server to serve Gzip-compressed file in a readable format to the browser.

The process of minifying your files is irreversible, so make sure you retain the version with the text in a readable format and all of your comments preserved. Most minifying and compression tools will make a backup of your original files.

You've completed your work on the design of the Pre-K Classes page for Trusted Friends Daycare. In the next session, you'll explore other uses of media queries by designing a page for printed output. You may close your files now.

Session 5.2 Quick Check

1. Provide code to display the body header as a flexbox. Include the browser extension for WebKit.
2. Provide a style to display flexbox items in a single line, oriented vertically starting from the bottom and moving up.
3. Provide a style that sets the initial size of a flex item to 250 pixels.
4. Provide a style that sets the growth rate of the flex item to 4.
5. What two things can happen when a flex item drops below its basis size?
6. Provide a style rule that sets the flex size of all `section` elements that are direct children of the page body be equal regardless of the size of the flexbox.
7. What property should be applied to reorder the placement of a flex item?
8. Provide a style to center the flex items along the flexbox's main axis.
9. Provide a style to center the flex items along the flexbox's cross axis.

Session 5.3 Visual Overview:

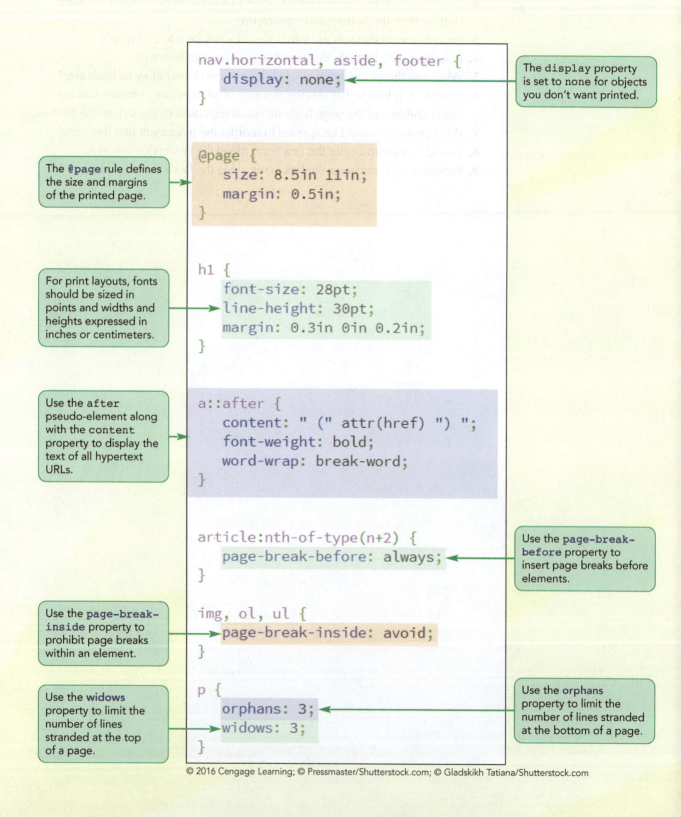

The @page rule defines the size and margins of the printed page.

For print layouts, fonts should be sized in points and widths and heights expressed in inches or centimeters.

Use the after pseudo-element along with the content property to display the text of all hypertext URLs.

Use the page-break-inside property to prohibit page breaks within an element.

Use the widows property to limit the number of lines stranded at the top of a page.

The display property is set to none for objects you don't want printed.

Use the page-break-before property to insert page breaks before elements.

Use the orphans property to limit the number of lines stranded at the bottom of a page.

```css
nav.horizontal, aside, footer {
    display: none;
}

@page {
    size: 8.5in 11in;
    margin: 0.5in;
}

h1 {
    font-size: 28pt;
    line-height: 30pt;
    margin: 0.3in 0in 0.2in;
}

a::after {
    content: " (" attr(href) ") ";
    font-weight: bold;
    word-wrap: break-word;
}

article:nth-of-type(n+2) {
    page-break-before: always;
}

img, ol, ul {
    page-break-inside: avoid;
}

p {
    orphans: 3;
    widows: 3;
}
```

Print Styles

> Page size is set at 8.5 inches by 11 inches with a 0.5 inch margin in portrait orientation.

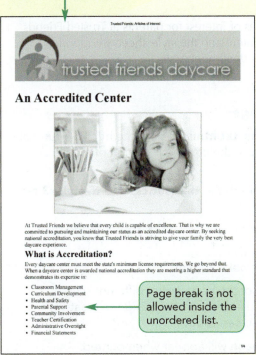

An Accredited Center

At Trusted Friends we believe that every child is capable of excellence. That is why we are committed to pursuing and maintaining our status as an accredited daycare center. By seeking national accreditation, you know that Trusted Friends is striving to give your family the very best daycare experience.

What is Accreditation?

Every daycare center must meet the state's minimum license requirements. We go beyond that. When a daycare center is awarded national accreditation they are meeting a higher standard that demonstrates its expertise in:

- Classroom Management
- Curriculum Development
- Health and Safety
- Parental Support
- Community Involvement
- Teacher Certification
- Administrative Oversight
- Financial Statements

> Page break is not allowed inside the unordered list.

page 1

Our commitment to accreditation gives you assurance we provide a positive educational experience for your child.

How does Accreditation Work?

Every other year we go through an intense review by recognized and esteemed national accreditation agencies. Their positive reports (available for inspection) confirm that we are providing a clean, safe, and positive environment for our children. Accreditation verifies that our teachers are qualified and fully engaged in giving our children a first-class educational experience.

Once we've completed the entire accreditation self-study process, trained professionals from our accrediting agencies conduct on-site visits to validate our compliance with national early childhood education standards. But accreditation doesn't just take place every two years. It's an ongoing process of self-evaluation, discussion, and parental reviews.

We encourage parents to help us improve our center and become better stewards for their children. You can part of the accreditation process as we work together to make Trusted Friends a great neighborhood center.

Who Provides Accreditation?

There are several national organizations that provide accreditation services. Who a center chooses for oversight is important. Trusted Friends pursues national accreditation from three of the most respected national early childhood accreditation agencies:

- National Association for Youth Care (**http://www.example.com/nayc**)
- United Accreditation for Early Care and Education (**http://www.example.com/uaece**)
- National Daycare Accreditation (**http://www.example.com/nda**)

Feel free to contact us to discuss accreditation and learn more about our standards for care and education.

> Hypertext URLs are displayed in bold after the hypertext link.

page 2

Our Community

> Page break is inserted before the article element, starting it on a new page.

Trusted Friends is committed to improving the lives of children in our community. Our expertise in caring for the children at our daycare center gives us a unique understanding of child development, education issues, and parenting. Trusted Friends has partnered with several community organizations that advocate for poor and needy children and families.

We don't think of it as charity. It's part of our calling.

Improving Literacy

Part of Trusted Friend's mission is to promote literacy, which is key to education and a fulfilling life. We support reading programs and national literacy efforts initiated at both the local and national level. These efforts include providing early access to books and other reading material. We are also in the Raised by Reading (**http://www.example.com/rbr**) program, helping parents share the reading experience with their children.

Promoting Partnerships

We are proud of our support for the Big Siblings (**http://www.example.com/bs**) organization. Several of our educators are Big Sibling mentors and we provide meeting space and monthly activities for this fine group. We are also deeply involved with the Young Care Nursery (**http://www.example.com/ycn**) organization, working to prevent child abuse and neglect. We partner with other caregivers committed to strengthening families in the community. For example we are a charter member of Sunflower Friends (**http://www.example.com/sf**) , which creates learning and enrichment opportunities for underprivileged children, helping them to realize their potential and recognize their inherent dignity.

Please contact us if you believe that Trusted Friends can be a partner with your group in improving the lives of children and families in our community.

page 3

Designing for Printed Media

So far your media queries have been limited to screens of different widths. In this session you'll explore how to apply media queries to print devices and work with several CSS styles that apply to printed output. To do this you'll create a **print style sheet** that formats the printed version of your web document.

Previewing the Print Version

Marjorie has created a page containing articles of interest for parents at Trusted Friends Daycare. She has already written the page content and the style sheets for mobile, tablet, and desktop devices. Open the articles document now.

To open the Articles of Interest page:

◗ **1.** Use your editor to open the **tf_articles_txt.html** file from the html05 ▶ tutorial folder. Enter *your name* and *the date* in the comment section of the file and save it as **tf_articles.html**.

◗ **2.** Within the document head, create links to the **tf_reset.css** and **tf_styles3.css** style sheet files in that order.

◗ **3.** Scroll through the document to become familiar with its contents and then save your changes to file, but do not close it.

◗ **4.** Open the **tf_articles.html** file in your web browser.

◗ **5.** Take some time to view the contents of the page under different screen resolutions, noting how Marjorie has used responsive design to create different page layouts based on the screen width.

Now, you'll examine how Marjorie's page will appear when printed.

◗ **6.** Use the Print Preview command within your browser to preview how this page will appear when printed. Figure 5-44 shows a preview of the first two pages of the print version using a black and white printer.

Figure 5-44	**Print version of the Articles of Interest page**

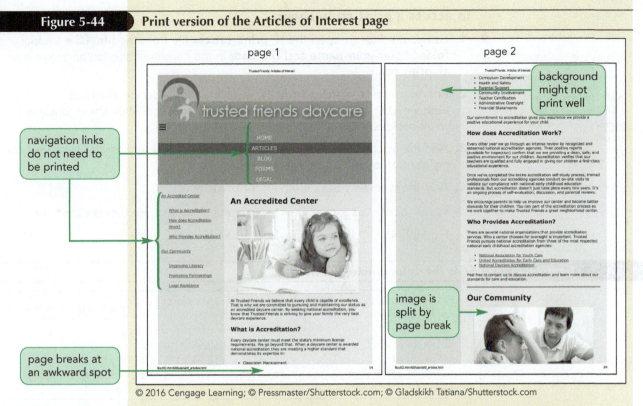

© 2016 Cengage Learning; © Pressmaster/Shutterstock.com; © Gladskikh Tatiana/Shutterstock.com

Trouble? Depending on your browser and printer, your print preview might appear different from the preview shown in Figure 5-44.

Browsers support their own internal style sheet to format the print versions of the web pages they encounter. However, their default styles might not always result in the best printouts. Marjorie points out that the print version of her page has several significant problems:

- The printed version includes two navigation lists, neither of which have a purpose in a printout.
- Page breaks have been placed in awkward places, splitting paragraphs and images in two.
- Background colors, while looking good on a screen, might not print well.

Marjorie would like you to design a custom print style sheet that fixes these problems by removing unnecessary page elements and choosing page breaks more intelligently.

Applying a Media Query for Printed Output

To apply a print style sheet, you use the `media` attribute in your `link` elements to target style sheets to either screen devices or print devices. Modify the tf_articles.html file now to access a new style sheet named tf_print.css into which you include your print styles.

To access a print style sheet:

1. Use your editor to open the **tf_print_txt.css** file from the html05 ▸ tutorial folder. Enter **your name** and **the date** in the comment section and save it as **tf_print.css**.

To avoid mixing screen styles with print styles, identify styles common to both devices with the media type *all*.

2. Return to the **tf_articles.html** file in your editor. Add the attribute media="all" to the link element for the tf_reset.css style sheet to apply it to all devices.

3. Add the attribute media="screen" to the link element for the tf_styles3.css style sheet to apply it only to screen devices.

4. Add the following link element for print styles:

```
<link href="tf_print.css" rel="stylesheet" media="print" />
```

Figure 5-45 highlights the revised link elements in the file.

Figure 5-45 Style sheets for different devices

```
<title>Trusted Friends: Articles of Interest</title>              styles for all devices
<meta charset="utf-8" />
<meta name="viewport" content="width=device-width, initial-scale=1" />
<link href="tf_reset.css" rel="stylesheet" media="all" />
<link href="tf_styles3.css" rel="stylesheet" media="screen" />
<link href="tf_print.css" rel="stylesheet" media="print" />
</head>
```

styles for print devices

styles for screen devices

5. Save your changes to the file and close it.

You'll start designing the print version of this page by hiding those page elements that should not be printed, including the navigation list, the aside element, and the body footer.

To hide elements in the print version:

1. Return to the **tf_print.css** file in your editor.

2. Go to the Hidden Objects section and add the following style rule:

```
nav.horizontal, aside, footer {
    display: none;
}
```

Figure 5-46 highlights the style rule to hide page elements.

Figure 5-46   **Hiding page elements for printing**

sets the display of the navigation list, aside element, and body footer to do not display

```
/* Hidden Objects */

nav.horizontal, aside, footer {
    display: none;
}
```

3. Save your changes to the file and then reload the tf_articles.html file in your browser and preview the printed output. Verify that the navigation lists, aside elements, and body footer are not displayed in the printed version.

Next, you'll define the page size of the print version of this document.

Working with the @page Rule

In CSS every printed page is defined as a **page box**, composed of two areas: the **page area**, which contains the content of the document, and the **margin area**, which contains the space between the printed content and the edges of the page.

Styles are applied to the page box using the following @page rule

```
@page {
    style rules
}
```

where `styles rules` are the styles applied to the page. The styles are limited to defining the page size and the page margin. For example, the following @page rule sets the size of the page margin to 0.5 inches:

```
@page {
        margin: 0.5in;
}
```

The page box does not support all of the measurement units you've used with the other elements. For example, pages do not support the em or ex measurement units. In general, you should use measurement units that are appropriate to the dimensions of your page, such as inches or centimeters.

Setting the Page Size

Because printed media can vary in size and orientation, the following size property allows web authors to define the dimensions of the printed page:

```
size: width height;
```

TIP

Users can override the page sizes and orientations set in @page rule by changing the options in their print dialog box.

where `width` and `height` are the width and height of the page. Thus to define a page that is 8.5 inches wide by 11 inches tall with a 1-inch margin, you would apply the following style rule:

```
@page {
    size: 8.5in 11in;
    margin: 1in;
}
```

You can replace the `width` and `height` values with the keyword `auto` (to let browsers determine the page dimensions) or `inherit` (to inherit the page size from the parent element). If a page does not fit into the dimensions specified in the @page rule, browsers will either rotate the page or rescale it to fit within the defined page size.

Using the Page Pseudo-Classes

By default, the @page rule is applied to every page of the printed output. However if the output covers several pages, you can define different styles for different pages by adding the following pseudo-class to the `@page` rule:

```
@page:pseudo-class {
      style rules
}
```

where *pseudo-class* is `first` for the first page of the printout, `left` for the pages that appear on the left in double-sided printouts, or `right` for pages that appear on the right in double-sided printouts. For example, if you are printing on both sides of the paper, you might want to create mirror images of the margins for the left and right pages of the printout. The following styles result in pages in which the inner margin is set to 5 centimeters and the outer margin is set to 2 centimeters:

```
@page:left {margin: 3cm 5cm 3cm 2cm;}
@page:right {margin: 3cm 2cm 3cm 5cm;}
```

Page Names and the Page Property

To define styles for pages other than the first, left, or right, you first must create a page name for those styles as follows

```
@page name {
    style rules
}
```

where *name* is the label given to the page. The following code defines a page style named wideMargins used for pages in which the page margin is set at 10 centimeters on every side:

```
@page wideMargins {
    margin: 10cm;
}
```

Once you define a page name, you can apply it to any element in your document. The content of the element will appear on its own page, with the browser automatically inserting page breaks before and after the element if required. To assign a page name to an element, you use the following `page` property

```
selector {
    page: name;
}
```

where *selector* identifies the element that will be displayed on its own page, and *name* is the name of a previously defined page style. Thus the following style rule causes all block quotes to be displayed on separate page(s) using the styles previously defined as the wideMargins page:

```
blockquote {
    page: wideMargins;
}
```

REFERENCE

Creating and Applying Page Styles

- To define a page box for the printed version of a document, use the CSS rule

```
@page {
    size: width height;
}
```

where *width* and *height* are the width and height of the page.
- To define the page styles for different output pages, use the rule

```
@page:pseudo-class {
    style rules
}
```

where *pseudo-class* is `first` for the first page of the printout, `left` for the pages that appear on the left in double-sided printouts, or `right` for pages that appear on the right in double-sided printouts.
- To create a named page for specific page styles, apply the rule

```
@page name {
    style rules
}
```

where *name* is the label assigned to the page style.
- To apply a named page style, use the rule

```
selector {
    page: name;
}
```

where *selector* identifies the element that will be displayed on its own page, and *name* is the name of a previously defined page style.

You'll use the `@page` rule to define the page size for the printed version of the Articles of Interest document. Marjorie suggests that you set the page size to 8.5 × 11 inches with 0.5-inch margins.

To define the printed page size:

1. Return to the **tf_print.css** file in your editor.

2. Go to the Page Box Styles section and add the following rule:

```
@page {
    size: 8.5in 11in;
    margin: 0.5in;
}
```

Figure 5-47 highlights the rule to set the page size.

Figure 5-47 Setting the page size

sets the page to 8.5 inches wide by 11 inches long

```
/* Page Box Styles */

@page {
    size: 8.5in 11in;
    margin: 0.5in;
}
```

sets the margin to 0.5 inches around the page content

3. Save your changes to the file.

With printed output, widths and heights are measured not in pixels but in inches or centimeters. Font sizes are not measured in pixels but rather in points. With that in mind, create styles to format the sizes of the text and graphics on the page.

To format the printed text:

1. Go to the Typography Styles section and insert the following styles to format the appearance of h1 and h2 headings and paragraphs:

```
h1 {
    font-size: 28pt;
    line-height: 30pt;
    margin: 0.3in 0in 0.2in;
}

h2 {
    font-size: 20pt;
    margin: 0.1in 0in 0.1in 0.3in;
}

p {
    font-size: 12pt;
    margin: 0.1in 0in 0.1in 0.3in;
}
```

2. Within the List Styles section, add the following style rules to format the appearance of unordered lists:

```
ul {
    list-style-type: disc;
    margin-left: 0.5in;
}
```

Figure 5-48 shows the typography and list styles in the print style sheet.

Figure 5-48   **Typographical formats**

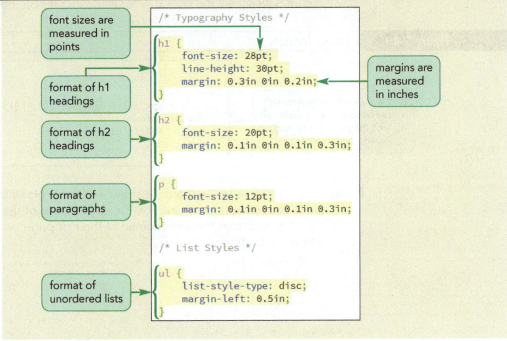

Next, you'll format the appearance of images on the page.

To format the printed images:

1. Within the Image Styles section, add the following style rule to format the appearance of inline images within each `article` element:

```
article img {
   border: 2px solid rgb(191, 191,191);
   display: block;
   margin: 0.25in auto;
   width: 65%;
}
```

Figure 5-49 shows the style rule for inline images on the printed page.

Figure 5-49   **Image formats**

displays all article images with a gray border, with a width of 65% of the page body, and centered horizontally

```
/* Image Styles */

article img {
   border: 2px solid rgb(191, 191, 191);
   display: block;
   margin: 0.25in auto;
   width: 65%;
}
```

2. Save your changes to the style sheet and then reload the tf_articles.html file in your browser and preview the appearance of the printed page. Figure 5-50 shows the appearance of the first page printed using a black and white printer.

| Figure 5-50 | **Preview of the first printed page** |

Trusted Friends: Articles of Interest

An Accredited Center

print version
of the images

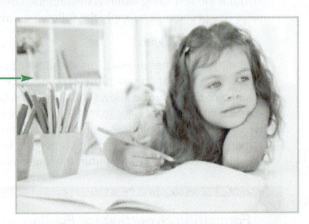

At Trusted Friends we believe that every child is capable of excellence. That is why we are committed to pursuing and maintaining our status as an accredited daycare center. By seeking national accreditation, you know that Trusted Friends is striving to give your family the very best daycare experience.

What is Accreditation?

Every daycare center must meet the state's minimum license requirements. We go beyond that. When a daycare center is awarded national accreditation they are meeting a higher standard that demonstrates its expertise in:

- Classroom Management
- Curriculum Development
- Health and Safety
- Parental Support
- Community Involvement
- Teacher Certification
- Administrative Oversight
- Financial Statements

file:///D:/html05/tutorial/tf_articles.html   1/4

Marjorie notices that all of the hyperlinks in the document appear in blue and underlined as determined by the default browser style. While this identifies the text as a hypertext link, it doesn't provide the reader any information about that link. She asks you to modify the style sheet to fix this problem.

Formatting Hypertext Links for Printing

Because printouts are not interactive, it's more useful for the reader to see the URL of a hypertext link so that he or she can access that URL at another time. To append the text of a link's URL to the linked text, you can apply the following style rule:

```
a::after {
    content: " (" attr(href) ") ";
}
```

TIP

Be sure to include blank spaces around the href value so that the URL does not run into the surrounding text.

This style rule uses the `after` pseudo-element along with the `content` property and the `attr()` function to retrieve the text of the `href` attribute and add it to the contents of the a element.

You should be careful when using this technique. Appending the text of a long and complicated URL will make your text difficult to read and might break your page layout if the text string extends beyond the boundaries of its container. One way to solve this problem is to apply the following `word-wrap` property to the URL text:

```
word-wrap: type;
```

where *type* is either `normal` (the default) or `break-word`. A value of `normal` breaks a text string only at common break points such as the white space between words. A value of `break-word` allows long text to be broken at arbitrary points, such as within a word, if that is necessary to make the text string fit within its container. Because a URL has no common break points such as blank spaces, applying the `break-word` option ensures that the text string of the URL will be kept to a manageable length by breaking it as needed to fit within the page layout.

REFERENCE

Formatting Hypertext for Printing

- To add the URL after a hypertext link, apply the style rule:

```
a::after {
    content: " (" attr(href) ") ";
}
```

- To automatically wrap the text of long URLs as needed, add the following style to the link text:

```
word-wrap: break-word;
```

Format the appearance of hypertext links in the document to display each link's URL and to display the hypertext links in a black bold font with no underlining, then use the `word-wrap` property to keep long URLs from extending beyond the boundaries of their container.

To format the hypertext links:

1. Return to the **tf_print.css** file in your editor and go to Hypertext Styles section, inserting the following styles to format the appearance of all hypertext links, appending the URL of each link:

```
a {
    color: black;
    text-decoration: none;
}

a::after {
    content: " (" attr(href) ") ";
    font-weight: bold;
    word-wrap: break-word;
}
```

Figure 5-51 describes the style rules used to format printed hypertext links.

Figure 5-51   **Formatting printed hypertext links**

```
/* Hypertext Styles */

a {
    color: black;
    text-decoration: none;
}

a::after {
    content: " (" attr(href) ") ";
    font-weight: bold;
    word-wrap: break-word;
}
```

displays hypertext links in black with no underlining

adds the URL of the hypertext link in a bold font

allows the URL to wrap in order to preserve page layout

2. Save your changes to the style sheet and then reload the tf_articles.html file in your browser and preview the page printout. Figure 5-52 shows the appearance of the printed hypertext links found on the second page of Marjorie's printout.

Figure 5-52   Preview of the hypertext links on page 2

Trusted Friends: Articles of Interest

How does Accreditation Work?

Every other year we go through an intense review by recognized and esteemed national accreditation agencies. Their positive reports (available for inspection) confirm that we are providing a clean, safe, and positive environment for our children. Accreditation verifies that our teachers are qualified and full engaged in giving our children a first-class educational experience.

Once we've completed the entire accreditation self-study process, trained professionals from our accrediting agencies conduct on-site visits to validate our compliance with national early childhood education standards. But accreditation doesn't just take place every two years. It's an ongoing process of self-evaluation, discussion, and parental reviews. We encourage our parents to help us improve our center and become better stewards for their children.

Who Provides Accreditation?

Trusted Friends pursues national accreditation from three of the most respected national early childhood accreditation agencies:

- National Association for Youth Care (**http://www.example.com/nayc**)
- United Accreditation for Early Care and Education (**http://www.example.com/uaece**)
- National Daycare Accreditation (**http://www.example.com/nda**)

Feel free to contact us to discuss accreditation and learn more about our standards for care and education.

URL of each hypertext link

Our Community

Trusted Friends is committed to improving the lives of children in our community. Our expertise in caring for the children at our daycare center gives us a unique understanding of child development, education issues, and parenting. Trusted Friends has partnered with several community organizations that advocate for poor and needy children and families. We don't think of it as charity. It's part of our calling.

2/3

© Gladskikh Tatiana/Shutterstock.com

You can search the web for several free scripting tools that give you more options for how your URLs should be printed, including scripts that automatically append all URLs as footnotes at the end of the printed document.

Working with Page Breaks

When a document is sent to a printer, the browser determines the location of the page breaks unless that information is included as part of the print style sheet. To manually insert a page break either directly before or directly after an element, apply the following `page-break-before` or `page-break-after` properties:

```
page-break-before: type;
page-break-after: type;
```

where `type` has the following possible values:

- `always` Use to always place a page break before or after the element
- `avoid` Use to never place a page break
- `left` Use to place a page break where the next page will be a left page
- `right` Use to place a page break where the next page will be a right page
- `auto` Use to allow the printer to determine whether or not to insert a page break
- `inherit` Use to insert the page break style from the parent element

For example, if you want each h1 heading to start on a new page you would apply the following style rule to insert a page break before each heading:

```
h1 {
    page-break-before: always;
}
```

REFERENCE

Adding a Page Break

- To set the page break style directly before an element, apply the property

  ```
  page-break-before: type;
  ```

  where `type` is always, avoid, left, right, auto, or inherit.
- To set the page break style directly after an element, apply

  ```
  page-break-after: type;
  ```

After the first article, Marjorie wants each subsequent article to start on a new page. To select every article after the initial article, use the selector

```
article:nth-of-type(n+2)
```

which selects the second, third, fourth, and so on article elements in the document (see "Exploring the nth-of-type Pseudo-class" in Tutorial 2.) To ensure that each of the selected articles starts on a new page, insert the page break before the article using the following style rule:

```
article:nth-of-type(n+2) {
    page-break-before: always;
}
```

Add this style rule to the print style sheet now.

To print each article on a new page:

1. Go to the Page Break Styles section and insert the following style rule:

```
article:nth-of-type(n+2) {
    page-break-before: always;

}
```

Figure 5-53 highlights the style rule to insert the article page breaks.

| Figure 5-53 | Adding page breaks before the document articles |

```
/* Page Break Styles */

article:nth-of-type(n+2) {
    page-break-before: always;
}
```

inserts a page break before the article

selects every article after the first one

2. Save your changes to the file and then reload the tf_articles.html file in your browser and preview the printed page. Verify that the second article in the document on Community Involvement starts on a new page.

Next, you'll explore how to remove page breaks from the printed version of your web page.

How Browsers Set Automatic Page Breaks

Browsers establish page breaks automatically, unless you manually specify the page breaks with a print style sheet. By default, browsers insert page breaks using the following guidelines:

- Insert all of the manual page breaks as indicated by the `page-break-before`, `page-break-after`, and `page-break-inside` properties
- Break the pages as few times as possible
- Make all pages that don't have a forced page break appear to have the same height
- Avoid page breaking inside page elements that have a border
- Avoid page breaking inside a web table
- Avoid page breaking inside a floating element

Other styles from the print style sheet are applied only after attempting to satisfy these constraints. Note that different browsers apply page breaks in different ways, so while you can apply general rules to your print layout, you cannot, at the current time, make the print versions completely consistent across browsers.

Preventing Page Breaks

You can prevent a page break by using the keyword `avoid` in the `page-break-after` or `page-break-before` properties. For example, the following style rule prevents page breaks from being added after any heading.

```
h1, h2, h3, h4, h5, h6 {
    page-break-after: avoid;
}
```

Unfortunately in actual practice, most current browsers don't reliably support prohibiting page breaks in this fashion. Thus, to prevent page breaks after an element, you will usually have to manually insert a page break before the element so that the element is moved to the top of the next page.

For other print layouts, you will want to prevent page breaks from being placed inside an element. This usually occurs when you have a long string of text that you don't want broken into two pages. You can prevent printers from inserting a page break by using the following `page-break-inside` property

```
page-break-inside: type;
```

where `type` is `auto`, `inherit`, or `avoid`. Thus, to prevent a page break from appearing within any image you can apply the following style rule:

```
img {
    page-break-inside: avoid;
}
```

Unlike the `page-break-before` and `page-break-after` properties, almost all current browsers support the use of the `avoid` keyword for internal page breaks.

REFERENCE

Preventing Page Breaks inside an Element

- To prevent a page break from occurring within an element, apply the style:

```
page-break-inside: avoid;
```

Marjorie asks you to revise the print style sheet to prevent page breaks from occurring within images, ordered lists, and unordered lists.

To avoid page breaks:

1. Return to the **tf_print.css** file in your editor and go to the Page Break Styles section and insert the following style rule:

```
img, ol, ul {
    page-break-inside: avoid;
}
```

Figure 5-54 highlights the style rule to avoid page breaks in lists and images.

Figure 5-54   **Avoiding line breaks within lists and images**

```
/* Page Break Styles */

article:nth-of-type(n+2) {
    page-break-before: always;
}

img, ol, ul {
    page-break-inside: avoid;
}
```

avoids line breaks within lists and images

2. Save your changes to the file.

Note that the `avoid` type does not guarantee that there will never be a page break within the element. If the content of an element exceeds the dimensions of the sheet of paper on which it's being printed, the browser will be forced to insert a page break.

Working with Widows and Orphans

Page breaks within block elements, such as paragraphs, can often leave behind widows and orphans. A widow is a fragment of text left dangling at the top of page, while an orphan is a text fragment left at the bottom of a page. Widows and orphans generally ruin the flow of the page text, making the document difficult to read. To control the size of widows and orphans, CSS supports the following properties:

```
widows: value;
orphans: value;
```

where `value` is the number of lines that must appear within the element before a page break can be inserted by the printer. The default value is 2, which means that a widow or orphan must have at least two lines of text before it can be preceded or followed by a page break.

If you wanted to increase the size of widows and orphans to three lines for the paragraphs in a document, you could apply the style rule

```
p {
    widows: 3;
    orphans: 3;
}
```

and the browser will not insert a page break if fewer than three lines of a paragraph would be stranded at either the top or the bottom of the page.

Controlling the Size of Widows and Orphans

- To set the minimum size of widows (lines stranded at the top of a page), apply the property

  ```
  widows: value;
  ```

  where `value` is the number of lines that must appear at the top of the page before the page break.

- To set the minimum size of orphans (lines stranded at the bottom of a page), apply the property

  ```
  orphans: value;
  ```

  where `value` is the number of lines that must appear at the bottom of the page before the page break.

Use the `widows` and `orphans` properties now, setting their size to 3 for paragraphs in the printed version of the Articles of Interest page.

To avoid widows and orphans:

1. Within the Page Break Styles section of the tf_print.css file, add the following style rule.

```
p {
    orphans: 3;
    widows: 3;
}
```

Figure 5-55 highlights the style rule for setting the size of widows and orphans.

Figure 5-55 Setting the size of widows and orphans

```
img, ol, ul {
    page-break-inside: avoid;
}

p {
    orphans: 3;
    widows: 3;
}
```

widows and orphans set to a minimum of 3 lines each

2. Save your changes to the file and then reload the **tf_articles.html** file in your browser. Preview the appearance of the printed document. Figure 5-56 shows the final appearance of the printed version of this document.

Figure 5-56 Final print version of the document

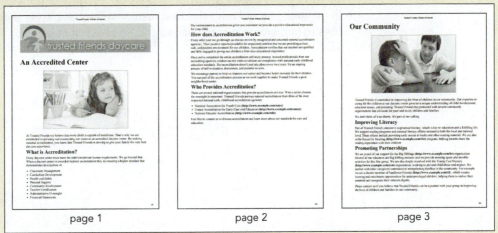

page 1   page 2   page 3

© 2016 Cengage Learning; © Pressmaster/Shutterstock.com; © Gladskikh Tatiana/Shutterstock.com;

Trouble? Depending on your browser and your default printer, your printed version may look slightly different from the one shown in Figure 5-56.

You've completed your work on the print styles for the Articles of Interest page. By modifying the default style sheet, you've created a printout that is easier to read and more useful to the parents and customers of the Trusted Friends Daycare Center.

PROSKILLS

Written Communication: Tips for Effective Printing

One challenge of printing a web page is that what works very well on the screen often fails when transferred to the printed page. For example, some browsers suppress printing background images, so that white text on a dark background, which appears fine on the computer monitor, is unreadable when printed. Following are some tips and guidelines you should keep in mind when designing the printed version of your web page:

- *Remove the clutter.* A printout should contain only information that is of immediate use to the reader. Page elements such as navigation lists, banners, and advertising should be removed, leaving only the main articles and images from your page.
- *Measure for printing.* Use only those measuring units in your style sheet that are appropriate for printing, such as points, inches, centimeters, and millimeters. Avoid expressing widths and heights in pixels because those can vary with printer resolution.
- *Design for white.* Because many browsers suppress the printing of background images and some users do not have access to color printers, create a style sheet that assumes black text on a white background.
- *Avoid absolute positioning.* Absolute positioning is designed for screen output. When printed, an object placed at an absolute position will be displayed on the first page of your printout, potentially making your text unreadable.
- *Give the user a choice.* Some readers will still want to print your web page exactly as it appears on the screen. To accommodate them, you can use one of the many JavaScript tools available on the web that allows readers to switch between your screen and print style sheets.

Finally, a print style sheet is one aspect of web design that works better in theory than in practice. Many browsers provide only partial support for the CSS print styles, so you should always test your designs on a variety of browsers and browser versions. In general, you will have the best results with a basic style sheet rather than one that tries to implement a complicated and involved print layout.

In this tutorial you've learned how to apply different styles to different types of devices and output formats. Marjorie appreciates the work you've done and will continue to rely on your knowledge of media queries, flexible layouts, and print styles as she redesigns the Trusted Friends website. You can close any open files or applications now.

REVIEW

Session 5.3 Quick Check

1. Create a `link` element that loads the myprint.css style sheet file but only for printed output.
2. Create a style rule that sets the size of the page box to 8.5 inches by 11 inches with a 1 inch margin.
3. Create a style rule for right-side pages with a top/bottom margin of 3 centimeters and a left/right margin of 5 centimeters.
4. Create a page style named smallMargins with a margin of 2 centimeters for every side.
5. Apply the smallMargins page style to a `section` element with the id *reviews*.
6. Create a style rule to insert a page break before every `section` element in the document.
7. Create a style rule to stop page breaks from being placed within any header or footer.
8. What style would you apply to allow the browser to wrap long strings of text to a new line whenever needed?
9. Create a style that limits the size of widows and for all `article` elements to 3 lines.

PRACTICE

Review Assignments

Data Files needed for the Review Assignments: tf_print2_txt.css, tf_styles4_txt.css, tf_tips_txt.html, 2 CSS files, 4 PNG files

Marjorie meets with you to discuss the redesign of the blog page showing parenting tips. As with the other pages you've worked on, she wants this page to be compatible with mobile devices, tablet and desktop devices, and printers. Marjorie has already written the page content and has done much of the initial design work. She needs you to complete the project by writing media queries for the different display options. Figure 5-57 shows a preview of the mobile design and the desktop design.

Figure 5-57   Parenting Tips page

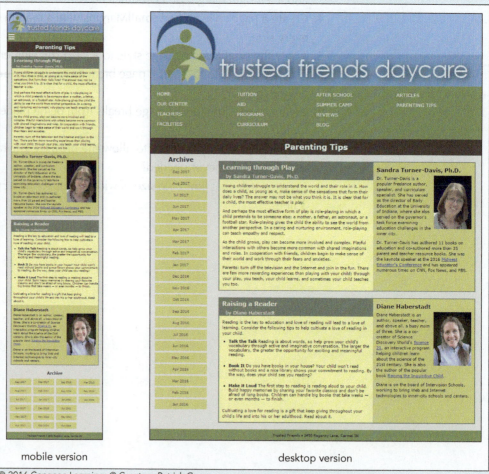

mobile version   desktop version

© 2016 Cengage Learning; © Courtesy Patrick Carey

You'll use several flexboxes to create the layout for these two designs so that the page content automatically rescales as the screen width changes.

Complete the following:

1. Use your HTML editor to open the **tf_tips_txt.html, tf_styles4_txt.css,** and **tf_print2_txt.css** files from the html05 ▸ review folder. Enter *your name* and *the date* in the comment section of each file, and save them as **tf_tips.html, tf_styles4.css,** and **tf_print2.css** respectively.

2. Go to the **tf_tips.html** file in your editor. Add a viewport `meta` tag to the document head to set the width of the layout viewport equal to the width of the device and set the initial scale of the viewport to 1.0.

3. Create links to the following style sheets: a) the tf_base.css file to be used with all devices, b) the tf_styles4.css file to be used with screen devices, and c) the tf_print2.css file to be used for printed output.

4. Take some time to study the contents and structure of the document, paying special attention to the IDs and class names of the elements, and then save your changes.

5. Go to the **tf_styles4.css** file in your editor. Note that Marjorie has placed all of her styles in the tf_designs.css file and imported them into this style sheet. You will not need to edit that style sheet file, but you might want to view it to become familiar with her style rules.

6. Go to the General Flex Styles section. Within this section, you'll create a flexible display layout that varies in response to changing screen widths. Note that when you use the different flex styles be sure you include the latest WebKit browser extension followed by the W3C specification.

7. In the General Flex Styles section create a style rule for the page body that displays the body as a flexbox oriented as a row, wrapping content to a new line as needed.

8. The page content is divided into two `section` elements with IDs of *left* and *right*. The left section does not need as much of the screen width. Create a style rule for the left section that sets its growth and shrink rates to 1 and 8 respectively and sets its basis size to 130 pixels.

9. The right section requires more screen width. Create a style rule for the right section that sets its growth and shrink values to 8 and 1 and sets its basis size to 351 pixels.

10. Next, you'll create a flexbox for the `section` element with class ID of tips that contains an article and a biographical aside, which will be displayed either in two columns or in a single column depending on the screen width. Add a style rule that displays the class of tips section elements as flexboxes in the row direction with wrapping.

11. The articles within each tips section need to occupy more of the screen width. Create a style rule for `article` elements that lays them out as flex items with a growth value of 2, shrink value of 1, and a basis size of 351 pixels.

12. The biographical asides within each tips section need to occupy less screen space. Create a style rule for `aside` elements that lays them out as flex items with a growth value of 1, shrink value of 2, and a basis size of 250 pixels.

13. Finally, the horizontal navigation list at the top of the page will also be treated as a flexbox. Create a style rule for the `ul` element within the horizontal navigation list displaying it as a flexbox in column orientation with wrapping. You do not have to define the sizes of the flex items because the width and height are set in the tf_designs.css style sheet.

14. Go to the Mobile Devices section and create a media query for screen devices with a maximum width of 480 pixels.

15. For mobile devices the vertical list of links to archived parenting tips should be displayed in several columns at the bottom of the page. Within the media query you created in the last step, add the following style rules to

   a. display the `ul` element within the vertical navigation list as a flexbox in column orientation with wrapping. Set the height of the element to 240 pixels.

   b. give the `section` element with an ID of *left* a flex order value of 99 to place it near the bottom of the page.

   c. give the body footer an order value of 100 to put it at the page bottom.

16. Marjorie wants to hide the navigation list at the top of the page when viewed on a mobile device unless the user hovers (or taps) a navicon. Using the technique shown in this tutorial, add the following style rules to set the behavior of the navicon within the media query for mobile devices:

   a. Display the navicon by creating a style rule for the `a#navicon` selector to display it as a block.

   b. Hide the contents of the navigation list by adding a style rule that sets the display of the `ul` element within the horizontal navigation list to `none`.

c. Display the navigation list contents in response to a hover or touch by creating a style rule for the `a#navicon:hover+ul, nav.horizontal ul:hover` selector that sets its display value to `block`.

17. Go to the Tablets and Desktop Devices section. Create a media query for screen devices with a width of at least 481 pixels. Under the wider screens, the contents of the horizontal navigation list at the top of the page should be displayed in several columns. In order to have the list items wrap to a new column, add a style rule to the media query that sets the height of the `ul` element within the horizontal navigation list to 160 pixels.

18. Save your changes to the style sheet and then open the **tf_tips.html** file in your browser or device emulator. Verify that as you change the screen width the layout of the page automatically changes to match the layout designs shown in Figure 5-57.

Next, you'll create the print styles for the Parenting Tips page. Figure 5-58 shows a preview of the output on a black and white printer.

Figure 5-58 **Parenting Tips print version**

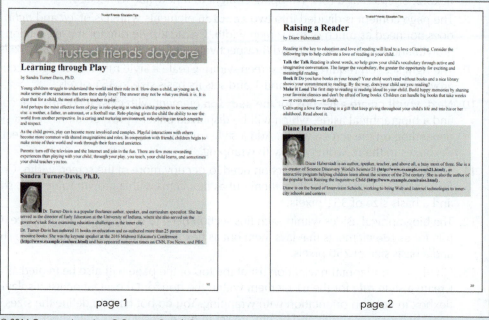

page 1 page 2

© 2016 Cengage Learning; © Courtesy Patrick Carey

19. Go to the **tf_print2.css** file in your editor. Go to the Hidden Objects section and hide the display of the following page elements: all navigation lists, the h1 heading in the body header, the left section element, and the body footer.

20. Go to the Page Box Styles section and set the page size to 8.5 inches by 11 inches with a margin of 0.5 inches.

21. Go the Header Styles section and add a style rule that displays the logo image as a block with a width of 100%.

22. Go to the Typography Styles section and add the following style rules for the text in the printed pages:

   a. For headers within the `article` element, set the bottom margin to 0.2 inches.

   b. For h1 headings within the `article` element, set the font size to 24 points and the line height to 26 points.

   c. For the `aside` element, set the background color to rgb(211, 211, 211) and add a top margin of 0.3 inches.

    d. For h1 headings in `aside` elements, set the font size to 18 points and the line height to 20 points.

    e. For images within `aside` elements, set the width to 0.8 inches.

    f. For paragraphs, set the font size to 12 points with a top and bottom margin of 0.1 inches.

23. Go to the Hypertext Styles section and add style rules to display all hypertext links in black with no underline. Also, insert a style rule that adds the text of the URL after the hypertext link in bold with the `word-wrap` property set to break-word.

24. Go to the Page Break Styles section and add the following style rules to

    a. insert page breaks after every `aside` element.

    b. never allow a page break within an `ol`, `ul`, or `img` element.

    c. set the size of widows and orphans within paragraphs to 3 lines each.

25. Save your changes to the file.

26. Reload the **tf_tips.html** file in your browser and preview its printed version. Verify that your pages resemble those shown in Figure 5-58 (there may be differences depending on your browser and your printer).

Case Problem 1

APPLY

Data Files needed for this Case Problem: gp_cover_txt.html, gp_page1_txt.html, gp_page2_txt.html, gp_page3_txt.html, gp_layout_txt.css, gp_print_txt.css, 2 CSS files, 21 PNG files

Golden Pulps   Devan Ryan manages the website *Golden Pulps*, where he shares tips on collecting and fun stories from the "golden age of comic books"—a period of time covering 1938 through the early 1950s. Devan wants to provide online versions of several classic comic books, which are now in the public domain.

He's scanned the images from the golden age comic book, *America's Greatest Comics 001*, published in March, 1941 by Fawcett Comics and featuring Captain Marvel. He's written the code for the HTML file and wants you to help him develop a layout design that will be compatible with mobile and desktop devices. Figure 5-59 shows a preview of the mobile and desktop version of a page you'll create.

Figure 5-59 Golden Pulps sample page

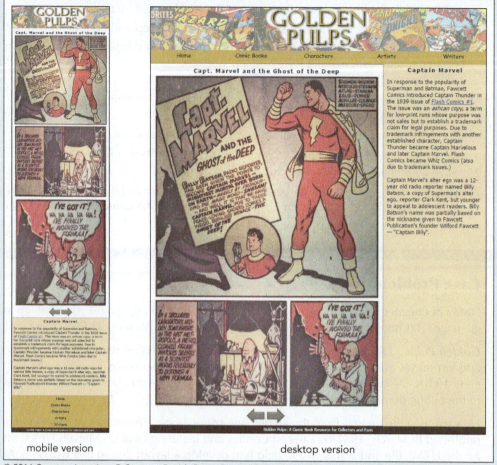

mobile version   desktop version

© 2016 Cengage Learning; © Courtesy Patrick Carey; Source: Comic Book Plus

Complete the following:

1. Using your editor, open the **gp_cover_txt.html, gp_page1_txt.html, gp_page2_txt.html, gp_page3_txt.html, gp_layout_txt.css,** and **gp_print_txt.css** files from the html05 ▸ case1 folder. Enter *your name* and *the date* in the comment section of each file, and save them as **gp_cover.html, gp_page1.html, gp_page2.html, gp_page3.html, gp_layout.css,** and **gp_print.css** respectively.

2. Go to the **gp_cover.html** file in your editor. Add a viewport `meta` tag to the document head, setting the width of the layout viewport to the device width and setting the initial scale of the viewport to 1.0.

3. Create links to the following style sheets: a) the gp_reset.css file to be used with all devices, b) the gp_layout.css file to be used with screen devices, and c) the gp_print.css file to be used for printed output.

4. Take some time to study the contents and structure of the file. Note each panel from the comic book is stored as a separate inline image with the class name *panel* along with class names of *size1* to *size4* indicating the size of the panel. Size1 is the largest panel down to size4, which is the smallest panel. Close the file, saving your changes.

5. Repeat Steps 2 through 4 for the gp_page1.html, gp_page2.html, and gp_page3.html files.

6. Go to the **gp_layout.css** file in your editor. In this style sheet, you'll create the layout styles for mobile and desktop devices. Note that Devan has used the `@import` rule to import the gp_designs.css file, which contains several graphical and typographical style rules.

7. Go to the Flex Layout Styles section and insert a style rule to display the page body as a flexbox oriented as rows with wrapping. As always, include the latest WebKit browser extension in all of your flex styles.

8. The page body content has two main elements. The `section` element with the ID *sheet* contains the panels from the comic book page. The `article` element contains information about the comic book industry during the Golden Age. Devan wants more of the page width to be given to the comic book sheet. Add a style rule that sets the growth and shrink rate of the sheet section to 3 and 1 respectively and set its basis size to 301 pixels.

9. Less page width will be given to the `article` element. Create a style rule to set its flex growth and shrink values to 1 and 3 respectively and set its basis size to 180 pixels.

10. Go to the Mobile Devices section and create a media query for screen devices with a maximum width of 480 pixels.

11. With mobile devices, Devan wants each comic book panel image to occupy a single row. Create a style rule that sets the width of images belonging to the panel class to 100%.

12. For mobile devices, Devan wants the horizontal navigation links to other pages on the Golden Pulps website to be displayed near the bottom of the page. Within the media query, set the flex order of the horizontal navigation list to 99.

13. Create a style rule to set the flex order of the body footer to 100. (Hint: There are two `footer` elements in the document, use a selector that selects the `footer` element that is a direct child of the `body` element.)

14. Go to the Tablet and Desktop Devices: Greater than 480 pixels section and create a media query that matches screen devices with widths greater than 480 pixels.

15. For tablet and desktop devices, you'll lay out the horizontal navigation list as a single row of links. Within the media query, create a style rule that displays the `ul` element within the horizontal navigation list as a flexbox, oriented in the row direction with no wrapping. Set the height of the element to 40 pixels.

16. For each `li` element within the `ul` element of the horizontal navigation list set their growth, shrink, and basis size values to 1, 1, and `auto` respectively so that each list items grows and shrinks at the same rate.

17. With wider screens, Devan does not want the panels to occupy their own rows as is the case with mobile devices. Instead, within the media query create style rules, define the width of the different classes of comic book panel images as follows:

    a. Set the width of size1 `img` elements to 100%.

    b. Set the width of size2 `img` elements to 60%.

    c. Set the width of size3 `img` elements to 40%.

    d. Set the width of size4 `img` elements to 30%.

18. Save your changes to the file and then open the **gp_cover.html** file in your browser or device emulator. Click the navigation links to view the contents of the cover and first three pages. Verify that with a narrow screen the panels occupy their own rows and with a wider screen the sheets are laid out with several panels per row. Further verify that the horizontal navigation list is placed at the bottom of the page for mobile devices.

19. Devan also wants a print style that displays each comic book sheet on its own page and with none of the navigation links. Go to the **gp_print.css** style sheet in your editor. Add style rules to

    a. hide the `nav`, `footer`, and `article` elements.

    b. set the width of the `section` element with the ID *sheet* to 6 inches. Set the top/bottom margin of that element to 0 inches and the left/right margin to `auto` in order to center it within the printed page.

    c. set the width of size1 images to 5 inches, size2 images to 3 inches, size3 images to 2 inches, and size4 images to 1.5 inches.

20. Save your changes to the file and then reload the contents of the comic book pages in your browser and preview the printed pages. Verify that the printed page displays only the website logo, the name of the comic book, and the comic book panels.

Case Problem 2

Data Files needed for this Case Problem: wc_styles_txt.css, 2 CSS files, 18 HTML files, 20 PNG files

Willet Creek   Michael Carpenter is an IT manager at the Willet Creek Resort in Ogden, Utah. You've recently been hired to work on the company's website. Many golfers have asked about mobile-friendly versions of the pages describing the Willet Creek golf course so they can easily view information about each hole on their mobile devices when they're out on the course. Michael would like you to use responsive design to create a mobile-friendly style sheet to be used by the pages describing the golf course holes. A preview of the completed design for one of the holes is shown in Figure 5-60.

Figure 5-60   **Willet Creek course website**

mobile version   desktop version

© 2016 Cengage Learning; © Courtesy Patrick Carey

The work on the HTML code for the 18 pages describing each hole has already been completed for you. Your job will be to write the style sheet that employs the techniques of responsive design.

Complete the following:

1. Using your editor, open the **wc_styles_txt.css** file from the html05 ▶ case2 folder. Enter *your name* and *the date* in the comment section of the file, and save it as **wc_styles.css**.

2. Open the **wc_hole01.html** file in your editor. For this case problem, you do not need to modify any HTML files, but you should take some time to study the contents and structure of this document (the other 17 HTML files have a similar structure). When you're finished studying the file, you may close it without saving any changes you may have inadvertently made.

3. Return to the **wc_styles.css** file in your editor. Use the `@import` rule to import the style rules from the wc_designs.css file. Write the rule so that the imported style sheet should only be used with screen devices.

4. You'll layout the golf course pages using a flex layout. Go to the Flex Layout Styles section and create a style rule for the page body that displays the body as a flexbox oriented in the row direction with wrapping. As always, include the WebKit browser extension in all of your flex styles.

5. Two of the child elements of the page body are a navigation list with the ID *hole_list* and an `article` element containing information about the current hole. Add a style rule that sets the flex growth, shrink, and basis size values of the hole_list navigation list to 1, 3, and 140 pixels.

6. Add a style rule that sets the flex growth, shrink, and basis size values of the `article` element to 3, 1, and 341 pixels.

7. The `article` element contains statistics and a summary about the current hole. Michael also wants this element to be treated as a flexbox. Add to the style rule for the `article` element styles that display the element as a flexbox oriented in the row direction with wrapping.

8. The two items within the `article` element are a `section` element with the ID *stats* and a `section` element with the ID *summary*. Create a style rule for the stats section that sets its flex growth, shrink, and basis values to 1, 4, and 120 pixels.

9. Create a style rule for the summary section that sets its flex growth, shrink, and basis values to 4, 1, and 361 pixels respectively.

10. The `aside` element contains an advertisement for other services offered by the Willet Creek Resort. Add a style rule that displays this element as a flexbox in row orientation with wrapping.

11. Information about individual services are saved in a `div` element within the `aside` element. Michael wants these `div` elements to be laid out with equal flex sizes. Create a style rule for every `div` element within the `aside` element that sets the flex growth and shrink values to 1 and the basis value to 180 pixels.

12. Next, you'll design the layout for the mobile version of the page. Go to the Mobile Styles section and add a media query for screen devices with a maximum width of 480 pixels.

13. Under the mobile layout, Michael wants the navigation list containing links to the 18 holes on the course to be displayed near the bottom of the page. Create a style rule that sets the flex order of the hole_list navigation list to 99. Create a style rule that sets the flex order of the footer to 100.

14. To reduce clutter, Michael wants the horizontal navigation list at the top of the page to be hidden unless the user taps a navicon. Create this hidden menu system by adding the following style rules to

    a. hide the display of the `ul` element within the horizontal navigation list.

    b. change the `display` property of the `ul` element to `block` if the user hovers over the navicon hypertext link or hovers over the unordered list within the horizontal navigation list. (Hint: Review the hover discussion in session 5.2 as needed.)

15. Michael also wants to hide the `aside` element when the page is viewed on a mobile device. Add a style rule to accomplish this.

16. Next, you'll create the styles that will be used for tablet and desktop devices. Create a media query for all screen devices with a width of at least 481 pixels.

17. Within the media query, create a style rule that hides the display of the navicon.

18. For these wider screens, Michael wants the horizontal navigation list to be laid out within a single row. Create a style rule that changes the display of the `ul` element within the horizontal navigation list to a flexbox that is oriented in the row direction with no wrapping.

19. For every list item in the `ul` element in the horizontal navigation list, set the growth and shrink values to 1 and the basis value to auto so that the list items grow and shrink together on the same row.

20. Save your changes to style sheet and then open the **wc_hole01.html** file in your browser or device emulator. Verify that when you reduce the screen width, the layout automatically changes to a single column layout and the `aside` element is hidden from the user. Further verify that for mobile-sized devices, the navigation links at the top of the page are hidden until the user hovers or touches the navicon.

21. Use the course navigation links on the page to view information on each of the 18 holes on the Willet Creek course. Verify that the layout matches that shown in Figure 5-60 for each page in both mobile and desktop size.

Case Problem 3

Data Files needed for this Case Problem: cw_home_txt.html, cw_styles_txt.css, 2 CSS files, 10 PNG files

Cauli-Wood Gallery   Sofia Fonte is the manager of the *Cauli-Wood Gallery*, an art gallery and coffee shop located in Sedona, Arizona. She has approached you for help in redesigning the gallery's website to include support for mobile devices and tablets. Your first project will be to redesign the site's home page following the principles of responsive design. A preview of the mobile and desktop versions of the website's home page is shown in Figure 5-61.

Figure 5-61   Cauli-Wood Gallery home page

mobile version   desktop version

Right: © 2016 Cengage Learning; © Tischenko Irina/Shutterstock.com; © re_bekka/Shutterstock.com; © Boyan Dimitrov/ Shutterstock.com; © rubtsov/Shutterstock.com; © Fotocrisis/Shutterstock.com; © Anna Ismagilova/Shutterstock.com; © DeepGreen/Shutterstock.com; Source: Facebook 2015; Source: 2015 Twitter; Left: © 2016 Cengage Learning; © Tischenko Irina/Shutterstock.com; © Courtesy Patrick Carey; © re_bekka/Shutterstock.com; © Anna Ismagilova/ Shutterstock.com; © rubtsov/Shutterstock.com; Source: Facebook 2015; Source: 2015 Twitter

Sofia has already written much of the HTML code and some of the styles to be used in this project. Your job will be to finish the redesign and present her with the final version of the page.

Complete the following:

1. Using your editor, open the **cw_home_txt.html** and **cw_styles_txt.css** files from the html05 ▶ case3 folder. Enter *your name* and *the date* in the comment section of each file, and save them as **cw_home.html** and **cw_styles.css** respectively.

2. Go to the **cw_home.html** file in your editor. Within the document head, insert a `meta` element that sets the browser viewport for use with mobile devices. Also, create links to cw_reset.css and cw_styles.css style sheets. Take some time to study the contents and structure of the document and then close the file saving your changes.

3. Return to the **cw_styles.css** file in your editor. At the top of the file, use the `@import` rule to import the contents of the cw_designs.css file, which contains several style rules that format the appearance of different page elements.

⊕ **Explore** 4. At the bottom of the home page is a navigation list with the id *bottom* containing several `ul` elements. Sofia wants these `ul` elements laid out side-by-side. Create a style rule for the bottom navigation list displaying it as a flexbox row with no wrapping. Set the `justify-content` property so that the flex items are centered along the main axis. Be sure to include the WebKit browser extension in all of your flex styles.

5. Define flex values for `ul` elements within the bottom navigation list so that the width of those elements never exceeds 150 pixels but can shrink below that value.

6. Sofia wants more highly contrasting colors when the page is displayed in a mobile device. Create a media query for mobile screen devices with maximum widths of 480 pixels. Within that media query, insert a style rule that sets the font color of all body text to rgb(211, 211, 211) and sets the body background color to rgb(51, 51, 51).

7. Sofia also wants to reduce the clutter in the mobile version of the home page. Hide the following elements for mobile users: the `aside` element, any `img` element within the `article` element, and the spotlight section element.

8. At the top of the web page is a navigation list with the ID *top*. For mobile devices, display the `ul` element within this navigation list as a flexbox row with wrapping. For each list item within this `ul` element, set the font size to 2.2em. Size the list items by setting their flex values to 1 for the growth and shrink rates and 130 pixels for the basis value.

9. Under the mobile layout, the six list items in the top navigation list should appear as square blocks with different background images. Using the selector `nav#top ul li:nth-of-type(1)` for the first list item, create a style rule that changes the background to the background image cw_image01.png. Center the background image with no tiling and size it so that the entire image is contained within the background.

10. Repeat the previous step for the next five list items using the same general format. Use the cw_image02.png file for background of the second list item, the cw_image03.png file for the third list item background, and so forth.

⊕ **Explore** 11. Sofia has placed hypertext links for the gallery's phone number and e-mail address in a paragraph with the id *links*. For mobile users, she wants these two hypertext links spaced evenly within the paragraph that is displayed below the top navigation list. To format these links, create a style rule that displays the links paragraph as a flexbox row with no wrapping, then add a style that sets the value of the `justify-content` property of the paragraph to `space-around`.

12. She wants the telephone and e-mail links to be prominently displayed on mobile devices. For each `a` element within the links paragraph, apply the following style rule that: a) displays the link text in white on the background color rgb(220, 27, 27), b) sets the border radius around each hypertext to 20 pixels with 10 pixels of padding, and c) removes any underlining from the hypertext links.

13. Next, you'll define the layout for tablet and desktop devices. Create a media query for screen devices whose width is 481 pixels or greater. Within this media query, display the page body as a flexbox in row orientation with wrapping.

14. The page body has four children: the header, the footer, the `article` element, and the `aside` element. The `article` and `aside` elements will share a row with more space given to the `article` element. Set the growth, shrink, and basis values of the `article` element to 2, 1, and 400 pixels. Set those same values for the `aside` element to 1, 2, and 200 pixels.

⊕ **Explore** 15. For tablet and desktop devices, the top navigation list should be displayed as a horizontal row with no wrapping. Enter a style rule to display the top navigation list `ul` as a flexbox with a background color of rgb(51, 51, 51) and a height of 50 pixels. Use the `justify-content` and `align-items` property to center the flex items both horizontally and vertically.

16. Define the flex size of each list item in the top navigation list to have a maximum width of 80 pixels but to shrink at the same rate as the width if the navigation list is reduced.

17. Sofia doesn't want the links paragraph displayed for tablet and desktop devices. Complete the media query for tablet and desktop devices by hiding this paragraph.

18. Save your changes to the style sheet and then open the **cw_home.html** file in your browser or device emulator. Verify that the layout and contents of the page switch between the mobile version and the tablet/desktop version shown in Figure 5-61 as the screen width is increased and decreased.

Case Problem 4

Data Files needed for this Case Problem: jb_home_txt.html, jb_styles_txt.css, 10 PNG files, 1 TXT file

Jersey Buoys   Tony Gallo is the owner of *Jersey Buoys*, a surfing school in Ocean City, New Jersey. Tony has hired you as part of a team that will redesign the school's website, putting more emphasis on supporting mobile devices. Tony wants you to start by redesigning the website's front page. He's supplied you with graphics and sample text. He needs you to write up the HTML code and CSS style sheets.

Complete the following:

1. Using your editor, open the **jb_home_txt.html** and **jb_styles_txt.css** files from the html05 ▸ case4 folder. Enter *your name* and *the date* in the comment section of each file and save them as **jb_home.html** and **jb_styles.css** respectively.

2. Using the content of the jb_info.txt file, create the content and structure of the jb_home.html page. You are free to supplement the material in these text files with additional textual content of your own if appropriate. The case4 folder includes public domain graphics that you may use with your website, but you should feel free to add your own non-copyrighted material appropriate to the case problem. Use the # symbol for the value of the href attribute in your hypertext links because you will be linking to pages that don't actually exist.

3. Be sure to include the viewport meta element so that your page is properly scaled on mobile devices.

4. Link your file to the jb_styles.css style sheet. If you need to create other style sheets for your project, such as a reset style sheet, link to those files as well. Indicate the type of device in your link element.

5. Go to the **jb_styles.css** file in your editor and create the layout and design styles to be used in your page. The design is up to you, but must include the following features:
   • Media queries that match devices of a specific width with a cutoff for mobile devices at 480 pixels in screen width.
   • Layout styles that vary based on the width of the device.
   • A navigation list that is initially hidden from the mobile user but that can be displayed in response to a hover or touch event over a navicon.
   • Telephone and email links that are reformatted to make them easier to use on mobile devices.
   • Tony does not want to display information on surfer slang in the mobile version of this page; exclude those elements in your media query for mobile devices.
   • Flex layouts oriented in either the row or column direction. Be sure to include the WebKit browser extension in all of your flex styles.
   • Flex items that grow and shrink from a defined initial size based on the width of the device screen.
   • Flex items that change their order from the default document order in the HTML file.
   • A flex layout that aligns the flex item content using the justify-content, align-items, align-content, or align-self properties.

6. Include comments in your style sheet to make it easy for other users to interpret.

7. Test your layout and design on a variety of devices, browsers, and screen resolutions to ensure that your sample page is readable under different conditions. If possible verify the behavior of the page on a mobile device or a mobile emulator.

TUTORIAL 6

Working with Tables and Columns

Creating a Program Schedule for a Radio Station

OBJECTIVES

Session 6.1
- Explore the structure of a web table
- Create table heading and data cells
- Apply CSS styles to a table
- Create cells that span multiple rows and columns
- Add a caption to a table

Session 6.2
- Create row and column groups
- Apply styles to row and column groups
- Display page elements in table form
- Create a multi-column layout

Case | *Dakota Listener Radio*

Kyle Mitchell is the program director at *DLR* (*Dakota Listener Radio*), a public radio station broadcasting out of Bismarck, North Dakota. Kyle has begun upgrading the DLR website to provide listeners with more information about the station's programs and policies.

The new website will include pages listing the DLR morning, afternoon, and evening schedules. Kyle believes that this information is best conveyed to the listener in a table, with days arranged in separate table columns and times within each day placed in separate table rows. Kyle has never created a web table, so he has come to you for help. He wants the table to be informative and easy to read so you enhance the appearance of the web page with CSS styles.

STARTING DATA FILES

html06 → **tutorial**

dlr_evenings_txt.html
dlr_lw0414_txt.html
dlr_columns_txt.css
dlr_tables_txt.css
+ 7 files

review

dlr_mornings_txt.html
dlr_columns2_txt.css
dlr_tables2_txt.css
+ 5 files

case1

mi_pricing_txt.html
mi_tables_txt.css
+ 8 files

case2

jpf_sudoku_txt.html
jpf_sudoku_txt.css
+ 4 files

case3

lht_feb_txt.html
lht_columns_txt.css
lht_tables_txt.css
+ 6 files

case4

hcc_schedule_txt.html
hcc_schedule_txt.css
hcc_styles_txt.css
+ 1 file

Session 6.1 Visual Overview:

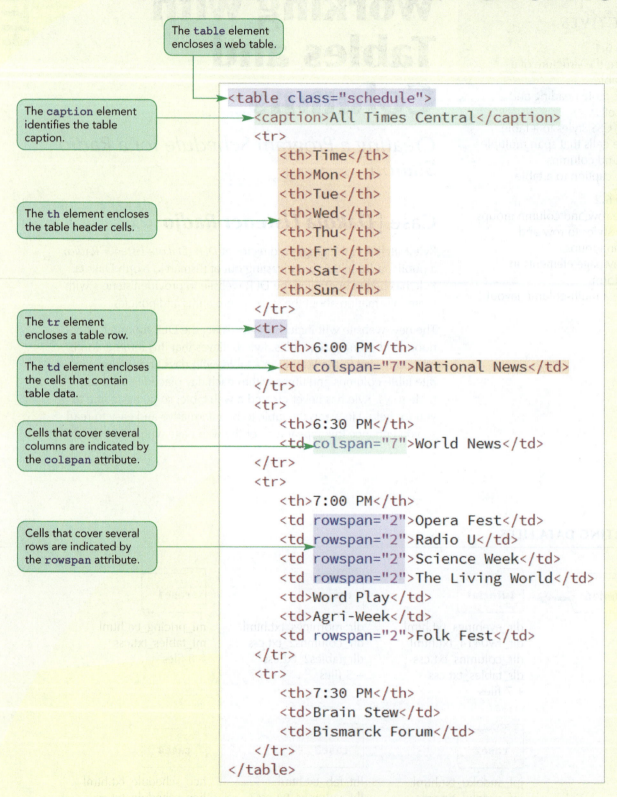

The **table** element encloses a web table.

The **caption** element identifies the table caption.

The **th** element encloses the table header cells.

The **tr** element encloses a table row.

The **td** element encloses the cells that contain table data.

Cells that cover several columns are indicated by the **colspan** attribute.

Cells that cover several rows are indicated by the **rowspan** attribute.

```
<table class="schedule">
   <caption>All Times Central</caption>
   <tr>
      <th>Time</th>
      <th>Mon</th>
      <th>Tue</th>
      <th>Wed</th>
      <th>Thu</th>
      <th>Fri</th>
      <th>Sat</th>
      <th>Sun</th>
   </tr>
   <tr>
      <th>6:00 PM</th>
      <td colspan="7">National News</td>
   </tr>
   <tr>
      <th>6:30 PM</th>
      <td colspan="7">World News</td>
   </tr>
   <tr>
      <th>7:00 PM</th>
      <td rowspan="2">Opera Fest</td>
      <td rowspan="2">Radio U</td>
      <td rowspan="2">Science Week</td>
      <td rowspan="2">The Living World</td>
      <td>Word Play</td>
      <td>Agri-Week</td>
      <td rowspan="2">Folk Fest</td>
   </tr>
   <tr>
      <th>7:30 PM</th>
      <td>Brain Stew</td>
      <td>Bismarck Forum</td>
   </tr>
</table>
```

Structure of a Web Table

The first table row is made up of all header cells.

The browser renders the web table with bold headers and spanning cells.

The two data cells span seven columns.

Time	Mon	Tue	Wed	Thu	Fri	Sat	Sun
6:00 PM	National News						
6:30 PM	World News						
7:00 PM	Opera Fest	Radio U	Science Week	The Living World	Word Play	Agri-Week	Folk Fest
7:30 PM					Brain Stew	Bismarck Forum	

All Times Central

These four data cells span two rows each.

The table caption is placed at the bottom-right corner of the table.

The border-collapse property determines which table borders are separated or collapsed into each other.

```css
table.schedule {
    background: white;
    border: 10px outset rgb(153, 0, 153);
    border-collapse: collapse;
    font-size: 0.75em;
    width: 100%;
}

table.schedule th, table.schedule td {
    border: 1px solid gray;
}

table.schedule caption {
    caption-side: bottom;
    text-align: right;
}
```

The caption-side property places the table caption at either the top or bottom of the web table.

Introducing Web Tables

In this tutorial, you explore how to use HTML to mark table data in the form of a web table. A **web table** is an HTML structure consisting of multiple table rows with each row containing one or more table cells. The cells themselves can contain additional HTML elements such as headings, paragraphs, inline images, and navigation lists. Thus, a web table is an effective tool for organizing and classifying your web page content.

Marking Tables and Table Rows

Each web table consists of a `table` element containing a collection of table rows marked using the `tr` (table row) element in the following general structure

```
<table>
    <tr>
        table cells
    </tr>
    <tr>
        table cells
    </tr>
    ...
</table>
```

where `table cells` are the cells within each row. Tables are considered block-level elements appearing by default on a new line within the web page. The dimension or size of the table is defined by the number of table rows and the number of cells within those rows.

To see how table content can be created using the `table` and `tr` elements, you meet with Kyle in his office at DLR to discuss the design for his page describing DLR's evening schedule. He wants you to place the schedule in a table, similar to the one shown in Figure 6-1.

> **TIP**
>
> Sketch your tables beforehand so that you can visualize the placement of the table rows and cells.

Figure 6-1 DLR nightly schedule

Time	Monday	Tuesday	Wednesday	Thursday	Friday	Saturday	Sunday
6:00	National News	National News	National News	National News	National News	National News	National News
6:30	World News	World News	World News	World News	World News	World News	World News
7:00	Opera Fest	Radio U	Science Week	The Living World	Word Play	Agri-Week	Folk Fest
7:30					Brain Stew	Bismarck Forum	
8:00	The Classical Music Connection				Old Time Radio	Saturday Nite Jazz	The Indie Connection
8:30					The Inner Mind		
9:00					Open Mike Nite		
9:30							
10:00	World News Feed	World News Feed	World News Feed	World News Feed	World News Feed	World News Feed	World News Feed

© 2016 Cengage Learning

Kyle's proposed table contains 10 rows: the first row contains headings for each of the table columns and the remaining rows list the DLR programs airing from 6:00 p.m. to 10:30 p.m. in half-hour intervals. Notice that some programs last longer than one-half hour and thus will cover multiple rows. Kyle has already created that web page that will contain this table and written style sheets for the page's layout, graphics, and typography.

REFERENCE

Marking a Web Table and Table Rows

• To mark a web table and the table rows, enter

```
<table>
   <tr>
      table cells
   </tr>
   <tr>
      table cells
   </tr>
   …
</table>
```

where `<table>` marks the `table` element, `<tr>` marks each table row, and *table cells* are the cells within each row.

You start working on his page by adding the first three rows of his proposed table within a `table` element. You also include a `class` attribute, placing the table in the schedule class to distinguish it from other tables that may exist on the DLR website.

To start working on the evening schedule page:

1. Use your editor to open the **dlr_evenings_txt.html** file from the html06 ▶ tutorial folder. Enter *your name* and *the date* in the comment section of the file and save it as **dlr_evenings.html**.

2. Scroll down the document to the `section` element with the `id` "main" and add the following `table` and `tr` elements after the initial paragraph in the section.

```
<table class="schedule">
   <tr>
   </tr>
   <tr>
   </tr>
   <tr>
   </tr>
</table>
```

Figure 6-2 shows the placement of the `table` and `tr` elements in the document.

Figure 6-2 **Marking a table and table rows**

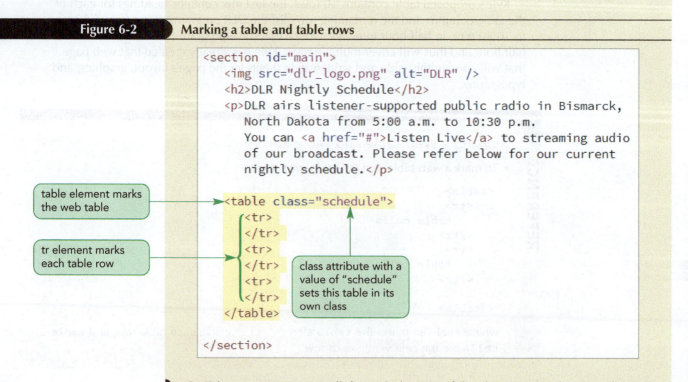

table element marks the web table

tr element marks each table row

```
<section id="main">
    <img src="dlr_logo.png" alt="DLR" />
    <h2>DLR Nightly Schedule</h2>
    <p>DLR airs listener-supported public radio in Bismarck,
        North Dakota from 5:00 a.m. to 10:30 p.m.
        You can <a href="#">Listen Live</a> to streaming audio
        of our broadcast. Please refer below for our current
        nightly schedule.</p>

<table class="schedule">
    <tr>
    </tr>
    <tr>
    </tr>
    <tr>
    </tr>
</table>

</section>
```

class attribute with a value of "schedule" sets this table in its own class

3. Take some time to scroll through the rest of the document to become familiar with its content and structure and then save your changes to the file, but do not close it.

At this point, you have a table with three rows but no content. Your next task is to add table cells to each of those rows.

Marking Table Headings and Table Data

Web tables support two types of table cells: header cells that contain content usually placed at the top of a column or the beginning of a row and data cells that contain content within those columns and rows. A header cell is marked using the th element. The default browser style for header cells is to display the text of the header in bold font and centered horizontally within the cell.

Kyle wants you to mark the cells in the first row of the radio schedule as header cells because those cells contain information describing the contents of each table column. He also wants the first cell in each of the remaining rows to be marked as a header cell because those cells identify the time of day in which each program airs. You start by adding header cells to the first three rows of the schedule table.

To mark table header cells:

1. In the first row of the table you just created in the dlr_evenings.html file, create header cells by inserting the following th elements:

```
<th>Time</th>
<th>Mon</th>
<th>Tue</th>
<th>Wed</th>
<th>Thu</th>
<th>Fri</th>
```

```
<th>Sat</th>
<th>Sun</th>
```

Note that since these headers cells are nested within a `tr` element, they will all appear within the same table row.

2. In the second row of the table, insert the following `th` element:

```
<th>6:00 PM</th>
```

3. In the third table row, insert the header cell:

```
<th>6:30 PM</th>
```

These cells are the headers for your table rows. Figure 6-3 highlights the newly added header cells in the table.

Figure 6-3   **Marking table header cells**

the th element marks header cells placed in the first row to identify the content of each column

```
<table class="schedule">
    <tr>
        <th>Time</th>
        <th>Mon</th>
        <th>Tue</th>
        <th>Wed</th>
        <th>Thu</th>
        <th>Fri</th>
        <th>Sat</th>
        <th>Sun</th>
    </tr>
    <tr>
        <th>6:00 PM</th>
    </tr>
    <tr>
        <th>6:30 PM</th>
    </tr>
</table>
```

header cells at the start of each row identifies the row content

4. Save your changes to the file and then load **dlr_evenings.html** in your browser. Verify that the table shows three rows: the first row contains the text "Time" followed by the days of the week. The second and third rows display the 6:00 PM and 6:30 PM times. All text is displayed in a bold font.

Data cells that do not function as headers for table rows or columns are marked using the `td` element. The default browser style for data cells is to display data cell text as unformatted text, left-aligned within the cell.

Marking Header Cells and Data Cells

- To mark a header cell, enter

  ```
  <th>content</th>
  ```

  where *content* is the content of the header cell, such as text or images.
- To mark a data cell, enter

  ```
  <td>content</td>
  ```

DLR airs national and world news at 6:00 and 6:30, respectively, every night of the week. You use table data cells to mark the names of these DLR programs.

To mark table data cells:

1. Within the second row of the table, add the following seven td elements after the initial th element:

   ```
   <td>National News</td>
   <td>National News</td>
   <td>National News</td>
   <td>National News</td>
   <td>National News</td>
   <td>National News</td>
   <td>National News</td>
   ```

2. Within the third table row, insert another seven td elements listing the World News program after the initial th element:

   ```
   <td>World News</td>
   <td>World News</td>
   <td>World News</td>
   <td>World News</td>
   <td>World News</td>
   <td>World News</td>
   <td>World News</td>
   ```

   Figure 6-4 highlights the newly added data cells in the second and third rows of the table.

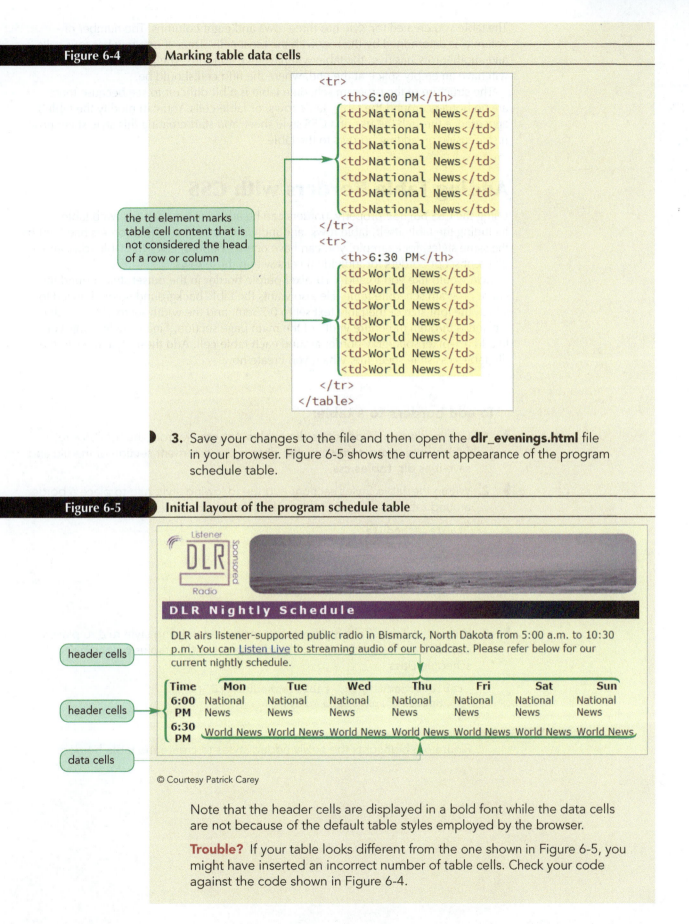

Figure 6-4   Marking table data cells

the td element marks table cell content that is not considered the head of a row or column

```
<tr>
   <th>6:00 PM</th>
   <td>National News</td>
   <td>National News</td>
   <td>National News</td>
   <td>National News</td>
   <td>National News</td>
   <td>National News</td>
   <td>National News</td>
</tr>
<tr>
   <th>6:30 PM</th>
   <td>World News</td>
   <td>World News</td>
   <td>World News</td>
   <td>World News</td>
   <td>World News</td>
   <td>World News</td>
   <td>World News</td>
</tr>
</table>
```

3. Save your changes to the file and then open the **dlr_evenings.html** file in your browser. Figure 6-5 shows the current appearance of the program schedule table.

Figure 6-5   Initial layout of the program schedule table

DLR Nightly Schedule

DLR airs listener-supported public radio in Bismarck, North Dakota from 5:00 a.m. to 10:30 p.m. You can Listen Live to streaming audio of our broadcast. Please refer below for our current nightly schedule.

header cells

header cells

data cells

Time	Mon	Tue	Wed	Thu	Fri	Sat	Sun
6:00 PM	National News	National News	National News	National News	National News	National News	National News
6:30 PM	World News	World News	World News	World News	World News	World News	World News

Note that the header cells are displayed in a bold font while the data cells are not because of the default table styles employed by the browser.

Trouble? If your table looks different from the one shown in Figure 6-5, you might have inserted an incorrect number of table cells. Check your code against the code shown in Figure 6-4.

The table you created for Kyle has three rows and eight columns. The number of columns is determined by the row with the most cells. Thus, if one row has four cells and another row has five, the table will have five columns. The row with only four cells will have an empty space at the end, where the fifth cell should be.

The structure of the program schedule table is a bit difficult to see because there are no borders around the table, table rows, or table cells. You can modify the table's appearance through the use of a CSS style sheet. You start creating this style sheet now, first focusing on adding borders to the table.

Adding Table Borders with CSS

Using the CSS border property, borders can be added to any part of a web table, including the table itself, table rows, and individual table cells. The borders need not be the same styles, for example, you can have one set of borders for the table rows and a different set of borders for individual cells within those rows.

Kyle would like you to add a 10-pixel purple border in the outset style around the entire program schedule table. He also wants the table background color changed to white, the font size of the table text set to 0.75em, and the width set to 100% so that it extends through the entire width of the main page section. Finally, Kyle wants you to add a 1-pixel solid gray border around each table cell. Add these style rules to the dlr_tables.css style sheet file, which you create now.

To add borders to a table:

1. Use your editor to open the **dlr_tables_txt.css** file from the html06 ▶ tutorial folder. Enter **your name** and **the date** in the comment section of the file and save it as **dlr_tables.css**.

2. Within the Table Styles section, add the following style rule to place a border around tables belonging to the schedule class:

```
table.schedule {
    background: white;
    border: 10px outset rgb(153, 0, 153);
    font-size: 0.75em;
    width: 100%;
}
```

3. Within the Table Cells Styles section, add the following style rule to place a border around each header cell and data cell within tables belonging to the schedule class.

```
table.schedule th, table.schedule td {
    border: 1px solid gray;
}
```

Figure 6-6 highlights the newly added styles to create the table borders.

Figure 6-6 ▶ **Adding styles to the table and table cells**

```
/* Table Styles */

table.schedule {
    background: white;
    border: 10px outset rgb(153, 0, 153);
    font-size: 0.75em;
    width: 100%;
}

/* Table Cell Styles */

table.schedule th, table.schedule td {
    border: 1px solid gray;
}
```

sets the table background to white

adds a 10-pixel purple outset border around the entire table

sets the table width to 100% of its parent element

sets the table font size to 0.75em

adds a 1-pixel solid gray border to every table cell

4. Save your changes to the style sheet and then reload to the dlr_evenings. html file in your editor.

5. Within the document head and directly before the closing </head> tag, add the following link element to link the document to the dlr_tables.css style sheet:

   `<link href="dlr_tables.css" rel="stylesheet" />`

6. Save your changes to the file and then reload the dlr_evenings.html file in your browser.

   Figure 6-7 shows the revised appearance of the table with the newly added borders.

Figure 6-7 ▶ **Program schedule with borders**

DLR Nightly Schedule

DLR airs listener-supported public radio in Bismarck, North Dakota from 5:00 a.m. to 10:30 p.m. You can Listen Live to streaming audio of our broadcast. Please refer below for our current nightly schedule.

border around the entire table

Time	Mon	Tue	Wed	Thu	Fri	Sat	Sun
6:00 PM	National News	National News	National News	National News	National News	National News	National News
6:30 PM	World News	World News	World News	World News	World News	World News	World News

borders around table cells

The default browser style is to separate the border around the entire table from the borders around individual table cells, creating additional space in the table layout. Another style choice is to collapse the borders into each other. Figure 6-8 shows the impact of both style choices.

Figure 6-8   Separate and collapsed borders

separate borders   collapsed borders

© 2016 Cengage Learning

To choose between the separate or collapsed borders model, apply the following `border-collapse` property to the `table` element

```
border-collapse: type;
```

where `type` is either `separate` (the default) or `collapse`. If the separate borders model is used, the spacing between the borders is set by adding the following `border-spacing` property to the `table` element

```
border-spacing: value;
```

where `value` is the space between the borders in one of the CSS units of measure. For example, the following style rule specifies that all borders within the table should be separated by a distance of 10 pixels:

```
table {
    border-collapse: separate;
    border-spacing: 10px;
}
```

In the collapsed borders model, borders from adjacent elements are merged together to form a single border, but the borders are not simply moved together, instead they are joined in a new style that combines features of both borders. For example, if two adjacent 1-pixel-wide borders are collapsed together, the resulting border is not 2-pixels wide, but only 1-pixel wide.

The situation is more complicated when adjacent borders have different widths, styles, or colors that cannot be easily combined. For example, how would you combine an outset red border and a solid blue border into a single border of only one color and style? To reconcile the differences between adjacent borders, CSS employs the following five rules, listed in order of decreasing precedence:

1. If either border has a border style of `hidden`, the collapsed border is hidden.
2. A border style of `none` is overridden by any other border style.
3. If neither border is hidden, the style of the wider border takes priority over the narrower border.
4. If the two borders have the same width but different styles, the border style with the highest priority is used. Double borders have the highest priority, followed by solid, dashed, dotted, ridge, outset, groove, and finally, inset borders.
5. If the borders differ only in color, the color of the element in the table with the higher priority takes precedence. Precedence is given first to borders around individual table cells, followed by borders for table rows, row groups, columns, and column groups; and finally, the border around the entire table. You will learn about row groups, columns, and column groups later in this tutorial.

Any situation not covered by these rules is left to browsers to determine which border dominates when collapsing the two borders. Figure 6-9 provides an example of the first rule in action. In this example, the border around the entire table is hidden but a 1-pixel blue border is assigned to the cells within the table. As shown in the image on the right, when collapsed, any cell borders adjacent to the table border adopt the hidden border property.

Figure 6-9   **Reconciling hidden borders**

in the collapsed borders model, the hidden border around the table takes precedence over the blue borders for individual cells

in the separate borders model, the border around the table is hidden and the border around each cell is shown in blue

separate borders

collapsed borders

```
table {border-style: hidden;
       border-collapse: separate;}
td    {border: 1px solid blue;}
```

```
table {border-style: hidden;
       border-collapse: collapse;}
td    {border: 1px solid blue;}
```

© 2016 Cengage Learning

Figure 6-10 shows what happens when two borders of the same width but different styles meet. In this case, because of Rule 4, the table cell borders with the double blue lines take precedence over the solid red line of the table border when the two borders are collapsed into one.

Figure 6-10   **Reconciling different border styles**

in the collapsed borders model, double borders around individual cells takes precedence over the singe border around the entire table

in the separate borders model, a single red border is placed around the entire table and a double blue border is placed around individual cells

separate borders

collapsed borders

```
table {border-style: 5px solid red;
       border-collapse: separate;}
td    {border: 5px double blue;}
```

```
table {border-style: 5px solid red;
       border-collapse: collapse;}
td    {border: 5px double blue;}
```

© 2016 Cengage Learning

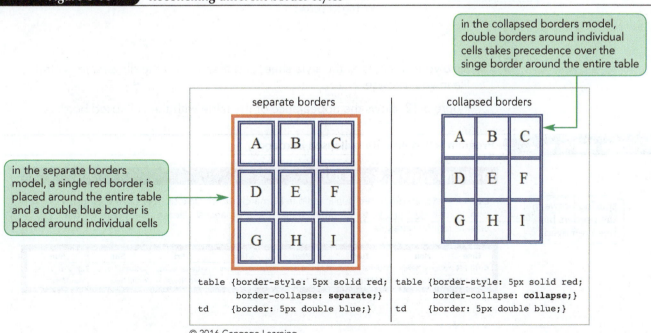

Although the collapsed borders model appears more complicated at first, the rules are reasonable and allow for a wide variety of border designs.

Styling Table Borders

- To define the table borders model, apply the style

  `border-collapse: type;`

  where *type* is `separate` (the default) to create separate borders or `collapse` to merge all adjacent borders.
- To set the space between separated borders, apply the style

  `border-spacing: value;`

  where *value* is the space between the borders in any of the CSS units of measure.

For the DLR evening program schedule, Kyle thinks the table would look better with collapsed borders and asks you to modify the table style sheet.

To collapse the table borders:

1. Return to the **dlr_tables.css** file in your editor.

2. Add the style `border-collapse: collapse;` to the style rule for the schedule table. Figure 6-11 highlights the newly added style.

Figure 6-11	Setting the border collapse style

```
table.schedule {
    background: white;
    border: 10px outset rgb(153, 0, 153);
    border-collapse: collapse;
    font-size: 0.75em;
    width: 100%;
}
```

sets the borders within the table to collapse into one another

3. Save your changes to the style sheet and then reload the dlr_evenings.html file in your browser.

Figure 6-12 shows the appearance of the table with the collapsed borders.

Figure 6-12	Program schedule with collapsed borders

DLR Nightly Schedule

DLR airs listener-supported public radio in Bismarck, North Dakota from 5:00 a.m. to 10:30 p.m. You can Listen Live to streaming audio of our broadcast. Please refer below for our current nightly schedule.

spacing between the borders has been removed

Time	Mon	Tue	Wed	Thu	Fri	Sat	Sun
6:00 PM	National News	National News	National News	National News	National News	National News	National News
6:30 PM	World News	World News	World News	World News	World News	World News	World News

Kyle remarks that the schedule information for the 6:00 p.m. and 6:30 p.m. timeslots is highly redundant because the *National News* and *World News* programs always air at those times every day of the week. He thinks that the schedule would be easier to read if those programs are entered only once with the table cell text extending across the week. You can achieve this effect using spanning cells.

Spanning Rows and Columns

A spanning cell is a single cell that occupies more than one cell row and/or column. Spanning cells are created by adding either or both of the following `rowspan` and `colspan` attributes to either `td` or `th` elements

```
rowspan="rows" colspan="cols"
```

where *rows* is the number of rows that the cell will occupy and *cols* is the number of columns. The spanning starts in the cell where you put the `rowspan` and `colspan` attributes, and goes to the right and downward from that location. For example, to create a data cell that spans three rows and two columns, enter the following `td` element:

```
<td rowspan="3" colspan="2" > ... </td>
```

It is important to remember that when a cell spans multiple rows or columns, it pushes other cells to the right or down. If you want to maintain the same number of rows and columns in your table, you must adjust the number of cells in a row or column that includes a spanning cell. To account for a column-spanning cell, you have to reduce the number of cells in the current row. For example, if a table covers five columns, but one of the cells in a row spans three columns, you need only three table cells in that row: two cells that occupy a single column each and the one cell that spans the other three columns.

REFERENCE

Creating Cells that Span Rows and Columns

- To create a cell that spans several columns, add the following attribute to `td` or `th` element

  ```
  colspan="cols"
  ```

  where *cols* is the number of columns covered by the cell.
- To create a cell that spans several rows, add the following attribute to `td` or `th` element

  ```
  rowspan="rows"
  ```

  where *rows* is the number of rows covered by the cell.

To see how column-spanning cells work, you replace the cells for the *National News* and *World News* programs that currently occupy seven cells each with a single cell spanning seven columns in each row.

To create a column-spanning cell:

1. Return to the **dlr_evenings.html** file in your editor.

2. Go to the schedule table and for the second table cell in both the second and third rows of the table, add the attribute

   ```
   colspan="7"
   ```

   to the opening **<td>** tag.

> You must remove cells from the table row when you add a column-spanning cell to ensure that the cell content aligns properly into columns.

3. Delete the remaining six table cells in both the second and third table rows to keep the size of those rows at eight total columns.

   Figure 6-13 highlights the revised code for the schedule table.

Figure 6-13 Spanning several columns with a single cell

```
<table class="schedule">
    <tr>
        <th>Time</th>
        <th>Mon</th>
        <th>Tue</th>
        <th>Wed</th>
        <th>Thu</th>
        <th>Fri</th>
        <th>Sat</th>
        <th>Sun</th>
    </tr>
    <tr>
        <th>6:00 PM</th>
        <td colspan="7">National News</td>
    </tr>
    <tr>
        <th>6:30 PM</th>
        <td colspan="7">World News</td>
    </tr>
</table>
```

remaining six td elements removed from the second and third rows to keep the size at 8 total columns

sets each cell to span 7 columns within its row

4. Save your changes to the file and then reload the dlr_evenings.html file in your browser.

   Figure 6-14 shows the revised appearance of the table with column-spanning cells in the second and third rows.

Figure 6-14 Column-spanning cells

the second cell in both rows 2 and 3 spans seven columns

DLR Nightly Schedule

DLR airs listener-supported public radio in Bismarck, North Dakota from 5:00 a.m. to 10:30 p.m. You can Listen Live to streaming audio of our broadcast. Please refer below for our current nightly schedule.

Time	Mon	Tue	Wed	Thu	Fri	Sat	Sun
6:00 PM	National News						
6:30 PM	World News						

The rest of the evening schedule shown earlier in Figure 6-1 includes programs that last longer than 30 minutes and thus will need to span several rows. To maintain a row layout with row-spanning cells, you need to remove extra cells from the rows below the spanning cell. Consider the table shown in Figure 6-15, which covers three rows and four columns. The first cell from the first row spans three rows. You need four table cells in the first row, but only three in the second and third rows. This is because the spanning cell from the first row occupies the position of the first cell in the second and third rows.

Figure 6-15	Row-spanning cells

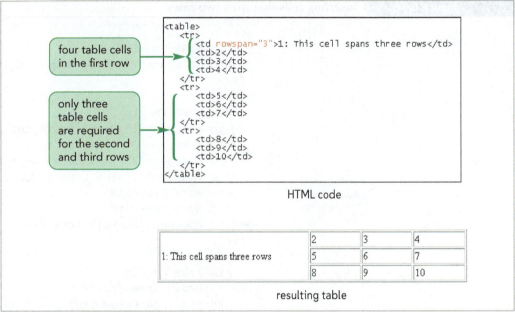

The 7:00 p.m. to 8:00 p.m. section of the DLR schedule contains several programs that run for an hour. To insert these programs, you create row-spanning cells that span two rows in the schedule table. To keep the columns lined up, you must reduce the number of cells entered in the subsequent row. Enter the next two rows of the program schedule table now.

To create row-spanning cells:

1. Return to the **dlr_evenings.html** file in your editor.

2. Directly above the closing `</table>` tag, insert the following table row:

```
<tr>
    <th>7:00 PM</th>
    <td rowspan="2">Opera Fest</td>
    <td rowspan="2">Radio U</td>
    <td rowspan="2">Science Week</td>
    <td rowspan="2">The Living World</td>
    <td>Word Play</td>
    <td>Agri-Week</td>
    <td rowspan="2">Folk Fest</td>
</tr>
```

3. Add the following row for the programs that start at 7:30 p.m.:

```
<tr>
    <th>7:30 PM</th>
    <td>Brain Stew</td>
    <td>Bismarck Forum</td>
</tr>
```

Figure 6-16 highlights the revised code for the schedule table.

Figure 6-16   Inserting cells that span two rows

```
<tr>
    <th>6:30 PM</th>
    <td colspan="7">World News</td>
</tr>
<tr>
    <th>7:00 PM</th>
    <td rowspan="2">Opera Fest</td>
    <td rowspan="2">Radio U</td>
    <td rowspan="2">Science Week</td>
    <td rowspan="2">The Living World</td>
    <td>Word Play</td>
    <td>Agri-Week</td>
    <td rowspan="2">Folk Fest</td>
</tr>
<tr>
    <th>7:30 PM</th>
    <td>Brain Stew</td>
    <td>Bismarck Forum</td>
</tr>
</table>
```

cells span
two rows

4. Save your changes to the file and then reload the dlr_evenings.html file in your browser.

Figure 6-17 shows the schedule for programs airing at 7:00 p.m. and 7:30 p.m.

Figure 6-17   Program schedule through 7:30 p.m.

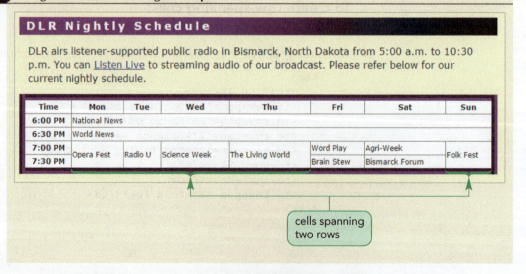

DLR Nightly Schedule

DLR airs listener-supported public radio in Bismarck, North Dakota from 5:00 a.m. to 10:30 p.m. You can Listen Live to streaming audio of our broadcast. Please refer below for our current nightly schedule.

Time	Mon	Tue	Wed	Thu	Fri	Sat	Sun
6:00 PM	National News						
6:30 PM	World News						
7:00 PM	Opera Fest	Radio U	Science Week	The Living World	Word Play	Agri-Week	Folk Fest
7:30 PM					Brain Stew	Bismarck Forum	

cells spanning
two rows

TIP

You can create even more complex layouts by nesting tables inside table cells.

The final part of the evening schedule includes the program *The Classical Musical Connection*, which spans two hours on Monday through Thursday. Like the news programs, you don't want to repeat the name of the show each day; and like the five hour-long programs you just entered, you don't want to repeat the name of the show in each half-hour cell. Kyle suggests that you use both the `rowspan` and `colspan` attributes to create a table cell that spans four rows and four columns.

Other programs in the 8:00 to 10:00 time slots, such as *Saturday Nite Jazz* and *The Indie Connection*, also span four rows, but only one column. The last program aired before KPAF signs off is the *World News Feed*, which is played every night from 10:00 to 10:30. You add these and the other late evening programs to the schedule table now.

To enter the remaining programs:

1. Return to the **dlr_evenings.html** file in your editor and, directly above the closing `</table>` tag, add the following table row for programs airing at 8:00 p.m.:

   ```
   <tr>
      <th>8:00 PM</th>
      <td rowspan="4" colspan="4">The Classical Music
   Connection</td>
      <td>Old Time Radio</td>
      <td rowspan="4">Saturday Nite Jazz</td>
      <td rowspan="4">The Indie Connection</td>
   </tr>
   ```

2. The *Inner Mind* is the only program starting at 8:30 p.m. during the week. Add the 8:30 p.m. starting time and the program listing as a new row in the schedule table:

   ```
   <tr>
      <th>8:30 PM</th>
      <td>The Inner Mind</td>
   </tr>
   ```

3. The only program that starts at 9:00 p.m. is the hour-long *Open Mike Nite* program. Add the following row to the table to display this program in the schedule:

   ```
   <tr>
      <th>9:00 PM</th>
      <td rowspan="2">Open Mike Nite</td>
   </tr>
   ```

4. There are no programs that start at 9:30 p.m. during the week. However, you still need to include this starting time in the schedule because the nightly schedule is broken down into half-hour increments. Add the following table row:

   ```
   <tr>
      <th>9:30 PM</th>
   </tr>
   ```

5. Complete the table by adding the last row, which lists the *World News Feed* program that airs every night starting at 10:00 p.m.:

   ```
   <tr>
      <th>10:00 PM</th>
      <td colspan="7">World News Feed</td>
   </tr>
   ```

Figure 6-18 highlights the newly added rows in the schedule table.

Figure 6-18   Adding the remaining DLR programs

program covers 4 half-hour slots on 4 consecutive days

programs cover 4 half-hour slots

only one program starts at 8:30 p.m.

program covers 2 half-hour slots

no program starts at 9:30 p.m.

program airs every night starting at 10:00 p.m.

```
   </tr>
   <tr>
      <th>8:00 PM</th>
      <td rowspan="4" colspan="4">The Classical Music Connection</td>
      <td>Old Time Radio</td>
      <td rowspan="4">Saturday Nite Jazz</td>
      <td rowspan="4">The Indie Connection</td>
   </tr>
   <tr>
      <th>8:30 PM</th>
      <td>The Inner Mind</td>
   </tr>
   <tr>
      <th>9:00 PM</th>
      <td rowspan="2">Open Mike Nite</td>
   </tr>
   <tr>
      <th>9:30 PM</th>
   </tr>
   <tr>
      <th>10:00 PM</th>
      <td colspan="7">World News Feed</td>
   </tr>
</table>
```

6. Save your changes to the file and then reload the dlr_evenings.html file in your browser.

Figure 6-19 shows the complete schedule for all of the DLR evening programs during the week.

Figure 6-19   The complete DLR evening schedule

Time	Mon	Tue	Wed	Thu	Fri	Sat	Sun
6:00 PM	National News						
6:30 PM	World News						
7:00 PM	Opera Fest	Radio U	Science Week	The Living World	Word Play	Agri-Week	Folk Fest
7:30 PM					Brain Stew	Bismarck Forum	
8:00 PM	The Classical Music Connection				Old Time Radio	Saturday Nite Jazz	The Indie Connection
8:30 PM					The Inner Mind		
9:00 PM					Open Mike Nite		
9:30 PM							
10:00 PM	World News Feed						

The web table you created matches the printout of DLR's evening schedule. Kyle likes the clear structure of the table. He notes that many DLR listeners tune into the station over the Internet, listening to DLR's streaming audio feed. Because those listeners might be located in different time zones, Kyle suggests that you add a caption to the table indicating that all times in the schedule are based on the Central Time Zone.

INSIGHT

Defining Borders in HTML

If you work with legacy websites, you might encounter web tables in which tables are formatted using HTML attributes. One such attribute is the following `border` attribute

```
<table border="value">
…
</table>
```

where `value` is the width of the table border in pixels. Adding a table border in this fashion also adds a border around individual table cells. HTML also supports two attributes, `frame` and `rules`, that allow you to specify exactly which table cells receive borders and which sides of those table cells are bordered.

These attributes are not supported in HTML5, but most browsers still support them for older websites. You should use CSS border styles whenever possible to format the appearance of your web table.

Creating a Table Caption

Table captions are another part of the basic table structure and are marked using the following `caption` element

```
<caption>content</caption>
```

where `content` is the content contained within the caption. Captions can contain additional text-level elements. For example, the following code marks the text Program Schedule using the `em` element, which marks it as emphasized text:

```
<caption><em>Program Schedule</em></caption>
```

Only one caption is allowed per web table, and the `caption` element must be listed directly after the opening `<table>` tag.

Add a caption to the program schedule.

To add a table caption:

▶ 1. Return to the **dlr_evenings.html** file in your editor.

▶ 2. Directly after the opening `<table>` tag, insert the following `caption` element:

```
<caption>All Times Central</caption>
```

Figure 6-20 highlights the table caption element.

Figure 6-20 Adding a caption to a web table

```
<table class="schedule">
    <caption>All Times Central</caption>
    <tr>
        <th>Time</th>
        <th>Mon</th>
        <th>Tue</th>
        <th>Wed</th>
        <th>Thu</th>
        <th>Fri</th>
        <th>Sat</th>
        <th>Sun</th>
    </tr>
```

3. Save your changes to the file.

By default, browsers place captions above the table, but you can specify the caption location using the `caption-side` property

```
caption-side: position;
```

where *position* is either `top` (the default) or `bottom` to place the caption below the table.

To align the caption text horizontally, you use the CSS `text-align` property. Thus, to place the schedule caption in the bottom-right corner of the table, you would enter the following CSS styles:

```
caption-side: bottom;
text-align: right;
```

Add styles to the dlr_tables.css style sheet to place the caption of the program schedule table to the bottom and right of the table.

To format the table caption:

1. Return to the **dlr_tables.css** file in your editor.

2. Go to the Table Caption Styles section and insert the following style rule:

   ```
   table.schedule caption {
       caption-side: bottom;
       text-align: right;
   }
   ```

   Figure 6-21 highlights the style rule for the table caption.

Figure 6-21	Adding a caption to a web table

```
/* Table Caption Styles */

table.schedule caption {
    caption-side: bottom;          places the caption
                                    at the bottom of
                                    the table
    text-align: right;             right-aligns the
}                                  caption text
```

3. Save your changes to the file and then reload the dlr_evenings.html file in your browser. Figure 6-22 shows the placement of the table caption below and to the right of the schedule table.

Figure 6-22	Placement of the table caption

Time	Mon	Tue	Wed	Thu	Fri	Sat	Sun
6:00 PM	National News						
6:30 PM	World News						
7:00 PM	Opera Fest	Radio U	Science Week	The Living World	Word Play	Agri-Week	Folk Fest
7:30 PM					Brain Stew	Bismarck Forum	
8:00 PM	The Classical Music Connection				Old Time Radio	Saturday Nite Jazz	The Indie Connection
8:30 PM					The Inner Mind		
9:00 PM					Open Mike Nite		
9:30 PM							
10:00 PM	World News Feed						

table caption ——► All Times Central

Table captions inherit the text styles associated with the table. For example, if you create a style for the `table` element that sets the font color to red, the caption text will also be displayed in a red font.

Problem Solving: Make your Tables Accessible

It is a challenge to make web tables accessible to users who rely on screen readers to access online content. Screen readers read table content linearly by moving left-to-right from the cells within each row and then down row-by-row through the table. To make the table content accessible, you must first structure the content so that it is easily interpreted even when read in a linear order.

Many screen readers include the ability to announce the row and column headers associated with each data cell, so you should always identify your row and column headers using the th element. You can also use the following scope attribute to explicitly associate a header cell with a row or column

```
<th scope="type">...</th>
```

where type is either row, column, rowgroup (for a group of rows), or colgroup (for a group of columns). For example, the following code explicitly associates the header cell with the content of its table row

```
<th scope="row">7:30 PM</th>
```

A screen reader encountering the scope attribute can use it to aurally identify a data cell with its row and column headers, making it easier for users to interpret the cell content.

Appendix D provides more information on making the web more accessible for users with special needs, including examples of other HTML attributes that can make your web tables more accessible.

You have completed your work on setting up the program schedule in a web table. In the next session, you will refine the table structure by grouping the rows and columns of the table. You will also further explore CSS styles designed specifically for tables and table data.

REVIEW

Session 6.1 Quick Check

1. How is the number of columns in a web table determined?

2. Provide code to create a table row with three header cells containing the text: *Morning*, *Afternoon*, and *Evening*.

3. Provide code to create a table row with three data cells containing the text *Tompkins*, *Ramirez*, and *Davis*.

4. Provide a style rule to display all `table` elements with collapsed borders.

5. Two table cells have adjacent borders. One cell has a 5-pixel-wide double border and the other cell has a 6-pixel-wide solid border. If the table borders are collapsed, what type of border will the two cells share?

6. A table data cell contains the text *Monday* and should stretch across two rows and three columns. Provide the HTML code for the cell.

7. What adjustment do you have to make to a table when a cell spans multiple columns to keep the column aligned?

8. What adjustment do you have to make to a table when a cell spans multiple rows to keep the columns aligned?

9. Provide the style rule to display all table captions at the lower-left corner of the table.

Session 6.2 Visual Overview:

The **colgroup** element identifies groups of columns in the web table.

Individual columns are identified with the **col** element.

The **thead** element identifies the row(s) in the table header.

The **tbody** element identifies the row(s) in the table body.

The **tfoot** element identifies the row(s) in the table footer.

```
<table class="schedule">
    <caption>All Times Central</caption>
    <colgroup>
        <col id="firstCol" />
        <col class="dayCols" span="5" />
    </colgroup>
    <thead>
        <tr>
            <th>Time</th>
            <th>Mon</th>
            <th>Tue</th>
            <th>Wed</th>
            <th>Thu</th>
            <th>Fri</th>
        </tr>
    </thead>
    <tbody>
        <tr>
            <th>6:00 PM</th>
            <td colspan="5">National News</td>
        </tr>
        <tr>
            <th>6:30 PM</th>
            <td colspan="5">World News</td>
        </tr>
        <tr>
            <th>7:00 PM</th>
            <td rowspan="2">Opera Fest</td>
            <td rowspan="2">Radio U</td>
            <td rowspan="2">Science Week</td>
            <td rowspan="2">The Living World</td>
            <td>Word Play</td>
        </tr>
        <tr>
            <th>7:30 PM</th>
            <td>Brain Stew</td>
        </tr>
    </tbody>
    <tfoot>
        <tr>
            <td colspan="6">DLR ends its broadcast day at 10:30 p.m.</td>
        </tr>
    </tfoot>
</table>
```

Rows and Column Groups

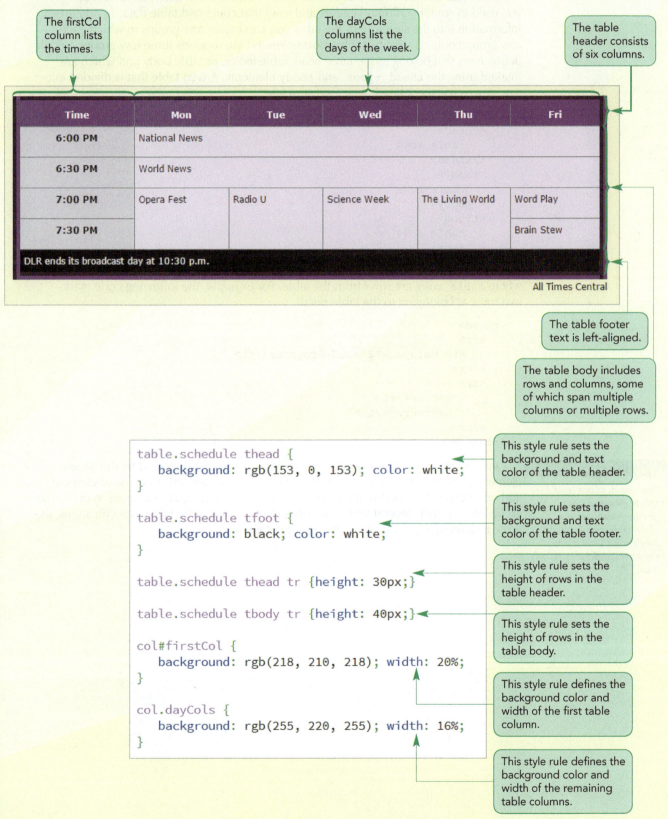

The firstCol column lists the times.

The dayCols columns list the days of the week.

The table header consists of six columns.

Time	Mon	Tue	Wed	Thu	Fri
6:00 PM	National News				
6:30 PM	World News				
7:00 PM	Opera Fest	Radio U	Science Week	The Living World	Word Play
7:30 PM					Brain Stew

DLR ends its broadcast day at 10:30 p.m.

All Times Central

The table footer text is left-aligned.

The table body includes rows and columns, some of which span multiple columns or multiple rows.

```
table.schedule thead {
    background: rgb(153, 0, 153); color: white;
}

table.schedule tfoot {
    background: black; color: white;
}

table.schedule thead tr {height: 30px;}

table.schedule tbody tr {height: 40px;}

col#firstCol {
    background: rgb(218, 210, 218); width: 20%;
}

col.dayCols {
    background: rgb(255, 220, 255); width: 16%;
}
```

This style rule sets the background and text color of the table header.

This style rule sets the background and text color of the table footer.

This style rule sets the height of rows in the table header.

This style rule sets the height of rows in the table body.

This style rule defines the background color and width of the first table column.

This style rule defines the background color and width of the remaining table columns.

Creating Row Groups

The table you created in the first session made no distinction between rows that you used to contain column headers and rows that contained table data. To add this information into the structure of the table you can create row groups in which each row group contains specific table information. HTML supports three row groups, which define rows that belong to the table head, table footer, or table body and which are marked using the thead, tfoot, and tbody elements. A web table that is divided into row groups has the following general structure:

```
<table>
   <thead>
      table rows
   </thead>
   <tbody>
      table rows
   </tbody>
   <tfoot>
      table rows
   </tfoot>
</table>
```

where *table rows* are rows from the table. For example, the following code marks two rows as belonging to the table head:

```
<thead>
   <tr>
      <th colspan="2">DLR Programs</th>
   </tr>
   <tr>
      <th>Time</th>
      <th>Program</th>
   </tr>
</thead>
```

Order is important. The thead element must appear first, followed by the tbody element and finally the tfoot element. A table can contain only one thead element and one tfoot element, but it can include any number of tbody elements to mark row groups that contain several topical sections. Note that in older HTML specifications, the tfoot element is placed before the tbody element.

Marking Row Groups

- To mark row groups in the table head, use

```
<thead>
   table rows
</thead>
```

where *table rows* are the rows in the table head.
- To mark row groups in the table footer, use

```
<tfoot>
   table rows
</tfoot>
```

where *table rows* are the rows in the table footer.
- To mark row groups in the table body, use

```
<tbody>
   table rows
</tbody>
```

where *table rows* are the rows in the table body.

To indicate the structure of the schedule table, you decide to use the `thead` element to mark the head row in the program schedule, the `tfoot` element to add a table footer, and the `tbody` element to mark the rows for the broadcast times of each program.

To create table row groups:

1. If you took a break after the last session, make sure the **dlr_evenings.html** file is open in your editor.

2. Enclose the first table row within an opening and closing set of `<thead>` tags to mark that row as the table header. Indent the HTML code for the row to make it easier to read.

3. Enclose the remaining table rows within an opening and closing set of `<tbody>` tags to mark those rows as belonging to the table body. Indent the HTML code for those rows to make them easier to read.

> The table footer row group should be placed after row groups marked with the tbody element.

4. Directly below the closing `</tbody>` tag, insert the following table footer consisting of a single row with one data cell spanning eight columns:

```
<tfoot>
   <tr>
      <td colspan="8">DLR ends its broadcast day at
10:30 p.m.</td>
   </tr>
</tfoot>
```

Figure 6-23 highlights the newly added code in the schedule table.

Figure 6-23   **Marking row groups**

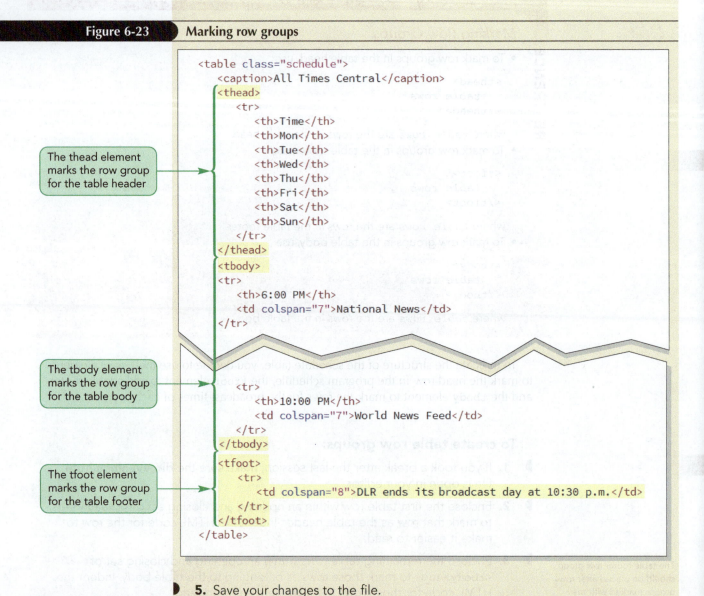

The thead element marks the row group for the table header

The tbody element marks the row group for the table body

The tfoot element marks the row group for the table footer

```
<table class="schedule">
    <caption>All Times Central</caption>
    <thead>
        <tr>
            <th>Time</th>
            <th>Mon</th>
            <th>Tue</th>
            <th>Wed</th>
            <th>Thu</th>
            <th>Fri</th>
            <th>Sat</th>
            <th>Sun</th>
        </tr>
    </thead>
    <tbody>
    <tr>
        <th>6:00 PM</th>
        <td colspan="7">National News</td>
    </tr>

        <tr>
            <th>10:00 PM</th>
            <td colspan="7">World News Feed</td>
        </tr>
    </tbody>
    <tfoot>
        <tr>
            <td colspan="8">DLR ends its broadcast day at 10:30 p.m.</td>
        </tr>
    </tfoot>
</table>
```

5. Save your changes to the file.

TIP

Row groups also are used for applications in which table body content is imported from external data sources, such as databases or XML documents.

One purpose of row groups is to allow you to create different styles for groups of rows in your table. Any style that you apply to the `thead`, `tbody`, or `tfoot` element is inherited by the rows those elements contain.

Kyle wants the rows within the table header to be displayed in a white font on a purple background. He wants the rows within the table footer to be displayed in a white font on a black background. Add these style rules to the dlr_tables.css file now.

To format the table row groups:

1. Return to the **dlr_tables.css** file in your editor.

2. Go to the Row Group Styles section and add the following style rule to format the content of the table header row group:

```
table.schedule thead {
    background: rgb(153, 0, 153);
    color: white;
}
```

3. Add the following style rule for the table footer row group:

```
table.schedule tfoot {
    background: black;
    color: white;
}
```

Figure 6-24 highlights the newly added style rules.

Figure 6-24   **Formatting row groups**

displays the rows from the table header row group in a white font on a purple background

displays the rows from the table footer row group in a white font on a black background

```
/* Row Group Styles */

table.schedule thead {
    background: rgb(153, 0, 153);
    color: white;
}

table.schedule tfoot {
    background: black;
    color: white;
}
```

4. Save your changes to the style sheet and then reopen the **dlr_evenings.html** file in your browser. Figure 6-25 shows the new appearance of the web table with the formatted row groups.

Figure 6-25   **Row groups in the schedule table**

table header

table body

table footer

Time	Mon	Tue	Wed	Thu	Fri	Sat	Sun
6:00 PM	National News						
6:30 PM	World News						
7:00 PM	Opera Fest	Radio U	Science Week	The Living World	Word Play	Agri-Week	Folk Fest
7:30 PM					Brain Stew	Bismarck Forum	
8:00 PM	The Classical Music Connection				Old Time Radio	Saturday Nite Jazz	The Indie Connection
8:30 PM					The Inner Mind		
9:00 PM					Open Mike Nite		
9:30 PM							
10:00 PM	World News Feed						

DLR ends its broadcast day at 10:30 p.m.

All Times Central

Next, Kyle wants to format the appearance of some of the columns in the table. You can define the appearance of a table column through the use of column groups.

Creating Column Groups

There is no HTML tag to mark table columns—the columns are determined implicitly based on the number of cells within the table rows. However, you can still reference those columns for the purposes of creating design styles through the following `colgroup` element

```
<table>
   <colgroup>
      columns
   </colgroup>
   table rows
</table>
```

where `columns` are the individual columns defined within the group and `table rows` are the table rows. The columns within the `colgroup` element are identified by the following `col` element:

```
<col span="value" />
```

where `value` is the number of columns spanned by the `col` element. If no `span` attribute is included, the `col` element references a single column. Thus, the following column structure defines a group of three columns with the first two columns grouped together:

```
<colgroup>
   <col span="2" />
   <col />
</colgroup>
```

TIP

The span attribute can also be added to the colgroup element to create column groups that span multiple columns.

Once you have defined your columns using the `colgroup` and `col` elements, you can identify individual columns using `id` and/or `class` attributes for the purposes of applying CSS styles to specific columns. For example, the following code defines a column group consisting of three columns, with the first two columns belonging to the firstCols class and the third column belonging has the ID lastCol.

```
<colgroup>
   <col span="2" class="firstCols" />
   <col id="lastCol" />
</colgroup>
```

REFERENCE

Identifying a Column Group

- To identify a group of columns from the web table, use

```
<colgroup>
   columns
</colgroup>
```

where `columns` are the individual columns defined within the group
- To identify a column within a column group, use

```
<col span="value" />
```

where `value` is the number of columns spanned by the `col` element.

Create a column group for the program schedule table with one `col` element used for the first column containing the list of broadcast times and the second `col` element used for the remaining seven columns containing the names of the DLR programs.

To define a column group:

1. Return to the **dlr_evenings.html** file in your editor.

2. Directly after the table caption, insert the following code to create a column group consisting of a first column with the ID firstcol followed by seven columns belonging to the dayCols class.

```
<colgroup>
   <col id="firstCol" />
   <col class="dayCols" span="7" />
</colgroup>
```

Figure 6-26 highlights the newly added style rules.

Figure 6-26   Defining a column group

| col element references the first column |
| col element references the next seven columns |

```
<table class="schedule">
   <caption>All Times Central</caption>
   <colgroup>
      <col id="firstCol" />
      <col class="dayCols" span="7" />
   </colgroup>
   <thead>
```

3. Save your changes to the file.

Once the column groups have been defined, you can create styles to format the appearance of the columns. The following style rule uses the class and id values defined in the previous example to set the background color of the column with the ID firstCol to red and the columns belonging to the dayCols class to yellow.

```
col#firstCol {background-color: red;}
col.dayCols {background-color: yellow;}
```

Note that columns and column groups accept only CSS style properties to modify the column borders, background, width, and visibility. Other styles are not supported. You cannot, for example, set the font size for all of the text within a particular column or column group.

Modify the dlr_tables.css style sheet to change the background color of the first column to gray and the background of the remaining columns (belonging to the dayCols class) to pink.

To format a column group:

1. Return to the **dlr_tables.css** file in your editor.

2. Go to the Column Group Styles section and insert the following style rules to format the appearance of the schedule table columns:

```
col#firstCol {
   background: rgb(218, 210, 218);
}

col.dayCols {
   background: rgb(255, 220, 255);
}
```

Figure 6-27 highlights the style rules for the two column groups.

Figure 6-27   **Formatting the table columns**

```
/* Column Group Styles */

col#firstCol {
    background: rgb(218, 210, 218);
}

col.dayCols {
    background: rgb(255, 220, 255);
}
```

displays the first column with a gray background

displays the day columns with a pink background

▶ **3.** Save your changes to the file and then reload the dlr_evenings.html file in your browser.

Figure 6-28 shows the appearance of the formatted columns.

Figure 6-28   **Column groups in the schedule table**

firstCol column

daysCol columns

Time	Mon	Tue	Wed	Thu	Fri	Sat	Sun
6:00 PM	National News						
6:30 PM	World News						
7:00 PM	Opera Fest	Radio U	Science Week	The Living World	Word Play	Agri-Week	Folk Fest
7:30 PM					Brain Stew	Bismarck Forum	
8:00 PM					Old Time Radio		
8:30 PM	The Classical Music Connection				The Inner Mind	Saturday Nite Jazz	The Indie Connection
9:00 PM					Open Mike Nite		
9:30 PM							
10:00 PM	World News Feed						
DLR ends its broadcast day at 10:30 p.m.							

All Times Central

You may have noticed that the new background colors have not been applied to all columns of the schedule table. The columns in the table header, for example, are still displayed on a medium purple background. To understand why, you need to explore how CSS handles style precedence for different parts of the table structure.

INSIGHT

Creating Banded Rows and Columns

A popular table design is to create table rows of alternating background colors to make it easier for users to locate table data. You can create banded rows using the `nth-of-type` pseudo-class. For example, to create a table in which the background colors alternate between yellow on the odd-numbered rows and gray on the even-numbered rows, apply the following style rules:

```
tr:nth-of-type(odd) {
    background: yellow;
}

tr:nth-of-type(even) {
    background: gray;
}
```

The same technique can be used to create banded columns of different background colors. The following style rules create odd-numbered columns that have a yellow background and even-numbered columns with a gray background:

```
colgroup col:nth-of-type(odd) {
    background: yellow;
}

colgroup col:nth-of-type(even) {
    background: gray;
}
```

Note that this technique assumes that none of the table `row` or `col` elements span more than one row or column.

Exploring CSS Styles and Web Tables

Table objects have different levels of precedence with styles for more specific table objects taking precedence over styles for less specific objects. Figure 6-29 diagrams the different levels of precedence in the table structure.

Figure 6-29   Levels of precedence in the table styles

- table cells — highest precedence
- rows
- row groups
- columns
- column groups
- table — lowest precedence

© 2016 Cengage Learning

The style rules with the highest precedence are those applied to individual table cells. Next are the style rules applied to table rows and table row groups. Then, are the style rules applied to columns and column groups. Finally, the style rules applied to the entire web table are the ones with the lowest precedence.

The order of precedence explains why the cells in the table header retained their medium purple background. That background color was defined in the style rule for the table header row group and thus took precedence over any background styles defined for a column or column group.

Working with Width and Height

By default, browsers will attempt to fit the most content possible within each column before wrapping the cell text to a new line. The result is that columns containing cells with more text are wider than those with less text. If the width of the entire table is set to be larger than the width required for individual columns, the extra space is divided equally among the columns. You can set the column widths to a different value by applying the width property to columns or column groups.

Kyle suggests you set the width of the first column to 16% of the width of the entire table and the widths of the remaining seven columns to 12% each, resulting in a total width of 100% divided among the eight columns. Add these styles to the style rules for the schedule table columns.

To set the width of a column:

1. Return to the **dlr_tables.css** file in your editor and go to the Column Group Styles section.

2. Add the style width: 16%; to the style rule for the firstCol column.

3. Add the style width: 12%; to the style rule for the columns of the dayCols class.

   Figure 6-30 highlights the width styles for the two column selectors.

Figure 6-30   Setting the column width

sets the width of the first column to 16% of the width of the table

sets the width of the day columns to 12%

```
col#firstCol {
    background: rgb(218, 210, 218);
    width: 16%;
}

col.dayCols {
    background: rgb(255, 220, 255);
    width: 12%;
}
```

Next, you explore how to work with row heights.

Creating Narrow Tables

As the width of a table decreases, the amount of space allotted to each column decreases proportionally. However, the column widths can be decreased only so far. Because browsers do not hyphenate words by default, the minimum column width is equal to the width of the longest word within the column. To allow the column widths to decrease below this limit, you can apply the following style rule to the `table` element:

```
table {table-layout: fixed;}
```

A `table-layout` value of `fixed` tells the browser to ignore cell content when reducing the width of the table columns. As the column width decreases, eventually the cell text will extend beyond the borders of the cell. To prevent this from happening, you can force the browser to insert line breaks within the individual words in your table cells by applying the following style rule:

```
th, td {word-wrap: break-word;}
```

By setting the `table-layout` property to `fixed` and allowing line breaks within words in the cell, your column widths can be reduced below the default limits set by the browser.

The height of each table row is based on the height of the tallest cell within the row. Because the cell height itself will increase as necessary to enclose its content, the result will be row heights that are not uniform across the table. You can define a uniform row height by applying the height style to table rows within each row group. Kyle suggest that you set the height of the table header row to 30 pixels and the height of each row in the table body to 40 pixels.

To set the height of the table rows:

1. Scroll up to the Row Group Styles section.

2. Add the following style rule to set the row height within the table header to 30 pixels:

```
table.schedule thead tr {
    height: 30px;
}
```

3. Add the following style rule to set the row height in the table body to 40 pixels:

```
table.schedule tbody tr {
    height: 40px;
}
```

Note that you don't apply the height property to the row groups themselves because that would set the height of the entire group and not the individual rows within the group.

Figure 6-31 highlights the height styles for the table rows.

Figure 6-31 Setting the row height

```
table.schedule tfoot {
        background: black;
        color: white;
}

table.schedule thead tr {
        height: 30px;
}

table.schedule tbody tr {
        height: 40px;
}
```

sets the height of the row in the table header to 30 pixels

sets the height of the rows in the table body to 40 pixels

4. Save your changes to the file and then refresh the **dlr_evenings.html** file in your browser.

Figure 6-32 shows the revised appearance of the table with the resized columns and rows.

Figure 6-32 Schedule table with resized columns and rows

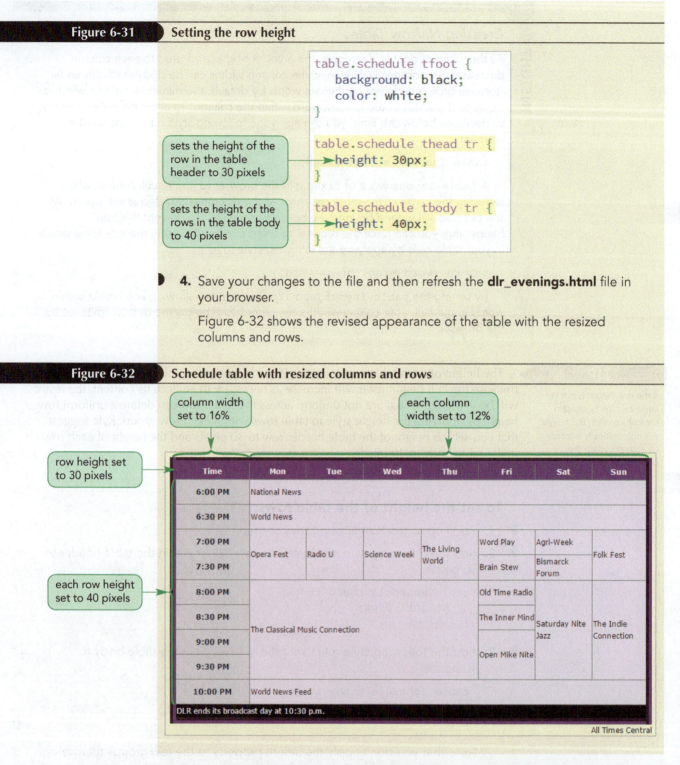

column width set to 16%

each column width set to 12%

row height set to 30 pixels

each row height set to 40 pixels

With the increased row height, Kyle would like all of the program names in the schedule to be vertically aligned with the tops of the cell borders. You can move the cell text using the `vertical-align` property introduced in Tutorial 2. Kyle also wants to increase the padding within each cell to add more space between the program names and the cell borders.

To increase the padding for the table cells:

1. Return to the **dlr_tables.css** file in your editor and go to the Table Cell Styles section.

2. Add the following styles to the style rule for the header and data cells in the schedule table:

   ```
   padding: 5px;
   vertical-align: top;
   ```

   Figure 6-33 highlights the new styles in the style sheet.

Figure 6-33   **Formatting the table cells**

adds 5 pixels of padding space to each table cell

aligns the content with the top of each table cell

```
/* Table Cell Styles */

table.schedule th, table.schedule td {
    border: 1px solid gray;
    padding: 5px;
    vertical-align: top;
}
```

3. Close the file, saving your changes.

4. Reload the dlr_evenings.html file in your browser.

   Figure 6-34 shows the completed design of the nightly schedule page.

Figure 6-34   **Completed design of the DLR Nightly Schedule page**

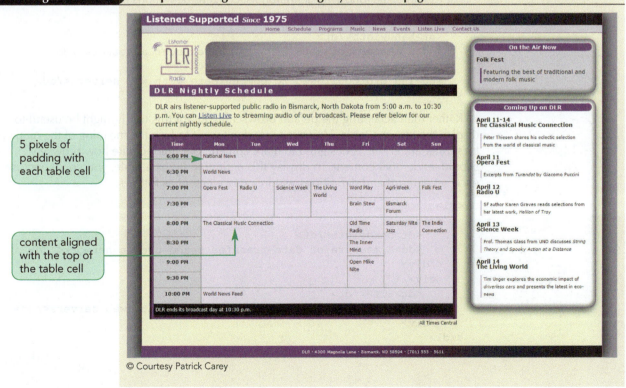

5 pixels of padding with each table cell

content aligned with the top of the table cell

© Courtesy Patrick Carey

You have completed work on DLR's nightly schedule page. However, you will continue to explore other issues that surround the use of web tables and table designs in the remainder of this session.

Applying Table Styles to Other Page Elements

Tables are useful for displaying information in an organized structure of rows and columns, but you are not limited to applying a table design only to web tables. Using the CSS `display` property, you can apply a table layout to other HTML elements, such as paragraphs, block quotes, or lists. Figure 6-35 list different CSS display styles and their equivalent HTML elements.

Figure 6-35   Table display styles

Display Style	Equivalent HTML Element
`display: table;`	table (treated as a block-level element)
`display: table-inline;`	table (treated as an inline element)
`display: table-row;`	tr
`display: table-row-group;`	tbody
`display: table-header-group;`	thead
`display: table-footer-group;`	tfoot
`display: table-column;`	col
`display: table-column-group;`	colgroup
`display: table-cell;`	td or th
`display: table-caption;`	caption

© 2016 Cengage Learning

For example, the following definition list contains definitions of two networking terms:

```
<dl>
   <dt>bandwidth</dt>
   <dd>A measure of data transfer speed over a network</dd>
   <dt>HTTP</dt>
   <dd>The protocol used to communicate with web servers</dd>
</dl>
```

Rather than accepting the default browser layout for this list, it might be useful to display the text in a table. However, you don't want to lose the meaning of the markup tags. After all, HTML is designed to mark content, but not indicate how browsers should render that content. To display this definition list as a table, you could enclose each set of terms and definitions within a `div` element as follows:

```
<dl>
   <div>
      <dt>bandwidth</dt>
      <dd>A measure of data transfer speed over a network</dd>
   </div>
   <div>
      <dt>HTTP</dt>
      <dd>The protocol used to communicate with web servers</dd>
   </div>
</dl>
```

You could then apply the following style sheet to the list, treating the entire definition list as a table—the `div` elements act as table rows, and the definition terms and descriptions act as table cells within those rows:

```
dl      {display: table; border-collapse: collapse; width: 300px;}
dl div {display: table-row;}
dt, dd {display: table-cell; border: 1px solid black;
          vertical-align: top; padding: 5px;}
```

As Figure 6-36 shows, when viewed in a web browser, the definition list looks exactly as if it were created using HTML table elements.

Figure 6-36   **Applying table styles to a definition list**

```
<dl>
    <div>
        <dt>bandwidth</dt>
        <dd>A measure of data transfer speed over
            a network</dd>
    </div>
    <div>
        <dt>HTTP</dt>
        <dd>The protocol used to communicate with
            web servers</dd>
    </div>
</dl>
```
definition list code

| bandwidth | A measure of data transfer speed over a network |
| HTTP | The protocol used to communicate with Web servers |

definition list displayed as table

```
dl {
    display: table;
    border-collapse: collapse;
    width: 300px;
}
dl div {
    display: table-row;
}
dt, dd {
    display: table-cell;
    border: 1px solid black;
    vertical-align: top;
    padding: 5px;
}
```
table styles

© 2016 Cengage Learning

In the same way, you can display other page elements in table form, as long as the markup tags are nested in a way that mimics a table structure.

Formatting a Table using HTML Attributes

If you work with legacy web pages, you might encounter web tables that use attributes to style the appearance of the table. For example, the width of the table can be set using the following width attribute

```
<table width="value"> … </table>
```

where *value* is the width of the table in pixels or as a percent of the width of the parent element.

The height of table rows can be set using the following height attribute

```
<tr height="value"> … </tr>
```

where value is the table row height in pixels.

The padding space within each table cell is set using the following cellpadding attribute

```
<table cellpadding="value"> … </table>
```

where *value* is the size of the padding space in pixels.

Finally, the space between table cells is set using the following cellspacing attribute

```
<table cellspacing="value"> … </table>
```

where *value* is the size of the space in pixels. The cellspacing attribute essentially sets the width of the borders around individual table cells.

Each of these attributes has been replaced by CSS styles; however you may still see them employed in older websites and if you are tasked with upgrading those sites you will need to understand those attribute's meaning and purpose.

Tables and Responsive Design

Tables do not scale well to mobile devices. Users will often be confronted with one of the following: a) a table in which the cell content is too small to be readable, b) a table that extends beyond the boundaries of the visual viewport, or c) table columns that are so narrow that the cell content is unreadable (see Figure 6-37).

Figure 6-37 **Web tables on mobile devices**

complete table
is too small to
read

table is easier to read but
does not fit within the
viewport

table fits within the viewport
but columns are too narrow
to read comfortably

BenBois/openclipart

What is often required is a new layout of the table data for mobile screens in which several table columns are reduced to two: one column containing all of the data labels and a second column containing the data associated with each label. Figure 6-38 shows an example of a mobile layout for the same table data shown in Figure 6-37.

Figure 6-38 **Two-column layout for a mobile device**

headings appear
in the first column
of the table

cell content appears
in the second column

BenBois/openclipart

There are several scripts and frameworks available on the web to design a table for use with mobile devices or you can use CSS to restructure the web table, which is based on an idea suggested by Chris Coyier at *https://css-tricks.com/responsive-data-tables/*.

The first step in creating a responsive web table that relies only on CSS is to add the text of data labels as attributes of all of the `td` elements in the table body. You can store these data labels using a **data attribute**, which is an attribute introduced in HTML5 that stores customized data. The general format of a data attribute is

```
data-text="value"
```

where `text` is the name of the data attribute and `value` is its value. Data attributes are often used for database applications that read the contents of HTML files. There are no standard names for data attributes, instead those names are specified by whatever application happens to be reading the HTML content.

For example, the following table uses a data attribute named `data-label` to store the text of the labels associated with each data cell.

```
<tr>
    <td data-label="Date">April 2, 2017</td>
    <td data-label="Program Title">Memories and Music</td>
    <td data-label="Featuring">Kelsey MacGraw, Mandy Dee,
        Young Irish
    </td>
    <td data-label="Venue">Folk City, Boise ID</td>
    <td data-label="Description">It's all about new music this
        week on Folk Fest. Scott Dirkens will preview new releases
        from Kelsey MacGraw and Mandy Dee. And then join us for
        a set from the always-popular group, Young Irish, from
        their recent tour.
    </td>
</tr>
```

Once you have assigned data labels to each `td` element, you need to change the table layout so that each table object is rendered as a block element. Because a responsive table design doesn't use a table header or footer, you hide those table features. Thus, within a media query for mobile devices, you establish the following style rules:

```
table, tbody, tr, td, th {
    display: block;
}

thead, tfoot {
    display: none;
}
```

Each data cell in the table body then needs to be placed using relative positioning with a large left padding space into which you insert the text of the data label. The following style rule creates a padding space that is 40% of the width of the data cell.

```
tbody td {
    position: relative;
    padding-left: 40%;
}
```

Finally, you need to insert the content of the `data-label` attribute directly before the data cell value. To accomplish that, you use the `before` pseudo-element along with the `content` property. The data label will be placed using absolute positioning at the top-left corner of the block. You can include some padding to offset the column heading from edges of the block. The width should be equal to the left padding space you set in the style rule for the `td` element. A basic style rule would appear as

```
td::before {
    content: attr(data-label);
    position: absolute;
    top: 0px;
    left: 0px;
    padding: 5px;
    width: 40%;
}
```

As shown earlier in Figure 6-38, the result is a list of data cells that are aligned as block elements and then, within each block element, the data label is followed by the data cell content. Note that the text of this web table is easier to read in the smaller viewport of the mobile device.

You can supplement these style rules with other styles to create a more pleasing design, but the goal is the same: to transform a table with multiple columns into a simpler two-column layout. Note that this approach doesn't work for more complex table layouts with cells spanning multiple rows and/or columns.

PROSKILLS

Written Communication: Designing Effective Web Tables

The primary purpose of a web table is to convey data in a compact and easily-interpreted way. You can apply several design principles to your web tables to make them more effective at presenting data to interested readers:

- *Contrast the data cells from the header cells.* Make it easy for readers to understand your data by highlighting the header column or row in a different color or font size.
- *Avoid spanning rows and columns unless necessary.* Usability studies have shown that information can be gleaned quickly when presented in a simple grid layout; don't break the grid by unnecessarily spanning a cell across rows and columns.
- *Break the monotony with icons.* If you are repeating the same phrase or word within a single row or column, consider replacing the text with an icon that conveys the same message. For example, in a table that describes the features of a product, use a check mark to indicate whether a particular feature is supported, rather than text.
- *Alternate the row colors.* A large table with dozens of rows can be difficult for readers to scan and interpret. Consider using alternative background colors for the table rows to break the monotony and reduce eye strain.
- *Don't overwhelm the eye with borders.* Cell borders should be used only when they aid users by separating one cell from another. If they're not needed for this purpose, they actually can distract from the data. Rather than using borders, apply ample spacing to your cells to differentiate the table's rows and columns.
- *Keep it brief.* A table should not extend beyond what will fit compactly within the user's browser window. If your table is too extensive, consider breaking it into several tables that focus on different areas of information.

A web table is judged primarily by its readability. This can best be accomplished by using a simple design whose features convey relevant information to readers, giving them the data they want as quickly as possible and making it easy to compare one value with another.

Designing a Column Layout

Tables are not the only way to add data columns to your web page. Starting with CSS3, web page designers were given the ability to create column layouts in which content is displayed side-by-side in the page. Column layouts differ from layouts that use floating elements or flexboxes in that content from a single element can flow from one column to the next in the same way that article text flows from one column to the next in a newspaper layout. If the page is resized, the flow of the content adjusts to match the new page width, retaining the column layout.

Setting the Number of Columns

The size of a column layout is established using the following `column-count` property

```
column-count: value;
```

where `value` is the number of columns in the layout. For example, the following style rule will lay out the content of the `article` element in three columns:

```
article {
    column-count: 3;
}
```

Browser support for the family of column styles is mixed at this time, so you will need to include browser extensions to ensure cross-browser compatibility. The following style rule will be supported by most current browsers:

```
article {
    -moz-column-count: 3;
    -webkit-column-count: 3;
    column-count: 3;
}
```

Other column styles described in this section employ the same browser extensions.

For each program aired by DLR, Kyle has created a page describing an upcoming episode. Kyle wants to apply a column layout to these pages. One of the pages that Kyle has created provides details of an upcoming episode of *The Living World*. Open that page now to view its current content and design.

To view the episode page:

1. Use your editor to open the **dlr_lw0414_txt.html** file from the html06 ▶ tutorial folder. Enter *your name* and *the date* in the comment section of the file and save it as **dlr_lw0414.html**.

2. Take some time to study the content and structure of the document.

3. Use your browser to open the **dlr_lw0414.html** file. Figure 6-39 shows the current layout of the page article on a desktop device.

| Figure 6-39 | Current layout of the driverless car article |

The Living World

April 14

Join host Tim Unger for this week's edition of *The Living World* where we discuss the future and economic impact of *autonomous vehicles*, otherwise known as *driverless cars*.

Rise of the Driverless Car and How It Will Impact You

Your world is about to change with widespread adoption of driverless cars. Driverless cars or autonomous vehicles that interact with their surroundings with radar, GPS, proximity sensors, and computer image enhancement. This information is fed into a control system that uses it to plot navigation paths and to respond to obstacles and road directions. A driverless car is capable of updating its status based on changing conditions. Driverless cars should be autonomous even when entering uncharted regions.

In the United States, the National Highway Traffic Safety Administration (NHTSA) has proposed the following levels of autonomy for motorized vehicles:

Level 0 The driver completely controls the vehicle at all times.

Level 1 Individual vehicle controls are automated, such as electronic stability control or automatic braking.

Level 2 At least two controls can be automated in unison, such as adaptive cruise control in combination with lane keeping.

Level 3 The driver can fully cede control of all safety-critical functions in certain conditions. The car senses when conditions require the driver to retake control and provides a "sufficiently comfortable transition time" for the driver to do so.

Level 4 The vehicle performs all safety-critical functions for the entire trip, with the driver not expected to control the vehicle at any time. Because this vehicle would control all functions from start to stop, including all parking functions, it could include unoccupied cars.

Currently, we are at Level 2 with many vehicles able to provide automated safety systems, such as automatic braking in response to input from collision sensors.

When Does Full Autonomy Arrive?

Level 4 autonomous vehicles are arriving and they're arriving quickly. The obstacles to adoption of a driverless economy are legal and technical. The United States traffic code does not prohibit autonomous vehicles, but it also does not specifically address them. Several states, including Nevada, Florida, California, and Michigan, have enacted traffic rules specifically tailored to driverless cars and more states are in the processing of enacting such legislation.

One area of legal entanglement is the laws against distracted driving. Google specifically requested an exemption to permit occupants to send text messages while sitting behind the wheel of an autonomous vehicle. Other similar regulations will need to be addressed as driverless cars move from the testing stage into general use.

Other countries have permitted the testing of autonomous vehicles on public roads. The United Kingdom enacted a testing phase in 2013, followed shortly by France in 2014.

© Courtesy Patrick Carey

long lines of text are difficult to read

Kyle is concerned that the article is difficult to read due to the long lines of text. In general, the optimal line of text should have about 60 characters or 12 words. However, the article on driverless cars averages about 140 characters and 24 words per line. He suggests you make the page a bit easier to read on desktop devices by splitting the article into two columns.

To apply a column layout:

1. Use your editor to open the **dlr_columns_txt.css** file from the html06 ▸ tutorial folder. Enter **your name** and **the date** in the comment section of the file and save it as **dlr_columns.css**.

2. Within the Column Styles section, insert the following media query to create column layout for the `article` element for devices with a minimum screen width of 641 pixels.

   ```
   @media only screen and (min-width: 641px) {
      article {
         -moz-column-count: 2;
         -webkit-column-count: 2;
          column-count: 2;
      }
   }
   ```

Figure 6-40 highlights the media query in the style sheet.

Figure 6-40 Applying a 2-column layout to the article element

applies the column style only to screen devices wider than 640 pixels

uses browser extensions to ensure compatibility across browsers

displays the article content across 2 columns

```
/* Column Styles */

@media only screen and (min-width: 641px) {
    article {
        -moz-column-count: 2;
        -webkit-column-count: 2;
        column-count: 2;
    }
}
```

3. Save your changes to the file.

4. Return to the **dlr_lw0414.html** file in your editor.

5. Within the document head, add a link to the **dlr_columns.css** style sheet.

6. Close the file, saving your changes.

7. Reload the dlr_lw0414.html file in your browser. Figure 6-41 shows the two column layout of the page article.

Figure 6-41 Article displayed across two columns

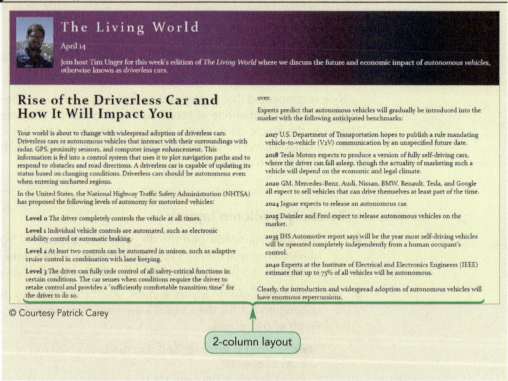

© Courtesy Patrick Carey

2-column layout

By splitting the page article across two columns, you have made the text easier to read.

Defining Columns Widths and Gaps

By default, columns are laid out evenly across the width of the parent element. Thus, with a 2-column layout, each column will occupy approximately half of the parent element width. Another way to define your column layout is to explicitly set the width of the columns and then allow the number of columns to be determined by what can fit within the allotted space. To set the column width, use the following column-width property

```
column-width: size;
```

where size is the minimum width of the column in one of the CSS units of measure. For example, the following style rule creates a column layout in which each column is at least 250-pixels wide:

```
article {
    column-width: 250px;
}
```

Column widths act like the basis value for items in a flexbox. The width is the initial size of each column, which will expand to match the available space. For example, if the parent element has a width of 500 pixels, this style rule will result in a 2-column layout. If the width is 750 pixels, the result is a 3-column layout. Between 500 and 750 pixels, the article will be laid out in 2-columns with increasing widths assigned to each column to fill up the parent element.

The column-width and column-count properties can be combined into the following shorthand columns property

```
columns: width count;
```

where width is the minimum width of each column and count is the maximum number of columns that will be fit into the allotted space. The following style rule creates a layout of 3 columns with a minimum width of 250 pixels each:

```
article {
    columns: 250px 3;
}
```

If the allotted space is larger than 750 pixels, the columns will increase in width to fill up the space. If the space is smaller than 750 pixels, the column count will decrease to 2.

These calculations assume that there is no space between the columns. However, by default browsers will create a gap of 1em between each column. To set a different gap size, apply the following column-gap property

```
column-gap: size;
```

where size is the width of the gap in one of the CSS units of measure. The following style rule creates a column layout in which each column is 250 pixels wide and the gap between the columns is 20 pixels:

```
article {
    column-gap: 20px;
    column-width: 250px;
}
```

Thus, to fit two columns under this style rule, the parent element must be at least 520-pixels wide. To fit three columns, the parent element must be at least 790-pixels wide (because there are two gaps of 20 pixels within the three columns), and so forth.

Kyle suggests you increase the width of the gap between the columns in his page to 30 pixels.

To set the column gap size:

▶ 1. Return to the **dlr_columns.css** file in your editor.

▶ 2. Within the style rule for the `article` element, add the following styles:

```
-moz-column-gap: 30px;
-webkit-column-gap: 30px;
column-gap: 30px;
```

Note that you include the browser extensions to provide cross-browser compatibility. Figure 6-42 highlights the new code in the style rule.

Figure 6-42 Setting the size of the column gap

```
@media only screen and (min-width: 641px) {
    article {
        -moz-column-count: 2;
        -webkit-column-count: 2;
        column-count: 2;

        -moz-column-gap: 30px;
        -webkit-column-gap: 30px;
        column-gap: 30px;
    }
}
```

sizes the size of the gap between the columns to 30 pixels

▶ 3. Save your changes to the file and then reload dlr_lw0414.html in your browser. Verify that the gap between the two columns has increased from its default gap size.

Another way to separate one column from the next is with a graphic dividing line, created using the following `column-rule` property

```
column-rule: border;
```

where *border* defines the style of the dividing line using the same CSS syntax employed to create borders around page elements. For example, the following style adds a 1-pixel solid red dividing line between the columns in a column layout:

```
column-rule: 1px solid red;
```

Like the `border` property you can break the `column-rule` property into the individual properties `column-rule-width`, `column-rule-style`, and `column-rule color` to set the dividing line's width, style, and color.

Kyle suggests that you add a 2-pixel solid gray dividing line to the column layout.

To create a column rule:

▶ 1. Return to the **dlr_columns.css** file in your editor and within the style rule for the `article` element add the following styles:

```
-moz-column-rule: 2px solid gray;
-webkit-column-rule: 2px solid gray;
column-rule: 2px solid gray;
```

Figure 6-43 highlights the code to create the gray dividing line between the columns.

Figure 6-43   Add a dividing line to the columns

```
@media only screen and (min-width: 641px) {
    article {
        -moz-column-count: 2;
        -webkit-column-count: 2;
        column-count: 2;

        -moz-column-gap: 30px;
        -webkit-column-gap: 30px;
        column-gap: 30px;

        -moz-column-rule: 2px solid gray;
        -webkit-column-rule: 2px solid gray;
        column-rule: 2px solid gray;
    }
}
```

adds a 2 pixel solid gray dividing line between the columns

2. Save your changes to the file and then reload dlr_lw0414.html in your browser. Figure 6-44 shows the revised appearance of the column layout.

Figure 6-44   Dividing line in the column layout

30 pixel gap between the column

a one line widow

Rise of the Driverless Car and How It Will Impact You

Your world is about to change with widespread adoption of driverless cars. Driverless cars or autonomous vehicles that interact with their surroundings with radar, GPS, proximity sensors, and computer image enhancement. This information is fed into a control system that uses it to plot navigation paths and to respond to obstacles and road directions. A driverless car is capable of updating its status based on changing conditions. Driverless cars should be autonomous even when entering uncharted regions.

In the United States, the National Highway Traffic Safety Administration (NHTSA) has proposed the following levels of autonomy for motorized vehicles:

over.

Experts predict that autonomous vehicles will gradually be introduced into the market with the following anticipated benchmarks:

2017 U.S. Department of Transportation hopes to publish a rule mandating vehicle-to-vehicle (V2V) communication by an unspecified future date.

2018 Tesla Motors expects to produce a version of fully self-driving cars, where the driver can fall asleep, though the actuality of marketing such a vehicle will depend on the economic and legal climate.

2020 GM, Mercedes-Benz, Audi, Nissan, BMW, Renault, Tesla, and Google all expect to sell vehicles that can drive themselves at least part of the time.

2024 Jaguar expects to release an autonomous car.

2-pixel solid gray dividing line

Column rules don't take up any space in the layout; if they are wider than the specified gap they will overlap the column content. Kyle notices that the column break in Google Chrome appears at an inconvenient location, leaving a single line and word at the start of the new column, making the text awkward to read. He would like you to revise the location of the column break.

Managing Column Breaks

By default, browsers automatically break the content within a column layout to keep the columns roughly the same height. As shown in Figure 6-44, this behavior can result in column breaks that make the text difficult to read. You can control the placement of column breaks through several CSS properties. As with page break styles discussed in Tutorial 5, you can control the size of column orphans (a line of text stranded at the bottom of a column) using the following orphans property:

```
orphans: value;
```

where *value* is the minimum number of lines stranded before a column break. Similarly, to control the size of column widows (a line of text placed at the top of a column), use the following widows property:

```
widows: value;
```

where *value* is the minimum number of lines placed after the column break. For example, the following style sets the column breaks within paragraphs to leave a minimum of 2 lines at the bottom and a minimum of 3 lines at the top of each column:

```
article p {
    orphans: 2;
    widows: 3;
}
```

Another way to define a column break before or after an element is to use the properties

```
break-before: type;
break-after: type;
```

where *type* is one of the following: auto (to allow the browser to automatically set the column break), always (to always place a column break), or avoid (to avoid placing a column break). To control the placement of column breaks within an element use the property

```
break-inside: type;
```

where *type* is either auto or avoid. For example, the following style rule always inserts a column break directly before any h2 heading that appears within an article:

```
article h2 {
    break-before: always;
}
```

Browser support for managing column breaks is mixed at the time of this writing. You can achieve the most cross-browser support by using the following browser extensions for the break-inside property:

```
-webkit-column-break-inside: type;
page-break-inside: type;
break-inside: type;
```

The extensions for the break-before and break-after properties follow a similar pattern.

Kyle asks you to add styles that limit the size of orphans and widows around the column break in the article element to at least three lines each.

To set the widows and orphans around the column breaks:

1. Return to the **dlr_columns.css** file in your editor and add the following styles to the style rule for the article element:

   ```
   widows: 3;
   orphans: 3;
   ```

   Figure 6-45 highlights the code to define the size of the widows and orphans.

Figure 6-45   **Defining widows and orphans around column breaks**

keeps at least three lines together after the column break

keeps at least three lines together before the column break

```
-moz-column-rule: 2px solid gray;
-webkit-column-rule: 2px solid gray;
column-rule: 2px solid gray;

widows: 3;
orphans: 3;
}
```

2. Save your changes to the file and then reload the dlr_lw0414.html file in your browser. Verify that the widows and orphans around the column break in the article are at least three lines apiece.

   Trouble? At the time of this writing, some browsers, such as the Firefox desktop browser, do not support the orphans and widows style properties as applied to column breaks.

The final edit that Kyle wants to make to the article is to have the article heading appear above the columns, rather than within the first column of the layout.

Spanning Cell Columns

For some layouts, you will want to have element content extend across all of the columns. You can create column-spanning content by applying the following column-span property

```
column-span: span;
```

where *span* is either none to prevent spanning or all to enable the content to span across all of the columns.

Creating a Column Layout

- To specify the number of columns in the layout, use

  `column-count: value;`

  where `value` is the number of columns in the layout.
- To specify the width of the columns, use

  `column-width: size;`

  where `size` is the minimum width of the columns expressed in one of the CSS units of measure or as a percentage of the width of the element.
- To set the size of the gap between columns, use

  `column-gap: size;`

  where `size` is the width of the gap.
- To add a dividing line between the columns, use

  `column-rule: border;`

  where `border` is the format of the border.
- To specify the width and number of columns in a single style property, use

  `columns: width count;`

  where `width` is the minimum width of each column and `count` is the total number of columns in the layout.
- To control the size of orphans or widows around a column break, use

  `orphans: value;`
  `widows: value;`

  where `value` is the number of lines in the column break orphan or widow.

Add a style rule so that the h1 heading, which currently appears in the first column of the article layout, spans across the columns.

To create a column-spanning heading:

1. Return to the **dlr_columns.css** file in your editor and, within the media query for desktop devices, add the following style rule for the h1 heading in the article element:

   ```
   article h1 {
      -moz-column-span: all;
      -webkit-column-span: all;
      column-span: all;
   }
   ```

   Figure 6-46 highlights the new style rule to create a column-spanning heading.

Figure 6-46   **Creating a column-spanning heading**

```
            widows: 3;
            orphans: 3;
        }

        article h1 {
            -moz-column-span: all;
            -webkit-column-span: all;
            column-span: all;
        }

    }
```

sets the heading so that it extends across all columns

2. Save your changes to the file and then reload dlr_lw0414.html in your browser. Figure 6-47 shows the final layout of page article.

Figure 6-47   **Final column layout of the article**

The Living World

April 14

Join host Tim Unger for this week's edition of *The Living World* where we discuss the future and economic impact of *autonomous vehicles*, otherwise known as *driverless cars*.

heading spans the two columns in the layout

Rise of the Driverless Car and How It Will Impact You

Your world is about to change with widespread adoption of driverless cars. Driverless cars or autonomous vehicles that interact with their surroundings with radar, GPS, proximity sensors, and computer image enhancement. This information is fed into a control system that uses it to plot navigation paths and to respond to obstacles and road directions. A driverless car is capable of updating its status based on changing conditions. Driverless cars should be autonomous even when entering uncharted regions.

In the United States, the National Highway Traffic Safety Administration (NHTSA) has proposed the following levels of autonomy for motorized vehicles:

Level 0 The driver completely controls the vehicle at all times.

Level 1 Individual vehicle controls are automated, such as electronic stability control or automatic braking.

Level 2 At least two controls can be automated in unison, such as adaptive cruise control in combination with lane keeping.

Level 3 The driver can fully cede control of all safety-critical functions in certain conditions. The car senses when conditions require the driver to retake control and provides a "sufficiently comfortable transition time" for the driver to do so.

Experts predict that autonomous vehicles will gradually be introduced into the market with the following anticipated benchmarks:

2017 U.S. Department of Transportation hopes to publish a rule mandating vehicle-to-vehicle (V2V) communication by an unspecified future date.

2018 Tesla Motors expects to produce a version of fully self-driving cars, where the driver can fall asleep, though the actuality of marketing such a vehicle will depend on the economic and legal climate.

2020 GM, Mercedes-Benz, Audi, Nissan, BMW, Renault, Tesla, and Google all expect to sell vehicles that can drive themselves at least part of the time.

2024 Jaguar expects to release an autonomous car.

2025 Daimler and Ford expect to release autonomous vehicles on the market.

2035 IHS Automotive report says will be the year most self-driving vehicles will be operated completely independently from a human occupant's control.

2040 Experts at the Institute of Electrical and Electronics Engineers (IEEE) estimate that up to 75% of all vehicles will be autonomous.

© Courtesy Patrick Carey

Trouble? At the time of this writing, the `column-span` property is not supported by the Firefox browser.

Kyle is pleased with the layout you created for the driverless car article. He'll continue to develop the new layout for the DLR website and get back to you for help on his future projects.

REVIEW

Session 6.2 Quick Check

1. What are the three table row group elements and in what order should they be entered in the HTML code?

2. Provide code to create a column group in which the first two columns belong to the introCol class and the next three columns belong to the col1, col2, and col3 classes respectively.

3. Provide code to change the background color of the 2 columns belonging to the introCol class to yellow.

4. What are the only CSS properties that can be applied to columns and column groups?

5. In the case of conflicting styles, which has the higher precedence: the style of the row group or the style of the column group?

6. Provide a style to set the height of every table row in the table header to 25 pixels.

7. Provide the code to display an unordered list as a table, the list items as table rows, and hypertext links within each list as table cells.

8. Provide code to display the content of all `div` elements in a column layout with the minimum width of each column set to 200 pixels. Use browser extensions in your code.

9. In the style rule you created in the last question, how many columns would be displayed and what would be their widths when the parent element is 500-pixels wide? Assume a column gap of 20 pixels.

Review Assignments

Data Files needed for the Review Assignments: dlr_mornings_txt.html, dlr_tables2_txt.css, dlr_columns2_txt.css, 2 CSS files, 3 PNG files

Kyle has reviewed your work on the DLR nightly schedule page. He wants you to make a few changes to the layout and apply those changes to a new page that describes the DLR morning schedule. Kyle already has entered much of the web page content and style. He wants you to complete his work by creating and designing the web table listing the times and programs for the morning schedule. Figure 6-48 shows a preview of the morning schedule page.

Figure 6-48   DLR Morning Schedule

© Courtesy Patrick Carey

Complete the following:

1. Use your HTML editor to open the **dlr_mornings_txt.html**, **dlr_tables2_txt.css** and **dlr_columns2_txt.css** files from the html06 ▶ review folder. Enter *your name* and *the date* in the comment section of each file, and save them as **dlr_mornings.html**, **dlr_tables2.css** and **dlr_columns2.css** respectively.

2. Go to the **dlr_mornings.html** file in your editor. Insert links to the dlr_tables2.css and dlr_columns2.css style sheets.

3. Scroll down the file and directly below the paragraph element, insert a web table with the class name **programs**.

4. Add a table caption containing the text **All Times Central**.

5. Below the caption, insert a `colgroup` element containing three columns. The first `col` element should have the `class` name **timeColumn**. The second `col` element should have the `class` name **wDayColumns** and span five columns in the table that will contain the weekday programs. The last `col` element should have the `class` name **wEndColumns** and span the last two columns containing the weekend programming.

6. Add the `thead` row group element containing a single table row with `th` elements containing the text shown in Figure 6-48.

7. Add the `tbody` row group element containing the times and names of the different DLR programs from 5:00 a.m. to 12:00 p.m., Monday through Sunday, in half-hour intervals. The times should be placed in `th` elements and the program names in `td` elements. Create row- and column-spanning cells to match the layout of the days and times shown in Figure 6-48.

8. Add the `tfoot` row group element containing a single row with a single `td` element that spans 8 columns and contains the text **Support your Public Radio Station**.

9. Close the dlr_mornings.html file, saving your changes.

10. Return to the **dlr_tables2.css** file in your editor and go to the Table Styles section. Create a style rule for the programs table that: a) sets the width of the table to 100%, b) adds a 15-pixel outset border with a color value of rgb(151, 151, 151), c) defines the borders so that they are collapsed around the table, and d) sets the font family to the font stack: Arial, Verdana, and sans-serif.

11. Create a style rule that sets the height of every table row to 25 pixels.

12. Create a style rule for every `th` and `td` element that: a) adds a 1-pixel solid gray border, b) aligns the cell content with the top of the cell, and c) sets the padding space 5 pixels.

13. Go to the Table Caption Styles section and create a style rule that places the `caption` element at the bottom of the table and centered horizontally.

14. Go to the Table Column Styles section. For `col` elements belonging to the timeColumn class, create a style rule that sets the column width to 10% and the background color to the value rgb(215, 205, 151).

15. For `col` elements of the wDayColumns class, create a style rule that sets the column width to 11% and the background color to rgb(236, 255, 211).

16. For `col` elements of the wEndColumns class, create a style rule that sets the column width to 17% and the background color to rgb(255, 231, 255).

17. Kyle wants you to format the table heading cells from the table header row. Go to the Table Header Styles section and create a style rule to set the font color of the text within the `thead` element to white and the background color to a medium green with the value rgb(105, 177, 60).

18. The different cells in the table header row should be formatted with different text and background colors. Using the `first-of-type` pseudo-class, create a style rule that changes the background color of the first `th` element with the `thead` element to rgb(153, 86, 7).

19. Using the `nth-of-type` pseudo-class, create style rules that change the background color of the 7th and 8th `th` elements within the `thead` element to rgb(153, 0, 153).

20. Kyle wants the table footer to be formatted in a different text and background color from the rest of the table. Go to the Table Footer Styles section. Create a style rule for the `tfoot` element that sets the font color to white and the background color to black.

21. Save your changes to the dlr_tables2.css style sheet.

22. Return to the **dlr_columns2.css** file in your editor. Kyle wants the introductory paragraph to appear in a three column layout for desktop devices. Within the Column Styles section, create a media query for screen devices with minimum widths of 641 pixels.

23. Within the media query, create a style rule for the paragraph element that: a) sets the column count to 3, b) sets the column gap to 20 pixels, and c) adds a 1-pixels solid black dividing line between columns. (Note: Remember to use web extensions to provide support for older browsers.)

24. Save your changes to the dlr_columns2.css style sheet and then open the **dlr_mornings.html** file in your browser and verify that the table layout and design resemble that shown in Figure 6-48.

Case Problem 1

APPLY

Data Files needed for this Case Problem: mi_pricing_txt.html, mi_tables_txt.css, 2 CSS files, 3 PNG files, 1 TXT file, 1 TTF file, 1 WOFF file

Marlin Internet   Luis Amador manages the website for Marlin Internet, an Internet service provider located in Crystal River, Florida. You have recently been hired to assist in the redesign of the company's website. Luis has asked you to complete work he's begun on a page describing different pricing plans offered by Marlin Internet. A preview of the page is shown in Figure 6-49.

Figure 6-49   **Marlin Internet Pricing page**

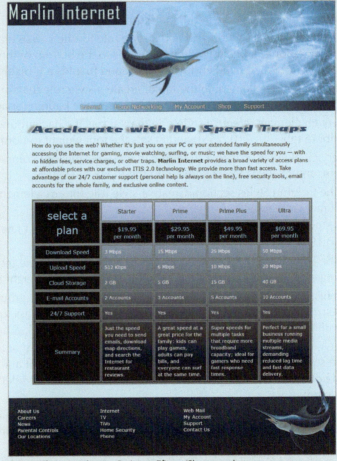

Luis has already finished most of the page design. Your job will be to add a web table describing the different service plans and to write the CSS code to format the table's appearance.

Complete the following:

1. Using your editor, open the **mi_pricing_txt.html** and **mi_tables_txt.css** files from the html06 ▶ case1 folder. Enter *your name* and *the date* in the comment section of each file, and save them as **mi_pricing.html** and **mi_tables.css** respectively.

2. Go to the **mi_pricing.html** file in your editor. Add a link to the mi_tables.css style sheet file to the document head.

3. Directly after the paragraph in the `article` element insert a web table with the ID **pricing**.

4. Add a `colgroup` element to the web table containing two `col` elements. The first `col` element should have the ID **firstCol**. The second `col` element should belong to the class **dataCols** and span 4 columns.

5. Add a `thead` row group element containing two rows. In the first row, insert five `th` elements containing the text shown in Figure 6-49. The first heading cell should span two rows. In the second row, add four headings cells containing the prices of the plans shown in Figure 6-49. Use a `br` element to display the price information on two separate lines.

6. Add a `tbody` row group element. In each row within the row group, add a `th` element containing the text shown in Figure 6-49 and four `td` elements containing the data values for each plan.

7. Add a `tfoot` row group element containing a single table row with a heading `th` element displaying the text **Summary**. Add four data `td` elements containing a description of each of the service plans. (Note: You can copy the summary text for each service plan from the mi_data.txt file in the html06/case1 folder.)

8. Save your changes to the file and then return to the **mi_tables.css** file in your editor.

9. Go to the Table Styles section and add a style rule for the `table` element that: a) sets the background color to a linear gradient that goes to the bottom of the table background starting from rgb(190, 215, 255) and ending in black and b) adds a 5-pixels solid gray border.

10. For every `th` and `td` element in the table, create a style rule that: a) adds a 3-pixel solid gray border, b) sets the line height to 1.4em, and c) sets the padding space to 8 pixels.

11. For every `th` element, create a style rule that: a) sets the background color to black, b) sets the font color to rgb(130, 210, 255), and c) sets the font weight to normal.

12. For every `td` element, create a style rule that: a) sets the font color to white, b) sets the font size to 0.9em, and c) aligns the cell text with the top of the cell.

13. Go to the Column Styles section. Create a style rule for `col` elements with the ID firstCol that sets the column width to 24%.

14. Create a style rule for `col` elements belonging to the dataCols class that sets the column width to 19%.

15. Go to the Table Header Styles section. Create a style rule for the table header row group including every row within that row group that sets the row height to 60 pixels.

16. For the first `th` element in the first row of the table header row group, create a style rule that sets its font size to 2em. (Hint: Use the `first-of-type` pseudo-class to select the first table row and first heading cell.)

17. For `th` elements in the first row of the table header row group that are not the first heading cell, create a style rule that sets the background color to transparent and the font color to black. (Hint: use the `not` selector with the `first-of-type` pseudo-class to select headings that are not first in the table row.)

18. Save your changes to the style sheet and then open the **mi_pricing.html** file in your browser and verify that the table layout and design resemble that shown in Figure 6-49.

Case Problem 2

APPLY

Data Files needed for this Case Problem: jpf_sudoku_txt.html, jpf_sudoku_txt.css, 2 CSS files, 2 PNG files

The Japanese Puzzle Factory   Rebecca Peretz has a passion for riddles and puzzles. Her favorites are the Japanese logic puzzles that have become very popular in recent years. Rebecca and a few of her friends have begun work on a new website called The Japanese Puzzle Factory where they plan to create and distribute Japanese-style puzzles. Eventually, the JPF website will include interactive programs to enable users to solve the puzzles online, but for now Rebecca is interested only in the design and layout of the pages. You have been asked to help by creating a draft version of the web page describing the Sudoku puzzle. Figure 6-50 shows a preview of the design and layout you will create for Rebecca.

Figure 6-50   **Japanese Puzzle Factor Sudoku page**

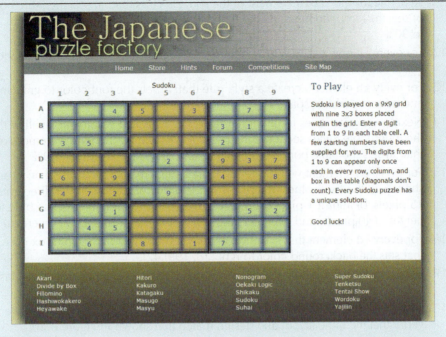

Rebecca has created some of the content and designs for this page. Your task is to complete the page by entering the HTML code and CSS styles for the Sudoku table. To create this table, you work with nested tables in which each cell of the outer 3×3 table itself contains a 3×3 table.

Complete the following:

1. Using your editor, open the **jpf_sudoku_txt.html** and **jpf_sudoku_txt.css** files from the html06 ▸ case2 folder. Enter *your name* and *the date* in the comment section of each file, and save them as **jpf_sudoku.html** and **jpf_sudoku.css** respectively.

2. Go to the **jpf_sudoku.html** file in your editor. Add a link to the jpf_sudoku.css style sheet file to the document head.

3. Within the `section` element, insert a `table` element that will be used to display the Sudoku puzzle. Give the table element the class name **spuzzle**.

4. Add a caption to the spuzzle table containing the text **Sudoku**.

5. Create a table header row group containing a single row. The row should display 10 heading cells. The first heading cell should be blank and the remaining nine cells should display the digits from 1 to 9.

6. Create the table body row group containing nine table rows with the first cell in each row containing a heading cell displaying the letters A through I.

7. After the initial table heading cell in the first, fourth, and seventh rows of the table body row group, insert three table data cells spanning three rows and three columns each. Altogether, these nine data cells will store the nine 3×3 boxes that are part of the Sudoku puzzle.

8. In the first row of the table body row, put the three table data cells you entered in the last step in the greenBox, goldBox, and greenBox classes, respectively. In the fourth row, the three data cells belong to the goldBox, greenBox, and goldBox classes. In the seventh row, the three data cells belong to the greenBox, goldBox, and greenBox classes.

9. Go to each of the nine table data cells you created in the last two steps. Within each data cell, insert a nested table belonging to the subTable class. Within each of these nested tables, insert three rows and three columns of data cells. Enter the digits from Figure 6-49 in the appropriate table cells. Where there is no digit, leave the data cell empty.

10. Save your changes to the file, and then return to the **jpf_sudoku.css** style sheet in your text editor.

11. You start by creating styles for the outer table. Go to the Table Styles section and create a style rule for the `table` element of the spuzzle class that: a) sets the table borders to collapse, b) sets the top/bottom margins to 0 pixels and the left/right margins to `auto`, and c) sets the width to 90%.

12. For every `td` element, create a style rule that: a) adds a 5-pixel outset gray border and b) sets the width to 33.3%.

13. For every `th` element, create a style rule that: a) sets the font color to gray and b) sets the right and bottom padding space to 10 pixels.

14. Next, you create styles for the inner table that is placed within each cell of the outer table. Go to the Inner Table Styles section and create a style rule for the `table` element of the subTable class that: a) sets the table borders to collapse and b) sets the width to 100%.

15. For every `td` element within the subTable table, create a style rule that: a) adds an inset box shadow with offset values of 0 pixels in the horizontal and vertical directions with a blur of 15 pixels, b) adds a 1-pixel solid black border, c) displays the text in a blue font, d) sets the cell height to 40 pixels, and e) centers the cell text in the horizontal and vertical directions.

16. For every `td` element that is nested within a `td` element of the goldBox class, create a style rule that sets the background color to rgb(228, 199, 42).

17. For every `td` element that is nested within a `td` element of the greenBox class, create a style rule that sets the background color to rgb(203, 229, 130).

18. Save your changes to the style sheet and then open the **jpf_sudoku.html** file in your browser and verify that the table layout and design match that shown in Figure 6-50.

Case Problem 3

CHALLENGE

Data Files needed for this Case Problem: lht_feb_txt.html, lht_tables_txt.css, lht_columns_txt.css, 2 CSS files, 3 PNG files, 1 TXT file

The Lyman Hall Theater Lewis Kern is an events manager at the Lyman Hall Theater in Brookhaven, Georgia. The theater is in the process of updating its website, and Lewis has asked you to work on the pages detailing events in the upcoming year. He's asked you to create a calendar page that lists the upcoming events for January, February, and March. A list of the events is stored in the lht_schedule.txt file.

Lewis wants a responsive design so that the calendar is readable for both mobile and desktop users. In addition to the calendar, Lewis wants the article describing the February events displayed in column layout. He suggests that you set the width of the columns, allowing the number of columns to be determined based on the width of the display screen. Figure 6-51 shows a preview of the page you will create for the theater viewed using mobile and desktop devices.

Figure 6-51   The Lyman Hall Theater February Calendar

mobile version   desktop version

© Stokkete/Shutterstock.com; © Studio10Artur/Shutterstock.com

Complete the following:

1. Using your editor, open the **lht_feb_txt.html**, **lht_tables_txt.css**, and **lht_columns_txt.css** files from the html06 ▸ case3 folder. Enter *your name* and *the date* in the comment section of each file, and save them as **lht_feb.html**, **lht_tables.css**, and **lht_columns.css** respectively.

2. Go to the **lht_feb.html** file in your editor. Add links to the lht_tables.css and lht_columns.css files to the document head.

3. Directly below the `article` element, insert a web table using the ID **calendar**.

4. Add a caption with the text **February 2018 Calendar**.

5. Add a column group containing two `col` elements. Give the first `col` element the class name **weekdays** and have it span five columns. Give the second `col` element the class name **weekends** and have it span 2 columns.

6. Add the table header row group with a single row with seven heading cells containing the three-letter day abbreviations **Sun** through **Sat**.

7. Add the table body row group with five rows and seven data cells within each row. Within each table cell, add the following code to create an h1 heading and description list:
```
<h1>day</h1>
<dl>
    <dt>event</dt>
    <dd>time</dd>
    <dd>price</dd>
</dl>
```

where *day* is the day of the month, *event* is the name of an event occurring on that day, *time* is the time of the event, and *price* is the admission price, using the days, events, times, and prices shown in the lht_schedule.txt file. If there is no event scheduled for the day, insert only the code for the h1 heading. Start your calendar with January 28 and conclude it with March 4.

✦ **Explore** 8. For each data cell you create in the table body, add an attribute in the opening td tab named **data-date** containing the date associated with the cell. For example, in the first table cell, enter data-date value "Sun, Jan 28, 2018", the second cell will have the data-date value "Mon, Jan 29, 2018" and so forth. (Note: This code will be used to display the date information in the mobile layout.)

9. Save your changes to the file and then return to the **lht_tables.css** file in your editor.

10. Within the Mobile Styles section, insert a media query for screen devices with a maximum width of 640 pixels.

✦ **Explore** 11. You want mobile devices to display the calendar information in two columns. To create this layout, add the style rules that: a) displays table, tbody, tr, td, th, and caption elements as blocks, b) does not display the thead h1 element, and c) displays the table caption in white on a medium gray background with a font size of 1.5em and a line height of 2em.

12. Create a style rule for every data cell that: a) adds a 1-pixel dotted gray border, b) changes the text color to rgb(11, 12, 145), c) places the cell using relative positioning, d) sets the left padding to 40%, and e) sets the minimum height to 40 pixels.

13. Create a style rule that uses the nth-of-type pseudo-class to display every odd-numbered table row with a background color of rgb(255, 235, 178) and a 2-pixel solid gray border.

14. Create a style rule that inserts the text of the data-date attribute before every data cell. Place the attribute text using absolute positioning at the coordinates (0, 0) with a width of 40% and padding space of 5 pixels.

15. Next, you design the layout of the calendar for tablet and desktop devices. Go to the Tablet and Desktop Styles section and insert a media query for screen devices with a minimum width of 641 pixels.

16. Create a style rule for the table element that: a) displays the background image lht_photo1. png with no tiling in the bottom-right corner of the table with a width of 40%, b) adds a 6-pixel double border with color value rgb(154, 64, 3), c) collapses the table borders, d) centers the table by setting the top/bottom margins to 20 pixels and the left/right margins to auto, e) uses a fixed layout for the table content, and f) sets the width of the table to 85%.

17. For every heading and data cell, create a style rule that: a) adds a 1-pixel solid gray border, b) sets the font size to 0.85em and with normal weight, c) adds a 5-pixel padding space, d) aligns the cell text with the top of the cell, e) sets the width to 14.28%, and f) allows the browser to wrap cell text within individual words. (Hint: Use the word-wrap property.)

18. For every data cell, create a style rule that: a) applies a semi-transparent background color with the value rgba(171, 171, 171, 0.6) and b) sets the text color to rgb(11, 12, 145).

✦ **Explore** 19. Lewis wants the February dates to appear in a different format from the January and March dates. Create a style rule for data cells whose data-date attribute contains the text "Feb" that: a) changes the background color to the semi-transparent value rgba(232, 214, 148, 0.6) and b) adds a gray inset box shadow with horizontal and vertical offsets of 0 pixels and a blur of 20 pixels. (Hint: See Figure 2-15 for a list of attribute selectors.)

20. Create a style rule for the table caption that: a) displays the caption at the top of the table, b) centers the caption text, c) adds 10 pixels to the bottom padding space, and d) sets the font size to 1.2em and the letter spacing to 3 pixels.

21. For heading cells within the table header, create a style rule to change the background color to rgb(154, 64, 3) and the text color to white.

22. Save your changes to the style sheet, then go to the **lht_columns.css** file in your editor and within the Column Styles section, create a style rule for the `article` element that: a) sets the column width to 260 pixels, b) sets the column gap to 20 pixels, c) adds a 1-pixel solid dividing line between columns with color value rgb(154, 64, 31), and d) sets the minimum size of widows and orphans to 2 lines.

23. Create a style rule for the h1 heading with the `article` element that extends the heading across all columns.

24. Save your changes to the style sheet and then open the **lht_feb.html** file in your browser. Verify that for desktop widths, the table appears as shown in right image of Figure 6-51 and the number of columns used in the introductory article changes from 2 to 3 based on the page width. Reduce the page width to below 640 pixels and verify that the calendar information is displayed in two columns as shown in the left image in Figure 6-51. (Note: At the time of this writing, the Firefox browser does not support the `column-span` property.)

Case Problem 4

CREATE

Data Files needed for this Case Problem: hcc_schedule_txt.html, hcc_styles_txt.css, hcc_schedule_txt.css, 1 TXT file

Hamilton Conference Center   Yancy Inwe is the facilities manager at the Hamilton Conference Center in Hamilton, Ohio. The conference center, a general-use facility for the community, hosts several organizations and clubs as well as special events and shows by local vendors. The center recently upgraded its intranet capabilities, and Yancy would like to create a website where employees and guests can easily track which conference rooms are available and which are being used. She would like this information displayed in a web table that lays out the room use for seven rooms and halls from 8:00 a.m. to 5:00 p.m. in half-hour increments. Eventually, this process will be automated by the conference's web server; but for now, she has come to you for help in setting up a sample web page layout and design.

Complete the following:

1. Using your editor, open the **hcc_schedule_txt.html**, **hcc_styles_txt.css**, and **hcc_schedule_txt.css** from the html06 ▸ case4 folder. Enter *your name* and *the date* in the comment section of each file and save them as **hcc_schedule.html**, **hcc_styles.css**, and **hcc_schedule.css** respectively.

2. Using the content of the hcc_rooms.txt file, create the content and structure of the hcc_schedule.html page. You are free to supplement the material in these text files with additional textual content of your own if appropriate. Use the # symbol for the value of the `href` attribute in your hypertext links because you will be linking to pages that don't actually exist.

3. Create a table containing the room reservation information. The table structure should contain the following elements:
    - a table caption
    - table row and column groups
    - examples of row- and/or column-spanning cells
    - examples of both heading and data cells

4. Place styles for the general page layout in the hcc_styles.css style sheet.

5. Add a column layout to one section of your document. The number of columns and its appearance are up to you. Include your column styles in the hcc_styles.css style sheet file.

6. Create a style for your table in the hcc_schedule.css style sheet. The layout and appearance of the table are up to you, but the table should include the following:
   - a border style applied to one or more table objects
   - a style that defines whether the table borders are separate or collapsed
   - styles applied to table rows and column groups
   - use of horizontal and vertical alignment of the table cell content
   - different widths applied to different table columns
   - styles applied to the table caption
7. Document your code in the HTML and CSS files with appropriate comments.

TUTORIAL **7**

Designing a Web Form

Creating a Survey Form

Case | *Red Ball Pizza*

Alice Nichols is a manager at *Red Ball Pizza*, a popular pizzeria in Ormond Beach, Florida. She wants to conduct an online survey of Red Ball customers using a web form that will be placed on the restaurant's website. She has asked you to help design a prototype for the survey form. The form should record customer information, as well as each customer's perception of his or her last experience at the restaurant. Alice wants the form to include different tools to ensure that each user enters valid data. Once a customer completes the form, the information will be sent to the Red Ball server for processing and analysis.

OBJECTIVES

Session 7.1
* Explore web forms
* Work with form servers
* Create forms and field sets
* Create labels and input boxes
* Explore form layout

Session 7.2
* Work with date and time fields
* Create a selection list
* Create option buttons
* Create check boxes and text area boxes

Session 7.3
* Create spinners and range sliders
* Use data lists
* Create form buttons
* Validate a form
* Apply validation styles

STARTING DATA FILES

html07 → tutorial

rb_survey_txt.html
rb_forms_txt.css
+ 9 files

review

rb_build_txt.html
rb_customer_txt.html
rb_validate_txt.css
+ 15 files

case1

cg_register_txt.html
cg_validate_txt.css
+ 9 files

case2

sb_payment_txt.html
sb_validate_txt.css
+16 files

case3

wm_demo_txt.html
wm_forms_txt.css
+ 5 files

case4

4 files

Session 7.1 Visual Overview:

The **action** attribute indicates the server program that processes the form.

The **input** element creates an input control based on the type attribute for entering data.

The **form** element encloses a web form.

The **fieldset** element groups the fields in the form.

The **legend** element provides the field set legend.

The **label** element associates a text string with an input control.

The **value** attribute provides a default value for the data field.

The **name** attribute provides the name of the data field.

The **for** attribute associates the label with an input control.

The **placeholder** attribute inserts descriptive text into the input control.

```
<form id="survey" action="http://www.example.com/redball/survey"
               method="post">

    <fieldset id="custInfo">
        <legend>Customer Information</legend>

        <label for="name">Name*</label>
        <input name="custName" id="name" type="text" placeholder="enter your name" />

        <label for="street">Street address</label>
        <input name="custStreet" id="street" type="text" />

        <label for="city">City</label>
        <input name="custCity" id="city" type="text" value="Ormond Beach" />

        <label for="state">State</label>
        <input name="custState" id="state" type="text" value="FL" />

        <label for="zip">Postal code</label>
        <input name="custZip" id="zip" type="text" placeholder="nnnnn (-nnnn)" />
    </fieldset>

</form>
```

Structure of a Web Form

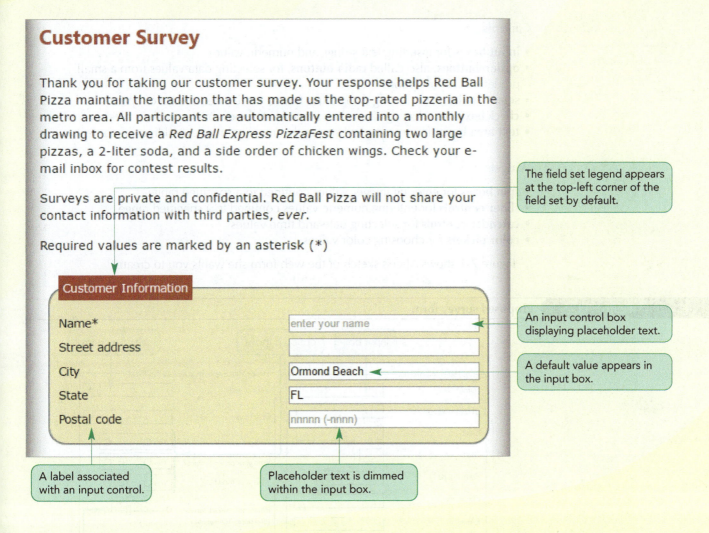

Customer Survey

Thank you for taking our customer survey. Your response helps Red Ball Pizza maintain the tradition that has made us the top-rated pizzeria in the metro area. All participants are automatically entered into a monthly drawing to receive a *Red Ball Express PizzaFest* containing two large pizzas, a 2-liter soda, and a side order of chicken wings. Check your e-mail inbox for contest results.

Surveys are private and confidential. Red Ball Pizza will not share your contact information with third parties, *ever*.

Required values are marked by an asterisk (*)

Customer Information

Name*   enter your name

Street address

City   Ormond Beach

State   FL

Postal code   nnnnn (-nnnn)

The field set legend appears at the top-left corner of the field set by default.

An input control box displaying placeholder text.

A default value appears in the input box.

A label associated with an input control.

Placeholder text is dimmed within the input box.

Introducing Web Forms

So far, the websites you have created have been passive: allowing the user to view information but not allowing him or her to directly interact with the page's content, except via hyperlinks. Starting with this tutorial, you will begin working with more interactive websites that allow for user feedback. The most common way of accepting user input is through a **web form**, which allows users to enter data that can be saved and processed.

Parts of a Web Form

A form contains **controls**, also known as **widgets**, which are the objects that allow the user to interact with the form. HTML supports several types of controls and widgets, including:

Controls

- **input boxes** for inserting text strings and numeric values
- **option buttons**, also called **radio buttons**, for selecting data values from a small predefined set of options
- **selection lists** for selecting data values from a more extensive list of options
- **check boxes** for selecting data values limited to two possibilities, such as "yes" or "no"
- **text area boxes** for entering text strings that may include several lines of content

Widgets

- **spin boxes** for entering integer values confined to a specified range
- **slider controls** for entering numeric values confined to a specified range
- **calendar controls** for selecting date and time values
- **color pickers** for choosing color values

Figure 7-1 shows Alice's sketch of the web form she wants you to create.

Figure 7-1	Proposed survey form

Alice's proposed form includes several of the controls discussed above, such as input boxes for entering the customer name, contact information, and e-mail address; option buttons for storing the customer's service experience; and a selection list from which customers can choose how they heard about Red Ball Pizza from a long list of options.

Each data entry control is associated with a **data field** or **field** in which data values supplied by the user are stored. For example, the input box in which a customer enters his or her name is associated with the custName field, the calendar control in which the customer enters the date he or she visited Red Ball Pizza is associated with the visitDate field, and so forth.

Forms and Server-Based Programs

Once the field values have been entered by the user, they are processed by a program running on the user's computer or on a web server in a secure location. For example, a web form is used to collect sales data from the customer for an order and the server program processes that data and handles the billing and delivery of the sales items. See Figure 7-2.

Figure 7-2   **Interaction between the web form and the server**

data from the web form is sent to a program running on the server

feedback from the server can be sent back to the browser

Alice is already working with a programmer on a web server program that will store and interpret the survey results. You will not have access to that program, so Alice just wants you to concentrate on the design of the web form. Your colleagues will test your form to verify that the information is being collected and processed correctly by the web server.

Restricting Access to Web Server Programs

Since the web form designer might not have permission to create or edit the programs running on the web servers, he or she will usually receive instructions about how to interact with the server programs. These instructions often include a list of fields that are required by the program and a description of the types of values expected in those fields.

There are several reasons to restrict direct access to these programs. The primary reason is that, when you run a server-based program, you are interacting directly with the server environment. Mindful of the security risks that computer hackers present and the drain on system resources caused by large numbers of programs running simultaneously, system administrators are understandably careful to maintain strict control over access to their servers and systems.

Server-based programs are written in a variety of languages. The earliest and most common of these programs is **Common Gateway Interface (CGI)**, which are scripts written in a language called **Perl**. Other popular languages widely used today for writing server-based programs include ASP, ColdFusion, C, Java, PHP, Python, and Ruby. You can check with your ISP or system administrator to find out what programs are available on your web server, and what rights and privileges you have in accessing them.

Starting a Web Form

All web forms are marked using the following `form` element

```
<form id="text" attributes>
    content
</form>
```

where the `id` attribute identifies the form (which is important when more than one form is being used on the web page), *attributes* specify how the form should be processed by the browser, and *content* is the form's content. Forms typically contain many of the controls that were listed earlier, but they also can contain page elements such as tables, paragraphs, inline images, and headings. A `form` element can be placed anywhere within the body of the page.

Inserting a Web Form

- To insert a web form, add

  ```
  <form id="text" attributes>
      content
  </form>
  ```

  where *text* identifies the form, *attributes* control how the form is processed, and *content* is the content of the form.

Add a form to Alice's survey page now with the ID survey.

To insert a web form:

1. Use your editor to open the **rb_survey_txt.html** file from the html07 ▸ tutorial folder. Enter **your name** and **the date** in the comment section of the file and save it as **rb_survey.html**.

2. Scroll down and, directly after the third paragraph in the section element, insert the following form element:

```
<form id="survey">
</form>
```

Figure 7-3 shows the placement of the web form.

Figure 7-3   Inserting a web form

form id identifies the form

```
<p>Required values are marked by an asterisk (*)</p>

<form id="survey">
</form>
```

form element marks the web form contents

Next, you will include attributes that tell the browser how the form should interact with the web server.

Interacting with the Web Server

To specify where to send the form data and how to send it, include the following `action`, `method`, and `enctype` attributes

```
<form action="url" method="type" enctype="type">
   content
</form>
```

where the `action` attribute provides the location of the web server program that processes the form, the `method` attribute specifies how the browser should send form data to the server, and the `enctype` attribute specifies how the form data should be encoded as it is sent to the server.

The `method` attribute has two possible values: `get` and `post`. The default is the **get method**, which tells the browser to append the form data to the end of the URL specified in the `action` attribute. The **post method** sends the form data in its own separate data stream. Each method has its uses, but the post method is considered to be a more secure form of data transfer. Your website administrator can supply the necessary information about which of the two methods you should use when accessing the scripts running on the server.

The `enctype` attribute has three possible values summarized in Figure 7-4.

Figure 7-4 **Values of the enctype attribute**

Value	Description
application/x-www-form-urlencoded	The default format in which the data is encoded as a long text string with spaces replaced by the + character and special characters (including tabs and line breaks) replaced with their hexadecimal code values
multipart/form-data	The format used when uploading files in which no encoding of the data values occurs
text/plain	The format in which data is transferred as plain text with spaces replaced with the + character but no other encoding of the data values occurs

Alice tells you that your survey form will be processed by the CGI script using the `action` attribute accessing a server program located at the fictional URL address http://www.example.com/redball/survey with the post method. You do not have to specify a value for the `enctype` attribute because the default value of application/x-www-form-urlencoded is sufficient. Add this information to your web form.

To specify how the form interacts with the server:

1. Return to the opening `<form>` tag and add the following attributes:

   ```
   action="http://www.example.com/redball/survey"
   method="post"
   ```

   Figure 7-5 highlights the newly added form attributes.

Figure 7-5 **Associating the web form with an action and a method**

```
<p>Required values are marked by an asterisk (*)</p>

<form id="survey" action="http://www.example.com/redball/survey" method="post">
</form>
```

location of server processing the form

method by which the form data is sent to the server

2. Save your changes to the file.

Because http://www.example.com/redball/survey does not correspond to a real CGI script running on the web and thus cannot process the survey form you will create in this tutorial, you will add a JavaScript program named rb_formsubmit.js to handle the form. The purpose of this JavaScript program is to intercept the content of the form before the browser attempts to contact the CGI script and report whether or not the data contained in the survey form has been correctly filled out. The Javascript program has already been created, so you will create a link to the file using the following `script` element:

```
<script src="rb_formsubmit.js"></script>
```

A `script` element is an HTML element used to access and run JavaScript programs that will run within the user's browser. You will learn more about scripts and their applications in Tutorial 9, but for now, you add this code to the document head so that it can be applied throughout this tutorial.

To insert a script:

▶ **1.** Scroll up to the document head and insert the following code directly above the closing `</head>` tag:

```
<script src="rb_formsubmit.js"></script>
```

Figure 7-6 highlights the code for the `script` element.

Figure 7-6	Using a script to manage the form submission

```
<title>Red Ball Survey</title>
<link href="rb_reset.css" rel="stylesheet" />
<link href="rb_styles.css" rel="stylesheet" />
<script src="rb_formsubmit.js"></script>
</head>
```

the script element runs JavaScript programs within the browser

external JavaScript file

▶ **2.** Save your changes to the file.

Now that you have added the `form` element to the survey page, you can start populating the survey form with controls and other form features. You will start by adding field sets.

Creating a Field Set

Because a web form can have dozens of different fields, you can make your form easier to interpret and more accessible by grouping fields that share a common purpose into a **field set**. Field sets are created using the following `fieldset` element

```
<fieldset id="id">
    content
</fieldset>
```

where `id` identifies the field set and `content` is the form content within the field set. An id is not required, but it is useful in distinguishing one field set from another.

Marking a Field Set

Alice wants you to organize the form into two field sets: the custInfo field set will enclose the fields containing contact information for *Red Ball Pizza* customers and the expInfo field set will enclose the fields that record those customers' impressions of the restaurant.

To add field sets to a form:

1. Scroll back to the web form and, within the `form` element, insert the following `fieldset` elements:

   ```
   <fieldset id="custInfo">
   </fieldset>

   <fieldset id="expInfo">
   </fieldset>
   ```

   Figure 7-7 highlights the code for the two new field sets.

Figure 7-7 **Inserting field sets**

```
<form id="survey" action="http://www.example.com/redball/survey" method="post">
   <fieldset id="custInfo">
   </fieldset>

   <fieldset id="expInfo">
   </fieldset>
</form>
```

id associated with each fieldset element

2. Save your changes to the file.

The default browser style is to place a border around the field set to set it off visually from other elements in the web form. Field sets act like block elements that expand to accommodate their content. Before viewing the two field sets in your browser, you will add a legend.

Adding a Field Set Legend

Every field set can contain a legend describing its content using the following `legend` element

```
<legend>text</legend>
```

where *text* is the text of the legend. The `legend` element contains only text and no nested elements. By default, legends are placed in the top-left corner of the field set box, though they can be moved to a different location using the CSS positioning styles.

Based on Alice's sketch from Figure 7-1, add the legend text "Customer Information" and "Share Your Experience at Red Ball Pizza" to the two field sets you just created.

To add legends to the field sets:

1. Within the custInfo field set, add the following legend element:

   `<legend>Customer Information</legend>`

2. Within the expInfo field set, add the legend:

   `<legend>Share Your Experience at Red Ball Pizza</legend>`

   Figure 7-8 highlights the code for the two legends.

Figure 7-8	Adding legends to the field sets

```
<form id="survey" action="http://www.example.com/redball/survey" method="post">
   <fieldset id="custInfo">
      <legend>Customer Information</legend>
   </fieldset>

   <fieldset id="expInfo">
      <legend>Share Your Experience at Red Ball Pizza</legend>
   </fieldset>
</form>
```

legend associated with each field set

3. Save your changes to the file and then open the **rb_survey.html** file in your browser. Figure 7-9 shows the appearance of the two field sets.

Figure 7-9	Legends displayed in the field set box

Customer Survey

Thank you for taking our customer survey. Your response helps Red Ball Pizza maintain the tradition that has made us the top-rated pizzeria in the metro area. All participants are automatically entered into a monthly drawing to receive a *Red Ball Express PizzaFest* containing two large pizzas, a 2-liter soda, and a side order of chicken wings. Check your e-mail inbox for contest results.

Surveys are private and confidential. Red Ball Pizza will not share your contact information with third parties, *ever*.

Required values are marked by an asterisk (*)

field set legend

field sets

┌─Customer Information───┐
│   │
└──┘
┌─Share Your Experience at Red Ball Pizza──────────────────────────────────┐
│   │
└──┘

The default browser style is to add a border around a field set

The field sets you added are currently empty, so they appear small and narrow on the survey page. Next, you will populate the field set with the controls that will be used to insert different field values.

Creating Input Boxes

Because most form controls are designed to receive user input, they are marked using the following input element

```
<input name="name" id="id" type="type" />
```

where the name attribute provides the name of the data field associated with the control, the id attribute identifies the control in which the user enters the field value, and the type attribute indicates the data type of the field. When the form is submitted to the server, the field name is paired with the field value; thus, you always need a name attribute if you are submitting the form to a server. The id attribute is required only when you need to reference the control, as would be the case when applying a CSS style to format the control's appearance.

Input Types

At the time of this writing, HTML supports twenty-two different values for the type attribute. Each input type is associated with a different form control, usually one that is tailored to make it easy for the user to enter data that matches the input type. For example, an input type of password is displayed as an input box that hides the input text for security purposes. Figure 7-10 describes the different type values for the input element and how their controls are typically displayed in most current browsers. If no type value is specified, the browser assumes a default value of text and adds a simple text input box to the web form.

Figure 7-10   Controls and the input type attribute

Type Value	Control Displayed by the Browser
button	A button that can be clicked to perform an action
checkbox	A check box for yes/no or true/false responses
color	A widget from which users can select a color
date	A widget from which users can select a calendar date
datetime-local	A widget from which users can select a calendar date and time
email	An input box used for e-mail addresses
file	A widget from which users can select a local file
hidden	A control that is hidden from the user
image	An image that can be clicked to perform an action
month	A widget from which users can select a calendar month and year
number	A spin box from which users can select a numeric value
password	An input box in which the entry value is hidden by * symbols
radio	A radio or option button that can be clicked by the user
range	A slider from which users can select a numeric value within a defined range
reset	A button that can be clicked to reset the web form
search	A widget that can be used to search for a defined term
submit	A button that can be clicked to submit the form for processing
tel	An input box used for telephone numbers
text (the default)	An input box used for text entries
time	A widget from which users can select a time value
url	An input box used for entering URLs
week	A widget from which users can select a week value

REFERENCE

Creating an Input Control

- To create an input control for data entry, add the element

  `<input name="name" id="id" type="type" />`

  where `name` provides the name of the field associated with the control, `id` identifies the control in which the user enters the field value, and `type` indicates the type of control displayed by the browser.

The first `input` elements you will add to the survey form will be input boxes in which the customer enters his or her name, street address, city, state, postal code, phone number, and e-mail address. For the program running on the web server, these input boxes with be associated with data fields named custName, custStreet, custCity, custState, custZip, custPhone, and custEmail, respectively. You will identify the controls for these fields with the ids: name, street, city, state, zip, phone, and mail. Before each `input` element, you will insert a text string that describes the content of the input box.

To add input elements:

1. Within the custInfo field set, add the following text strings and `input` elements:

```
Name*
<input name="custName" id="name" type="text" />

Street address
<input name="custStreet" id="street" type="text" />

City
<input name="custCity" id="city" type="text" />

State
<input name="custState" id="state" type="text" />

Postal code
<input name="custZip" id="zip" type="text" />

Phone number
<input name="custPhone" id="phone" type="tel" />

E-mail*
<input name="custEmail" id="mail" type="email" />
```

Figure 7-11 highlights the code for the newly inserted `input` elements.

Figure 7-11   **Adding input elements to the form**

name of the field associated with the input box

id of the input box control for entering the customer name

```
<fieldset id="custInfo">
    <legend>Customer Information</legend>
    Name*
    <input name="custName" id="name" type="text" />

    Street address
    <input name="custStreet" id="street" type="text" />

    City
    <input name="custCity" id="city" type="text" />

    State
    <input name="custState" id="state" type="text" />

    Postal code
    <input name="custZip" id="zip" type="text" />

    Phone number
    <input name="custPhone" id="phone" type="tel" />

    E-mail*
    <input name="custEmail" id="mail" type="email" />
</fieldset>
```

input boxes for general text entries

input box for telephone numbers

input box for e-mail addresses

TIP

You can prevent users from entering data into a control by adding the attribute disabled to the element tag.

2. Save your changes to the file and then reload the rb_survey.html file in your browser.

3. Click the **Name*** input box on the form to make it active and type *your name* in the input box. Press the **Tab** key to move the insertion point to the next input box.

4. Complete the form by entering *your contact information* in the remainder of the form, pressing the **Tab** key to move from one input box to the next. Figure 7-12 shows the completed data entry for the form.

| Figure 7-12 | Displaying input boxes |

input box used to enter the customer street address

Required values are marked by an asterisk (*)

┌─Customer Information───┐
│ Name* Alice Nichols   Street address 811 Beach Drive   City Ormond Beach   State │
│ FL   Postal code 32175   Phone number (386) 555-7499   E-mail* │
│ anichols@example.com   │
└──┘
┌─Share Your Experience at Red Ball Pizza──────────────────────────────────────┐
│   │
└──┘

By default, browsers display input boxes as inline elements with a default length of 20 characters. Later, you will explore how to format these controls to make them easier to read and work with.

INSIGHT

Navigating Forms with Access Keys

You activate controls like input boxes either by clicking them with your mouse or by tabbing from one control to another. As your forms get longer, you might want to give users the ability to jump to a particular input box. This can be done with an access key. An **access key** is a single key on the keyboard that you press in conjunction with another key, commonly the Alt key for Windows users or the control key for Mac users, to jump to a spot in the web page. You create an access key by adding the accesskey attribute to the HTML element that creates the control. For example, to create an access key for the custName input box, you would enter the following code:

```
<input name="custName" id="custName" accesskey="1" />
```

If a user types Alt+1 (or control+1 for Mac users), the insertion point automatically moves to the custName input box. Note that you must use letters that are not reserved by your browser. For example, Alt+f is used by many browsers to access the File menu and thus should not be used as an access key. Access keys also can be used with hypertext links and are particularly helpful to users with impaired motor skills who find it difficult to use a mouse or others who prefer not to use a mouse.

Note that you should test your access keys with different browsers since a keyboard shortcut on one browser might not work with another. Your form can be enhanced through the use of access keys but it should not rely on them.

Input Types and Virtual Keyboards

Most mobile and tablet devices do not have physical keyboards; instead, they use **virtual keyboards** that exist as software representations of the physical device. One way that web forms can be made responsive to the needs of mobile and touch devices is by displaying different virtual keyboards for each input type. With an input box for telephone numbers, it is more convenient to have digits (instead of alphabetic characters) prominently displayed on the keyboard. Figure 7-13 shows the virtual keyboards that will be displayed based on the value of the `type` attribute.

Figure 7-13 **Virtual keyboards for different input types**

type="text" type="email" type="number"

type="tel" type="url"

Note that for e-mail addresses the `@` key is prominently displayed as well as a key that inserts the `.com` character string. Similarly, for url data, the virtual keyboard includes a key that inserts the `www.` character string. The choice and layout of the virtual keyboard is determined by the operating system of the device.

Adding Field Labels

In the last set of steps, you entered a descriptive text string above each `input` element to indicate what content should be entered into the input box. However, nothing in the HTML code explicitly associates that descriptive text with the input box. To associate a text string with a control, you enclose the text string within the following `label` element

```
<label for="id">label text</label>
```

where *id* is the id of the control that you want associated with the label, and *label text* is the text of the label. For example, the following code associates the label text "Street address" with the input box for the custStreet control:

```
<label for="street">Street address</label>
<input name="custStreet" id="street" type="text" />
```

You also can make this association implicitly by nesting the control, such as an `input` element, within the `label` element as in the following code:

```
<label>
    Street address
    <input name="custStreet" id="street" />
</label>
```

Notice that you do not need to include a `for` attribute when you nest the control since the association is made implicit.

Which approach you use depends on how you want to lay out a form's content. When you use the `for` attribute, you can place the label text anywhere within the page and it will still be associated with the control. However, by nesting the control within the label, you can treat both the control and its label as a single object, which can make form layout easier because you can move both the label text and the control as a single unit around the page. Depending on the layout of your form, you might use both approaches.

Creating a Field Label

- To explicitly associate a text label with a control, use the following `label` element and the `for` attribute

  ```
  <label for="id">label text</label>
  ```

  where `id` identifies the control associated with the label.
- To implicitly associate a text label with a control, nest the control within the `label` element as follows

  ```
  <label>
      label text
      control
  </label>
  ```

  where `control` is the HTML code for the form control.

Once you associate a label with a control, clicking the label activates the control. In the case of input boxes, clicking the label would automatically move the insertion point into the input box, making it ready for data entry. With date or color types, clicking the label will display the calendar or color picker widget.

Use the `label` element and `for` attribute now to associate the text strings you entered in the last set of steps with their corresponding input boxes.

To insert form labels:

The value of the `for` attribute should match the value of the `id` attribute for the control.

1. Return to the **rb_survey.html** file in your editor.

2. Go to the custInfo field set and enclose the text string *Name** within the following `label` element:

   ```
   <label for="name">Name*</label>
   ```

3. Repeat Step 2 for the remaining descriptive text strings in the custInfo field set, using the `for` attribute to associate each text string with the id of the subsequent `input` element. Figure 7-14 highlights the newly added code in the web form.

Figure 7-14   **Adding form labels**

> for attribute associates the label with the name input box

> label element →

```
<legend>Customer Information</legend>
<label for="name">Name*</label>
<input name="custName" id="name" type="text" />

<label for="street">Street address</label>
<input name="custStreet" id="street" type="text" />

<label for="city">City</label>
<input name="custCity" id="city" type="text" />

<label for="state">State</label>
<input name="custState" id="state" type="text" />

<label for="zip">Postal code</label>
<input name="custZip" id="zip" type="text" />

<label for="phone">Phone number</label>
<input name="custPhone" id="phone" type="tel" />

<label for="mail">E-mail*</label>
<input name="custEmail" id="mail" type="email" />
```

▶ **4.** Save your changes to the file and then reload the rb_survey.html file in your browser.

▶ **5.** Test the labels by clicking each label and verifying that the insertion point appears within the corresponding input box, making that control active on the form.

Alice stops by to see your progress on the survey form. In its current state, the form is difficult to read. She wants you to design a layout that will be easier to read and that will be responsive to both mobile and desktop devices.

Designing a Form Layout

To be effective, the layout of your form should aid the user in interpreting the form and navigating easily from one input control to the next. There are two general layouts: one in which the labels are placed directly above the input controls in a single column and the other in which the labels and controls are placed side-by-side in two columns. See Figure 7-15.

Figure 7-15   Form layouts

one-column layout   two-column layout

TIP

In a two-column layout, you can move the label text even closer to the input controls by right aligning the label text.

Usability studies have shown that a single column layout is more accessible because the labels are placed more closely to their input controls. However, for long forms involving many fields, a single column layout can be difficult to work with due to the extensive vertical space required.

Alice wants you to use a single column layout for mobile devices due to the limited horizontal space on those devices, but she wants a two-column layout for devices with larger screen widths. To accomplish this, you will use a flex layout that will allow the labels and controls to assume flexible widths based on the available screen width of the device being used.

First, you will nest each label and input box within a `div` element that will act as a flexbox container.

To create a flexbox for the `label` and `input` elements:

1. Return to the **rb_survey.html** file in your editor and scroll down to the custInfo field set.

2. Nest the label and input box for the custName field within the following `div` element, indenting the code to make it easier to read:

```
<div class="formRow">
    <label for="name">Name*</label>
    <input name="custName" id="name" type="text" />
</div>
```

3. Repeat Step 2 for the remaining label and input box pairs, nesting each pair within a `div` element belonging to the formRow class. Figure 7-16 highlights the new code in the file.

Figure 7-16 Nesting labels and input controls within div elements

```
<div class="formRow">
    <label for="name">Name*</label>
    <input name="custName" id="name" type="text" />
</div>

<div class="formRow">
    <label for="street">Street address</label>
    <input name="custStreet" id="street" type="text" />
</div>

<div class="formRow">
    <label for="city">City</label>
    <input name="custCity" id="city" type="text" />
</div>

<div class="formRow">
    <label for="state">State</label>
    <input name="custState" id="state" type="text" />
</div>

<div class="formRow">
    <label for="zip">Postal code</label>
    <input name="custZip" id="zip" type="text" />
</div>

<div class="formRow">
    <label for="phone">Phone number</label>
    <input name="custPhone" id="phone" type="tel" />
</div>

<div class="formRow">
    <label for="mail">E-mail*</label>
    <input name="custEmail" id="mail" type="email" />
</div>
```

Next, you will create a style rule that displays each `div` element of the formRow class as a flexbox and the objects that are direct children of those `div` elements as flex items.

To add styles for a flexible form layout:

▶ 1. Scroll to the top of the rb_survey.html file and then, within the document head and, directly above the `script` element, add a link to the **rb_forms.css** style sheet.

▶ 2. Save your changes to the file and then use your editor to open the **rb_forms_txt.css** file from the html07 ▶ tutorial folder. Enter *your name* and *the date* in the comment section of the file and save it as **rb_forms.css**.

3. Within the Forms Layout Styles section, add the following style rule to display the formRow `div` element as a flexbox with row orientation and a 7-pixel top and bottom margin:

```
div.formRow {
    display: -webkit-flex;
    display: flex;
    -webkit-flex-flow: row wrap;
    flex-flow: row wrap;
    margin: 7px 0px;
}
```

4. Add the following style rules to set the growth, shrink, and basis values of the objects that are direct children of the formRow `div` element:

```
div.formRow > * {
    -webkit-flex: 1 1 150px;
    flex: 1 1 150px;
}
```

Figure 7-17 shows the new style rules in the style sheet.

Figure 7-17 **Adding styles to create a flexible layout**

displays the div element with the class formRow as a horizontal flexbox

sets the top/bottom margins to 7 pixels

sets the flex sizes of objects that are direct children of the formRow div element

```
/* Form Layout Styles */

div.formRow {
    display: -webkit-flex;
    display: flex;
    -webkit-flex-flow: row wrap;
    flex-flow: row wrap;
    margin: 7px 0px;
}

div.formRow > * {
    -webkit-flex: 1 1 150px;
    flex: 1 1 150px;
}
```

5. Save your changes to the style sheet and then reload rb_survey.html file in your browser.

6. Resize your screen width to verify that the form layout changes between one and two columns as the screen changes width. See Figure 7-18.

Figure 7-18	Flex layout of the labels and text input controls

Required values are marked by an asterisk (*)

┌─Customer Information─────────────
│ Name*
│ [   ]
│
│ Street address
│ [   ]
│
│ City
│ [   ]
│
│ State
│ [   ]
│
│ Postal code
│ [   ]
│
│ Phone number
│ [   ]
│
│ E-mail*
│ [   ]

Required values are marked by an asterisk (*)

┌─Customer Information─────────────────────
│ Name*   [   ]
│ Street address [   ]
│ City   [   ]
│ State   [   ]
│ Postal code   [   ]
│ Phone number   [   ]
│ E-mail*   [   ]

narrow screen layout   wide screen layout

Another way to set the width of an input box is by adding the following `size` attribute to the `input` element in the HTML file

```
size="chars"
```

where `chars` is the width of the input box in characters. For example, the following `input` element sets the width of the input box for the custState field to two characters:

```
<input id="state" size="2" type="text" />
```

Note that this is not an exact measure because the width of individual characters varies depending on the typeface and font style.

Alice suggests that you also use a flexible layout for the two field sets so that they are displayed side-by-side for wider screen devices and stacked for narrow screens. Create style rules now that will change the web form to a flexbox and the field sets as items within that flexbox. You will also add styles to change the appearance of the field set boxes themselves.

To create a flexible layout for the form:

1. Return to the **rb_forms.css** file in your editor.

2. At the top of the Form Layout Styles section, insert the following style rule to display the survey form as a flexbox:

```
form#survey {
    display: -webkit-flex;
    display: flex;
    -webkit-flex-flow: row wrap;
    flex-flow: row wrap;
}
```

3. Add the following style rule to display the field sets within the survey form as flex items:

```
form#survey > fieldset {
    background-color: rgb(241, 232, 181);
    border-radius: 20px;
    -webkit-flex: 1 1 300px;
    flex: 1 1 300px;
    font-size: 0.85em;
    padding: 10px;
    margin: 10px;
}
```

Figure 7-19 shows the new style rules in the style sheet.

Figure 7-19   **Creating a flexible layout for the form field sets**

```
/* Form Layout Styles */

form#survey {
    display: -webkit-flex;
    display: flex;
    -webkit-flex-flow: row wrap;
    flex-flow: row wrap;
}

form#survey > fieldset {
    background-color: rgb(241, 232, 181);
    border-radius: 20px;
    -webkit-flex: 1 1 300px;
    flex: 1 1 300px;
    font-size: 0.85em;
    padding: 10px;
    margin: 10px;
}
```

displays the survey form as a flexbox

sets the field set background color to yellow-gold

applies rounded corners to the field set

defines the font size, padding, and margin spaces of the field set

sets the flex size of the field set

4. Save your changes to the style sheet and then reload rb_survey.html file in your browser.

5. Resize your screen width and verify that the form layout changes from one column to two columns, with both field sets side by side as shown in Figure 7-20 when the screen width is larger, to one column, with the field sets stacked vertically when the screen width is reduced.

Figure 7-20   **Flex layout of the field sets for a wide screen layout**

Customer Information

Name*

Street address

City

State

Postal code

Phone number

E-mail*

Share Your Experience at Red Ball Pizza

Finally, Alice wants the field set legends to stand out from the border. She suggests you change the text and background color of the legends.

To set the style of the field set legend:

1. Return to the **rb_forms.css** file in your editor.

2. Go to the Legend Styles section and insert the following style rule:

   ```
   legend {
       background-color: rgb(179, 20, 25);
       color: white;
       padding: 5px;
   }
   ```

   Figure 7-21 highlights the style rule for the field set legend.

Figure 7-21   **Style rule for the field set legend**

sets the background color to red

sets the text color to white

```
/* Legend Styles */

legend {
    background-color: rgb(179, 20, 25);
    color: white;
    padding: 5px;
}
```

adds 5 pixels of padding around the legend text

3. Save your changes to the style sheet and then reload rb_survey.html file in your browser. Verify that the two field set legends appear in white font on a red background.

Using the `autocomplete` Attribute

Many browsers include an autocomplete feature that automatically completes an input control based on previous user entries. For example, a user who routinely fills in his or her street address in a multitude of web forms can enable the browser to remember that information and to insert it automatically into any address field from a web form.

The autocomplete feature is a useful time-saver in most cases, but it also can be a security risk when using a computer located in a public place. After all, you may not want to have a private credit card number or password automatically filled in by a browser on a computer that other people will be using.

One way to prevent this problem is through the `autocomplete` attribute which enables or disables the browser's autocomplete function. For example, the following `input` element prevents the browser from automatically filling out the creditCard field.

```
<input name="creditCard" autocomplete="false" type="text" />
```

To enable the browser's autocomplete capability, set the value of the `autocomplete` attribute to `true`.

It is easier to use the form with the new layout. However, more than 90% of Red Ball Pizza customers come from Ormond Beach in Florida. Rather than forcing these customers to enter that data, it would be simpler to have those values entered for them. You can do that using default values.

Defining Default Values and Placeholders

To specify a default field value, you add the following `value` attribute to the HTML element for the form control

```
value="value"
```

where *value* is the value that will be entered by default into the control unless the user enters a different value. For example, the following `input` element sets the default value of the custCity field to Ormond Beach:

```
<input name="custCity" id="city" type="text" value="Ormond Beach" />
```

Set the default values for the custCity and custState fields to *Ormond Beach* and *FL* respectively.

TIP

You can replace the default field value by entering a new value for the field.

To define a default field value:

1. Return to the **rb_survey.html** file in your editor and scroll down to the custInfo field set.

2. Add the attribute **value="Ormond Beach"** to the `input` element for the custCity input control.

3. Add the attribute **value="FL"** to the `input` element for the custState input control.

   Figure 7-22 highlights the attributes that add default values to the custCity and custState fields.

Figure 7-22   Defining the default field value

```
<div class="formRow">
    <label for="city">City</label>
    <input name="custCity" id="city" type="text" value="Ormond Beach" />
</div>

<div class="formRow">
    <label for="state">State</label>
    <input name="custState" id="state" type="text" value="FL" />
</div>
```

sets the default value for the custCity field

sets the default value for the custState field

4. Save your changes to the file and then reload rb_survey.html file in your browser. Verify that the City and State input boxes show the text strings *Ormond Beach* and *FL* respectively.

   Trouble? If the form does not reload with the replacement text, close the file and reopen it in your browser, which clears all fields and opens a new copy of the form.

Placeholders are text strings that appear within a form control, providing a hint about the kind of data that should be entered into the field. However, unlike a default field value, a placeholder is not stored in the control as the field's value. Placeholders are defined using the following `placeholder` attribute

```
placeholder="text"
```

where *text* is the text of the placeholder. For example, the following `placeholder` attribute provides guidance about the format users should use when entering values for the custPhone field:

```
<input name="custPhone" id="phone" placeholder="(nnn) nnn-nnnn" />
```

When the browser displays the form, the text *(nnn) nnn-nnnn* appears grayed out in the input box indicating to the user that he or she should enter a phone number, including both the area code and the seven-digit number. The placeholder automatically disappears as soon as a user selects the control and begins to enter a value.

Alice asks you to add placeholders to the input boxes for the custName, custZip, and custPhone fields.

To define a placeholder:

1. Return to the **rb_survey.html** file in your editor.

2. Add the attribute `placeholder="first and last name"` to the input element for the custName field.

3. Add the attribute `placeholder="nnnnn (-nnnn)"` to the input element for the custZip field.

4. Add the attribute `placeholder="(nnn) nnn-nnnn"` to the input element for the custPhone field.

Figure 7-23 highlights the `placeholder` attributes added to the form.

Figure 7-23　　**Defining placeholder text**

5. Save your changes to the file and then reload rb_survey.html file in your browser. As shown in Figure 7-24, placeholder text has been added to the Name, Postal code, and Phone input boxes.

Figure 7-24   **Viewing default values and placeholder text**

The style of the placeholder text is determined by the browser. There are no CSS styles to format the appearance of the placeholder but all major browsers include their own browser extensions for placeholders. Depending on the browser, the placeholder is treated either as a pseudo-class or a pseudo-element named either `input-placeholder` for the `webkit` and `ms` extensions or `placeholder` for the `moz` extension.

The following code shows a cross-browser style sheet that changes the text color of the placeholder text for every input box to light red.

```
input::-webkit-input-placeholder {
    color: rgb(255, 151, 151);
}

input:-ms-input-placeholder {
    color: rgb(255, 151, 151);
}

input::-moz-placeholder {
    color: rgb(255, 151, 151);
}
```

Note that you cannot place different browser extensions within the same style rule because if style rule contains a selector that the browser doesn't recognize, the entire rule will be ignored.

Decision Making: Creating Cross-Browser Compatible Forms

Several form attributes, such as the `placeholder` attribute, might not be supported by older browsers. This poses a problem for designers who must decide whether or not to use such attributes. One school of thought holds that a web form should look and function the same across all browsers and browser versions. Thus, a feature like the `placeholder` attribute should not be used. If a placeholder is needed, it should be created using a JavaScript program that can be applied uniformly across browsers and browser versions. The opposing view holds that the best design is one that uses each browser to its utmost capabilities, and that the web will only improve in the long run if the most current features are employed because their use will encourage their more rapid adoption across the browser market.

To decide between these two approaches, you must evaluate whether the form feature you're adding is critical to understanding and using your web form. If it is, you need to include workarounds so that all users are supported regardless of their browser. On the other hand, if the feature enhances the user's experience but is not essential to working with the web form, it can be safely added without leaving older browsers behind.

You have finished the initial stage of developing the survey form. Alice is pleased with the form's appearance and content. In the next session, you will extend the form by adding new fields and controls, including calendar widgets, selection lists, option buttons, and check boxes.

REVIEW

Session 7.1 Quick Check

1. Provide the code to create a form with the `id` "registration" that employs the `action` attribute to access the CGI script at *www.example.com/cgi-bin/registration* using the `post` method.

2. What different roles do the `name` and `id` attributes assume when applied with the following `input` element?
   ```
   <input name="lastName" id="lName" type="text" />
   ```

3. Provide the code to create a field set containing the legend text "Contact Information".

4. Provide the code to create an input box for a data field named custPassword, with an input type suitable for a field containing password data.

5. For mobile devices that use virtual keyboards, what is the advantage of using a `type` attribute value of "tel" for an input box in which users enter telephone numbers?

6. What are two ways of associating a field label with a form control?

7. Provide the code to create a field label with the text "User Name" that is associated with an input box with the ID username.

8. Provide the code to create an input box for the country field with the default text "United States".

9. Provide the code to create an input box for the socialSecurity field displaying the placeholder text "nnn-nn-nnnn".

Session 7.2 Visual Overview:

The **select** element creates a drop-down list box control.

The **size** attribute sets the number of visible options.

The **multiple** attribute allows for multiple selections from the drop-down list.

Each option in a selection list is marked with the **option** element.

The **checkbox** data type creates a checkbox control.

The **selected** attribute identifies the default option in a selection list.

Each radio button within an option group belongs to the same data field.

The **textarea** element marks a text area box control.

The **radio** data type creates an option button control.

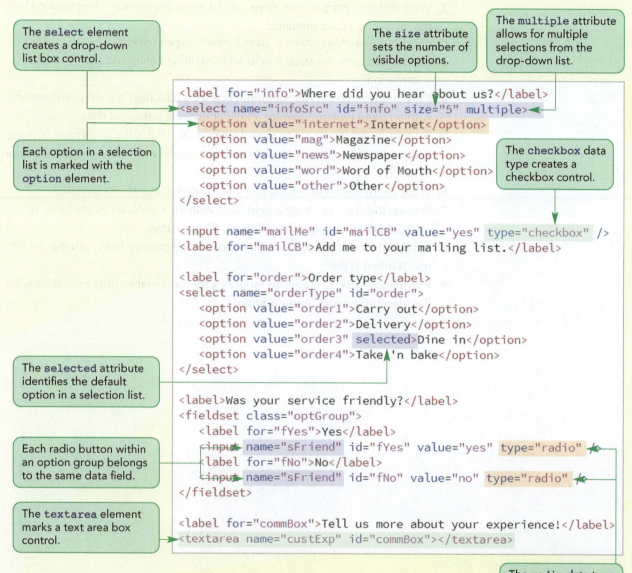

```html
<label for="info">Where did you hear about us?</label>
<select name="infoSrc" id="info" size="5" multiple>
    <option value="internet">Internet</option>
    <option value="mag">Magazine</option>
    <option value="news">Newspaper</option>
    <option value="word">Word of Mouth</option>
    <option value="other">Other</option>
</select>

<input name="mailMe" id="mailCB" value="yes" type="checkbox" />
<label for="mailCB">Add me to your mailing list.</label>

<label for="order">Order type</label>
<select name="orderType" id="order">
    <option value="order1">Carry out</option>
    <option value="order2">Delivery</option>
    <option value="order3" selected>Dine in</option>
    <option value="order4">Take 'n bake</option>
</select>

<label>Was your service friendly?</label>
<fieldset class="optGroup">
    <label for="fYes">Yes</label>
    <input name="sFriend" id="fYes" value="yes" type="radio"
    <label for="fNo">No</label>
    <input name="sFriend" id="fNo" value="no" type="radio"
</fieldset>

<label for="commBox">Tell us more about your experience!</label>
<textarea name="custExp" id="commBox"></textarea>
```

Web Form Widgets

Customer Survey

Thank you for taking our customer survey. Your response helps Red Ball Pizza maintain the tradition that has made us the top-rated pizzeria in the metro area. All participants are automatically entered into a monthly drawing to receive a *Red Ball Express PizzaFest* containing two large pizzas, a 2-liter soda, and a side order of chicken wings. Check your e-mail inbox for contest results.

Surveys are private and confidential. Red Ball Pizza will not share your contact information with third parties, *ever*.

Required values are marked by an asterisk (*)

Customer Information

Name*	first and last name
Street address	
City	Ormond Beach
State	FL
Postal code	nnnnn (-nnnn)
Where did you hear about us?	Internet / Magazine / Newspaper / Word of Mouth / Other

☐ Add me to your mailing list.

Share Your Experience at Red Ball Pizza

Date of visit	mm / dd / yyyy
Order type	Dine in ▼
Was your service friendly?	Yes ○ No ○

Tell us more about your experience!

Selection list displayed as a drop-down list box control with the default option displayed.

The user can select only one option button control.

A check mark appears when the user clicks the checkbox control.

Selection list box control showing five items; the user can select more than one option.

The user can type in the text area box control.

Entering Date and Time Values

To ensure that users enter data in the correct format, you can use controls specifically designed for the field's data type. Consider, for example, the following code that creates an input box for a birthdate field:

```
<label for="bdate">Date of Birth</label>
<input name="bdate" id="bdate" />
```

There is nothing to prevent users from entering the same date in a wide variety of formats such as September 14, 1996, 9/14/96, or 1996-09-14. The lack of uniformity in these date formats makes it difficult for a web server program to store and analyze the data.

Starting with HTML5, date and time fields could be indicated using one of the following `type` attributes: `date`, `time`, `datetime-local`, `month`, and `week`. Each of these `type` attribute values has a different control associated with it, enabling the user to select the date, time, month, or week value. The text into the input box is based on the user's selection in the control widget, ensuring the date or time text is entered in the same format for every user. Figure 7-25 shows examples of the widgets used by the Google Chrome browser.

TIP

If a browser does not support date and time controls, it will display an input box, leaving the user free to enter the date or time value in whatever format he or she wishes.

Figure 7-25 Date and time controls

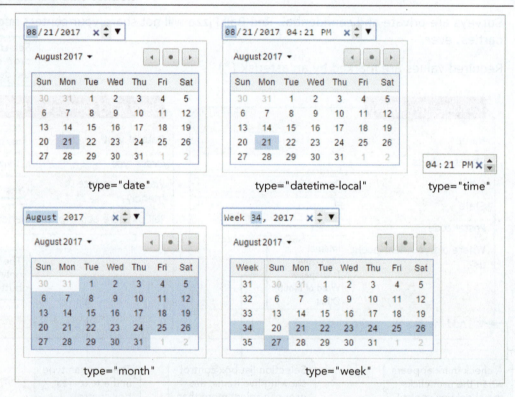

The explnfo field set will contain fields in which the customer can describe his or her experience at the pizzeria. Alice wants the field set to include a calendar control that users can use to enter the date of their visit to Red Ball Pizza.

To create a date field:

1. If you took a break after the previous session, make sure **rb_survey.html** is open in your editor.

2. Go to the expInfo field set and insert the following `label` and `input` element:

```
<div class="formRow">
   <label for="visit">Date of visit</label>
   <input name="visitDate" id="visit" type="date" />
</div>
```

Figure 7-26 highlights the code for the `label` and `input` elements.

Figure 7-26   Creating a date field

```
<fieldset id="expInfo">
   <legend>Share Your Experience at Red Ball Pizza</legend>

   <div class="formRow">
      <label for="visit">Date of visit</label>
      <input name="visitDate" id="visit" type="date" />
   </div>
                              sets the data type of the
                              visitDate field to "date"
</fieldset>
```

3. Save your changes to the file and then reload rb_survey.html file in your browser.

4. Click the Date of visit control and select a date to verify that the text of the date is entered into the input box.

Trouble? At the time of this writing, the Firefox and Internet Explorer browsers do not support the date type and will simply display an input box.

Creating a Selection List

The next part of the survey form records how customers place their orders from Red Ball Pizza. A customer order can be placed in one of four ways: pickup, delivery, dine in, or, in the case of pizzas, uncooked pizzas that customers can take home and bake. Alice doesn't want customers to enter their order types into an input box because customers will enter this information in different ways, and the large variety of spellings and text will make it difficult to group and analyze the survey results. Instead, she wants each user to select the order type from a predetermined group of options. This can be accomplished using a selection list.

A selection list is a list box that presents users with a group of possible values for the data field and is created using the following `select` and `option` elements

```
<select name="name">
   <option value="value1">text1</option>
   <option value="value2">text2</option>
   ...
</select>
```

where *name* is the name of the data field, *value1*, *value2*, and so on are the possible field values, and *text1*, *text2*, and so on are the text of the entries in the selection list that users see on the web form. Note that the field value does not have to match the option text. In most cases, the option text will be expansive and descriptive, while the corresponding field value will be brief and succinct for use with the server program analyzing the form data.

The first option in the selection list is selected by default and thus contains the field's default value. To make a different option the default, add the `selected` attribute to the `option` element as follows:

```
<option value="value" selected>text</option>
```

Note that XHTML documents require the attribute `selected="selected"` to be compliant with XHTML standards for attribute values.

Creating a Selection List

- To create a selection list, add the elements

```
<select name="name">
   <option value="value1">text1</option>
   <option value="value2">text2</option>
   ...
</select>
```

where *name* is the name of the data field, *value1*, *value2*, and so on are the possible field values; and *text1*, *text2*, and so on are the text entries displayed in the selection list on the web form.

- To allow users to make multiple selections, add the attribute `multiple` to the `select` element.
- To set the number of options displayed at one time in the selection list, add the following attribute to the `select` element

```
size="value"
```

where *value* is the number of options displayed in the selection list at any one time.

- To specify the default value, add the `selected` attribute to the `option` element that you want to set as the default.

Add a selection list to the Red Ball Pizza survey form to record the type of order placed by the customer, storing the value in the orderType field. Identify the selection list control with ID order. Alice knows that most of the survey respondents dine in at the restaurant. Although she wants the options for the orderType field listed in alphabetical order, she would like the Dine in option selected by default.

To create a selection list:

1. Return to the **rb_survey.html** file in your editor.

2. Within the expInfo field set, add the following code to create the label and selection list:

```
<div class="formRow">
   <label for="order">Order type</label>
   <select name="orderType" id="order">
      <option value="order1">Carry out</option>
      <option value="order2">Delivery</option>
      <option value="order3" selected>Dine in</option>
      <option value="order4">Take 'n bake</option>
   </select>
</div>
```

TIP

The default width of the selection box is equal to the width of the longest option text unless the width is set using a CSS style.

Figure 7-27 highlights the code for the selection list.

| Figure 7-27 | Creating a selection list for the orderType field |

```html
<div class="formRow">
   <label for="visit">Date of visit</label>
   <input name="visitDate" id="visit" type="date" />
</div>

<div class="formRow">
   <label for="order">Order type</label>
   <select name="orderType" id="order">
      <option value="order1">Carry out</option>
      <option value="order2">Delivery</option>
      <option value="order3" selected>Dine in</option>
      <option value="order4">Take 'n bake</option>
   </select>
</div>
```

field name associated with the selection list

id of the selection list control

order3 (Dine in) is the default selected value of the orderType field

possible values of the orderType field

text strings displayed in the selection list for each option

3. Save your changes to the file and then reload the rb_survey.html file in your browser.

4. Click the Order type selection list and verify that the list of order types appears in the drop-down list box and that Dine in is the default selected option. See Figure 7-28.

| Figure 7-28 | Viewing the selection list options |

Share Your Experience at Red Ball Pizza

Date of visit   mm/dd/yyyy

Order type   Dine in
                       Carry out
                       Delivery
                       Dine in
                       Take 'n bake

calendar control for selecting the date of the customer's visit

Dine in is the default selected option

a drop-down list box displays the text of the four options

Working with Select Attributes

By default, a selection list appears as a drop-down list box. To display a selection list as a scroll box with more than one option visible in the web form, add the following size attribute to the select element

```html
<select size="value"> ... </select>
```

where *value* is the number of options that the selection list displays at one time. For example, a size value of 5 would display 5 items in the scroll box.

The default behavior of the selection list is to allow only one selection from the list of options. To allow more than one item to be selected, add the following `multiple` attribute to the `select` element:

```
<select multiple> ... </select>
```

There are two ways for users to select multiple items from a selection list. For noncontiguous selections, users can press and hold the Ctrl key (or the command key on a Mac) while making the selections. For a contiguous selection, users can select the first item, press and hold the Shift key, and then select the last item in the range. This selects the two items, as well as all the items between them.

Alice has another selection list to add to the survey form, which will record how a customer heard about Red Ball Pizza. The survey presents the user with five options: Internet, Magazine, Newspaper, Word of Mouth, or Other. Alice wants the form to display all of the options, so you set the value of the `size` attribute to 5. She also wants customers to be able to select multiple options from the selection list.

To apply the size and multiple attributes:

1. Return to the **rb_survey.html** file in your editor and go to the custInfo field set.

2. At the bottom of the field set, insert the following code:

```
<div class="formRow">
<label for="info">Where did you hear about us?
<br />(select all that apply)
</label>
<select name="infoSrc" id="info" size="5" multiple>
    <option value="internet">Internet</option>
    <option value="mag">Magazine</option>
    <option value="news">Newspaper</option>
    <option value="word">Word of Mouth</option>
    <option value="other">Other</option>
</select>
</div>
```

Figure 7-29 highlights the code for the selection list.

Figure 7-29   **Inserting a selection list for the infoSrc field**

```
<div class="formRow">
    <label for="mail">E-mail*</label>
    <input name="custEmail" id="mail" type="email" />
</div>

<div class="formRow">
    <label for="info">Where did you hear about us?<br />(select all that apply)</label>
    <select name="infoSrc" id="info" size="5" multiple>
        <option value="internet">Internet</option>
        <option value="mag">Magazine</option>
        <option value="news">Newspaper</option>
        <option value="word">Word of Mouth</option>
        <option value="other">Other</option>
    </select>
</div>

</fieldset>
```

field name

displays 5 options in the selection list

allows the user to make multiple selections

3. Save your changes and then reload the rb_survey.html file in your browser. Figure 7-30 shows the infoSrc selection list box.

   Viewing the selection list for the infoSrc field

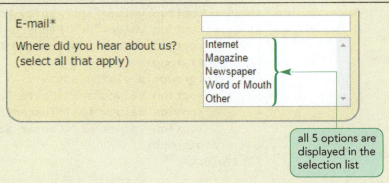

4. Verify that you can now select multiple values for the infoSrc field by using the Ctrl+click, Command+click, Shift+click keyboard and mouse combinations.

If you use a multiple selection list in a form, be aware that the form sends a name/value pair to the server for each option the user selects from the list. Verify that your server-based program can handle a single field with multiple values before using a multiple selection list.

Grouping Selection Options

In long selection lists, it can be difficult for users to locate a particular option value. You can organize selection list options by placing them in option groups using the `optgroup` element

```
<select>
    <optgroup label="label1">
        <option>text1</option>
        <option>text2</option>
    </optgroup>
    <optgroup label="label2">
        <option>text3</option>
        <option>text4</option>
    </optgroup>
</select>
```

where *label1*, *label2*, and so forth are the labels for the different groups of options. The text of the label appears in the selection list above each group of items but it is not a selectable item from the list. Figure 7-31 shows an example of a selection list in which the options are divided into two groups.

Figure 7-31 **Grouping options in a selection list**

```
<label for="appetizers">Starter Menu</label>
<select name="meal">
    <optgroup label="Appetizers">
        <option value="sms">Spicy Mozzarella Sticks</option>
        <option value="pr">Pepperoni Rolls</option>
        <option value="tr">Toasted Ravioli</option>
    </optgroup>
    <optgroup label="Salads">
        <option value="sms">Pasta Salad</option>
        <option value="tbs">Tuscan Bread Salad</option>
        <option value="pr">Caesar Salad</option>
    </optgroup>
</select>
```

option group labels

Starter Menu — Spicy Mozzarella Sticks ▼

Appetizers
- Spicy Mozzarella Sticks
- Pepperoni Rolls
- Toasted Ravioli

Salads
- Pasta Salad
- Tuscan Bread Salad
- Caesar Salad

The appearance of the option group label is determined by the browser. You can apply a style to an entire option group including its label, but there is no CSS style to change the appearance of the option group label alone.

Hidden Fields

Some fields have predefined values that do not require user input and are often not displayed within the web form. You create a **hidden field** by setting the value of the type attribute to hidden as follows:

```
<input name="name" value="value" type="hidden" />
```

where *name* is the name of the data field and *value* is the value stored in the field. With a hidden field, both the field value and the input control are hidden from the user. Even though hidden fields are not displayed by browsers, the field values still can be read by examining the source code; for this reason, you should not put any sensitive information in a hidden field.

Creating Option Buttons

Option buttons, also called radio buttons, are like selection lists in that they limit fields to a set of possible values; but, unlike selection lists, the options appear as separate controls in the web form. Option buttons are created with a group of input elements with a type attribute value of "radio", sharing a common data field name as follows

```
<input name="name" value="value1" type="radio" />
<input name="name" value="value2" type="radio" />
<input name="name" value="value3" type="radio" />
...
```

TIP

To show that a group of radio buttons are associated with the same field, place the radio button controls within a field set.

where *name* is the name of the data field and *value1*, *value2*, *value3*, and so on are the field values associated with each option. While a user can select multiple items in a selection list, a user can only click or check one option in a group of radio buttons. Selecting one radio button automatically deselects the others and sets the value of the field to the value of the checked radio button.

For example, the following code creates a group of option buttons for the sFriend field, limiting the possible field values to "yes" or "no".

```
Was your service friendly?
<label for="fYes">Yes</label>
<input name="sFriend" value="yes" id="fYes" type="radio" />
<label for="fYes">No</label>
<input name="sFriend" value="no" id="fNo" type="radio" />
```

Note that the two radio button controls are given different ids and field values to distinguish them from each other, however they share the same field name, "sFriend".

By default, an option button is unselected; however, you can set an option button to be selected as the default by adding the following checked attribute to the input element:

```
<input name="name" type="radio" checked />
```

REFERENCE

Creating an Option List

- To create a group of option buttons associated with the same field, add the input elements

```
<input name="name" value="value1" type="radio" />
<input name="name" value="value2" type="radio" />
<input name="name" value="value3" type="radio" />
...
```

where *name* is the name of the data field, and *value1*, *value2*, *value3*, and so on are the field values associated with each option.
- To specify the default option, add the checked attribute to the input element.

In the next part of the form, Alice wants to ask customers general questions about their experiences at the restaurant. She wants to know whether the service was friendly, whether orders were recorded correctly, and if the food was delivered hot. She suggests that you present these questions using radio buttons, placing each group of radio buttons within a fieldset element belonging to the optGroup class.

To create a set of option buttons:

1. Return to the **rb_survey.html** file in your editor and go to the expInfo field set.

2. At the bottom of the expInfo field set, add the following code to create radio buttons for the sFriend field:

```
<div class="formRow">
   <label>Was your service friendly?</label>
   <fieldset class="optGroup">
      <label for="fYes">Yes</label>
      <input name="sFriend" id="fYes" value="yes"
type="radio" />
      <label for="fNo">No</label>
      <input name="sFriend" id="fNo" value="no"
type="radio" />
   </fieldset>
</div>
```

The value of the name attribute must be the same for all option buttons within a group.

3. Add the following group of radio buttons for the oCorrect field:

```
<div class="formRow">
   <label>Was your order correct?</label>
   <fieldset class="optGroup">
      <label for="cYes">Yes</label>
      <input name="oCorrect" id="cYes" value="yes"
type="radio" />
      <label for="cNo">No</label>
      <input name="oCorrect" id="cNo" value="no"
type="radio" />
   </fieldset>
</div>
```

4. Finally, add the following group of radio buttons for the foodHot field:

```
<div class="formRow">
   <label>Was your food hot?</label>
   <fieldset class="optGroup">
      <label for="hYes">Yes</label>
      <input name="foodHot" id="hYes" value="yes"
type="radio" />
      <label for="hNo">No</label>
      <input name="foodHot" id="hNo" value="no"
type="radio" />
   </fieldset>
</div>
```

Figure 7-32 highlights the code for the set of option buttons.

Figure 7-32	Creating option groups for the sFriend, oCorrect, and foodHot fields

options for the sFriend field

label for the option group

field value

radio button controls

```
<div class="formRow">
    <label>Was your service friendly?</label>
    <fieldset class="optGroup">
        <label for="fYes">Yes</label>
        <input name="sFriend" id="fYes" value="yes" type="radio" />
        <label for="fNo">No</label>
        <input name="sFriend" id="fNo" value="no" type="radio" />
    </fieldset>
</div>
```

options for the oCorrect field

```
<div class="formRow">
    <label>Was your order correct?</label>
    <fieldset class="optGroup">
        <label for="cYes">Yes</label>
        <input name="oCorrect" id="cYes" value="yes" type="radio" />
        <label for="cNo">No</label>
        <input name="oCorrect" id="cNo" value="no" type="radio" />
    </fieldset>
</div>
```

options for the foodHot field

```
<div class="formRow">
    <label>Was your food hot?</label>
    <fieldset class="optGroup">
        <label for="hYes">Yes</label>
        <input name="foodHot" id="hYes" value="yes" type="radio" />
        <label for="hNo">No</label>
        <input name="foodHot" id="hNo" value="no" type="radio" />
    </fieldset>
</div>

    </fieldset>
</form>
```

5. Save your changes to the file and then reload rb_survey.html in your browser. Figure 7-33 shows the appearance of the three groups of radio buttons in the survey form.

Figure 7-33	Option buttons for the serve field

radio buttons for the sFriend field

option group labels

radio buttons for the oCorrect field

radio buttons for the foodHot field

6. Click the radio buttons with each option group and verify that if you select one radio button, the other button in that group is automatically deselected.

Creating Check Boxes

Check boxes are designed for fields that record the presence or absence of an object or event. The check box control is created using the following `input` element with the `type` attribute set to "checkbox"

```
<input name="name" value="value" type="checkbox" />
```

TIP

The default field value for a check box control is "On".

where the `value` attribute contains the value of the field when the check box is checked, and the `type` attribute indicates that the input box is a check box. By default, the check box is not checked, however you can make a check box selected automatically by adding the `checked` attribute to the `input` element.

For example, the following code creates a check box for the orderDone field, recording whether an order has been completed:

```
<label for="orderCB">Order Completed</label>
<input name="orderDone" id="orderCB" value="yes" type="checkbox" />
```

If the check box is selected by the customer, the browser will send a name/value pair of orderDone/yes to the script running on the web server when the form is submitted. A name/value pair is sent to the server only when the check box is checked by the user. If the control is not checked, then no name/value pair is sent when the form is submitted.

REFERENCE

Creating a Check Box

• To create a check box, add the element

```
<input name="name" value="value" type="checkbox" />
```

where `type` is the type of input control, *name* is the name of the data field, and *value* is the data field value if the check box is selected.
• To specify that a check box is selected by default, add the `checked` attribute to the `input` element.

Alice wants her survey form to include a check box that customers can select if they wish to be added to the pizzeria's e-mail list for specials and promotions. Add a check box for the mailMe field to the custInfo field set now.

To add a `checkbox` control:

1. Return to the **rb_survey.html** file in your editor and go to the end of the custInfo field set.

2. Add the following code to create a check box followed by the label for the checkbox control:

```
<input name="mailMe" id="mailCB" value="yes" type="checkbox" />
<label for="mailCB">Add me to your mailing list for great
coupons and specials!</label>
```

Figure 7-34 highlights the code for the check box and label.

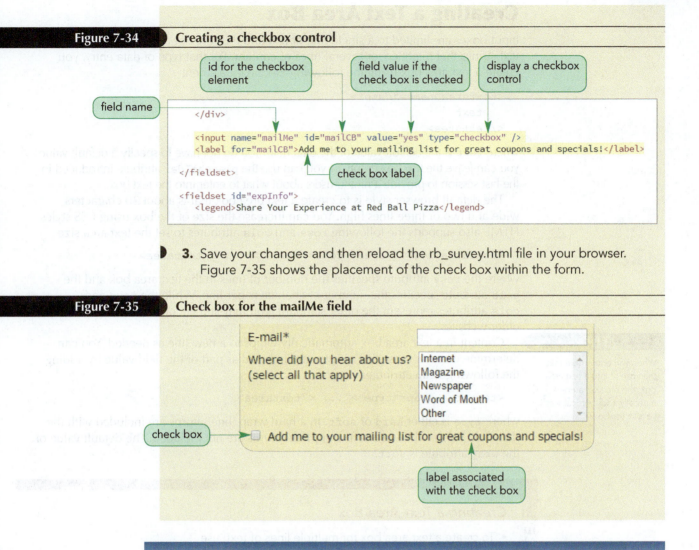

Figure 7-34   Creating a checkbox control

field name

id for the checkbox element

field value if the check box is checked

display a checkbox control

```
    </div>

    <input name="mailMe" id="mailCB" value="yes" type="checkbox" />
    <label for="mailCB">Add me to your mailing list for great coupons and specials!</label>

</fieldset>

<fieldset id="expInfo">
    <legend>Share Your Experience at Red Ball Pizza</legend>
```

check box label

3. Save your changes and then reload the rb_survey.html file in your browser. Figure 7-35 shows the placement of the check box within the form.

Figure 7-35   Check box for the mailMe field

E-mail*

Where did you hear about us? (select all that apply)

Internet
Magazine
Newspaper
Word of Mouth
Other

check box

☐ Add me to your mailing list for great coupons and specials!

label associated with the check box

Tab Indexing and Autofocus

INSIGHT

Typically, users navigate through a form using the Tab key, which moves the insertion point from one field to another in the order that the form controls are entered into the HTML file.

You can specify an alternate order by adding the `tabindex` attribute to any control in your form. When each control is assigned a tab index number, the insertion point moves through the fields from the lowest index number to the highest. For example, to assign the tab index number 1 to the custName field from the survey form, you add the following `tabindex` attribute to the control:

```
<input name="custName" tabindex="1" />
```

This code places the insertion point in the custName field when the form is first opened. (Fields with 0 or negative tab indexes are omitted from the tab order entirely.)

Another way to place the insertion point in a field when the form is initially opened is to use the following `autofocus` attribute:

```
<input name="custName" autofocus />
```

Older browsers that do not support tab indexing or the `autofocus` attribute simply ignore them and open a file without giving the focus to any form control. When a user tabs through the form in those older browsers, the tab order will reflect the order of the elements in the HTML file.

Creating a Text Area Box

Input boxes are limited to a single line of text and thus are not appropriate for extended text strings that might cover several lines of content. For that type of data entry, you create a text area box using the following textarea element

```
<textarea name="name">
    text
</textarea>
```

where text is the default value of the data field. You do not have to specify a default value; you can leave the text box empty or you can use the placeholder attribute introduced in the last session to provide a hint to users about what to enter into the text box.

The default browser style is to create a text area box that is about 20 characters wide and two or three lines high. You can increase the size of the box using CSS styles. HTML also supports the following rows and cols attributes to set the text area size

```
<textarea rows="value" cols="value"> ... </textarea>
```

where the rows attribute specifies the number of lines in the text area box and the cols attribute specifies the number of characters per line. While the rows and cols attributes represent the older standard, you may still encounter their use in older websites.

Content in a text area box automatically wraps to a new line as needed. You can determine whether those line returns are included as part of the field value by adding the following wrap attribute:

```
<textarea wrap="type"> ... </textarea>
```

where type is either hard or soft. In a hard wrap, line returns are included with the data field value, while in a soft wrap, line returns are not included. The default value of the wrap attribute is soft.

> **TIP**
>
> When you enter more text than can fit into a text area box, the browser automatically adds vertical scroll bars to the box.

REFERENCE

Creating a Text Area Box

- To create a text area box for multiple lines of text, use

  ```
  <textarea name="name">
      text
  </textarea>
  ```

  where name is the name of the field associated with the text area box and text is the default text that appears in the box.
- To specify the dimensions of the box, use a CSS style or apply the following attributes

  ```
  rows="value" cols="value"
  ```

  where the rows attribute specifies the number of lines in the text area box and the cols attribute specifies the number of characters per line.
- To specify how the field value should handle wrapped text, use the attribute

  ```
  wrap="type"
  ```

  where type is either hard (to include the locations of the line wraps) or soft (to ignore line wrap locations).

Alice wants to include a text area box where customers can enter extended commentary about the pizzeria, storing their comments in the custExp field. You will set the dimensions of the text area box using CSS.

To add a text area box:

1. Return to the **rb_survey.html** file in your editor and go to the end of the expInfo field set.

2. Add the following code to create a text area box at the bottom of the field set:

```
<label for="commBox">Tell us more about your
    experience!</label>
<textarea name="custExp" id="commBox"></textarea>
```

Figure 7-36 highlights the code for the text area box and label.

Figure 7-36 **Creating a text area box**

displays a text area box

```
    </div>

    <label for="commBox">Tell us more about your experience!</label>
    <textarea name="custExp" id="commBox"></textarea>

    </fieldset>
</form>
```

field name

id of the text area box

3. Save your changes and then return to the **rb_forms.css** file in your editor.

4. Go to the Text Area Styles section and insert the following style rule to set the size and top margin of the text area box.

```
textarea {
    margin-top: 10px;
    height: 100px;
    width: 95%;
}
```

Figure 7-37 shows the style rule for the text area box.

Figure 7-37 **Styles for the text area box**

```
/* Text Area Styles */

textarea {
    margin-top: 10px;
    height: 100px;
    width: 95%;
}
```

5. Save your changes and then reload rb_survey.html in your browser. Figure 7-38 shows the appearance of the text area box.

Figure 7-38 **Text area box in the web form**

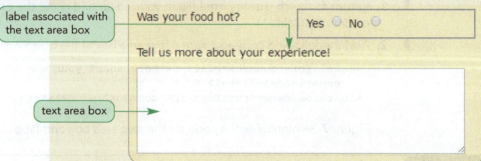

label associated with the text area box

Was your food hot?   Yes ○ No ○

Tell us more about your experience!

text area box

6. Test the text area box by clicking it and then typing a sample comment inside of the box.

Written Communication: Creating Effective Forms

Web forms are one of the main ways of getting feedback from your users, so it is important for the forms to be easily accessible. A well-designed form often can be the difference between a new customer and a disgruntled user who leaves your site to go elsewhere. Here are some tips to remember when designing a form:

- Keep your forms short and to the point.
- Mark fields that are required but also limit their number. Don't overwhelm your users with requests for information that is not really essential.
- Use the `autofocus` attribute to place users automatically into the first field of your form, rather than forcing them to click that field.
- Many users will navigate through your form using the Tab key. Make sure that your tab order is logical and easy for users to follow.
- Provide detailed instructions about what users are expected to do. Don't assume that your form is self-explanatory.
- If you ask for personal data and financial information, provide clear assurances that the data will be secure. If possible, provide a link to a web page describing your security practices.
- If you need to collect a lot of information, break the form into manageable sections spread out over several pages. Allow users to easily move backward and forward through the form without losing data. Provide information to users indicating where they are as they progress through your pages.
- Clearly indicate what users will receive once a form is submitted, and provide feedback on the website and through e-mail that tells them when their data has been successfully submitted.

Finally, every form should undergo usability testing before it is made available to the general public. Weed out any mistakes and difficulties before your users see the form.

You have greatly extended the scope of the survey form through the use of a calendar control, selection lists, option button groups, a check box, and a text area box. In the next session, you will continue to work on the survey form by exploring how to design a form that verifies the user enters valid data before it is submitted to the web server for processing.

REVIEW

Session 7.2 Quick Check

1. Provide code to create a calendar control to store date values for the expireDate field.

2. Provide code to create a date/time control that stores both date and time values for the orderDelivery field.

3. Provide code to create a selection list for the shipState field limited to the values "CA", "NV", "OR", and "WA" with the option text "California", "Nevada", "Oregon", and "Washington". Make "OR" the default value and display two values at a time in the selection list and allow the user to make multiple selections.

4. Provide code to create a selection list named orderDay containing the values and option text SAT and SUN placed in the Weekend option group, and the option text MON, TUE, WED, THU, and FRI placed in the Weekday option group.

5. Provide code to create two radio buttons for the compType field with the values PC and Mac. Make PC the default value.

6. Kelsey has written the following code to create a data field for users to select a food type using radio buttons. What mistake did she make in her coding?
```
<input name="French" value="Fr" type="radio" />
<input name="Italian" value="It" type="radio" />
<input name="Chinese" value="Ch" type="radio" />
```

7. Provide code to enter the value of a data field named compType using a check box. Set the value of the Computer field to "yes" if the check box is checked. Associate the check box with the label text "I use a PC.".

8. Provide code to create a text area box for the memoMsg field. Add the placeholder text, "Enter your memo message" to the text area box.

Session 7.3 Visual Overview:

The **required** attribute indicates that a field value is required.

The **pattern** attribute specifies the general pattern that the characters in the field value must follow.

The **min** and **max** attributes define the range of possible field values; the **step** sets the interval between values.

The **datalist** element defines a set of suggested field values.

The **submit** data type creates a button to submit the form for processing.

```
<label for="name">Name*</label>
<input name="custName" id="name" type="text" required />

<label for="phone">Phone number</label>
<input name="custPhone" id="phone" type="tel"
  pattern="^\d{10}$|^(\(\d{3}\)\s*)?\d{3}[\s-]?\d{4}$" />

<label for="dineSpin">How often do you dine out per month?</label>
<input name="dineOut" id="dineSpin" type="number"
       value="1" step="1" min="0" max="20" />

<label for="dish">What's your favorite dish?</label>
<input name="favDish" id="dish" type="text" list="dishType" />
<datalist id="dishType">
   <option value="Big Kahuna Pizza" />
   <option value="BBQ Chicken Pizza" />
   <option value="Pasta Rolls" />
   <option value="Pasto Artichoke Pizza" />
</datalist>

<label for="rangeBox">Rate the service at Red Ball<br />
(0=poor; 10=great)</label>
0 <input name="serviceRate" id="rangeBox" type="range"
         value="5" step="1" min="1" max="10"    /> 10

<input type="submit" value="Submit My Survey" />
<input type="reset" value="Cancel" />
```

The **number** data type creates a spin box control for data entry.

The **reset** data type creates a button that restores the form to its default values.

The **range** data type creates a range slider for data entry.

Data Validation

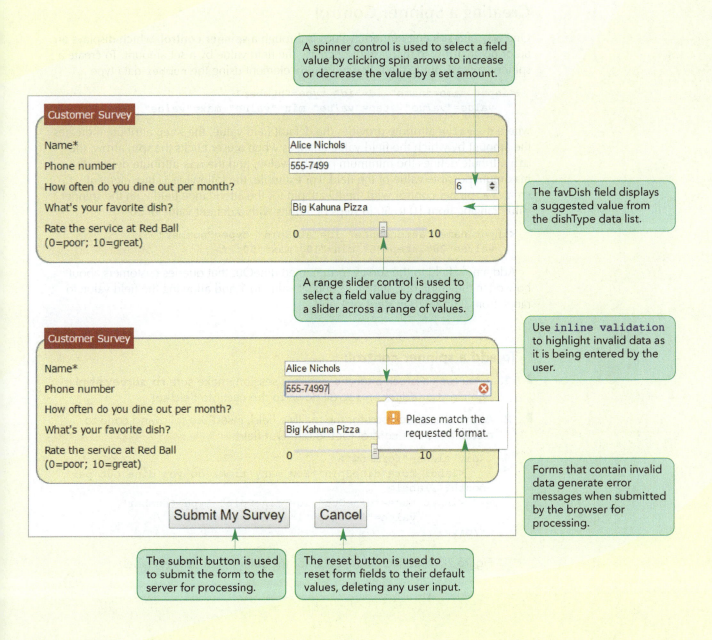

A spinner control is used to select a field value by clicking spin arrows to increase or decrease the value by a set amount.

Customer Survey

Name*   Alice Nichols

Phone number   555-7499

How often do you dine out per month?   6

What's your favorite dish?   Big Kahuna Pizza

Rate the service at Red Ball
(0=poor; 10=great)   0   10

The favDish field displays a suggested value from the dishType data list.

A range slider control is used to select a field value by dragging a slider across a range of values.

Use **inline validation** to highlight invalid data as it is being entered by the user.

Customer Survey

Name*   Alice Nichols

Phone number   555-74997

How often do you dine out per month?

What's your favorite dish?   Big Kahuna Pizza
                                                    Please match the
                                                    requested format.
Rate the service at Red Ball
(0=poor; 10=great)   0   10

Forms that contain invalid data generate error messages when submitted by the browser for processing.

Submit My Survey   Cancel

The submit button is used to submit the form to the server for processing.

The reset button is used to reset form fields to their default values, deleting any user input.

Entering Numeric Data

In the last session, you worked with several form controls that restricted field values to a set of possible values, ensuring that the user submits valid data to the server for processing. HTML also supports restrictions on numeric values by specifying that the values must fall within a defined range.

Creating a Spinner Control

One way of restricting numeric values is through a **spinner control**, which displays an up or down arrow to increase or decrease the field value by a set amount. To create a spinner control, apply the following `input` element using the `number` data type

```
<input name="name" id="id" type="number"
    value="value" step="value" min="value" max="value" />
```

where the `value` attribute provides the default field value, the `step` attribute indicates the amount by which the field value changes when a user clicks the spin arrow, the `min` attribute defines the minimum possible value, and the `max` attribute defines the maximum possible value of the field. For example, the following `input` element creates a spinner control with the ID attSpin for the attendance field with the spinner value ranging from 10 to 50 in steps of 5 units with a default value of 20:

```
<input name="attendance" id="attSpin" type="number"
    value="20" step="5" min="10" max="50" />
```

Add a new field to the survey form named dineOut that queries customers about how often they dine out, setting its default value to 1 and allowing the field value to range from 0 up to 20 in steps of 1 unit.

To add a spinner control:

1. If you took a break after the previous session, make sure **rb_survey.html** is open in your editor and scroll down to the custInfo field set.

2. Above the check box for the mailMe field, insert the following code to create a spinner control for the dineOut field:

```
<div class="formRow">
    <label for="dineSpin">How many times do you dine out per
month?</label>
    <input name="dineOut" id="dineSpin" type="number"
            value="1" step="1" min="0" max="20" />
</div>
```

Figure 7-39 highlights the code for the spinner control and label.

Figure 7-39   Creating a spinner control for the dineOut field

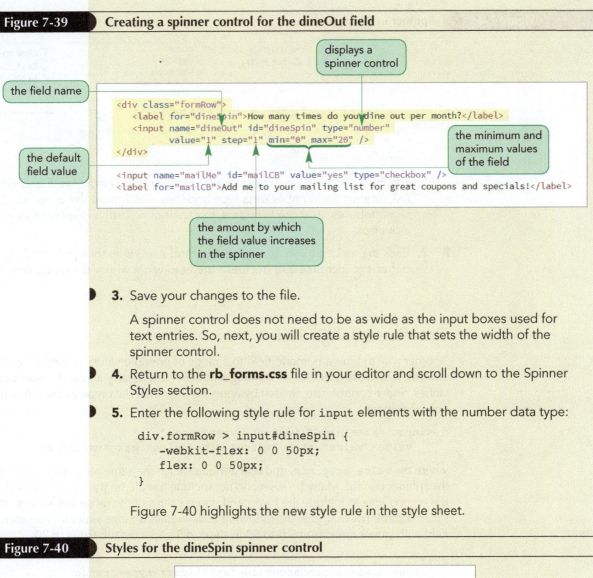

the field name

displays a
spinner control

the default
field value

the minimum and
maximum values
of the field

the amount by which
the field value increases
in the spinner

```
<div class="formRow">
    <label for="dineSpin">How many times do you dine out per month?</label>
    <input name="dineOut" id="dineSpin" type="number"
           value="1" step="1" min="0" max="20" />
</div>

<input name="mailMe" id="mailCB" value="yes" type="checkbox" />
<label for="mailCB">Add me to your mailing list for great coupons and specials!</label>
```

3. Save your changes to the file.

A spinner control does not need to be as wide as the input boxes used for text entries. So, next, you will create a style rule that sets the width of the spinner control.

4. Return to the **rb_forms.css** file in your editor and scroll down to the Spinner Styles section.

5. Enter the following style rule for `input` elements with the number data type:

```
div.formRow > input#dineSpin {
    -webkit-flex: 0 0 50px;
    flex: 0 0 50px;
}
```

Figure 7-40 highlights the new style rule in the style sheet.

Figure 7-40   Styles for the dineSpin spinner control

```
/* Spinner Styles */

div.formRow > input#dineSpin {
    -webkit-flex: 0 0 50px;
    flex: 0 0 50px;
}
```

fixes the size of the
dineSpin spinner
control at 50 pixels

6. Save your changes to the style sheet and then reload rb_survey.html in your browser. Figure 7-41 shows the layout and appearance of the spinner control.

Figure 7-41   **Spinner in the web form**

> **Trouble?** At the time of this writing, some browsers (such as IE and Edge) do not support the number data type and they also ignore the `step`, `min`, and `max` attributes. In those browsers, the spinner control is displayed as a text input box.

 7. Click the input box for the spinner control and verify that you use the arrow buttons to increase and decrease the field value within the range 0 to 20.

Creating a Range Slider

Another way to limit a numeric field to a range of possible values is through a **slider control**, which the user can use to drag a marker horizontally across the possible field values. Slider controls are created by applying the range data type in the following input element

```
<input name="name" id="id" type="range"
    value="value" step="value" min="value" max="value" />
```

where the `value`, `step`, `min`, and `max` attributes have the same meanings as they did for the spinner control. Many browsers do not include a scale on the range slider widget, so it is a good idea to include the lower and upper values of the range before and after the slider control. For example, the following code creates a range slider for the attendance field with values range from 10 to 50 in steps of 5 and a default value of 20.

```
10
<input name="attendance" id="attSlider" type="range"
    value="20" step="5" min="10" max="50" />
50
```

REFERENCE

Creating Spinner Controls and Range Sliders

- To create a spinner control for numeric data, enter the input element with a type value of "number"

```
<input name="name" id="id" type="number"
    value="value" step="value" min="value" max="value" />
```

where the value attribute provides the default field value, the step attribute indicates the amount by which the field value changes when a user clicks the spin arrow, the min attribute defines the minimum value, and the max attribute defines the maximum value of the field.

- To create a range slider control for numeric data, use the following input element with a type value of "range":

```
<input name="name" id="id" type="range"
    value="value" step="value" min="value" max="value" />
```

Add a range slider to the survey form now, which customers can use to rate their experience at Red Ball Pizza from 0 (poor) up to 10 (great).

To add a range slider control:

1. Return to the **rb_survey.html** file in your editor and scroll down to the expInfo field set.

2. Directly above the text area control, add the following code to create a range slider control for the serviceRate field:

```
<div class="formRow">
    <label for="rangeBox">Rate the overall service<br />
            (0=poor; 10=great)</label>
    0
    <input name="serviceRate" id="rangeBox" type="range"
            value="5" step="1" min="0" max="10" />
    10
</div>
```

Figure 7-42 highlights the code for the range slider control and label.

Figure 7-42   Creating a range slider control for the serviceRate field

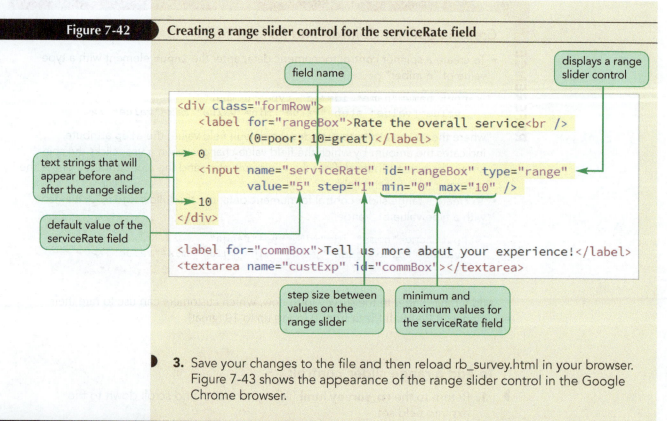

displays a range slider control

field name

text strings that will appear before and after the range slider

default value of the serviceRate field

```
<div class="formRow">
    <label for="rangeBox">Rate the overall service<br />
        (0=poor; 10=great)</label>
    0
    <input name="serviceRate" id="rangeBox" type="range"
        value="5" step="1" min="0" max="10" />
    10
</div>

<label for="commBox">Tell us more about your experience!</label>
<textarea name="custExp" id="commBox"></textarea>
```

step size between values on the range slider

minimum and maximum values for the serviceRate field

3. Save your changes to the file and then reload rb_survey.html in your browser. Figure 7-43 shows the appearance of the range slider control in the Google Chrome browser.

Figure 7-43   Viewing the range slider control

range slider label

minimum field value

maximum field value

click and drag to change the field value

Rate the overall service
(0=poor; 10=great)   0   10

Tell us more about your experience!

Trouble? Other browsers will display different styles for the range slider widget. For example, Microsoft Edge and Internet Explorer will display a colored bar with a pop-up window showing the current value of the serviceRate field. If your browser does not support the range slider widget, it will display a text input box.

4. Verify that you can drag the marker on the range slider to the left and right.

Styles for Widgets

The appearance of a form widget is largely determined by the browser and there are no CSS styles to alter it. However, most browsers do provide style extensions that allow you to modify their widgets. One useful browser extension is the following appearance extension that defines the widget associated with the form control

```
-moz-appearance: type;
-webkit-appearance: type;
```

where *type* is the type of widget including none (for no widget), button, checkbox, listbox, radio, range, spinner, textfield, and many other types depending on the browser. For example, to display a selection list as an input box, you would apply the following style rule:

```
select {
    -moz-appearance: textfield;
    -webkit-appearance: textfield;
}
```

The selection list options will still appear but as pop-ups for the input box. You should use these browser extensions with care because they are not part of the CSS standard, and thus respond unpredictably.

The next data field that Alice wants added to the survey form is a text box, which customers can use to indicate their favorite Red Ball Pizza dish. There are a lot of possible answers and Alice doesn't want to limit the options to a selection list, but she does want to provide suggestions to customers as they type their entries. You can add these suggestions with a data list.

Suggesting Options with Data Lists

A **data list** is a list of possible data values that a form field can have. When applied to an input box, the data values appear as a pop-up list of suggested values. Data lists are defined using the following datalist element

```
<datalist id="id">
   <option value="value" />
   <option value="value" />
...
</datalist>
```

where the value assigned to the different option elements provides the suggested entry in the list for its associated option element. To apply a data list, add the following list attribute to the input element

```
<input list="id" />
```

where *id* references the id of the datalist element. For example, to create an input box for the favDish field that offers a few suggested items, you could enter the following code:

```
<input name="favDish" type="text" list="dishes" />
<datalist id="dishes">
   <option value="Antipasto Pizza" />
   <option value="Big Kahuna Pizza" />
   <option value="BBQ Chicken Pizza" />
</datalist>
```

The options in the dishes data list are just suggestions. The customer is not obligated to accept any options and can type a dish of his or her own choosing.

Creating and Applying a Data List

- To create a data list of possible values, enter

```
<datalist id="id">
   <option value="value" />
   <option value="value" />
…
</datalist>
```

where each `value` attribute provides the text of a possible value in the data list.
- To reference the data list from an input control, add the `list` attribute

```
<input name="name" list="id" />
```

where `id` references the ID of the data list structure.

Add an input box for the favDish field to the survey form now and augment it with a data list of suggested Red Ball Pizza dishes.

To apply a data list to an input control:

1. Return to the **rb_survey.html** file in your editor and go to the custInfo field set.

2. Directly above the div element that encloses the spinner control for the dineOut field, enter the following code to create the input box for the favDish field along with the field's data list of suggested values.

```
<div class="formRow">
   <label for="dish">What's your favorite dish?</label>
   <input name="favDish" id="dish" type="text" list="dishType"
/>
   <datalist id="dishType">
      <option value="Anitpasto Pizza" />
      <option value="Big Kahuna Pizza" />
      <option value="BBQ Chicken Pizza" />
      <option value="Mediterranean Herb Pizza" />
      <option value="Pasta Rolls" />
      <option value="Pasto Artichoke Pizza" />
   </datalist>
</div>
```

Figure 7-44 highlights the code for the input box and data list.

Figure 7-44   Applying a data list to the favDish field

```
<div class="formRow">
   <label for="dish">What's your favorite dish?</label>
   <input name="favDish" id="dish" type="text" list="dishType" />
   <datalist id="dishType">
      <option value="Anitpasto Pizza" />
      <option value="Big Kahuna Pizza" />
      <option value="BBQ Chicken Pizza" />
      <option value="Mediterranean Herb Pizza" />
      <option value="Pasta Rolls" />
      <option value="Pasto Artichoke Pizza" />
   </datalist>
</div>

<div class="formRow">
   <label for="dineSpin">How many times do you dine out per month?</label>
   <input name="dineOut" id="dineSpin" type="number"
          value="1" step="1" min="0" max="20" />
</div>
```

data list containing suggested values

links the favDish field to the dishType data list

3. Save your changes to the file and reload rb_survey.html in your browser.

4. Click the input box for the favDish field and type the letter **p**. Note that the browser displays the list of dishes that start with the letter "p". See Figure 7-45.

Figure 7-45   Viewing suggested data values

suggested values from the data list starting with the letter "p"

Trouble? Currently the Firefox browser will display any data list entry that contains the letter "p" as opposed to only those data list values starting with the letter "p".

Now that you have entered most of the survey form fields, you will examine how to submit the form for processing. To do that, you will create a form button.

Working with Form Buttons

So far, all of your form controls have been used to enter field values. Another type of control is one that performs an action. This is usually done with **form buttons**, which can perform the following actions:

- Run a command from a program linked to the web form.
- Submit the form to a program running on the web server.
- Reset the form fields to their default values.

The first type of button you will examine is the command button.

Creating a Command Button

A **command button** is a button that runs a program, which affects the content of the page or the actions of the browser. Command buttons are created using the following `input` element with the `type` attribute set to `button`

```
<input value="text" onclick="script" type="button" />
```

where `text` is the text that appears on the button and `script` is the name of the program or the program code that is run when the button is clicked by the user. For example, the following `input` element creates a command button containing the text "Run Program", which runs the setup() program when the button is clicked:

```
<input value="Run Program" onclick="setup()" type="button" />
```

There is no need to use command buttons in the Red Ball Pizza survey form.

Creating Submit and Reset Buttons

The two other kinds of form buttons are submit and reset buttons. A **submit button** submits the form to the server for processing when clicked. A **reset button** resets the form, changing all fields to their original default values and deleting any field values that the user might have entered. Submit and reset buttons are created using the following `input` elements with the `type` attribute set to "submit" and "reset" respectively

```
<input value="text" type="submit" />
<input value="text" type="reset" />
```

where once again `text` is the text string that appears on the button.

REFERENCE

Creating Form Buttons

- To create a form button to run a command, use

  ```
  <input value="text" onclick="program" type="button" />
  ```

  where `text` is the text that appears on the button and `program` is the program that is run in response to the user clicking the button.
- To create a form button to submit the form and its fields and values to a script, use

  ```
  <input value="text" type="submit" />
  ```

- To create a form button to reset the form to its default values and appearance, use

  ```
  <input value="text" type="reset" />
  ```

Alice wants the survey form to include both a submit button and a reset button. The submit button, which she wants labeled "Submit My Survey", will send the form data to the server for processing when clicked. The reset button, which she wants labeled

"Cancel", will erase the user's input and reset the fields to their default values. Add these two buttons at the bottom of the form within a div element with the ID buttons.

To create submit and reset buttons:

1. Return to the **rb_survey.html** file in your editor and scroll down to the closing </form> tag.

2. Directly above the closing </form> tag, insert the following code:

```
<div id="buttons">
    <input type="submit" value="Submit My Survey" />
    <input type="reset" value="Cancel" />
</div>
```

Figure 7-46 highlights the code to create the submit and reset buttons.

Figure 7-46   **Creating submit and reset buttons**

creates a submit button

creates a reset button

the text on the button control

```
</fieldset>

<div id="buttons">
    <input type="submit" value="Submit My Survey" />
    <input type="reset" value="Cancel" />
</div>
</form>
```

3. Save your changes to the file.

Next, you will format the appearance of the div element and the two buttons it contains.

4. Return to the **rb_forms.css** file in your editor and go to the Form Button Styles section.

5. Add the following style rule to set the width of the div element to 100% and to horizontally center its content.

```
div#buttons {
    text-align: center;
    width: 100%;
}
```

6. Add the following style rule to set the font size, padding, and margins for all submit and reset buttons in the page.

```
input[type='submit'], input[type='reset'] {
    font-size: 1.2em;
    padding: 5px;
    margin: 15px;
}
```

Figure 7-47 shows the style rules for the form buttons on the page.

Figure 7-47 **Styles for the form buttons**

```
/* Form Button Styles */

div#buttons {
    text-align: center;
    width: 100%;
}

input[type='submit'], input[type='reset'] {
    font-size: 1.2em;
    padding: 5px;
    margin: 15px;
}
```

sets the width of the div element to 100% and centers its contents

sets the font size, padding, and margins of the submit and reset buttons

7. Save your changes to the file and then reload rb_survey.html in your browser. Figure 7-48 shows the layout and content of the completed web form.

Figure 7-48 **Completed design and layout of the survey form**

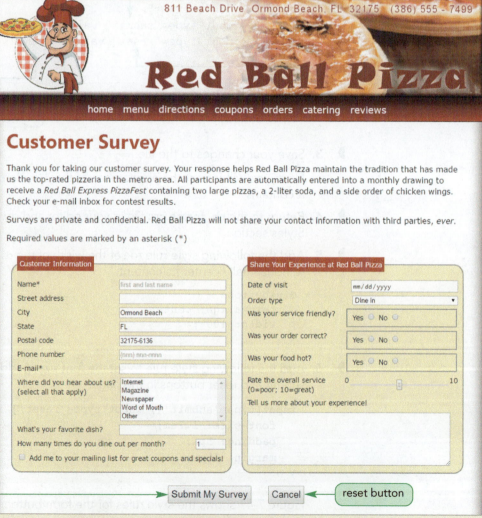

submit button

reset button

▶ **8.** Enter some sample data into the form and then click the **Cancel** button to test the actions of your reset button. Verify that the form is reset to its initial state and the data fields return to their default values. You will test the actions of the submit button shortly.

Designing a Custom Button

The appearance of a command, submit, and reset button is determined by the browser. While you can modify some basic properties such as the button border, font, or background color, you can't add clipart graphics or other features. For more control over a button's appearance use the following `button` element

```
<button type="text">
   content
</button>
```

where the `type` attribute specifies the button type (`submit`, `reset`, or `button`—for creating a command button) and *content* are HTML elements placed within the button, including formatted text, inline images, and other design elements supported by HTML. For example, the following code demonstrates how an inline image and text marked as a paragraph can be nested within a submit button.

```
<button type="submit">
   <img src="orderImg.png" alt="" />
   <p>Place your order now</p>
</button>
```

You do not need a custom button in the survey form.

Validating a Web Form

The most important part of form design is ensuring that users enter reasonable values in the correct format. Part of this is accomplished through the use of form controls, such as option buttons and selection lists, which limit the user to a set of pre-approved values. However, there are other data fields that do not easily fit into those types of input controls. For example, how can you ensure that the user has entered a valid credit card number or an e-mail address in the proper format?

The process of ensuring that the user has supplied valid data is called **validation** and can take place on the web server where it is known as **server-side validation** or within the user's own browser where it is referred to as **client-side validation**. Whenever possible, you should supplement server-side validation with client-side validation to reduce the server's workload. In a payment form, you should verify that the customer correctly completed all of the fields *before* submitting the data to the server so that the server does not have to deal with an improperly completed form.

TIP

You can turn off client-validation by adding the attribute `novalidate` to the `form` element.

Identifying Required Values

The first validation test you should perform is to verify that data has been supplied for all required data fields. To identify those fields that are required (as opposed to those that are optional), add the `required` attribute to the control. For example, the following code specifies that the custName field is required and cannot be left blank by the user:

```
<input name="custName" required />
```

In the same way, the `required` attribute can be added to the `select` element or the `textarea` area to make those data fields required. If a required field is left blank, the browser will not submit the form but will return an error message instead, indicating that the required data field has not been filled out.

For the Red Ball Pizza survey form, Alice wants every customer to enter a name and an e-mail address, so she asks you to make the custName and custEmail fields required.

To create submit and reset buttons:

1. Return to the **rb_survey.html** file in your editor.

2. Add the attribute **required** to the input element for both the custName and custEmail fields.

   Figure 7-49 highlights the newly added required attribute.

Figure 7-49	Making custName and custEmail required fields

marks custName as a required field

marks custEmail as a required field

3. Save your changes to the file and then reload rb_survey.html in your browser.

4. Test your form by clicking the **Submit My Survey** button without entering any values into the form itself. As shown in Figure 7-50, the browser fails to submit the form and instead displays a bubble containing the message that the custName field needs to be filled out.

Figure 7-50	Validation error message in Google Chrome

the form fails the validation test when no customer name is provided

Trouble? Figure 7-50 shows the error message rendered using the Google Chrome browser. The exact text and format of the validation bubble will vary from one browser to the next.

▶ **5.** Enter *your name* into the custName field and then resubmit the form (without entering an e-mail address). Verify that the custName field now passes validation but a bubble with a validation error message appears next to the blank e-mail box.

▶ **6.** Enter *your e-mail address* into the custEmail field and then resubmit the form. Verify that the browser displays an alert message indicating that no invalid data have been detected.

▶ **7.** Click the **OK** button to dismiss the dialog box.

The dialog box you encountered in Step 6 is not part of HTML or your browser. It was generated from the rb_formsubmit.js script file that you linked the web page to in Session 1. The confirmation dialog box only appears when no validation errors have been detected in the submitted form. Also, note that all of your data values have been preserved in the survey form. This is also a feature of the script file to avoid re-typing field values as you continue to test the web form. If you want to clear the form to see the default values, reopen the file in your browser.

Validating Based on Data Type

A form will fail the validation test if the data values entered into a field do not match the field type. For example, a data field with the number type will be rejected if non-numeric data is entered. Similarly, fields marked using the email and url types will be rejected if a user provides an invalid e-mail address or text that does not match the format of a URL.

You have already specified data types for the survey form fields. Verify that the form will not accept invalid data for the custEmail field.

To verify the form does not accept invalid data:

▶ **1.** Click the input box for the custEmail field in the survey form and type the text **Alice Nichols** (or any text string that does not represent an e-mail address).

▶ **2.** Click the **Submit My Survey** button to submit the form.

As shown in Figure 7-51, the browser rejects the form based on the invalid data entered for the custEmail field.

Figure 7-51 | Rejecting an invalid e-mail address

the form fails the validation test when an improper text string is entered for the e-mail address

3. Change the field value to **alice.nichols@example.com** and resubmit the form. Verify that the form now passes the validation test.

4. Click the **OK** button to close the JavaScript dialog box.

Accepting the e-mail address does not mean that the e-mail address is real; it only means that the text field value follows the proper general pattern for e-mail addresses, which is a string of characters with no blank spaces followed by the @ symbol and then followed by another string of nonblank characters. For validation tests that involve more complicated text patterns, you can do a pattern test.

Testing for a Valid Pattern

To test whether a field value follows a valid pattern of characters, you can test the character string against a regular expression. A **regular expression** or **regex** is a concise description of a character pattern. It is beyond the scope of this tutorial to discuss the syntax of regular expressions, but to validate a text value against a regular expression, add the following `pattern` attribute to the `input` element

```
pattern="regex"
```

where _regex_ is the regular expression pattern. For example, the following code tests the value of the custZip field against the regular expression pattern $\verb|^\d{5}$|$

```
<input name="custZip" pattern="^\d{5}$" />
```

where the regular expression $\verb|^\d{5}$|$ represents any string of 5 numeric characters. Thus, the value 85017 would match this regular expression, but values like 850177 or X8514 would not. Regular expressions are based on a rich language and can be written to match credit card numbers, phone numbers, e-mail addresses, and so forth.

Validating Field Values

- To indicate that a field is required, add the `required` attribute to the form control.
- To validate an e-mail address, set the data type to `email`.
- To validate a web address, set the data type to `url`.
- To validate that a text input box follows a character pattern, add the attribute

  ```
  pattern="regex"
  ```

  where *regex* is a regular expression that defines the character pattern.

Alice has obtained regular expressions for phone numbers and 5- or 9-digit postal codes. Add the pattern attribute now to the custZip and custPhone fields to validate those field values. Note that some regular expressions are long and complicated, and you must type them exactly as written. If you make a mistake, you can copy the text of the regular expressions from the rb_regex.txt file in the tutorial.07/tutorial folder.

To test a field value against a regular expression:

1. Return to the **rb_survey.html** file in your editor and scroll down to the `input` element for the custZip field.

2. Add the following attribute to create a regular expression that matches 5- and 9-digit zip codes to the `input` element:

   ```
   pattern="^\d{5}(-\d{4})?$"
   ```

3. Go to the `input` element for the custPhone field and add the following attribute to create a regular expression that matches phone numbers with or without an area code:

   ```
   pattern="^\d{10}$|^(\(\d{3}\)\s*)?\d{3}[\s-]?\d{4}$"
   ```

   Figure 7-52 highlights the `pattern` attribute for both the custZip and custPhone fields.

| Figure 7-52 | Pattern matching with regular expressions |

```
<div class="formRow">
    <label for="zip">Postal code</label>
    <input name="custZip" id="zip" type="text" placeholder="nnnnn (-nnnn)"
    pattern="^\d{5}(-\d{4})?$" />
</div>

<div class="formRow">
    <label for="phone">Phone number</label>
    <input name="custPhone" id="phone" type="tel" placeholder="(nnn) nnn-nnnn"
    pattern="^\d{10}$|^(\(\d{3}\)\s*)?\d{3}[\s-]?\d{4}$" />
</div>
```

regular expression pattern that matches 5- or 9-digit postal codes

regular expression pattern that matches phone numbers with or without area codes

4. Save your changes to the file and then reload rb_survey.html in your browser.

5. Enter **your e-mail address** in the input box for the custEmail field so that the two required fields have a value.

6. Type **321** in the input box for the postal code and then submit the form. As shown in Figure 7-53, the browser rejects the field value because it does not match the pattern of either a 5-digit or 9-digit postal code.

Figure 7-53 ▶ **Rejecting an invalid postal code**

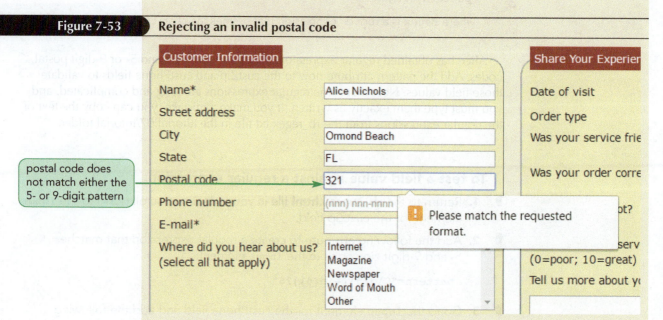

postal code does not match either the 5- or 9-digit pattern

7. Change the postal code value to **32175** and resubmit the form. Verify that the form now passes the validation test.

8. Test the custPhone field by entering **5-7499** in the input box for the customer phone number and then submitting the form. Verify that the browser rejects the data as invalid.

9. Change the phone number to **555-7499** and resubmit the form, verifying that it now passes the validation test.

Defining the Length of the Field Value

Because older browsers might not support the `pattern` attribute, you can do a simple test based on character length using the following `maxlength` attribute

```
maxlength="value"
```

where `value` is the maximum number of characters in the field value. For example, the following `input` element limits the number of characters in the custZip field to 5, which means that field values with more than 5 characters will not be validated.

```
<input name="custZip" maxlength="5" />
```

Note that the `maxlength` attribute does not distinguish between characters and digits. A user could enter the text string *abcde* as easily as *32175* and have the field values pass validation.

INSIGHT

WebKit Styles for Validation Messages

Like widgets, the appearance of the bubble containing the validation message is determined by the browser. There is no standard CSS style to format the error message but there are browser extensions that give you more control over the error message style. For Google Chrome, the validation message is organized into the following pseudo-elements selectors:

- `::-webkit-validation-bubble:` Selecting the entire bubble containing the validation message
- `::-webkit-validation-bubble-arrow:` Selecting the pointing arrow above the validation bubble
- `::-webkit-validation-bubble-message:` Selecting the validation message within the bubble
- `::-webkit-validation-bubble-arrow-clipper:` Selecting the bubble behind the top arrow

To modify the appearance of the validation message, you can apply the following style rule, which displays the message in a gray font on an ivory background.

```
::-webkit-validation-bubble-message {
    color: gray;
    background: ivory;
}
```

Other browsers support their own collection of extensions to modify the appearance of the validation bubble. Because these are not part of the CSS standards, there is no common syntax yet for modifying the validation message. You can learn more about these extensions by viewing the documentation on the browser manufacturer's website.

Applying Inline Validation

One disadvantage with the validation tests you have applied is that they all occur after a user has completed and submitted the form. It is extremely annoying for the user to go back to an already completed form to fix an error. Studies have shown that users are less likely to make errors and can complete a form faster if they are informed of data entry errors as they occur. The technique of immediate data validation and reporting of errors is known as **inline validation**.

Using the focus Pseudo-Class

One way of integrating inline validation with a web form is to change the display style of fields that currently contain invalid data. This can be done using some of the pseudo-classes described in Figure 7-54.

Figure 7-54 **Pseudo-classes for form controls and fields**

Pseudo-Class	Matches
checked	A check box or option button that is selected or checked
default	A default control, such as the default option in a selection list
disabled	A control that is disabled
enabled	A control that is enabled
focus	A control that has the focus (is actively selected) in the form
indeterminate	A check box or option button whose toggle states (checked or unchecked) cannot be determined
in-range	A field whose value lies within the allowed range (between the min and max attribute values)
invalid	A field whose value fails the validation test
optional	A field that is optional (not required) in the form
out-of-range	A field whose value lies outside the allowed range (outside the min and max attribute values)
required	A field that is required in the form
valid	A field whose value passes the validation test

For example, to create styles for all of the checked option buttons in the form, you could apply the checked pseudo-class, as in the following style rule

```
input[type="radio"]:checked {
    styles
}
```

where *styles* are the CSS styles applied to checked option buttons. Note that option buttons that are not checked will not receive these styles.

The first pseudo-class you will apply to the survey form will be used to change the background color of any element that has the focus. **Focus** refers to the state in which an element has been clicked by the user, making it the active control on the form. You may have noticed that some browsers highlight or add a glowing border around input boxes that have the focus.

Alice would like the input boxes, selection lists, and text area boxes that have the focus to be displayed with a light green background color.

To create style rules for elements that have the focus:

1. Return to the **rb_forms.css** file in your editor and scroll down to the Validation Styles section.

2. Add the following style rule to change the background color to light green for all **input**, **select**, and **textarea** elements that have the focus.

```
input:focus, select:focus, textarea:focus {
    background-color: rgb(220, 255, 220);
}
```

Figure 7-55 highlights the style rule to change the background color.

Figure 7-55   **Creating a style rule for the focus pseudo-class**

change the background color to light green when the control element has the focus

```
/* Validation styles */

input:focus, select:focus, textarea:focus {
    background-color: rgb(220, 255, 220);
}
```

> **3.** Save your changes to the file and then reload rb_survey.html in your browser.

> **4.** Click the input box for the customer name and verify that the background color changes to a light green as shown in Figure 7-56.

Figure 7-56   **Text inbox box with the focus**

background color changes to light green when the text input box has the focus

Customer Information

Name*   first and last name

Street address

City   Ormond Beach

> **5.** Press the **Tab** key repeatedly to change the focus to the remaining input controls. Verify the background color changes to light green when an input control has the focus and has a background.

Pseudo-Classes for Valid and Invalid Data

The `valid` and `invalid` pseudo-classes are used to format controls based on whether their field values pass a validation test or not. For example, the following style rule displays all `input` elements containing invalid data with a light red background

```
input:invalid {
    background-color: rgb(255, 232, 233);
}
```

while the following style rule displays all `input` elements containing valid data with a light green background:

```
input:valid {
    background-color: rgb(220, 255, 220);
}
```

Both of these style rules set the background color whether the `input` element has the focus or not. Displaying a form full of input backgrounds with different background colors can be confusing and distracting to the user. As a result, it is better practice to highlight invalid field values only when those input controls have the focus, as in the following style rule that combines both the `focus` and `invalid` pseudo-classes:

```
input:focus:invalid {
    background-color: rgb(255, 232, 233);
}
```

Alice suggests that the form perform inline validation for the input boxes with IDs of "name", "zip", "phone", and "mail". For valid data, she wants those input boxes to be displayed with a light green background along with a green check mark image. For invalid data, she wants the background to be light red with a red X image. Use the rb_valid.png and rb_invalid.png image files for the green check mark and red X images.

To perform inline validation:

1. Return to the **rb_forms.css** file in your editor and scroll to the bottom of the file.

Include the focus pseudo-class so that the validation style is only applied when the control is active in the form.

2. Add the following style rule to display a light green background and a green check mark image when valid data is entered in the custName, custZip, custPhone, and custEmail fields:

```
input#name:focus:valid,
input#zip:focus:valid,
input#phone:focus:valid,
input#mail:focus:valid {
   background: rgb(220, 255, 220) url(rb_valid.png) bottom
right/contain no-repeat;
}
```

3. Add the following style rule to display a light red background and a red X image when invalid data is entered in those same fields:

```
input#name:focus:invalid,
input#zip:focus:invalid,
input#phone:focus:invalid,
input#mail:focus:invalid {
   background: rgb(255, 232, 233) url(rb_invalid.png) bottom
right/contain no-repeat;
}
```

Figure 7-57 highlights the style rules to style valid and invalid data.

Figure 7-57	Creating styles for valid and invalid field values

```
input:focus, select:focus, textarea:focus {
   background-color: rgb(220, 255, 220);
}

input#name:focus:valid,
input#zip:focus:valid,
input#phone:focus:valid,
input#mail:focus:valid {
   background: rgb(220, 255, 220) url(rb_valid.png) bottom right/contain no-repeat;
}

input#name:focus:invalid,
input#zip:focus:invalid,
input#phone:focus:invalid,
input#mail:focus:invalid {
   background: rgb(255, 232, 233) url(rb_invalid.png) bottom right/contain no-repeat;
}
```

style for valid data values in the selected fields that have the focus

display a green check mark image in the input box background

style for invalid data values in the selected fields that have the focus

display a red X image in the input box background

4. Save your changes to the style sheet and then reload rb_survey.html in your browser.

5. Test inline validation by typing the zip code value **32175-6136** into the input box for the customer's zip code. Note that the input box provides immediate visual feedback on whether the current field value passes the validation test. See Figure 7-58.

Figure 7-58   **Inline validation on the customer postal code**

Postal code 321|	the initial text string does not pass the validation test
Postal code 32175	the 5-digit postal code passes validation
Postal code 32175-61|	entering more digits causes the field value to once again fail validation
Postal code 32175-6136|	the final 9-digit postal code value passes validation

6. Continue to test the web form by entering data into the other input boxes, noting how the form automatically performs a validation test on your data values.

PROSKILLS

Problem Solving: Using Form Building Tools

One of the limitations of CSS is that it does not provide an easy way to format the form controls other than basic styles for text and background colors. To gain more control over your form controls, you may want to explore third party frameworks that provide customized widgets and form design tools. Some popular frameworks include:

- Google Forms (*docs.google.com/forms*): A free service for form design that also automatically tabulates the user responses in an online spreadsheet
- Wufoo (*wufoo.com*): A paid service that supplies a powerful form builder engine and tools for uploading documents and images
- Jotform (*www.jotform.com*): A paid service with form tools and the ability to automatically upload completed forms to your website
- Form Stack (*www.formstack.com*): A paid service with form building software and tools to manage workflow, data analysis, and tabulation

Form building tools can speed up the process of designing and testing your web forms. However, like all frameworks they are best used when you have a good understanding of the underlying HTML and CSS code that they employ.

You have finished your work on the survey form. Alice will place a copy of your files in a folder on the company's web server and from there the form can continue to be tested to verify that the server program and the web form work well together. Alice is pleased with your work on this project and will get back to you to create other web forms for the Red Ball Pizza website.

Session 7.3 Quick Check

1. Provide the code to create a spinner control for the partySize field ranging from 20 to 200 in increments of 20 units with a default value of 50.
2. Provide the code to create a range slider for the redColor field that ranges from 0 to 255 in increments of 5 units with a default value of 255.
3. Provide the code to create an input box for the custState field that has the suggested options Alabama, Alaska, Arizona, Arkansas, California, and Colorado from a data list with the ID stateList.
4. Create a submit button displaying the text "Send Donation".
5. Provide the code to create an input box for the socSecNum field and make the field required.
6. The userAccount field must follow the regular expression pattern `^\user\-d{4}$`. Provide the code for a text input box validating the field value against this pattern.
7. Provide a style rule to display all `textarea` elements with the background color rgb(220, 220, 255) when they have the focus.
8. Provide a style rule for the input box with ID userAccount that changes the background color to pink when the input box has the focus and is invalid.
9. Provide a style rule for the input box with ID userAccount that changes the background color to the value rgb(211, 255, 211) when the input box has the focus and is valid.

Review Assignments

Data Files needed for the Review Assignments: rb_build_txt.html, rb_customer_txt.html, rb_validate_txt.css, 3 CSS files, 1 JavaScript file, 10 PNG files, 1 TXT file

Alice wants you to start work on an online order form for customers to place orders through the Red Ball Pizza website. The form will span several pages in which customers will specify whether the order is for pickup or delivery and will indicate the toppings they want on their pizza(s). Figure 7-59 shows a preview of the form customers will use to indicate their delivery option (including an address or pickup and at what time they want their order).

Figure 7-59   Red Ball Pizza form for Customer Data

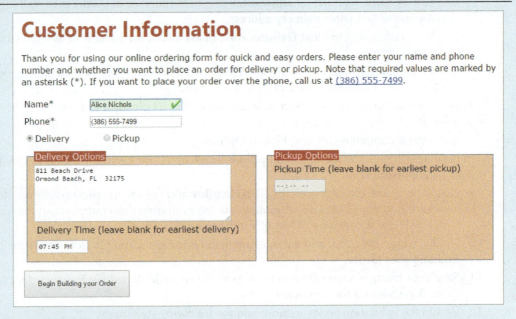

Alice has already written some of the HTML code for the web pages and designed many of the style sheets. Your job will be to write the code for the form elements and validation styles.

Complete the following:

1. Use your HTML editor to open the **rb_customer_txt.html**, **rb_build_txt.html**, and **rb_validate_txt.css** files from the html07 ▸ review folder. Enter *your name* and *the date* in the comment section of each file, and save them as **rb_customer.html**, **rb_build.html** and **rb_validate.css** respectively.

2. Return to the **rb_customer.html** file in your editor. Within the document head, insert links to the rb_forms2.css and rb_validate.css files.

3. Still within the document head, use the `script` element to link the file to the rb_formsubmit2.js file.

4. Scroll down to the `section` element and, directly after the initial paragraph, insert a `form` element that employs the action at the fictional address *http://www.example.com/redball/ customer* using the post method.

5. Within the `form` element, insert a `div` element that encloses a label with the text **Name*** associated with the nameBox control. Also, within the `div` element, add an input text box with the ID **nameBox**, field name **custName**, and placeholder text **First and Last Name**. Make custName a required field.

6. Create a second `div` element in the web form that encloses a label with the text **Phone*** associated with the phoneBox control. Within the `div` element, add an input box with the ID **phoneBox**, field name **custPhone,** and placeholder text **(nnn) nnn-nnnn**. Make custPhone

a required field and have any text entry follow the regular expression pattern **^\d{10}$ | ^(\ (\d{3}\)\s*)?\d{3}[\s-]?\d{4}$**. (Note: You can copy the regular expression code from the rb_regex2.txt file.)

7. Add another `div` element to the web form containing the following code:

   a. Insert an `input` element to create an option button for the **orderType** field with the ID **delivery**. Make the option button checked by default. After the option button, insert a label associated with the delivery control containing the text **Delivery**.

   b. Add an `input` element to create a second option button for the **orderType** field with the ID **pickup**, followed by a label associated with the pickup control containing the text **Pickup**.

8. Next within the form, create a field set with the ID **deliveryInfo**. Within this field set, add the following:

   a. A legend containing the text **Delivery Options**.

   b. A text area box with the ID **addressBox** and field name of **delAddress** containing the placeholder text **Enter delivery address**.

   c. A label containing the text **Delivery Time (leave blank for earliest delivery)** associated with the delBox control.

   d. Add an `input` element with the ID **delBox** and field name **delTime** for storing delivery time values. Use a data type of "time" for the control.

9. Next within the web form, create a field set with the ID **pickupInfo** containing the following information for pickup orders:

   a. A legend containing the text **Pickup Options**.

   b. A label containing the text **Pickup Time (leave blank for earliest pickup)** associated with pickupBox control.

   c. Add an `input` element with the ID **pickupBox** and field name **pickupTime** for storing time values. Add the `disabled` attribute to the tag to disable this control when the form is initially opened. Use a data type of "time" for the control.

10. Finally, within the form, add a `div` element containing a submit button displaying the text **Begin Building your Order**.

11. Save your changes to the file and then go to the **rb_validate.css** file in your editor to add validation styles for the web form.

12. Within the Validation Styles section, add the following style rules:

    a. A rule that displays `input`, `select`, and `textarea` elements that have the focus with a background color of rgb(255, 255, 180).

    b. A rule that displays the nameBox and phoneBox controls that have the focus and contain valid data with a background color of rgb(220, 255, 220) and the background image file rb_okay.png at the right with no tiling contained within the background.

    c. A rule that displays the nameBox and phoneBox controls that have the focus and invalid data with a background color of rgb(255, 230, 230) and the background image file rb_warning.png at the right with no tiling contained within the background.

13. Save your changes to the style sheet and then open the **rb_customer.html** file in your browser. Verify the following:

    a. The content and the layout of the form resemble the form shown in Figure 7-59.

    b. If you submit the form by clicking the Begin Building your Own button with no customer name or phone number, the browser warns you of the missing values.

    c. As you enter text into the custName field, the input box background changes to show that the field value is valid.

    d. When you enter a phone number into the custPhone field, the input box provides inline validation to indicate whether a valid phone number has been entered.

    e. When you click the submit button for a successfully completed form, the browser displays the alert message that the form data passes the initial validation test.

    (Note: The script file used with this web page is written to enable only either the delivery option or the pickup option but not both.)

Next, you will create a form that customers will use to build their customized pizzas. A preview of the form is shown in Figure 7-60.

Figure 7-60   **Red Ball Pizza form to Build a Pizza**

14. Return to the **rb_build.html** file in your editor. Insert a link to the rb_forms2.css file and add a `script` element to link the file to the rb_formsubmit2.js file.

15. Scroll down to the `section` element, insert a `form` element below the paragraph element that employs the action at the fictional address *http://www.example.com/redball/build* using the `post` method.

16. Within the `form` element, add a `div` element containing a label with the text **Quantity** associated with the quantityBox control. Add a spinner control with the ID **quantityBox** and the field name **pizzaQuantity**. Have the value of the field range from 1 to 10 with a default value of 1.

17. Add a `div` element that displays images of the pizza sizes, containing the following:

    a. The inline image rb_sizes.png.

    b. The label **Pizza Size** associated with the sizeBox control.

    c. A range slider with the ID **sizeBox** and the field name **pizzaSize** ranging from 10 to 16 in steps of 2 with a default value of 14.

18. Add a `div` element that provides the selection of pizza crusts containing the following:

    a. The label **Pizza Crust** associated with the crustBox control.

    b. A selection list for the **pizzaCrust** field with the ID **crustBox** and containing the following option values and text: **Thin**, **Thick**, **Stuffed**, and **Pan**.

19. Add a `div` element containing a check box with the ID **cheeseBox** for the **doubleCheese** field followed by the label **Double Cheese** associated with the cheeseBox control. Then, add a second check box with the ID **sauceBox** for the **doubleSauce** field followed by the label **Double Sauce** also associated with that check box.

20. Customers can choose what to place on their pizzas. Create a field set containing the legend **Meat Toppings**. Add the following content to the field set.

 a. A `div` element containing the label **Location** but not associated with any form control. Next to the label, place the inline images full.png, left.png, right.png, and none.png with the alternate text "full", "left", "right", and "none" used to graphically indicate where the meat ingredients should be placed on the pizza (on the full pie, the left side, the right side, or nowhere).

 b. A `div` element containing the label **Pepperoni** and followed by four option buttons belonging to the **pepperoni** field and with the values "full", "left", "right", and "none". Make "none" checked by default.

 c. Repeat Step b to insert `div` elements with the values used in Step b but associated with the ham, pork, sausage, and chicken fields.

21. Using Figure 7-60 as your guide, repeat Step 20 to create a field set with the legend **Vegetable Toppings**, followed by `div` elements with the values used in Step 20 but associated with the mushrooms, peppers, onions, tomatoes, and jalapenos fields.

22. At the bottom of the form, add a `div` element containing a submit button with the text **Add to your Order**.

23. Save your changes to the file and then open **rb_build.html** in your browser. Verify that the content and layout of the form resemble that shown in Figure 7-60. Verify that all of the form controls work as expected, that is, you can only select one location for each ingredient option at a time.

Case Problem 1

Data Files needed for this Case Problem: cg_register_txt.html, cg_validate_txt.css, 3 CSS files, 1 JavaScript file, 4 PNG files, 1 TXT file

APPLY

ACGIP Conference   Professor Darshan Banerjee is the project coordinator for the annual conference of the Association of Computer Graphics and Image Processing (*ACGIP*), which takes place this year in Sante Fe, New Mexico. Darshan has asked you to work on the conference's website, starting with the registration form for conference attendees. The initial form will collect contact information for people attending the conference. Figure 7-61 shows a preview of the form you will create for Darshan.

Figure 7-61 **Registration form for the ACGIP Conference**

© IgorGolovniov/Shutterstock.com; © Jason Winter/Shutterstock.com

Professor Banjerjee has already written the HTML code for the page and the styles for the form elements. He wants you to write the HTML code for the web form and the CSS validation styles. Complete the following:

1. Using your editor, open the **cg_register_txt.html** and **cg_validate_txt.css** files from the html07 ▸ case1 folder. Enter *your name* and *the date* in the comment section of each file, and save them as **cg_register.html** and **cg_validate.css** respectively.

2. Return to the **cg_register.html** file in your editor. Add a link to the cg_forms.css and cg_validate.css style sheet files to the document head.

3. Add a `script` element to the document head that loads the cg_script.js file.

4. Scroll down to the `section` element and insert a web `form` element that employs the action at *http://www.example.com/cg/register* via the `post` method.

5. Add the labels and input boxes shown previously in Figure 7-61 and described in Figure 7-62. Place the input boxes directly after the labels and associate each label with its input box control. You do not need to enclose the `label` and `input` elements with `div` elements.

Figure 7-62   Fields and controls from the registration form

Label	Data Field	Control ID	Type	Required	Placeholder
Title	title	titleBox	text	no	
First Name*	firstName	fnBox	text	yes	
Last Name*	lastName	lnBox	text	yes	
Address*	address	addBox	text	yes	
Company or University	group	groupBox	text	no	
E-mail*	email	mailBox	email	yes	
Phone Number*	phoneNumber	phoneBox	tel	yes	(nnn) nnn-nnnn
ACGIP Membership Number	acgipID	idBox	text	no	acgip-nnnnnn

6. Create a data list named **titleList** containing the suggestions: Mr., Mrs., Ms., Prof., Dr., Assist. Prof., and Assoc. Prof. Apply the titleList data list to the titleBox control.

7. Apply the regular expression pattern **^\d{10}$ | ^(\(\d{3}\)\s*)?\d{3}[\s-]?\d{4}$** to the phoneNumber field. Apply the regular expression pattern **^acgip\-\d{6}$** to the acgipID field. (Note: You can copy the regular expression code for the phoneNumber field from the cg_regex.txt file.)

8. Add the **Registration Category** label associated with the regList control. Add a selection list with the ID **regList** that stores values in the **registerType** field. Populate the selection list with the option text: "ACGIP Member ($695)", "Non-Member ($795)", "Student ($310)", "Poster ($95)", and "Guest ($35)". Make the corresponding option values equal to "member", "nonmember", "student", "poster", and "guest".

9. Within the form, add a paragraph containing a submit button with the text **continue**.

10. Save your changes to the file and return to the **cg_validate.css** file in your editor to create styles for validating data entry.

11. Within the Validation Style section, add the following style rules:

   a. Display all `input`, `select`, and `textarea` elements that have the focus with a background color of rgb(245, 245, 140).

   b. When the fnBox, lnBox, addBox, mailBox, phoneBox, and idBox controls have the focus and are valid, change the background color to rgb(220, 255, 220) and display the cg_valid.png image with no tiling in the right side of the background contained within the box.

   c. When the fnBox, lnBox, addBox, mailBox, phoneBox, and idBox controls have the focus and are not valid, change the background color to rgb(255, 232, 232) and display the image cg_invalid.png with no tiling in the right side of the background contained within the box.

12. Save your changes to the style sheet and then open **cg_register.html** in your browser. Verify that the content and layout of the form resemble that shown in Figure 7-61. Verify that you must enter all required field values in the proper format for the form to be submitted successfully. Confirm that the browser performs inline validation on the firstName, lastName, address, email, phoneNumber, and acgipID fields.

Case Problem 2

APPLY

Data Files needed for this Case Problem: sb_payment_txt.html, sb_validate_txt.css, 3 CSS files, 1 JavaScript file, 10 PNG files, 2 TXT files

The Spice Bowl Rita Sato is the manager of the web development team for *The Spice Bowl*, an online grocery store specializing in gourmet spices. She has asked you to create web forms for the site. You will start your work by developing a payment form used to collect billing and credit data from the store's customers. The form should include validation tests for credit card numbers to ensure that the card numbers match the correct credit card number patterns. The page should also include a form in which users can log into their *Spice Bowl* account. Figure 7-63 shows a preview of the page you will create for Rita.

Figure 7-63   Payment form for the Spice Bowl

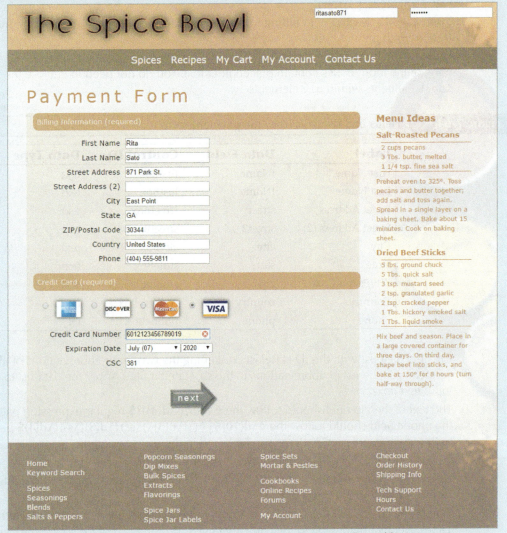

© Natalia Klenova/Shutterstock.com; Sources: American Express Company; Discover Financial Services; MasterCard Inc.; Visa, Inc.

Complete the following:

1. Using your editor, open the **sb_payment_txt.html** and **sb_validate_txt.css** files from the html07 ▸ case2 folder. Enter *your name* and *the date* in the comment section of each file, and save them as **sb_payment.html** and **sb_validate.css** respectively.

2. Return to the **sb_payment.html** file in your editor. Add links to the sb_forms.css and sb_validate.css style sheet files to the document head. Add a `script` element to load the sb_script.js file.

3. The page will contain a form in which customers can log into their account. Directly after the sb_logo.png image, insert a `form` element with the ID **login**. Have the form use the *http://www.example.com/sb/login* via the post method.

4. Within the login form, insert the following fields and controls:

   a. A text input box with the ID **userBox** for the **username** field. Add the placeholder text **username**.

   b. A text input box with the ID **pwdBox** for the **password** field. Add the placeholder text **password**.

5. Next, insert a payment form. Directly below the Payment Form h1 header, insert a `form` element that employs action at http://www.example.com/sb/payment via the post method. Assign the web form the id **payment**.

6. Insert a field set with the id **billing** to the payment form. Add the legend **Billing Information (required)** to the field set.

7. Within the billing field set, add the labels and input boxes specified in Figure 7-64. Note that none of the input boxes contain placeholder text. You do not need to enclose the `label` or `input` elements within `div` elements.

Figure 7-64   **Fields and controls from the payment form**

Label	Data Field	Control ID	Data Type	Required
First Name	fName	firstBox	text	yes
Last Name	lName	lastBox	text	yes
Street Address	street	streetBox	text	yes
Street Address (2)	street2	streetBox2	text	no
City	city	cityBox	text	yes
State	state	stateBox	text	yes
ZIP/Postal Code	zip	zipBox	text	no
Country	country	countryBox	text	yes
Phone	phone	phoneBox	tel	yes

8. Create a data list with the ID **stateList** containing the two-letter abbreviations of all the states. (You can use the list of abbreviations in the sb_state.txt file.) Apply the data list to the stateBox input text box.

9. The text of the zip field should follow the `^\d{5}(-\d{4})?$` regular expression pattern. The text of the phone field should follow the `^\d{10}$|^(\(\d{3}\)\s*)?\d{3}[\s-]?\d{4}$` pattern. Note that both regular expression patterns can be found in the sb_regex.txt file.

10. Set the default value of the country field to **United States**.

11. Create a field set with the ID **creditCard**, which you use to insert credit card fields. Add the legend **Credit Card (required)**.

12. Within the creditCard field set, insert another field set containing four `label` elements, with each `label` element belonging to the cardLabel class. Within each of the four `label` elements, insert an option button from the cCard field with the value **amex**, **discover**, **master**, and **visa**. Make cCard a required field. Follow each option button with an `image` element containing the image of its corresponding credit card image using the sb_amex.png, sb_discover.png, sb_master.png, and sb_visa.png files.

13. After the creditCard field set, insert a label containing the text **Credit Card Number** associated with the cardBox input control. Create an input text box with the ID **cardBox** for the cardNumber field. Make the field cardNumber required and have the field value follow the regular expression pattern for credit card numbers (using the regular expression in the sb_regex.txt file).

14. Create the **Expiration Date** label associated with the monthList control.

15. Add a selection list with the ID **monthList** for the cardMonth field. Make the cardMonth field required. Populate the selection list with the option text "--Month--", "January (01)", "February (02)" and so forth up to "December (12)". For the "--Month--", set the field value to an empty text string. For the month options, insert the month value from 1 up to 12.

16. Add a selection list with the ID **yearList** for the cardYear field. Make the cardYear field required. Populate the selection list with the option text "--Year--", "2017", "2018", "2019", "2020", and "2021". For the "--Year--", set the field value to an empty text string and, for the year options, insert the 4-digit year value.

17. Create a label with the text **CSC** associated with the cscBox. Add a text input box with the ID **cscBox** for the required **csc** field. Have the csc field value follow the regular expression pattern `^\d{3}$`. Set the maximum length of the field value to 3 characters and display the placeholder text **nnn**.

18. After the creditCard field set, insert a `button` element of the submit type. Within the button, insert the sb_button.png inline image with the alternate text **next**. (Note: The text for the button is part of the button image, so the `value` attribute is not needed.)

19. Save your changes to the file and then go to sb_validate.css file in your editor to design the validation styles for the web form.

20. Within the Validation Styles section, insert the following style rules to perform inline validation:

   a. For every `input` element that is not a radio type and that has the focus, change the background color to rgb(255, 218, 165). (Hint: Use the attribute selector `input:not([type='radio'])` to select `input` elements that are not radio types.)

   b. For every `input` element that is not a radio type and that has the focus with a valid value, change the background color to rgb(215, 255, 215) and display the image file sb_valid.png with no tiling in the right edge of the input box.

   c. For every `input` element that is not a radio type and that has the focus with an invalid value, change the background color to rgb(255, 245, 215) and display the image file sb_invalid.png with no tiling in the right edge of the input box.

21. Save your changes to the style sheet and then open **sb_payment.html** in your browser.

22. Verify that you cannot submit the form without all required fields entered in the proper format.

23. Verify the validation checks for the credit card number by confirming that the form rejects the following credit card number 6012123456789019 (which does not follow a valid card number pattern). Further verify that the form accepts the following credit card number 6011123456789019 (which follows a valid card number pattern).

Case Problem 3

Data Files needed for this Case Problem: wm_demo_txt.html, wm_forms_txt.css, 2 CSS files, 1 JavaScript file, 2 PNG files

WidgetMage   Anna Lopez is the founder of WidgetMage, a website that specializes in designing teaching materials and demos for people learning how to program. Anna has asked you to work on a page users can use to explore CSS typographical styles. Anna already has the JavaScript code written to make the demo page work and a style sheet for the page. She wants you to finish her project by writing the form controls for the demo. A preview of the page you will create is shown in Figure 7-65.

CHALLENGE

Figure 7-65   **Form for CSS demo**

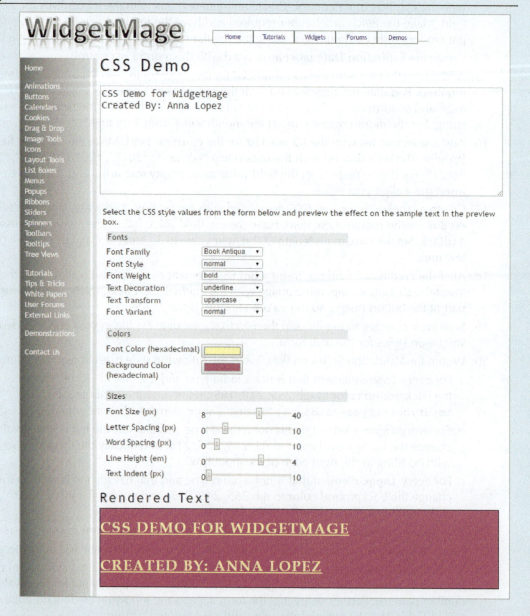

Complete the following:

1. Using your editor, open the **wm_demo_txt.html** and **wm_forms_txt.css** files from the html07 ▸ case3 folder. Enter *your name* and *the date* in the comment section of each file, and save them as **wm_demo.html** and **wm_forms.css** respectively.

2. Return to the **wm_demo.html** file in your editor. Add a link to the wm_forms.css style sheet file to the document head. Add a `script` element to load the wm_script.js file.

3. Scroll down to the h1 heading and insert a `form` element. You do not need to specify an `action` or `method` attribute.

⊕ **Explore** 4. Insert a text area box with the ID **sampleBox** for the field **sampleText**. Add the following attributes to the text area box:

   a. Add the placeholder text **Enter sample text and press the Tab key**.

   b. Use the `autofocus` attribute so that the text area box receives the focus when the page is opened by the user.

c. Set the `tabindex` attribute of the `textarea` control to 1.

d. Set the `wrap` attribute to `hard` so that line returns are retained as part of the field value.

Note: Do *not* include a blank space between the opening and closing `<textarea>` tags or else the placeholder text will not appear within the text area box.

5. After the text area box, insert a paragraph containing the text **Select the CSS style values from the form below and preview the effect on the sample text in the preview box**.

6. Directly after the paragraph, insert a field set with the legend Fonts that will be used to insert controls the user can use to select font styles.

Note: In the steps that follow, make sure you add both a `name` attribute and an `id` attribute to each selection list giving the same value to both attributes. Also, make sure that you enter the name and ID values in lowercase letters. Finally, make sure that every selection list has both option text and option values set to the same text string.

7. Within the Fonts field set, insert the label **Font Family** followed by a selection list for the fontfamily field. Add the following options to the selection list: **default, serif, sans-serif, monospace, cursive, fantasy, Arial, 'Book Antiqua', 'Courier New', Geneva, Helvetica, Impact, Palatino, Tahoma,** and **'Times New Roman'**. Set the option values equal to the option text, including the single quotes in the option value where required for the font name.

⟁ **Explore** 8. For the options created for the fontfamily selection list, enclose the generic font names in an option group named generic and the specific fonts within an option group named specific.

9. After the fontfamily selection list, insert the **Font Style** label followed by a selection list for the fontstyle field with the option text and option values equal to **normal, italic,** and **oblique**.

10. Add the **Font Weight** label followed by a selection list for the fontweight field containing the option values and option text normal and bold.

11. Add the **Text Decoration** label followed by the selection list for the textdecoration field containing the option values and option text **none, line-through, overline,** and **underline**.

12. Add the **Text Transform** label followed by the selection list for the texttransform field containing the option values and option text **none, capitalize, lowercase,** and **uppercase**.

13. Add the **Font Variant** label followed by the selection list for the fontvariant field containing the option text and values **normal** and **small-caps**.

Next, you insert controls the user can use to select both the text and background colors that will be applied to the demo text.

⟁ **Explore** 14. Create a field set with the legend **Colors** and containing the following labels and `input` elements:

a. The **Font Color (hexadecimal)** label followed by an input box with the data type set to **color**, the field name and ID set to **color**, and the default value set to **#000000**.

b. The **Background Color (hexadecimal)** label followed by an input box with the color data type, the field name and ID set to **backgroundcolor**, a placeholder value of **#rrggbb**, and the default value set to **#FFFFFF**.

Finally, you create controls that define the typographical sizes.

15. Create a field set with the legend **Sizes**.

16. Within the Sizes field set, insert the **Font Size (px)** label. Following the label, insert a `div` element belonging to the slider class. Within the `div` element, insert a range slider with the field name and ID fontsize. Have the value of the fontsize field range from 8 to 40 in steps of 1. Give the fontsize field a default value of **14**. Directly before and after the `input` element opening and closing tags, insert the text **8** and **40** respectively so that the user can see the range of values in the range slider control.

17. Repeat the previous step to create range sliders for the other typographical sizing styles and that include text before and after the slider input control opening and closing tabs to show the range of the slider:

    a. The **Letter Spacing (px)** label followed by a letterspacing field that ranges from **0** to **10** in steps of **1** with a default value of **0**.

    b. The **Word Spacing (px)** label followed by a wordspacing field that ranges from **0** to **10** in steps of **1** with a default value of **0**.

    c. The **Line Height (em)** label followed by a lineheight field that ranges from **0** to **4** in steps of **0.2** with a default value of **1**.

    d. The **Text Indent (px)** label followed by a textindent field that ranges from **0** to **10** in steps of **1** with a default value of **0**.

18. Save your changes to the file and then return to the **wm_forms.css** file in your editor to create the form styles.

19. Go to the Field Set Styles section and create a style for all `fieldset` elements that removes the field set border, sets the width to 60%, and sets the top/bottom margin to 10 pixels and the left/right margin to 0 pixels.

20. For every field set legend, create a style rule that sets the background color to rgb(232, 232, 232), sets the width to 100%, and sets the top/bottom margin to 2 pixels and the left/right margin to 0 pixels.

21. Go to the DIV Styles section and create a style rule for `div` elements of the slider class that floats the element on the left, sets the width to 60%, and sets the top/bottom margin to 2 pixels and the left/right margin to 0 pixels.

22. Go to the Control Styles section and create the following style rules:

    a. For all labels, create a style rule that floats the label on the left margin once the left margin is clear, displays the label as a block with a width of 40%, and sets the top/bottom margin to 2 pixels and the left/right margin to 0 pixels.

    b. For all `input` and `select` elements, create a style rule that sets the top/bottom margin to 2 pixels and the left/right margins to 0 pixels.

    c. For all range slider input elements, create a style rule that sets the width to 60%.

    d. For all selection lists, create a style rule that displays the selection list as a block floated on the left and sets the width to 120 pixels.

    e. For all input boxes of the `color` type, create a style rule that displays the color box as a block floated on the left and sets the width to 75 pixels.

    f. For all text area boxes, create a style rule that sets the font size to 1.5em, the width to 100%, the height to 200 pixels, and the bottom margin to 15 pixels.

✛ **Explore** 23. Go to the Placeholder Styles section. In this section, you will create a style for the placeholder text within the text area box. Using the WebKit, Moz, and MS browser extensions, create three style rules for placeholder text within text area boxes that sets the background color to rgb(255, 255, 191), sets the font color to rgb(255, 151, 151), and sets the font size to 1.5em.

24. Save your changes to the style sheet and open the **wm_demo.html** file in your browser. Test the form by entering sample text into the text area box near the top of the form. Verify that when you tab out of the text area box, the text appears in the rendering box at the bottom of the page. Change the style of the rendered text by selecting options and values from the style controls on the form. If your browser does not support the color data type, change the colors by entering hexadecimal values for the font color and background color fields.

Case Problem 4

Data Files needed for this Case Problem: 1 JavaScript file, 3 PNG files

Millennium Computers   You are employed at Millennium Computers, a discount mail-order company specializing in computers and computer components. Your supervisor, Sandy Walton, has asked you to create an order form web page so that customers can purchase products online. Your order form is for computer purchases only. There are several options for customers to consider when purchasing computers from Millennium. Customers can choose from the following:

- Processor Speed: 3.2 GHz, 4.0 GHz, 5.2 GHz
- Memory: 1 GB, 2 GB, 4 GB, 8 GB
- Monitor Size: 15", 17", 19", 21"
- Hard Drive: 240 GB, 500 GB, 750 GB, 1 TB
- DVD Burner: yes/no
- Tuner Card: yes/no
- Media Card Reader: yes/no

Complete the following:

1. Use your text editor to create an HTML file named **mc_pc.html** and two style sheets named **mc_styles.css** and **mc_forms.css**. Enter *your name* and *the date* in a comment section in each file. Include any other comments you think will aptly document the purpose and content of the files. Save the files in the html07 ▶ case4 folder.

2. Go to the **mc_pc.html** file and link your page to the mc_styles.css and mc_forms.css styles. Add a script element that attaches the page to the mc_script.js file that you will use to confirm whether or not the form fields are successfully submitted.

3. Add a web `form` element named cForm. Add attributes so the form is submitted using the `post` method employing the action http://www.mill_computers.com/orders/process.cgi.

4. Design a page for Millennium Computers. Insert any styles you create in the mc_styles.css style sheet. You are free to use the mc_logo.png file and whatever text or images you want in order to complete the look and content of the page.

5. Be sure the form contains the following elements:
   - Input boxes for the customer's first name, last name, street address, city, state, zip code, and phone number. The field names should be **fName**, **lName**, **street**, **city**, **state**, **zip**, and **phone**, respectively.
   - Add validation checks marking all of the customer contact fields as required.
   - Use regular expression patterns to ensure that each user enters his or her zip code and phone number in the correct format.

- Selection lists for the processor speed, memory, monitor size, and hard drive size. The field names should be **pSpeed**, **mem**, **monitor**, and **hd**, respectively. The option values should match the option text.
- Option buttons for the DVD burner, tuner card, and media card reader options. The field names should be **dvd**, **tuner**, and **mcard**, respectively.
- A check box for the warranty field that asks customers if they want the 24-month extended warranty.
- A text area box requesting additional information or comments on the order.
- Three form buttons: a submit button with the text **Send Order**, a reset button with the text **Cancel Order**, and a command button with the text **Contact Me**.

6. Create a style for your form in the **mc_forms.css** style sheet. The layout and appearance of the form are up to you. It should include style rules to highlight input boxes that receive the focus, and it should employ inline validation for missing or incorrectly entered data.

7. Test your website on a variety of browsers to ensure your design works under different conditions.

TUTORIAL 8

Enhancing a Website with Multimedia

Working with Sound, Video, and Animation

OBJECTIVES

Session 8.1
- Understand audio and video formats
- Insert an HTML audio clip
- Support multiple audio formats

Session 8.2
- Insert an HTML video clip
- Write a video caption track
- Format video captions

Session 8.3
- Create a CSS transition
- Explore transition attributes
- Create a CSS key frame animation
- Apply a CSS animation

Case | *Cinema Penguin*

Maxine Michaels runs the movie blog *Cinema Penguin* containing reviews, articles, and stories about classic movies from the golden era of Hollywood. She wants to enhance the user experience of her website by adding sound and video clips of famous movie moments.

Maxine has asked for your help to develop a sample page describing the 1951 classic movie musical *Royal Wedding*, starring Fred Astaire and Jane Powell. Maxine has collected audio and video clips from the movie that she wants added to the page. The page also includes a short article describing a famous piece of cinema trickery in which Astaire appears to dance on the ceiling. Maxine wants you to use CSS animation styles to demonstrate how this effect was achieved.

STARTING DATA FILES

html08 → **tutorial**

cp_royal_txt.html
cp_animate_txt.css
cp_media_txt.css
cp_captions_txt.vtt
+ 11 files

review

cp_astaire_txt.html
cp_animate2_txt.css
cp_media2_txt.css
cp_captions2_txt.vtt
+ 9 files

case1

ws_jfk_txt.html
ws_media_txt.css
ws_captions_txt.vtt
+ 8 files

case2

ba_physics_txt.html
ba_animate_txt.css
+ 6 files

case3

paa_game_txt.html
paa_animate_txt.css
+ 10 files

case4

rnt_poetry_txt.html
rnt_audio_txt.css
+ 8 files

Session 8.1 Visual Overview:

The **audio** element embeds an audio file in the web page.

```
<aside>
   <h1>Listen Up</h1>
   <p>The music for <cite>Royal Wedding</cite> was composed by Burton Lane,
      who is best known for his work in <cite>Finian's Rainbow </cite>(1947)
      and his Grammy Award-winning <cite>On a Clear Day You Can See
      Forever</cite>(1965).</p>
   <p>Lane's greatest musical accomplishment may
      very well be his discovery of an 11-year-old singing sensation named
      Frances Gumm, whom the world now knows better as Judy Garland.
   </p>
   <p>Click the play button below to hear the opening of the musical overture
      for Burton Lane's <cite>Royal Wedding</cite>.</p>
   <audio controls>
      <source src="cp_overture.mp3" type="audio/mp3" />
      <source src="cp_overture.ogg" type="audio/ogg" />
      <p><em>To play this audio clip, your browser needs to support HTML5.</em></p>
   </audio>
</aside>
```

The **controls** attribute displays media player controls for the audio clip.

The **source** element provides the source of the multimedia file.

Browsers that do not support HTML5 multimedia elements will display this text as a fallback message to the user.

The **type** attribute provides the format of the multimedia file.

Playing Web Audio

Listen Up

The music for *Royal Wedding* was composed by Burton Lane, who is best known for his work in *Finian's Rainbow* (1947) and his Grammy Award-winning *On a Clear Day You Can See Forever*(1965).

Lane's greatest musical accomplishment may very well be his discovery of an 11-year-old singing sensation named Frances Gumm, whom the world now knows better as Judy Garland.

Click the play button below to hear the opening of the musical overture for Burton Lane's *Royal Wedding*.

Audio player controls are part of the browser's media player.

Native media player provided by the browser to play audio files.

Introducing Multimedia on the Web

The original purpose of the web and HTML was to deliver textual information via interconnected hypertext documents. HTML was a perfect tool for academic researchers needing to share text and data. Once graphical capabilities were added to the HTML language, developers were free to create documents with images and arresting page layouts that opened up the web's potential for commerce and business. The next major phase in the language was the introduction of multimedia support in the form of streaming audio, video, and interactive games, making the web a dominant entertainment platform.

It is estimated that by 2019, online video will account for 80% of global Internet traffic, rising to 85% within the United States alone (*Cisco Visual Networking Index: Forecast and Methodology, 2014–2019,* May 2015). Thus, web developers need to consider how to best utilize multimedia in making their websites attractive to the public. One of the biggest challenges in delivering multimedia content is putting that content in a form that can be retrieved quickly and easily without loss of quality.

Understanding Codecs and Containers

To achieve fast and easy transmission of multimedia content, that content is stored using a **codec**, which is a computer program that encodes and decodes streams of data. Codecs compress data so that it can be transmitted in a fast and efficient manner and then decompress it when it is to be read or played back. The compression method can be either lossy or lossless.

Using **lossy compression**, nonessential data are removed in order to achieve a smaller file size. An audio file might be compressed by removing sounds that the human ear can barely hear. A video file might be compressed by removing frames from the video playback. The more the file is compressed, the more content is lost. The sound from a highly compressed audio file can become muddy and indistinct. A highly compressed video clip can become blurry or jerky in its movements. Thus, one consideration in lossy compression is determining at what point essential data has been removed because, once that data is lost, it cannot be recovered.

Using **lossless compression**, data is compressed by removing redundant information. For example, the following text string, consisting of 4 As followed by 5 Bs, and then 6 Cs requires 15 characters of information:

AAAABBBBBCCCCCC

Yet, this content can be rewritten using the following 6 characters with no loss of information:

4A5B6C

This same general technique can be applied to digital audio and video, which can contain long stretches of redundant sound and images. The disadvantage of lossless compression is that you cannot achieve the same level of compression as with lossy compression. Most codecs involve some combination of lossy and lossless techniques. Web developers can choose from dozens of different codecs to compress their multimedia content.

Codecs are placed within a **container** that handles the packaging, transportation, and presentation of the data. The container is essentially the file format, which is identified by a file extension. The web supports a multitude of container and codec combinations but not all containers and codecs are equally supported. For example, Google Chrome uses the WebM container for video content, compressing that data with the VP8 codec; however, that combination of container and codec is not supported by Internet Explorer or any Apple device, such as iPods or iPads.

Thus, web developers have to account for browser support before making any multimedia content available to the user.

Understanding Plug-Ins

Once multimedia has been stored within a container file, a **media player** is required to decode and play that content. Because multimedia was not part of the original HTML specifications, browsers, for many years, used a **plug-in**, which is a software program accessed by the browser to provide a feature or capability not native to the browser. The most commonly used plug-ins for multimedia content included Adobe Flash, Apple's QuickTime player, and the Windows Media Player. A plug-in either opens in its own external window or runs within the web page as an **embedded object**, in much the same way that a graphic image appears embedded within the page.

There are several problems with the plug-in approach for delivery of multimedia content:

- Plugs-ins require users to install a separate application in addition to their web browsers.
- There is not a common plug-in that is available across all browsers, operating systems, and devices.
- HTML documents that support multiple plug-ins are difficult to create and maintain.
- Plug-ins consume valuable system resources, resulting in slow and unreliable performance.
- Plug-ins are a security risk with some of the most prominent Internet attacks working their way into browsers via a plug-in.

Starting with HTML5, support for audio and video content was added to the HTML language, providing a common framework for delivering multimedia content without the need for plug-ins. HTML5 is now an accepted and well-supported standard, but if you need to work with older browsers or maintain a legacy website, you might still encounter code that utilizes plug-ins. In this tutorial, you review code to access those plug-ins but your focus will be on working with the HTML5 audio and video elements and attributes.

Before exploring these elements and attributes in depth, open the page for Cinema Penguin that Maxine has created for you.

To open Maxine's web page:

▶ 1. Use your editor to open the **cp_royal_txt.html** file from the html08 ▸ tutorial folder. Enter *your name* and *the date* in the comment section of the file and save it as **cp_royal.html**.

▶ 2. Review the rest of the document to become familiar with its contents and structure.

▶ 3. Open **cp_royal.html** in your browser. The initial page describing the movie *Royal Wedding* is shown in Figure 8-1.

Figure 8-1 **Initial Royal Wedding page**

Sources: openclipart.org; wiki

Royal Wedding is one of a handful of Metro-Goldwyn-Mayer productions from the early 1950s whose original copyrights were never renewed, which places the movie in the public domain. Maxine can add production stills, sound clips, and video clips from the film to her website without worrying about copyright infringement. One of her audio clips contains the first few seconds from the film's overture. She would like to add that clip to the Listen Up box in the lower-left corner of the web page. To do that, you use the audio element.

Working with the audio Element

Audio clips are embedded within a web page using the following audio element

```
<audio src="url" attributes />
```

where *url* specifies the source of the audio file and *attributes* define how the audio clip should be handled by the browser. Figure 8-2 describes some of the attributes associated with HTML audio and video elements.

Figure 8-2	Attributes of HTML audio and video elements

Attribute	Description
autoplay	Starts playing the media clip as soon as it is loaded by the browser
controls	Displays the player controls in the web page
loop	Automatically restarts the media clip when it is finished playing
muted	Specifies that the audio output should be muted
preload="auto|metadata|none"	Specifies whether the media clip should be preloaded by the browser, where type is auto (to load the entire clip), metadata (to preload only descriptive data about the clip), or none (not to preload the media clip)
src="url"	Specifies the source of the media clip, where url is the location and name of the media file

TIP

Because XHTML requires values for every attribute, enter the controls attribute as controls="controls" to display media player controls on a page written in XHTML.

For example, the following tag loads audio from the cp_overture.mp3 file and displays the media player controls, which allows the user to interact with the audio clip from within the web page:

```
<audio src="cp_overture.mp3" controls />
```

If you don't include a controls attribute, the audio clip is embedded within the page but without the browser's native media player. This can be used to create a soundtrack that automatically starts and plays in the background. The following tag uses the cp_overture.mp3 file as background music, automatically starting when the page is loaded and looping back to the beginning when the clip is finished:

```
<audio src="cp_overture.mp3" autoplay loop />
```

Adding background sounds to a web page is generally discouraged because they can quickly become annoying with no easy way of turning them off!

Browsers and Audio Formats

HTML does not specify any particular audio format and thus, developers are free to pick a format that meets the needs of their customers and clients. The most popular formats for web-based audio are described in Figure 8-3.

Figure 8-3   **Audio formats in HTML**

Format	Description	Codec	File Extension(s)	MIME Type
MP3	**MPEG-1 Audio Layer 3** or **MP3** is one of the most widely used audio types and is the standard format for digital audio players	MP3	.mp3	audio/mpeg
AAC	**Advanced Audio Coding** or **AAC** is the encoding standard for all Apple products, as well as YouTube and several gaming systems and mobile devices; AAC was introduced as the successor to MP3 with the goal of achieving better sound quality at similar compression ratios	AAC	.aac .mp4 .m4a	audio/mp4
OGG	A file compression format designed for web audio, **Ogg** is an open source and royalty-free format; in general, Ogg provides better sound quality than MP3, especially at lower bit rates	Vorbis	.ogg	audio/ogg
WAV	The original audio format for Windows PCs, **WAV** is commonly used for storing uncompressed audio, making it impractical for all but the shortest audio clips	PCM	.wav	audio/wav

Because there is not a defined audio format, browsers and devices differ on the types of audio formats they support. For example, Apple devices do not support the Ogg format. Thus, before choosing an audio format, you need to determine whether or not your user's browser will be able to play it. Figure 8-4 lists the browser support for different audio formats at the time of this writing, but, because browser support of audio and video is constantly evolving, you should always check the current levels of support on the browser market.

Figure 8-4   **Browser support for audio formats**

Browser	MP3	AAC	Ogg	WAV
Chrome (desktop)	✓	✓	✓	✓
Chrome (mobile)	✓	✓	✓	✓
Firefox (desktop)	✓	✓	✓	✓
Firefox (mobile)			✓	✓
Microsoft Edge (desktop)	✓	✓		
Internet Explorer (desktop)	✓	✓		
Internet Explorer (mobile)	✓	✓		
Opera (desktop)			✓	✓
Opera (mobile)			✓	✓
Safari (desktop)	✓	✓		✓
Safari (mobile)	✓	✓		✓

You can provide the most cross-browser support by supplying multiple versions of the same audio clip and letting the browser choose which one to play. To provide several versions of the same media file, nest several `source` elements within a single `audio` element as follows

```
<audio>
    <source src="url1" type="mime-type" />
    <source src="url2" type="mime-type" />
…
</audio>
```

TIP

If no type attribute is provided, the browser will download a section of the file to determine whether it corresponds to a recognized format.

where *url1*, *url2*, and so on are the URLs for each audio file and *mime-type* specifies the audio format associated with each file. The browser goes through the `source` elements starting from the top, stopping once it encounters an audio format that it can play, so that even though multiple audio files are listed, only one audio file will be completely downloaded by the browser.

The following `audio` element provides two choices for the *Royal Wedding* overture clip:

```
<audio controls>
    <source src="cp_overture.mp3" type="audio/mp3" />
    <source src="cp_overture.ogg" type="audio/ogg" />
</audio>
```

The browser will first attempt to play the cp_overture.mp3 file but, if that is not a supported format, it will try to play the cp_overture.ogg file. Notice that including the `type` attribute, while not required, informs the browser of the file type and speeds up the process of choosing a compatible audio source.

Exploring MIME Types

INSIGHT

The **Multipurpose Internet Mail Extension** or **MIME type** was first introduced as a way of attaching nontextual content to e-mail messages. With the growth of the web, the use of MIME types expanded to include the flow of information across the web. Each MIME type includes the following header:

type/subtype

where *type* is the general data type and *subtype* is a special classification of data within that type. The possible values for type are application, audio, image, message, model, multipart, text, and video. Within these types, there can be dozens or hundreds of subtypes. For example, HTML text files have the MIME type text/html while CSS files have the MIME type text/css. Audio files include MIME types such as audio/mp3, audio/ogg, and audio/wav among dozens of others.

When a web server sends content to the browser, it includes the MIME type so that the browser is able to interpret and render that content for the user. The file extension given to a file should correspond to its MIME type. Thus, an MP3 file should be delivered by the server with the audio/mp3 MIME type and the mp3 file extension.

Maxine has created two audio files of the overture music for *Royal Wedding* stored in the MP3 and Ogg format. Add these audio clips to her web page now.

To add an audio clip:

▶ **1.** Return to the **cp_royal.html** file in your editor.

▶ **2.** Scroll down to the `aside` element for the Listen Up content.

3. Directly before the closing `</aside>` tag, insert the following content:

```
<p>Click the play button below to hear the musical overture
   for Burton Lane's <cite>Royal Wedding</cite>.
</p>
<audio controls>
   <source src="cp_overture.mp3" type="audio/mp3" />
   <source src="cp_overture.ogg" type="audio/ogg" />
</audio>
```

Figure 8-5 highlights the newly added code.

Figure 8-5   Inserting an audio clip

```
<p>Lane's greatest musical accomplishment may
   very well be his discovery of an 11-year-old singing sensation named
   Frances Gumm, whom the world now knows better as Judy Garland.
</p>
<p>Click the play button below to hear the musical overture
   for Burton Lane's <cite>Royal Wedding</cite>.</p>
<audio controls>
   <source src="cp_overture.mp3" type="audio/mp3" />
   <source src="cp_overture.ogg" type="audio/ogg" />
</audio>
</aside>
```

displays the controls
for the audio player

two possible
sources for
the audio file

4. Save your changes to the file.

Before running this audio clip, you will format the appearance of the browser's native media player that will run the audio.

Applying Styles to the Media Player

The appearance of the media player is determined by the browser itself. Figure 8-6 shows the default media player for several major browsers.

Figure 8-6   Native audio player for different browsers

Google Chrome

Microsoft Internet Explorer

Microsoft Edge

Opera

Firefox

You can use CSS to set the width of the media player, add borders and drop shadows, and apply filters and transformations to the player's appearance but, if you want a completely customized player, you need to build it yourself using the form controls introduced in the last tutorial along with a JavaScript program to set the behavior and operation of each control. There are also many third-party HTML5 players available to allow you to create a customized media player adapted to the needs of your company or organization.

For the Cinema Penguin website, you will use the native media player supplied by the browser but you will use CSS to make some minor changes to the player's appearance.

To apply styles to the Media Player:

1. Scroll to the document head of the **cp_royal.html** file in your editor and add a link to the **cp_media.css** style sheet directly before the closing </head> tag.

2. Save your changes to the file and then use your editor to open the **cp_media_txt.css** file from the html08 ▸ tutorial folder. Enter *your name* and *the date* in the comment section of the file and save it as **cp_media.css**.

3. Go to the Audio and Video Player Styles section and insert the following style rule:

```
audio {
    box-shadow: rgb(51, 51, 51) 8px 8px 15px;
    display: block;
    margin: 10px auto;
    width: 90%;
}
```

Figure 8-7 highlights the newly added styles for the audio element.

Figure 8-7	Styles for the native media player

```
/* Audio and Video Player Styles */

audio {
    box-shadow: rgb(51, 51, 51) 8px 8px 15px;
    display: block;
    margin: 10px auto;
    width: 90%;
}
```

4. Save your changes to the style sheet.

Test the audio clip you entered into the Cinema Penguin web page.

To play the audio clip:

1. Reload the cp_royal.html file in your web browser.

2. Scroll to the bottom of the page and click the play button on the media player to play the embedded audio clip.

Figure 8-8 shows the appearance of the media player within the Google Chrome browser.

Figure 8-8   **Appearance of the native media player within Google Chrome**

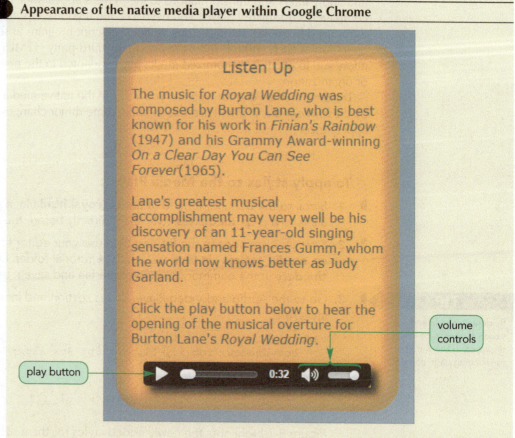

Listen Up

The music for *Royal Wedding* was composed by Burton Lane, who is best known for his work in *Finian's Rainbow* (1947) and his Grammy Award-winning *On a Clear Day You Can See Forever* (1965).

Lane's greatest musical accomplishment may very well be his discovery of an 11-year-old singing sensation named Frances Gumm, whom the world now knows better as Judy Garland.

Click the play button below to hear the opening of the musical overture for Burton Lane's *Royal Wedding*.

volume controls

play button   0:32

3. The clip will run for about 32 seconds. Press the stop button on the media player to halt the playback.

Trouble? Depending on your browser and device, you may see a different media player in your web page.

Maxine likes the audio clip but asks what would happen if the user opens this page in an older browser that doesn't support the `audio` element. In that situation, the browser would not display any media player, but you can provide alternate content for the user.

Providing a Fallback to an Audio Clip

It is considered bad design to add a feature to a web page without also providing some fallback option to users who cannot take advantage of that feature. You already used one type of fallback option by specifying two audio sources so that, if the browser cannot play the MP3 version of the audio clip, it can attempt to play the OGG version.

If the browser can't play either version or doesn't support the `audio` element at all, you can follow the `source` elements with HTML code that the browser will recognize. The simplest fallback option is a text string indicating that the user needs to upgrade the browser to take advantage of the feature you added to the page.

Add a paragraph within the `audio` element to display a message for users who are unable to play either of the two source files you provided.

To provide alternate text to the audio clip:

1. Return to the **cp_royal.html** file in your editor.

2. Scroll down to the `audio` element and insert the following code directly before the closing `</audio>` tag:

```
<p><em>To play this audio clip, your browser needs to support HTML5.</em></p>
```

Figure 8-9 highlights the fallback text for the audio clip.

Figure 8-9 | Adding fallback text to the audio element

```
<audio controls>
    <source src="cp_overture.mp3" type="audio/mp3" />
    <source src="cp_overture.ogg" type="audio/ogg" />
    <p><em>To play this audio clip, your browser needs to support HTML5.</em></p>
</audio>
</aside>
```

displays this paragraph when the audio element is not supported

3. Save your changes to the file.

You can test this feature by opening the page in an older browser or using the developer tools provided with your browser to emulate an earlier browser version. Figure 8-10 shows how the page might look when the `audio` element is not supported.

Figure 8-10 | Fallback text displayed within the web page

Click the play button below to hear the opening of the musical overture for Burton Lane's *Royal Wedding*.

fallback text displayed for browsers that don't support the audio element

To play this audio clip, your browser needs to support HTML5.

Another way of supporting older browsers is to provide code that will work with multimedia plug-ins.

PROSKILLS

Verbal Communication: Tips for Effective Web Audio

Enhancing your website with audio clips can be an effective way to provide information and entertainment for your users and customers. However, it must be used judiciously to avoid annoying users. Here are some tips to keep in mind when using web audio:

- *Avoid background music.* Remember that many customers multitask when using the web and are often listening to their own music and audio files. Don't annoy them by inserting your audio clip over theirs.
- *Give users control.* Turn off the autoplay feature of your audio player. Let each user choose whether or not to play your audio clip. Your users might be accessing your site at work or in a public place where audio is inappropriate. Always give users the ability to pause, stop, and—above all—mute the audio.
- *Keep it short.* If you use sound to supplement different visual effects in your page, keep the clips short in duration. Don't force your users to listen to long clips.
- *Accommodate hearing-impaired customers.* The web is an important source of information for the hard of hearing. Always provide alternatives for those who can't hear your site's audio content.

Finally, every feature on your website, including sound, should have a reason for being there. An audio clip should provide users with important information that cannot be conveyed in any other way.

Exploring Embedded Objects

As you learned earlier, older browsers relied on plug-ins to play audio and video files. The plug-ins were marked using the following embed element

```
<embed src="url" type="mime-type"
       width="value" height="value" />
```

where url is the location of the media file, the type attribute provides the mime-type, and the width and height attributes set the width and height of the media player. For example, the following code loads the cp_overture.mp3 file into a media player 250 pixels wide by 50 pixels high:

```
<embed src="cp_overture.mp3" type="audio/mp3"
       width="250" height="50" />
```

The plug-in associated with this particular media file is defined within the user's browser. One user might associate MP3 files with Apple's QuickTime Player while another user might associate them with the Windows Media Player. One of the challenges with plug-ins is that they relied on the user installing a specific piece of software, which some users were either unable or reluctant to do. HTML5 avoids this problem and makes inserting audio and video content as seamless as inserting inline images.

Plug-In Attributes

The src, type, height, and width attributes are generic attributes and can be applied to the embed element for any plug-in. The embed element also allows for attributes that are tailored to specific plug-ins. For example, the following embed element adds attributes that are recognized by Apple's QuickTime Player to display the media player controls and prevent the playback from starting automatically:

```
<embed src="cp_overture.mp3" width="250" height="50"
       controller="yes" autoplay="no" />
```

Other plug-ins might use different attributes or attribute values to achieve the same effect. For Windows Media Player, the equivalent tag is as follows:

```
<embed src="cp_overture.mp3" width="250" height="50"
       showcontrols="yes" autostart="no" />
```

Both plug-ins can be supported by including both sets of attributes within the same tag as follows:

```
<embed src="cp_overture.mp3" width="250" height="50"
       controller="yes" autoplay="no"
       showcontrols="yes" autostart="no" />
```

Each plug-in will use the attributes designed for it and ignore the others, enabling a single tag to work across multiple plug-ins.

Plug-Ins as Fallback Options

Plug-ins can act as a fallback option for browsers that don't support the HTML5 multimedia elements by adding the embed element to the end of the audio element as the last option for the browser. The following code demonstrates how to employ a plug-in as a fallback to the audio element you inserted earlier into the cp_royal.html file:

```
<audio controls>
   <source src="cp_overture.mp3" type="audio/mp3" />
   <source src="cp_overture.ogg" type="audio/ogg" />
   <embed src="cp_overture.mp3" width="250" height="50"
          controller="yes" autoplay="no"
          showcontrols="yes" autostart="no" />
</audio>
```

TIP

Browsers that don't support HTML5 ignore the audio and source elements but apply the embed element to insert the media player via a plug-in.

The use of plug-ins has steadily declined since the widespread adoption of the HTML5 standard. Maxine decides against including support for plug-in media players, instead she will rely on the fallback message directing users to upgrade older browsers.

You have completed your work to add a sound clip to the *Royal Wedding* page. In the next session, you insert a video clip of a famous dance from that movie.

Session 8.1 Quick Check

REVIEW

1. What is the difference between a codec and a container?
2. What is the difference between lossy and lossless compression?
3. What are four sound formats used for web audio?
4. Provide code to play the audio clip soundtrack.mp3 as a background sound that plays continuously when the page is opened by a browser.
5. Provide code to insert the cp_dance.mp3 audio file. Have the browser display the media player controls.
6. Supplement the code from the previous step to allow the browser to choose between the cp_dance.mp3 and cp_dance.ogg audio files.
7. Supplement the code from the previous step to have the browser apply the code <p>Your browser must support HTML5 to play this audio.</p> if the browser does not support the HTML audio element.
8. Provide the HTML code to insert the cp_dance.mp3 file using the embed element. Assume that the file will be played by Apple's QuickTime Player, displaying the play controls on the page. Set the width of the player to 350 pixels and the height to 40 pixels.

Session 8.2 Visual Overview:

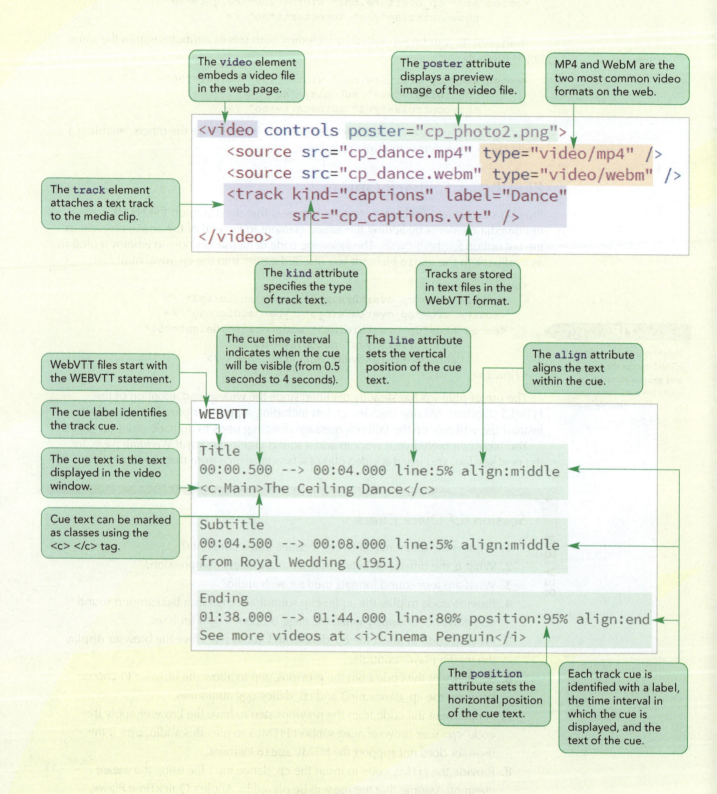

The video element embeds a video file in the web page.

The poster attribute displays a preview image of the video file.

MP4 and WebM are the two most common video formats on the web.

```
<video controls poster="cp_photo2.png">
    <source src="cp_dance.mp4" type="video/mp4" />
    <source src="cp_dance.webm" type="video/webm" />
    <track kind="captions" label="Dance"
           src="cp_captions.vtt" />
</video>
```

The track element attaches a text track to the media clip.

The kind attribute specifies the type of track text.

Tracks are stored in text files in the WebVTT format.

The cue time interval indicates when the cue will be visible (from 0.5 seconds to 4 seconds).

The line attribute sets the vertical position of the cue text.

The align attribute aligns the text within the cue.

WebVTT files start with the WEBVTT statement.

The cue label identifies the track cue.

The cue text is the text displayed in the video window.

Cue text can be marked as classes using the <c> </c> tag.

```
WEBVTT

Title
00:00.500 --> 00:04.000 line:5% align:middle
<c.Main>The Ceiling Dance</c>

Subtitle
00:04.500 --> 00:08.000 line:5% align:middle
from Royal Wedding (1951)

Ending
01:38.000 --> 01:44.000 line:80% position:95% align:end
See more videos at <i>Cinema Penguin</i>
```

The position attribute sets the horizontal position of the cue text.

Each track cue is identified with a label, the time interval in which the cue is displayed, and the text of the cue.

Playing Web Video

The cue pseudo-element selects the cues from the media track.

```css
::cue {
    background: rgba(0, 0, 0, 0.3);
    color: orange;
    font: 1.2em serif;
}

::cue(.Main) {
    text-shadow: black 3px 3px 0px;
    font: 2.5em serif;
}
```

The cue text is from the Main class.

In Focus

The high point of *Royal Wedding* is the C
Astaire appears to dance on the ceiling a
room. The effect was accomplished by p
inside of a rotating cage with fixed came
turned, Astaire would seamlessly dance
the box, creating the illusion of weightlessness.

Click the play button to view this classic dance sequence.

The Ceiling Dance

The Title cue text as rendered in the video window.

Native media player provided by the browser to play video files.

CC (closed captioning) button is used to display captions within the video player.

0:03

Source: wiki

The media player displays controls for video playback.

Exploring Digital Video

In this session, you explore how to embed video within your web pages. Before exploring the HTML `video` elements, you examine some of the issues involved with producing video files suitable for the web.

Video Formats and Codecs

A video file typically contains two codecs: one codec for audio and another for the video images. The audio codecs are the same ones you examined in the last session. Figure 8-11 describes the most commonly used video codecs on the web.

Figure 8-11 **Video codecs used on the web**

Codec	Description
H.264	Developed by the MPEG group, the **H.264** codec is the industry standard for high-definition video streams, movie sharing websites such as YouTube, and video plug-ins
Theora	**Theora** is a royalty-free codec developed by the Xiph.org Foundation that produces video streams that can be used with almost any container
VP8	**VP8** is an open-source royalty-free codec owned by Google for use in Google's WebM video format
VP9	**VP9** is Google's successor to the VP8 codec, offering the same video quality as VP8 at half the download size

The most popular video codec is H.264 used by YouTube and most commercial vendors; however, because H.264 is a commercial product, it is not royalty free. This is not an issue if you are creating a video that is not actually being sold. If you are creating a commercial video that uses the H.264 codec, you might have to pay licensing fees depending on the number of subscribers to your video content. The Theora, VP8, and VP9 codecs are royalty free, but they are not as widely supported at the time of this writing.

Browser support for video containers is focused on three formats: MP4, Ogg, and WebM, with multiple combinations of video and audio codecs available within each container. Figure 8-12 summarizes these formats and their use on the web.

Figure 8-12 **Video formats used on the web**

Format	Description	Video Codec	File Extension(s)	MIME Type
MPEG-4	**MPEG-4** or **MP4** is a widely used proprietary format developed by Apple based on the Apple QuickTime movie format	H.264	.mp4 .m4v	video/mp4
Ogg	**Ogg** is an open source format developed by the Xiph.org Foundation using the Theora codec as an alternative to the MPEG-4 codec	Theora	.ogg	video/ogg
WebM	**WebM** is an open source format introduced by Google to provide royalty-free video and audio to be used with the HTML5 video element	VP8 VP9	.webm	video/webm

Video content suffers the same limitation as audio content in that no single format has universal support among all browsers and devices. Thus, as with audio content, you may have to supply multiple versions of the same video if you want the widest cross-browser support. See Figure 8-13.

Figure 8-13   **Browser support for video formats**

Browser	MPEG-4	Ogg	WebM
Chrome (desktop)	✓	✓	✓
Chrome (mobile)	✓	✓	✓
Firefox (desktop)	✓	✓	✓
Firefox (mobile)	✓	✓	✓
Microsoft Edge (desktop)	✓		
Internet Explorer (desktop)	✓		
Internet Explorer (mobile)	✓		
Opera (desktop)	✓	✓	✓
Opera (mobile)	✓		✓
Safari (desktop)	✓		
Safari (mobile)	✓		

The level of support for video formats is constantly changing as are the video formats themselves. As always, the best way to determine whether a browser supports a particular video format is to test the video file on that browser.

Using the HTML5 `video` Element

Videos are embedded into a web page using the following `video` element

```
<video attributes>
   <source src="url1" type="mime-type" />
   <source src="url2" type="mime-type" />
   …
</video>
```

where `attributes` are the HTML attributes that control the behavior and appearance of the video playback, `url1`, `url2`, and so on are the possible sources of the video, and `mime-type` specifies the format associated with each video file. As with sources for the `audio` element, a browser uses the first source it finds in a format it supports. Fallback content can also be added after the list of video sources for browsers that don't support HTML5 video. The `video` element supports many of the same attributes used within the `audio` element shown earlier in Figure 8-2.

The following code embeds two possible video files on the web page with a fallback message for browsers that don't support the `video` element:

```
<video controls>
   <source src="cp_dance5.mp4" type="video/mp4" />
   <source src="cp_dance5.webm" type="video/webm" />
   <p><em>To play this video clip, your browser needs
   to support HTML5.</em></p>
</video>
```

Maxine has a video clip of a classic dance sequence from *Royal Wedding* in which Fred Astaire appears to dance on the walls and ceiling of his hotel room. She has two versions of the clip: one in MP4 format and the other in the WebM format. Use the `video` element now to embed these videos on her web page.

To embed a video file into the web page:

1. If you took a break after the previous session, make sure the **cp_royal.html** file is open in your editor.

2. Scroll down to the aside element titled In Focus and add the following code directly before the closing </aside> tag:

```
<p>Click the play button to view this classic dance
sequence.</p>
<video controls>
   <source src="cp_dance.mp4" type="video/mp4" />
   <source src="cp_dance.webm" type="video/webm" />
   <p><em>To play this video clip, your browser needs to
      support HTML5.</em></p>
</video>
```

Figure 8-14 highlights the code for the embedded video.

Figure 8-14	Adding a video clip to a web page

```
<aside>
  <h1>In Focus</h1>
  <p>The high point of <cite>Royal Wedding</cite> is the <cite>Ceiling Dance</cite>
     in which Astaire appears to  dance on the ceiling and walls
     of his hotel room. The effect was accomplished by putting the whole set
     inside of a rotating cage with fixed camera mount.
     As the cage turned, Astaire
     would seamlessly dance across the four sides of the box, creating the
     illusion of weightlessness.
  </p>
  <p>Click the play button to view this classic dance sequence.</p>
  <video controls>
    <source src="cp_dance.mp4" type="video/mp4" />
    <source src="cp_dance.webm" type="video/webm" />
    <p><em>To play this video clip, your browser needs to support HTML5.</em></p>
  </video>
</aside>
```

displays the browser's native media player

sources for the video clip

fallback text for browsers that don't support HTML5 video

3. Save your changes to the file.

   Next, you modify the cp_media.css style sheet file to format the appearance of the video media player for your browser.

4. Go to the **mp_media.css** file in your editor.

5. Modify the style rule for the audio element by adding the **video** selector.

   Figure 8-15 highlights the modified style rule.

Figure 8-15   Defining the video player styles

add video to the
style rule selector

```css
audio, video {
    box-shadow: rgb(51, 51, 51) 8px 8px 15px;
    display: block;
    margin: 10px auto;
    width: 90%;
}
```

6. Save your changes to the style sheet and then reopen the **cp_royal.html** file in your browser.

7. Click the play button on your browser's media player to play the video clip.

Figure 8-16 shows the video clip in action as it replays the ceiling dance sequence from *Royal Wedding*.

Figure 8-16   Video clip embedded in the web page

In Focus

The high point of *Royal Wedding* is the *Ceiling Dance* in which Astaire appears to dance on the ceiling and walls of his hotel room. The effect was accomplished by putting the whole set inside of a rotating cage with fixed camera mount. As the cage turned, Astaire would seamlessly dance across the four sides of the box, creating the illusion of weightlessness.

Click the play button to view this classic dance sequence.

first frame of the
video is used as
the preview image

1:44

video player
controls

When the media player initially loads a video file, the player shows the first video frame as a preview of the video's content. Maxine would like to replace that preview image with an image of Astaire dancing on his apartment room's wall. To define the video's preview image, you apply the following `poster` attribute to the `video` element

```
<video poster="url">
...
</video>
```

where `url` points to an image file containing the preview image. The `poster` attribute is also used as a placeholder image that is displayed when the video is still being downloaded or used in place of the video if the browser fails to download the video file at all.

Maxine suggests you use the cp_photo2.png file as the poster image for the video clip.

To set the video's poster image:

1. Return to the **cp_royal.html** file in your editor.

2. Add the following attribute to the `video` element: **poster="cp_photo2.png"**.

   Figure 8-17 highlights the poster attribute.

Figure 8-17 Defining a poster image for the video

preview image of the video clip

```
<video controls poster="cp_photo2.png">
   <source src="cp_dance.mp4" type="video/mp4" />
   <source src="cp_dance.webm" type="video/webm" />
   <p><em>To play this video clip, your browser needs to support HTML5.</em></p>
</video>
```

3. Save your changes to the file and then reload cp_royal.html in your browser.

   Figure 8-18 shows the poster image applied to the video of the ceiling dance sequence.

Figure 8-18 Video clip poster image

image displayed prior to playing the video

Source: wiki

Maxine suggests that the video clip would benefit from some descriptive captions. Rather than modifying the video clip itself, you can add those captions using media tracks.

Adding a Text Track to Video

With the increased reliance on multimedia on the web comes the responsibility of making audio and video content accessible to all users. This can be done by adding a text track to the media clip that can be read or recited to visually impaired users. Text tracks are added to an audio or video clip using the following `track` element

```
<track kind="type" src="url" label="text" srclang="lang" />
```

where the `kind` attribute defines the `track` type, the `src` attribute references a file containing the track text, the `label` attribute gives the track name, and the `srclang` attribute indicates the language of the track. A single media clip might be associated with multiple track types as indicated by the value of the `kind` attribute. Figure 8-19 lists the different kinds of tracks that can be associated with an audio or video file.

Figure 8-19	Values of the kind attribute

Kind Value	Description
captions	Brief text descriptions synced to specified time points within the media clip; designed for hearing impaired users
chapters	Chapter titles used by the media player to navigate the user to specific time points within the media clip
descriptions	Longer descriptions synced to specified time points within the media clip; designed for visually impaired users
subtitles	(the default) Translation of dialog from the media clip; the language of the subtitle must be specified in the srclang attribute
metadata	Metadata content used by external scripts accessing the media file

For example, the following code attaches six tracks to the story.mp4 video file:

```
<video controls>
   <source src="story.mp4" type="video/mp4" />
   <track kind="captions" src="captions.vtt" label=" Captions" />
   <track kind="chapters" src="chapters.vtt" label="Chapters" />
   <track kind="subtitles" src="english.vtt" srclang="en"
default />
   <track kind="subtitles" src="french.vtt" srclang="fr" />
   <track kind="subtitles" src="spanish.vtt" srclang="es" />
   <track kind="descriptions" src="summary.vtt" label="Summary" />
</video>
```

The tracks contain captions, chapter titles, subtitles in English, French, and Spanish, and finally a track that summarizes the contents of the video. The media player can only show one of these tracks at a time. The active track by is marked with the `default` attribute, which enables that track and disables all of the other tracks. In this case, the track English subtitles is enabled while all of the other tracks are disabled. The user can choose a different track from the media player, usually by selecting the track from one of the media player controls. Note that the `default` attribute is required, even if the track list contains only one track.

Making Tracks with WebVTT

Tracks are stored as simple text files written in the **Web Video Text Tracks** or **WebVTT** language. The format of a WebVTT file follows the structure

```
WEBVTT

cue1

cue2
…
```

where *cue1*, *cue2*, and so on are cues matched with specific time intervals within the media clip. Note that the list of cues is separated by a single blank line after the cue text. Unlike HTML, white space is not ignored in WebVTT files.

Each cue has the general form

```
label
start --> stop
cue text
```

where *label* is the name assigned to the cue, *start* and *stop* define the time interval associated with the cue, and *cue text* is the text of the cue. Times are entered in the format *mm:ss.ms* for the minutes, seconds, and milliseconds values. For longer clips, you can include an hours value, writing the time in the form *hh:mm:ss.ms*.

The following code adds two cues to the WebVTT file:

```
WEBVTT

Intro
00:00.500 --> 00:09.000
Once upon a time

Conclusion
14:20.000 --> 14:30.000
And they all lived happily ever after
```

The Intro cue, "Once upon a time", starts at the half-second mark and runs through the 9-second mark; the Conclusion cue, "And they all lived happily ever after", covers the time interval from 14 minutes 20 seconds through 14 minutes 30 seconds of the clip.

Create a track file now for the ceiling dance video displaying a title and subtitle at the start of the video and an advertisement for Cinema Penguin near the end.

To create a track file:

1. Use a text editor to open the **cp_captions_txt.vtt** file from the html08 ▶ tutorial folder. Save this blank text file as **cp_captions.vtt**.

2. In the first line of the file, enter **WEBVTT**.

3. Insert a blank line followed by the text for the Title cue spanning the interval from the first half-second up to the fourth second:

   ```
   Title
   00:00.500 --> 00:04.000
   The Ceiling Dance
   ```

4. Insert a blank line followed by the Subtitle cue in the interval from 4.5 seconds through 8 seconds:

```
Subtitle
00:04.500 --> 00:08.000
from Royal Wedding (1951)
```

5. Insert a blank line followed by the Ending cue in the interval from 1 minute 38 seconds through 1 minute 44 seconds:

```
Ending
01:38.000 --> 01:44.000
See more videos at Cinema Penguin
```

Figure 8-20 describes the contents of the cp_captions.vtt file.

Figure 8-20   WebVTT file to define track text

6. Save your changes to the file.

Next, you apply the cp_captions.vtt file to the dance sequence video. If you are testing your page on Google Chrome or Opera, be aware that you will have to upload your files to a web server. Neither of these browsers will open track files stored locally.

To add captions to a video clip:

1. Return to the **cp_royal.html** file in your editor and scroll down to the video element.

2. Directly after the second source element, insert the following track:

```
<track kind="captions" label="Dance Captions"
  src="cp_captions.vtt" default />
```

Figure 8-21 highlights the HTML code for the track.

Figure 8-21 Applying a track to a video clip

displays the track text as a caption

caption label

source of caption text

enables the track for display in the media player

```
<video controls poster="cp_photo2.png">
   <source src="cp_dance.mp4" type="video/mp4" />
   <source src="cp_dance.webm" type="video/webm" />
   <track kind="captions" label="Dance Captions" src="cp_captions.vtt" default />
   <p><em>To play this video clip, your browser needs to support HTML5.</em></p>
</video>
```

3. Save your changes to the file and then reload cp_royal.html in your browser. If you are using Google Chrome or Opera, upload your files to a web server for testing.

4. Click the play button on your browser's media player and, if necessary, click the Closed Captioning button to display the video captions. Verify that captions appear at the half-second, 4.5 second, and 1 minute 38 second marks in the video.

Figure 8-22 shows the final caption from the video clip.

Figure 8-22 Caption in the ceiling dance movie

ending caption

select to display captions in the media player

Trouble? If you don't see any captions, check the code in your WebVTT file against the code shown in Figure 8-20. Make sure your text matches that figure because the WebVTT syntax must be strictly followed.

By default, the caption cues are centered at the bottom of the video window. To change the position of the cues, you can edit the settings in the WebVTT file, as discussed next.

Placing the Cue Text

The size and position of the cue text can be set by adding the following cue settings directly after the cue's time interval

```
setting1:value1 setting2:value2 …
```

where *setting1*, *setting2*, and so on define the size and position of the cue text and *value1*, *value2*, and so on are the setting values. Note that there is no space between the setting name and value. Figure 8-23 describes the different settings supported in the WebVTT language.

Figure 8-23   Cue attributes in WebVTT

Cue Setting	Description
align:*value*	Sets the horizontal alignment of the text within the cue, where *value* is start (left-aligned), middle (center-aligned), or end (right-aligned)
line:*value*	Sets the vertical position of the cue within the video window, where *value* ranges from 0% (top) to 100% (bottom)
position:*value*	Sets the horizontal position of the cue within the video window, where *value* ranges from 0% (left) to 100% (right)
size:*value*	Sets the width of the cue as a percentage of the width of the video window
vertical:*type*	Displays the cue text vertically rather than horizontally where *type* is rl (writing direction is right to left) or lr (writing direction is left to right)

TIP

To center the cue in the video window, set the line and position values to 50% and the align value to middle.

By applying the line and align settings, the Intro cue in the following track is placed at the top of the video window and centered horizontally. By applying the line, position, and align settings, the Conclusion cue is placed at the bottom-left corner of the video window with the cue text left-aligned. Note that the default placement of the cue is the bottom center of the video window.

```
Intro
00:00.500 --> 00:09.000 line:0% align:middle
Once upon a time

Conclusion
14:20.000 --> 14:30.000 line:100% position:0% align:start
And they all lived happily ever after
```

Maxine suggests that you center the Title and Subtitle cues for the ceiling dance video near the top of the video window and place the Ending cue near the bottom-right corner with the text right-aligned.

To position the track cues:

1. Return to the **cp_captions.vtt** file in your editor.

2. After the time intervals for the Title and Subtitle cues, insert the attributes:

   ```
   line:5% align:middle
   ```

3. After the time interval for the Ending cue, insert the attributes:

   ```
   line:80% position:95% align:end
   ```

   Figure 8-24 highlights the attributes for each cue within the track.

Figure 8-24 **Placing the cue text**

places the Title and Subtitle cues near the top of the video window with the text centered

```
Title
00:00.500 --> 00:00:04.000 line:5% align:middle
The Ceiling Dance

Subtitle
00:04.500 --> 00:00:08.000 line:5% align:middle
from Royal Wedding (1951)

Ending
01:38.000 --> 00:01:44.000 line:80% position:95% align:end
See more videos at Cinema Penguin
```

places the Ending cue near the bottom-right corner of the video window with the text right-aligned

4. Save your changes to the file and then reload the cp_royal.html file in your browser. If you are using Google Chrome or Opera, upload your files to a web server for testing.

5. Play the video clip and verify that the Title and Subtitle cues appear centered near the top of the video window and the Ending cue appears near the bottom-right corner of the window.

   Trouble? If the cues have not changed position, check your code against the code in Figure 8-24. Make sure you have not entered a space between the attribute name and the attribute value or placed the values on a new line. At the time of this writing, Microsoft Edge and Internet Explorer do not support positioning the track cues.

The WebVTT settings do not include styles to format the appearance of the cue text, but you can create such styles using CSS. Note that browser support for such styles is mixed; therefore you should not make these styles crucial to users' interpretation of the video cues text.

Applying Styles to Track Cues

CSS supports the following cue pseudo-element to format the appearance of the cues appearing within a media clip:

```
::cue {
    styles
}
```

Styles for the cue pseudo-element are limited to the background, color, font, opacity, outline, text-decoration, text-shadow, visibility, and white-space properties. For example, the following style rule displays all cues in a 2em yellow serif font on a red background:

```
::cue {
    background: red;
    color: yellow;
    font: 2em serif;
}
```

Use the cue pseudo-element to change the format of the captions in the ceiling dance video to an orange color on a semi-transparent black background. Set the size and type of the caption text to a 1.2em serif font.

To format the cue text:

1. Return to the **cp_media.css** file in your editor and scroll down to the Track Styles section.

2. Add the following style rule:

```
::cue {
    background: rgba(0, 0, 0, 0.3);
    color: orange;
    font: 1.2em serif;
}
```

Figure 8-25 highlights the style rule for cue text.

Figure 8-25 ▸ **Applying styles to cue text**

selects the cue text from the media clip

changes the background to semi-transparent black

```
/* Track Styles */

::cue {
    background: rgba(0, 0, 0, 0.3);
    color: orange;
    font: 1.2em serif;
}
```

3. Save your changes to the style sheet and then reload the cp_royal.html file in your browser. If you are using Google Chrome or Opera, upload your files to a web server for testing.

4. Play the video clip and verify that the captions appear in a serif orange font on a semi-transparent black background.

   Trouble? At the time of this writing, only Google Chrome and Opera support styles that modify the color and typeface of the cue text. Safari supports styles to change the font size. Internet Explorer and Firefox do not support any cue styles.

The cue pseudo-element selects all of the cue text in the media clip. To format specific cues or text strings within a cue you identify sections of the cue text using the following markup tags:

- <i></i> for italicized text
- <b></b> for bold-faced text
- <u></u> for underlined text
- <span></span> to mark spans of text
- <ruby></ruby> to mark ruby text
- <rt></rt> to mark ruby text

For example, the following code italicizes the name of the website using the <i></i> tag

```
Ending
01:38.000 --> 01:44.000
See more videos at <i>Cinema Penguin</i>
```

TIP

Ruby text refers to annotative characters placed above or to the right of other characters and is often used with Chinese or Japanese symbols.

WebVTT also supports tags that are not part of the HTML library, such as the following <c></c> tag used to mark text strings belonging to a particular class

```
<c.classname></c>
```

where *classname* defines the class.

And for captions that distinguish between one voice and another, WebVTT supports the following <v></v> tag

```
<v name></v>
```

where *name* is the name of the voice associated with the caption. The following track shows how to apply the <c></c> and <v></v> tags to mark scenes and the voices of Bernardo and Francisco from the opening of *Hamlet*.

```
Cue1
00:00.000 --> 00:05.000
<c.scene>Elsinore. A platform before the castle</c>

Cue2
00:05.500 --> 00:12.000
<v Bernardo>Who's there?</v>
<v Francisco>Nay, answer me: stand, and unfold yourself.</v>

Cue3
00:12.500 --> 00:18.000
<v Bernardo>Long live the king!</v>
<v Francisco>Bernardo?</v>
```

For cues based on their class name, add the class name to the cue pseudo-element as follows

```
::cue(.classname) {
    style rules
}
```

where *classname* is the class marked within in the <c></c> tag.

To format voice text, use the style rule

```
::cue(v[voice=name]) {
    style rules
}
```

where *name* is the name assigned in the <v></v> tag.

Thus, the following style rules display the scene and voices from the opening scene in *Hamlet* using red for the scene direction text, blue for Bernardo's voice, and green for Francisco's voice:

```
::cue(.scene) {color: red;}
::cue(v[voice=Bernardo]) {color: blue;}
::cue(v[voice=Francisco]) {color: green;}
```

Maxine suggests that the opening Title caption be displayed in a larger font with a drop shadow and that the website in the ending cue be italicized. Mark the caption text using the <c></c> tag belonging to the Main class and italicize the name of the website. Then, add the appropriate style rule to your style sheet.

To apply styles to cue text:

▶ **1.** Return to the **cp_captions.vtt** file in your editor.

▶ **2.** Enclose the cue text for the Title cue within <c> tags with the class name **Main**.

3. Go to the Ending cue and enclose *Cinema Penguin* within opening and closing `<i>` tags.

Figure 8-26 highlights the revised code in the file.

Figure 8-26   **Applying a class to cue text**

```
WEBVTT


Title
00:00.500 --> 00:04.000 line:5% align:middle
<c.Main>The Ceiling Dance</c>

Subtitle
00:04.500 --> 00:08.000 line:5% align:middle
from Royal Wedding (1951)

Ending
01:38.000 --> 01:44.000 line:80% position:95% align:end
See more videos at <i>Cinema Penguin</i>
```

markup tag for the Main class

displays the website title in italics

4. Save your changes to the file and then return to the **cp_media.css** in your editor.

5. Scroll to the bottom of the file and add the following style rule:

```
::cue(.Main) {
   text-shadow: black 3px 3px 0px;
   font: 2.5em serif;
}
```

Figure 8-27 highlights the style rule for cues belonging to the Main class.

Figure 8-27   **Styling cues based on class name**

```
::cue {
   background: rgba(0, 0, 0, 0.3);
   color: orange;
   font: 1.2em serif;
}

::cue(.Main) {
   text-shadow: black 3px 3px 0px;
   font: 2.5em serif;
}
```

selector for cue text belonging to the Main class

6. Save your changes to the file and then reload the cp_royal.html file in your browser. If you are using Google Chrome or Opera, upload your files to a web server for testing.

7. Play the ceiling dance video and note that the first caption is displayed in a larger font with a black drop shadow. See Figure 8-28.

Figure 8-28 **Formatted text from the Title cue**

Title cue is displayed in a larger font with a black text shadow

Click the play button to view this classic dance sequence.

The Ceiling Dance

0:02

Trouble? At the time of this writing, only Google Chrome and Opera support all of the text styles used to format captions. Safari will apply the larger font size. Internet Explorer and Firefox do not support styling caption text.

Maxine likes your work in creating and formatting the ceiling dance video clip. However, she would like to review other options for embedding multimedia content on her website.

Using Third-Party Video Players

Prior to the widespread adoption of HTML5 for embedded video, browsers used plug-ins using the following `object` element

```
<object attributes>
   parameters
</object>
```

where *attributes* define the object and *parameters* are values passed to the object controlling the object's appearance and actions. The `object` element, which replaced the `embed` element introduced in the last session, could be used for any type of content—from sound and video clips to graphic images, PDF files, and even the content of other web pages.

The parameters of the object are defined using the following `param` element

```
<param name="name" value="value" />
```

where the *name* is the name of the parameter and the *value* is the parameter's value. There is no standard list of parameter names and values because they are based on the plug-in used to display the object. For example, the following `object` element could be used in place of the `embed` element you studied in the first session to insert the cp_overture.mp3 audio clip:

```
<object data="overture.mp3" type="audio/mp3"
        height="20" width="250">
   <param name="src" value="cp_overture.mp3" />
</object>
```

The presumption is that content of the audio/mp3 mime-type would be associated with a plug-in that the browser would run to play the audio clip using the `src` and `value` attributes of the `param` element. Thus, the page's author would have to know how to work with the individual plug-ins and provide workarounds for the different plug-ins the user may have installed.

Exploring the Flash Player

Perhaps the most-used plug-in for video playback was the Adobe Flash player, which was embedded using the following `object` element

```
<object data="url"
        type="application/x-shockwave-flash"
        width="value" height="value">
   <param name="movie" value="url" />
   parameters
</object>
```

where *url* is the location and filename of the file containing the Flash video, and *parameters* are the other `param` elements that manage the appearance and actions of the player. Notice that you must always include at least the movie parameter to identify the video file to be played in the Flash player. Figure 8-29 lists some of the other parameters recognized by the Adobe Flash Player.

Figure 8-29   **Parameters of the Flash player**

Name	Value(s)	Description
bgcolor	*color value*	Sets the background color of the player
flashvar	*text*	Contains text values that are passed to the player as variables to control the behavior and content of the movie
id	*text*	Identifies the movie so that it can be referenced
loop	true | false	Plays the movie in a continuous loop
menu	true | false	Displays a popup menu when a user right-clicks the player
name	*text*	Names the movie so that it can be referenced
play	true | false	Starts the player when the page loads
quality	low | autolow | autohigh | medium | high | best	Sets the playback quality of the movie; low values favor playback speed over display quality; high values favor display quality over playback speed
scale	showall | noborder | exactfit	Defines how the movie clip is scaled within the defined space; a value of showall makes the entire clip visible in the specified area without distortion; a value of noborder scales the movie to fill the specified area without distortion but possibly with some cropping; a value of exactfit makes the entire movie visible in the specified area without trying to preserve the original aspect ratio
wmode	window | opaque | transparent	Sets the appearance of the player against the page background; a value of window causes the movie to play within its own window; a value of opaque hides everything behind the player; a value of transparent allows the page background to show through transparent colors in the player

The Flash player can act as a fallback for older browsers that don't support HTML5 by nesting the `object` element within the `audio` or `video` element. The following code demonstrates how the Flash video from the cp_dance.swf file can be set as a fallback video for browsers that can't play either the cp_dance.mp4 or cp_dance.webm files using a native media player:

```
<video controls>
    <source src="cp_dance.mp4" type="video/mp4" />
    <source src="cp_dance.webm" type="video/webm" />
    <object data="cp_dance.swf"
            type="application/x-shockwave-flash"
            width="320" height="240">
        <param name="movie" value="cp_dance.swf" />
        <param name="quality" value="high" />
        <p>You must have the Flash Player to play
           the video clip</p>
    </object>
</video>
```

TIP

To hide the Flash player, set the width and height values to 0.

Note that within the `object` element is a final fallback message for users with browsers that cannot play the video clip in any of the formats.

Maxine decides against providing a Flash version of the ceiling dance movie because she feels that the browser support for HTMl5 video is sufficient for users of her website.

Embedding Videos from YouTube

The biggest supplier of online videos is YouTube with over 1 billion users and 4 billion views per day. YouTube videos are easy to embed in your web page using YouTube's HTML5 video player, which supports a wide variety of video formats and codecs including H.264, WebM VP8, and WebM VP9.

To share a YouTube video, bring up the video on the YouTube site and click the Share button below the video player. YouTube provides options to post a hypertext link to the video to a multitude of social media sites or to share the link via e-mail. To embed the video within your website, click Embed, which brings up a preview of the embedded player and the HTML code you need to add to your web page. Figure 8-30 shows the embed options on the YouTube website for the full movie version of *Royal Wedding*.

Figure 8-30   Sharing a YouTube video

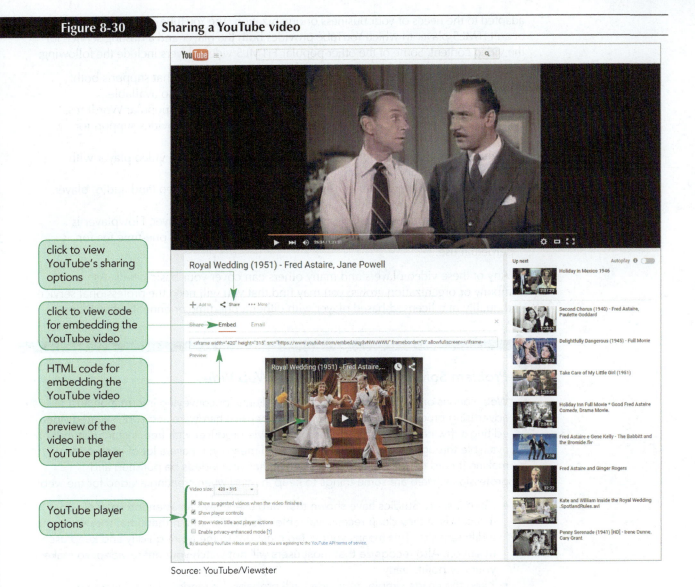

click to view YouTube's sharing options

click to view code for embedding the YouTube video

HTML code for embedding the YouTube video

preview of the video in the YouTube player

YouTube player options

Source: YouTube/Viewster

The general code for the embedded player is

```
<iframe width="value" height="value" src="url"
        frameborder="0" allowfullscreen>
</iframe>
```

where *url* provides the link to the YouTube video, while the width and height attributes define the dimensions of the player embedded on your web page. The frameborder attribute sets the width of the border around the player in pixels. The allowfullscreen attribute allows the user to play the video in fullscreen mode. Finally, the **iframe element** itself is used to mark **inline frames**, which are windows embedded within the web page that display the content of another page or Internet resource. Please note that any videos submitted to YouTube are still subject to copyright restrictions and might be removed if those restrictions are violated.

HTML5 Video Players

Rather than using your browser's native video player, you can use one of the many commercial and free HTML5 video players on the market. Unlike plug-ins, which are applications distinct from your browser, an HTML5 video player works within your browser with CSS and JavaScript files to present a customizable player that can be adapted to the needs of your business or organization. The YouTube player is one example of an HTML5 player in which YouTube provides both the player and a hosting service for the video content. Some of the other popular HTML5 video players include the following:

- **JWPlayer** (*www.jwplayer.com*) A popular commercial player that supports both HTML5 and Flash video. A free non-commercial version is also available.
- **Video.js** (*www.videojs.com*) A free player that works with the popular WordPress HTML framework. Video.js is extremely customizable and provides support for captions and subtitles.
- **MediaElement.js** (*mediaelementjs.com*) An HTML5 audio and video player with support for Flash and Microsoft Silverlight.
- **Projekktor** (*www.projekktor.com*) A free and open source video (and audio) player. Projekktor also includes support for embedded playlists.
- **Flowplayer** (*flowplayer.org*) Originally marketed as a Flash player, Flowplayer is a commercially licensed audio and video player, payable as a one-time fee for perpetual use.

Any of these video players and many others can cover your basic needs. As your company or organization grows, you may find that you will need the professional service and quality of a licensed-based player with either a one-time or annual subscription.

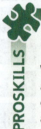

PROSKILLS

Problem Solving: Tips for Effective Web Video

Web video is one of the most important mediums for conveying information and advertising products and services. With inexpensive hardware and sophisticated video editing software, almost anyone can be a movie producer with free, instant distribution available through the web. However, this also means you have a lot of competition, making it hard to get noticed; it is essential that your videos be polished and professional. Here are some things to keep in mind when creating a video for the web:

- *Keep it short.* Studies have shown that web users have an attention span of about 4 seconds. If they don't receive valuable information within that time, they will go to a different site. This means your video must get to the point quickly and keep users' attention. Also recognize that most users will not watch your entire video, so make your key points early.
- *Keep the image simple.* Your video will probably be rendered in a tiny frame, so make your content easier to view by shooting close-ups. Avoid wide-angle shots that will make your subject even smaller to the user's eye. Avoid complex backgrounds and distracting color schemes.
- *Keep the human element.* Eye-tracking studies have shown that people naturally gravitate to human faces for information and emotional content. Use tight shots in which the narrator speaks directly into the camera.
- *Use effective lighting.* Light should be projected onto the subject. Avoid relying solely on overhead lights, which can create distracting facial shadows. Video compression can result in loss of detail; thus, make sure you use bright lighting on key areas to highlight and focus users' attention on the important images in your video.
- *Follow the rule of thirds.* Avoid static layouts by imagining the frame divided into a 3 × 3 grid. Balance items of interest along the lines of the intersection in the grid rather than centered within the frame. If interviewing a subject, leave ample headroom at the top of the frame.
- *Avoid pans and zooms.* Excessive panning and zooming can make your video appear choppy and distorted, and unnecessary movement slows down the video stream.

Finally, consider investing in professional video services that can storyboard an idea for you and that have the experience and expertise to create a finished product that will capture and keep the attention of users and customers.

Maxine is pleased with the work you have done embedding the dance sequence video in the *Royal Wedding* page. In the next session, you will explore how to make your websites come alive with transitions and interactive animation.

REVIEW

Session 8.2 Quick Check

1. Provide code to embed the chapter1.mp4 or chapter1.webm videos into the web page. Have the browser's native media player displayed on the page.
2. Provide the code to display the image file dickens.png as the preview image for a video clip.
3. Provide the code to insert a subtitle track named "Spanish Version" using the track text in the spanish.vtt file and the Spanish source language. Make this the active track in the video clip.
4. Provide the code for a track cue in the WebVTT language with the name "Intro" and spanning the time interval from 1 second to 8.3 seconds. Have the cue contain the text "It was the best of times …"
5. Revise the code in the previous question using the `line`, `position`, and `align` attributes so that the Intro cue is displayed in the top-left corner of the video window and the cue text left-aligned.
6. Provide a style rule to display cue text in a red 1.3em cursive font on a gray background.
7. Provide the code to mark the cue text "It was the best of times …" as belonging to the voice of the narrator.
8. Provide the code to display text in the narrator voice with a white font.

Session 8.3 Visual Overview:

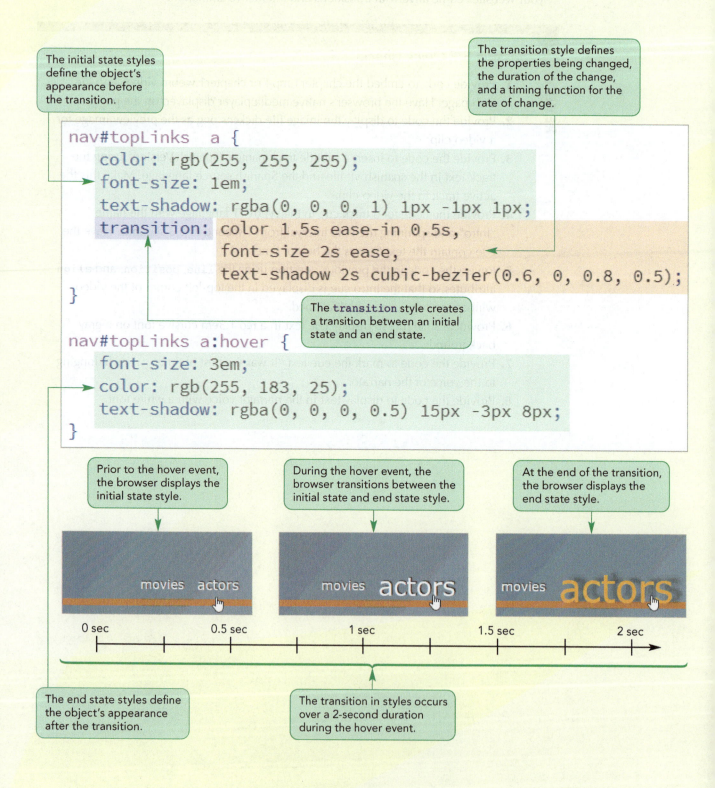

The initial state styles define the object's appearance before the transition.

The transition style defines the properties being changed, the duration of the change, and a timing function for the rate of change.

```
nav#topLinks  a {
    color: rgb(255, 255, 255);
    font-size: 1em;
    text-shadow: rgba(0, 0, 0, 1) 1px -1px 1px;
    transition: color 1.5s ease-in 0.5s,
                font-size 2s ease,
                text-shadow 2s cubic-bezier(0.6, 0, 0.8, 0.5);
}

nav#topLinks a:hover {
    font-size: 3em;
    color: rgb(255, 183, 25);
    text-shadow: rgba(0, 0, 0, 0.5) 15px -3px 8px;
}
```

The **transition** style creates a transition between an initial state and an end state.

Prior to the hover event, the browser displays the initial state style.

During the hover event, the browser transitions between the initial state and end state style.

At the end of the transition, the browser displays the end state style.

movies actors

movies actors

movies actors

0 sec   0.5 sec   1 sec   1.5 sec   2 sec

The end state styles define the object's appearance after the transition.

The transition in styles occurs over a 2-second duration during the hover event.

Transitions and Animations

Each key frame has a progress value and a style rule.

The @keyframes rule defines the key frame styles used in an animation.

A name of "spin" is assigned to the animation.

The spin animation rotates the video player.

```css
@keyframes spin {
    0%      {transform: rotate(0deg);}
    23%     {transform: rotate(0deg);}
    28%     {transform: rotate(90deg);}
    39%     {transform: rotate(90deg);}
    42%     {transform: rotate(180deg);}
    68%     {transform: rotate(180deg);}
    72%     {transform: rotate(270deg);}
    90%     {transform: rotate(270deg);}
    94%     {transform: rotate(360deg);}
    100%    {transform: rotate(360deg);}
}

video {
    animation: spin 104.04s linear infinite;
}

input#rotateVideo:checked~video {
    animation-play-state: running;
}

input#rotateVideo:not(:checked)~video {
    animation-play-state: paused;
}
```

The spin animation is applied to the video element.

Linear timing applies the transition at a constant rate.

The animation lasts 104.04 seconds.

The animation style applies a key frame animation to an object.

The animation-play-state style defines whether the animation is running or is paused.

A value of "infinite" causes the animation to run continuously.

Source: wiki

Creating Transitions with CSS

In this session, you explore how to use CSS transitions and animations to add movement and action to your websites without relying on video files or external plug-ins. You start by examining how to create a CSS transition.

Introducing Transitions

A **transition** is a change in an object's style from an initial state to an ending state, usually in response to an event initiated by the user or the browser. You have already worked with this type of effect starting in Tutorial 2 when you employed the `hover` pseudo-class to change the style of a hypertext link in response to the user moving the mouse pointer over a hypertext link. However, the hover effect is instantaneous with no intermediate steps. If the background color of the link were to change from white to black, there is no instant in which the background is gray. A transition on the other hand, slows down that change and provides intermediate styles so that a white background gradually changes into black, passing through different shades of gray (see Figure 8-31).

Figure 8-31 Transition from an initial state to an end state

no transition in color between the initial and end states

gradual transition in color between the initial and end state

To create this type of transition, you employ the following `transition` style

```
transition: property duration;
```

where *property* is a property of the object that changes between the initial and end states and *duration* is the transition time in seconds or milliseconds. The following style rules use the `transition` style to create a transition for the background style as the hypertext link goes from an initial state to an end state (hovered) over a 4-second interval:

TIP

To specify a time in milliseconds, use the "ms" unit.

```
a {
   background: white;
   color: black;
   transition: background 4s;
}
```

```
a:hover {
   background: green;
   color: white;
}
```

In this example, the background color gradually changes from white to light green and then progressively to darker shades of green. This transition happens over the 4-second transition, during which the intermediate states showing the changes in color are displayed (see Figure 8-32).

Figure 8-32   Applying a transition to the background

Note that only the background changes in the intermediate states. The text color stays black until the end state is reached because the `color` property is not included in the transition. To apply the transition to more than one property, enter the properties and their duration times in the following comma-separated list:

```
transition: background 4s, color 4s;
```

In this example, the background color changes gradually from white to dark green at the same time that the font color changes gradually from black to white (see Figure 8-33).

Figure 8-33   Applying a transition to the background and text color

The duration values for multiple properties does not need to be the same: one property could change over a 4-second interval while another property might change over 3 seconds (in which case it would reach its end state a full second before the other property).

Rather than writing each property individually, you can apply the transition to all properties by using the keyword `all`. Figure 8-34 shows a transition applied to all of the properties that change between the initial and end states, creating an effect in which the object changes background, text color, and rotates 90° over a 4-second interval.

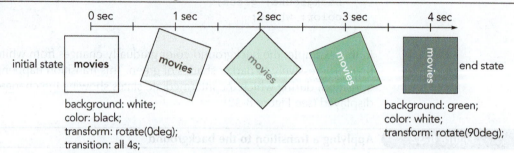

In general, it is more efficient to explicitly list the properties that are changing rather than using the `all` keyword; otherwise, the browser must keep track of all of the style properties to determine which ones are changing and which are not.

Properties Affected by Transitions

Not every property is a candidate for the `transition` style. A general rule of thumb is that, if the property allows for an intermediate value between its initial and end states, it can be used in a transition. Your browser can calculate an intermediate value for properties such as width, height, color, or font size. However, the following style rule can't be used in a transition because there is no in-between state between no display and a block display. Either the image is displayed or it is not.

```
div img {
   display: none;
}
div:hover img {
   display: block;
}
```

To create an effect where an object gradually comes into view, you would apply the transition to the object's opacity, changing the object from completely transparent (opacity = 0) to completely opaque (opacity = 1).

TIP

You can also set the properties affected by the transition and their duration using the transition-property and transition-duration styles.

All current browsers support the `transition` style, but if you need to support older browsers you should include the following browser extensions:

```
-ms-transition: background 4s;
-o-transition: background 4s;
-moz-transition: background 4s;
-webkit-transition: background 4s;
transition: background 4s;
```

In this session, you use the `transition` style without the browser extensions.

Setting the Transition Timing

TIP

You can also define the timing-function using the transition-timing-function property.

The speed of the transition does not need to be constant; it can vary, with some parts of the transition occurring at a faster rate than others. To define the varying speed of the transition, add the following *timing-function* value to the transition style

```
transition: property duration timing-function;
```

where *timing-function* is one of the following keywords:

- `ease`: (the default) The transition occurs more rapidly at the beginning and slows down near the end
- `ease-in`: The transition starts slowly and maintains a constant rate until the finish
- `ease-out`: The transition starts at a constant rate and then slows down toward the finish
- `ease-in-out`: The transition starts slowly, reaches a constant rate, and then slows down toward the finish
- `linear`: The transition is applied at a constant rate throughout the duration

Figure 8-35 compares the linear, ease-in, and ease-out timings when applied to a 4-second transition in the background color. The linear timing changes the color at a constant rate, the ease-in timing changes the background slowly at first and rapidly at the end, and the ease-out timing does the opposite with the most rapid change occurring in the first seconds.

Figure 8-35	Comparing transition timings

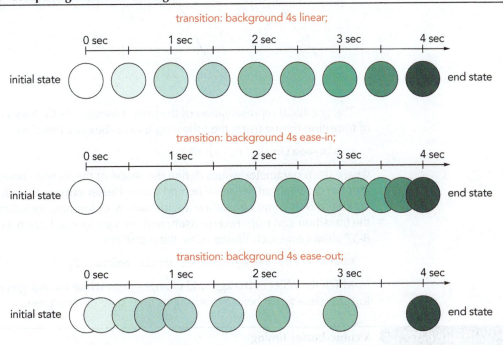

Another way to visualize a timing function is as a graph, which can show the progress of the transition vs. the duration. Figure 8-36 charts the five timing functions where the vertical axis measures the progress of the transition toward completion and the horizontal axis measures the duration. For example, the linear timing is expressed as a straight line because the transition occurs at a constant rate while the other timings contain intervals where the rate of change slows down or speeds up.

Figure 8-36 Graphing the transition timings

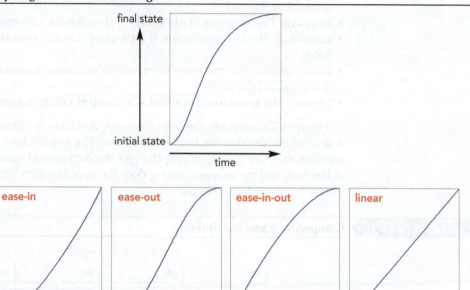

The graphical representation of the timing function is the basis of another measure of transition timing using the following `cubic-bezier` function

```
cubic-bezier(n, n, n, n)
```

where the *n* parameter values define the shape of the timing curve. Without going into the detail about the math behind Cubic Bézier curves, the advantage of this approach is that you can define a wide variety of timings, including timings in which the transition can stop, reverse itself, and then go forward again to its end state. Figure 8-37 shows one such timing using the transition

```
transition: background 4s cubic-bezier(0, 2, 1, -1)
```

in which the object's background changes from white toward green and then back toward white again before reaching its final state of dark green.

Figure 8-37 A cubic-bezier timing

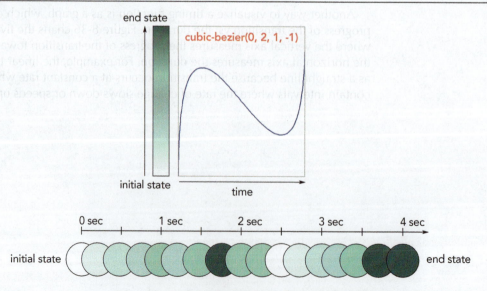

transition: background 4s cubic-Bezier(0, 2, 1, -1);

You can generate your own Cubic Bézier curves using the graphing tool at *cubic-bezier.com*.

Delaying a Transition

A transition does not need to start immediately after the event that triggers it. By adding the following *delay* value to the `transition` style you can delay the start of the transition

```
transition: property duration timing-function delay;
```

where *delay* is measured in seconds or milliseconds. The following style creates a 4-second transition for the background style and a 2-second transition for the text color that starts after a 2-second delay (see Figure 8-38):

```
transition: background 4s linear,
            color 2s ease-out 2s;
```

Figure 8-38   Delaying a transition

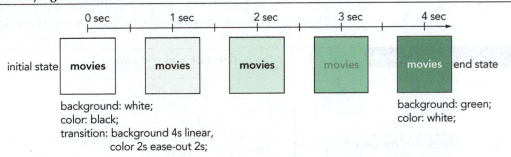

By using a transition delay you can create interesting effects in which your transitions start and end at different times.

Creating a Hover Transition

Now that you have reviewed the CSS styles for creating transitions, Maxine wants to apply a transition effect to the navigation list at the top of the *Royal Wedding* page. When the user hovers the pointer over the items in the navigation list, she wants the links to appear to jump out of the page, increasing in size as they move "toward" the reader. Before writing the `transition` styles, you must first define styles for the initial and end states of these links.

To define the initial and end state for the navigation links:

1. If you took a break after the previous session, make sure the **cp_royal.html** file is open in your editor.

2. Directly above the closing `</head>` tag, insert a link to the **cp_animate.css** style sheet file.

3. Save your changes to the workbook and then use your editor to open the **cp_animate_txt.css** file from the html08 ▸ tutorial folder. Enter *your name* and *the date* in the comment section of the file and save it as **cp_animate.css**.

4. Go to the Transition Styles section and insert the following style rule that defines the initial state of hypertext links in the navigation list:

```
nav#topLinks a {
    color: rgb(255, 255, 255);
    font-size: 1em;
    letter-spacing: 0em;
    text-shadow: rgba(0, 0, 0, 1) 1px -1px 1px;
}
```

5. Next, add the following style rule that defines the end state for those links in response to the hover event:

```
nav#topLinks a:hover {
    color: rgb(255, 183, 25);
    font-size: 3em;
    letter-spacing: 0.1em;
    text-shadow: rgba(0, 0, 0, 0.5) 15px -3px 8px;
}
```

Figure 8-39 shows the style rules for the initial and end states.

Figure 8-39 **Style rules for the initial state and end state**

```
/* Transition Styles */

nav#topLinks a {
    color: rgb(255, 255, 255);
    font-size: 1em;
    letter-spacing: 0em;
    text-shadow: rgba(0, 0, 0, 1) 1px -1px 1px;
}

nav#topLinks a:hover {
    color: rgb(255, 183, 25);
    font-size: 3em;
    letter-spacing: 0.1em;
    text-shadow: rgba(0, 0, 0, 0.5) 15px -3px 8px;
}
```

initial state displays the hypertext links in white with a small text shadow

end state displays the hypertext links in light orange with a larger font and a larger text shadow

6. Save your changes to the style sheet and then reopen the **cp_royal.html** file in your browser.

7. Hover your mouse pointer over links at the top of the page and verify that the hover event causes the style of the links to change. See Figure 8-40.

Figure 8-40   **Effect of the hover event on the links at the top of the page**

Sources: openclipart.org; wiki

The links change instantaneously from the initial state to the end state and the effect that Maxine wants to achieve of links jumping out of the page is lost. Add the `transition` property to slow down the transition from initial to end state for the `color`, `font-size`, `letter-spacing`, and `text-shadow` properties.

To define styles for the navigation links:

1. Return to the cp_animate.css file and, within the style rule for the nav#topLinks a selector, add a new line containing the text `transition:` to insert the `transition` style.

   Maxine wants you to add a different transition method to each of the four properties that are changing.

2. Within the transition style, add **color 1.5s ease-in 0.5s,** which applies an `ease-in` transition to the change in the `color` property with a duration of 1.5 seconds after a half-second delay.

3. To the transition style, add **font-size 2s ease,** which applies a 2-second transition to the change in font size.

4. Add **letter-spacing 2s ease-out**, which applies a 2-second **ease-out** transition to the change in letter spacing.

5. Complete the transition style by adding **text-shadow 2s cubic-bezier (0.6, 0, 0.8, 0.5);**, which applies a 2-second transition to the **text-shadow** property using the **cubic-bezier** function.

Figure 8-41 highlights the transition style.

Figure 8-41 **Setting the transition styles values**

```
/* Transition Styles */

nav#topLinks a {
    color: rgb(255, 255, 255);
    font-size: 1em;
    letter-spacing: 0em;
    text-shadow: rgba(0, 0, 0, 1) 1px -1px 1px;
    transition: color 1.5s ease-in 0.5s,
                font-size 2s ease,
                letter-spacing 2s ease-out,
                text-shadow 2s cubic-bezier(0.6, 0, 0.8, 0.5);
}
```

1.5-second transition with the ease-in transition and a half-second delay

2-second transition with the ease timing

2-second transition with the ease-out timing

2-second transition using a Cubic Bezier function

6. Save your changes to the style sheet and then reload cp_royal.html in your browser.

7. Hover the mouse pointer over the links in the top navigation list and verify that each link changes state over a 2-second duration. Note that the transition works in both directions, repeating the transition in reverse as you move the mouse pointer away from the links.

Figure 8-42 shows the change in the hypertext link over the 2-second duration of the transition.

Figure 8-42   Running the transition

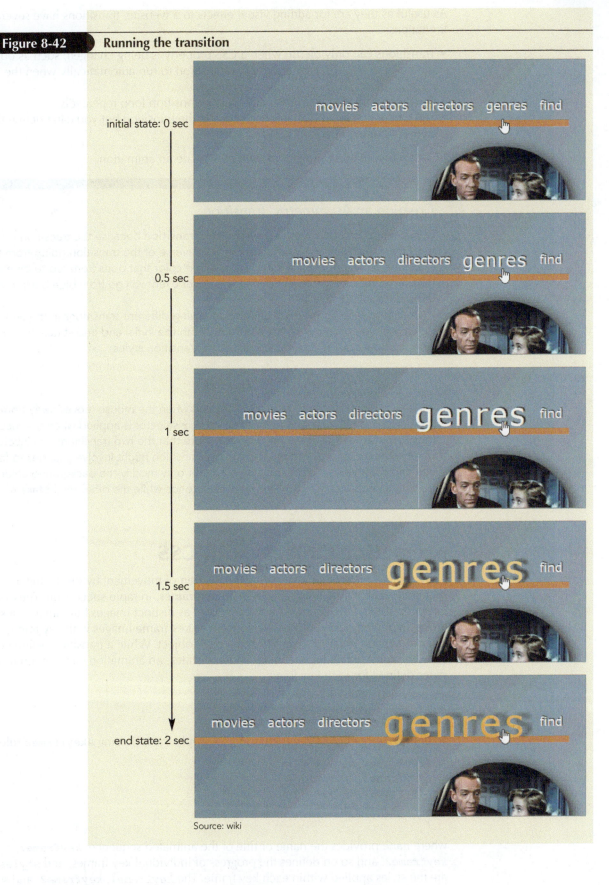

Source: wiki

As useful as they are for adding visual effects to a website, transitions have several limitations:

- Transitions can only be run when a CSS property is being changed, such as during the hover event. You cannot design a transition to run automatically when the page loads.
- Transitions are run once. You can't have a transition loop repeatedly.
- You can define the initial and end states of the transition but you can't define the styles of the intermediate states.

To overcome these limitations, you can create an animation.

Creating an Asymmetric Transition

By default, a CSS transition is a **symmetric transition** because the transition going from the initial state to the end state is the reverse of the transition going from the end state back to the initial state. Thus, a text color that goes from red to blue as the mouse moves over an object during the hover event will go from blue back to red as the mouse moves away.

To create an **asymmetric transition** involving different transitions in the two directions, you must define transitions for both the initial and end states. For example, with the hover event you would create two transition styles:

```
a {transition: properties}
a:hover {transition: properties}
```

The style rule for the a selector is applied when the mouse moves away from the page object and the style rule for the a:hover selector is applied when the mouse moves toward and over the page object. Note that the two transitions can involve totally different effects and durations. One transition might involve changes to font size and color while the other transition might only modify the background color. One transition can take place over a span of 2 seconds while the other might take 4 seconds.

Animating Objects with CSS

Animation is a technique of creating the illusion of movement by displaying a sequence of changing images, known as **key frames**, in rapid succession. The brain interprets the rapidly changing key frames not as distinct images but rather as a single image in motion. CSS replaces the concept of key frame images with key frame styles that are applied in rapid succession to a page object. While a transition is limited to two style rules defined at the initial and end states, an animation can contain multiple styles defined for each key frame.

The @keyframes Rule

To define a sequence of key frames in CSS, apply the following @keyframes rule

```
@keyframes name {
  keyframe1 {styles;}
  keyframe2 {styles;}
  …
}
```

where *name* provides the name or title of the animated sequence, *keyframe1*, *keyframe2*, and so on defines the progress of individual key frames, and *styles* are the styles applied within each key frame. The *keyframe1*, *keyframe2*, and so on values are expressed as percentages where 0% indicates a key frame at the start of the sequence and 100% represents the sequence's last frame. The 0% and 100% values can also be replaced with the keywords `from` and `to`. At the time of this writing, some browsers require a browser extension to define the key frames. For example, if you are using Safari, you might have to add the following WebKit extension to your code:

```
@-webkit-keyframes name {
    keyframe1 {styles;}
    keyframe2 {styles;}
}
```

Check with your browser documentation to determine its level of support for CSS3 key frames.

Key frames can be used to move objects across the page as in the following `@keyframes` rule that traces out an object's flight path (see Figure 8-43).

```
@keyframes flight {
    from {left: 0px;   top: 0px;}
    5%   {left: 50px; top: 80px;}
    10%  {left: 70px; top: 80px;}
    20%  {left: 90px; top: 25px;}
    to   {left: 60px; top: 10px;}
}
```

Figure 8-43   **A path animation over a ten-second duration**

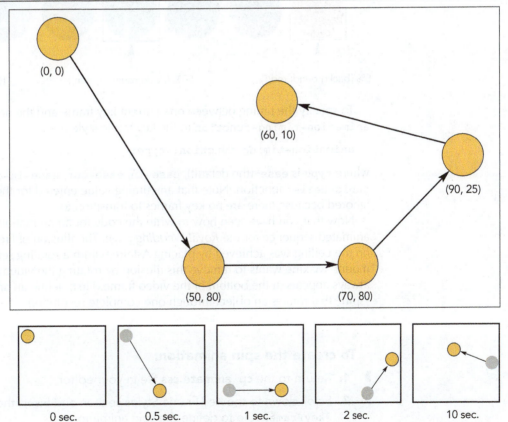

The pace at which the object moves through this path is determined by the percentages assigned to each key frame, allowing the same animation to be run at any speed by changing the total duration of the sequence. With the 10-second duration shown in Figure 8-43, the object would take 2 seconds to reach the (90, 25) coordinate and 8 more seconds to complete the circuit to the (60, 10) point. If the total duration were 20 seconds, the (90, 25) point would be reached after 4 seconds and 16 more seconds would be required to reach the last point.

Each pair of key frames can be treated as a transition with the browser providing the in-between styles, such as in the rainbow animation shown in the following code:

```
@keyframes rainbow {
   0%   {background: red;}
   50%  {background: green;}
   100% {background: violet;}
}
```

Figure 8-44 shows the frames of the rainbow animated sequence in which the key frames define the background color at the 0%, 50%, and 100% mark while the in-between colors are added by the browser to create a smooth transition from one key frame to the next.

Figure 8-44	Transitions between key frames

0% {background: red;}   50% {background: green;}   100% {background: violet;}

To specify the timing between one current key frame and the next, add the following `animation-timing-function` to the key frame style rule

```
animation-timing-function: type;
```

where `type` is `ease` (the default), `ease-in`, `ease-out`, `ease-in-out`, `linear`, or the `cubic-bezier` function. Note that any timing value entered for the last key frame is ignored because there are no key frames to transition to.

Now that you have seen how to write the code for an animation, you will create an animated sequence for the *Royal Wedding* page. The illusion of Fred Astaire dancing on the ceiling was achieved by placing Astaire within a rotating set with a fixed camera mount. Maxine wants to remove this illusion by rotating the video player so that Astaire always appears at the bottom of the video frame. First, define an animation named "spin" that rotates an object through one complete revolution.

To create the spin animation:

1. Return to the **cp_animate.css** file in your editor.

2. Scroll down to the Key Frame Styles section and insert the following `@keyframes` rule to define the spin animation:

```
@keyframes spin {
   0%   {transform: rotate(0deg);}
   100%   {transform: rotate(360deg);}
}
```

Figure 8-45 highlights the initial code for the spin animation.

Figure 8-45 Defining animation key frames

3. Save your changes to the style sheet.

Now that you have defined the animation sequence, you apply it to the video player.

Applying an Animation

A key frames animation is applied to an object using the following `animation-name` and `animation-duration` properties

```
animation-name: keyframes;
animation-duration: times;
```

where `keyframes` is a comma-separated list of animations applied to the object using the names from the `@keyframes` rule and `times` are the lengths of each animation expressed in seconds or milliseconds. The following style rule applies the rainbow animation defined earlier to the web page body, creating an effect where the page background changes from red to green to violet over an interval of 5 seconds.

```
body {
   animation-name: rainbow;
   animation-duration: 5s;
}
```

Figure 8-46 describes other CSS properties used to control the behavior and style of the animation.

Figure 8-46 **Animation Properties**

Property	Description
animation-name = keyframes	Assigns the keyframes animation to the object
animation-duration = time	Sets the length of the animation in seconds or milliseconds (default = 0s)
animation-timing-function = ease|ease-in|ease-out| ease-in-out|linear| cubic-bezier(n,n,n,n)	Defines the default timing between key frames in the animation (default = ease)
animation-delay = time	Sets the delay time in seconds and milliseconds before animation is started (default = 0s)
animation-iteration-count = value|infinite	Specifies the number of times the animation is played, where value is an integer and infinite repeats the animation without stopping (default = 1)
animation-direction = normal|reverse|alternate| alternate-reverse	Defines the direction of the animation, where normal plays the animation as defined in the @keyframes rule, reverse reverses the order, alternate plays the animation in the normal direction followed by the reverse direction (for multiple iterations), and alternate-reverse plays the animation in reverse direction followed by normal direction (default=normal)
animation-fill-mode = none|backwards|forwards|both	Defines what styles from the animation are applied to the object outside the time it is running, where none does not apply any styles, backwards applies the styles from the first key frame, forwards applies the styles from the last key frame, and both applies styles in both directions (default=none)
animation-play-state = running|paused	Defines whether the animation is running or paused (default = running)

The following style rule applies to two animations applied to the img element:

```
img {
   animation-name: rainbow, spin;
   animation-duration: 6s, 2s;
   animation-timing-function: ease-in, linear;
   animation-iteration-count: 1, 3;
}
```

The rainbow animation is applied for 6 seconds using ease-in timing between the key frames and lasting 1 iteration. The spin animation is applied for 2 seconds using linear timing and repeated three times.

All of the animation properties can be combined into the following shortcut animation style

```
animation: name duration timing-function delay iteration-count
   direction fill-mode play-state
```

where the name, duration, timing-function, and so on values match the values for the corresponding properties listed in Figure 8-46. The animation name must be listed first, then the other properties can be listed in any order; except, if both a duration and a delay time are specified, the first time value is assumed to refer to the duration and the second to the delay. Omitted values are assumed to have their default value. For example, the following style plays the rainbow animation for 4 seconds using linear timing, repeating that animation twice:

```
animation: rainbow 4s linear 2;
```

As with transitions, you can support older browsers by using browser extensions. Thus, the preceding style would be entered as:

```
-ms-animation: rainbow 4s linear 2;
-o-animation: rainbow 4s linear 2;
-moz-animation: rainbow 4s linear 2;
-webkit-animation: rainbow 4s linear 2;
animation: rainbow 4s linear 2;
```

In this session, you use the `animation` styles without browser extensions.

Once an animation has been defined and applied to an object, it will run automatically when the page is loaded. Apply the spin animation to the video player for 4 seconds using linear timing and set the iteration count to infinite so that the video player spins continuously.

To apply the spin animation:

▶ **1.** Scroll down to the Animation Styles section within the cp_animate.css file and insert the following style rule:

```
video {
    animation: spin 4s linear infinite;
}
```

Figure 8-47 highlights the code used to spin the video player.

| **Figure 8-47** | **Applying the spin animation** |

▶ **2.** Save your changes to the style sheet.

▶ **3.** Reload the cp_royal.html file in your browser. Verify that when the page loads, the animation rotating the video player starts automatically. See Figure 8-48.

Figure 8-48   **Rotating the video player**

Trouble? Videos played on some mobile devices will automatically be displayed in full screen mode so that you cannot see any animation effects on the video player.

Rather than having the video player rotate continuously when the page loads, Maxine wants the spin animation to be initiated and paused by the user. You can do this using web form controls.

INSIGHT

Stepping between Key Frames

To create a smooth transition between states or key frames, the browser will automatically generate a set of intermediate frames. You can specify the number of intermediate frames using the following `steps()` function

```
steps(number)
```

where *number* is the number of frames between each key frame. The `steps()` function is useful when you want to apply a specific number of discrete frames. The following style applies the clock animation for a duration of 60 seconds broken into 60 frames, each of which would occupy 1 second of time:

```
animation: clock 60s steps(60);
```

One application of the `steps()` function is to create animated images, known as **sprites**, made of several frames shown in rapid succession at timed steps. You can explore sprites in Case Problem 3 at the end of this tutorial.

Controlling an Animation

In many applications, you will not want your animation to start automatically when the page loads but rather in response to the user clicking a form button. You can control an animation using JavaScript, but for this project, you limit yourselves to a CSS solution.

Because an animation can have two states of operation—play or pause—you can use a check box to control the animation. If the check box is selected the animation will play; if the check box is not selected the animation will be paused. First, you will create the check box alongside an empty label. Note that you will write the content of the label shortly.

To create the animation check box:

▶ **1.** Return to the **cp_royal.html** file in your editor.

▶ **2.** Scroll down to the video element and, directly before the `<video>` tag, insert the following checkbox and label elements:

```
<input type="checkbox" id="rotateVideo" />
<label for="rotateVideo"></label>
```

Figure 8-49 highlights the HTML code.

Figure 8-49   **Creating a check box and label to run the animation**

```
<input type="checkbox" id="rotateVideo" />
<label for="rotateVideo"></label>
<video controls poster="cp_photo2.png">
   <source src="cp_dance.mp4" type="video/mp4" />
   <source src="cp_dance.webm" type="video/webm" />
   <track kind="captions" label="Dance Captions" src="cp_captions.vtt" default />
   <p><em>To play this video clip, your browser needs to support HTML5.</em></p>
</video>
```

▶ **3.** Save your changes to the file.

Next, you will define two style rules for the check box: one in which the check box is checked and other in which it is not. If the check box is checked, you want the video clip to be played; you do this by setting the value of animation-play-state property for the video to running as in the following style rule:

```
input#rotateVideo:checked~video {
   animation-play-state: running;
}
```

Remember that this style rule only affects the animation that rotates the video player, it has no effect on the playing of the video itself. The style rule uses the ~ symbol as a sibling selector to select the video that follows the rotateVideo check box in the document. (See Figure 2-12 for a description of the ~ symbol.)

To pause the animation, you use the same selector but include the following not pseudo-class. (See Figure 2-43 for a discussion of the not pseudo-class.) You use the not pseudo-class in order to apply the animation-play-state property with a value of pause to the video player when the rotateVideo check box is not checked:

```
input#rotateVideo:not(:checked)~video {
   animation-play-state: paused;
}
```

Thus, depending on whether the rotateVideo check box is checked or not, the animation will either be running or paused. Add these two styles to the cp_animate.css style sheet.

To create styles for animation playback:

▶ **1.** Return to the **cp_animate.css** file in your editor.

▶ **2.** Directly after the style rule for the video element, insert the following style rule to run the animation:

```
input#rotateVideo:checked~video {
   animation-play-state: running;
}
```

3. Add the following style rule to pause the animation:

```
input#rotateVideo:not(:checked)~video {
    animation-play-state: paused;
}
```

Figure 8-50 highlights the style rules to run and pause the animation.

Figure 8-50   **Creating a check box and label to run the animation**

the rotateVideo check box is checked

```
video {
    animation: spin 4s linear infinite;
}

input#rotateVideo:checked~video {
    animation-play-state: running;
}

input#rotateVideo:not(:checked)~video {
    animation-play-state: paused;
}
```

plays the spin animation

the rotateVideo check box is not checked

pauses the spin animation

4. Save your changes to the file and then reload the cp_royal.html file in your browser.

5. Check the check box next to the video player to start the spin animation. Uncheck the check box to pause the animation. See Figure 8-51.

Figure 8-51   **Using a check box to control the animation playback**

check to play the spin animation and uncheck to pause it

Click the play button to view this classic dance sequence.

1:44

Cinema Penguin © 2018 English (US) A

Source: wiki

Maxine wants to replace the check box with a more attractive icon that displays the ↻ symbol to run the animation and the ✋ symbol to pause the animation. The two symbols have the Unicode values \21bb and \270b respectively. This is where you use the blank label by adding text to the label displaying either the ↻ symbol when the check box is not checked or the ✋ symbol when the check box is checked. You will add this text using the `after` pseudo-element and `content` property in the following style rules:

```
input#rotateVideo:not(:checked)+label::after {
   content: "\21bb";
}
```

to add the ↻ symbol when the check box is not checked. Then use the style rule that follows to insert the ✋ symbol when the check box label is checked:

```
input#rotateVideo:checked+label::after {
   content: "\270b";
}
```

Add both of these style rules to the style sheet and hide the rotateVideo check box so that only the icons are displayed.

To create styles for animation playback:

1. Return to the **cp_animate.css** file in your editor.

2. Go to the Animation Icon Styles section and insert the following style rule to hide the rotateVideo check box:

```
input#rotateVideo {
   display: none;
}
```

3. Add the following style rule to insert the ↻ symbol after the check box label if the check box is not checked:

```
input#rotateVideo:not(:checked)+label::after {
   content: "\21bb";
}
```

4. Add the following style rule to insert the ✋ symbol if the check box is checked:

```
input#rotateVideo:checked+label::after {
   content: "\270b";
}
```

Figure 8-52 highlights the style rules to insert the ↻ and ✋ icons.

Figure 8-52 Displaying playback icons

```
/* Animation Icon Styles */

input#rotateVideo {
    display: none;
}

input#rotateVideo:not(:checked)+label::after {
    content: "\21bb";
}

input#rotateVideo:checked+label::after {
    content: "\270b";
}
```

hides the rotateVideo check box

inserts the ↻ symbol when the rotateVideo check box is not checked

inserts the ✋ symbol when the rotateVideo check box is checked

5. Save your changes to the file and then reload the cp_royal.html file in your browser.

6. Verify that the ↻ symbol appears at the top left of the video player. Click the ↻ icon and verify that the video player starts to rotate and the icon changes to ✋. Confirm that as you continue to click the ↻ and ✋ icons the animation alternately plays and pauses.

Maxine wants you to modify the format of the icons to make them larger and more attractive. She also wants the icons to always appear above the video player. She also wants to make sure the icon is never obscured by the rotating video player. You can ensure this by setting the z-index value of the label to 2.

To format the play and pause icons:

1. Return to the **cp_animate.css** file in your editor.

2. Add the following style rule at the bottom of the file:

```
label {
    background: rgb(56, 87, 119);
    border-radius: 65px;
    color: rgba(255, 255, 255, 0.7);
    display: block;
    font-size: 35px;
    font-weight: bold;
    line-height: 50px;
    margin: 10px auto;
    position: relative;
    text-align: center;
    width: 50px;
    z-index: 2;
}
```

Figure 8-53 shows the style rules for the check box label text.

Figure 8-53   **CSS style rule for the play and pause icons**

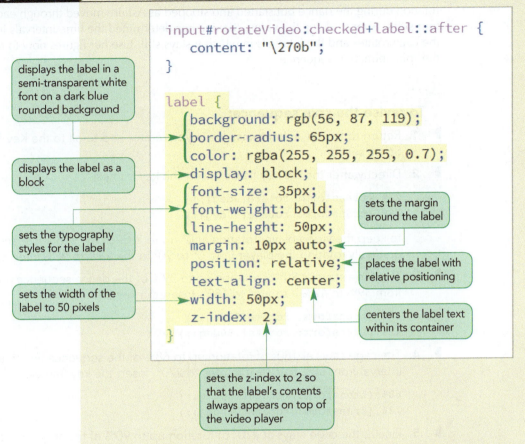

```
input#rotateVideo:checked+label::after {
    content: "\270b";
}

label {
    background: rgb(56, 87, 119);
    border-radius: 65px;
    color: rgba(255, 255, 255, 0.7);
    display: block;
    font-size: 35px;
    font-weight: bold;
    line-height: 50px;
    margin: 10px auto;
    position: relative;
    text-align: center;
    width: 50px;
    z-index: 2;
}
```

displays the label in a semi-transparent white font on a dark blue rounded background

displays the label as a block

sets the typography styles for the label

sets the width of the label to 50 pixels

sets the margin around the label

places the label with relative positioning

centers the label text within its container

sets the z-index to 2 so that the label's contents always appears on top of the video player

3. Save your changes to the file and then reload cp_royal.html in your browser.

4. Click the ↻ and ✋ icons to play and pause the animation. Figure 8-54 shows the revised format of the two icons.

Figure 8-54   **Revised play and pause icons**

play icon

pause icon

Source: wiki

Now that you have created controls that play and pause the spin animation, your next task is to revise the spin animation so that the rotating of the video player matches the rotation of the cage in which Fred Astaire danced. The cage was not in constant rotation during the dance but started and stopped as Astaire moved through each of its four sides. After studying the video, Maxine has determined the time intervals in which the cage rotates and the intervals in which it stays still. Use her figures now to revise the spin animation sequence.

To revise the spin sequence:

1. Return to the **cp_animate.css** file in your editor and scroll to the Key Frames Styles section.

2. Directly after the 0% key frame, insert the key frames:

   ```
   23% {transform: rotate(0deg);}
   28% {transform: rotate(90deg);}
   ```

   to keep the video player rotation at 0° up to 23% of the sequence and then gradually rotating the player from 0° to 90° in the 23% to 28% interval.

3. The cage stays at 90° of rotation up to 39% of the dance sequence and then from 39% to 42% it rotates to 180°. Insert the key frames:

   ```
   39% {transform: rotate(90deg);}
   42% {transform: rotate(180deg);}
   ```

4. The cage stays at 180° of rotation up to 68% of the sequence and in the interval from 68% to 72% it rotates to 270°. Insert the key frames:

   ```
   68% {transform: rotate(180deg);}
   72% {transform: rotate(270deg);}
   ```

5. Finally, the cage stays at 270° of rotation up to 90% of the sequence and then rotates to 360° at the 94% mark. Insert the key frames:

   ```
   90% {transform: rotate(270deg);}
   94% {transform: rotate(360deg);}
   ```

   The length of the animation needs to match the length of the video clip to ensure that the rotation of the video player matches the rotation of the cage used in the video.

6. Change the duration of the animation from 4s to **104.04s**, which is the length of the Ceiling Dance video clip.

   Figure 8-55 highlights the new and revised code in the style sheet.

Figure 8-55   Defining the key frames to match the video

```
@keyframes spin {
    0%      {transform: rotate(0deg);}
    23%     {transform: rotate(0deg);}
    28%     {transform: rotate(90deg);}
    39%     {transform: rotate(90deg);}
    42%     {transform: rotate(180deg);}
    68%     {transform: rotate(180deg);}
    72%     {transform: rotate(270deg);}
    90%     {transform: rotate(270deg);}
    94%     {transform: rotate(360deg);}
    100%    {transform: rotate(360deg);}
}

/* Animation Styles */

video {
    animation: spin 104.04s linear infinite;
}
```

new key frames that rotate the video player at different intervals

animation duration set to 104.04 seconds to match the length of the video clip

▶ **7.** Save your changes to the file.

Your final task is to keep the animation and the video player in sync so that when the animation starts, the video player starts and when the animation pauses, the video player pauses. Because there are no CSS styles that control video playback, this task requires an external JavaScript program. Maxine gives you the cp_spin.js file that contains a JavaScript program that will play and pause the video whenever the spin animation runs or pauses.

To link to the cp_spin.js file:

▶ **1.** Return to the **cp_royal.html** file in your editor.

▶ **2.** Directly before the closing </head> tag, insert the following script element:

```
<script src="cp_spin.js"></script>
```

Figure 8-56 highlights the script element in the document head.

Figure 8-56 | Using a script to keep the animation and the video in sync

```
<link href="cp_animate.css" rel="stylesheet" />

<script src="cp_spin.js"></script>
</head>
```

> script file used to start and pause the video playback in sync with the animation

You need to provide instructions to the user about how to use the animation you created.

3. Scroll down to the paragraph directly before the rotateVideo check box and within the paragraph, add the following text:

To see the dance as it appeared on the movie set, go to the start of the clip and click ↻ to rotate and play the video. Click ✋ to pause the rotation and the playback.

Figure 8-57 highlights the newly added text.

Figure 8-57 | Instructions to run the animation

```
<p>Click the play button to view this classic dance sequence. To see the dance
  as it appeared on the movie set, go to the start of the clip and click &#8635;
  to rotate and play the video. Click &#9995; to pause the rotation and
  the playback.
</p>

<input type="checkbox" id="rotateVideo" />
<label for="rotateVideo"></label>
```

> character code for the ✋ symbol

> character code for the ↻ symbol

4. Save your changes to the file and then reload cp_royal.html in your browser.

5. Click the ↻ icon to start both the animation and the video player. Verify the rotation of the player is synchronized to the dance so that Astaire always appears upright within the video window.

6. Click the ✋ icon and verify that it pauses both the animation and the video playback.

Figure 8-58 shows the rotated video player in sync with the rotation of the movie set.

Figure 8-58   Final version of the Ceiling Dance animation

click to start the animation and the video playback

video playback syncs with the animation rotating the player

Trouble?   Do not use the controls on the video player itself to pause or play the video; the animation will not sync up with the dance.

You have completed your work on the *Royal Wedding* page for the Cinema Penguin website. Maxine is very pleased with the enhancements you have made to the page and feels that with the audio, video, and animation you have added, the page has really come alive and provided useful insight regarding how the illusion of the Ceiling Dance was achieved. Maxine will continue to work on developing new pages of interest for her website and will contact you for help on future projects.

Problem Solving: Safe Animation and Motion Sensitivity

One area of web accessibility that is too often overlooked is the health impact that flashy animated effects can have on large segments of the population. For individuals afflicted with migraines, epilepsy, or vestibular disorders such as vertigo, large and rapidly changing animations can induce symptoms of nausea, headaches, and dizziness. Some of the most adverse reactions occur in response to large movement across an entire screen such as might occur with a full screen wipe of page content. Other areas of concern are animations involving apparent rapid motion, twisting in 3D space, or unexpected shifts in the direction of motion—all of which can leave viewers feeling disoriented.

In designing a safe animation for all of your users, keep in mind the following principles:

- *Keep the Animation Restrained.* Don't have your animation dominate the user experience. It should augment your design, not overwhelm it.
- *Give the User Control.* Whenever possible, give users the ability to ignore or turn off an animated sequence.
- *Test your Page Animation-Free.* Some users may need to turn off your animated sequences. Make sure your website is still useful and informative for them.

All of which is not to say that animation should be eliminated from website designs. A well-designed animation can provide useful information to the viewer and augment the user experience. Good design is inviting to everyone.

REVIEW

Session 8.3 Quick Check

1. Provide code to change the background color of a hypertext link from yellow to blue over a 3-second interval in response to the hover event.

2. Provide a style that changes the font size over a 2-second interval and the font color over a 3-second interval.

3. Which timing function should you use to start the transition at a constant rate and then slow down toward the end state?

4. Provide the style that creates a transition on all properties over a 5-second interval using linear timing and a half-second delay.

5. Name three ways in which animations differ from transitions.

6. Provide an animation named biggerText that sets the font size to 1em, 1.2em, 1.5em, and 2em at key frames located at 0%, 10%, 20%, and 100% of the animation duration.

7. Provide code to run the biggerText animation in the `header` element over an interval of 4.5 seconds.

8. Provide the style to run an animation in reverse.

9. Provide code to apply the flip animation to the `img` element in the page header. Have the animation run repeatedly over a 4-second interval in alternating directions using ease-out timing.

PRACTICE

Review Assignments

Data Files needed for the Review Assignments: cp_astaire_txt.html, cp_animate2_txt.css, cp_media2_txt.css, cp_captions2_txt.vtt, 2 CSS files, 3 PNG files, 1 MP3 file, 1 MP4 file, 1 OGG file, 1 WebM file

Maxine has been working on new pages at the *Cinema Penguin* website. She has returned for help on a page featuring a profile of Fred Astaire. Maxine created a sound clip from one of Astaire's songs in the *Royal Wedding* and a video clip of a dance in that movie featuring Astaire's duet with a hat rack. She wants both clips embedded on the page. In addition, Maxine wants you to try a new hover transition for the links at the top of the page. Finally, she wants you to create an animation that displays a scrolling marquee of the Fred Astaire filmography. Figure 8-59 shows a preview of the final page.

Figure 8-59   Fred Astaire biography page

Sources: openclipart.org; wiki

Complete the following:

1. Use your HTML editor to open the **cp_astaire_txt.html**, **cp_media2_txt.css**, and **cp_animate2_txt.css** files from the html08 ▶ review folder. Enter *your name* and *the date* in the comment section of each file, and save them as **cp_astaire.html**, **cp_media2.css** and **cp_animate2.css** respectively. In addition, use your text editor to open the **cp_captions2_txt.vtt** file from the same folder and save it as **cp_captions2.vtt**.

2. Go to the **cp_astaire.html** file in your editor. Insert a link to the cp_media2.css and cp_animate2css files. Take some time to study the contents and structure of the document.

3. Scroll down to the `aside` element titled "Listen up". Directly after the introductory paragraph, insert an audio clip with the audio controls displayed in the browser. Add two possible source files to the audio clip: cp_song.mp3 and cp_song.ogg. Identify the mime-type of each audio source. If the browser does not support HTML5 audio, display a paragraph with the message **Upgrade your browser to HTML5**.

4. Scroll down to the `aside` element titled "In Focus" and after the introductory paragraph insert a video clip with the video controls enabled and display the poster image cp_poster.png. Add two possible sources to the video clip: cp_hatrack.mp4 and cp_hatrack.webm. Include the mime-type for each video source. If the user's browser does not support HTML5 video, display a paragraph with the message **Upgrade your browser to HTML5**.

5. Directly after the two video sources in the `video` element you created in the last step, insert a caption track using the captions you will specify in the cp_captions2.vtt file in later steps. Give the caption track the label **Movie Captions** and set it as the default track for the video clip.

6. Save your changes to the file and then open the **cp_caption2.vtt** file in your text editor. Add an initial line to the text file indicating that this file is in WEBVTT format.

7. Add the following track cues to the cp_caption2.vtt file:
   a. A Title cue appearing in the 0.5 seconds to 5-second interval containing the text **The Hat Rack Dance** enclosed in a class tag with the name **Title**. Set the `line` and `align` attributes for the caption to **10%** and **middle** respectively to place the caption centered and near the top of the video window.
   b. A Subtitle cue in the 5.5 to 9-second interval with the text **from Royal Wedding (1951)**. Enclose "Royal Wedding (1951)" within `<i>` tags to italicize it. Place the caption at the 10% line and align the caption text in the middle.
   c. A Finish cue displayed from the 1 minute 5 second mark to the 1 minute 11 second mark and containing the text **See more videos at Cinema Penguin**. Enclose "Cinema Penguin" within `<i>` tags and place the caption at the 80% line and 90% position with the caption text aligned at the end.

8. Save your changes to the file and then go to the **cp_media2.css** file in your editor. Within the Media Styles section, insert a style rule for all `audio` and `video` elements that displays them as blocks with a width of 95%. Center the `audio` and `video` elements by setting the top/bottom margins to 20 pixels and left/right margins set to `auto`.

9. Go to the Track Styles section and create a style rule for track cues that: a) sets the background color to `transparent`, b) adds a black text shadow with horizontal and vertical offsets of 1 pixel and a blur of 2 pixels, c) sets the text color to rgb(255, 177, 66), and d) sets the font size to 1.2 em using the sans serif font family.

10. Create a style rule for track cues belonging to the Title class that sets the font size to 2em and font family to serif.

11. Save your changes to the style sheet and then open the **cp_astaire.html** file in your browser. Verify that you can play the audio and video clips and the layout matches that shown in Figure 8-59. Verify that captions are added to the video clip providing the title and subtitle of the clip at the start of the video and a message about *Cinema Penguin* at the end. (*Note*: If you are using Google Chrome or Opera, you will have to upload your files to a server if you want to see the captions and the styles you created for the video clip.)

12. Maxine wants to create a transition for the links at the top of the page that enlarges the link text and moves it out and above its default position. Return to the **cp_animate2.css** file in your editor, go to the Transition Styles section and create a style rule for the `nav#topLinks a` selector that: a) sets the text color to rgb(255, 255, 255), b) adds a text shadow with the color rgba(0, 0, 0, 1), a horizontal offset of 1 pixel, a vertical offset of –1 pixel, and a blur of 1 pixel, and c) uses the `transform` style to apply the functions `scale(1,1)` and `translateY(0px)`.

13. Within the style rule you created in the last step, add a transition that applies to all of the properties of the selected element over an interval of 1.2 seconds using linear timing.

14. Create a style rule for the `nav#topLinks a:hover` selector that: a) sets the text color to rgb(255, 183, 25), b) sets the text shadow to the color rgba(0, 0, 0, 0.5) with a horizontal offset of 0 pixels, a vertical offset of 15 pixels, and a blur of 4 pixels, and c) uses the `transform` style with `scale(2,2)` and `translateY(-15px)` to double the scale of the object and translate it –15 pixels in the vertical direction.

15. Save your changes to the style sheet and then reload cp_astaire.html in your browser. Hover your mouse pointer over the links at the top of the page and verify that your browser applies a transition over a 1.2 second duration as each link increases in size and appears to move upward and outward from the page in response to the hover event.

The list of Fred Astaire's films has been stored within a table nested within a `div` element with the ID Marquee. The table is long and Maxine wants to only display a portion of it at a time, allowing the contents of the table to automatically scroll upward as in a theater marquee. To create this animated effect, you change the `top` position style of the table over a specified time interval, moving the table upward through the marquee.

16. Return to the **cp_animate2.css** file in your editor and go to the Marquee Styles section and insert a style rule that places the marquee `div` element with relative positioning. Add a style rule for the table nested within the marquee `div` element that places the table using absolute positioning. Do not specify any coordinates for either element.

17. Go to the Keyframe Styles section and create an animation named **scroll** with the following two key frames: a) at 0%, set the value of the `top` property to **250px** and b) at 100%, set the value of the `top` property to **–1300px**.

18. Go to the Animation Styles section and apply the scroll animation to the table within the marquee `div` element over a duration of 50 seconds using linear timing within infinite looping.

19. Maxine wants the marquee to stop scrolling whenever the user hovers the mouse pointer over it. Add a style rule for the `div#marquee:hover table` selector that pauses the animation during the hover event.

20. Save your changes to the file and then reload the cp_astaire.html file in your browser. Verify that the marquee listing the Fred Astaire films starts scrolling automatically when the page loads, goes back to the beginning after the last film is listed, and stops whenever the user hovers the mouse pointer over the marquee. (*Note*: On touchscreen devices, tap the marquee to initiate the hover event and pause the scrolling text, and then tap elsewhere on the page to remove the hover and restart the marquee.)

APPLY

Case Problem 1

Data Files needed for this Case Problem: ws_jfk_txt.html, ws_media_txt.css, ws_captions_txt.vtt, 2 CSS files, 1 MP4 file, 4 PNG files, 1 WebM file

Rhetoric in the United States   Professor Annie Cho teaches rhetoric and history at White Sands College. She has asked for your help in designing a companion website for her course. The page you will work on contains portions of the inaugural address delivered by President John F. Kennedy in 1961. She has obtained a video excerpt of the speech that she wants you to augment with captions. A preview of the page you will create is shown in Figure 8-60.

Figure 8-60   **Rhetoric in the United States page**

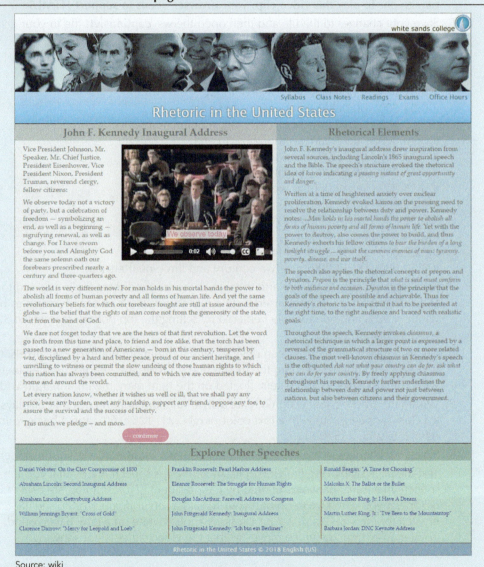

Source: wiki

Complete the following:

1. Using your editor, open the **ws_jfk_txt.html**, **ws_media_txt.css**, and **ws_captions_txt.vtt** files from the html08 ▸ case1 folder. Enter *your name* and *the date* in the comment section of each file, and save them as **ws_jfk.html**, **ws_media.css**, and **ws_captions.vtt** files respectively.

2. Go to the **ws_jfk.html** file in your editor. Insert a link to the ws_media.css style sheet file. Take some time to study the content and structure of the document.

3. Scroll down to the `article` element and directly below the h1 heading, insert a video clip with the controls enabled, displaying the poster image ws_jfk_poster.png file. Add two possible sources to the video clip: ws_jfk_speech.mp4 and ws_jfk_speech.webm, including the mime-type for each video source.

4. After the two video sources, add a captions track with the label **Speech Captions** using the source file ws_captions.vtt. If the browser does not support embedded video, display the paragraph: **To play this video clip, your browser needs to support HTML5**.

5. Save your changes to the file and then open the **ws_captions.vtt** file in your text editor. Add an initial line to the text file indicating that this file is in WEBVTT format.

6. Add the following track cues to the ws_captions.vtt file, labeling the captions 1 through 12 (times are in parenthesis):

   (00:01.00 - 00:004.000) We observe today
   (00:04.000 - 00:06.000) not a victory of party,
   (00:06.000 - 00:10.000) but a celebration of freedom –
   (00:10.000 - 00:12.000) symbolizing an end,
   (00:12.000 - 00:15.000) as well as a beginning –
   (00:15.000 - 00:17.000) signifying renewal,
   (00:17.000 - 00:19.000) as well as change.
   (00:19.000 - 00:22.000) For I have sworn before you
   (00:22.000 - 00:24.000) and Almighty God
   (00:24.000 - 00:27.000) the same solemn oath
   (00:27.000 - 00:30.000) our forebears prescribed
   (00:30.000 - 00:33.000) nearly a century and three-quarters ago.

7. Save your changes to the file and then go to the **ws_media.css** file in your editor. Within the Video Player Styles section, insert a style rule that displays `video` elements as blocks with a width of 90% and horizontally centered by setting the top/bottom margins to 5 pixels and the left/right margins to `auto`.

8. Create a media query for screen devices with a minimum width of 521 pixels. (See Tutorial 5 to review media queries.) Within the media query, create a style for `video` elements that sets the width of the player to 360 pixels, floated on the right margin with a margin width of 10 pixels.

9. Within the Track Styles section, create a style rule for caption cues that displays the text in a 1.3em sans-serif font with a text color of rgb(221, 128, 160), and a background color of rgba(255, 255, 255, 0.8).

10. Save your changes to the file and then load the **ws_jfk.html** file in your browser.

11. Test the page by playing the video clip of Kennedy's speech. Verify that captions are added to the speech, matching the words uttered by the president. (*Notes*: If you are using Google Chrome or Opera, you will have to upload your files to a server if you wish to see the caption styles you created for the video clip. If your captions appear white on a gray background, move the mouse pointer away from the video player so that the video slider is not showing.)

APPLY

Case Problem 2

Data Files needed for this Case Problem: ba_physics_txt.html, ba_animate_txt.css, 2 CSS files, 4 PNG files

Big Apple Physics   Jason Tompkins runs the online physics website *Big Apple Physics,* providing physics instruction and help for homeschoolers and independent learners. In order to teach physics concepts such as motion and mechanics better, he would like to supplement his written material with animated demos. He has come to you for help in creating an animated demo teaching the concepts of the Law of the Conservation of Momentum. A preview of the page you will create is shown in Figure 8-61.

Figure 8-61   **Big Apple Physics page**

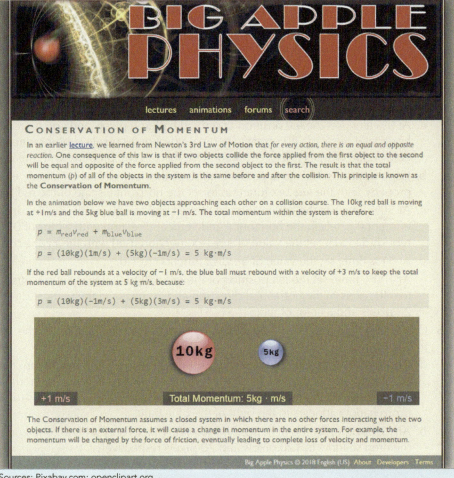

Sources: Pixabay.com; openclipart.org

Complete the following:

1. Using your editor, open the **ba_physcis_txt.html** and **ba_animate_txt.css** files from the html08 ▸ case2 folder. Enter *your name* and *the date* in the comment section of each file, and save them as **ba_physics.html** and **ba_animate.css** respectively.

2. Go to the **ba_physics.html** file in your editor. Add a link to the ba_animate.css style sheet file to the document head. Take some time to study the content of the file. Note that a `div` element with the name "animBox" will be used to store the animation you create. The animation box has two image files representing balls that will move across the screen and five `div` elements that will contain text describing the velocity and momentum of those moving objects.

3. Save your changes and go to the **ba_animate.css** file in your editor. Jason wants you to create a transition effect for the navigation list in which a semicircle grows behind each link when it is hovered over. Within the Transition Styles section, add a style rule for the `nav a` selector that: a) displays the background image file ba_target.png centered horizontal and vertically with no tiling, b) sets the size of the background image to 0%, c) sets the hypertext font color to rgb(253, 240, 133), and d) adds a transition that changes the background size over 0.3 seconds and the font color over 0.8 seconds.

4. Create a style rule for the `nav a:hover` selector to set the background size to 100% and the font color to rgb(244, 130, 130).

5. Next, you will animate the effect of two balls caroming off each other. You will start with the red ball, which moves from the left to the right across the animation box. Within the Animation Styles section, create the **moveRed** animation containing the following key frames:

   a. At 0% time, set the left position of the red ball to 0 pixels and add a drop shadow with a horizontal offset of −40 pixels, a vertical offset of 20 pixels, a blur radius of 25 pixels, and a color value of rgb(51, 51, 51). (*Hint*: Use the `filter` property with the `drop-shadow`.)

   b. Jason wants the balls to appear to squish as they collide. At 49% time, use the `transform` property with the `scaleX` function to set the horizontal scale of the red ball to 1.

   c. At 50% time, set the left position of the red ball to 380 pixels. Set the drop shadow to an offset of 0 pixels in the horizontal and vertical direction with a blur of 0 pixels and a color of rgb(51, 51, 51). Set the value of `scaleX` function used with the `transform` property to 0.4.

   d. At 51% time, set the value of `scaleX` function to 1.0.

   e. At 100% time, set the left position of the red ball to 0 pixels. Set the offset of the drop shadow to −40 pixels in the horizontal direction and 20 pixels in the vertical direction with a blur of 25 pixels and a color of rgb(51, 51, 51).

6. Create an animation named **moveBlue** that moves the blue ball across the animation box. Add the following:

   a. Copy the 0% to 51% key frames you used for the moveRed animation, changing the `left` property to `right`, so that all coordinates of the blue ball are measured from its right edge. Also change the horizontal offset of the drop shadow from −40 pixels to 40 pixels, so that the drop shadow appears to the right of the blue ball.

   b. At 100% time, set the right position to −700 pixels, and set horizontal and vertical offsets of the drop shadow to 120 pixels and 20 pixels respectively.

7. In the animation, Jason wants to alternately hide and display information about the velocity of the moving balls. Create an animation named **showText** that sets the opacity to 0 at 0% and 49% time and sets the opacity to 1 at 51% and 100% time.

8. Create an animation named **hideText** that sets the opacity to 1 at 0% and 49% time and sets the opacity to 0 at 51% and 100% time.

9. Apply the moveRed animation to the redBall image over a 5-second interval with linear timing and infinite looping. Apply the moveBlue animation to the blueBall image over a 5-second interval also with linear timing and infinite looping. Apply the hideText animation to the redSpeed1 and blueSpeed1 `div` elements using the same timing parameters as the previous two animations. Finally, apply the showText animation to the redSpeed2 and blueSpeed2 `div` elements using the same timing parameters as with the other three animations.

10. Save your changes to the style sheet and then open **ba_physics.html** in your browser.

11. Test the hover transition by moving your mouse pointer over the navigation list links. Verify that the semicircle grows behind the hovered link and that the link color gradually changes from yellow to light red.

12. Verify that the animation demo shows two balls colliding, with the blue ball recoiling at the faster rate of speed off the screen. Further verify that drop shadows move behind the balls, disappearing at the moment of collision. Finally, verify that at the moment of collision, the two balls appear to squish together momentarily. (*Note:* If you are using Internet Explorer, you will not see any drop shadows.)

Case Problem 3

Data Files needed for this Case Problem: paa_game_txt.html, paa_animate_txt.css, 2 CSS files, 6 PNG files, 1 TTF file, 1 WOFF file

Pixal Arts and Entertainment   Heather Neidell manages the website for Pixal Arts and Entertainment, a company specializing in games and entertainment apps. She has asked you to work on the initial page for the company's new game, *Frustrated Fox*. To make the page come alive, she wants you to enhance the page with animation using sprites from several characters in the game. A preview of the page you will create is shown in Figure 8-62.

Figure 8-62   **Frustrated Fox page**

Complete the following:

1. Using your editor, open the **paa_game_txt.html** and **paa_animate_txt.css** files from the html08 ▶ case3 folder. Enter *your name* and ***the date*** in the comment section of each file, and save them as **paa_game.html** and **paa_animate.css** respectively.

2. Go to the **paa_game.html** file in your editor. Add a link to the paa_animate.css style sheet file to the document head.

3. Scroll down to the gameBox `div` element. Within this element, insert three `div` elements with the ids **butterfly**, **bat**, and **fox** and belonging to the **sprite** class. These `div` elements will contain animated backgrounds showing three characters from the game.

4. Save your changes to the file and then return to the **paa_animate.css** file in your editor.

5. Within the Transition Effects section, insert a style rule for the `nav#gameLinks a` selector that: a) places the links using relative positioning, b) sets the font color to white, and c) transitions the font color over a 0.5-second interval.

6. Insert a style rule for the `nav#gameLinks a:hover` selector that sets the font color to rgb(255, 194, 99).

⊕ **Explore** 7. Heather wants a transition effect applied to the links in the gameLinks list in which a gradient-colored bar gradually expands under each link during the hover event. To create this effect, you will use the `after` pseudo-element and the `content` property to insert the bar. Create a style rule for the `nav#gameLinks a::after` selector that: a) places an empty text string as the value of the `content` property, b) places the content with absolute positioning with a top value of 100% and a left value of 0 pixels, c) sets the width to 0% and the height to 8 pixels, d) changes the background to a linear gradient that moves `to right` from the color value rgb(237, 243, 71) to rgb(188, 74, 0), e) sets the border radius to 4 pixels, and f) hides the bar by setting the opacity to 0.

8. When the links are hovered over, change the appearance of the bar by adding a style rule for the `nav#gameLinks a:hover::after` selector that changes the opacity to 1 and the width to 100%.

9. Return to the style rule for the `nav#gameLinks a::after` selector and add a transition style that applies the opacity and width changes over a half-second interval.

10. To create animated cartoons, Heather has stored frames of the images in the **paa_bat.png**, **paa_bfly.png**, and **paa_fox.png** image files. View these files to see the different frames to be displayed in the animation.

11. Return to the **paa_animate.css** file and, within the Sprite Styles section, create a style rule that displays all `div` elements of the sprite class with absolute positioning.

12. For the `div` element with the ID bat, create a style rule that: a) sets the width and height to 40 pixels by 50 pixels, b) sets the top and left coordinates to 100 pixels and –50 pixels, and c) displays the paa_bat.png as the background image placed at the left center of the background with no tiling and sized to cover the background.

13. Create a similar style rule for the `div` element with the ID butterfly, setting the width and height at 35 pixels, the top-left coordinates at 60 pixels and –50 pixels, and using the paa_bfly.png as the background image. Create another style rule for the `div` element with the ID fox, setting the width and height at 280 and 260 pixels, the bottom and right coordinates at 10 pixels, and the paa_fox.png file as the background image. (*Note*: The background image in all aminations should place the image at the left center with no tiling and sized to cover the background.)

14. Sprites are animated by moving the background image file across the background of the object. Go to the Animation Styles section and create an animation named **playSprite** that sets the background image position to right center at 100% time.

15. Heather wants the bat and butterfly to flutter as they move across the animation box. Create an animation named **flyRight** with the following key frames: a) at 25% time, set the top coordinate to 150 pixels, b) at 50% time, set the top coordinate to 55 pixels, c) at 65% time, set the top coordinate to 120 pixels, d) at 90% time, set the top coordinate to 50 pixels, and e) at 100% time, set the top and left coordinates to 80 pixels and 100%.

⊕ **Explore** 16. Sprites achieve the animation effect by changing the background image in $n - 1$ discrete steps, where n is the number of frames in the sprite. Apply the `playSprite` animation to the fox `div` element after a 4-second delay over a time interval of 3.5 seconds and a steps value of 27. Set the animation to loop infinitely.

17. Apply the `playSprite` animation to the bat `div` element over a 2-second interval with 39 steps. Apply the `flyRight` animation over an 8-second interval with linear timing. Set both animations to loop infinitely.

18. Apply the `playSprite` animation to the butterfly `div` element after a 3-second delay, with a playing time of 1 second spaced out in 33 steps. Apply the `flyRight` animation over a 6-second interval. Make the butterfly appear to hover by applying a Cubic Bézier curve to the `flyRight` timing with the function `cubic-bezier(0,1,0.73,0)`. Set both animations to loop infinitely.

19. Save your changes to the file and then open the **paa_game.html** file in your browser.

20. Hover your mouse pointer over the four links below the Frustrated Fox logo and verify that a gradient-filled bar grows beneath the links in response to the hover event.

21. Verify that the animation box shows an animated bat and then a butterfly moving across the sky and that, after a short delay, an animated fox jumps up toward the bat and butterfly trying to catch them.

CHALLENGE

Case Problem 4

Data Files needed for this Case Problem: rnt_poetry_txt.html, rnt_audio_txt.css, 2CSS files, 2 PNG files, 2 MP3 files, 2 OGG files

Roads Not Taken   Debra Li runs a poetry website called *Roads Not Taken*. She has asked for your help in creating a page on the poetry of Robert Frost. She wants to augment the page with a video clip of the Frost poem, *The Road Not Taken*, as well as audio clips of the poems, *Fire and Ice* and *Devotion*. A preview of the page you will create is shown in Figure 8-63.

Figure 8-63   Roads Not Taken page

Sources: wiki; YouTube/aweblackbough

Complete the following:

1. Using your editor, open the **rnt_poetry_txt.html** and **rnt_audio_txt.css** files from the html08 ▶ case4 folder. Enter *your name* and *the date* in the comment section of each file, and save them as **rnt_poetry.html** and **rnt_audio.css** respectively.

2. Go to the **rnt_poetry.html** file in your editor. Add a link to the rnt_audio.css style sheet file to the document head.

⊕ **Explore** 3. The video clip that Debra wants to use is from the YouTube website. Scroll down to the `figure` element and directly above the figure caption insert an `iframe` element loading the video from *http://www.youtube.com/v/ie2Mspukx14*. You do not have to specify the width, height, or frame border size of the inline frame.

4. Scroll down and directly under the h2 heading, Fire and Ice, insert an audio clip with the player controls displayed. Within the audio clip provide two possible audio file sources: rnt_fireice. mp3 and then rnt_fireice.ogg.

⊕ **Explore** 5. For browsers that do not support HTML5 audio but do support plug-ins, nest an `embed` element within the `audio` element, loading the rnt_fireice.mp3 file. Set the width of the embedded player to 250 pixels and the height to 50 pixels using the `width` and `height` attributes of the `embed` element. Display the embedded player controls but do not start the player automatically. Use the `controller`, `autoplay`, `showcontrols`, and `autostart` attributes so the audio file works across multiple plug-ins.

6. If the browser does not support either HTML5 audio or embedded players, display a paragraph tag indicating that no embedded audio is supported.

7. Go to the h2 heading for Devotion and repeat Steps 4 through 6 using the audio files rnt_devotion.mp3 and rnt_devotion.ogg.

8. Save your changes to the file and then return to **rnt_audio.css** file in your editor.

9. Within the Audio Styles section, add a style rule for the `audio` element that: a) displays the audio clip as a block, b) adds a dark gray box shadow with a horizontal and vertical offset of 8 pixels and a blur of 15 pixels, c) sets the top/bottom margin to 20 pixels and the left/right margin to `auto`, and d) sets the width of the player to 80%.

⊕ **Explore** 10. Some browsers allow for custom styles to modify the appearance of the audio and video players. WebKit supports several selectors to select parts of the audio player including the control button, control panel, and forward and rewind buttons. Using the selector `audio::-webkit-media-controls-panel` change the background color of the audio player to rgb(128, 128, 255).

11. Save your changes to the file and then load **rnt_poetry.html** in your browser. Verify that you can play the video and audio clips embedded in the document. Depending on your browser, you might be prompted to load or update the Adobe Flash plug-in. If you are using Google Chrome, verify that the control panel of the two audio players is displayed in a medium blue color.

TUTORIAL 9

Getting Started with JavaScript

Creating a Countdown Clock

Case | *Tulsa's New Year's Bash*

Every year on December 31st, Tulsa, Oklahoma, rings in the New Year with a daylong celebration that includes races, circus performers, tasting booths, live bands, and dances. The celebration is capped by fireworks at midnight. The bash has become so big that partygoers come from miles away to join in the fun, and planning for the celebration starts early.

Hector Sadler manages promotion for the New Year's Bash. One of his responsibilities is to maintain a website that advertises the event and builds anticipation for it. Hector wants to include a countdown clock on the site's home page that displays the current time and the number of days, hours, minutes, and seconds remaining before the fireworks go off. You will write the JavaScript code to create this clock for Hector.

OBJECTIVES

Session 9.1
- Insert a script element
- Write JavaScript comments
- Display an alert dialog box
- Use browser debugging tools

Session 9.2
- Reference browser and page objects
- Use JavaScript properties and methods
- Write HTML code and text content into a page
- Work with a Date object

Session 9.3
- Use JavaScript operators
- Create a JavaScript function
- Create timed commands

STARTING DATA FILES

html09 → **tutorial**
tny_clock_txt.html
tny_script_txt.js
+ 5 files

review
tny_july_txt.html
tny_timer_txt.js
+ 5 files

case1
sd_map_txt.html
sd_mapper_txt.js
+ 30 files

case2
bc_union_txt.html
bc_today_txt.js
+ 6 files

case3
ja_vynes_txt.html
ja_quote_txt.js
+ 8 files

case4
ph_pay_txt.html
ph_clock_txt.js
+ 12 files

Session 9.1 Visual Overview:

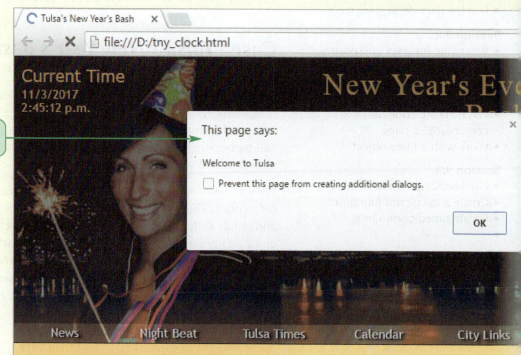

An alert dialog box created by JavaScript.

Tulsa's New Year's Eve Bash is back for the 26th year of fun and excitement. Be sure to arrive early for all of the festivities and the final countdown. The party starts on December 31 at noon with the *FrostiRun* 5K and 10K races. Sign up now or the morning of the race.

Family fun is available at the *Kid's Korner* with booths and free activities for the whole family, including performances from clowns, jugglers, and the wheel walkers of *Dominic J.*

The fun continues with *A Taste of Tulsa* from Tulsa's best eateries, and the artistically inclined should plan on attending the *Winter Art Fair* on Tulsa's downtown square.

Music from *Lester's Blues Band* and *The Jazz Express* brings us into the New Year. The dancing starts at 7 p.m. and continues until midnight. From 10 to 11 p.m. we say goodbye to the old year (and ring in the new) with the famous New Year's Eve Bash fireworks spectacular.

© altafulla/Shutterstock.com; © jbdphotography/Shutterstock.com

Creating a JavaScript File

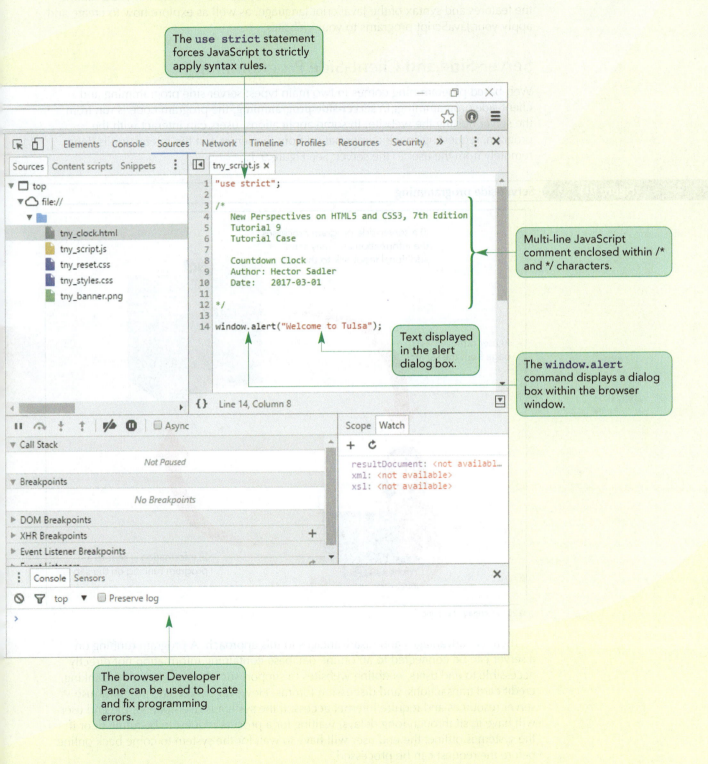

The `use strict` statement forces JavaScript to strictly apply syntax rules.

Multi-line JavaScript comment enclosed within /* and */ characters.

Text displayed in the alert dialog box.

The `window.alert` command displays a dialog box within the browser window.

The browser Developer Pane can be used to locate and fix programming errors.

```javascript
1  "use strict";
2
3  /*
4     New Perspectives on HTML5 and CSS3, 7th Edition
5     Tutorial 9
6     Tutorial Case
7
8     Countdown Clock
9     Author: Hector Sadler
10    Date:   2017-03-01
11
12 */
13
14 window.alert("Welcome to Tulsa");
```

Introducing JavaScript

In the last two tutorials, you read about JavaScript as a programming tool for creating interactive web forms and animated graphics. Starting with this tutorial, you examine the features and syntax of the JavaScript language, as well as explore how to create and apply your JavaScript programs to your websites.

Server-Side and Client-Side Programming

Web-based programming comes in two main types: server-side programming and client-side programming. In **server-side programming**, the program code is run from the server hosting the website. In some applications, users can interact with the program, requesting specific information from the server, but the interaction is done remotely from the user to the server. See Figure 9-1.

Figure 9-1   Server-side programming

3) a server-side program processes the information and may send additional feedback to the user

1) user retrieves web page from the server

2) information is sent to a program running on the server

© 2016 Cengage Learning

There are advantages and disadvantages to this approach. A program running on a server can be connected to an online database containing information not directly accessible to end users, enabling websites to support such features as online banking, credit card transactions, and discussion forums. However, server-side programs use server resources and require Internet access. If the system is over-loaded, the end user will have to sit through long delays, waiting for a process request to be fulfilled; or if the system is offline, the end user will have to wait for the system to come back online before the request can be processed.

In **client-side programming**, programs are run on the user's computer using scripts that are downloaded along with the HTML and CSS files. See Figure 9-2.

Figure 9-2   Client-side programming

1) user retrieves web page from the server

2) user runs the program locally, receiving instant feedback

© 2016 Cengage Learning

Client-side programming distributes the load so that one server is not overloaded with program-related requests; it tends to be more responsive because users do not have to wait for a response from a remote server. However, client-side programs can never completely replace server-side programming. For example, tasks such as running a search or processing a purchase order must be run from a central server because only the server can access the database needed to complete these types of operations.

In many cases, a combination of server-side and client-side programming is used. For example, data entry forms typically use client-side programs to validate some data entries, such as contact information, and server-side programs to submit the validated form for further processing that can only be done from a central server. In this tutorial, you will work only with client-side programming. However, it is important to be aware that in many cases, a complete web programming environment includes both client-side and server-side elements.

The Development of JavaScript

The programming language for client-side programs is **JavaScript**. JavaScript is an **interpreted language**, meaning that the program code is executed directly without requiring an application known as a **compiler** to translate the code into machine language. You need only two things to use JavaScript: a text editor to write the JavaScript code and a browser to run the commands. This means that JavaScript code can be inserted directly into an HTML file, or it can be placed in a separate text file that is linked to the HTML file.

Through the years, JavaScript has undergone several revisions, which include new components and features that might not be supported by older browsers. Because of this, you need to test your JavaScript code on a variety of browsers and platforms in the same way you test your HTML and CSS code to ensure the widest compatibility.

Working with the `script` Element

JavaScript code is attached to an HTML file using the following `script` element

```
<script src="url"></script>
```

where *url* is the URL of the external file containing the JavaScript code. Thus, the following code loads the contents of the tny_script.js file:

```
<script src="tny_script.js"></script>
```

If you don't want to use an external file, you can create an **embedded script** by omitting the `src` attribute and placing all of the JavaScript code within the `script` element as follows

```
<script>
   code
</script>
```

where *code* is the code of the JavaScript program.

REFERENCE

Inserting the `script` Element

- To link a web page to an external script file, add the following `script` element to the HTML file

  ```
  <script src="url"></script>
  ```

  where *url* is the URL of the external file containing the JavaScript code.
- To embed a script within the HTML file, add the following `script` element

  ```
  <script>
     code
  </script>
  ```

  where *code* is the code of the JavaScript program.
- To load an external script file asynchronous with the HTML file, add the attribute `async` to the `script` element.
- To load an external script file after the HTML file has finished loading, add the attribute `defer` to the `script` element.

Loading the `script` Element

The `script` element can be placed anywhere within the HTML document. When the browser encounters a script, it immediately stops loading the page and begins loading and then processing the script commands. Only when the script is completely processed does the browser continue to load the rest of the HTML file.

With larger and more complicated scripts, this loading sequence can degrade the user's experience because the page is literally stalled as it waits for the script to be processed. You can modify this sequence by adding the `async` or `defer` attributes to the `script` element. The `async` attribute tells the browser to parse the HTML and JavaScript code together, only pausing to process the script before returning to the HTML file. The `defer` attribute defers script processing until after the page has been completely parsed and loaded. See Figure 9-3.

Figure 9-3   Loading HTML and JavaScript code

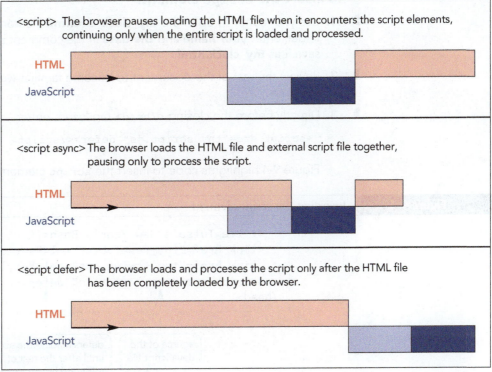

<script> The browser pauses loading the HTML file when it encounters the script elements, continuing only when the entire script is loaded and processed.

HTML

JavaScript

<script async> The browser loads the HTML file and external script file together, pausing only to process the script.

HTML

JavaScript

<script defer> The browser loads and processes the script only after the HTML file has been completely loaded by the browser.

HTML

JavaScript

© 2016 Cengage Learning

The `async` and `defer` attributes are ignored for embedded scripts and the code nested within the `script` element is executed as soon as it is encountered within the HTML file.

Inserting the `script` Element

Hector wants you to create a script that will display a running countdown clock for use with his page on Tulsa's New Year's Bash website. You will start working on his page by inserting a `script` element in the document head that will load the contents of the tny_script.js file. You will use the `defer` attribute to ensure that the script will not execute until all the page content is loaded by the browser.

To insert the `script` element:

1. Use your editor to open the **tny_clock_txt.html** file from the html09 ▸ tutorial folder. Enter **your name** and **the date** in the comment section of the file and save it as **tny_clock.html**.

2. Review the rest of the document to become familiar with its contents and structure.

3. Directly before the closing `</head>` tag insert, enter:

   ```
   <script src="tny_script.js" defer></script>
   ```

   Figure 9-4 highlights code to insert the `script` element.

Figure 9-4	Inserting the script element

```
<title>Tulsa's New Year's Bash</title>
<link href="tny_reset.css" rel="stylesheet" />
<link href="tny_styles.css" rel="stylesheet" />
<script src="tny_script.js" defer></script>
</head>
```

source of the JavaScript file

defers loading the script file until after the rest of the page is loaded by the browser

4. Open **tny_clock.html** in your browser. The initial page is shown in Figure 9-5.

Figure 9-5	Initial countdown clock

date and time values

Current Time
11/3/2017
2:45:12 p.m.

New Year's Eve Bash

58 DAYS   18 HOURS   14 MINUTES   48 SECONDS

© altafulla/Shutterstock.com; © jbdphotography/Shutterstock.com

days, hours, minutes, and seconds until January 1st

At the top of the page, Hector has inserted placeholder text showing the current date and time and the number of days, hours, minutes, and seconds until January 1st of 2018. However, this text is static and will not change to reflect the current date and time. Hector wants you to create a script that will update the date and time values every second and continually calculate the amount of time left until midnight on New Year's Eve. You will put the commands to create this countdown clock in a JavaScript file named tny_script.js.

Using Other Scripting Languages

The `script` element can be used with programming languages other than JavaScript. Other client-side scripting languages are identified by including the MIME type of the language. For example, the scripting language VBScript from Microsoft has the MIME type `text/vbscript` and can be accessed using the following code:

```
<script src="url" type="text/vbscript"></script>
```

You do not have to include a `type` attribute for JavaScript files because browsers assume JavaScript's MIME type, `text/javascript,` by default.

Creating a JavaScript Program

Because JavaScript files are simple text files, you can create and edit them using a standard text editor. You will start your study of JavaScript by first learning how to insert comments that describe the contents and goals of the script.

Adding Comments to your JavaScript Code

Adding comments to your code is an important programming practice. It helps other people who examine your code understand what your programs are designed to do and how they work. It can even help you in the future when you return to edit the programs and need to recall the programming choices you made. JavaScript comments can be entered on single or multiple lines. The syntax of a single-line comment is

```
// comment text
```

where `comment text` is the JavaScript comment. Single-line comments can be placed on the same line containing a JavaScript command in the general format:

```
command; // comment text
```

Multiple-line comments include several comments with each comment on its own line and are inserted using the following format:

```
/*
   comment text spanning
   several lines
*/
```

REFERENCE

Adding a JavaScript Comment

- To add a comment on a single line or inline with other JavaScript commands, enter

  `// comment text`

  where *comment text* is the JavaScript comment.
- To create a comment the spans multiple lines, enter:

  ```
  /*
      comment text spanning
      several lines
  */
  ```

Hector has already started a JavaScript file with a multiple-line comment describing the file and its authorship. Open this file now and complete the initial comment lines.

To edit JaveScript comments:

1. Use your editor to open the **tny_script_txt.js** file from the html09 ▸ tutorial folder.

2. Enter **your name** and **the date** in the comment section of the file as shown in Figure 9-6.

| Figure 9-6 | Adding a JavaScript comment |

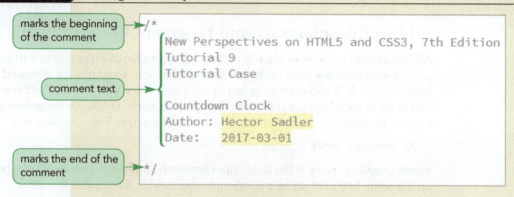

marks the beginning of the comment

comment text

marks the end of the comment

```
/*
    New Perspectives on HTML5 and CSS3, 7th Edition
    Tutorial 9
    Tutorial Case

    Countdown Clock
    Author: Hector Sadler
    Date:   2017-03-01
*/
```

3. Save the file as **tny_script.js**.

Next, you insert your first JavaScript command.

Writing a JavaScript Command

Every JavaScript program consists of a series of commands or statements. Each command is a single line that indicates an action for the browser to take. A command should end in a semicolon, employing the following syntax:

`JavaScript command;`

To test your understanding of JavaScript, you will add the following command to the tny_script.js file in the steps that follow:

`window.alert("Welcome to Tulsa");`

This command displays a dialog box to the user containing the message "Welcome to Tulsa". Note that the text of the message is enclosed in double quotes.

To add a command to the script:

Be sure to enclose the text of the alert dialog box within both opening and closing quotes or else an error will result.

1. Directly below the comments and after the `*/` line, enter:

   ```
   window.alert("Welcome to Tulsa");
   ```

   Figure 9-7 highlights the JavaScript command.

Figure 9-7	Displaying a dialog box

runs an alert dialog box in the browser window

text displayed in the dialog box

2. Save your changes to the file and then reload the tny_clock.html file in your browser. As shown in Figure 9-8, the browser displays a dialog box with the message you specified.

Figure 9-8	Google Chrome dialog box

Note that the dialog box style is determined by the browser. The dialog box in Figure 9-8 is the one displayed by Google Chrome.

Trouble? If you are using Internet Explorer, you might have to click the Allow Blocked Content button to allow results from your JavaScript program to appear in the browser window.

3. Click the **OK** button to close the dialog box.

The JavaScript command you just wrote is a very simple one. Before writing more complicated commands, you should first review some of the basics of JavaScript syntax and how to locate mistakes that might appear in your programs.

Understanding JavaScript Syntax

In addition to always including semicolons at the end of each command, there are some other syntax rules you should keep in mind when writing a JavaScript command. JavaScript is case sensitive, so you must pay attention to whether or not the letters of a JavaScript command are capitalized. For example, the command below improperly capitalizes the dialog box command as `Window.Alert` and, as a result, an error will occur when the script is run.

Example of improper capitalization:

```
Window.Alert("Welcome to Tulsa");
```

Example of proper capitalization:

```
window.alert("Welcome to Tulsa");
```

Like HTML, JavaScript ignores occurrences of extra white space between commands, so you can indent your code to make it easier to read. However, unlike HTML, you must be careful about line breaks within commands. A line break placed within the name of a JavaScript command or within a quoted text string will cause an error when the script is run. Thus, the following code will cause the program to fail.

Example of improper line break:

```
window.alert("Welcome
to Tulsa");
```

If you want to break a text string into several lines, you can indicate that the text string continues on the next line by using the following backslash \ character.

Example of proper line break:

```
window.alert("Welcome \
to Tulsa");
```

To see how your browser will handle errors in your JavaScript code, modify the `window.alert` command you just wrote, adding an intentional error using improper capitalization.

To insert an intentional error:

1. Return to the **tny_script.js** file in your editor and change the command to display an alert dialog box to the following incorrect syntax:

```
Window.Alert("Welcome to Tulsa");
```

2. Save your changes to the file and then reload the tny_clock.html file in your browser. Verify that the dialog box is not displayed by the browser.

At this point, you know the dialog box did not display because of the intentional error you entered in the code. But, what if the dialog box did not display as intended and you don't know the reason? Then, you can use your browser's debugging tools to track the error to its source.

Debugging your Code

As you work with JavaScript, you will inevitably encounter scripts that fail to work because of an error in the code. To fix those problems, you need to debug your program. **Debugging** is the process of locating and fixing a programming error. To debug a program, you must first determine the type of error present in your code.

There are three types of errors: load-time errors, run-time errors, and logical errors. A **load-time error** occurs when a script is first loaded by a browser. As the page loads, the browser reads through the code looking for mistakes in syntax. If a syntax error is uncovered, the browser halts loading the script before trying to execute it.

A **run-time error** occurs after a script has been successfully loaded with no syntax errors and is being executed by a browser. In a run-time error, the mistake occurs when the browser cannot complete a line of code. For example, if a command includes a mathematical expression involving division by zero (something that is not allowed), the program will fail with a run-time error even though proper syntax is used.

A **logical error** is free from syntax and executable mistakes, but results in an incorrect result, such as the wrong name being returned from a database or an incorrect value being returned from a calculation. A logical error is often the hardest to fix and will require meticulous tracing of every step of the code to detect the mistake.

Opening a Debugger

Every major browser includes debugging tools to locate and fix errors in your JavaScript code. For most browsers, you can open the debugging tool by pressing the F12 key on your keyboard or by selecting Developer Tools from the browser menu. To see a browser debugger, you will open the developer tools for Google Chrome. If you don't have access to Google Chrome, use the developer tools for your browser, reading the browser's online documentation to learn how to the use your browser's tools.

To open the Google Chrome developer tools:

1. With the browser window still open, press the **F12** key to view the Google Chrome developer tools.

2. Reload the tny_clock.html file.

3. From the menu list at the top of the Developer Tools pane, click **Sources** to show the list of files used in the current page.

4. Click **tny_script.js** from the Sources file list to show the program code in that file. See Figure 9-9.

Figure 9-9 **Google Chrome developer tools**

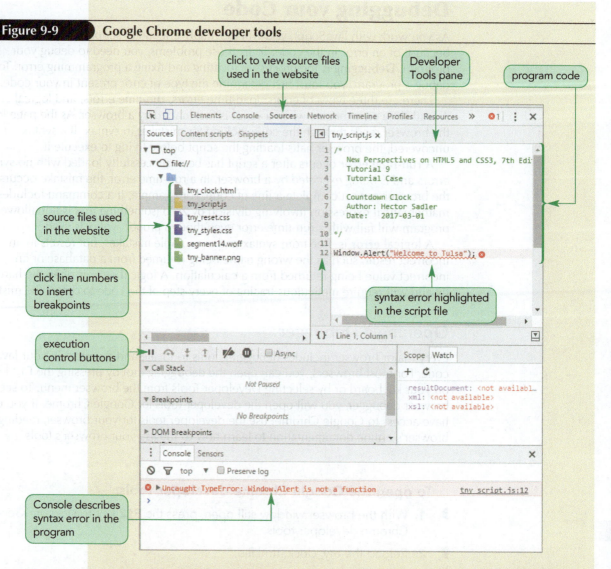

click to view source files used in the website

Developer Tools pane

program code

source files used in the website

click line numbers to insert breakpoints

execution control buttons

syntax error highlighted in the script file

Console describes syntax error in the program

Trouble? Depending on your browser setup, the location and size of your Google Chrome Developer pane might not match the one shown in Figure 9-9. If you do not see the Console shown in Figure 9-9 at the bottom of the pane, click Console to show the errors.

The syntax error you introduced in the script file is highlighted and the Console pane at the bottom of the window provides the error message, "Uncaught TypeError: Window.Alert is not a function"—a message indicating that the browser cannot process this command due to its improper syntax. At this point, you correct the syntax error by rewriting the code.

To fix the syntax error:

1. Return to the **tny_script.js** file in your editor and change the command to display the alert dialog box back to:

   ```
   window.alert("Welcome to Tulsa");
   ```

2. Save your changes and then reload the tny_clock.html file in your browser with the developer tools still visible. Verify that no syntax errors are reported and that the alert dialog box is once again displayed to the user.

3. Click the **OK** button to close the dialog box.

Inserting a Breakpoint

Debuggers contain a wealth of tools to aid you as you create more complex and involved programs. A script might work flawlessly except for one line that causes all subsequent commands to fail. One useful technique for locating the source of an error is to set up **breakpoints**, which are locations where the browser will pause the program, allowing the programmer to determine whether the error has already occurred at that point in the script's execution. To set a breakpoint in the Google Chrome browser, click the line number next to the line where you want the browser to pause execution of the script. Try this now by setting up a breakpoint in the line where the alert dialog box is displayed.

To place a breakpoint:

1. In the pane showing the source code of the tny_script.js file, click the line number corresponding to the line containing the `window.alert` command.

Notice that a blue arrow highlights the line, indicating that a breakpoint has been established at this location in the script.

2. Reload the tny_clock.html file in your browser. Verify that the browser halts execution of the script prior to displaying the alert dialog box and that a message is displayed with a control that allows the user to resume execution of the script. See Figure 9-10.

| Figure 9-10 | Setting a breakpoint in Google Chrome |

message displayed because of breakpoint; click to resume executing the script

breakpoint in the script

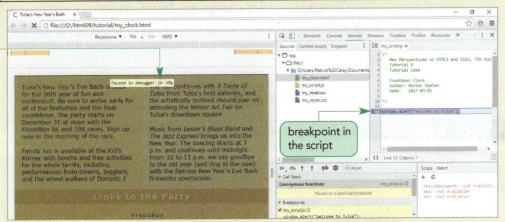

3. Click the **Play/Pause** button ▶ to resume execution of the script and then click the **OK** button to close the alert dialog box.

4. Click the line number next to the line containing the `window.alert` command to remove the breakpoint.

In this tutorial, you won't be adding any more intentional errors, but you might make your own mistakes in typing the JavaScript commands for the countdown clock program. If you do, you can use the debugging tools in your browser to locate and fix the mistake. For now, you close the Developer Tools pane and remove the command you created to display an alert dialog box. You won't need it in the final version of the program.

To close the browser's developer tools:

1. Within the browser window, press the **F12** key to close the developer tools.

2. Return to the **tny_script.js** file in your editor.

3. Select the line `window.alert("Welcome to Tulsa");` and delete it, removing it from the script.

Applying Strict Usage of JavaScript

JavaScript was designed to be easy for novice programmers to use. For that reason, JavaScript differs from some other programming languages, such as Java, which demand strict application of rules for syntax and program structure. Some JavaScript lapses in syntax are resolved in a way that it is not fatal to the program's execution. While this is attractive to novice programmers, it does encourage a certain degree of laxness in coding.

Many developers advocate that JavaScript be run in **strict mode** in which all lapses in syntax result in load-time or run-time errors. Using strict mode encourages good programming technique and also makes the script run more efficiently and faster. To run a script in strict mode, add the following statement to the first line of the file:

```
"use strict";
```

For this and future projects, you apply strict mode to the JavaScript code you create.

To apply strict usage to JavaScript:

1. Go to the top of the tny_script.js file in your editor and directly before the initial comment line /*, insert the line:

```
"use strict";
```

and press **Enter**. Figure 9-11 shows the revised code in the file.

Figure 9-11   Applying strict usage to JavaScript

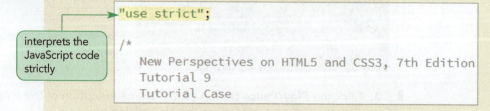

interporets the
JavaScript code
strictly

```
"use strict";

/*
    New Perspectives on HTML5 and CSS3, 7th Edition
    Tutorial 9
    Tutorial Case
```

2. Save your changes to the file.

Be aware that operating JavaScript in strict mode applies not just to your code but to any third-party scripts that your program accesses. This can cause fatal errors if the authors of those scripts did not write all of their commands following strict guidelines. You can avoid this problem by applying the "use strict" statement locally only to functions that you create rather than globally as the first line of your script file. The issues of JavaScript functions and local and global scope are discussed in the next two sessions.

PROSKILLS

Written Communication: Writing Better JavaScript Code

In working environments, the maintenance of a program or script is often shared among several individuals. The program you write today might be the responsibility of one of your colleagues next month. Thus, an important goal in writing program code is to make it intelligible to other users so that they can easily maintain and update it. Here are some tips to help you write better JavaScript code:

- **Use consistent names:** One common source of error is misnamed variables and functions. You can avoid this problem by being consistent in the use of uppercase and lowercase letters in your variable and function names.
- **Make the code easier to read with whitespace:** Crowded commands and statements are difficult to read and edit. Use whitespace and indented text generously to make your code more legible to others.
- **Keep your lines compact:** Long text strings can wrap to new lines in your text editor, making the text difficult to read. Strive to keep your lines to 80 characters or less. When a statement doesn't fit on a single line, break it to a new line at a point that maximizes readability.
- **Comment your work:** Always add comments to your work, documenting the purpose of each command and expression.

As your scripts become longer and more complicated you can also simplify your code by breaking it up into several JavaScript files dedicated to a specific task. Such files can be shared among several web pages, freeing you from having to rewrite the same code several times.

REVIEW

Session 9.1 Quick Check

1. What is a server-side program? What is a client-side program?
2. Provide code to attach your HTML file to a script located in the tny_functions.js file. Assume that the script file is loaded asynchronously.
3. What is the difference between asynchronously loading a script file and deferring the loading of the script file?
4. Provide code to insert the following comment text in a JavaScript file:
   Tulsa New Year's Bash
   Clock Functions
5. Provide the command to display an alert dialog box with the message "Happy New Year!".
6. What will be the result of running the following JavaScript command:
   WINDOW.ALERT("Page Loaded");
7. What is a breakpoint and why would you use a breakpoint in debugging your code?
8. What statement would be added to your JavaScript file to ensure that your code is strictly interpreted?

Session 9.2 Visual Overview:

The **Date object** stores a date value and a time value.

The **toLocaleDateString()** method returns a text string containing the date using local conventions.

The **var** keyword declares a JavaScript variable. Here the currentDay, dateStr, and timeStr variables are declared by the script.

The **toLocaleTime-String()** method returns a text string containing the time using local conventions.

The **getElementById()** method selects the element with the ID "dateNow".

```javascript
/* Store the current date and time */
var currentDay = new Date("May 23, 2018 14:35:05");
var dateStr = currentDay.toLocaleDateString();
var timeStr = currentDay.toLocaleTimeString();

/* Display the current date and time */
document.getElementById("dateNow").innerHTML =
dateStr + "<br />" + timeStr;

/* Display the time left until New Year's Eve */
document.getElementById("days").textContent = "dd";
document.getElementById("hrs").textContent = "hh";
document.getElementById("mins").textContent = "mm";
document.getElementById("secs").textContent = "ss";
```

© altafulla/Shutterstock.com;
© jbdphotography/Shutterstock.com

The **textContent** property defines the text within the referenced element.

The **innerHTML** property defines the HTML code within the referenced element.

JavaScript Variables and Dates

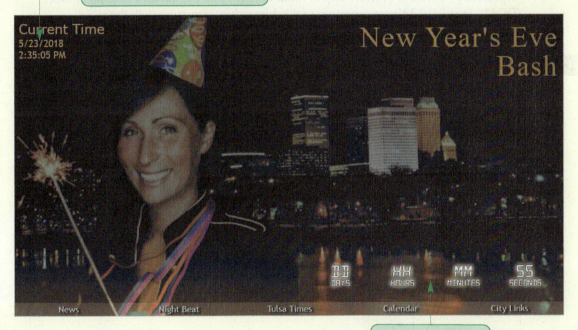

Date and time values generated with the `toLocaleDateString()` and `toLocaleTimeString()` methods.

Countdown clock text generated using the `textContent` property.

Introducing Objects

In the last session, you limited your use of JavaScript to creating an alert dialog box, but you left the content of the web page unchanged. In this session, you will use JavaScript to write content into the web page itself. To do that, you have to work with objects. An **object** is an entity within the browser or web page that has **properties** that define it and **methods** that can be acted upon it. For example, a video embedded on a web page is an object and has properties such as source of the video file or the width and height of the video player. It also has methods such as playing or pausing the video.

JavaScript is an **object-based language** that manipulates an object by changing one or more of its properties or by applying a method that affects the object's behavior within the web page or web browser. There are four kinds of JavaScript objects: **built-in objects** that are intrinsic to the JavaScript language, **browser objects** that are part of the browser, **document objects** that are part of the web document, and **customized objects** that are created by the programmer for use in his or her application.

Browser objects and document objects are organized in hierarchical structures respectively called the **browser object model (BOM)** and the **document object model (DOM)**. Figure 9-12 shows a portion of this hierarchical structure with the window object, representing the browser window, as the topmost object in the hierarchy.

Figure 9-12 **Object hierarchy**

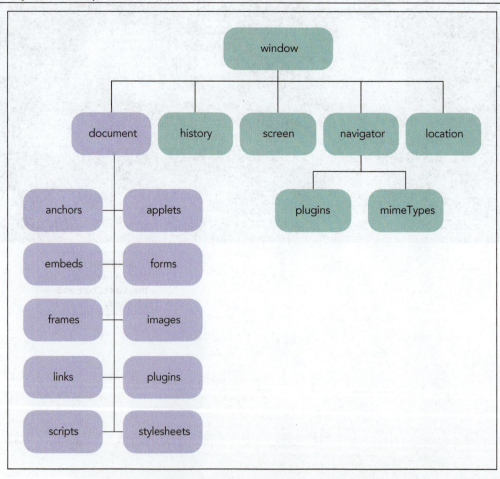

The following are contained within the `window` object:

- the `document` object containing objects found within the web page document
- the `history` object containing the browser's history list
- the `screen` object containing information about the computer screen
- the `navigator` object containing information about the browser application
- the `location` object containing information about the current URL

These objects themselves might contain other objects. For example, the `forms` object contained in the `document` object contains objects for each element within a web form.

It is important to note that document objects can be referenced only after the browser has finished parsing the page content. Any command that references a document object before the browser has parsed the HTML code will result in an error because those objects do not yet reside in memory. To ensure that an object can be referenced within a JavaScript program, apply the `defer` attribute to the `script` element so that JavaScript code is run only after the page is completed loaded.

Object References

Each object within the hierarchy is referenced by its object name such as `window`, `document`, or `navigator`. Because every object aside from the `window` object is nested within other objects, you can reference an object within the hierarchy using the notation

```
object1.object2.object3 ...
```

where *object1* is at the top of the hierarchy, *object2* is a child of *object1*, and so on. Thus, to reference the `images` object nested within the `window` and `document` object, you would use the JavaScript expression

```
window.document.images
```

You do not always have to use a complete reference detailing the entire object hierarchy. By default, JavaScript will assume that object references point to the current browser window. Thus, you can also refer to the `images` object in the current browser window using the expression:

```
document.images
```

Referencing Object Collections

Objects are organized into groups called **object collections**. Thus, the following object reference

```
document.images
```

references all of the inline images in the document marked with the `<img />` tag. Figure 9-13 describes some other object collections found within the document object model.

Figure 9-13	Document object collections

Object Collection	References
document.anchors	All elements marked with the `<a>` tag
document.applets	All `applet` elements
document.embeds	All `embed` elements
document.forms	All web forms
document.frames	All `frame` elements
document.images	All inline images
document.links	All hypertext links
document.plugins	All plug-ins supported by the browser
document.scripts	All `script` elements
document.styleSheets	All `stylesheet` elements

To reference a specific member of an object collection, you can use either

```
collection[idref]
```

or

```
collection.idref
```

where *collection* is a reference to the object collection, and *idref* is either an index number representing the position of the object in the collection or the value of the `id` attribute assigned to the element. The first object in the collection has an index number of 0 with subsequent objects given index numbers of 1, 2, 3, and so on. Thus, if the first inline image within a document has the tag

```
<img src="tny_logo.jpg" id="logoImg" />
```

you can reference that image using any of the following expressions:

```
document.images[0]
document.images["logoImg"]
document.images.logoImg
```

Object collections can also be based on tag names using the expression

```
document.getElementsByTagName(tag)
```

where *tag* is the name of an HTML element. For instance, the expression

```
document.getElementsByTagName("h1")
```

returns an object collection of all `h1` elements within the current document, while the expression

```
document.getElementsByTagName("h1")[0]
```

references only the first `h1` element found in the document.

Object collections can also be formed from HTML elements belonging to the same class by using the expression

```
document.getElementsByClassName(class)
```

where *class* is the value of the `class` attribute from the HTML document. Thus, the expression

```
document.getElementsByClassName("newGroup")
```

returns the collection of all elements that contain the attribute `class="newGroup"`. Because there is no distinction between HTML elements in this expression, the object collection might contain elements with different tag names as long as they all share a common value for the `class` attribute.

Finally, you also can create references to objects by the value of their `name` attribute using the expression

```
document.getElementsByName(name)
```

where `name` is the value of the `name` attribute associated with the element. Note that because more than one element can share the same name—such as radio buttons within a web form—this method returns an object collection rather than a single object.

Referencing an Object by ID and Name

One of the problems with object collections is that JavaScript will have to search through the entire collection to locate a specific item. If the object collection is large, this can be a time-consuming task and slow down the program. Another, more efficient approach, is to reference an element by its `id` attribute, using the expression

```
document.getElementById(id)
```

where `id` is the value of the `id` attribute. Thus, the expression

```
document.getElementById("dateNow")
```

references the element with the ID dateNow in the document. Note that only one object is returned, not a collection, because each `id` value is unique within an HTML document.

REFERENCE

Referencing Objects

- To reference an object as part of the collection in a document, use either

  collection[idref]

  or

  collection.idref

  where *idref* is either an index number representing the position of the object in the collection or the value of the `id` attribute assigned to that element.
- To reference a collection of elements based on the tag name, use

  ```
  document.getElementsByTagName(tag)
  ```

  where *tag* is the name of the element tag.
- To reference a collection of elements based on the value of the `class` attribute, use

  ```
  document.getElementsByClassName(class)
  ```

  where *class* is the `class` attribute value.
- To reference a collection of elements based on the value of the `name` attribute, use

  ```
  document.getElementsByName(name)
  ```

  where *name* is the value of the `name` attribute.
- To reference a document object based on the value of its `id` attribute, use

  ```
  document.getElementById(id)
  ```

  where *id* is the `id` attribute value.

Now that you have explored multiple ways to reference objects within a web page document, you will look at how to modify those objects.

Changing Properties and Applying Methods

An object can be modified in two ways: either by changing the object's properties or by applying a method. First, you examine how to modify an object property.

Object Properties

An object property is accessed using the following expression

```
object.property
```

where *object* is a reference to an object and *property* is a property associated with that object. For example, in Tutorial 8 you learned that input box controls have the `value` property, which sets the values displayed in the input box. To return the value of the input box control with the ID firstName, you would apply the expression:

```
document.getElementById("firstName").value
```

Thus, if the input box control displays the value "Hector", this expression will return the text string "Hector".

To change the value of an object property, run the command

```
object.property = value;
```

where *value* is the new value of the property for the referenced object. For example, to change the value in the firstName input box to "Diane", you would run the command:

```
document.getElementById("firstName").value = "Diane";
```

Not every property can be changed. Some properties are **read-only properties** and cannot be modified. For example, the `navigator` object representing the browser supports the `appVersion` property, which returns the version number of the browser program. So, while you can use the expression `navigator.appVersion` to view the version number of your browser, you certainly cannot use JavaScript to change your browser version.

Applying a Method

The other way to modify an object is by applying a method to it. A method can be thought of as an action operating on an object to produce a result. Methods are applied using the expression

```
object.method(values)
```

where *object* is a reference to an object, *method* is the name of the method that can be applied to the object, and *values* is a comma-separated list of values associated with that method. You applied an object method in the previous session when you ran the command:

```
window.alert("Welcome to Tulsa")
```

In this command, the `window` object represents the browser window and the `alert()` method is a method that displays a dialog box within the browser window. The text string "Welcome to Tulsa" is the *value* associated with the `alert()` method that sets the text of the dialog box.

Similarly, the `getElementById()` expression is a method applied to the `document` object in order to reference a particular object within the document based on its ID value.

Now that you have learned the basic syntax of objects, properties, and methods, you can use JavaScript to write content into a web page.

Writing HTML Code

The HTML code that is stored within a page element can be referenced using the following innerHTML property

```
element.innerHTML
```

where *element* is an object reference to an element within the web document. For example, if the document contains the following div element

```
<div id="daysLeft">58<br /><span>Days</span></div>
```

then the expression

```
document.getElementById("daysLeft").innerHTML
```

returns the text string "58
Days". Notice that both HTML tags and text content are returned by the innerHTML property. To change the content of this div element so that it contains the HTML code "45
Days", you could change the value of the innerHTML property in the following command:

```
document.getElementById("daysLeft").innerHTML =
"45<br /><span>Days</span>";
```

Changing the value of the innerHTML property overwrites whatever content is currently contained within the selected object, so you should be careful when using it to rewrite the content of elements that already exist in your document.

Hector has set up his web page with the following div element containing date and time values:

```
<div id="dateNow">11/3/2017<br />2:45:12 p.m.</div>
```

Use the innerHTML property to change the content of this div element to the text string "m/d/y
h:m:s". Note that you will replace this text string later with calculated values representing the current date and time.

To write HTML code with JavaScript:

1. If you took a break after the previous session, make sure the **tny_script.js** file is open in your editor.

2. Directly below the */ line in the comments area, insert the following code:

```
/* Display the current date and time */
document.getElementById("dateNow").innerHTML =
"m/d/y<br />h:m:s";
```

Figure 9-14 highlights the newly added code.

| Figure 9-14 | Changing the value of the HTML code within an element |

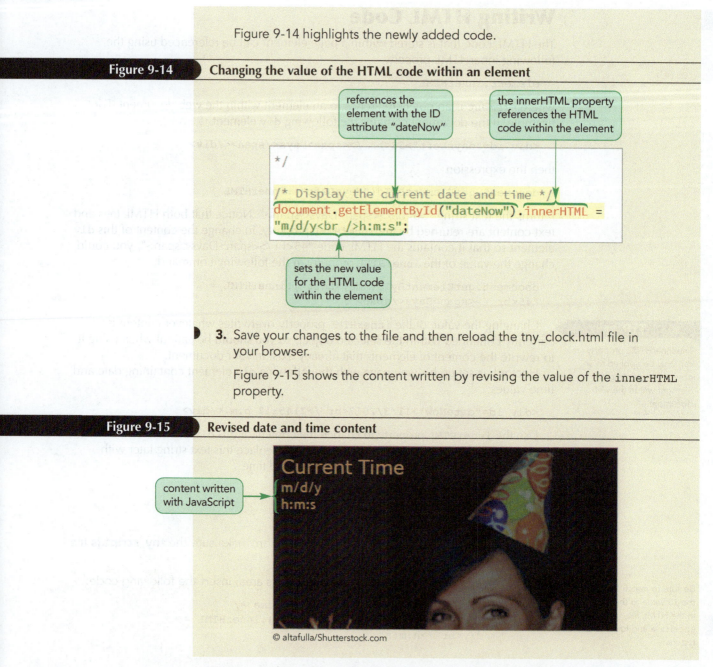

references the element with the ID attribute "dateNow"

the innerHTML property references the HTML code within the element

```
*/

/* Display the current date and time */
document.getElementById("dateNow").innerHTML =
"m/d/y<br />h:m:s";
```

sets the new value for the HTML code within the element

3. Save your changes to the file and then reload the tny_clock.html file in your browser.

Figure 9-15 shows the content written by revising the value of the innerHTML property.

| Figure 9-15 | Revised date and time content |

content written with JavaScript

Current Time
m/d/y
h:m:s

© altafulla/Shutterstock.com

Figure 9-16 lists other JavaScript properties and methods that can be used to modify the content of page elements.

Figure 9-16   Properties and methods to insert content

Property or Method	Description
element.innerHTML	Returns the HTML code within element
element.outerHTML	Returns the HTML code within element as well as the HTML code of element itself
element.textContent	Returns the text within element disregarding any HTML tags
element.insertAdjacentHTML (position, text)	Inserts HTML code defined by text into element at position, where position is one of the following: 'beforeBegin' (before the element's opening tag), 'afterBegin' (right after the element's opening tag), 'beforeEnd' (just before the element's closing tag), or 'afterEnd' (after the element's closing tag)

For example, if a page element contains only text and no HTML markup, you can modify its content more efficiently using the textContent property. In the tny_clock.html file, Hector has placed the countdown values in the following span elements:

```
<div><span id="days">58</span><br />Days</div>
<div><span id="hrs">10</span><br />Hours</div>
<div><span id="mins">14</span><br />Minutes</div>
<div><span id="secs">48</span><br />Seconds</div>
```

Use the textContent property now to change the days, hours, minutes, and seconds values to the text strings "dd", "hh", "mm", and "ss".

To write text content with JavaScript:

1. Return to the **tny_script.js** file in your editor.

2. At the bottom of the file, insert the following code:

```
/* Display the time left until New Year's Eve */
document.getElementById("days").textContent = "dd";
document.getElementById("hrs").textContent = "hh";
document.getElementById("mins").textContent = "mm";
document.getElementById("secs").textContent = "ss";
```

Figure 9-17 highlights the newly added code.

Figure 9-17   Revised text content

```
/* Display the current date and time */
document.getElementById("dateNow").innerHTML =
"m/d/y<br />h:m:s";

/* Display the time left until New Year's Eve */
document.getElementById("days").textContent = "dd";
document.getElementById("hrs").textContent = "hh";
document.getElementById("mins").textContent = "mm";
document.getElementById("secs").textContent = "ss";
```

references the element with the IDs "days", "hrs", "mins", and "secs"

property for the text content within each element

new text content within each element

3. Save your changes to the file and reload the tny_clock.html file in your browser.

Figure 9-18 shows the placeholder text used for countdown clock values.

Figure 9-18 | **Revised text content**

countdown clock text generated by JavaScript using the textContent property

© jbdphotography/Shutterstock.com; Source: www.1001fonts.com

Note that if you want to insert HTML code along with the text content, you must use the `innerHTML` property. The `textContent` property should only be used when no markup tags are involved.

INSIGHT

Writing Content with `document.write()`

Another way to write HTML content to the web page document is with the following method

```
document.write(text)
```

where *text* is the text of the content. The `document.write()` method is most often used with embedded scripts, writing content directly into the document as it is being loaded by the browser. For example, the following code uses an embedded script to write an h1 heading directly into the page header:

```
<header>
   <script>
      document.write("<h1>Welcome to Tulsa</h1>");
   </script>
</header>
```

Note that if this method is applied after the HTML file is completely loaded by the browser, it will *overwrite all of the HTML content in the document*, replacing the HTML code with the text specified in the `document.write()` method. If you want to modify the page after it has been loaded by the browser, you should only use the `innerHTML` or `textContent` properties.

Next, you will begin replacing the current date, time, and countdown placeholder values with calculated values. To do that, you must learn how to work with JavaScript variables.

Working with Variables

Because you used a specific text string with the `innerHTML` and `textContent` properties, your script did little more than what you could have accomplished by entering the HTML code directly into the web page document. JavaScript is much more powerful and versatile when used in conjunction with variables. A **variable** is a named item in a program that stores a data value, such as a number or text string, or an object, such as a part of the web browser or browser window. Variables are useful because they can store information created in one part of the script and use that information elsewhere.

Declaring a Variable

Variables are introduced into a script by **declaring** the variable using the following var keyword

```
var variable = value;
```

where *variable* is the name assigned to the variable and *value* is the variable's initial value. For example, the following statement declares a variable named currentDay and assigns it an initial value of "May 3, 2018".

```
var currentDay = "May 3, 2018";
```

You do not have to provide an initial value to a variable. You can leave the variable's value undefined as in the following command which declares the currentDay variable but does not provide a value.

```
var currentDay;
```

You can declare multiple variables by entering the variable names in a comma-separated list. The following statement declares two variables named currentMonth, and currentYear, assigning them the values of "May" and 2018 respectively.

```
var currentMonth = "May", currentYear = 2018;
```

JavaScript imposes the following limits on variable names:

- The first character must be either a letter or an underscore character (_).
- The remaining characters can be letters, numbers, or underscore characters.
- Variable names cannot contain spaces.
- You cannot use names that are part of the JavaScript language itself; for example, you cannot name a variable "document" or "window" or "textContent".

TIP

To avoid programming errors, use a consistent pattern of case for variable names and give your variables descriptive names that are easy to interpret.

Like other aspects of the JavaScript language, variable names are case sensitive. The variable names currentDay and currentday represent two different variables. One common programming mistake is to forget this important fact and to use uppercase and lowercase letters interchangeably in variable names.

After a variable is declared, its value can be changed by assigning a new value using the following command

```
variable = value;
```

where *variable* is the variable name and *value* is a new value assigned to the variable. Thus, the following command changes the value of the currentDay variable to "May 4, 2018":

```
currentDay = "May 4, 2018";
```

One of the advantages of using variables is that you can change their values several times throughout the program, often in response to user actions within the web page.

Variables and Data Types

JavaScript variables can store different types of information known as the variable's **data type**. JavaScript supports the following data types:

- numeric value
- text string
- Boolean value
- object
- null value

A **numeric value** is any number, such as 13, 22.5, or 3.14159. Numbers can also be expressed in scientific notation, such as 5.1E2 for the value 5.1×10^2 (or 510). Thus, if you wish to store the value 2018 in the currentYear variable, you would run the command

```
currentYear = 2018;
```

A **text string** is any group of characters enclosed within either double or single quotation marks. The following statement stores the text "May" in the currentMonth variable.

```
currentMonth = "May";
```

A **Boolean value** indicates the truth or falsity of a statement. There are only two possible Boolean values: `true` or `false`. For example, the following statement sets the value of the isMay variable to `true` and the value of the isApril variable to `false`:

```
var isMay = true, isApril = false;
```

Boolean values are most often used in programs that must respond differently to different conditions. The isMay variable cited above might be used in a program that tests whether the current month is May. If the value is set to `true`, the program runs differently than if the value is set to `false`. Note that if no value is assigned to a Boolean variable, it is interpreted as having a value of false.

Variables that represent objects can be used to simplify code by removing the need to rewrite long and sometimes complicated object references. Thus, the following dateDiv variable will store the reference to the document element with the `ID` dateNow:

```
var dateDiv = document.getElementById("dateNow");
```

Finally, a `null` value indicates that no value has yet been assigned to a variable. This can be done explicitly assigning the keyword `null` to a variable, as in the statement

```
var currentDate = null;
```

or implicitly by simply declaring the variable without assigning it a value.

INSIGHT

JavaScript and Weakly Typed Languages

In JavaScript, a variable's data type can be changed by the context in which it is used. In the following two statements, the currentMonth variable starts out as a numeric variable with an initial value of 4, but then becomes a text string variable containing the text "May":

```
var currentMonth = 4;

currentMonth = "May";
```

A programming language like JavaScript, in which variables are not strictly tied to specific data types, is referred to as a **weakly typed language**. Some other programming languages, known as **strongly typed languages**, force the programmer to explicitly identify a variable's data type. In strongly typed languages, the above code would result in an error because variables are not allowed to switch from one data type to another.

While a strongly typed language might seem restricting, it has the advantage of flagging programming errors, such as might occur when your program inadvertently switches the data type of a variable from a number to a text string.

Using a Variable

After you have created a variable, you can use it in JavaScript statements in place of the value it contains by inserting the variable name into a command or expression. For example, the following code uses the dateDiv variable to reference the page element with ID dateNow and then applies the innerHTML property to that object:

```
var dateDiv = document.getElementById("dateNow");
dateDiv.innerHTML = "May 3, 2018";
```

The effect is the same as if you had inserted the following command into your program:

```
document.getElementById("dateNow").innerHTML = "May 3, 2018";
```

The advantage of using a variable is that having defined the dateDiv variable, you can use it throughout the program without having to reenter a long and complicated object reference every time, which speeds up the execution of the code and makes your program easier to read and manage.

Working with Date Objects

One type of object you can store in a variable is a **Date object**, which is a built-in JavaScript object used to store information about dates and times. Date objects are defined using the following expression

```
new Date("month day, year hrs:mins:secs");
```

where *month*, *day*, *year*, *hrs*, *mins*, and *secs* provide the Date object's date and time. For example, the following command stores a Date object containing a date of May 23, 2018 and a time of 2:35:05 p.m. in the thisDate variable:

```
var thisDate = new Date("May 23, 2018 14:35:05");
```

Note that time values are based on 24-hour time so that a time of 2:35 p.m. would be entered as 14:35. If you omit the hours, minutes, and seconds values, JavaScript assumes that the time is 0 hours, 0 minutes, and 0 seconds—in other words, midnight of the specified day. If you omit both a date and time value, the Date object returns the current date and time based on the computer's system clock. Thus, the following command stores a `Date` object containing the current date and time in the thisDate variable:

```
var thisDate = new Date();
```

You can also define a date using the expression

```
new Date(year, month, day, hrs, mins, secs);
```

where *year*, *month*, *day*, *hrs*, *mins*, and *secs* are numeric values for the date and time. The *month* value is entered as an integer from 0 to 11, where 0 = January, 1 = February, and so forth. Time values are again expressed in 24-hour time. Thus, the following command also creates a variable storing the date and time May 23, 2018, at 2:35:05 p.m.:

```
var thisDate = new Date(2018, 4, 23, 14, 35, 5);
```

REFERENCE

Creating and Storing a Date

- To create a `Date` object, use

  ```
  new Date("month day, year hrs:mins:secs")
  ```

  where *month*, *day*, *year*, *hrs*, *mins*, and *secs* indicate the date and time to be stored in the `Date` object. Time values are entered in 24-hour time.
- To create a `Date` object using numeric values, use

  ```
  new Date(year, month, day, hrs, mins, secs)
  ```

  where *year*, *month*, *day*, *hrs*, *mins*, and *secs* are numeric values of the date and time with *month* an integer from 0 to 11, where 0 = January, 1 = February, and so forth. Time values are entered in 24-hour time.
- To create a `Date` object containing the current date and time, use:

  ```
  new Date()
  ```

Creating a `Date` Object

Now that you have seen how to store date and time information in a variable, you will create a variable named currentDay that stores a Date object. You use May 23, 2018 as the initial date and 2:35:05 p.m. as the initial time. Later in this tutorial, you will set the value of the currentDay variable to the current date and time. For now, using a preset date and time lets you check that any calculations based on the date and time are correct.

To create the currentDay variable:

1. Return to the **tny_script.js** file in your editor.

2. Directly below the closing */ line near the top of the file, insert:

   ```
   /* Store the current date and time */
   var currentDay = new Date("May 23, 2018 14:35:05");
   ```

   Figure 9-19 highlights the newly added code.

Figure 9-19	Creating a Date object

Next, you apply JavaScript's `Date` methods to extract information about this `Date` object.

Applying Date Methods

JavaScript dates are stored as numeric values equal to the number of milliseconds between the specified date and January 1, 1970 at midnight. For example, a `Date` object for May 23, 2018 at 2:35:05 p.m. has a hidden value equal to 1,527,104,105,000 milliseconds. Fortunately, you don't have to work directly with this value! Instead, Figure 9-20 describes some of the JavaScript methods used to extract information from a Date object.

Figure 9-20	Methods of the Date object

Date	Method	Description	Result
var thisDay = new Date("May 23, 2018 14:35:05");	thisDay.getSeconds()	seconds	5
	thisDay.getMinutes()	minutes	35
	thisDay.getHours()	hours	14
	thisDay.getDate()	day of the month	23
	thisDay.getMonth()	month number, where January = 0, February =1, etc.	4
	thisDay.getFullYear()	year	2018
	thisDay.getDay()	day of the week, where Sunday = 0, Monday = 1, etc.	3
	thisDay.toLocaleDateString()	text of the date using local conventions	"5/23/2018"
	thisDay.toLocaleTimeString()	text of the time using local conventions	"2:35:05 PM"

Hector wants to display the date and time on separate lines in the page header. To accomplish this, you create two new variables. The following dateStr variable will store the text string of the date portion of the `Date` object and the timeStr variable will store the text string of the time portion:

```
var dateStr = currentDay.toLocaleDateString();
var timeStr = currentDay.toLocaleTimeString();
```

Both the `toLocaleDateString()` and `toLocaleTimeString()` methods return text strings based on local conventions for rendering dates and times. Thus, in the United States the dateStr and timeStr variables will store the text "5/23/2018" and "2:35:05 PM" respectively. Other countries, with different local conventions, will use different text representations of these dates and times.

The dateStr and timeStr variables can be used with the `innerHTML` property for the dateNow div element to change the code inserted into the page element:

```
document.getElementById("dateNow").innerHTML =
dateStr + "<br />" + timeStr;
```

The + symbol is used in this command to combine two or more text strings in a single text string. Thus, in this command if the dateStr variable stores the text "5/23/2018" and the timeStr variable stores the text string "2:35:05 PM", the text string "5/23/2018
 2:35:05 PM" will be added to the inner HTML of the dateNow element.

Using Date Methods

- To retrieve the year, month, day, hours, minutes, and seconds value from a `Date` object, use the following methods

  ```
  date.getFullYear()
  date.getMonth()
  date.getDate()
  date.getHours()
  date.getMinutes()
  date.getSeconds()
  ```

  where *date* is a Date object.
- To retrieve the date as a text string using local conventions, apply the method:

  ```
  date.toLocaleDateString()
  ```

- To retrieve the time as a text string using local conventions, apply the method:

  ```
  date.toLocaleTimeString()
  ```

Rewrite the code in the tny_script.js file now to use `Date` objects and methods to display dates and times.

To apply date variables and methods:

1. Directly after the line declaring the currentDay variable, insert:

```
var dateStr = currentDay.toLocaleDateString();
var timeStr = currentDay.toLocaleTimeString();
```

2. Change the line that displays the current date and time to:

```
document.getElementById("dateNow").innerHTML =
dateStr + "<br />" + timeStr;
```

Figure 9-21 highlights the new code in the file.

Figure 9-21   Displaying dates and times

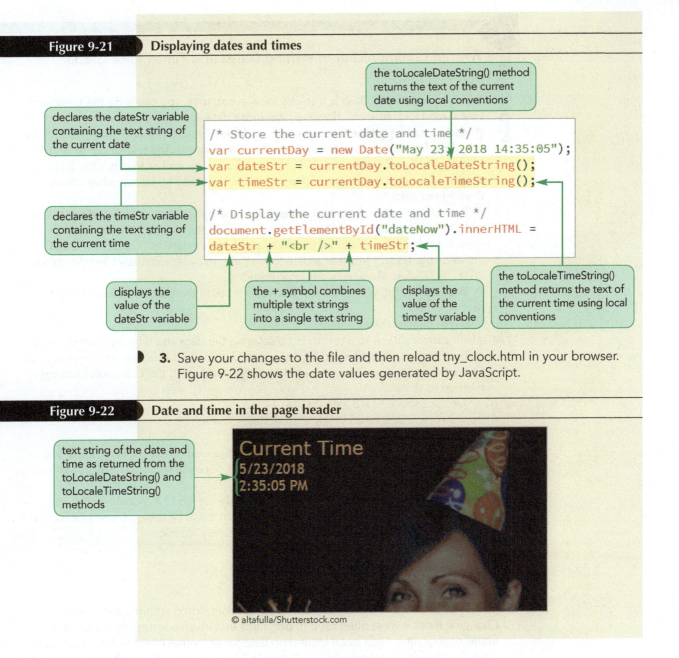

the toLocaleDateString() method returns the text of the current date using local conventions

declares the dateStr variable containing the text string of the current date

```
/* Store the current date and time */
var currentDay = new Date("May 23, 2018 14:35:05");
var dateStr = currentDay.toLocaleDateString();
var timeStr = currentDay.toLocaleTimeString();

/* Display the current date and time */
document.getElementById("dateNow").innerHTML =
dateStr + "<br />" + timeStr;
```

declares the timeStr variable containing the text string of the current time

displays the value of the dateStr variable

the + symbol combines multiple text strings into a single text string

displays the value of the timeStr variable

the toLocaleTimeString() method returns the text of the current time using local conventions

▶ **3.** Save your changes to the file and then reload tny_clock.html in your browser. Figure 9-22 shows the date values generated by JavaScript.

Figure 9-22   Date and time in the page header

text string of the date and time as returned from the toLocaleDateString() and toLocaleTimeString() methods

Current Time
5/23/2018
2:35:05 PM

© altafulla/Shutterstock.com

Written Communication: Writing Dates and Times for a Global Marketplace

The Tulsa New Year's Bash is a strictly local event; thus, you can write the dates and times using local formats. However, America's date and time conventions are not shared across the globe. If you are not careful with your dates and times, you run the risk of confusing your international readers. For example, the text string 10/3/2018 is interpreted as October 3rd, 2018 in some countries, and as March 10th, 2018 in others. Some countries express times in a 12-hour (AM/PM) format while others use the 24-hour clock.

If you expect your dates and times to be read by an international audience, you need to ensure that your text corresponds to local standards. One way to do this is to spell out the month portion of the date, expressing a date as "October 3, 2018". Other designers suggest that a date format with the year expressed first (for example, 2018-10-3) is less likely to be misinterpreted.

With JavaScript, you can write dates and times in the user's own local format using method

    date.toLocaleString()

which converts *date* to a text string displaying the date and time formatted based on the conventions employed by the user's computer. Thus, a date and time such as October 3rd, 2018 at 2:45 p.m. would be displayed using the `toLocaleString()` method as

    Tue, October 3, 2018 2:45:00 PM

from a computer located in the United States and as

    mardi 3 octobre 2018 1714:45:00

from a computer located in France. Note that the exact appearance of the string generated by the `toLocaleString()` method depends on the date/time settings on the computer and the settings of the browser.

As businesses continue to expand to meet the needs of a global market, you should use JavaScript's Date object in a way that makes it easier to communicate with your international customers and clients in a "timely" fashion.

Setting Date and Time Values

JavaScript also supports methods to change the date stored within a `Date` object. Changing dates is most often used in programs that involve setting the value of a future date or time, such as an expiration date for an online membership or an online calendar used for event scheduling. Figure 9-23 summarizes the methods supported by the JavaScript `Date` object used for setting date and time values.

| Figure 9-23 | JavaScript methods to set values of the Date object |

Date Method	Description
date.setDate(*value*)	Sets the day of the month of *date*, where *value* is an integer, ranging from 1 up to 31 (for some months)
date.setFullYear(*value*)	Sets the four-digit year value of *date*, where *value* is an integer
date.setHours(*value*)	Sets the 24-hour value of *date*, where *value* is an integer ranging from 0 to 23
date.setMilliseconds(*value*)	Sets the millisecond value of *date*, where *value* is an integer between 9 and 999
date.setMinutes(*value*)	Sets the minutes value of *date*, where *value* is an integer ranging from 0 to 59
date.setMonth(*value*)	Sets the month value of *date*, where *value* is an integer ranging from 0 (January) to 11 (December)
date.setSeconds(*value*)	Sets the seconds value of *date*, where *value* is an integer ranging from 0 to 59
date.setTime(*value*)	Sets the time value of *date*, where *value* is an integer representing the number of milliseconds since midnight on January 1, 1970

For example, the following code uses the `setFullYear()` method to change the date stored in the thisDate variable from May 23, 2017 to May 23, 2018:

```
var thisDate = new Date("May 23, 2017");
thisDate.setFullYear(2018);
```

In the next session, you will use the `setFullYear()` method in the countdown clock to calculate the number of days, hours, minutes, and seconds remaining until the New Year's Bash. If you want to take a break, you can close your editor and your browser now.

REVIEW

Session 9.2 Quick Check

1. What are the four types of JavaScript objects?
2. Provide the expression to reference all paragraph elements in the document.
3. Provide the expression to reference an element with the ID sidebar.
4. Provide the command to change the HTML code within the sidebar element to <h1>More Stories</h1>.
5. Provide the command to change the text within the sidebar element to "Current News".
6. Provide the command to declare the variable totalMonths with an initial value of 12.
7. What are Boolean values?
8. Provide the command to create a variable named expDate containing the date April 4, 2018 at 8:38:14 a.m.
9. Provide the expression to extract the hours value from the expDate variable.

Session 9.3 Visual Overview:

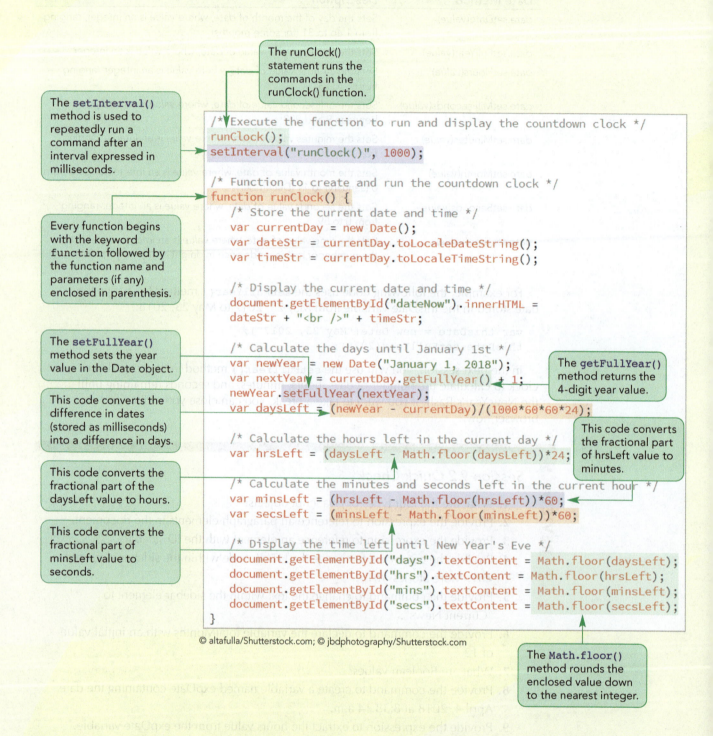

The runClock() statement runs the commands in the runClock() function.

The setInterval() method is used to repeatedly run a command after an interval expressed in milliseconds.

Every function begins with the keyword function followed by the function name and parameters (if any) enclosed in parenthesis.

The setFullYear() method sets the year value in the Date object.

This code converts the difference in dates (stored as milliseconds) into a difference in days.

This code converts the fractional part of the daysLeft value to hours.

This code converts the fractional part of minsLeft value to seconds.

The getFullYear() method returns the 4-digit year value.

This code converts the fractional part of hrsLeft value to minutes.

The Math.floor() method rounds the enclosed value down to the nearest integer.

```javascript
/* Execute the function to run and display the countdown clock */
runClock();
setInterval("runClock()", 1000);

/* Function to create and run the countdown clock */
function runClock() {
   /* Store the current date and time */
   var currentDay = new Date();
   var dateStr = currentDay.toLocaleDateString();
   var timeStr = currentDay.toLocaleTimeString();

   /* Display the current date and time */
   document.getElementById("dateNow").innerHTML =
   dateStr + "<br />" + timeStr;

   /* Calculate the days until January 1st */
   var newYear = new Date("January 1, 2018");
   var nextYear = currentDay.getFullYear() + 1;
   newYear.setFullYear(nextYear);
   var daysLeft = (newYear - currentDay)/(1000*60*60*24);

   /* Calculate the hours left in the current day */
   var hrsLeft = (daysLeft - Math.floor(daysLeft))*24;

   /* Calculate the minutes and seconds left in the current hour */
   var minsLeft = (hrsLeft - Math.floor(hrsLeft))*60;
   var secsLeft = (minsLeft - Math.floor(minsLeft))*60;

   /* Display the time left until New Year's Eve */
   document.getElementById("days").textContent = Math.floor(daysLeft);
   document.getElementById("hrs").textContent = Math.floor(hrsLeft);
   document.getElementById("mins").textContent = Math.floor(minsLeft);
   document.getElementById("secs").textContent = Math.floor(secsLeft);
}
```

JavaScript Functions and Expressions

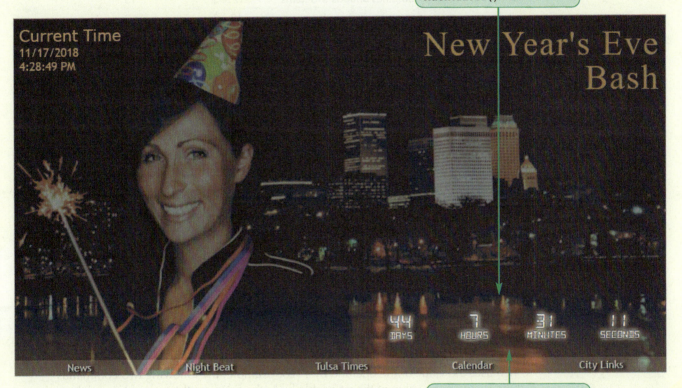

The days, hours, minutes, and seconds values are displayed as whole numbers due to the `Math.floor()` method.

The days, hours, minutes, and seconds left values are updated every second due to the `setInterval()` method.

Working with Operators and Operands

In the previous session, you worked with Date objects to display specified dates and times on a web page. In this session, you will learn how to perform calculations with dates and JavaScript variables. To perform a calculation, you need to insert a JavaScript statement that contains an operator. An **operator** is a symbol used to act upon an item or a variable within an expression. The variables or expressions that operators act upon are called **operands**. Figure 9-24 describes the operators supported by JavaScript.

Figure 9-24 JavaScript operators

Operator	Description	Expression	Returns
+	Combines or adds two items	12 + 3	15
–	Subtracts one item from another	12 – 3	9
*	Multiplies two items	12*3	36
/	Divides one item by another	12/3	4
%	Returns the remainder after dividing one item by another	18%5	3
++	Increases a value by 1	12++	13
– –	Decreases a value by 1	12– –	11
–	Changes the sign of a value	–12	–12

Note that the + operator is used to add two or more numbers to calculate a sum, but as you saw in the last session it can also be used to combine two or more text strings into a single text string. The following command shows an expression that uses the + operator to combine several text strings.

```
"<img src='" + imgFile + "' alt='' />"
```

TIP

To insert single quotation marks into a text string, you must enclose the text string with double quotation marks.

If the imgFile variable stores the text string "logo.png", this expression would return the text string "<img src='logo.png' alt='' />".

Operators are organized into **binary operators**, like + and –, which work with two operands in an expression and **unary operators**, which work on only one operand. One such unary operator is ++ (also known as the **increment operator**), which increases the value of the operand by 1. For example, the following two commands both increase the value of the x variable by 1; the first uses the + operator and the second uses the increment ++ operator:

```
x = x + 1;
x++;
```

A similar operator is the **decrement operator**, indicated by the – – symbol, which decreases the operand's value by 1.

Using Assignment Operators

Another type of operator is the **assignment operator**, which is used to assign a value to an item. Figure 9-25 lists the different JavaScript assignment operators.

Figure 9-25   **JavaScript assignment operators**

Operator	Example	Equivalent To
=	x = y	x = y
+=	x += y	x = x + y
−=	x −= y	x = x − y
*=	x *= y	x = x * y
/=	x /= y	x = x /y
%=	x %= y	x = x % y

The most common assignment operator is the equal sign (=), which assigns the value of one expression to another. JavaScript also allows you to combine the act of assigning a value and changing a value within a single operator. For example, both of the following expressions increase the value of the x variable by 2 but the += operator does so more efficiently.

```
x = x + 2;
x += 2;
```

TIP

Do not insert a space between the symbols in the += operator or JavaScript will report a syntax error.

After you master the syntax, you can use assignment operators to create efficient and compact expressions.

Calculating the Days Left in the Year

You will use operators and Date objects to calculate the number of days remaining until the New Year's Bash. To calculate this value, you need to do the following:

1. Create a Date object for January 1st of the next year
2. Calculate the difference between the current date and the upcoming January 1st

To create the January 1st Date object, you first declare the following newYear variable:

```
var newYear = new Date("January 1, 2018");
```

Using 2018 for the year is only a temporary step. The end goal is to create a Date object for January 1st of the upcoming year (whenever that may be). You can determine this value by extracting the year value from the currentDay variable you created in the last session and adding 1 to it using the following command:

```
var nextYear = currentDay.getFullYear() + 1;
```

Then, by applying the setFullYear() method, change the year of the newYear Date object to the coming year as follows:

```
newYear.setFullYear(nextYear);
```

With the newYear variable now containing a date matching the upcoming January 1st, the following command calculates the time difference between that date and the current day:

```
var daysLeft = newYear - currentDay;
```

However, because JavaScript measures time difference in milliseconds, not days, the daysLeft variable stores the number of milliseconds between January 1st and the current date. To express this value in days, you need to divide the difference by the number of milliseconds in one day. Because there are 1000 milliseconds in one second, 60 seconds in one minute, 60 minutes in one hour, and 24 hours are in one day, the revised command becomes:

```
var daysLeft = (newYear - currentDay)/(1000*60*60*24);
```

Add all of these commands to the tny_script.js file to calculate the days between the current date and upcoming January 1st.

To calculate the days left until the new year:

1. If you took a break after the previous session, make sure the **tny_script.js** file is open in your editor.

2. Directly above the comment /* Display the time left until New Year's Eve */, insert the following code:

   ```
   /* Calculate the days until January 1st */
   var newYear = new Date("January 1, 2018");
   var nextYear = currentDay.getFullYear() + 1;
   newYear.setFullYear(nextYear);
   var daysLeft = (newYear - currentDay)/(1000*60*60*24);
   ```

3. Replace the text string "dd" in the first line below the "Display the time left until New Year's Eve" comment with the daysLeft variable.

   Figure 9-26 describes the newly added code.

Figure 9-26 | Calculating the days left before the next January 1st

- sets the initial value of the newYear variable
- changes the year value of the newYear Date variable so that it contains the next January 1 date after currentDay
- calculates days left by converting the time difference from milliseconds to days
- adds 1 to the year value of the currentDay variable
- replaces the "dd" text string with the daysLeft variable

```
/* Display the current date and time */
document.getElementById("dateNow").innerHTML =
dateStr + "<br />" + timeStr;

/* Calculate the days until January 1st */
var newYear = new Date("January 1, 2018");
var nextYear = currentDay.getFullYear() + 1;
newYear.setFullYear(nextYear);
var daysLeft = (newYear - currentDay)/(1000*60*60*24);

/* Display the time left until New Year's Eve */
document.getElementById("days").textContent = daysLeft;
```

---

4. Save your changes to the file and then reload tny_clock.html in your browser.

   Figure 9-27 shows the calculated days until January 1st for the sample date of May 23, 2018.

Figure 9-27 **Days left until January 1st**

calculated value of the daysLeft variable

© jbdphotography/Shutterstock.com; Source: www.1001fonts.com

Trouble? If no value appears for the daysLeft variable, you might have made an error when entering the code. Use your browser debugger to check your code against the code shown in Figure 9-26, making corrections as needed. Save the file and then reload the web page.

The value displayed in the daysLeft field is 222.43396... (the clock font displays a decimal point as --), indicating that almost 222 and a half days are left until the start of the New Year's Bash. The fractional part of the value represents how much of the current day is remaining, which in this case is about 0.434 days. Since Hector wants the countdown clock to display the days, hours, minutes, and seconds until the party begins as integers, you have to modify the results by converting the fractional values to integer values expressed in hours, minutes, and seconds. You can do this by using some of the built-in JavaScript functions for mathematical calculations.

Working with the Math Object

One way of performing these types of calculations is to use JavaScript's `Math` object. The **Math object** is a built-in object used for performing mathematical tasks and storing mathematical values.

Using Math Methods

The `Math` object supports several different methods for calculating logarithms, extracting square roots, returning trigonometric values, and so forth. The syntax for applying a `Math` method is

```
Math.method(expression)
```

where *method* is the method you apply to a mathematical expression. Figure 9-28 lists the JavaScript `Math` methods and their descriptions.

Figure 9-28 Methods of the Math object

Method	Description	Example	Returns
Math.abs(x)	Returns the absolute value of x	Math.abs(−5)	5
Math.ceil(x)	Rounds x up to the next highest integer	Math.ceil(3.58)	4
Math.exp(x)	Raises e to the power of x	Math.exp(2)	e^2 (approximately 7.389)
Math.floor(x)	Rounds x down to the next lowest integer	Math.floor(3.58)	3
Math.log(x)	Returns the natural logarithm of x	Math.log(2)	0.693
Math.max(x, y)	Returns the larger of x and y	Math.max(3, 5)	5
Math.min(x, y)	Returns the smaller of x and y	Math.min(3, 5)	3
Math.pow(x, y)	Returns x raised to the power of y	Math.pow(2,3)	2^3 (or 8)
Math.rand()	Returns a random number between 0 and 1	Math.rand()	Random number between 0 and 1
Math.round(x)	Rounds x to the nearest integer	Math.round(3.58)	4
Math.sqrt(x)	Returns the square root of x	Math.sqrt(2)	approximately 1.414

Because the countdown clock will display only the integer portion of the days left, you will apply the `Math.floor()` method, which rounds a value down to the next lowest integer, to the daysLeft variable. For the 222.4339… value currently in the countdown clock, this method returns the integer value 222.

To apply the Math.floor() method:

1. Return to the **tny_script.js** file in your editor.

2. Apply the Math.floor method to the command that displays the value of the daysLeft variable, changing it to:

   ```
   document.getElementById("days").textContent =
   Math.floor(daysLeft);
   ```

   Figure 9-29 highlights the revised code in the command.

Figure 9-29 Applying the Math.floor() method

```
/* Display the time left until New Year's Eve */
document.getElementById("days").textContent = Math.floor(daysLeft);
```

rounds the daysLeft value down to the next lowest integer

3. Save your changes to the file and then reload the tny_clock.html file in your browser. Verify that 222 days with no decimal places are now shown in the countdown clock.

The difference between the exact days left in the year 222.43396… and the rounded value 222 is 0.43396…, which represents the fractional part of the current day left until the New Year's Eve Bash. Hector wants this value expressed in hours, which you can calculate by multiplying the fraction part by 24 (the number of hours in a single day) using the following command:

```
var hrsLeft = (daysLeft - Math.floor(daysLeft))*24;
```

As with the daysLeft variable in the previous set of steps, you need to round this value down to the next lowest integer using the `Math.floor()` method so that the integer portion only is displayed in the countdown clock.

To calculate the hours left:

1. Return to the **tny_script.js** file in your editor.

2. Directly below the line declaring the daysLeft variable, insert:

```
/* Calculate the hours left in the current day */
var hrsLeft = (daysLeft - Math.floor(daysLeft))*24;
```

> Be sure that the number of opening parentheses symbols matches the number of closing parentheses symbols.

3. Change the command that displays the text string "hh" as the hours left to:

```
document.getElementById("hrs").textContent =
Math.floor(hrsLeft);
```

Figure 9-30 highlights the code to calculate and displays the hrsLeft variable.

Figure 9-30	Calculating the hours left in the current day

```
var daysLeft = (newYear - currentDay)/(1000*60*60*24);

/* Calculate the hours left in the current day */
var hrsLeft = (daysLeft - Math.floor(daysLeft))*24;


/* Display the time left until New Year's Eve */
document.getElementById("days").textContent = Math.floor(daysLeft);
document.getElementById("hrs").textContent = Math.floor(hrsLeft);
document.getElementById("mins").textContent = "mm";
document.getElementById("secs").textContent = "ss";
```

> calculates the fractional part of the current day in terms of hours

> displays the integer part of hours left

4. Save your changes to the file and then reload tny_clock.html in your browser. Figure 9-31 shows the hours left in the current day.

Figure 9-31	Days and hours left until January 1st

> number of hours left in the current day

> number of days left in the current year

© jbdphotography/Shutterstock.com; Source: www.1001fonts.com

You may have noticed that JavaScript appears to have reported an extra hour in the day. The total is accurate since the current time is given as 2:35:05 PM but JavaScript reports that 10 hours are left. The extra hour comes from daylight savings time, which moves the clock backward one hour in the autumn, adding an extra hour to the overall calculation. Because the time interval between May 23 and January 1st includes the switch to daylight savings time, the extra hour appears in the hours part of the countdown clock.

Complete the countdown clock by calculating the minutes left in the current hour and the seconds left in the current minute. The technique to calculate the minutes left in the current hour is similar to the one you used to calculate the hours left in the current day. You multiply the difference between the hrsLeft value and the whole hours value by 60 (the number of minutes in an hour) to express the fractional part in terms of minutes, as shown in the following command:

```
var minsLeft = (hrsLeft - Math.floor(hrsLeft))*60;
```

Finally, to calculate the seconds left in the current minute, you multiply the fractional part of the minsLeft variable by 60 (the number of seconds in a minute), as follows:

```
var secsLeft = (minsLeft - Math.floor(minsLeft))*60;
```

As with the daysLeft and hrsLeft variables, you want to display only the integer part of the minsLeft and secsLeft variables by using the `Math.floor()` method. Add these commands to the script.

To calculate the minutes and seconds left:

1. Return to the **tny_script.js** file in your editor.

2. Directly below the command to declare the hrsLeft variable, add the following code:

```
/* Calculate the minutes and seconds left in the current hour
*/
var minsLeft = (hrsLeft - Math.floor(hrsLeft))*60;
var secsLeft = (minsLeft - Math.floor(minsLeft))*60;
```

3. Replace the "mm" and "ss" text strings in the countdown clock commands with values for the minsLeft and secsLeft variables rounded down to the next lowest integer using the `Math.floor()` method. The revised commands should appear as:

```
document.getElementById("mins").textContent =
Math.floor(minsLeft);
document.getElementById("secs").textContent =
Math.floor(secsLeft);
```

Figure 9-32 highlights the code to calculate the minutes and seconds left in the year.

| Figure 9-32 | Calculating the minutes and seconds left |

calculates the fractional part of the hours left in terms of minutes

calculates the fractional part of the minutes left in terms of seconds

```
/* Calculate the hours left in the current day */
var hrsLeft = (daysLeft - Math.floor(daysLeft))*24;

/* Calculate the minutes and seconds left in the current hour */
var minsLeft = (hrsLeft - Math.floor(hrsLeft))*60;
var secsLeft = (minsLeft - Math.floor(minsLeft))*60;


/* Display the time left until New Year's Eve */
document.getElementById("days").textContent = Math.floor(daysLeft);
document.getElementById("hrs").textContent = Math.floor(hrsLeft);
document.getElementById("mins").textContent = Math.floor(minsLeft);
document.getElementById("secs").textContent = Math.floor(secsLeft);
```

displays minutes left and seconds left as whole numbers

4. Save your changes to the file and then reload tny_clock.html in your browser. The countdown clock values for the specified date are shown in Figure 9-33.

| Figure 9-33 | Days, hours, minutes, and seconds left until January 1st |

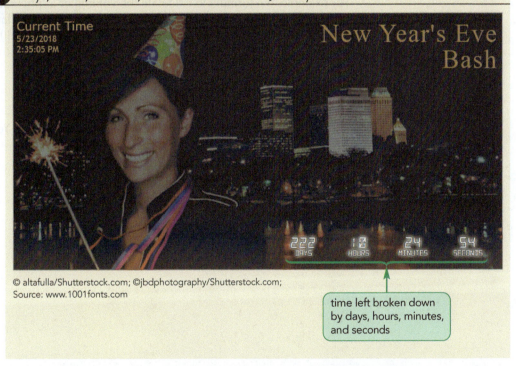

© altafulla/Shutterstock.com; ©jbdphotography/Shutterstock.com;
Source: www.1001fonts.com

time left broken down by days, hours, minutes, and seconds

Another factor in time calculations is that the day is not evenly divided into seconds. A fraction of a second is always left over each day. As the days accumulate, these fractions of a second add up. Most time devices, such as atomic clocks, account for this accumulation by adding a leap second on certain days of the year. JavaScript includes leap seconds in its time calculations as well and thus, it may sometimes appear that the seconds value in the countdown clock is off by a second.

Using Math Constants

Many functions require the use of mathematical constants, such as π and e. Rather than entering the numeric values of these constants directly into the code, you can reference the built-in constants stored in the JavaScript `Math` object. The syntax to access one of these mathematical constants is

```
Math.CONSTANT
```

where *CONSTANT* is the name of one of the mathematical constants supported by the `Math` object, shown in Figure 9-34.

Figure 9-34 Math constants

Constant	Description
Math.E	The base of the natural logarithms (2.71828…)
Math.LN10	The natural logarithm of 10 (2.3026…)
Math.LN2	The natural logarithm of 2 (0.6931…)
Math.LOG10E	The base 10 logarithm of e (0.4343…)
Math.LOG2E	The base 2 logarithm of e (1.4427…)
Math.PI	The value of π (3.14159…)
Math.SQRT1_2	The value of 1 divided by the square root of 2 (0.7071…)
Math.SQRT2	The square root of 2 (1.4142 …)

For example, the formula to calculate the volume of a sphere is $4\pi r^3/3$, where r is the radius of the sphere. To reference the value of π in the calculation of a sphere's volume, you would apply the `Math.PI` constant. To cube the value of r, you would use the method `Math.pow(r, 3)`. Putting these together, the code to calculate the volume of a sphere of 10 units would be as follows:

```
var radius = 10;
var volume = 4*Math.PI*Math.pow(radius, 3)/3;
```

You don't need to use any `Math` object constants for the New Year's Bash website.

Generating Random Numbers

One of the most useful applications of JavaScript is to create dynamic pages that can change in a random fashion. A commercial website might need to display banner ads in a random order so that customers see a different ad each time they access the page. To create these kinds of effects, you need a script that generates a random value. JavaScript accomplishes this using the `Math.random()` method, which returns a random value between 0 and 1. You can change the range of possible random values using the expression

```
lowest + size*Math.random()
```

where `lowest` is the lower boundary of the range and `size` is the size of the range. For example, to generate a random number from 20 to 30, you could apply the following expression:

```
10*Math.random() + 20;
```

In many cases, you want to limit a random number to integer values. To do so, enclose the random value within the `Math.floor()` method as follows

```
Math.floor(lowest + size*Math.random())
```

where `lowest` is the smallest integer in the range and `size` is the number of integer values in the range. Thus, to generate a random integer from 21 to 30, you would apply the following expression:

```
Math.floor(21 + 10*Math.random());
```

Note that using the `Math.floor()` method guarantees that the random number is rounded down to the next lowest integer, which in this example limits it to a range of integers from 21 to 30.

You will complete the calculations on the countdown clock so that instead of the sample date and time you used in this session, you will display the actual date and time based on your computer's clock. Recall that you can create a `Date` object showing the current date and time by using the expression

```
new Date()
```

with no parameter value for the object constructor.

To use the current date and time:

1. Return to the **tny_script.js** file in your editor.

2. Change the command declaring the currentDay variable to:

   ```
   var currentDay = new Date();
   ```

   Figure 9-35 highlights the revised command.

Figure 9-35   **Storing the current date and time**

stores the current date and time in the currentDay variable

```
/* Store the current date and time */
var currentDay = new Date();
var dateStr = currentDay.toLocaleDateString();
var timeStr = currentDay.toLocaleTimeString();
```

3. Save your changes and then reload tny_clock.html in your browser. Verify that the browser displays the current date and time.

4. Continue to reload the web page and verify that each time you reload the page, the time and countdown clock are updated with the current values.

Reloading the page updates the time and countdown values, but Hector would like your script to automatically update those values every second without requiring the user to reload the page. To create this effect, you first need to place all of the code you have written within a function.

Working with JavaScript Functions

When you want to reuse the same JavaScript commands throughout your web page, you store the commands in a function. A **function** is a collection of commands that performs an action or returns a value. Every function includes a function name that identifies it and a set of commands that are run when the function is called. Some functions also require **parameters**, which are variables associated with the function. The general syntax of a JavaScript function is

```
function function_name(parameters){
    commands
}
```

where *function_name* is the name of the function, *parameters* is a comma-separated list of variables used in the function, and *commands* is the set of statements run by the function. As with variable names, a function name must begin with a letter or underscore (_) and cannot contain any spaces. Also, like variable names, function names are case sensitive and thus, JavaScript treats names such as runClock and runclock as different functions.

For example, the following showDay function sets the innerHTML property of the dateNow element to the text string "11/3/2017
2:45:12 p.m."

```
function showDay() {
    document.getElementById("dateNow").innerHTML =
    "11/3/2017<br />2:45:12 p.m.";
}
```

Note that there are no parameters for this function, which means it always writes the same HTML code into the dateNow element. However, you could store the date and time text strings as parameters named dateStr and timeStr as the following function demonstrates:

```
function showDay(dateStr, timeStr) {
    document.getElementById("dateNow").innerHTML =
    dateStr + "<br />" + timeStr;
}
```

Note that parameters are treated as variables within the function. By defining the parameter values elsewhere in the JavaScript file, you can run this function to write different HTML code into the dateNow element.

Create a new function now named runClock() containing the code you have written to create and display the countdown clock.

To insert the runClock() function:

1. Return to the **tny_script.js** file in your editor.

2. Directly below the initial comment section, insert the following comment:

   ```
   /* Function to create and run the countdown clock */
   ```

3. Next, add the following code as the initial line of the runClock() function:

   ```
   function runClock() {
   ```

4. Scroll to the bottom of the file and insert a closing } to close the runClock() function.

5. Indent the code within the function to make it easier to read.

   Figure 9-36 shows the code and structure of the runClock() function.

Figure 9-36	Complete the runClock() function

there are no parameters in this function

opening { marks the start of the function commands

function name

```
/* Function to create and run the countdown clock */
function runClock() {
   /* Store the current date and time */
   var currentDay = new Date();
   var dateStr = currentDay.toLocaleDateString();
   var timeStr = currentDay.toLocaleTimeString();

   /* Display the current date and time */
   document.getElementById("dateNow").innerHTML =
   dateStr + "<br />" + timeStr;

   /* Calculate the days until January 1st */
   var newYear = new Date("January 1, 2018");
   var nextYear = currentDay.getFullYear() + 1;
   newYear.setFullYear(nextYear);
   var daysLeft = (newYear - currentDay)/(1000*60*60*24);

   /* Calculate the hours left in the current day */
   var hrsLeft = (daysLeft - Math.floor(daysLeft))*24;

   /* Calculate the minutes and seconds left in the current hour */
   var minsLeft = (hrsLeft - Math.floor(hrsLeft))*60;
   var secsLeft = (minsLeft - Math.floor(minsLeft))*60;

   /* Display the time left until New Year's Eve */
   document.getElementById("days").textContent = Math.floor(daysLeft);
   document.getElementById("hrs").textContent = Math.floor(hrsLeft);
   document.getElementById("mins").textContent = Math.floor(minsLeft);
   document.getElementById("secs").textContent = Math.floor(secsLeft);
}
```

function code is indented to make it easier to read

closing } marks the end of the function commands

Next, you explore how to run a function within your program.

Calling a Function

To run a function, you have to call it. If the function has any parameters, the initial values of the parameters are set when the function is called. The expression to call a function and run the commands it contains has the general form

```
function_name(parameter values)
```

where *function_name* is the name of the function and *parameter values* is a comma-separated list of values that match the parameters of the function. If no parameters are used with the function, leave the parameter values blank as follows:

```
function_name()
```

For example, to call the showDay() function described earlier with the text string "11/3/2017" for the `dateStr` parameter and "2:45:12 p.m." as the value of the timeStr parameter, you would run the following command:

```
showDay("11/3/2017", "2:45:12 p.m.");
```

resulting in the following HTML code being written into the dateNow element:

```
11/3/2017<br />2:45:12 p.m.
```

Parameter values can also be variables. The following code calls the showDay() function using the values stored in the text1 and text2 variables:

```
var text1="11/3/2017";
var text2="2:45:12 p.m.";
showDay(text1, text2);
```

resulting in the same code written to the `innerHTML` property of the dateNow element. One of the great advantages of functions is that they can be repeatedly called with different parameter values to achieve different results. Another advantage is that functions break long and complicated scripts into manageable chunks. It's also good programming practice to include oft-used functions in a separate JavaScript file so that they can be accessed and used by multiple scripts throughout the website.

Execute the runClock() function now by adding a line to call it.

To call the runClock() function:

1. Directly above the runClock() function, insert the following command:

   ```
   /* Execute the function to run and display the countdown clock */
   runClock();
   ```

2. Compare your code to Figure 9-37, which highlights the code to run the runClock() function.

Figure 9-37   Calling the runClock() function

command to execute the runClock() function →

```
/* Execute the function to run and display the countdown clock */
runClock();


/* Function to create and run the countdown clock */
function runClock() {
   /* Store the current date and time */
```

3. Save your changes to the file and then reload tny_clock.html in your browser. Verify that the page once again displays the current date and time and calculates the time interval until the New Year's Bash.

Creating a Function to Return a Value

You created the runClock() function to perform the action of writing HTML code to elements on the countdown clock web page. The other use of a function is to return a calculated value. For a function to return a value, it must conclude with a `return` statement as follows

```
function function_name(parameters){
   commands
   return value;
}
```

where *value* is the calculated value that is returned by the function. For example, the following calcArea() function returns the area of a rectangle for a given length and width:

```
function calcArea(length, width) {
   var rectArea = length*width;
   return rectArea;
}
```

In this function, the value of the rectArea variable is returned by the function. The following code demonstrates how to call the calcArea() function for an 8×6 rectangle, storing the calculated area in the totalArea variable:

```
var x = 8;
var y = 6;
var totalArea = calcArea(x,y);
```

The first two commands assign the values 8 and 6 to the *x* and *y* variables, respectively. The values of both of these variables are then sent to the calcArea() function as the values of the length and width parameters. The calcArea() function uses these values to calculate the area, which is stored in the totalArea variable.

Functions that return a value can be placed within larger expressions. For example, the following code calls the calcArea() function within an expression that multiplies the area value by 2 and store it as the variable z2:

```
var z2 = calcArea(x,y)*2;
```

You do not need to create a function that returns a value for Hector's countdown clock page.

INSIGHT

Functions and Variable Scope

As you have seen, the commands within a function are run only when the function is called. This has an impact on how variables within the function are treated. Every variable you create has a property known as **scope**, which indicates where you can reference the variable within the JavaScript file. A variable's scope can be either local or global. A variable declared within a function has **local scope** and can be referenced only within that function. Variables with local scope are sometimes referred to as **local variables**. All of the variables you created in this session have local scope and can only be referenced from within the runClock() function. Function parameters also have local scope and are not recognized outside of the function in which they are used.

Variables not declared within functions have **global scope** and can be referenced from anywhere within the script file or from within other script files. Variables with global scope are often referred to as **global variables**.

Running Timed Commands

You have completed the functions required for the countdown clock, but the clock is largely static, changing only when the page is reloaded by the browser. Hector wants the clock to be updated constantly so that it always shows the current time and the time remaining until the New Year's Bash. To do this, you need to rerun the runClock() function at specified times. JavaScript provides two methods for doing this: time-delayed commands and timed-interval commands.

Working with Time-Delayed Commands

A **time-delayed command** is a JavaScript command that is run after a specified amount of time has passed. The time delay is defined using the following setTimeout() method

```
setTimeout("command", delay);
```

where *command* is a JavaScript command and *delay* is the delay time in milliseconds before a browser runs the command. The command must be placed within either double or single quotation marks. For example, the following command sets a 5-millisecond delay before a browser runs the runClock() function:

```
setTimeout("runClock()", 5);
```

In some JavaScript programs, you may want to cancel a time-delayed command. This can be necessary when other user actions remove the need to run the command. Time-delayed commands are canceled using the following statement:

```
clearTimeout();
```

There is no limit to the number of time-delayed commands a browser can process. To distinguish one time-delayed command from another, you assign a unique identification to each command using the statement

```
var timeID = setTimeout("command", delay);
```

where *timeID* is a variable that stores the ID of the time-delayed command. After you have assigned an ID to the command, you can cancel it using the following clearTimeout() method

```
clearTimeout(timeID);
```

where once again *timeID* is the variable that stores the ID of the command.

Running Commands at Specified Intervals

The other way to time JavaScript commands is by using a timed-interval command, which instructs browsers to run the same command repeatedly at a specified interval. Timed-interval commands are applied using the following setInterval() method

```
setInterval("command", interval);
```

TIP

With timed-interval commands, the first execution of the command occurs after a delay equal to the size of the time interval.

where *interval* is the interval in milliseconds before the command is run again. Timed-interval commands are halted using the following statement:

```
clearInterval();
```

As with time-delayed commands, you may have several timed-interval commands running simultaneously. To distinguish one timed-interval command from another, you store the time ID in a variable as follows

```
var timeID = setInterval("command", interval);
```

and halt the timed-interval command by applying the `clearInterval()` method with `timeID` as the parameter value:

```
clearInterval(timeID);
```

An important point to remember about the `setTimeout()` and `setInterval()` methods is that after a browser processes a request to run a command at a later time, the browser doesn't stop. Instead, the browser processes the next commands in the script without delay. For example, you might try to run three functions at 50-millisecond intervals using the following structure:

```
setTimeout("function1()", 50);
setTimeout("function2()", 50);
setTimeout("function3()", 50);
```

However, a browser would execute this code by running all three functions almost simultaneously. To run the functions with a separation of about 50 milliseconds between one function and the next, you would need to use three different delay times, as follows:

```
setTimeout("function1()", 50);
setTimeout("function2()", 100);
setTimeout("function3()", 150);
```

In this case, a user's browser would run the first function after 50 milliseconds, the second function 50 milliseconds after that, and the third function after another 50 milliseconds have passed.

REFERENCE

Running Timed Commands

- To run a command after a delay, use the method

  `var timeID = setTimeout("command", delay)`

  where *command* is the command to be run, *delay* is the delay time in milliseconds, and *timeID* is a variable that stores the ID associated with the time-delayed command.
- To repeat a command at set intervals, use the method

  `var timeID = setInterval("command", interval)`

  where *interval* is the time, in milliseconds, between repetitions of the command.
- To cancel a specific time-delayed command, use the method

  `clearTimeout(timeID)`

  where *timeID* is the ID of the time-delayed command.
- To clear all time-delayed commands, use the following method:

  `clearTimeout()`

- To cancel a repeated command, use the method

  `clearInterval(timeID)`

  where *timeID* is the ID of the repeated command.
- To clear all repeated commands, use the following method:

  `clearInterval()`

Use the `setInterval()` method to repeatedly run the runClock() function. Because the function should run once every second, set the interval length to 1000 milliseconds using the command:

```
setInterval("runClock()", 1000);
```

Add this command to the tny_script.js file now.

To run the runClock() function every second:

▶ **1.** Return to the **tny_script.js** file in your editor and, directly below the runClock() command, insert the following:

```
setInterval("runClock()", 1000);
```

Figure 9-38 highlights the code to run the timed-interval command.

Figure 9-38   **Repeating the runClock() function**

```
/* Execute the function to run and display the countdown clock */
runClock();
setInterval("runClock()", 1000);
```

repeats the runClock()
function every second

▶ **2.** Save your changes to the file and then reload tny_clock.html in your browser.

▶ **3.** Verify that every second the time value and the countdown value change as the date of the New Year's Eve Bash comes ever closer.

You have completed the countdown clock for the New Year's Bash. Hector will continue to work on the event's website and get back to you with any new projects or concerns.

Controlling How JavaScript Works with Numeric Values

As you perform mathematical calculations using JavaScript, you will encounter situations in which you need to work with the properties of numeric values themselves. JavaScript provides several methods that allow you to examine the properties of numbers and specify how they are displayed on a web page.

Handling Illegal Operations

Some mathematical operations can return results that are not numeric values. For example, you cannot divide a number by a text string. An expression such as `5/"A"` will return the value `NaN`, which stands for "Not A Number" and is JavaScript's way of indicating an illegal operation that should involve only numeric values, but doesn't. You can check for the presence of this particular error using the following `isNaN()` function

```
isNaN(value)
```

where *value* is the value or variable you want to test for being numeric. The `isNaN()` function returns a Boolean value of `true` if the value is not numeric and `false` otherwise. The use of the `isNaN()` function is one way to locate illegal operations in code in which non-numeric values are treated as numeric.

Another illegal operation is dividing a number by 0, which returns a value of `Infinity`, indicating a numeric calculation whose result is greater than the largest numeric value supported by JavaScript. An `Infinity` value is also generated for an operation whose result is less than the smallest numeric value. JavaScript is limited to numeric values that fall between approximately 1.8×10^{-308} and 1.8×10^{308}. Any operation that exceeds those bounds, such as attempting to divide a number by 0, causes JavaScript to assign a value of `Infinity` to the result. You can check for this outcome using the function

```
isFinite(value)
```

where *value* is the value you want to test for being finite. Like the `isNaN()` function, the `isFinite()` function returns a Boolean value of `true` if the value is a finite number falling within JavaScript's acceptable range and `false` if the numeric value falls outside that range or if the value is not a number at all.

Defining a Number Format

When JavaScript displays a numeric value, it stores that value to 16 decimal places of accuracy. This can result in long numeric strings of digits being displayed by browsers. For example, a value such as 1/3 is stored as 0.3333333333333333.

It is rare that will you need to display a calculated value to 16 decimal places. To control the number of digits displayed by browsers, you can apply the following `toFixed()` method

```
value.toFixed(n)
```

where *value* is the value or variable and *n* is the number of decimal places that should be displayed in the output. The following examples show the `toFixed()` method applied to different numeric values:

```
var testValue = 2.835;
testValue.toFixed(0)   // returns "3"
testValue.toFixed(1)   // returns "2.8"
testValue.toFixed(2)   // returns "2.84"
```

Note that the `toFixed()` method limits the number of decimals displayed by a value and converts the value into a text string. Also, the `toFixed()` method rounds the last digit in an expression rather than truncating it.

Converting Between Numbers and Text

Sometimes, you might need to convert a number to a text string and vice versa. One way to convert a number to a text string is by using the + operator to add a text string to a number. For example, the following code uses the + operator to concatenate a numeric value with an empty text string. The result is a text string containing the characters 123.

```
testNumber = 123;          // numeric value
testString = testNumber + ""; // text string
```

To convert a text string to a number, you can apply an arithmetic operator (other than the + operator) to the text string. The following code takes the text string 123 and multiplies it by 1. JavaScript converts the text string "123" to the numeric value 123.

```
testString = "123";        // text string
testNumber = testString*1; // numeric value
```

Another way of converting a text string to a numeric value is to use the following `parseInt()` function, which extracts the leading integer value from a text string

```
parseInt(text)
```

where `text` is the text string or variable from which you want to extract the leading integer value. The `parseInt()` function returns the integer value from the text string, discarding any non-integer characters. If a text string does not begin with an integer, the function returns the value `NaN`, indicating that the text string contains no accessible number. The following are some sample values returned by the `parseInt()` method:

```
parseInt("120 lbs");                   // returns 120
parseInt("120.88 lbs");                // returns 120
parseInt("weight equals 120 lbs");     // returns NaN
```

Figure 9-39 summarizes the different JavaScript functions and methods used to work with numeric values.

TIP

You can use the parse-Float() method to extract decimal values from text strings.

Figure 9-39   **Numerical functions and methods**

Numerical Function	Description
`isFinite(value)`	Indicates whether *value* is finite and a real number
`isNaN(value)`	Indicates whether *value* is a number
`parseFloat(string)`	Extracts the first numeric value from the text *string*
`parseInt(string)`	Extracts the first integer value from the text *string*

Numerical Method	Description
`value.toExponential(n)`	Returns a text string displaying *value* in exponential notation with *n* digits to the right of the decimal point
`value.toFixed(n)`	Returns a text string displaying *value* to *n* decimal places
`value.toPrecision(n)`	Returns a text string displaying *value* to *n* significant digits either to the left or to the right of the decimal point

You don't need to use the `parseInt()` or other numeric methods in your code. At this point, you can close any open files or applications.

PROSKILLS

Problem Solving: Fixing Common Programming Mistakes

When you begin writing JavaScript programs, you will invariably encounter mistakes in your code. Some common sources of programming errors include:

- **Misspelling a variable name:** For example, if you named a variable ListPrice, then misspellings or incorrect capitalization—such as listprice, ListPrice, or list_price—will result in the program failing to run correctly.
- **Mismatched parentheses or braces:** The following code results in an error because the function lacks the closing brace:

```
function Area(width, height) {
    var size = width*height;
```

- **Mismatched quotes:** If you neglect the closing quotes around a text string, JavaScript treats the text string as an object or variable, resulting in an error. The following code results in an error because the closing double quote is missing from the firstName variable:

```
var firstName = "Sean';
var lastName = "Lee";
```

- **Missing quotes:** When you combine several text strings using the + symbol, you might neglect to quote all text strings. For example, the following code generates an error because of the missing quotes around the <br /> tag:

```
document.write("MidWest Student Union" + <br />);
```

As you become more experienced, you will be able to quickly spot these types of errors, making it easier for you to debug your programs.

REVIEW

Session 9.3 Quick Check

1. Provide the command to increase the value of the thisDay variable by 1, using the increment operator.
2. Rewrite the following command using an assignment operator:
   `income = income - taxes;`
3. Provide the expression to return the value of dailyIncome, rounded up to the next highest integer.
4. The area of a circle is πr^2 where r is the circle's radius. Provide a JavaScript expression to return a circle's area where the radius has been stored in a variable named radius.
5. Provide code to create a function named calcCirArea() that returns the area of a circle for a given radius.
6. Provide the command to call the calcCirArea() function using a value of 15 for the circle's radius and storing the result in a variable named finalArea.
7. What is the difference between variables with local scope and variables with global scope?
8. Provide the command to run the init() function after a 5-second delay. There are no parameter values for the init() function.
9. Provide the command the run the init() function once every 5 seconds.

Review Assignments

Data Files needed for the Review Assignments: tny_july_txt.html, tny_timer_txt.js, 2 CSS files, 1 PNG file, 1 TTF file, 1 WOFF file

Hector wants you to create a countdown clock page for the Tulsa Summer Party held on July 4th of every year. He wants the page to show the current date and time and to include a timer that counts down to the start of the fireworks at 9 p.m. on the 4th. Hector has already completed the page content and needs you to write the JavaScript code. A preview of the completed page for a sample date and time is shown in Figure 9-40.

Figure 9-40 **Tulsa Summer Party**

© jbdphotography/Shutterstock.com; © Aija Lehtonen/Shutterstock.com; Source: www.1001fonts.com

Complete the following:

1. Use your editor to open the **tny_july_txt.html** and **tny_timer_txt.js** files from the html09 ▶ review folder. Enter *your name* and *the date* in the comment section of each file, and save them as **tny_july.html** and **tny_timer.js** respectively.

2. Go to the **tny_july.html** file in your editor. Directly above the closing `</head>` tag, insert a `script` element that links to the tny_timer.js file. Defer the loading of the script file until the web page loads.

3. Take some time to study the content and structure of the file, paying close attention to the id attributes applied to different page elements. Save your changes to the document.

4. Go to the **tny_timer.js** file in your editor. At the top of the file, insert a statement to tell the browser to apply strict usage of the JavaScript code in the file.

5. Directly above the nextJuly4() function, insert a function named **showClock()** that has no parameters. Within the showClock() function, complete Steps a through g.

   a. Declare a variable named **thisDay** that stores a Date object containing the date May 19, 2018 at 9:31:27 a.m.

   b. Declare a variable named **localDate** that contains the text of the date from the thisDay variable using local conventions. Declare another variable named **localTime** that contains the text of the time stored in the thisDay variable using local conventions.

   c. Within the inner HTML of the page element with the ID currentTime, write the following code
   ```
   <span>date</span><span>time</span>
   ```
   where *date* and *time* are the values of the localDate and localTime variables.

   d. Hector has supplied you with a function named nextJuly4() that returns the date of the next 4th of July. Call the nextJuly4() function using thisDay as the parameter value and store the date returned by the function in the **j4Date** variable.

   e. The countdown clock should count down to 9 p.m. on the 4th of July. Apply the setHours() method to the j4Date variable to change the hours value to 9 p.m. (*Hint*: Express the value for 9 p.m. in 24-hour time.)

   f. Create variables named **days**, **hrs**, **mins**, and **secs** containing the days, hours, minutes, and seconds until 9 p.m. on the next 4th of July. (*Hint*: Use the code from the tny_script.js file in the tutorial case as a guide for calculating these variable values.)

   g. Change the text content of the elements with the IDs "dLeft", "hLeft", "mLeft", and "sLeft" to the values of the days, hrs, mins, and secs variables rounded down to the next lowest integer.

6. Directly after the opening comment section in the file, insert a command to call the showClock() function.

7. After the command that calls the showClock() function, insert a command that runs the showClock() function every second.

8. Document your work in this script file with comments.

9. Save your changes to the file and then open the **tny_july.html** file in your browser. Verify that the page shows the date and time of May 19, 2018 at 9:31:27 a.m., and that the countdown clock shows that Summer Party fireworks will begin in 46 days, 11 hours, 28 minutes, and 33 seconds. The countdown clock will not change because the script uses a fixed date and time for the thisDay variable.

10. Return to the **tny_timer.js** file in your editor. Change the statement that declares the thisDay variable so that it contains the current date and time rather than a specific date and time.

11. Save your changes to the file and then reload the tny_july.html file in your browser. Verify that the countdown clock changes every second as it counts down the time until the start of the fireworks at 9 p.m. on the 4th of July.

Case Problem 1

Data Files needed for this Case Problem: sd_map_txt.html, sd_mapper_txt.js, 2 CSS files, 28 PNG files

Star Dust Stories Dr. Andrew Weiss of Thomas & Lee College maintains an astronomy page called *Star Dusk Stories*. One of the tools of the amateur stargazer is a planisphere, which is a handheld device composed of two flat disks: one disk shows a map of the constellations, and the other disk contains a window corresponding to the part of the sky that is visible at a given time and date. When a user rotates the second disk to the current date and time, the constellations that appear in the window correspond to the constellations currently visible in the nighttime sky.

Dr. Weiss has asked for your help in writing a JavaScript program to display a planisphere showing the constellations visible at the current date and time. He has created 24 different sky chart image files, named sd_sky0.png through sd_sky23.png, that represent 24 different rotations of the nighttime sky. He has also created an image containing a transparent window through which a user can view a selected sky chart. A preview of the completed web page is shown in Figure 9-41.

Figure 9-41 | Star Dust Stories planisphere

Patrick Carey

Complete the following:

1. Use your editor to open the **sd_map_txt.html** and **sd_mapper_txt.js** files from the html09 ▶ case1 folder. Enter *your name* and *the date* in the comment section of each file, and save them as **sd_map.html** and **sd_mapper.js** respectively.

2. Go to the **sd_map.html** file in your editor. Directly above the closing `</head>` tag, insert a `script` element that links the page to the sd_mapper.js file. Defer the loading of the script file until after the rest of the web page is loaded by the browser.

3. Study the contents of the file and then save your changes.

4. Go to the **sd_mapper.js** file in your editor. At the top of the file, insert a statement to apply your JavaScript code with strict usage.

5. Declare a variable named **thisTime** containing a `Date` object for February 3, 2018 at 3:15:28 a.m.

6. Use the `toLocaleString()` method to save the text of the thisTime variable in the **timeStr** variable.

7. Change the inner HTML code of the page element with the ID timestamp to the value of the timeStr variable.

8. Next, you will determine which sky map to show in the web page. First, create a variable named **thisHour**, using the `getHours()` method to extract the hour value from the thisTime variable.

9. Create a variable named **thisMonth** using the `getMonth()` method to extract the month number from the thisTime variable.

10. The number of the map to use with the given hour and month is calculated with the formula

    (2×*month* + *hour*) % 24

    where *month* is the value of the thisMonth variable and *hour* is the value of the thisHour variable. Store the value of this formula in the **mapNum** variable.

11. You will use JavaScript to write the HTML code for the inline element showing the sky image to use in the web page. Create a variable named **imgStr** that stores the following text string

    `<img src='sd_skyMap.png' />`

    where *Map* is the value of the mapNum variable. (*Hint*: Use the + operator to combine text strings together and be sure to include the single quote character within the text strings.)

12. For the page element with the ID planisphere, use the `insertAdjancentHTML()` to insert the value of the imgStr variable directly after the element's opening tag.

13. Add descriptive comments to the file, documenting your work.

14. Save your changes to the file and then open **sd_map.html** in your browser. Verify that your planisphere map and date and time resemble that shown in Figure 9-41.

15. Return to the **sd_mapper.js** file in your editor. Modify the command that creates the thisTime variable so that it uses the current date and time, whatever that may be.

16. Reload sd_map.html in your browser and verify that it shows the current date and time along with the star map for the sky at that moment.

APPLY

Case Problem 2

Data Files needed for this Case Problem: bc_union_txt.html, bc_today_txt.css, 2 CSS files, 4 PNG files

Bridger College Student Union   Sean Baris manages the website for the student union at Bridger College in Bozeman, Montana. The student union provides daily activities for the students on campus. As website manager, part of Sean's job is to keep the site up to date on the latest activities sponsored by the union. At the beginning of each week, he revises a set of seven web pages detailing the events for each day in the upcoming week.

Sean would like the website to display the current day's schedule within an `aside` element. To do this, the page must determine the day of the week and then load the appropriate HTML code into the element. He would also like the Today at the Union page to display the current day and date. Figure 9-42 shows a preview of the page he wants you to create.

Figure 9-42	Daily events at the Bridger College Student Union

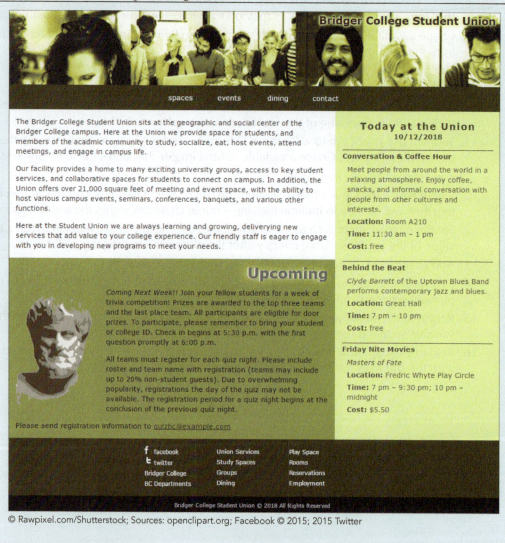

© Rawpixel.com/Shutterstock; Sources: openclipart.org; Facebook © 2015; 2015 Twitter

Complete the following:

1. Use your editor to open the **bc_union_txt.html** and **bc_today_txt.js** files from the html09 ▶ case2 folder. Enter *your name* and *the date* in the comment section of each file, and save them as **bc_union.html** and **bc_today.js** respectively.

2. Go to the **bc_union.html** file in your editor. Directly above the closing `</head>` tag, insert a `script` element that links the page to the bc_today.js file. Defer the loading of the script until after the rest of the page is loaded by the browser.

3. Study the contents of the file and then save your changes.

4. Go to the **bc_today.js** file in your editor. At the top of the file, insert a statement indicating that the code will be handled by the browser assuming strict usage.

   Note that within the file is the getEvent() function, which returns the HTML code for the daily events at the union given a day number ranging from 0 (Sunday) to 6 (Saturday).

5. Declare the **thisDate** variable containing the `Date` object for the date October 12, 2018.

6. Declare the **dateString** variable containing the text of the thisDate variable using local conventions.

7. Declare the **dateHTML** variable containing the following text string

   `<h2>date</h2>`

   where *date* is the value of the dateString variable.

8. Create the **thisDay** variable containing the day of the week number from the thisDate variable. (*Hint*: Use the `getDay()` method.)

9. Using the thisDay variable as the parameter value, call the getEvent() function to get the HTML code of that day's events and store that value in a variable named **eventHTML**.

10. Applying the `insertAdjacentHTML()` method to the page element with the ID unionToday, insert the value of the dateHTML plus the eventHTML variables before the end of the element contents.

11. Document your code with descriptive comments.

12. Save your changes to the file and then load **bc_union.html** in your browser. Verify that the sidebar shows both the date "10/12/2018" formatted as an h2 heading and the daily events for that date formatted as a description list. Your content should resemble that shown in Figure 9-42.

13. Return to the **bc_today.js** file and test your code by changing the date in the thisDate variable from 10/13/2018 up to 10/19/2018. Verify that a different set of events is listed for each date when you refresh the page in your browser.

14. Return to the **bc_today.js** file and change the value of the thisDate variable so that it uses the current date and time.

15. Reload the bc_union.html file in your browser to show the date and the events for the current day of the week.

Case Problem 3

Data Files needed for this Case Problem: ja_vynes_txt.html, ja_quote_txt.js, 2 CSS files, 4 PNG files, 1 TTF file, 1 WOFF file

Austen Vynes   Emelia Dawes shares her passion for the works of Jane Austen by managing a website named Austen Vynes dedicated to the writer and her works. Emelia is revising the layout and design of her website and would like your assistance in redesigning the front page. She wants the front page to display a random Jane Austen quote every time the page is loaded by the browser. Emelia asks you to write a JavaScript program to supply a randomly selected quote. A preview of the page is shown in Figure 9-43.

Figure 9-43   Random quote on the Austen Vynes page

Sources: openclipart.org; Patrick Carey; British National Archives; A Memoir of Jane Austen by her nephew J. E. Austen-Leigh, Vicar of Bray, Berks. London: Richard Bentley, New Burlington Street, Publisher in Ordinary to her Majesty, 1870

Complete the following:

1. Use your editor to open the **ja_vynes_txt.html** and **ja_quote_txt.js** files from the html09 ▸ case3 folder. Enter *your name* and *the date* in the comment section of each file, and save them as **ja_vynes.html** and **ja_quote.js** respectively.

2. Go to the **ja_vynes.html** file in your editor. Directly above the closing `</head>` tag, insert a `script` element that links the page to the ja_quote.js file. Defer the loading of the script file until the rest of the page is loaded by the browser.

3. Study the contents of the file and then save your changes.

4. Go to the **ja_quote.js** file in your editor. At the top of the file, insert a statement indicating that the code will be handled by the browser assuming strict usage.

✛ **Explore** 5. Directly below the comment section, insert a function named **randomInt** that will be used to generate a random integer. Specify two parameters for the function named **lowest** and **size**. The lowest parameter will specify the lowest possible value for the random integer and the size parameter will set the number of integers to be generated. Use those two parameter values and the `Math.floor()` and `Math.random()` methods to return a random integer within the specified range.

6. Above the randomInt() function insert a command to call the function, generating a random integer from 0 to 9. (*Hint*: Remember that the size of this interval is 10 because it includes 0 in its range.) Store the result from the function in the **randomQ** variable.

✛ **Explore** 7. Create a variable named **quoteElem** that references the first element in the document that has the quote tag name.

8. Call the getQuote() function using the randomQ variable as the parameter value to generate a random Jane Austen quote. Display the text of the quote as the inner HTML code of the quoteElem variable.

9. Add appropriate comments to your code to document your work.

10. Save your changes to the file and then open the **ja_vynes.html** file in your browser. Verify that a random Jane Austen quote appears at the top of the page.

11. Reload the page several times and verify that with each reloading, a different Austen quote appears on the page.

CHALLENGE

Case Problem 4

Data Files needed for this Case Problem: ph_pay_txt.html, ph_clock_txt.js, 2 CSS files, 8 PNG files, 1 TTF file, 1 WOFF file

Philip Henslowe Classic Theatre Randall Chen, the media director for the *Philip Henslowe Classic Theatre* of Coeur d'Alene, Idaho, has asked you to work on redesigning the ticket purchasing pages for the theater's website. The page you will focus on today contains a countdown clock for ticket reservations. Once a customer has reserved seats for a show, he or she has 30 minutes to complete the order or else the seats will revert back to the general public. Randall wants you to program a countdown clock showing the time left before the reservation is voided when the time has run out for submitting the order. You will not be asked to program the script to handle an order submitted within the allotted time. A preview of the page you will create is shown in Figure 9-44.

Figure 9-44 Ticket order page

© Matusciac Alexandru/Shutterstock.com; © Christian Bertrand/Shutterstock.com; Sources: American Express Company; Discover Financial Services; MasterCard Inc.; Visa, Inc.; Patrick Carey

Complete the following:

1. Use your editor to open the **ph_pay_txt.html** and **ph_clock_txt.js** files from the html09 ▶ case4 folder. Enter *your name* and *the date* in the comment section of each file, and save them as **ph_pay.html** and **ph_clock.js** respectively.

2. Go to the **ph_pay.html** file in your editor. Directly above the closing `</head>` tag, insert a `script` element that links the page to the ph_clock.js file. Defer the loading of the script file until the rest of the page is loaded by the browser.

3. Study the contents of the file and then save your changes.

4. Go to the **ph_clock.js** file in your editor. At the top of the file, insert a statement indicating that the code will be handled by the browser assuming strict usage.

5. To begin testing your clock, you will assume a time-to-order of only 15 seconds. Directly below the initial comment section, insert a global variable named **minsLeft** setting its initial value to **0**. The purpose of this variable will be to track the number of minutes left to submit the ticket order.

6. Declare a global variable named **secsLeft**, setting its initial value to **15**. The purpose of this variable will be to track the number of seconds left within each minute to order.

7. Declare a global variable named **timeLeft**, which will store the number of seconds left to submit the ticket order. Set the initial value of the variable equal to the number of minutes left multiplied by 60 plus the number of seconds left.

8. Create the **countdown()** function, which will be used to update the minsLeft, secsLeft, and timeLeft variables every second. The function has no parameters. Add the commands specified in Steps a through g to the function.

   a. Calculate a new value for the minsLeft variable by dividing the timeLeft variable by 60 and using the `Math.floor()` method to round that value down to the next lowest integer.

   b. Calculate a new value for the secsLeft variable equal to the value of the timeLeft variable minus 60 times the minsLeft variable.

   c. Randall wants the countdown clock to display leading zeroes when the minsLeft or secsLeft values are between 0 and 9. The addLeadingZero() function has been provided for you to add these zeroes if necessary. Create a new variable named **minsString** and set it equal to the value returned by the addLeadingZero() function using minsLeft as the parameter value.

   d. Call the addLeadingZero() function again using secsLeft as the parameter value and store the result in the **secsString** variable.

   e. Within the element with the ID minutes, change text content to the value of the minsString variable. Within the element with the ID seconds, change the text content to the value of the secsString variable.

   f. Randall has supplied you with a function named checkTimer() that will check whether there is any time left to submit the order. Add a command to call this function. The function has no parameters.

   ⊕ **Explore** g. Use the decrement operator to decrease the value of the timeLeft variable by 1.

⊕ **Explore** 9. Scroll back to the top of the file and, directly below the statement that declares the timeLeft variable, insert a command to run the countdown() function every second. Store this timed command in a variable named **clockID**.

10. Scroll back down the file and, directly below the countdown() function, insert a function named **stopClock()**. The purpose of this function is to stop the clock once the time to submit the order has run out and to notify the user that the time has expired. The function has no parameters. Add the commands specified in Steps a and b to the function.

    a. Use the `insertAdjacentHTML()` method to insert the following HTML code `<br />(Order Expired)`, directly before the end of the page element with the ID TimeHead.

    ⊕ **Explore** b. Use the `clearInterval()` method to clear the timed command stored in the clockID and stop it from continuing to run.

11. Document your code with descriptive comments.

12. Save your changes to the file and then open **ph_pay.html** in your browser. Verify that a 15-second countdown commences once the page is loaded and continues counting down to zero. Further verify that seconds values between 0 and 9 are displayed with leading zeroes.

13. Return to the **ph_clock.js** file in your editor. Change the initial value of the minsLeft and secsLeft variables to **30** and **0** respectively.

14. Save your changes and reload ph_clock.html in your browser. Verify that the countdown clock now starts from 30 minutes and counts down every second to the end of the time allotted for the order.

TUTORIAL 10

OBJECTIVES

Session 10.1
- Create an array
- Work with array properties and methods

Session 10.2
- Create a program loop
- Work with the `for` loop
- Write comparison and logical operators

Session 10.3
- Create a conditional statement
- Use the `if` statement

Exploring Arrays, Loops, and Conditional Statements

Creating a Monthly Calendar

Case | *The Lyman Hall Theater*

With first-class concerts, performances from Broadway touring companies, and shows from famous comics, singers, and other entertainers, the Lyman Hall Theater is a popular attraction in Brookhaven, Georgia. Lewis Kern is the center's events manager tasked with the job of updating the theater's website.

Lewis wants your help with developing an event calendar application. Rather than constructing the calendar manually, he wants you to write a JavaScript program to automatically generate a web table for a given calendar month, listing the events occurring at the theater during that month. The application should be flexible enough to work with any month so that Lewis only has to enter the event list each month. He wants you to develop a prototype for the August calendar.

STARTING DATA FILES

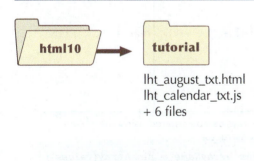

html10 → **tutorial**

lht_august_txt.html
lht_calendar_txt.js
+ 6 files

review

lht_events_txt.html
lht_table_txt.js
+ 6 files

case1

tc_cart_txt.html
tc_cart_txt.js
tc_order_txt.js
+ 10 files

case2

hg_game_txt.html
hg_report_txt.js
+ 7 files

case3

ah_report_txt.html
ah_report_txt.js
+ 4 files

case4

vw_election_txt.html
vw_results_txt.js
+ 4 files

Session 10.1 Visual Overview:

```
/* Set the date displayed in the calendar */
var thisDay = new Date("August 24, 2018");

/* Write the calendar to the element with the id 'calendar' */
document.getElementById("calendar").innerHTML = createCalendar(thisDay);

/* Function to generate the calendar table */
function createCalendar(calDate) {
    var calendarHTML = "<table id='calendar_table'>";
    calendarHTML += calCaption(calDate);
    calendarHTML += "</table>";
    return calendarHTML;
}

/* Function to write the calendar caption */
function calCaption(calDate) {
    // montName array contains the list of month names
    var monthName = ["January", "February", "March", "April",
                     "May", "June", "July", "August", "September",
                     "October", "November", "December"];

    // Determine the current month
    var thisMonth = calDate.getMonth();

    // Determine the current year
    var thisYear = calDate.getFullYear();

    // Write the caption
    return "<caption>" + monthName[thisMonth] + " " + thisYear + "</caption>";

}
```

© Nejron Photo/Shutterstock

The createCalendar() function writes the HTML code of the calendar table.

The calCaption() function writes the calendar caption.

An **array** is a collection of values organized under a single name.

Values within an array are referenced using the format

array[i]

where *array* is the array name and *i* is the index number of the value within the array.

Arrays can be created using the object constructor

var *arrayName* = new Array(*values*);

or using an array literal

var *arrayName* = [*values*];

Creating and Using Arrays

The Lyman Hall Theater

home   events   box office   facilities   directions   contact

August at the Lyman Hall Theater

Broadway closes out a great summer at the LHT with seven performances of Hamilton, starring Tre Dawes. These performances are sure to sell out, so order your seats today.

We're not done with Broadway yet, as popular singer Toni Trindle provides a great evening of jazz standards in Stardust Memories and Ted Gilliam

presents his one-man show, The Future is Prologue based on the writings of George Orwell.

The young will enjoy Have Spacesuit, Will Travel – a stage production using more than 500 images to create a living graphic novel of Robert A. Heinlein's classic science fiction story.

School's in session with our continuing

lecture series. Mary Dees presents the latest developments in cognitive research with Hacking your Dreams and David Wu discusses gravity waves in What Einstein Got Wrong.

Join us on Sunday for Classics Brunch with music provided by the Carson Quartet. Seating is limited, so please reserve your table for this popular series.

August 2018

The Lyman Hall Theater
414 Leeward Drive
Brookhaven, GA 30319
Office: (404) 555 - 4140

Box Office
Group Rates
Events

Staff
Employment Info
Directions & Parking

The code written to the web page is:

```
<table id='calendar _ table'>
  <caption>August 2018</caption>
</table>
```

Introducing the Monthly Calendar

You and Lewis meet to discuss his idea for a monthly events calendar. He wants the calendar to appear in the form of a web table with links to specific events placed within the table cells. The appearance and placement of the calendar will be set using a CSS style sheet. Figure 10-1 shows a preview of the monthly calendar you will create for the Lyman Hall Theater website.

Figure 10-1   Monthly events calendar

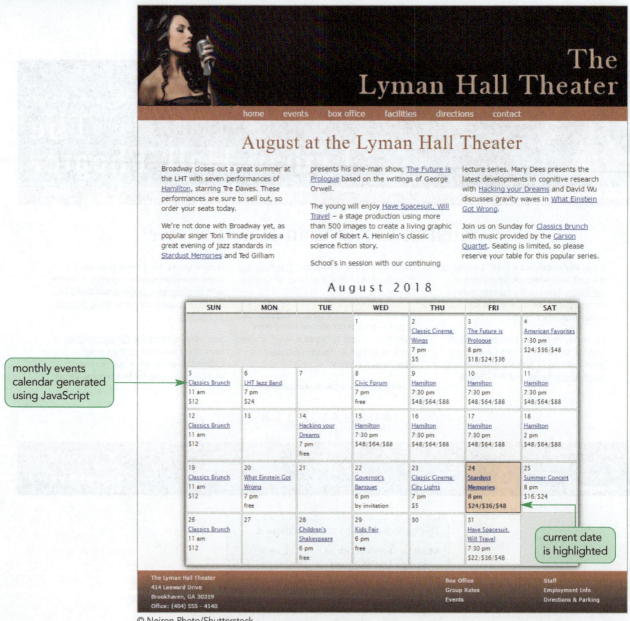

© Nejron Photo/Shutterstock

The program you create should be easily adaptable so that it can be used to create other monthly calendars. Lewis wants the code that generates the calendar placed in the lht_calendar.js file. The events listed in the calendar will be placed in the lht_events.js file. Finally, the styles for the calendar will be placed in the lht_calendar.css style sheet file. Lewis already has created the styles required for the calendar table, but he has left the JavaScript coding to you. You will start by adding links to the lht_calendar.js and lht_calendar.css files to a web page describing the August events at the Lyman Hall Theater. You will work with the lht_events.js file later in this tutorial.

To access the August Events web page:

1. Use your editor to open the **lht_august_txt.html** and **lht_calendar_txt.js** files from the html10 ▸ tutorial folder. Enter *your name* and *the date* in the comment section of each file and save them as **lht_august.html** and **lht_calendar.js** respectively.

2. Return to the **lht_august.html** file in your editor, and then add the following code above the closing </head> tag to create links to both the calendar style sheet and the JavaScript file that will generate the HTML code for the calendar:

```
<link href="lht_calendar.css" rel="stylesheet" />
<script src="lht_calendar.js" defer></script>
```

Figure 10-2 highlights the revised code in the document head.

Figure 10-2	Linking to the style sheet and JavaScript file

style sheet for the calendar table

JavaScript file that will generate the HTML code for the calendar table

```
<title>Lyman Hall Theater in August</title>
<link href="lht_base.css" rel="stylesheet" />
<link href="lht_layout.css" rel="stylesheet" />
<link href="lht_calendar.css" rel="stylesheet" />
<script src="lht_calendar.js" defer></script>
</head>
```

The calendar will be placed within a div element with the ID calendar.

3. Scroll down the file and, and, directly below the closing </article> tag, insert the following div element:

```
<div id="calendar"></div>
```

Figure 10-3 highlights the location where the calendar will be placed.

Figure 10-3	Location of the calendar table

```
</section>
</article>

<div id="calendar"></div>
```

HTML code for the calendar table will be placed within this div element

4. Save your changes to the file.

Reviewing the Calendar Structure

The calendar you create will be constructed as a web table. Before you start writing the code to create this table, you should understand the table's structure. Lewis wants the following class names and IDs assigned to the different parts of the table:

- The entire calendar is set in a web table with the ID *calendar_table*.
- The cell containing the calendar title has the ID *calendar_head*.

- The seven cells containing the days of the week abbreviations all belong to the class *calendar_weekdays*.
- The cells containing the dates of the month all belong to the class *calendar_dates*.
- The cell containing the current date has the ID *calendar_today*.

These class and ID designations make it easier for page developers to assign different styles to the different parts of the calendar. If developers want to change the table's appearance, they will not have to edit the JavaScript code to do so; instead, they only will have to modify the style sheet.

Adding the calendar() Function

You will place the commands that generate the calendar within a single function named createCalendar(). The initial code to generate the calendar follows:

```
var thisDay = new Date("August 24, 2018");
document.getElementById("calendar").innerHTML =
createCalendar(thisDay);

function createCalendar(calDate) {
   var calendarHTML = "<table id='calendar_table'>";
   calendarHTML += "</table>";
   return calendarHTML;
}
```

The thisDay variable stores the current date. For the purposes of this example, you will set the date to August 24, 2018. The next line of the function stores the HTML code for the calendar in the `div` element with the ID calendar that you have just created. Initially this HTML code, taken from the createCalendar() function, consists only of the opening and closing tags of the `table` element. Note that you place the value of the `id` attribute within single quotes because the entire text string of HTML code is already enclosed within double quotes.

To insert the initial code of the calendar app:

1. Return to the **lht_calendar.js** file in your editor. Insert following code at the bottom of the file to set the calendar date:

   ```
   /* Set the date displayed in the calendar */
   var thisDay = new Date("August 24, 2018");
   ```

2. Next, add the following code to insert the HTML code of the calendar into the web page:

   ```
   /* Write the calendar to the element with the id "calendar" */
   document.getElementById("calendar").innerHTML =
   createCalendar(thisDay);
   ```

3. Finally, enter the initial code for the createCalendar() function that generates the HTML code:

   ```
   /* Function to generate the calendar table */
   function createCalendar(calDate) {
      var calendarHTML = "<table id='calendar_table'>";
      calendarHTML += "</table>";
      return calendarHTML;
   }
   ```

When writing attribute values, you need to enclose the values within single quotes while the text of the HTML code is enclosed within double quotes.

Figure 10-4 describes the code in the file.

| Figure 10-4 | Initial code for the calendar app |

the createCalendar() function writes the HTML code for the calendar table

sample date for the calendar

writes the calendar table to the web page

the += assignment operator adds a text string to the value of the calendarHTML variable

initial value of the calendarHTML variable

```
*/

/* Set the date displayed in the calendar */
var thisDay = new Date("August 24, 2018");

/* Write the calendar to the element with the id "calendar" */
document.getElementById("calendar").innerHTML = createCalendar(thisDay);

/* Function to generate the calendar table */
function createCalendar(calDate) {
    var calendarHTML = "<table id='calendar_table'>";
    calendarHTML += "</table>";
    return calendarHTML;
}
```

4. Save your changes to the file.

Next, you will start to write the code to create the contents of the calendar table. The three main tasks to complete the calendar table are as follows:

- Create a caption displaying the month and the year
- Create the table row containing the names of the days of the week
- Create rows for each week in the month with cells for each day in the week

In this session, you will learn how to create a calendar table caption. In the next session, you will complete the rest of the table.

Introducing Arrays

Lewis wants the calendar table caption to display the text *Month Year*, where *Month* is the name of the month and *Year* is the four-digit year value. In the last tutorial, you learned that you can use the getMonth() method of the JavaScript Date object to extract a month number and the getFullYear() method to extract the four-digit year value. For example, a Date object storing the date March 18, 2018 has a month value of 2 (because month values start with 0 for the month of January) and a four-digit year value of 2018. However, Lewis wants the month name rather than the month number to appear in the table but, because no Date method returns the name of the month, you will have to write code to associate each month number with a month name. One way of doing this is by using an array.

An array is a collection of values organized under a single name. Each individual value is associated with a number known as an **index** that distinguishes it from other values in the array. Array values are referenced using the expression

```
array[i]
```

where *array* is the name of the array and *i* is the index of a specific value in the array. Index values start with 0 so that the initial item in an array has an index value of 0, the second item has an index value of 1, and so on. For example, the expression

```
monthName[4]
```

references the fifth (not the fourth) item in the monthName array.

Creating and Populating an Array

To create an array, you can apply the object constructor

```
var array = new Array(length);
```

where *array* is the name of the array and *length* is the number of items in the array. The *length* value is optional; if you omit this parameter, the array expands automatically as more items are added to it. However, by defining the length of an array, JavaScript will allot only the amount of memory needed to generate the array so that the code runs more efficiently. Thus, to create an array named monthName for the 12 month names, you would enter the following statement:

```
var monthName = new Array(12);
```

Alternatively, you could omit the array length and enter the statement as follows:

```
var monthName = new Array();
```

Once you have created an array, you can populate it with values using the same commands you use for any variable. The only difference is that you must specify both the array name and the index number of the array item. The command to set the value of a specific item in an array is

```
array[i] = value;
```

where *value* is the value assigned to the array item with the index value *i*. For example, to insert month names in the monthName array, starting with January, you could enter the following statements:

```
monthName[0] = "January";
monthName[1] = "February";
...
monthName[11] = "December";
```

Rather than writing each array value in a separate statement, you can populate the entire array in a single statement using the following command

```
var array = new Array(values);
```

where *values* is a comma-separated list of the values in the array. The following command places twelve month names into the monthName array in a single statement:

```
var monthName = new Array("January", "February", "March", "April",
"May", "June", "July", "August", "September", "October", "November",
"December");
```

The index numbers are based on the position of the values in the list. The first item in the list ("January") would have an index number 0, the second ("February") would have an index of 1, and so forth.

A final way to create an array is with an **array literal**, in which the array values are a comma-separated list within a set of square brackets. The expression to create an array literal is

```
var array = [values];
```

where *values* are the values of the array. The following command uses the array literal form to store an array of month names:

```
var monthName = ["January", "February", "March", "April", "May",
"June", "July", "August", "September", "October", "November",
"December"];
```

TIP

To create an empty array literal that you populate later in the program, leave the brackets blank as in the command var x = [];

If you know the contents of your array, it is usually quicker and easier to set up your array using the array literal notation.

Array values do not need to be the same data type. You can mix numeric values, text strings, and other data types within a single array, as demonstrated by the following statement:

```
var x = ["April", 3.14, true, null];
```

REFERENCE

Creating and Populating Arrays

- To create an array, use the object constructor

  ```
  var array = new Array(length);
  ```

  where *array* is the name of the array and *length* is the number of items in the array. The optional *length* value sets the array to a specified size; if omitted, the array expands as new items are added to it.
- To set the value of an item within an array, use the command

  ```
  array[i] = value;
  ```

  where *i* is the index of the array item and *value* is the value assigned to the item.
- To create and populate an array within a single command, use

  ```
  var array = new Array(values);
  ```

  where *values* is a comma-separated list of values.
- To create an array using the array literal format, use the following statement:

  ```
  var array = [values];
  ```

Now that you have seen how to create and populate an array, you will create an array of month names to use in your calendar application. You will insert the array in a function named calCaption() whose purpose is to write the HTML code of the calendar caption. The function has a single parameter named calDate that stores a `Date` object containing the current date.

To create the calCaption() function:

1. Return to the **lht_calendar.js** file in your editor.

2. At the bottom of the file, insert the following function to write the caption of the calendar table and create the monthName array:

```
/* Function to write the çalendar caption */
function calCaption(calDate) {
   // monthName array contains the list of month names
   var monthName = ["January", "February", "March", "April",
                    "May", "June", "July", "August", "September",
                    "October", "November", "December"];
```

3. Next, within the function, use the `getMonth()` and `getFullYear()` methods to extract the month number and 4-digit year number from the calDate parameter by entering the following commands:

```
// Determine the current month
var thisMonth = calDate.getMonth();

// Determine the current year
var thisYear = calDate.getFullYear();
```

4. Finally, complete the function by returning the caption tag for the calendar containing the month name and 4-digit year number. To display the month name, use the monthName array with the value of the thisMonth variable as the index number. Enter the code:

```
// Write the caption
return "<caption>" + monthName[thisMonth] + " " + thisYear
+ "</caption>";
}
```

5. Scroll up to the createCalendar() function and insert the following statement directly before the command `calendarHTML += "</table>";`:

```
calendarHTML += calCaption(calDate);
```

This code calls the calCaption() function, which returns the HTML code of the table caption. Figure 10-5 describes the newly added code.

Figure 10-5	The calCaption() function

```
/* Function to generate the calendar table */
function createCalendar(calDate) {
    var calendarHTML = "<table id='calendar_table'>";
    calendarHTML += calCaption(calDate);
    calendarHTML += "</table>";
    return calendarHTML;
}

/* Function to write the calendar caption */
function calCaption(calDate) {
    // monthName array contains the list of month names
    var monthName = ["January", "February", "March", "April",
                     "May", "June", "July", "August", "September",
                     "October", "November", "December"];
    // Determine the current month
    var thisMonth = calDate.getMonth();

    // Determine the current year
    var thisYear = calDate.getFullYear();

    // Write the caption
    return "<caption>" + monthName[thisMonth] + " " + thisYear + "</caption>";
}
```

calls the calCaption() function to insert the HTML code for the table caption

the calCaption() function writes the HTML code for the table caption

creates an array of the month names

extracts the month number of the current month

extracts the 4-digit year value

returns the HTML code for the table caption

displays the name of the month drawn from the monthName array

displays the year based on the extracted 4-digit year value

6. Save your changes to the file, and then open **lht_august.html** in your browser. Verify that the web page now shows the caption of the calendar table with the August 2018 date as shown in Figure 10-6.

Figure 10-6   **Calendar caption displayed in the web page**

Broadway closes out a great summer at the LHT with seven performances of Hamilton, starring Tre Dawes. These performances are sure to sell out, so order your seats today.

We're not done with Broadway yet, as popular singer Toni Trindle provides a great evening of jazz standards in Stardust Memories and Ted Gilliam

presents his one-man show, The Future is Prologue based on the writings of George Orwell.

The young will enjoy Have Spacesuit, Will Travel – a stage production using more than 500 images to create a living graphic novel of Robert A. Heinlein's classic science fiction story.

School's in session with our continuing

lecture series. Mary Dees presents the latest developments in cognitive research with Hacking your Dreams and David Wu discusses gravity waves in What Einstein Got Wrong.

Join us on Sunday for Classics Brunch with music provided by the Carson Quartet. Seating is limited, so please reserve your table for this popular series.

August 2018

calendar table caption written using JavaScript

Trouble? If the caption does not appear in the page, your code might contain a mistake. Check your code against the code shown in the previous figures. Common sources of error include forgetting to close all quoted text strings, failing to match the use of uppercase and lowercase letters in function names and variable names, misspelling function names and variable names, and failing to close parentheses and brackets when required.

Next, you will explore the properties and methods associated with arrays.

Working with Array Length

A JavaScript array automatically expands in length as more items are added. To determine the array's current size, apply the following `length` property

```
array.length
```

where `array` is the name of the array. The value returned by the `length` property is equal to one more than the highest index number in the array (because array indices start at 0 rather than 1), so, if the highest number in the index is 11, then the value returned would be 12.

JavaScript allows for the creation of **sparse arrays**, in which some array values are undefined. As a result, the `length` value is not always the same as the number of array values. For example, the following commands create a sparse array in which only the first and last items have defined values:

```
var x = new Array();
x[0] = "Lewis";
x[99] = "80517";
```

TIP

You can add new items to the end of any array using the command *array*[*array.length*] = *value;*

The value of the `length` property for this array is 100 even though it only contains two values. Sparse arrays occur frequently in database applications involving customer records where items such as mobile phone numbers or postal codes have not been entered for every person.

REFERENCE

Specifying Array Length

- To determine the size of an array, use the property

  `array.length`

  where `array` is the name of the array and `length` is one more than the highest index number in the array.
- To add an item to the end of an array, run the command

  `array[i] = value;`

  where `i` is an index value higher than the highest index currently in the array. If you don't know the highest index number, use the property `array.length` in place of `i`.
- To remove items from an array, run the command

  `array.length = value;`

  where `value` is an integer that is smaller than the highest index currently in the array.

Note that you cannot reduce the value of the `length` property without removing items from the end of your array. For example, the following command would reduce the monthName array to the first three months—January, February, and March:

`monthName.length = 3;`

Increasing the value of the `length` property adds more items to an array, but the items have null values until they are defined.

PROSKILLS

Problem Solving: Using Multidimensional Arrays

Many database applications need to store data in a rectangular format known as a **matrix**, in which the values are arranged in a rectangular grid. The following is an example of a matrix laid out in a grid of three rows and four columns:

$$\begin{bmatrix} 4 & 15 & 8 & 2 \\ 1 & 3 & 18 & 6 \\ 3 & 7 & 10 & 4 \end{bmatrix}$$

The rows and columns in a matrix form the basis for indices. For example, the value 18 from this matrix is referenced using the index pair (2, 3) because the value 18 appears at the intersection of the second row and third column.

Although matrices are commonly used in databases (where each row might represent an individual and each column a characteristic of that individual), JavaScript does not support matrices. However, you can mimic the behavior of matrices in JavaScript by nesting one array within another in a structure called a **multidimensional array**. For example, the following code creates the array *mArray*, which contains a collection of nested arrays:

```
var mArray =
   [
      [4, 15, 8, 2],
      [1, 3, 18, 6],
      [3, 7, 10, 4]
   ];
```

Note that the values of this array match the values of the matrix shown above. In this case, the first nested array matches the first row of the matrix, the second array matches the second row, and the third array matches the third row. The values of the nested arrays are matched with each of the four columns.

Values within a multidimensional array are referenced by the expression

```
array[x][y]
```

where *x* contains the index of the outer array (the row) and *y* contains the index of the nested array (the column). Thus, the expression

```
mArray[1][2]
```

returns the value 18 from the matrix's second row and third column (remember that indices start with 0, not 1). The number of rows in a multidimensional array is given by the `length` property. The number of columns can be determined by retrieving the `length` property for the first row of the table. For example, the expression

```
mArray[1].length
```

would return a value of 4 for the fours columns in mArray. Note that this approach presumes that every row has the same number of columns. You can continue to nest arrays in this fashion to create matrices of even higher dimensions.

Reversing an Array

Arrays are associated with a collection of methods that allow you to change their content, order, and size. You can also use these methods to combine different arrays into a single array and to convert arrays into text strings. Although you will not need to use these methods in the calendar app, you will examine them for future projects.

By default, items are placed in an array either in the order in which they are defined or explicitly by index number. JavaScript supports two methods for changing the order of these items: `reverse()` and `sort()`. The `reverse()` method, as the name suggests, reverses the order of items in an array, making the last items first and the first items last. In the following set of commands, the `reverse()` method is used to change the order of the values in the weekDay array:

```
var weekDay = ["Sun", "Mon", "Tue", "Wed", "Thu", "Fri", "Sat"];
weekDay.reverse();
```

After running the `reverse()` method, the weekDay array would contain the items in the following order: "Sat", "Fri", "Thu", "Wed", "Tue", "Mon", and finally, "Sun".

Sorting an Array

The `sort()` method rearranges array items in alphabetical order. This can cause unexpected results if you apply the `sort()` method to data values that are not usually sorted alphabetically. Applying the `sort()` method to numeric values, will sort the values in order by their leading digits, rather than by their numerical values. Thus, applying the `sort()` method in the following set of commands

```
var x = [3, 45, 1234, 24];
x.sort();
```

would result in the order 1234, 24, 3, 45 because this is the order of those numbers when sorted by their leading digits. To correctly sort numeric data, you must create a **compare function** that compares the values of two adjacent array items. The general form of a compare function is

```
function fname(a, b) {
    return a negative, positive, or 0 value
}
```

where *fname* is the name of the compare function, and *a* and *b* are parameters that represent a pair of array values. The function then returns a negative, positive, or zero value based on the comparison of those values. If a negative value is returned, then *a* is placed before *b* in the array. If a positive value is returned, then *b* is placed before *a*, and finally, if a zero value is returned, *a* and *b* retain their original positions. The compare function is applied to every pair of values in the array to ensure they are sorted in the proper order.

The following compare function could be used to sort numeric values in ascending order

```
function ascending(a, b) {
    return a - b;
}
```

whereas to sort numbers in a descending order, you could apply the following function, which subtracts *a* from *b*, rather than *b* from *a*:

```
function descending(a, b) {
    return b - a;
}
```

Other compare functions are possible to deal with a wide variety of sorting rules, but these two are the simplest for sorting arrays of numeric values.

The compare function is applied to the `sort()` method as follows

```
array.sort(fname)
```

TIP

You can also sort an array in descending order by sorting it first in ascending order and then by applying the `reverse()` method to reverse the sorted order of the array.

where *fname* is the name of the compare function. For example, to use the ascending() compare function to sort the x array described earlier in ascending numeric order, you would run the following command:

```
x.sort(ascending)
```

After applying the sort() method with the ascending function, the values in the x array would be sorted in ascending numeric order as: 3, 24, 45, and finally, 1234.

INSIGHT

Performing a Random Shuffle

For some applications, you will want to randomly rearrange the contents of an array. For example, you might be writing a program to simulate a randomly shuffled deck of cards. You can shuffle an array using the same sort() method you use to place the array in a defined order; however, to place the items in a random order, you use a compare function that randomly returns a positive, negative, or 0 value. The following compare function employs a simple approach to this problem:

```
function randOrder(){
   return 0.5 - Math.random();
}
```

The following code demonstrates how this compare function could be used to randomly shuffle an array of poker cards:

```
var pokerDeck = new Array(52);
pokerDeck[0] = "2 of Clubs";
pokerDeck[1] = "3 of Clubs";
…
pokerDeck[51] = "Ace of Spades";
pokerDeck.sort(randOrder)
```

After running this command, the contents of the pokerDeck array will be placed in random order. To reshuffle the array, you would simply rerun the sort() method with the randOrder() function.

Extracting and Inserting Array Items

In some scripts, you might want to extract a section of an array, known as a **subarray**. One way to create a subarray is with the following slice() method

```
array.slice(start, stop)
```

where *start* is the index value of the array item at which the slicing starts and *stop* is the index value at which the slicing ends. Note that the stop index value is not included in the subarray. The *stop* value is optional; if it is omitted, the array is sliced to its end. The original contents of the array are unaffected after slicing, but the extracted items can be stored in another array. For example, the following command slices the monthName array, extracting only three summer months—June, July, August—and storing them in the summerMonths array:

```
summerMonths = monthName.slice(5, 8);
```

Remember that arrays start with the index value 0, so the sixth month of the year (June) has an index value of 5 and the ninth month of the year (September) has an index value of 8.

Related to the slice() method is the following splice() method

```
array.splice(start, size, values)
```

which is a general-purpose method for removing and inserting array items, where *start* is the starting index in the array, *size* is the number of array items to remove after the *start* index, and *values* is an optional comma-separated list of values to insert into the array. If no *values* are specified, the splice method simply removes items from the array.

The following statement employs the splice() method to remove the summer months from the monthName array:

```
summerMonths = monthName.splice(5, 3);
```

However, to insert new abbreviations of month names into the monthName array, you could apply the following splice() method which places the values "Jun", "Jul", and "Aug" into the array starting with the 5th index number:

```
monthName.splice(5, 3, "Jun", "Jul", "Aug");
```

The important difference between the slice() and splice() methods is that the splice() method always alters the original array, so you should not use the splice() method if you want the original array left unaffected.

Using Arrays as Data Stacks

Arrays can be used to store information in a data structure known as a **stack** in which new items are added to the top of the stack—or to the end of the array—much like a person clearing a dinner table adds dishes to the top of a stack of dirty plates. A stack data structure employs the **last-in first-out (LIFO)** principle in which the last items added to the stack are the first ones removed. You encounter stack data structures when using the Undo feature of some software applications, in which the last command you performed is the first command that is undone.

JavaScript supports several methods to allow you to work with a stack of array items. For example, the push() method appends new items to the end of an array. It has the syntax

```
array.push(values)
```

where *values* is a comma-separated list of values to be appended to the end of the array. To remove—or **unstack**—the last item, you apply the pop() method, as follows:

```
array.pop()
```

The following set of commands demonstrates how to use the push() and pop() methods to employ the LIFO principle by adding and then removing items from a data stack:

```
var x = ["a", "b", "c"];
x.push("d", "e"); // x = ["a", "b", "c", "d", "e"]
x.pop();          // x = ["a", "b", "c", "d"]
x.pop();          // x = ["a", "b", "c"]
```

In this code, the push() method adds two items to the end of the array, and then the pop() method removes those last items one at a time.

A **queue**, which employs the **first-in-first-out (FIFO)** principle in which the first item added to the data list is the first removed, is similar to a stack. You see the FIFO principle in action in a line of people waiting to be served. For array data that should be treated as a queue, you use the shift() method, which is similar to the pop() method except that it removes the first array item, not the last item. JavaScript also supports the unshift() method, which inserts new items at the front of the array.

REFERENCE

Using Array Methods

- To reverse the order of items in an array, use the method

  `array.reverse()`

  where *array* is the name of the array.
- To sort an array in alphabetical order, use the following method:

  `array.sort();`

- To sort an array in any order, use

  `array.sort(fname)`

  where *fname* is the name of a compare function that returns a positive, negative, or 0 value.
- To extract items from an array without affecting the array contents, use

  `array.slice(start, stop)`

  where *start* is the index of the array item at which the slicing starts and *stop* is the index at which the slicing ends. If no *stop* value is provided, the array is sliced to the end of the array.
- To remove items from an array, use

  `array.splice(start, size)`

  where *start* is the index of the array item at which the splicing starts and *size* is the number of items to remove from the array. If no *size* value is specified, the array is spliced to its end.
- To replace items in an array, use

  `array.splice(start, size, values)`

  where *values* is a comma-separated list of new values to replace the old values in the array.
- To add new items to the end of an array, use

  `array.push(values)`

  where *values* is a comma-separated list of values.
- To remove the last item from an array, use the following method:

  `array.pop()`

Figure 10-7 summarizes several other methods that can be applied to arrays. Arrays are a powerful and useful feature of the JavaScript language. The methods associated with arrays can be used to simplify and expand the capabilities of web page scripts.

Figure 10-7	Array methods

Method	Description
copyWithin(target, start[, end])	Copies items within the array to the target index, starting with the start index and ending with the optional end index
concat(array1, array2,...)	Joins the array to two or more arrays, creating a single array containing the items from all the arrays
fill(value[, start][, end])	Fills the array with items having the value value, starting from the start index and ending at the end index
indexOf(value[, start])	Searches the array, returning the index number of the first element equal to value, starting from the optional start index
join(separator)	Joins all items in the array into a single text string; the array items are separated using the text in the separator parameter; if no separator is specified, a comma is used
lastIndexOf(value[, start])	Searches backward through the array, returning the index number of the first element equal to value, starting from the optional start index
pop()	Removes the last item from the array
push(values)	Appends the array with new items, where values is a comma-separated list of item values
reverse()	Reverses the order of items in the array
shift()	Removes the first item from the array
slice(start, stop)	Extracts the array items starting with the start index up to the stop index, returning a new subarray
array.splice(start, size, values)	Extracts size items from the array starting with the item with the index start; to insert new items into the array, specify the array items in a comma-separated values list
array.sort(fname)	Sorts the array where fname is the name of a function that returns a positive, negative, or 0 value; if no function is specified, array is sorted in alphabetical order
array.toString()	Converts the contents of the array to a text string with the array values in a comma-separated list
array.unshift(values)	Inserts new items at the start of the array, where values is a comma-separated list of new values

You set up the first parts of the online calendar in this session. In the next sessions, you will complete the monthly calendar by working with loops and conditional statements.

REVIEW

Session 10.1 Quick Check

1. What is an array?
2. Provide a command to create an array named dayNames using the object constructor form.
3. Provide a command to create and populate the dayNames array with the abbreviations of the seven days of the week (starting with Sun and going through Sat). Use the array literal form.
4. Provide a command to return the third value from the dayNames array.
5. Provide a command to sort the dayNames array in alphabetical order.
6. Provide a command to extract the middle five values from the dayNames array.
7. Provide a command to create a multidimensional array named myArray for the following matrix:

$$\begin{bmatrix} 3 & 0 & -2 \\ 12 & -8 & 1 \\ 4 & 1 & -3 \end{bmatrix}$$

Session 10.2 Visual Overview:

The **continue expression** is a Boolean expression that must be true for the loop to continue.

The **update expression** updates the counter variable each time through the loop.

The **start expression** provides the starting value of the counter variable, i.

A **for loop** is a programming structure in which a set of commands is repeated based on the changing values of a **counter variable**.

```
/* Function to write a table row of weekday abbreviations */
function calWeekdayRow() {

    // Array of weekday abbreviations
    var dayName = ["SUN", "MON", "TUE", "WED", "THU", "FRI", "SAT"];
    var rowHTML = "<tr>";

    // Loop through the dayName array
    for (var i = 0; i < dayName.length; i++) {
        rowHTML += "<th class='calendar_weekdays'>" + dayName[i] + "</th>";
    }

    rowHTML += "</tr>";
    return rowHTML;
}
```

The same command block is executed with different values of the counter variable during each iteration of the **for** loop.

Applying a Program Loop

August at the Lyman Hall Theater

Broadway closes out a great summer at the LHT with seven performances of Hamilton, starring Tre Dawes. These performances are sure to sell out, so order your seats today.

We're not done with Broadway yet, as popular singer Toni Trindle provides a great evening of jazz standards in Stardust Memories and Ted Gilliam

presents his one-man show, The Future is Prologue based on the writings of George Orwell.

The young will enjoy Have Spacesuit, Will Travel – a stage production using more than 500 images to create a living graphic novel of Robert A. Heinlein's classic science fiction story.

School's in session with our continuing

lecture series. Mary Dees presents the latest developments in cognitive research with Hacking your Dreams and David Wu discusses gravity waves in What Einstein Got Wrong.

Join us on Sunday for Classics Brunch with music provided by the Carson Quartet. Seating is limited, so please reserve your table for this popular series.

August 2018

SUN	MON	TUE	WED	THU	FRI	SAT

> The days of the week are written using a **program loop** that repeats a set of similar commands until a stopping condition is met.

> The code created for the table row is as follows:
>
> ```
> <tr>
>     <th class='calendar _ weekdays'>SUN</th>
>     <th class='calendar _ weekdays'>MON</th>
>     <th class='calendar _ weekdays'>TUE</th>
>     <th class='calendar _ weekdays'>WED</th>
>     <th class='calendar _ weekdays'>THU</th>
>     <th class='calendar _ weekdays'>FRI</th>
>     <th class='calendar _ weekdays'>SAT</th>
> </tr>
> ```

Working with Program Loops

Now that you are familiar with the properties and methods of arrays, you will return to working on the calendar app. So far, you have created only the table caption displaying the calendar's month and year. The first row of the table will contain the three-letter abbreviations of the seven days of the week, starting with SUN and continuing through SAT. Each abbreviation needs to be placed within an element with the class name calendar_weekdays using the following code:

```
<tr>
   <th class='calendar_weekdays'>SUN</th>
   <th class='calendar_weekdays'>MON</th>
   <th class='calendar_weekdays'>TUE</th>
   <th class='calendar_weekdays'>WED</th>
   <th class='calendar_weekdays'>THU</th>
   <th class='calendar_weekdays'>FRI</th>
   <th class='calendar_weekdays'>SAT</th>
</tr>
```

This code contains a lot of repetitive text with the same th element and class name repeated seven times. Imagine if you had to repeat essentially the same string of code dozens, hundreds, or even thousands of times—the code would become unmanageably long. Programmers deal with this kind of situation by creating program loops. A **program loop** is a set of commands executed repeatedly until a stopping condition is met. Two commonly used program loops in JavaScript are for loops and while loops.

Exploring the for Loop

In a for loop, a variable known as a counter variable is used to track the number of times a block of commands is run. Each time through the loop, the value of the counter variable is increased or decreased by a set amount. When the counter variable reaches or exceeds a specified value, the for loop stops. The general structure of a for loop is

```
for (start; continue; update) {
   commands
}
```

where start is an expression that sets the initial value of a counter variable, continue is a Boolean expression that must be true for the loop to continue, update is an expression that indicates how the value of the counter variable should change each time through the loop, and commands are the JavaScript statements that are run for each loop.

Suppose you want to set a counter variable to range in value from 1 to 4 in increments of 1. You could use the following expression to set the initial value of the counter variable:

```
var i = 1;
```

The name of the counter variable in this example is i, which is a common variable name often applied in program loops.

The next expression in the for loop structure defines the condition under which the program loop continues. The following expression sets the loop to continue as long as the value of the counter variable is less than or equal to 4:

```
i <= 4;
```

Finally, the following update expression uses the increment operator to indicate that the value of the counter variable increases by 1 each time through the program loop:

```
i++;
```

Putting all of these expressions together, you get the following `for` loop:

```
for (var i = 1; i <= 4; i++) {
    commands
}
```

The collection of commands that is run each time through a loop is known collectively as a **command block**, a feature you have already worked with in functions. A command block is indicated by its opening and closing curly braces { }. The following is an example of a `for` loop that adds the HTML code for four `td` elements to a table row:

```
var htmlCode = "<tr>";
for (var i = 1; i <= 4; i++) {
    htmlCode += "<td>" + i + "</td>";
}
htmlCode += "</tr>";
```

As shown in Figure 10-8, each time through the loop, the value displayed in the table cell is changed by 1.

Figure 10-8 **Writing HTML code with a for loop**

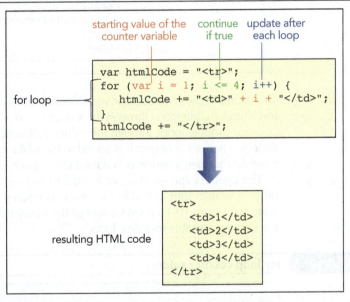

One `for` loop can be nested within another. Figure 10-9 shows the code used to create a table with two rows and three columns.

Figure 10-9 Nested for loop

```
var htmlCode = "<table>";
for (var rowNum = 1; rowNum <= 2; rowNum++) {
   htmlCode += "<tr>";
      for (var colNum = 1; colNum <= 3; colNum++) {
         htmlCode += "<td>" + rowNum + "," + colNum + "</td>";
      }
   htmlCode += "</tr>";
}
htmlCode += "</table>";
```

nested for loop

```
<table>
   <tr>
      <td>1,1</td><td>1,2</td><td>1,3</td>
   </tr>
   <tr>
      <td>2,1</td><td>2,2</td><td>2,3</td>
   </tr>
</table>
```

resulting HTML code

This example uses two counter variables named rowNum and colNum. The rowNum variable loops through the values 1 and 2 and for each of those values, the colNum variable loops through the values 1, 2, and 3. Each time the value of the colNum variable changes, a new cell is added to the table. Each time the value of the rowNum variable changes, a new row is added to the table.

The update expression is not limited to increasing the counter by 1. You can use the other operators introduced in the previous tutorial to create a wide variety of increment patterns. Figure 10-10 shows a few of the many different ways of updating the value of the counter variable in a `for` loop.

Figure 10-10 for loop counter values

for Loop	Counter Values
`for (var i = 1; i <= 5; i++)`	i = 1, 2, 3, 4, 5
`for (var i = 5; i > 0; i--)`	i = 5, 4, 3, 2, 1
`for (var i = 0; i <= 360; i+=60)`	i = 0, 60, 120, 180, 240, 360
`for (var i = 1; i <= 64; i*=2)`	i = 1, 2, 4, 8, 16, 32, 64

Exploring the while Loop

The `for` loop is only one way of creating a program loop in JavaScript. The **while loop**, in which a command block is run as long as a specific condition is met, is similar to the `for` loop. However, unlike the `for` loop, the condition in a `while` loop does not depend on the value of a counter variable. The `while` loop has the general syntax

```
while (continue) {
   commands
}
```

where *continue* is a Boolean expression that must be true for the command block to be run; otherwise, the command block is skipped and the program loop ends.

The following code shows how to create the table shown earlier in Figure 10-8 as a while loop:

```
var htmlCode = "<tr>";
var i = 1;
while (i <= 4) {
    htmlCode += "<td>" + i + "</td>";
    i++;
}
```

The while loop continues as long as the value of the i variable remains less than or equal to 4. Each time through the command block, the loop writes the value of i into a table cell and then increases the counter by 1.

Like for loops, while loops can be nested within one another. The following code demonstrates how to create the 2 × 3 table shown earlier in Figure 10-9 using nested while loops:

```
var htmlCode = "<table>";
var rowNum = 1;
while (rowNum <= 2) {
    htmlCode += "<tr>";
    var colNum = 1;
    while (colNum <= 3) {
        htmlCode += "<td>" + rowNum + "," + colNum + "</td>";
        colNum++;
    }
    htmlCode += "</tr>";
    rowNum++;
}
```

Again, the initial values of the counter variables are set before the while loops are run and are updated within the command blocks.

Because for loops and while loops share many of the same characteristics, which one you choose for a given application is often a matter of personal preference. In general, for loops are used whenever you have a counter variable and while loops are used for conditions that don't easily lend themselves to using counters. For example, you could construct a while loop that runs as long as the current time falls within a specified time interval.

TIP

Use a for loop when your loop contains a counter variable. Use a while loop for a more general stopping condition.

Exploring the do/while Loop

In the for and while loops, the test to determine whether to continue the loop is made before the command block is run. JavaScript also supports a program loop called do/while that tests the condition to continue the loop right after the latest command block is run. The structure of the do/while loop is as follows:

```
do {
    commands
    }
while (continue);
```

For example, the following code is used to create the table shown earlier in Figure 10-8 as a do/while loop:

```
var htmlCode = "<tr>";
var i = 1;
do {
    htmlCode += "<td>" + i + "</td>";
    i++;
}
while (i <= 4);
htmlCode += "</tr>";
```

The do/while loop is usually used when the program loop should run at least once before testing for the stopping condition.

The <= symbol used in these program loops is an example of a comparison operator. Before continuing your work on the calendar app, you examine the different types of comparison operators supported by JavaScript.

Comparison and Logical Operators

A **comparison operator** is an operator that compares the value of one expression to another returning a Boolean value indicating whether the comparison is true or not. Thus, the following expression uses the < comparison operator to test whether the value of the x variable is less than 100:

```
x < 100
```

If this comparison is true, the expression returns the Boolean value `true` and, if otherwise, `false`. Figure 10-11 lists the comparison operators supported by JavaScript.

| Figure 10-11 | Comparison operators |

Operator	Example	Description
==	x == y	Tests whether x is equal in value to y
===	x === y	Tests whether x is equal in value to y and has the same data type
!=	x != y	Tests whether x is not equal to y
>	x > y	Tests whether x is greater than y
>=	x >= y	Tests whether x is greater than or equal to y
<	x < y	Tests whether x is less than y
<=	x <= y	Tests whether x is less than or equal to y

When you want to test whether two values are equal, you use either a double equal sign (==) or a triple equal sign (===). The double equal sign tests whether two items are equal in value while the triple equal sign tests whether the two items are equal in value and also in data type. Thus, the following expression tests whether x is equal in value to 100 and is a number:

```
x === 100
```

Using the single equal sign (=) for the comparison operator is a common programming mistake; remember that the equal sign is an assignment operator and is reserved for setting one value equal to another, not for testing whether two values are equal.

JavaScript also supports **logical operators** that allow you to connect several expressions. For example, the logical operator && returns a value of true only if both of the expressions are true. Figure 10-12 lists the JavaScript logical operators.

Figure 10-12	**Logical operators**

Operator	Definition	Example	Description
`&&`	and	`(x === 5) && (y === 8)`	Tests whether x is equal to 5 and y is equal to 8
`||`	or	`(x === 5) || (y === 8)`	Tests whether x is equal to 5 or y is equal to 8
`!`	not	`!(x < 5)`	Tests whether x is not less than 5

Program Loops and Arrays

Program loops can be used to cycle through the different values contained within an array. The general structure for accessing each value from an array using a `for` loop is

```
for (var i = 0; i < array.length; i++) {
    commands involving array[i]
}
```

where `array` is the array containing the values to be looped through and `i` is the counter variable used in the loop. The counter variable in this case represents the index number of an item from the array. The `length` property is used to determine the size of the array. The last item in the array has an index value of one less than the array's length—because array indices start with zero—so you continue the loop only when the array index is less than the length value.

REFERENCE

Creating Program Loops

- To create a `for` loop, use looping structure

  ```
  for (start; continue; update) {
      commands
  }
  ```

  where *start* is an expression that sets the initial value of a counter variable, *continue* is a Boolean expression that must be true for the loop to continue, *update* is an expression that indicates how the value of the counter variable should change each time through the loop, and *commands* is the JavaScript commands that are run each time through the loop.

- To create a `while` loop, use the following structure:

  ```
  while (continue) {
      commands
  }
  ```

- To create a `do/while` loop, use the following:

  ```
  do {
      commands
      }
  while (continue);
  ```

- To loop through the contents of an array, enter the `for` loop

  ```
  for (var i = 0; i < array.length; i++) {
      commands involving array[i]
  }
  ```

  where `i` is a counter variable representing the indices of the array items and `array` is the array to be looped through.

With this information, you can create a function that employs arrays and a `for` loop to create a row displaying the names of the seven days of the week. First, you will place the three-letter abbreviation of each weekday in an array and then loop through that array, writing a table heading cell for each day. You will place these commands in a function named calWeekdayRow().

To create the calWeekdayRow() function:

1. If you took a break after the previous session, make sure the **lht_calendar.js** file is open in your text editor.

2. At the bottom of the file, insert the following commands to begin creating the function by inserting an array named *dayName* containing the three-letter abbreviations of the seven days of the week:

```
/* Function to write a table row of weekday abbreviations */
function calWeekdayRow() {
   // Array of weekday abbreviations
   var dayName = ["SUN", "MON", "TUE", "WED", "THU", "FRI",
"SAT"];
```

3. Next, create the rowHTML variable containing the opening tag for the table row by inserting the following command:

```
var rowHTML = "<tr>";
```

You must enclose all commands in a `for` loop within a set of opening and closing curly braces so that each command is run every time through the loop.

4. Add the following `for` loop to loop through the contents of the dayName array, adding HTML code for each `th` element:

```
// Loop through the dayName array
for (var i = 0; i < dayName.length; i++) {
   rowHTML += "<th class='calendar_weekdays'>" + dayName[i] +
"</th>";
}
```

5. Finally, complete the calWeekdayRow() function by adding a closing </tr> tag to the value of the rowHTML variable and return that variable's value. Add the code that follows:

```
   rowHTML += "</tr>";
   return rowHTML;
}
```

Figure 10-13 shows the complete contents of the calWeekdayRow() function.

Figure 10-13   The calWeekdayRow() function

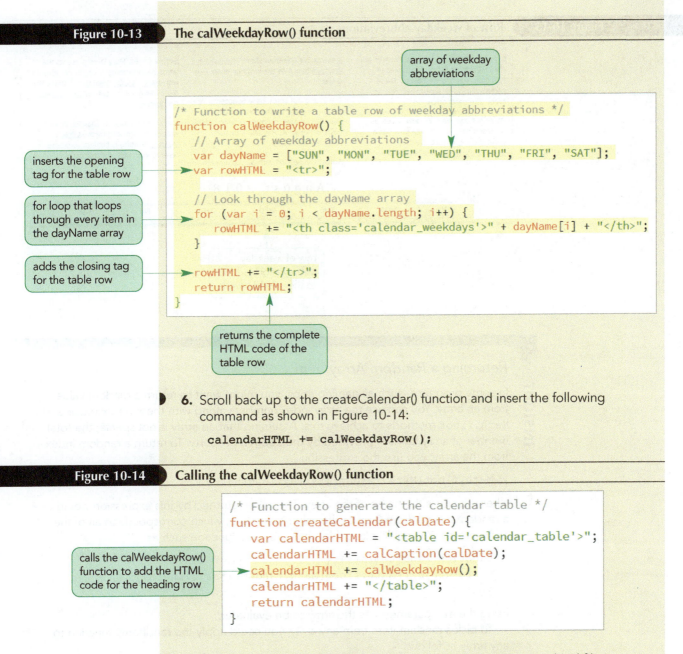

array of weekday
abbreviations

```
/* Function to write a table row of weekday abbreviations */
function calWeekdayRow() {
    // Array of weekday abbreviations
    var dayName = ["SUN", "MON", "TUE", "WED", "THU", "FRI", "SAT"];
    var rowHTML = "<tr>";

    // Look through the dayName array
    for (var i = 0; i < dayName.length; i++) {
        rowHTML += "<th class='calendar_weekdays'>" + dayName[i] + "</th>";
    }

    rowHTML += "</tr>";
    return rowHTML;
}
```

inserts the opening
tag for the table row

for loop that loops
through every item in
the dayName array

adds the closing tag
for the table row

returns the complete
HTML code of the
table row

> **6.** Scroll back up to the createCalendar() function and insert the following
> command as shown in Figure 10-14:
>
> ```
> calendarHTML += calWeekdayRow();
> ```

Figure 10-14   Calling the calWeekdayRow() function

```
/* Function to generate the calendar table */
function createCalendar(calDate) {
    var calendarHTML = "<table id='calendar_table'>";
    calendarHTML += calCaption(calDate);
    calendarHTML += calWeekdayRow();
    calendarHTML += "</table>";
    return calendarHTML;
}
```

calls the calWeekdayRow()
function to add the HTML
code for the heading row

> **7.** Save your changes to the file, and then reload the lht_august.html file in
> your browser.
>
> Figure 10-15 shows the revised appearance of the page with the calendar
> table now showing a row of weekday abbreviations.

Figure 10-15 **Row of weekday abbreviations**

Broadway closes out a great summer at the LHT with seven performances of Hamilton, starring Tre Dawes. These performances are sure to sell out, so order your seats today.

We're not done with Broadway yet, as popular singer Toni Trindle provides a great evening of jazz standards in Stardust Memories and Ted Gilliam

presents his one-man show, The Future is Prologue based on the writings of George Orwell.

The young will enjoy Have Spacesuit, Will Travel – a stage production using more than 500 images to create a living graphic novel of Robert A. Heinlein's classic science fiction story.

School's in session with our continuing

lecture series. Mary Dees presents the latest developments in cognitive research with Hacking your Dreams and David Wu discusses gravity waves in What Einstein Got Wrong.

Join us on Sunday for Classics Brunch with music provided by the Carson Quartet. Seating is limited, so please reserve your table for this popular series.

A u g u s t   2 0 1 8

SUN	MON	TUE	WED	THU	FRI	SAT

row of weekday abbreviations added to the calendar table

INSIGHT

Returning a Random Array Item

In some programs, such as gaming apps, you might want to return a random value from an array. You can use the array index numbers along with the `Math.random` and `Math.floor` methods to achieve this. Assuming that an array is not sparse, the total number of array items is provided by the `length` property. To return a random index from the array, you use the expression

```
Math.floor(Math.random()*array.length);
```

where *array* is the name of the array. The value returned by this expression would be a random integer from 0 up to the value `length-1`, which corresponds to all of the array indices. You could place this expression in a function such as

```
function randItem(arr) {
   return arr[Math.floor(Math.random()*arr.length)];
}
```

using the `arr` parameter as the array to be evaluated.

To pick a random item from any array, you could apply the randItem() function to any array as follows

```
var color = ["red", "blue", "green", "yellow"];
var randColor = randItem(color);
```

and the randColor variable would contain one of the four colors chosen at random from the color array.

Array Methods to Loop Through Arrays

JavaScript supports several methods to loop through the contents of an array without having to create a program loop structure. Because these methods are built into the JavaScript language, they are faster than program loops; however, older browsers might not support them, so you should apply them with caution.

Each of these methods is based on calling a function that will be applied to each item in the array. The general syntax is

```
array.method(callback [, thisArg])
```

where *array* is the array, *method* is the array method, and *callback* is the name of the function that will be applied to each array item. An optional argument, *thisArg*, can be included to pass a value to the callback function. The general syntax of the callback function is

```
function callback(value [, index, array]) {
    commands
}
```

where *value* is the value of the array item during each pass through the array, *index* is the numeric index of the current array item, and *array* is the name of the array. Only the *value* parameter is required; the others are optional.

Running a Function for Each Array Item

The first method you will explore is `forEach()`, which is used to run a function for each item in the array. The general syntax is

```
array.forEach(callback [, thisArg])
```

where *callback* is the function that is applied to each item in the array. For example, the following `forEach()` method applies the sumArray() function with each item in the x array:

```
var sum = 0;
var x = [2, 5, 7, 12];

x.forEach(sumArray);

function sumArray(value) {
    sum += value;
}
```

Note that the sumArray() function has a single parameter named `value`, representing the current array item. The result of running the `forEach()` method with the sumArray() function is that the value of each item in the x array is added to the sum variable, resulting in a final value of 26 in this example. The `forEach()` method can also be used to modify the values of individual array items.

The following code calls the stepUp() function to increase the value of each item in the x array by 1:

```
var x = [4, 7, 11];

x.forEach(stepUp);

function stepUp(value, i, arr) {
    arr[i] = value + 1;
}
```

Notice that in this case, the stepUp() function has three parameters, with the second parameter (`i`) representing the array index and the third parameter (`arr`) representing the array itself. After running this code, the x array would contain the values [5, 8, 12].

Mapping an Array

The `map()` method performs an action similar to the `forEach()` method except that the function it calls returns a value that can be used to map the contents of an existing array into a new array. The following code demonstrates how to use the `map()`

method to create a new array in which each item is equal to twice the value of the corresponding item in the original array:

```
var x = [3, 8, 12];

var y = x.map(DoubleIt);

function DoubleIt(value) {
    return 2*value;
}
```

After running this code, the y array contains the values [6, 16, 24]. Note that the `map()` method does not affect the contents or structure of the original array, and the new array will have the same number of array items as the original. If the original array is sparse with several missing indices, the mapped array will have the same sparseness.

Filtering an Array

Often when working with arrays, you will want to extract array items that match some specified condition. For example, in an array of test scores, you might want to extract only those test scores with a value of 90 or above. The following `filter()` method can be used to create such arrays

```
array.filter(callback [, thisArg])
```

where *callback* is a function that returns a Boolean value of `true` or `false` for each item in the array. The array items that return a value of `true` get copied into the new array. The following code demonstrates how to use the `filter()` method to create a subarray of items whose value is greater than 90:

```
var scores = [92, 68, 83, 95, 91, 65, 77];

var highScores = scores.filter(gradeA);

function gradeA(value) {
    return value > 90;
}
```

After running this code, the highScores array would contain the values [92, 95, 91].

Another common use of arrays is to examine an array's contents to determine whether every array item satisfies a specified condition. The following `every()` method returns the value `true` if every item in the array matches the condition specified by the callback function and, if otherwise, returns `false`:

```
array.every(callback [, thisArg])
```

As with the `filter()` method, the function used by the `every()` method must return a Boolean value of `true` or `false`. For example, the following code uses the `every()` method to test whether every test score exceeds a value of 70:

```
var scores = [92, 68, 83, 95, 91, 65, 77];

var allPassing = scores.every(passTest);

function passTest(value) {
    return value > 70;
}
```

In this example, the value of the allPassing variable would be `false` because not every value in the scores array is greater than 70. Similarly, the following `some()` method

```
array.some(callback [,thisArg])
```

returns a value of `true` if some—but not necessarily all—array items match a condition specified in the function and a value of `false` if none of the array items match the condition specified in the function. Applying the `some()` method to the above array would return a value of true because some (but not all) of the scores are greater than 70.

Figure 10-16 summarizes the different JavaScript array methods that can be used to work with the collection of items within an array.

Figure 10-16 **Array methods to loop through arrays**

Array Method	Description
every(*callback* [, *thisArg*])	Tests whether the condition returned by the *callback* function holds for all items in *array*; in all array methods, the optional *thisArg* parameter is used to pass values to the *callback* function
filter(*callback* [, *thisArg*])	Creates a new array populated with the elements of *array* that return a value of *true* from the *callback* function
forEach(*callback* [, *thisArg*])	Applies the *callback* function to each item in *array*
map(*callback* [, *thisArg*])	Creates a new array by passing the original array items to the *callback* function, which returns the mapped value of the array items
reduce(*callback* [, *thisArg*])	Reduces *array* by keeping only those items that return a value of *true* from the *callback* function
reduceRight(*callback* [, *thisArg*])	Reduces *array* from the last element by keeping only those items that return a value of *true* from the *callback* function
some(*callback* [, *thisArg*])	Tests whether the condition returned by the *callback* function holds for at least one item in *array*
find(*callback* [, *thisArg*])	Returns the value of the first element in the array that passes a test in the *callback* function
findIndex(*callback* [, *thisArg*])	Returns the index of the first element in the array that passes a test in the *callback* function

Decision Making: Efficient Loops

As your programs increase in size and complexity, the ability to write efficient code becomes essential. Bloated, inefficient code is particularly noticeable with program loops that might repeat the same set of commands hundreds or thousands of times. A millisecond wasted due to one poorly written command can mean an overall loss of dozens of seconds when it is part of a loop. Because studies show that users will rarely wait more than a few seconds for program results, it is important to shave off as many milliseconds as you can. Here are some ways to speed up your loops:

- **Calculate outside the loop**. There is no reason to repeat the exact same calculation hundreds of times within a loop. For example, the following code unnecessarily recalculates the same Math.log(cost) value a thousand times in the `for` loop:

```
for (i = 0; i < 1000; i++) {
   x[i] = i*Math.log(cost);
}
```

Instead, place that calculation outside the loop, where it will be calculated only once:

```
var costLog = Math.log(cost);
for (i = 0; i < 1000; i++) {
   x[i] = i*costLog;
}
```

- **Determine array lengths once**. Rather than forcing JavaScript to count up the length of a large array each time through the loop, calculate the length before the loop starts:

```
var x = myArray.length;
for (var i = 0; i < x; i++) {
   commands
}
```

- **Decrement rather than increment**. Instead of counting up to an array length, count down from the array length to 0, as in the following `for` loop:

```
var x = myArray.length;
for (var i = x; i--) {
   commands
}
```

When the counter variable equals 0, the loop will stop.

- **Unroll the loop**. When only a few items are being iterated in a loop, it is actually faster not to use a program loop. Instead, enter each counter value explicitly in separate statements.

- **Manage Loop size**: A long command block is a red flag warning you that you might be trying to do too much each time through a loop. Look for ways to reduce the number of tasks and calculations in the command block to a bare minimum.

In the next session, you will explore how to work with JavaScript's conditional statements and put together everything you have learned to complete the calendar app.

Session 10.2 Quick Check

1. What is a program loop? Name three types of program loops supported by JavaScript.
2. Provide a `for` statement to use a counter variable named i that starts with the value 0 and continues up to 100 in increments of 10.
3. Provide a `for` statement that stores the HTML code for a table row consisting of five table cells in a variable named tableCode. Assume the table cells display the text `Column` *i*, where *i* is the value of the counter variable, and the value of the counter variable increases from 1 to 5 in increments of 1.
4. Provide code to duplicate the task in the previous question using a while loop.
5. Provide code, using an array method, to increase the value of each item in the array x = [2, 14, -3, 7] by 10.
6. Provide code, using an array method, to map the value of items in the array x = [2, 14, -3, 7] into a new array named y in which each of the values is increased by 10.
7. Provide code, using an array method, to return a Boolean value indicating whether every value in the array x = [2, 14, -3, 7] is positive.
8. Provide code, using an array method, to store only the positive values from the array x = [2, 14, -3, 7] in a new array named y.

Session 10.3 Visual Overview:

A **conditional expression** is an expression that is either true or false.

In an **if statement**, an expression is tested for being true or false; if true, a specified command is run.

In an **if else statement** one command block is run if the statement is true, while a second command block is run if the statement is false.

The command in a simple if statement is run if the condition is true.

The first command block in an if else statement is run if the condition is true.

```
for (var i = 1; i <= totalDays; i++) {
    day.setDate(i);
    weekDay = day.getDay();

    if (weekDay === 0) htmlCode += "<tr>";

    if (i === highlightDay) {
        htmlCode += "<td class='calendar_today'>" + i + "</td>";
    } else {
        htmlCode += "<td class='calendar_dates'>" + i + "</td>";
    }

    if (weekDay === 6) htmlCode += "</tr>";
}
```

The equals operator (===) tests whether two items share the same value and data type.

The second command block in an if else statement is run if the condition is false.

Conditional Statements

```javascript
function daysInMonth(calDate) {
   var dayCount = [31,28,31,30,31,30,31,31,30,31,30,31];

   var thisYear = calDate.getFullYear();
   var thisMonth = calDate.getMonth();

   if (thisYear % 4 === 0) {
      if ((thisYear % 100 != 0) || (thisYear % 400 === 0)) {
         dayCount[1] = 29;
      }
   }

   return dayCount[thisMonth];

}
```

The or operator (||) is used when either of two conditions may be true for the entire conditional expression to be true.

In a nested if structure, one if statement is placed within another; the nested if statement is run only if the conditional expressions of both the outer and inner if statements are true.

Introducing Conditional Statements

Your next task in your calendar app is to create a program loop that writes the days of the month, entered within different table cells arranged in separate table rows. The process should end when the last day of the month is reached. Because months have different numbers of days, you first need to create a function named daysInMonth() that determines the number of days in a given month.

Like the calCaption() function you created earlier, the daysInMonth() function will have a single parameter, calDate, containing a Date object on which your calendar will be based. The function will also store the year value and month value in the variables thisYear and thisMonth, respectively, and will contain the following array that stores the number of days in each month:

```
var dayCount = [31,28,31,30,31,30,31,31,30,31,30,31];
```

This array is an example of a **parallel array** because each entry in the array matches—or is parallel to—an entry in the monthName array you created in the first session. To return the days of the month from the calendar date, the function will use the value of the thisMonth variable to reference the corresponding day value in the dayCount array with the following expression:

```
dayCount[thisMonth]
```

So, for instance, given the date July 6, 2018, the function would return the value 31. You add the daysInMonth() function now.

To start creating the daysInMonth() function:

1. If you took a break after the previous session, make sure the **lht_calendar.js** file is open in your text editor.

2. At the bottom of the file, insert the following code, as shown in Figure 10-17:

```
 * Function to calculate the number of days in the month */
function daysInMonth(calDate) {
   // Array of days in each month
   var dayCount = [31,28,31,30,31,30,31,31,30,31,30,31];

   // Extract the four digit year and month value
   var thisYear = calDate.getFullYear();
   var thisMonth = calDate.getMonth();

   // Return the number of days for the current month
   return dayCount[thisMonth];
}
```

Figure 10-17 **Inserting the daysInMonth() function**

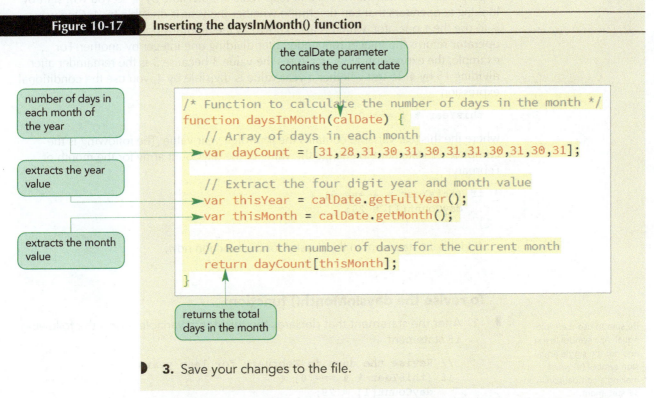

the calDate parameter contains the current date

number of days in each month of the year

extracts the year value

extracts the month value

```
/* Function to calculate the number of days in the month */
function daysInMonth(calDate) {
    // Array of days in each month
    var dayCount = [31,28,31,30,31,30,31,31,30,31,30,31];

    // Extract the four digit year and month value
    var thisYear = calDate.getFullYear();
    var thisMonth = calDate.getMonth();

    // Return the number of days for the current month
    return dayCount[thisMonth];
}
```

returns the total days in the month

▶ **3.** Save your changes to the file.

Perhaps you have already noticed a problem with the dayCount array: February has 29 days during a leap year, not 28 days as shown in the array. For the daysInMonth() function to return the correct value for the month of February, it must examine the year value and then set the value for the number of days in February to either 28 or 29 based on whether the current year is a leap year. You can do this through a conditional statement. A **conditional statement** is a statement that runs a command or command block only when certain circumstances are met.

Exploring the `if` Statement

The most common conditional statement is the `if` statement, which has the structure

```
if (condition) {
    commands
}
```

where *condition* is a Boolean expression that is either true or false, and *commands* is the command block that is run if *condition* is true. If only one command is run, you can eliminate the command block and enter the `if` statement as follows:

```
if (condition) command;
```

A conditional statement uses the same comparison and logical operators you used with the program loops in the last session. For example, the following `if` statement would set the value of the dayCount array for February to 29 if the year value were 2020 (a leap year):

```
if (thisYear === 2020) {
    dayCount[1] = 29;
}
```

For the calendar app, you will need to create a conditional expression that tests whether the current year is a leap year and then sets the value of dayCount[1] appropriately. The general rule is that leap years are divisible by 4, so you will start by looking at operators that can determine whether the year is divisible by 4. One way is to use the % operator, which is also known as the modulus operator. The **modulus operator** returns the integer remainder after dividing one integer by another. For example, the expression 15 % 4 returns the value 3 because 3 is the remainder after dividing 15 by 4. To test whether a year value is divisible by 4, you use the conditional expression

```
thisYear % 4 === 0
```

where the thisYear variable contains the four-digit year value. The following is the complete if statement to change the value of the dayCount array for the month of February:

```
if (thisYear % 4 === 0) {
   dayCount[1] = 29;
}
```

Add this if statement to the daysInMonth() function now.

To revise the daysInMonth() function:

Be sure to use the triple equal sign symbol (===) and not the single equal sign symbol (=) when making a comparison in an if statement.

1. After the statement that declares the thisMonth variable, insert the following if statement:

```
// Revise the days in February for leap years
if (thisYear % 4 === 0) {
   dayCount[1] = 29;
}
```

Figure 10-18 highlights the newly added code in the function.

Figure 10-18   Inserting an if statement

```
/* Function to calculate the number of days in the month */
function daysInMonth(calDate) {
   // Array of days in each month
   var dayCount = [31,28,31,30,31,30,31,31,30,31,30,31];

   // Extract the four digit year and month value
   var thisYear = calDate.getFullYear();
   var thisMonth = calDate.getMonth();

   // Revise the days in February for leap years
   if (thisYear % 4 === 0) {
      dayCount[1] = 29;
   }

   // Return the number of days for the current month
   return dayCount[thisMonth];

}
```

tests whether thisYear is evenly divisible by 4

if it is, sets the value of dayCount[1] (February) to 29

2. Save your changes to the file.

Assigning Values with Conditional Operators

When you want to simply assign a value to a variable rather than run a command block, you can write a more compact conditional expression using a **conditional operator** or a **ternary operator**, which has the syntax

```
condition ? value1 : value2;
```

where `condition` is a Boolean expression, `value1` is the value if the expression is true and `value2` is the value if the expression is false. For example, the following statement assigns a value of "Morning" to the session variable if the hour variable is less than 12 and "Afternoon" if otherwise:

```
var session = hour < 12 ? "Morning" : "Afternoon";
```

Conditional operators can test more than one possible condition by adding a second conditional operator to the last term in the expression as follows

```
condition1 ? value1 : condition2 ? value2 : value3;
```

where `value1` is assigned if `condition1` is true, `value2` is assigned if `condition2` is true (but not `condition1`), and `value3` is assigned if neither `condition1` nor `condition2` are true. Thus, the following statement assigns one of three possible values to the session variable based on the value of the hour variable:

```
var session = hour < 12 ? "Morning" : hour < 16 ? "Afternoon" :
"Evening";
```

If hour is less than 12, the session variable has the value "Morning"; if hour is less than 16 (but greater than 12), the value is "Afternoon"; and otherwise, the value of the session variable is "Evening".

Note that conditional operators can only be used to assign a value. If you need to do more than one action in response to a conditional expression, use an `if` statement.

Nesting `if` Statements

The `if` statement you wrote for the daysInMonth() function works as a simple approximation, but it is not completely accurate. In most cases, a year that is evenly divisible by 4 is a leap year. The only exceptions are years that occur at the turn of the century, which are evenly divisible by 100. These years are not leap years unless they are also evenly divisible by 400. Thus, years such as 1800, 1900, and 2100 are not leap years even though they are evenly divisible by 4. Years such as 2000 and 2400 are leap years because they are evenly divisible by 400. Figure 10-19 shows the complete process used to determine whether a particular year is a leap year.

Figure 10-19   Process to calculate leap years

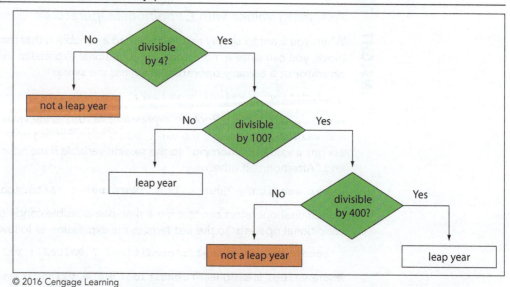

© 2016 Cengage Learning

To translate these rules into our calendar app, you need to nest one `if` statement inside another one. The general structure of this nested `if` statement is as follows:

```
if (thisYear % 4 === 0) {
    further test for century years
}
```

The nested `if` statement needs to add two more conditions: (1) the year is not divisible by 100, and (2) the year is divisible by 400. The expressions for these two conditions are as follows:

```
thisYear % 100 != 0
thisYear % 400 === 0
```

If either of those two conditions is true for a year evenly divisible by 4, then the year is a leap year. Note that you will use the not equal to operator (`!=`) to test for an inequality in the first expression. You will then combine these two expressions into a single expression using the or operator (`||`), as follows:

```
(thisYear % 100 != 0) || (thisYear % 400 === 0)
```

Finally, you will nest this conditional expression as follows:

```
if (thisYear % 4 === 0) {
    if ((thisYear % 100 != 0) || (thisYear % 400 === 0)) {
        dayCount[1] = 29;
    }
}
```

Under this set of nested `if` statements, the number of days in February is 29 only if the thisYear variable is divisible by 4, and then only if it is also divisible by 400 or not divisible by 100. Take some time to compare this set of nested `if` statements with the chart shown earlier in Figure 10-19 to confirm that it satisfies all possible conditions for leap years. After incorporating this set of nested `if` statements, the daysInMonth() function returns the correct number of days for any month in any given year.

To complete the daysInMonth() function:

1. Within the `if` statement you entered in the last set of steps, delete the statement

```
dayCount[1] = 29
```

2. Replace the statement you just deleted with the following nested `if` statement:

```
if ((thisYear % 100 != 0) || (thisYear % 400 === 0)) {
   dayCount[1] = 29;
}
```

Figure 10-20 highlights the newly inserted nested `if` statement.

| Figure 10-20 | Inserting a nested if statement |

if the year is divisible by 4 and either not divisible by 100 or divisible by 400, it's a leap year

```
// Revise the days in February for leap years
if (thisYear % 4 === 0) {
   if ((thisYear % 100 != 0) || (thisYear % 400 === 0)) {
      dayCount[1] = 29;
   }
}
```

3. Save your changes to the file.

Exploring the `if else` Statement

The `if` statement runs a command or a command block only if the conditional expression returns the value `true`; it does nothing if the condition is false. On some occasions, you might want to choose between alternate command blocks so that one command block is run if the conditional expression is true, and a different command block is run if the expression is false. The general structure of an `if else` statement follows:

```
if (condition) {
   commands if condition is true
} else {
   commands if condition is false
}
```

If only a single command is run in response to the `if` statement, you can use the following abbreviated form:

```
if (condition) command if condition is true
else command if condition is false;
```

The following example shows an `if else` statement that displays two possible alert boxes depending on whether the value of the day variable is Friday or not:

```
if (day === "Friday") alert("Thank goodness it's Friday")
else alert("Today is " + day);
```

Like `if` statements, `if else` statements can be nested as in the following code, which chooses between three possible alert boxes:

```
if (day === "Friday") alert("Thank goodness it's Friday")
else {
    if (day === "Monday") alert("Blue Monday")
    else alert("Today is " + day);
}
```

Some programmers advocate always using curly braces even if the command block contains only a single command. This practice visually separates one `else` clause from another. Also, when reading through nested statements, it can be helpful to remember that an `else` clause usually pairs with the nearest preceding `if` statement.

Using Multiple `else` `if` Statements

For more complex scripts, you might need to choose from several alternatives. In these cases, you can specify multiple `else` clauses, each with its own `if` statement. This is not a new type of conditional structure, but rather a way of taking advantage of the syntax rules inherent in the `if else` statement. The general structure for choosing from several alternatives is

```
if (condition1) {
    commands1
} else if (condition2) {
    commands2
} else if (condition3) {
    commands3
...
} else {
    default commands
}
```

where `condition 1`, `condition 2`, `condition 3`, and so on are the different conditions to be tested. This construction should always include a final `else` clause that is run by default if none of the preceding conditional expressions is true. When a browser runs a series of statements like this one, it stops examining the remaining `else` clauses at the first true condition. The structure in the following example employs multiple `else if` conditions:

```
if (day === "Friday") {
    alert("Thank goodness it's Friday");
} else if (day === "Monday") {
    alert("Blue Monday");
} else if (day === "Saturday") {
    alert("Sleep in today");
} else {
    alert("Today is " + day);
}
```

Working with Conditional Statements

- To test a single condition, use the construction

```
if (condition) {
    commands
}
```

where *condition* is a Boolean expression and *commands* is a command block run if the conditional expression is true.

- To test between two conditions, use the following construction:

```
if (condition) {
    commands if condition is true
} else {
    commands if not true
}
```

- To test multiple conditions, use the construction

```
if (condition1) {
    commands1
} else if (condition2) {
    commands2
} else if (condition3) {
    commands3
...
} else {
    default commands
}
```

where *condition 1*, *condition 2*, *condition 3*, and so on are the different conditions to be tested. If no conditional expressions return the value true, the *default command block* is run.

You now have all of the tools you need to complete the calendar app. The only remaining task involves writing out the table cells containing the calendar days so that they are organized into separate rows. You will complete the calendar app in the next section.

Exploring the switch Statement

Another way to handle multiple conditions is with the **switch statement**—also known as the **case statement**—in which different commands are run based upon different possible values of a specified variable. The syntax of the switch statement is

```
switch (expression) {
    case label1: commands1; break;
    case label2: commands2; break;
    case label3: commands3; break;
    ...
    default: default commands
}
```

where *expression* is an expression that returns a value; *label1*, *label2*, and so on are possible values of that expression; *commands1*, *commands2*, and so on are the commands associated with each label; and *default commands* is the set of commands to be run if no label matches the value returned by expression. The following switch statement demonstrates how to display a different alert box based on the value of the day variable:

```
switch (day) {
    case "Friday": alert("Thank goodness it's Friday"); break;
    case "Monday": alert("Blue Monday"); break;
    case "Saturday": alert("Sleep in today"); break;
    default: alert("Today is " + day);
}
```

The break statement is optional and is used to halt the execution of the switch statement once a match has been found. For programs with multiple matching cases, you can omit the break statements and JavaScript will continue moving through the switch statements, running all matching commands.

Because of its simplicity, the switch statement is often preferred over a long list of else if statements that can be confusing to read and to debug.

Completing the Calendar App

The last part of creating the calendar involves writing table cells for each day of the month. The completed calendar app must do the following:

- Calculate the day of the week in which the month starts.
- Write blank table cells for the days before the first day of the month.
- Loop through the days of the current month, writing each date in a different table cell and starting a new table row on each Sunday.

You will place all of these commands in a function named calDays(). The function will have a single parameter named calDate storing a Date object for the current date. You add this function to the lht_calendar.js file.

To start the calDays() function:

1. At the bottom of the lht_calendar.js file, insert the following function:

```
/* Function to write table rows for each day of the month */
function calDays(calDate) {
    // Determine the starting day of the month

    // Write blank cells preceding the starting day

    // Write cells for each day of the month
}
```

Figure 10-21 highlights the initial code of the function, as well as comments to help explain the code that will be added.

Figure 10-21 | Inserting the calDays() function and comments

```
/* Function to write  table rows for each day of the month */
function calDays(calDate) {
    // Determine the starting day of the month

    // Write blank cells preceding the starting day

    // Write cells for each day of the month
}
```

2. Save your changes to the file.

Setting the First Day of the Month

To loop through all of the days of the month, you need to keep track of each day as its table cell is written into the calendar table. You will store this information in a Date object named day. The initial value of the day variable will be set to match the first day of the calendar month using the following expression:

```
var day = new Date(calDate.getFullYear(), calDate.getMonth(), 1);
```

Note that the new Date() object constructor uses the four-digit year value and month value from the calDate parameter to set the year and month, and then sets the day value to 1 to match the first day of the month. For example, if the current date is August 12, 2017, the date stored in the day variable will be August 1, 2017; that is, no matter what current day is, the date stored in the day variable will be the first day for that month and year.

Next, to determine the day of the week on which the month starts, you use the following getDay() method:

```
var weekDay = day.getDay();
```

Recall that the getDay() method returns an integer ranging from 0 (Sunday) to 6 (Saturday). You add these two commands to the calDays() function now.

To create the day and weekDay variables:

▶ **1.** Below the first comment in the calDays() function, insert the following commands:

```
var day = new Date(calDate.getFullYear(), calDate.getMonth(), 1);
var weekDay = day.getDay();
```

Figure 10-22 highlights the newly added code.

Figure 10-22   **Calculating the start day of the month**

sets the first day of the month

determines the weekday on which the month begins

```
/* Function to write  table rows for each day of the month */
function calDays(calDate) {
   // Determine the starting day of the month
   var day = new Date(calDate.getFullYear(), calDate.getMonth(), 1);
   var weekDay = day.getDay();

   // Write blank cells preceding the starting day

   // Write cells for each day of the month
}
```

▶ **2.** Save your changes to the file.

Placing the First Day of the Month

Before the first day of the month, the calendar table should show only empty table cells that represent the days from the previous month. The value of the weekDay variable indicates how many empty table cells you need to create. For example, if the value of the weekDay variable is 4, indicating that the month starts on a Thursday, you know that there are four blank table cells—corresponding to Sunday, Monday, Tuesday, and Wednesday—that need to be written at the start of the first table row. The following loop writes the HTML code for the empty table cells to start the table row:

```
var htmlCode = "<tr>";
for (var i = 0; i < weekDay; i++) {
   htmlCode += "<td></td>";
}
```

Note that if weekDay equals 0—indicating that the month starts on a Sunday—then no blank table cells will be written because the value of the counter variable is never less than the value of the weekDay variable and thus, the command block in the `for` loop is completely skipped.

To write the initial blank cells of the first table row:

▶ **1.** Below the second comment line, insert the following `for` loop:

```
var htmlCode = "<tr>";
for (var i = 0; i < weekDay; i++) {
   htmlCode += "<td></td>";
}
```

Figure 10-23 highlights the code for the `for` loop.

Figure 10-23	Inserting blank cells for the days that precede the start of the month

```
/* Function to write  table rows for each day of the month */
function calDays(calDate) {
   // Determine the starting day of the month
   var day = new Date(calDate.getFullYear(), calDate.getMonth(), 1);
   var weekDay = day.getDay();

   // Write blank cells preceding the starting day
   var htmlCode = "<tr>";
   for (var i = 0; i < weekDay; i++) {
      htmlCode += "<td></td>";
   }

   // Write cells for each day of the month

}
```

inserts opening <tr> tag for the initial table row

inserts a blank table cell for each weekday prior to the first of the month

▶ **2.** Save your changes to the file.

Writing the Calendar Days

Finally, you will write the table cells for each day of the month using the following for loop:

```
var totalDays = daysInMonth(calDate);

for (var i = 1; i <= totalDays; i++) {
   day.setDate(i);
   weekDay = day.getDay();

   if (weekDay === 0) htmlCode += "<tr>";
   htmlCode += "<td class='calendar_dates'>" + i + "</td>";
   if (weekDay === 6) htmlCode += "</tr>";
}
```

The code starts by determining the total days in the month using the daysInMonth() function you created earlier. It then loops through those days, and each time through the loop it changes the day and weekDay variables to match the current day being written. If the day is a Sunday, a new table row is started; if the day is a Saturday, the current table row is ended. Each table cell displays the day number and belongs to the calendar_dates class, which allows it to be styled using the style rule from the lht_calendar.css style sheet.

To write the calendar days:

▶ **1.** Below the last comment in the calDays() function, add the following commands:

```
var totalDays = daysInMonth(calDate);

for (var i = 1; i <= totalDays; i++) {
   day.setDate(i);
   weekDay = day.getDay();
```

```
        if (weekDay === 0) htmlCode += "<tr>";
        htmlCode += "<td class='calendar_dates'>" + i + "</td>";
        if (weekDay === 6) htmlCode += "</tr>";
    }

    return htmlCode;
```

Figure 10-24 highlights the code to write the table cells for each day of the month.

Figure 10-24 Writing the HTML code for the table row and cells

calculates the total number of days in the current month

loops through the total number of days

if the day is a Sunday, starts a new table row

creates a table cell for each day, displaying the day number

```
// Write cells for each day of the month
var totalDays = daysInMonth(calDate);

for (var i = 1; i <= totalDays; i++) {
    day.setDate(i);
    weekDay = day.getDay();

    if (weekDay === 0) htmlCode += "<tr>";
    htmlCode += "<td class='calendar_dates'>" + i + "</td>";
    if (weekDay === 6) htmlCode += "</tr>";
}

return htmlCode;
}
```

for each day, determines the weekday on which it falls

if the day is a Saturday, ends the table row

returns the HTML code for the table row and cells

Next, you call the calDays() function from within the createCalendar() function and view the results.

2. Scroll up to the createCalendar() function, and then insert the following statement directly above the command that writes the closing </table> tag.

```
calendarHTML += calDays(calDate);
```

Figure 10-25 highlights the code in the function.

Figure 10-25 Calling the calDays() function

calls the calDays function, which adds the HTML code for the table row and cells that display the days of the month

```
/* Function to generate the calendar table */
function createCalendar(calDate) {
    var calendarHTML = "<table id='calendar_table'>";
    calendarHTML += calCaption(calDate);
    calendarHTML += calWeekdayRow();
    calendarHTML += calDays(calDate);
    calendarHTML += "</table>";
    return calendarHTML;
}
```

3. Save your changes to the file, and then reload the lht_august.html file in your browser. As shown in Figure 10-26, the page should now display the monthly calendar for August, 2018.

Figure 10-26   **Monthly calendar for August, 2018**

We're not done with Broadway yet, as popular singer Toni Trindle provides a great evening of jazz standards in Stardust Memories and Ted Gilliam

than 500 images to create a living graphic novel of Robert A. Heinlein's classic science fiction story.

School's in session with our continuing

Join us on Sunday for Classics Brunch with music provided by the Carson Quartet. Seating is limited, so please reserve your table for this popular series.

days from the preceding month are displayed as blank cells

days from the next month are displayed as blank cells

Trouble? If you do not see a calendar, you might have made a mistake in the code. Common mistakes include misspelling variable names, forgetting to close quoted text strings, inconsistently using uppercase and lowercase letters in variable names, and omitting closing braces in command blocks. Compare your code to the complete code of the calDays() function shown in Figures 10-23 and 10-24.

Highlighting the Current Date

Lewis likes the calendar's appearance but mentions that the calendar should also highlight the current day: August 24, 2018. Recall that Lewis has created a special style rule for the current day, identified using the HTML id value "calendar_today". Thus, to highlight that table cell, the calDays() function should test each day as it is being written; and if the date matches the calendar day, the function should write the table cell as

```
<td class='calendar_dates' id='calendar_today'>day</td>
```

where *day* is the day number. Otherwise, the function should write the table cell without the id attribute as follows:

```
<td class='calendar_dates'>day</td>
```

To determine the day number of the calendar day, you create the highlightDay variable, using the getDate() method to extract the day value from the calDate parameter. When the counter in the for loop matches the value of this variable, the loop will write the table cell including the calendar_today id attribute.

To highlight the current date in the calendar:

1. Return to the **lht_calendar.js** file in your editor, and then scroll down to the calDays() function.

TIP

Calculations such as the getDate() method that need to be performed once should always be placed outside the program loop to avoid unnecessarily repeating the same calculation each time through the loop.

2. In the Write cells for each day of the month section and directly above the for loop in that section, insert the following statement to calculate the day value of the current day:

```
var highlightDay = calDate.getDate();
```

3. Replace the statement that writes the table cell in the for loop with the following code:

```
if (i === highlightDay) {
   htmlCode += "<td class='calendar_dates' id='calendar_
today'>" + i + "</td>";
} else {
   htmlCode += "<td class='calendar_dates'>" + i + "</td>";
}
```

Figure 10-27 highlights the newly added if statement in the function.

Figure 10-27 **Highlighting the current date in the calendar**

```
// Write cells for each day of the month
var totalDays = daysInMonth(calDate);

var highlightDay = calDate.getDate();
for (var i = 1; i <= totalDays; i++) {
   day.setDate(i);
   weekDay = day.getDay();

   if (weekDay === 0) htmlCode += "<tr>";
   if (i === highlightDay) {
      htmlCode += "<td class='calendar_dates' id='calendar_today'>" + i + "</td>";
   } else {
      htmlCode += "<td class='calendar_dates'>" + i + "</td>";
   }
   if (weekDay === 6) htmlCode += "</tr>";
}

return htmlCode;
}
```

- stores the current day in the highlightDay variable
- if the day is the highlight day, write a table cell with the id 'calendar_today'
- otherwise write a table cell with no id value

4. Save your changes to the file, and then reload lht_august.html in your browser. The table cell corresponding to August 24, 2018 should now be highlighted as shown in Figure 10-28.

Figure 10-28   **Calendar with the current date highlighted**

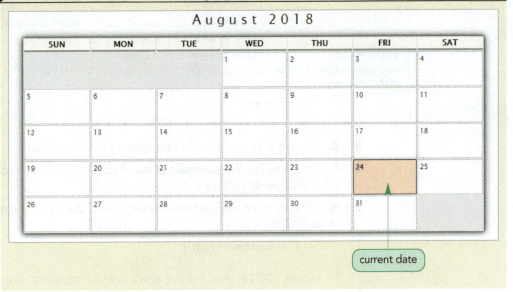

current date

Displaying Daily Events

The final piece of your calendar app is to display the daily events in August. Lewis already has created an array of daily event text, part of which is shown in Figure 10-29.

Figure 10-29   **The dayEvent array**

```
var dayEvent = new Array();

dayEvent[1] = "";
dayEvent[2] = "<br /><a href='#'>Classic Cinema: Wings</a><br />7 pm<br />$5";
dayEvent[3] = "<br /><a href='#'>The Future is Prologue</a><br />8 pm<br />$18/$24/$36";
dayEvent[4] = "<br /><a href='#'>American Favorites</a><br />7:30 pm<br />$24/$36/$48";
dayEvent[5] = "<br /><a href='#'>Classics Brunch</a><br />11 am<br />$12";
dayEvent[6] = "<br /><a href='#'>LHT Jazz Band</a><br />7 pm<br />$24";
dayEvent[7] = "";
```

The dayEvent array has 31 items to match the 31 days in August. Array items that match days on which no event is scheduled contain a blank text string, while daily events are written in the HTML code that will be inserted into the calendar table. To display this content, you create a link to the lht_events.js file and then, within the calDays() function, you add an expression to write the contents of the dayEvent array into the individual table cells.

To display the daily events:

1. Return to the **lht_august.html** file in your text editor. Directly above the script element for the lht_calendar.js file, insert the following script element for the lht_events.js file:

   ```
   <script src="lht_events.js" defer></script>
   ```

   Figure 10-30 highlights the newly added code.

Figure 10-30	Linking to the lht_events.js file

links to the script file containing the dayEvents array →

```
<link href="lht_base.css" rel="stylesheet" />
<link href="lht_layout.css" rel="stylesheet" />
<link href="lht_calendar.css" rel="stylesheet" />
<script src="lht_events.js" defer></script>
<script src="lht_calendar.js" defer></script>
</head>
```

2. Close the lht_august.html file, saving your changes.

3. Return to the **lht_calendar.js** file in your text editor, and then scroll down to the calDays() function.

4. Within the `if else` statement conditions, change the expression `+ i +` in two places to:

   ` + i + dayEvent[i] +`

   Figure 10-31 highlights the newly added code that displays the events on each day.

Figure 10-31	Displaying events for each day of the month

```
if (weekDay === 0) htmlCode += "<tr>";
if (i === highlightDay) {
    htmlCode += "<td class='calendar_dates' id='calendar_today'>" + i + dayEvent[i] + "</td>";
} else {
    htmlCode += "<td class='calendar_dates'>" + i + dayEvent[i] + "</td>";
}
if (weekDay === 6) htmlCode += "</tr>";
```

displays the event for the day

5. Save your changes to the file.

6. Reload the **lht_august.html** file in your browser. Verify that the calendar now shows the daily events as displayed in Figure 10-32.

Figure 10-32	Final version of the August 2018 calendar

You complete your work on the app by modifying the code so that it shows the calendar for the current month.

To display the calendar for the current month:

1. Return to the **lht_calendar.js** file in your editor.

2. Change the statement setting the value of the thisDay variable to:

   ```
   var thisDay = new Date();
   ```

   Figure 10-33 highlights the changed code in the file.

Figure 10-33	Displaying a calendar for the current month and date

```
/* Set the date displayed in the calendar */
var thisDay = new Date();
```

sets the thisDay variable to the current date and time

3. Close the file, saving your changes.

4. Reload the **lht_august.html** file in your browser. Verify that the page shows the calendar for the current month and that the current date is highlighted within the calendar (the events listed in the calendar will still be based on the entries in the dayEvent array).

Managing Program Loops and Conditional Statements

Although you are finished with the calendar app, you still should become familiar with some features of program loops and conditional statements for future work with these JavaScript structures. You examine three features in more detail—the `break`, `continue`, and `label` statements.

Exploring the `break` Command

Although you briefly saw how to use the `break` statement when creating a `switch` statement, the `break` statement can be used anywhere within program code. Its purpose is to terminate any program loop or conditional statement. When a `break` statement is encountered, control is passed to the statement immediately following it. It is most often used to exit a program loop before the stopping condition is met. For example, consider a loop that examines an array for the presence or absence of a particular value, such as a customer ID number. The code for the loop might look as follows:

```
for (var i = 0; i< ids.length; i++) {
   if (ids[i] === "C-14281") {
      alert("C-14281 is in the list");
   }
}
```

What would happen if the ids array had tens of thousands of entries? It would be time consuming to keep examining the array once the C-14281 ID has been encountered. To address this, the following `for` loop breaks off when it encounters the ID value, keeping the browser from needlessly examining the rest of the array:

```
for (var i = 0; i< ids.length; i++) {
   if (ids[i] === "C-14281") {
      alert("C-14281 is in the list");
      break;   // stop processing the for loop
   }
}
```

Exploring the `continue` Command

The **continue statement** is similar to the `break` statement except that instead of stopping the program loop altogether, the `continue` statement stops processing the commands in the current iteration of the loop and continues on to the next iteration. For example, your program might employ the following `for` loop to add the values from an array:

```
var total = 0;
for (var i = 0; i < data.length; i++) {
   total += data[i];
}
```

Each time through the loop, the value of the current entry in the data array is added to the total variable. When the `for` loop is finished, the total variable is equal to the sum of the values in the data array. However, what would happen if this were a sparse array containing several empty entries? In that case, when a browser encountered a missing or null value, that value would be added to the total variable, resulting in a null total. One way to fix this problem would be to use the `continue` statement, jumping out of the current iteration if a missing or null value were encountered. The revised code would look like the following:

```
var total = 0;
for (var i = 0; i < data.length; i++) {
   if (data[i] === null) continue;  // continue to next iteration
   total += data[i];
}
```

Exploring Statement Labels

`Statement` **labels** are used to identify statements in JavaScript code so that you can reference those lines elsewhere in a program. The syntax of the `statement` label is

```
label: statements
```

where `label` is the text of the label and `statements` are the statements identified by the label. You have already seen labels with the `switch` statement, but labels can also be used with other program loops and conditional statements to provide more control over how statements are processed. Labels often are used with `break` and `continue` statements in order to break off or continue a program loop. The syntax to reference a label in such cases is simply

```
break label;
```

or

```
continue label;
```

For example, the following `for` loop uses a `statement` label not only to jump out of the programming loop when the text string C-14281 is found but also to jump to the location in the script identified by the next_report label and to continue to process the statements found there:

```
for (var i = 0; i< ids.length; i++) {
   if (ids[i] === "C-14281") {
      document.write("C-14281 is in the list.");
      break next_report;
   }
}

next_report:
JavaScript statements
```

Teamwork: The Danger of Spaghetti Code

Spaghetti code is a pejorative programming term that refers to convoluted or poorly written code. One hallmark of spaghetti code is the frequent branching from one section of code to another, making it difficult to track the program line-by-line as it is executed. A change in one part of the program could lead to unpredictable changes in a completely different section of the code.

Most developers discourage the use of break, continue, and label statements unless absolutely necessary. They can confuse a programmer trying to debug code in which a program loop can end before its stopping condition, or code in which statements are not processed in the order that they are written in a document. Almost all of the tasks you perform with these statements can also be performed by carefully setting up the conditions for program loops.

Even with the best of intentions, spaghetti code can easily occur in environments in which the same code is maintained by several people or passed from one employee to another. Each programmer adds a particular feature that is needed today without adequately documenting the changes made to the code and without considering the impact of those changes on the larger program.

To avoid or at least reduce the occurrence of spaghetti code, you should always document your code and develop a structure that is easy to follow. Break up tasks into smaller functions that are easier to manage and can be reused in other parts of your programs. Also, avoid global variables whenever possible because a change in the value of a global variable can have repercussions throughout the entire code. Instead, use local variables with their scope limited to small, compact functions. If a variable must be used elsewhere in your code, it should be passed as a parameter value with the meaning and purpose of the parameter well documented within the program.

By practicing good coding techniques, you can make your programs more accessible to your colleagues and make it easier to pass your code on to your successors.

Lewis is pleased with the final version of the calendar app. Because of the way the function and the style sheets were designed, he can use this utility in many other pages on the website with only a minimal amount of recoding in the documents.

REVIEW

Session 10.3 Quick Check

1. What is a conditional statement? What is the most commonly used conditional statement?

2. Provide code to display an alert box with the message "Good Morning" if the value of the thisHour variable is less than 9.

3. Provide code to display an alert box with the message "Good Morning" if the value of the thisHour variable is less than 9 and the alert box message "Good Day" if otherwise.

4. Provide code to display an alert box with four possible messages: "Good Morning", "Good Day", "Good Afternoon", or "Good Evening" depending on whether the value of the thisHour variable is less than 9, less than 12, less than 16, or otherwise.

5. Provide the expression to extract the day of the week value from a `Date` object variable named thisDate.

6. Use a conditional operator to assign a value of "Weekend" to the thisWeek variable if thisDate equals 0 or 6 and a value of "Weekday" if otherwise.

7. What command can be used to break out of the current iteration in a `for` loop?

8. What command forces a script to go to the next iteration of the current program loop?

PRACTICE

Review Assignments

Data Files needed for the Review Assignments: lht_events_txt.html, lht_table_txt.js, 3 CSS files, 1 JS file, 2 PNG files

Lewis wants you to write another script that shows a table of events at the Lyman Hall Theater over the next two weeks from the current date. He has already created three arrays for use with the script:

- The eventDates array containing a list of dates and time at which theater events are scheduled
- The eventDescriptions array containing the description of those events
- The eventPrices array containing the admission prices of those events

Lewis has already written the page content and provided style sheets for use with the page. Your job will be to write a script that selects the events that occur in the two-week window from the current date and display them in the web page. A preview of the page you will create is shown in Figure 10-34.

Figure 10-34   Upcoming events at the Lyman Hall Theater

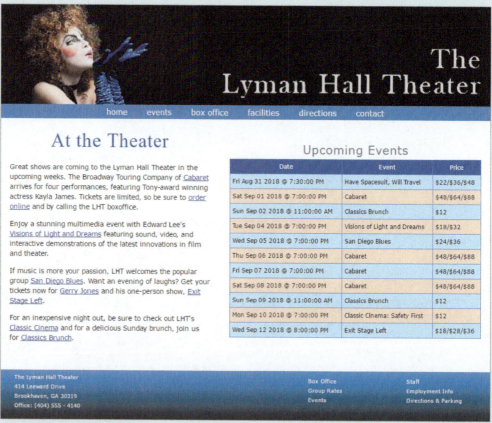

© Igor Borodin/Shutterstock.com

Complete the following:

1. Use your editor to open the **lht_events_txt.html** and **lht_table_txt.js** files from the html10 ▸ review folder. Enter *your name* and *the date* in the comment section of each file, and save them as **lht_events.html** and **lht_table.js** respectively.

2. Go to the **lht_events.html** file in your editor. Directly above the closing `</head>` tag, insert `script` elements that link the page to the **lht_list.js** and **lht_table.js** files in that order. Defer the loading and running of both script files until after the page has loaded.

3. Scroll down the document and, directly after the closing `</article>` tag, insert a `div` element with the ID eventList. It is within this element that you will write the HTML code for the table of upcoming theater events. Close the file saving your changes. (*Hint*: Be sure to review this file and all the support files, noting especially the names of variables that you will be using in the code you create.)

4. Go to the **lht_table.js** file in your editor. Below the comment section, declare a variable named **thisDay** containing the date August 30, 2018. You will use this date to test your script.

5. Create a variable named **tableHTML** that will contain the HTML code of the events table. Add the text of the following HTML code to the initial value of the variable:

```
<table id='eventTable'>
    <caption>Upcoming Events</caption>
    <tr><th>Date</th><th>Event</th><th>Price</th></tr>
```

6. Lewis only wants the page to list events occurring within 14 days after the current date. Declare a variable named **endDate** that contains a `Date` object that is 14 days after the date stored in the thisDay variable. (*Hint*: Use the `new Date()` object constructor and insert a time value that is equal to thisDay.getTime() + 14*24*60*60*1000.)

7. Create a `for` loop that loops through the length of the eventDates array. Use `i` as the counter variable.

8. Within the `for` loop insert the following commands in a command block:

   a. Declare a variable named **eventDate** containing a `Date` object with the date stored in the ith entry in the eventDates array.

   b. Declare a variable named **eventDay** that stores the text of the eventDate date using the `toDateString()` method.

   c. Declare a variable named **eventTime** that stores the text of the eventDate time using the `toLocaleTimeString()` method.

   d. Insert an `if` statement that has a conditional expression that tests whether thisDay is ≤ eventDate and eventDate ≤ endDate. If so, the event falls within the two-week window that Lewis has requested and the script should add the following HTML code text to the value of the tableHTML variable.

   ```
   <tr>
       <td>eventDay @ eventTime</td>
       <td>description</td>
       <td>price</td>
   </tr>
   ```

   where *eventDay* is the value of the eventDay variable, *eventTime* is the value of the eventTime variable, *description* is the ith entry in the eventDescriptions array, and *price* is the ith entry in the eventPrices array.

9. After the `for` loop, add the text of the HTML code `</table>` to the value of the tableHTML variable.

10. Insert the value of the tableHTML variable into the inner HTML of the `page` element with the ID eventList.

11. Document your code in the script file using appropriate comments.

12. Save your changes to the file, and then load the **lht_events.html** file in your browser. Verify that the page shows theater events over a two-week period starting with Friday, August 31, 2018 and concluding with Wednesday, September 12, 2018.

Case Problem 1

Data Files needed for this Case Problem: tc_cart_txt.html, tc_cart_txt.js, tc_order_txt.js, 2 CSS files, 8 PNG files

Trophy Case Sports Sarah Nordheim manages the website for Trophy Case Sports, a sports memorabilia store located in Beavercreek, Ohio. She has asked you to work on creating a script for the shopping cart page. The script should take information on the items that the customer has purchased and present it in table form, calculating the total cost of the order. A preview of the page you will create is shown in Figure 10-35.

Figure 10-35 Trophy Case Sports shopping cart

voyeg3r/openclipart; © Marie C Fields/Shutterstock; Sources: Courtesy of the Gerald R. Ford Presidential Museum; Vintagecardprices.com; Library of Congress Prints and Photographs Division; facebook.com

Sarah has already designed the page layout. Your job will be to use JavaScript to enter the order information (this task will later be handled by a script running on the website) and to write a script that generates the HTML code for the shopping cart table.

Complete the following:

1. Use your editor to open the **tc_cart_txt.html**, **tc_cart_txt.js** and **tc_order_txt.js** files from the html10 ▸ case1 folder. Enter *your name* and *the date* in the comment section of each file, and save them as **tc_cart.html**, **tc_cart.js** and **tc_order.js** respectively.

2. Go to the **tc_cart.html** file in your editor. Directly above the closing `</head>` tag, insert `script` elements to link the page to the tc_order.js and tc_cart.js files in that order. Defer the loading and running of both script files until after the page has loaded.

3. Scroll down the file and directly below the h1 heading titled "Shopping Cart" insert a `div` element with the ID cart.

4. Save your changes to the file and go to the **tc_order.js** file in your editor.

5. Within the tc_order.js file, you will create arrays containing information on a sample customer order. Create an array named **item** that will contain the ID numbers of the items purchased by the customer. Add the following four item numbers to the array: 10582, 23015, 41807, and 10041.

6. Create an array named **itemDescription** containing the following item descriptions:
   - 1975 Green Bay Packers Football (signed), Item 10582
   - Tom Landry 1955 Football Card (unsigned), Item 23015
   - 1916 Army-Navy Game, Framed Photo (signed), Item 41807
   - Protective Card Sheets, Item 10041

7. Create an array named **itemPrice** containing the following item prices: 149.93, 89.98, 334.93, and 22.67.

8. Create an array named **itemQty** containing the following quantities that the customer ordered of each item: 1, 1, 1, and 4.

9. Save your changes to the file, and then open the **tc_cart.js** file in your editor.

10. In your script, you will calculate a running total of the cost of the order. Declare a variable named **orderTotal** and set its initial value to 0.

11. Declare a variable named cartHTML that will contain the HTML code for the contents of the shopping cart, which will be displayed as a table. Set its initial value to the text string:

```
<table>
<tr>
<th>Item</th><th>Description</th><th>Price</th><th>Qty</th><th>Total</th>
</tr>
```

12. Create a `for` loop that loops through the entries in the item array. Each time through the loop, execute the commands described in Steps a through e.

   a. Add the following HTML code to the value of the cartHTML variable

   ```
   <tr>
   <td><img src='tc_item.png' alt='item' /></td>
   ```

   where *item* is the current value from the item array.

b. Add the following HTML code to the cartHTML variable to display the description, price, and quantity ordered of the item

```
<td>description</td>
<td>$price</td>
<td>quantity</td>
```

where *description* is the current value from the itemDescription array, *price* is the current value from the itemPrice array preceded by a $ symbol, and *quantity* is the current value from the itemQty array.

c. Declare a variable named **itemCost** equal to the *price* value multiplied by the *quantity* value for the current item.

d. Add the following HTML code to the cartHTML variable to display the cost for the item(s) ordered, completing the table row

```
<td>$cost</td></tr>
```

where *cost* is the value of the itemCost variable, preceded by a $ symbol.

e. Add the value of the itemCost variable to the orderTotal variable to keep a running total of the total cost of the customer order.

13. After the `for` loop has completed, add the following HTML code to the value of the cartHTML variable, completing the shopping cart table

```
<tr>
<td colspan='4'>Subtotal</td>
<td>$total</td>
</tr>
</table>
```

where *total* is the value of the orderTotal variable, preceded by a $ symbol.

14. Apply the cartHTML value to the inner HTML of the `div` element with the ID cart.

15. Document your script file with appropriate comments, and then save your work.

16. Open the **tc_cart.html** file in your browser and verify that the page now shows the shopping cart data for the sample customer order.

APPLY

Case Problem 2

Data Files needed for this Case Problem: hg_game_txt.html, hg_report_txt.js, 2 CSS files, 1 JS file, 4 PNG files

Harpe Gaming Sean Greer manages the development of the website for Harpe Gaming, a store chain specializing in digital games and entertainment. He is working on a redesign of the website and has asked you to work on the design of product pages. Each product page contains a description of a game and a few sample customer reviews. Figure 10-36 shows a preview of the page you will work on.

Figure 10-36	Harpe Gaming product page

Source: sixsixfive/openclipart; © Courtesy Patrick Carey

You work on a page for a digital game called *Dance Off*. The information about the game and customer reviews is stored in an external JavaScript file. Your job will be to extract that data from the JavaScript file and write it into the HTML code of the web page.

Complete the following:

1. Use your editor to open the **hg_game_txt.html** and **hg_report_txt.js** files from the html10 ▶ case2 folder. Enter *your name* and *the date* in the comment section of each file, and save them as **hg_game.html** and **hg_report.js** respectively.

2. Go to the **hg_game.html** file in your editor. Directly above the closing `</head>` tag, insert `script` elements to link the page to the hg_product.js and hg_report.js files in that order. Defer the loading and running of both script files until after the page has loaded.

3. Scroll down the document and insert an empty `article` element and an empty `aside` element directly above the closing `</section>` tag. The `article` element will contain information about the game. The `aside` element will contain a list of customer reviews.

4. Save your changes to the file, and then open the **hg_product.js** file in your editor. Take some time to review the variables and values stored in the file but do not make any changes to the file content.

5. Go to the **hg_report.js** file in your editor. First, you write information about the game that will be displayed in the web page. Declare a variable named gameReport. Within the **gameReport** variable, store the following HTML code

```
<h1>title</h1>
<h2>By: manufacturer</h2>
<img src="hg_id.png" alt="id" id="gameImg" />
<table>
  <tr><th>Product ID</th><td>id</td></tr>
  <tr><th>List Price</th><td>price</td></tr>
  <tr><th>Platform</th><td>platform</td></tr>
  <tr><th>ESRB Rating</th><td>esrb</td></tr>
  <tr><th>Condition</th><td>condition</td></tr>
  <tr><th>Release</th><td>release</td></tr>
</table>
summary
```

where `title`, `manufacturer`, `id`, `price`, `platform`, `esrb`, `condition`, `release` and `summary` use the values from corresponding variables in the hg_product.js file.

6. Display the value of the gameReport variable in the inner HTML of the first (and only) `article` element in the document. (*Hint*: Use the `getElementsByTagName()` method, referencing the first item in the array of `article` elements.)

7. Next, you write the information from the customer ratings. Start by calculating the average customer rating of the game. Declare a variable named **ratingsSum** setting its initial value to 0.

8. Declare a variable named **ratingsCount** equal to the length of the ratings array.

9. Create a `for` loop to loop through the contents of the ratings array. Each time through the loop, add the value of current ratings value to the value of the ratingsSum variable.

10. After the `for` loop, declare the **ratingsAvg** variable, setting its value equal to the value of the ratingsSum variable divided by the value of ratingsCount.

11. Declare a variable named **ratingReport**. Set its initial value to the text string

```
<h1>Customer Reviews</h1>
<h2> average out of 5 stars (count reviews)</h2>
```

where *average* is the value of the ratingsAvg variable and *count* is the value of ratingsCount.

12. Next, you display the content of the first three customer reviews. Create a `for` loop in which the counter goes from 0 to 2 in steps of 1. Within the `for` loop, insert the commands described in Steps a through c:

    a. Add the following HTML code to the value of the ratingReport variable

    ```
    div class="review">
    <h1>title</h1>
      <table>
      <tr><th>By</th><td>author</td></tr>
      <tr><th>Review Date</th><td>date</td></tr>
      <tr><th>Rating</th><td>
    ```

    where *title* is the value of the ratingTitles array item for current review, *author* is the value of the current ratingAuthors array item, and *date* is the value of the current ratingDates item.

    b. Each customer rates the game on a scale of 1 to 5 stars. Sean would like to have the stars displayed graphically. Add a nested `for` loop where the counter goes from 1 up to the value of the current customer rating of the game in increments of one. Each time through the nested `for` loop, add the following HTML code to the value of the ratingReport variable:

    ```
    <img src="hg_star.png" />
    ```

    c. Directly after the nested for loop, but still within the outer `for` loop, insert commands to add the following HTML code to the value of the ratingReport variable

    ```
    </td></tr></table>
    summary
    </div>
    ```

    where *summary* is the value from the ratingSummaries array for the current customer review.

13. Write the value of the ratingReport variable to the inner HTML of the first and only `aside` element in the document. (*Hint*: As you did with the `article` element in Step 6, use the `getElementsByTagName()` method and reference the first item from the array of `aside` elements.)

14. Document your code with informative comments throughout, and then save the file.

15. Open the **hg_game.html** file in your browser. Verify that the page shows the game summary and contents of the first three customer reviews. The page should also correctly calculate an average customer rating of 3.79 for the *Dance Off* game based on a total of 19 customer reviews.

Case Problem 3

Data Files needed for this Case Problem: ah_report_txt.html, ah_report_txt.js, 2 CSS files, 1 JS file, 1 PNG file

Appalachian House   Kendrick Thorne is the fundraising coordinator for Appalachian House, a charitable organization located in central Kentucky. One of his responsibilities is to report on the progress Appalachian House is making in soliciting donations. On an administration web page available only to Appalachian House staff, Kendrick wants to display a list of information on recent donations. The data on the donations has been made available to him in a multidimensional array within a JavaScript file. Kendrick wants your help in retrieving the data from this array and writing a script to produce the HTML code summarizing the result. Figure 10-37 shows a preview of the page you will create.

Figure 10-37   **Donors page at Appalachian House**

© Courtesy Patrick Carey

As part of writing the script for Kendrick, you work with some of the JavaScript array methods used to filter and loop through the contents of an array.

Complete the following:

1. Use your editor to open the **ah_report_txt.html** and **ah_report_txt.js** files from the html10 ▸ case3 folder. Enter *your name* and *the date* in the comment section of each file, and save them as **ah_report.html** and **ah_report.js** respectively.

2. Go to the **ah_report.html** file in your editor. Directly above the closing `</head>` tag, insert `script` elements to link the page to the ah_donors.js and ah_report.js files in that order. Defer the loading and running of both script files until after the page has loaded.

3. Scroll down the file to the h1 heading entitled "Donor Report". Directly below this h1 heading, insert the following `div` elements into which you will insert the donation summary:

   ```
   <div id="donationSummary"></div>
   <div id="donorTable"></div>
   ```

4. Save your changes to the file, and then open the **ah_donors.js** file in your editor. Study the content of the multidimensional array named donors. Note that the first column of the array (with an index of 0) contains the ID of each donor, the second column (index 1) contains the donor's first name, the third column (index 2) contains the donor's last name, and so forth. The amount of each donation is stored in the tenth column (index 9). Do not make any changes to the content of this file.

5. Go to the **ah_report.js** file in your editor. The file contains four callback functions at the end of the file that you will use in generating the donation report. Take some time to study the content of these functions.

6. Create a variable named **donationTotal** in which you will calculate the total amount of the donations to Appalachian House. Set its initial value to 0.

✣ **Explore** 7. Apply the `forEach()` method to the donors array, using the callback function calcSum(). This statement will calculate the donation total.

8. Create a variable named **summaryTable** storing the text of the following HTML code

   ```
   <table>
    <tr><th>Donors</th><td> donors </td></tr>
    <tr><th>Total Donations</th><td>$total</td></tr>
   </table>
   ```

   where *donors* is the length of the donors.array, and *total* is the value of the donationTotal variable, preceded by a $. Apply the `toLocaleString()` method to the donationTotal variable so that the total amount of donations is displayed with a thousands separator in the report.

9. Set the innerHTML property of the `div` element with the ID donationSummary to the value of the summaryTable variable.

✣ **Explore** 10. Kendrick wants the report to show a list of the donors who contributed $1000 or more to Appalachian House. Using the `filter()` method with the callback function findMajorDonors(), create an array named **majorDonors**.

✣ **Explore** 11. Kendrick wants the major donors list sorted in descending order. Apply the `sort()` method to the majorDonors variable using the callback function donorSortDescending().

12. Create a variable named **donorTable** that will store the HTML code for the table of major donors. Set the initial value of the variable to the text of the following HTML code:

```
<table>
 <caption>Major Donors</caption>
 <tr>
  <th>Donation</th><th>Donor ID</th>
  <th>Date</th><th>Name</th><th>Address</th>
  <th>Phone</th><th>E-mail</th>
 </tr>
```

13. Create the HTML code for each donor row by applying the `forEach()` method to the majorDonors variable, using writeDonorRow() as the callback function.

14. Add the text string `</table>` to the value of the donorTable variable.

15. Set the `innerHTML` property of the `div` element with the ID donorTable to the value of the donorTable variable.

16. Add comments to your script, documenting your work.

17. Save your changes to the file, and then open **ah_report.js** in your browser. Verify that the page shows a total donation to Appalachian House of $125,200 from 87 donors. Also, verify that the page shows a list, in descending order, of 15 donors who contributed $1000 or more to the charity.

Case Problem 4

Data Files needed for this Case Problem: vw_election_txt.html, vw_results_txt.js, 2 CSS files, 1 JS file, 1 PNG file

VoterWeb Pam Carls is a manager for the website Voter Web, which compiles voting totals and statistics from local and national elections. Pam has the results of recent congressional elections from eight districts in Minnesota stored as multidimensional arrays in a JavaScript file. Pam wants you to create a script displaying these results and calculating the vote percentage for each candidate within each race. A preview of the page is shown in Figure 10-38.

Figure 10-38   **Election results at VoterWeb**

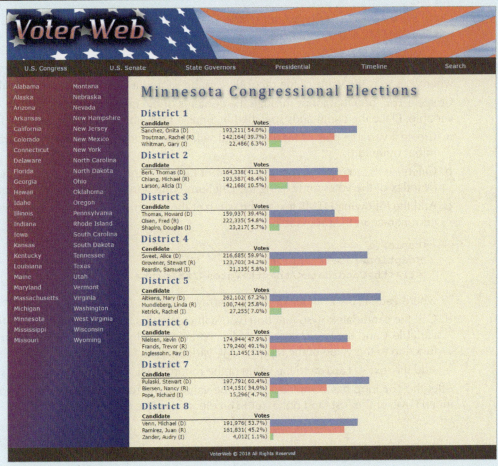

Complete the following:

1. Use your editor to open the **vw_election_txt.html** and **vw_results_txt.js** files from the html10 ▶ case4 folder. Enter *your name* and *the date* in the comment section of each file, and save them as **vw_election.html** and **vw_results.js** respectively.

2. Go to the **vw_election.html** file in your editor. Directly above the closing `</head>` tag, insert `script` elements to link the page to the vw_congminn.js and vw_results.js files in that order. Defer the loading and running of both script files until after the page has loaded.

3. Scroll down the file and, directly above the footer, insert an empty `section` element. You will write the HTML code of the election report in this element. Save your changes to the file.

4. Open the **vw_congminn.js** file in your editor and study the contents. Note that the file contains the results of 8 congressional elections in Minnesota. The candidate information is stored in multidimensional arrays named candidate, party, and votes. Do not make any changes to this file.

5. Go to the **vw_results.js** file in your editor. Declare a variable named **reportHTML** containing the following HTML text

   ```
   <h1>title</h1>
   ```

   where `title` is the value of the raceTitle variable stored in the vw_congminn.js file.

6. Create a `for` loop that loops through the contents of the race array using `i` as the counter variable. Place the commands specified in Steps a through e within this program for loop:

   a. Create a variable named **totalVotes** that will store the total votes cast in each race. Set its initial value to 0.

   b. Calculate the total votes cast in the current race by applying the `forEach()` method to i^{th} index of the votes array using the calcSum() function as the callback function.

   c. Add the following HTML text to the value of the reportHTML variable to write the name of the current race in the program loop

   ```
   <table>
    <caption>race</caption>
    <tr><th>Candidate</th><th>Votes</th></tr>
   ```

   where `race` is the ith index of the race array.

   d. Call the candidateRows() function (you will create this function shortly) using the counter variable `i` and the totalVotes variable as parameter values. Add the value returned by this function to the value of the reportHTML variable.

   e. Add the text `</table>` to the value of the reportHTML variable.

7. After the `for` loop has completed, write the value of the reportHTML variable into the innerHTML of the first (and only) `section` element in the document.

8. Next, create the **candidateRows()** function. The purpose of this function is to write individual table rows for each candidate, showing the candidate's name, party affiliation, vote total, and vote percentage. The candidateRows() function has two parameters named **raceNum** and **totalVotes**. Place the commands in Steps a through c within this function.

   a. Declare a local variable named **rowHTML** that will contain the HTML code for the table row. Set the initial value of this variable to an empty text string.

   ⊕ **Explore** b. Create a `for` loop in which the counter variable j goes from 0 to 2 in steps of 1 unit. Within the `for` loop do the following:

   i. Declare a variable named **candidateName** that retrieves the name of the current candidate and the current race. (*Hint*: Retrieve the candidate name from the multidimensional candidate array using the reference, candidate[raceNum][j].)

   ii. Declare a variable named **candidateParty** that retrieves the party affiliation of the current candidate in the current race from the multidimensional party array.

   iii. Declare a variable named **candidateVotes** that retrieves the votes cast for the current candidate in the current race from the multidimensional votes array.

   iv. Declare a variable named **candidatePercent** equal to the value returned by the calcPercent() function, calculating the percentage of votes received by the current candidate in the loop. Use candidateVotes as the first parameter value and totalVotes as the second parameter value.

   v. Add the following HTML code to the value of the rowHTML variable

   ```
   <tr>
   <td>name (party)</td>
   <td>votes (percent)</td>
   </tr>
   ```

   where *name* is the value of candidateName, *party* is the value of candidateParty, *votes* is the value of candidateVotes, and *percent* is the value of candidatePercent. Apply the `toLocaleString()` method to *votes* in order to display the vote total with a thousands separator. Apply the `toFixed(1)` method to *percent* in order to display percentage values to 1 decimal place.

   c. Return the value of the rowHTML variable.

9. Save your changes to the file, and then load **vw_election.html** in your browser. Verify that the three candidate names, party affiliations, votes, and vote percentages are shown for each of the eight congressional races.

10. Pam also wants the report to display the vote percentages as bar charts with the length of the bar corresponding to the percentage value. Return to the **vw_results.js** file in your editor. At the bottom of the file, create a function named **createBar()** with one parameter named partyType. Add the commands described in Steps a through b to the function:

   a. Declare a variable named **barHTML** and set its initial value to an empty text string.

   ⊕ **Explore** b. Create a `switch/case` statement that tests the value of the partyType parameter. If partyType equal "D" set barHTML equal to:

   ```
   <td class='dem'></td>
   ```

   If partyType equals "R" set barHTML equal to:

   ```
   <td class='rep'></td>
   ```

   Finally, if partyType equals "I" set barHTML to:

   ```
   <td class='ind'></td>
   ```

11. Return the value of barHTML.

   Next, add these empty data cells to the race results table, with one cell for every percentage point cast for the candidate.

12. Scroll up to the candidateRows() function. Directly before the line that adds the HTML code `</tr>` to the value of the rowHTML variable, insert a `for` loop with a counter variable k that goes from 0 up to a value less than candidatePercent in increments of 1 unit. Each time through the loop call the createBar() function using candidateParty and candidatePercent as the parameter values.

13. Add comments throughout the file with descriptive information about the variables and functions.

14. Save your changes to the file, and then reload **vw_election.html** in your browser. Verify that each election table shows a bar chart with different the length of bars representing each candidate's vote percentage.

TUTORIAL 11

Working with Events and Styles

Designing an Interactive Puzzle

OBJECTIVES

Session 11.1
- Create an event handler
- Reference an attribute from a page element
- Change the inline style of a page element

Session 11.2
- Create code for mouse events
- Create code for keyboard events
- Design and apply custom cursors

Session 11.3
- Create and apply anonymous functions
- Work with alert, confirm, and prompt dialog boxes

Case | *The Japanese Puzzle Factory*

The Japanese Puzzle Factory, a website owned and operated by Rebecca Peretz, is created for people who, like her, love Japanese logic puzzles. Rebecca has asked you to create an interactive version of the Hanjie puzzle for her website. Hanjie is played on a square grid; cells in the grid can be either filled-in or left empty based on puzzle hints. A solved puzzle displays a pixelated image of a person, place, or thing. Rebecca already has designed three sample puzzles but needs your help with writing the JavaScript code that will enable users to interact with the puzzle and its contents. Your code should also provide hints and useful feedback for users who need help.

STARTING DATA FILES

tutorial

jpf_hanjie_txt.html
jpf_hanjie_txt.js
+ 9 files

review

jpf_hitori_txt.html
jpf_hitori_txt.js
+ 8 files

case1

bw_review_txt.html
bw_review_txt.js
+ 7 files

case2

mt_calc_txt.html
mt_calc_txt.js
+ 5 files

case3

pc_cword_txt.html
pc_cword_txt.js
+ 8 files

case4

kg_search_txt.html
kg_search_txt.js
+ 9 files

Session 11.1 Visual Overview:

This command runs the init() function when the page is loaded.

The **onload** event handler runs when the page is loaded by the browser.

```
window.onload = init;

function init() {
   // Insert the title for the first puzzle
   document.getElementById("puzzleTitle").innerHTML = "Puzzle 1";

   // Insert the HTML code for the first puzzle table
   document.getElementById("puzzle").innerHTML =
       drawPuzzle(puzzle1Hint, puzzle1Rating, puzzle1);

   //Add event handlers for the puzzle buttons
   var puzzleButtons = document.getElementsByClassName("puzzles");
   for (var i = 0; i < puzzleButtons.length; i++) {
       puzzleButtons[i].onclick = swapPuzzle;
   }

   setupPuzzle();
}

function setupPuzzle() {
   /* Match all of the data cells in the puzzle */
   puzzleCells = document.querySelectorAll("table#hanjieGrid td");

   /* Set the initial color of each cell to gold */
   for (var i = 0; i < puzzleCells.length; i++) {
       puzzleCells[i].style.backgroundColor = "rgb(233, 207, 29)";
   }
}
```

The **onclick** event handler runs when the object is clicked.

This command runs the swapPuzzle() function when the button is clicked.

The **querySelectorAll()** method creates an object collection based on a CSS selector.

This command references all of the td elements within the hanjieGrid table.

To apply an inline style to an object, use the style property.

This command changes the value of the background-color style.

Event Handlers and Event Objects

The **event object** stores properties and methods associated with an event.

Click the Puzzle 1 through Puzzle 3 buttons to swap puzzles.

The **target** property returns a reference to the object in which the event was initiated.

```
function swapPuzzle(e) {
   var puzzleID = e.target.id;
   var puzzleTitle = e.target.value;


   document.getElementById("puzzleTitle").innerHTML =
      puzzleTitle;
   switch (puzzleID) {
   case "puzzle1":
      document.getElementById("puzzle").innerHTML =
        drawPuzzle(puzzle1Hint, puzzle1Rating, puzzle1);
      break;
    case "puzzle2":
      document.getElementById("puzzle").innerHTML =
        drawPuzzle(puzzle2Hint, puzzle2Rating, puzzle2);
      break;
   case "puzzle3":
      document.getElementById("puzzle").innerHTML =
        drawPuzzle(puzzle3Hint, puzzle3Rating, puzzle3);
      break;
   }
   setupPuzzle();
}
```

Introducing JavaScript Events

JavaScript programs are often run in response to **events**, which are actions initiated by the user or by the browser, such as clicking an object on a form or closing a web page. Rebecca Peretz of the Japanse Puzzle Factory, wants you to develop an interactive game based on the Japanese puzzle, Hanjie.

   A Hanjie puzzle is laid out on a grid in which each grid cell is either filled or left empty. Within each column and row heading is a series of numbers indicating how the filled cells in that column or row are arranged. For example, a row heading containing the text 4 7 2 indicates that the row contains three groups of filled cells of lengths 4, 7, and 2. The groups are separated by gaps, but the size of the gaps is not specified. The exact location of the filled cells and the size of the gaps must be derived using logic and the clues provided by the other column and row headings. A successfully solved puzzle will display a pixelated image, such as the one shown in Figure 11-1.

Figure 11-1   **A Hanjie puzzle showing the profile of Sherlock Holmes**

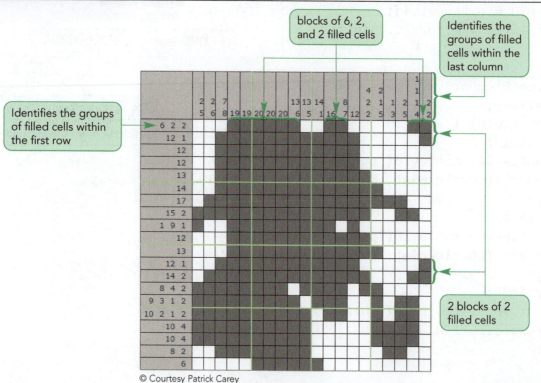

© Courtesy Patrick Carey

   Figure 11-2 previews the application—or app—that you will develop for Rebecca. Users are given the choice of 3 puzzles; the corresponding puzzle is displayed by clicking the Puzzle 1 through Puzzle 3 buttons at the top of the page. Initially, the puzzle contents are hidden, with all cells displayed in gold. By clicking or dragging the mouse pointer over the table grid, users mark cells as being filled or empty. Rebecca wants users to be able to check their progress, so she provided a button that enables them to preview their solution, which also highlights any mistakes. Finally, when a user wants to see the solution, he or she is able to click the Show Solution button. Thus, to make the puzzle an interactive experience, your app needs to respond to several events including clicking a form button, moving a mouse pointer, clicking a grid cell, and pressing keyboard keys.

Figure 11-2   Preview of the Hanjie Puzzle page

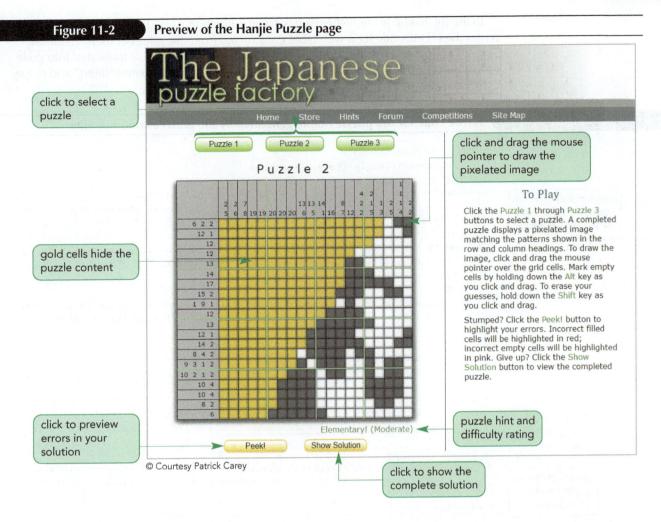

click to select a puzzle

click and drag the mouse pointer to draw the pixelated image

gold cells hide the puzzle content

click to preview errors in your solution

puzzle hint and difficulty rating

click to show the complete solution

© Courtesy Patrick Carey

Rebecca has already done some of the programming work for you. She has saved three Hanjie puzzles in the jpf_grids1.js file as multidimensional arrays under the variable names puzzle1, puzzle2, and puzzle3. Hints and difficulty ratings for the puzzles have been stored in the puzzle1Hint through puzzle3Hint, and puzzle1Rating through puzzle3Rating variables. Figure 11-3 shows the variable values for the first puzzle, which is a simple triangle created when the cells in the upper-left corner of a 5×5 grid are filled and the lower-right cells are empty.

Figure 11-3   puzzle1Hint, puzzle1Rating, and puzzle1 variables

filled cells are indicated by the # character

empty cells are indicated by a blank text string

```
var puzzle1Hint = "Triangle";
var puzzle1Rating = "Easy";
var puzzle1 = [
                ['#', '#', '#', '#', '#'],
                ['#', '#', '#', '#', ' '],
                ['#', '#', '#', ' ', ' '],
                ['#', '#', ' ', ' ', ' '],
                ['#', ' ', ' ', ' ', ' ']
              ];
```

In the jpf_hanjie.js file, Rebecca has saved a function named drawPuzzle() that writes the HTML code for a web table constructed from the values of these variables. Figure 11-4 shows how the puzzle information from Figure 11-3 is translated into code for a web table. Note that filled cells are indicated by the class name "filled" and empty cells have the class name "empty".

Figure 11-4 **HTML code for the puzzle1 table generated by the drawPuzzle() function**

```
<table id="hanjieGrid">
   <caption>Triangle (Easy)</caption>
   <tr>
      <th></th><th class="cols">5</th><th class="cols">4</th>
      <th class="cols">3</th><th class="cols">2</th><th class="cols">1</th>
   </tr>
   <tr>
      <th class="rows">5</th><td class="filled"></td><td class="filled"></td>
      <td class="filled"></td><td class="filled"></td><td class="filled"></td>
   </tr>
   <tr>
      <th class="rows">4</th><td class="filled"></td><td class="filled"></td>
      <td class="filled"></td><td class="filled"></td><td class="empty"></td>
   </tr>
   <tr>
      <th class="rows">3</th><td class="filled"></td><td class="filled"></td>
      <td class="filled"></td><td class="empty"></td><td class="empty"></td>
   </tr>
   <tr>
      <th class="rows">2</th><td class="filled"></td><td class="filled"></td>
      <td class="empty"></td><td class="empty"></td><td class="empty"></td>
   </tr>
   <tr>
      <th class="rows">1</th><td class="filled"></td><td class="empty"></td>
      <td class="empty"></td><td class="empty"></td><td class="empty"></td>
   </tr>
</table>
```

column and row totals are calculated by the drawPuzzle() function

filled cells are placed in the filled class

empty cells are placed in the empty class

Open Rebecca's files now and load the code from the jpf_grids1.js and jpf_hanjie.js files.

To load the puzzle files:

1. Use your editor to open the **jpf_hanjie_txt.html** and **jpf_hanjie_txt.js** files from the html11 ► tutorial folder. Enter **your name** and **the date** in the comment section of each file and save them as **jpf_hanjie.html** and **jpf_hanjie.js** respectively.

2. Return to the **jpf_hanjie.html** file in your editor. Within the head element, insert a link to the **jpf_hanjie.css** style sheet file containing the styles that will be applied to the puzzle table.

3. Add the following script elements to link the page to the jpf_grids1.js and jpf_hanjie.js files, loading both files asynchronously so that the browser does not pause when it encounters the external JavaScript files:

   ```
   <script src="jpf_grids1.js" async></script>
   <script src="jpf_hanjie.js" async></script>
   ```

   Figure 11-5 highlights the revised code in the document head.

Figure 11-5   Loading the Hanjie files

style sheet containing styles for the puzzle table

code containing the content of three Hanjie puzzles

```html
<title>The Hanjie Puzzle</title>
<link href="jpf_base.css" rel="stylesheet" />
<link href="jpf_layout.css" rel="stylesheet" />
<link href="jpf_hanjie.css" rel="stylesheet" />

<script src="jpf_grids1.js" async></script>
<script src="jpf_hanjie.js" async></script>
</head>
```

code for generating the interactive Hanjie puzzle

loads the JavaScript files asynchronously as the HTML file loads

4. Take some time to study the contents of the HTML file. Note that the file has two currently empty elements: the h1 element with the ID "puzzleTitle", which will display the title of the puzzle and the figure element with the ID "puzzle", which will store the puzzle table code.

5. Close the file, saving your changes.

Currently, no puzzle table is displayed in the web page. To insert the HTML code for the table, you will create the init() function, running the function automatically when the page is loaded by the browser. You can achieve this using an event handler.

Creating an Event Handler

An **event handler** is a property that controls how an object will respond to an event, waiting until the event occurs and then responding by running a function or command block to execute an action. Event handlers can be added to a page element using the following attribute

```
<element onevent = "script">
```

where *element* is the element in which the event occurs, *event* is the name of the event, and *script* are the commands that the browser runs in response to the event. For example, the following code adds the onload event handler to the page's body element, running the init() function once the page body has been completely loaded by the browser:

```
<body onload = "init()">
```

Event handlers can also be defined as object properties using the command

```
object.onevent = function;
```

where *object* is the object in which the event occurs, *event* is the name of the event, and *function* is the name of a function run in response to the event. Thus, to run the init() function in response to the page load event, you could also apply the following command:

```
window.onload = init;
```

Figure 11-6 describes some of the many other event handlers supported by JavaScript that can be applied to actions occurring within the web browser.

Figure 11-6 Event handlers for the browser window

Event Handler	Run Script
onbeforeunload	when page is about to be unloaded by the browser
oncopy	when the user copies the content of an element
oncut	when the user cuts the content of an element
onerror	when an error occurs while loading an external file, such as an image or a video clip
onload	after the page has finished loading
onpaste	when the user pastes some content into an element
onresize	when the browser window is resized
onunload	when the page is unloaded by the browser (or the browser window is closed)

REFERENCE

Applying an Event Handler

- To apply an event handler as an HTML attribute, use

  ```
  <element onevent = "script">
  ```

  where *element* is the element in which the event occurs, *event* is the name of the event, and *script* are the commands that the browser runs in response to the event.
- To apply an event handler as an object property, use

  ```
  object.onevent = function;
  ```

  where *object* is the object in which the event occurs, *event* is the name of the event, and *function* is the name of a function run in response to the event.
- To run a function when the page is loaded, use

  ```
  window.onload = function;
  ```

Add the init() function now to load the contents of the first Hanjie puzzle, and include an event handler to run the function in response to the load event.

To assign an onload event handler:

1. Return to the **jpf_hanjie.js** file in your editor. Directly below the initial comment section, insert the following code for the init() function:

   ```
   function init() {
      // Insert the title for the first puzzle
      document.getElementById("puzzleTitle").innerHTML = "Puzzle 1";

      // Insert the HTML code for the first puzzle table
      document.getElementById("puzzle").innerHTML =
         drawPuzzle(puzzle1Hint, puzzle1Rating, puzzle1);
   }
   ```

2. Directly above the init() function, inset the following statement to run the function when the page is loaded by the browser.

   ```
   // Run the init() function when page loads
   window.onload = init;
   ```

   Figure 11-7 highlights the newly added code for the onload event handler.

Specify only the name of the function invoked by the event handler, do not include parentheses or parameters.

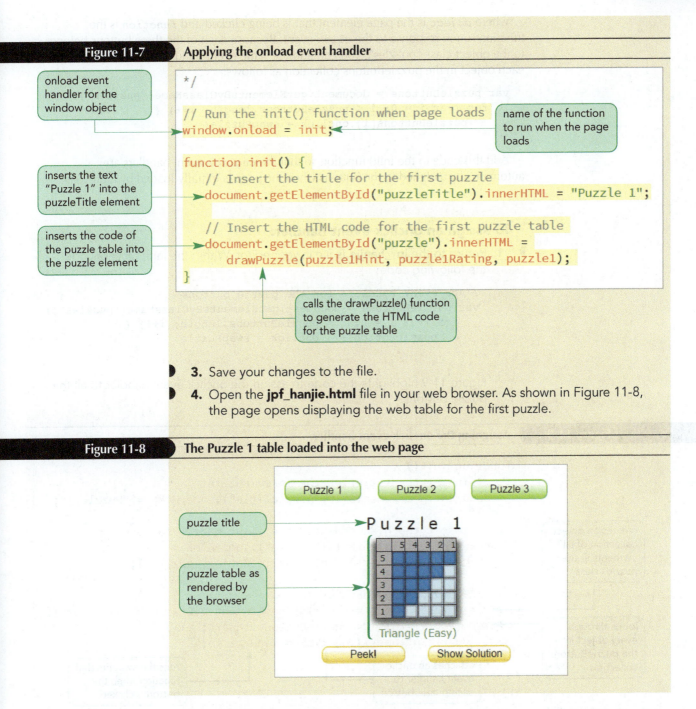

| Figure 11-7 | Applying the onload event handler |

onload event handler for the window object

```
*/

// Run the init() function when page loads
window.onload = init;

function init() {
    // Insert the title for the first puzzle
    document.getElementById("puzzleTitle").innerHTML = "Puzzle 1";

    // Insert the HTML code for the first puzzle table
    document.getElementById("puzzle").innerHTML =
        drawPuzzle(puzzle1Hint, puzzle1Rating, puzzle1);
}
```

name of the function to run when the page loads

inserts the text "Puzzle 1" into the puzzleTitle element

inserts the code of the puzzle table into the puzzle element

calls the drawPuzzle() function to generate the HTML code for the puzzle table

3. Save your changes to the file.

4. Open the **jpf_hanjie.html** file in your web browser. As shown in Figure 11-8, the page opens displaying the web table for the first puzzle.

| Figure 11-8 | The Puzzle 1 table loaded into the web page |

puzzle title

puzzle table as rendered by the browser

Puzzle 1   Puzzle 2   Puzzle 3

Puzzle 1

Triangle (Easy)

Peek!   Show Solution

Above the puzzle table, Rebecca has inserted three form buttons created with the following HTML code:

```
<input type="button" class="puzzles" id="puzzle1" value="Puzzle 1" />
<input type="button" class="puzzles" id="puzzle2" value="Puzzle 2" />
<input type="button" class="puzzles" id="puzzle3" value="Puzzle 3" />
```

Rebecca wants you to add an event handler to each of these buttons to run the swapPuzzle() function when the button is clicked, thereby loading a different puzzle into the web page. To respond to a mouse click, you apply the following onclick event handler

```
object.onclick = function;
```

where *object* is the page element that is being clicked and *function* is the function run in response to the click event. Because each of the three buttons belongs to the object class "puzzles", you can add the same event handler by looping through each object in the puzzleButtons collection as follows:

```
var puzzleButtons = document.getElementsByClassName("puzzles");
    for (var i = 0; i < puzzleButtons.length; i++) {
        puzzleButtons[i].onclick = swapPuzzle;
    }
```

Add this code to the init() function so that the onclick event handlers are automatically assigned to the buttons when the page is initially loaded by a browser.

To assign an onclick event handler:

1. Return to the **jpf_hanjie.js** file in your editor. Within the init() function, add the following code:

```
//Add event handlers for the puzzle buttons
var puzzleButtons = document.getElementsByClassName("puzzles");
    for (var i = 0; i < puzzleButtons.length; i++) {
        puzzleButtons[i].onclick = swapPuzzle;
    }
```

Figure 11-9 highlights the code to assign the onclick event handler to all the puzzle buttons.

Figure 11-9	Assigning the onclick event handler

```
function init() {
    // Insert the title for the first puzzle
    document.getElementById("puzzleTitle").innerHTML = "Puzzle 1";

    // Insert the HTML code for the first puzzle table
    document.getElementById("puzzle").innerHTML =
        drawPuzzle(puzzle1Hint, puzzle1Rating, puzzle1);

    //Add event handlers for the puzzle buttons
    var puzzleButtons = document.getElementsByClassName("puzzles");
    for (var i = 0; i < puzzleButtons.length; i++) {
        puzzleButtons[i].onclick = swapPuzzle;
    }
}
```

creates an object collection of all elements in the puzzles class

loops through every object in the puzzleButtons collection

attaches an onclick event handler to each puzzle button

runs the swapPuzzle() function when the button is clicked

2. Save your changes to the file.

The advantage of assigning the same onclick event handler to each object in the puzzleButtons collection is that Rebecca can add as many puzzles and as many puzzle buttons to her page as she wishes; and, as long as each of those buttons belongs to the puzzles class, it will be associated with the swapPuzzle() function. The challenge lies in determining which button was clicked. Without knowing which button activated the onclick event handler, there is no way of knowing which puzzle to load into the page. You can determine this information using the event object.

Using the Event Object

The event object is an object that contains properties and methods associated with an event. For example, the action of clicking a mouse button generates an event object containing information such as which mouse button was clicked, where in the page it was clicked, the time at which it was clicked, and so forth. To retrieve this information, the event object is passed as an argument to the function handling the event. Thus, in the following event handler statement

```
myButton.onclick = myFunction;
```

the event object can be included as the parameter for myFunction()

```
function myFunction(evt) {
    function code
}
```

where *evt* is the name assigned to the parameter receiving the event object from the event handler. You can give the event object any parameter name, but the standard practice is to name the parameter "e" or "evt" or "event". Once the event object has been included as a parameter, it can be referenced within the handler function. For example, the following code assigns the name "e" to the event object and displays an alert dialog box identifying which button was click:

```
function myFunction(e) {
    alert(e.button);
}
```

Note that different events will support different properties and methods. The button property, for example, is associated only with mouse or pointer events. Figure 11-10 lists some of the core properties and methods associated with almost all events.

Figure 11-10   Event object properties and methods

Property	Description
evt.bubbles	Returns a Boolean value indicating whether the event is bubbling up through the object hierarchy, where *evt* is the event object for the event
evt.cancelable	Returns a Boolean value indicating whether the event can have its default action canceled
evt.currentTarget	Returns the object that is currently experiencing the event
evt.defaultPrevented	Returns a Boolean value indicating whether the preventDefault() method was called for the event
evt.eventPhase	Returns the phase of the event propagation the event object is currently at, where 0 = NONE, 1 = CAPTURING_PHASE, 2 = AT_TARGET, and 3 = BUBBLING_PHASE
evt.isTrusted	Returns a Boolean value indicating whether the event is trusted by the browser
evt.target	Returns the object in which the event was initiated
evt.timeStamp	Returns the time (in milliseconds) when the event occurred
evt.type	Returns the type of the event
evt.view	Reference the browser window in which the event occurred

Method	Description
evt.preventDefault()	Cancels the default action associated with the event
evt.stopImmediatePropagation()	Prevents other event listeners of the event from being called
evt.stopPropagation()	Prevents further propagation of the event in the capturing and bubbling phase

To determine which of the three puzzle buttons initiated the `click` event, you will use the following `target` property that identifies the source of the event:

```
evt.target
```

In this case, the `target` property returns a reference to the button that was clicked by the user. To reference the button's ID, add the following `id` property to the expression

```
evt.target.id
```

which returns the text string "puzzle1", "puzzle2", or "puzzle3".

Using an Event Object

- To reference an event object within an event handler function, add the following parameter to the function

```
function function(evt) {
    function code
}
```

where *function* is the function assigned to the event, *evt* is the name given to the event object, and *function code* are the commands run in response to the event.
- To determine the source of an event, use the following `target` property

```
evt.target
```

where *evt* is the event object.
- To determine the ID of the event target, use the following:

```
evt.target.id
```

Use an event object now in writing the swapPuzzle() function.

To create the swapPuzzle() function:

1. Directly below the init() function, insert the following code to begin creating the swapPuzzle() function:

```
function swapPuzzle(e) {
    var puzzleID = e.target.id;
```

2. Next, extract the title of the puzzle from the value attribute in the puzzle buttons by adding the command:

```
var puzzleTitle = e.target.value;
document.getElementById("puzzleTitle").innerHTML =
puzzleTitle;
```

3. Finally, insert the following switch statement that calls the drawPuzzle() function for each of the three possible puzzle ID values:

```
switch (puzzleID) {
case "puzzle1":
    document.getElementById("puzzle").innerHTML =
    drawPuzzle(puzzle1Hint, puzzle1Rating, puzzle1);
    break;
```

```
case "puzzle2":
   document.getElementById("puzzle").innerHTML =
    drawPuzzle(puzzle2Hint, puzzle2Rating, puzzle2);
   break;
case "puzzle3":
   document.getElementById("puzzle").innerHTML =
    drawPuzzle(puzzle3Hint, puzzle3Rating, puzzle3);
   break;
}
```

4. Enter a closing **}** to close off the function. Figure 11-11 highlights the completed code.

Figure 11-11	Creating the swapPuzzle() function

```
//Add event handlers for the puzzle buttons
var puzzleButtons = document.getElementsByClassName("puzzles");
   for (var i = 0; i < puzzleButtons.length; i++) {
      puzzleButtons[i].onclick = swapPuzzle;
   }
}
```

the target property references the button that was clicked

event object for the event handler

```
function swapPuzzle(e) {
   var puzzleID = e.target.id;
```

retrieves the ID of the clicked button

retrieves the value of the clicked button

```
   var puzzleTitle = e.target.value;
   document.getElementById("puzzleTitle").innerHTML = puzzleTitle;

   switch (puzzleID) {
   case "puzzle1":
      document.getElementById("puzzle").innerHTML =
       drawPuzzle(puzzle1Hint, puzzle1Rating, puzzle1);
      break;
   case "puzzle2":
      document.getElementById("puzzle").innerHTML =
       drawPuzzle(puzzle2Hint, puzzle2Rating, puzzle2);
      break;
   case "puzzle3":
      document.getElementById("puzzle").innerHTML =
       drawPuzzle(puzzle3Hint, puzzle3Rating, puzzle3);
      break;
   }
}
```

displays the puzzle based on the value of the puzzleID variable

5. Save your changes to the file and then reload **jpf_hanjie.html** in your browser.

6. Click the **Puzzle 1**, **Puzzle 2**, and **Puzzle 3** buttons and verify that you can switch between any of the three Hanjie puzzles. Figure 11-12 shows the contents of the third puzzle.

Figure 11-12 **Contents of the third puzzle table**

Four Score and Seven (Moderate)

© Courtesy Patrick Carey

Trouble? If you can't switch between the puzzles, check your code. Common mistakes are mistyping the methods such as the `document.getElementById()` method, forgetting to close double quotation marks, and incorrect use of upper-case and lowercase letters.

Now that you have loaded the puzzles into the web page, your next task is to hide the puzzle solution from the user. To do this, you must modify the display styles of the cells in the puzzle table.

Using the this *Keyword with Event Handlers*

Another way of locating the object that called an event handler is with the `this` keyword. The **this** keyword is a JavaScript keyword that references the owner of an object or function. You can think of `this` as acting like a pronoun in a sentence. For example, in the following phrase

"I bought a vase; this is the one I bought."

the word "this" acts as a pronoun or reference to the word "vase". Of course, context is important because, in the following sentence, "this" references the word "store":

"I bought a vase at the store; this is where I bought it."

In a similar way, context or scope is essential when determining the owner referenced by the `this` keyword. With event handlers, the owner is the object in which the event occurred. Thus, in the following code, the keyword `this` refers to the button that invoked the swapPuzzle() function in response to the click event:

```
puzzleButtons[i].onclick = swapPuzzle;
…


function swapPuzzle(e) {
    var puzzleID = this.id;
}
```

You can use either `this` or `e.target` to reference the owner of the event. In Tutorial 14, you will learn how to apply the `this` keyword with customized objects created by the programmer.

Exploring Object Properties

In the swapPuzzle() function, you used the `id` and `value` properties to extract the values of the `id` and `value` attributes from the `input` elements for the three puzzle buttons. Most HTML attributes can be accessed as properties of document objects. For example, setting the `src` attribute in the following `img` element

```
<img id="logoImg" src="logo.png" />
```

can also be done by setting the `src` property of the `document.images` object:

```
document.images["logoImg"].src = "logo.png";
```

The JavaScript object properties that mirror HTML attributes follow certain conventions. All JavaScript properties must begin with a lowercase letter. If the HTML attribute consists of multiple words, then the initial word in the JavaScript property is lowercase but the first letter of each subsequent word is an uppercase letter—a format known as **camel case**. For example, HTML's `maxlength` attribute in the following HTML input element

```
<input type="text" id="fName" maxlength="15" />
```

is expressed in the following JavaScript code in camel case as

```
document.getElementById("fName").maxLength = 15;
```

If the name of the HTML attribute is a reserved JavaScript name or keyword, the corresponding JavaScript property is often prefaced with the text string `html`. Thus, the `for` attribute in the following HTML `label` element

```
<label id="fLabel" for="fName"> … </label>
```

is mirrored by the following JavaScript statement:

```
document.getElementById("fLabel").htmlFor = "fName";
```

One exception to this convention is the `class` attribute. Because the class name is reserved by JavaScript for other purposes, references to the HTML class attribute use the `className` property. Thus, the HTML code that sets the value of the `class` attribute

```
<div id="menu1" class="menu">
```

would have the following equivalent JavaScript expression:

```
document.getElementById("menu1").className = "menu";
```

Once you are comfortable with these conventions, you can apply your knowledge of HTML elements and attributes to their equivalent JavaScript expressions involving object names and properties.

INSIGHT

Working with Form Fields

You can use JavaScript to access and modify the values stored in form fields using the `value` attribute of the input control. For example, the value of the following HTML input element

```
<input type="text" id="custName" />
```

can be accessed using the following JavaScript reference:

```
document.getElementById("custName").value
```

Input controls, such as radio buttons or selection lists, support the checked property to indicate whether the control has been checked by the user. To determine the checked status of the control, use the expression

```
object.checked
```

where *object* is a reference to the control element.

Finally, to direct the user to a specific control on the form, you can give the control the focus using the following `focus()` method

```
object.focus()
```

where *object* is the control that will receive the focus, becoming the active element in the form.

Object Properties and Inline Styles

Much of the Hanjie puzzle interface involves changing the styles applied to each cell in the Hanjie table. You can do this by applying inline styles using the following `style` attribute

```
<element style = "property:value"> …
```

where *element* is the page element, *property* is a CSS style property, and *value* is the value assigned to that property. The equivalent command in JavaScript is

```
object.style.property = "value";
```

with the *property* style written in camel case. For example, the following JavaScript command sets the font size of the first h1 heading in the document to 1.4em:

```
document.getElementsByTagName("h1")[0].style.fontSize = "1.4em";
```

Notice that because JavaScript does not support hyphens in property names, the CSS `font-size` style is entered as the `fontSize` property.

Setting an Inline Style with JavaScript

- To set the inline style of a page element, use

  `object.style.property = "value";`

  where *object* is a reference to the page element, *property* is the CSS style written in camel case, and *value* is the value of the style property.

Because the `style` property is applied as an inline style, it does not alter any style rules from the page's style sheet. However, because inline styles have precedence over style sheets, the inline styles will be reflected in the page appearance.

Problem Solving: Choosing Between Classes and Inline Styles

JavaScript allows styles to be changed in two ways. One approach is to modify the object's appearance by setting or changing the object's inline style as in the following command, which changes an object's font color:

`document.getElementById("main").style.color = "red";`

The other approach is to keep all styles in an external style sheet marked with different class names. A part of an external CSS style sheet that changes the font color to red might look like

`.redText {color: red}`

Using class names allows the programmer to change the font color by using the class name as follows:

`document.getElementById("main").className = "redText";`

There are several good reasons to use classes for the task of changing styles rather than the `style` property. First, using classes makes it easier to maintain consistent styles within a website because all styles are confined to a style sheet rather than being spread across several style sheets and within JavaScript programs. Second, it is usually easier to use commands to modify a style in a style sheet rather than in what might be a long and complex JavaScript program. Finally, speed tests have shown that browsers are more responsive and apply style changes more quickly by changing the element's class rather than by modifying the `style` property.

Still, situations exist when you would not want to create a different class for every change in an object's appearance, such as when that class value contains important structural information regarding the object's use or position in the document. For that reason, most JavaScript programmers use a combination of classes and inline styles to modify the appearance of their documents.

Creating Object Collections with CSS Selectors

Rebecca suggests that you hide the solution to the Hanjie puzzle by changing the background color of all table cells to the gold color value rgb(233, 207, 29). To accomplish this in CSS, you could apply the following style rule for all td elements within the hanjieGrid table:

```
table#hanjieGrid td {
    background-color: rgb(233, 207, 29);
}
```

To do the same thing in JavaScript, you must first define an object collection based on a CSS selector using the following querySelectorAll() method

```
document.querySelectorAll(selector)
```

where *selector* is the CSS selector that the object collection is based on. Thus, the following statement creates an object collection named puzzleCells, which stores each of the td elements from the hanjieGrid table:

```
var puzzleCells = document.querySelectorAll("table#hanjieGrid td");
```

Once the object collection has been defined, you can change the background-color style of each td element by applying the following backgroundColor property to the objects in the puzzleCells collection:

```
for (var i = 0; i < puzzleCells.length; i++) {
    puzzleCells[i].style.backgroundColor = "rgb(233, 207, 29)";
}
```

TIP

The querySelector() or querySelectorAll() methods do not support the use of pseudo-elements or pseudo-classes.

If you wanted to reference only the first element that matches a selector pattern, you could use the following JavaScript method

```
document.querySelector(selector)
```

where *selector* is once again a CSS selector.

REFERENCE

Creating an Object Collection based on a CSS Selector

- To reference an object collection using a CSS selector, apply the method

  ```
  document.querySelectorAll(selector)
  ```

  where *selector* is the CSS selector that the object collection is based upon.
- To return only the first object from the selector, use:

  ```
  document.querySelector(selector)
  ```

Use the querySelectorAll() method now as part of the setupPuzzle() function that sets the background color of the td elements in the puzzle table.

To create the setupPuzzle() function:

1. Return to the **jpf_hanjie.js** file in your editor and, directly above the init() function, insert the following statement to declare the puzzleCells variable.

   ```
   var puzzleCells;
   ```

   Note that by defining the puzzleCells variable outside of a function, you will give it global scope, making it available to every function in this application.

2. Scroll down the file and, directly below the swapPuzzle() function, insert the following code for the setupPuzzle() function:

```
function setupPuzzle() {
    /* Match all of the data cells in the puzzle */
    puzzleCells = document.querySelectorAll("table#hanjieGrid
td");

    /* Set the initial color of each cell to gold */
    for (var i = 0; i < puzzleCells.length; i++) {
        puzzleCells[i].style.backgroundColor = "rgb(233, 207,
29)";
    }
}
```

Figure 11-13 describes the code for the setupPuzzle() function.

Figure 11-13	Creating the setupPuzzle() function

creates an object collection of all of the td elements in the hanjieGrid table

loops through every td element in the puzzleCells collection

changes the value of the background-color inline style for each td element to gold

```
}

function setupPuzzle() {
    /* Match all of the data cells in the puzzle */
    puzzleCells = document.querySelectorAll("table#hanjieGrid td");

    /* Set the initial color of each cell to gold */
    for (var i = 0; i < puzzleCells.length; i++) {
        puzzleCells[i].style.backgroundColor = "rgb(233, 207, 29)";
    }
}
```

3. Add the **setupPuzzle();** command to the init() function so that it runs when the page loads, hiding the solution of the first puzzle. See Figure 11-14.

Figure 11-14	Revising the init() function

defines puzzleCells as a global variable so it can be used in all functions

sets up the initial puzzle displayed in the web page

```
var puzzleCells;

function init() {
    // Insert the title for the first puzzle
    document.getElementById("puzzleTitle").innerHTML = "Puzzle 1";

    // Insert the HTML code for the first puzzle table
    document.getElementById("puzzle").innerHTML =
        drawPuzzle(puzzle1Hint, puzzle1Rating, puzzle1);

    //Add event handlers for the puzzle buttons
    var puzzleButtons = document.getElementsByClassName("puzzles");
    for (var i = 0; i < puzzleButtons.length; i++) {
        puzzleButtons[i].onclick = swapPuzzle;
    }

    setupPuzzle();
}
```

4. The setupPuzzle() function should also be run whenever the user switches from one puzzle to another. Add the **setupPuzzle();** command to the end of the swapPuzzle() function. See Figure 11-15.

Figure 11-15 Revising the swapPuzzle() function

changes the puzzle to Puzzle 3 as part of the swapPuzzle function

sets up the puzzle swap as the result of a button click

```
        case "puzzle3":
            document.getElementById("puzzle").innerHTML =
              drawPuzzle(puzzle3Hint, puzzle3Rating, puzzle3);
            break;
    }

    setupPuzzle();
}
```

5. Save your changes to the file and then reload **jpf_hanjie.html** in your browser.

6. Click the Puzzle buttons to verify that the cells of the Hanjie puzzles are now displayed in gold with no visual indication of each puzzle's solution. Figure 11-16 shows the appearance of the first puzzle with the solution hidden from the user.

Figure 11-16 Hiding the puzzle solution

puzzle solution hidden from the user

You have completed your first part of the Hanjie Puzzle app by loading the puzzles into Rebecca's web page and hiding their solutions. In the next session, you will explore how to use mouse and keyboard events to aid the user in solving the puzzles.

Session 11.1 Quick Check

1. Provide the HTML code to run the setup() function when the page is loaded by the browser.
2. Provide the JavaScript code to run the setup() function when the page is loaded by the browser.
3. Provide an expression that returns the ID of the object initiating an event. Assume that the name of your event object is evt.
4. Provide an expression that returns the time that an event occurred in milliseconds. Assume that the name of your event object is evt.
5. Provide JavaScript code to change the source of the first inline image in the document to introImg.png.
6. Provide JavaScript code to change the font family of the first h1 heading in the document to Arial.
7. Provide the expression to create an object collection of all objects referenced by the CSS selector `div#intro p`.
8. Provide the expression to return only the first paragraph referenced by the CSS selector `div#intro p`.

Session 11.2 Visual Overview:

The **altKey** property indicates whether the Alt key is pressed.

The **shiftKey** property indicates whether the Shift key is pressed.

The **addEventListener()** method listens for events as they propagate through the object hierarchy.

The **preventDefault()** method prevents the browser from performing its default response to an event.

The **removeEventListen-er()** method removes an event listener.

```javascript
function setBackground(e) {
    var cursorType;

    if (e.shiftKey) {
        cellBackground = "rgb(233, 207, 29)";
        cursorType = "url(jpf_eraser.png), cell";
    } else if (e.altKey) {
        cellBackground = "rgb(255, 255, 255)";
        cursorType = "url(jpf_cross.png), crosshair";
    } else {
        cellBackground = "rgb(101, 101, 101)";
        cursorType = "url(jpf_pencil.png), pointer";
    }

    e.target.style.backgroundColor = cellBackground;

    for (var i = 0; i < puzzleCells.length; i++) {
        puzzleCells[i].addEventListener("mouseenter", extendBackground);
        puzzleCells[i].style.cursor = cursorType;
    }

    e.preventDefault();
}

function extendBackground(e) {
    e.target.style.backgroundColor = cellBackground;
}

function endBackground() {
    for (var i = 0; i < puzzleCells.length; i++) {
        puzzleCells[i].removeEventListener("mouseenter", extendBackground);
        puzzleCells[i].style.cursor = "url(jpf_pencil.png), pointer";
    }
}
```

The **mouseenter** event fires when the pointer enters a page element.

This code runs the extendBackground() function in response to the mouseenter event.

The **cursor** style defines the cursor for a page element.

This is the image file for a cursor.

This is the generic cursor used if the image file is not supported.

© Courtesy Patrick Carey

Event Listeners and Cursors

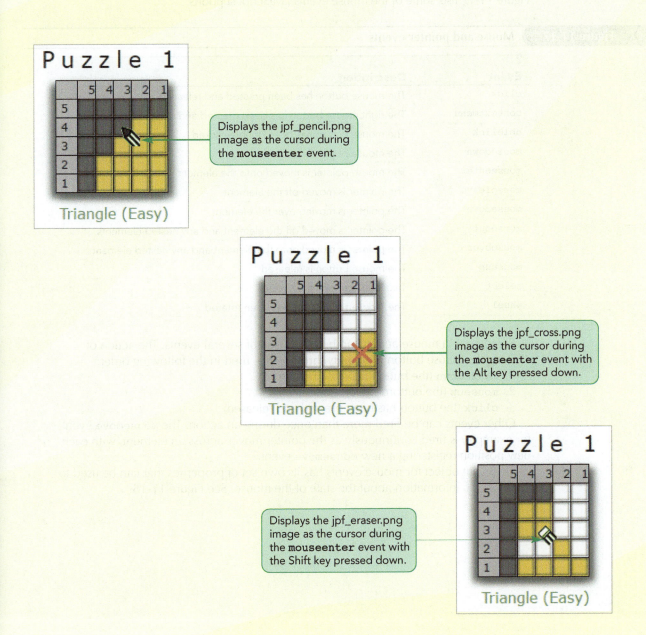

Puzzle 1

Triangle (Easy)

Displays the jpf_pencil.png image as the cursor during the **mouseenter** event.

Puzzle 1

Triangle (Easy)

Displays the jpf_cross.png image as the cursor during the **mouseenter** event with the Alt key pressed down.

Puzzle 1

Triangle (Easy)

Displays the jpf_eraser.png image as the cursor during the **mouseenter** event with the Shift key pressed down.

Working with Mouse Events

In the last session, you used the `onclick` event handler to respond to the action of clicking one of the three puzzle buttons on Rebecca's web page. JavaScript supports other events associated with the mouse such as right-clicking, double-clicking, and moving the pointer over and out of page elements. For each action, you can script a response. Figure 11-17 lists some of the mouse events JavaScript supports.

Figure 11-17   **Mouse and pointer events**

Event	Description
`click`	The mouse button has been pressed and released
`contextmenu`	The right mouse button has been pressed and released
`dblclick`	The mouse button has been double-clicked
`mousedown`	The mouse button is pressed
`mouseenter`	The mouse pointer is moved onto the element
`mouseleave`	The pointer is moved off the element
`mousemove`	The pointer is moving over the element
`mouseout`	The pointer is moved off the element and any nested elements
`mouseover`	The pointer is moved onto the element and any nested elements
`mouseup`	The mouse button is released
`select`	Text is selected by the pointer
`wheel`	The mouse scroll wheel has been rotated

Sometimes, a mouse action can be comprised of several events. The action of clicking the mouse button is actually three events, fired in the following order:

1. `mousedown` (the button is pressed down)
2. `mouseup` (the button is released)
3. `click` (the button has been pressed and released)

Other events can be fired more than once during an action. The `mousemove` event, for example, is fired continuously as the pointer moves across an element, with each new position registering a new `mousemove` event.

The event object for mouse events has its own set of properties that can be used to give specific information about the state of the mouse. See Figure 11-18.

Figure 11-18   Mouse event object properties

Event Property	Description
evt.button	Returns a number indicating the mouse button that was pressed, where 0 = left, 1 = wheel or middle, and 3 = right and *evt* is event object for the mouse event
evt.buttons	Returns a number indicating the mouse button or buttons that were pressed, where 1 = left, 2 = right, 4 = wheel or middle, 8 = back, 16 = forward, and other multiple buttons are indicated by the sum of their numbers
evt.clientX	Returns the horizontal coordinate (in pixels) of the mouse pointer relative to the browser window
evt.clientY	Returns the vertical coordinate (in pixels) of the mouse pointer relative to the browser window
evt.detail	Returns the number of times the mouse button was clicked
evt.pageX	Returns the horizontal coordinate (in pixels) of the mouse pointer relative to the document
evt.pageY	Returns the vertical coordinate (in pixels) of the mouse pointer relative to the document
evt.relatedTarget	References the secondary target of the event; for the mouseover event this is the element that the pointer is leaving and for the mouseout event this is the element that the pointer is entering
evt.screenX	Returns the horizontal coordinate (in pixels) of the mouse pointer relative to the physical screen
evt.screenY	Returns the vertical coordinate (in pixels) of the mouse pointer relative to the physical screen
evt.which	Returns a number indicating the mouse button that was pressed, where 0 = none, 1 = left, 2 = wheel or middle, and 3 = right

The following code shows how an event handler can be used to record the exact window position of the mouse pointer as it moves across the drawImg element:

```
document.getElementById("drawImg").onmousemove = trackPointer;

function trackPointer(e) {
   var hPos = e.clientX;
   var vPos = e.clientY;
   document.getElementById("imgLoc").innerText =
      " (" + hPos + ", " + vPos + ")";
}
```

TIP

Use care with mouse-move events because they can slow down your page's performance as the browser continuously responds to the movement of the pointer.

As the mouse moves across the drawImg element, the trackPointer() function is fired with each change in location of the mouse pointer and the current location is displayed within the imgLoc element.

REFERENCE

Creating Event Handlers for Mouse Events

- To apply an event handler for the action of pressing the mouse button down, use

  `object.onmousedown = function;`

  where `object` is the element in which the mousedown event occurs and `function` is the function that is run in response to the event.
- To apply an event handler for the action of releasing the mouse button, use:

  `object.onmouseup = function;`

- To apply an event handler when the mouse pointer enters an element, use

  `object.onmouseenter = function;`

  or

  `object.onmouseover = function;`

  where the `mouseenter` event fires only for the element and the `mouseover` event fires for the element and its nested elements.
- To apply an event handler when the mouse pointer leaves an element, use

  `object.onmouseleave = function;`

  or

  `object.onmouseout = function;`

  where the `mouseleave` event fires only for the element and the `mouseout` event fires for the element and its nested elements.
- To apply an event handler when the mouse pointer moves, use:

  `object.onmousemove = function;`

You will use the `mousedown` event handler to enable the user to draw the solution on the puzzle grid. As the user presses the mouse pointer down on any puzzle table cell, the browser runs the setBackground() function to change the value of that cell's `background-color` style to the gray background color, rgb(101, 101, 101).

To create an event handler for the mousedown event:

1. If you took a break after the previous session, make sure **jpf_hanjie.js** is open in your editor.

2. Directly below the init() function, insert the following statement to declare cellBackground as a global variable that will be available to all functions in the file:

   `var cellBackground;`

3. Scroll down to the setupPuzzle() function. Within the `for` loop, add the following command to add an event handler for every occurrence of the mousedown event within a puzzle cell:

   ```
   // Set the cell background color in response to the mousedown
   event
   puzzleCells[i].onmousedown = setBackground;
   ```

4. Directly below the setupPuzzle() function, insert the following code for the setBackground() function to change the background color of the target of the mousedown event.

```
function setBackground(e) {
    cellBackground = "rgb(101, 101, 101)";
    e.target.style.backgroundColor = cellBackground;
}
```

Figure 11-19 highlights the newly added code in the file.

Figure 11-19   **Applying the onmousedown event handler**

```
var puzzleCells;
var cellBackground;                          global variable for
                                             storing the cell
                                             background color

function setupPuzzle() {
    /* Match all of the data cells in the puzzle */
    puzzleCells = document.querySelectorAll("table#hanjieGrid td");

    /* Set the initial color of each cell to gold */
    for (var i = 0; i < puzzleCells.length; i++) {
        puzzleCells[i].style.backgroundColor = "rgb(233, 207, 29)";
        // set the cell background color in response to the mousedown event
        puzzleCells[i].onmousedown = setBackground;
    }
}

function setBackground(e) {
    cellBackground = "rgb(101, 101, 101)";
    e.target.style.backgroundColor = cellBackground;
}
```

adds an event handler to every mousedown event in the puzzle cells

runs the setBackground() function in response to the mousedown event

sets the background-color style to the value of the cellBackground variable

5. Save your changes to the file and then reload **jpf_hanjie.html** in your web browser.

6. Move the mouse pointer over cells in the first puzzle table and verify that, as you press the mouse button down, the cell color under the pointer changes from gold to gray. See Figure 11-20.

Figure 11-20 **Changing the cell background color**

pressing the mouse pointer down over each puzzle cell changes the background color to gray

7. Click the **Puzzle 2** and **Puzzle 3** buttons to verify that you can also mark the cells in those tables.

Using the `mousedown` action, a user can change the color of each cell in the puzzle table but the process will quickly become tedious with larger puzzles. Rebecca suggests you modify the program to allow the user to draw on the puzzle grid by dragging the pointer over large table cell ranges with the mouse button pressed down. When the button is released, the drawing processing ends, not to be started again until the next `mousedown` event.

To write this section of the code, you will first examine the JavaScript Event Model in detail.

Introducing the Event Model

An event doesn't touch only one object; instead, it interacts with a whole hierarchy of objects. When you clicked within a puzzle cell, you were also clicking within the table row in which the cell resided, the table containing the table row, the figure box containing the table, the document containing the figure, and then finally, the browser window containing the document. The process in which a single event is applied to a hierarchy of objects is part of the **event model**, which describes how events and objects interact within the web page and web browser.

TIP

You can determine the event phase using the `eventPhase` property of the event object. You can determine whether the event is bubbling using the event object's `bubbles` property.

Once an event has been initiated, it propagates through the object hierarchy in three phases. In the **capture phase**, the event moves down the object hierarchy starting from the root element (the browser window) and moving inward until it reaches the object that initiated the event, such as a cell within the puzzle table. In the **target phase**, the event has reached the target of the event object and no longer moves down the object hierarchy. Finally, in the **bubbling phase**, the event propagates up the object hierarchy back to the root element (browser window) where the propagation stops. See Figure 11-21.

Figure 11-21	Event propagation in the event model

© Courtesy Patrick Carey

Event handlers, like `onclick` and `onmousedown`, respond to events during the target phase, but they do not recognize the propagation of events through the capture and bubbling phases. Another limitation of event handlers is that only one function can be applied to an event handler at a time. In the following code, the second event handler supersedes the first so that only function2() is run when the page is loaded by the browser.

```
window.onload = function1;
window.onload = function2;
```

Because of these limitations with event handlers, a more robust way of scripting events is often needed.

Adding an Event Listener

Another way of responding to an event is with an **event listener**, which listens for events as they propagate through the capture, target, and bubble phases, allowing the script to respond to an event within any phase. For example, one function could be run during the capture phase of the event and a second function could be run in the bubbling phase.

To add an event listener to an object, apply the following `addEventListener()` method

```
object.addEventListener(event, function [, capture = false]);
```

where *object* is the object in which the event occurs, *event* is the event, *function* is the function that is run in response to the event, and *capture* is an optional Boolean value where `true` indicates that the function is executed during the capture phase and `false` (the default) indicates that the function is run during the bubbling phase.

TIP

The prefix "on" is not used with event listeners for events such as the `click` event; the "on" prefix is only used with event handlers, such as `onclick`.

Unlike event handlers, more than one function can be applied to an event using the `addEventListener()` method. In the following code, both function1() and function2() run when the page is loaded by the browser:

```
window.addEventListener("load", function1);
window.addEventListener("load", function2);
```

With event listeners, the programmer can combine several scripts designed to do different tasks or create a script to run a function and not worry that it will block another function loaded from a different script.

Rebecca suggests that you create an event listener for `mouseenter` events occurring within the puzzle cells to extend the background color to each cell that the pointer enters. To do this, you will place the commands to extend the background color in the extendBackground() function.

To create an event listener for the mouseenter event:

Do not include the prefix "on" when specifying the event using the `addEventListener()` method.

1. Return to the **jpf_hanjie.js** file in your editor and go to the setBackground() function.

2. Add the following `for` loop to the setBackground() function, creating an event listener for every puzzle cell touched by the `mouseenter` event to call the extendBackground() function.

   ```
   // Create an event listener for every puzzle cell
   for (var i = 0; i < puzzleCells.length; i++) {
       puzzleCells[i].addEventListener("mouseenter",
   extendBackground);
   }
   ```

3. Directly below the setBackground() function, insert the following extendBackground() function to set the `background-color` style to the value currently stored in the global cellBackground variable.

   ```
   function extendBackground(e) {
       e.target.style.backgroundColor = cellBackground;
   }
   ```

   Figure 11-22 highlights the code that adds the event listener to the puzzle app.

Figure 11-22	Extending the cell background color

```
function setBackground(e) {
    cellBackground = "rgb(101, 101, 101)";
    e.target.style.backgroundColor = cellBackground;

    // Create an event listener for every puzzle cell
    for (var i = 0; i < puzzleCells.length; i++) {
        puzzleCells[i].addEventListener("mouseenter", extendBackground);
    }
}

function extendBackground(e) {
    e.target.style.backgroundColor = cellBackground;
}
```

adds an event listener to every mouseenter event in the puzzle cells

runs the extendBackground() function in response to the mouseenter event

sets the background-color style to the value of the cellBackground variable

> 4. Save your changes to the file and then reload **jpf_hanjie.html** in your browser.
>
> 5. Press the pointer button down within any puzzle cell in the Puzzle 1 table and verify that as the pointer enters other puzzle cells, the browser changes their background color to gray.

Once you press the pointer button down within a puzzle cell, there is no way to stop the drawing process. The extendBackground() function will be run whenever the mouse pointer enters a puzzle cell. You can correct this problem by removing the event listener.

Understanding Mouseenter and Mouseover

JavaScript supports two types of events – mouseenter and mouseover – that are triggered by the mouse pointer entering a page element. However, these two events differ in how they propagate through the object hierarchy. Consider the following HTML code:

```
<div id="outer">
   <div id="inner"></div>
</div>
```

If you create a mouseenter event listener for the outer div element, the event will be triggered only for the outer div element. This is because the mouseenter event does not bubble through the object hierarchy. On the other hand, the mouseover event does bubble and thus will be fired when the pointer enters either outer div element or inner div elements. Unless you want the event triggered for an element and all its descendants, you should listen only for the mouseenter event.

There is a similar distinction between the mouseleave and mouseout events in which the mouseleave event does not bubble and the mouseout event does.

Removing an Event Listener

The event model is extremely dynamic and allows for event listeners to be removed from the document. To remove an event listener, apply the following removeEventListener() method

```
object.removeEventListener(event, function [, capture = false]);
```

where *object*, *event*, *function*, and *capture* have the same meanings as they did for the addEventListener() method. Once the event listener has been removed, the event will no longer trigger a response from the script.

Adding and Removing an Event Listener

- To add an event listener to an element, apply the method

```
object.addEventListener(event, function [, capture = false]);
```

where *object* is the object in which the event occurs, *event* is the event, *function* is the function run in response to the event, and *capture* indicates whether the function is executed during the capture phase (true) or during the bubbling phase (false).

- To remove an event listener from an element, apply the method:

```
object.removeEventListener(event, function [, capture = false]);
```

Rebecca suggests that you revise the script so that the extendBackground() function is run only as long as the pointer button is pressed down, but once the user releases the mouse button anywhere in the document, the event listener for the mousemove event that runs the extendBackground() function is removed.

To remove an event listener:

▶ 1. Return to the **jpf_hanjie.js** file in your editor and scroll to the end of the init() function.

▶ 2. Add the following code to run the endBackground() function whenever the mouseup event is fired anywhere within the document.

```
// Add an event listener for the mouseup event
document.addEventListener("mouseup", endBackground);
```

Figure 11-23 highlights the new code in the init() function.

Figure 11-23 **Adding an event listener for the mouseup event**

```
//Add event handlers for the puzzle buttons
var puzzleButtons = document.getElementsByClassName("puzzles");
for (var i = 0; i < puzzleButtons.length; i++) {
    puzzleButtons[i].onclick = swapPuzzle;
}

setupPuzzle();

// Add an event listener for the mouseup event
document.addEventListener("mouseup", endBackground);
}
```

runs the endBackground() function in response to the mouseup event

listens for the mouseup event occurring anywhere within document

---

▶ 3. Scroll down the document and, directly after the extendBackground() function, add the following endBackground() function that removes the event listener for the mouseenter event from the puzzle cells.

```
function endBackground() {
    // Remove the event listener for every puzzle cell
    for (var i = 0; i < puzzleCells.length; i++) {
        puzzleCells[i].removeEventListener("mouseenter",
    extendBackground);
    }
}
```

Figure 11-24 highlights the code for the endBackground() function.

Figure 11-24	Removing an event listener

```
function extendBackground(e) {
   e.target.style.backgroundColor = cellBackground;
}

function endBackground() {
   // Remove the event listener for every puzzle cell
   for (var i = 0; i < puzzleCells.length; i++) {
      puzzleCells[i].removeEventListener("mouseenter", extendBackground);
   }
}
```

removes the event listener that runs the extendBackground() function in response to the mouseenter event

4. Save your changes to the file and then reload **jpf_hanjie.html** in your browser.

5. Press the mouse button and drag the pointer over the puzzle cells in the Puzzle 1 table. Verify that table cells are marked as the button is pressed while dragging the pointer. See Figure 11-25.

Figure 11-25	Testing the event listener

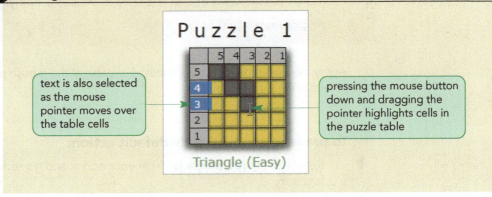

text is also selected as the mouse pointer moves over the table cells

pressing the mouse button down and dragging the pointer highlights cells in the puzzle table

Rebecca notices that when she clicks and drags the pointer over the puzzle table the text within the row headings is selected and highlighted. She wants you to prevent this action.

Controlling Event Propagation

The browser has its own default responses to events. For example, when a submit button is clicked in a web form, the browser will submit the form for processing. When the mouse pointer is dragged over a section of the web page with the mouse button pressed down, the text in that section is selected and highlighted. To prevent the browser's default actions from occurring, apply the following `preventDefault()` method to the event object:

```
evt.preventDefault()
```

TIP

To determine whether a default action is preventable, use an if statement that tests whether an event object's `cancelable` property equals true.

The following code demonstrates how the `preventDefault()` method can be applied to prevent a submit button from submitting a web form when clicked:

```
document.querySelector("input[type='submit']").onclick = runForm;
function runForm(e) {
    function commands
    e.preventDefault();
}
```

You can also prevent the browser's default action by returning the value `false` from the event handler function as in the following code, which also prevents the submit button from submitting the web form when clicked:

```
document.querySelector("input[type='submit']").onclick = runForm;
function runForm(e) {
    function commands
    return false;
}
```

TIP

Preventing the default action does not stop the propagation of the event through the object hierarchy. To keep the event from propagating through the hierarchy, apply the `stopPropagation()` method to the event object.

Note that the `return false;` statement does not prevent default actions if event listeners are used in place of event handlers.

REFERENCE

Controlling Event Propagation

- To prevent an event from propagating through the object hierarchy, apply:

  `evt.stopPropagation()`

  where *evt* is the event object for the event.
- To cancel the browser's default response to the event, apply:

  `evt.preventDefault();`

Apply the `preventDefault()` method to prevent the mouse pointer from selecting cells within the puzzle table.

To prevent the browser's default action:

1. Return to the **jpf_hanjie.js** file in your editor and go to the setBackground() function.

2. Add the following code to the setBackground() function to prevent the default action of the browser.

   ```
   // Prevent the default action of selecting table text
   e.preventDefault();
   ```

   Figure 11-26 highlights the new code in the setBackground() function.

Figure 11-26	Preventing the default browser action

```
function setBackground(e) {
   cellBackground = "rgb(101, 101, 101)";
   e.target.style.backgroundColor = cellBackground;

   // Create an event listener for every puzzle cell
   for (var i = 0; i < puzzleCells.length; i++) {
      puzzleCells[i].addEventListener("mouseenter", extendBackground);
   }

   // Prevent the default action of selecting table text
   e.preventDefault();
}
```

prevents the default browser action of selecting text in the table

3. Save your changes to the file and then reload **jpf_hanjie.html** in your browser.

4. Click and drag the mouse pointer over the cells in the puzzle table, verifying that you can still draw on the puzzle grid and that the text in the table rows is no longer selected.

Rebecca wants users not only to mark those cells they think should be filled in but also mark cells they think should be left empty. To give users the ability to choose whether a cell should be marked as filled or empty, you will work with keyboard events and properties.

Exploring Keyboard Events

Another way for users to interact with the web page and browser is through their keyboard. JavaScript supports the keydown, keypress, and keyup events described in Figure 11-27.

Figure 11-27	Keyboard Events

Event	Description
keydown	A key is pressed down
keypress	A key is pressed down and released, resulting in a character being typed
keyup	A key is released

When the user types a keyboard key, the three events rapidly occur in the following order:

1. keydown — The user presses the key down
2. keypress — A character is generated based on the key
3. keyup — The key is released

TIP

The keypress event will only be fired when a key that produces a printable character is pressed, keys such as the Shift and Ctrl keys do not fire the keypress event because they do not generate printable characters.

Although the keydown and keypress events are similar in name, the difference between them lies in the difference between the physical keyboard keys and the characters they generate. The keydown and keyup events are fired in response to the physical act of pressing the key down and of a key moving up when it is no longer held down. The keypress event is fired in response to the computer generating a character.

Figure 11-28 describes the properties associated with the event object for key events.

Figure 11-28 **Keyboard Event Properties**

Event Property	Description
evt.altKey	Returns a Boolean value indicating whether the Alt key was used in the event object, *evt*
evt.ctrlKey	Returns a Boolean value indicating whether the Ctrl key was used in the event
evt.charCode	Returns the Unicode character code of the key used in the keypress event
evt.key	Returns the text of the key used in the event (not supported by the Safari browser)
evt.keyCode	Returns the Unicode character code of the key used in the keypress event or the key code used in the keydown or keyup events
evt.location	Returns the location number of the key where 0 = key located in the standard position, 1 = a key on the keyboard's left edge, 2 = a key on the keyboard's right edge, and 3 = a key on the numeric keypad
evt.metaKey	Returns a Boolean value indicating whether the meta key (the Command key on Mac keyboards or the Windows key on PC keyboards) was used in the event
evt.shiftKey	Returns a Boolean value indicating whether the Shift key was used in the event
evt.which	Returns the Unicode character code of the key used in the keypress event or the key code used in the keydown or keyup events

The value associated with a key event property is affected by the event itself. For the keypress event, which is fired only after a character is generated, the charCode, keyCode, and which properties all return a Unicode character number. For the keydown and keyup events, which are fired in response to the physical actions of the key, the keyCode and which properties return a keyboard code number identifying the key and the charCode property returns a value of 0. Figure 11-29 shows sample values of the charCode, keyCode, which, and key properties for different keyboard keys and events.

Figure 11-29   **Keyboard Event Properties**

Key(s)	Values with keypress	Values with keydown and keyup
a, z	charCode = 97, 122 keyCode = 97, 122 which = 97, 122 key = "a", "z"	charCode = 0, 0 keyCode = 65, 90 which = 65, 90 key = "a", "z"
1, 9 (on numeric keypad)	charCode = 49, 57 keyCode = 49, 57 which = 49, 57 key = "1", "9"	charCode = 0, 0 keyCode = 97, 105 which = 97, 105 key = "1", "9"
1, 9 (on top keyboard row)	charCode = 49, 57 keyCode = 49, 57 which = 49, 57 key = "1", "9"	charCode = 0, 0 keyCode = 49, 57 which = 49, 57 key = "1", "9"
Shift, Ctrl, Alt, Meta (Mac Command key; PC Window key) Command	*no event detected*	charCode = 0, 0, 0, 0 keyCode = 16, 17, 18, 91 which = 16, 17, 18, 91 key = "Shift", "Control", "Alt", "Meta"
←, ↑, →, ↓	*no event detected*	charCode = 0, 0, 0, 0 keyCode = 37, 38, 39, 40 which = 37, 38, 39, 40 key = "ArrowLeft", "ArrowUp", "ArrowRight", "ArrowDown"

In addition to character keys, JavaScript supports the **modifier keys** Alt, Ctrl, Shift, and Command through the use of the `altKey`, `ctrlKey`, `shiftKey`, and `metaKey` properties, returning `true` if those keys are used in the event. These properties are also associated with mouse events so that event handlers and listeners can be written for events involving both mouse actions and modifier keys.

REFERENCE

Responding to Keyboard Events

- To respond to the action of pressing down a keyboard key, use the `keydown` event.
- To respond to the action of pressing a keyboard key generating a character, use the `keypress` event.
- To respond to the action of releasing a keyboard key, use the `keyup` event.
- To return the character code of the key typed in the `keypress` event, use

   `evt.charCode`

   where `evt` is the event object for the keypress event.
- To return the keyboard code for the key used in the `keydown` or `keyup` event, use either of the following:

   `evt.keyCode`

   or

   `evt.which`

- To determine whether the Alt, Shift, Ctrl, or Command keys are used in the event, use

   `evt.altKey`
   `evt.shiftKey`
   `evt.ctrlKey`
   `evt.metaKey`

   which will return `true` if those keys are used and `false` otherwise.

Rebecca suggest you modify the setBackground() function so that, if the user is pressing down the Alt key while dragging the mouse, the cell's background color changes to white, indicating an empty cell. Users can erase false guesses by holding down the Shift key as the mouse is dragged, changing the puzzle cell's background color back to its original gold. Finally, if no modifier key is pressed down, the puzzle cell's background color is changed to gray, indicating a filled cell that is part of the puzzle image.

To respond to keyboard events and properties:

1. Return to the **jpf_hanjie.js** file in your editor and go to the setBackground() function.

2. Within the setBackground() function, delete the initial command in the function that sets the value of the cellBackground variable: `cellBackground = "rgb(101, 101, 101)";`

3. Replace the deleted command with the following conditional statements that set the value of the cellBackground variable based on which, if any, modifier key are pressed down.

```
// Set the background based on the keyboard key
if (e.shiftKey) {
    cellBackground = "rgb(233, 207, 29)";
} else if (e.altKey) {
    cellBackground = "rgb(255, 255, 255)";
} else {
    cellBackground = "rgb(101, 101, 101)";
}
```

Figure 11-30 highlights the new code in the setBackground() function.

Figure 11-30   Changing the background color for different modifier keys

if the Shift key is pressed down, changes the background to gold

if the Alt key is pressed down, changes the background to white

otherwise, changes the background to gray

```
function setBackground(e) {
   // Set the background based on the keyboard key
   if (e.shiftKey) {
      cellBackground = "rgb(233, 207, 29)";
   } else if (e.altKey) {
      cellBackground = "rgb(255, 255, 255)";
   } else {
      cellBackground = "rgb(101, 101, 101)";
   }

   e.target.style.backgroundColor = cellBackground;
```

sets the background-color style to the value of the cellBackground variable

4. Save your changes to the file and then reload **jpf_hanjie.html** in your browser.

5. Start drawing the puzzle solution by clicking and dragging the mouse pointer over the puzzle. Then, mark cells you think are empty in the solution by holding down the Alt key as you click and drag the pointer over the puzzle. Finally, erase your guesses by holding down the Shift key as you click and drag the mouse pointer over the puzzle.

Figure 11-31 shows the Puzzle 1 table with filled cells in gray, empty cells in white, and erased cells back to their original gold.

Figure 11-31   Puzzle table with cells of gold, white, and gray

the gray color is applied by clicking and dragging the mouse pointer

return the cell color to gold by holding down the Shift key while clicking and dragging the mouse pointer over a white or gray cell

the white color is applied by pressing down the Alt key while dragging the mouse pointer

Rebecca wants users to have a visual indication when the Shift or Alt keys are in use. She suggests you change the appearance of the mouse pointer when the user is pressing down the Shift or Alt keys.

Changing the Cursor Style

Cursors can be defined using the following CSS cursor style

```
cursor: cursorTypes;
```

where *cursorTypes* is a comma-separated list of cursor types. The equivalent JavaScript command is:

```
object.style.cursor = cursorTypes;
```

where *object* is the page object that will display the cursor style when hovered over by the mouse pointer. Figure 11-32 lists some of the different generic cursor types built into the browser.

Figure 11-32	Cursor Styles

Cursor	Style	Cursor	Style
╋	crosshair	↕	n-resize
▷	default	⤢	ne-resize
▷?	help	⟷	e-resize
✛	move	⤡	se-resize
🖑	pointer	↕	s-resize
I	text	⤢	sw-resize
◯	wait	⟷	w-resize
		⤡	nw-resize

For example, the following code changes the cursor style for the hanjieGrid object to the pointer cursor.

```
document.getElementById("hanjieGrid").style.cursor = "pointer";
```

Note that the actual appearance of the cursor is dependent on the browser and operating system. If none of the generic types fit the design of your project, you can create a customized cursor from an image file using

```
url(image)
```

TIP

Cursor image files should be 32 × 32 pixels in size for the best appearance and browser support.

where *image* is an image file. Most browsers currently support the PNG, GIF, JPG, CUR, and SVG image formats. At the time of this writing Microsoft Edge and Internet Explorer only support cursors created in the CUR and ANI formats. Custom cursors should be listed first and the generic cursor should always be listed last so that the browser can display something if it can't support a custom cursor image. For example, the following style applies the cursor image in the jpf_pencil.png file but if that is not supported, the browser will display a cursor using the generic pointer image:

```
cursor: url(jpf_pencil.png), pointer;
```

By default, the click point for a cursor is located in the top-left corner of the cursor image at the coordinates (0, 0). To specify a different location, add the (x, y) coordinates of the click point to the cursor definition as follows

```
url(image) x y
```

where *x* is the *x*-coordinate of the click point and *y* is the *y*-coordinate in pixels. Thus, the following cursor sets the click point for jpf_pencil.png image at the coordinates (12, 6):

```
cursor: url(jpf_pencil.png) 12 6, pointer;
```

Appying a Cursor Style

- To define the cursor used for an element, apply the CSS style

  ```
  cursor: cursorTypes;
  ```

  where *cursorTypes* is a comma-separated list of cursor types.
- To create a customized cursor based on an image, use the cursor type

  ```
  url(image) x y
  ```

  where *image* is the image file and *x* and *y* are optional values that specify the (*x*, *y*) coordinate of the cursor's click point.

Rebecca has created three custom images for use as cursors in the Hanjie puzzle. The jpf_pencil.png file displays a pencil image, which she wants used as a cursor when the user is marking filled cells. The jpf_cross.png file should be applied when the user is marking empty cells. Finally, the jpf_eraser.png file should be applied when the user is erasing filled and empty cells. Before and after marking up the puzzle table, the cursor should display the pencil image within the puzzle cells.

To define the cursor styles:

1. Return to the **jpf_hanjie.js** file in your editor and go to the setupPuzzle() function.

2. Within the setupPuzzle() function, set up the default cursor for the puzzle cells. Within the for loop that defines the properties of the puzzle cells, add the following code:

   ```
   // Use a pencil image as the cursor
   puzzleCells[i].style.cursor = "url(jpf_pencil.png), pointer";
   ```

   Figure 11-33 highlights the added code in the setupPuzzle() function.

Figure 11-33   **Setting cursor style for the puzzle cells**

```
function setupPuzzle() {
   /* Match all of the data cells in the puzzle */
   puzzleCells = document.querySelectorAll("table#hanjieGrid td");

   /* Set the initial color of each cell to gold */
   for (var i = 0; i < puzzleCells.length; i++) {
      puzzleCells[i].style.backgroundColor = "rgb(233, 207, 29)";
      // Set the cell background color in response to the mousedown event
      puzzleCells[i].onmousedown = setBackground;
      // Use a pencil image as the cursor
      puzzleCells[i].style.cursor = "url(jpf_pencil.png), pointer";
   }
}
```

uses the pencil image as the cursor for puzzle cells

if the image file is not supported, uses the generic pointer cursor

3. Next, insert commands to change the cursor based on which keyboard key is pressed down. Scroll down to the setBackground() function. At the top of the function (just after the opening curly brace), insert the following line that declares the cursorType variable:

```
var cursorType;
```

4. If the Shift key is pressed down, add the following command to the `if` condition:

```
cursorType = "url(jpf_eraser.png), cell";
```

5. If the Alt key is pressed down, add the following command to the `else if` condition:

```
cursorType = "url(jpf_cross.png), crosshair";
```

6. Finally, if no key is pressed down, add the following command to the `else` condition:

```
cursorType = "url(jpf_pencil.png), pointer";
```

7. Within the for loop in the setBackground() function, add the following command to change the cursor style of all puzzle cells to the value of cursorType.

```
puzzleCells[i].style.cursor = cursorType;
```

Figure 11-34 highlights the revised code in the setBackground() function.

Figure 11-34	Applying different cursor styles for marking the puzzle

declares a variable to store the cursor type

if the Shift key is pressed, displays the eraser image or the generic cell cursor

if the Alt key is pressed, displays the cross image or the generic crosshair cursor

otherwise, displays the pencil image or the generic pointer cursor

applies the cursorType cursor to all puzzle cells

```javascript
function setBackground(e) {
   var cursorType;

   // Set the background based on the keyboard key
   if (e.shiftKey) {
      cellBackground = "rgb(233, 207, 29)";
      cursorType = "url(jpf_eraser.png), cell";
   } else if (e.altKey) {
      cellBackground = "rgb(255, 255, 255)";
      cursorType = "url(jpf_cross.png), crosshair";
   } else {
      cellBackground = "rgb(101, 101, 101)";
      cursorType = "url(jpf_pencil.png), pointer";
   }

   e.target.style.backgroundColor = cellBackground;

   // Create an event listener for every puzzle cell
   for (var i = 0; i < puzzleCells.length; i++) {
      puzzleCells[i].addEventListener("mouseenter", extendBackground);
      puzzleCells[i].style.cursor = cursorType;
   }

   // Prevent the default action of selecting table text
   e.preventDefault();
}
```

8. Finally, when the mouse button is released, the cursor style for the puzzle cells should go back to the pencil pointer. Go to the endBackground() function and add the following command to the `for` loop:

```
puzzleCells[i].style.cursor = "url(jpf_pencil.png), pointer";
```

Figure 11-35 highlights the new code in the endBackground() function.

Figure 11-35	Restoring the cursor image

```
function endBackground() {
    // Remove the event listener for every puzzle cell
    for (var i = 0; i < puzzleCells.length; i++) {
        puzzleCells[i].removeEventListener("mouseenter", extendBackground);
        puzzleCells[i].style.cursor = "url(jpf_pencil.png), pointer";
    }
}
```

after the mouse button is released, sets the cursor styles for the puzzle cells to the pencil or pointer cursor

9. Save your changes to the file and then reload **jpf_hanjie.html** in your browser. Verify: a) the default cursor within the puzzle table is a pencil, b) holding down the Alt key while clicking and dragging within the table changes the cursor to a cross, and c) holding down the Shift key while clicking and dragging turns the cursor to an eraser. See Figure 11-36.

Figure 11-36	Cursors displayed when solving the puzzle

pencil cursor used to mark filled cells

cross cursor used to mark cells as empty

eraser cursor used to erase marked cells

© Courtesy Patrick Carey

Trouble? If you are using Microsoft Edge or Internet Explorer, you will see the generic pointer, crosshair, and cell pointers in place of the pencil, cross, and eraser images.

You have completed your work in designing a mouse and keyboard interface for the Hanjie puzzle. Using the event handlers and listeners you developed, users can more easily work toward solving the puzzle.

Problem Solving: Object Detection with the IE Event Model

If you are working with older browsers, you might need to make your scripts compatible with the **Internet Explorer event model**, which was the event model used by the IE browser prior to IE 9. There are several crucial differences between the standard model and the IE event model. Under the IE event model, the event object is referenced with the object:

```
window.event
```

or more simply:

```
event
```

The IE browser did not support the addEventListener() and removeEventListener() methods. Instead it used

```
attachEvent(onevent, function)
```

and

```
detachEvent(onevent, function)
```

where *event* is the name of the event and *function* is the function run in response. Events in the IE event model were only attached during the bubbling phase. There was no control of events during the capture phase. The names used for event properties and methods often differed between the standard and IE event models. For example, the *evt*.target property in the standard event model is replaced with `event.srcElement` in the IE event model.

To support both event models, programmers use **object detection** within an `if` structure that determines whether the browser supported a particular object, property, or method. The general structure is

```
if (object) {
   commands
}
```

where *object* is an object or property or method and *commands* are the commands that will be run only if the browser recognizes the object. An `if` structure that tests for the support of the IE event model would appear as follows:

```
if (window.event) {
   IE event model commands
} else {

   standard event model commands
}
```

If `window.event` is recognized as a JavaScript object by the browser, the IE commands are run; otherwise commands for the standard event model are run.

You can learn more about the IE event model at the website for the Internet Explorer browser. With more recent versions of Internet Explorer supporting the standard event model and with the introduction of Microsoft Edge, it is less crucial to support the IE event model; however, it may still be an issue if your work involves managing legacy websites.

In the next session, you will complete the puzzle app by developing functions to test whether the user has successfully completed the puzzle and to provide helpful hints to those users who are stuck.

REVIEW

Session 11.2 Quick Check

1. Which mouse event is fired when the right mouse button is pressed and released?
2. Provide the expression to return the *x*-coordinate of the mouse event relative to the document. Assume that the name of your event object is evt.
3. What is the difference between an event handler and an event listener?
4. Write an event listener to run the showFinal() function in response to the click event in the document body during the capture phase.
5. Provide code to remove the event listener described in the previous question.
6. What character code value is supplied by the `charCode` property during the `keyup` event?
7. Provide code to return a Boolean value indicating whether the Command or Windows key was used in an event. Assume a name of evt for the event object.
8. Provide a JavaScript command to set the cursor style of the document to the image file dragMe.png with the click point at the coordinates (12, 15). Use the generic cursor named "move" for browsers that don't support the cursor image file.

Session 11.3 Visual Overview:

An **anonymous function** is a function without a name that can be used as the function definition called within a method or another function.

This command listens for the click event on the Show Solution button.

The `confirm()` method creates a dialog box that returns a value of true or false.

The commands within the anonymous function remove the inline background-color styles from every puzzle cell.

This is the message displayed in the confirm dialog box.

```
// Add an event listener to the Show Solution button
document.getElementById("solve").addEventListener("click",

    function() {
        if (confirm("You will lose your work on the puzzle. Continue?")) {

            // Remove the inline backgroundColor style from each cell
            for (var i = 0; i < puzzleCells.length; i++) {
                puzzleCells[i].style.backgroundColor = "";
            }

        }
    }
);
```

Anonymous Functions and Dialog Boxes

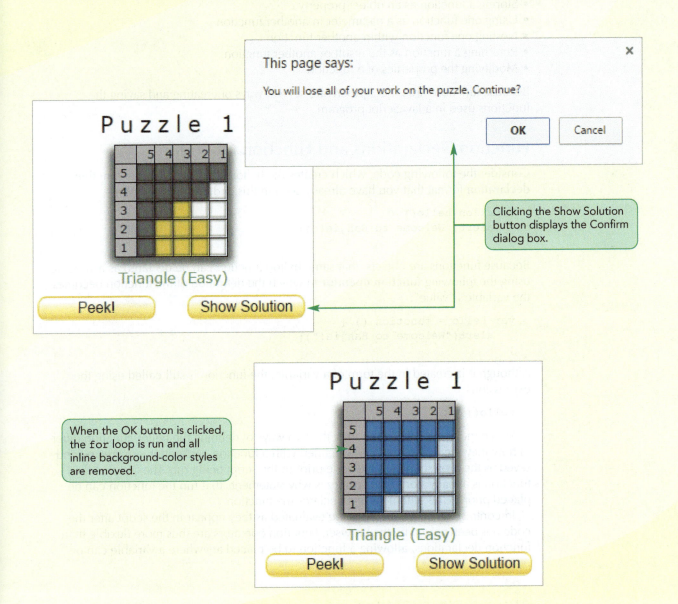

This page says:

You will lose all of your work on the puzzle. Continue?

OK   Cancel

Clicking the Show Solution button displays the Confirm dialog box.

When the OK button is clicked, the `for` loop is run and all inline background-color styles are removed.

Puzzle 1
Triangle (Easy)
Peek!   Show Solution

Working with Functions as Objects

Thus far, functions have been treated simply as blocks of code that execute a series of tasks or return a calculated value. However, almost everything in JavaScript is an object and functions are no exception. The fact that functions are objects means that anything you can do with a regular object you can do with a function, including

- Storing a function as variable
- Storing a function as an object property
- Using one function as a parameter in another function
- Nesting one function within another function
- Returning a function as the result of another function
- Modifying the properties of a function

Because functions are objects, there are several ways of creating and saving the functions used in a JavaScript program.

Function Declarations and Function Operators

Consider the following code, which creates the hello() function using the **function declaration** format that you have already seen in this and previous tutorials:

```
function hello() {
    alert("Welcome to Hanjie!");
}
```

Because functions are objects, that same hello() function can be declared as a variable using the following **function operator** in which the definition of the function becomes the variable's "value":

```
var hello = function () {
    alert("Welcome to Hanjie!");
}
```

Although it is created in the form of a variable, the function is still called using the expression:

```
hello()
```

While the end result is the same, the two ways of defining the hello() function differ in how they are stored. Functions defined with a function declaration are created and saved as the browser parses the code prior to the script being run. The fact that the function is already stored in memory is why statements that run the function can be placed prior to the statement that declares the function.

In contrast, function operators are evaluated as they appear in the script after the code has been parsed by the browser. Function operators are thus more flexible than function declarations, allowing a function to be placed anywhere a variable can be placed.

Anonymous Functions

You may have noticed that in the function operator format, the definition of the hello() function was specified in the following structure:

```
function() {
    commands
}
```

The structure is known as an anonymous function because it has the form of a function declaration but without the function name. By contrast, functions that are named are called **named functions**. An anonymous function can be inserted into any expression where a function reference is required. For example, the following code that calls the hello() function in response to the load event

```
function hello() {
    alert("Welcome to Hanjie!");
}

window.onload = hello;
```

could be replaced with an anonymous function that inserts the function directly in the event handler:

```
window.onload =
    function () {
        alert("Welcome to Hanjie!");
    };
```

If an event listener is used, an anonymous function could be inserted as a parameter indicating what actions should be performed in response to the event:

```
window.addEventListener("load",
    function() {
        alert("Welcome to Hanjie!");
    }
);
```

Anonymous functions have several advantages over named functions. For example, they are more concise and easier to manage because the function is directly included with the expression that invokes it, thus limiting the scope of the function to exactly where it is needed.

REFERENCE

Using an Anonymous Function with Events

- To use an anonymous function as an event handler, apply the following code:

  object.on*event* = function() {*commands*}

- To use an anonymous function with an event listener, apply:

  object.addEventListener(*event*, function() {*commands*}
  [, *capture*]);

Rebecca wants you to create an event listener that will display the solution for the Hanjie puzzle when the Show Solution button is clicked. To display the solution, you will remove any inline styles that the user might have already applied to the puzzle cells with the mouse and keyboard. Rather than declaring a named function to perform this operation, insert the commands as an anonymous function.

To use an anonymous function:

1. If you took a break after the previous session, make sure **jpf_hanjie.js** is open in your editor.

2. Add the following code at the end of the init() function:

```
// Add an event listener to the Show Solution button
document.getElementById("solve").addEventListener("click",
    function() {
    }
);
```

3. Within the anonymous function, insert the following `for` loop:

```
// Remove the inline backgroundColor style from each cell
for (var i = 0; i < puzzleCells.length; i++) {
   puzzleCells[i].style.backgroundColor = "";
}
```

Note that by setting the value of the `background-color` style to an empty text string, that inline style is erased, leaving only those styles defined in the jpf_hanjie.css style sheet. Figure 11-37 highlights the code for the event listener.

Figure 11-37   Using an anonymous function

```
setupPuzzle();

// Add an event handler for the mouseup event
document.addEventListener("mouseup", endBackground);

// Add an event listener to the Show Solution button
document.getElementById("solve").addEventListener("click",
   function() {
      // Remove the inline backgroundColor style from each cell
      for (var i = 0; i < puzzleCells.length; i++) {
         puzzleCells[i].style.backgroundColor = "";
      }
   }
);
}
```

listens for the Show Solution button click event

inserts the response to the click event as an anonymous function

erases the inline background-color style from each puzzle cell by setting the style value to an empty text string

4. Save your changes to the file and then reload **jpf_hanjie.html** in your browser.

5. Mark up the contents of the Puzzle 1 table using filled and empty cells and then click the **Show Solution** button to erase the inline styles, leaving only the styles from the jpf_hanjie.css style sheet file. See Figure 11-38.

Figure 11-38   **Showing the puzzle solution**

puzzle cell colors set using the mouse and keyboard

click the Show Solution button to erase the inline styles, leaving only the external style sheet styles

Solving Hanjie puzzles can be extremely difficult because a mistake in one cell can cause multiple mistakes across the puzzle. Rebecca wants you to write a function that highlights user mistakes without revealing the complete solution to the puzzle.

Passing Variable Values into Anonymous Functions

Recall that JavaScript supports two types of variables: global variables, which are declared outside of any function and thus are accessible throughout the app, and local variables, which are declared within a function and are only accessible to code within that function. The Hanjie puzzle app contains two global variables: the puzzleCells array referencing the puzzle cells and the cellBackground variable storing the color value applied by the mouse pointer to the puzzle cells.

While those variables are necessary for this assignment, global variables should be avoided when possible. The problem is that, because global variables are accessible to every function in the application, the task of tracking which functions are using and modifying them becomes increasingly difficult as the application grows in size and complexity. Good coding practice dictates that variables should be limited to local scope, so they are confined within the function in which they are used.

An advantage of using anonymous functions is that they reduce the need for global variables because they perform their actions locally within a function. The following code demonstrates how an anonymous function can access the local msgText variable for use in an event handler:

```
var init() {
   var msgText = "Welcome to Hanjie!");
   document.getElementById("startUp").onclick =
      function () {
         alert(msgText);
      };
}
```

If the event handler in this example were referencing a named function defined elsewhere in the file, the msgText variable would have to be made global to be accessible.

You will use this aspect of anonymous functions to write a function providing puzzle hints to the user. Rebecca suggests that all cells that the user has incorrectly marked as filled (with the gray background) should be displayed in red, while all cells that the user has incorrectly marked as empty (with the white background) should be displayed in pink.

Recall from Figure 11-4 that cells that are part of the puzzle image belong to the filled class and cells that are not belong to the empty class. Thus, you can create object collections for both classes of cells using the following commands:

```
var filled = document.querySelectorAll("table#hanjieGrid
td.filled");
var empty = document.querySelectorAll("table#hanjieGrid td.empty");
```

Add these two variables as local variables within the setupPuzzle() function.

To create the local variables:

1. Return to the **jpf_hanjie.js** file in your editor.

2. At the end of the setupPuzzle() function, insert the following statements to declare the filled and empty variables:

```
// Create object collections of the filled and empty cells
var filled = document.querySelectorAll("table#hanjieGrid
td.filled");
var empty = document.querySelectorAll("table#hanjieGrid
td.empty");
```

Figure 11-39 highlights the new code in the file.

Figure 11-39	Declaring the filled and empty variables

```
function setupPuzzle() {
   /* Match all of the data cells in the puzzle */
   puzzleCells = document.querySelectorAll("table#hanjieGrid td");

   /* Set the initial color of each cell to gold */
   for (var i = 0; i < puzzleCells.length; i++) {
      puzzleCells[i].style.backgroundColor = "rgb(233, 207, 29)";
      // Set the cell background color in response to the mousedown event
      puzzleCells[i].onmousedown = setBackground;
      // Use a pencil image as the cursor
      puzzleCells[i].style.cursor = "url(jpf_pencil.png), pointer";
   }

   // Create object collections of the filled and empty cells
   var filled = document.querySelectorAll("table#hanjieGrid td.filled");
   var empty = document.querySelectorAll("table#hanjieGrid td.empty");
}
```

collection of cells that should be filled by the user

collection of cells that should be left empty by the user

You will use the filled and empty variables to highlight user mistakes. Cells incorrectly marked in white should be displayed in pink, while cells incorrectly marked in gray should be displayed in red. Add code to change the background colors of the puzzle cell to an anonymous function running within an event listener.

To highlight incorrectly marked cells:

1. Add the following event listener immediately after the declaration of the filled and empty variables, to run an anonymous function in response to clicking the Peek button.

```
// Create an event listener to highlight incorrect cells
document.getElementById("peek").addEventListener("click",
   function() {
   }
);
```

Figure 11-40 highlights the code.

Figure 11-40	Creating an event listener for the Peek button

```
// Create object collections of the filled and empty cells
var filled = document.querySelectorAll("table#hanjieGrid td.filled");
var empty = document.querySelectorAll("table#hanjieGrid td.empty");

// Create an event listener to highlight incorrect cells
document.getElementById("peek").addEventListener("click",
   function() {
   }
);
}
```

runs anonymous function in response to the event

creates an event listener for the click event with the Peek! button

2. The anonymous function needs to loop through the filled and empty collections and identify the incorrectly marked cells. A cell from the filled class is incorrect if the user has marked it in white when it should have been filled with gray. If a filled cell is incorrectly marked white, change the background color to pink by inserting the following code into the anonymous function:

```
// Display incorrect white cells in pink
for (var i = 0; i < filled.length; i++) {
   if (filled[i].style.backgroundColor === "rgb(255, 255,
255)"){
      filled[i].style.backgroundColor = "rgb(255, 211, 211)";
   }
}
```

3. Next, loop through the cells in the empty class. An empty cell is incorrect if the user has marked it gray when it should have been filled with white. If an empty cell is incorrectly marked gray, change the background color to red by adding the following code to the anonymous function.

```
// Display incorrect gray cells in red
for (var i = 0; i < empty.length; i++) {
   if (empty[i].style.backgroundColor === "rgb(101, 101,
101)"){
      empty[i].style.backgroundColor = "rgb(255, 101, 101)";
   }
}
```

Figure 11-41 highlights and describes the code within the anonymous function.

Figure 11-41	Highlighting incorrect cells

```
// Create an event listener to highlight incorrect cells
document.getElementById("peek").addEventListener("click",
    function() {
        // Display incorrect white cells in pink
        for (var i = 0; i < filled.length; i++) {
            if (filled[i].style.backgroundColor === "rgb(255, 255, 255)"){
                filled[i].style.backgroundColor = "rgb(255, 211, 211)";
            }
        }

        // Display incorrect gray cells in red
        for (var i = 0; i < empty.length; i++) {
            if (empty[i].style.backgroundColor === "rgb(101, 101, 101)"){
                empty[i].style.backgroundColor = "rgb(255, 101, 101)";
            }
        }
    }
);
```

if a cell is incorrectly displayed in white ...

If cell is incorrectly displayed in gray ...

... change the background color to pink

... change the background color to red

4. Save your changes and then reload **jpf_hanjie.html** in your browser.

5. Mark up Puzzle 1 as shown in Figure 11-42 and then click the **Peek!** button. Verify that the incorrectly marked cells are highlighted in pink and red.

Figure 11-42	Viewing incorrect cells

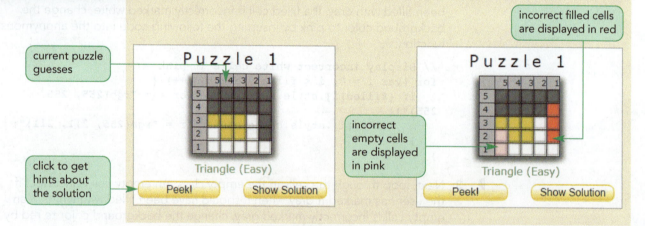

current puzzle guesses

click to get hints about the solution

incorrect filled cells are displayed in red

incorrect empty cells are displayed in pink

Creating Timed Commands with Anonymous Functions

REFERENCE

- To run an anonymous function after a time delay, use:

  ```
  setTimeout(function() {commands}, delay);
  ```

- To run an anonymous function at specific time intervals, use:

  ```
  setInterval(function() {commands}, interval);
  ```

Rebecca wants the red and pink color hints to appear only briefly. Create an anonymous function that changes all red cells in the puzzle table back to gray and all pink cells back to white and insert the function as a parameter value of the `setTimeout()` method. Set the time delay to 500 milliseconds so that the anonymous function is run after a half-second delay.

To remove the puzzle hints:

▶ **1.** Return to the **jpf_hanjie.js** file in your editor and scroll as needed to the setupPuzzle() function.

▶ **2.** Directly after the `for` loop that marks incorrect cells in red, insert the following `setTimeout()` method:

```
// Remove the hints after 0.5 seconds
setTimeout(
    function() {
    }, 500);
```

Figure 11-43 highlights the code for the `setTimeout()` method.

Figure 11-43	Using an anonymous function with the setTimeout() method

```
        // Display incorrect gray cells in red
        for (var i = 0; i < empty.length; i++) {
            if (empty[i].style.backgroundColor === "rgb(101, 101, 101)"){
                empty[i].style.backgroundColor = "rgb(255, 101, 101)";
            }
        }

        // Remove the hints after 0.5 seconds
        setTimeout(
            function() {
            }, 500);
    }
);
```

runs anonymous function after a 0.5 second delay

sets the delay time in milliseconds

▶ **3.** Within the anonymous function, insert the following commands to change all pink cells back to white and all red cells back to gray.

```
// Change pink cells to white and red cells to gray
for (var i = 0; i < puzzleCells.length; i++) {
    if (puzzleCells[i].style.backgroundColor === "rgb(255, 211, 211)") {
        puzzleCells[i].style.backgroundColor = "rgb(255, 255, 255)";
    }
    if (puzzleCells[i].style.backgroundColor === "rgb(255, 101, 101)") {
        puzzleCells[i].style.backgroundColor = "rgb(101, 101, 101)";
    }
}
```

Figure 11-44 highlights the code within the anonymous function.

Figure 11-44 **Removing the puzzle hints**

```
// Remove the hints after 0.5 seconds
setTimeout(
    function() {
        // Change pink cells to white and red cells to gray
        for (var i = 0; i < puzzleCells.length; i++) {
            if (puzzleCells[i].style.backgroundColor === "rgb(255, 211, 211)") {
                puzzleCells[i].style.backgroundColor = "rgb(255, 255, 255)";
            }
            if (puzzleCells[i].style.backgroundColor === "rgb(255, 101, 101)") {
                puzzleCells[i].style.backgroundColor = "rgb(101, 101, 101)";
            }
        }
    }
}, 500);
```

changes all pink cells back to white

changes colors after a half-second delay

changes all red cells back to gray

4. Save your changes and then reload **jpf_hanjie.html** in your browser.

5. Complete Puzzle 1 with some correct and incorrect guesses and then click the **Peek!** button. Verify that the hints highlighting your mistakes appear only briefly before your guesses are restored.

One of the challenges of anonymous functions is keeping track of all of the nested levels of functions and procedures. In this last task, the setupPuzzle() function contained an event listener, which contained an anonymous function, which contained the `setTimeout()` method, which contained another anonymous function, which contained a `for` loop, which contained an `if` statement! So, while the code is efficient, it is easy to misplace a curly brace or forget a closing parenthesis. Many JavaScript editors use color coding to make it easier to note when functions and methods have not been properly closed and you should indent your code as a visual aid to tracking the nested levels. Finally, you can avoid coding errors by gradually drilling down into the lower levels of the code. Do not insert a new nested level of procedures and functions until the outer levels are free of syntax errors.

INSIGHT

Storing Data using the `data-*` Attribute

In some page elements, you might want to include data values along with the element text, such as including personnel information within the element tag that marks the employee name. You can insert a data value into an element using the following `data-*` attribute

```
<element data-name="value"> …
```

where *name* is a user-defined name for the data and *value* is the data's value. For example, the following code stores three data values labeled `data-section`, `data-position`, and `data-hire-date` within a span element that marks the employee's name.

```
<span id="employee"
    data-section="IT" data-position="Manager"
    data-hire-date="2015-08-01">
    Rebecca Peretz
</span>
```

Each `data-*` attribute becomes part of the element's **dataset object** and can be accessed in JavaScript with the following reference

```
object.dataset.name
```

where *name* is the name portion of the `data-*` attribute. If `data-name` contains several hyphenated words, reference the data set name using camel case. The following code demonstrates how to access the three `data-*` attribute values that provide information about Rebecca Peretz:

```
var employee = document.getElementById("employee");
var section = employee.dataset.section;
var position = employee.dataset.position;
var hireDate = employee.dataset.hireDate;
```

Be aware that the `dataset` property is not supported by older browsers, such as Internet Explorer prior to IE 11. If you need to support older browser versions, consider using the `getAttribute()` method instead.

Rebecca likes the work you have done but she is concerned that when a user switches from one puzzle to another, the work on the current puzzle will be completely lost. She would like the app to display a warning message to users. You can do this with an alert dialog box.

Displaying Dialog Boxes

You have already created alert dialog boxes in Tutorial 9 by using the following `alert()` method

```
alert(text)
```

TIP

You can add a line return to the dialog box message text by including the character code \n within the text string.

where *text* is the message displayed in the alert dialog box. When an alert dialog box is displayed, the execution of the program code halts until the user clicks the OK button in the dialog box. The alert message is limited to plain text and cannot include HTML-formatted text. For more elaborate alert dialog boxes, you would have to use JavaScript to construct the appearance and content of a custom dialog box; that topic is beyond the scope of this tutorial.

JavaScript also supports confirmation and prompt dialog boxes. The description of each type of dialog box is displayed in Figure 11-45.

Figure 11-45 JavaScript dialog boxes

Dialog Box	Description	Example
alert(*text*)	Displays an alert message	alert("Welcome to Hanjie!");
		This page says: ✕ Welcome to Hanjie! OK
confirm(*text*)	Displays a confirmation box, returning a value of true if the user clicks the OK button and false if the Cancel button is clicked	var quitGame = confirm("Quit the Game?");
		This page says: ✕ Quit the Game? OK Cancel
prompt(*text* [, *defaultInput*])	Displays a prompt box, prompting the user to enter input text, where *defaultInput* is an optional attribute specifying the default input value; if the user clicks OK the input text is returned, if the Cancel button is clicked a value of null is returned	var gameType = prompt("Enter your Game", "Hanjie");
		This page says: ✕ Enter your Game Hanjie OK Cancel

The exact appearance of the dialog boxes is determined by the operating system and the browser. There are no JavaScript properties or CSS styles to modify the dialog box aside from specifying the text of the dialog box message.

REFERENCE

Displaying Browser Dialog Boxes

- To display a message in an alert box, apply

  alert(*text*)

  where *text* is the text of the dialog box message.
- To display a confirmation dialog box that returns a value of true or false, apply:

  confirm(*text*)

- To display a dialog box in which the user can enter a text string, apply

  prompt(*text* [, *defaultInput*])

  where *defaultInput* is an optional attribute specifying the default input value.

Rebecca suggests that the puzzle app display a confirm dialog box before swapping one puzzle for another by adding the following `if` structure to the swapPuzzle() function:

```
if (confirm(prompt)) {
   swap puzzle commands
}
```

Because the confirm() method returns a value of either true or false, placing the dialog box within an `if` statement causes the command block to be run only when a user clicks the OK button. If the user clicks the Cancel button, the swap puzzle commands are skipped. Add this structure to the swapPuzzle() function now.

To use a confirm dialog box:

1. Return to the **jpf_hanjie.js** file in your editor and go to the swapPuzzle() function.

2. Directly after the opening function line, insert the following statement:

   ```
   if (confirm("You will lose all of your work on the puzzle!
   Continue?")) {
   ```

3. Scroll down to the bottom of the swapPuzzle() function. Before the closing curly brace, insert the closing curly brace **}** to close off the `if` statement and close the rest of the commands within a command block.

4. Indent the lines within the command block three spaces to make your code easier to read. Figure 11-46 shows the revised swapPuzzle() function.

| Figure 11-46 | Applying a confirm dialog box |

5. Save your changes to the file and then reload **jpf_hanjie.html** in your browser.

6. Click the **Puzzle 2** button to switch from Puzzle 1 to Puzzle 2. Verify that the browser displays a confirm dialog box. See Figure 11-47.

Figure 11-47   Switching from Puzzle 1 to Puzzle 2

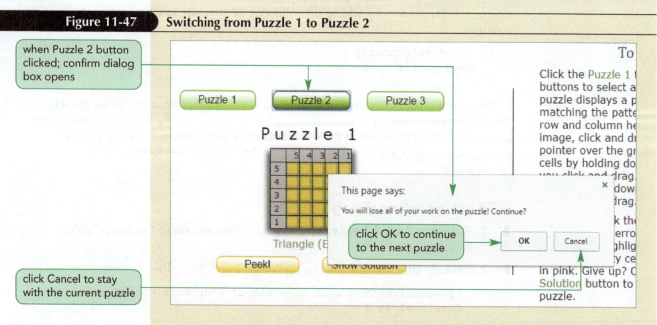

7. Click the **OK** button to load the second puzzle.

8. Click the **Puzzle 3** button to load the third puzzle; but, in response to the confirmation dialog box, click the **Cancel** button. Verify that the second puzzle remains displayed on the page.

Trouble? If the puzzle app fails to switch puzzles, check your code and verify that you enclosed all of the command block within the swapPuzzle() function within the curly braces.

The last task remaining for the Hanjie puzzle app is to notify the user when the puzzle has been successfully solved. A puzzle is solved when the user has correctly drawn the puzzle image without missing any cells or including cells that aren't part of the puzzle image. If even one cell violates either of these two conditions, then the puzzle is not yet solved.

Rebecca suggest you test the puzzle solution at every occurrence of a mouseup event within the puzzle table. If the puzzle is solved, Rebecca wants the browser to display an alert box with the message "You Solved the Puzzle" displayed to the user.

To test the puzzle solution:

1. Return to the **jpf_hanjie.js** file in your editor and go to the setupPuzzle() function.

2. Directly before the closing brace within the setupPuzzle() function, insert the following code adding an event handler to the puzzle table:

```
// Check the puzzle solution
document.getElementById("hanjieGrid").
addEventListener("mouseup",
    function() {
    });
```

Figure 11-48 highlights the newly added code.

| Figure 11-48 | Adding a mouseup event listener to the setupPuzzle() function |

```
/* Set the initial color of each cell to gold */
for (var i = 0; i < puzzleCells.length; i++) {
    puzzleCells[i].style.backgroundColor = "rgb(233, 207, 29)";
    // Set the cell background color in response to the mousedown event
    puzzleCells[i].onmousedown = setBackground;
    // Use a pencil image as the cursor
    puzzleCells[i].style.cursor = "url(jpf_pencil.png), pointer";
}

// Check the puzzle solution
document.getElementById("hanjieGrid").addEventListener("mouseup",
    function() {
    });
}
```

runs the anonymous function in response to the mouseup event within the puzzle table

inserts the anonymous function

3. Within the anonymous function, insert the following statement to set the initial value of the solved variable to `true`:

```
var solved = true;
```

4. Next, add the following `for` loop that examines every cell in the puzzle table to determine if the cell comes from the filled class and is not gray or comes from the empty class and is gray. If either of these conditions is true, then the puzzle solution is wrong and the value of the solved variable is changed to false and the loop stops. (There is no reason to continue the loop after the first incorrect cell is found.)

```
for (var i = 0; i< puzzleCells.length; i++) {
    if ((puzzleCells[i].className === "filled" &&
        puzzleCells[i].style.backgroundColor !== "rgb(101,
101, 101)")
        ||
        (puzzleCells[i].className === "empty" &&
        puzzleCells[i].style.backgroundColor === "rgb(101, 101,
101)")) {

            solved = false;
            break;
    }
}
```

5. After the `for` loop, display an alert box if solved is `true`, with a congratulatory message:

```
if (solved) alert("You Solved the Puzzle");
```

Figure 11-49 describes the newly added code in the anonymous function.

Figure 11-49	Check for the puzzle solution

tracks whether the puzzle is solved or not

loops through every cell in the puzzle table

if a cell from the filled class is not gray or a cell from the empty class is gray, changes the solved value to false and breaks off the loop

```javascript
// Check the puzzle solution
document.getElementById("hanjieGrid").addEventListener("mouseup",
    function() {
    var solved = true;
    for (var i = 0; i< puzzleCells.length; i++) {
        if ((puzzleCells[i].className === "filled" &&
            puzzleCells[i].style.backgroundColor !== "rgb(101, 101, 101)")
            ||
            (puzzleCells[i].className === "empty" &&
            puzzleCells[i].style.backgroundColor === "rgb(101, 101, 101)")) {

            solved = false;
            break;
        }
    }
    if (solved) alert("You Solved the Puzzle");
    }
);
```

if the loop ends with the value of the solved variable still true, display an alert dialog box

6. Save your changes to the file and then reload **jpf_hanjie.html** in your browser.

7. Use your mouse to solve Puzzle 1 and verify that when the puzzle is correctly solved, an alert box is automatically displayed on the `mouseup` event occurring within the puzzle table. See Figure 11-50.

Figure 11-50	A successfully completed puzzle

The complete puzzle image drawn with no missing or extra cells

dialog box notifying the user of the solved puzzle

8. Click the **OK** button to close the dialog box.

PROSKILLS

Problem Solving: Principles of Puzzle Design

Puzzles are among the oldest forms of entertainment, starting with the mazes and labyrinths created almost 4000 years ago and leading to the popular Sudoku and interactive puzzles of the present day. Puzzle games are a huge part of the game market. For example, the popular puzzle game Angry Birds topped a half-billion downloads within a year of its release, with gamers worldwide spending about 300 million minutes each day playing it. Puzzles can be placed within the following general categories:

- mathematics and logic (*Sudoku*, *Minesweeper*, *Rubik's Cube*)
- physics (*Angry Birds*, *Cut the Rope*)
- visual (*Where's Waldo?*, hidden objects)
- language (crosswords, anagrams, word search)
- situational (riddles, adventure games, *Twenty Questions*)

Regardless of its category, a successful puzzle needs well-defined rules with a clear over-all objective. One great challenge in puzzle design is to find the balance between making a puzzle too easy, which can be boring, and too hard, which users might find frustrating. Few users read tutorials; so, beginning puzzle levels should act as a training ground for success at higher levels. To keep gamers motivated, many designers stagger the difficulty levels so that after a particularly difficult level, an easier level follows—giving players a "mental breather" before moving on to new challenges.

Play testing is a key component in puzzle development. Testing should be done

- early in the development process and continuously as the puzzle is changed and modified
- with people who have not played the game before
- without providing extraneous hints or information to users

After each test, the user should be interviewed to learn which features of the game were successful, and which need more work and development. Compile statistics on the amount of time needed to complete each step. You might find that you need to add more training levels, or that your puzzle has unnecessary distractions or false clues. Finally, don't be afraid to remove a level from your design if it is stalling the user's progress through the game. Remember that the most successful puzzle game is one that teaches users how to solve it by playing it.

You have completed your work on the Hanjie puzzle app. Rebecca has left some other puzzles in the jpf_grids2.js file as a challenge if you want to try your hand at solving a new puzzle. However, that is not required to complete the assignment.

Rebecca wants to add other types of Japanese logic puzzles to the website. After working on this project, she is confident that you can develop more apps for her in the future.

Session 11.3 Quick Check

1. Provide the general code to create a function named showReport() using the function declaration format.

2. Provide the general code to create the showReport() function using a function operator.

3. What is an anonymous function?

4. Provide the general code that runs an anonymous function in response to the click event on the form button with the ID "formReport".

5. Provide the general code to run an anonymous function every 2 seconds.

6. Provide code to display a confirm dialog box with the message, "Export Report?". Store the results of the dialog box in the exportRep variable.

7. Provide code to display a prompt dialog box with the message "Enter Report Name". Set the default value to the text string "Income Statement" and store the results of the dialog box in the reportName variable.

8. Provide code to reference the `data-*` attributes for the following HTML element:

```
<div id="report" data-title="Earnings Report"
     data-author="Sam Browne"
     data-report-date="2018-07-01">
     …
</div>
```

PRACTICE

Review Assignments

Data Files needed for the Review Assignments: jpf_hitori_txt.html, jpf_hitori_txt.js, 3 CSS files, 1 JS file, 4 PNG files

Rebecca has asked for your help with another puzzle page. This page involves solving the Hitori puzzle. The Hitori puzzle is played on a grid of numbers. Each number is either circled or darkened; a darkened cell is referred to as a block. A successful solution will meet these three criteria:

1. The same number cannot be circled more than once in any row or column.
2. Blocks cannot touch horizontally or vertically, though they may be placed diagonally to one another.
3. Circled numbers must complete a continuous path throughout the grid; no circled number or group of circled numbers can be isolated from the others by a line of blocks.

Figure 11-51 shows a preview of the Hitori page you will create for Rebecca, with the solution of a sample Hitori puzzle.

Figure 11-51   **The Hitori Puzzle Page**

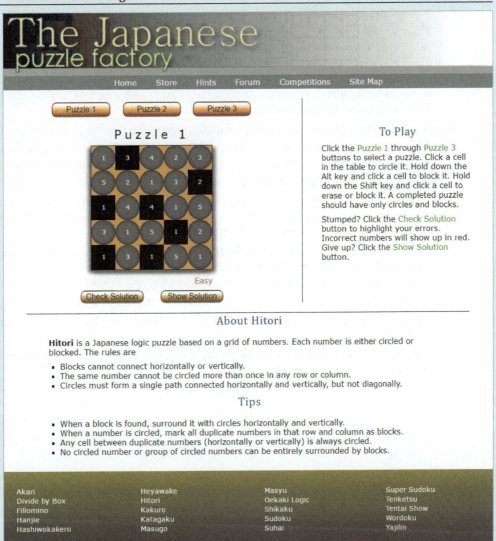

© Courtesy Patrick Carey

Rebecca wants you to create an interface for this puzzle similar to the one you created for the Hanjie puzzle. She already has stored three puzzles in a JavaScript file named jpf_grids3.js, and within that file she has created the following variables:

- hitori1Rating through hitori3Rating containing the difficulty ratings of the puzzles
- hitori1Numbers through hitori3Numbers containing the numbers in the puzzle grids
- hitori1Blocks through hitori3Blocks specifying the location of the blocks in the puzzle grids

Rebecca has provided you with the following functions:

- drawHitori(), which writes the HTML code of the puzzle table given the puzzle numbers, location of the puzzle blocks, and the puzzle rating
- checkSolution(), which returns an alert box indicating whether the puzzle has been solved
- showSolution(), which displays the puzzle solution

Your job will be to complete the application by writing the code that displays the puzzle and provides users with an interface to solve it.

Complete the following:

1. Use your editor to open the **jpf_hitori_txt.html** and **jpf_hitori_txt.js** files from the html11 ►
   review folder. Enter *your name* and *the date* in the comment section of each file, and save them
   as **jpf_hitori.html** and **jpf_hitori.js** respectively.

2. Go to the **jpf_hitori.html** file in your editor. Directly above the closing `</head>` tag, link the
   page to the **jpf_hitori.css** style sheet and to the **jpf_grids3.js** and **jpf_hitori.js** JavaScript files. Load
   both JavaScript files asynchronously. Take some time to study the contents of the HTML file and
   then close it, saving your changes.

3. Go to the **jpf_hitori.js** file in your editor. Directly below the comment section, declare the global
   allCells variable, which you will use to store an array of the puzzle cells in the Hitori table. Do
   not define a value for the variable yet.

4. Insert a command to run the startUp() function when the page is loaded by the browser.

5. Add the startUp() function, which displays the contents of Puzzle 1 after the page is loaded and
   sets up the initial event handlers. Within the function, add the following commands:

   a. Change the inner HTML of the element with the ID, "puzzleTitle" to the text "Puzzle 1".

   b. Call the drawHitori() function using the hitori1Numbers, hitori1Blocks, and hitori1Rating
      variables as parameter values and store the HTML code returned by the function in the inner
      HTML of the page element with the ID "puzzle".

   c. Declare a variable named **puzzleButtons** referencing the page elements with the class name
      "puzzles". Loop through the puzzleButtons object collection and for each button add an event
      handler that runs the switchPuzzle() function when the button is clicked.

   d. Call the setupPuzzle() function that defines the initial appearance of the first puzzle.

   e. Add an event handler to the Check Solutions button to run the findErrors() function when
      clicked.

   f. Add an event handler to the Show Solutions button to run the showSolution() function when
      clicked.

6. Add the switchPuzzle() function, which switches the page between the three possible Hitori puzzles. Include the event object **e** as a parameter of the function and add the following commands:

   a. Declare the **puzzleID** variable equal to the ID of the event object target.

   b. Change the inner HTML of the element with the ID "puzzleTitle" to the value of the `value` attribute of the event object target.

   c. Create a `switch-case` structure with the puzzleID variable that loads the appropriate HTML code for each of the three puzzles into the page element with the ID "puzzle". Use the drawHitori() function to generate the HTML code and assume that puzzleID is limited to the values "puzzle1", "puzzle2", and "puzzle3".

   d. After the `switch-case` structure, call the setupPuzzle() function to set up the features of the selected puzzle.

   e. Enclose all of the commands in the switchPuzzle() function within an `if` statement that displays a confirm dialog box asking users whether they want to switch puzzles even though their work will be lost. If the confirm dialog box returns a value of true, run the commands within the `if` statement command block.

7. Create the **setupPuzzle()** function to set up the features of the puzzle table. Within the function add the following commands:

   a. Use the `querySelectorAll()` method to create an object collection of all of the `td` elements within the hitoriGrid table and save the object collection in the allCells variable.

   b. Create a `for` loop that loops the allCells object collection and, for each cell, change the `background-color` style to white, the font color to black, and the `border-radius` value to 0.

   c. Within the `for` loop, add a `mousedown` event listener for each cell in the allCells collection that changes the cell's appearance depending on whether the Shift key, the Alt key, or no key is pressed by the user. Add the following commands to the anonymous function for the `mousedown` event:

      i. Change the background color to white, the font color to black, and the border radius to 0 if the user is pressing the Shift key.

      ii. Change the background color to black, the font color to white, and the border radius to 0 if the user is pressing the Alt key.

      iii. Otherwise, change the background color to rgb(101, 101, 101), the font color to white, and the border radius to 50%.

      iv. To avoid inadvertently selecting the text of the table cells, include a command to prevent the default action of the browser in response to the mousedown event.

   d. Rebecca wants a different mouse cursor depending on whether the user is pressing the Shift key, the Alt key, or no key when the mouse pointer moves over a puzzle cell. Within the `for` loop, add a `mouseover` event listener for each puzzle cell that runs an anonymous function that

      i. Changes the cursor to the jpf_eraser.png image or the generic cursor named "alias" if the user is pressing the Shift key.

      ii. Changes the cursor to the jpf_block.png image or the generic cursor named "cell" if the user is pressing the Alt key.

      iii. Otherwise, changes the cursor to the jpf_circle.png image or the generic cursor named "pointer".

   e. Finally, within the `for` loop, add an event listener that runs the checkSolution() function in response to the `mouseup` event to test whether the user has solved the puzzle.

8. Create the findErrors() function that will highlight incorrect cells by displaying the cell number of an incorrect cell in a red font. Add the following commands:

   a. Create a `for` loop that goes through all of the cells in the allCells object collection. If the cell belongs to the blocks class but has a background color of rgb(101, 101, 100) or if it belongs to the circles class but has a black background, change the font color to red.

   b. The red font colors should appear only briefly. After the `for` loop, insert a `setTimeout()` method with a 1-second interval. Within the `setTimeout()` method, add an anonymous function that loops through every cell in the allCells collection, changing all cells with a font color of red back to white.

9. Document your code in the JavaScript file with descriptive comments throughout.

10. Save your changes to the file and then load **jpf_hitori.html** in your browser.

    a. Verify that you can switch puzzles by clicking the Puzzle buttons at the top of the page, and that you are prompted to confirm whether you want to change your puzzle. Verify that you can view the complete solution to each puzzle by clicking the Show Solution button.

    b. Verify than you can change a cell to a gray circle by clicking the cell. Verify that you can change a cell to a solid black block by clicking the cell with the Alt key pressed down. Finally, verify that you can restore a cell to black text on a white background by clicking a previously selected cell with the Shift key pressed down.

    c. Verify that the cursor changes shape as you move the mouse pointer over the puzzle cells, changing from a circular cursor to a block cursor when the Alt key is pressed or to an eraser cursor when the Shift key is pressed.

    d. Verify that you can test for errors by clicking the Check Solution button, and that your errors are displayed in a red font for one second.

    e. Solve the first puzzle using the solution provided in Figure 11-51. Verify that you receive a congratulatory message upon successfully completing the puzzle.

11. You are welcome to solve the second and third puzzles on your own, but they are not part of the assignment.

Case Problem 1

Data Files needed for this Case Problem: bw_review_txt.html, bw_review_txt.js, 2 CSS files, 5 PNG files

Online Bookworms   Daniel Palmer is a content manager of Online Bookworms, a website dedicated to lovers of books and reading. One of Daniel's tasks is to create a comments page in which users can enter short comments in a text area box about books they have read. To keep the comments short and to the point, Daniel wants to limit each comment to 1000 words. He asks you to write a script that will update a character counter that shows the user how much of the 1000 characters has already been typed.

Daniel also wants users to be able to rate the books by moving a mouse pointer over a row of five stars. If the user moves the mouse pointer over the third star, the first three stars should be lit. If the user moves the mouse pointer over the fourth star, the first four stars should be lit and so forth. Clicking a star image, enters that rating into an input box for processing.

A preview of the page you will create is shown in Figure 11-52.

Figure 11-52   Online Bookworms Review Page

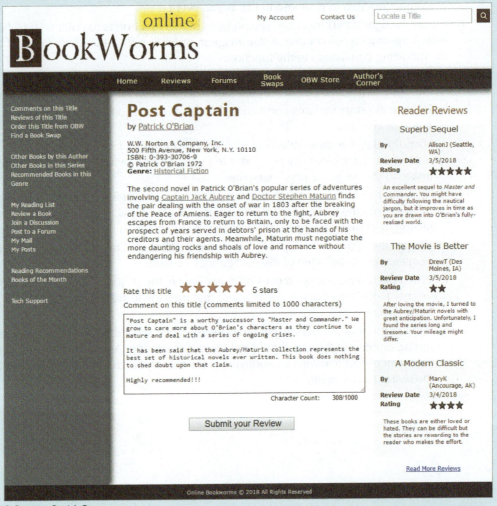

Complete the following:

1. Use your editor to open the **bw_review_txt.html** and **bw_review_txt.js** files from the html11 ▶ case1 folder. Enter *your name* and *the date* in the comment section of each file, and save them as **bw_review.html** and **bw_review.js** respectively.

2. Return to the **bw_review.html** file in your editor. Go to the document head and add a script element for the **bw_review.js** file. Load the file asynchronously.

3. Take some time to study the contents of the file, paying close attention to the form elements and their IDs. Save your changes to the file.

4. Return to the **bw_review.js** file in your editor. Directly after the initial comment section, insert an event handler that runs the init() function when the page is loaded by the browser.

5. Create the **init()** function. The purpose of the function is to define the event listeners used in the page. Add the following commands to the function:

   a. Declare the **stars** variable that stores an object collection of the reviewing stars, referenced by the `span#stars img` selector.

   b. Loop through the star collection and for each star image in the collection change the cursor style to `pointer` and add an event listener to run the lightStars() function in response to the `mouseenter` event occurring over each star image.

   c. After the `for` loop, add an event listener to the comment text area box that runs the updateCount() function in response to the `keyup` event.

6. Create the **lightStars()** function. The purpose of this function is to color a star when the user moves the mouse pointer over a star image in order to reflect the user's rating of the book. Add the following commands to the function:

   a. Daniel has stored the rating value of each star image in the img element's `alt` attribute. Store the value of the `alt` attribute of the target of the event object in the **starNumber** variable.

   b. Declare the **stars** variable containing the object collection referenced by the selector `span#stars img`.

   c. Loop through the stars collection with an index ranging from 0 up to less than the value of the starNumber variable. Light every star in the collection by changing the `src` attribute of the star image to the bw_star2.png image file.

   d. After the `for` loop, create another loop that loops through the stars collection with the index ranging from the value of the starNumber variable to less than 5. Unlight every star in this collection by changing the `src` attribute of the star image to the bw_star.png image file.

   e. Change the value of the input box with the `id` attribute "rating" to *starNumber* **stars**, where *starNumber* is the value of the starNumber variable.

   f. When the mouse pointer moves off a star image, the lit stars should be unlit. Add an event listener to the target of the event object that runs the turnOffStars() function in response to the `mouseleave` event.

   g. If the user clicks the star image, the selected rating should be set, which means moving the mouse pointer off the star should not remove the rating. Add an event listener for the target of the event object that runs an anonymous function removing the turnOffStars() function from the `mouseleave` event.

7. Create the **turnOffStars()** function. The purpose of this function is to unlight the stars when the user moves the mouse pointer off the star images. Add the following commands to the function:

    a. Declare the **stars** variable containing the object collection referenced by the selector `span#stars img`.

    b. Loop through all images in the stars collection and change the `src` attribute of each image to the bw_star.png file.

    c. Change the value of the rating input box to an empty text string.

8. Create the **updateCount()** function that keeps a running total of the number of characters that the user has typed into the comment text area box. Add the following commands to the function:

    a. Declare the **commentText** variable that references the value stored in the comment text area box.

    b. Use the countCharacters() function with commentText as the parameter value to calculate the number of characters in commentText. Store the value in the **charCount** variable.

    c. Declare the **wordCountBox** that references the wordCount input box.

    d. Change the value stored in the wordCount input box to the text string *charCount*/1000 where *charCount* is the value of the charCount variable.

    e. If charCount is greater than 1000, change the style of the wordCount input box to a white font on a red background, otherwise set the style to a black font on a white background.

9. Document your work with descriptive comments throughout the file and save the script file.

10. Open **bw_review.html** in your browser. Verify that as you move your mouse pointer over the stars below the book description, the rating value automatically matches your selection. Also verify that moving the mouse pointer off the star images removes the rating unless you have clicked one of the stars. Finally, verify that as you type characters into the text area box, a running count of the character total is shown below the box and, if the number of characters exceeds 1000, the total is displayed in a white font on a red background.

Case Problem 2

Data Files needed for this Case Problem: mt_calc_txt.html, mt_calc_txt.js, 3 CSS files, 2 PNG files

The Math Table Theresa Kaine runs The Math Table, a website containing math resources for home-schooling families and educators. Theresa wants to add an online calculator to the site and has asked for your help in designing a simple prototype. A preview of her page is shown in Figure 11-53.

Figure 11-53 **The Math Table Online Calculator**

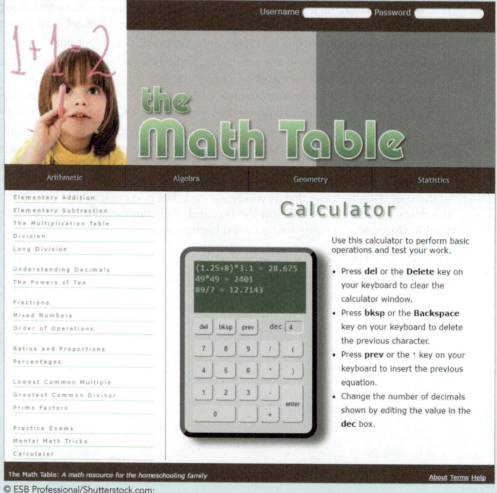

© ESB Professional/Shutterstock.com;
© Courtesy Patrick Carey

The calculator is created using different form widgets. The calculator window is a text area box and form buttons are used for each of the calculator buttons. The calculator window displays several lines of equations so that students can view multiple equations at once. To use the calculator:

- Enter expressions by clicking the calculator buttons or by typing the expression into the calculator window
- Evaluate an expression by clicking the enter button or pressing the Enter key
- Clear the calculator window by clicking the del button or pressing the Delete key
- Remove the last character from an expression by clicking the bksp button or pressing the Backspace key

- Copy the previous equation listed in the window by clicking the prev button or pressing the up-arrow key on the keyboard
- Change the number of decimal places used in the answer by changing the value in the dec box

To aid you in programming the script for the calculator, Theresa has supplied the following functions:

- eraseChar(textStr), which erases the last character from the text string, textStr
- evalEq(textStr, decimals), which evaluates the equation in textStr, returning a value to the number of decimals specified by the decimals parameter
- lastEq(textStr), which returns the previous expression from the list of expressions in the textStr parameter

Your job will be creating a fully functioning online calculator by adding the event handlers that respond to the user's mouse and keyboard actions.

Complete the following:

1. Use your editor to open the **mt_calc_txt.html** and **mt_calc_txt.js** files from the html11 ▶ case2 folder. Enter *your name* and *the date* in the comment section of each file, and save them as **mt_calc.html** and **mt_calc.js** respectively.
2. Go to the **mt_calc.html** file in your editor. In the head section, create a link to the **mt_calc.css** style sheet. Add a `script` element for the **mt_calc.js** file, loading the file asynchronously. Take some time to study the contents of the HTML file noting the element IDs and attributes and then save your changes to the file.
3. Return to the **mt_calc.js** file in your editor. Directly below the initial comment section, insert a command that runs the init() function when the page is loaded by the browser.
4. Create the init() function, which sets up the event handlers for the page. Within the init() function, add the following commands:
   a. Declare the **calcButtons** variable containing the collection of page elements belonging to the calcButton class.
   b. Loop through the calcButtons object collection and, for each button in that collection, run the buttonClick() function in response to the `click` event.
   c. After the `for` loop, add a command that runs the calcKeys() function in response to the `keydown` event occurring within the element with the ID "calcWindow".
5. Create the buttonClick() function. The purpose of this function is to change what appears in the calculator window when the user clicks the calculator buttons. Add the following commands to the function:
   a. Declare the **calcValue** variable equal to the `value` attribute of the calcWindow text area box.
   b. Declare the **calcDecimal** variable equal to the `value` attribute of the decimals input box.
   c. Each calculator button has a `value` attribute that defines what should be done with that button. Declare the **buttonValue** attribute equal to the `value` attribute of the event object target.
   d. Create a `switch-case` structure for the following possible values of the buttonValue variable:
      i. For "del", delete the contents of the calculate window by changing calcValue to an empty text string.
      ii. For "bksp", erase the last character in the calculator window by changing calcValue to the value returned by the eraseChar() function using calcValue as the parameter value.
      iii. For "enter", calculate the value of the current expression by changing calcValue to:

      ```
      " = " + evalEq(calcValue, calcDecimal) + "\n"
      ```

      Note that \n is used to add a line return at the end of the answer.
      iv. For "prev", copy the last equation in the calculator window by changing calcValue to the value returned by the lastEq() function using calcValue as the parameter value.
      v. Otherwise, append the calculator button character to the calculator window by letting, calcValue equal calcValue plus buttonValue.

     e. After the `switch-case` structure, set the `value` attribute of the calcWindow text area box to calcValue.

     f. Run the command `document.getElementById("calcWindow").focus()` to put the cursor focus within the calculator window.

6. Next, you will control the keyboard actions within the calculator window. Theresa wants you to program the actions that will happen when the user presses the Delete, Enter, and up arrow keys. Add the calcKeys() function containing the following commands:

     a. As you did in the buttonClick() function, declare the **calcValue** and **calcDecimal** variables.

     b. Create a `switch-case` structure for different values of the key attribute of the event object as follows:

        i. For "Delete", erase the contents of the calculator window by changing calcValue to an empty text string.

        ii. For "Enter", add the following expression to calcValue:

```
" = " + evalEq(calcValue, calcDecimal)
```

        iii. For "ArrowUp", add the following expression to calcValue

```
lastEq(calcWindow.value)
```

        iv. And then enter a command that prevents the browser from performing the default action in response to the user pressing the up-arrow key.

     c. After the `switch-case` structure, set the `value` attribute of the calcWindow text area box to calcValue.

7. Document your work by commenting your program commands and then save your changes to the file.

8. Open the **mt_calc.html** file in your browser. Click the different calculator buttons and verify that you can enter a mathematical expression into the calculator and evaluate that expression by clicking the enter button. Verify that you can erase the last character by clicking the bksp button. Verify that you can copy the last expression by clicking the enter button followed by the prev button. Show that you can clear the contents of the calculator window by clicking the del button. Finally verify that you can change the number of decimal places in the answer by changing the value in the dec input box.

9. Click within the calculator window and, using the keyboard, directly type a mathematical expression. Verify that pressing the Enter key evaluates the current expression and moves the cursor to a new line. Show that you can copy the previous expression by pressing the Enter key followed by the up-arrow key on your keyboard. Finally verify that pressing the Delete key clears the contents of the calculator window. **Note:** Keyboard commands might not work in the Safari browser since Safari does not support the key property at the time of this writing.

Case Problem 3

Data Files needed for this Case Problem: pc_cword_txt.html, pc_cword.js, 3 CSS files, 5 PNG files

Park City Gazette   Bernard Mills is a website manager for the Park City Gazette located in Ennis, Montana. He has asked for your help in developing a crossword puzzle page. The puzzle interface should include support for both keyboard and mouse events and provide hints to users about their mistakes. A preview of the page is shown in Figure 11-54.

CHALLENGE

Figure 11-54   **Park City Gazette crossword puzzle**

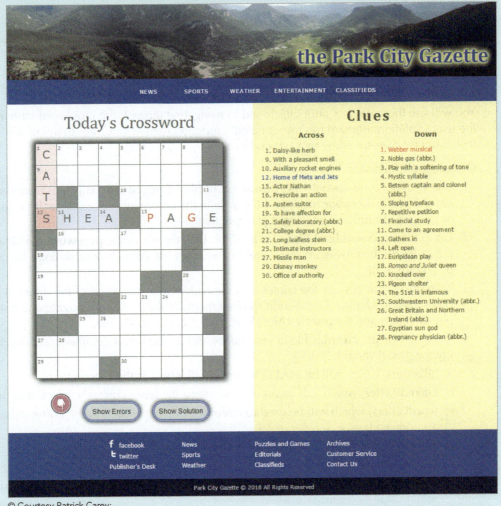

© Courtesy Patrick Carey;
Source: Perhelion/Public Domain;
Source: Facebook © 2015;
Source: 2015 © Twitter

The puzzle needs to support the following features:

- Letters are entered from the keyboard in either the horizontal or vertical direction; letters can be removed by pressing either the Delete or Backspace keys.
- The active cell is highlighted in the puzzle; the across and down cells that intersect with the active cell are also highlighted and the clues associated with the highlighted cells are shown in colored text as well as the clue for that cell and the other letters in the clue answers.
- The user can navigate through the puzzle using either the mouse button or by pressing the Tab, Enter, and arrow keys on the keyboard.
- If the user clicks the Show Errors button, any mistakes are briefly displayed in a red font.
- If the user clicks the Show Solution button, the puzzle solution is shown.

Bernard has already created a sample puzzle in which each crossword letter is placed within a separate table cell. He has also put information about the puzzle within each cell using the following `data-*` attributes:

- `data-letter` stores the letter for the crossword puzzle solution
- `data-left`, `data-up`, `data-right`, and `data-down` store the IDs of the letters to the left, above, to the right, and below the current letter
- `data-clue-a` stores the ID of the puzzle clue for the across word
- `data-clue-d` stores the ID of the puzzle clue for the down word

You will use these `data-*` attributes to aid in navigating through the crossword table and checking the user's solution. Bernard has also created a function named getChar() that you will use to retrieve the character corresponding to a key code value.

Complete the following:

1. Use your editor to open the **pc_cword_txt.html** and **pc_cword_txt.js** files from the html11 ► case3 folder. Enter *your name* and *the date* in the comment section of each file, and save them as **pc_cword.html** and **pc_cword.js** respectively.

2. Go to the **pc_cword.html** file in your editor. Link the file to the **pc_cword.css** file containing the styles for the crossword puzzle table and clues list. Asynchronously load the script from **pc_cword.js** file.

3. Take some time to study the contents of the table. Note the values of the different `data-*` attributes used to identify the different span elements of the crossword puzzle and note the IDs of the puzzle letters and the puzzle clues. Save your changes to the file.

4. Return to the **pc_cword.js** file in your editor. Below the initial comment section, declare the following global variables:

   a. **allLetters**, which will be used to reference all letters in the crossword puzzle

   b. **currentLetter**, which will be used to reference the letter currently selected in the puzzle

   c. **wordLetters**, which will be used to reference the letters used in the currently selected across and down clues

   d. **acrossClue**, which will be used to reference the across clue currently selected in the puzzle

   e. **downClue**, which will be used to reference the down clue currently selected in the puzzle

   f. **typeDirection**, which stores the current typing direction (either to the right or down); set its initial value to "right"

5. Add a command to run the init() function when the page loads.

6. Create the **init()** function, which sets up the initial conditions of the puzzle. Add the following commands to the function:

   a. Set allLetters to reference the elements using the selector `table#crossword span`.

   b. Set currentLetter to reference the first object in allLetters collection

   c. ✥ **Explore** Declare the **acrossID** variable, setting its value equal to the value of the `data-clue-a` attribute for currentLetter. Declare the **downID** variable, setting its value equal to the value of the `data-clue-d` attribute for currentLetter.

   d. Set the value of acrossClue to reference the element with the `id` attribute "acrossID". Set the value of downClue to reference the element with the `id` attribute "downID".

7. Next, create the formatPuzzle() function. This function will format the colors of the crossword table cells and the clues in the clues list based on the letter that is selected by user. The function has a single parameter named **puzzleLetter**. Add the following commands to the function:

   a. Change the value of currentLetter to puzzleLetter.

   b. Remove the current colors in the puzzle by looping through all items in the allLetters object collection, changing the `background-color` style of each to an empty text string.

   c. After the `for` loop, remove the highlighting of the current clues by changing the `color` style of acrossClue and downClue to an empty text string.

   d. ✥ **Explore** Determine whether there exists an across clue for the current letter by testing whether `currentLetter.dataset.clueA` is not equal to `undefined`. If true, then do the following:

      i. Set acrossClue to reference the element with the ID value of `currentLetter.dataset.clueA` in order to reference the across clue for the current letter.

      ii. Change the `color` style of acrossClue to blue.

      iii. Set wordLetters to reference all elements selected by the CSS selector `[data-clue-A = clue]` where *clue* is the value of `data-clue-a` for currentLetter.

      iv. Change the `background-color` style of every item in wordLetters to the light blue color value rgb(231, 231, 255).

   e. Repeat Step d for the down clue indicated by the `data-clue-d` attribute, changing the `color` style of downClue to red and the `background-color` style of the items in wordLetters to the light red color value rgb(255, 231, 231).

   f. Indicate the typing direction for the current letter. If typeDirection = "right", change the background color of currentLetter to the blue color value rgb(191, 191, 255); otherwise, change the background color to the red color value rgb(255, 191, 191).

8. Return to the init() function and add the following commands to apply the formatPuzzle() function:

   a. Color the crossword puzzle's first letter by calling the formatPuzzle() function using currentLetter as the parameter value.

   b. Users should be able to select a puzzle cell using their mouse. Loop through the items in the allLetters object collection and for each item:

      i. Change the cursor style to pointer.

      ii. Add `onmousedown` event handler that runs an anonymous function calling the formatPuzzle() function using the event object target as the parameter value.

9. Create the selectLetter() function. The purpose of this function is to allow users to select puzzle cells using the keyboard. Add the following commands to the function:

   a. Declare the **leftLetter**, **upLetter**, **rightLetter**, and **downLetter** variables and set their values to reference the letters to the left, above, to the right, and below the current letter selected in the table. (*Hint*: use the `dataset.left`, `dataset.up`, `dataset.right`, and `dataset.down` properties of currentLetter.)

   b. ⊕ **Explore** Store the code of the key pressed by the user in the **userKey** variable. (*Hint*: use the `keyCode` property of the event object to retrieve the key code value.)

   c. Add the following `if-else` structure to determine the program response based on the value of userKey:

      i. If userKey equals 37 (the left arrow key), call the formatPuzzle() function using leftLetter as the parameter value.

      ii. If userKey equals 38 (the up arrow key), call formatPuzzle() with the upLetter variable.

      iii. If userKey equals 39 or 9 (the right arrow and tab keys), call formatPuzzle() with the rightLetter variable.

      iv. If userKey equals 40 or 13 (the down arrow and enter keys), call formatPuzzle() with the downLetter variable.

      v. If the userKey equals 8 or 46 (the backspace or delete keys), delete the text content of currentLetter.

      vi. If userKey equals 32 (the spacebar key), run the switchTypeDirection() function to change the typing direction.

      vii. If the code value is between 65 and 90 (the letters a through z), write the character into the cell by changing the text content of currentLetter to the value returned by the getChar() function using userKey as the parameter value and then move to the next cell in the puzzle. If typeDirection is "right", move to the next cell by calling the formatPuzzle() function with the rightLetter variable; otherwise, go down to the next cell by calling the format-Puzzle() variable with the downLetter variable.

   d. After the `if-else` structure, enter a command to prevent the browser from performing the default action in response to the keyboard event.

10. Return to the init() function and add an event handler to run the selectLetter() function in response to the `keydown` event occurring within the document.

11. Create the switchTypeDirection() function to toggle the typing direction between right and down. Add the following commands to the function:

    a. Declare the variable **typeImage** that points to the element with the ID "directionImg".

    b. Create an `if-else` structure that tests the value of the typeDirection global variable.

    c. If typeDirection = "right", then change typeDirection to "down", change the src attribute of typeImage to "pc_right.png", and change the background color of currentLetter to the red color value rgb(255, 191, 191); otherwise change the typeDirection to "right", change the src attribute of typeImage to "pc_down.png", and change the background color of current letter to rgb(191, 191, 255).

12. Users can change the typing direction either by using the keyboard or by clicking the pointer on an image located below the crossword puzzle. Return to the init() function and add the following commands:

    a. Declare the variable **typeImage** referencing the element with the ID "directionImg".

    b. Change the `cursor` style of type Image to "pointer".

    c. Run the switchTypeDirection() function when the typeImage is clicked.

13. Bernard wants users to be able to briefly view their mistakes. Add an `onclick` event handler to the init() function that runs the following commands when the user clicks the Show Errors button:

    a. Loop through all items in the allLetters object collection. If the text content of an item does not match the value of the letter's `dataset.letter` property, change the color style of the letter to red.

    b. After a 3-second interval, set the `color` style for the items in the allLetters collection to an empty text string, restoring the letters to the default font color.

14. Complete the init() function by adding an `onclick` event handler to the Show Solution button. In response to the `click` event, run an anonymous function containing a `for` loop that goes through all items in the allLetters collection, setting the text content of each item to the value of the letter's `dataset.letter` property.

15. Document your solution by commenting your code and then save your file.

16. Open the **pc_cword.html** file in your browser. Verify your solution by doing the following:

    a. Navigate through the puzzle using the arrow keys, Tab key, and Enter key

    b. Select a puzzle cell using the mouse

    c. Confirm that the across cells and across numbered clue for the selected cell are highlighted in blue and the down cells and down numbered clue are highlighted in red

    d. Press the spacebar or click the direction image to verify that the typing direction and image toggles between right and down and that the color of the active cell indicates the typing direction

    e. Delete the current letter by either pressing the Delete key or the Backspace key

    f. Briefly highlight puzzle mistakes by clicking the Show Errors button

    g. View the complete solution by clicking the Show Solution button

Case Problem 4

Data Files needed for this Case Problem: kg_search_txt.html, kg_search_txt.js, 3 CSS files, 1 JS file, 5 PNG files

CREATE

Kidder Garden   Pete Burnham of the Kidder Garden website has asked for help in developing an interactive word search game. He envisions a page in which children can select letters from the word search table using a mouse pointer. When all the words in the list have been found, a congratulatory message is displayed. A preview of the page is shown in Figure 11-55.

Figure 11-55   **Kidder Garden Word Search**

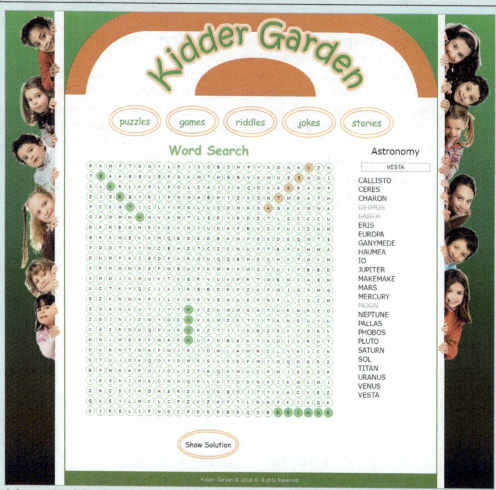

Peter has already provided the style sheet and HTML code for the page. He has also supplied you with the following JavaScript variables:

- A title for the puzzle stored in the wordSearchTitle variable
- The word list stored in the wordArray variable
- The grid of the puzzle letters stored in the letterGrid array
- The grid of the location of words within the puzzle stored in the wordGrid array

He has also supplied you with the following functions:

- The drawWordSearch() function, which writes the HTML code for a web table with the ID "wordSearchTable" containing the letters in the word search puzzle. Table cells that contain letters are part of the word list belonging to the wordCell class.
- The showList() function, which writes the HTML code for an unordered list with the ID "wordSearchList" containing the words to be found in the puzzle

Pete wants you to write an app that does the following:

- Writes the HTML code for word search table into the `figure` element with the ID "wordTable".
- Writes the HTML code for the word list into the `figure` element with the ID "wordList".
- Users select letters by pressing the mouse pointer down and moving over each table cell. As the pointer enters the table cell for the letter, the background color should change to pink and the letter within the cell should be added to text displayed in the pickedLetter input box.
- When the mouse button is released, the entry in the pickedLetter input box should be checked against the word list. If there is a match, the word is crossed out in the list and the letters selected in the table should change to a light green background.
- If there is no match, the selected letters in the background table should have their background colors removed. After each word selection, the contents of the pickedLetter input box should be removed in preparation for the next selection of letters.
- As an aid to the user, the mouse pointer should be displayed using the pointer icon for cells in the word search table. (*Note*: The pointer looks like a hand with a pointing finger.)
- When moving the mouse pointer over the table cells, the text within those cells should not be selected by the browser.
- Once a letter is displayed with a green background, its background color should never change.
- Once all the words have been found, an alert dialog box should display a congratulatory message to the user.
- The complete list of word locations can be displayed by clicking the Show Solution button.

The final form of the solution and your JavaScript program is left to you.

Complete the following:

1. Use your editor to open the **kg_search_txt.html** and **kg_search_txt.js** files from the html11 ▶ case4 folder. Enter *your name* and *the date* in the comment section of each file, and save them as **kg_search.html** and **kg_search.js** respectively.

2. Link the kg_search.html file to the **kg_search.css** style sheet file and to the **kg_maketable.js** and **kg_search.js** JavaScript files. Load both JavaScript files asynchronous. Save your changes to the file.

3. Within the kg_search.js file have a function run when the page is loaded that inserts the contents of the word search table and word search list into the web page, and sets up the event handlers and event listeners for the document.

4. Declare whatever global variables you feel are needed to complete the assignment.

5. Write the code that will satisfy Pete's condition for the word search app. Your code should contain at least one example of the following:

   a. An application of an event handler

   b. An application of an event listener

   c. Removing an event listener from a page element

   d. Application of a CSS inline style to a page element

   e. An alert dialog box

   f. A command that prevents a default browser action in response to an event

6. Document your solution with comments throughout the code.

7. Test your solution in your browser. Verify that it satisfies the conditions that Pete has set out.

TUTORIAL 12

Working with Document Nodes and Style Sheets

Creating a Dynamic Document Outline

Case | *Bridger College*

Norene Somerville, a professor of history at Bridger College, is putting the text of important historic documents online for her students to download and study. She wants each document to be available in HTML format on a single page, however, she is concerned that some of the documents are very long and difficult to view within a single page.

Norene believes that a document outline would be a great aid to her students, allowing them to quickly view the main topics of interest for each document. She also wants the outline to contain hypertext links to each topic heading in the source article. Norene doesn't have the time to create such an outline for each document in her website and so she has asked you to create a JavaScript program that automatically generates an outline and hypertext links for any document she wishes to post for her students.

OBJECTIVES

Session 12.1
- Explore nodes and the node tree
- Create element and text nodes
- Append nodes to a web document

Session 12.2
- Work with the properties and methods of element nodes
- Create attribute nodes
- Add attribute nodes to page elements

Session 12.3
- Create external and embedded style sheets with JavaScript
- Add style sheets to a web document
- Create a style rule for an embedded style sheet
- Enable and disable style sheets

STARTING DATA FILES

html12

tutorial
bc_const_txt.html
bc_outline_txt.js
bc_switch_txt.js
+ 5 files

review
bc_fed_txt.html
bc_keys_txt.js
+ 4 files

case1
na_home_txt.html
na_styler_txt.js
+ 23 files

case2
sub_menu_txt.html
sub_cart_txt.js
+ 11 files

case3
js_nodes_txt.html
js_tree_txt.js
+ 4 files

case4
gi_qbs_txt.html
gi_sort_txt.js
+ 3 files

Session 12.1 Visual Overview:

A **node** is any object within the HTML file; the nodes are organized in a hierarchical structure called a **node tree**.

An **text node** is a node that matches a text string contained within an element node.

An **element node** is a node that matches an element in the HTML file.

Exploring the Node Tree

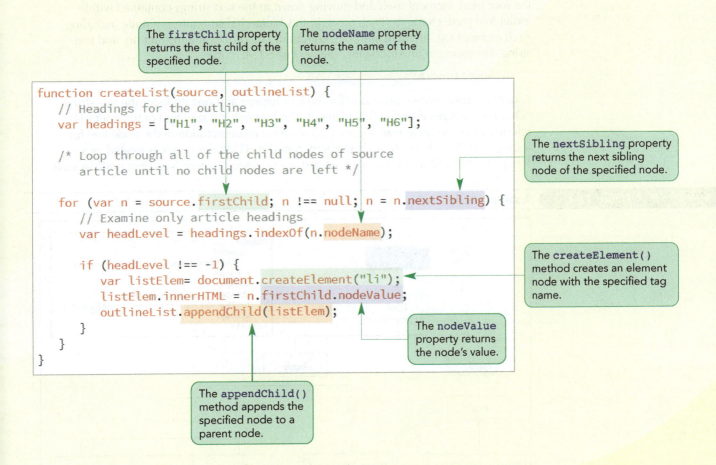

The firstChild property returns the first child of the specified node.

The nodeName property returns the name of the node.

The nextSibling property returns the next sibling node of the specified node.

```
function createList(source, outlineList) {
   // Headings for the outline
   var headings = ["H1", "H2", "H3", "H4", "H5", "H6"];

   /* Loop through all of the child nodes of source
      article until no child nodes are left */

   for (var n = source.firstChild; n !== null; n = n.nextSibling) {
      // Examine only article headings
      var headLevel = headings.indexOf(n.nodeName);

      if (headLevel !== -1) {
         var listElem= document.createElement("li");
         listElem.innerHTML = n.firstChild.nodeValue;
         outlineList.appendChild(listElem);
      }
   }
}
```

The createElement() method creates an element node with the specified tag name.

The nodeValue property returns the node's value.

The appendChild() method appends the specified node to a parent node.

Introducing Nodes

So far, you have generated the HTML content for web pages by explicitly inserting the text of the HTML code into page elements via the `innerHTML` property. While effective for smaller fragments of HTML code, the `innerHTML` property becomes unwieldly for larger document structures as the browser needs to parse increasingly longer text strings. An HTML text string can also be more difficult to debug because it does not present the structure of the content that is being inserted into the document. Another approach, which you will explore in this tutorial, is to build a document structure using nodes.

Nodes and Document Structure

The contents of an HTML file are arranged in a hierarchical structure, starting from the root `html` element itself and moving down to the text strings contained within individual page elements. Each piece in this hierarchal structure is a **node** including each element tag, element attribute, comment tag, processing instruction, and text string. For example, the following fragment of HTML code

```
<h1>Outline</h1>
```

consists of two nodes—one node for the h1 element and one node for the text string, "Outline" contained within that element. The hierarchical structure of the nodes is referred to as the **node tree**. Figure 12-1 shows a representation of the node tree for a sample HTML file. Note each element from the HTML document is treated as a separate node within the tree and the text within each element is its own node as well.

Figure 12-1 A sample node tree

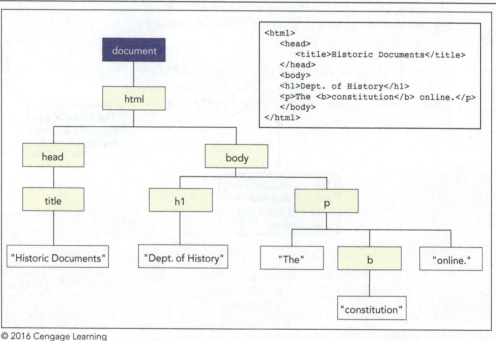

© 2016 Cengage Learning

Nodes in the node tree have a familial relationship—each node can be a parent, child, and/or sibling of other nodes. This relationship is indicated using the expression

$node$`.relationship`

where $node$ is a currently selected node or object, and $relationship$ is the relationship of another node to the current node. For example, the expression

$node$`.parentNode`

refers to the parent of $node$. In the node tree shown in Figure 12-1, the parent of the body node is the `html` node, and the parent of the `html` node is the document node, which is also known as the **root node**.

Each node can contain one or more **child nodes**. To reference the first child of the current node, apply the following expression:

$node$`.firstChild`

In the node tree shown in Figure 12-1, the `h1` node is the first child of the `body` node, and the text node "Dept. of History" is the first (and only) child of the `h1` node. All of the child nodes are organized into the following object collection:

$node$`.childNodes`

As with other object collections, a particular item from the `childNodes` collection can be referenced using the following index number

$node$`.childNodes[`i`]`

where i is the index number, starting with 0 for the first child node.

To determine the total number of child nodes for a given node, apply the following `length` property:

$node$`.childNodes.length`

For example, the length of the `childNodes` collection for the paragraph element in Figure 12-1 is 3 (the two text nodes and the `b` element). Figure 12-2 summarizes the rest of the familial relationships in the node tree.

Figure 12-2	Node relationships

Expression	Description
$node$`.firstChild`	The first child of $node$
$node$`.lastChild`	The last child of $node$
$node$`.childNodes`	A collection of all of the nodes that are direct children of $node$
$node$`.previousSibling`	The sibling prior to $node$
$node$`.nextSibling`	The sibling after $node$
$node$`.ownerDocument`	The root node of the document
$node$`.parentNode`	The parent of $node$

The properties in Figure 12-2 make no distinction between nodes that represent elements and nodes that represent other parts of the HTML document, such as text strings, white space, and HTML comment tags. Thus, an expression such as *node*.childNodes.length returns the number of child nodes of all types. If you are interested only in working with element nodes, this property does not provide the information you need. Figure 12-3 lists the properties that are applicable only to element nodes.

Figure 12-3   **Element node relationships**

Property	Description
node.children	A collection of all of the element nodes contained within *node*
node.firstElementChild	The first element within *node*
node.lastElementChild	The last element within *node*
node.nextElementSibling	The next sibling element to *node*
node.previousElementSibling	The previous sibling element to *node*
node.childElementCount	The number of child elements within *node*
node.children.length	The number of child elements within *node*

TIP

You can also count the number of child nodes that are elements using the childElementCount property.

For example, in the HTML fragment

```
<article>
   <h1>The U.S. Constitution</h1>
   <h2>Preamble</h2>
   <p>We the People of the United States, in Order to form a
      more perfect Union …
   </p>
</article>
```

the children.length property for the article element node returns a value of 3, indicating that the article element contains three child element nodes—the h1, h2, and p element nodes. Note that the element node properties are not supported by versions of Internet Explorer before IE9, though they are supported by all current browsers.

REFERENCE

Specifying Node Relationships

- To access the parent of a node, use the reference

  node.parentNode

  where *node* is a node object in the node tree.
- To reference the first child and last child of a node, use the following references:

  node.firstChild
  node.lastChild

- To reference the collection of all child nodes, use the following reference:

  node.childNodes

- To reference the previous and next siblings, use the following references:

  node.previousSibling
  node.nextSibling

Restructuring the Node Tree

One of the reasons to work with nodes rather than simply write HTML code through the `innerHTML` property is that you can take a current node tree and rearrange it into a new structure. You will explore how to do this with the outlining program that Norene wants you to create.

Norene has provided you with a sample page containing the text of the United States Constitution. She feels that this would pose an ideal challenge for a script that generates outlines because the document is very long and divided into different topical sections. Figure 12-4 shows Norene's sketch of her idea for the document outline in which the outline is generated as an ordered list.

Figure 12-4   **Proposed outline**

© 2016 Cengage Learning

Ideally, any outlining app you create for this document should be applicable to a wide selection of other source documents in her library. Norene wants to base her outline on the `h1` through `h6` heading elements often used to mark the topical sections in HTML documents. The `h1` heading usually marks a primary section in the document, `h2` marks a secondary heading, and so on. Figure 12-5 shows the type of HTML code the outlining app would generate. The app would search the document article for heading elements, copying the text of each heading into a nested list with higher-level headings placed in the outer lists. Thus, all `h1` headings would be placed in the outermost list of the outline, `h2` headings would be nested within the `h1` headings, and so forth down to any `h6` headings.

Figure 12-5 **Document headings restructured as an outline**

document content

nested list generated by the outlining function

© 2016 Cengage Learning

The JavaScript code to generate this node tree will be located in an external JavaScript file. The style design will be stored in an external CSS style sheet. Using external files will allow Norene to easily apply the finished app to other documents in her library.

To open the U.S. Constitution file:

▶ 1. Use your editor to open the **bc_const_txt.html** and **bc_outline_txt.js** files from the html12 ▸ tutorial folder. Enter *your name* and *the date* in the comment section of each file and save them as **bc_const.html** and **bc_outline.js** respectively.

▶ 2. Return to the **bc_const.html** file in your editor. Within the head element, insert a link to the **bc_outline.css** style sheet file, which contains the styles that will be applied to the document outline you will generate.

▶ 3. Add a `script` element to asynchronously load the **bc_outline.js** file.

▶ 4. Study the contents of the HTML file and then save your changes to the file.

The document contains an `aside` element with the ID "outline", into which you will place the node tree containing the document outline. It also contains an `article` element with ID "doc" that will be the basis for that outline. When the page is initially loaded by a browser, you want it to run the makeOutline() function to generate the code for the document outline. Start adding this function to the bc_outline.js file now.

To begin creating the makeOutline() function:

1. Go to the **bc_outline.js** file in your editor.

2. Below the initial comment section, insert the following code:

```
/* Generate an outline based on h1 through h6 headings in the
source document */

window.addEventListener("load", makeOutline);

function makeOutline() {
    // Location of the document outline
    var outline = document.getElementById("outline");

    // Source document for the outline
    var source = document.getElementById("doc");
}
```

Figure 12-6 describes the newly added code to the document.

Figure 12-6   Adding the makeOutline() function

runs the makeOutline() function when the page is loaded

```
*/
/* Generate an outline based on h1 through h6 headings
   in the source document */

window.addEventListener("load", makeOutline);

function makeOutline() {
    // Location of the document outline
    var outline = document.getElementById("outline");

    // Source document for the outline
    var source = document.getElementById("doc");
}
```

event listener for the load event

defines the location of the outline and source variables

3. Save your changes to the file.

To insert the contents of the document outline, your program will need to generate nodes and attach them to the HTML file.

Problem Solving: Nodes and White Space

One source of confusion when working with nodes is the treatment of white space within an HTML file. The document object model specifies that the white space between element tags should be treated as a text node. Therefore, the following HTML fragment

```
<h1>The U.S. Constitution</h1>
<h2>Preamble</h2>
```

contains five nodes: two element nodes (for the h1 and h2 elements), two text nodes (for the text strings "The U.S. Constitution" and "Preamble"), and one more text node you don't see representing the line return between the closing </h1> tag and the opening <h2> tag.

One source of confusion is that versions of Internet Explorer before IE9 did not count white space nodes as text nodes, so the above HTML fragment would have only four nodes under the IE document object model. This has been corrected in IE9, and all current browsers should count both text nodes and white space nodes the same. If you need to write programs for legacy websites viewed under older browsers, you might have to deal with the different node counts calculated by different browsers.

Creating and Appending Nodes

JavaScript's document object model supports several methods to create nodes of different types. These methods are described in Figure 12-7.

Figure 12-7 Methods to create nodes

Method	Description
`document.createAttribute(att)`	Creates an attribute node with the name `att`
`document.createComment(text)`	Creates a comment node containing the comment `text`
`document.createElement(elem)`	Creates an element node with the name `elem`
`document.createTextNode(text)`	Creates a text node containing the text string `text`
`node.cloneNode(deep)`	Creates a copy of `node` where `deep` is a Boolean value that indicates whether to copy all descendants of `node` (`true`) or only `node` itself (`false`)

Using these methods, you can create a wide variety of document objects. For example, the following code creates an element node for the h1 element and a text node containing the text "Outline", storing those nodes in the mainHeading and headingText variables:

```
var mainHeading = document.createElement("h1");
var headingText = document.createTextNode("Outline");
```

Cloning Nodes

All of the methods described in Figure 12-7 create single nodes, with the exception of the `cloneNode()` method. The `cloneNode()` method is useful when you need to create a copy of an existing node, including any descendants of that node. Thus, the following command creates a copy of the title node, including any descendants of that node:

```
var newtitle = title.cloneNode(true);
```

If you only want to clone a single node and not its descendants as well, set the value of the `cloneNode()` method to `false`.

The `cloneNode()` method provides a quick and easy way to create elements and their content without having to create each node individually.

Create element and text nodes for an `h1` element, an ordered list `ol` element, and the text string "Outline", and add those nodes to the makeOutline() function under the variable names, mainHeading, outlineList, and headingText.

To create element and text nodes:

▶ **1.** Within the makeOutline() function, add the following commands:

```
var mainHeading = document.createElement("h1");
var outlineList = document.createElement("ol");
var headingText = document.createTextNode("Outline");
```

Figure 12-8 describes the code to create the element and text nodes.

Figure 12-8	Creating element and text nodes

```
function makeOutline() {
    // Location of the document outline
    var outline = document.getElementById("outline");

    // Source document for the outline
    var source = document.getElementById("doc");

    var mainHeading = document.createElement("h1");
    var outlineList = document.createElement("ol");
    var headingText = document.createTextNode("Outline");
}
```

creates element nodes for the h1 and ol elements

creates a text node containing the text string "Outline"

▶ **2.** Save your changes to the file.

When a node is created, it is added to the computer memory as a **document fragment**, but it is not a part of the document's node tree until it is appended to a node within the tree. Figure 12-9 describes several methods for appending one node to another.

Figure 12-9 **Methods to append and replace nodes**

Method	Description
node.appendChild(*new*)	Appends *new* node as a child of *node*
node.insertBefore(*new*, *child*)	Inserts *new* node directly before *child* node (if no *child* node is specified then *new* node is added as the last child node)
node.normalize()	Traverses all of the child nodes of *node*; any adjacent text nodes are merged into a single text node
node.removeChild(*old*)	Removes *old* node from *node*
node.replaceChild(*new*, *old*)	Replaces *old* node with *new* node.

Using the methods described in Figures 12-7 and 12-9, you can create elaborate document fragments that contain several levels of different nodes. Figure 12-10 shows the process by which you would create the following HTML fragment using those methods:

```
<p><em>Historic</em> Documents</p>
```

Figure 12-10 **Creating an HTML document fragment**

Code	Node Tree

`newEM = document.createElement("em");`
`text1 = document.createTextNode("Historic");`
 	
`newP = document.createElement("p");`
`text2 = document.createTextNode(" Documents");`
	em — "Historic" p — "Documents"

`newEM.appendChild(text1);` `newP.appendChild(text2);`	em / "Historic" p / "Documents"
`newP.insertBefore(newEM,text2);`	p → em / "Historic", "Documents" `<p><em>Historic</em> Documents</p>`

© 2016 Cengage Learning

TIP

When applied to a node that already is a child of the current node, the `appendChild()` and `insertBefore()` methods move the child node from its current location to its new location.

The approach shown in Figure 12-10 first uses the `createElement()` and `createTextNode()` methods to create four nodes: an element node for emphasized text, an element node for a paragraph, a text node containing the text string Historic, and a text node containing a blank space followed by the text string Documents. The `appendChild()` method is then employed to attach the text nodes to the element nodes. The last line of code uses the `insertBefore()` method to insert the emphasized text before the second text node. Although at first glance this approach might seem more cumbersome than simply using the `innerHTML` method, the advantage of using nodes is that you can work with individual elements and text strings with more detail and flexibility than is possible with other approaches.

REFERENCE

Creating Nodes

- To create an element node, use the method

  ```
  document.createElement(elem)
  ```

  where *elem* is the name of the element.
- To create an attribute node, use the method

  ```
  document.createAttribute(att)
  ```

  where *att* is the name of the attribute.
- To create a text node, use the method

  ```
  document.createTextNode(elem)
  ```

  where *elem* is the text string within the text node.
- To create a comment node, use the method

  ```
  document.createComment(elem)
  ```

  where *elem* is the text of the comment.
- To copy a preexisting node, use the method

  ```
  node.cloneNode(deep)
  ```

  where *node* is the preexisting node, and *deep* is a Boolean value indicating whether to copy all descendants of *node* (`true`) or only *node* itself (`false`).

Use the `appendChild()` method now to append the element and text nodes you have already created in the makeOutline() function to the `aside` element in Norene's document.

To attach nodes to the document:

1. Add the following commands to the makeOutline() function:

```
mainHeading.appendChild(headingText);
outline.appendChild(mainHeading);
outline.appendChild(outlineList);
```

Element nodes must be appended to the document before the content of the nodes can be viewed in rendered page.

Figure 12-11 highlights the code to attach nodes to the document.

Figure 12-11 **Attaching element and text nodes**

```
var mainHeading = document.createElement("h1");
var outlineList = document.createElement("ol");
var headingText = document.createTextNode("Outline");

mainHeading.appendChild(headingText);
outline.appendChild(mainHeading);
outline.appendChild(outlineList);
}
```

appends the text node to the h1 element

appends an ordered list to the outline

appends the h1 heading to the outline

2. Save your changes to the file and then load the **bc_const.html** file in your browser. Figure 12-12 shows the page with the outline heading added to the page aside.

Figure 12-12 **Outline heading**

outline h1 heading

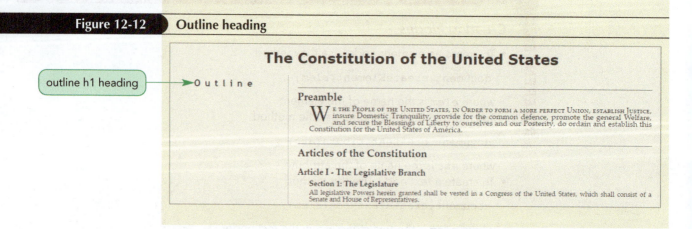

As you build the outline by adding nodes to the document, you can view the revised structure with your browser's developer tools. Explore how to view the node structure using the Google Chrome browser.

To view the attached elements:

1. Within the Google Chrome browser, click the **F12** key to open the Developer pane.

2. Click the **Sources** menu entry at the top of the pane and click **bc_const.html** from the list of source files.

3. Click the **Elements** menu option at the top of the pane to view the elements within the web page document.

4. Click the **black triangle** next to the aside element within the element tree in the top pane to expand it and view its contents.

   Figure 12-13 shows the elements that have been created using the commands in the makeOutline() function.

Figure 12-13 **Viewing elements within the developer window**

click to expand or collapse an element

elements created using the makeOutline() function

Trouble? If you are using Microsoft Edge or Internet Explorer, you can view the element tree in the DOM Explorer window. If you are using Firefox, you can view the element tree in the Inspector window. Finally, if you are using Safari, you can view the element tree by first enabling the developer tools and then viewing the Web Inspector window.

5. Press **F12** again to close the Developer pane.

The `ol` element has been attached to the `aside` element on the page. Next, you will add items to that list.

Appending and Removing Nodes

- To append a new node as a child of a preexisting node, use

  `node.appendChild(new)`

  where *node* is the preexisting node and *new* is the new child. The new child node is appended to the end of the child nodes collection. If *new* is already a child of *node*, it is moved from its current location to the new location.
- To insert a new node at a specific location in the child nodes collection, use

  `node.insertBefore(new, child)`

  where *child* is the child node in front of which the *new* node should be placed. If *new* already exists as a node in the document fragment, it is moved from its current location to the new location.
- To remove a child node, use

  `node.removeChild(old)`

  where *old* is the child node to be removed.
- To replace one child node with another, use

  `node.replaceChild(new, old)`

  where *old* is the child node to be replaced and *new* is the new child.

Working with Node Types, Names, and Values

The text for each entry in the outline list needs to match the text of a heading in the source article. The outlining app will do the following:

1. Loop through the child nodes of the source article.
2. For each child node, test whether it represents an `h1` through `h6` element node.
3. If it is a heading, extract the element's text and create a list item containing that same text string.
4. Append the list item as a new child of the outline's ordered list.

For simplicity's sake, assume that each heading element is a direct child of the `article` element rather than being nested within other elements, and that the heading elements contain only text and no nested elements.

Looping through the Child Nodes Collection

There are two ways of looping through a collection of child nodes. One approach uses a counter variable starting with a value of 0 and increasing by 1 for each node, up to the length of the `childNodes` collection. The general form of this loop follows:

```
for (var i = 0; i < node.childNodes.length; i++) {
   commands
}
```

In this form, the child nodes in the `for` loop have the object reference

```
node.childNodes[i]
```

where *node* is the parent node of the child nodes collection, and *i* is the value of the counter variable in the `for` loop.

The second approach uses familial references, starting with the first child of the parent node and then moving to each subsequent sibling until no siblings remain. The general form of this `for` loop is as follows:

```
for (var n = node.firstChild; n !== null; n = n.nextSibling) {
    commands
}
```

In this form, the child nodes in the `for` loop are referenced using the `n` variable defined within the `for` loop expression. The loop examines each node until no next sibling is available, at which point the value of `n` is null and the loop stops.

Although both approaches yield the same results, using familial references has the advantage that it does not require a browser to calculate the total length of the child nodes collection. For large documents containing thousands of nodes, this can speed up the processing time. This method also provides the flexibility to insert new nodes into a document within the `for` loop without having to recalculate the length of the child nodes collection.

You will use familial references in the following createList() function to create the list of heading elements from the source article. The initial code for the function follows:

```
function createList(source, outlineList) {
    for (var n = source.firstChild; n !== null; n = n.nextSibling) {
    }
}
```

The source parameter is the source article containing the heading on which you will base the outline. The outlineList parameter specifies the ordered list into which the list items are to be inserted. The initial code for this function uses a `for` loop to move through the children of the source article parameter, sibling by sibling.

To start the createList() function:

▶ 1. Return to the **bc_outline.js** file in your editor.

▶ 2. Below the makeOutline() function, insert the following code:

```
function createList(source, outlineList) {
    /* Loop through all of the child nodes of source
       article until no child nodes are left */

    for (var n = source.firstChild; n !== null; n =
    n.nextSibling) {

    }
}
```

Figure 12-14 highlights the initial code of the createList() function.

Figure 12-14   Using sibling nodes in a for loop

```
    outline.appendChild(outlineList);
}

function createList(source, outlineList) {
    /* Loop through all of the child nodes of source
       article until no child nodes are left */

    for (var n = source.firstChild; n !== null; n = n.nextSibling) {

    }
}
```

| starts the loop with the first child node | runs the loop as long as the current node is not null | goes to the next sibling node each time through the loop |

3. Save your changes to the file.

Next, you will work with the properties of the nodes within the `for` loop.

Node Properties

Because a node is another type of JavaScript object, it has properties that define it. The following properties indicate the type of node, the node name, and the node value for a *node* in the document:

```
node.nodeType
node.nodeName
node.nodeValue
```

The `nodeType` property returns an integer indicating whether the node refers to an element, an attribute, a text string, a comment, a document, or another type of node. The `nodeName` property returns the name of the node within the document. Finally, the `nodeValue` property returns the node's value. Figure 12-15 displays the values of these three properties for the different types of nodes you will typically encounter in a web document.

Figure 12-15   Node types, names, and values

Node	node.nodeType	node.nodeName	node.nodeValue
Element	1	ELEMENT NAME	null
Attribute	2	attribute name	attribute value
Text	3	#text	text string
Comment	8	#comment	comment text
Document	9	#document	null

To see how these properties, compare with a node tree, Figure 12-16 displays the `nodeType`, `nodeName`, and `nodeValue` property values for each of the nodes shown earlier in Figure 12-1.

Figure 12-16 Node properties for the node tree shown in Figure 12-1

Node	node.nodeType	node.nodeName	node.nodeValue
Document	9	#document	null
html	1	HTML	null
head	1	HEAD	null
body	1	BODY	null
title	1	TITLE	null
"Historic Documents"	3	#text	Historic Documents
h1	1	H1	null
"Dept. of History"	3	#text	Dept. of History
p	1	P	null
"The "	3	#text	The
b	1	B	null
"constitution"	3	#text	constitution
" online"	3	#text	online

In the `for` loop from the createList() function, you want to examine only those child nodes that are from heading elements whose element name is H1 through H6. Notice that you use capital letters for the element name because that is how the element name is represented in the `nodeName` property. You can place these possible headings in the following array variable:

```
var headings = ["H1", "H2", "H3", "H4", "H5", "H6"];
```

To test whether a particular value is found within the headings array use the following `indexOf()` function (introduced in Figure 10-7)

```
array.indexOf(value)
```

where *array* is the array and *value* is a value to be searched for within the array. The `indexOf()` function returns the index number of the value within the array, or if no value can be found, it returns the value 1. For example, the following expression

```
headings.indexOf("H3")
```

would return the value 2, because the index of the H3 entry in the headings array is 2. However, the expression

```
headings.indexOf("h3")
```

would return the value -1 because that specific text string is not found within the headings array.

You can store the heading level for an element node, n, using the following expression

```
var headLevel = headings.indexOf(n.nodeName);
```

so that element nodes for `h1` elements would have a headLevel value of 0, `h2` elements would have a value of 1, and so forth. Element nodes that are not one of the 6 heading elements would have a headLevel value of -1.

Determining Node Properties

- To determine the type of object a node represents, use

  `node.nodeType`

  where *node* is a node object in the node tree. The `nodeType` property returns the value 1 for elements, 2 for attributes, and 3 for text nodes.
- To return the value of a node, use the following:

  `node.nodeValue`

  For an element, the value of the `nodeValue` property is `null`. For an attribute, the value represents the attribute's value. For a text node, the value represents the text string contained in the node.
- To return the name of a node, use the following:

  `node.nodeName`

  For elements, the name of the node matches the name of the element in uppercase letters. For attributes, the node name matches the attribute name. For text nodes, the node name is `#text`.

Add commands to the createList() function to create the headings array and to use the `indexOf()` function to test whether a node is one of the six heading elements.

To test for article heading nodes:

1. Directly after the opening line of the createList() function, insert the code:

```
// Headings for the outline
var headings = ["H1", "H2", "H3", "H4", "H5", "H6"];
```

2. Within the `for` loop, add the following code:

```
// Examine only article headings
var headLevel = headings.indexOf(n.nodeName);

if (headLevel !== -1) {
}
```

Figure 12-17 highlights the newly added code in the createList() function.

Figure 12-17 Checking for article headings

array of headings to be displayed in the outline

retrieves the index of the element node name

tests whether the element node name appears in the headings array

```
function createList(source, outlineList) {
   // Headings for the outline
   var headings = ["H1", "H2", "H3", "H4", "H5", "H6"];

   /* Loop through all of the child nodes of source
      article until no child nodes are left */
   for (var n = source.firstChild; n !== null; n = n.nextSibling) {
      // Examine only article headings
      var headLevel = headings.indexOf(n.nodeName);

      if (headLevel !== -1) {
      }
   }
}
```

From Figure 12-16, you may have noticed that element nodes don't have a value for the nodeValue property. It might seem that an element node's value should be the content it contains, but that content is itself a text node. Therefore, to access the text contained within an element, you can reference the text node within the element. For the following code,

```
<h1 id="title">History Online</h1>
```

the text of the h1 heading can be accessed with

```
document.getElementById("title").firstChild.nodeValue;
```

Note that this expression assumes the element text is the first child of the element. If there are other nested nodes, a different reference is required.

In the outlining app, you will assume that the headings only contain text and no nested elements. Using this assumption, retrieve the text from each heading and add it as a list item to the outline.

To add the list item headings:

1. Within the if statement in the createList() function, insert the following code to retrieve the text of each heading and append that text to a list item in the outline list.

```
var listElem = document.createElement("li");
listElem.innerHTML = n.firstChild.nodeValue;
outlineList.appendChild(listElem);
```

Figure 12-18 describes the code to create the list item text.

Figure 12-18   Adding a list item to the outline list

creates an li element

sets the inner HTML of the li element to the value of the heading's text node

```
if (headLevel !== -1) {
    var listElem = document.createElement("li");
    listElem.innerHTML = n.firstChild.nodeValue;
    outlineList.appendChild(listElem);
}
```

appends the li element to the outline list

2. Return to the makeOutline() function and add the following code to run the createList() function using the source and outlineList variables as the parameter values.

```
createList(source, outlineList);
```

Figure 12-19 shows the revised code of the makeOutline() function.

Figure 12-19   Displaying the outline

```
    mainHeading.appendChild(headingText);
    outline.appendChild(mainHeading);
    outline.appendChild(outlineList);

    createList(source, outlineList);
}
```

populates the outline list

source of the outline headings

node containing the outline list

3. Save your changes to the file and then reload **bc_const.html** in your browser. Figure 12-20 shows the outline generated from the text of all of the headings in the source article.

| Figure 12-20 | Displaying the outline |

list generated after checking for h1 through h6 headings

You have completed your initial work on the outlining app. By navigating through the node tree, you have created list items matching the headings in the U.S. Constitution document. However, these list entries make no distinction between the headings so that an h1 heading appears the same way as an h2 or h3 heading. In the next session, you will modify the outline to distinguish main headings from minor headings and subheadings.

REVIEW

Session 12.1 Quick Check

1. What are nodes? What objects of an HTML file do they represent?
2. What property references the parent of a node?
3. What object references the third child node of an object?
4. What property would you use to reference child nodes that are elements?
5. For an element node representing a `blockquote` element, what values are returned by the `nodeType`, `nodeName`, and `nodeValue` properties?
6. Provide a command to create a node containing the text string "U.S. Constitution". Store the node in the docText variable. Provide another command to create an `h2` element node, storing the node in the mainTitle variable. Provide a command to append the docText variable to the mainTitle variable.
7. The elemArr variable contains the following array:

   ```
   var elemArr = ["H1", "H2", "H3", "H4", "H5", "H6"];
   ```

   Provide the value returned by the following expression:

   ```
   elemArr.indexOf("H4");
   ```

Session 12.2 Visual Overview:

An **attribute node** represents an attribute that can be associated with an element node.

Exploring Attribute Nodes

The `hasAttribute()` method returns a Boolean value indicating whether the node has the specified attribute.

```javascript
// Add an id to the heading if it is missing
if (n.hasAttribute("id") === false) {
   n.setAttribute("id", "head" + headNum);
}

var listElem= document.createElement("li");

// Add an id to the list item
listElem.setAttribute("id", "list" + n.id);

linkElem.setAttribute("href", "#" + n.id);

// Append the hypertext link to the list item
listElem.appendChild(linkElem);
```

To add an attribute node to an HTML element, you can also use the **attribute name** as the node's property name and the property value to represent the attribute value.

The `setAttribute()` method sets the value of an attribute node that is attached to an element.

Creating a Nested List

Norene reviewed the initial outline you created in the previous session. She is pleased that the outline extracts the text from the heading elements in the Constitution document. However, it doesn't distinguish between main headings and subheadings. Recall that Norene wants you to make the outline a nested list in which lower-level headings are nested within upper-level headings. Figure 12-21 shows how the current HTML fragment generated by the createList() function needs to be modified to create a nested list of headings. All entries that match the h1 heading are placed at the top level of the table of contents, the entries for h2 headings are placed at the next lower level, and so forth.

Figure 12-21	Creating a nested list

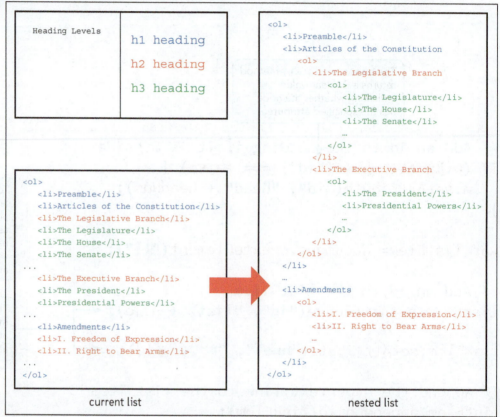

© 2016 Cengage Learning

You need to modify the createList() function so that every time a new list item is added to the outline, it is placed at the appropriate level in the table of contents. There are three possibilities:

1. The new list item is at the same level as the previous list item (such as when an h2 element follows another h2 element).
2. The new list item is at a lower level than the previous list item (such as when an h3 element follows an h2 element).
3. The new list item is at a higher level than the previous list item (such as when an h1 element follows an h3 element).

To determine the level of each list item, you can use the information returned by the indexOf() function that you used in the previous session. The function returns a value of 0 for all h1 headings it encounters, 1 for all h2 headings, 2 for all h3 headings, and so forth. With that information, you can apply the following three rules to determine how a new list item should be placed in the table of contents:

1. A list item at the same level as the previous item is simply appended to the current ordered list.
2. A list item at a lower level than the previous item is placed in a new ordered list that is nested within the current ordered list.
3. A list item at a higher level than the previous item is appended to the corresponding ordered list higher up in the table of contents.

The key to these conditions is to store the index number of the previous heading within the prevLevel. Then, as the program loops through all the element headings, it compares the headLevel value of the current node to the index value of prevLevel. The following `if` condition tests the three possibilities for the comparison of the index numbers:

TIP

Since the headings array lists the higher-level headings first, lower-level headings have higher index numbers.

```
if (headLevel === prevLevel) {
    // Append the list item to the current list
} else if (headLevel > prevLevel) {
    // Start a new nested list
} else {
    // Append the entry to a higher list
}
```

Add this `if` structure to the code of the createList() function.

To insert the `if` conditions:

1. If you took a break after the previous session, go to the **bc_outline.js** file in your editor.

2. Scroll down to the statement that creates the headings array and, after the headings array, insert the following command to declare the prevLevel variable, setting its initial value to 0:

   ```
   // Previous Level of the Headings
   var prevLevel = 0;
   ```

3. Within the `if` statement, replace the command `outlineList.appendChild(listElem);` with the following if-else structure:

   ```
   if (headLevel === prevLevel) {
       // Append the list item to the current list
   } else if (headLevel > prevLevel) {
       // Start a new nested list
   } else {
       // Append the list item to a higher list
   }
   ```

4. Directly after the if-else structure, add the following command to update the value of the prevLevel variable to reflect the level of the current list item.

   ```
   // Update the value of prevLevel
   prevLevel = headLevel;
   ```

   Figure 12-22 describes the newly added code.

Figure 12-22   **Creating the if-else structure for different heading levels**

```
function createList(source, outlineList) {
    // Headings for the outline
    var headings = ["H1", "H2", "H3", "H4", "H5", "H6"];

    // Previous Level of the Headings
    var prevLevel = 0;

    /* Loop through all of the child nodes of source
       article until no child nodes are left */

    for (var n = source.firstChild; n !== null; n = n.nextSibling) {
    // Examine only article headings
        var headLevel = headings.indexOf(n.nodeName);

        if (headLevel !== -1) {
            var listElem = document.createElement("li");
            listElem.innerHTML = n.firstChild.nodeValue;

            if (headLevel === prevLevel) {
                // Append the list item to the current list
            } else if (headLevel > prevLevel) {
                // Start a new nested list
            } else {
                // Append the list item to a higher list
            }

            // Update the value of prevLevel
            prevLevel = headLevel;
        }
    }
}
```

sets the initial value of the prevLevel variable → `var prevLevel = 0;`

replaces the statement and appends the list item with the if structure → (if structure block)

updates the value of the prevLevel variable each time through the loop → `prevLevel = headLevel;`

Next, you will enter the code for each `if` condition. First, if prevLevel equals headLevel, then the current node is at the same level as the previous entry and you add the new entry to the current list. Figure 12-23 shows how creating and appending such a node to the node tree corresponds directly to inserting the code in an HTML fragment.

Figure 12-23   **Appending a list item**

© 2016 Cengage Learning

Revise the code for the createList() function.

To append the list item:

1. Add the following command to the first nested `if` condition:

   ```
   outlineList.appendChild(listElem);
   ```

   Figure 12-24 highlights the newly added code.

Figure 12-24   **Appending the list item to the current list**

```
if (headLevel === prevLevel) {
    // Append the list item to the current list
    outlineList.appendChild(listElem);
} else if (headLevel > prevLevel) {
    // Start a new nested list
} else {
    // Append the list item to a higher list
}
```

2. Save your changes to the file.

3. Reload **bc_const.html** in your browser and verify that the outline is still displayed to the left of the source article and that no errors are reported by your browser.

   Trouble? A few headings from the source document do not appear in the outline. This will be corrected as you add more code to the createList() function.

The `else if` condition responds to the situation where the new heading is at a lower level than the previous heading. In those cases, you want to insert the list item within a new nested list appended to the current list. Figure 12-25 shows the HTML fragment and node tree of the resulting new content in the table of contents.

Figure 12-25   Appending a nested list

© 2016 Cengage Learning

To do this in JavaScript, create a new ordered list and then append the list item to it using the following commands:

```
var nestedList = document.createElement("ol");
nestedList.appendChild(listElem);
```

The nested list is then appended as a child of the previous—and currently last—entry in the current list, which can be done with

```
outlineList.lastChild.appendChild(nestedList);
```

Finally, the nested list needs to be set as the new outline list using

```
outlineList = nestedList;
```

so that the text of subsequent headings is added to it.

Revise the `else if` condition in the createList() function.

To append the nested list:

1. Return to the **bc_outline.js** file in your editor.

2. Within the `else if` condition of the createList() function, insert the following code to create a new nested list.

```
var nestedList = document.createElement("ol");
nestedList.appendChild(listElem);
```

3. Next, add the following code to add the nested list to the current outline list.

```
// Append nested list to last item in the current list
outlineList.lastChild.appendChild(nestedList);
```

4. Finally, add the following code to designate the nested list as the new outline list.

```
// Change the current list to the nested list
outlineList = nestedList;
```

Figure 12-26 describes the code within the else `if` condition.

Figure 12-26   **Creating a nested list**

creates the nested list and appends the list item to it

appends the nested list to the current outline list

makes the nested list the current outline list

```
if (headLevel === prevLevel) {
    // Append the list item to the current list
    outlineList.appendChild(listElem);
} else if (headLevel > prevLevel) {
    // Start a new nested list
    var nestedList = document.createElement("ol");
    nestedList.appendChild(listElem);
    // Append nested list to last item in the current list
    outlineList.lastChild.appendChild(nestedList);
    // Change the current list to the nested list
    outlineList = nestedList;
} else {
    // Append the list item to a higher list
}
```

5. Save your changes to the file.

6. Reload **bc_const.html** in your browser and verify that the outline is still displayed to the left of the source article and that no errors are reported by your browser. Figure 12-27 shows part of the outline with the list items nested by heading level.

Figure 12-27   **Viewing the nested list**

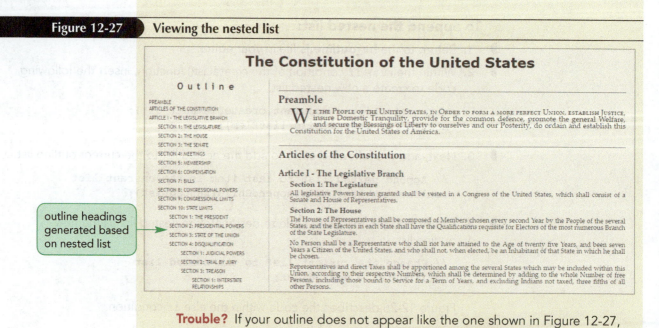

outline headings
generated based
on nested list

Trouble? If your outline does not appear like the one shown in Figure 12-27, check your code against the code shown in Figure 12-26 for errors.

At this point, the createList() function only works going across the current level or down to the next level of headings. There are no commands to go back up to the higher-level headings.

To move up one or more levels in the outline, you append the new list item to a preexisting list. Figure 12-28 shows an HTML fragment and the corresponding node tree for adding a new list item to a higher-level list.

Figure 12-28   **Appending an item to an upper level list**

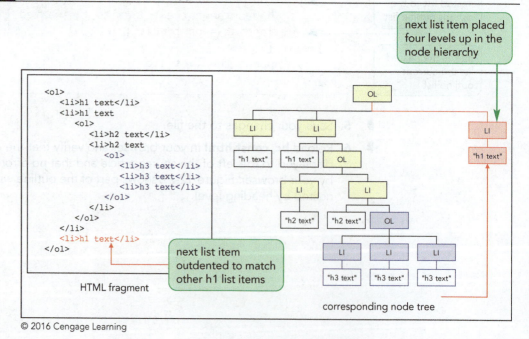

next list item placed
four levels up in the
node hierarchy

next list item
outdented to match
other h1 list items

HTML fragment

corresponding node tree

The challenge is to calculate how many levels to go up in the node tree to find the correct list for the new entry. Examine Figure 12-28 and notice that for each level you go up in the section headings, you go up two levels in the node tree—past the parent `ol` element of the current outline list and then past that element's `li` parent. For example, to go from `h3` headings back up to `h1` headings, you go up four levels in the node tree. Thus, you must first calculate the difference between the index number of the previous heading and the index number of the current heading, which is simply the difference between the prevLevel variable and the headLevel variable. You can store that difference in the following levelUp variable:

```
var levelUp = prevLevel - headLevel;
```

To move up the node tree, you apply the `parentNode` property twice for each difference in level between the two headings using the following `for` loop:

```
for (var i = 1; i <= levelUp; i++) {
   outlineList = outlineList.parentNode.parentNode;
}
```

On each iteration, the `for` loop changes the table of contents list to the outline list two levels up on the node tree. The loop stops when it has gone up the correct number of levels as indicated by the levelUp variable. Once it is at the correct level, the list item is appended to the outline list.

Complete the `else` condition in the changeList() function now.

To complete the `else` condition:

▶ 1. Return to the **bc_outline.js** file in your editor.

▶ 2. Within the `else` condition of the createList() function, add the following commands to calculate the difference between the current level and the previous level:

```
// Calculate the difference between the current and previous
level
var levelUp = prevLevel - headLevel;
```

▶ 3. Add the following command for loop to move up the levels of nested lists:

```
// Go up to the higher level
for (var i = 1; i <= levelUp; i++) {
   outlineList = outlineList.parentNode.parentNode;
}
```

▶ 4. Finally, append the list item to the higher-order list:

```
outlineList.appendChild(listElem);
```

Figure 12-29 highlights the code in the `else` condition.

Figure 12-29 **Populating a higher ordered list**

the levelUp variable calculates the difference between the levels

moves the outlineList object up two levels for each iteration in the for loop

appends the list item to the outlineList node

```
} else {
   // Append the list item to a higher list
   // Calculate the difference between the current and previous level
   var levelUp = prevLevel - headLevel;
   // Go up to the higher level
   for (var i = 1; i <= levelUp; i++) {
      outlineList = outlineList.parentNode.parentNode;
   }
   outlineList.appendChild(listElem);
}
```

applies the parentNode property twice to move up two levels

5. Save your changes to the file and then reload **bc_const.html** in your browser. Figure 12-30 shows the final layout of the outline with different headings placed at different levels within the list.

Figure 12-30 **Layout of the nested lists**

h1 headings

h2 headings

h3 headings

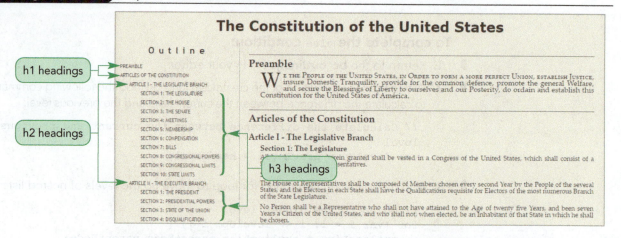

Norene likes that the layout of the outline makes it clear which are the main headings, lower headings, and subheadings. Next, she wants you to make a dynamic outline in which users can jump to different sections of the document by clicking links in the outline list. To do that, you will use attribute nodes.

INSIGHT

Traversing the Node Tree with Recursion

In creating the document outline, you made several simplifying assumptions. One was that all of the section headings in each historic document would be siblings and children of the source document. You did not allow for the possibility that a section heading would be further nested within another element. However, some applications that involve working with the node tree require a script to traverse the entire tree, touching each node. One way of doing this is through recursion.

Recursion is a programming technique in which a function calls itself repeatedly until a stopping condition is met. The following is an example of a recursive function that counts the number of child nodes descending from a given node:

```
function countNodes(node, nodeCount) {
    for (var n = node.firstChild; n !== null; n = n.nextSibling)
    {
        nodeCount++;
        countNodes(n, nodeCount);
    }
    return nodeCount;
}
```

Notice that the countNodes() function includes a `for` loop that loops through every child node of the given node object. For each child node, the function increases the value of the nodeCount parameter by 1 and then calls itself to add the number of children of that child node to the total. This process of drilling down the node tree by repeatedly calling the countNodes() function continues until no descendant nodes remain in the node tree.

Every recursive function needs a starting point. If you wanted to count all of the nodes in Norene's source article, you would point the node parameter to the source article and set the initial value of the nodeCount variable to 0. The expression to count all of the nodes would be as follows:

```
countNodes(source, 0);
```

If you applied this command to Norene's U.S. Constitution document, you would discover that the article contains 435 text, element, and white space nodes.

Working with Attribute Nodes

An attribute node contains an attribute that can be attached to an element node. However, unlike element and text nodes, attribute nodes are not part of the node tree because they are not the child or parent of any node and thus cannot be placed within a hierarchy. Instead, an attribute node is associated with an element node as shown in Figure 12-31 in which the attribute node for the `href` attribute is associated with the element node for the `a` element.

Figure 12-31   **Attribute nodes**

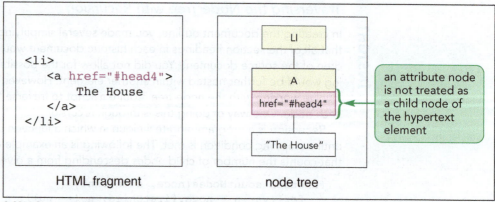

© 2016 Cengage Learning

The document object model supports several methods to create, attach, and set the values of attributes. Some of these are listed in Figure 12-32.

Figure 12-32   **Methods of attribute nodes**

Method	Description
`node.attributes`	Returns the collection of attributes associated with *node*
`node.attributes[i].nodeName`	Returns the attribute name from an item in the attributes collection where *i* is the index number
`node.attributes[i].nodeValue`	Returns the attribute value from an item in the attributes collection
`document.createAttribute(att)`	Creates an attribute node with the name *att*
`node.getAttribute(att)`	Returns the value of the *att* attribute associated with *node*
`node.hasAttribute(att)`	Returns a Boolean value indicating whether *node* is associated with the *att* attribute
`node.removeAttribute(att)`	Removes the *att* attribute from the *node*
`node.removeAttributeNode(att)`	Removes *att* attribute node from the node
`node.setAttribute(att, value)`	Creates or changes the value of the *att* attribute of the *node*

To create or set an attribute for an element, you use the `setAttribute()` method. The following code creates a list item element and then uses the `setAttribute()` method to set the ID value of the list item to the text string listHead1:

```
var listElem = document.createElement("li");
listElem.setAttribute("id","listHead1");
```

The net effect is to create the following HTML fragment:

```
<li id="listHead1"></li>
```

For HTML attributes, however, it is still simpler to set an attribute value by applying the HTML attribute as a property of the object as you did in the last tutorial.

In some cases, you need to determine whether an element has an attribute, such as the `id` attribute. In these situations, use the `hasAttribute()` method, which returns the Boolean value `true` if the element contains the attribute. For example, the expression

```
listElem.hasAttribute("id")
```

would return the value `true` if the list item had an `id` attribute, and would return `false` otherwise.

REFERENCE

Working with Attribute Nodes

- To set the value of an attribute node, apply

  ```
  node.setAttribute(att, value)
  ```

  where *node* is a node object in the node tree, *att* is an attribute of that node, and *value* is the attribute's value.
- To determine whether a node contains an attribute, apply the following:

  ```
  node.hasAttribute(att)
  ```

- To remove an attribute from a node, apply the following:

  ```
  node.removeAttribute(att)
  ```

- To create an attribute node, apply the following:

  ```
  document.createAttribute(att)
  ```

Creating Heading IDs

Norene wants you to revise the createList() function so that the entries in the U.S. Constitution outline are linked to the headings they represent. Again, it is useful to write out the HTML code for the proposed change so that you know what nodes need to be created by the function. Creating the hypertext links involves two steps, which are listed next and illustrated in Figure 12-33:

1. Add an `id` attribute to each heading (if it doesn't already have one) to mark its location within the web page.
2. Change the content of each list item to a hypertext link pointing to the corresponding heading.

Figure 12-33   Linking list items to their headings

headings with id values	```<h1 id="head1">Preamble</h1>```
	…
	```<h1 id="head2">Articles of the Constitution</h1>```
	…
	```<h2 id="head3">Legislative Branch</h2>```
	…
	```<h3 id="head4">Section 1: The Legislature</h3>```
	…
	```<h3 id="head5">Section 2: The House</h3>```
	…
	```<h3 id="head6">Section 3: The Senate</h3>```
	…

outline with links to each heading tag	```<ol>```
	    ```<li><a href="#head1">Preamble</a></li>```
	    ```<li><a href="#head2">Articles of the Constitution</a></li>```
	    ```<ol>```
	        ```<li><a href="#head3">Legislative Branch</a></li>```
	        ```<ol>```
	            ```<li><a href="#head4">Section 1: The Legislature</a></li>```
	            ```<li><a href="#head5">Section 2: The House</a></li>```
	            ```<li><a href="#head6">Section 3: The Senate</a></li>```
	    ...

Because each ID must be unique, you will create a counter variable named headNum that increases by 1 for each heading found in the source document. Add the headNum variable to the createList() function, setting its initial value to 0.

To create the headNum variable:

1. Return to the **bc_outline.js** file in your editor.

2. Within the createList() function, insert the following code directly after the command to declare the prevLevel variable:

```
// Running total of the article headings
var headNum = 0;
```

Figure 12-34 highlights the code to create the headNum variable.

| Figure 12-34 | Creating the headNum variable |

```
function createList(source, outlineList) {
    // Headings for the outline
    var headings = ["H1", "H2", "H3", "H4", "H5", "H6"];

    // Previous Level of the Headings
    var prevLevel = 0;

    // Running total of the article headings
    var headNum = 0;
```

sets the initial value of the headNum variable to 0

Next, use the headNum variable to write the ID of each article heading using the reference

```
headingi
```

where *i* is the value of the headNum variable. You must be careful not to overwrite any preexisting IDs. Therefore, the code should first test whether an ID already exists for the element and then insert an id attribute only if it doesn't.

To insert the heading IDs:

Attribute names and values must be enclosed within quotation marks.

1. Directly after the `if` condition that tests whether the value of the headLevel variable is not equal to -1, insert the following commands:

```
// Add an id to the heading if it is missing
headNum++;
if (n.hasAttribute("id") === false) {
    n.setAttribute("id", "head" + headNum);
}
```

Figure 12–35 highlights the code to insert the heading IDs.

Figure 12-35   **Inserting heading ids**

increases the value of headNum by 1

tests whether an id attribute already exists for the heading

if no id attribute exists, adds one using the headNum variable

```
if (headLevel !== -1) {
   // Add an id to the heading if it is missing
   headNum++;
   if (n.hasAttribute("id") === false) {
      n.setAttribute("id", "head" + headNum);
   }
   var listElem= document.createElement("li");
   listElem.innerHTML = n.firstChild.nodeValue;
```

2. Save your changes to the file and then reload **bc_const.html** in your browser.

3. Use your browser's developer tools to view the elements within the U.S. Constitution article and verify that the headings now contain the IDs head1 through head58. Figure 12-36 shows the element hierarchy from the Google Chrome Developer tab.

Figure 12-36   **Viewing heading IDs**

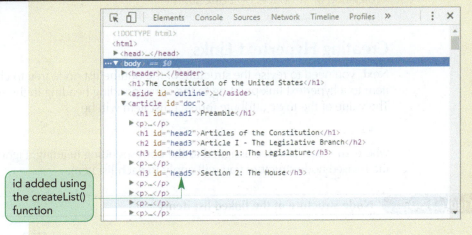

id added using the createList() function

INSIGHT

Looping through the Attributes Collection

You can examine each HTML attribute associated with an element using the following attributes collection:

```
node.attributes
```

Each attribute's name is referenced using the `nodeName` property, and each attribute's value is referenced using the `nodeValue` property. For example, the following `for` loop writes a text string containing each attribute's name and value, enclosed in quotes, for the document's first `section` element:

```
var s1 = document.getElementsByTagName("section")[0];
var attText = "";

for (var i = 0; i < s1.attributes.length; i++) {
    attText += s1.attributes[i].nodeName;
    attText += "=";
    attText += "'" + s1.attributes[i].nodeValue + "' ";

}
```

The attributes collection is an example of a **named node map**, which is an unordered list of nodes that can be referenced by their names—in this case, attribute names. You also can reference the `attributes` collection using an index number, as the previous code demonstrates. However, be aware that there is no standard ordering of attributes by index number.

Creating Hypertext Links

Next, you need to revise the structure of the outline list node tree to change each list item to a hypertext link pointing to the corresponding heading in the source document. The value of the `href` attribute for each list item will be

```
#id
```

where *id* is the ID value assigned to the corresponding heading. Figure 12-37 shows the revised node structure you will apply to each list item.

Figure 12-37 **Node structure of the linked list items**

© 2016 Cengage Learning

To create the new node structure, you will replace the old commands that inserted the text of the link items with new code that inserts the text for each item as a hyperlink using the following code:

```
var linkElem = document.createElement("a");
linkElem.innerHTML = n.innerHTML;
linkElem.setAttribute("href", "#" + n.id);
```

Note that the value of the hypertext link is set to point to the id attribute of the matching heading node from the source article. Finally, append the hypertext link to the list item, as follows:

```
listElem.appendChild(linkElem);
```

Add these commands to the createList() function now.

To create the hypertext links:

1. Return to the **bc_outline.js** file in your editor and go to the createList() function.

2. Delete the line `listElem.innerHTML = n.firstChild.nodeValue;` from the code in the createList() function:

3. Replace the deleted line with the following code to create the hypertext link and set its href attribute:

   ```
   // Create hypertext links to the document headings
   var linkElem = document.createElement("a");
   linkElem.innerHTML = n.innerHTML;
   linkElem.setAttribute("href", "#" + n.id);
   ```

4. Append the hypertext link to the list item by adding the command:

   ```
   // Append the hypertext link to the list item
   listElem.appendChild(linkElem);
   ```

   Figure 12-38 shows the revised code to create the hypertext links.

Figure 12-38   Creating hypertext links

```
if (headLevel !== -1) {
   // Add an id to the heading if it is missing
   headNum++;
   if (n.hasAttribute("id") === false) {
      n.setAttribute("id", "head" + headNum);
   }

   var listElem= document.createElement("li");

   // Create hypertext links to the document headings
   var linkElem = document.createElement("a");
   linkElem.innerHTML = n.innerHTML;
   linkElem.setAttribute("href", "#" + n.id);

   // Append the hypertext link to the list item
   listElem.appendChild(linkElem);
```

creates a hypertext link within each list item

appends the hypertext link to the list item

5. Save your changes to the file and then reload **bc_const.html** in your browser. The list entries now appear as hypertext links, as shown in Figure 12-39.

Figure 12-39   Hypertext links in the outline

The Constitution of the United States

Outline

PREAMBLE
ARTICLES OF THE CONSTITUTION
   ARTICLE I - THE LEGISLATIVE BRANCH
      SECTION 1: THE LEGISLATURE
      SECTION 2: THE HOUSE
      SECTION 3: THE SENATE
      SECTION 4: MEETINGS
      SECTION 5: MEMBERSHIP
      SECTION 6: COMPENSATION
      SECTION 7: BILLS
      SECTION 8: CONGRESSIONAL POWERS
      SECTION 9: CONGRESSIONAL LIMITS
      SECTION 10: STATE LIMITS
   ARTICLE II - THE EXECUTIVE BRANCH
      SECTION 1: THE PRESIDENT

outline list items are linked to their headings

Preamble

W E THE PEOPLE OF THE UNITED STATES, IN ORDER TO FORM A MORE PERFECT UNION, ESTABLISH JUSTICE, insure Domestic Tranquility, provide for the common defence, promote the general Welfare, and secure the Blessings of Liberty to ourselves and our Posterity, do ordain and establish this Constitution for the United States of America.

Articles of the Constitution

Article I - The Legislative Branch

Section 1: The Legislature
All legislative Powers herein granted shall be vested in a Congress of the United States, which shall consist of a Senate and House of Representatives.

Section 2: The House
The House of Representatives shall be composed of Members chosen every second Year by the People of the several States, and the Electors in each State shall have the Qualifications requisite for Electors of the most numerous Branch of the State Legislature.

6. Click a link from the outline and verify that you are jumped to that heading within the U.S. Constitution.

7. Use your browser's developer tools to view the elements and attributes you have generated for the outline. Figure 12-40 displays the code for the outline list as displayed in the Google Chrome Developer pane.

Figure 12-40   **Viewing the elements in the outline list**

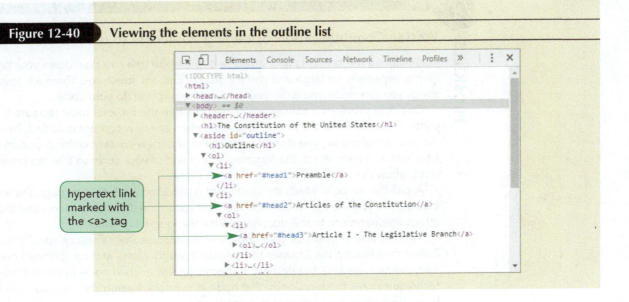

hypertext link marked with the <a> tag

PROSKILLS

Written Communication: Speeding up Access to the DOM

Manipulating the contents and structure of the node tree can slow down your programs, especially for large and complicated document structures. There are several things you can do as you write your code to help speed up your code.

One core problem is **reflow**, which occurs when the browser must recreate the content and layout of the entire document when any new content is added. To reduce the amount of reflow, you should create all of your new content within a document fragment and then attach the fragment at the end of your code so that the browser must reflow the page only once.

Avoid `for` loops in which the document is modified each time through the loop. Instead, manipulate the document fragment each time through the loop and then attach that fragment to the document once the loop has finished.

Another way to optimize your code is with variables that reference specific nodes. Rather than forcing the browser to navigate through a long and complicated node tree, define a variable to reference a specific parent or child node within that tree. This technique stores the location of that node in memory, freeing the browser from having to locate it again the next time it is used.

Another place where the browser can be slowed down is in the creation of **node lists** that reference collections of objects. Node lists can be memory intensive because the browser must keep them updated as the document is modified. For example, the following code creates a node list named allP, which consists of all paragraphs in the document:

```
var allP = document.getElementsByTagName("P");
for (var i = 0; i < allP.length; i++) {
    thisP = allP[i];
}
```

You can optimize this code with the following `for` loop, which avoids the creation of this node list:

```
for (var i = 0; (thisP = document.getElementsByTagName("P")
[i]); i++) {

}
```

The advantage is that the browser doesn't create a separate node list that must be constantly updated and revised whenever the document changes. Instead, the browser examines those nodes only within the context of the `for` loop. Once the loop is finished, there is nothing for the browser to keep track of.

Used together, these techniques can speed up your program and make it operate more efficiently, especially when manipulating the contents of long and complicated documents.

You have finished making the outline into a nested list of hypertext links. In the next session, you will explore how to work with CSS style sheets and style sheet rules.

REVIEW

Session 12.2 Quick Check

1. Provide the code to create two `ul` list elements—one nested inside the other. Use the variable name topList for the upper list element and the variable name bottomList for the bottom list element.

2. In the previous question, what is the node reference to the topList object from a list item found within the bottom list?

3. Why are attribute nodes not part of the document node tree?

4. Provide the node method to determine whether an element node contains the `type` attribute.

5. Provide the command to create a web form check box, storing the element node in the CBox variable. Use an attribute node method to define the `type` attribute.

6. What expression would you use in the previous question to determine whether the CBox `input` element has a `value` attribute?

Session 12.3 Visual Overview:

Before you can use the style sheet link, you must define the `href` and `rel` attributes.

To add an external style sheet, create a `link` element.

To add the `link` element to the style sheets collection, append it to the document head.

To disable a style, set its `disabled` property to `true`.

```javascript
var pageStyle = document.createElement("link");
pageStyle.setAttribute("href", "bc_page.css");
pageStyle.setAttribute("rel", "stylesheet");
pageStyle.setAttribute("disabled", "disabled");
document.head.appendChild(pageStyle);
pageStyle.disabled = true;

var buttonDIV = document.createElement("div");
buttonDIV.setAttribute("id", "styleButtons");
var webButton = document.createElement("input");
webButton.setAttribute("type", "button");
webButton.setAttribute("value", "Web View");
var pageButton = document.createElement("input");
pageButton.setAttribute("type", "button");
pageButton.setAttribute("value", "Page View");

buttonDIV.appendChild(webButton);
buttonDIV.appendChild(pageButton);
document.body.insertBefore(buttonDIV, document.body.firstChild);

var buttonStyles  = document.createElement("style");
document.head.appendChild(buttonStyles);

document.styleSheets[document.styleSheets.length-1].insertRule(
   "div#styleButtons {position: fixed;}", 0);

document.styleSheets[document.styleSheets.length-1].insertRule(
   "div#styleButtons input { \
      height: 40px; \
      margin: 5px 10px; \
      width: 100px;}", 1);

webButton.onclick = function() {pageStyle.disabled = true;};
pageButton.onclick = function() {pageStyle.disabled = false;};
```

To add an embedded style sheet, create a `style` element and append it to the document head.

Style rules are added by specifying the text of the CSS rule.

The `insertRule()` method adds a style rule to a style sheet.

Click the Web View and Page View buttons to disable and enable the pageStyle style sheet.

Style Sheets and Style Rules

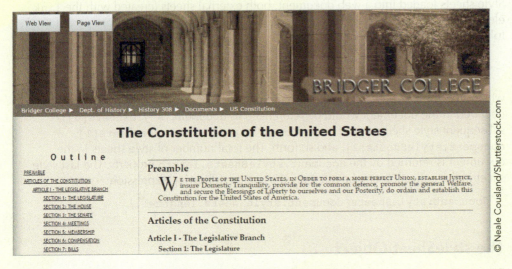

website under the Web View style

website under the Page View style

Working with Style Sheets

In the last tutorial, you created inline styles by modifying the `style` property of various page elements. Inline styles are hampered by the fact that the `style` property is applied to specific elements in the document rather than globally through a CSS style rule. In this session, you will explore how to use JavaScript to create and modify style sheets that can be applied to an entire document.

The styleSheets Collection

Style sheets loaded into a web document, both external sheets (created with the `link` element) and embedded style sheets (created with the `style` element), are part of the following object collection:

```
document.styleSheets
```

The arrangement of style sheets within the collection reflects the order in which they are declared within the document head. Thus, the first style sheet declared in the document would be referenced as `document.styleSheets[0]`; subsequent style sheets would be referenced as `document.styleSheets[1]`, `document.styleSheets[2]`, and so forth. The total number of style sheets in the document is returned by the `document.styleSheets.length` property. The last style sheet in the collection can be referenced using the following expression:

```
document.styleSheets[document.styleSheets.length-1]
```

The styleSheet Object

Each style sheet in the `styleSheets` collection is a `styleSheet` object and supports the properties displayed in Figure 12-41.

Figure 12-41	styleSheet object properties

Property	Description
`sheet.cssRules`	The object collection of style rules within the style sheet
`sheet.disabled`	A Boolean value indicating whether the style sheet is disabled (`true`) or enabled (`false`)
`sheet.href`	The URL of the style sheet file or an empty text string for an embedded style sheet (read-only)
`sheet.media`	A text string containing the list of media types associated with the style sheet (read-only)
`sheet.ownerNode`	The embed or `link` element node that created the style sheet (read-only)
`sheet.parentStyleSheet`	The styleSheet object containing the style sheet inserted via the `@import` rule (read-only)
`sheet.title`	The title of the style sheet (read-only)
`sheet.type`	The MIME type of the style sheet (read-only)

TIP

You can also reference a style sheet property by adding an ID to the `link` or `style` element and using the `getElementsById()` method to access the element node itself.

For example, the following expression returns the URL of the third style sheet in the current document:

```
document.styleSheets[2].href
```

Note that many of the style sheet properties are read-only and thus cannot be changed in JavaScript.

Norene knows that her students may not want to view her documents in the default web page view, so she has asked you to create an app known as a **style sheet switcher** in which users can choose among different style sheets to display the web document. Norene proposes two style sheets shown in Figure 12-42: the web view sheet that displays the source article as well as a page heading, document outline, and page footer; and a page view sheet that displays only the text of the document with no other page elements.

Figure 12-42	Viewing the document in web and page view

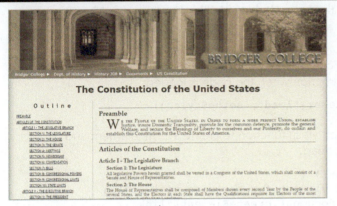

web view   page view

© Neale Cousland/Shutterstock.com

Norene has already created a page view style sheet and saved it in the bc_page.css file. As you have done in previous tutorials, you can apply the style sheet by adding the following tag to the document head:

```
<link href="bc_page.css" rel="stylesheet" />
```

However, rather than inserting the `link` element directly into the HTML file, you will add the `link` element through a JavaScript app that will also be used to enable the user to switch between the web view and page view style sheets.

To create the hypertext links:

1. If you took a break after the previous session, go to the **bc_const.html** file in your editor and add the following script element to the document head to load the bc_switch.js file:

   ```
   <script src="bc_switch.js" async></script
   ```

2. Save your changes to the file.

3. Use your editor to open the **bc_switch_txt.js** files from the html12 ▸ tutorial folder. Enter **your name** and **the date** in the comment section the file and save it as **bc_switch.js**.

4. Directly below the initial comment section, add the following event listener to run the setupStyles() function when the page is loaded.

   ```
   window.addEventListener("load", setupStyles);
   ```

5. Insert the following setupStyles() function to create a link element and append it the document head.

   ```
   function setupStyles() {
      // Create a link element for the page view styles
      var pageStyle = document.createElement("link");
      pageStyle.setAttribute("href", "bc_page.css");
      pageStyle.setAttribute("rel", "stylesheet");

      // Append the link element to the document head
      document.head.appendChild(pageStyle);
   }
   ```

   Figure 12-43 describes the newly added code in the bc_switch.js file.

Figure 12-43   **Inserting the setupStyles() function**

runs the setupStyles() function when the page is loaded

creates a link element

defines the source of the style sheet file

defines the link element as pointing to a style sheet file

```
*/

window.addEventListener("load", setupStyles);

function setupStyles() {
   // Create a link element for the page view styles
   var pageStyle = document.createElement("link");
   pageStyle.setAttribute("href", "bc_page.css");
   pageStyle.setAttribute("rel", "stylesheet");

   // Append the link element to the document head
   document.head.appendChild(pageStyle);
}
```

appends the link element to the document head, adding it to the styleSheets collection

6. Save your changes to the file and then reload **bc_const.html** in your browser. Verify that the document is displayed using the page view styles.

TIP

A disabled style sheet is removed from the `styleSheets` object collection.

By creating and appending the `link` element to the document head, you have also added the bc_page.css style sheet to the document's style sheet collection. Because the bc_page.css file is loaded last, its rules supersede the rules from earlier style sheets. Since you will be writing code to switch between web view and page view, you must disable this style sheet by adding the `disabled` attribute to the `link` element or by applying the `disabled` property to the style sheet object itself. Disable this style sheet now using JavaScript.

To disable a style sheet:

1. Return to the **bc_switch.js** file in your editor and go to the setupStyles() function.

2. Directly after the statement that sets the `rel` attribute, add the following command to set the `disabled` attribute of the `link` element to the value "disabled":

   ```
   pageStyle.setAttribute("disabled", "disabled");
   ```

3. Some browsers, such as Firefox, do not support HTML's `disabled` attribute for `link` elements. Create a cross-browser solution by adding the following command after the `appendChild()` statement to disable the pageStyle style sheet using the `disabled` object property.

   ```
   pageStyle.disabled = true;
   ```

   Figure 12-44 describes the code to disable the style sheet.

Figure 12-44   Disabling a style sheet

```
function setupStyles() {
   // Create a link element for the page view styles
   var pageStyle = document.createElement("link");
   pageStyle.setAttribute("href", "bc_page.css");
   pageStyle.setAttribute("rel", "stylesheet");
   pageStyle.setAttribute("disabled", "disabled");

   // Append the link element to the document head
   document.head.appendChild(pageStyle);
   pageStyle.disabled = true;
}
```

adds the `disabled` attribute to the link element

disables the page view style sheet object for browsers that don't support the disabled attribute

4. Save your changes and reload **bc_const.html** in your browser, verifying that the page view style is no longer being applied and that the web view style is active.

5. Use your browser's developer tools to view the `link` elements within the document head, verifying that the `link` element for the bc_page.css style is listed last and is disabled. See Figure 12-45.

Figure 12-45 **Style sheet links in the document head**

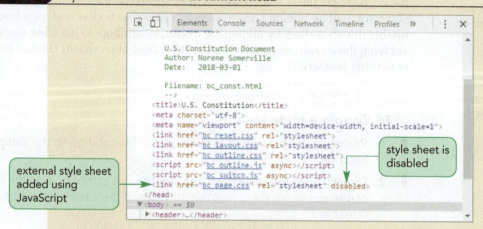

Trouble? If you don't see the `link` element for the bc_page.css file, you might be viewing the bc_const.html source file. Try the Elements or DOM Explorer tab of your Developer Tools pane.

To switch between the two views of the page you will create form buttons that will alternately enable and disable the bc_page.css style sheet. The HTML code for the form buttons is as follows:

```
<div id="styleButtons">
    <input type="button" value="Web View" />
    <input type="button" value="Page View" />
</div>
```

Use element and attribute nodes to insert this HTML fragment at the very top of the page body.

To insert the style buttons:

1. Return to the **bc_switch.js** file in your editor and go to the setupStyles() function.

2. Directly before the closing brace of the setupStyles() function, add the following commands to create the `div` element container for the style buttons.

   ```
   // Insert buttons for the style switcher
   var buttonDIV = document.createElement("div");
   buttonDIV.setAttribute("id", "styleButtons");
   ```

3. Add the following commands to create the Web View button:

   ```
   var webButton = document.createElement("input");
   webButton.setAttribute("type", "button");
   webButton.setAttribute("value", "Web View");
   ```

4. Add the following commands to create the Page View button:

   ```
   var pageButton = document.createElement("input");
   pageButton.setAttribute("type", "button");
   pageButton.setAttribute("value", "Page View");
   ```

5. Append the two buttons to the `div` element with the commands:

```
buttonDIV.appendChild(webButton);
buttonDIV.appendChild(pageButton);
```

6. Finally, use the following command to insert the `div` element at the top of the page body directly before the first child element:

```
document.body.insertBefore(buttonDIV,
document.body.firstChild);
```

Figure 12-46 describes the newly added code in the setupStyle() function.

Figure 12-46	Adding style buttons using the setupStyles() function

```
// Append the link element to the document head
document.head.appendChild(pageStyle);
pageStyle.disabled = true;

// Insert buttons for the style switcher
var buttonDIV = document.createElement("div");
buttonDIV.setAttribute("id", "styleButtons");

var webButton = document.createElement("input");
webButton.setAttribute("type", "button");
webButton.setAttribute("value", "Web View");

var pageButton = document.createElement("input");
pageButton.setAttribute("type", "button");
pageButton.setAttribute("value", "Page View");

buttonDIV.appendChild(webButton);
buttonDIV.appendChild(pageButton);

document.body.insertBefore(buttonDIV, document.body.firstChild);
}
```

- div element containing the style buttons
- input button for Web View
- input button for Page View
- append the buttons to the div element
- insert the div element at the start of the page body

7. Save your changes and reload **bc_const.html** in your browser. As shown in Figure 12-47, the Web View and Page View buttons are inserted at the top of the page body.

Figure 12-47	Style buttons in the page

- style buttons

© Neale Cousland/Shutterstock.com

The Web View and Page View buttons are displayed using the browser's default style sheet. Norene doesn't have a style sheet file that formats the two buttons and would like you to create such a style sheet within the Style Switcher app. You will write the contents of the style sheet using JavaScript.

Using Preferred and Alternate Style Sheets

Some browsers contain built-in style sheet switchers. To use those built-in style sheet switchers, the style sheets must be created by the user as persistent, preferred, or alternate style sheets where

- A **persistent style sheet** is the default style sheet and can't be turned off. It has a `rel` attribute value of "stylesheet" and does not have a `title` attribute.
- A **preferred style sheet** is identical to a persistent style sheet except that it does contain a `title` attribute, which allows it to be turned on and off by the end user.
- An **alternate style sheet** has a `rel` attribute value of "alternate stylesheet" and is also identified by its `title` attribute. Alternate style sheets are not turned on by default, but end users can switch to them as alternates to the preferred style sheet.

For example, the following HTML code contains persistent, preferred, and alternate style sheets. The bc_base.css style sheet is the default style sheet and is always active. The bc_web.css style sheet is the preferred style sheet and is also active. The bc_page.css style sheet is the alternate style sheet and can be turned on by the end user in preference to the bc_web.css style sheet.

```
<link href="bc_base.css" rel="stylesheet" />
<link href="bc_web.css" rel="stylesheet" title="Web View" />
<link href="bc_page.css" rel="alternate stylesheet"
      title="Page View" />
```

The method by which the end user chooses between the preferred and alternate style sheets varies by browser. The Firefox browser displays the list of preferred and alternate sheets in the View > Page Style menu while the Internet Explorer browser lists those style sheets in the View > Style menu. Google Chrome provides support for preferred and alternate style sheets through a browser extension. To determine what your browser supports, you need to check your browser documentation.

For browsers that don't support alternate style sheets, use JavaScript to create an interface for style sheet switching.

Working with Style Sheet Rules

Just as every style sheet is part of an object collection, the style rules within the sheet are part of the following object collection:

```
stylesheet.cssRules
```

where stylesheet is a reference to a sheet within the `document.styleSheets` object collection. For example, if the first style sheet contains the following rules

```
<style id="hStyles">
   h1 {color: red;}
   h2 {color: blue;}
</style>
```

then the following object reference

```
document.styleSheets[0].cssRules[1]
```

points to the second style rule:

```
h2 {color: blue;}
```

The order of the style rules matches the order in which they appear within the style sheet.

Style Rule Objects

Each individual rule within the `cssRules` collection is treated as an object with the properties described in Figure 12-48.

Figure 12-48   **cssRule object properties**

Property	Description
rule.cssText	The contents of *rule* as a text string (read-only)
rule.parentRule	The style rule containing *rule* as a parent (read-only)
rule.parentStyleSheet	The style sheet containing *rule* (read-only)
rule.selectorText	The text of the selector for *rule*
rule.style.*property*	The value of a specific style *property* within *rule*
rule.type	An integer representing the type of *rule* where 0=unknown, 1=style rule, 2=@charset, 3=@import, 4=@media, 5=@font-face, and 6=@page (read-only)

The following expression returns the text of the second style rule from the first style sheet in the `document.styleSheets` collection:

```
document.styleSheets[0].cssRules[1].cssText
```

For the style sheet described above, this expression returns the text string "h2 {color: blue;}"

The `cssText` property can only be used to read the text of a CSS rule, it cannot be used to change the rule's contents. Instead, to change an existing rule, use the `style` and `selectorText` properties. In the last tutorial, you applied the `style` property to inline styles. It can also be used with style rules and with style sheets. To change the second CSS rule in the first style sheet from

TIP

You can remove a style property by setting its value to an empty string.

```
h2 {
    color: blue;
}
```

to

```
h3 {
    color: green;
    font-size: 1.2em;
}
```

apply the following commands:

```
document.styleSheets[0].cssRules[1].selectorText = "h3";
document.styleSheets[0].cssRules[1].style.color = "green";
document.styleSheets[0].cssRules[1].style.fontSize = "1.2em";
```

For security reasons, the Google Chrome browser allows access to style rules only within embedded style sheets or style sheets loaded on servers.

Adding and Removing Style Rules

New style rules are added to a style sheet using the following `insertRule()` method

```
sheet.insertRule(rule, index)
```

where `rule` is the text of the rule to be inserted and `index` is the position of the new rule within the style sheet. Inserting a new rule within the style sheet moves the placement of other rules down in the `cssRules` collection. An index value of 0 inserts the rule at the beginning of the style sheet, moving all other rules down one line, changing their index values. To add a new rule at the end of the style sheet, use `sheet.cssRules.length` as the index value.

For example, the following command

```
document.styleSheets[0].insertRule("h3 {color: green;}", 2);
```

inserts the style rule

```
h3 {
    color: green;
}
```

as the new third rule in the first style sheet, moving the previous third rule (if it exists) down one position. To remove a style rule, apply the command

```
sheet.deleteRule(index)
```

where `index` is the index number of the style rule. Once a rule has been removed, all subsequent rules move up in the `cssRules` collection and their index values subsequently change.

REFERENCE

Working with Style Sheet Rules

- To reference a style rule within a style sheet, use the object collection

  ```
  sheet.cssRules[index] = true;
  ```

  where `sheet` is a style sheet object and `index` is the index number of the rule, starting with 0 for the first style rule.
- To reference the selector text of a style rule, use

  ```
  rule.selectorText
  ```

  where `rule` is the style sheet rule.
- To reference the style property of a style rule, use

  ```
  rule.style.property
  ```

  where `property` is the style property.
- To reference the text of a style rule, use

  ```
  rule.cssText
  ```

- To insert a new style rule into a style sheet, apply

  ```
  sheet.insertRule(rule, index)
  ```

  where `sheet` is the style sheet, `rule` is the text of the style rule, and `index` is the index value of the new rule.
- To remove a rule from a style sheet, apply

  ```
  sheet.deleteRule(index)
  ```

  where `index` is the index value of the rule.

Norene wants you to create styles for the Web View and Page View buttons and the buttonStyle `div` element. First, use JavaScript to append an embedded style sheet to the end of the document head.

To insert an embedded style sheet:

▸ **1.** Return to the **bc_switch.js** file in your editor.

▸ **2.** At the bottom of the setupStyles() function, insert the following command to create a style element:

```
// Append an embedded style sheet to the document head
var buttonStyles = document.createElement("style");
```

▸ **3.** Append the `style` element to the end of the document head using the command:

```
document.head.appendChild(buttonStyles);
```

Figure 12-49 highlights the code to create the embedded style sheet.

Figure 12-49   Creating an embedded style sheet

creates the style element

appends the style element to the end of the document head

```
document.body.insertBefore(buttonDIV, document.body.firstChild);

// Append an embedded style sheet to the document head
var buttonStyles = document.createElement("style");
document.head.appendChild(buttonStyles);
}
```

Next, use the `insertRule()` method to add style rules to the embedded style sheet. Because the embedded style sheet is listed last in the document head, it can be referenced using the expression `document.styleSheets[document.styleSheets.length-1]`. The argument values for the `insertRule()` method will extend over several lines, so you will end each line with the \ character. (See Tutorial 9 for a discussion of extended text strings in JavaScript commands.)

To insert the style rules:

▸ **1.** Within the setupStyle() function, add the following command to insert a style rule that places the styleButtons `div` element with fixed positioning.

```
// Add style rules to the embedded style sheet
document.styleSheets[document.styleSheets.length-1].
insertRule(
  "div#styleButtons { \
    position: fixed; \
  }", 0);
```

An argument value that extends over several lines must have each line end with the \ character with no blank spaces following that character.

▶ **2.** Insert a new rule to format the Web View and Page View buttons using the following command:

```
document.styleSheets[document.styleSheets.length-1].
insertRule(
   "div#styleButtons input { \
      background-color: rgba(68, 94, 186, 0.6); \
      border: 3px solid rgba(0, 24, 123, 0.6); \
      border-radius: 50%; \
      cursor: pointer; \
      color: white; \
      display: inline-block; \
      font-size: 1.2em; \
      height: 60px; \
      margin: 5px 10px; \
      width: 100px; \
   }", 1);
```

▶ **3.** Finally, Norene doesn't want the Web View and Page View buttons displayed when the page is printed. Add the following @media rule to hide the styleButtons div element for print media:

```
document.styleSheets[document.styleSheets.length-1].
insertRule(
"@media print { \
   div#styleButtons { \
      display: none; \
   } \
}",2);
```

Figure 12-50 describes the code to add style rules to the embedded style sheet.

Figure 12-50   **Adding style rules to the embedded style sheet**

references the last sheet in the document.styleSheets collection

places the styleButtons div element with fixed positioning

```
// Append an embedded style sheet to the document head
var buttonStyles = document.createElement("style");
document.head.appendChild(buttonStyles);

// Add style rules to the embedded style sheet
document.styleSheets[document.styleSheets.length-1].insertRule(
  "div#styleButtons { \
     position: fixed; \
  }", 0);
```

inserts a new rule at the start of the style sheet

inserts a new rule in the last style sheet

formats the Web View and Page View buttons

```
document.styleSheets[document.styleSheets.length-1].insertRule(
  "div#styleButtons input { \
     background-color: rgba(68, 94, 186, 0.6); \
     border: 3px solid rgba(0, 24, 123, 0.6); \
     border-radius: 50%; \
     cursor: pointer; \
     color: white; \
     display: inline-block; \
     font-size: 1.2em; \
     height: 60px; \
     margin: 5px 10px; \
     width: 100px; \
  }", 1);
```

the \ character extends the text string to the next line

places the new rule in the second position of the last style sheet

hides the styleButtons div element under print media

```
document.styleSheets[document.styleSheets.length-1].insertRule(
  "@media print { \
     div#styleButtons { \
        display: none; \
     } \
  }", 2);
}
```

places the new rule in the third position of the last style sheet

> **4.** Save your changes to the file and then reload **bc_const.html** in your browser. Figure 12-51 displays the appearance of the style buttons using the embedded style sheet rules you created.

Figure 12-51   **Formatted style buttons**

buttons formatted with the embedded style sheet

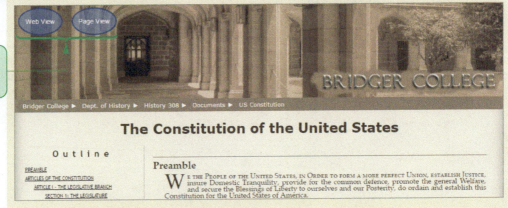

© Neale Cousland/Shutterstock.com

5. Open the Print Preview window in your browser and confirm that the style buttons do not appear under print media.

The last task for the style sheet switcher is to add event handlers to the Web View and Page View buttons to enable and disable the bc_page.css style sheet.

To add event handlers to the style buttons:

1. Return to the **bc_switch.js** file in your editor.

2. At the end of the setupStyles() function, insert the following event handler to disable the pageStyle style sheet when the Web View button is clicked.

```
// Turn the Page View style off and on
webButton.onclick = function() {
    pageStyle.disabled = true;
}
```

3. Insert the following event handler to enable the pageStyle style sheet when the Page View button is clicked.

```
pageButton.onclick = function() {
    pageStyle.disabled = false;
};
```

Figure 12-52 highlights the final code in the file.

Figure 12-52 **Disabling and enabling the Style Sheet**

```
                        display: none; \
                    } \
            }", 2);

            // Turn the Page View style off and on
            webButton.onclick = function() {
                pageStyle.disabled = true;
            }

            pageButton.onclick = function() {
                pageStyle.disabled = false;
            };

        }
```

disables the Page View style sheet when clicked

enables the Page View style sheet when clicked

4. Save your changes to the file and reload **bc_const.html** in your browser. Verify that you can switch between web view and page view by clicking the style buttons.

Exploring Calculated Styles

In this session, you've worked with style sheets and style rules, but the final appearance of any page element isn't usually determined from one style sheet or rule, it is a **calculated style** based on all of the styles found within external style sheets, embedded sheets, inline styles, and the styles built into the browser itself. In some applications, you might want to retrieve these calculated styles. For example, a program that works with the page layout might need to retrieve the height of page columns in pixels and the width of a page article as it is rendered by the browser. You can retrieve that information using the following getComputedStyle() method

```
document.getComputedStyle(object, pseudo)
```

where *object* is a page object and *pseudo* is a text string containing a pseudo-element that is applied to the page object. If no pseudo-element is used, set the *pseudo* value to null.

The getComputedStyle() method returns a CSSStyleDeclaration object containing all the calculated styles for that page object. For example, the following code retrieves the calculated styles for the first paragraph of the current document:

```
var p1 = document.getElementsByTagName("p")[0];
var p1Styles = document.getComputedStyle(p1, null);
```

To retrieve the calculated value of a specific style, use

```
styleDeclaration.getPropertyValue(styleText)
```

or

```
styleDeclaration.style
```

where *styleDeclaration* is a CSSStyleDeclaration object, *styleText* is a text string containing a CSS style property, and *style* is the JavaScript name of a style property. Thus, to view the font size of the first paragraph from the previous code, you could use either of the following:

```
p1Styles.getPropertyValue("font-size")
```

or

```
p1Styles.fontSize
```

TIP

You cannot access the calculated value of a short-cut property, such as the margin or border style; you can only access style values that are calculated, such as margin-left or border-width.

Calculated styles are read-only values and cannot be changed via JavaScript. The values are expressed in absolute units based on how the browser renders the object. Thus, a calculated property that measures a size is expressed only in pixels.

Decision Making: Programming Styles under Older Browsers

If you need to work with older browsers or are updating a legacy website, you may encounter code written for versions of Internet Explorer prior to IE 9. The earlier versions of the IE browser used a different document object model for accessing and modifying style sheets. Under the older IE model:

- Style sheet rules are referenced using the `rules` object collection rather than `cssRules`
- New rules are added with the `addRule()` method rather than `insertRule()`
- Existing rules are deleted with the `removeRule()` method rather than `deleteRule()`
- Calculated styles are accessed using the `currentStyle()` method rather than `getComputedStyle()`

You can resolve these differences using object detection to determine which DOM the user's browser supports. IE 9 and higher and Microsoft Edge both support the W3C model for managing style sheets and style rules.

You have completed your work on Norene's U.S. Constitution document. With a minimal amount of recoding, Norene can apply both scripts you have developed to other articles that she wishes to post on her website.

Session 12.3 Quick Check

1. Provide the object reference to the last style sheet in the document.
2. Provide code to add an external style sheet linked to the newstyles.css file to the end of the document head.
3. Provide code to disable the first style sheet in the document
4. Provide the object reference to the last style rule for the *sheet* object.
5. Provide code to change the first style rule for the *sheet* object to the following:

```
h1 {
    font-size: 2.2em;
    text-align: center;
}
```

6. Provide code to insert the following style rule into the third position of the *sheet* object.

```
h2 {
    font-size: 1.8em;
}
```

7. Provide code to remove the second style rule from the *sheet* object.
8. Provide code to retrieve the calculated height of the first aside element in the document.

Review Assignments

Data Files needed for the Review Assignments: bc_fed_txt.html, bc_keys_txt.js, 3 CSS files, 1 PNG file

Many of Norene's documents have essential keywords that highlight important ideas and themes. Norene has marked these keywords with a `dfn` (definition) element. She wants you to create an app that searches the document text and locates these keywords and lists them in a keyword box displayed alongside the document. The entries in the keyword box should be inserted as hypertext, linked to that section of the document where the keyword is used. The display styles for the keyword box will be entered as part of the JavaScript program. Figure 12-53 shows a preview of the page created for the tenth Federalist paper written by James Madison in 1787 on the danger of factions to the republic.

Figure 12-53 | **Keyword list for the Federalist 10 article**

© Neale Cousland/Shutterstock.com

Complete the following:

1. Use your editor to open the **bc_fed_txt.html** and **bc_keys_txt.js** files from the html12 ▸ review folder. Enter *your name* and *the date* in the comment section of each file, and save them as **bc_fed.html** and **bc_keys.js** respectively.

2. Go to the **bc_fed.html** file in your editor. Directly above the closing `</head>` tag, link the page to the **bc_keys.js** JavaScript file, loading the file asynchronously. Take some time to study the contents of the HTML file and then close it, saving your changes.

3. Go to the **bc_keys.js** file in your editor. Add event listeners to run the findKeyWords() and makeKeyStyles() functions when the page is loaded.

4. Create the findKeyWords() function to locate the keywords from the document and generate the keyword list. Within the findKeyWords() function, perform the tasks described in steps 5 through 10.

5. Create an `aside` element with the ID "keywords" and containing an `h1` heading with the text "Keyword List".

6. Create an `ol` element and append it to the keywords `aside` element.

7. Next, generate the list of keywords and add IDs to each keyword entry in the source article. Create an object collection named **keyWordElems** referencing all `dfn` elements within the doc article (*Hint*: Use the `querySelectorAll()` method.) Create an array named **keyWords** with a length equal to the length of the keyWordElems collection. Add a `for` loop that loops through all the items in the keyWordElems object collection, and for each item do the following:

   a. Set the value of each item in the keyWords array to the text of the corresponding item in the keyWordElems object collection.

   b. Next, set the ID of the current item in the keyWords array. However, the ID cannot contain blank spaces. Norene has supplied you with the replaceWS() function to replace blank spaces with the "_" character. Call the replaceWS() function with the current keyword as the parameter value and store the value returned by the function in the **linkID** variable.

   c. Set the ID of current item in the keyWordElems object collection to `"keyword_linkID"` where `linkID` is the value of the linkID variable.

8. Sort the keyWords array in alphabetical order.

9. Next, generate the list items in the keyword list. Add a `for` loop that loops through each item in the keyWords array, doing the following for each item:

   a. Declare the **keyWordListItem** variable, storing an `li` element.

   b. Declare the **keyWordLink** variable storing an `a` element.

   c. Change the innerHTML of keyWordLink to the value of the text of the current keyword.

   d. Declare the **linkID** variable containing the value returned by the replaceWS() function using the current keyword as the parameter value.

   e. Change the `href` attribute of keyWordLink to `"#keyword_linkID"` where `linkID` is the value of the linkID variable.

   f. Append keyWordLink to keyWordList and then append keyWordList to the ordered list you created in Step 6.

10. Insert the keywords list box you defined in Step 5 as the first child of the `article` element with the ID "doc".

11. Next, create the makeKeyStyles() function that will define the style sheet for the keywords box. Add the following commands to the function:

    a. Create an embedded style sheet and append it to the document head.

    b. Add the following style rules to the style sheet:

    ```
    aside#keywords {
        border: 3px solid rgb(101, 101, 101);
        float: right;
        margin: 20px 0px 20px 20px;
        padding: 10px;
        width: 320px;
    }
    aside#keywords h1 {
        font-size: 2em;
        margin: 5px;
        text-align: center;
    }
    aside#keywords ol {
        margin-left: 20px;
        font-size: 1.2em;
    }
    aside#keywords ol li {
        line-height: 1.5em;
    }
    aside#keywords ol li a {
        color: rgb(101, 101, 101);
        text-decoration: none;
    }
    ```

12. Document your code with comments throughout the JavaScript file and then save your changes.

13. Open the **bc_fed.html** file in your browser and verify that the page resembles the content and layout shown in Figure 12-53. Verify that you can click the entries in the keyword list to go to the corresponding term in the Federalist 10 article.

Case Problem 1

Data Files needed for this Case Problem: na_home_txt.html, na_styler_txt.js, 7 CSS files, 16 PNG files

New Accents Photography   Christine Drake is the owner and chief photographer at New Accents Photography, a photography studio in Ashland, Oregon, that specializes in wedding photos. Wedding portraiture is a competitive business, and Christine wants to improve the design of her website's opening page. Christine is proud of the many and varied styles of portraiture that New Accents Photography offers, and she would like to create an interactive style sheet switcher that loads different style designs selected by the user.

Christine wants your help with writing a JavaScript app that examines the list of style sheets in the site's home page and creates a figure box of clickable thumbnail images for each sheet design. A preview of the page you will create for Christine is shown in Figure 12-54.

Figure 12-54   **Styles for New Accents Photography**

© Lana K/Shutterstock.com; © ArtFamily/Shutterstock.com; © Kuznetcov_Konstantins/Shutterstock.com;
© My Good Images/Shutterstock.com; © Daniel Dupuis/Shutterstock.com; © BuketGvozdey/Shutterstock.com;
© naddi/Shutterstock.com; © ninanaina/Shutterstock.com; © Marina Zakharova/Shutterstock.com; Source: Patrick Carey

Complete the following:

1. Use your editor to open the **na_home_txt.html** and **na_styler_txt.js** files from the html12 ▶ case1 folder. Enter *your name* and *the date* in the comment section of each file, and save them as **na_home.html** and **na_styler.js** respectively.

2. Go to the **na_home.html** file in your editor. Go to the document head and add a `script` element for the **na_styler.js** file. Load the file asynchronously. Save your changes to the file.

3. Go to the **na_styler.js** file in your editor. Add an event listener that runs the setStyles() function when the page loads.

4. Create the setStyles() function using the commands listed in Steps 5 through 10.

5. Christine wants one of five fancy style sheets to be randomly used when the page is opened. Declare the **styleNum** variable equal to the value returned by the randInt() function, using 5 as the parameter value.

6. Create an element node for the `link` element and set its `rel` attribute to "stylesheet", its `id` attribute to "fancySheet", and its `href` attribute to "na_style_*num*.css" where *num* is the value of the styleNum variable. Append the fancySheet `style` element to the document head, adding it to the document's style sheets collection.

7. Christine wants users to be able to choose between the five fancy style sheet themes she has created by clicking thumbnail images from a figure box. Create an element node named **figBox** for the `figure` element. Set its `id` attribute to "styleThumbs" and append it to the `div` element with the ID "box".

8. Next, populate the figure box with preview images of the five fancy style sheets. Insert a `for` loop with an index that goes from 0 up through 4 and each time through the loop do the following:

   a. Create an `img` element node named **sheetImg** with a `src` attribute of "na_small_*num*.png" and an `alt` attribute value of "na_style_*num*.css" where *num* is the value of the index in the `for` loop.

   b. Have the browser load a different style sheet when the user clicks one of the thumbnail images by adding an event handler to sheetImg that runs an anonymous function changing the `href` attribute of the `link` element with the ID "fancySheet" to the value of the `alt` attribute of the event target.

   c. Append sheetImg to the figBox element node.

9. Next, design the appearance of the thumbnail figure box. Create an embedded style sheet named **thumbStyles** and append it to the document head.

10. Add the following style rules to the thumbStyles style sheet:

```
figure#styleThumbs {
   position: absolute;
   left: 0px;
   bottom: 0px;
}

figure#styleThumbs img {
   outline: 1px solid black;
   cursor: pointer;
   opacity: 0.75;
}
figure#styleThumbs img:hover {
   outline: 1px solid red;
   opacity: 1.0;
}
```

11. Document your work with informative comments and then save the JavaScript file.

12. Open the **na_home.html** file in your browser. Verify that by clicking the thumbnail images in the lower-left corner of the page, the document is displayed in a different style theme. Further verify that reloading the page randomly selects a style theme from one of the five style sheet files.

Case Problem 2

Data Files needed for this Case Problem: sub_menu_txt.html, sub_cart_txt.js, 2 CSS files, 9 PNG files

Subsistence   Maria Torres manages the website for Subsistence, a popular chain of sandwich shops located in southern Indiana. She has asked you to work on the interface for the store's shopping cart. Maria has supplied you with a web page highlighting the store's daily specials. She would like customers to be able to add items to the shopping cart by clicking a button next to the item description; once the button is clicked, then the description and image are added to a shopping cart panel located on the right side of the page. The shopping cart should keep a running total of the number of each item ordered. Figure 12-55 shows a preview of the page you will work on for Maria.

Figure 12-55   Subsistence shopping cart items

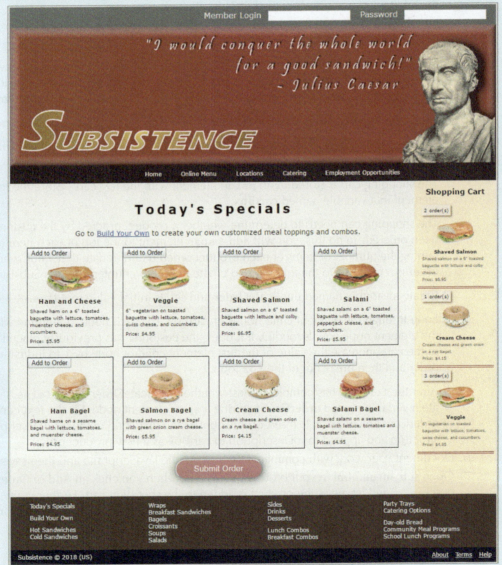

© Markus Mainka/Shutterstock.com; Source: Wikimedia Commons/public domain; Source: Patrick Carey

Complete the following:

1. Use your editor to open the **sub_menu_txt.html** and **sub_cart_txt.js** files from the html12 ▸ case2 folder. Enter *your name* and *the date* in the comment section of each file, and save them as **sub_menu.html** and **sub_cart.js** respectively.

2. Go to the **sub_menu.html** file in your editor. Add a `script` element to the document head for the **sub_cart.js** file, loading it asynchronously. Take some time to study the contents and structure of the file and then save your changes.

3. Return to the **sub_cart.js** file in your editor. Add an event listener that runs the setupCart() function when the page is loaded.

4. Create the **setupCart()** function. The purpose of this function is to define the event handlers for the Add to Order buttons on the page. Add the following commands to the function:

   a. Create a variable named **addButtons**, which contains the collection of elements belonging to the addButton class.

   b. Loop through the addButtons collection and for each button, add an event handler that runs the addItem() function when the button is clicked.

5. Create the **addItem()** function, which adds items to the shopping cart on the page. Add the following commands to the function:

   a. The description of the food item is the next sibling element to the button that was clicked by the customer. Use the `nextElementSibling` property to reference the next sibling element to the target of the event object. Store the sibling element in the variable **foodItem**.

   b. Create the **foodID** variable, which contains the value of the `id` attribute for foodItem.

   c. Use the `cloneNode()` method to create a copy of the foodItem element and all of its descendants. Store this node structure in the **foodDescription** variable.

   d. The shopping cart is stored in an `aside` element with the ID "cart". Store the reference to this element in a variable named **cartBox**.

   The shopping cart needs to determine whether a product ordered by the customer has already been ordered. To do this, you will add a `span` element to the top of each item in the cart containing the number of items of each product ordered and update that value when a product order is repeated. Do the following to create the order counter for each Subsistence product.

   e. Create a variable named **duplicateOrder** and set its initial value to `false`.

   f. Loop through the element child nodes of cartBox. For each node, determine whether the ID of the element node equals foodID. If it does, the customer has previously placed that menu item in the cart. Increase the value of the first element child of node by 1 to indicate an additional order and then break out of the `for` loop.

   g. After the `for` loop has completed, test whether duplicateOrder is still `false`. If it is, then create a variable named **orderCount** storing a `span` element node. Set the text content of the orderCount element to 1. Insert orderCount as the first child of the foodDescription node structure and append foodDescription to cartBox as a new product order.

6. Document your work with comments throughout the JavaScript file and then save your work.

7. Open **sub_menu.html** in your browser. Verify that when you click an Add to Order button, the description and image of the product is added to the shopping cart. Further verify that when you click the same food product several times, a running total of the number of items ordered is displayed in the shopping cart.

CHALLENGE

Case Problem 3

Data Files needed for this Case Problem: js_nodes_txt.html, js_tree_txt.js, 3 CSS files, 1 PNG file

JSWorks   Jorge Soto is the owner and administrator of JSWorks, a website containing JavaScript tutorials, tips, and specialized apps. Jorge is working on a multipage tutorial concerning the creation and use of document nodes. You are helping Jorge maintain his website and have volunteered to work on a page describing the appearance of the document node tree. Jorge would like you to include a node tree that is based on the article he is writing so that visitors to his site can see the complete appearance of the node tree for a sample HTML fragment. Figure 12-56 shows a preview of the page.

Figure 12-56	Node tree diagram for JSWorks

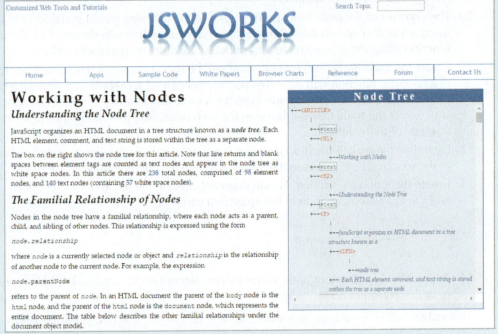

Source: Patrick Carey

The JavaScript program you will design will need to use recursion to navigate through the entire structure of Jorge's article. As it proceeds through the article, it will record each element node and text node, displaying them in a nested list alongside the article text. The CSS styles for the nested list already have been created for you; your only job will be to generate the HTML code of the nested list. Jorge also wants your code to keep a running count of the total number of element and text nodes, including text nodes containing only white space.

Complete the following:

1. Use your editor to open the **js_nodes_txt.html** and **js_tree_txt.js** files from the html12 ▸ case3 folder. Enter **your name** and **the date** in the comment section of each file, and save them as **js_nodes.html** and **js_tree.js** respectively.

2. Go to the **js_nodes.html** file in your editor. Within the document head, create links to the **js_tree.css** style sheet file and the **js_tree.js** JavaScript file. Load the js_tree.js file asynchronously.

3. Take some time to study the code of the HTML file and then save your changes to the document.

4. Return to the **js_tree.js** file in your editor. Jorge wants you to keep track of the total count of nodes, element nodes, text nodes, and white-space nodes. Below the comment section, create the following global variables: **nodeCount**, **elemCount**, **textCount**, and **wsCount** and set their initial values to 0.

5. Create an event handler that runs the makeTree() function when the page loads.

6. The makeTree() function will be used to create the node tree for the source article on the page. Create the makeTree() function, adding the commands described in Steps 7 through 10.

7. Within the makeTree() function, create the following `aside` element fragment

```
<aside id="treeBox">
   <h1>Node Tree</h1>
</aside>
```

and append it to the `section` element with the ID "main".

8. The node tree will be created within an ordered list. Declare a variable named **nodeList** containing the initial `ol` element node that will be the foundation of the node tree and append it to the `aside` element fragment.

9. The node tree will be based on the contents of the elements matching the CSS selector "#main article". Declare a variable named **sourceArticle** that points to these elements. (*Hint*: Use the `querySelectorAll()` method.)

10. The contents of the node tree and the count of the different global variables will be updated using a function named makeBranches(), which you will create shortly. Call the makeBranches() function using the sourceArticle and nodeList variables as parameter values.

11. Create the makeBranches() function that will be used to append node branches to the node tree diagram. The function will have two parameters named **treeNode** and **nestedList**. The treeNode parameter stores the current node from the source article and the nestedList parameter stores the structure of the node tree displayed in the web page. Add the commands described in Steps 12 through 17 to the function.

12. Each time the makeBranches() function is called, it is because a new node has been discovered in the source article. Increase the value of the nodeCount variable by 1.

13. Create the following list item HTML fragment, storing the list item element in the **liElem** variable and the `span` element node in the **spanElem** variable:

```
<li>
   +--<span></span>
</li>
```

14. Append the spanElement node to the liElem element node; append the liElem node to the nestedList element node.

✛ **Explore** 15. If treeNode represents an element node, then do the following:

    a. Increase the value of the elemCount variable by 1.

    b. Add the `class` attribute to the spanElem node, setting its value to "elementNode".

    c. Append the text string "*<element>*" to the spanElem node, where *element* is the name of the HTML element. (*Hint*: Use the `textContent` property to append the text of the element tag and not the element tag itself.)

✛ **Explore** 16. Else if treeNode represents a text node, do the following:

    a. Increase the value of the textCount variable by 1.

    b. Declare the variable **textString** equal to the value of the text node.

    c. Jorge has provided a function named isWhiteSpaceNode() to determine whether a text node represents white space or not. Call the isWhiteSpaceNode() function using textString as the parameter value. If the function returns the value `true`, then do the following:

       i. Increase the value of the wsCount variable by 1

      ii. Change the `class` attribute of the spanElem node to "whiteSpaceNode"

     iii. Append the text string "#text" to the spanElem node

    d. If the isWhiteSpaceNode() function returns the value `false`, then do the following:

       i. Change the class attribute of the spanElem node to "textNode"

      ii. Append the text string "*text*" to the spanElem node where *text* is the value of the textString variable

⊕ **Explore** 17. The makeBranches() function should recursively move through the different levels of nodes in the source article. To apply recursion, test whether the number of child nodes of treeNode is greater than zero. If it is, then do the following:

    a. Create the following HTML fragment as an element node with the name **newList**:

```
<ol>|</ol>
```

    b. Append newList to the nestedList element node.

    c. Loop through the child nodes of treeNode using **n** to represent each child node and, for each child node, call the makeBranches() function using n and newList as the parameter values.

18. Return to the makeTree() function and add commands to display the total count of nodes, element nodes, text nodes, and whitespace nodes within the `span` elements whose IDs are "totalNodes", "elemNodes", "textNodes", and "wsNodes", respectively.

19. Document your work with informative comments throughout the JavaScript file.

20. Save your changes to the file and load **js_nodes.html** in your browser. Verify that the browser displays the schematic diagram of the node tree for the Working with Nodes article. Further verify that the second paragraph of the article reports 238 total nodes in the document, comprised of 98 element nodes, and 140 text nodes (of which 57 are whitespace nodes).

Case Problem 4

Data Files needed for this Case Problem: gi_qbs_txt.html, gi_sort_txt.js, 2 CSS files, 1 PNG file

Gridirony   Jeremy Howard is the owner and operator of the fantasy football website, Gridirony. The Gridirony website provides a gaming environment for fantasy football players, including pages and pages of in-depth statistics and analysis. Much of Gridirony's data is arranged in tables and Jeremy wants an app that will turn any of his web tables into a sortable table in which users can sort the table data in ascending or descending order by clicking a table column heading. Figure 12-57 shows a preview of a table in which the quarterback statistics are sorted in descending order by the quarterback rating.

Figure 12-57	Sortable web table for Gridirony

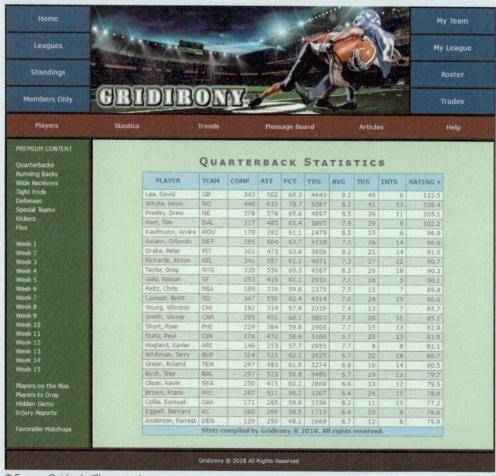

© Eugene Onishenko/Shutterstock.com

Jeremy has already written the HTML and CSS code for the page, but he wants your help in writing the JavaScript code to create the sortable table app.

Complete the following:

1. Use your editor to open the **gi_qbs_txt.html** and **gi_sort_txt.js** files from the html12 ▸ case4 folder. Enter *your name* and *the date* in the comment section of each file, and save them as **gi_qbs.html** and **gi_sort.js** respectively.

2. Go to the **gi_qbs.html** file in your editor. Within the document head, create a link to the **gi_sort.js** JavaScript file, loading the file asynchronously.

3. Scroll down the file and locate the web table containing the quarterback statistics. Add a class attribute to the opening `<table>` tag with the value "sortable" to indicate that this table can be sorted by the user.

4. Save your changes to the file and then go to the **gi_sort.js** file in your editor.

5. Below the initial comment section, declare the following global variables:

   a. The empty array **tableData**, which will store the data values in the web table

   b. The empty array **dataCategories**, which will store the text of the column headings

   c. The **sortIndex** variable, which will store the index number of the table column used for sorting; set its initial value to **0** (the first table column)

   d. The **sortDirection** variable, which will store whether the column is sorted in ascending order (1) or descending order (-1); set its initial value to **1** (to sort in ascending order)

6. Add an event listener that runs an anonymous function when the page is loaded. Within the anonymous function, call and run the defineDataArray() and writeTableData() functions.

🔷 **Explore** 7. Create a function named **defineDataArray()**. The purpose of this function is to populate the tableData array as a two-dimensional array with values taken from the rows and cells of the web table body. Add the following commands to the function:

   a. Declare the **tableRows** variable, which references all of the `tr` elements within the table body of the sortable table. (*Hint*: Use the `querySelectorAll()` method with "`table.sortable tbody tr`" as the selector.)

   b. Create a `for` loop that loops through the contents of tableRows. Within the `for` loop, declare a variable named **rowCells** containing the child element nodes of the current table row (*Hint*: Use the `children()` method.) and declare an empty array named **rowValues** with a size equal to the length of rowCells.

   c. Within the `for` loop, insert a nested `for` loop that loops through the contents of the rowCells variable. For each row cell, add the text content of the row cell to the rowValues array.

   d. After the nested `for` loop has finished, add the rowValues array to the tableData array.

   e. After the outer `for` loop has finished, the tableData array will contain a two-dimensional array of all of the data in the table body. Sort the tableData array using the dataSort2D() function as the compare function.

Explore 8. Create the **writeTableData()** function. The purpose of this function is to create the table body based on the sorted data. Add the following commands to the function:

a. Create a set of nested `for` loops that builds the following node structure

```
<tbody>
   <tr>
      <td>tableData[0][0]</td>
      <td>tableData[0][1]</td>
...
   </tr>
   <tr>
      <td>tableData[1][0]</td>
      <td>tableData[1][1]</td>
...
</tbody>

where tableData[0][0], tableData[0][1], tableData[1][0], tableData[1][1],
and so on are the values from the two-dimensional tableData array. Store
the node structure in a variable named newTableBody.
```

b. Use the `replaceChild()` method to replace the `tbody` element from the current web table with newTableBody.

9. Save your changes to the file and then load the **gi_qbs.html** file in your browser. Verify that the table is sorted in alphabetical order by the player names (from the first column).

10. Return to the **gi_sort.js** file in your editor. Next, you will add controls to allow the table to be sorted by any column just by clicking a column heading. Within the anonymous function for the "load" event, add a command to call the defineColumns() function.

Explore 11. Create the **defineColumns()** function. The purpose of this function is to set up the appearance and behavior of the column headings. Add the following commands to the function:

a. Append a new embedded style sheet to the document head

b. Within the new style sheet, add the following rule to display a pointer cursor over the column headings:

```
table.sortable thead tr th {
   cursor: pointer;
}
```

c. The column headings should display an icon that indicates that they are sortable. The initial content will be a blank space indicated by the character code \\00a0. Add the following style rule to the new style sheet:

```
table.sortable thead tr th::after {
   content: '\\00a0';
   font-family: monospace;
   margin-left: 5px;
}
```

d. The first column is already sorted in ascending order. Change the icon for the first column heading to a ▲ by adding the following style rule to the new style sheet:

```
table.sortable thead tr th:nth-of-type(1)::after {
   content: '\\25b2';
}
```

e. Next, populate the dataCategories array so that it contains the text of all of the column headings. Create a `for` loop that loops through the `th` elements in the table heading. For each table heading cell, do the following:

   i. Store the text content of the table heading cell in the dataCategories array

   ii. Add an event handler that calls the columnSort() function when the table heading cell is clicked

12. Create the **columnSort()** function. The purpose of this function is to sort the web table based on the column heading that was clicked by the user. Add the following commands to the function:

   a. You first must determine which column was clicked by the user. Declare a variable named **columnText** equal to the text content of the event object target.

   b. Retrieve the index number of the column by applying the `indexOf()` method to the dataCategories array, using the value of columnText as the array value to be found. Store the index number in the **columnIndex** variable.

   c. If the user clicks the column heading currently used for sorting, the sorting direction is toggled between ascending and descending. If the user clicks a new column heading, the table should be sorted by the values in that column. Test whether columnIndex is equal to sortIndex. If it is, multiply the sortDirection variable by -1 (to change the sort direction); otherwise set sortIndex equal to columnIndex.

   d. Next, you have to move the icon into the column heading cell used for sorting. First, declare the **columnNumber** variable equal to columnIndex plus 1.

   e. Declare the **columnStyles** variable referencing the last style sheet in the document and then delete the third rule from that style sheet (the one that adds the sorting icon to the table heading cell.)

f. If sortDirection = 1 (ascending), add the following style rule to columnStyles to display the ▲ icon

```
table.sortable thead tr th:nth-of-type(col)::after {
    content: '\\25b2';
}
```

otherwise, add the following style rule to display the ▼ icon for a descending sort order:

```
table.sortable thead tr th:nth-of-type(col)::after {
    content: '\\25bc';
}
```

where *col* is the value of the columnNumber variable.

g. Sort the values in the tableData array using the dataSort2D() function as the compare function.

h. Create and append the newly sorted table body to the web table by calling the writeTable-Data() function.

13. Document your work with comments throughout the file and then save your file.

14. Reopen **gi_qbs.html** in your browser. Verify that you can sort the table in different order by clicking each column heading and that an arrow icon indicates the sort column and the current sorting direction. Further verify that you can toggle between an ascending and descending sort by clicking the same column heading more than once.

TUTORIAL 13

Programming for Web Forms

Creatings Forms for Orders and Payments

Case | *Coctura Home Kitchen*

Aisha Jahlan manages the website for Coctura Home Kitchen, a company that sells kitchen appliances for the modern kitchen. She has recently hired you to assist in redesigning the company's website. She wants you to begin focusing on the forms used for product orders and information. Aisha wants you write a form that automatically calculates the cost of a customer order and then transfers that data into a payment form located on another page. Finally, she wants to validate the credit card data in the payment form with customized validation messages. To develop these forms, you will use the form tools built into JavaScript.

OBJECTIVES

Session 13.1
- Reference forms and form fields
- Create calculated fields
- Retrieve field values from selection lists and radio buttons
- Format numeric and currency data

Session 13.2
- Append field names and data to URLs
- Explore the syntax of regular expressions
- Use a regular expression to extract data from the URL query string

Session 13.3
- Work with the validityState object
- Create custom validation messages
- Validate credit card numbers

STARTING DATA FILES

html13 → **tutorial**

co_order_txt.html
co_order_txt.js
co_payment_txt.html
co_payment_txt.js
+ 13 files

review

co_cart_txt.html
co_cart_txt.js
co_credit_txt.html
co_credit_txt.js
+ 13 files

case1

mpl_links_txt.html
mpl_links_txt.js
+ 5 files

case2

dl_expense_txt.html
dl_expense_txt.js
+ 4 files

case3

mas_register_txt.html
mas_register_txt.js
mas_reg2_txt.html
mas_reg2_txt.js
+ 7 files

case4

ws_cloud_txt.js
ws_lincoln_txt.html
+ 7 files

demo

demo_regexp.html
+ 5 files

Session 13.1 Visual Overview:

To reference a web form, use `document.forms.form` where *form* is the ID or name of the web form.

The `selectedIndex()` method returns the index of the selected option from a selection list.

The `value` property returns the field value from a web form control.

To determine which option from an option button was clicked, use the `querySelector` method.

```javascript
function calcOrder() {
    var orderForm = document.forms.orderForm;

    // Calculate the inital cost of the order
    var mIndex = orderForm.elements.model.selectedIndex;
    var mCost = orderForm.elements.model.options[mIndex].value;
    var qIndex = orderForm.elements.qty.selectedIndex;
    var quantity = orderForm.elements.qty[qIndex].value;

    // Initial cost = model cost x quantity
    var initialCost = mCost*quantity;
    orderForm.elements.initialCost.value = formatUSCurrency(initialCost);

    // Retrieve the cost of the user's protection plan
    var pCost = document.querySelector('input[name="protection"]:checked').value*quantity;
    orderForm.elements.protectionCost.value = formatNumber(pCost, 2);

    // Calculate the order subtotal
    orderForm.elements.subtotal.value = formatNumber(initialCost + pCost, 2);

    // Calculate the sales tax
    var salesTax = 0.05*(initialCost + pCost);
    orderForm.elements.salesTax.value = formatNumber(salesTax, 2);

    // Calculate the cost of the total order
    var totalCost = initialCost + pCost + salesTax;
    orderForm.elements.totalCost.value = formatUSCurrency(totalCost);
}
```

Forms and Elements

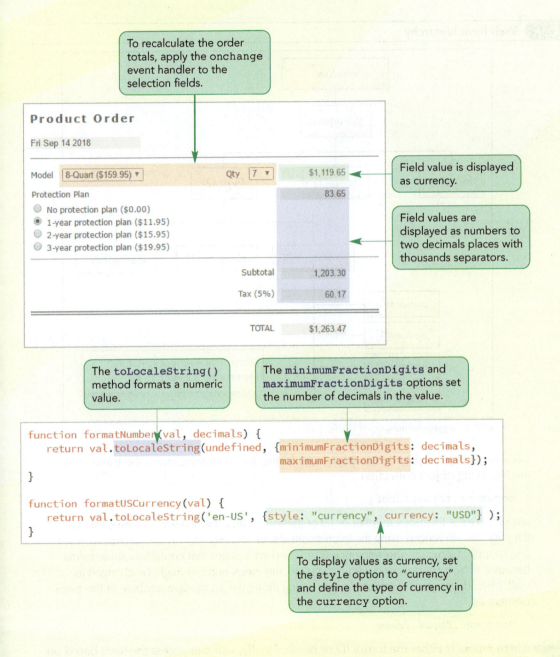

To recalculate the order totals, apply the onchange event handler to the selection fields.

Product Order

Fri Sep 14 2018

Model 8-Quart ($159.95) ▾   Qty 7 ▾ $1,119.65

Protection Plan   83.65

○ No protection plan ($0.00)
◉ 1-year protection plan ($11.95)
○ 2-year protection plan ($15.95)
○ 3-year protection plan ($19.95)

Subtotal   1,203.30

Tax (5%)   60.17

TOTAL $1,263.47

Field value is displayed as currency.

Field values are displayed as numbers to two decimals places with thousands separators.

The `toLocaleString()` method formats a numeric value.

The `minimumFractionDigits` and `maximumFractionDigits` options set the number of decimals in the value.

```
function formatNumber(val, decimals) {
    return val.toLocaleString(undefined, {minimumFractionDigits: decimals,
                                          maximumFractionDigits: decimals});
}

function formatUSCurrency(val) {
    return val.toLocaleString('en-US', {style: "currency", currency: "USD"} );
}
```

To display values as currency, set the `style` option to "currency" and define the type of currency in the `currency` option.

Exploring the Forms Object

To program the behavior and contents of a web form, you must work with the properties and methods of the `form` object and the elements it contains. As shown in Figure 13-1, web forms and their elements are part of the hierarchy of objects within the web document.

Figure 13-1   Web form hierarchy

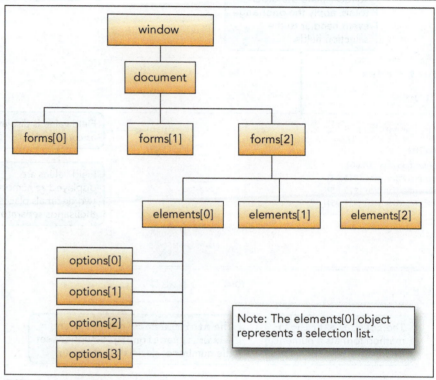

© 2016 Cengage Learning

Because a page can contain multiple web forms, JavaScript organizes the forms into the following object collection

    `document.forms[idref]`

where `idref` is the index number or ID of the form. Thus, the first several forms listed in the page are referenced using the expressions `document.forms[0]`, `document.forms[1]`, and so forth. Generally, this reference is not used with pages that contain multiple forms because, if the form is moved within the page, the index number might be changed as well. Instead, you can reference the form using either the `id` or `name` attribute of the `form` element as

    `document.forms.fname`

TIP

If an ID value exists, you can always reference a form or an element within a form using the `getElementById()` attribute.

where `fname` is either the form's ID or name. Finally, you can access the form based on the `name` attribute (not the `id` attribute) using the expression

    `document.form`

where `form` is the name assigned to the form.

Figure 13-2 describes some of the properties and methods associated with the form object.

Figure 13-2	Form properties and methods

Property or Method	Description
form.action	Sets or returns the action attribute of the web *form*
form.autocomplete	Sets or returns the autocomplete attribute; allows the browser to automatically complete form fields
form.enctype	Sets or returns the enctype attribute
form.length	Returns the number of elements in the form
form.method	Sets or returns the method attribute
form.name	Sets or returns the name attribute
form.target	Sets or returns the target attribute
form.reset()	Resets the web form
form.submit()	Submits the web form
form.requestAutocomplete()	Triggers the browser to initiate autocompletion of those form fields that have autocomplete activated

Aisha has supplied you with a sample page that will be a model for product orders. The page has a form in which customers can log into their membership accounts and a form used to select a product to order. View her page now.

To open the product order page:

1. Use your editor to open the **co_order_txt.html** and **co_order_txt.js** files from the html13 ▶ tutorial folder. Enter **your name** and **the date** in the comment section of each file and save them as **co_order.html** and **co_order.js** respectively.

2. Return to the **co_order.html** file in your editor. Within the head element, insert a script element to asynchronously load the **co_order.js** file.

3. Study the contents of the HTML file, noting the placement of the two forms within the document and then save your changes to the file.

4. Close the file, saving your changes and then open the **co_order.html** file in your browser. Figure 13-3 describes the content of the order form.

Figure 13-3   **Fields in the order form**

In this session, you will only work with the properties and methods of the order form, which Aisha has laid out within a web table. The order form includes a selection list for the model field containing a list of three sizes for the cooking pot (4-quart ($89.95), 6-quart ($129.95), 8-quart ($159.95)) and a selection list for the number of pots of the selected model the user wants to order. Customers can choose one of four protection plan options for each item they purchase ranging from no protection plan ($0.00) up to a 3-year protection plan ($19.95). A 5% sales tax will be added to any order. In the last column of the table are input fields to calculate the subtotals, taxes, and total cost of the order.

Working with Form Elements

A form's input controls, selection lists, text area boxes, and field sets are organized into the following `elements` collection

    `form.elements[idref]`

where `form` is the reference to the web form and `idref` is the index number or ID of the element. You can also reference an element using its name or `id` attribute using the following expression

    `form.elements.ename;`

where `ename` is either the element's ID or name. For example, to reference the orderDate field from the orderForm, you apply the following object reference:

    `document.orderForm.elements.orderDate`

Finally, you can reference a field using the value of the field name attribute in the following expression

    `form.field`

where `field` is the value of the field name. Note that this does not work with the `id` attribute, only with the `name` attribute.

REFERENCE

Referencing Form Objects

- To access a web form, use the object reference

  `document.forms[idref]`

  where `idref` is the ID or index number of the form. You can also use

  `document.fname`

  where `fname` is the name or ID of the form.
- To reference a field within a form, use the object reference

  `form.elements[idref]`

  where `form` is the object reference to the form and `idref` is the ID or index number of the form element. You can also use

  `form.elements.ename`

  where `ename` is the value of the `id` or `name` attribute associated with the element in the form.
- To reference an element within a form, based on the field name, use

  `form.field`

  where `field` is the value of the field name.

Working with Input Fields

The first task on Aisha's list is to display the current date in the order form. To change the value of the orderDate field, you need to work with the properties and methods of input controls.

Setting the Field Value

To set the value of an input control, apply the following expression

```
element.value = value;
```

where `element` is a reference to a form element and `value` is the value to be stored in the element. For example, to store the text string "2018-03-10" in the orderDate field, apply the command:

```
document.orderForm.orderData.value = "2018-03-10";
```

The `value` property is one of many properties and methods associated with input fields. Figure 13-4 describes some of the others.

Figure 13-4   **Properties and methods of input boxes**

Property or Method	Description
input.autocomplete	The value of the input box's autocomplete attribute
input.defaultValue	The default value for the input box
input.form	The form containing the input box
input.maxLength	The maximum number of characters allowed in the input box
input.name	The name of the field associated with the input box
input.pattern	The value of the input box's pattern attribute
input.placeholder	The value of the input box's placeholder attribute
input.readOnly	Returns whether the input box is read-only or not
input.required	Returns whether the input box is required or not
input.size	The value of the input box's size attribute
input.type	The data type associated with the input box
input.value	The current value displayed in the input box
input.blur()	Removes the focus from the input box
input.focus()	Gives focus to the input box
input.select()	Selects the contents of the input box

REFERENCE

Working with Fields

- To set the value of a form field, use the object property

  `element.value = value`

  where `element` is the reference to the form field and `value` is the value you want to assign to the field.
- To move the focus to a form field, apply the method:

  `element.focus()`

- To remove the focus from a form field, apply the method:

  `element.blur()`

Add an event listener to the co_order.js file to display the current date in the orderDate field when the page is loaded by the browser.

To set the value of the orderDate field:

1. Return to the **co_order.js** file in your editor.

2. Directly below the comment section, insert the following code:

```
window.addEventListener("load", function() {
    var orderForm = document.forms.orderForm;
    orderForm.elements.orderDate.value =
    new Date().toDateString();
});
```

Figure 13-5 describes the newly added code in the file.

Figure 13-5   **Displaying the current date**

3. Save your changes to the file and then reload **co_order.html** in your browser. Figure 13-6 shows the order form with the current date.

Figure 13-6   **Displaying the current date**

Navigating between Fields

Aisha wants the model field to be selected automatically when the form opens so that it is ready for data entry. When a form field is selected either by clicking it or by moving it using keyboard buttons or arrows, it receives the focus of the browser. To program this action, you use the following `focus()` method:

```
element.focus();
```

Add a command to move the focus to the model field in the order form.

TIP

You can remove the focus by applying the `blur()` method to the element, but the `blur()` method will not select any other element in the form.

To select the qty field:

1. Return to the **co_order.js** file in your text editor.

2. Within the anonymous function for the `load` event, add the following command:

```
orderForm.elements.model.focus();
```

Figure 13-7 highlights the newly added code in the file.

Figure 13-7   **Setting the form focus**

```
window.addEventListener("load", function() {
    var orderForm = document.forms.orderForm;
    orderForm.elements.orderDate.value = new Date().toDateString();
    orderForm.elements.model.focus();
});
```

applies the focus
to the model field

3. Save your changes to the file and then reload **co_order.html** in your browser. Verify that the selection list box for the model field has the focus in the order form (as indicated by the highlighted border around the selection list in the Google Chrome browser).

Trouble? Browsers differ in how they highlight the active field. Your browser might not highlight the border around the field with the focus.

In the rest of the form, you will calculate the cost of a customer's order. This involves (1) determining the price of the order (equal to the price of the selected cooking pot model multiplied by the quantity ordered); (2) adding the cost of the protection plan, if any, for each item; (3) calculating the sales tax; and (4) adding all these costs to determine the grand total. Start with a function to calculate the cost of the order.

Working with Selection Lists

The model prices and quantities are both placed within selection lists. Figure 13-8 lists the properties associated with the selection list object.

Figure 13-8   **Selection list properties**

Property	Description
select.length	The number of options in the selection list, select
select.multiple	Returns true if more than one option can be selected from the list
select.name	The selection list field name
select.options	The object collection of the selection list options
select.selectedIndex	The index number of the currently selected option
select.size	The number of options displayed in the selection list
select.add(option)	Adds option to the selection list
select.remove(index)	Removes the option with the index number, index, from the selection list

The value of a selection list is determined by which option has been selected by the user. The selection list options are organized into the following `options` object collection

```
select.options[idref]
```

where *select* is the reference to the selection list object and *idref* is the index number or ID of the option. Figure 13-9 describes the properties associated with the selection list and its individual options.

Figure 13-9	Properties of selection list options

Property	Description
option.defaultSelected	Returns true if *option* is selected by default
option.index	The index number of *option* within the options collection
option.selected	Returns true if the option has been selected by the user
option.text	The text associated with *option*
option.value	The field value of *option*

TIP

If no option is selected, the selectedIndex property returns the value -1.

To return the value from a selection list field, you must first determine which option button has been selected using the `selectedIndex` property. The following code demonstrates how to return the value of the selected option from the model selection list.

```
var orderForm = document.forms.orderForm;
var model = orderForm.elements.model;
var modelIndex = model.selectedIndex;
var modelValue = model.options[modelIndex].value;
```

REFERENCE

Working with Selection Lists

- To determine the index of the selected option in the selection list, use

  `select.selectedIndex`

  where *select* is the selection list object.
- To extract the text of an option in a selection list, use

  `select.options[idref].text`

  where *idref* is the index number or ID of the option.
- To extract the value of an option in a selection list, use:

  `select.options[idref].value`

The initial cost of the customer's order is equal to the price of the selected model multiplied by the quantity of items ordered. Because both the model and qty fields are entered as selection lists, you will retrieve the value of the two selected options. Add the code into the calcOrder() function, which will run when the page loads.

To enter the calcOrder() function:

1. Return to the **co_order.js** file in your editor.

2. Below the event listener for the `load` event, insert the following code for the calcOrder() function:

```
function calcOrder() {
    var orderForm = document.forms.orderForm;

    // Calculate the initial cost of the order
    var mIndex = orderForm.elements.model.selectedIndex;
    var mCost = orderForm.elements.model.options[mIndex].value;
    var qIndex = orderForm.elements.qty.selectedIndex;
    var quantity = orderForm.elements.qty[qIndex].value;

    // Initial cost = cost x quantity
    var initialCost = mCost*quantity;
    orderForm.elements.initialCost.value = initialCost;
}
```

3. Scroll up to the anonymous function for the `load` event and add the following code to call the calcOrder() function when the page is loaded:

```
// Calculate the cost of the order
calcOrder();
```

Figure 13-10 describes the newly added code in the file.

| Figure 13-10 | Calculating the cost of models ordered |

```
    orderForm.elements.model.focus();

    // Calculate the cost of the order
    calcOrder();
});

function calcOrder() {
    var orderForm = document.forms.orderForm;

    // Calculate the initial cost of the order
    var mIndex = orderForm.elements.model.selectedIndex;
    var mCost = orderForm.elements.model.options[mIndex].value;
    var qIndex = orderForm.elements.qty.selectedIndex;
    var quantity = orderForm.elements.qty[qIndex].value;

    // Initial cost = model cost x quantity
    var initialCost = mCost*quantity;
    orderForm.elements.initialCost.value = initialCost;
}
```

calculates the cost of the order when the page loads

determines the index of the selected model option

retrieves the value of the selected model option

retrieves the value of the selected qty option

calculates the cost of the models ordered

4. Save your changes to the file and then reload **co_order.html** in your browser. Figure 13-11 shows the initial cost of the order.

Figure 13-11   **Calculating the cost of models ordered**

A value of 129.95 appears in the initialCost field, which is equal to the cost of the 6-quart pot ($129.95) multiplied by the quantity purchased (1).

Selection Lists with Multiple Values

Some selection lists are set up to collect multiple selections. In those cases, the `selectedIndex` property returns only the index number of the first selected item. If you want to determine the indices of all the selected items, you must create a `for` loop that runs through the options in the list, checking each to determine whether the `selected` property is `true` (indicating that the option was selected by the user). If the option is selected, it can then be added to an array of the selected options using the `push()` method. The general structure of the `for` loop is

```
var selectedOpt = new Array();
for (var i = 0; i < select.options.length; i++) {
    if (select.options[i].selected) {
        selectedOpt.push(select.options[i]);
    }
}
```

where `select` is a selection list object. After this code is run, the selectedOpt array will contain all the options within the selection list that have been chosen by the user. To work with the selected options, you can create another `for` loop that loops through the items in the selectedOpt array to extract the text and value properties from each.

To the initial cost, add the cost of the protection plan, if any, selected by the customer. To retrieve the cost of the protection plan, you will need to work with the values stored in option buttons associated with the protection plans.

Working with Options Buttons and Check Boxes

Option or radio buttons are grouped by a common field name placed within the following array

```
options[idref]
```

where *options* is the common field name used by all the option buttons and *idref* is either the index number or ID of the option button. For example, the first option button for the protection field from the customer order form would have the reference:

```
document.forms.orderForm.elements.protection[0]
```

Figure 13-12 describes some of the properties associated with an individual option button object.

| Figure 13-12 | Properties of option or radio buttons |

Property	Description
option.checked	Boolean value indicating whether the option button, *option*, is currently checked by the user
option.defaultChecked	Boolean value indicating whether *option* is checked by default
option.disabled	Boolean value indicating whether *option* is disabled or not
option.name	The field name associated with *option*
option.value	The field value associated with *option*

To determine which option button has been checked by the user, you have to examine the checked property of each button. For example, the following code uses a for loop to go through each option button associated with the protection field, storing the value of the selected option in the pCost variable, and breaking off the for loop once the checked button has been located:

```
var orderForm = document.forms.orderForm;
var protection = orderForm.elements.protection;
for (var i = 0; i < protection.length; i++) {
   if (protection[i].checked === true) {
      var pCost = protection[i].value;
      break;
   }
}
```

Working with Option Button Groups

- To reference a specific option button within a group, use the object reference

  `options[idref]`

  where *options* is the common field name used by all the option buttons and *idref* is the ID or index number of the option button.
- To determine whether an option button is currently checked, use the object property

  `options[idref].checked`

  which returns the Boolean value `true` if the button is checked.
- To determine which button in the option button group is checked, create a `for` loop that examines each option button's checked property, returning the index of the checked button or referencing the checked option button using the expression

  `document.querySelector('input[name="field"]:checked')`

  where *field* is the common field name for all option buttons in the group.

Another way to retrieve the value of the checked option button without using a `for` loop is to use the following CSS selector. The following selector returns the option button that is checked within the protection field:

```
input[name="protection"]:checked
```

You can then place this selector within a `querySelector()` method to retrieve the value of the checked option:

```
var pCost =
document.querySelector('input[name="protection"]:checked').value;
```

Aisha wants to calculate the total cost of the protection plans, which is equal to the cost of the selected protection plan multiplied by the quantity of items ordered. Use the `querySelector()` method to indicate which protection option is selected by the customer.

To retrieve the cost of the selected protection plan:

1. Return to the **co_order.js** file in your editor.

2. Within the calcOrder() function, add the following commands:

```
// Retrieve the cost of the user's protection plan
var pCost = document.querySelector('input[name="protection"]:
checked').value*quantity;
orderForm.elements.protectionCost.value = pCost;
```

Figure 13-13 highlights the code in the function.

Figure 13-13   **Retrieving the cost of the selected protection plan**

```
// Initial cost = model cost x quantity
var initialCost = mCost*quantity;
orderForm.elements.initialCost.value = initialCost;

// Retrieve the cost of the user's protection plan
var pCost = document.querySelector('input[name="protection"]:checked').value;
orderForm.elements.protectionCost.value = pCost;
}
```

shows the protection plan cost in the order form

query to select the option button that is checked for the protection field

▶ **3.** Save your changes to the file.

Working with Check Boxes

Check box controls work the same way as option buttons in which the checked property indicates whether the box is checked and the value associated with a checked box is stored in the value property of the check box object. However, this value is applied only when the check box is checked; otherwise there is no field value associated with the element.

INSIGHT

Combining Field Values

JavaScript treats field values as text strings; therefore, you cannot simply use the + operator to add two or more field values because JavaScript will concatenate the text strings rather than adding the numeric values. For example, if one field contains the value "129.95" and a second field contains the value "11.95", then the + operator returns the text string "129.9511.95". This is not an issue with other mathematical operators. For example, multiplying two field values will return a numeric value and not a text string.

One way of converting a text string to a numeric value is to apply either the parseFloat() or parseInt() function introduced in Figure 9-39 to extract the field value as a number. Thus, the following expression

```
parseFloat(form.element1.value)+
parseFloat(form.element2.value)
```

will return the numeric sum of the values in element1 and element2, rather than the combination of the two text strings.

To complete the order form, calculate the order subtotal, taxes due, and the total cost of the order.

To complete the order form calculations:

1. Return to the **co_order.js** file in your editor and scroll down to the calcOrder() function.

2. Add the following commands to the calcOrder() function to calculate and display the order subtotal:

```
// Calculate the order subtotal
orderForm.elements.subtotal.value = initialCost + pCost;
```

3. Add the following commands to calculate the sales tax, which is 5% of the subtotal value:

```
// Calculate the sales tax
var salesTax = 0.05*(initialCost + pCost);
orderForm.elements.salesTax.value = salesTax;
```

4. Finally, calculate the total cost of the order which is equal to the sum of the initialCost, pCost, and salesTax variables.

```
// Calculate the cost of the total order
var totalCost = initialCost + pCost + salesTax;
orderForm.elements.totalCost.value = totalCost;
```

Figure 13-14 describes the newly added code in the calcOrder() function.

Figure 13-14	Completing the calculations in the order form

adds the cost of the models ordered and the cost of the protection plan

```
// Calculate the order subtotal
orderForm.elements.subtotal.value = initialCost + pCost;

// Calculate the sales tax
var salesTax = 0.05*(initialCost + pCost);
orderForm.elements.salesTax.value = salesTax;

// Calculate the cost of the total order
var totalCost = initialCost + pCost + salesTax;
orderForm.elements.totalCost.value = totalCost;
}
```

adds the initial cost, the cost of the protection plan, and the sales tax

calculates the sales tax at 5% of the order subtotal

5. Save your changes to the file and then reload the **co_order.html** file in your browser. Figure 13-15 shows the calculated values from the initial order form.

Figure 13-15   Initial totals from the order form

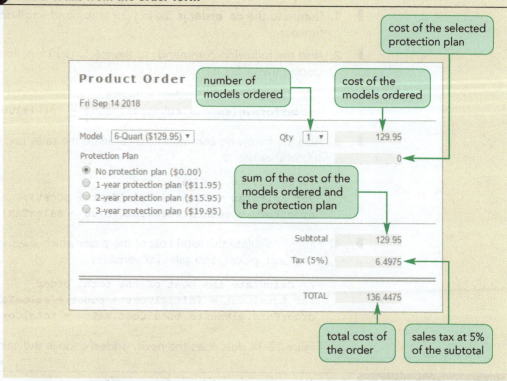

Figure 13-15   Initial totals from the order form

Aisha has examined your work on the order form and finds the numeric values difficult to read. She wants the numbers formatted to two decimal places and commas used as thousands separators. She also wants the initial cost and the total order cost displayed as U.S. currency.

Formatting Numeric Values

Numeric values are displayed by JavaScript to 16 decimal place accuracy. As discussed earlier in Tutorial 9, you can control the number of digits displayed by the browser using the `toFixed()` method. However, the `toFixed()` method is limited to only defining the decimal place accuracy; it does not format numbers as currency or separate thousands with the comma symbol. To have more control over the numeric format, apply the following `toLocaleString()` method

```
value.toLocaleString(locale, {options})
```

TIP

You can also set the *locale* value to undefined to apply the numeric format of the user's computer.

where *locale* is a comma-separated list of location and language codes that indicate the locale for displaying numeric values, and *options* is a comma-separated list of formatting options for numeric values. With no arguments, the `toLocalString()` method displays the numeric value using the local standards on the user's computer.

The following code demonstrates the format applied to a sample number assuming the default English format:

```
var testValue = 14281.4756;
testValue.toLocalString();    // returns the text "14,281.4756"
```

Different locales use different number formats. In France, the convention is to use spaces as thousands separators and commas to mark the decimal place. Thus, a French format of the same sample value appears as:

```
var testValue = 14281.4756;
testValue.toLocalString("fr");   // returns the text "14 281,4756"
```

Figure 13-16 describes the options that can be applied to numerical values for even more control over the number formatting.

Figure 13-16	Options from the toLocaleString() method

Option	Description
style: *type*	Formatting style to use where *type* is "decimal", "currency", or "percent"
currency: *code*	Currency symbol to use for currency formatting where *code* designates the country or language
currencyDisplay: *type*	Currency text to display where *type* is "symbol" for a currency symbol, "code" for the ISO currency code, or "name" for the currency name
useGroup: *Boolean*	Indicates whether to use a thousands grouping symbol (true) or not (false)
minimumIntegerDigits: *num*	The minimum number of digits to display where *num* ranges from 1 (the default) to 21
minimumFractionDigits: *num*	The minimum number of fraction digits where *num* varies from 0 to 20; 2 digits are used for currency and 0 digits are used for plain number and percentages
maximumFractionDigits: *num*	The maximum number of fraction digits where *num* varies from 0 to 20; 2 digits are used for currency and 0 digits are used for plain number and percentages
minimumSignficantDigits: *num*	The minimum number of significant digits where *num* varies from 1 (the default) to 21
maximumSignificantDigits: *num*	The maximum number of significant digits where *num* varies from 1 (the default) to 21

The following code demonstrates how to display a numeric value as currency using U.S. dollars:

```
var testValue = 14281.5;
testValue.toLocalString("en-US", {style: "currency", currency: "USD"})
// returns the text "$14,281.50"
```

To display a numeric value to exactly two decimal places, set the minimumFractionDigits and maximumFractionDigits values to "2" as in the following code:

```
var testValue = 14281.4756;
testValue.toLocalString(undefined, {minimumFractionDigits: 2,
maximumFractionDigits: 2})
// returns the text "14,281.48"
```

TIP

The toLocalString() method will round the missing digits to the nearest value.

Note that, when undefined is used as the locale value, the browser applies the thousands separator using whatever local conventions are applied on the user's computer.

REFERENCE

Formatting Numeric Values

- To display a numeric value with thousands separators, apply

  `value.toLocaleString()`

  where *value* is the numeric value.
- To display a numeric value as U.S. currency, apply:

  `value.toLocaleString("en-US", {style: "currency", currency: "USD"})`

- To set the number of decimal places for a numeric value, apply:

  `value.toFixed(n)`

- To apply the thousands separator and to set the number of decimal places for a numeric value, apply

  `value.toLocaleString(undefined, {minimumFractionDigits: n, maximumFractionDigits: n})`

  where `undefined` applies the thousands separator per local convention and *n* is the number of decimal places.

Aisha wants to display the values in the order form to two decimals places with thousands separators and she wants the initial cost and the total order cost displayed in currency format. To create these formats, you will add two new functions to the JavaScript file.

To create functions to format numerical values:

1. Return to the **co_order.js** file in your editor and scroll to the bottom of the file.

2. Add the following function to format numeric values as a text string using local standards:

   ```
   function formatNumber(val, decimals) {
      return val.toLocaleString(undefined,
         {minimumFractionDigits: decimals,
          maximumFractionDigits: decimals});
   }
   ```

   Note that the val parameter contains the numeric value to format and the decimals parameter specifies the number of decimal places to display.

3. Add the following function to format numeric values as U.S. currency:

   ```
   function formatUSCurrency(val) {
      return val.toLocaleString('en-US',
        {style: "currency", currency: "USD"} );
   }
   ```

Options for the `toLocaleString()` method must be enclosed with curly braces and separated by commas.

Figure 13-17 describes the newly added code in the file.

Figure 13-17 | Defining functions to format numeric values

```
            orderForm.elements.totalCost.value = totalCost;
}
function formatNumber(val, decimals) {
    return val.toLocaleString(undefined,
        {minimumFractionDigits: decimals,
         maximumFractionDigits: decimals});
}

function formatUSCurrency(val) {
    return val.toLocaleString('en-US',
        {style: "currency", currency: "USD"} );
}
```

number of decimals to display

does not apply a locale number format

numeric value

applies the English United States number format

sets the currency style to U.S. dollars

sets the minimum and maximum number of decimals places to the value of decimals

Next, apply these functions to the values displayed in the order form.

To apply the number format functions:

1. Scroll up to the calcOrder() function and change the command to display the initial cost of the order to:

   ```
   orderForm.elements.initialCost.value =
   formatUSCurrency(initialCost);
   ```

2. Change the command to display the cost of the protection plan to:

   ```
   orderForm.elements.protectionCost.value = formatNumber(pCost, 2);
   ```

3. Change the commands to display the subtotal and sales tax values to:

   ```
   orderForm.elements.subtotal.value = formatNumber(initialCost +
   pCost, 2);
   ```

   and

   ```
   orderForm.elements.salesTax.value = formatNumber(salesTax, 2);
   ```

4. Finally, change the command to display the order total to:

   ```
   orderForm.elements.totalCost.value =
   formatUSCurrency(totalCost);
   ```

Figure 13-18 highlights the changed code in the function.

Figure 13-18   **Applying the number format functions**

formats the initial cost as U.S. currency

```
// Initial cost = model cost x quantity
var initialCost = mCost*quantity;
orderForm.elements.initialCost.value = formatUSCurrency(initialCost);

// Retrieve the cost of the user's protection plan
var pCost = document.querySelector('input[name="protection"]:checked').value*quantity;
orderForm.elements.protectionCost.value = formatNumber(pCost, 2);

// Calculate the order subtotal
orderForm.elements.subtotal.value = formatNumber(initialCost + pCost, 2);

// Calculate the sales tax
var salesTax = 0.05*(initialCost + pCost);
orderForm.elements.salesTax.value = formatNumber(salesTax, 2);

// Calculate the cost of the total order
var totalCost = initialCost + pCost + salesTax;
orderForm.elements.totalCost.value = formatUSCurrency(totalCost);
}
```

formats the total cost as U.S. currency

displays the other form values as numbers to 2 decimal places

5. Save your changes to the file and then reload **co_order.html** in your browser. Figure 13-19 shows the formatted values in the order form.

Figure 13-19   **Formatted form values**

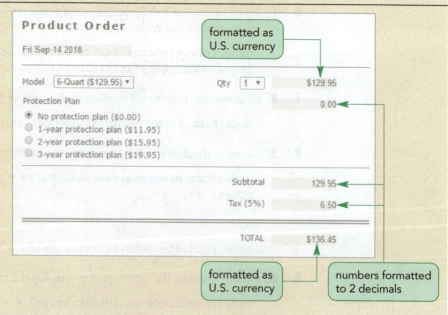

formatted as U.S. currency

Product Order

Fri Sep 14 2018

| Model | 6-Quart ($129.95) ▾ | Qty | 1 ▾ | $129.95 |

Protection Plan   0.00

○ No protection plan ($0.00)
○ 1-year protection plan ($11.95)
○ 2-year protection plan ($15.95)
○ 3-year protection plan ($19.95)

Subtotal   129.95
Tax (5%)   6.50

TOTAL $136.45

formatted as U.S. currency

numbers formatted to 2 decimals

Next, add code to recalculate the costs whenever the customer changes an option in the order form.

PROSKILLS

Written Communication: Making a Website International Friendly

On the World Wide Web, your customers and associates can come from anywhere. You need to plan your website for your international visitors as well as your domestic clients. Consider the following tips as you plan to go "international":

- Support international conventions for dates, times, numbers, and currency using country and language codes in your HTML content and JavaScript programs.
- Avoid images that contain text strings. A picture is a worth a thousand words but not if that picture includes language foreign to your audience.
- Make your layout flexible. The translated version of your content might contain more words or fewer words than your web page. Ensure that the page layout can adapt to different text content. Remember that in some countries, text is read from right to left.
- Optimize your site for international searches, including using country-specific domain names and keywords tailored to international customers.
- Provide customers with a way to convert their payments into their own currency or provide information on exchange rates.
- Be aware of cultural differences: color, working hours, holidays, and so forth have different meanings and different impact in different countries.

Once you have established an international website, monitor its usage with various analytical tools such as Google Webmaster and Analytics. A poor traffic report might indicate a problem with the international content of your website.

Applying Form Events

JavaScript supports the event handlers described in Figure 13-20 for responding to user actions within a form.

Figure 13-20	Form event handlers

Event Handler	Description
element.onblur	The form element has lost the focus
element.onchange	The value of element has changed
element.onfocus	The element has received the focus
element.oninput	The element has received user input
element.oninvalid	The element value is invalid
form.onreset	The form has been reset
element.onsearch	The user has entered something into a search field
element.onselect	Text has been selected within the element
form.onsubmit	The form has been submitted

Thus, to rerun the calcOrder() function when the user changes the quantity of items to order, you could apply the event handler:

```
orderForm.elements.qty.onchange = calcOrder;
```

For options buttons and check boxes, use the onclick event handler in response to the user clicking those elements.

onchange vs. oninput

The `oninput` and `onchange` event handlers can both be used when the user changes the content of an input box. Their difference is in when they are initiated by the browser. The `oninput` event handler is fired immediately when the text content is entered by the user. The `onchange` event handler is fired when the input box content changes and the input box loses the focus. Note that the `oninput` event handler is not applicable to selection lists or option buttons because no text content is modified by the user.

Aisha wants the form to be recalculated whenever the user changes the order quantity, model, or protection plan. Apply the `onchange` event handler to the selection lists and the `onclick` event handler to the option buttons for the protection field.

To apply event handlers to the form:

1. Return to the **co_order.js** file in your text editor.

2. Within the anonymous function for the `load` event, add the following commands to run the calcOrder() function in response to changing values in the model and qty fields:

   ```
   // Event handlers for the web form
   orderForm.elements.model.onchange = calcOrder;
   orderForm.elements.qty.onchange = calcOrder;
   ```

3. Add the following code to add `onclick` event handlers to every option button in the protection field:

   ```
   var planOptions =
   document.querySelectorAll('input[name= "protection"]');
   for (var i = 0; i < planOptions.length; i++) {
      planOptions[i].onclick = calcOrder;
   }
   ```

Figure 13-21 highlights the event handlers for the order form.

Figure 13-21 Adding event handlers to form elements

```
// Calculate the cost of the order
calcOrder();

// Event handlers for the web form
orderForm.elements.model.onchange = calcOrder;
orderForm.elements.qty.onchange = calcOrder;

var planOptions = document.querySelectorAll('input[name="protection"]');
for (var i = 0; i < planOptions.length; i++) {
   planOptions[i].onclick = calcOrder;
}
});
```

runs the calcOrder() function when the value of the model or qty field changes

loops through the option buttons for the protection field adding onclick event handlers to each button

4. Save your changes to the file and then reload **co_order.html** in your browser. Test the form by changing the model to the **8-Quart ($159.95)** pot, the quantity value to **7**, and the protection plan to the **3-year** option. Verify that the total cost of the order is $1,322.27 with a subtotal value of 1,259.30 and a tax value of 62.97.

Working with Hidden Fields

In many web forms, important data is stored within hidden fields so that the data is available to programmers but removed from the user's control. Aisha has placed the following two hidden fields in the order form to store the model ordered by the user and the name of the selected protection plan:

```
<input type="hidden" id="modelName" name="modelName" />
<input type="hidden" id="protectionName" name="protectionName" />
```

The model name is stored as the text of the options in the model selection list and can be stored in the modelName field using the text attribute in the following command:

```
orderForm.elements.modelName.value =
orderForm.elements.model.options[mIndex].text;
```

However, because the protection plans are selected using option buttons, you have to retrieve the text that follows the checked option. You can retrieve the value of that text node using the nextSibling and nodeValue properties in the following command:

```
orderForm.elements.protectionName.value = document.querySelector
('input[name="protection"]:checked').nextSibling.nodeValue;
```

Add these two commands to the calcOrder() function.

To apply event handlers to the form:

1. Return to the **co_order.js** file in your text editor and scroll to the bottom of the calcOrder() function.

2. Add the following code to the function:

```
// Store the order details
orderForm.elements.modelName.value =
    orderForm.elements.model.options[mIndex].text;

orderForm.elements.protectionName.value =
    document.querySelector('input[name="protection"]:checked')
.nextSibling.nodeValue;
```

Figure 13-22 highlights the revised code in the function.

Figure 13-22 Storing data in hidden fields

```
// Calculate the cost of the total order
var totalCost = initialCost + pCost + salesTax;
orderForm.elements.totalCost.value = formatUSCurrency(totalCost);

// Store the order details
orderForm.elements.modelName.value =
    orderForm.elements.model.options[mIndex].text;
orderForm.elements.protectionName.value =
    document.querySelector('input[name="protection"]:checked').nextSibling.nodeValue;
}
```

hidden fields

retrieves the text of the selected option in the selection list

references the checked option button for the protection field

retrieves the text in the text node next to the checked option button

3. Save your changes to the file and then reload **co_order.html** in your browser to verify that no errors are reported. Because the modelName and protectionName fields are hidden, they will not appear in the web page, but you can view them and their values using the developer tools in your browser.

You have completed your work on the calculations involved with the order form. In the next session, you will learn how to copy the order form data to a new page in the Coctura website.

REVIEW

Session 13.1 Quick Check

1. Provide the object reference to the third web form in the page.
2. Provide the object reference to the second element within the first web form.
3. Provide code to change the value of the input box with the ID "country" to "Mexico".
4. Provide code to change the focus to the element with the field name "country" in the web form named "registration".
5. Provide code to retrieve the value of the selected option in the selection list with the ID "state", storing the value in the variable stateName.
6. Provide code to retrieve the value of the checked option in the option group for the field "shipping".
7. Provide code to display the value of the payment variable as United States currency.
8. Provide code to run the calcShipping() function when the value of the state field in the shoppingCart form is changed.

Session 13.2 Visual Overview:

These attributes append the field *name/value* pairs to the query string portion of the URL in the payment page.

```html
<section id="orderSection">
  <form id="orderForm" name="orderForm" method="get" action="co_payment.html">

    <table id="orderTable">
      <caption>Product Order</caption>
      <tr>
        <td colspan="3">
          <input type="text" id="orderDate" name="orderDate" readonly />
        </td>
```

The `replace()` method replaces a character or character pattern with a specified text string.

The `slice()` method slices the text starting with the second character.

The `location.search` object returns the query string portion of the current page's URL.

This regular expression matches every occurrence of the + character.

```javascript
window.addEventListener("load", function(){
    var formData = location.search.slice(1);
    formData = formData.replace(/\+/g," ");
    formData = decodeURIComponent(formData);
    var formFields = formData.split(/[&=]/g);

    document.forms.order.elements.orderDate.value = formFields[1];
    document.forms.order.elements.modelName.value = formFields[5];
    document.forms.order.elements.qty.value = formFields[7];
    document.forms.order.elements.initialCost.value = formFields[9];
    document.forms.order.elements.protectionName.value = formFields[13];
    document.forms.order.elements.protectionCost.value = formFields[15];
    document.forms.order.elements.subtotal.value = formFields[17];
    document.forms.order.elements.salesTax.value = formFields[19];
    document.forms.order.elements.totalCost.value = formFields[21];
} );
```

The `decodeURIComponent()` method decodes every URI character codes with its character values.

This regular expression matches every occurrence of the & or = characters.

The `split()` method splits a text string into an array of substrings at every occurrence of a character or character pattern.

Passing data between forms

The query string portion of the URL contains the field *name/value* pairs from the calling form.

Data retrieved from the calling form.

These are the data stored in the calling form.

© Courtesy Patrick Carey; Sources: American Express Company; Discover Financial Services; MasterCard, Inc.; Visa, Inc.

Sharing Data between Forms

In many applications, you will want to share data that has been input among several forms and spread across several web pages. In those situations, you might want to copy the data entered in one form to another form on a separate page. In this session, you will explore how to do that by appending data to a web page URL.

Appending Form Data

To append form data to the URL, add the following `method` and `action` attributes to the `form` element

```
<form method="get" action="url">
```

where *url* is the URL of the page to which you want to append the form data.

Edit the co_order.html file to open the co_payment.html file when the order form is submitted.

To modify the order form attribute:

1. If you took a break after the previous session, reopen the **co_order.html** file in your text editor.

2. Scroll down and edit the opening `<form>` tag for the order form by adding the following attributes:

   ```
   method="get" action="co_payment.html"
   ```

   Figure 13-23 highlights the revised code.

Figure 13-23 | **Appending form data to a URL**

appends the form data to the URL of the action page

```
<section id="orderSection">
   <form id="orderForm" name="orderForm" method="get" action="co_payment.html">

      <table id="orderTable">
         <caption>Product Order</caption>
         <tr>
            <td colspan="3">
               <input type="text" id="orderDate" name="orderDate" readonly />
            </td>
```

opens the co_payment.html file when the form is submitted

3. Close the file, saving your changes.

Next, submit a completed order form, verifying that it opens the co_payment file with the data fields and values appended to the URL.

To submit the order:

1. Use your editor to open the **co_payment_txt.html** and **co_payment_txt.js** files from the html13 ▸ tutorial folder. Enter *your name* and *the date* in the comment section of each file and save them as **co_payment.html** and **co_payment.js** respectively.

2. Go to the **co_payment.html** file in your editor and within the document head, add a `script` element to load the **co_payment.js** file asynchronously. Save your changes to the file.

3. Reopen the **co_order.html** file in your browser. Select the **6-Quart** model, with a quantity of **2** and the **1-year protection** plan. Click the **add to cart** button to submit the order form and open the **co_payment.html**.

   As shown in Figure 13-24, the address bar in the browser shows the URL with form field names and data values from the order form appended to the URL.

Figure 13-24	The payment page

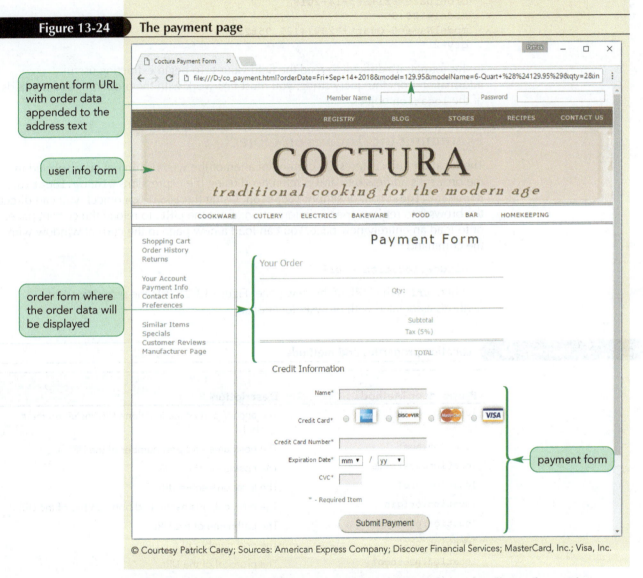

payment form URL with order data appended to the address text

user info form

order form where the order data will be displayed

payment form

© Courtesy Patrick Carey; Sources: American Express Company; Discover Financial Services; MasterCard, Inc.; Visa, Inc.

At the top of the payment page is a blank order form that you will populate with values taken from the co_order.html page and currently appended to the page's URL. The URL has the general format

```
http://server/path/file?field1=value1&field2=value2&field3=value3...
```

where *server* and *path* are the server and path names for the web page and *file* is the filename of the web page. Next is the ? character, followed by the **query string**, which contains field names and data values appended to the URL in which *field1*, *field2*, and so on are the names of the fields, and *value1*, *value2*, and so on are the corresponding field values. Note that each field/value pair is separated by the & character. The following text string contains the complete text of a query string appended to the URL of the co_payment.html file:

```
orderDate=Fri+Sep+14+2018&model=129.95&modelName=6-Quart+%28%2412
9.95%29&qty=2&initialCost=%24259.90&protection=11.95&protectionName=
+1-year+protection+plan+%28%2411.95%29&protectionCost=23.90&subtotal
=283.80&salesTax=14.19&totalCost=%24297.99
```

Thus, the first few field/value pairs come from the order form in the co_order.html file with values for the orderDate, model, modelName, and qty fields:

```
orderDate=Fri+Sep+14+2018
model=129.95
modelName=6-Quart+%28%24129.95%29
qty=2
```

In this format, it's difficult to read the field values. To begin extracting useful information from the query string, you must first work with the properties and methods of the location object.

Examining the `location` Object

The **location object** stores the current location of the web document (as displayed in the browser's address bar) and is referenced using the expressions `window.location`, `document.location`, or simply `location`. Using the `location` object, you can direct the browser to retrieve specific information about the URL, to reload the current page, or to load an entirely new page. You can load a new page in the current window with the command

```
window.location = url
```

where *url* is the URL of the new page. Figure 13-25 lists the properties and methods associated with browser locations.

Figure 13-25   Location properties and methods

Property or Method	Description
location.hash	The anchor part of the location's URL including the # symbol
location.host	The hostname and port number of the URL
location.hostname	The hostname of the URL
location.href	The location's entire URL
location.origin	The protocol, hostname, and port number of the URL
location.pathname	The pathname of the URL
location.port	The port number of the URL
location.protocol	The protocol of the URL
location.search	The query string portion of the URL (all the text after the ? symbol)
location.assign(*newurl*)	Loads a new document with the URL, *newurl*
location.reload(*fromServer*)	Reloads the current location from the server where *fromServer* is false to load the location from the browser's cache (the default) or true to reload from the server
location.replace(*newurl*)	Loads a new document with the URL, *newurl* and replaces the current location in the browser history with *newURL*
location.toString()	Returns the href portion of the location's URL

Use the `location.search` property to extract the query string from the URL, storing the query string text in a variable named formQuery.

To extract the query string from the page location:

1. Return to the **co_payment.js** file in your editor.

2. Directly below the initial comment section, add the following event listener for the `load` event:

```
window.addEventListener("load", function(){
    // Retrieve the field/value pairs from the URL
    var formData = location.search;
});
```

Figure 13-26 highlights the newly added code in the file.

Figure 13-26   Extracting the field/value pairs from the location URL

```
*/

window.addEventListener("load", function(){
    // Retrieve the field/value pairs from the URL
    var formData = location.search;
});
```

references the location of the current page

returns the query string portion of the location URL

3. Save your changes to the file.

The formData variable contains the following text string (with a different date in your page):

```
?orderDate=Fri+Sep+14+2018&model=129.95&modelName…
```

To extract information from this text string, you must work with the properties and methods of text strings.

Working with Text Strings

Text string objects are created implicitly when storing any text string value within a variable or by extracting a text string from a web form field or a location URL. They can also be created explicitly using the following object constructor

```
var stringVar = new String(text);
```

where *stringVar* is a variable that stores the text string, and *text* is the text of the string. Figure 13-27 lists the JavaScript methods for extracting text from a text string object.

Figure 13-27	**String object properties and methods**

Property or Method	Description
`str.length`	Returns the number of characters in the text string, `str`
`str.charAt(i)`	Returns the character at index, `i`, where the first character has index 0, the second character has index 1, …
`str.charCodeAt(i)`	Returns the Unicode of the character at index, `i`
`str.concat(str1, str2, …)`	Appends the substrings `str1`, `str2`, … to the text string, `str`
`str.endsWith(text [,length])`	Returns `true` if `str` ends with the substring `text`; the optional `length` property specifies the length of the string to search
`String.fromCharCode(n1, n2, …)`	Constructs a `String` object using the Unicode character codes `n1`, `n2`, …
`str.includes(text [,start])`	Returns `true` if `str` contains the substring `text`; the optional `start` property specifies the index of the starting character for the search
`str.indexOf(text [,start])`	Returns the first index of substring `text` within the text string, `str`; a value of -1 is returned if `text` is not present within `str`
`str.lastIndexOf(text [,start])`	Returns the last index of substring `text` within the text string, `str`
`str.repeat(n)`	Repeats the text string, `str`, `n` times
`str.slice(start [,end])`	Extracts a substring from `str`, between the `start` and `end` index values, if no `end` value is specified the substring extend to the end of `str`
`str.split(text [,limit])`	Splits `str` into an array of string values for each occurrence of `text`; the optional `limit` attribute specifies an upper limit for the length of the array
`str.startsWith(text [,start])`	Returns `true` if `str` starts with the substring `text`
`str.substr(start [,length])`	Extracts a substring from `str`, starting at the index value `start` and continuing for the next `length` characters; if no `length` value is specified the substring extends to the end of `str`
`str.substring(start [,end])`	Extracts a substring from `str`, between the `start` and `end` index values; if no `end` value is specified the substring extends to the end of `str`
`str.toLowerCase()`	Converts `str` to lowercase letters
`str.toUpperCase()`	Converts `str` to uppercase letters
`str.trim()`	Removes white-space characters from the start and end of `str`

Extracting Substrings from a Text String

JavaScript supports methods that allow you to examine the individual characters within a text string. Like arrays and object collections, the first character in the text string has an index value of 0, the second has an index value of 1, and so on. To reference a character use the `charAt()` method

```
string.charAt(i)
```

where *string* is the string object and *i* is the index value of the character. For example, the following expression returns the fourth character from the text string, which is the character "d":

```
"Traditional Cooking".charAt(3)
```

The charAt() method extracts only a single character. To extract longer text strings, known as **substrings**, use the following slice() method

```
string.slice(start [,end])
```

TIP

Blank spaces are counted as characters within a text string.

where *start* is the starting index value and *end* is the index value at which the slicing stops. If you do not specify an *end* value, the substring is extracted to the end of the text string. The following expression extracts the substring "Cook" from the text string:

```
"Traditional Cooking".slice(12, 15)
```

The slice() method creates a single substring. To create an array of substrings, apply the following split() method

```
strArray = string.split(str)
```

TIP

The delimiter character is not placed in the array generated by the split() method, so in this example, the blank space delimiter is part of the sub-strings in the words array.

where *strArray* is the array that will store the substrings and *str* is a **delimiter** that marks the break between one substring and another. Thus, the following command creates the substring array ["traditional", "cooking", "for", "the", "modern", "age"] by splitting the text string at each occurrence of a blank space:

```
var words = "traditional cooking for the modern age".split(" ")
```

Searching within a Text String

Other string object methods are used to search for the occurrence of substrings within larger text strings. The most often used method is the following indexOf() method

```
string.indexOf(str [,start])
```

TIP

If the substring is not found, the indexOf() method returns a value of -1.

returning the index value of the first occurrence of the substring *str*. The *start* value is optional and indicates the index value where the search starts; the default is from the first character. For example, the following expression locates the first occurrence of a blank character, returning the index value 11:

```
"Traditional Cooking".indexOf(" ")
```

REFERENCE

Working with String Objects

- To determine the number of characters in a text string, use

  ```
  string.length
  ```

  where *string* is a text string object.
- To extract one character from a text string, use

  ```
  string.chartAt(i)
  ```

  where *i* is the index value of character, starting with 0 for the first character.
- To extract a substring from a text string, use

  ```
  string.slice(start [,end])
  ```

  where *start* is the index value of the starting character and *end* is the index value of the ending character.
- To split a string into several substrings, use

  ```
  strArray = string.split(str)
  ```

  where *strArray* is an array containing the substrings, and *str* is the text string that marks the break between one substring and the next.
- To search a text string, use

  ```
  index = string.indexOf(str [,start])
  ```

  where *index* is the index value of the found substring, *str* is the substring to search for and *start* is the index value of the character from which to start the search; if you do not specify a starting value the search starts from the first character. If the search fails, a value of -1 is returned.

The value of the formData variable containing the field/value pairs starts with the ? character. Remove the character by applying the `slice()` method to the formData expression.

To split a text string:

1. Within the anonymous function for the page the `load` event, apply the method `slice(1)` to the value of the `location.search` object.

   Figure 13-28 highlights the revised code in the function.

Figure 13-28   **Extracting a substring using the slice() method**

```
window.addEventListener("load", function(){
    // Retrieve the field/value pairs from the URL
    var formData = location.search.slice(1);
} );
```

extracts a substring starting with the second character

2. Save your changes to the file.

All the examples you have examined have involved explicitly specified characters and substrings. However, these strings methods also support substrings that match character patterns. Before continuing with the code to retrieve the form data, you will examine how to work with regular expressions.

INSIGHT

Storing Data with Session or Local Storage

Another way of saving data from a web form is by using session or local storage, which stores data in a **storage object** named sessionStorage or localStorage. **Session storage objects** store data for the current browser session and are deleted when the session ends. **Local storage objects** store data locally on the user's computers with no expiration date and thus can be accessed from previous browser sessions. To store data in a session storage object, apply the commands

```
sessionStorage.variable = value;
```
or
```
sessionStorage[variable] = value;
```

where *variable* is the name of the session storage variable and *value* is the variable's value. The same commands can be used for local storage except that localStorage replaces the sessionStorage in the code. For example, the following expression stores a date string in the orderDate local storage variable:

```
localStorage.orderDate = "Fri, Sept 14 2018";
```

You can also set and retrieve storage values using the following setItem() method:

```
localStorage.setItem("variable", value)
```

Once a value has been stored, it can be accessed by applying the following getItem() method for session or local storage:

```
sessionStorage.getItem("variable")
```
or
```
localStorage.getItem("variable")
```

You can free up memory by removing items from session or local storage. To remove a specific variable from session storage, apply the following removeItem() method:

```
sessionStorage.removeItem("variable")
```
or
```
localStorage.removeItem("variable")
```

and to remove all items from session storage, run:

```
sessionStorage.clear();
```
or
```
localStorage.clear()
```

The amount of space allotted for session and local storage varies between browsers. For example, Google Chrome allots about 5 megabytes for local storage but places no restriction on session storage. Note that the Microsoft Edge and Microsoft Internet Explorer browsers require that the web page be loaded on a server; they will not apply local or session storage for web pages on the local file system of your computer.

Introducing Regular Expressions

A **regular expression** is a text string that defines a character pattern. Regular expressions have the following general form

```
/pattern/
```

where *pattern* is the regular expression code that defines a character pattern. For example, the following regular expression defines a character pattern in which 5 digits are followed by a dash and another 4 digits:

```
/\d{5}-\d{4}/
```

Thus, a text string such as "13472-0912" matches this pattern but text strings such as "13472" or "134720912" do not.

Matching a Substring

The most basic regular expression is simply a substring of characters entered as

```
/chars/
```

where *chars* is the substring text. To help you understand regular expressions, you will apply this regular expression pattern in a demo page.

To use the regular expression demo:

1. Use your web browser to open the **demo_regexp.html** file from the html13 ▶ demo folder.

2. Type **Coctura Products Are Prepared With Care** in the text area box located in the upper-left corner of the page.

3. Click the **Or enter one directly** text box located directly below the drop-down list box and type **/are/** as the regular expression.

4. Click the **Pattern Test** button. The first occurrence of the "are" substring is highlighted and the Pattern Test Result field displays the word "match", indicating that a matching character pattern has been found in the text string. See Figure 13-29.

Figure 13-29	Matching a substring

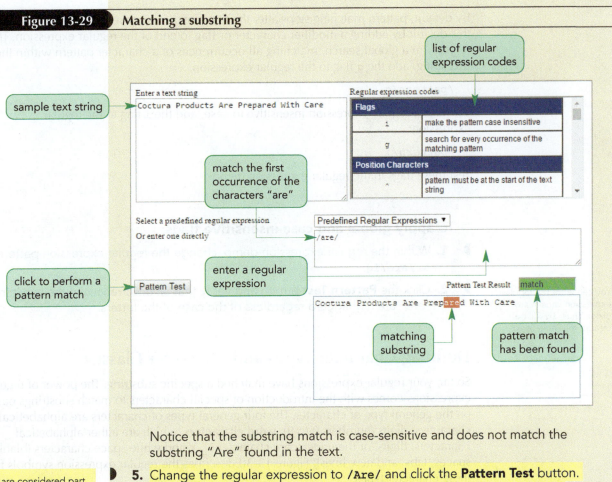

sample text string

list of regular expression codes

match the first occurrence of the characters "are"

enter a regular expression

click to perform a pattern match

matching substring

pattern match has been found

Notice that the substring match is case-sensitive and does not match the substring "Are" found in the text.

5. Change the regular expression to **/Are/** and click the **Pattern Test** button. The pattern now matches the word "Are" found earlier in the text string.

Spaces are considered part of a regular expression substring. Thus, the regular expression /Are/ is different from the regular expression /Are/.

To specify the beginning or end, regular expressions mark the beginning and end of a text string with the ^ and $ characters, respectively. Thus the following expression will match the substring "Coctura" but only if it comes at the start of the text.

```
/^Coctura/
```

while the regular expression

```
/Coctura$/
```

matches the substring "Coctura" only if it comes at the end of the text string. Finally, the expression

```
/^Coctura$/
```

only matches text strings that contain the word "Coctura" and *nothing else*.

Setting Regular Expression Flags

By default, pattern matching stops after the first match is discovered. You can override this default by adding a modifier character or **flag** to end of the regular expression. Thus to perform a global search, matching all occurrences of a character pattern within the text string, add the g flag to the regular expression:

    /pattern/g

To make a regular expression insensitive to case, add the i flag to the regular expression:

    /pattern/i

Test these flags in the regular expression demo.

To apply global and case-insensitive flags:

▶ **1.** Within the regular expression demo, change the regular expression pattern to /are/ig.

▶ **2.** Click the **Pattern Test** button and verify that all occurrences of the substring "are" are highlighted regardless of the case of the letters.

You can enter the regular expression flags in any order. Thus, ig will be treated the same as gi.

Defining Character Types and Character Classes

So far, your regular expressions have matched a specific substring. The power of regular expressions comes with the introduction of special characters to match substrings based on the general type of character. The four general types of characters are alphabetical characters; digits (numbers 0 to 9), **word characters**, which are either alphabetical characters, digits, or the underscore character (_); and white-space characters (blank spaces, tabs, and new lines). Figure 13-30 describes the regular expression symbols for these character types.

Figure 13-30	Character types

Character	Description
\b	a word boundary
\B	not a word boundary
\d	a digit from 0 to 9
\D	any non-digit character
\w	an alphabetical character (in uppercase or lowercase letters), a digit, or an underscore
\W	any non-word character
\s	a white-space character (a blank space, tab, new line, carriage return, or form feed)
\S	any non-white-space character
.	any character

The term **word** has a special meaning in the regular expression language and refers to any string of symbols consisting solely of word characters. The string "R2D2" is considered a single word, but "R2D2&C3PO" is considered two words, with the & symbol marking the boundary between the words. Word boundaries are indicated by the \b symbol. The following pattern matches any word that starts with the characters "art" such as "artful", "artist", or "article".

TIP

Regular expression symbols have opposite meanings when expressed in uppercase letters. Thus, the symbol \B means the absence of a word boundary and the symbol \W means the absence of a word character.

```
/\bart/
```

On the other hand, the following pattern matches any word that ends with "art" such as "smart", "dart", or "heart".

```
/art\b/
```

Finally, the following pattern matches only the word "art" and nothing else.

```
/\bart\b/
```

To view the effect of word boundaries on regular expressions:

1. Within the regular expression demo, change the regular expression pattern to /\bare\b/ig to match all character strings containing the text string "are" surrounded by word boundaries.

2. Click the **Pattern Test** button. Figure 13-31 shows the matched substring in the text string.

| Figure 13-31 | Using word boundaries in regular expressions |

4. Change the regular expression to /\Bare\B/ig to match only those words that do not start or end with "are". Then, press the **Pattern Test** button and verify that only the word "Prepared" contains a matching text string.

3. Change the regular expression to /\Bare\b/ig to match only those words that end with "are" but do not begin with "are". Press the **Pattern Test** button. Only the word "Care" matches the regular expression. Remember, a space is not considered a character and so the word "Are" is not a match.

4. Change the regular expression to /\Bare\B/ig to match only those words that do not start or end with "are". Then, press the **Pattern Test** button and verify that only the word "Prepared" contains a matching text string.

Digits are represented by the \d character. To match any occurrence of a single digit, apply the regular expression

/\d/

which finds matches in text strings such as 105, 6, or U2 because these examples all contain an instance of a single digit. To match several consecutive digits, simply repeat the \d symbol. Thus, the following regular expression matches the occurrence of any five digits:

/\d\d\d\d\d/

To match words consisting only of five-digit numbers, mark the word boundaries with the \b character as follows:

/\b\d\d\d\d\d\b/

Finally, to match a text string that consists solely of 5-digit numbers with no other characters, apply the regular expression:

/^\d\d\d\d\d$/

Test this pattern now on the demo page.

To test the five-digit pattern:

1. Within the regular expression demo, change the text in the Enter a text string box to **51523**.

2. Change the regular expression pattern to /^\d\d\d\d\d$/ and click the **Pattern Test** button. The demo page highlights all the digits in the test indicating a complete match.

3. Change the sample text string to **51,523** and click the **Pattern Test** button. The demo reports no match because the text string does not consist of only 5 digits and no other characters.

There is no character type that matches only alphabetical characters. However, you can specify a collection of characters known as a **character class** to limit the regular expression to a select group of characters. The regular expression pattern for a character class is

[chars]

where chars are characters in the class. Thus, to create a character class matching all vowels in the text string regardless of case, apply the following regular expression pattern:

/[aeiou]/gi

Larger character classes are defined by a range of characters in sequential order. To create a character class for all lowercase letters, use

[a-z]

for uppercase letters, use

[A-Z]

and for both uppercase and lowercase letters, use

[a-zA-Z]

In this fashion, you can continue to add ranges of characters to a character class. The following character class matches only digits, lowercase letters, and uppercase letters:

```
[0-9a-zA-Z]
```

To create a negative character class that matches any character not in the class, preface the list of characters with the caret symbol (^). The following regular expression matches all characters that are *not* vowels, regardless of case:

```
/[^aeiou]/gi
```

Note that the negative character set uses the same ^ symbol that is used to mark the beginning of a text string. Although the symbol is the same, the meaning is very different in this context. Figure 13-32 summarizes the syntax for creating regular expression character classes.

Figure 13-32   **Character classes**

Pattern	Description
[*chars*]	Match any character in the *chars* list
[^*chars*]	Do not match any character in the *chars* list
[*char1-charN*]	Match characters in the range *char1* through *charN*
[^*char1-charN*]	Do not match any characters in the range *char1* through *charN*
[a-z]	Match any lowercase letter
[A-Z]	Match any uppercase letter
[a-zA-Z]	Match any lowercase or uppercase letter
[0-9]	Match any digit
[0-9a-zA-Z]	Match any digit or letter

To explore working with a character class, you will use the demo page to create character classes that match vowels and consonants.

To create a character class pattern:

1. Within the regular expression demo, change the text in the Enter a text string box to **traditional cooking for the modern age**.

2. Change the regular expression pattern to /[aeiou]/gi and click the **Pattern Test** button. All the vowels in the text string are highlighted.

   Next, highlight only the consonants in the text string.

3. Change the regular expression pattern to /[^aeiou\s]/gi and click the **Pattern Test** button.

   The regular expression selects all the characters in the text string that are not vowels or white-space characters. See Figure 13-33.

Figure 13-33   **All matched consonant characters**

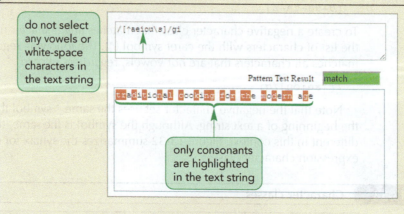

do not select any vowels or white-space characters in the text string

only consonants are highlighted in the text string

Specifying Repeating Characters

Regular expressions can include symbols that indicate the number of times to repeat a character type. To specify the exact number of times to repeat a character, append the character with the following

```
{n}
```

where *n* is the number of times to repeat the character. The following regular expression defines a character pattern consisting of five digits and nothing else:

```
/^\d{5}$/
```

If it is unclear how many times to repeat a character, use the symbol * for 0 or more repetitions, + for 1 or more repetitions, or ? for 0 repetitions or 1 repetition. Figure 13-34 describes these and other repetition characters in the regular expression language.

Figure 13-34   **Repetition characters**

Repetition Characters	Description
*	Repeat 0 or more times
?	Repeat 0 or 1 time
+	Repeat 1 or more times
{n}	Repeat exactly *n* times
{n,}	Repeat at least *n* times
{n,m}	Repeat at least *n* times but no more than *m* times

To apply a repetition pattern:

1. Within the regular expression demo, change the text in the Enter a text string box to **To be or not to be. That is the question**.

2. Change the regular expression pattern to **/\bt[a-zA-Z]*\b/gi** to match all words that begin with the letter "t" followed by any number of uppercase or lowercase letters. Click the **Pattern Test** button. Figure 13-35 shows the words matched by the regular expression pattern.

Figure 13-35   **Regular expression with repetitive characters**

```
/\bt[a-zA-Z]*\b/gi
```

select any word beginning with the letter "t" followed by 0 or more letters

Pattern Test Result   match

To be or not to be. That is the question.

matching patterns

3. Change the regular expression to /\bt[a-zA-Z]{2}\b/gi to revise the regular expression to limit the number of letters after the initial letter "t" to two. Click the **Pattern Test** button and verify that the only word matching the regular expression is "the".

Using Escape Sequences

Many commonly used characters are reserved by the language used in a regular expression. For example, the forward slash character / is reserved to mark the beginning and end of a regular expression. The ?, +, and * characters are used to specify the number of times a character can be repeated. But, what if you need to use one of these characters in a regular expression? For example, how do you create a regular expression matching the date pattern *mm/dd/yyyy* when the / character is already reserved for other uses?

In cases such as this, you use an **escape sequence** by prefacing the character with the backslash character \ to indicate that the character that follows should be interpreted as a character and not a command. For example, the escape sequence \$ represents the $ character while the escape sequence \\ represents a single \ character. Figure 13-36 provides a list of escape sequences for other special characters.

Figure 13-36   **Escape sequences**

Escape Sequence		Represents
\/		/
\\		\
\.		.
*		*
\+		+
\?		?
|			
\(	\)	( )
\{	\}	{ }
\^		^
\$		$
\n		a new line
\r		a carriage return
\t		a tab

To apply an escape sequence:

1. Within the regular expression demo, change the text in the Enter a text string box to the date **3/14/2018**

2. Change the regular expression pattern to /^\d{1,2}\/\d{1,2}\/\d{4}$/ to match date text strings of the form *mm/dd/yyyy*. Click the **Pattern Test** button. Figure 13-37 shows that the date is matched by the regular expression pattern.

Figure 13-37   Regular expression with repetitive characters

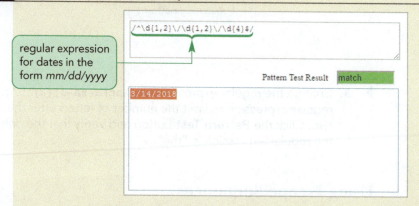

regular expression for dates in the form *mm/dd/yyyy*

/^\d{1,2}\/\d{1,2}\/\d{4}$/

Pattern Test Result   match

3/14/2018

TIP

Explore the date expressions available from the selection list on the demo page to learn about other regular expressions involving dates.

3. Test the regular expression against other data strings; note that matches invalidate date strings such as 23/99/0007 or 0/0/0000, which do not represent real dates.

Specifying Alternate Patterns and Grouping

In some regular expressions, you may want to define two possible patterns for the same text string. You can do this by joining different patterns using the | character. The general form is

  pattern1|*pattern2*

where *pattern1* and *pattern2* are two distinct patterns. For example, the following expression matches a text string that contains either only 5 digits or 5 digits followed by a dash and another 4 digits:

  /^\d{5}$|^\d{5}-\d{4}$/

Explore how to use the alternate character on the demo page by creating a regular expression that matches the titles Mr., Mrs., or Miss.

To specify alternate regular expression patterns:

1. Within the regular expression demo, change the text in the Enter a text string box to **Mr. Hughes**

2. Change the regular expression pattern to /Mr\.|Mrs\.|Miss/ Click the **Pattern Test** button to verify that the regular expression matches "Mr.".

3. Change the text string box to **Mrs. Hughes** and then to **Miss Hughes**, verifying that the regular expression matches those text strings as well.

Another useful technique in regular expressions is to group character symbols so they can be treated as a single unit. The syntax to create a group is

```
(pattern)
```

where `pattern` is a regular expression pattern. Groups are often used with the | character to create regular expressions that match different variations of the same text. For example, a phone number might be entered with or without an area code. The pattern for the phone number without an area code, such as 555-1234, is as follows:

```
/^\d{3}-\d{4}$/
```

If an area code is included in the number, such as 800-555-1234, the pattern for the phone number is as follows:

```
/^\d{3}-\d{3}-\d{4}$/
```

To treat the area code as optional, place it within a group using the `()` symbols and apply the `?` repetition character to the entire area code group. The regular expression is

```
/^(\d{3}-)?\d{3}-\d{4}$/
```

which matches either 555-1234 or 800-555-1234.
Try this now in the regular expression demo.

To specify alternate regular expression patterns:

▶ **1.** Within the Regular Expression Demo, change the text in the Enter a text string box to **555-1234**.

▶ **2.** Change the regular expression pattern to `/^(\d{3}-)?\d{3}-\d{4}$/`. Click the **Pattern Test** button to verify that the phone number matches the regular expression pattern. See Figure 13-38.

Figure 13-38   **Regular expression with repetitive characters**

▶ **3.** Change the phone number text string to **800-555-1234** and click the **Pattern Test** button to verify that the regular expression also matches this phone number.

▶ **4.** Continue to explore other text strings and regular expression patterns and then close the demo page when finished.

Problem Solving: Avoiding Regular Expression Errors

The language of regular expressions is beautifully terse and powerful, but because of that, it is easy to fall into syntax mistakes and processing errors. Here are some typical errors that may creep into your regular expressions:

- Including spaces in the regular expression. While in other programming languages, such as JavaScript, white space can be used to make your code more readable, a blank space in a regular expression is treated as a character and will be evaluated as such.
- Forgetting to escape special characters, such as (and).
- Forgetting to include the ^ and $ characters when you want your regular expression to test the entire text string as a single unit.
- Excessive backtracking. **Backtracking** occurs when the regular expression contains quantifiers such as the * or + characters, which forces the parser to examine each possible substring within a larger text string. A text string consisting of no more than 20 characters might result in millions of individual searches, slowing down the program's execution. You can avoid such catastrophic backtracking by not overusing quantifiers and tightly writing your regular expressions to limit the number of possible matches.

Always test your regular expressions before committing them to your JavaScript program. There are several free and fee-based regular expression testers available on the web that can highlight syntax errors and help you avoid catastrophic backtracking by reporting on the processing time required by your regular expression.

Programming with Regular Expressions

The code of a regular expression can be directly entered in JavaScript as a **regular expression literal**. For example, the following command stores a regular expression in the regx variable:

```
var regx = /\d{5}-\d{4}/g;
```

A regular expression can also be defined using the following new `RegExp()` object constructor

```
new RegExp(pattern, flags);
```

where *pattern* is the regular expression pattern and *flags* are any modifiers added to the pattern. The following command stores a regular expression in the regx variable using an object constructor:

```
var regx = new RegExp("\d{5}-\d{4}", "g");
```

One of the advantages of using an object constructor is that you can store regular expressions as variables. For example, the following code creates a regular expression based on the value of the patternTest variable:

```
var patternTest = "\d{5}-\d{4}"
var regx = new RegExp(patternTest, "g");
```

Creating a Regular Expression

- To create a regular expression literal, use

`/pattern/flags`

where *pattern* is the regular expression pattern and *flags* are the optional modifiers assigned to the regular expression.
- To create a regular expression object constructor, use:

`new RegExp(pattern, flags)`

Regular Expression Methods

Because regular expressions are another type of JavaScript object, they have their own collection of methods. For example, you can search a text string to determine whether a character pattern defined by a regular expression is present within the text. You can replace or remove characters within the text string that match a regular expression pattern. You can also split a text string into several substrings at each occurrence of a regular expression character pattern. Because of their flexibility in defining character patterns, regular expressions are an indispensable tool for managing textual data. Figure 13-39 lists the regular expression methods supported in JavaScript.

Figure 13-39 Regular expression methods

Method	Description
`re.exec(str)`	Searches the text string, `str`, for the character pattern expressed in the regular expression `re`, returning data about the search results in an array
`re.test(str)`	Searches `str` for the character pattern `re`; if a match is found returns the Boolean value `true`
`re.toString()`	Converts the regular expression `re` to a text string
`str.match(re)`	Searches `str` for the character pattern expressed in the regular expression `re`, returning the search results in an array
`str.search(re)`	Searches `str` for a substring matching the regular expression `re`; returns the index of the match, or -1 if no match is found
`str.replace(re, newsubstr)`	Replaces the characters in `str` defined by the regular expression `re` with the text string `newsubstr`
`str.split(re)`	Splits `str` at each point indicated by the regular expression `re`, storing each substring as an item in an array

One method associated with regular expressions is the following `test()` method, which determines whether a text string contains a substring that matches a regular expression

`re.test(str)`

where `re` is a regular expression and `str` is the text string to be tested. The `test()` method returns the Boolean value `true` if a match is located within the text string and `false` otherwise. For example, the following code uses the `test()` method to compare the text string stored in the zipCode variable with the regular expression object stored in the regx variable:

```
var zipCode = document.forms[0].zip.value;
var regx = /^\d{5}$/;
var testValue = regx.test(zipCode);
```

To determine where within the text string the regular expression match occurs, apply the following `search()` method:

```
str.search(re)
```

The `search()` method returns the index of the first matching substring from the string. If no match is found, it returns the value –1, just like the `indexOf()` method discussed earlier in the session. However, unlike the `indexOf()` method, you cannot begin the `search()` method at a location other than the start of the text string. All `search()` method searches occur from the start of the text string.

You can apply the following `match()` method to create an array of substrings from the characters within the text string that match a regular expression pattern

```
var results = str.match(re)
```

TIP

The global flag must be set to locate all matches in the text string. Without the g flag, only the first match is returned.

where `results` is an array containing each matched substring. For example, the following command extracts the individual words from the text string, placing each word in the words array:

```
var words = "traditional cooking for the modern age".match(/\b\
w+\b/g)
```

A method that is similar to the `match()` method is the `split()` method, which breaks a text string into substrings at each location where a pattern match is found, placing the substrings into an array. You saw how to use the `split()` method earlier in the session when it was applied to string objects. It can also be used with regular expressions. The following code shows how to split a text string at each word boundary followed by one or more white-space characters:

```
words = "traditional cooking for the modern age".split(/\b\s*/g);
```

In this example, each element in the words array contains a word from the sample text string.

Besides pattern matching and extracting substrings, regular expressions can also be used to replace text with the following `replace()` method

```
str.replace(re,newsubstr)
```

where `str` is a text string containing text to be replaced, `re` is a regular expression defining the pattern of a substring, and `newsubstr` is the replacement substring. The following code shows how to apply the `replace()` method to replace "Kitchen & Dining" with "Kitchen and Dining":

```
var oldtext = "Coctura Kitchen & Dining";
var newtext = oldtext.replace(/&/g, "and");
```

REFERENCE

Working with Regular Expressions

- To test whether a string matches a regular expression, use

  `re.test(str)`

  where *re* is the regular expression and *str* is the text string to be tested.
- To search a text string, use

  `index = str.search(re)`

  where *index* is the index of the first found substring that matches the regular expression.
- To replace a substring with a new text string, use

  `str.replace(re, newsubstr)`

  where *newsubstr* is the replacement text for characters found matching the regular expression.
- To split a string into substrings, use

  `var strArray = str.split(re)`

  where *strArray* is a text array created by splitting the text string at ever occurrence of characters matching the regular expression pattern.

You will use the `replace()` method to extract information from the query string in the URL for the co_payment.html page. Because URLs cannot have spaces, query strings use the + character in place of blank spaces. Use the `replace()` method now to replace all + characters with blank spaces.

To apply the replace() method:

1. Return to the **co_payment.js** file in your editor.

2. Within the anonymous function for the `load` event, add the following command:

   `formData = formData.replace(/\+/g," ");`

   > You must use the escape character \+ to match occurrences of the + character.

   Figure 13-40 highlights the new code in the file.

Figure 13-40   Applying the replace() method

```
window.addEventListener("load", function(){
    // Retrieve the field/value pairs from the URL
    var formData = location.search.slice(1);
    formData = formData.replace(/\+/g," ");
} );
```

replaces every + character with a blank space

regular expression matching every + character in the text string

3. Save your changes to the file.

Replacing URI Encoded Characters

In addition to blank spaces, there are other characters that are not allowed in the URL's query string. For example, the / and : characters are not allowed because they are reserved for use in the URL pathname. When the browser encounters a character in a field name or value that is reserved for other purposes, it replaces the character with a character code known as the **URI encoded character**. A list of reserved characters and their corresponding URI character codes is displayed in Figure 13-41.

Figure 13-41	URI Character Codes

Character	URI Character Code
!	%21
#	%23
$	%24
&	%26
`	%27
(	%28
)	%29
*	%2A
+	%2B
,	%2C
/	%2F
:	%3A
;	%3B
=	%3D
?	%3F
@	%40
[	%5B
]	%5D

Thus, when a field value such as "6-Quart ($129.95)" is appended to a URL, it gets encoded as "6-Quart+%28%24129.95%29" with %28 replacing the (character, %24 replacing the $ character, and %29 replacing the) character. To decode the field value back into its original values, apply the following decodeURIComponent() function

    decodeURIComponent(string)

where *string* is a text string containing URI-encoded characters. Thus, the expression

    decodeURIComponent("%28%24129.95%29")

returns the text string "($129.95)". Apply the decodeURIComponent() function to the URL containing the form data now.

TIP

A text string can be encoded with URI character codes by applying the encodeURIComponent() function to the text string.

To decode the URL:

▶ **1.** Within the anonymous function for the load event, add the following command:

    formData = decodeURIComponent(formData);

Figure 13-42 highlights the command added to the anonymous function.

Figure 13-42   **Decoding the URI character codes**

```
window.addEventListener("load", function(){
    // Retrieve the field/value pairs from the URL
    var formData = location.search.slice(1);
    formData = formData.replace(/\+/g," ");
    formData = decodeURIComponent(formData);
} );
```

decodes the text string in formData, replacing URI character codes with their character strings

> **2.** Save your changes to the file.

Writing URL Data to a Web Form

The final step in extracting the form data from the URL is to split the query string at each occurrence of a field name or field value. Recall that the general form of the appended form data is

   field1=value1&field2=value2&field3=value3...

with the = and & characters marking the separation between field names and field values. To split the query string at each occurrence of the & or = character, apply the following `split()` method to the formData variable

```
var formFields = formData.split(/&=/g);
```

where `/&=/g` is a regular expression that matches every & and = character in the formData text string. If formData stores the following text string

```
orderDate=Fri Sep 14 2018&model=129.95&modelName=6-Quart ($129.95)...
```

then the formFields array will store the following values:

```
formFields[0]="orderDate";
formFields[1]="Fri Sep 14 2018";
formFields[2]="model";
formFields[3]="129.95";
formFields[4]="modelName";
formFields[5]="6-Quart ($129.95)";
...
```

Create the formFields array now within the anonymous function for the `load` event.

To split the values in the URL:

> **1.** Within the anonymous function for the `load` event, add the following command:

```
var formFields = formData.split(/[&=]/g);
```

Figure 13-43 highlights the command to split the values in the formData text string.

| Figure 13-43 | Splitting field names and values |

```javascript
window.addEventListener("load", function(){
    // Retrieve the field/value pairs from the URL
    var formData = location.search.slice(1);
    formData = formData.replace(/\+/g," ");
    formData = decodeURIComponent(formData);
    var formFields = formData.split(/[&=]/g);
} );
```

> field names and
> values stored in the
> formFields array

> splits the data at every
> occurrence of an &
> and an = character

▶ **2.** Save your changes to the file.

The final step is to write the values stored in the formFields array to specified fields in the order form stored in the co_payment.html file. By inspecting the contents of the formFields array, you learn that the values stored in the formFields array are:

- formFields[1]   the date of the customer order
- formFields[5]   the name of the model ordered by the customer
- formFields[7]   the quantity of items ordered
- formFields[9]   the initial cost of the order
- formFields[13]   the name of the protection plan chosen by the customer
- formFields[15]   the cost of the selected protection plan
- formFields[17]   the order subtotal
- formFields[19]   the amount of sales tax owed
- formFields[21]   the total cost of the order

Add these values to the corresponding fields in the order form.

To store the field values:

▶ **1.** Within the anonymous function for the `load` event, add the following commands to store the field values:

```javascript
// Write the field values to the order form
document.forms.order.elements.orderDate.value = formFields[1];
document.forms.order.elements.modelName.value = formFields[5];
document.forms.order.elements.qty.value = formFields[7];
document.forms.order.elements.initialCost.value =
formFields[9];
document.forms.order.elements.protectionName.value =
formFields[13];
document.forms.order.elements.protectionCost.value =
formFields[15];
document.forms.order.elements.subtotal.value = formFields[17];
document.forms.order.elements.salesTax.value = formFields[19];
document.forms.order.elements.totalCost.value =
formFields[21];
```

Figure 13-44 highlights the commands to write the field values into the corresponding fields in the order form.

Figure 13-44	Storing the field values in the order form elements

```javascript
window.addEventListener("load", function(){
   // Retrieve the field/value pairs from the URL
   var formData = location.search.slice(1);
   formData = formData.replace(/\+/g," ");
   formData = decodeURIComponent(formData);
   var formFields = formData.split(/[&=]/g);

   // Write the field values to the order form
   document.forms.order.elements.orderDate.value = formFields[1];
   document.forms.order.elements.modelName.value = formFields[5];
   document.forms.order.elements.qty.value = formFields[7];
   document.forms.order.elements.initialCost.value = formFields[9];
   document.forms.order.elements.protectionName.value = formFields[13];
   document.forms.order.elements.protectionCost.value = formFields[15];
   document.forms.order.elements.subtotal.value = formFields[17];
   document.forms.order.elements.salesTax.value = formFields[19];
   document.forms.order.elements.totalCost.value = formFields[21];
} );
```

2. Save your changes to the file.

   Now that you have finished the code to write the order values into the pay-ment page, test your code with a sample order.

3. Reopen the **co_order.html** file in your browser and enter an order for three 4-quart DigiPots with a 2-year protection plan. Click the **add to cart** button to submit the order data and open the payment page. Figure 13-45 shows the content of the payment page with the order data retrieved from the URL query string and written to the order form.

Figure 13-45	Order values written into the payment page

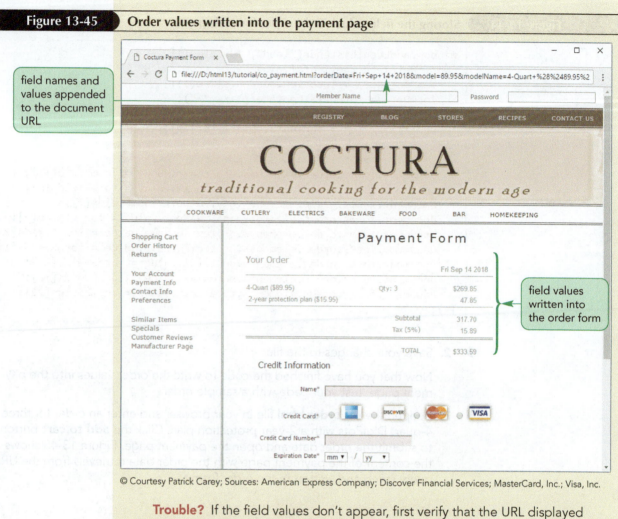

field names and values appended to the document URL

field values written into the order form

© Courtesy Patrick Carey; Sources: American Express Company; Discover Financial Services; MasterCard, Inc.; Visa, Inc.

Trouble? If the field values don't appear, first verify that the URL displayed in the address bar includes the *name/value* pairs from the completed order. Then, check your code against the code shown in Figures 13-43 and 13-44 to verify that you have not made any typing errors and use your browser's debugging tools to check for syntax errors.

4. Return to the **co_order.html** file in your browser and submit different sample orders, verify that for each sample order, the details of the order are automatically written to the payment page.

You have completed the work on the copying the field values from the order page to the payment page. In the next session, you will continue to work with the payment page by writing JavaScript routines to validate the payment information.

Session 13.2 Quick Check

1. What JavaScript object and property returns the query string from the URL of the current page?

2. Provide the regular expression to match every occurrence of the word "the".

3. Social security numbers can be entered either as ddddddddd or ddd-dd-dddd. Write a regular expression to match either pattern.

4. Write a regular expression to match the words "street", "avenue", or "lane". Make the match case insensitive and match every occurrence in the text string.

5. Write the JavaScript command to test whether the text string "444-128" matches the regular expression /\d{3}-\d{3}/

6. Provide the JavaScript command to split the text string stored in the orderDate variable at every occurrence of the / character.

7. Provide the command to decode the URI-encoded characters in the urlString variable.

8. Provide the command to store the value "11-04-2018" in the orderDate object using local storage.

Session 13.3 Visual Overview:

The `valueMissing` property tests if a required value is missing.

The `setCustomValidity()` method defines the validation message.

This code sets the validation message to an empty text string to mark the field as valid.

```
function validateName() {
  var cardName = document.getElementById("cardName");
  if (cardName.validity.valueMissing) {
    cardName.setCustomValidity("Enter your name");
  } else {
    cardName.setCustomValidity("");
  }
}

function validateNumber() {
  var cardNumber = document.getElementById("cardNumber");
  if (cardNumber.validity.valueMissing) {
    cardNumber.setCustomValidity("Enter a card number");
  } else if (cardNumber.validity.patternMismatch) {
    cardNumber.setCustomValidity("Enter a valid number");
  } else {
    cardNumber.setCustomValidity("");
  }
}

function validateCVC() {
  var cvc = document.getElementById("cvc");
  var card = document.querySelector('input[name="credit"]:checked').value;

  if (cvc.validity.valueMissing) {
    cvc.setCustomValidity("Enter the CVC number");
  } else if ((card === "amex") && (/^\d{4}$/.test(cvc.value) === false)) {
    cvc.setCustomValidity("Enter a 4-digit CVC number");
  } else if ((card !== "amex") && (/^\d{3}$/.test(cvc.value) === false)) {
    cvc.setCustomValidity("Enter a 3-digit CVC number");
  } else {
    cvc.setCustomValidity("");
  }
}
```

The `patternMismatch` property tests if the value doesn't match the regular expression pattern.

The `test()` method tests if a value matches a specified regular expression.

Validating form data

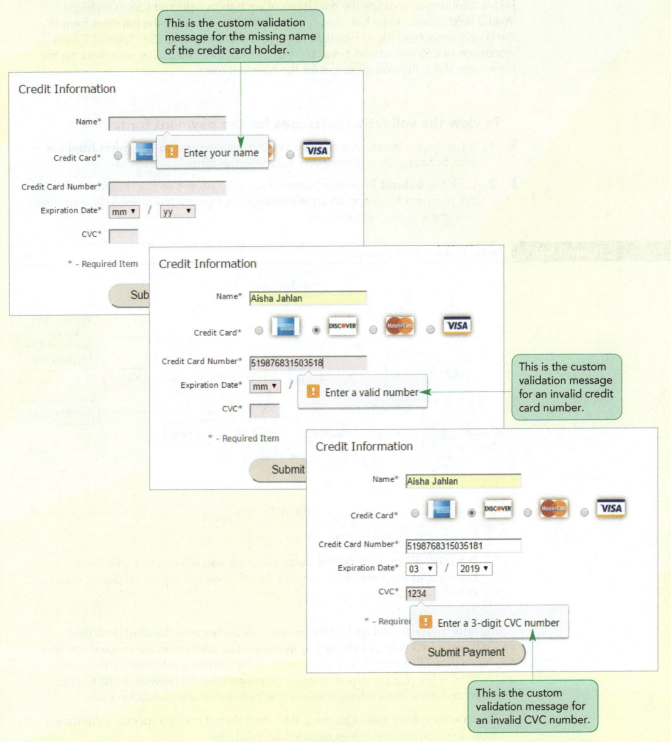

This is the custom validation message for the missing name of the credit card holder.

This is the custom validation message for an invalid credit card number.

This is the custom validation message for an invalid CVC number.

Sources: American Express Company; Discover Financial Services; MasterCard, Inc.; Visa, Inc.

Validating Data with JavaScript

In Tutorial 7, you learned how to use HTML and CSS to validate form data, using HTML attributes to indicate the data types of each form field and CSS to highlight invalid field values. Aisha has already added validation rules to the payment form in the co_payment.hmtl file to highlight missing or incorrect data. (See Tutorial 7 for a discussion of CSS `valid` and `invalid` selectors.) Before continuing your work on the form, view the validation messages for the payment form.

To view the validation messages for the payment form:

1. If you took a break after the last session, reopen the **co_payment.html** file in your browser. Do not enter any data into the form.

2. Click the **Submit Payment** button. Figure 13-46 shows the different fields in the payment form and an error message created by the browser in response to a missing cardName value.

Figure 13-46	Payment form field names

Source: American Express Company; Visa, Inc.

Trouble? If you running the Safari browser, you will not see a validation error because, at the time of this writing, Safari does not report validation errors within the browser.

The error message displayed by the browser occurs because the cardName field, which is a required field as indicated by the `required` attribute in the co_payment.html file, had a data value provided by the user when the form was submitted. The appearance and content of the pop-up error message is determined by the browser. Aisha has the following concerns about relying solely on the browser's native validation tools:

1. The validation error messages are generic and do not contain specific information about the field and the values required for validation.
2. The validation tests are based solely on a single field value and do not include tests that involve several data fields.
3. The validation tests are limited to what was entered (or not entered) into the data field and thus cannot be generalized to work with calculated items or functions.

You can supplement the native browser validation tools using the form validation properties and methods built into JavaScript, which are known collectively as the **Constraint Validation API**. Aisha wants you to write a validation script that does the following:

1. Verifies that the customer has entered the name that appears on the credit card
2. Verifies that one of four credit card brands has been selected
3. Verifies that a valid credit card number has been entered
4. Verifies that the card's expiration date has been selected from the drop-down lists
5. Verifies that a valid CVC credit number has been entered

You will start by exploring how to work with JavaScript's validation properties and methods.

Introducing the Constraint Validation API

The Constraint Validation API includes the properties and methods listed in Figure 13-47.

Figure 13-47   **Constraint Validation API properties and methods**

Property or Method	Description
`form.noValidate`	Set to `true` to prevent the native browser tools from validating the web form `form`
`form.reportValidity()`	Reports on the validation status of `form` using the native browser validation tools
`element.willValidate`	Returns `true` if `element` is capable of being validated by the browser (regardless of whether the data itself is actually valid)
`element.valid`	Returns `true` if `element` contains valid data
`element.validationMessage`	Returns the text of the validation message returned by the browser when `element` fails validation
`element.validity`	Returns a `ValidityState` object containing specific information about the validation of `element`
`element.setCustomValidity(msg)`	Sets the validity message displayed by the browser where `msg` is the text displayed when `element` fails validation (set `msg` to an empty text string to indicate that the element does not have a validation error)
`element.checkValidity()`	Returns `true` if `element` is valid and `false` if it is not valid; a `false` value also fires the `invalid` event

For example, the following expression returns the Boolean value `true` if the cardName field from the payment form contains valid data:

```
document.forms.payment.elements.cardName.valid
```

You can also test for valid data using the following `checkValidity()` method:

```
document.forms.payment.elements.cardName.checkValidity()
```

The `checkValidity()` method returns a value of `true` for valid data; but, if the field is invalid, the method returns a value of `false` while firing the `invalid` event, which can be managed using an event handler or event listener.

TIP

To turn off the browser's native validation tools, run the command `form.noValidate = true;` where `form` references the web form.

Exploring the ValidityState Object

There are several reasons a data field might be invalid. JavaScript stores the reason for failing validation in the **ValidityState** object. To determine why a data value failed validation, apply the expression

```
element.validity.ValidityState
```

where `ValidityState` is one the validation states described in Figure 13-48.

Figure 13-48	Validity properties

Validation State	Description
`element.validity.badInput`	The field element, `element`, contains data that the browser is unable to convert, such as when an e-mail address lacks the @ character
`element.validity.customError`	A custom validation message has been set to a non-empty text string using the `setCustomValidity()` method
`element.validity.patternMismatch`	The `element` contains data that does not match the character pattern specified in the `pattern` attribute
`element.validity.rangeOverflow`	The `element` contains data greater than the value specified by the `max` attribute
`element.validity.rangeUnderflow`	The `element` contains data less than the value specified by the `min` attribute
`element.validity.stepMismatch`	The `element` contains a data value that does not fit the rules determined by the `step` attribute
`element.validity.tooLong`	The `element` contains data whose character length exceeds the value of the `length` attribute
`element.validity.typeMismatch`	The `element` contains data that does not match the data type specified by the `type` attribute
`element.validity.valid`	The `element` contains valid data, satisfying all constraints
`element.validity.valueMissing`	The `element` does not contain data though it is marked with the `required` attribute

TIP

The typeMismatch property only tests whether the value of the userMail field has the correct format for an e-mail address, not whether such an e-mail address exists.

For example, if data type of the userMail field is set to "mail", the following code uses the `typeMismatch` property to return a value of `true` if the user enters a proper e-mail address and `false` if otherwise.

```
var mailAddress = document.getElementById("userMail");
mailAddress.value = "testmail.com";
return mailAddress.validity.typeMismatch;
```

Creating a Custom Validation Message

When a data field fails validation, the browser displays a pop-up message notifying the user. Different browsers may display different messages. For example, Google Chrome displays the message "Please fill out this field" for missing data values while the Microsoft Edge browser displays the message "This is a required field.". To display the same error message across all browsers, apply the following `setCustomValidity()` method

```
element.setCustomValidity(msg)
```

where *msg* is the custom message displayed by the browser, not the browser's default message, when an element is invalid. If an element is valid, then set the `setCustomValidity` property to an empty text string. If no `msg` text is specified, the element is considered valid.

Creating a Custom Validation Message

- To set the validation message when the field data is invalid, use

  `element.setCustomValidity(`*msg*`)`

  where msg is the text that is displayed when the field is invalid
- To remove the validation message and define the field data as valid, use:

  `element.setCustomValidity("")`

If the customer neglects to specify the name on the credit card, Aisha wants the browser to display the message "Enter your name as it appears on the card" when the user leaves this input box blank. Use the `valueMissing` property of the `validity` object to test whether a value has been entered into the cardName field. If no value has been entered display the message "Enter your name as it appears on the card".

To create a custom validation message:

1. Go the **co_payment.js** file in your editor.

2. After the anonymous function for the `load` event, add the following validateName() function:

   ```
   function validateName() {
      var cardName = document.getElementById("cardName");
      if (cardName.validity.valueMissing) {
         cardName.setCustomValidity("Enter your name as it
   appears on the card");
      } else {
         cardName.setCustomValidity("");
      }
   }
   ```

Always include a custom validation message with an empty text string for fields that pass the validation test so that those fields are marked as valid.

Figure 13-49 describes the code in the function.

Figure 13-49   Creating the validateName() function

```
    document.forms.order.elements.salesTax.value = formFields[19];
    document.forms.order.elements.totalCost.value = formFields[21];
} );

function validateName() {
   var cardName = document.getElementById("cardName");
   if (cardName.validity.valueMissing) {
      cardName.setCustomValidity("Enter your name as it appears on the card");
   } else {
      cardName.setCustomValidity("");
   }
}
```

tests if the required value is missing from the cardName field

no pop-up error message when the field is valid

pop-up error message when the field is invalid

Preventing Validation Error Messages

Another way to control the native browser validation messages is by preventing action of an `invalid` event, which is fired when the browser notes an invalid data value during form submission. The following code uses the `addEventListener()` method to listen for an occurrence of the invalid event within a form field, running an anonymous function in response:

```
element.addEventListener("invalid", function(e) {
    e.preventDefault();
    e.stopPropagation();
    commands;
});
```

The anonymous function uses the `preventDefault()` method to prevent the browser's default action of reporting the error and the `stopPropagation()` method to stop the invalid event from propagating through the document tree. Having captured the `invalid` event, the programmer can then run a set of custom *commands* to respond to the invalid event.

Responding to Invalid Data

Form data can be tested when the user inserts a value into a form field and just before the form data is submitted for processing. To check the validity of form data as it's being inserted, use an event handler or event listener for the `input` event. To catch invalid data before the form is submitted, add an event handler or event listener for the `click` event of the form's submit button.

Run the validateName() function in response to changing input within the cardName field and after the user clicks the Submit Payment button on the payment form.

To call the validateName() function:

1. Directly below the event listener for the `load` event, insert another event listener, that is to run when the page is loaded by the browser, containing the following code:

```
window.addEventListener("load", function() {
    document.getElementById("subButton").onclick = runSubmit;
    document.getElementById("cardName").oninput = validateName;
});
```

2. Add the following function to run when the user clicks the Submit Payment button:

```
function runSubmit() {
    validateName();
}
```

Figure 13-50 describes the newly added code in the file.

| Figure 13-50 | Calling the validateName() function |

calls the runSubmit() function when the Submit Payment button is clicked

```
        document.forms.order.elements.totalCost.value = formFields[21];
} );

window.addEventListener("load", function() {
    document.getElementById("subButton").onclick = runSubmit;
    document.getElementById("cardName").oninput = validateName;
});

function runSubmit() {
    validateName();
}
```

runs when the user clicks the Submit button

calls the validateName() function when the user inputs data into the cardName field

> **3.** Save your changes to the file and then reload **co_payment.html** in your browser. Click the **Submit Payment** button and verify that the revised pop-up error message shown in Figure 13-51 appears next to the input box for the cardName field.

| Figure 13-51 | Custom pop-up error message for missing cardName data |

no data entered into the required cardName field

custom validation error message

Credit Information

Name*

Credit Card*   ▣   ! Enter your name as it appears on the card

Credit Card Number*

Source: American Express Company

> **4.** Enter sample text into the cardName field and click the **Submit Payment** button again. Verify that no pop-up error message appears for the cardName field.

The next field on the payment form is the credit field, which is laid out as a set of option buttons. This is also a required field; however, with option buttons clicking one option button automatically sets the values of all the option buttons in the group, therefore the `required` attribute is only applied to the first option button and validation tests only need to be done on the first option button.

Testing for Validation Errors

- To test whether a form field is missing a required value, use:

  `element.validity.valueMissing`

- To test whether a form field is storing the wrong data type, use:

  `element.validity.typeMismatch`

- To test whether a form field fails the pattern match, use:

  `element.validity.patternMismatch`

Create the validateCredit() function now to test whether the user has selected an option button from the group and if no option button is selected, display the custom validation message "Select your credit card".

To create the validateCredit() function:

1. Return to the **co_payment.js** file in your editor and within the runSubmit() function add the following command:

   ```
   validateCredit();
   ```

2. Next, insert the following validateCredit() function after the runSubmit() function.

   ```
   function validateCredit() {
      var creditCard = document.forms.payment.elements.credit[0];
      if (creditCard.validity.valueMissing) {
         creditCard.setCustomValidity("Select your credit card");
      } else {
         creditCard.setCustomValidity("");
      }
   }
   ```

Note that you do not have to include an `oninput` event handler for the credit field because the user is only clicking the option buttons, not entering a field value. Figure 13-52 describes the new code in the file.

Figure 13-52   Creating the validateCredit() function

```
function runSubmit() {
   validateName();
   validateCredit();
}

function validateCredit() {
   var creditCard = document.forms.payment.elements.credit[0];
   if (creditCard.validity.valueMissing) {
      creditCard.setCustomValidity("Select your credit card");
   } else {
      creditCard.setCustomValidity("");
   }
}
```

validates the credit card option

tests whether the first option button is missing a value

no error message displayed if credit card is selected

custom error message if no credit card is selected

3. Save your changes to the file and then reload **co_payment.html** in your browser. Enter a sample name in the creditName field and then click the **Submit Payment** button without specifying a credit card type. Verify that the browser displays the pop-up error message "Select your credit card" next to the unselected credit card options.

4. Click one of the credit card images and then click the **Submit Payment** button again. Verify that the pop-up error message shifts down to the next field in the form for credit card numbers.

The next field in the payment form is the cardNumber field in which credit card numbers must match a specific pattern of characters.

Validating Data with Pattern Matching

In Tutorial 7, you learned that text strings can be matched against a regular expression pattern by adding the following `pattern` attribute to the `input` element

```
pattern = "regex"
```

where `regex` is the regular expression.

Aisha has already entered a regular expression pattern in the co_payment.html file for the cardNumber field to ensure that card numbers entered by the user have the correct numerical pattern. She wants the form to display the error message "Enter your card number" if the customer leaves the card number field blank and the error message "Enter a valid credit card number" if the customer enters a credit card number that does not match the correct pattern. Use the `valueMissing` property to test if the field has been left blank and `patternMismatch` property to confirm that the card number follows the correct pattern.

To validate the credit card number:

1. Return to the **co_payment.js** file in your editor and, directly below the runSubmit() function, insert the following validateNumber() function to specify the custom validation message for credit cards.

```
function validateNumber() {
   var cardNumber = document.getElementById("cardNumber");
   if (cardNumber.validity.valueMissing) {
      cardNumber.setCustomValidity("Enter your card number");
   } else if (cardNumber.validity.patternMismatch) {
      cardNumber.setCustomValidity("Enter a valid card
number");
   } else {
      cardNumber.setCustomValidity("");
   }
}
```

2. Add the following command to the second anonymous function for the `load` event, to run the validateNumber() function whenever the user enters data into the cardNumber field.

```
document.getElementById("cardNumber").oninput =
validateNumber;
```

3. Add the following command to the runSubmit() function to run the validateNumber() function when the user clicks the Submit Payment button.

```
validateNumber();
```

Figure 13-53 describes the newly added code in the file.

Figure 13-53 Creating the validateNumber() function

```
window.addEventListener("load", function() {
    document.getElementById("subButton").onclick = runSubmit;
    document.getElementById("cardName").oninput = validateName;
    document.getElementById("cardNumber").oninput = validateNumber;
});

function runSubmit() {
    validateName();
    validateCredit();
    validateNumber();
}

function validateNumber() {
    var cardNumber = document.getElementById("cardNumber");
    if (cardNumber.validity.valueMissing) {
        cardNumber.setCustomValidity("Enter your card number");
    } else if (cardNumber.validity.patternMismatch) {
        cardNumber.setCustomValidity("Enter a valid card number");
    } else {
        cardNumber.setCustomValidity("");
    }
}
```

runs validateNumber() when the user clicks the Submit Payment button

runs validateNumber() when the user types a value into the field

validation message when no credit card number is entered

tests for a pattern mismatch

validation message when an invalid card number is entered

no message is displayed if the data is valid

4. Save your changes to the file and then reload **co_payment.html** in your browser. Complete the creditName and select a credit card and then click the **Submit Payment** button. Verify that the browser displays the pop-up message, "Enter your card number".

5. Enter the invalid credit card number **1234567890** into the cardNumber field and click the **Submit Payment** button. Verify that the browser displays the message "Enter a valid card number", as shown in Figure 13-54.

Figure 13-54 Custom pop-up error message for an invalid card number

an invalid card number

custom validation error message

6. Enter the valid credit card number **6011280768434856** into the cardNumber field and click the **Submit Payment** button. Verify that the browser accepts this number and does not display an error message for the cardNumber field.

The next part of the payment form contains two drop-down list boxes for the credit card expiration date.

Validating a Selection List

Aisha has placed the possible expiration date values in two selection lists named expMonth and expYear. The first entry in each of the two selection lists is "mm" and "yy", respectively. Aisha wants you to validate these two fields so that if a user leaves the first entry in either of the selection lists unchanged, then the entry will be flagged as invalid. Use the selectedIndex property introduced in the last session to determine if the selected index is 0 (the first entry) or else, if not 0, then which entry in each selection list has been selected. If the index is 0, then the browser will declare the field value as invalid.

To validate the expiration date:

1. Return to the **co_payment.js** file in your editor and, directly below the runSubmit() function, insert the following validateMonth() function:

```
function validateMonth() {
   var cardMonth = document.getElementById("expMonth");
   if (cardMonth.selectedIndex === 0) {
      cardMonth.setCustomValidity("Select the expiration
month");
   } else {
      cardMonth.setCustomValidity("");
   }
}
```

2. Add the following validateYear() function:

```
function validateYear() {
   var cardYear = document.getElementById("expYear");
   if (cardYear.selectedIndex === 0) {
      cardYear.setCustomValidity("Select the expiration
year");
   } else {
      cardYear.setCustomValidity("");
   }
}
```

3. Add the following commands to the second anonymous function, which is part of the load event, to run the validateMonth() and validateYear() functions when the user changes the select option in the expMonth and expYear selection lists:

```
document.getElementById("expMonth").onchange = validateMonth;
document.getElementById("expYear").onchange = validateYear;
```

4. Add the following commands to the runSubmit() function:

```
validateMonth();
validateYear();
```

Figure 13-55 describes the newly added code in the file.

Figure 13-55 Creating the validateMonth() and validateYear() functions

> runs validateMonth() and validateYear() when the user changes the selected option in the selection list

> runs validateMonth() and validateYear() when the Submit Payment button is clicked

> if the first option is selected, declares that expMonth value is invalid

> if the first option is selected, declares that expYear value is invalid

```javascript
   document.getElementById("cardNumber").oninput = validateNumber;
   document.getElementById("expMonth").onchange = validateMonth;
   document.getElementById("expYear").onchange = validateYear;
});

function runSubmit() {
   validateName();
   validateCredit();
   validateNumber();
   validateMonth();
   validateYear();
}

function validateMonth() {
   var cardMonth = document.getElementById("expMonth");
   if (cardMonth.selectedIndex === 0) {
      cardMonth.setCustomValidity("Select the expiration month");
   } else {
      cardMonth.setCustomValidity("");
   }
}

function validateYear() {
   var cardYear = document.getElementById("expYear");
   if (cardYear.selectedIndex === 0) {
      cardYear.setCustomValidity("Select the expiration year");
   } else {
      cardYear.setCustomValidity("");
   }
}
```

5. Save your changes to the file and then reload **co_payment.html** in your browser. Complete the payment form with valid values up to the expMonth selection list and then click the **Submit Payment** button. Verify that unless you select a month and a year from the selection lists, validation error messages appear.

The last field remaining in the payment form is the CVC field, which is the card verification code printed on credit cards to provide additional security in financial transactions.

Testing a Form Field Against a Regular Expression

Credit card CVC numbers are either 3-digit numbers or 4-digit numbers depending on the card being used. American Exchange cards use 4-digit CVC numbers while Discover, MasterCard, and Visa use 3-digit numbers. Thus, the regular expression for 4-digit CVC numbers used by American Express card holders is

```
/^\d{4}$/
```

while for the other card holders, the regular expression is

```
/^\d{3}$/
```

You can test for these regular expression patterns using the `test()` method. For example, the following code returns a Boolean value indicating whether the value in the cardCVC field matches the 4-digit pattern:

```
var cardCVC = document.getElementById("cvc");
return /^\d{4}$/.test(cardCVC.value)
```

While for 3-digit CVC numbers, the code is:

```
var cardCVC = document.getElementById("cvc");
return /^\d{3}$/.test(cardCVC.value)
```

Create the validateCVC() function now to test whether the user has entered the correct number of CVC digits for his or her credit card type.

To validate the CVC number:

▶ **1.** Return to the **co_payment.js** file in your editor and, directly below the runSubmit() function, insert the following code to start creating the validateCVC() function by inserting a reference to the cvc field and extracting the value of the currently selected credit card:

```
function validateCVC() {
   var cardCVC = document.getElementById("cvc");
   var creditCard = document.querySelector('input[name=
"credit"]:checked').value;
```

▶ **2.** Complete the validateCVC() function by inserting the following if structure that tests whether a CVC number has been entered and, if it has been entered, whether it is a valid pattern for the selected credit card:

```
if (cardCVC.validity.valueMissing) {
  cardCVC.setCustomValidity("Enter your CVC number");
  } else if ((creditCard === "amex") &&
(/^\d{4}$/.test(cardCVC.value) === false)) {
  cardCVC.setCustomValidity("Enter a 4-digit CVC number");
  } else if ((creditCard !== "amex") &&
(/^\d{3}$/.test(cardCVC.value) === false)) {
    cardCVC.setCustomValidity("Enter a 3-digit CVC number");
  } else {
  cardCVC.setCustomValidity("");
  }
}
```

▶ **3.** Add the following command to the second anonymous function, which is part of the load event, to run the validateCVC() function when the user changes the field value:

```
document.getElementById("cvc").oninput = validateCVC;
```

4. Add the following command to the runSubmit() function to run the validateCVC() function when the user clicks the Submit Payment button:

```
validateCVC();
```

Figure 13-56 highlights the code in the file.

Figure 13-56 **Creating the validateCVC() function**

```
        document.getElementById("expYear").onchange = validateYear;
        document.getElementById("cvc").oninput = validateCVC;
});

function runSubmit() {
    validateName();
    validateCredit();
    validateNumber();
    validateMonth();
    validateYear();
    validateCVC();
}

function validateCVC() {
    var cardCVC = document.getElementById("cvc");
    var creditCard = document.querySelector('input[name="credit"]:checked').value;

    if (cardCVC.validity.valueMissing) {
        cardCVC.setCustomValidity("Enter your CVC number");
    } else if ((creditCard === "amex") && (/^\d{4}$/.test(cardCVC.value) === false)) {
    cardCVC.setCustomValidity("Enter a 4-digit CVC number");
    } else if ((creditCard !== "amex") && (/^\d{3}$/.test(cardCVC.value) === false)) {
    cardCVC.setCustomValidity("Enter a 3-digit CVC number");
    } else {
    cardCVC.setCustomValidity("");
    }
}
```

- gets the value of the checked credit card
- tests whether a value has been entered
- tests whether a 4-digit CVC value was entered for the American Express card
- tests whether a 3-digit CVC value was entered for other credit cards

5. Save your changes to the file and then reload **co_payment.html** in your browser. Complete the payment form with valid values up to the CVC input box and then test the input box with a missing value, a 3-digit CVC number for the American Express card, and a 4-digit CVC number for other credit cards. See Figure 13-57.

Figure 13-57 **Custom pop-up error message for invalid CVC numbers**

Sources: American Express Company; Discover Financial Services; MasterCard, Inc.; Visa, Inc.

6. Enter a valid CVC and then click the **Submit Payment** button again. Verify that the browser accepts the number without showing an error message.

Aisha has examined your work on the form and notes that a credit card number might fit the numeric pattern but still be invalid. She asks you to add one more validation check that tests whether the credit card numbers themselves are legitimate.

Testing for Legitimate Card Numbers

In addition to a specified pattern of characters, all legitimate credit card numbers must satisfy the **Luhn Algorithm** also known as the **Mod10 Algorithm**, which is an algorithm developed in the 1960's to provide a quick validation check on an account number by ensuring that the sum of the digits in the number meet certain mathematical criteria. Almost all institutions that issue unique identification numbers employ the Luhn Algorithm or some variation of it. Figure 13-58 shows how the Luhn Algorithm is applied to a sample identification number.

Figure 13-58   The Luhn Algorithm

Luhn Algorithm

1. Separate the number into two alternating groups starting from the last digit on the right

   ID Number
   1 2 3 4 5 6 7 8 9 7
   Hans Peter Luhn

   2 4 6 8 7   1 3 5 7 9

2. Double the digits in the second group   2 6 10 14 18

3. Sum up the digits in both groups   2 + 4 + 6 + 8   2 + 6 + 1 + 0 + 1 + 4
                                        + 7 = 27   + 1 + 8 = 23

4. Total the sums from both groups   27 + 23 = 50

5. If the total sum is evenly divisible by   50/10 = 5   ✓ The ID Number is
   10, the number is legitimate   legitimate

© Courtesy Patrick Carey

The steps in testing whether an ID number satisfies the Luhn Algorithm are as follows:

1. Starting from the last digit and moving to the left, divide the alternating digits of the ID number into two groups.
2. Add the digits in the first group.
3. Double the digits in the second group and then add the sum of the doubled digits (not the sum of the numbers themselves so, if one of the digits is 10, then add 1 + 0, or if one of the digits is 18, then add 1 + 8.)
4. Calculate the total of the sums from the two groups.
5. If the total sum is evenly divisible by 10, the ID number satisfies the Luhn Algorithm and is considered legitimate, otherwise the ID number is illegitimate.

Aisha wants you to include the Luhn Algorithm in your validation check of the customer's credit card. Start by creating the sumDigits() function that sums the digits found within a text string.

To insert the sumDigits() function:

1. Return to the **co_payment.js** file in your editor and at the bottom of the file, insert the following function:

```javascript
function sumDigits(numStr) {
    var digitTotal = 0;
    for (var i = 0; i < numStr.length; i++) {
        digitTotal += parseInt(numStr.charAt(i));
    }
    return digitTotal;
}
```

Figure 13-59 describes the code in the function.

Figure 13-59 **Creating the sumDigits() function**

the numStr parameter contains the text string of the ID number

the digitTotal variable keeps a running total of the sum of the digits in the number string

loops through every character in the number string

returns the numeric sum of the digits in the string

for every character in the number string, adds the integer value of the character to digitTotal

2. Save your changes to the file.

Next, create the luhn() function that adds the digits in the two alternating groups of digits, doubling the values in the second digit list.

To insert the luhn() function:

1. After the sumDigits() function, begin inserting the luhn() function by adding the following code that defines two variables: the string1 variable containing one set of digits and the string2 variable containing the digits that will be doubled:

```
function luhn(idNum) {
    var string1 = "";
    var string2 = "";
```

2. Next, loop through the first group of digits, adding the alternating set of digit characters to string1. Note that the counting variable starts with the last character and decreases by two units, skipping every other digit in the idNum text string, until it reaches the beginning of the text string:

```
// Retrieve the odd-numbered digits
for (var i = idNum.length - 1; i >= 0; i-= 2) {
    string1 += idNum.charAt(i);
}
```

3. Next, loop through the second group of digits, adding double the digits to the string2 varaible:

```
// Retrieve the even-numbered digits and double them
for (var i = idNum.length - 2; i >= 0; i-= 2) {
    string2 += 2*idNum.charAt(i);
}
```

TIP

See Figure 9-24 for a discussion of the modulus % operator.

4. Finally, call the sumDigits() function to return the sum of the digit characters in string1 and string2 and use the modulus operator to determine whether that sum is divisible by 10:

```
// Return whether the sum of the digits is divisible by 10
return sumDigits(string1 + string2) % 10 === 0;
}
```

Figure 13-60 Creating the luhn() function

```
        return digitTotal;
}

function luhn(idNum) {
    var string1 = "";
    var string2 = "";

    // Retrieve the odd-numbered digits
    for (var i = idNum.length - 1; i >= 0; i-= 2) {
        string1 += idNum.charAt(i);
    }
    // Retrieve the even-numbered digits and double them
    for (var i = idNum.length - 2; i >= 0; i-= 2) {
        string2 += 2*idNum.charAt(i);
    }

    // Return whether the sum of the digits is divisible by 10
    return sumDigits(string1 + string2) % 10 === 0;
}
```

loops through the alternate digit characters starting with the last digit

adds each digit in the string1 variable

adds the double of each digit to the string2 variable

returns a Boolean value indicating whether the total sum is divisible by 10

loops through the alternate digit characters starting with the second-to-last digit

5. Save your changes to the file.

Validate the credit card number data by adding another condition that tests whether the value of the cardNumber field passes the Luhn test.

To validate the credit card number:

1. Scroll up to the validateNumber() function and add the following condition directly before the final `else` condition:

```
} else if (luhn(cardNumber.value) === false) {
    cardNumber.setCustomValidity("Enter a legitimate card
number");
```

Figure 13-61 describes the code in the function.

Figure 13-61   **Validating with the Luhn algorithm**

tests whether the card number passes the Luhn test

if the number fails validation, displays the validation error message

```
function validateNumber() {
   var cardNumber = document.getElementById("cardNumber");
   if (cardNumber.validity.valueMissing) {
      cardNumber.setCustomValidity("Enter your card number");
   } else if (cardNumber.validity.patternMismatch) {
      cardNumber.setCustomValidity("Enter a valid card number");
   } else if (luhn(cardNumber.value) === false) {
      cardNumber.setCustomValidity("Enter a legitimate card number");
   } else {
      cardNumber.setCustomValidity("");
   }
}
```

2. Save your changes to the file and the reload the **co_payment.html** file in your browser.

TIP

You can find lists of test credit card numbers in a variety of sites on the web.

3. Complete the payment form with valid data values but enter the credit card number **6011280768434850**, which fits the required pattern but is not a legitimate card number.

4. Click the **Submit Payment** button and verify that the form is rejected due to the illegitimate card number. See Figure 13-62.

Figure 13-62   **An illegitimate credit card number**

credit card number does not pass the Luhn test

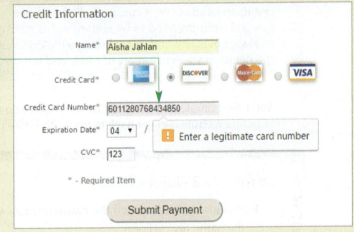

Sources: American Express Company; Discover Financial Services; MasterCard, Inc.; Visa, Inc.

5. Change the credit card number to the sample number **6011280768434856** and click the **Submit Payment** button. Verify that the form data passes all validation tests with the new card number.

Written Communication: Designing an E-Commerce Website

When customers shop online, they are looking for what every customer looks for: good products at a good price in a shopping experience that is pleasant and easy. While both of these things are important, you cannot forget that your competition is only a click away and, if your customers don't have confidence in your website design, they might also not have confidence in the products you sell.

Here are some tips to keep in mind as you build your e-commerce website:

- Don't burden your customers with a long and complicated registration process. Provide guest users with easy access to your catalog because they will be more likely to register after viewing all you have to offer.
- Provide robust search tools. Make it easy to match your customers with the products they are most likely to purchase.
- Make it easy to navigate the purchasing process. Customers should be able to easily move forward and backward in the purchase process so mistakes can be easily fixed. Provide information to the customer at each step in the process about what is being purchased and how much it will cost. Don't hide fees or taxes until later in the shopping process or you run the risk of irritating your customer.
- Put discount options and membership deals front and center in any purchasing process so that your customers can take advantage of deals that make a final purchase more likely.
- Use validation tests and security measures to reassure your customer that their credit information is safe and secure.
- Incorporate social media in your e-commerce website, providing your customers the opportunity to discuss with you and other customers your products and services.

A successful e-commerce site is never static: it should always be evolving to meet the changing needs of your customer. Technology and customer tastes are constantly in flux and websites need to be current with a quickly changing market. Thus, you need to always evaluate and re-evaluate your e-commerce design to ensure that it meets the needs of your customers of today and tomorrow.

You have completed your work on the payment page. Aisha will continue to work on the Coctura website and get back to you with future projects and programming tasks.

Session 13.3 Quick Check

1. Provide code to turn off the native browser validation for the web form with the name reviewForm.
2. Provide an expression to report on the validation status of the reviewForm web form.
3. Provide code to indicate whether there is a type mismatch for data entered in the input box with the ID "reviewDate".
4. Provide code to indicate whether the input field with the ID "reviewRating" has a value greater than allowed by the max attribute.
5. Provide code to change the validation message for the reviewRating input box to "Value larger than allowed.".
6. Provide code to test whether the value entered in the customerID input box matches the regular expression /^[A-Z]{3}-\d{2}$/
7. Does the ID number "383" satisfy the Luhn Algorithm? Explain.
8. Does the ID number "380" satisfy the Luhn Algorithm? Explain.

Review Assignments

Data Files needed for the Review Assignments: co_cart_txt.html, co_cart_txt.js, co_credit_txt.html, co_credit_txt.js, 3 CSS files, 1 HTML file, 9 PNG files

Aisha wants you to work on another version of the shopping cart and payment pages. As with the version you completed in this tutorial, she wants you to add code to the shopping cart page that calculates the total cost of the order and transfers that data to the credit card payment page when the shopping cart form is submitted. On the credit card payment page, she wants to display the contents of the order and provide validation checks for the credit card payment. Figure 13-63 shows a preview of the forms on the two pages. Some of the code for both pages have already been created for you. Your job will be to finish the code.

Figure 13-63	Espresso machine order

Shopping Cart Form

Credit Card Payment Form

rces: American Express Company; Discover Financial Services; MasterCard, Inc.; Visa, Inc.

Complete the following:

1. Use your editor to open the **co_cart_txt.html**, **co_cart_txt.js**, **co_credit_txt.html**, and **co_credit_txt.js** files from the html13 ▸ review folder. Enter *your name* and *the date* in the comment section of each file, and save them as **co_cart.html**, **co_cart.js**, **co_credit.html**, and **co_credit.js** respectively.

2. Go to the **co_cart.html** file in your editor. Link the page to the **co_cart.js** file, loading the file asynchronously. Study the contents of the file and the cart form. Take note of the field names and IDs of the files in the form.

3. Within the `<form>` tag for the cart form, add attributes to open the **co_credit.html** file using the `get` method when the cart form is submitted. Save your changes to the file.

4. Go to the **co_cart.js** file in your editor. Directly below the initial comment section, add an event listener for the window `load` event that does the following when the page is loaded:

   a. Runs the calcCart() function.

   b. Runs the calcCart() function when the field value is changed. (*Hint*: Apply an onchange event handler to the modelQty field in the cart form.)

   c. Uses a `for` loop that loops through every option in the group of shipping option buttons, adding an event handler to run the calcCart() function when each option button is clicked.

5. Create the calcCart() function to calculate the cost of the customer's order using field values in the cart form. Within the calcCart() function, do the following:

   a. Create a variable named **orderCost** that is equal to the cost of the espresso machine stored in the modelCost field multiplied by the quantity of machines ordered as stored in the modelQty field. Display the value of the orderCost variable in the orderCost field, formatted as U.S. currency. (*Hint*: Use the formatUSCurrency() function.)

   b. Create a variable named **shipCost** equal to the value of the selected shipping option from the group of shipping option buttons multiplied by the quantity of machines ordered. Display the value of the shipCost variable in the shippingCost field, formatted with a thousands separator and to two decimals places. (*Hint*: Use the formatNumber() function.)

   c. In the subTotal field, display the sum of orderCost and shipCost formatted with a thousands separator and to two decimal places.

   d. Create a variable named **salesTax** equal to 0.05 times the sum of the orderCost and shipCost variables. Display the value of the salesTax variable in the salesTax field, formatted with a thousands separator and to two decimal places.

   e. In the cartTotal field, display the sum of the orderCost, shipCost, and salesTax variables. Format the value as U.S. currency.

   f. Store the label text of the shipping option selected by the user from the shipping field in the hidden shippingType field.

6. Save your changes to the file and then open **co_cart.html** in your browser. Verify that the page correctly calculates and displays the total cost of the order as shown in Figure 13-63 and that the totals are automatically updated as you change the order options.

7. Go to the **co_credit.html** file in your editor. Link the page to the **co_credit.js** file, loading the file asynchronously. Study the contents of the file and the forms and fields it contains. Close the file, saving your changes.

8. Go to the **co_credit.js** file in your editor. Create an event listener for the window `load` event that retrieves the field values attached to the query string of the page's URL. Add the following to the event listener's anonymous function:

   a. Create the **orderData** variable that stores the query string text from the URL. Slice the orderData text string to remove the first ? character, replace every occurrence of the + character with a blank space, and decode the URI-encoded characters.

   b. Split the orderData variable at every occurrence of a & or = character and store the substrings in the **orderFields** array variable.

   c. Write the following values from the orderFields array into the indicated fields of the order form:

      i. orderFields[3] into the modelName field

      ii. orderFields[5] into the modelQty field

      iii. orderFields[7] into the orderCost field

      iv. orderFields[9] into the shippingType field

      v. orderFields[13] into the shippingCost field

      vi. orderFields[15] into the subTotal field

      vii. orderFields[17] into the salesTax field

      viii. orderFields[19] into the cartTotal field

9. Add another event listener for the window `load` event that runs different validation event handlers when the page is loaded by the browser. Add code to the anonymous function for the `load` event that does the following:

   a. Runs the runSubmit() function when the subButton is clicked.

   b. Runs the validateName() function when a value is input into the cardHolder field.

   c. Runs the validateNumber() function when a value is input into the cardNumber field.

   d. Runs the validateDate() function when a value is input into the expDate field.

   e. Runs the validateCVC() function when a value is input into the cvc field.

10. Create the runSubmit() function that is run when the form is submitted. Within the function, add commands to run the validateName(), validateCredit(), validateNumber(), validateDate(), and validateCVC() functions.

11. Create the validateDate() function. The purpose of this function is to validate the credit card expiration date stored in the expDate field. Within the function, insert an if-else structure that tests the following:

   a. If no value has been entered for the expiration date, set the custom validation message to "Enter the expiration date".

   b. If the expiration date does not match the regular expression pattern:
     `/^(0[1-9]|1[0-2])\/20[12]\d$/`
     set the custom validation message to "Enter a valid expiration date". (*Hint*: Use the `test()` method.)

   c. Otherwise set the custom validation message to an empty text string.

12. The remaining functions have already been entered for you. Save your changes to the file.

13. Return to the **co_cart.html** file in your browser and enter a sample customer order and click the **Checkout** button to submit the order and load the co_credit.html file. Verify the following:

   a. The field values from the customer order are displayed in the order form.

   b. You cannot submit the payment unless you entered the name of the card holder, selected a credit card company, entered a valid credit card number (you can find lists of sample test credit card numbers on the web), entered a valid expiration date, and entered a valid CVC number.

Case Problem 1

Data Files needed for this Case Problem: mpl_links_txt.html, mpl_links_txt.js, 2 CSS files, 3 PNG files

Monroe Public Library   Denise Kruschev manages the website for the Monroe Public Library in Monroe, Ohio. One of her responsibilities is to add content and links to the site that will be of interest to the library's patrons. Denise has asked you to create a web page containing links to hundreds of government websites. She knows that a long list of links will fill the page, making navigation within the page difficult. Denise wants to use "select and go" navigation in which the links are placed within a selection list. When a patron selects a website from the list, the linked site should open automatically. Denise has already set up the selection list and the URLs for each government site; she wants you to write the JavaScript code to load the website chosen via the selection list. Figure 13-64 shows a preview of the web page you will create.

Figure 13-64   **Monroe Public Library links to government sites**

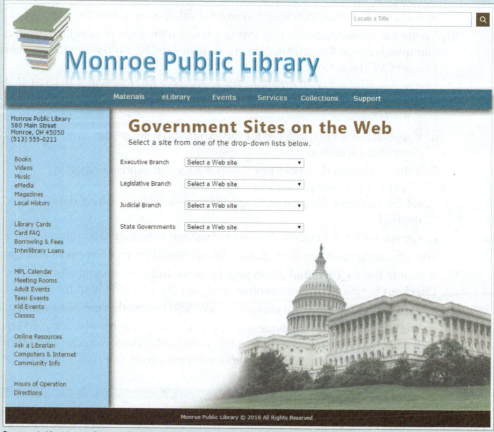

Source: J_Alves/openclipart; Lubos Houska/Public Domain; © Courtesy Patrick Carey

Complete the following:

1. Use your editor to open the **mpl_links_txt.html** and **mp_links_txt.js** files from the html13 ►
   case1 folder. Enter *your name* and *the date* in the comment section of each file, and save them
   as **mpl_links.html** and **mpl_links.js** respectively.

2. Go to the **mpl_links.html** file in your editor. Within the document head, add a `script` element
   for the **mpl_links.js** file. Load the file asynchronously. Take some time to study the content of the
   file. Note that the selection lists are placed within a form element named "govLinks". Save your
   changes to the file.

3. Return to the **mp_links.js** file in your editor and create an event listener for the load event that
   runs an anonymous function.

4. Within the anonymous function, create the **allSelect** variable referencing all `select` elements
   nested within the govLinks form.

5. Loop through the allSelect object collection and for each selection list in the collection create
   an anonymous function for the `onchange` event. Within this anonymous function, use the `href`
   property of the `location` object to change the page shown in the browser window to the value
   of the target of the event object that initiated the `onchange` event.

6. Document your commands with JavaScript comments.

7. Save your changes to the file and then open the **mpl_links.html** file in your browser. Verify that
   you can load different government websites by selecting the website name from the entries in the
   four selection lists.

Case Problem 2

Data Files needed for this Case Problem: dl_expense_txt.html, dl_expense_txt.js, 2 CSS files, 1 HTML file, 1 PNG file

DeLong Enterprises   Kay Ramirez is a human resources manager at DeLong Enterprises, a manufacturer of computer components and digital equipment located in Plano, Texas. The company has been busy putting corporate information on the company's intranet. Kay is heading a project to put all payroll-related forms and reports online. She asks you to help write a program for an online travel expense form. The form requires employees to list their various travel expenses for corporate-sponsored trips. Kay wants a script added to the form to ensure that all the required data is entered in the correct format. She also wants the form to automatically total the expense costs for transportation, lodging, meals, and other miscellaneous items for each travel day for the entire trip. A preview of the page is shown in Figure 13-65.

Figure 13-65	DeLong Enterprises travel expense report

© Courtesy Patrick Carey

Complete the following:

1. Use your editor to open the **dl_expense_txt.html** and **dl_expense_txt.js** files from the html13 ▶ case2 folder. Enter *your name* and *the date* in the comment section of each file, and save them as **dl_expense.html** and **dl_expense.js** respectively.

2. Go to the **dl_expense.html** file in your editor. Add a `script` element for the **dl_expense.js** file. Load the file asynchronously.

3. Scroll down to the empInfo table and add `pattern` attributes to the following fields using regular expressions (*Note*: Regular expressions in the HTML `pattern` attribute do not include the opening and closing / character):

   a. The accID field should consist only of the letters "ACT" followed by exactly 6 digits.

   b. The deptID field should consist only of the letters "DEPT" followed by 4 to 6 digits.

   c. The projID field should consist only of the letters "PROJ" followed by a dash and then two lowercase letters followed by another dash and 3 digits.

   d. The ssn field should consist only of 3 digits followed by a dash followed by 2 more digits followed by a dash, ending with 4 more digits.

4. Take some time to study the class names for the `input` elements in the travelExp table. This table will be used to calculate the total travel expenses for each day and across all categories. Note that input elements that contribute to the total are placed in the sum class. Input elements belonging to a common date are placed in the date0 through date5 classes. Finally, input elements belonging to different expense categories are placed in the trans, lodge, meal, and other classes. Save your changes to the file.

5. Return to the **dl_expense.js** file in your editor. Directly below the initial comment section, add an event listener for the `load` event. Apply an anonymous function to the `load` event that does the following:

   a. Declares a variable named **changingCells** that matches all `input` elements in the travelExp table that belong to the sum class.

   b. For every item in the changingCells collection, adds an onchange event handler that runs calcExp() function.

   c. For the button with the ID "submitButton", adds an event handler for the click event that runs the validateSummary() function when the button is clicked.

6. Kay wants a customized validation message if employees neglect to fill out the summary field that provides a summary of the travel expenses. Create the validateSummary() function that displays the message "**You must include a summary of the trip in your report.**" if the validation state of the summary field value is missing; otherwise set the custom validation message to an empty text string.

7. Create the calcClass() function with a single parameter **sumClass**. The purpose of this function is to sum the values of input elements belonging to the sumClass class of elements. Add the following commands to the function:

   a. Create a variable named **sumFields** containing the object collection of all elements belonging to the sumClass class.

   b. Create a variable named **sumTotal** that will be used to keep a running total of the total values in the input elements in the sumFields object collection. Set the initial value of sumTotal to 0.

c. Loop through the items in the sumFields object collection. For each item, declare a variable named **itemValue** equal to the numeric value of the current input element in the sumFields array. (*Hint*: Use the `parseFloat()` function to extract the numeric value.) If itemValue is a numeric value, add it to itemValue. (*Hint*: Use the isNaN() function to determine whether itemValue is or is not a number.)

d. After the `for` loop, return the value of sumTotal.

8. Create the calcExp() function. The purpose of this function is to calculate the row and column totals from the travelExp table. Add the following commands to the function:

a. Create the **expTable** variable referencing all the table row (`tr`) elements within the table body of the travelExp table.

b. Loop through the rows in the expTable collection and, for each table row, set the value of the input element with the ID subtotal*Index* to the value returned by the calcClass() function using the parameter value date*Index*. Where *Index* is the value of the index counter in the `for` loop. Format the value returned by the calcClass() function as a text string using the formatNumber() function to 2 decimals.

c. After the `for` loop, set the values of the transTotal, lodgeTotal, mealTotal, and otherTotal `input` elements by calling the calcClass() function using parameter values "trans", "lodge", "meal", and "other". Format the values using the formatNumber() to 2 decimal places.

d. Set the value of the expTotal `input` element to the value returned by the calcClass() function using "sum" as the parameter value. Format the returned value using the formatUSCurrency() function.

9. Document your work with comments through the newly added code.

10. Save your changes to the file and load **dl_expense.html** in your browser. Verify the following:

a. You cannot submit the form without adding a travel summary, a name, a social security number, and account, department, and project IDs in the correct format.

b. If you fail to enter a travel summary, the customized message, "You must include a summary of the trip in your report." is displayed.

c. When you enter or change values in the expense report table, the column and row totals are automatically updated and the column and row totals are formatted to 2 decimals places with a thousands separator. The overall travel expense total should be shown in currency format. (*Note*: At the time of this writing, Firefox does not support the `date` data type, so you will not see the mm/dd/yyyy value in the travel date column.)

CHALLENGE

Case Problem 3

Data Files needed for this Case Problem: mas_register_txt.html, mas_register_txt.js, mas_reg2_txt.html, mas_reg2_txt.js, 2 CSS files, 5 PNG files

Media Arts Society Gary Unwin manages the promotion for the Media Arts Society annual conference – a popular conference for people who develop multimedia applications and technology. He has asked you to work on the conference website. One of your first jobs will be to work on the registration page. You will start by designing the page in which conference-goers enter their contact information and choose which session packages to purchase. Figure 13-66 shows a preview of the page you will create.

Figure 13-66 Media Arts Society registration page

© Elesey/Shutterstock.com;
Source: public domain image/RR Auction

To create this page, you will save the choices of the user in session storage variables and then display those values and their totals on the right side of the page. You will also use those session storage variables in another page in the MAS conference website.

Complete the following:

1. Use your editor to open the **mas_register_txt.html**, **mas_register_txt.js**, **mas_reg2_txt.html**, and **mas_reg2_txt.js** from the html13 ▸ case3 folder. Enter *your name* and *the date* in the comment section of each file, and save them as **mas_register.html**, **mas_register.js**, **mas_reg2.html**, and **mas_reg2.js** respectively.

2. Go to the **mas_register.html** file in your editor. Add a `script` element for the **mas_register.js** file. Load the file asynchronously.

3. Take some time to study the contents of the file, taking note of the field names and IDs assigned to different form controls. Save your changes to the file.

4. Return to the **mas_register.js** file in your editor. Directly below the initial comment section, insert an event listener for the window `load` event. Run an anonymous function in response to the event containing the following commands:

   a. Call the calcCart() function (which you will create shortly).

   b. Create an `onclick` event handler for the regSubmit button that runs the sessionTest() function when the button is clicked.

   c. Create `onblur` event handlers for the input boxes with the IDs: fnBox, lnBox, groupBox, mailBox, phoneBox, and banquetBox, running the calcCart() function in response to each event.

   d. Create an `onchange` event handler for the sessionBox selection list, running the calcCart() function when the selection list is changed.

   e. Create an `onclick` event handler for the mediaCB check box, running the calcCart() function in response.

5. Create the sessionTest() function. The purpose of this function is to provide a validation test for the conference session selection list. Add the following commands to the function:

   a. Test whether the selected index of the sesssionBox selection list is equal to -1. If it is, the user has not selected a session package. Display the custom validation message "Select a Session Package".

   b. If the selected index is equal to -1 set the custom validation message to an empty text string.

⊕ **Explore** 6. Create the calcCart() function. The purpose of this function is to calculate the registration cost and to save information about the customer's choices in session storage. Add the following commands to the function:

   a. In the session storage variable **confName**, store the value "*firstName lastName*" where *firstName* and *lastName* are the values of the firstName and lastName fields in the regForm form.

   b. Store the values of the group, email, phoneNumber, and banquetGuests fields in the session storage variables: **confGroup**, **confMail**, **confPhone**, and **confBanquet**.

   c. The cost of the banquet is $55 per guest. Multiply the value of the banquetGuests field by 55 and store the result in the session storage variable **confBanquetCost**.

   d. Record which session the user has selected. If the selected index of the sessionBox selection list is not equal to -1, store the text of the selected option in the session storage variable **confSession** and the value of the selected option in the **confSessionCost** sesson storage variable; otherwise store an empty text string and the value 0 respectively.

e. The user can opt to purchase a media pack for $115 containing gifts from the conference. If the user has clicked the mediaCB check box, store the values "yes" and 115 in the **confPack** and **confPackCost** session storage variables; otherwise store the values "no" and 0.

f. Calculate the total registration cost by storing the value

session + *banquet* + *media*

in the **confTotal** session storage variable, where *session*, *banquet*, and *media* are the values of the confSessionCost, confBanquetCost, and confPackCost session storage variables. (*Hint*: Use the parseFloat() method to add the numeric values of the data fields.)

g. Call the writeSessionValues() function.

✛ **Explore** 7. Display the values of the session storage variables in the current web page by creating the writeSessionValues() function, adding the following commands:

a. Set the text content of span elements with the IDs "regName", "regGroup", "regEmail", "reg-Phone", "regSession", "regBanquet", and "regPack", to the values of the session storage variables, confName, confGroup, confMail, confPhone, confSession, confBanquet, and confPack.

b. Set the text content of the span element with the ID "regTotal" to the value $*total* where *total* is the value of the confTotal session storage variable.

8. Document your work in the file with comments and then save the file.

9. Open the **mas_reg2.html** file in your editor. Add a script element for the **mas_reg2.js** file. Load the file asynchronously. Save your changes to the document.

10. Open the **mas_reg2.js** file in your editor. Directly below the comment section, copy and paste the writeSessionValues() function from the mas_register.js file.

11. Add an event listener that runs the writeSessionValues() variable when the page loads. Save your changes to the file.

12. Open the **mas_register.html** file in your browser. Verify the following:

a. Values and selected options from the registration form are automatically displayed in the page as you tab from one control element to the next.

b. You cannot submit the form unless a conference session packet has been selected.

c. When the form is submitted, the browser displays the content of the mas_reg2.html file with the user's choices automatically retrieved from the session storage variables and displayed at the top of the page.

Note: If you are testing your code on the Edge or Internet Explorer browsers, you must load the solution files to a server. Session storage will not be activated for files loaded on your local computer.

Case Problem 4

Data Files needed for this Case Problem: ws_lincoln_txt.html, ws_cloud_txt.js, 3 CSS files, 1 JS file, 3 PNG files

Rhetoric in the United States   Professor Annie Cho, who teaches rhetoric and history at White Sands College, wants your help in developing her website on great American speeches. She has asked you to create a word cloud of Abraham Lincoln's first inaugural address. A **word cloud** is a chart of several words, in which each word's size is based on the frequency of use in a selected text. Word clouds highlight the most important themes and concepts in the given text. A preview of the word cloud for Lincoln's first inaugural address is shown in Figure 13-67.

Figure 13-67   **Word cloud of Lincoln's first inaugural address**

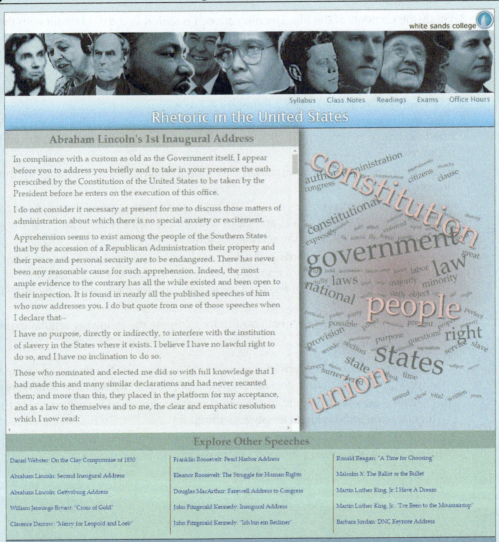

Sources: Lincoln by Thomas Le Mere (1863); Eleanor Roosevelt (1947); Daniel Webster - photographer unknown; Dr. Martin Luther King (1963); Ronald Reagan – archives photo (1984); Barbara Joran (1976); J. F. Kennedy – www.nara.gov (1961); Calvin Coolidge – Notman Photo Co (1919); Rebecca L Felton (1922); William Jennings Bryan (1901) All Public Domain Images.; © Courtesy Patrick Carey

By viewing the word cloud, it is clear to Professor Cho's students that the first inaugural address was primarily focused on government and constitutional issues, while topics such as slavery and war were not as prominent. To create a word cloud, you will work with the JavaScript methods and properties for manipulating text strings. You will also work with regular expressions to remove commonly used words such as "it" or "this", also known as **stop words**. Professor Cho has provided you with an array of stop words as well as some JavaScript functions that will aid you in writing the word cloud code.

Complete the following:

1. Use your editor to open the **ws_lincoln_txt.html** and **ws_cloud_txt.js** from the html13 ▸ case4 folder. Enter *your name* and *the date* in the comment section of each file, and save them as **ws_lincoln.html** and **ws_cloud.js** respectively.

2. Go to the **ws_lincoln.html** file in your editor. Link the page to the **ws_cloud.css** style sheet and the **ws_stopwords.js** and **ws_clouds.js** JavaScript files (in that order). Load the JavaScript files asynchronously.

3. Study the contents of the file. Lincoln's speech is stored in a `div` element with the ID "speech". The word cloud text will be placed in the `aside` element with the ID "cloud". Close the file, saving your changes.

4. Go to the **ws_cloud.js** file. Directly below the comment section, insert an event listener for the windows `load` event. Have the event listener run the anonymous function containing the commands described in Steps 5 through 18.

5. Declare the **wordContent** variable containing the text content of the speech `div` element, using the `textContent` property to retrieve only the speech text and not any of the HTML tags in the element.

✦ **Explore** 6. Apply the `toLowerCase()` method to wordContent to change all the words to lowercase.

7. Use the regular expression `/[!\.,:;\?\'"\(\)\{\}\d\-]/` and the `replace()` method to replace punctuation characters and digits with empty text strings: (*Hint*: Use the g flag in your regular expression to apply the search globally.)

✦ **Explore** 8. The ws_stopwords.js file that you loaded in Step 2 includes an array named **stopWords** containing a list of common words that should *not* be included in the word cloud. Loop through the contents of the stopwords array and for each entry in the array do the following:

   a. Use the `new RegExp()` object constructor to create the following regular expression

      `\\bstopword\\b`

      where *stopword* is the current stop word in the array. Set the flag of this regular expression to g for a global search and save the regular expression in the variable **stopWordsRE**.

   b. Use the `replace()` method to replace every occurrence of words matching the stopWordsRE regular expression with an empty text string.

✦ **Explore** 9. There may be blank spaces at the beginning and end of the text in the wordContent variable. Apply the `trim()` method to remove excess blank spaces.

10. Apply the `split()` method to split wordContent at every occurrence of one or more white-space characters. Save the array of words in the **wordArray** variable.

Professor Cho has supplied you with the findUnique() function, which creates an array of unique values in a given array, returning a 2-dimensional array of the form

`array[i][j]`

where

`array[i][0]`

displays the text of the ith word, while

`array[i][1]`

displays the count or number of times the ith word is used in the text.

11. Call the findUnique() function with the wordArray variable as the parameter value and store the 2-dimensional array of unique words and their counts in the **uniqueWords** array.

12. Sort the contents of the uniqueWords array in decreasing order of word count, using the sortByCount() function as the compare function for the `sort()` method.

13. Professor Cho wants only the top 100 words displayed in the word count. Reduce the length of the uniqueWords array to 100.

14. To format the words in the word cloud you will need to know the count for the least-used word. Store the count of the least-used word in the **minimumCount** variable. (*Hint*: Use the reference uniqueWords[99][1].)

15. Professor Cho wants the top-three words highlighted in the word count. Store the count of the third highest-used word in the **top3Count** variable. (*Hint*: Use the reference uniqueWords[2][1].)

16. The word cloud should list the words alphabetically. Sort the uniqueWords variable alphabetically by applying the sortByWord() function as the compare function.

17. With the words that will be displayed in the word count stored in the correct order in the uniqueWords array, you are ready to format and display the words in the cloud. Each word will be placed within a `span` element and formatted according to its use in the speech. Create a `for` loop that loops through the uniqueWords array and for each word do the following:

   a. Create a `span` element, stored in the **cloudWord** variable.

   b. Set the text content of cloudWord to the value of the current word in the uniqueWord array. (*Hint*: Use uniqueWords[i][0] where *i* is your counter variable.)

   c. Next, determine the font size of the word, proportional to how often it is used. Professor Cho wants words displayed with a font-size of

   $$0.45 \times \frac{count}{minimum}$$

   where *count* is the word count for the current word in the uniqueWord array and *minimum* is the value of the minimumCount variable, up to a maximum value of 6em. Declare the **wordSize** variable and set it equal to the minimum value of 6 in the equation above. (*Hint*: Use uniqueWords[i][1] to retrieve the word count.)

   d. Set the `font-size` style of cloudWord to "*size*em" where *size* is the value of the wordSize variable in em units.

   e. For visual interest, Professor Cho wants the cloud words to be randomly rotated within the word cloud. Set the `transform` style of cloudWord to "rotate(*random*deg)" where *random* is a random integer between -30 and +30. (*Hint*: Use the randomValue() function to generate the random angle.)

   f. Professor Cho wants to highlight the top 3 words. If the current word in the uniqueWord array has a word count value greater than or equal to the value of top3Count, set the `color` style of cloudWord to rgb(251, 191, 191) and the `text-shadow` style to "2px 2px 5px rgb(51, 51, 51)".

   g. Append cloudWord as a new child of the cloud `aside` element.

18. Document your work with comments throughout and then save your changes to the file.

19. Load **ws_lincoln.html** in your browser and verify that a word cloud of the top 100 words from Lincoln's 1st inaugural address appears on the page and that the top three words (constitution, people, and union) appear in pink with a shadow. Verify that the words are different font sizes, indicating their status within the group of top one-hundred words used.

TUTORIAL 14

OBJECTIVES

Session 14.1
- Use nested functions
- Create an object literal
- Define object properties and methods

Session 14.2
- Define an object class
- Use object constructor functions
- Instantiating an object
- Define an object prototype

Session 14.3
- Explore prototype chains
- Use the `apply()` and `call()` methods
- Work with objects and arrays
- Create a `for...in` loop

Exploring Object-Based Programming

Designing an Online Poker Game

Case | *Arthur's Games*

Bob Voiklund supervises programming at a new gaming website, Arthur's Games. The website will go online next month and Bob has asked you to develop a sample web application for an online poker game. Bob has already designed the layout and content of the sample page; he wants you to write the code to make the game work.

Because the website will eventually offer several poker-style games, Bob wants your code to be easily adapted to the other games your colleagues at Arthur's Games will develop. One way to create reusable objects and code is with object-based programming. Bob asks you to explore this technique by creating customized objects designed for card games.

STARTING DATA FILES

html14 → **tutorial**

ag_poker_txt.html
ag_poker_txt.js
ag_cards_txt.js
+ 60 files

review

ag_squares_txt.html
ag_cards2_txt.js
ag_squares_txt.js
+ 62 files

case1

bu_home_txt.html
bu_bubbles_txt.js
+ 13 files

case2

cc_staff_txt.html
cc_staff_txt.js
+ 41 files

case3

rb_pizza_txt.html
rb_build_txt.js
+ 20 files

case4

kg_stamps_txt.html
kg_stamps_txt.js
+ 41 files

Session 14.1 Visual Overview:

An **object literal** creates a custom object by storing the properties of the object within a comma-separated list of *name:value* pairs enclosed within a set of curly braces.

Name/value pair creating the currentBank and currentBet properties of the pokerGame object.

name:value pair creating the custom placeBet() method for the pokerGame object.

The this keyword references the current object, pokerGame.

```
var pokerGame = {
    currentBank: null,
    currentBet: null,

    placeBet: function() {
        this.currentBank -= this.currentBet;
        return this.currentBank;
    }
};
```

This code uses the dot operator to reference the currentBank and currentBet properties of the pokerGame object.

This code calls the placeBet() method to change the value of the currentBank property of the pokerGame object.

```
// Set the initial values of the pokerGame object
pokerGame.currentBank = 500;
pokerGame.currentBet = 25;

// Restart the game when the Reset button is clicked
resetButton.addEventListener("click", function() {
    pokerGame.currentBank = 500;
    bankBox.value = pokerGame.currentBank;
});

// Enable the Draw and Stand buttons after the deal
dealButton.addEventListener("click", function() {
    if (pokerGame.currentBank >= pokerGame.currentBet) {
        bankBox.value = pokerGame.placeBet();
    } else {
        alert("Reduce the size of your bet");
    }
});
```

Custom Objects, Properties, and Methods

When the Deal button is clicked, the placeBet() method is applied to the pokerGame object.

Bank input box shows the current value of pokerGame.currentBank.

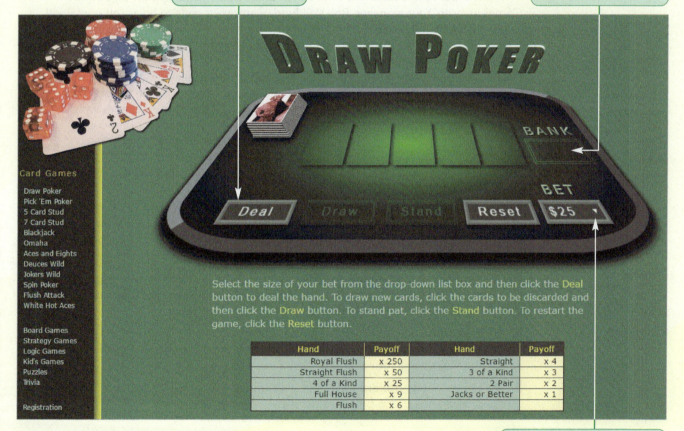

Select the size of your bet from the drop-down list box and then click the Deal button to deal the hand. To draw new cards, click the cards to be discarded and then click the Draw button. To stand pat, click the Stand button. To restart the game, click the Reset button.

Hand	Payoff	Hand	Payoff
Royal Flush	x 250	Straight	x 4
Straight Flush	x 50	3 of a Kind	x 3
4 of a Kind	x 25	2 Pair	x 2
Full House	x 9	Jacks or Better	x 1
Flush	x 6		

Value of pokerDeck.currentBet changes by selecting an option from the Bet selection list.

Working with Nested Functions

In Tutorial 11, you nested anonymous functions within event handlers and event listeners. However, any function, including named functions, can be nested within another function as in the following structure

```
function outsideFn() {
   commands
   function insideFn() {
      commands
   }
   commands
}
```

where *outsideFn()* is the outer or containing function and *insideFn()* is the inner or nested function. A nested function is limited in scope to the commands within the containing function in the same way that variables defined within the function are local in scope. The nested function is thus hidden from other code in the script, making the code contained and easier to manage.

You will use nested functions in developing the poker game app for the Arthur's Games website. Your manager, Bob Voiklund, wants your code to be as self-contained as possible so that it is easily portable to other pages on the website, removing the danger of code in one app interfering with code in another app.

Bob presents you with the files for the poker app. He wants you to work with two JavaScript files. The ag_poker.js file will store commands to play the poker game that you will design and the ag_cards.js file will store commands to create the objects used in your poker game and other poker games available on the Arthur's Games website. Open his documents now and view the page he has designed in your browser.

To open the product order page:

1. Use your editor to open the **ag_poker_txt.html**, **ag_cards_txt.js**, and **ag_poker_txt.js** files from the html14 ▸ tutorial folder. Enter *your name* and *the date* in the comment section of each file and save them as **ag_poker.html**, **ag_cards.js**, and **ag_poker.js** respectively.

2. Return to the **ag_poker.html** file in your editor. Within the head element, insert script elements to asynchronously load the **ag_cards.js** and **ag_poker.js** files in that order.

3. Take some time to study the contents of the file, taking note of the id attributes used to identify different parts of the poker game and then close the file, saving your changes.

4. Open the **ag_poker.html** file in your browser. Figure 14-1 shows the initial appearance of the poker game app.

Figure 14-1   **Draw Poker web page**

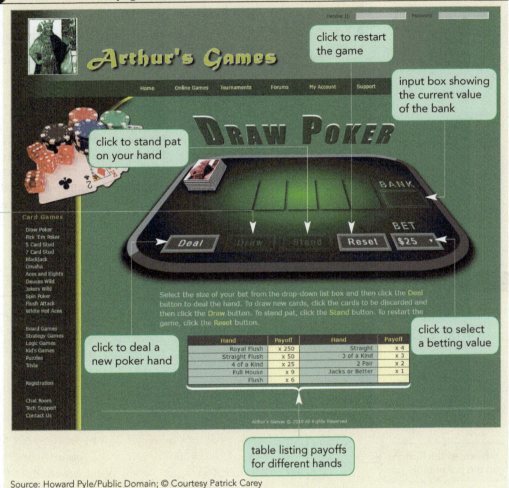

Source: Howard Pyle/Public Domain; © Courtesy Patrick Carey

The app displays the poker table on which users will play a game of draw poker. Bob sets up the following conditions for the game play:

1. The player starts the game with $500 (play money) in the bank.
2. Before each hand is dealt, the player chooses an amount to bet from the selection list. The bank is reduced by the amount bet. Bob has entered four betting values into the selection list: $25, $50, $75, and $100.
3. The player clicks the Deal button and is dealt five cards from a poker deck.
4. The player can replace any or all cards in the hand with new cards drawn from a randomly shuffled deck. New cards are retrieved by clicking the Draw button.
5. After one draw, the poker hand is considered final and it is evaluated by the program. To win back the bet, the hand needs to contain at least a pair of jacks or better. Higher-valued hands result in higher payoffs. For example, a full house (three of a kind and a pair) pays off at nine times the amount bet so that a $50 bet returns $450. Bob has included a table of the payoffs for each of nine possible winning hands.
6. After the player's winnings (if any) are added to the bank, a new round begins. The player can choose a new amount to bet and then click the Deal button to be dealt the next hand.
7. The game continues until the bank is empty or the player quits.

All these operations will be stored within the playDrawPoker() function that automatically runs when the page loads. Start creating the playDrawPoker() function by adding references to all the buttons on the poker table.

To begin the playDrawPoker() function:

1. Go to the **ag_poker.js** file in your editor.
2. Directly below the initial comment section, insert the following code:

```
window.addEventListener("load", playDrawPoker);

function playDrawPoker() {
    var dealButton = document.getElementById("dealB");
    var drawButton = document.getElementById("drawB");
    var standButton = document.getElementById("standB");
    var resetButton = document.getElementById("resetB");
    var handValueText = document.getElementById("handValue");
    var betSelection = document.getElementById("bet");
    var bankBox = document.getElementById("bank");
}
```

Figure 14-2 highlights the new code in the file.

Figure 14-2	Inserting the playDrawPoker() function

Elements on the Draw Poker page perform the following tasks:

- The Deal button deals five cards from the poker deck into the player's hand.
- The Draw button replaces all selected cards in the player's hand with new cards from the deck.
- The Stand button signals to the dealer that the player wants to keep all the cards in the dealt hand.
- The Reset button restarts the game with a fresh pot, resetting the bank value to $500.
- The Bet selection list places the bet before the next hand is dealt.

The Deal, Draw, and Stand buttons and the Bet selection list will be turned on and off depending on the state of the game. Both the Draw and Stand buttons are disabled before the deal so that a player can only draw new cards or stand pat after a hand has been dealt. The Deal button and Bet selection list are disabled while the current hand is in play so that a new hand cannot be dealt and a bet cannot be placed until play on the current hand is completed.

To disable and enable these buttons nest the following functions within the playDrawPoker() function:

```
function disableObj(obj) {
   obj.disabled = true;
   obj.style.opacity = 0.25;
}

function enableObj(obj) {
   obj.disabled = false;
   obj.style.opacity = 1;
}
```

In addition to disabling or enabling the selected object, the functions also set the opacity style so that disabled objects are semi-transparent on the page. By nesting the functions, you limit their use to within the playDrawPoker() function, ensuring that the functions do not conflict with functions or variables defined in other scripts that this website might employ.

To nest the functions within the playDrawPoker() function:

▶ **1.** Within the playDrawPoker() function, insert the following nested functions:

```
// Disable Poker Button
function disableObj(obj) {
   obj.disabled = true;
   obj.style.opacity = 0.25;
}

// Enable Poker Button
function enableObj(obj) {
   obj.disabled = false;
   obj.style.opacity = 1;
}
```

Figure 14-3 highlights the code for the nested functions.

Figure 14-3	Creating nested functions

```
function playDrawPoker() {
   var dealButton = document.getElementById("dealB");
   var drawButton = document.getElementById("drawB");
   var standButton = document.getElementById("standB");
   var resetButton = document.getElementById("resetB");
   var handValueText = document.getElementById("handValue");
   var betSelection = document.getElementById("bet");
   var bankBox = document.getElementById("bank");

   // Disable Poker Button
   function disableObj(obj) {
      obj.disabled = true;
      obj.style.opacity = 0.25;
   }

   // Enable Poker Button
   function enableObj(obj) {
      obj.disabled = false;
      obj.style.opacity = 1;
   }
}
```

function that disables a button on the form

makes the button semi-transparent

function that enables a button on the form

makes the button opaque

2. Save your changes to the file.

Next, use the disableObj() and enableObj() functions to turn off and on the poker table buttons. When a new hand is ready to be dealt, only the Deal button and the Bet selection list should be enabled. After the hand has been dealt, those two objects should be disabled and only the Draw and Stand buttons should be enabled. Add event listeners to the playDrawPoker() function now.

To add event listeners to the playDrawPoker() function:

1. Directly before the nested disableObj() function, insert the following command to enable only the Draw and Stand buttons after the user clicks the Deal button:

```
// Enable the Draw and Stand buttons after the deal
dealButton.addEventListener("click", function() {
   disableObj(dealButton);
   disableObj(betSelection);
   enableObj(drawButton);
   enableObj(standButton);
});
```

2. After the event listener for the `click` event, add the following commands to enable only the Deal button and the Bet selection list after the user has either drawn new cards or stood pat on the hand, thus ending the current play of the hand:

```
// Enable the Deal and Bet options when the current hand ends
drawButton.addEventListener("click", function() {
    enableObj(dealButton);
    enableObj(betSelection);
    disableObj(drawButton);
    disableObj(standButton);
});
standButton.addEventListener("click", function() {
    enableObj(dealButton);
    enableObj(betSelection);
    disableObj(drawButton);
    disableObj(standButton);
});
```

Figure 14-4 highlights the event listeners in the function.

Figure 14-4	Enabling and disabling the poker buttons

```
var betSelection = document.getElementById("bet");
var bankBox = document.getElementById("bank");

// Enable the Draw and Stand buttons after the deal
dealButton.addEventListener("click", function() {
    disableObj(dealButton);
    disableObj(betSelection);
    enableObj(drawButton);
    enableObj(standButton);
});

// Enable the Deal and Bet options when the current hand ends
drawButton.addEventListener("click", function() {
    enableObj(dealButton);
    enableObj(betSelection);
    disableObj(drawButton);
    disableObj(standButton);
});
standButton.addEventListener("click", function() {
    enableObj(dealButton);
    enableObj(betSelection);
    disableObj(drawButton);
    disableObj(standButton);
});
```

clicking the Deal button starts a new hand and enables only the Draw and Stand buttons

clicking the Draw or Stand buttons ends the current hand and enables only the Deal button and the Bet selection list

3. Save your changes to the file and then reload **ag_poker.html** in your web browser.

4. Click the **Deal** button and verify that the Deal button and Bet selection list are disabled, allowing the user only the options of clicking the Draw or Stand buttons. (*Note*: Code for the Reset button will be added later.)

5. Click the **Draw** button and **Stand** buttons when they are enabled and verify that they re-enable the Deal button and the Bet selection list.

Now that you have defined the behavior of the Deal, Draw, and Stand buttons and the Bet selection list, you will begin working on designing custom objects, properties, and methods for the poker game.

Executable Code and the eval() Function

JavaScript supports three types of executable code: global code, function code, and eval code. Each type of code has a different scope and is executed in a different manner. **Global code** is any code that lies outside of a function and is automatically executed when encountered by the browser. As the name implies, global code has global scope. **Function code** is any code placed within a function and must be called to be executed. As you have seen, function code can be either local or global in scope, depending on whether the function is nested within another function. **Eval code** is any code that is passed to the browser using the `eval()` function. The scope of eval code is limited within the `eval()` function itself. The syntax of the eval() function is

```
eval(string)
```

where *string* is a text string containing executable code. The `eval()` function is used whenever an application needs to create executable code during run time, usually in response to an action by the user or another application. For example, the following code employs the `eval()` function to display the value of a variable specified by the user through a prompt dialog box:

```
var varName = prompt("Enter a variable name");
var runCmd = "alert(" + varName + ")";
eval(runCmd);
```

In this code, the user is prompted for a variable name, which is stored in the varName variable. The text of the `alert()` method is then stored in the runCmd variable. Finally, the `eval()` function is called to run the stored JavaScript command, running the `alert()` method with the text string specified in the runCmd variable.

The `eval()` function should be used with caution because it opens an application to untested code retrieved from outside sources. Many programmers refuse to use the `eval()` function because of this security risk and argue that any tasks done with the `eval()` function could be done just as well with more secure JavaScript methods. However, you may see it employed in various legacy websites and program code.

Introducing Custom Objects

As you have seen, JavaScript is an object-based programming language that involves working with the properties and methods associated with objects. There are three kinds of JavaScript objects. **Native objects,** such as the `Date` or `Array` objects, are part of the JavaScript language. **Host objects** are objects provided by the browser for use in interacting with the web document and browser, such as the `window`, `document`, or `form` objects. **Custom objects**, also known as **user-defined objects**, are objects created by the user for specific programming tasks.

For the poker game application, you will create the following four custom objects, representing objects commonly found in card games:

- A poker game object containing information about the card game being played.
- A poker deck object containing information about the cards used in the game.
- A poker hand object containing information about the hand played by the user in the game.
- Poker card objects containing information about the individual cards in the poker hand.

A custom object can be defined in one of three ways: 1) creating it as an object literal, 2) using an object constructor, or 3) applying the object `create()` method. In this session, you will explore how to create objects using object literals.

Object Literals

To create a custom object as an object literal, you store the properties of the object within a comma-separated list of *name:value* pairs enclosed within a set of curly braces. The general syntax of the object literal is

```
var objName = {
    name1: value1,
    name2: value2,
    ...
};
```

where *objName* is the name of the object, *name1*, *name2*, and so on are the names associated with that object, and *value1*, *value2*, and so on are the values assigned to those names. The following code creates an object named cardGame

```
var cardGame = {
    title: "Draw Poker",
    createdBy: "Bob Voiklund",
    yearCreated: 2018,
    lastRevised: null,
    programmers: ["Tom Devlan", "Chanda Bhasin"]
};
```

Each *name:value* pair contains a property and property value associated with the object. The cardGame object has five properties: title, createdBy, yearCreated, lastRevised, and programmers. Note that properties can contain any JavaScript data type, including other objects. For example, the programmers property of the cardGame object contains an `Array` object.

One object can be nested within another. In the following code, the creators object is nested within the cardGame object.

```
var cardGame = {
    title: "Draw Poker",
    creators: {
        supervisor: "Bob Voiklund",
        programmers: programmers: ["Tom Devlan", "Chanda Bhasin"]
    }
    yearCreated: 2018,
    lastRevised: null
};
```

TIP

A property can be assigned the `null` value if no data value has been set yet.

Bob asks you to create a pokerGame object containing properties and methods associated with the draw poker game. Initially, the object will have two properties: the currentBank property storing the amount currently in the bank and the currentBet property storing the size of the current bet. You will set the initial values of both properties to `null`. Bob wants the pokerGame object placed in the ag_cards.js file so that it can be used by other card games that will be posted on the Arthur's Games website.

To create the pokerGame object:

▶ **1.** Go to the **ag_cards.js** file in your editor.

2. Directly below the comment section, insert the following code to create the pokerGame object.

```
/*     The pokerGame Object   */
var pokerGame = {
    currentBank: null,
    currentBet: null
};
```

The code for the pokerGame object is displayed in Figure 14-5.

Figure 14-5	Creating the pokerGame object literal

3. Save your changes to the file.

Dot Operators and Bracket Notation

Accessing a custom object property uses the by-now familiar *object.property* notation involving the **dot operator**, connecting the object name with an object property. However, object properties can also be written using the following **bracket notation**

```
object["property"]
```

where *object* is the object name and *property* is the object property. Thus, the value of the currentBank property of the pokerGame object could be set with either

```
pokerGame.currentBank = 500;
```

or

```
pokerGame["currentBank"] = 500;
```

You saw this dot operator syntax in Tutorial 13 where form elements could be referenced using either document.forms.*id* or document.forms["*id*"] where *id* is the ID of the form element. In both cases, *id* is a property of the form, expressed either with a dot operator or in bracket notation. You will have an opportunity to use the bracket notation in Session 14-3 of this tutorial.

Data Storage with Associative Arrays

INSIGHT

The object literal structure is often referred to as an **associative array** in which a group of items is referenced not by an array index but by a descriptive text string known as a **key**. The general structure is

```
var array = {key1:value1, key2:value2, …}
```

where *key1*, *key2*, and so on are the associate array keys and *value1*, *value2*, and so on are the values for each key. For example, the following associative array defines several key values for describing the properties of an employee:

```
var employee = {
   name: "Robert Voiklund",
   position: "manager",
   email: "rvoiklund@example.com"
};
```

To reference the employee's e-mail address, use the bracket notation `employee["email"]` with the key value "email" rather than an array index. Other key values would be referenced in a similar way.

Despite the term, associative arrays are *not* part of the class of `Array` objects and do not support JavaScript's `Array` object properties and methods. For example, there is no `length` property for associative arrays that would return the number of items within the object nor is there a `sort()` method for sorting the associative array's contents.

TIP

Associate arrays are called hash tables or hashes in other programming languages such as C# or Perl.

For the Draw Poker game, Bob wants you to set the values of the currentBank and currentBet properties of the pokerGame object to 500 and 25 respectively. Set these values now using the dot operator format.

To set the currentBank and currentBet properties:

1. Return to the **ag_poker.js** file in your editor and go to the playDrawPoker() function.

2. Directly below the command that defines the bankBox variable, add the following commands to set the value of the currentBank and currentBet properties of the pokerGame object:

   ```
   // Set the initial values of the pokerGame object
   pokerGame.currentBank = 500;
   pokerGame.currentBet = 25;
   ```

3. Add the following command to display the value of currentBank property in the bankBox element:

   ```
   bankBox.value = pokerGame.currentBank;
   ```

4. Finally, the value of the currentBet property should be updated every time the user changes the selected option in the Bet selection list. Add the following event listener to change the value of the currentBet property:

   ```
   betSelection.onchange = function(e) {
      pokerGame.currentBet =
   parseInt(e.target.options[e.target.selectedIndex].value);
   };
   ```

Figure 14-6 describes the newly added code.

Figure 14-6	Setting values for the currentBank and currentBet properties

references the property using the dot operator notation

runs the anonymous function when the Bet selection value is changed

```
var betSelection = document.getElementById("bet");
var bankBox = document.getElementById("bank");

// Set the initial values of the pokerGame object
pokerGame.currentBank = 500;
pokerGame.currentBet = 25;

bankBox.value = pokerGame.currentBank;
betSelection.onchange = function(e) {
   pokerGame.currentBet = parseInt(e.target.options[e.target.selectedIndex].value);
};
```

sets the bank value to the value of the currentBank property

uses the parseInt() function to change the text value to an integer

returns the text value of the selected item in the Bet selection list

5. Save your changes to the file and then reload **ag_poker.html** in your browser. Verify that a bank value of 500 appears in the BANK box and a value of 25 appears in the BET box on the page.

Trouble? If the page doesn't work, check your code against that shown in Figure 14-5 and Figure 14-6.

Next, you will add custom methods to the pokerGame object.

PROSKILLS

Written Communication: Dot Operators vs Bracket Notation

You can reference an object property using either the dot operator form *object.property* or the bracket notation form *object*[*"property"*]. Why the two approaches? The dot operator form is easier to read and interpret, however, it is limited because it is not able to handle properties referenced as variables. For example, the following employee object contains the name and position properties:

```
var employee = {name: "Robert Voiklund",
                position: "manager"}
```

If you wished to pick which employee property to view using the following prompt dialog box

```
var empInfo = prompt("Specify an employee property");
```

you could not retrieve the specified property using the following expression

```
employee.empInfo
```

because there is no empInfo property associated with the employee object. However, because property names are treated as text strings in bracket notation, you could apply the following expression to retrieve the desired employee information:

```
employee[empInfo]
```

If the empInfo variable equals "position", then this expression would be equivalent to

```
employee["position"]
```

and would return the text string, "manager".

Creating a Custom Method

Methods are added to a custom object by including a function name and its commands as the following *name:value* pair

```
var objName = {
    method: function() {
        commands
    }
}
```

where `method` is the name of the method and `commands` are commands run by the method. Thus, the following code adds the placeBet() method to the pokerDeck object:

```
var pokerDeck = {
    currentBank: null,
    currentBet: null,
    placeBet: function() {
        this.currentBank -= this.currentBet;
        return currentBank;
    }
}
```

TIP

For a discussion of the -= assignment operator, see Figure 9-25.

The placeBet() method uses the `this` keyword to reference the current object, which, in this case, is the pokerDeck object itself. The `-=` assignment operator is used to subtract the value of the current bet from the current bank value. The method concludes by returning the value of the currentBank property.

To apply the placeBet() method to the pokerDeck object, run the expression

```
pokerDeck.placeBet()
```

and whatever value has been stored in the currentBet property will be subtracted from the value of currentBank and the new bank value will be returned by the method.

REFERENCE

Creating an Object Literal

- To define an object as an object literal, use the structure

```
var objName = {
    property: value,
    ...
    method: function() {
        commands
    }
};
```

where *objName* is the name of the object, *property* is the name of an object property, *value* is the property's value, and *method* is the name of a method associated with the object.
- To reference an object property, use either *objName*.*property* or *objName*["*property*"].
- To call an object method, apply *objName*.*method*().

Add the placeBet() method to the pokerGame object to reduce the bank value by the size of the bet.

To define the placeBet()methods:

1. Return to the **ag_cards.js** file in your editor.

2. Go to the code for the pokerGame object and add a **,** (comma) to the end of the line defining the currentBet property.

3. Add the following code defining the placeBet() method:

```
placeBet: function() {
    this.currentBank -= this.currentBet;
    return this.currentBank;
}
```

Figure 14-7 describes the code for the newly added placeBet() method for the pokerGame object.

Figure 14-7   Inserting the placeBet() method

the comma separates the property from the method that follows

```
/*     The pokerGame Object   */
var pokerGame = {
    currentBank: null,
    currentBet: null,

    placeBet: function() {
        this.currentBank -= this.currentBet;
        return this.currentBank;
    }
};
```

the this keyword references the current object (pokerGame)

the placeBet() method reduces the bank by the size of the bet

4. Save your changes to the file.

The placeBet() method should be run whenever the user clicks the Deal button, which initiates a new poker hand only if the current bank has sufficient funds to cover the bet. Add an `if-else` condition to the event listener for the Deal button that tests whether the bet can be placed and if so, reduces the bank value in response.

To apply the placeBet() method:

1. Return to the **ag_poker.js** file in your editor.

2. At the top of the anonymous function for the `click` event of the Deal button, insert the following `if` condition

```
if (pokerGame.currentBank >= pokerGame.currentBet) {
```

3. Indent the next 4 lines that enable or disable the buttons on the poker game page.

4. On the line after the four lines you just indented, add the following statement to change the value in the bank based on the size of the bet placed by the user.

```
bankBox.value = pokerGame.placeBet();
```

5. Complete the `if-else` structure by adding the following code covering the condition when the size of the bet exceeds the bank value.

```
} else {
    alert("Reduce the size of your bet");
}
```

Figure 14-8 shows the newly added code to the anonymous function.

Figure 14-8   Testing whether the bank can cover the size of the bet

```
// Enable the Draw and Stand buttons after the deal
dealButton.addEventListener("click", function() {
    if (pokerGame.currentBank >= pokerGame.currentBet) {
        disableObj(dealButton);
        disableObj(betSelection);
        enableObj(drawButton);
        enableObj(standButton);
        bankBox.value = pokerGame.placeBet();
    } else {
        alert("Reduce the size of your bet");
    }
});
```

tests whether the bank covers the size of the bet

after the Deal button is clicked, reduces the bank by the size of the bet

displays a message if the bank can't cover the bet

6. Save your changes to the file and then reload **ag_poker.html** in your browser.

7. Select **75** from the Bet selection list and click the **Deal** button. Verify the bank is reduced to 425. See Figure 14-9.

Figure 14-9   Changing the bank value

... the bank is reduced by the size of the bet

BANK
425

every time the Deal button is clicked ...

Draw   Stand   Reset

BET

bet size

Source: Howard Pyle/Public Domain; © Courtesy Patrick Carey

8. Click either the **Draw** or **Stand** buttons to verify that the Deal button and Bet selection list are re-enabled, ready for the next game hand and bet.

9. Continue to click the **Deal** button followed by the **Draw** or **Stand** button to reduce the bank amount, verifying that the browser displays an alert dialog box when the user attempts to deal a new hand with a bank that cannot cover the size of the bet.

The remaining button on the Draw Poker page is the Reset button, which restarts the game with a fresh bankroll. Add an event listener for this button to restore the bank value to 500 and enable the Deal button and Bet selection list in preparation for a new game.

To create an event listener for the Reset button:

▶ 1. Return to the **ag_poker.js** file in your editor.

▶ 2. Directly above the event listener for the Deal button, insert the following code:

```
//Restart the game when the Reset button is clicked
resetButton.addEventListener("click", function() {
   pokerGame.currentBank = 500;
   bankBox.value = pokerGame.currentBank;
   enableObj(dealButton);
   enableObj(betSelection);
   disableObj(drawButton);
   disableObj(standButton);
});
```

The code for the event listener is described in Figure 14-10.

Figure 14-10 **Resetting the game**

runs the anonymous function when the Reset button is clicked

```
};

// Restart the game when the Reset button is clicked
resetButton.addEventListener("click", function() {
   pokerGame.currentBank = 500;
   bankBox.value = pokerGame.currentBank;
   enableObj(dealButton);
   enableObj(betSelection);
   disableObj(drawButton);
   disableObj(standButton);
});

// Enable the Draw and Stand buttons after the deal
dealButton.addEventListener("click", function() {
```

changes the bank value to 500

enables only the Deal button and the Bet selection list

▶ 3. Save your changes to the file and reload **ag_poker.html** in your browser.

▶ 4. Click the **Deal** and **Draw** button to simulate betting that would be done in a game. Verify that when you click the **Reset** button, the bank value returns to 500 and only the Deal and Reset buttons and the Bet selection list are enabled.

You have completed the initial work on programming the Draw Poker game by creating a custom object for the game and adding event listeners for the game buttons. In the next session, you will study how to create object classes for the cards and hands in the poker deck.

REVIEW

Session 14.1 Quick Check

1. What is the scope of a nested function?
2. What are three types of objects supported by JavaScript?
3. Provide code to create a custom object named pokerCard containing the suit property with a value of "Spades" and a rank property with a value of "King".
4. Provide the code to add the custom dropRank() method to the pokerCard object that changes the value of the rank property to "Queen". (*Hint*: Create the dropRank() function and use the `this` keyword to reference the current object.)
5. Provide code to return the value of the rank property of the pokerCard object in bracket notation.
6. When would you use bracket notation in place of the dot operator with object properties?
7. What is the difference between associative arrays and index arrays?
8. Why are associative arrays not true arrays in JavaScript?

Session 14.2 Visual Overview:

A **constructor function** defines the properties and methods associated with the object type or class.

These are parameters used in the construction of pokerCard objects.

These are the properties associated with the pokerCard class of objects.

The cardImage() method returns the name of the image file for the pokerCard object.

```
function pokerCard(cardSuit, cardRank) {
    this.suit = cardSuit;
    this.rank = cardRank;
    this.rankValue = null;
}
```

A **prototype** is a template object containing all of the properties and methods associated with the object's class.

```
pokerCard.prototype.cardImage = function() {
    var suitAbbr = this.suit.substring(0, 1).toLowerCase();
    return suitAbbr + this.rankValue + ".png";
};
```

The replaceFromDeck() method replaces the pokerCard object with the first card from the cards array in the pokerDeck object.

```
pokerCard.prototype.replaceFromDeck = function(pokerDeck) {
    this.suit = pokerDeck.cards[0].suit;
    this.rank = pokerDeck.cards[0].rank;
    this.rankValue = pokerDeck.cards[0].rankValue;
    pokerDeck.cards.shift();
}
```

This code calls the replaceFromDeck() method for the current card in the user's hand.

```
// Enable the Deal and Bet options when the current hand ends
drawButton.addEventListener("click", function() {

    // Replace the cards selected for discarding
    for (var i = 0; i < cardImages.length; i++) {
        if (cardImages[i].discard) {
            myHand.cards[i].replaceFromDeck(myDeck);
            cardImages[i].src = myHand.cards[i].cardImage();
            cardImages[i].discard = false;
        }
    }
});
```

This code calls the cardImage() method for the current card in the user's hand.

Object Classes and Prototypes

A new hand is dealt with 5 cards removed from the poker deck.

Cards selected for removal from the hand are turned over.

Selected cards are replaced by clicking the Draw button.

New cards from the poker deck replace the selected cards.

Source: Howard Pyle/Public Domain; Copyright © 1997 John Fitzgibbon; Copyright © 1997 Jochen Tuchbreiter; Copyright © 1998 Markus F.X.J. Oberhumer; © Courtesy Patrick Carey

Defining an Object Type

In the last session, you created the pokerGame object as an object literal. In this session, you will explore how to create objects that belong to object types, sharing common properties and methods.

Creating an Object with the new Operator

In previous tutorials, you created native objects using the new operator. For example, you can create an Array object with the expression

```
var array = new Array();
```

or a regular expression object with the expression:

```
var regex = new RegExp();
```

To create a custom object using the new operator, apply the following commands

```
var objName = new Object();
object.property = value;
object.method = function() {
   commands
};
```

where *objName* is the object name, *property* is a property defined for that object, and *method* is a method assigned to that object. For example, the following code defines the pokerGame object and its properties and methods using the new Object() operator:

```
var pokerGame = new Object();
pokerGame.currentBank = null;
pokerGame.currentBet = null;
pokerGame.placeBet = function() {
   this.currentBank -= this.currentBet;
   return this.currentBank;
};
```

The new Object() statement is equivalent to an empty object literal {} in that it creates an object devoid of properties and methods. Any properties or methods must be added in separate JavaScript statements, as in the example above.

The biggest limitation of an object created either as an object literal or with the new Object() command is that the object is not reusable. Any custom properties or methods apply to that object and no others.

Constructor Functions

The power of object-based programming lies in creating objects that belong to a specific type or class with shared properties and methods. To create such object classes, you apply a function known as an object constructor or a constructor that defines the properties and methods associated with the object type. A specific object that is based on an object class is known as an **object instance** or **instance**. Creating an object instance based on an object class is known as **instantiating** an object. For example, when you created an array object using the new Array() command you were instantiating an object based on the properties and methods associated with the class of Array objects.

Object constructors are defined with the following constructor function

```
function objClass(parameters) {
   this.prop1 = value1;
   this.prop2 = value2;
   ...
   this.method1 = function1;
   this.method2 = function2;
   ...
}
```

where *objClass* is the name of the object class; *parameters* are the parameters used by the constructor function; *prop1*, *prop2*, and so on are the properties associated with that object class; and *method1*, *method2*, and so on are the methods associated with that object class. The `this` keyword in this context refers to any object instance of this particular object class.

For example, the constructor function for an object class of poker cards might appear as follows:

```
function pokerCard(cardSuit, cardRank) {
   this.suit = cardSuit;
   this.rank = cardRank;
   this.rankValue = null;
   this.showCard() function() {
      return "Your card is a " + this.rank + " of " + this.suit;
   }
}
```

The suit and rank properties will store the suit and rank of the poker card that is created based on the values specified by the cardSuit and cardRank parameters. The rankValue property is used to store the numeric value of the card's rank. The showCard() function returns a text string describing the card. The `this` keyword refers to objects of the pokerCard class.

Once the constructor function for the object class is defined, instances of the object are created with the command

```
var objInstance = new objClass(parameters);
```

where *objInstance* is a specific instance of the object, *objClass* is the object class as defined by the constructor function, and *parameters* are the values of any parameters included in the constructor function. Thus, the following code creates two instances of the class of pokerCard objects, one for the king of hearts and the other for the seven of spades:

```
var card1 = new pokerCard("Hearts", "King");
card1.rankValue = 13;
var card2 = new pokerCard("Spades", "7");
card2.rankValue = 7;
```

The rankValue property is assigned directly based on the rankValue of an Ace = 14, King = 13, Queen = 12, and so on.

The showCard() method is attached to both object instances so that the command

```
card1.showCard()
```

returns the text string "Your card is a King of Hearts".

Defining and Instantiating an Object Class

- To define a class of objects, use the constructor function

```
function objClass(parameters) {
   this.prop1 = value1;
   this.prop2 = value2;
   …

   this.method1 = function1;
   this.method2 = function2;
   …
}
```

where *objClass* is the name of the object class; *parameters* are the parameters associated with the class; *prop1*, *prop2*, and so on are the object properties; and *method1*, *method2*, and so on are the object methods.

- To instantiate an object from an object class, apply

```
var objInstance = new objClass(parameters);
```

where *objInstance* is a specific instance of the object.

Create a constructor class for poker cards in the ag_cards.js file that defines properties for the card suit, card rank, and value of the card.

To create an object constructor for poker cards:

1. If you took a break after the previous session, make sure the **ag_cards.js** file is open in your editor.

2. Below the object literal for the pokerGame object, insert the following constructor for the class of poker card objects:

```
/* Constructor function for poker cards */
function pokerCard(cardSuit, cardRank) {
   this.suit = cardSuit;
   this.rank = cardRank;
   this.rankValue = null;
}
```

Figure 14-11 describes the code in the constructor function.

Figure 14-11   **Constructor function for pokerCard object class**

defines the parameters
for the object class

suit property of the
pokerCard class

rank property of the
pokerCard class

```
};

/* Constructor function for poker cards */
function pokerCard(cardSuit, cardRank) {
    this.suit = cardSuit;
    this.rank = cardRank;
    this.rankValue = null;
}
```

rankValue property stores
the value of the card rank

3. Save your changes to the file.

Next, you will create an object class for an entire deck of cards.

Combining Object Classes

One object class can include objects defined in other classes. For the Draw Poker game, you will create an object class named pokerDeck, which itself contains an array of 52 objects from the pokerCard class. The code for the constructor function follows:

```
function pokerDeck() {
    this.cards = new Array(52);

    var suits = ["Clubs", "Diamonds", "Hearts", "Spades"];
    var ranks = ["2", "3", "4", "5", "6",
                 "7", "8", "9", "10",
                 "Jack", "Queen", "King", "Ace"];

    var cardCount = 0;
    for (var i = 0; i < 4; i++) {
        for (var j = 0; j < 13; j++) {
            this.cards[cardCount] = new pokerCard(suits[i], ranks[j]);
            this.cards[cardCount].rankValue = j+2;
            cardCount++;
        }
    }
}
```

To instantiate an object from the pokerDeck class, create a variable named "myDeck" using the following command:

```
var myDeck = new pokerDeck();
```

Objects created in the pokerDeck class have a single property named "cards", which is the array of 52 pokerCard objects populated with a `for` loop going through all possible combinations of suits and ranks. The array of pokerCard objects for the myDeck variable is referenced with the expression:

```
myDeck.cards
```

The cards array contains the following objects:

```
[
   {suit: "Clubs", rank: "2", rankValue: 2},
   {suit: "Clubs", rank: "3", rankValue: 3},
   {suit: "Clubs", rank: "4", rankValue: 4},
   {suit: "Clubs", rank: "5", rankValue: 5},
   ...
   {suit: "Spades", rank: "Ace", rankValue: 14}
]
```

Each card in the deck can be retrieved by referencing an index in the cards array. The following expression retrieves the fourth card from the deck

```
myDeck.cards[4]
```

which, in this case, is the pokerCard object for the 5 of Clubs with a rank value of 5.

Add the constructor function for the pokerDeck object class to the ag_cards.js file.

To create an object constructor for poker cards:

1. Below the constructor function for the pokerCard object class in the ag_cards.js file, insert the following constructor for the class of pokerDeck objects:

```
/* Constructor function for poker decks */
function pokerDeck() {
   this.cards = new Array(52);

   var suits = ["Clubs", "Diamonds", "Hearts", "Spades"];
   var ranks = ["2", "3", "4", "5", "6",
                "7", "8", "9", "10",
                "Jack", "Queen", "King", "Ace"];

   var cardCount = 0;
   for (var i = 0; i < 4; i++) {
      for (var j = 0; j < 13; j++) {
         this.cards[cardCount] = new pokerCard(suits[i],
   ranks[j]);
         this.cards[cardCount].rankValue = j+2;
         cardCount++;
      }
   }
}
```

Figure 4-12 describes the code in the constructor function for the pokerDeck object class.

Figure 14-12	Constructor function for pokerDeck object class

```
function pokerCard(cardSuit, cardRank) {
    this.suit = cardSuit;
    this.rank = cardRank;
    this.rankValue = null;
}

/* Constructor function for poker decks */
function pokerDeck() {
    this.cards = new Array(52);

    var suits = ["Clubs", "Diamonds", "Hearts", "Spades"];
    var ranks = ["2", "3", "4", "5", "6",
                 "7", "8", "9", "10",
                 "Jack", "Queen", "King", "Ace"];

    var cardCount = 0;
    for (var i = 0; i < 4; i++) {
        for (var j = 0; j < 13; j++) {
            this.cards[cardCount] = new pokerCard(suits[i], ranks[j]);
            this.cards[cardCount].rankValue = j+2;
            cardCount++;
        }
    }
}
```

defines the cards property containing an array of 52 items

defines arrays of card suits and ranks

loops through all possible combinations of suits and ranks

for each combination of suits and ranks, places a pokerCard object in the cards array

increases the cardCount variable by one each time through the nested loops

sets the rank value of each card in the deck

   2. Save your changes to the file.

Almost all card games require the deck of cards to be randomly sorted. You can add the following shuffle() method to the pokerDeck object class that randomizes the order of items in the cards array:

```
this.shuffle = function() {
    this.cards.sort(function() {
        return 0.5 - Math.random();
    });
};
```

The code uses the `sort()` method of Array objects with a compare function that returns a random arrangement of the array items. (See Chapter 10's *Performing a Random Shuffle* Insight box for more information on random sorting and using compare functions with the `sort()` method.)

Add the shuffle() method to the constructor function for the pokerDeck object class.

To add the shuffle() method to the pokerDeck object class:

   1. Within the constructor function for the pokerDeck object class in the ag_cards.js file, add the following code:

```
// Method to randomly sort the deck
this.shuffle = function() {
    this.cards.sort(function() {
        return 0.5 - Math.random();
    });
};
```

Figure 4-13 describes the code used in the shuffle() method.

| Figure 14-13 | Defining the shuffle() method for pokerDeck objects |

```
for (var i = 0; i < 4; i++) {
    for (var j = 0; j < 13; j++) {
        this.cards[cardCount] = new pokerCard(suits[i], ranks[j]);
        this.cards[cardCount].rankValue = j+2;
        cardCount++;
    }
}

// Method to randomly sort the deck
this.shuffle = function() {
    this.cards.sort(function() {
        return 0.5 - Math.random();
    });
};
}
```

defines the shuffle() method for the pokerDeck object class

compare function for the sort() method that returns array items in a randomly sorted order

2. Save your changes to the **ag_cards.js** file.

Create an instance of the pokerDeck object class and then apply the shuffle() method to randomly sort the contents of that deck.

To create an instance of the pokerDeck class:

1. Return to the **ag_poker.js** file in your editor.

2. Directly after the command that sets the initial value of the currentBet property of the pokerGame object to 25, insert the following command to create and shuffle a new deck of cards:

```
// Create a new deck of cards and shuffle it
var myDeck = new pokerDeck();
myDeck.shuffle();
```

3. You can view the contents of the myDeck object using the console feature of your browser debugger. Add the following command to place the myDeck contents in the debugger console:

```
console.log(myDeck);
```

Figure 14-14 describes the newly added code in the application.

Figure 14-14   Creating an instance of the pokerDeck object class

creates an instance of the pokerDeck object

randomly shuffles the contents of the cards array in the myDeck object

```
// Set the initial values of the pokerGame object
pokerGame.currentBank = 500;
pokerGame.currentBet = 25;

// Create a new deck of cards and shuffle it
var myDeck = new pokerDeck();
myDeck.shuffle();
console.log(myDeck);
```

displays the contents of the myDeck object in the browser's debugging console

▶ **4.** Save your changes to the file and then reopen the **ag_poker.html** file in your browser.

▶ **5.** Press the **F12** key or open your browser's debugger using your browser's menu commands and click the **Console** menu on the debugger menu.

▶ **6.** Click the **arrow** icons within the Console window, expanding the pokerDeck object to view the contents of the items in the cards array. Figure 14-15 shows the expanded version of the cards array in the developer pane of the Google Chrome browser with the first five cards (Queen of Clubs, Ace of Clubs, 7 of Hearts, Jack of Clubs, and 2 of Diamonds) randomly ordered by the shuffle() method.

Figure 14-15   Viewing the poker deck contents in the Google Chrome debugger console

Console window in the Google Chrome debugger

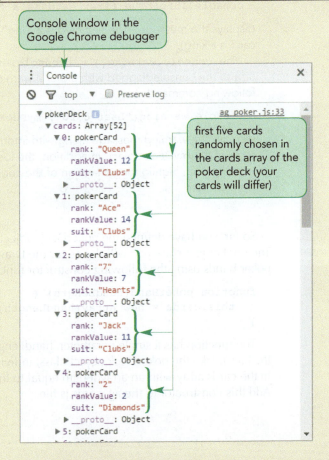

first five cards randomly chosen in the cards array of the poker deck (your cards will differ)

Trouble? Each browser is slightly different in how it accesses the Console window. If you are not sure how to access the Console window in your browser, check your browser's documentation or talk to your technical resource person.

7. Reload **ag_poker.html** in your browser several times and verify that the order of the cards in the cards array changes with each page load.

PROSKILLS

Problem Solving: Using the Console Object

The **console** is a host object used to access the contents of the browser's debugging console. While different browsers manage their debugging console differently, the JavaScript methods and properties for accessing the Console are shared by all browsers. To write information directly into the console, apply the following `console.log()` method

```
console.log(object1, object2, …);
```

where *object1*, *object2*, and so on are objects to be displayed in the console. For example, the following code displays both a text string object and information about the myDeck object.

```
console.log("The cards in myDeck are: ", myDeck);
```

Similar to the `console.log()` method is the `console.info()`, which sends a message to the console in which object information can be attached. The following `console.info` command

```
console.info("The first card is a " + myDeck.cards[0].rank);
```

displays the message "The first card is a King" in the console (assuming that the first card is a king).

The `console.warning()` and `console.error()` methods write object information to the console flagged with either a warning or an error icon. For example, the following command

```
console.warning("Last card", myDeck.cards[51]);
```

displays the warning message along with information about the last card in the cards array of the myDeck object. In addition, the location in the code is flagged with a warning icon, highlighting a section of the code that may need attention from the programmer.

So far, you have defined the pokerDeck object class and the pokerCard object class. The final object class you will define for the Draw Poker game is an object class for poker hands using the following constructor function:

```
function pokerHand(handLength) {
   this.cards = new Array(handLength);
}
```

The function has a single parameter, handLength, specifying the number of cards in the hand. Like the pokerDeck object class, individual pokerCard objects will be placed in the cards array with an array length equal to the value of the handLength parameter. Add this constructor to the ag_cards.js file.

To create the pokerHand constructor:

▶ **1.** Return to the **ag_cards.js** file in your editor.

▶ **2.** Directly below the constructor for the pokerDeck class, insert the following constructor function for poker hands:

```
/* Constructor function for poker hands */
function pokerHand(handLength) {
   this.cards = new Array(handLength);
}
```

Figure 14-16 describes the code to create an object instance using the constructor function.

| Figure 14-16 | Defining the constructor function for the pokerHand object class |

```
this.shuffle = function() {
   this.cards.sort(function() {
      return 0.5 - Math.random();
   });
};
}
```

parameter that defines the size of the poker hand

```
/* Constructor function for poker hands */
function pokerHand(handLength) {
   this.cards = new Array(handLength);
}
```

creates an array for the cards in the poker hand

▶ **3.** Save your changes to the file.

To insert pokerCard objects into the cards array, you will add a dealTo() method to the pokerDeck object class that moves poker cards from the cards array in a pokerDeck object to the cards array in the pokerHand object. The code for the dealTo() method is

```
function pokerDeck() {
   ...
   this.dealTo = function(pokerHand) {
      for (var i = 0; i < pokerHand.cards.length; i++) {
         pokerHand.cards[i] = this.cards.shift();
      }
   };
}
```

The dealTo() method has a single parameter, pokerHand, which references the pokerHand object that will receive the cards from the poker deck. The code then loops through the array of cards in the poker deck and uses the `shift()` method to remove the first items from the array and place them in the cards array of the poker hand. (For a discussion of the `shift()` method, see Figure 10-7 in Tutorial 10.) After the `for` loop, the size of the poker deck is reduced by the number of cards placed into the poker hand. The ability to mimic the actions of real-world objects is one attraction of object-based programming.

To create the dealTo() method:

1. Scroll up to the pokerDeck constructor in the ag_cards.js file.

2. Within the constructor function, add the following code to define the dealTo() method:

   ```
   // Method to deal cards from the deck into a poker hand
   this.dealTo = function(pokerHand) {
      for (var i = 0; i < pokerHand.cards.length; i++) {
         pokerHand.cards[i] = this.cards.shift();
      }
   };
   ```

   Figure 14-17 highlights the code for the dealTo() method.

Figure 14-17	Creating the dealTo() method for the pokerDeck object class

```
this.shuffle = function() {
   this.cards.sort(function() {
      return 0.5 - Math.random();
   });
};

// Method to deal cards from the deck into a poker hand
this.dealTo = function(pokerHand) {
   for (var i = 0; i < pokerHand.cards.length; i++) {
      pokerHand.cards[i] = this.cards.shift();
   }
};
}
```

parameter referencing a pokerHand object

loop through the cards array in the poker hand

the shift() method takes the first card from the pokerDeck object and inserts it into the cards array of the pokerHand object

3. Save your changes to the file.

Next, create an instance of the pokerHand object for the Draw Poker game and then deal cards into that hand when the Deal button is clicked. Because the deck size is reduced with each deal, verify that the deck contains at least 10 cards before dealing the hand; otherwise create a newly shuffled deck and deal the hand from that deck.

To create an instance of a pokerHand object:

1. Return to the **ag_poker.js** file in your editor and go to the playDrawPoker() function.

2. Directly below the `console.log()` command that displays the contents of the myDeck object, insert the following code to create an instance of a pokerHand object.

   ```
   // Create a pokerHand object
   var myHand = new pokerHand(5);
   ```

Figure 14-18 highlights the code to instantiate the pokerHand object.

| Figure 14-18 | Creating an instance of the pokerHand object class |

```
// Create a new deck of cards and shuffle it
var myDeck = new pokerDeck();
myDeck.shuffle();
console.log(myDeck);

// Create a pokerHand object
var myHand = new pokerHand(5);
```

number of cards
in the poker hand

3. Scroll down to the event listener for the Deal button. Directly after the command to apply the placeBet() method to the pokerGame object, add the following code:

```
// Deal cards into the poker hand after confirming
// there are at least 10 cards in the deck
if (myDeck.cards.length < 10) {
    myDeck = new pokerDeck();
    myDeck.shuffle();
}
myDeck.dealTo(myHand);
```

4. Add the following command to display the contents of the myDeck and myHand objects in the browsers debugger console window:

```
console.log(myDeck, myHand);
```

Figure 14-19 describes the newly added code in the file.

Figure 14-19	Dealing from the deck into the poker hand

```
// Enable the Draw and Stand buttons after the deal
dealButton.addEventListener("click", function() {
    if (pokerGame.currentBank >= pokerGame.currentBet) {
        disableObj(dealButton);
        disableObj(betSelection);
        enableObj(drawButton);
        enableObj(standButton);
        bankBox.value = pokerGame.placeBet();

        // Deal cards into the poker hand after confirming
        // there are at least 10 cards in the deck
        if (myDeck.cards.length < 10) {
            myDeck = new pokerDeck();
            myDeck.shuffle();
        }
        myDeck.dealTo(myHand);
        console.log(myDeck, myHand);

    } else {
        alert("Reduce the size of your bet");
    }
});
```

if there are less than 10 cards in the deck, creates a new shuffled deck

deals cards from the deck into the hand

displays the myDeck and myHand objects in the debugger console

5. Save your changes to the file and then reload **ag_poker.html** in your browser.

6. Click the **Deal** button.

7. Open the Console window on your browser's debugger and view the contents of the poker hand. Verify that there are five cards in the pokerHand and the length of the cards array in the pokerDeck has been reduced from 52 to 47 because the first five cards from pokerDeck object were placed in the pokerHand object. See Figure 14-20.

Figure 14-20	**Cards shifted from the poker deck to the poker hand**

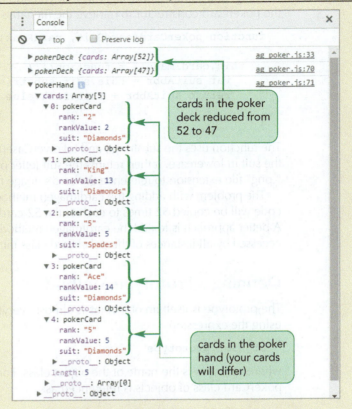

Trouble? If you are using the Firefox browser, you may have to reload the page rather than simply refresh the page to see the results in the debugger console.

8. Continue to click the **Draw** button followed by the **Deal** button, verifying that with each new deal, the number of cards in the poker deck is reduced by 5 cards. Further verify that when the size of the poker deck drops below 10 cards, a new full deck is used with the next deal of the cards.

9. Return to the **ag_poker.js** file in your editor and delete both occurrences of the `console.log()` method. Save your changes to the file.

The Draw Poker game doesn't yet show the actual cards in the page. You will correct this now by displaying the card images on the poker table. To accomplish this, you will use an object prototype.

Working with Object Prototypes

Every object has a prototype, which is a template for all the properties and methods associated with the object's class. If the constructor function is a machine to create object instances, then the prototype is the blueprint for the objects that are created. When an object is instantiated from a constructor function, it copies the properties and methods from the prototype into the new object.

However, this can result in inefficient use of memory and resources. For example, Bob wants a method that will retrieve the source file for each card's image. He has stored 52 separate image files for each card with the filename *svalue*.png, where *s* is the first letter of the card's suit and *value* is the card's rank value. Thus, the image file for the 7 of clubs is named c7.png, the image file for the king of diamonds is named d13.png, and so forth. Bob suggests that you add the following cardImage() method to the pokerCard constructor to retrieve the filename for a given card's image.

```
function pokerCard(cardSuit, cardRank) {
    ...
    this.cardImage() = function() {
      var suitAbbr = this.suit.substring(0, 1).toLowerCase();
      return suitAbbr + this.rankValue + ".png";
    }
}
```

The function uses the substring() and toLowerCase() methods to extract the first letter of the suit in lowercase. It then returns the suit letter plus the rank value appended with the ".png" file extension to reference the card's image file.

The problem with adding the cardImage() method to the constructor is that the same code will be copied 52 times to each of the 52 cards, wasting valuable system resources. A better approach is to add the cardImage() method to the prototype so that it can be accessed by all instances of the pokerCard class rather than copied to each instance.

Defining a Prototype Method

The prototype is itself an object (as is almost everything in JavaScript) and is referenced using the expression

   objName.prototype

where *objName* is the name of the object class. For example, the prototype for the pokerCard class of objects is referenced as:

   pokerCard.prototype

To add a method to a prototype, apply the command

   objName.prototype.*method* = *function*;

where *method* is the name of the method and *function* is the function applied by the method. To add the cardImage() method to the pokerCard prototype, apply the following command:

TIP

A general programming practice to ensure clean and efficient code is to add custom methods only to the object prototype.

```
pokerCard.prototype.cardImage = function() {
    var suitAbbr = this.suit.substring(0, 1).toLowerCase();
    return suitAbbr + this.rankValue + ".png";
};
```

Now, every instance of a pokerCard object will have access to this method.

REFERENCE

Working with Object Prototypes

- To reference the prototype of an object class, use

   objName.prototype

   where *objName* is the name of the object class.
- To add a method to an object prototype, use

   objName.prototype.*method* = *function*;

   where *method* is the name of the method and *function* is the function applied by the method.

Create the cardImage() method as a part of the pokerCard prototype in ag_cards.js file.

To add a method to an object prototype:

1. Return to the **ag_cards.js** file in your editor and scroll to the pokerCard constructor.

2. Directly below the pokerCard constructor, add the following code to define the cardImage() method:

```
/* Method to reference the image source file for a card */
pokerCard.prototype.cardImage = function() {
   var suitAbbr = this.suit.substring(0, 1).toLowerCase();
   return suitAbbr + this.rankValue + ".png";
};
```

Figure 4-21 describes the code for the cardImage() method.

Figure 14-21   Adding the cardImage() method to the prototype

```
function pokerCard(cardSuit, cardRank) {
   this.suit = cardSuit;
   this.rank = cardRank;
   this.rankValue = null;
}

/* Method to reference the image source file for a card */
pokerCard.prototype.cardImage = function() {
   var suitAbbr = this.suit.substring(0, 1).toLowerCase();
   return suitAbbr + this.rankValue + ".png";
};
```

prototype of the pokerCard object

retrieves the first character of the card suit in lowercase

returns the text string *svalue*.png where *s* is the suit letter and *value* is the rank value (2 – 14)

3. Save your changes to the file.

Native objects such as the `Array`, `Date`, and `string` objects can be extended with new methods added to those object's prototypes. For example, to make the shuffle() method, defined earlier for the pokerDeck object, available to all arrays, apply the following expression:

```
Array.prototype.shuffle = function() {
   this.sort(function() {
      return 0.5 - Math.random();
   });
}
```

Now, any array can be sorted in random order by applying the shuffle() method.

Bob has placed five transparent images, created with the ag_trans.gif file, on the card table in the Draw Poker page. Each image belongs to the cardImg class. Bob wants you to change the source of these five images to a card image from the user's hand. Apply the cardImage() method in the ag_poker.js file to display the image for each card.

To display the card images:

1. Return to the **ag_poker.js** file in your editor and go to the playDrawPoker() function.

2. Directly below the command that defines the bankBox variable, add the following code to create an object collection for all inline images in the cardImg class.

```
var cardImages = document.querySelectorAll("img.cardImg");
```

Figure 14-22 highlights the newly added code.

Figure 14-22	Creating the cardImages object collection

```
function playDrawPoker() {
   var dealButton = document.getElementById("dealB");
   var drawButton = document.getElementById("drawB");
   var standButton = document.getElementById("standB");
   var resetButton = document.getElementById("resetB");
   var handValueText = document.getElementById("handValue");
   var betSelection = document.getElementById("bet");
   var bankBox = document.getElementById("bank");
   var cardImages = document.querySelectorAll("img.cardImg");
```

references all images belonging to the cardImg class →

3. Scroll down to the event listener for the Deal button. Directly after the command to deal cards from the myDeck object into the myHand object, add the following code to change the source of the card images on the page.

```
// Display the card images on the table
for (var i = 0; i < cardImages.length; i++) {
   cardImages[i].src = myHand.cards[i].cardImage();
}
```

Figure 14-23 shows the code to display the card images.

Figure 14-23	Setting the image filenames for each card in the poker hand

```
      // Deal cards into the poker hand after confirming
      // there are at least 10 cards in the deck
      if (myDeck.cards.length < 10) {
         myDeck = new pokerDeck();
         myDeck.shuffle();
      }
      myDeck.dealTo(myHand);

      // Display the card images on the table
      for (var i = 0; i < cardImages.length; i++) {
         cardImages[i].src = myHand.cards[i].cardImage();
      }

   } else {
      alert("Reduce the size of your bet");
   }
});
```

applies the cardImage() method to each card, retrieving the name of the image file

loops through all of the images in the cardImages collection →

4. Save the file and then reload **ag_poker.html** in your browser.

5. Click the **Deal** button and verify that images of the poker hand are displayed on the poker table. See Figure 14-24.

| Figure 14-24 | Cards in the current poker hand |

card images for the current hand (your hand will vary)

Source: Howard Pyle/Public Domain; Copyright © 1997 John Fitzgibbon; Copyright © 1997 Jochen Tuchbreiter; Copyright © 1998 Markus F.X.J. Oberhumer; © Courtesy Patrick Carey

Trouble? If you are using the Firefox browser, you may have to reload the page rather than simply refreshing the page to see the results in the debugger console.

6. Repeatedly click the **Draw** button followed by the **Deal** button to deal a new hand, verifying a different hand appears on the table with each deal.

You programmed the actions of the Deal button. Next, you will program the actions of the Draw button. When a card is drawn, it is taken from the top of the deck, replacing the selected card on the table. To simulate the action of replacing a poker card with a drawn card, add the following replaceFromDeck() method to the pokerCard prototype.

```
pokerCard.prototype.replaceFromDeck = function(pokerDeck) {
    this.suit = pokerDeck.cards[0].suit;
    this.rank = pokerDeck.cards[0].rank;
    this.rankValue = pokerDeck.cards[0].rankValue;
    pokerDeck.cards.shift();
}
```

The method replaces the suit, rank, and rankValue from the pokerCard object with the corresponding values from the first card of the poker deck. The method then applies the shift() method to remove the first card from the cards array in the pokerDeck object.

To add replaceFromDeck() method to the pokerCard prototype:

1. Return to the **ag_cards.js** file in your editor.

2. Directly below the cardImage() method for the pokerCard object prototype add:

```
/* Method to replace a card with a one from the deck */
pokerCard.prototype.replaceFromDeck = function(pokerDeck) {
    this.suit = pokerDeck.cards[0].suit;
    this.rank = pokerDeck.cards[0].rank;
    this.rankValue = pokerDeck.cards[0].rankValue;
    pokerDeck.cards.shift();
}
```

Figure 14-25 describes the code in the method.

Figure 14-25   Creating the replaceFromDeck() method

```
pokerCard.prototype.cardImage = function() {
   var suitAbbr = this.suit.substring(0, 1).toLowerCase();
   return suitAbbr + this.rankValue + ".png";
};

/* Method to replace a card with a one from the deck */
pokerCard.prototype.replaceFromDeck = function(pokerDeck) {
   this.suit = pokerDeck.cards[0].suit;
   this.rank = pokerDeck.cards[0].rank;
   this.rankValue = pokerDeck.cards[0].rankValue;
   pokerDeck.cards.shift();
}
```

replaces the properties of the current card with the properties of the deck's first card

removes the first card from the poker deck

3. Save your changes to the file.

Players will choose which cards to replace by clicking the card image on the poker table. When the card image is clicked: 1) the card is turned facedown, showing the card back, and 2) the card is marked for being discarded by adding a discard property with a value of `true` to the inline image. The code to add event handlers to each card image follows:

```
for (var i = 0; i < cardImages.length; i++) {
   cardImages[i].index = i;
   cardImages[i].onclick = function(e) {
      if (e.target.discard !== true) {
         e.target.discard = true;
         e.target.src = "ag_cardback.png";
      } else {
         e.target.discard = false;
         e.target.src = myHand.cards[e.target.index].cardImage();
      }
   };
}
```

The code loops through every card image and adds an `index` property to the image object. The purpose of the index property is to store the position of the card image in the poker hand so that the event listener will access the correct card in the pokerHand object. With each click, the card image toggles between showing the card face and the card back and between setting the discard property to true and to false.

Nest this event handler within the event listener for the Deal button to allow users to choose which cards to discard once the hand has been dealt.

To create event listeners for each card image:

1. Return to the **ag_poker.js** file in your editor and scroll as needed to the event handler for the Deal button.

You must store the index number prior to the event listener because the counter variable is outside the scope of the event listener function.

2. Within the `for` loop that defines the card images for the dealt hand, add the following code:

```
// Event handler for each card image
cardImages[i].index = i;
cardImages[i].onclick = function(e) {
    if (e.target.discard !== true) {
        e.target.discard = true;
        e.target.src = "ag_cardback.png";
    } else {
        e.target.discard = false;
        e.target.src = myHand.cards[e.target.index].cardImage();
    }
};
```

Figure 14-26 describes the code for the card image event listeners.

| Figure 14-26 | Creating an event handler for each card image |

```
myDeck.dealTo(myHand);
// Display the card images on the table
for (var i = 0; i < cardImages.length; i++) {
    cardImages[i].src = myHand.cards[i].cardImage();

    // Event handler for each card image
    cardImages[i].index = i;
    cardImages[i].onclick = function(e) {
        if (e.target.discard !== true) {
            e.target.discard = true;
            e.target.src = "ag_cardback.png";
        } else {
            e.target.discard = false;
            e.target.src = myHand.cards[e.target.index].cardImage();
        }
    };
}
```

stores the index of the current card image

event handler handles the click event on the card image

if the card is not marked to be discarded, marks it to be discarded and changes the image to the card back

if the card is marked to be discarded, marks it not to be discarded and changes the image to the card front

3. Save your changes to the file and then reload **ag_poker.html** in your browser. Click each of the card images and verify that each image toggles between the card face and the card back. See Figure 14-27.

| Figure 14-27 | Marking cards to be discarded |

cards marked to be discarded

After the player has selected the cards to be discarded, clicking the Draw button replaces the selected cards with new cards from the top of the deck. Because the player is allowed only one round of discards, edit the event listener for the Draw button to replace the selected cards and then remove the event handler for the cards shown in the hand.

To replace the discarded cards:

1. Return to the **ag_poker.js** file in your editor and scroll down to the event listener for the Draw button.

2. Within the event listener, add the following code:

```
// Replace the cards selected for discarding
for (var i = 0; i < cardImages.length; i++) {
  if (cardImages[i].discard) {
    myHand.cards[i].replaceFromDeck(myDeck);
    cardImages[i].src = myHand.cards[i].cardImage();
    cardImages[i].discard = false;
  }
  cardImages[i].onclick = null;
}
```

Figure 14-28 describes the new code in the event listener.

Figure 14-28	Discarding cards when the Draw button is clicked

```
// Enable the Deal and Bet options when the current hand ends
drawButton.addEventListener("click", function() {
    enableObj(dealButton);
    enableObj(betSelection);
    disableObj(drawButton);
    disableObj(standButton);

    // Replace the cards selected for discarding
    for (var i = 0; i < cardImages.length; i++) {
        if (cardImages[i].discard) {
            myHand.cards[i].replaceFromDeck(myDeck);
            cardImages[i].src = myHand.cards[i].cardImage();
            cardImages[i].discard = false;
        }
        cardImages[i].onclick = null;
    }
});
```

tests whether the card is selected to be discarded

replaces the card with the next card from the deck

changes the card image for the new card

loops through every card image

marks the card as no longer to be discarded

removes the event handler for every card in the hand

3. Save your changes to the file and then reload **ag_poker.html** in your browser. Click the **Deal** button to deal a new hand and then click one or more cards to select for discarding. Click the **Draw** button to replace the selected cards with new cards from the top of the deck. See Figure 14-29.

Figure 14-29   **New cards drawn from the deck**

original hand

cards selected to be discarded

click the Draw button to replace the selected cards

new cards replace the discarded cards

click the Deal button to start a new hand

Source: Howard Pyle/Public Domain; Copyright © 1997 John Fitzgibbon; Copyright © 1997 Jochen Tuchbreiter; Copyright © 1998 Markus F.X.J. Oberhumer; © Courtesy Patrick Carey

Understanding Public, Private, and Privileged Methods

In developing methods for custom objects, you need to decide whether those methods are public, private, or privileged. A **public method** is defined for the object prototype and may be called outside of the object. The cardImage() method you developed in this session is an example of a public method.

A **private method** is a method that is accessible only within the object itself. The following code shows an example of a private method used within the pokerCard constructor:

```
function pokerCard() {
   function getFilename() {
      var fileName = this.suit.substring(0,1);
      if (this.rank == "10") {
         fileName += "10";
      } else {
         fileName += this.rank.substring(0,1);
         return fileName + ".png";
      }
      this.cardImage() = function() {
       return getFilename().toLowerCase();
   }
}
```

The getFilename() function nested within the cardImage() method is private because its scope is limited to the constructor function and is not accessible to any code outside of that function.

A **privileged method** is a method that is able to access private variables and methods but is also accessible to the public. In the code sample above, the cardImage() function is available to the public but it is also privileged because it relies on the value returned by calling the private getFilename() function.

Private and privileged methods can be made only within the constructor function itself. Public methods can be made at any time using the object's prototype. Knowing which methods are public, private, and privileged is important to ensure that your code does not conflict with code existing elsewhere in your application.

You have completed your work programming the card interface for Arthur's Games Draw Poker page. In the next session, you will continue your exploration of custom objects and object prototypes by creating methods to evaluate the player's hand and calculating the payoff for a winning hand.

REVIEW

Session 14.2 Quick Check

1. Provide code to create a custom object named bounceBall using the new operator. Include a property named ballColor with a value named "red" and a ballSpeed property value of 3.

2. Provide the code to replace the bouncBall object with an object class where the color and speed values are defined in the constructor function parameters.

3. Provide code to create an instance of the bounceBall object in the myBall variable, using a color of green and a speed of 5.

4. Provide code to display information about the myBall object in the browser's debugging console log.

5. Provide code to loop through all the properties in the myBall object.

6. What is a prototype?

7. Why should a method be defined with a prototype rather than within a constructor function?

8. Provide code to add the moveBall() method to the bounceBall prototype.

Session 14.3 Visual Overview:

The `forEach()` method loops through each item in an array, applying the commands in the command block.

This statement creates an empty object literal.

```javascript
pokerHand.prototype.hasSets = function() {
    var handSets = {};
    this.cards.forEach(function(card) {
        if (handSets.hasOwnProperty(card.rankValue)) {
            handSets[card.rankValue]++;
        } else {
            handSets[card.rankValue] = 1;
        }
    });

    var sets = "none";
    var pairRank;

    for (var cardRank in handSets){
        if (handSets[cardRank] === 4) {sets = "Four of a Kind";}
        if (handSets[cardRank] === 3) {
            if (sets === "Pair") {sets = "Full House";}
            else {sets = "Three of a Kind";}
        }
        if (handSets[cardRank] === 2) {
            if (sets === "Three of a Kind") {sets = "Full House";}
            else if (sets === "Pair") {sets = "Two Pair";}
            else {sets = "Pair"; pairRank = cardRank;}
        }
    }

    if (sets === "Pair" && pairRank >= 11) {
        sets = "Jacks or Better";
    }

    return sets;
};
```

The bracket notation references object properties in the form *object[prop]* where *object* is the object name and *prop* is the property name.

The for...in structure loops through all of the enumerable properties within an object.

The cardRank variable represents the property names in the handSets object.

The sets variable returns the type of poker hand.

Objects and Arrays

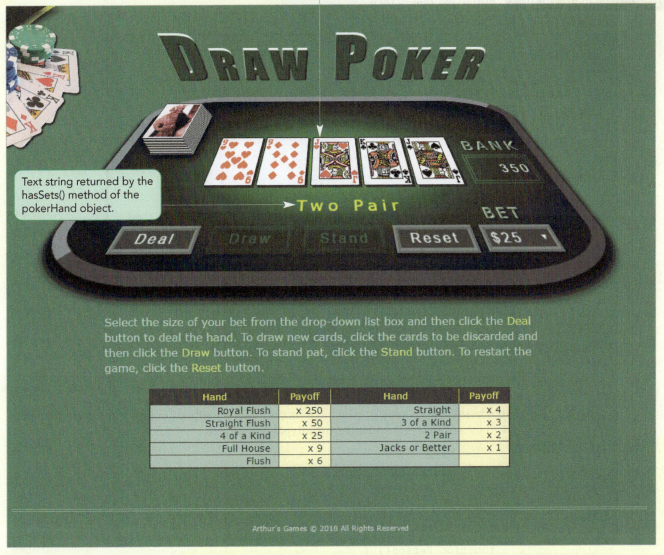

The poker hand contains a pair of 9's and a pair of Jacks.

Text string returned by the hasSets() method of the pokerHand object.

DRAW POKER

BANK
350

Two Pair

BET
$25

Deal   Draw   Stand   Reset $25

Select the size of your bet from the drop-down list box and then click the Deal button to deal the hand. To draw new cards, click the cards to be discarded and then click the Draw button. To stand pat, click the Stand button. To restart the game, click the Reset button.

Hand	Payoff	Hand	Payoff
Royal Flush	x 250	Straight	x 4
Straight Flush	x 50	3 of a Kind	x 3
4 of a Kind	x 25	2 Pair	x 2
Full House	x 9	Jacks or Better	x 1
Flush	x 6		

Arthur's Games © 2018 All Rights Reserved

Combining Objects

Using prototypes, any object class can inherit the properties and methods from another class. Figure 14-30 shows a diagram of three object classes named Person, Employee, and Staff, which share common properties and methods. The Person object class contains descriptive and biographical information about individual persons. The Employee object class inherits the properties and methods of the Person prototype and adds others pertaining to employees. Finally, the Staff class inherits properties and methods from both the Person and Employee prototypes, adding its own set of properties and methods.

Figure 14-30	Prototypal Inheritance

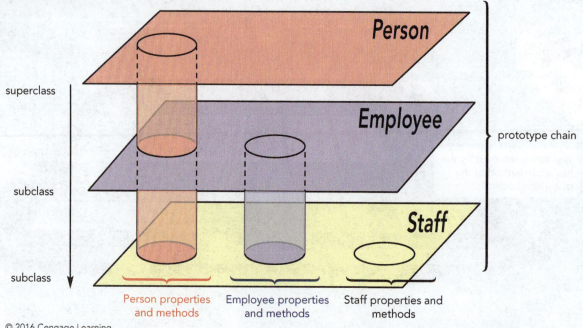

superclass

subclass

subclass

prototype chain

Person properties and methods   Employee properties and methods   Staff properties and methods

© 2016 Cengage Learning

This hierarchy of object classes creates a **prototype chain** ranging from the base object class in the chain, known as the **superclass** down to the lower classes or **subclasses**. The process by which the properties and methods of base classes are shared with the subclasses is known as **prototypal inheritance**.

Creating a Prototype Chain

A prototype chain is created by defining an object prototype as an instance of an object class. To create the prototype chain shown in Figure 14-30, first define the constructor functions and prototypes for the Person, Employee, and Staff objects:

```
function Person() {
   this.showName = function() {
      console.log(this.lastName + ", " + this.firstName;)
   }
}

function Employee() {
   this.empEMail = null;
}
```

```
function Staff(fName, lName) {
   this.firstName = fName;
   this.lastName = lName;
}
```

Next, since every staff member is an employee and every employee is a person, you define the prototypes for the Employee and Staff objects as follows:

```
Employee.prototype = new Person();
Staff.prototype = new Employee();
```

Because the Staff prototype is part of a prototype chain that extends to the Person object, it inherits the showName() method originating in the Person prototype. Thus, the following showName() can be used with the myStaff object to display the text string "Voiklund, Bob" in the debugger console.

```
var myStaff = new Staff("Bob", "Voiklund")
myStaff.showName(); // Returns "Voiklund, Bob"
```

Order is important when defining the prototype chain. Start at the top of the hierarchy and move down to the lower subclasses. When JavaScript encounters code that references an object property or method, it attempts to resolve it in the following order:

1. Check for the property or method within the current object instance
2. Check for the property or method with the object's prototype
3. If the prototype is an instance of another object, check for the property or method in that object
4. Continue moving down the chain until the property or method is located or the end of the chain is reached

All prototype chains ultimately find their source in the base object.

The Base Object

The **base object** or Object is the fundamental JavaScript object whose methods are available to all objects. When you create a custom object using an object literal or by applying the new Object() command, you were creating a subclass of the base object. Figure 14-31 describes some of the properties and methods that all objects inherit from the Object prototype.

Figure 14-31	Common object properties and methods

Property or Method	Description
object.constructor	References the constructor function that creates object
object.hasOwnProperty(prop)	Returns true if object has the specified property, prop
object.isPrototypeOf(obj)	Returns true if object exists in object obj prototype chain
object.propertyIsEnumerable(prop)	Returns true if the prop property is enumerable
object.toLocaleString()	Returns a text string representation of object using local standards
object.toString()	Returns a text string representation of object
object.valueOf()	Returns the value of object as a text string, number, Boolean value, undefined, or null

For example, you can determine whether an object supports a particular property using the hasOwnProperty() method. Thus, the following code returns true if the pokerCard object supports the rank property:

```
pokerCard.hasOwnProperty("rank");
```

The constructor for Object also supports methods that can be used to retrieve and define properties for any object. Figure 14-32 lists some of the methods associated with the Object constructor.

Figure 14-32 **Methods of the Object constructor**

Method	Description
Object.assign(target, sources)	Copies all of the enumerable properties from the sources objects into the target object
Object.create(proto, properties)	Creates an object using the prototype, proto; where properties is an optional list of properties added to the object
Object.defineProperty(obj, prop, descriptor)	Defines or modifies the property, prop, for the object, obj; where descriptor describes the property
Object.defineProperties(obj, props)	Defines or modifies the properties, prop, for the object, obj
Object.freeze(obj)	Freezes obj so that it cannot be modified by other code
Object.getPrototypeOf(obj)	References the prototype of the object, obj
Object.isFrozen(obj)	Return true if obj is frozen
Object.keys(obj)	Returns an array of the enumerable properties found in obj

For example, the expression

```
Object.keys(myStaff)
```

will return the array ["firstName", "lastName"], which are the keys defined for the myStaff object above.

The Object.create() method provides another way to create objects that are based on existing prototypes. Thus, the expression

```
var myIntern = Object.create(Staff.prototype);
```

creates a new object using the Staff prototype, copying the properties and methods associated with that prototype. The following code applies the showName() method, copied from the Staff prototype via the prototypal chain, to the myIntern object:

```
myIntern.firstName = "Sandi";
myIntern.lastName = "Ghang";
myIntern.showName();   // Returns the text string "Ghang, Sandi"
```

Note that while myIntern copied the showName() method, the myIntern object is not part of the prototypal chain that traces back to the Person object because it is not defined as an instance of an object prototype; instead it is a copy of that prototype.

Using the apply() and call() Methods

Another way of sharing methods between objects is by applying or calling a method from one object for use in another object. To borrow a method from one object class use the following apply() method

```
function.apply(thisObj [,argArray])
```

where *function* is a reference to a function, *thisObj* is the object that receives the actions of the function, and *argArray* is an optional array of argument values sent to the function. Depending on the function involved, *argArray* might include an explicit reference to the object receiving the function.

In the following code, the showRank() method is defined for the pokerCard object prototype

```
function pokerCard(rankValue) {
    this.rank = rankValue;
}

pokerCard.prototype.showRank = function() {
    console.log(this.rank);
};
```

but it could be applied to any object that supports the rank property by using the `apply()` method as follows:

```
function UnoCard(rank) {
    this.rank = rank;
}

var myUnoCard = new UnoCard("8 green");
pokerCard.prototype.showRank.apply(myUnoCard);
```

The result of this code will be an entry in the debugger console with the text "8 green", which is the rank assigned to the myUnoCard object.

The `call()` method is similar to the `apply()` method except that the argument values are placed in a comma-separated list of values instead of an array. The syntax of the `call()` method is

```
function.call(thisObj, arg1, arg2, arg3, ...)
```

where *arg1*, *arg2*, *arg3*, and so on is the comma-separated list of argument values for *function*.

TIP

The apply() method is used with arrays (think "a" for "array") while the call() method is used for a comma-separated list of values (think "c" for "comma").

REFERENCE

Applying or Calling a Function

- To apply a function to an object, use

  ```
  function.apply(thisObj [, argArray])
  ```

  where *function* is a reference to a function, *thisObj* is the object that receives the actions of the function, and *argArray* is an array of argument values sent to the function.

- To call a function to an object, use

  ```
  function.call(thisObj, arg1, arg2, arg3, ...)
  ```

  where *arg1*, *arg2*, *arg3*, and so on is the comma-separated list of argument values for *function*.

To evaluate hands from a poker game, you will create a method that checks the rankValue of all cards in the hand and then returns the rank of the hand's highest card. A maximum value is determined using the `max()` method from the `Math` object. You can use the call() method to apply the max() method to the pokerHand object prototype, creating the following highCard() method

```
pokerHand.prototype.highCard = function() {
    return Math.max.call(pokerHand,
        this.cards[0].rankValue,
        this.cards[1].rankValue,
        this.cards[2].rankValue,
        this.cards[3].rankValue,
        this.cards[4].rankValue);
};
```

which will the return the maximum value of the rankValue property in the cards array of the pokerHand object class. Add the highCard() method to the ag_cards.js file.

To create the highCard() method:

1. If you took a break after the previous session, make sure the **ag_cards.js** file is open in your editor.

2. Directly after the constructor for the pokerHand object, add the following code to define the highCard() method:

```
/* Return the highest ranked card in the hand */
pokerHand.prototype.highCard = function() {
    return Math.max.call(pokerHand,
        this.cards[0].rankValue,
        this.cards[1].rankValue,
        this.cards[2].rankValue,
        this.cards[3].rankValue,
        this.cards[4].rankValue);
};
```

Figure 14-33 describes the code in the highCard() method.

Figure 14-33 Creating the highCard() method

adds the highCard() method to the pokerHand object prototype

calls the max() method from the Math object

returns the maximum rank value from the five cards in the poker hand

```
/* Constructor function for poker hands */
function pokerHand(handLength) {
    this.cards = new Array(handLength);
}

/* Return the highest ranked card in the hand */
pokerHand.prototype.highCard = function() {
    return Math.max.call(pokerHand,
        this.cards[0].rankValue,
        this.cards[1].rankValue,
        this.cards[2].rankValue,
        this.cards[3].rankValue,
        this.cards[4].rankValue);
};
```

3. Save your changes to the file.

Next, you will create methods that evaluate the player's hand to determine whether the hand is a winning one.

Introducing the Function Object

Almost everything in JavaScript is an object, including functions themselves. The `Function` object supports its own collection of properties and methods. You have already learned about two methods: `apply()` and `call()`.

`Function` object properties include the following:

`func.name`	returns the name of the function, `func`
`func.caller`	returns the function that called the function
`func.length`	returns the number of arguments used by the function

For example, the commands

```
var myHand = newPokerHand(5);
console.log(myHand.constructor.length);
```

will report on the number of arguments required by the constructor function for the myHand object, which, in this case, is 1 because the pokerHand constructor has a single argument.

Because functions are objects, new functions can be created using the following new `Function` constructor

```
var func = new Function(arg1, arg2, … , body);
```

where *func* is the name of the function, *arg1*, *arg2*, and so on are the function arguments, and *body* is the function code. The following code creates the adder() function used for returning the sum of two values:

```
var adder = new Function("x", "y", "return x + y");
```

The adder() function is equivalent to the following:

```
function adder(x, y) {
   return x + y;
}
```

The advantage of the new `Function` constructor is that it can be used to construct dynamic functions whose properties and methods are themselves variables.

Combining Objects and Arrays

While a custom object contains data stored in arrays, you can speed up the efficiency of your code by using many of JavaScript's built-in `Array` object methods to loop through the contents of an array. For a discussion of `Array` object methods for program loops, see Figure 10-16 in Tutorial 10.

To win at Draw Poker, a player needs to have one of the following hands (listed in decreasing order of value):

1. Royal Flush (10, Jack, Queen, King, Ace of one suit)
2. Straight Flush (Any five cards of the same suit in consecutive order)
3. Four of a Kind (Four cards of the same rank)
4. Full House (Three cards of the same rank and a pair of cards of the same rank)
5. Flush (Five cards of the same suit)
6. Straight (Any five cards in consecutive order)
7. Three of a Kind (Three cards of the same rank)
8. Two Pair (Two pairs of cards not of the same rank)
9. Jacks or Better (A pair of Jacks, Queens, Kings, or Aces)

Any other hand is a losing one. To evaluate whether the player's hand matches one of these types, you will start by creating methods to determine whether the player's hand has a flush or a straight.

Applying the every() Array method

To determine whether the poker hand matches a flush, you will use the every() method to test whether every item in an array matches a specified condition. In this case, you want to test whether every card in the cards array of the pokerHand object has the same value for the suit property. The following hasFlush() method tests for that condition:

TIP

See Figure 10-16 for a discussion of the every() method.

```
pokerHand.prototype.hasFlush = function() {
   var firstSuit = this.cards[0].suit;
   return this.cards.every(function(card) {
      return card.suit === firstSuit;
   });
};
```

The hasFlush() method stores the suit of the first card in the hand in the firstSuit variable. It then applies the every() method to every card in the cards array of the poker hand, testing whether every card has the same suit as the first card. If all cards pass that test, the method returns the value true (indicating that hand is a flush), otherwise it returns the value false. Add the hasFlush() method to the prototype of the pokerHand object.

To create the hasFlush() method:

1. Directly after the code for the highCard() method in the ag_cards.js file, add the following code:

   ```
   /* Test for the presence of a flush */
   pokerHand.prototype.hasFlush = function() {
      var firstSuit = this.cards[0].suit;
      return this.cards.every(function(card) {
         return card.suit === firstSuit;
      });
   };
   ```

   Figure 14-34 highlights the code of the hasFlush() method.

Figure 14-34   Creating the hasFlush() method

```
                this.cards[3].rankValue,
                this.cards[4].rankValue);
};
```
stores the suit of the first card in the hand

the every() method loops through every item in an array testing whether every item returns a value of true

```
/* Test for the presence of a flush */
pokerHand.prototype.hasFlush = function() {
   var firstSuit = this.cards[0].suit;
   return this.cards.every(function(card) {
      return card.suit === firstSuit;
   });
};
```

returns true if the suit of each card matches the suit of the first card

2. Save your changes to the file.

Next, test for the presence of a straight. For a straight, the five cards must be in unbroken ascending order such as 2, 3, 4, 5, 6 or 8, 9, 10, Jack, Queen. However, because the cards in the poker hand are not sorted you must first sort the cards array in ascending order using the following sort() method and anonymous compare function:

```
this.cards.sort(function(a, b) {
   return a.rankValue - b.rankValue;
});
```

Once the cards array is sorted, use the following every() method to test whether rank value is one more than the preceding rank in the array (skipping the first card in the array).

```
return this.cards.every(function(card, i, cards) {
   if (i > 0) {
      return (cards[i].rankValue - cards[i-1].rankValue === 1);
   } else {
      return true;
   }
});
```

Note that the compare function for the every() method uses the i variable to reference the index of every item as the program loops through the cards array. If the difference between consecutive rank values is 1 for every pair of cards (after the first card), the function returns the value true.

Add the complete code for the hasStraight() method to the pokerHand object prototype.

To create the hasStraight() method:

▶ **1.** Directly after the code for the hasFlush() method in ag_cards.js file, add:

```
/* Test for the presence of a straight */
pokerHand.prototype.hasStraight = function() {
  this.cards.sort(function(a, b) {
    return a.rankValue - b.rankValue;
  });
  return this.cards.every(function(card, i, cards) {
    if (i > 0) {
        return (cards[i].rankValue - cards[i-1].rankValue ===
1);
    } else {
      return true;
    }
  });
};
```

Figure 14-35 describes the hasStraight() method.

Figure 14-35	Creating the hasStraight() method

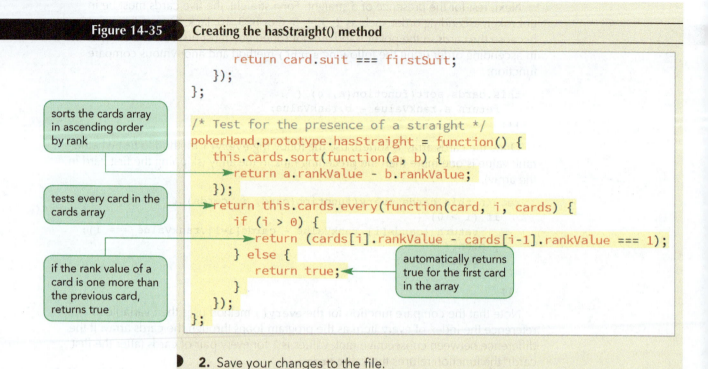

sorts the cards array in ascending order by rank

tests every card in the cards array

if the rank value of a card is one more than the previous card, returns true

automatically returns true for the first card in the array

```
        return card.suit === firstSuit;
    });
};

/* Test for the presence of a straight */
pokerHand.prototype.hasStraight = function() {
    this.cards.sort(function(a, b) {
        return a.rankValue - b.rankValue;
    });
    return this.cards.every(function(card, i, cards) {
        if (i > 0) {
            return (cards[i].rankValue - cards[i-1].rankValue === 1);
        } else {
            return true;
        }
    });
};
```

▶ **2.** Save your changes to the file.

You can combine the highCard(), hasFlush(), and hasStraight() methods to test for the presence of a Straight Flush or Royal Flush. A Royal Flush is simply a Straight Flush whose high card is an Ace with a rank value of 14.

To create the hasStraightFlush() and hasRoyalFlush() methods:

▶ **1.** Directly after the code for the hasStraight() method in the ag_cards.js file, add the following code defining the hasStraightFlush() method:

```
/* Test for the presence of a straight flush */
pokerHand.prototype.hasStraightFlush = function() {
    return this.hasFlush() && this.hasStraight();
};
```

▶ **2.** Next, add the following code defining the hasRoyalFlush() method:

```
/* Test for the presence of a royal flush */
pokerHand.prototype.hasRoyalFlush = function() {
    return this.hasStraightFlush() && this.highCard() === 14;
};
```

Figure 14-36 describes newly added code in the file.

Figure 14-36   **Creating the hasStraightFlush() and hasRoyalFlush() methods**

```
        });
    };

    /* Test for the presence of a straight flush */
    pokerHand.prototype.hasStraightFlush = function() {
        return this.hasFlush() && this.hasStraight();
    };

    /* Test for the presence of a royal flush */
    pokerHand.prototype.hasRoyalFlush = function() {
        return this.hasStraightFlush() && this.highCard() === 14;
    };
```

returns true if the hand is both a straight and a flush

returns true if the hand is a straight flush with an Ace high card (rank value = 14)

▶ **3.** Save your changes to the file.

With the completion of these methods, the only remaining hands to be tested are those hands containing cards of duplicate ranks. These are (in decreasing order of value): Four of Kind, Full House, Three of a Kind, Two Pair, and Jacks or Better. To test for these hands, you will use an array to generate an object literal.

Creating an Object Literal with the `forEach()` Method

For the Draw Poker game, you will generate an object literal named handSets that summarizes the content of the card ranks in the hand. For example, if the hand contains the following cards:

- Queen of Spades
- 3 of Clubs
- Jack of Hearts
- Queen of Hearts
- 3 of Diamonds

the handSets object would be

```
handSets {
    3: 2;
    11: 1:
    12: 2;
}
```

in which the key is the rank value of each card (where Jack = 11 and Queen = 12) and the key value is the number of times that rank value appears in the hand. Thus, the 3 and 12 (Queen) each appear twice, while the Jack (11) appears only once. With the content of the hand summarized in the handSets object, you can then determine what kind of hand it represents.

To create the handSets object, use the `forEach()` method to run a command block for each item in the card array. The code to generate the handSets array is

TIP

See Figure 10-16 for more information on the `forEach()` method.

```
var handSets = {};
this.cards.forEach(function(card) {
    if (handSets.hasOwnProperty(card.rankValue)) {
        handSets[card.rankValue]++;
    } else {
        handSets[card.rankValue] = 1;
    }
});
```

The code begins by creating handSets as an empty object. It then uses the forEach() method to loop through every item in the cards array. For every card, the code tests whether the handSets object already has a key matching the card's rank value. If true, then that card is already in the hand and the value of that rank for the handSets object is increased by one; otherwise the code creates a property for that rank with a value of 1. Note that the code uses the bracket notation for object properties as discussed in Session 1 in which the following expression referencing the "12" property of the handSets object

```
handSets[12]
```

is equivalent to

```
handSets.12
```

Start creating the hasSets() method for the pokerHand object in the ag_cards.js file.

To create the hasSets() method:

1. Directly after the code for the hasRoyalFlush() method in the ag_cards.js file, add the following code for the hasSets() method:

```
/* Test for duplicates in the hand */
pokerHand.prototype.hasSets = function() {
   // handSets summarizes the duplicates in the hand
   var handSets = {};
   this.cards.forEach(function(card) {
      if (handSets.hasOwnProperty(card.rankValue)) {
         handSets[card.rankValue]++;
      } else {
         handSets[card.rankValue] = 1;
      }
   });
};
```

Figure 14-37 describes newly added code in the file.

Figure 14-37 Creating the hasSets() method

```
   return this.hasStraightFlush() && this.highCard() === 14;
};


/* Test for duplicates in the hand */
pokerHand.prototype.hasSets = function() {
   // handSets summarizes the duplicates in the hand
   var handSets = {};
   this.cards.forEach(function(card) {
      if (handSets.hasOwnProperty(card.rankValue)) {
         handSets[card.rankValue]++;
      } else {
         handSets[card.rankValue] = 1;
      }
   });
};
```

the forEach() method loops through each entry in the cards array

creates an empty object

tests whether a card of that rank has already been found in the hand

if so, increases the count for that rank by 1

otherwise, sets the count to 1

2. Save your changes to the file.

To determine what kind of hand is stored in the handSets object go through each property or key in the object. However, JavaScript objects (or associative arrays) don't support `for` loops like arrays do. To examine the properties and keys of an object, use a `for…in` loop.

Applying a `for…in` loop

Because objects or associative arrays do not use indices, you cannot loop through the properties and keys with a counter variable. Instead, use the following **for…in loop**:

```
for (prop in obj) {
    commands
}
```

where *prop* references the properties contained within the *obj* object. For example, to loop through the contents of the following employee object

```
var employee = {
    name: "Robert Voiklund",
    position: "manager",
    email: "rvoiklund@example.com"
};
```

apply the following `for … in` loop

```
for (prop in employee) {
    console.info(prop + " is " + employee[prop]);
}
```

and the debugger console will display the messages:

"name is Robert Voiklund"
"position is manager"
"email is rvoiklund@example.com"

Note that `for…in` loops do not follow a specific order because properties can be listed and read out in any order. For item collections in which order is important, use an `Array` object with array values assigned index numbers. Only properties that are countable or **enumerable** are accessible to `for…in` loops. You can determine whether a property is enumerable using the following `propertyIsEnumerable()` method

```
obj.propertyIsEnumerable(prop)
```

where *obj* is the object and *prop* is the property.

You will use a `for…in` loop to loop through every property in the handSets object, testing each card for its count of duplicates. If a card has four duplicates, you know that the hand is Four of a Kind. If there are three duplicates, the hand may be a Full House or Three of a Kind, depending on whether the remaining two cards are paired. Finally, if a pair is found, the hand may contain only that one pair or two pairs, depending on the contents of the other three cards. The `for…in` loop needs to account for each possibility.

To create a for...in loop:

1. Within the hasSets() method of the pokerHand object prototype, add the following variables:

```
var sets = "none";
var pairRank;
```

The sets variable will be used to keep track of whatever sets have been found in the hand. The pairRank variable will record the rank of any pairs found in the hand to determine later whether the pair is a part of a pair of Jacks or better.

2. Add the following for...in loop:

```
for (var cardRank in handSets){
}
```

The cardRank variable will reference the properties of the handSets object, which, in this case, is the rank value of each card found in the deck.

> To reference a property as a variable, you must place the variable using bracket notation.

3. Within the for...in loop, add the following command to test whether a card appears four times in the hand, changing the value of the sets variable to "Four of a Kind":

```
if (handSets[cardRank] === 4) {sets = "Four of a Kind";}
```

4. Next, within the for...in loop, add the following if condition that tests whether three of a kind appears in the hand. If so, it may be part of a full house. If a pair has already been found, change the sets value to "Full House", otherwise change the sets value to "Three of a Kind".

```
if (handSets[cardRank] === 3) {
   if (sets === "Pair") {sets = "Full House";}
   else {sets = "Three of a Kind";}
}
```

5. Finally, within the for...in loop, add the following if condition that tests whether a pair has been found. If so, it is part of a full house, a two pair, or a single pair in which you will store the rank value in the pairRank variable (to determine later if it's a pair of Jacks or better.)

```
if (handSets[cardRank] === 2) {
   if (sets === "Three of a Kind") {sets = "Full House";}
   else if (sets === "Pair") {sets = "Two Pair";}
   else {sets = "Pair"; pairRank = cardRank;}
}
```

6. After the for...in loop has completed examining the cards in the hand, add the following if condition that tests whether the sets variable is equal to "Pair" and the pairRank value is greater than or equal to 11. If so, change the sets variable to "Jacks or Better".

```
if (sets === "Pair" && pairRank >= 11) {
   sets = "Jacks or Better";
}
```

7. After the if condition, complete the hasSets() method by adding the following command to return the value of sets variable.

```
return sets;
```

Figure 14-38 describes the completed code in the hasSets() method.

Figure 14-38	Adding a for...in loop

```
/* Test for duplicates in the hand */
pokerHand.prototype.hasSets = function() {
   // handSets summarizes the duplicates in the hand
   var handSets = {};
   this.cards.forEach(function(card) {
      if (handSets.hasOwnProperty(card.rankValue)) {
         handSets[card.rankValue]++;
      } else {
         handSets[card.rankValue] = 1;
      }
   });

   var sets = "none";
   var pairRank;

   for (var cardRank in handSets){
      if (handSets[cardRank] === 4) {sets = "Four of a Kind";}
      if (handSets[cardRank] === 3) {
         if (sets === "Pair") {sets = "Full House";}
         else {sets = "Three of a Kind";}
      }
      if (handSets[cardRank] === 2) {
         if (sets === "Three of a Kind") {sets = "Full House";}
         else if (sets === "Pair") {sets = "Two Pair";}
         else {sets = "Pair"; pairRank = cardRank;}
      }
   }

   if (sets === "Pair" && pairRank >= 11) {
      sets = "Jacks or Better";
   }

   return sets;
};
```

Annotations:

- stores the rank value of the first pair found in the hand
- stores the sets found in the hand
- the for...in loop goes through each of the properties in the handSets object
- the hand contains a set of four duplicates
- the hand contains a set of three duplicates which may be part of a full house or three of a kind
- the hand contains a pair which may be part of a two pair hand
- if hand only contains a pair, tests whether it is a pair of Jacks or better
- returns the sets in the hand

8. Save your changes to the file.

Using all the methods you have created in this session, you can create a single handType() method that returns a text string describing the type of hand the player owns or returns the text string "No Winner" if the hand is not a winning one. Add the handType() method to the ag_cards.js file.

To create the handType() method:

1. Directly after the code for the hasSets() method in the ag_cards.js file, add the following code for the handType() method:

```
/* Returns the type of poker hand */
pokerHand.prototype.handType = function() {
   if (this.hasRoyalFlush()) {return "Royal Flush";}
   else if (this.hasStraightFlush()) {return "Straight
Flush";}
   else if (this.hasFlush()) {return "Flush";}
   else if (this.hasStraight()) {return "Straight";}
   else {
      var sets = this.hasSets();
      if (sets === "Pair" || sets === "none") {sets = "No
Winner";}
      return sets;
   }
};
```

Figure 14-39 describes handType() method.

Figure 14-39   Creating the handType() method

```
      return sets;
};

/* Returns the type of poker hand */
pokerHand.prototype.handType = function() {
   if (this.hasRoyalFlush()) {return "Royal Flush";}
   else if (this.hasStraightFlush()) {return "Straight Flush";}
   else if (this.hasFlush()) {return "Flush";}
   else if (this.hasStraight()) {return "Straight";}
   else {
      var sets = this.hasSets();
      if (sets === "Pair" || sets === "none") {sets = "No Winner";}
      return sets;
   }
};
```

returns the hand type for flushes and straights

if hand contains only a low pair or no sets, returns "No Winner"

2. Save your changes to the file.

Bob has created a div element with the ID "handValueText" to display the text returned by the handType() method. Add code to the event listeners for the Draw and Stand buttons to display the hand type that the player has in the hand.

To display the hand type:

1. Return to the **ag_poker.js** file in your editor.

2. Scroll to the event listener for the Draw button and add the following code:

```
// Evaluate the hand drawn by user
handValueText.textContent = myHand.handType();
```

3. Go to the event listener for the Stand button and add the following code:

```
// Evaluate the hand dealt to the user
handValueText.textContent = myHand.handType();
```

Figure 14-40 highlights the newly added code.

Figure 14-40   **Displaying the hand type**

```
                cardImages[i].onclick = null;
        }

        // Evaluate the hand drawn by user
        handValueText.textContent = myHand.handType();
    });

    standButton.addEventListener("click", function() {
        enableObj(dealButton);
        enableObj(betSelection);
        disableObj(drawButton);
        disableObj(standButton);

        // Evaluate the hand dealt to the user
        handValueText.textContent = myHand.handType();
    });
```

displays the hand type after the Draw button is clicked

displays the hand type when the play stands pat

4. Save your changes to the file.

When the Deal button is clicked to deal a new hand, the handValue text should be reset to an empty text string. Add code to the event listener for the Deal button to reset the text string, and then test your changes to the poker game application.

To remove the hand value text string:

1. Scroll up to the event listener for the Deal button.

2. Remove the text shown in the handValueText div element by adding the following code as the first line of code in the initial if condition that tests whether the current bank is greater than or equal to the current bet:

```
handValueText.textContent = "";
```

Figure 14-41 highlights the newly added code.

Figure 14-41   **Removing the hand value text**

```
// Enable the Draw and Stand buttons after the deal
dealButton.addEventListener("click", function() {
    if (pokerGame.currentBank >= pokerGame.currentBet) {
        handValueText.textContent = "";
        disableObj(dealButton);
        disableObj(betSelection);
```

removes the hand value text when a new hand is dealt

3. Save your changes to the file and then reload **ag_poker.html** in your browser.

4. Click the **Deal** button to deal a new hand, then select cards for discarding and click the **Draw** button. Verify that the page displays the correct value of the played hand. See Figure 14-42.

Figure 14-42 A winning poker hand

three of a kind

Source: Howard Pyle/Public Domain; Copyright © 1997 John Fitzgibbon; Copyright © 1997 Jochen Tuchbreiter; Copyright © 1998 Markus F.X.J. Oberhumer; © Courtesy Patrick Carey

Trouble? If your program doesn't work, compare your code against the figures shown in this session. Common errors include: forgetting to close braces, brackets, and quotation marks; misspelling variable names and methods; and improper use of uppercase and lowercase letters. For logical errors, use the `console.log()` method to display intermediate results in your browser debugger's console.

Teamwork: Trying, Throwing, and Catching Errors

When you create custom objects and methods that will be used by others, you may need to guard against errors introduced by other users improperly applying your objects and methods. One way is to apply the `throw new Error()` command, which reports an error to the browser. For example, the following code uses the `arguments.length` property to verify that the user has supplied both arguments when applying the pokerCard() constructor function. If two arguments are not provided, the code reports an error and halts further execution of the code.

```
function pokerCard(suit, rank) {
   if (arguments.length != 2) {
      throw new Error("This function requires 2 arguments");
   }
   …
}
```

The `throw new Error()` command is only one part of a larger structure of error testing. The general structure for catching run-time errors is

```
try {
   code
}
catch(err) {
   handle errors
}
```

where *code* is JavaScript code to be tested for errors, *err* is the JavaScript `Error` object used for storing information about run-time errors, and *handle errors* is JavaScript code indicating how the browser should respond to the error. The following code demonstrates the use of the `try … catch` structure to capture an error where a required username variable is missing a value:

```
try {
   if (username == "") throw new Error("Missing username");
}
catch(err) {
   console.error("You must supply a username");
}
```

The error is caught and the program displays an error message in the debugger console. If you throw an error without a corresponding `catch` command block, the error is sent directly to the browser, which, in this case, halts the program and displays the error message in its JavaScript debugger.

By including such error control structures in your custom objects and methods, you can provide other users valuable information in how they should apply your work in their code.

The only thing remaining for the game is to update the bank value for winning hands. Recall that different hands provide different payouts. To start, you will add a handOdds() method to the pokerHand object prototype that returns the payout multiplier for hands of differing values, starting from a 250× multiplier for Royal Flushes to a 1× for hands containing only a pair of Jacks or Better. The payout multiplier for non-winning hands is 0.

To create the handOdds() method:

1. Return to the **ag_cards.js** file in your editor.

2. Directly below the handType() method, add the following handOdds() method for the pokerHand object prototype:

```
/* Return the payout multiplier for each hand */
pokerHand.prototype.handOdds = function() {
   switch (this.handType()) {
      case "Royal Flush" : return 250;
      case "Straight Flush" : return 50;
      case "Four of a Kind" : return 25;
      case "Full House" : return 9;
      case "Flush" : return 6;
      case "Straight" : return 4;
      case "Three of a Kind" : return 3;
      case "Two Pair" : return 2;
      case "Jacks or Better" : return 1;
      default: return 0;
   }
};
```

Figure 14-43 highlights the newly added code.

Figure 14-43   **Creating the handOdds() method**

You also must add the following payout() method to the pokerGame object literal to update the bank value in response to a winning hand:

```
payout: function(odds) {
   this.currentBank += this.currentBet*odds;
   return this.currentBank;
}
```

The odds parameter will be based on the odds returned by the handOdds() method, which is then multiplied by the current bet and added to the bank value.

To create the handOdds() method:

1. Scroll up to the pokerGame object literal in the **ag_cards.js** file.

2. Type a **,** (comma) at the end of the placeBet() method and press **Enter** twice.

3. Enter the following payout() method:

```
payout: function(odds) {
    this.currentBank += this.currentBet*odds;
    return this.currentBank;
}
```

Figure 14-44 highlights the code for the payout() method.

Figure 14-44   Creating the payout() method

```
/*      The pokerGame Object   */
var pokerGame = {
    currentBank: null,
    currentBet: null,

    placeBet: function() {
        this.currentBank -= this.currentBet;
        return this.currentBank;          ⟵ separates the placeBet()
    },                                       and payout() methods
                                             with a comma

    payout: function(odds) {        ⟵ increases the bank
        this.currentBank += this.currentBet*odds;   value by the size of
        return this.currentBank;                    the bet multiplied
    }                                               by the odds value
};
```

4. Save your changes to the file.

Finally, apply the payout() method after the Draw or Stand button has been clicked when the final evaluation of the hand takes place and update the value displayed in the player's bank.

To display the bank value after the payout:

1. Return to the **ag_poker.js** file in your editor.

2. Add the following code at the end of the event listener function for both the Draw and Stand buttons.

```
// Pay off the final hand
bankBox.value = pokerGame.payout(myHand.handOdds());
```

Figure 14-45 highlights the newly added code.

Figure 14-45 Changing the displayed bank value

uses the handOdds() method to return the payout odds for the current hand

updates the bank value based on the pokerGame object payout() method

```
     // Evaluate the hand drawn by user
     handValueText.textContent = myHand.handType();

     // Pay off the final hand
     bankBox.value = pokerGame.payout(myHand.handOdds());
});

standButton.addEventListener("click", function() {
     enableObj(dealButton);
     enableObj(betSelection);
     disableObj(drawButton);
     disableObj(standButton);

     // Evaluate the hand dealt to the user
     handValueText.textContent = myHand.handType();

     // Pay off the final hand
     bankBox.value = pokerGame.payout(myHand.handOdds());
});
```

3. Save your changes to the file and then reload **ag_poker.html** in your browser.

4. Play the game, verifying that winning hands increase the value of the bank.

Bob plays the final version of your poker game. He is pleased with the results and appreciates the work you have done creating customized objects for the game. Those objects will be made available to your colleagues at the Arthur's Games website to be reused in other card game applications.

Session 14.3 Quick Check

REVIEW

1. What is the prototype chain?
2. How do you create a prototype chain?
3. Why would you use the `Object.create()` method to create an object?
4. Provide an expression to test whether the myCard object contains a property named "suit".
5. What is the difference between the `apply()` and `call()` methods?
6. How do you loop through the properties or keys of an object?
7. Provide code to write all the properties of the myCard object to the debugger console log.

Review Assignments

PRACTICE

Data Files needed for the Review Assignments: ag_squares_txt.html, ag_squares_txt.js, ag_cards2_txt.js, 2 CSS files, 1 GIF file, 57 PNG files, 1 TTF file, 1 WOFF file

After your work on the Draw Poker game, Bob wants you to work on programming the page for the Poker Squares game. Poker Squares is played on a 5×5 grid in which players place a card from the deck on one of 25 grid cells. When all 25 cells are filled, five rows and five columns of poker hands are evaluated. Points are given for the following hands:

- Royal Flush (30 pts)
- Straight Flush (30 pts)
- Four of Kind (16 pts)
- Full House (10 pts)
- Flush (5 pts)
- Straight (12 pts)
- Three of a Kind (6 pts)
- Two Pair (3 pts)
- One Pair (1 pt)

A winning grid has ten hands totaling 50 points or more. Bob has created the page design and made available many of the custom objects and methods you developed for the Draw Poker game. Your task will be to complete the application by writing the code for the game interface and providing methods to evaluate the hands in each row and column, as well as calculate the final game total.

Because the cards are laid out in a grid, your code will store pokerHand objects in a 2-dimensional array named cardGrid. Each item of the cardGrid array will contain a single pokerHand object and each hand object will contain a cards array consisting of 5 pokerCard objects.

A preview of a completed page is shown in Figure 14-46.

Figure 14-46   **Poker Squares game**

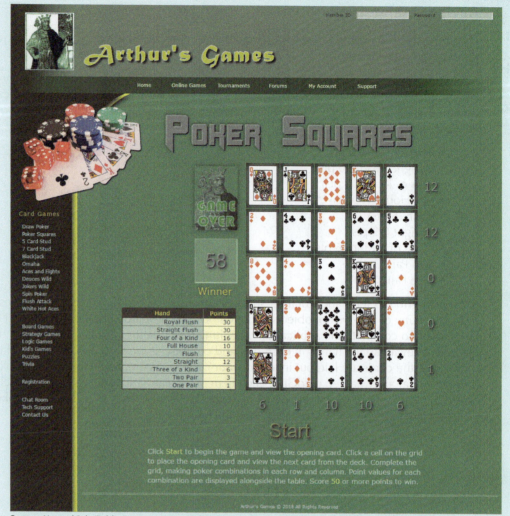

Source: Howard Pyle/Public Domain; Copyright © 1997 John Fitzgibbon; Copyright © 1997 Jochen Tuchbreiter; Copyright © 1998 Markus F.X.J. Oberhumer; © Courtesy Patrick Carey

Complete the following:

1. Use your editor to open the **ag_squares_txt.html**, **ag_squares_txt.js**, and **ag_cards2_txt.js** files from the html14 ► review folder. Enter *your name* and *the date* in the comment section of each file, and save them as **ag_squares.html**, **ag_squares.js**, and **ag_cards2.js** respectively.

2. Go to the **ag_squares.html** file in your editor. Link the page to the **ag_card2.js** and **ag_squares.js** files in that order, loading the files asynchronously. Take some time to study the HTML code in the file and then close it, saving your changes.

3. Go to the **ag_cards2.js** file in your editor. Bob has already created an object literal for the squareGame object containing the cardGrid array for storing five poker hands and two methods: the calcRowPoints() method for calculating the point total for a poker hand in a row indicated by an index argument, and the calcColumnPoints() method for calculating the point total for a poker hand in a column indicated by an index. Complete the squareGame object by adding the following properties and methods (make sure you separate the properties and methods with a comma.)

   a. The **gameTotal** property of the squareGame variable, which stores the total points achieved in the Poker Squares game. Set its value to **0**.

   b. The **winTotal** property of the squareGame variable, which stores the point total required for winning the game. Set its value to **50**.

   c. The **gameResult()** method, which returns the text string "Winner" if gameTotal is greater than or equal to winTotal; otherwise returns the text string "No Winner".

4. Below the squareGame object, insert code for the **insertCard()** method of the pokerHand object prototype. The purpose of this method is to insert a card into a poker hand at a specified index. The method has two arguments: the **card** argument referencing a pokerCard object and the **index** argument specifying the location where the card should be placed. Insert a command into the function to make `this.cards[index]` equal to the value of the card argument.

5. Document your work with comments, and save your changes to the file.

6. Open the **ag_squares.js** file in your editor.

7. Go to the playPokerSquares() function. Within the function add an `onclick` event handler to the startButton object that runs an anonymous function when the user clicks the Start Button on the web page. Within the anonymous function, do the tasks laid out in Steps 8 through 13.

8. Set up the initial game board by doing the following:
   a. Set the gameTotal property of the squareGame object to 0.
   b. Remove the current game score by changing the value of the gameScore input box on the page to an empty text string.
   c. Remove the current game result by changing the text content of the gameResult element on the page to an empty text string.
   d. Remove the current row and column totals by looping through the contents of the rowSumCells and columnSumCells object collections, setting the text content of each cell to an empty text string.
   e. Remove the current card images by looping through the cardImages object collection, setting the source of every inline image to the "ag_trans.gif" file.

9. Create a new pockerDeck object named **myDeck** and use the shuffle() method to randomize the order of its cards.

10. Create a new pokerCard object named **myStarterCard**. Apply the `shift()` method to the cards array of myDeck to store the first card from the deck in myStarterCard. Change the `src` attribute of the newCard inline image by calling the cardImage() method for the myStarterCard object.

11. The starter card is added to the board by clicking a cell in the grid table where the user wants the card placed. For every image in the cardImages collection, create an `onclick` event handler that does the following:
   a. Applies the cardImage() method to the myStarterCard object to display the image of the current card in the event object target.
   b. Stores the row number and column number of the clicked image in the **rowNum** and **colNum** variable. (*Hint*: Use the `charAt()` method to retrieve the second and third characters of the `id` attribute of the event object target.)
   c. Applies the insertCard() method to the `squareGame.cardGrid[rowNum]` object to insert a card into the new grid. Use myStarterCard as the poker card and colNum as the location in the insertCard() method.
   d. After the card has been placed within the grid, it cannot be changed. Set the `onclick` event handler of the event target to `null` to prevent the user from re-clicking the cell later in the game.

12. Finally, test whether the user has completed the grid table. Within the `onclick` event handler of the previous step, test whether there are more than 27 cards left in the deck. If there are more than 27 cards left, the game continues. Shift the next card from myDeck into the myStarterCard object and change the `src` attribute of newCard to display the image of the next starter card.

13. Otherwise, if the grid table is completed and the game is over, calculate the game score and totals for the poker hands in each row and column as follows:

   a. Indicate that the game is over by changing the `src` attribute of the newCard image to the "ag_cardback3.png" file.

   b. Calculate the row poker hand totals by creating a `for` loop with a counter variable that goes from 0 to 4. Declare the **rowTotal** variable equal to the value returned by the calcRowPoints() method of squareGame object, using your counter variable as the parameter value. Add rowTotal to the value of the gameTotal property of the squareGame object. Display the rowTotal value in the element with the ID `rowindexsum` where *index* is the value of your counter variable.

   c. Calculate the column totals with another `for` loop as you did in the previous step for the row totals. Use the calcColumnPoints() method to calculate the totals for each column poker hand, adding the column total to the gameTotal property and displaying column total value in the element with the ID `colindexsum`.

   d. Change the value of the gameScore input box to the value of the gameTotal property of the squareGame object.

   e. Show whether the user won or lost by changing the text content of the gameResult element to the text returned by the squareGame object's gameResult() method.

14. Document your work with comments and save the file.

15. Open the **ag_squares.html** file in your browser. Click the **Start** button to begin a game. Verify that you can add cards to the grid by clicking cells within the table. Play a complete game by filling out the grid and verify that when all cells are filled, the page displays: a) row and column totals for every hand, b) the overall point total for the game, c) a message indicating whether the player won or lost, and d) a card image showing that the game is over.

Case Problem 1

APPLY

Data Files needed for this Case Problem: bu_home_txt.html, bu_bubbles_txt.js, 2 CSS files, 11 PNG files

Bubbla Party Supplies   Drew Evans is a manager at Bubbla Party Supplies, a company that specializes in party favors, decorations, and costumes. He's asked you to work on the home page for the company website. Drew would like to add some fun bubble shapes that appear to drift, bounce, spin and change hue as part of the company logo. You can create these effects using custom objects in JavaScript. A preview of the home page is shown in Figure 14-47.

Figure 14-47   Bubbla Party Supplies home page

Christophe BOISSON/Shutterstock.com; Rehan Qureshi/Shutterstock.com; glitch/openclipart.org; pixabella/openclipart.org; lemmling/openclipart.org; naoshika/openclipart.org; Machovka/openclipart.org: mi_brami/openclipart.org; jhnri4/openclipart.org; rdevris/openclipart.crg; LiL_Mermaid_Girl/openclipart.org; gmad/openclipart.org; © Courtesy Patrick Carey

To create the animated bubbles, you will create a custom class of "bubble" objects that contains several useful properties such as a bubble's position and velocity on the page, its speed of rotation, and its hue. You will also create an effect that makes the bubbles bounce off the "walls" of the container.

Complete the following:

1. Use your editor to open the **bu_home_txt.html** and **bu_bubbles_txt.js** files from the html14 ▶ case1 folder. Enter *your name* and *the date* in the comment section of each file, and save them as **bu_home.html** and **bu_bubbles.js** respectively.

2. Go to the **bu_bubbles.html** file in your editor. Within the document head, add a `script` element for the **bu_bubbles.js** file. Load the file asynchronously.

3. Scroll down to the `section` element with the ID "logosection" and insert a `div` element with the ID "bubbleBox" in which you will display the bubble images.

4. Save your changes and go to the **bu_bubbles.js** file in your editor. Directly below the comment section, create an object literal for the **box** object. Add the following properties to the object: the **width** property with a value **1024** that defines the width of the box containing the bubbles, and the **height** property with a value of **500** defining the box's height.

5. Create an object constructor function for the **bubble** class of objects. Include two arguments with the function: the **size** argument specifying the radius of the bubble, and the **img** property specifying the URL of the image file of the bubble image. Add the following properties to the bubble object class:
   a. The **radius** property, setting it to the value of the size argument.
   b. The **imageURL**, setting it to the value of the img argument.

    c. The **xVelocity** property, storing the horizontal velocity of the bubble and the **yVelocity** property storing the vertical velocity. Set both values to `null`.

    d. The **xPos** property, storing the horizontal position of the bubble and the **yPos** property storing the vertical position. Set both values to `null`.

    e. The **opacity** property, storing the bubble's opacity. Set its value to **1**.

    f. The **hue** property, storing the bubble's hue value. Set its value to **0**.

    g. The **rotate** property, storing the speed of the bubble's spin. Set its value to **0**.

    h. The **rotateDirection** property, storing the direction in which the bubble spins. Set its value to **1**.

6. After the bubble constructor function, create the following methods for the bubble prototype:

    a. The **fadeBubble()** method that causes the bubble to fade by reducing its opacity. Insert a command to decrease the value of the bubble's opacity property by 0.0005.

    b. The **changeColor()** method that changes the hue of the bubble. Insert a command that increases the value of the bubble's hue property by 3 and then calculates the remainder by dividing that sum by 360, storing the result in the hue property. (*Hint:* Use the % operator described in Figure 9-24 to calculate the remainder.)

    c. The **rotateBubble()** that rotates the bubble. Insert a command that increases the value of the rotate property by the value of the rotateDirection property and then calculate the remainder by dividing that sum by 360, storing the result in the rotate property. (*Hint:* Once again use the % operator.)

7. Create the **moveBubble()** method for the bubble prototype that moves the bubble across the bubble box, bouncing the bubble off the box's wall if necessary. The method has two arguments: **height** and **width** defining the height and width of the box. Insert the following commands into the method:

    a. Create the following variables to define the extent of the bubble: **bubbleTop** equal to the value of the yPos property, **bubbleBottom** equal to the sum of the yPos and radius properties, **bubbleLeft** equal to the value of the xPos property, and **bubbleRight** equal to the sum of the xPos and radius properties.

    b. If bubbleTop is less than zero or bubbleBottom is greater than the height argument, then the bubble has hit the top or bottom wall; if so, change the direction of the vertical velocity by letting `this.yVelocity` equal `this.yVelocity`.

    c. If bubbleLeft is less than zero or bubbleRight is greater than the width argument, the bubble has hit the left or right wall; if so, change the direction of the horizontal velocity by letting `this.xVelocity` equal `this.xVelocity`.

    d. Move the bubble to its new location by adding the value of the yVelocity property to yPos and adding the value of the xVelocity property to xPos.

8. Scroll down to the event listener for the `load` event. Drew has already inserted a `setInterval()` method that is set up to create a new bubble every half-second as long as there are no more than 20 bubbles already in the box. Drew has also nested the randInt() function within the event handler that returns a random integer within a specified range. You will use the randInt() function to create bubbles of random appearance, velocity, hue, and spin. Within the `if` condition, add the commands specified in Steps 9 through 15.

9. Declare the **newBubble** variable using the `new bubble()` object constructor to create a bubble. Set the size of the bubble to a random size between 50 and 120 and the image file to "bu_bubble*int*.png", where *int* is a random integer from 1 to 10. (*Hint:* Use the randInt() function to generate the random integers for both the size and img arguments.)

10. Define the following property values for the newBubble object:

    a. Set the xPos and yPos properties to half of the box.width and box.height properties respectively, placing the new bubble in the center of the bubble box.

    b. Set the xVelocity and yVelocity properties to a random integer between 5 and 5.

c. Set the rotate and hue properties to a random integer between 0 and 360.

d. Set the rotateDirection property to a random integer between 2 and 2.

11. Next, you will create an inline image displaying the bubble image within the bubble box. Add the following commands to create the bubble image:

a. Create an img element named **bubbleImg** with its `position` property set to `absolute`.

b. Set the `src` property of bubbleImg to the value of the imageURL property of the newBubble object.

c. Set the `width` style of bubbleImg to *radius*px, where *radius* is the value of the radius property of newBubble.

d. Set the `left` and `top` styles of bubbleImg to *xPos*px and *yPos*px respectively, where *xPos* and *yPos* are the values of the xPos and yPos properties of newBubble.

e. Append bubbleImg to the bubbleBox element.

12. Now, that you've created the bubble image, you will insert commands to animate its appearance. Within the `if` statement, add a setInterval() method that repeats an anonymous function every 25 milliseconds, storing the ID of the `setInterval()` method in the bubbleInterval variable. Add the commands specified in Steps 13 through 15 to the anonymous function.

13. Apply the fadeBubble() method to the newBubble object to decrease the bubble's opacity.

14. If the opacity property of newBubble is less than 0, remove the bubble by

a. Removing bubbleImg element from bubbleBox.

b. Applying the `clearInterval()` method to stop the animation effects for the bubble, using bubbleInterval as the ID of the repeated command.

15. Otherwise, animate the bubble by adding the following the commands:

a. Set the value of the `opacity` style of bubbleImg to the value of the opacity property of the newBubble object.

b. Change the hue of the bubble by applying the changeColor() method to the newBubble object and applying the `filter` style

```
hue-rotate(huedeg)
```

to bubbleImg where *hue* is the value of the newBubble's hue property.

c. Spin the bubble by applying the rotateBubble() method to the newBubble object and applying the transform style

```
rotate(rotatedeg)
```

to bubbleImg, where *rotate* is the value of the newBubble's rotate property.

d. Move the bubble by applying the moveBubble() method with box.height and box.width as the argument values. Set the `top` and `left` styles of bubbleImg to the values of the yPos and xPos properties of the newBubble object.

16. Document your work by commenting your code throughout the file.

17. Save your changes to the file and then load **bu_home.html** in your browser. Verify that the animated bubbles are displayed in the company logo that spin, move, bounce off the wall, and change colors in random fashion. Verify that the bubbles eventually fade out, to be replaced by new bubbles of varying sizes and shapes.

Case Problem 2

Data Files needed for this Case Problem: cc_staff_txt.html, cc_staff_txt.js, 2 CSS files, 1 JS file, 38 PNG files

Crescent Credit Union League Richard Coates is the IT manager at the Crescent Credit Union League (CCUL), an advocacy group for credit unions, providing a political voice for credit unions and offering education and training for CCUL members. Richard wants you to work on the CCUL's staff directory page for its website. He wants users to be able to search the directory, retrieving contact information for specific employees at CCUL.

The staff directory is stored in an object literal named "staff" that contains a single object named "directory". The directory object contains an array of objects that displays each employee's id, first and last name, position, department, e-mail address, phone number, and image file. Your job is to create a search tool that searches the staff object directory array for employees whose last name, position, and/or department matches the user's search conditions. A preview of the page you will create is shown in Figure 14-48.

Figure 14-48 Crescent Credit Union League staff directory

Almeidah/openclipart.org; Rawpixel.com/Shutterstock.com; © Courtesy Patrick Carey

Complete the following:

1. Use your editor to open the **cc_staff_txt.html** and **cc_staff_txt.js** files from the html14 ▸ case2 folder. Enter *your name* and *the date* in the comment section of each file, and save them as **cc_staff.html** and **cc_staff.js** respectively.

2. Go to the **cc_staff.html** file in your editor. Within the document head, add `script` elements for the **cc_data.js** and **cc_staff.js** files in that order. Load the files asynchronously. Take some time to study the contents of the file and then close it, saving your changes.

3. Use your editor to open the **cc_data.js** file and study the data stored in the staff object to become familiar with its contents and structure. Close the file, but do not make any changes to the document.

4. Go to the **cc_staff.js** file in your editor. Richard has already created a constructor function for the class of employee objects storing each employee's id, name, department, position, e-mail, phone, and photo. He has also already created an object literal named **searchResult** that will be used to store the search results in an employees array.

5. Go to the event listener for the `click` event. This event listener will run the code that displays the search results in a staff table. Within this event listener, add the code specified in Steps 6 through 19.

6. Richard has added the removeChildren() method to the prototype of the `HTMLElement` object that removes all children from a DOM element. Apply this method to the tableBody variable to remove all table rows that might still be present in the staff table from previous searches.

7. Erase previous search results by setting the employees array of the searchResult object to the empty array [].

8. Next, you will write the code that returns the employee records that match search conditions set by the user. Apply the `forEach()` array method to loop through the contents of the directory array in the staff object. For each employee object in the directory array, run an anonymous function with the parameter, **record**, that represents each record in the array. Add the commands specified in Steps 9 through 15 to the anonymous function within the `forEach()` array method.

9. Create the **nameSearch** variable equal to the value entered in the nameSearch input box.

10. Users can search for names in three ways: 1) Matching an employee's last name if it contains the text string specified in nameSearch, 2) Matching an employee's last name if it begins with the nameSearch text string, and 3) Matching an employee's last name only if it exactly matches the nameSearch text string. Richard has supplied you with code to add the selectedValue() method to the prototype of the `HTMLSelectElement` object class in order to return the value of the selected option in any selection list. Apply the selectedValue() method to the nameSearchType selection list to return the option selected by the user, storing the value in the **nameSearchType** variable.

11. Create a `switch-case` structure for the following possible values of the nameSearchType variable:
    a. If nameSearchType equals "contains", use the `new RegExp()` constructor to create a regular expression object named **nameRegExp** containing the regular expression *nameSearch* where *nameSearch* is the value of the nameSearch variable. Include the "`i`" flag with the regular expression object so that the regular expression matches lowercase or uppercase characters.
    b. If nameSearchType equals "beginsWith", set nameRegExp object to the regular expression ^*nameSearch*, once again with the "`i`" flag.
    c. If nameSearchType equals "exact", set nameRegExp object to the regular expression ^*nameSearch*$ with the "`i`" flag to allow for uppercase and lowercase matches.

12. Using nameRegExp as the regular expression, apply the `test()` method to the record.Lastname property (the last name stored in the employee record currently being examined in the `forEach()` loop). Store the results of the `test()` method in the **foundName** variable.

13. Repeat Steps 9 through 12 to determine whether the employee's position property matches the value entered into the positionSearch input box on the web form. Store the value of the positionSearch input box in the **positionSearch** variable, the type of search in the **positionSearchType** variable, the regular expression in the **positionRegExp** variable, and the result of the regular expression test in the **foundPosition** variable.

14. The final search condition in the web form allows the user to specify the employee's department. Users can leave the department blank (to match any department) or they can specify the department from the deptSearch selection list. Apply the selectedValue() method that Richard created for `select` elements to the deptSearch selection list to retrieve the department value selected by the user, storing the value in the **deptSearch** variable. If deptSearch equals "" or the value of record.dept (the value of the dept property for the current employee record currently being examined in the `forEach()` loop), store the Boolean value `true` in the **foundDept** variable.

15. For an employee record to be displayed in the staff table, it must match the search condition set by the user. Insert an `if` statement that tests whether foundName, foundPosition, and foundDept are all `true`. If so, use the `push()` method to add a new employee object to the employees array in the searchResult object. (*Hint*: use record.id, record.firstName, record.lastName, and so on as the parameter values in the new employee() statement.)

16. After the `forEach` loop has finished and the employees array in the searchResult object contains all of the employee records matching the user's search conditions, change the text content of the tableCaption object to "*total* records found" where *total* is the value of the length of the employees array in the searchResult object.

17. Apply the sortById() method to the searchResult object, which will sort the content of the employees array by the employee ID number.

18. Finally, add a table row to the body of the staff table: one row for each employee record. Apply the `forEach()` method to employees array in the searchResult object and for each record in the array, append the following document fragment to the tableBody object

    ```
    <tr>
        <td><img src="photo" /></td>
        <td>first last</td>
        <td>dept</td>
        <td>position</td>
        <td><a href="mailto:email">email</a></td>
        <td><a href="tel:phone">phone</a></td>
    </tr>
    ```

    where *photo*, *first*, *last*, *dept*, *position*, *email*, and *phone* are the values of the photo, firstName, lastName, dept, position, email, and phone property of the current record in the employees array of the searchResult object.

19. Document your work on the application with descriptive comments and then save your work.

20. Open the **cc_staff.html** file in your browser. Verify that you can use the Search form to search for employees based on their last name, department, and position. Further verify that you can apply the Contains, Begin With, and Exact options for matching the employee's last name and position in the company.

Case Problem 3

Data Files needed for this Case Problem: rb_pizza_txt.html, rb_build_txt.js, 2 CSS files, 18 PNG files

CHALLENGE

Red Ball Pizza   Alice Nichols, the manager at *Red Ball Pizza*, in Ormond Beach, Florida, wants to add online ordering to the store's website. She's asked your help in writing the code for a page in which customers can select options from a web form to create a custom pizza and add their selections to a shopping cart. As they select what to put on the pizza, a preview of the completed pizza appears on the web page. A preview of the page is shown in Figure 14-49.

Figure 14-49   **Build a pizza at Red Ball Pizza**

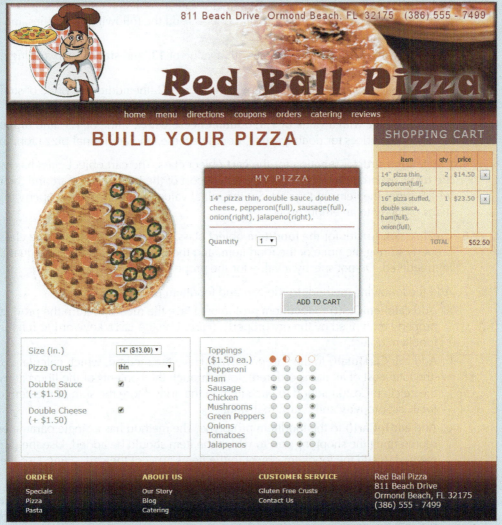

Maksim Denisenko/Shutterstock.com; Maxim Maksutov/Shutterstock.com; Shebeko/Shutterstock.com; © Courtesy of Patrick Carey

Alice has already designed the page and included some of the code for the web page. Your job will be to complete the programming by adding custom objects, properties, and methods for the pizza and the shopping cart.

Complete the following:

1. Use your editor to open the **rb_pizza_txt.html** and **rb_build_txt.js** files from the html14 ▸ case3 folder. Enter *your name* and *the date* in the comment section of each file, and save them as **rb_pizza.html** and **rb_build.js** respectively.

2. Go to the **rb_pizza.html** file in your editor. Link the file to the **rb_build.js** file, loading that file asynchronously.

3. Take some time to study the elements in the web form, noting the IDs and classes associated with each element. Save your changes to the file and then go to the **rb_build.js** file in your editor.

4. Directly below the initial comment section, create an object literal named **pizzaPrice** that will store the price of individual pizza components. Add the following properties and values to the object literal:
   - **size12** with a value of 11, **size14** with a value of **13**, and **size16** with a value of **16** (the prices of 12", 14", and 16" pizzas)
   - **stuffed** with a value of **3** and **pan** with a value of **2** (the additional price of stuff-crust and pan-style pizzas)
   - **doubleSauce** with a value of **1.5**, **doubleCheese** with a value of **1.5**, and **topping** with a value of **1.5** (the prices for double sauce, double cheese, and additional pizza toppings.)

5. Create a constructor function for the **cart** object class. The cart object class has two properties: the **totalCost** property, which stores the total cost of the items in the cart and the **items** array, which stores the items in the cart. Set the initial value of the totalCost property to 0 and set the items property to an empty array.

6. Create a constructor for the **foodItem** object class. Add two properties to the class: the **price** property storing the price of the food item, and the **qty** property storing the quantity of the food item ordered. Do not specify a value for the properties.

7. Add the following methods to the cart and foodItem prototypes:
   a. Add **calcItemCost()** to foodItem prototype. Have the method return the product of the price property multiplied by the qty property. (*Hint*: Use the `this` keyword to reference the foodItem object.)
   b. Add **calcCartTotal()** to the cart prototype. Have the method, which calculates the cartTotal (the total cost of all items ordered), loop through the contents of the items array and apply the calcItemCost() method to each item in the array. Store the sum of the item costs in the totalCost property and return that value.
   c. Add **addToCart()** to the foodItem prototype. The method has a single parameter named **cart** representing the shopping cart to which the item should be added. Use the `push()` Array method to add the foodItem object to the items array of the cart. (*Hint*: Use the `this` keyword to reference the foodItem object.)
   d. Add **removeFromCart()** to the foodItem prototype. The method has a single parameter named **cart** representing the shopping cart from which the item should be removed. Loop through the items array in the cart object and for each item test whether it is equal to the foodItem object. If it is, use the `splice()` method to remove the object from the items array and break off the `for` loop. (*Hint*: Use the `this` keyword to reference the foodItem object and use the `splice(index, 1)` to remove the foodItem where *index* is the counter variable in the `for` loop.)

8. Create the following constructors for pizzas and toppings on pizzas:
   a. Create a constructor for the **pizza** object class. Add the following properties to the class: **size** (for the size of the pizza), **crust** (for the crust style), **doubleSauce** and **doubleCheese**

(to indicate whether pizza has double sauce or double cheese), and the **toppings** property (for storing the array of topping items on the pizza). Do not set an initial value for the size, crust, doubleSauce, or doubleCheese properties. Set toppings to an empty array.

b. Create a constructor for the **topping** object class. Add the **name** property for storing the name of the topping, and the **side** property for recording whether the topping should be across the full pizza, or only on the left or right side. Do not set an initial value for either property.

⊕ **Explore** 9. Have both the pizza and topping object class inherit the properties and methods of any food item by making their prototypes instances of the foodItem object.

10. Add the **addTopping()** method to the pizza object prototype. The method has a single parameter named "topping". Use the `push()` Array method to add topping to the toppings array of the pizza.

11. Add the **calcPizzaPrice()** method to the pizza prototype. The purpose of this method is to calculate the total price of the pizza with all of its selected options. Add the following commands to the method:

a. Based on the value of the size property, set the value of the pizza's price property to either the value of the size12, size14, or size16 property of the pizzaPrice object you created in Step 4.

b. If the pizza crust equals "stuffed" or "pan", increase the value of the price property by the corresponding value of the stuffed or pan properties of the pizzaPrice object.

c. If the doubleSauce or doubleCheese values are `true`, increase the price by the corresponding value of the doubleSauce or doubleCheese properties of the pizzaPrice object.

d. Loop through the contents of the toppings array and for each topping, calculate the qty property of the topping multiplied by the value of the topping property of pizzaPrice. Add the value to the pizza's price.

e. Return the final calculated value of the price property.

12. Now that you've defined the custom objects for ordering pizzas, scroll down to the event listener for the `load` event. Alice has already nested the buildPizza() and addPizzaToCart() functions in the event listener but you will have to complete these functions to create a working shopping cart page. Directly before the buildPizza() function, insert the following commands:

a. Declare the **myCart** variable as an instance of a cart object.

b. Run the addPizzaToCart() function when the addToCartButton form button is clicked.

⊕ **Explore** 13. Go to the buildPizza() function that builds the pizza based on the values entered into the web form. The function has a single parameter, newPizza, which represents a new pizza that will be created based on the customer's choices. Add commands described in Steps 14 through 18 to the function.

14. Set the qty property of newPizza to the selected value in the pizzaQuantityBox selection list. (*Hint*: Use the selectedValue() method that has been added to the `Array` prototype to return the value of the selected option in a selected list.)

15. Set the size property of newPizza to the selected value in the pizzaSizeBox selection list. Set the crust property of newPizza to the selected value in the pizzaCrustBox selection list.

16. Set the doubleSauce and doubleCheese properties of newPizza to the `checked` properties of the doubleSauceBox and doubleCheeseBox check boxes.

17. Declare the variable **checkedToppings**, which contains all the topping option buttons that have been checked by the user. (*Hint*: Use the CSS selector `input.topping:checked` to create the object collection.)

18. Loop through the option buttons in checkedToppings and for each option, test whether the option button value is not equal to "none". If true, then do the following:

a. Declare **myTopping** as an instance of the topping object class.

b. Set the name property of myTopping to the name of the option button and set the side property of myTopping to the value of the option button.

c. If option button value is "full", then set the qty property of myTopping to 1, otherwise set the value of the qty property to 0.5.

d. Apply the addTopping() method to add myTopping to newPizza.

Explore 19. Next, you will complete the function that adds a pizza to the shopping cart. Go to the addPizzaToCart() function and insert the commands described in Steps 20 through 26.

20. Declare the **myPizza** variable as an instance of the pizza object class. Call the buildPizza() function to build the ingredients of myPizza and then apply the addToCart() method to myPizza to add myPizza to myCart.

21. Items in the shopping cart are displayed in table rows of the body section of the cartTable table. Create the following table row structure, saved under the variable **newItemRow**

```
<tr>
    <td>summary</td>
    <td>qty</td>
    <td>price</td>
    <td>
        <input type="button" value="X" />
    </td>
</tr>
```

where summary is the text content of the pizzaSummary element, qty is the value of the qty property for myPizza, and $price$ is the value returned by the calcPizzaPrice() method applied to myPizza. Format $price$ as U.S. currency using the `toLocaleString()` method described in Tutorial 13. Give the element node for the input button, the variable name **removeButton**.

22. Append newItemRow to the cartTableBody element.

23. The cartTotalBox input box displays the total cost of the order. Set the value of cartTotalBox to the value returned by the calcCartTotal() method applied to my cart. Format the total cost as U.S. currency.

24. Display the contents of myCart in the console log of your browser's debugger.

25. Alice wants customers to be able to remove items from the shopping cart by clicking the removeItem button created in Step 21. Add an `onclick` event handler to removeButton that does the following:

a. Applies the removeFromCart() method to myPizza to remove myPizza from myCart.

b. Removes the newItemRow from cartTableBody.

c. Changes the value of cartTotalBox to the value returned by the calcCartTotal() method applied to myCart (now with the removed pizza item). Displays the new total as U.S. currency.

d. Displays the revised contents of myCart in the debugger console log.

26. Call the resetDrawPizza() function to restore the web form controls to their original appearances.

27. Document your work on the order application with descriptive comments and then save your work.

28. Open **rb_pizza.html** in your browser. Verify that you can add pizza selections to the shopping cart using the web form controls and that they will appear in the shopping cart table. Further verify that as you add and remove items from the shopping cart by clicking the "X" button, the contents of myCart, as displayed in the debugger console, are similarly updated to reflect the new shopping cart contents.

CREATE

Case Problem 4

Data Files needed for this Case Problem: kg_stamps_txt.html, kg_stamps_txt.js, 2 CSS files, 39 PNG files

Kidder Garden   Pete Burnham of the Kidder Garden website wants you to develop an application for drawing images or "stamps". As a proof of concept, he wants you to create a web page in which users can choose stamps of a specified size and shade (opacity) and then place those stamp images on a canvas using the mouse. The user can then modify the size, position, rotation, or shading (opacity) by clicking tools from a toolbar and applying that tool to a stamp image. Pete has already designed the web page. He needs you to write the code to create the stamp objects and place them as images on the page's canvas. Figure 14-50 shows a preview of a completed page with stamp images created and modified by the user.

Figure 14-50   **Stamps game at Kidder Garden**

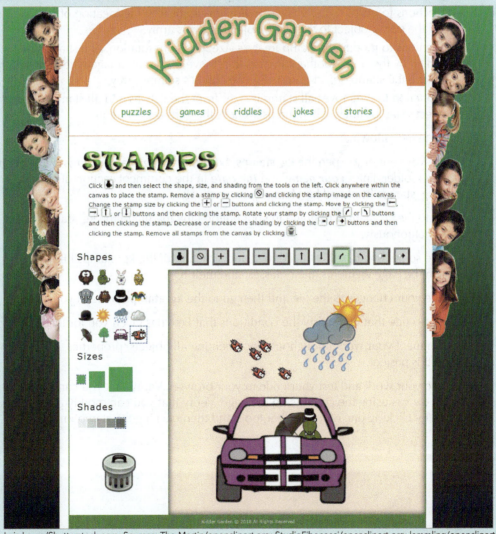

Luis Louro/Shutterstock.com; Sources: The Martin/openclipart.org; StudioFibonacci/openclipart.org; lemmling/openclipart.org; asrafil/openclicpart.org; uroesch/openclipart.org; dominquechappard/openclipart.org; ivak/openclipart.org; frankes/openclipart.org; GR8DAN/openclipart.org; LX/openclipart.org; alekids/openclipart.org; Gerald_G/openclipart.org; Firkin/openclipart.org; Andy/openclipart.org; © Courtesy Patrick Carey

Pete has also supplied you with the following object methods that will be useful to you:

- The elementX() method for the Event object prototype that returns the x-coordinate of a mouse click event occurring within an element.
- The elementY() method for the Event object prototype that returns the y-coordinate of a mouse click event occurring within an element.
- The removeChildren() method that removes all child nodes from an element.

The final form of the code is up to you and may include enhancements that you think will add to the value of the final application, but it must include the following:

- An interface that shows the currently selected shape, size, and shading (opacity) controls and the currently selected tool from the toolbar.
- A custom stamp object that stores the shape, size, and shade (opacity) of a stamp.
- A custom game object that stores the current control and tool option selected by the user and includes an array of all stamp objects created by the user.
- A custom method for the class of stamp objects to add the stamp to the stamps array within the game object and another method to empty out the game object's stamps array.
- Functions to place stamp images on the page canvas at the location of the user's mouse click and add the stamp object to the game object's stamps array.
- Functions to modify the stamp image's size, position, rotation, and shading when the image is clicked by the user. Another function to remove the stamp image when clicked by the user and to remove the stamp object from the game object's stamps array.
- A function that removes all stamp images from the canvas and all stamp objects from the game object's stamps array, when the user clicks the garbage can icon.

Complete the following:

1. Use your editor to open the **kg_stamps_txt.html** and **kg_stamps_txt.js** files from the html14 ▶ case4 folder. Enter *your name* and *the date* in the comment section of each file, and save them as **kg_stamps.html** and **kg_stamps.js** respectively.

2. Go to the **kg_stamps.html** file in your editor. Link the file to the **kg_stamps.js** file, loading that file asynchronously.

3. Take some time to study the content and structure of the kg_stamps.html file, becoming familiar with the page elements, their classes, and their IDs.

4. Save your changes to the file and then go to the **kg_stamps.js** file in your editor.

5. Write code that will satisfy the conditions that Pete has given you for the final application.

6. Comment your work throughout, documenting all objects, properties, and methods you created for this project.

7. Save your work and test your code in your browser. Verify that you can place stamp images on the canvas using the controls on the page. Verify that you can modify a stamp image on the canvas by clicking one of the toolbar tools and then clicking the stamp image.

Color Names with Color Values, and HTML Character Entities

Both HTML and XHTML allow you to define colors using either color names or color values. HTML and XHTML support a list of 16 basic color names. Most browsers also support an extended list of color names, which are listed in Table A-1 in this appendix, along with their RGB and hexadecimal values.

Table A-2 in this appendix lists the extended character set for HTML, also known as the ISO Latin-1 Character Set. You can specify characters by name or by numeric value. For example, you can use either ® or ® to specify the registered trademark symbol, ®.

STARTING DATA FILES

There are no starting Data Files needed for this appendix.

Table A-1:
Color names and corresponding values

Color Name	RGB Value	Hexadecimal Value
aliceblue	(240,248,255)	#F0F8FF
antiquewhite	(250,235,215)	#FAEBD7
aqua	(0,255,255)	#00FFFF
aquamarine	(127,255,212)	#7FFFD4
azure	(240,255,255)	#F0FFFF
beige	(245,245,220)	#F5F5DC
bisque	(255,228,196)	#FFE4C4
black	(0,0,0)	#000000
blanchedalmond	(255,235,205)	#FFEBCD
blue	(0,0,255)	#0000FF
blueviolet	(138,43,226)	#8A2BE2
brown	(165,42,42)	#A52A2A
burlywood	(222,184,135)	#DEB887
cadetblue	(95,158,160)	#5F9EA0
chartreuse	(127,255,0)	#7FFF00
chocolate	(210,105,30)	#D2691E
coral	(255,127,80)	#FF7F50
cornflowerblue	(100,149,237)	#6495ED
cornsilk	(255,248,220)	#FFF8DC
crimson	(220,20,54)	#DC1436
cyan	(0,255,255)	#00FFFF
darkblue	(0,0,139)	#00008B
darkcyan	(0,139,139)	#008B8B
darkgoldenrod	(184,134,11)	#B8860B
darkgray	(169,169,169)	#A9A9A9
darkgreen	(0,100,0)	#006400
darkkhaki	(189,183,107)	#BDB76B
darkmagenta	(139,0,139)	#8B008B
darkolivegreen	(85,107,47)	#556B2F
darkorange	(255,140,0)	#FF8C00
darkorchid	(153,50,204)	#9932CC
darkred	(139,0,0)	#8B0000
darksalmon	(233,150,122)	#E9967A
darkseagreen	(143,188,143)	#8FBC8F
darkslateblue	(72,61,139)	#483D8B
darkslategray	(47,79,79)	#2F4F4F
darkturquoise	(0,206,209)	#00CED1
darkviolet	(148,0,211)	#9400D3
deeppink	(255,20,147)	#FF1493
deepskyblue	(0,191,255)	#00BFFF
dimgray	(105,105,105)	#696969
dodgerblue	(30,144,255)	#1E90FF
firebrick	(178,34,34)	#B22222
floralwhite	(255,250,240)	#FFFAF0
forestgreen	(34,139,34)	#228B22
fuchsia	(255,0,255)	#FF00FF

Color Name	RGB Value	Hexadecimal Value
gainsboro	(220,220,220)	#DCDCDC
ghostwhite	(248,248,255)	#F8F8FF
gold	(255,215,0)	#FFD700
goldenrod	(218,165,32)	#DAA520
gray	(128,128,128)	#808080
green	(0,128,0)	#008000
greenyellow	(173,255,47)	#ADFF2F
honeydew	(240,255,240)	#F0FFF0
hotpink	(255,105,180)	#FF69B4
indianred	(205,92,92)	#CD5C5C
indigo	(75,0,130)	#4B0082
ivory	(255,255,240)	#FFFFF0
khaki	(240,230,140)	#F0E68C
lavender	(230,230,250)	#E6E6FA
lavenderblush	(255,240,245)	#FFF0F5
lawngreen	(124,252,0)	#7CFC00
lemonchiffon	(255,250,205)	#FFFACD
lightblue	(173,216,230)	#ADD8E6
lightcoral	(240,128,128)	#F08080
lightcyan	(224,255,255)	#E0FFFF
lightgoldenrodyellow	(250,250,210)	#FAFAD2
lightgreen	(144,238,144)	#90EE90
lightgrey	(211,211,211)	#D3D3D3
lightpink	(255,182,193)	#FFB6C1
lightsalmon	(255,160,122)	#FFA07A
lightseagreen	(32,178,170)	#20B2AA
lightskyblue	(135,206,250)	#87CEFA
lightslategray	(119,136,153)	#778899
lightsteelblue	(176,196,222)	#B0C4DE
lightyellow	(255,255,224)	#FFFFE0
lime	(0,255,0)	#00FF00
limegreen	(50,205,50)	#32CD32
linen	(250,240,230)	#FAF0E6
magenta	(255,0,255)	#FF00FF
maroon	(128,0,0)	#800000
mediumaquamarine	(102,205,170)	#66CDAA
mediumblue	(0,0,205)	#0000CD
mediumorchid	(186,85,211)	#BA55D3
mediumpurple	(147,112,219)	#9370DB
mediumseagreen	(60,179,113)	#3CB371
mediumslateblue	(123,104,238)	#7B68EE
mediumspringgreen	(0,250,154)	#00FA9A
mediumturquoise	(72,209,204)	#48D1CC
mediumvioletred	(199,21,133)	#C71585
midnightblue	(25,25,112)	#191970
mintcream	(245,255,250)	#F5FFFA
mistyrose	(255,228,225)	#FFE4E1

Color Name	RGB Value	Hexadecimal Value
moccasin	(255,228,181)	#FFE4B5
navajowhite	(255,222,173)	#FFDEAD
navy	(0,0,128)	#000080
oldlace	(253,245,230)	#FDF5E6
olive	(128,128,0)	#808000
olivedrab	(107,142,35)	#6B8E23
orange	(255,165,0)	#FFA500
orangered	(255,69,0)	#FF4500
orchid	(218,112,214)	#DA70D6
palegoldenrod	(238,232,170)	#EEE8AA
palegreen	(152,251,152)	#98FB98
paleturquoise	(175,238,238)	#AFEEEE
palevioletred	(219,112,147)	#DB7093
papayawhip	(255,239,213)	#FFEFD5
peachpuff	(255,218,185)	#FFDAB9
peru	(205,133,63)	#CD853F
pink	(255,192,203)	#FFC0CB
plum	(221,160,221)	#DDA0DD
powderblue	(176,224,230)	#B0E0E6
purple	(128,0,128)	#808080
red	(255,0,0)	#FF0000
rosybrown	(188,143,143)	#BC8F8F
royalblue	(65,105,0)	#4169E1
saddlebrown	(139,69,19)	#8B4513
salmon	(250,128,114)	#FA8072
sandybrown	(244,164,96)	#F4A460
seagreen	(46,139,87)	#2E8B57
seashell	(255,245,238)	#FFF5EE
sienna·	(160,82,45)	#A0522D
silver	(192,192,192)	#C0C0C0
skyblue	(135,206,235)	#87CEEB
slateblue	(106,90,205)	#6A5ACD
slategray	(112,128,144)	#708090
snow	(255,250,250)	#FFFAFA
springgreen	(0,255,127)	#00FF7F
steelblue	(70,130,180)	#4682B4
tan	(210,180,140)	#D2B48C
teal	(0,128,128)	#008080
thistle	(216,191,216)	#D8BFD8
tomato	(255,99,71)	#FF6347
turquoise	(64,224,208)	#40E0D0
violet	(238,130,238)	#EE82EE
wheat	(245,222,179)	#F5DEB3
white	(255,255,255)	#FFFFFF
whitesmoke	(245,245,245)	#F5F5F5
yellow	(255,255,0)	#FFFF00
yellowgreen	(154,205,50)	#9ACD32

Character	Code	Code Name	Description
	&#09;		Tab
	&#10;		Line feed
	&#32;		Space
!	&#33;		Exclamation mark
"	&#34;	&quot;	Double quotation mark
#	&#35;		Pound sign
$	&#36;		Dollar sign
%	&#37;		Percent sign
&	&#38;	&amp;	Ampersand
'	&#39;		Apostrophe
(	&#40;		Left parenthesis
)	&#41;		Right parenthesis
*	&#42;		Asterisk
+	&#43;		Plus sign
,	&#44;		Comma
-	&#45;		Hyphen
.	&#46;		Period
/	&#47;		Forward slash
0 - 9	0–9		Numbers 0–9
:	&#58;		Colon
;	&#59;		Semicolon
<	&#60;	&lt;	Less than sign
=	&#61;		Equal sign
>	&#62;	&gt;	Greater than sign
?	&#63;		Question mark
@	&#64;		Commercial at sign
A - Z	A–Z		Letters A–Z
[	&#91;		Left square bracket
\	&#92;		Back slash
]	&#93;		Right square bracket
^	&#94;		Caret
_	&#95;		Horizontal bar (underscore)
`	&#96;		Grave accent
a - z	a–z		Letters a–z
{	&#123;		Left curly brace
|	|		Vertical bar
}	&#125;		Right curly brace
~	&#126;		Tilde
,	&#130;		Comma
ƒ	&#131;		Function sign (florin)
"	&#132;		Double quotation mark
…	&#133;		Ellipsis
†	&#134;		Dagger

Character	Code	Code Name	Description
‡	&#135;		Double dagger
ˆ	&#136;		Circumflex
‰	&#137;		Permil
Š	&#138;		Capital S with hacek
‹	&#139;		Left single angle
Œ	&#140;		Capital OE ligature
	–		Unused
'	&#145;		Single beginning quotation mark
'	&#146;		Single ending quotation mark
"	&#147;		Double beginning quotation mark
"	&#148;		Double ending quotation mark
•	&#149;		Bullet
–	&#150;		En dash
—	&#151;		Em dash
~	&#152;		Tilde
™	&#153;	&trade;	Trademark symbol
š	&#154;		Small s with hacek
›	&#155;		Right single angle
œ	&#156;		Lowercase oe ligature
Ÿ	&#159;		Capital Y with umlaut
			Non-breaking space
¡	&#161;	&iexcl;	Inverted exclamation mark
¢	&#162;	&cent;	Cent sign
£	&#163;	&pound;	Pound sterling
¤	&#164;	&curren;	General currency symbol
¥	&#165;	&yen;	Yen sign
¦	&#166;	&brvbar;	Broken vertical bar
§	&#167;	&sect;	Section sign
¨	&#168;	&uml;	Umlaut
©	&#169;	&copy;	Copyright symbol
ª	&#170;	&ordf;	Feminine ordinal
«	&#171;	&laquo;	Left angle quotation mark
¬	&#172;	&not;	Not sign
	&#173;	&shy;	Soft hyphen
®	&#174;	&reg;	Registered trademark
¯	&#175;	&macr;	Macron
°	&#176;	&deg;	Degree sign
±	&#177;	&plusmn;	Plus/minus symbol
²	&#178;	&sup2;	Superscript 2
³	&#179;	&sup3;	Superscript 3
´	&#180;	&acute;	Acute accent
µ	&#181;	&micro;	Micro sign
¶	&#182;	&para;	Paragraph sign

Character	Code	Code Name	Description
·	&#183;	&middot;	Middle dot
ç	&#184;	&cedil;	Cedilla
¹	&#185;	&sup1;	Superscript 1
º	&#186;	&ordm;	Masculine ordinal
»	&#187;	&raquo;	Right angle quotation mark
¼	&#188;	&frac14;	Fraction one-quarter
½	&#189;	&frac12;	Fraction one-half
¾	&#190;	&frac34;	Fraction three-quarters
¿	&#191;	&iquest;	Inverted question mark
À	&#192;	&Agrave;	Capital A, grave accent
Á	&#193;	&Aacute;	Capital A, acute accent
Â	&#194;	&Acirc;	Capital A, circumflex accent
Ã	&#195;	&Atilde;	Capital A, tilde
Ä	&#196;	&Auml;	Capital A, umlaut
Å	&#197;	&Aring;	Capital A, ring
Æ	&#198;	&Aelig;	Capital AE ligature
Ç	&#199;	&Ccedil;	Capital C, cedilla
È	&#200;	&Egrave;	Capital E, grave accent
É	&#201;	&Eacute;	Capital E, acute accent
Ê	&#202;	&Ecirc;	Capital E, circumflex accent
Ë	&#203;	&Euml;	Capital E, umlaut
Ì	&#204;	&Igrave;	Capital I, grave accent
Í	&#205;	&Iacute;	Capital I, acute accent
Î	&#206;	&Icirc;	Capital I, circumflex accent
Ï	&#207;	&Iuml;	Capital I, umlaut
Ð	&#208;	&ETH;	Capital ETH, Icelandic
Ñ	&#209;	&Ntilde;	Capital N, tilde
Ò	&#210;	&Ograve;	Capital O, grave accent
Ó	&#211;	&Oacute;	Capital O, acute accent
Ô	&#212;	&Ocirc;	Capital O, circumflex accent
Õ	&#213;	&Otilde;	Capital O, tilde
Ö	&#214;	&Ouml;	Capital O, umlaut
×	&#215;	&times;	Multiplication sign
Ø	&#216;	&Oslash;	Capital O, slash
Ù	&#217;	&Ugrave;	Capital U, grave accent
Ú	&#218;	&Uacute;	Capital U, acute accent
Û	&#219;	&Ucirc;	Capital U, circumflex accent
Ü	&#220;	&Uuml;	Capital U, umlaut
Ý	&#221;	&Yacute;	Capital Y, acute accent
Þ	&#222;	&THORN;	Capital THORN, Icelandic
ß	&#223;	&szlig;	Small sz, ligature
à	&#224;	&agrave;	Small a, grave accent
á	&#225;	&aacute;	Small a, acute accent

Character	Code	Code Name	Description
â	&#226;	&acirc;	Small a, circumflex accent
ã	&#227;	&atilde;	Small a, tilde
ä	&#228;	&auml;	Small a, umlaut
å	&#229;	&aring;	Small a, ring
æ	&#230;	&aelig;	Small ae, ligature
ç	&#231;	&ccedil;	Small c, cedilla
è	&#232;	&egrave;	Small e, grave accent
é	&#233;	&eacute;	Small e, acute accent
ê	&#234;	&ecirc;	Small e, circumflex accent
ë	&#235;	&euml;	Small e, umlaut
ì	&#236;	&igrave;	Small i, grave accent
í	&#237;	&iacute;	Small i, acute accent
î	&#238;	&icirc;	Small i, circumflex accent
ï	&#239;	&iuml;	Small i, umlaut
ð	&#240;	&eth;	Small eth, Icelandic
ñ	&#241;	&ntilde;	Small n, tilde
ò	&#242;	&ograve;	Small o, grave accent
ó	&#243;	&oacute;	Small o, acute accent
ô	&#244;	&ocirc;	Small o, circumflex accent
õ	&#245;	&otilde;	Small o, tilde
ö	&#246;	&ouml;	Small o, umlaut
÷	&#247;	&divide;	Division sign
ø	&#248;	&oslash;	Small o, slash
ù	&#249;	&ugrave;	Small u, grave accent
ú	&#250;	&uacute;	Small u, acute accent
û	&#251;	&ucirc;	Small u, circumflex accent
ü	&#252;	&uuml;	Small u, umlaut
ý	&#253;	&yacute;	Small y, acute accent
þ	&#254;	&thorn;	Small thorn, Icelandic
ÿ	&#255;	&yuml;	Small y, umlaut

APPENDIX **B**

HTML Elements and Attributes

This appendix provides descriptions of the major elements and attributes of HTML. The elements and attributes represent the specifications of the W3C; therefore, they might not all be supported by the major browsers. Also, in some cases, an element or attribute is not part of the W3C specifications, but instead is an extension offered by a particular browser. Where this is the case, the element or attribute is listed with the supporting browser indicated in parentheses.

Many elements and attributes have been deprecated by the W3C. Deprecated elements and attributes are supported by most browsers, but their use is discouraged. In addition, some elements and attributes have been marked as *obsolete*. The use of both deprecated and obsolete items is not recommended. However, while deprecated items are in danger of no longer being supported by the browser market, obsolete items will probably still be supported by the browser market for the foreseeable future.

Finally, elements and attributes that are new with HTML5 are indicated by (HTML5) in the text. Note that some of these elements and attributes are not supported by all browsers and browser versions.

The following data types are used throughout this appendix:

- *char* A single text character
- *char code* A character encoding
- *color* An HTML color name or value
- *date* A date and time in the format: *yyyy-mm-dd*T*hh:mm:ss*TIMEZONE
- *id* An id value
- *lang* A language type
- *media* A media type equal to all, aural, braille, handheld, print, projection, screen, tty, or tv
- *integer* An integer value
- *mime-type* A MIME data type, such as "text/html"
- *mime-type list* A comma-separated list of mime-types
- **option1**|*option2*| … The value is limited to the specified list of *options*, with the default in **bold**
- *script* A script or a reference to a script
- *styles* A list of style declarations
- *text* A text string
- *text list* A comma-separated list of text strings
- *url* The URL for a web page or file
- *value* A numeric value
- *value list* A comma-separated list of numeric values

STARTING DATA FILES

There are no starting Data Files needed for this appendix.

General Attributes

Several attributes are common to many page elements. Rather than repeating this information each time it occurs, the following tables summarize these attributes.

Core Attributes

The following attributes apply to all page elements and are supported by most browser versions.

Attribute	Description
class="text"	Specifies the class or group to which an element belongs
contenteditable= "text list"	Specifies whether the contents of the element are editable (HTML5)
contextmenu="id"	Specifies the value of the id attribute on the menu with which to associate the element as a context menu
draggable="true|false"	Specifies whether the element is draggable (HTML5)
dropzone= "copy|move|link"	Specifies what types of content can be dropped on the element and which actions to take with content when it is dropped (HTML5)
hidden="hidden"	Specifies that the element is not yet, or is no longer, relevant and that the element should not be rendered (HTML5)
id="text"	Specifies a unique identifier to be associated with the element
spellcheck="true|false"	Specifies whether the element represents an element whose contents are subject to spell checking and grammar checking (HTML5)
style="styles"	Defines an inline style for the element
title="text"	Provides an advisory title for the element

Language Attributes

The web is designed to be universal and has to be adaptable to languages other than English. Thus, another set of attributes provides language support. This set of attributes is not as widely supported by browsers as the core attributes are. As with the core attributes, they can be applied to most page elements.

Attribute	Description
dir="**ltr**|rtl"	Indicates the text direction as related to the lang attribute; a value of ltr displays text from left to right; a value of rtl displays text from right to left
lang="lang"	Identifies the language used in the page where lang is the language code name

Form Attributes

The following attributes can be applied to most form elements or to a web form itself, but not to other page elements.

Attribute	Description
accesskey="char"	Indicates the keyboard character that can be pressed along with the accelerator key to access a form element
disabled="disabled"	Disables a form field for input
tabindex="integer"	Specifies a form element's position in a document's tabbing order

Event Attributes

To make web pages more dynamic, HTML supports event attributes that identify scripts to be run in response to an event occurring within an element. For example, clicking a main heading with a mouse can cause a browser to run a program that hides or expands a table of contents. Each event attribute has the form

```
onevent = "script"
```

where *event* is the name of the event attribute and *script* is the name of the script or command to be run by the browser in response to the occurrence of the event within the element.

Core Events

The core event attributes are part of the specifications for HTML. They apply to almost all page elements.

Attribute	Description
onabort	Loading of the element is aborted by the user. (HTML5)
onclick	The mouse button is clicked.
oncontextmenu	The user requested the context menu for the element. (HTML5)
ondblclick	The mouse button is double-clicked.
onerror	The element failed to load properly. (HTML5)
onkeydown	A key is pressed down.
onkeypress	A key is initially pressed.
onkeyup	A key is released.
onload	The element finishes loading. (HTML5)
onmousedown	The mouse button is pressed down.
onmousemove	The mouse pointer is moved within the element's boundaries.
onmouseout	The mouse pointer is moved out of the element's boundaries.
onmouseover	The mouse pointer hovers over the element.
onmouseup	The mouse button is released.
onmousewheel	The user rotates the mouse wheel.
onreadystatechange	The element and its resources finish loading. (HTML5)
onscroll	The element or document window is being scrolled. (HTML5)
onshow	The user requests that the element be shown as a context menu. (HTML5)
onsuspend	The browser suspends retrieving data. (HTML5)

Document Events

The following list of event attributes applies not to individual elements within the page, but to the entire document as it is displayed within the browser window or frame.

Attribute	Description
onafterprint	The document has finished printing (IE only).
onbeforeprint	The document is about to be printed (IE only).
onload	The page is finished being loaded.
onunload	The page is finished unloading.

Form Events

The following list of event attributes applies to either an entire web form or fields within a form.

Attribute	Description
onblur	The form field has lost the focus.
onchange	The value of the form field has been changed.
onfocus	The form field has received the focus.
onformchange	The user made a change in the value of a form field in the form. (HTML5)
onforminput	The value of a control in the form changes. (HTML5)
oninput	The value of an element changes. (HTML5)
oninvalid	The form field fails to meet validity constraints. (HTML5)
onreset	The form has been reset.
onselect	Text content has been selected in the form field.
onsubmit	The form has been submitted for processing.

Drag and Drop Events

The following list of event attributes applies to all page elements and can be used to respond to the user action of dragging and dropping objects in the web page.

Attribute	Description
ondrag	The user continues to drag the element. (HTML5)
ondragenter	The user ends dragging the element, entering the element into a valid drop target. (HTML5)
ondragleave	The user's drag operation leaves the element. (HTML5)
ondragover	The user continues a drag operation over the element. (HTML5)
ondragstart	The user starts dragging the element. (HTML5)
ondrop	The user completes a drop operation over the element. (HTML5)

Multimedia Events

The following list of event attributes applies to embedded multimedia elements such as audio and video clips and is used to respond to events initiated during the loading or playback of those elements.

Attribute	Description
oncanplay	The browser can resume playback of the video or audio, but determines when the playback will have to stop for further buffering.
oncanplaythrough	The browser can resume playback of the video or audio, and determines the playback can play through without further buffering. (HTML5)
ondurationchange	The DOM duration of the video or audio element changes. (HTML5)
onemptied	The video or audio element returns to the uninitialized state. (HTML5)
onended	The end of the video or audio is reached. (HTML5)
onloadeddata	The video or audio is at the current playback position for the first time. (HTML5)

Attribute	Description
onloadedmetadata	The duration and dimensions of the video or audio element are determined. (HTML5)
onloadstart	The browser begins looking for media data in the video or audio element. (HTML5)
onpause	The video or audio is paused. (HTML5)
onplay	The video or audio playback is initiated. (HTML5)
onplaying	The video or audio playback starts. (HTML5)
onprogress	The browser fetches data for the video or audio. (HTML5)
onratechange	The video or audio data changes. (HTML5)
onseeked	A seek operation on the audio or video element ends. (HTML5)
onseeking	Seeking is initiated on the audio or video. (HTML5)
onstalled	An attempt to retrieve data for the video or audio is not forthcoming. (HTML5)
ontimeupdate	The current playback position of the video or audio element changes. (HTML5)
onvolumechange	The volume of the video or audio element changes. (HTML5)
onwaiting	Playback of the video or audio stops because the next frame is unavailable. (HTML5)

HTML Elements and Attributes

The following table contains an alphabetic listing of the elements and attributes supported by HTML. Some attributes are not listed in this table but instead, they are described in the general attributes tables presented in the previous section of this appendix.

Element/Attribute	Description
`<!-- text -->`	Inserts a comment into the document (comments are not displayed in the rendered page)
`<!doctype>`	Specifies the Document Type Definition for a document
`<a> </a>`	Marks the beginning and end of a link
`charset="text"`	Specifies the character encoding of the linked document (obsolete)
`coords="value list"`	Specifies the coordinates of a hotspot in a client-side image map; the value list depends on the shape of the hotspot: shape="rect" "*left, right, top, bottom*" shape="circle" "*x_center, y_center, radius*" shape="poly" "*x1, y1, x2, y2, x3, y3, ...*" (obsolete)
`href="url"`	Specifies the URL of the link
`hreflang="text"`	Specifies the language of the linked document
`name="text"`	Specifies a name for the enclosed text, allowing it to be a link target (obsolete)
`rel="text"`	Specifies the relationship between the current page and the link specified by the href attribute
`rev="text"`	Specifies the reverse relationship between the current page and the link specified by the href attribute (obsolete)
`shape="rect|circle|polygon"`	Specifies the shape of the hotspot (obsolete)
`title="text"`	Specifies the pop-up text for the link
`target="text"`	Specifies the target window or frame for the link
`type="mime-type"`	Specifies the data type of the linked document
`<abbr> </abbr>`	Marks abbreviated text

Element/Attribute	Description
`<acronym> </acronym>`	Marks acronym text (deprecated)
`<address> </address>`	Marks address text
`<applet> </applet>`	Embeds an applet into the browser (deprecated)
`align="align"`	Specifies the alignment of the applet with the surrounding text where *align* is absmiddle, absbottom, baseline, bottom, center, left, middle, right, texttop, or top
`alt="text"`	Specifies alternate text for the applet (deprecated)
`archive="url"`	Specifies the URL of an archive containing classes and other resources to be used with the applet (deprecated)
`code="url"`	Specifies the URL of the applet's code/class (deprecated)
`codebase="url"`	Specifies the URL of all class files for the applet (deprecated)
`datafld="text"`	Specifies the data source that supplies bound data for use with the data source
`datasrc="text"`	Specifies the ID or URL of the applet's data source
`height="integer"`	Specifies the height of the applet in pixels
`hspace="integer"`	Specifies the horizontal space around the applet in pixels (deprecated)
`mayscript="mayscript"`	Permits access to the applet by programs embedded in the document
`name="text"`	Specifies the name assigned to the applet (deprecated)
`object="text"`	Specifies the name of the resource that contains a serialized representation of the applet (deprecated)
`src="url"`	Specifies an external URL reference to the applet
`vspace="integer"`	Specifies the vertical space around the applet in pixels (deprecated)
`width="integer"`	Specifies the width of the applet in pixels (deprecated)
`<area />`	Marks an image map hotspot
`alt="text"`	Specifies alternate text for the hotspot
`coords="value list"`	Specifies the coordinates of the hotspot; the value list depends on the shape of the hotspot: shape="rect" "*left, right, top, bottom*" shape="circle" "*x_center, y_center, radius*" shape="poly""*x1, y1, x2, y2, x3, y3, …*"
`href="url"`	Specifies the URL of the document to which the hotspot points
`hreflang="lang"`	Language of the hyperlink destination
`media="media"`	The media for which the destination of the hyperlink was designed
`rel="text"`	Specifies the relationship between the current page and the destination of the link
`nohref="nohref"`	Specifies that the hotspot does not point to a link
`shape="rect|circle|polygon"`	Specifies the shape of the hotspot
`target="text"`	Specifies the target window or frame for the link
`<article> </article>`	Structural element marking a page article (HTML5)
`<aside> </aside>`	Structural element marking a sidebar that is tangentially related to the main page content (HTML5)
`<audio> </audio>`	Marks embedded audio content (HTML5)
`autoplay="autoplay"`	Automatically begins playback of the audio stream
`preload="none|metadata|auto"`	Specifies whether to preload data to the browser
`controls="controls"`	Specifies whether to display audio controls

Element/Attribute	Description
loop="loop"	Specifies whether to automatically loop back to the beginning of the audio clip
src="url"	Provides the source of the audio clip
<b> </b>	Marks text offset from its surrounding content without conveying any extra emphasis or importance
<base />	Specifies global reference information for the document
href="url"	Specifies the URL from which all relative links in the document are based
target="text"	Specifies the target window or frame for links in the document
<basefont />	Specifies the font setting for the document text (deprecated)
color="color"	Specifies the text color (deprecated)
face="text list"	Specifies a list of fonts to be applied to the text (deprecated)
size="integer"	Specifies the size of the font range from 1 (smallest) to 7 (largest) (deprecated)
<bdi> </bdi>	Marks text that is isolated from its surroundings for the purposes of bidirectional text formatting (HTML5)
<bdo> </bdo>	Indicates that the enclosed text should be rendered with the direction specified by the dir attribute
<big> </big>	Increases the size of the enclosed text relative to the default font size (deprecated)
<blockquote> </blockquote>	Marks content as quoted from another source
cite="url"	Provides the source URL of the quoted content
<body> </body>	Marks the page content to be rendered by the browser
alink="color"	Specifies the color of activated links in the document (obsolete)
background="url"	Specifies the background image file used for the page (obsolete)
bgcolor="color"	Specifies the background color of the page (obsolete)
link="color"	Specifies the color of unvisited links (obsolete)
marginheight="integer"	Specifies the size of the margin above and below the page (obsolete)
marginwidth="integer"	Specifies the size of the margin to the left and right of the page (obsolete)
text="color"	Specifies the color of page text (obsolete)
vlink="color"	Specifies the color of previously visited links (obsolete)
 	Inserts a line break into the page
clear="none|left|right|all"	Displays the line break only when the specified margin is clear (obsolete)
<button> </button>	Creates a form button
autofocus="autofocus"	Gives the button the focus when the page is loaded (HTML5)
disabled="disabled"	Disables the button
form="text"	Specifies the form to which the button belongs (HTML5)
formaction="url"	Specifies the URL to which the form data is sent (HTML5)
formenctype="mime-type"	Specifies the encoding of the form data before it is sent (HTML5)
formmethod="get|post"	Specifies the HTTP method with which the form data is submitted
formnovalidate="formnovalidate"	Specifies that the form should not be validated during submission (HTML5)
formtarget="text"	Provides a name for the target of the button (HTML5)
name="text"	Provides the name assigned to the form button
type="submit|reset|button"	Specifies the type of form button
value="text"	Provides the value associated with the form button

Element/Attribute	Description
`<canvas> </canvas>`	Marks a resolution-dependent bitmapped region that can be used for dynamic rendering of images, graphs, and games (HTML5)
`height="integer"`	Height of canvas in pixels
`width="integer"`	Width of canvas in pixels
`<caption> </caption>`	Creates a table caption
`align="align"`	Specifies the alignment of the caption where *align* is bottom, center, left, right, or top (deprecated)
`valign="top|bottom"`	Specifies the vertical alignment of the caption
`<center> </center>`	Centers content horizontally on the page (obsolete)
`<cite> </cite>`	Marks citation text
`<code> </code>`	Marks text used for code samples
`<col> </col>`	Defines the settings for a column or group of columns (obsolete)
`align="align"`	Specifies the alignment of the content of the column(s) where *align* is left, right, or center
`char="char"`	Specifies a character in the column used to align column values (obsolete)
`charoff="integer"`	Specifies the offset in pixels from the alignment character specified in the char attribute (obsolete)
`span="integer"`	Specifies the number of columns in the group
`valign="align"`	Specifies the vertical alignment of the content in the column(s) where *align* is top, middle, bottom, or baseline
`width="integer"`	Specifies the width of the column(s) in pixels (obsolete)
`<colgroup> </colgroup>`	Creates a container for a group of columns
`align="align"`	Specifies the alignment of the content of the column group where *align* is left, right, or center (obsolete)
`char="char"`	Specifies a character in the column used to align column group values (obsolete)
`charoff="integer"`	Specifies the offset in pixels from the alignment character specified in the char attribute (obsolete)
`span="integer"`	Specifies the number of columns in the group
`valign="align"`	Specifies the vertical alignment of the content in the column group where *align* is top, middle, bottom, or baseline (obsolete)
`width="integer"`	Specifies the width of the columns in the group in pixels (obsolete)
`<command> </command>`	Defines a command button (HTML5)
`checked="checked"`	Selects the command
`disabled="disabled"`	Disables the command
`icon="url"`	Provides the URL for the image that represents the command
`label="text"`	Specifies the text of the command button
`radiogroup="text"`	Specifies the name of the group of commands toggled when the command itself is toggled
`type="command| radio|checkbox"`	Specifies the type of command button
`<datalist> </datalist>`	Encloses a set of option elements that can act as a dropdown list (HTML5)
`<dd> </dd>`	Marks text as a definition within a definition list

Element/Attribute	Description
`<del> </del>`	Marks text as deleted from the document
`cite="url"`	Provides the URL for the document that has additional information about the deleted text
`datetime="date"`	Specifies the date and time of the text deletion
`<details> </details>`	Represents a form control from which the user can obtain additional information or controls (HTML5)
`open="open"`	Specifies that the contents of the details element should be shown to the user
`<dfn> </dfn>`	Marks the defining instance of a term
`<dir> </dir>`	Contains a directory listing (deprecated)
`compact="compact"`	Permits use of compact rendering, if available (deprecated)
`<div> </div>`	Creates a generic block-level element
`align="left|center right|justify"`	Specifies the horizontal alignment of the content (obsolete)
`datafld="text"`	Indicates the column from a data source that supplies bound data for the block (IE only)
`dataformatas="html |plaintext|text"`	Specifies the format of the data in the data source bound with the the button (IE only)
`datasrc="url"`	Provides the URL or ID of the data source bound with the block (IE only)
`<dl> </dl>`	Encloses a definition list using the dd and dt elements
`compact="compact"`	Permits use of compact rendering, if available (obsolete)
`<dt> </dt>`	Marks a definition term in a definition list
`nowrap="nowrap"`	Specifies whether the content wraps using normal HTML line-wrapping conventions
`<em> </em>`	Marks emphasized text
`<embed> </embed>`	Defines external multimedia content or a plugin (HTML5)
`align="align"`	Specifies the alignment of the object with the surrounding content where align is bottom, left, right, or top (obsolete)
`height="integer"`	Specifies the height of the object in pixels
`hspace="integer"`	Specifies the horizontal space around the object in pixels (obsolete)
`name="text"`	Provides the name of the embedded object (obsolete)
`src="url"`	Provides the location of the file containing the object
`type="mime-type"`	Specifies the mime-type of the embedded object
`vspace="integer"`	Specifies the vertical space around the object in pixels (obsolete)
`width="integer"`	Specifies the width of the object in pixels
`<fieldset> </fieldset>`	Places form fields in a common group
`disabled="disabled"`	Disables the fieldset
`form="id"`	The id of the form associated with the fieldset
`name="text"`	The name part of the name/value pair associated with this element
`<figure> </figure>`	A structural element that represents a group of media content that is self-contained along with a caption (HTML5)
`<figcaption> </figcaption>`	Represents the caption of a figure (HTML5)
`<font> </font>`	Formats the enclosed text (deprecated)
`color="color"`	Specifies the color of the enclosed text (deprecated)
`face="text list"`	Specifies the font face(s) of the enclosed text (deprecated)
`size="integer"`	Specifies the size of the enclosed text, with values ranging from 1 (smallest) to 7 (largest); a value of +integer increases the font size relative to the font size specified in the basefont element (deprecated)

Element/Attribute	Description
`<footer> </footer>`	A structural element that represents the footer of a section or page (HTML5)
`<form> </form>`	Encloses the contents of a web form
`accept="mime-type list"`	Lists mime-types that the server processing the form will handle (deprecated)
`accept-charset="char code"`	Specifies the character encoding that the server processing the form will handle
`action="url"`	Provides the URL to which the form values are to be sent
`autocomplete="on|off"`	Enables automatic insertion of information in fields in which the user has previously entered data (HTML5)
`enctype="mime-type"`	Specifies the mime-type of the data to be sent to the server for processing; the default is "application/x-www-form-urlencoded"
`method="get|post"`	Specifies the method of accessing the URL specified in the action attribute
`name="text"`	Specifies the name of the form
`novalidate="novalidate"`	Specifies that the form is not meant to be validated during submission (HTML5)
`target="text"`	Specifies the frame or window in which output from the form should appear
`<frame> </frame>`	Marks a single frame within a set of frames (deprecated)
`bordercolor="color"`	Specifies the color of the frame border
`frameborder="1|0"`	Determines whether the frame border is visible (1) or invisible (0); Netscape also supports values of yes or no
`longdesc="url"`	Provides the URL of a document containing a long description of the frame's contents
`marginheight="integer"`	Specifies the space above and below the frame object and the frame's borders, in pixels
`marginwidth="integer"`	Specifies the space to the left and right of the frame object and the frame's borders, in pixels
`name="text"`	Specifies the name of the frame
`noresize="noresize"`	Prevents users from resizing the frame
`scrolling="auto|yes|no"`	Specifies whether the browser will display a scroll bar with the frame
`src="url"`	Provides the URL of the document to be displayed in the frame
`<frameset> </frameset>`	Creates a collection of frames (deprecated)
`border="integer"`	Specifies the thickness of the frame borders in the frameset in pixels (not part of the W3C specifications, but supported by most browsers)
`bordercolor="color"`	Specifies the color of the frame borders
`cols="value list"`	Arranges the frames in columns with the width of each column expressed either in pixels, as a percentage, or using an asterisk (to allow the browser to choose the width)
`frameborder="1|0"`	Determines whether frame borders are visible (1) or invisible (0); (not part of the W3C specifications, but supported by most browsers)
`framespacing="integer"`	Specifies the amount of space between frames in pixels (IE only)
`rows="value list"`	Arranges the frames in rows with the height of each column expressed either in pixels, as a percentage, or using an asterisk (to allow the browser to choose the height)

Element/Attribute	Description
`<hi> </hi>`	Marks the enclosed text as a heading, where *i* is an integer from 1 (the largest heading) to 6 (the smallest heading)
`align="align"`	Specifies the alignment of the heading text where *align* is left, center, right, or justify (obsolete)
`<head> </head>`	Encloses the document head, containing information about the document
`profile="url"`	Provides the location of metadata about the document
`<header> </header>`	Structural element that represents the header of a section or the page (HTML5)
`<hgroup> </hgroup>`	Structural element that groups content headings (HTML5)
`<hr />`	Draws a horizontal line (rule) in the rendered page
`align="align"`	Specifies the horizontal alignment of the line where *align* is left, center, or right (obsolete)
`color="color"`	Specifies the color of the line (obsolete)
`noshade="noshade"`	Removes 3D shading from the line (obsolete)
`size="integer"`	Specifies the height of the line in pixels or as a percentage of the enclosing element's height (obsolete)
`width="integer"`	Specifies the width of the line in pixels or as a percentage of the enclosing element's width (obsolete)
`<html> </html>`	Encloses the entire content of the HTML document
`manifest="url"`	Provides the address of the document's application cache manifest (HTML5)
`xmlns="text"`	Specifies the namespace prefix for the document
`<i> </i>`	Represents a span of text offset from its surrounding content without conveying any extra importance or emphasis
`<iframe> </iframe>`	Creates an inline frame in the document
`align="align"`	Specifies the horizontal alignment of the frame with the surrounding content where *align* is bottom, left, middle, top, or right (obsolete)
`datafld="text"`	Indicates the column from a data source that supplies bound data for the inline frame (IE only)
`dataformatas="html|plaintext|text"`	Specifies the format of the data in the data source bound with the inline frame (IE only)
`datasrc="url"`	Provides the URL or ID of the data source bound with the inline frame (IE only)
`frameborder="1|0"`	Specifies whether to display a frame border (1) or not (0) (obsolete)
`height="integer"`	Specifies the height of the frame in pixels
`longdesc="url"`	Indicates the document contains a long description of the frame's content (obsolete)
`marginheight="integer"`	Specifies the space above and below the frame object and the frame's borders, in pixels (obsolete)
`marginwidth="integer"`	Specifies the space to the left and right of the frame object and the frame's borders, in pixels (obsolete)
`name="text"`	Specifies the name of the frame
`sandbox="allow-forms|allow-scripts|allow-top-navigation|allow-same-origin"`	Defines restrictions to the frame content (HTML5)
`seamless="seamless"`	Displays the inline frame as part of the document (HTML5)
`scrolling="auto|yes|no"`	Determines whether the browser displays a scroll bar with the frame (obsolete)

Element/Attribute	Description
src="*url*"	Indicates the document displayed within the frame
srcdoc="*text*"	Provides the HTML code shown in the inline frame (HTML5)
width="*integer*"	Specifies the width of the frame in pixels
<img> </img>	Inserts an inline image into the document
align="*align*"	Specifies the alignment of the image with the surrounding content where *align* is left, right, top, text textop, middle, absmiddle, baseline, bottom, absbottom (obsolete)
alt="*text*"	Specifies alternate text to be displayed in place of the image
border="*integer*"	Specifies the width of the image border (obsolete)
datafld="*text*"	Names the column from a data source that supplies bound data for the image (IE only)
dataformatas="html| plaintext|text"	Specifies the format of the data in the data source bound with the image (IE only)
datasrc="*url*"	Provides the URL or ID of the data source bound with the image (IE only)
dynsrc="*url*"	Provides the URL of a video or VRML file (IE and Opera only)
height="*integer*"	Specifies the height of the image in pixels
hspace="*integer*"	Specifies the horizontal space around the image in pixels (deprecated)
ismap="ismap"	Indicates that the image can be used as a server-side image map
longdesc="*url*"	Provides the URL of a document containing a long description of the image (obsolete)
name="*text*"	Specifies the image name (obsolete)
src="*url*"	Specifies the image source file
usemap="*url*"	Provides the location of a client-side image associated with the image (not well-supported when the URL points to an external file)
vspace="*integer*"	Specifies the vertical space around the image in pixels (obsolete)
width="*integer*"	Specifies the width of the image in pixels
<input> </input>	Marks an input field in a web form
align="*align*"	Specifies the alignment of the input field with the surrounding content where *align* is left, right, top, texttop, middle, absmiddle, baseline, bottom, or absbottom (obsolete)
alt="*text*"	Specifies alternate text for image buttons and image input fields
checked="checked"	Specifies that the input check box or input radio button is selected
datafld="*text*"	Indicates the column from a data source that supplies bound data for the input field (IE only)
dataformatas="html|. plaintext|text"	Specifies the format of the data in the data source bound with the input field (IE only)
datasrc="*url*"	Provides the URL or ID of the data source bound with the input field (IE only)
disabled="disabled"	Disables the input control
form="*text*"	Specifies the form to which the button belongs (HTML5)
formaction="*url*"	Specifies the URL to which the form data is sent (HTML5)
formenctype="*mime-type*"	Specifies the encoding of the form data before it is sent (HTML5)
formmethod="get|post"	Specifies the HTTP method with which the form data is submitted
formnovalidate= "formnovalidate"	Specifies that the form should not be validated during submission (HTML5)

Element/Attribute	Description
formtarget="*text*"	Provides a name for the target of the button (HTML5)
height="*integer*"	Specifies the height of the image input field in pixels (HTML5)
list="*id*"	Specifies the id of a data list associated with the input field (HTML5)
max="*value*"	Specifies the maximum value of the field (HTML5)
maxlength="*integer*"	Specifies the maximum number of characters that can be inserted into a text input field
min="*value*"	Specifies the minimum value of the field (HTML5)
multiple="multiple"	Specifies that the user is allowed to specify more than one input value (HTML5)
name="text"	Specifies the name of the input field
pattern="*text*"	Specifies the required regular expression pattern of the input field value (HTML5)
placeholder="*text*"	Specifies placeholder text for the input field (HTML5)
readonly="readonly"	Prevents the value of the input field from being modified
size="*integer*"	Specifies the number of characters that can be displayed at one time in an input text field
src="*url*"	Indicates the source file of an input image field
step="any|*value*"	Specifies the value granularity of the field value (HTML5)
type="*text*"	Specifies the input type where *text* is button, checkbox, color, date, datetime, datetime-local, email, file, hidden, image, month, number, password, radio, range, reset, search, submit, tel, text, time, url, or week (HTML5)
value="*text*"	Specifies the default value of the input field
width="*integer*"	Specifies the width of an image input field in pixels (HTML5)
<ins> </ins>	Marks inserted text
cite="*url*"	Provides the URL for the document that has additional information about the inserted text
datetime="*date*"	Specifies the date and time of the text insertion
<kbd> </kbd>	Marks keyboard-style text
<keygen> </keygen>	Defines a generate key within a form (HTML5)
autofocus="autofocus"	Specifies that the element is to be given the focus when the form is loaded
challenge="*text*"	Provides the challenge string that is submitted along with the key
disabled="disabled"	Disables the element
form="*id*"	Specifies the id of the form associated with the element
keytype="rsa"	Specifies the type of key generated
name="*text*"	Specifies the name part of the name/value pair associated with the element
<label> </label>	Associates the enclosed content with a form field
datafld="text"	Indicates the column from a data source that supplies bound data for the label (IE only)
dataformatas="html| plaintext|text"	Specifies the format of the data in the data source bound with the label (IE only)
datasrc="*url*"	Provides the URL or ID of the data source bound with the label (IE only)
for="text"	Provides the ID of the field associated with the label
form="*id*"	Specifies the id of the form associated with the label (HTML5)

Element/Attribute	Description
`<legend> </legend>`	Marks the enclosed text as a caption for a field set
`align="bottom|left |top|right"`	Specifies the alignment of the legend with the field set; Internet Explorer also supports the center option (deprecated)
`<li> </li>`	Marks an item in an ordered (ol), unordered (ul), menu (menu), or directory (dir) list
`value="integer"`	Sets the value for the current list item in an ordered list; subsequent list items are numbered from that value
`<link />`	Creates an element in the document head that establishes the relationship between the current document and external documents or objects
`charset="char code"`	Specifies the character encoding of the external document (obsolete)
`href="url"`	Provides the URL of the external document
`hreflang="text"`	Indicates the language of the external document
`media="media"`	Indicates the media in which the external document is presented
`rel="text"`	Specifies the relationship between the current page and the link specified by the href attribute
`rev="text"`	Specifies the reverse relationship between the current page and the link specified by the href attribute (obsolete)
`sizes="any|value"`	Specifies the sizes of icons used for visual media (HTML5)
`target="text"`	Specifies the target window or frame for the link (obsolete)
`type="mime-type"`	Specifies the mime-type of the external document
`<map> </map>`	Creates an element that contains client-side image map hotspots
`name="text"`	Specifies the name of the image map
`<mark> </mark>`	Defines marked text (HTML5)
`<menu> </menu>`	Represents a list of commands
`compact="compact"`	Reduces the space between menu items (obsolete)
`label="text"`	Defines a visible label for the menu (HTML5)
`type="context|list| toolbar"`	Defines which type of list to display
`<meta />`	Creates an element in the document's head section that contains information and special instructions for processing the document
`charset="char code"`	Defines the character encoding for the document (HTML5)
`content="text"`	Provides information associated with the name or http-equiv attributes
`http-equiv="text"`	Provides instructions to the browser to request the server to perform different http operations
`name="text"`	Specifies the type of information specified in the content attribute
`scheme="text"`	Supplies additional information about the scheme used to interpret the content attribute (obsolete)
`<meter> </meter>`	Defines a measurement within a predefined range (HTML5)
`high="value"`	Defines the high value of the range
`low="value"`	Defines the low value of the range
`max="value"`	Defines the maximum value
`min="value"`	Defines the minimum value
`optimum="value"`	Defines the optimum value from the range
`value="value"`	Defines the meter's value
`<nav> </nav>`	Structural element defining a navigation list (HTML5)

Element/Attribute	Description
`<nobr> </nobr>`	Disables line wrapping for the enclosed content (not part of the W3C specifications, but supported by most browsers)
`<noembed> </noembed>`	Encloses alternate content for browsers that do not support the embed element (not part of the W3C specifications, but supported by most browsers)
`<noframe> </noframe>`	Encloses alternate content for browsers that do not support frames (obsolete)
`<noscript> </noscript>`	Encloses alternate content for browsers that do not support client-side scripts
`<object> </object>`	Places an embedded object (image, applet, sound clip, video clip, etc.) into the page
`archive="url"`	Specifies the URL of an archive containing classes and other resources preloaded for use with the object (obsolete)
`align="align"`	Aligns the object with the surrounding content where *align* is absbottom, absmiddle, baseline, bottom, left, middle, right, texttop, or top (obsolete)
`border="integer"`	Specifies the width of the border around the object (obsolete)
`classid="url"`	Provides the URL of the object (obsolete)
`codebase="url"`	Specifies the base path used to resolve relative references within the embedded object (obsolete)
`codetype="mime-type"`	Indicates the mime-type of the embedded object's code (obsolete)
`data="url"`	Provides the URL of the object's data file
`datafld="text"`	Identifies the column from a data source that supplies bound data for the embedded object (IE only)
`dataformatas="html|` `plaintext|text"`	Specifies the format of the data in the data source bound with the embedded object (IE only)
`datasrc="url"`	Provides the URL or ID of the data source bound with the embedded object (IE only)
`declare="declare"`	Declares the object without embedding it on the page (obsolete)
`form="id"`	Specifies the id of the form associated with the object (HTML5)
`height="integer"`	Specifies the height of the object in pixels
`hspace="integer"`	Specifies the horizontal space around the image in pixels (obsolete)
`name="text"`	Specifies the name of the embedded object
`standby="text"`	Specifies the message displayed by the browser while loading the embedded object (obsolete)
`type="mime-type"`	Indicates the mime-type of the embedded object
`vspace="integer"`	Specifies the vertical space around the embedded object (obsolete)
`width="integer"`	Specifies the width of the object in pixels
`<ol> </ol>`	Contains an ordered list of items
`reversed="reversed"`	Specifies that the list markers are to be displayed in descending order (HTML5)
`start="integer"`	Specifies the starting value in the list
`type="A|a|I|i|1"`	Specifies the bullet type associated with the list items (deprecated)
`<optgroup> </optgroup>`	Contains a group of option elements in a selection field
`disabled="disabled"`	Disables the option group control
`label="text"`	Specifies the label for the option group
`<option> </option>`	Formats an option within a selection field
`disabled="disabled"`	Disables the option control
`label="text"`	Supplies the text label associated with the option
`selected="selected"`	Selects the option by default
`value="text"`	Specifies the value associated with the option

Element/Attribute	Description
`<output> </output>`	Form control representing the result of a calculation (HTML5)
`name="text"`	Specifies the name part of the name/value pair associated with the field
`form="id"`	Specifies the id of the form associated with the field
`for="text list"`	Lists the id references associated with the calculation
`<p> </p>`	Marks the enclosed content as a paragraph
`align="align"`	Horizontally aligns the contents of the paragraph where *align* is left, center, right, or justify (obsolete)
`<param> </param>`	Marks parameter values sent to an object element or an applet element
`name="text"`	Specifies the parameter name
`type="mime-type"`	Specifies the mime-type of the resource indicated by the value attribute (obsolete)
`value="text"`	Specifies the parameter value
`valuetype="data|ref|object"`	Specifies the data type of the value attribute (obsolete)
`<pre> </pre>`	Marks the enclosed text as preformatted text, retaining white space from the document
`<progress> </progress>`	Represents the progress of completion of a task (HTML5)
`value="value"`	Specifies how much of the task has been completed
`max="value"`	Specifies how much work the task requires in total
`<q> </q>`	Marks the enclosed text as a quotation
`cite="url"`	Provides the source URL of the quoted content
`<rp> </rp>`	Used in ruby annotations to define what to show browsers that do not support the ruby element (HTML5)
`<rt> </rt>`	Defines explanation to ruby annotations (HTML5)
`<ruby> </ruby>`	Defines ruby annotations (HTML5)
`<s> </s>`	Marks the enclosed text as strikethrough text
`<samp> </samp>`	Marks the enclosed text as a sequence of literal characters
`<script> </script>`	Encloses client-side scripts within the document; this element can be placed within the head or the body element or it can refer to an external script file
`async="async"`	Specifies that the script should be executed asynchronously as soon as it becomes available (HTML5)
`charset="char code"`	Specifies the character encoding of the script
`defer="defer"`	Defers execution of the script
`language="text"`	Specifies the language of the script (obsolete)
`src="url"`	Provides the URL of an external script file
`type="mime-type"`	Specifies the mime-type of the script
`<section> </section>`	Structural element representing a section of the document (HTML5)
`<select> </select>`	Creates a selection field (drop-down list box) in a web form
`autofocus="autofocus"`	Specifies that the browser should give focus to the selection field as soon as the page loads (HTML5)
`datafld="text"`	Identifies the column from a data source that supplies bound data for the selection field (IE only)

Element/Attribute	Description
dataformatas="html| plaintext|text"	Specifies the format of the data in the data source bound with the selection field (IE only)
datasrc="*url*"	Provides the URL or ID of the data source bound with the selection field (IE only)
disabled="disabled"	Disables the selection field
form="*id*"	Provides the id of the form associated with the selection field (HTML5)
multiple="multiple"	Allows multiple sections from the field
name="*text*"	Specifies the selection field name
size="*integer*"	Specifies the number of visible items in the selection list
<small> </small>	Represents "final print" or "small print" in legal disclaimers and caveats
<source />	Enables multiple media sources to be specified for audio and video elements (HTML5)
media="*media*"	Specifies the intended media type of the media source
src="*url*"	Specifies the location of the media source
type="*mime-type*"	Specifies the MIME type of the media source
<span> </span>	Creates a generic inline element
datafld="*text*"	Identifies the column from a data source that supplies bound data for the inline element (IE only)
dataformatas="html| plaintext|text"	Specifies the format of the data in the data source bound with the inline element (IE only)
datasrc="*url*"	Provides the URL or ID of the data source bound with the inline element (IE only)
<strong> </strong>	Marks the enclosed text as strongly emphasized text
<style> </style>	Encloses global style declarations for the document
media="*media*"	Indicates the media of the enclosed style definitions
scoped="scoped"	Indicates that the specified style information is meant to apply only to the style element's parent element (HTML5)
type="*mime-type*"	Specifies the mime-type of the style definitions
<sub> </sub>	Marks the enclosed text as subscript text
<summary> </summary>	Defines the header of a detail element (HTML5)
<sup> </sup>	Marks the enclosed text as superscript text
<table> </table>	Encloses the contents of a web table
align="*align*"	Aligns the table with the surrounding content where *align* is left, center, or right (obsolete)
bgcolor="*color*"	Specifies the background color of the table (obsolete)
border="*integer*"	Specifies the width of the table border in pixels (obsolete)
cellpadding= "integer"	Specifies the space between the table data and the cell borders in pixels (obsolete)
cellspacing= "integer"	Specifies the space between table cells in pixels (obsolete)
datafld="*text*"	Indicates the column from a data source that supplies bound data for the table (IE only)
dataformatas="html| plaintext|text"	Specifies the format of the data in the data source bound with the table (IE only)

Element/Attribute	Description
datapagesize="*integer*"	Sets the number of records displayed within the table (IE only)
datasrc="*url*"	Provides the URL or ID of the data source bound with the table (IE only)
frame="*frame*"	Specifies the format of the borders around the table where *frame* is above, below, border, box, hsides, lhs, rhs, void, or vside (obsolete)
rules="*rules*"	Specifies the format of the table's internal borders or gridlines where *rules* is all, cols, groups, none, or rows (obsolete)
summary="*text*"	Supplies a text summary of the table's content
width="*integer*"	Specifies the width of the table in pixels (obsolete)
<tbody> </tbody>	Encloses the content of the web table body
align="*align*"	Specifies the alignment of the contents in the cells of the table body where *align* is left, center, right, justify, or char (obsolete)
char="*char*"	Specifies the character used for aligning the table body contents when the align attribute is set to "char" (obsolete)
charoff="*integer*"	Specifies the offset in pixels from the alignment character specified in the char attribute (obsolete)
valign="*align*"	Specifies the vertical alignment of the contents in the cells of the table body where *align* is baseline, bottom, middle, or top (obsolete)
<td> </td>	Encloses the data of a table cell
abbr="*text*"	Supplies an abbreviated version of the contents of the table cell (obsolete)
align="*align*"	Specifies the horizontal alignment of the table cell data where *align* is left, center, or right (obsolete)
bgcolor="*color*"	Specifies the background color of the table cell (obsolete)
char="*char*"	Specifies the character used for aligning the table cell contents when the align attribute is set to "char" (obsolete)
charoff="*integer*"	Specifies the offset in pixels from the alignment character specified in the char attribute (obsolete)
colspan="*integer*"	Specifies the number of columns the table cell spans
headers="*text*"	Supplies a space-separated list of table headers associated with the table cell
height="*integer*"	Specifies the height of the table cell in pixels (obsolete)
nowrap="nowrap"	Disables line-wrapping within the table cell (obsolete)
rowspan="*integer*"	Specifies the number of rows the table cell spans
scope="col|colgroup |row|rowgroup"	Specifies the scope of the table for which the cell provides data (obsolete)
valign="*align*"	Specifies the vertical alignment of the contents of the table cell where *align* is top, middle, or bottom (obsolete)
width="*integer*"	Specifies the width of the cell in pixels (obsolete)
<textarea> </textarea>	Marks the enclosed text as a text area input box in a web form
autofocus="autofocus"	Specifies that the text area is to receive the focus when the page is loaded (HTML5)
datafld="*text*"	Specifies the column from a data source that supplies bound data for the text area box (IE only)
dataformatas="html| plaintext|text"	Specifies the format of the data in the data source bound with the text area box (IE only)

Element/Attribute	Description
datasrc="url"	Provides the URL or ID of the data source bound with the text area box (IE only)
cols="integer"	Specifies the width of the text area box in characters
disable="disable"	Disables the text area field
form="id"	Associates the text area with the form identified by id (HTML5)
maxlength="integer"	Specifies the maximum allowed value length for the text area
name="text"	Specifies the name of the text area box
placeholder="text"	Provides a short hint intended to aid the user when entering data (HTML5)
readonly="readonly"	Specifies the value of the text area box, cannot be modified
required="required"	Indicates whether the text area is required for validation (HTML5)
rows="integer"	Specifies the number of visible rows in the text area box
wrap="soft|hard"	Specifies how text is wrapped within the text area box and how that text-wrapping information is sent to the server-side program
<tfoot> </tfoot>	Encloses the content of the web table footer
align="align"	Specifies the alignment of the contents in the cells of the table footer where align is left, center, right, justify, or char (obsolete)
char="char"	Specifies the character used for aligning the table footer contents when the align attribute is set to "char" (obsolete)
charoff="integer"	Specifies the offset in pixels from the alignment character specified in the char attribute (obsolete)
valign="align"	Specifies the vertical alignment of the contents in the cells of the table footer where align is baseline, bottom, middle, or top (obsolete)
<th> </th>	Encloses the data of a table header cell
abbr="text"	Supplies an abbreviated version of the contents of the table cell (obsolete)
align="align"	Specifies the horizontal alignment of the table cell data where align is left, center, or right (obsolete)
axis="text list"	Provides a list of table categories that can be mapped to a table hierarchy (obsolete)
bgcolor="color"	Specifies the background color of the table cell (obsolete)
char="char"	Specifies the character used for aligning the table cell contents when the align attribute is set to "char" (obsolete)
charoff="integer"	Specifies the offset in pixels from the alignment character specified in the char attribute (obsolete)
colspan="integer"	Specifies the number of columns the table cell spans
headers="text"	A space-separated list of table headers associated with the table cell
height="integer"	Specifies the height of the table cell in pixels (obsolete)
nowrap="nowrap"	Disables line-wrapping within the table cell (obsolete)
rowspan="integer"	Specifies the number of rows the table cell spans
scope="col|colgroup|row|rowgroup"	Specifies the scope of the table for which the cell provides data
valign="align"	Specifies the vertical alignment of the contents of the table cell where align is top, middle, or bottom (obsolete)
width="integer"	Specifies the width of the cell in pixels (obsolete)

Element/Attribute	Description
`<thead> </thead>`	Encloses the content of the web table header
`align="align"`	Specifies the alignment of the contents in the cells of the table header where *align* is left, center, right, justify, or char (obsolete)
`char="char"`	Specifies the character used for aligning the table header contents when the align attribute is set to "char" (obsolete)
`charoff="integer"`	Specifies the offset in pixels from the alignment character specified in the char attribute (obsolete)
`valign="align"`	Specifies the vertical alignment of the contents in the cells of the table header where *align* is baseline, bottom, middle, or top (obsolete)
`<time> </time>`	Represents a date and/or time (HTML5)
`<title> </title>`	Specifies the title of the document, placed in the head section of the document
`<tr> </tr>`	Encloses the content of a row within a web table
`align="align"`	Specifies the horizontal alignment of the data in the row's cells where *align* is left, center, or right (obsolete)
`char="char"`	Specifies the character used for aligning the table row contents when the align attribute is set to "char" (obsolete)
`charoff="integer"`	Specifies the offset in pixels from the alignment character specified in the char attribute (obsolete)
`valign="align"`	Specifies the vertical alignment of the contents of the table row where *align* is baseline, bottom, middle, or top (obsolete)
`<track> </track>`	Enables supplementary media tracks such as subtitles and captions (HTML5)
`default="default"`	Enables the track if the user's preferences do not indicate that another track would be more appropriate
`kind="kind"`	Specifies the kind of track, where *kind* is subtitles, captions, descriptions, chapters, or metadata
`label="text"`	Provides a user-readable title for the track
`src="url"`	Provides the address of the track
`srclang="lang"`	Provides the language of the track
`<tt> </tt>`	Marks the enclosed text as teletype or monospaced text (deprecated)
`<u> </u>`	Marks the enclosed text as underlined text (deprecated)
`<ul> </ul>`	Contains an unordered list of items
`compact="compact"`	Reduces the space between unordered list items (obsolete)
`type="disc│square│circle"`	Specifies the bullet type associated with the list items (obsolete)
`<var> </var>`	Marks the enclosed text as containing a variable name
`<video> </video>`	Defines an embedded video clip (HTML5)
`audio="text"`	Defines the default audio state; currently only "muted" is supported
`autoplay="autoplay"`	Specifies that the video should begin playing automatically when the page is loaded
`controls="controls"`	Instructs the browser to display the video controls
`height="value"`	Provides the height of the video clip in pixels
`loop="loop"`	Instructs the browser to loop the clip back to the beginning
`preload="auto│metadata│none"`	Indicates whether to preload the video clip data
`poster="url"`	Specifies the location of an image file to act as a poster for the video clip
`width="value"`	Provides the width of the video clip in pixels

Element/Attribute	Description
`<wbr />`	Indicates a line-break opportunity (HTML5)
`<xml> </xml>`	Encloses XML content (also referred to as a *data island*) or references an external XML document (IE only)
`ns="url"`	Provides the URL of the XML data island (IE only)
`prefix="text"`	Specifies the namespace prefix of the XML content (IE only)
`src="url"`	Provides the URL of an external XML document (IE only)
`<xmp> </xmp>`	Marks the enclosed text as preformatted text, preserving the white space of the source document; replaced by the pre element (deprecated)

APPENDIX **C**

Cascading Styles and Selectors

This appendix describes the selectors, units, and attributes supported by Cascading Style Sheets (CSS). Features from CSS3 are indicated by (CSS). Note that not all CSS3 features are supported by all browsers and all browser versions, so you should always check your code against different browsers and browser versions to ensure that your page is being rendered correctly. Also, many CSS3 styles are still in the draft stage and will undergo continuing revisions and additions. Additional information about CSS can be found at the World Wide Web Consortium website at *www.w3.org*.

STARTING DATA FILES

There are no starting Data Files needed for this appendix.

Selectors

The general form of a style declaration is:

```
selector {attribute1:value1; attribute2:value2; ...}
```

where *selector* is the selection of elements within the document to which the style will be applied; *attribute1*, *attribute2*, and so on are the different style attributes; and *value1*, *value2*, and so on are values associated with those styles. The following table shows some of the different forms that a selector can take.

Selector	Matches
`*`	All elements in the document
`e`	An element, *e*, in the document
`e1, e2, e3, …`	A group of elements, *e1*, *e2*, *e3*, in the document
`e1 e2`	An element, *e2*, nested within the parent element, *e1*
`e1 > e2`	An element, *e2*, that is a child of the parent element, *e1*
`e1+e2`	An element, *e2*, that is adjacent to element, *e1*
`e1.class`	An element, *e1*, belonging to the *class* class
`.class`	Any element belonging to the *class* class
`#id`	An element with the id value *id*
`[att]`	The element contains the *att* attribute
`[att="val"]`	The element's *att* attribute equals "*val*"
`[att~="val"]`	The element's *att* attribute value is a space-separated list of "words," one of which is exactly "*val*"
`[att|="val"]`	The element's *att* attribute value is a hyphen-separated list of "words" beginning with "val"
`[att^="val"]`	The element's *att* attribute begins with "*val*" (CSS3)
`[att$="val"]`	The element's *att* attribute ends with "*val*" (CSS3)
`[att*="val"]`	The element's *att* attribute contains the value "*val*" (CSS3)
`[ns|att]`	References all *att* attributes in the *ns* namespace (CSS3)

Pseudo-Elements and Pseudo-Classes

Pseudo-elements are elements that do not exist in HTML code but whose attributes can be set with CSS. Many pseudo-elements were introduced in CSS2.

Pseudo-Element	Matches
`e::after {content: "text"}`	Text content, *text*, that is inserted at the end of an element, *e*
`e::before {content: "text"}`	Text content, *text*, that is inserted at the beginning of an element, *e*
`e::first-letter`	The first letter in the element *e*
`e::first-line`	The first line in the element *e*
`::selection`	A part of the document that has been highlighted by the user (CSS3)

Pseudo-classes are classes of HTML elements that define the condition or state of the element in the web page. Many pseudo-classes were introduced in CSS2.

Pseudo-Class	Matches
`:canvas`	The rendering canvas of the document
`:first`	The first printed page of the document (used only with print styles created with the @print rule)
`:last`	The last printed page of the document (used only with print styles created with the @print rule)
`:left`	The left side of a two-sided printout (used only with print styles created with the @print rule)
`:right`	The right side of a two-sided printout (used only with print styles created with the @print rule)
`:root`	The root element of the document
`e:active`	The element, *e*, that is being activated by the user (usually applies only to hyperlinks)
`e:checked`	The checkbox or radio button, *e*, that has been checked (CSS3)
`e:disabled`	The element, *e*, that has been disabled in the document (CSS3)
`e:empty`	The element, *e*, that has no children
`e:enabled`	The element, *e*, that has been enabled in the document (CSS3)
`e:first-child`	The element, *e*, which is the first child of its parent element
`e:first-node`	The first occurrence of the element, *e*, in the document tree
`e:first-of-type`	The first element of type *e* (CSS3)
`e:focus`	The element, *e*, that has received the focus of the cursor
`e:hover`	The mouse pointer is hovering over the element, *e*
`e:lang(text)`	Sets the language, *text*, associated with the element, *e*
`e:last-child`	The element, *e*, that is the last child of its parent element (CSS3)
`e:last-of-type`	The last element of type *e* (CSS3)
`e:link`	The element, *e*, has not been visited yet by the user (applies only to hyperlinks)
`e:not`	Negates the selector rule for the element, *e*, applying the style to all *e* elements that do not match the selector rules
`e:nth-child(n)`	Matches n^{th} child of the element, *e*; *n* can also be the keywords odd or even (CSS3)
`e:nth-last-child(n)`	Matches n^{th} child of the element, *e*, counting up from the last child; *n* can also be the keywords odd or even (CSS3)
`e:nth-of-type(n)`	Matches n^{th} element of type *e*; *n* can also be the keywords odd or even (CSS3)
`e:nth-last-of-type(n)`	Matches n^{th} element of type *e*, counting up from the last child; *n* can also be the keywords odd or even (CSS3)
`e:only-child`	Matches element *e* only if it is the only child of its parent (CSS3)
`e:only-of-type`	Matches element *e* only if it is the only element of its type nested within its parent (CSS3)
`e:target`	Matches an element, *e*, that's the target of the identifier in the document's URL (CSS3)
`e:visited`	The element, *e*, has been already visited by the user (to only the hyperlinks)

@ Rules

CSS supports different "@ rules" designed to run commands within a style sheet. These commands can be used to import other styles, download font definitions, or define the format of printed output.

@ Rule	Description
@charset "*encoding*"	Defines the character set encoding used in the style sheet (this must be the very first line in the style sheet document)
@font-face {*font descriptors*}	Defines custom fonts that are available for automatic download when needed (CSS3)
@import url(*url*) *media*	Imports an external style sheet document into the current style sheet, where *url* is the location of the external stylesheet and *media* is a comma-separated list of media types (optional)
@media *media* {*style declaration*}	Defines the media for the styles in the *style declaration* block, where *media* is a comma-separated list of media types
@namespace *prefix* url(*url*)	Defines the namespace used by selectors in the style sheet, where *prefix* is the local namespace prefix (optional) and *url* is the unique namespace identifier; the @namespace rule must come before all CSS selectors (CSS3)
@page *label pseudo-class* {*styles*}	Defines the properties of a printed page, where *label* is a label given to the page (optional), *pseudo-class* is one of the CSS pseudo-classes designed for printed pages, and *styles* are the styles associated with the page

Miscellaneous Syntax

The following syntax elements do not fit into the previous categories but are useful in constructing CSS style sheets.

Item	Description
style !important	Places high importance on the preceding *style*, overriding the usual rules for inheritance and cascading
/* *comment* */	Attaches a *comment* to the style sheet

Units

Many style attribute values use units of measurement to indicate color, length, angles, time, and frequencies. The following table describes the measuring units used in CSS.

Units	Description
Color	**Units of Color**
currentColor	The computed value of the color property (CSS3)
flavor	An accent color chosen by the user to customize the user interface of the browser (CSS3)
name	A color name; all browsers recognize 16 base color names: aqua, black, blue, fuchsia, gray, green, lime, maroon, navy, olive, purple, red, silver, teal, white, and yellow
#*rrggbb*	A hexadecimal color value, where *rr* is the red value, *gg* is the green value, and *bb* is the blue value
#*rgb*	A compressed hexadecimal value, where the *r, g,* and *b* values are doubled so that, for example, #A2F = #AA22FF
hsl(*hue, sat, light*)	Color value based on hue, saturation, and lightness, where *hue* is the degree measure on the color wheel ranging from 0° (red) up to 360°, *sat* is the saturation range from 0% to 100%, and *light* is the lightness range from 0% to 100% (CSS3)
hsla(*hue, sat, light, alpha*)	Semi-transparent color based on the HSL model with *alpha* representing the opacity of the color ranging from 0 (transparent) up to 1 (completely opaque) (CSS3)
rgb(*red, green, blue*)	The decimal color value, where *red* is the red value, *green* is the green value, and *blue* is the blue value
rgb(*red%, green%, blue%*)	The color value percentage, where *red*% is the percent of maximum red, *green*% is the percent of maximum green, and *blue*% is the percent of maximum blue
rgba(*red, green, blue, alpha*)	Semi-transparent color based on the RGB model with *alpha* representing the opacity of the color ranging from 0 (transparent) up to 1 (completely opaque) (CSS3)
Length	**Units of Length**
auto	Keyword that allows the browser to automatically determine the size of the length
ch	Width of the "0" glyph found in the font (CSS3)
em	A relative unit indicating the width and the height of the capital "M" character for the browser's default font
ex	A relative unit indicating the height of the small "x" character for the browser's default font
px	A pixel, representing the smallest unit of length on the output device
in	An inch
cm	A centimeter
mm	A millimeter
pt	A point, approximately 1/72 inch
pc	A pica, approximately 1/12 inch
%	A percent of the width or height of the parent element
rem	A relative unit basing its size relative to the size in the root (html) element

Units	Description
xx-small	Keyword representing an extremely small font size
x-small	Keyword representing a very small font size
small	Keyword representing a small font size
vw	A percentage of the viewport width
vh	A percentage of the viewport height
vmin	The smaller value between vw and vh
medium	Keyword representing a medium-sized font
large	Keyword representing a large font
x-large	Keyword representing a very large font
xx-large	Keyword representing an extremely large font
Angle	**Units of Angles**
deg	The angle in degrees
grad	The angle in gradients
rad	The angle in radians
turns	Number of complete turns (CSS3)
Time	**Units of Time**
ms	Time in milliseconds
s	Time in seconds
Frequency	**Units of Frequency**
hz	The frequency in hertz
khz	The frequency in kilohertz

Attributes and Values

The following table describes the attributes and values for different types of elements. The attributes are grouped into categories to help you locate the features relevant to your particular design task.

Attribute	Description
Aural	**Styles for Aural Browsers**
cue: url(url1) url(url2)	Adds a sound to an element: if a single value is present, the sound is played before and after the element; if two values are present, the first is played before and the second is played after
cue-after: url(url)	Specifies a sound to be played immediately after an element
cue-before: url(url)	Specifies a sound to be played immediately before an element
elevation: location	Defines the vertical location of the sound, where location is below, level, above, lower, higher, or an angle value
mark: before after	Adds a marker to an audio stream (CSS3)
mark-before: text	Marks an audio stream with the text string (CSS3)
mark-after: text	Marks an audio stream afterwards with the text string (CSS3)
pause: time1 time2	Adds a pause to an element: if a single value is present, the pause occurs before and after the element; if two values are present, the first pause occurs before and the second occurs after
pause-after: time	Adds a pause after an element
pause-before: time	Adds a pause before an element

Attribute	Description
phonemes: *text*	Specifies the phonetic pronunciation for the audio stream (CSS3)
pitch: *value*	Defines the pitch of a speaking voice, where *value* is x-low, low, medium, high, x-high, or a frequency value
pitch-range: *value*	Defines the pitch range for a speaking voice, where *value* ranges from 0 to 100; a low pitch range results in a monotone voice, whereas a high pitch range sounds very animated
play-during: url(*url*) mix repeat *type*	Defines a sound to be played behind an element, where *url* is the URL of the sound file; mix overlays the sound file with the sound of the parent element; repeat causes the sound to be repeated, filling up the available time; and *type* is auto to play the sound only once, none to play nothing but the sound file, or inherit
rest: *before after*	Specifies the rest-before and rest-after values for the audio (CSS3)
rest-before: *type*	Specifies a rest to be observed before speaking the content, where *type* is none, x-weak, weak, medium, strong, x-strong, or inherit (CSS3)
rest-after: *type*	Specifies a rest to be observed after speaking the content, where *type* is none, x-weak, weak, medium, strong, x-strong, or inherit (CSS3)
richness: *value*	Specifies the richness of the speaking voice, where *value* ranges from 0 to 100; a low value indicates a softer voice, whereas a high value indicates a brighter voice
speak: *type*	Defines how element content is to be spoken, where *type* is normal (for normal punctuation rules), spell-out (to pronounce one character at a time), none (to suppress the aural rendering), or inherit
voice-balance: *type*	Specifies the voice balance, where *type* is left, center, right, leftwards, rightwards, inherit, or a *number* (CSS3)
voice-duration: *time*	Specifies the duration of the voice (CSS3)
voice-family: *text*	Defines the name of the speaking voice, where *text* is male, female, child, or a text string indicating a specific speaking voice
voice-rate: *type*	Specifies the voice rate, where *type* is x-slow, slow, medium, fast, x-fast, inherit, or a *percentage* (CSS3)
voice-pitch: *type*	Specifies the voice pitch, where *type* is x-low, low, medium, high, x-high, inherit, a *number*, or a *percentage* (CSS3)
voice-pitch-range: *type*	Specifies the voice pitch range, where *type* is x-low, low, medium, high, x-high, inherit, or a *number* (CSS3)
voice-stress: *type*	Specifies the voice stress, where *type* is strong, moderate, none, reduced, or inherit (CSS3)
voice-volume: *type*	Specifies the voice volume, where *type* is silent, x-soft, soft, medium, loud, x-loud, inherit, a *number*, or a *percentage* (CSS3)
Backgrounds	**Styles Applied to an Element's Background**
background: *color* url(*url*) *repeat attachment position*	Defines the background of the element, where *color* is a CSS color name or value, *url* is the location of an image file, *repeat* defines how the background image should be repeated, *attachment* defines how the background image should be attached, and *position* defines the position of the background image

Attribute	Description
background: url(url) position size repeat attachment origin clip color	Defines the background of the element, where url is the location of the image file, position is the position of the image, size is the size of the image, repeat defines how the image should be repeated, attachment defines how the image should be attached, origin defines the origin of the image, clip defines the location of the clipping box, and color defines the background color (CSS3)
background-attachment: type	Specifies how the background image is attached, where type is inherit, scroll (move the image with the page content), or fixed (fix the image and not scroll)
background-clip: location	Specifies the location of the background box, where location is border-box, padding-box, content-box, no-clip, a unit of length, or a percentage (CSS3)
background-color: color	Defines the color of the background, where color is a CSS color name or value; the keyword "inherit" can be used to inherit the background color of the parent element, or "transparent" can be used to allow the parent element background image to show through
background-image: url(url)	Specifies the image file used for the element's background, where url is the URL of the image file
background-origin: box	Specifies the origin of the background image, where box is border-box, padding-box, or content-box (CSS3)
background-position: x y	Sets the position of a background image, where x is the horizontal location in pixels, as a percentage of the width of the parent element, or the keyword "left", "center", or "right", y is the vertical location in pixels, as a percentage of the height and of the parent element, or the keyword "top", "center", or "bottom"
background-repeat: type	Defines the method for repeating the background image, where type is no-repeat, repeat (to tile the image in both directions), repeat-x (to tile the image in the horizontal direction only), or repeat-y (to tile the image in the vertical direction only)
background-size: size	Sets the size of the background image, where size is auto, cover, contain, a length, or a percentage (CSS3)
Block-Level Styles	**Styles Applied to Block-Level Elements**
border: length style color	Defines the border style of the element, where length is the border width, style is the border design, and color is the border color
border-bottom: length style color	Defines the border style of the bottom edge of the element
border-left: length style color	Defines the border style of the left edge of the element
border-right: length style color	Defines the border style of the right edge of the element
border-top: length style color	Defines the border style of the top edge of the element
border-color: color	Defines the color applied to the element's border using a CSS color unit
border-bottom-color: color	Defines the color applied to the bottom edge of the element
border-left-color: color	Defines the color applied to the left edge of the element
border-right-color: color	Defines the color applied to the right edge of the element
border-top-color: color	Defines the color applied to the top edge of the element

Attribute	Description
`border-image: url(url) size`	Sets an image file for the border, where *url* is the location of the image file and *size* is stretch, repeat, round, none, a *length*, or a *percentage* (CSS3)
`border-style: style`	Specifies the design of the element's border where `style` is dashed, dotted double, groove, inset, none, outset, ridge, or solid
`border-style-bottom: style`	Specifies the design of the element's bottom edge
`border-style-left: style`	Specifies the design of the element's left edge
`border-style-right: style`	Specifies the design of the element's right edge
`border-style-top: style`	Specifies the design of the element's top edge
`border-radius: tr br bl tl`	Specifies the radius of the border corners in pixels, where *tr* is the top-right corner, *br* is the bottom-right corner, *bl* is the bottom-left corner, and *tl* is the top-left corner (CSS3)
`border-top-right-radius: horiz vert`	Specifies the horizontal and vertical radius for the top-right corner (CSS3)
`border-bottom-right-radius: horiz vert`	Specifies the horizontal and vertical radius for the bottom-right corner (CSS3)
`border-bottom-left-radius: horiz vert`	Specifies the horizontal and vertical radius for the bottom-left corner (CSS3)
`border-top-left-radius: horiz vert`	Specifies the horizontal and vertical radius for the top-left corner (CSS3)
`border-width: length`	Defines the width of the element's border, in a unit of measure or using the keyword "thick", "medium", or "thin"
`border-width-bottom: length`	Defines the width of the element's bottom edge
`border-width-left: length`	Defines the width of the element's left edge
`border-width-right: length`	Defines the width of the element's right edge
`border-width-top: length`	Defines the width of the element's top edge
`box-shadow: top right bottom left color`	Adds a box shadow, where *top*, *right*, *bottom*, and *left* set the width of the shadow and *color* sets the shadow color (CSS3)
`margin: top right bottom left`	Defines the size of the margins around the top, right, bottom, and left edges of the element, in one of the CSS units of length
`margin-bottom: length`	Defines the size of the element's bottom margin
`margin-left: length`	Defines the size of the element's left margin
`margin-right: length`	Defines the size of the element's right margin
`margin-top: length`	Defines the size of the element's top margin
`padding: top right bottom left`	Defines the size of the padding space within the top, right, bottom, and left edges of the element, in one of the CSS units of length
`padding-bottom: length`	Defines the size of the element's bottom padding
`padding-left: length`	Defines the size of the element's left padding
`padding-right: length`	Defines the size of the element's right padding
`padding-top: length`	Defines the size of the element's top padding
Browser	**Styles to Affect the Appearance of the Browser**
`appearance: type`	Specifies that an element should be displayed like a standard browser object, where *type* is normal, button, push-button, hyperlink, radio-button, checkbox, pop-up-menu, list-menu, radio-group, checkbox-group, field, or password (CSS3)

Attribute	Description
cursor: *type*	Defines the cursor image used, where *type* is n-resize, ne-resize, e-resize, se-resize, s-resize, sw-resize, w-resize, nw-resize, crosshair, pointer, move, text, wait, help, auto, default, inherit, or a URL pointing to an image file
icon: *value*	Specifies that an element should be styled with with an iconic equivalent, where *value* is auto, a *url*, or inherit (CSS3)
nav-down: *position*	Specifies where to navigate using the arrow-down and arrow-up navigation keys, where *position* is auto, a *target-name*, or an element *id* (CSS3)
nav-index: *value*	Specifies the tabbing order, where *value* is auto, inherit, or a *number* (CSS3)
nav-left: *position*	Specifies where to navigate using the arrow-left and arrow-right navigation keys, where *position* is auto, a *target-name*, or an element *id* (CSS3)
nav-right: *position*	Specifies where to navigate using the arrow-left and arrow-right navigation keys, where *position* is auto, a *target-name*, or an element *id* (CSS3)
nav-up: *position*	Specifies where to navigate using the arrow-down and arrow-up navigation keys, where *position* is auto, a *target-name*, or an element *id* (CSS3)
resize: *type*	Specifies whether an element is resizable and in what direction, where *type* is none, both, horizontal, vertical, or inherit (CSS3)
Column	**Styles for Multi-Column Layouts**
column-count: *value*	Specifies the number of columns, where *value* is the column number or auto (CSS3)
column-fill: *type*	Specifies whether to balance the content of the columns, where *type* is auto or balance (CSS3)
column-gap: *value*	Sets the size of the gap between the columns, where *value* is the width of the gap or auto (CSS3)
column-rule: *width style color*	Adds a dividing line between the columns, where *width*, *style*, and *color* define the style of the line (CSS3)
column-rule-color: *color*	Defines the color of the dividing line (CSS3)
column-rule-style: *style*	Defines the border style of the dividing line (CSS3)
column-rule-width: *width*	Sets the width of the dividing line (CSS3)
columns: *width count*	Sets the width and number of columns in the multi-column layout (CSS3)
column-span: *value*	Sets the element to span across the columns, where *span* is 1 or all (CSS3)
column-width: *value*	Sets the width of the columns (CSS3)
Content	**Styles to Generate Content**
bookmark-label: *value*	Specifies the label of a bookmark, where *value* is content, an *attribute*, or a text *string* (CSS3)
bookmark-level: *value*	Specifies the bookmark level, where *value* is an *integer* or none (CSS3)
bookmark-target: *value*	Specifies the target of a bookmark link, where *value* is self, a *url*, or an *attribute* (CSS3)
border-length: *value*	Describes a way of separating footnotes from other content, where *value* is a *length* or auto (CSS3)
content: *text*	Generates a text string to attach to the content of the element

Attribute	Description
content: attr(*attr*)	Returns the value of the *attr* attribute from the element
content: close-quote	Attaches a close quote using the characters specified in the quotes style
content: counter(*text*)	Generates a counter using the text string *text* attached to the content (most often used with list items)
content: counters(*text*)	Generates a string of counters using the comma-separated text string *text* attached to the content (most often used with list items)
content: no-close-quote	Prevents the attachment of a close quote to an element
content: no-open-quote	Prevents the attachment of an open quote to an element
content: open-quote	Attaches an open quote using the characters specified in the quotes style
content: url(*url*)	Attaches the content of an external file indicated in the *url* to the element
counter-increment: *id integer*	Defines the element to be automatically incremented and the amount by which it is to be incremented, where *id* is an identifier of the element and *integer* defines by how much
counter-reset: *id integer*	Defines the element whose counter is to be reset and the amount by which it is to be reset, where *id* is an identifier of the element and *integer* defines by how much
crop: *value*	Allows a replaced element to be a rectangular area of an object instead of the whole object, where *value* is a shape or auto (CSS3)
hyphenate-after: *value*	Specifies the minimum number of characters after the hyphenation character, where *value* is an *integer* or auto (CSS3)
hyphenate-before: *value*	Specifies the minimum number of characters before the hyphenation character, where *value* is an *integer* or auto (CSS3)
hyphenate-character: *string*	Specifies the hyphenation character, *string* (CSS3)
hyphenate-line: *value*	Specifies the maximum number of hyphenated lines, where *value* is an *integer* or no-limit (CSS3)
hyphenate-resource: url(*url*)	Provides an external resource at *url* that defines hyphenation points (CSS3)
hyphens: *type*	Defines the hyphenation property, where *type* is none, manual, or auto (CSS3)
image-resolution: *value*	Defines the image resolution, where *value* is normal, auto, or the dpi of the image (CSS3)
marks: *type*	Defines an editor's mark, where *type* is crop, cross, or none (CSS3)
quotes: *text1 text2*	Defines the text strings for the open quotes (*text1*) and the close quotes (*text2*)
string-set: *values*	Accepts a comma-separated list of named strings, where *values* is the list of text strings (CSS3)
text-replace: *string1 string2*	Replaces *string1* with *string2* in the element content (CSS3)
Display Styles	**Styles that Control the Display of the Element's Content**
box-sizing: *type*	Specifies how the width and height properties should be interpreted for a block element where *type* is content-box, border-box, initial, or inherit (CSS3)
clip: rect(*top, right, bottom, left*)	Defines what portion of the content is displayed, where *top*, *right*, *bottom*, and *left* are distances of the top, right, bottom, and left edges from the element's top-left corner; use a value of auto to allow the browser to determine the clipping region

Attribute	Description
display: *type*	Specifies the display type of the element, where *type* is one of the following: block, inline, inline-block, inherit, flex, list-item, none, run-in, table, inline-table, table-caption, table-column, table-cell, table-column-group, table-header-group, table-footer-group, table-row, or table-row-group
flex: *grow shrink basis*	Sets the growth rate, shrink rate, and basis size for items within a flexbox (CSS3)
flex-basis: *length*	Sets the basis size for items within a flex box (CSS3) .
flex-direction: *direction*	Sets the direction of items within a flexbox where *direction* is row, row-reverse, column, column-reverse, initial, or inherit (CSS3)
flex-flow: *direction wrap*	Sets the flow of items within a flexbox where *direction* is the flex direction and *wrap* indicates whether items are wrapped to a new line (CSS3)
flex-grow: *value*	Sets the growth rate of a flex item where *value* is a numeric value (CSS3)
flex-shrink: *value*	Sets the shrink rate of a flex item where *value* is a numeric value (CSS3)
flex-wrap: *type*	Sets whether flex items wrap to a new line where *type* is nowrap, wrap, wrap-reverse, initial, or inherit (CSS3)
height: *length*	Specifies the height of the element in one of the CSS units of length
min-height: *length*	Specifies the minimum height of the element
min-width: *length*	Specifies the minimum width of the element
max-height: *length*	Specifies the maximum height of the element
max-width: *length*	Specifies the maximum width of the element
overflow: *type*	Instructs the browser how to handle content that overflows the dimensions of the element, where *type* is auto, inherit, visible, hidden, or scroll
overflow-style: *type*	Specifies the preferred scrolling method for overflow content, where *type* is auto, marquee-line, or marquee-block (CSS3)
overflow-x: *type*	Instructs the browser how to handle content that overflows the element's width, where *type* is auto, inherit, visible, hidden, or scroll (IE only)
overflow-y: *type*	Instructs the browser on how to handle content that overflows the element's height, where *type* is auto, inherit, visible, hidden, or scroll (IE only)
text-overflow: *type*	Instructs the browser on how to handle text overflow, where *type* is clip (to hide the overflow text) or ellipsis (to display the … text string) (IE only)
visibility: *type*	Defines the element's visibility, where *type* is hidden, visible, or inherit
width: *length*	Specifies the width of the element in one of the CSS units of length
Fonts and Text	**Styles that Format the Appearance of Fonts and Text**
color: *color*	Specifies the color of the element's foreground (usually the font color)
direction: *type*	Specifies the direction of the text flow, where *type* equals ltr, rtl, or inherit (CSS3)

Attribute	Description
`font: style variant weight size/line-height family`	Defines the appearance of the font, where *style* is the font's style, *variant* is the font variant, *weight* is the weight of the font, *size* is the size of the font, *line-height* is the height of the lines, and *family* is the font face; the only required attributes are *size* and *family*
`font-effect: type`	Controls the special effect applied to glyphs where *type* is none, emboss, engrave, or outline (CSS3)
`font-emphasize: emphasize position`	Sets the style of the font emphasis and decoration (CSS3)
`font-emphasize-position: position`	Sets the font emphasis position, where *position* is before or after (CSS3)
`font-emphasize-style: style`	Sets the emphasis style, where *style* is none, accent, dot, circle, or disc (CSS3)
`font-family: family`	Specifies the font face used to display text, where *family* is sans-serif, serif, fantasy, monospace, cursive, or the name of an installed font
`font-size: value`	Specifies the size of the font in one of the CSS units of length
`font-size-adjust: value`	Specifies the aspect *value* (which is the ratio of the font size to the font's ex unit height) (CSS3)
`font-smooth: type`	Specifies the type of font smoothing, where *type* is auto, never, always, or a specified size (CSS3)
`font-stretch: type`	Expands or contracts the font, where *type* is narrower, wider, ultra-condensed, extra-condensed, condensed, semi-condensed, normal, semi-expanded, extra-expanded, or ultra-expanded (CSS3)
`font-style: type`	Specifies a style applied to the font, where *type* is normal, italic, or oblique
`font-variant: type`	Specifies a variant of the font, where *type* is inherit, normal, or small-caps
`font-weight: value`	Defines the weight of the font, where *value* is 100, 200, 300, 400, 500, 600, 700, 800, 900, normal, lighter, bolder, or bold
`hanging-punctuation: type`	Determines whether a punctuation mark may be placed outside the text box, where *type* is none, start, end, or end-edge (CSS3)
`letter-spacing: value`	Specifies the space between letters, where *value* is a unit of length or the keyword "normal"
`line-height: value`	Specifies the height of the lines, where *value* is a unit of length or the keyword "normal"
`punctuation-trim: type`	Determines whether or not a full-width punctuation character should be trimmed if it appears at the start or end of a line, where *type* is none, start, end, or adjacent (CSS3)
`text-align: type`	Specifies the horizontal alignment of text within the element, where *type* is inherit, left, right, center, or justify
`text-align-last: type`	Specifies how the last line of a block is aligned for fully justified text, where *type* is start, end, left, right, center, or justify (CSS3)
`text-decoration: type`	Specifies the decoration applied to the text, where *type* is blink, line-through, none, overline, or underline
`text-emphasis: type location`	Specifies the emphasis applied to the text, where *type* is none, accent, dot, circle, or disk and *location* is before or after (CSS3)
`text-indent: length`	Specifies the amount of indentation in the first line of the text, where *length* is a CSS unit of length

Attribute	Description
text-justify: *type*	Specifies the justification method applied to the text, where *type* is auto, inter-word, inter-ideograph, inter-cluster, distribute, kashida, or tibetan (CSS3)
text-outline: *value1 value2*	Specifies a text outline, where *value1* represents the outline thickness and *value2* represents the optional blur radius (CSS3)
text-shadow: *color x y blur*	Applies a shadow effect to the text, where *color* is the color of the shadow, *x* is the horizontal offset in pixels, *y* is the vertical offset in pixels, and *blur* is the size of the blur radius (optional); multiple shadows can be added with shadow effects separated by commas (CSS3)
text-transform: *type*	Defines a transformation applied to the text, where *type* is capitalize, lowercase, none, or uppercase
text-wrap: *type*	Specifies the type of text wrapping, where *type* is normal, unrestricted, none, or suppress (CSS3)
unicode-bibi: *type*	Allows text that flows left-to-right to be mixed with text that flows right-to-left, where *type* is normal, embed, bibi-override, or inherit (CSS3)
vertical-align: *type*	Specifies how to vertically align the text with the surrounding content, where *type* is baseline, middle, top, bottom, text-top, text-bottom, super, sub, or one of the CSS units of length
white-space: *type*	Specifies the handling of white space (blank spaces, tabs, and new lines), where *type* is inherit, normal, pre (to treat the text as preformatted text), or nowrap (to prevent line-wrapping)
white-space-collapse: *type*	Defines how white space inside the element is collapsed, where *type* is preserve, collapse, preserve-breaks, or discard (CSS3)
word-break: *type*	Controls line-breaks within words, where *type* is normal, keep-all, loose, break-strict, or break-all (CSS3)
word-spacing: *length*	Specifies the amount of space between words in the text, where *length* is either a CSS unit of length or the keyword "normal" to use normal word spacing
Layout	**Styles that Define the Layout of Elements**
bottom: *y*	Defines the vertical offset of the element's bottom edge, where *y* is either a CSS unit of length or the keyword "auto" or "inherit"
clear: *type*	Places the element only after the specified margin is clear of floating elements, where *type* is inherit, none, left, right, or both
float: *type*	Floats the element on the specified margin with subsequent content wrapping around the element, where *type* is inherit, none, left, right, or both
float-offset: *horiz vert*	Pushes floated elements in the opposite direction of where they would have been, where *horiz* is the horizontal displacement and *vert* is the vertical displacement (CSS3)
left: *x*	Defines the horizontal offset of the element's left edge, where *x* is either a CSS unit of length or the keyword "auto" or "inherit"
move-to: *type*	Causes the element to be removed from the page flow and reinserted at later point in the document, where *type* is normal, here, or an *id* value (CSS3)
position: *type*	Defines how the element is positioned on the page, where *type* is absolute, relative, fixed, static, and inherit
right: *x*	Defines the horizontal offset of the element's right edge, where *x* is either a CSS unit of length or the keyword "auto" or "inherit"

Attribute	Description
`top: y`	Defines the vertical offset of the element's top edge, where *y* is a CSS unit of length or the keyword "auto" or "inherit"
`z-index: value`	Defines how overlapping elements are stacked, where *value* is either the stacking number (elements with higher stacking numbers are placed on top) or the keyword "auto" to allow the browser to determine the stacking order
Lists	**Styles that Format Lists**
`list-style: type image position`	Defines the appearance of a list item, where *type* is the marker type, *image* is the URL of the location of an image file used for the marker, and *position* is the position of the marker
`list-style-image: url(url)`	Defines image used for the list marker, where *url* is the location of the image file
`list-style-type: type`	Defines the marker type used in the list, where *type* is disc, circle, square, decimal, decimal-leading-zero, lower-roman, upper-roman, lower-alpha, upper-alpha, or none
`list-style-position: type`	Defines the location of the list marker, where *type* is inside or outside
`marker-offset: length`	Defines the distance between the marker and the enclosing list box, where *length* is either a CSS unit of length or the keyword "auto" or "inherit" (CSS3)
Outlines	**Styles to Create and Format Outlines**
`outline: color style width`	Creates an outline around the element content, where *color* is the color of the outline, *style* is the outline style, and *width* is the width of the outline
`outline-color: color`	Defines the color of the outline
`outline-offset: value`	Offsets the outline from the element border, where *value* is the length of the offset (CSS3)
`outline-style: type`	Defines the style of the outline, where *type* is dashed, dotted, double, groove, inset, none, outset, ridge, solid, or inherit
`outline-width: length`	Defines the width of the outline, where *length* is expressed in a CSS unit of length
Printing	**Styles for Printed Output**
`fit: type`	Indicates how to scale an element to fit on the page, where *type* is fill, hidden, meet, or slice (CSS3)
`fit-position: vertical horizontal`	Sets the position of the element in the page, where *vertical* is top, center, or bottom; *horizontal* is left or right; or either or both positions are auto, a *value*, or a *percentage* (CSS3)
`page: label`	Specifies the page design to apply, where *label* is a page design created with the @page rule
`page-break-after: type`	Defines how to control page breaks after the element, where *type* is avoid (to avoid page breaks), left (to insert a page break until a left page is displayed), right (to insert a page break until a right page is displayed), always (to always insert a page break), auto, or inherit
`page-break-before: type`	Defines how to control page breaks before the element, where *type* is avoid left, always, auto, or inherit
`page-break-inside: type`	Defines how to control page breaks within the element, where *type* is avoid, auto, or inherit
`marks: type`	Defines how to display crop marks, where *type* is crop, cross, none, or inherit

Attribute	Description
size: *width height orientation*	Defines the size of the page, where *width* and *height* are the width and the height of the page and *orientation* is the orientation of the page (portrait or landscape)
orphans: *value*	Defines how to handle orphaned text, where *value* is the number of lines that must appear within the element before a page break is inserted
widows: *value*	Defines how to handle widowed text, where *value* is the number of lines that must appear within the element after a page break is inserted
Special Effects	**Styles to Create Special Visual Effects**
animation: *name duration timing delay iteration direction*	Applies an animation with the specified *duration*, *timing*, *delay*, *iteration*, and *direction* (CSS3)
animation-delay: *time*	Specifies the animation delay *time* in milliseconds (CSS3)
animation-direction: *direction*	Specifies the animation direction, where *direction* is normal or alternate (CSS3)
animation-duration: *time*	Specifies the duration of the animation *time* in milliseconds (CSS3)
animation-iteration-count: *value*	Specifies the number of iterations in the animation (CSS3)
animation-name: *text*	Provides a name for the animation (CSS3)
animation-play-state: *type*	Specifies the playing state of the animation, where *type* is running or paused
animation-timing-function: *function*	Provides the timing function of the animation, where *function* is ease, linear, ease-in, ease-out, ease-in-out, cubic-Bezier, or a *number* (CSS3)
backface-visibility: *visible*	Specifies whether the back side of an element is visible during a transformation, where *visible* is hidden or visible (CSS3)
filter: *type parameters*	Applies transition and filter effects to elements, where *type* is the type of filter and *parameters* are parameter values specific to the filter (IE only)
image-orientation: *angle*	Rotates the image by the specified *angle* (CSS3)
marquee-direction: *direction*	Specifies the direction of a marquee, where *direction* is forward or reverse (CSS3)
marquee-play-count: *value*	Specifies how often to loop through the marquee (CSS3)
marquee-speed: *speed*	Specifies the speed of the marquee, where *speed* is slow, normal, or fast (CSS3)
marquee-style: *type*	Specifies the marquee style, where *type* is scroll, slide, or alternate (CSS3)
opacity: *alpha*	Sets opacity of the element, ranging from 0 (transparent) to 1 (opaque) (CSS3)
perspective: *value*	Applies a perspective transformation to the element, where *value* is the perspective length (CSS3)
perspective-origin: *origin*	Establishes the origin of the perspective property, where *origin* is left, center, right, top, bottom, or a *position* value (CSS3)
rotation: *angle*	Rotates the element by *angle* (CSS3)
rotation-point: *position*	Sets the location of the rotation point for the element (CSS3)
transform: *function*	Applies a 2D or a 3D transformation, where *function* provides the transformation parameters (CSS3)

Attribute	Description
transform-origin: *position*	Establishes the origin of the transformation of an element, where *position* is the position within the element (CSS3)
transform-style: *type*	Defines how nested elements are rendered in 3D space, where *type* is flat or preserve-3d (CSS3)
transition: *property duration timing delay*	Defines a timed transition of an element, where *property*, *duration*, *timing*, and *delay* define the appearance and timing of the transition (CSS3)
transition-delay: *time*	Sets the delay time of the transition in milliseconds (CSS3)
transition-duration: *time*	Sets the duration time of the transition in milliseconds (CSS3)
transition-property: *type*	Defines the name of the CSS property modified by the transition, where *type* is all or none (CSS3)
transition-timing-function: *type*	Sets the timing function of the transition, where *type* is ease, linear, ease-in, ease-out, ease-in-out, cubic-Bezier, or a *number* (CSS3)
Tables	**Styles to Format the Appearance of Tables**
border-collapse: *type*	Determines whether table cell borders are separate or collapsed into a single border, where *type* is separate, collapse, or inherit
border-spacing: *length*	If separate borders are used for table cells, defines the distance between borders, where *length* is a CSS unit of length or inherit
caption-side: *type*	Defines the position of the caption element, where *type* is bottom, left, right, top, or inherit
empty-cells: *type*	If separate borders are used for table cells, defines whether to display borders for empty cells, where *type* is hide, show, or inherit
table-layout: *type*	Defines the algorithm used for the table layout, where *type* is auto (to define the layout once all table cells have been read), fixed (to define the layout after the first table row has been read), or inherit

APPENDIX D

Making the Web More Accessible

Studies indicate that about 20% of the population has some type of disability. Many of these disabilities do not affect an individual's ability to interact with the web. However, other disabilities can severely affect an individual's ability to participate in the web community. For example, on a news website, a blind user could not see the latest headlines. A deaf user would not be able to hear a news clip embedded in the site's main page. A user with motor disabilities might not be able to move a mouse pointer to activate important links featured on the site's home page.

Disabilities that inhibit an individual's ability to use the web fall into four main categories:

- **Visual disability:** A visual disability can include complete blindness, color-blindness, or an untreatable visual impairment.
- **Hearing disability:** A hearing disability can include complete deafness or the inability to distinguish sounds of certain frequencies.
- **Motor disability:** A motor disability can include the inability to use a mouse, to exhibit fine motor control, or to respond in a timely manner to computer prompts and queries.
- **Cognitive disability:** A cognitive disability can include a learning disability, attention deficit disorder, or the inability to focus on large amounts of information.

While the web includes some significant obstacles to full use by disabled people, it also offers the potential for contact with a great amount of information that is not otherwise cheaply or easily accessible. For example, before the web, in order to read a newspaper, a blind person was constrained by the expense of Braille printouts and audio tapes, as well as the limited availability of sighted people willing to read the news out loud. As a result, blind people would often only be able to read newspapers after the news was no longer new. The web, however, makes news available in an electronic format and in real-time. A blind user can use a browser that converts electronic text into speech, known as a **screen reader**, to read a newspaper website. Combined with the web, screen readers provide access to a broader array of information than was possible through Braille publications alone.

> "The power of the Web is in its universality. Access by everyone regardless of disability is an essential aspect."
>
> — Tim Berners-Lee, W3C Director and inventor of the World Wide Web

STARTING DATA FILES

There are no starting Data Files needed for this appendix.

In addition to screen readers, many other programs and devices—known collectively as **assistive technology** or **adaptive technology**—are available to enable people with different disabilities to use the web. The challenge for the web designer, then, is to create web pages that are accessible to everyone, including (and perhaps especially) to people with disabilities. In addition to being a design challenge, for some designers, web accessibility is the law.

Working with Section 508 Guidelines

In 1973, Congress passed the Rehabilitation Act, which aimed to foster economic independence for people with disabilities. Congress amended the act in 1998 to reflect the latest changes in information technology. Part of the amendment, **Section 508**, requires that any electronic information developed, procured, maintained, or used by the federal government be accessible to people with disabilities. Because the web is one of the main sources of electronic information, Section 508 has had a profound impact on how web pages are designed and how web code is written. Note that the standards apply to federal websites, but not to private sector websites; however, if a site is provided under contract to a federal agency, the website or portion covered by the contract has to comply. Required or not, though, you should follow the Section 508 guidelines not only to make your website more accessible, but also to make your HTML code more consistent and reliable. The Section 508 guidelines are of interest not just to web designers who work for the federal government, but to all web designers.

The Section 508 guidelines encompass a wide range of topics, covering several types of disabilities. The part of Section 508 that impacts web design is sub-section 1194.22, titled

§ 1194.22   Web-based intranet and internet information and applications.

Within this section are 15 paragraphs, numbered (a) through (p), which describe how each facet of a website should be designed so as to maximize accessibility. Let's examine each of these paragraphs in detail.

Graphics and Images

The first paragraph in sub-section 1194.22 deals with graphic images. The standard for the use of graphic images is that

§1194.22 (a)   A text equivalent for every nontext element shall be provided (e.g., via "alt", "longdesc", or in element content).

In other words, any graphic image that contains page content needs to include a text alternative to make the page accessible to visually impaired people. One of the simplest ways to do this is to use the `alt` attribute with every inline image that displays page content. For example, in Figure D-1, the `alt` attribute provides the text of a graphical logo for users who can't see the graphic.

Figure D-1	Using the alt attribute

```
<img src="jkson.jpg" alt="Jackson Electronics" />
```

Not every graphic image requires a text alternative. For example, a decorative image such as a bullet does not need a text equivalent. In those cases, you should include the `alt` attribute, but set its value to an empty text string. You should never neglect to include the `alt` attribute. If you are writing XHTML-compliant code, the `alt` attribute is required. In other cases, screen readers and other nonvisual browsers will recite the filename of a graphic image file if no value is specified for the `alt` attribute. Since the filename is usually of no interest to the end-user, this results in needless irritation.

The `alt` attribute is best used for short descriptions that involve five words or fewer. It is less effective for images that require long descriptive text. You can instead link these images to a document containing a more detailed description. One way to do this is with the `longdesc` attribute, which uses the syntax

```
<img src="url" longdesc="url" />
```

where *url* for the `longdesc` attribute points to a document containing a detailed description of the image. Figure D-2 shows an example that uses the `longdesc` attribute to point to a web page containing a detailed description of a sales chart.

Figure D-2	Using the alt attribute

```
<img src="chart.jpg" alt="Sales Chart"
     longdesc="sales.html" />
```

In browsers that support the `longdesc` attribute, the attribute's value is presented as a link to the specified document. However, since many browsers do not yet support this attribute, many web designers currently use a D-link. A **D-link** is an unobtrusive "D" placed next to the image on the page, which is linked to an external document containing a fuller description of the image. Figure D-3 shows how the sales chart data can be presented using a D-link.

Figure D-3   Using a D-link

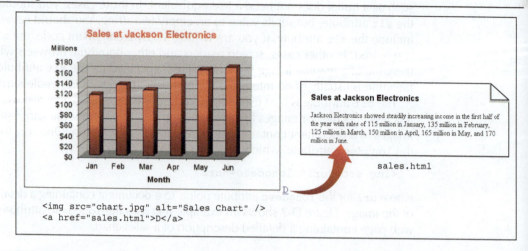

```
<img src="chart.jpg" alt="Sales Chart" />
<a href="sales.html">D</a>
```

To make your pages accessible to visually-impaired users, you will probably use a combination of alternative text and linked documents.

Multimedia

Audio and video have become important ways of conveying information on the web. However, creators of multimedia presentations should also consider the needs of deaf users and users who are hard of hearing. The standard for multimedia accessibility is

§1194.22 (b)   Equivalent alternatives for any multimedia presentation shall be synchronized with the presentation.

This means that any audio clip needs to be accompanied by a transcript of the audio's content, and any video clip needs to include closed captioning. Refer to your multimedia software's documentation on creating closed captioning and transcripts for your video and audio clips.

Color

Color is useful for emphasis and conveying information, but when color becomes an essential part of the site's content, you run the risk of shutting out people who are color blind. For this reason the third Section 508 standard states that

§1194.22 (c)   Web pages shall be designed so that all information conveyed with color is also available without color, for example from context or markup.

About 8% of men and 0.5% of women are afflicted with some type of color blindness. The most serious forms of color blindness are

- **deuteranopia**: an absence of green sensitivity; deuteranopia is one example of red-green color blindness, in which the colors red and green cannot be easily distinguished.
- **protanopia**: an absence of red sensitivity; protanopia is another example of red-green color blindness.
- **tritanopia**: an absence of blue sensitivity; people with tritanopia have much less loss of color sensitivity than other types of color blindness.
- **achromatopsia**: absence of any color sensitivity.

The most common form of serious color blindness is red-green color blindness. Figure D-4 shows how each type of serious color blindness would affect a person's view of a basic color wheel.

| Figure D-4 | Types of color blindness |

Color combinations that are easily readable for most people may be totally unreadable for users with certain types of color blindness. Figure D-5 demonstrates the accessibility problems that can occur with a graphical logo that contains green text on a red background. For people who have deuteranopia, protanopia, or achromatopsia, the logo is much more difficult to read.

| Figure D-5 | The effect of color blindness on graphical content |

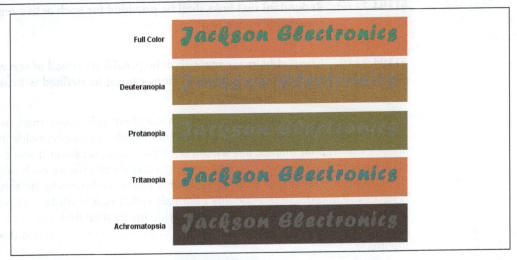

To make your page more accessible to people with color blindness, you can do the following:

- Provide noncolor clues to access your page's content. For example, some web forms indicate required entry fields by displaying the field names in a red font. You can supplement this for color blind users by marking required fields with a red font *and* with an asterisk or other special symbol.
- Avoid explicit references to color. Don't instruct your users to click a red button in a web form when some users are unable to distinguish red from other colors.
- Avoid known areas of color difficulty. Since most color blindness involves red-green color blindness, you should avoid red and green text combinations.

- Use bright colors, which are the easiest for color blind users to distinguish.
- Provide a grayscale or black and white alternative for your color blind users, and be sure that your link to that page is easily viewable.

Several sites on the web include tools you can use to test your website for color blind accessibility. You can also load color palettes into your graphics software to see how your images will appear to users with different types of color blindness.

Style Sheets

By controlling how a page is rendered in a browser, style sheets play an important role in making the web accessible to users with disabilities. Many browsers, such as Internet Explorer, allow a user to apply their own customized style sheet in place of the style sheet specified by a web page's designer. This is particularly useful for visually impaired users who need to display text in extra large fonts with a high contrast between the text and the background color (yellow text on a black background is a common color scheme for such users). In order to make your pages accessible to those users, Section 508 guidelines state that

§1194.22 (d)   Documents shall be organized so they are readable without requiring an associated style sheet.

To test whether your site fulfills this guideline, you should view the site without the style sheet. Some browsers allow you to turn off style sheets; alternately, you can redirect a page to an empty style sheet. You should modify any page that is unreadable without its style sheet to conform with this guideline.

Image Maps

Section 508 provides two standards that pertain to image maps:

§1194.22 (e)   Redundant text links shall be provided for each active region of a server-side image map.

and

§1194.22 (f)   Client-side image maps shall be provided instead of server-side image maps except where the regions cannot be defined with an available geometric shape.

In other words, the *preferred* image map is a client-side image map, unless the map uses a shape that cannot be defined on the client side. Since client-side image maps allow for polygonal shapes, this should not be an issue; however if you must use a server-side image map, you need to provide a text alternative for each of the map's links. Because server-side image maps provide only map coordinates to the server, this text is necessary in order to provide link information that is accessible to blind or visually impaired users. Figure D-6 shows a server-side image map that satisfies the Section 508 guidelines by repeating the graphical links in the image map with text links placed below the image.

| Figure D-6 | Making a server-side image map accessible |

Client-side image maps do not have the same limitations as server-side maps because they allow you to specify alternate text for each hotspot within the map. For example, if the image map shown in Figure D-6 were a client-side map, you could make it accessible using the following HTML code:

```
<img src="servermap.jpg" alt="Jackson Electronics"
 usemap="#links" />
<map name="links">
   <area shape="rect" href="home.html" alt="home"
    coords="21,69,123,117" />
   <area shape="rect" href="products.html" alt="products"
    coords="156,69,258,117" />
   <area shape="rect" href="stores.html" alt="stores"
    coords="302,69,404,117" />
   <area shape="rect" href="support.html" alt="support"
    coords="445,69,547,117" />
</map>
```

Screen readers or other nonvisual browsers use the value of the alt attribute within each <area /> tag to give users access to each area. However, because some older browsers cannot work with the alt attribute in this way, you should also include the text alternative used for server-side image maps.

Tables

Tables can present a challenge for disabled users, particularly for those who employ screen readers or other nonvisual browsers. To render a web page, these browsers employ a technique called **linearizing**, which processes web page content using a few general rules:

1. Convert all images to their alternative text.
2. Present the contents of each table one cell at a time, working from left to right across each row before moving down to the next row.
3. If a cell contains a nested table, that table is linearized before proceeding to the next cell.

Figure D-7 shows how a nonvisual browser might linearize a sample table.

Figure D-7   Linearizing a table

table							linearized content
Desktop PCs	**Model**	**Processor**	**Memory**	**DVD Burner**	**Modem**	**Network Adapter**	Desktop PCs Model Processor Memory DVD Burner Modem Network Adapter Paragon 2.4 Intel 2.4GHz 256MB No Yes No Paragon 3.7 Intel 3.7GHz 512MB Yes Yes No Paragon 5.9 Intel 5.9GHz 1024MB Yes Yes Yes
	Paragon 2.4	Intel 2.4GHz	256MB	No	Yes	No	
	Paragon 3.7	Intel 3.7GHz	512MB	Yes	Yes	No	
	Paragon 5.9	Intel 5.9GHz	1024MB	Yes	Yes	Yes	

One way of dealing with the challenge of linearizing is to structure your tables so that they are easily interpreted even when linearized. However, this is not always possible, especially for tables that have several rows and columns or may contain several levels of nested tables. The Section 508 guidelines for table creation state that

§1194.22 (g)   Row and column headers shall be identified for data tables.

and

§1194.22 (h)   Markup shall be used to associate data cells and header cells for data tables that have two or more logical levels of row or column headers.

To fulfill the 1194.22 (g) guideline, you should use the `<th>` tag for any table cell that contains a row or column header. By default, header text appears in a bold centered font; however, you can override this format using a style sheet. Many nonvisual browsers can search for header cells. Also, as a user moves from cell to cell in a table, these browsers can announce the row and column headers associated with each cell. In this way, using the `<th>` tag can significantly reduce some of the problems associated with linearizing.

You can also use the `scope` attribute to explicitly associate a header with a row, column, row group, or column group. The syntax of the `scope` attribute is

```
<th scope="type"> … </th>
```

where `type` is either `row`, `column`, `rowgroup`, or `colgroup`. Figure D-8 shows how to use the `scope` attribute to associate the headers with the rows and columns of a table.

Providing a Text-Only Equivalent

If you cannot modify a page to match the previous accessibility guidelines, as a last resort you can create a text-only page:

§1194.22 (k) **A text-only page, with equivalent information or functionality, shall be provided to make a Web site comply with the provisions of this part, when compliance cannot be accomplished in any other way. The content of the text-only pages shall be updated whenever the primary page changes.**

To satisfy this requirement, you should

- provide an easily accessible link to the text-only page.
- make sure that the text-only page satisfies the Section 508 guidelines.
- duplicate the essential content of the original page.
- update the alternate page when you update the original page.

By using the Section 508 guidelines, you can work toward making your website accessible to everyone, regardless of disabilities.

Understanding the Web Accessibility Initiative

In 1999, the World Wide Web Consortium (W3C) developed its own set of guidelines for web accessibility called the **Web Accessibility Initiative (WAI)**. The WAI covers many of the same points as the Section 508 rules, and expands on them to cover basic website design issues. The overall goal of the WAI is to facilitate the creation of websites that are accessible to all, and to encourage designers to implement HTML in a consistent way.

The WAI sets forth 14 guidelines for web designers. Within each guideline is a collection of checkpoints indicating how to apply the guideline to specific features of a website. Each checkpoint is also given a priority score that indicates how important the guideline is for proper web design:

- **Priority 1:** A web content developer **must** satisfy this checkpoint. Otherwise, one or more groups will find it impossible to access information in the document. Satisfying this checkpoint is a basic requirement for some groups to be able to use web documents.
- **Priority 2:** A web content developer **should** satisfy this checkpoint. Otherwise, one or more groups will find it difficult to access information in the document. Satisfying this checkpoint will remove significant barriers to accessing web documents.
- **Priority 3:** A web content developer **may** address this checkpoint. Otherwise, one or more groups will find it somewhat difficult to access information in the document. Satisfying this checkpoint will improve access to web documents.

The following table lists WAI guidelines with each checkpoint and its corresponding priority value. You can learn more about the WAI guidelines and how to implement them by going to the World Wide Web Consortium Web site at *www.w3.org*.

WAI Guidelines	Priority
1. Provide equivalent alternatives to auditory and visual content	
1.1 Provide a text equivalent for every nontext element (e.g., via `alt`, `longdesc`, or in element content). *This includes:* images, graphical representations of text (including symbols), image map regions, animations (e.g., animated GIFs), applets and programmatic objects, ascii art, frames, scripts, images used as list bullets, spacers, graphical buttons, sounds (played with or without user interaction), stand-alone audio files, audio tracks of video, and video.	1
1.2 Provide redundant text links for each active region of a server-side image map.	1
1.3 Until user agents can automatically read aloud the text equivalent of a visual track, provide an auditory description of the important information of the visual track of a multimedia presentation.	1
1.4 For any time-based multimedia presentation (e.g., a movie or animation), synchronize equivalent alternatives (e.g., captions or auditory descriptions of the visual track) with the presentation.	1
1.5 Until user agents render text equivalents for client-side image map links, provide redundant text links for each active region of a client-side image map.	3
2. Don't rely on color alone	
2.1 Ensure that all information conveyed with color is also available without color, for example from context or markup.	1
2.2 Ensure that foreground and background color combinations provide sufficient contrast when viewed by someone having color deficits or when viewed on a black and white screen. [Priority 2 for images, Priority 3 for text].	2
3. Use markup and style sheets and do so properly	
3.1 When an appropriate markup language exists, use markup rather than images to convey information.	2
3.2 Create documents that validate to published formal grammars.	2
3.3 Use style sheets to control layout and presentation.	2
3.4 Use relative rather than absolute units in markup language attribute values and style sheet property values.	2
3.5 Use header elements to convey document structure and use them according to specification.	2
3.6 Mark up lists and list items properly.	2
3.7 Mark up quotations. Do not use quotation markup for formatting effects such as indentation.	2
4. Clarify natural language usage	
4.1 Clearly identify changes in the natural language of a document's text and any text equivalents (e.g., captions).	1
4.2 Specify the expansion of each abbreviation or acronym in a document where it first occurs.	3
4.3 Identify the primary natural language of a document.	3
5. Create tables that transform gracefully	
5.1 For data tables, identify row and column headers.	1
5.2 For data tables that have two or more logical levels of row or column headers, use markup to associate data cells and header cells.	1
5.3 Do not use a table for layout unless the table makes sense when linearized. If a table does not make sense, provide an alternative equivalent (which may be a linearized version).	2
5.4 If a table is used for layout, do not use any structural markup for the purpose of visual formatting.	2

WAI Guidelines	Priority
5.5 Provide summaries for tables.	3
5.6 Provide abbreviations for header labels.	3
6. Ensure that pages featuring new technologies transform gracefully	
6.1 Organize documents so they may be read without style sheets. For example, when an HTML document is rendered without associated style sheets, it must still be possible to read the document.	1
6.2 Ensure that equivalents for dynamic content are updated when the dynamic content changes.	1
6.3 Ensure that pages are usable when scripts, applets, or other programmatic objects are turned off or not supported. If this is not possible, then provide equivalent information on an alternative accessible page.	1
6.4 For scripts and applets, ensure that event handlers are input device-independent.	2
6.5 Ensure that dynamic content is accessible or provide an alternative presentation or page.	2
7. Ensure user control of time-sensitive content changes	
7.1 Until user agents allow users to control flickering, avoid causing the screen to flicker.	1
7.2 Until user agents allow users to control blinking, avoid causing content to blink (i.e., change presentation at a regular rate, such as turning on and off).	2
7.3 Until user agents allow users to freeze moving content, avoid movement in pages.	2
7.4 Until user agents provide the ability to stop the refresh, do not create periodically auto-refreshing pages.	2
7.5 Until user agents provide the ability to stop auto-redirect, do not use markup to redirect pages automatically. Instead, configure the server to perform redirects.	2
8. Ensure direct accessibility of embedded user interfaces	
8.1 Make programmatic elements such as scripts and applets directly accessible or compatible with assistive technologies [Priority 1 if functionality is important and not presented elsewhere, otherwise Priority 2.]	2
9. Design for device-independence	
9.1 Provide client-side image maps instead of server-side image maps except where the regions cannot be defined with an available geometric shape.	1
9.2 Ensure that any element with its own interface can be operated in a device-independent manner.	2
9.3 For scripts, specify logical event handlers rather than device-dependent event handlers.	2
9.4 Create a logical tab order through links, form controls, and objects.	3
9.5 Provide keyboard shortcuts to important links (including those in client-side image maps), form controls, and groups of form controls.	3
10. Use interim solutions	
10.1 Until user agents allow users to turn off spawned windows, do not cause pop-ups or other windows to appear and do not change the current window without informing the user.	2
10.2 Until user agents support explicit associations between labels and form controls, ensure that labels are properly positioned for all form controls with implicitly associated labels.	2
10.3 Until user agents (including assistive technologies) render side-by-side text correctly, provide a linear text alternative (on the current page or some other) for *all* tables that lay out text in parallel, word-wrapped columns.	3
10.4 Until user agents handle empty controls correctly, include default, place-holding characters in edit boxes and text areas.	3
10.5 Until user agents (including assistive technologies) render adjacent links distinctly, include nonlink, printable characters (surrounded by spaces) between adjacent links.	3

WAI Guidelines	Priority
11. Use W3C technologies and guidelines	
11.1 Use W3C technologies when they are available and appropriate for a task and use the latest versions when supported.	2
11.2 Avoid deprecated features of W3C technologies.	2
11.3 Provide information so that users may receive documents according to their preferences (e.g., language, content type, etc.).	3
11.4 If, after best efforts, you cannot create an accessible page, provide a link to an alternative page that uses W3C technologies, is accessible, has equivalent information (or functionality), and is updated as often as the inaccessible (original) page.	1
12. Provide context and orientation information	
12.1 Title each frame to facilitate frame identification and navigation.	1
12.2 Describe the purpose of frames and how frames relate to each other if this is not obvious from frame titles alone.	2
12.3 Divide large blocks of information into more manageable groups where natural and appropriate.	2
12.4 Associate labels explicitly with their controls.	2
13. Provide clear navigation mechanisms	
13.1 Clearly identify the target of each link.	2
13.2 Provide metadata to add semantic information to pages and sites.	2
13.3 Provide information about the general layout of a site (e.g., a site map or table of contents).	2
13.4 Use navigation mechanisms in a consistent manner.	2
13.5 Provide navigation bars to highlight and give access to the navigation mechanism.	3
13.6 Group related links, identify the group (for user agents), and, until user agents do so, provide a way to bypass the group.	3
13.7 If search functions are provided, enable different types of searches for different skill levels and preferences.	3
13.8 Place distinguishing information at the beginning of headings, paragraphs, lists, etc.	3
13.9 Provide information about document collections (i.e., documents comprising multiple pages).	3
13.10 Provide a means to skip over multiline ASCII art.	3
14. Ensure that documents are clear and simple	
14.1 Use the clearest and simplest language appropriate for a site's content.	1
14.2 Supplement text with graphic or auditory presentations where they will facilitate comprehension of the page.	3
14.3 Create a style of presentation that is consistent across pages.	3

Checking Your Web Site for Accessibility

As you develop your website, you should periodically check it for accessibility. In addition to reviewing the Section 508 and WAI guidelines, you can do several things to verify that your site is accessible to everyone:

- Set up your browser to suppress the display of images. Does each page still convey all of the necessary information?
- Set your browser to display pages in extra large fonts and with a different color scheme. Are your pages still readable under these conditions?
- Try to navigate your pages using only your keyboard. Can you access all of the links and form elements?
- Open your page in a screen reader or other nonvisual browser. (The W3C website contains links to several alternative browsers that you can download as freeware or on a short-term trial basis in order to evaluate your site.)
- Use tools that test your site for accessibility. (The WAI pages at the W3C website contain links to a wide variety of tools that report on how well your site complies with the WAI and Section 508 guidelines.)

Following the accessibility guidelines laid out by Section 508 and the WAI will result in a website that is not only more accessible to a wider audience, but whose design is also cleaner, easier to work with, and easier to maintain.

Checking Your Web Site for Accessibility

As you develop your web site, you should periodically check it for accessibility. In addition to reviewing the Section 508 and WAI guidelines, you can do several things to verify that your site is accessible to everyone.

- Set up your browser to suppress the display of images. Does each page still convey all of the necessary information?
- Set your browser to display in extra-large fonts and with a different color scheme. Are your pages still readable under these conditions?
- Try to navigate your pages using only your keyboard. Can you access all of the links and form elements?
- Open your page in as many reader or other nonvisual browsers at the W3C website contains links to several alternative browsers that you can download as freeware are open (a short-term trial basis in order to evaluate your site).
- Use tools that test your site for accessibility. The WAI pages at the W3C website contain links to a wide variety of tools that report on how well your site complies with the WAI and Section 508 guidelines.

Following the accessibility guidelines laid out by Section 508 and the WAI will result in a website that is not only more accessible to a wide audience, but whose design is also cleaner, easier to work with, and easier to maintain.

APPENDIX **E**

Designing for the Web

Before you begin creating links between your website pages, it's worthwhile to use a technique known as storyboarding to map out exactly how you want the pages to relate to each other. A **storyboard** is a diagram of a website's structure, showing all the pages in the site and indicating how they are linked together. Because websites use a variety of structures, it's important to storyboard your website before you start creating your pages. This helps you determine which structure works best for the type of information your site contains. A well-designed structure ensures that users will be able to navigate the site without getting lost or missing important information.

Every website should begin with a single home page that acts as a focal point for the website. It is usually the first page that users see. From that home page, you add links to other pages in the site, defining the site's overall structure. The websites you commonly encounter as you navigate the web employ several different web structures. You'll examine some of these structures to help you decide how to design your own sites.

Linear Structures

If you wanted to create an online version of a famous play, like Shakespeare's *Hamlet*, one method would be to link the individual scenes of the play in a long chain. Figure E-1 shows the storyboard for this **linear structure**, in which each page is linked with the pages that follow and precede it. Readers navigate this structure by moving forward and backward through the pages, much as they might move forward and backward through the pages of a book.

STARTING DATA FILES

There are no starting Data Files needed for this appendix.

Figure E-1   **A linear structure**

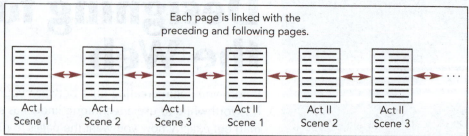

© 2016 Cengage Learning

Linear structures work for websites that are small in size and have a clearly defined order of pages. However, they can be difficult to work with as the chain of pages increases in length. An additional problem is that in a linear structure, you move farther and farther away from the home page as you progress through the site. Because home pages often contain important general information about a site and its author, this is usually not the best design technique.

You can modify this structure to make it easier for users to return immediately to the home page or other main pages. Figure E-2 shows this online play with an **augmented linear structure**, in which each page contains an additional link back to the opening page of each act.

Figure E-2   **An augmented linear structure**

© 2016 Cengage Learning

Hierarchical Structures

Another popular structure is the **hierarchical structure**, in which the home page links to pages dedicated to specific topics. Those pages, in turn, can be linked to even more specific topics. A hierarchical structure allows users to easily move from general to specific and back again. In the case of the online play, you could link an introductory page containing general information about the play to pages that describe each of the play's acts, and within each act you could include links to individual scenes. See Figure E-3.

Figure E-3	A hierarchical structure

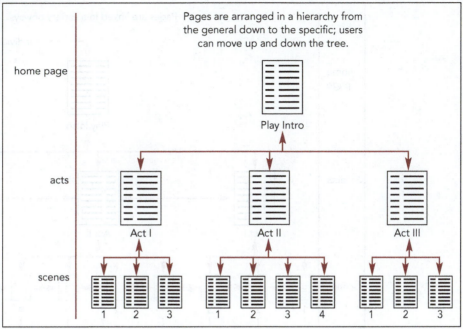

© 2016 Cengage Learning

Mixed Structures

Within this structure, a user could move quickly to a specific scene within the play, bypassing the need to move through each scene that precedes it.

With larger and more complex websites, you often need to use a combination of structures. Figure E-4 shows the online play using a mixture of hierarchical and linear structures. The overall form is hierarchical, as users can move from a general introduction down to individual scenes; however, users can also move through the site in a linear fashion, going from act to act and scene to scene. Finally, each individual scene contains a link to the home page, allowing users to jump to the top of the hierarchy without moving through the different levels.

Figure E-4   **A mixed structure**

© 2016 Cengage Learning

As these examples show, a little foresight can go a long way toward making your website easier to use. Also keep in mind that search results from a web search engine such as Google or Yahoo! can point users to any page in your website—not just your home page—so users will need to be able to quickly understand what your site contains and how to navigate it. At a minimum, each page should contain a link to the site's home page or to the relevant main topic page. In some cases, you might want to supply your users with a **site index**, which is a page containing an outline of the entire site and its contents. Unstructured websites can be difficult and frustrating to use. Consider the storyboard of the site displayed in Figure E-5.

Figure E-5   **Website with no coherent structure**

© 2016 Cengage Learning

This confusing structure makes it difficult for users to grasp the site's contents and scope. The user might not even be aware of the presence of some pages because there are no connecting links, and some of the links point in only one direction. The web is a competitive place; studies have shown that users who don't see how to get what they want within the first few seconds often leave a website. How long would a user spend on a site like the one shown in Figure E-5?

Protected Structures

Sections of most commercial websites are often off-limits except to subscribers and registered customers. Storyboarding a protected structure is particularly important to ensure that no unauthorized access to the protected area is allowed in the site design. As shown in Figure E-6, these sites have a password-protected web page that users must go through to get to the off-limits areas.

Figure E-6 **A protected structure**

public site · protected section

© 2016 Cengage Learning

The same website design principles apply to the protected section as the regular, open section of the site. As always, you want to create and maintain detailed storyboards to improve your site's performance and accessibility to all users.

Page Validation with XHTML

Introducing XHTML

In these tutorials, you have worked with documents written to correspond with the specifications of HTML5. However, other versions of HTML have applications both on the web and in the business world. One of these versions is XHTML. To understand what XHTML is, you will look at the XML language first.

XML

Extensible Markup Language or **XML** is a language for designing specialized markup languages called **XML vocabularies**, which can be used for a variety of document needs. Some popular XML vocabularies include MathML for mathematical content, CML for documenting chemical structures, and MusicML for describing musical scores. Individual users and businesses can also create markup languages tailored for their specific needs. The content of XML documents resembles what you have seen for HTML documents in which content is marked with element tags that can contain element attributes. For example, the following code is an excerpt from a MusicML document describing Mozart's *Piano Sonata in A Major*:

```
<work>
   <work-number>K. 331</work-number>
   <work-title>Piano Sonata in A Major</work-title>
</work>
<identification>
   <creator type="composer">Wolfgang Amadeus
    Mozart</creator>
   <rights>Copyright 2018 Recordare LLC</rights>
</identification>
```

XHTML is another XML vocabulary in which the content and structure is written in XML but uses the tags and attributes associated with HTML. However, the structure of an XHTML document differs from an HTML document in ways you will explore next.

STARTING DATA FILES

There are no starting Data Files needed for this appendix.

Starting an XHTML Document

All XML documents, and thus all XHTML documents, must begin with a **prolog** that indicates the document adheres to the syntax rules of XML. The form of the XML prolog is

```
<?xml version="value" encoding="type" ?>
```

where the `version` attribute indicates the XML version of the document and the `encoding` attribute specifies its character encoding. For XHTML documents, set the version to "1.0". The encoding depends on the character set being used. For example, if a document is saved using the UTF-8 character set, you would start the XHTML document with the following prolog:

```
<?xml version="1.0" encoding="UTF-8" ?>
```

With XHTML documents, you can define the character encoding within the XML prolog or with the following `meta` element, added to the document head

```
<meta http-equiv="Content-type" content="text/html;charset=type" />
```

where `type` is once again the character encoding. Thus, the `meta` element

```
<meta http-equiv="Content-type" content="text/html;charset=UTF-8" />
```

defines the content type as using the UTF-8 character set.

Creating Well-Formed Documents

Once an XML document has been created, a program called an **XML parser** checks the file for errors in syntax and content. An XML document that employs the correct syntax is known as a **well-formed document**. Browsers usually accept HTML documents that violate HTML syntax as long as the violation is not too severe; however, an XML parser rejects any XML document that is not well formed. See Figure F-1.

| Figure F-1 | Testing for well formedness |

the parser checks for syntax errors in the XML document

the document author writes the code of the XML document

if the document is well formed, it is passed by the parser and its content is displayed by the browser or other XML application

© 2016 Cengage Learning

For example, the following code is an example of code that is not well formed because it violates the basic rule that every two-sided tag must have both an opening and closing tag:

Not well-formed code:

```
<body>
    <h1>Web Page Title
</body>
```

An XML parser rejects documents that are not well formed and thus the document content will not be displayed by the browser. To correct this error and make the code well formed, you need to add the closing tag as shown next.

Well-formed code:

```
<body>
    <h1>Web Page Title </h1>
</body>
```

When you write XHTML code, it is important to be familiar with all of the rules of proper syntax. Figure F-2 lists seven syntax requirements that all XML documents (and therefore all XHTML documents) must follow.

| Figure F-2 | Rules for well-formed XML code |

Rule	Incorrect	Correct
Element names must be lowercase.	`<P>This is a paragraph.</P>`	`<p>This is a paragraph.</p>`
Elements must be properly nested.	`<p>This text is <b>bold</p>.</b>`	`<p>This text is <b>bold</b>.</p>`
All elements must be closed.	`<p>This is a paragraph.`	`<p>This is a paragraph.</p>`
Empty elements must be terminated.	`This is a line break.  `	`This is a line break.  `
Attribute names must be lowercase.	`<td COLSPAN="3">`	`<td colspan="3">`
Attribute values must be quoted.	`<td colspan=3>`	`<td colspan="3">`
Attributes must have values.	`<option selected>`	`<option selected="selected">`

In addition to the rules specified in Figure F-2, all XML documents must also include a single **root element** that contains all other elements. For XHTML, that root element is the `html` element. You should already be familiar with many of these rules because you have been working with well-formed HTML since Tutorial 1. However, on older websites, you may find document code that violates this basic syntax but which most browsers still support.

In some older HTML documents, you might find cases of attribute minimization, a situation in which an element attribute lacks a value. XHTML does not allow attribute minimization so XHTML uses the name of the attribute as the attribute value. Figure F-3 lists the minimized attributes found in some HTML documents, along with the XHTML-compliant versions of these attributes.

| Figure F-3 | Attribute minimization in HTML and XHTML |

HTML	XHTML
compact	compact="compact"
checked	checked="checked"
declare	declare="declare"
readonly	readonly="readonly"
disabled	disabled="disabled"
selected	selected="selected"
defer	defer="defer"
ismap	ismap="ismap"
nohref	nohref="nohref"
noshade	noshade="noshade"
nowrap	nowrap="nowrap"
multiple	multiple="multiple"
noresize	noresize="noresize"

For example, in HTML, the following code can be used to indicate that a radio button should be selected by default:

```
<input type="radio" checked>
```

In XHTML, this code would be rewritten as follows:

```
<input type="radio" checked="checked" />
```

Failure to make this change would cause the XHTML document to be rejected as not well formed. Note that in HTML, either form is accepted: You can write a minimized attribute either with the attribute value or without it.

Creating Valid XHTML Documents

In addition to being tested for well formedness, XML documents can also be checked to see if they are valid. A **valid document** is a well-formed document that also contains only those elements, attributes, and other features that have been defined for its XML vocabulary. For example, if the code

```
<body>
    <mainhead>Web Page Title</mainhead>
</body>
```

was entered into an XHTML file, the code would be considered well formed because it complies with the syntax rules of XML—but it would not be valid because XHTML does not support a mainhead element. To specify the correct content and structure for a document, the developers of an XML-based language can create a collection of rules called the **document type definition** or **DTD**, which are stored either within the XML file or externally in a text file known as a **DTD file**. As shown in Figure F-4, an XML parser tests the content of a document against the rules in the DTD file. If the document does not conform to those rules, the parser rejects the document as not valid.

© 2016 Cengage Learning

For example, an XML vocabulary designed for a business might contain elements naming each product in its inventory. The DTD for that document could require that each product name element be accompanied by an `id` attribute value and that no products share the same name or id. An XML parser would reject any XML document that didn't satisfy those rules, even if the document was well formed. In this way, XML differs from HTML, which does not include a mechanism to force web page authors to adhere to rules for syntax and content.

Transitional, Frameset, and Strict DTDs

There are several different DTDs associated with HTML and XHTML documents. Some DTDs represent older versions of HTML. For example, if you want to create a document that is validated only against the standards of HTML5, a DTD is available for this purpose.

For XHTML 1.0, there are three DTDs available for testing the validity of XHTML documents:

- **transitional DTD**: The transitional DTD supports many presentational features of HTML, including elements and attributes that have been deprecated in HTML5. It is best used with websites that need to support older standards.
- **frameset DTD**: The frameset DTD is used for documents containing frames, as well as deprecated elements and attributes. It is best used with older websites that rely on frames.
- **strict DTD**: The strict DTD does not allow for any deprecated HTML elements and attributes, and it does not support frames or inline frames. It is best used for documents that must conform strictly to the latest standards.

All three DTDs require that every valid XHTML document include the following elements: `html`, `head`, `title`, and `body`. If these elements are omitted, the document will be rejected by the XML parser.

There are elements that are allowed in one DTD but not in another. For example, the following elements are allowed under the transitional DTD but they are not allowed under the strict DTD for XHTML 1.0:

- applet
- basefont
- center
- dir
- font
- isindex
- menu
- noframes
- s
- strike
- u

In addition to using these elements in the transitional DTD, you often will encounter them in older websites.

The frameset DTD supports these elements as well as the `frame`, `frameset`, and `noframes` elements. Therefore, the following code, which uses the deprecated `font` element and `color` attribute,

```
<font color="red">Wizard Works</font>
```

would be considered valid code under the transitional and frameset DTDs but not under the strict DTD.

In addition to prohibiting the use of certain elements, the strict DTD also requires a particular document structure. For example, you cannot nest a block-level element within an inline element. Figure F-5 lists the prohibited child elements under the strict DTD.

Figure F-5	Child elements prohibited under the XHTML strict DTD

Element	Prohibited Children
inline elements	*any block-level element*
body	a, abbr, acronym, b, bdo, big, br, button, cite, code, dfn, em, i, img, input, kbd, label, map, object, q, samp, select, small, span, strong, sub, sup, textarea, tt, var
button	button, form, fieldset, iframe, input, isindex, label, select, textarea
blockquote	a, abbr, acronym, b, bdo, big, br, button, cite, code, dfn, em, i, img, input, kbd, label, map, object, q, samp, select, small, span, strong, sub, sup, textarea, tt, var
form	a, abbr, acronym, b, bdo, big, br, cite, code, dfn, em, form, i, img, kbd, map, object, q, samp, small, span, strong, sub, sup, tt, var
label	label
pre	big, img, object, small, sub, sup

Thus, the following code would be disallowed under the strict DTD because it places an inline image as a child of the `body` element:

```
<body>
    <img src="logo.jpg" alt="Wizard Works" />
</body>
```

However, you could make this code compliant with the strict DTD by placing the inline image within a paragraph, as follows:

```
<body>
   <p>
      <img src="logo.jpg" alt="Wizard Works" />
   </p>
</body>
```

The goal of this rule is to enforce the inline nature of the img element. Because an inline image is displayed inline within a block element such as a paragraph, it should not be found outside of that context. For the same reason, form elements (such as the input or select elements) should be found only within a form, not outside of a form, under the strict DTD.

The Valid Use of Attributes

DTDs also include different rules for attributes and their use. Under the strict DTD, deprecated attributes are not allowed. A list of these prohibited attributes with their corresponding elements is displayed in Figure F-6.

Figure F-6 | **Attributes prohibited under the XHTML strict DTD**

Element	Prohibited Attribute(s)
a	target
area	target
base	target
body	alink, bgcolor, link, text, vlink
br	clear
caption	align
div	align
dl	compact
form	name, target
hn	align
hr	align, noshade, size, width
img	align, border, hspace, name, vspace
input	align
li	type, value
link	target
map	name
object	align, border, hspace, vspace
ol	compact, start
p	align
pre	width
script	language
table	align, bgcolor
td	bgcolor, height, nowrap, width
th	bgcolor, height, nowrap, width
tr	bgcolor
ul	type, compact

Many of the attributes listed in Figure F-6 are called presentational attributes because they define how browsers should render the element. Note that all of the attributes listed in Figure F-6 are supported in the transitional and frameset DTDs. Therefore, the following code, which uses the `align` attribute to float an inline image on the left margin of the page, would not be valid under the strict DTD because the `align` attribute is prohibited; however, it would be allowed under the frameset and transitional DTDs.

```
<img src="logo.jpg" alt="Wizard Works" align="left" />
```

The strict DTD also requires the use of the `id` attribute in place of the `name` attribute for several elements. For example, the following tag that you might see in older HTML code

```
<img name="logo" alt="logo image" />
```

would be written in XHTML under the strict DTD using the `id` attribute as follows:

```
<img id="logo" alt="logo image" />
```

Whereas some attributes are prohibited, others are required. A list of the required attributes and the elements they are associated with is shown in Figure F-7.

| Figure F-7 | Required attributes for XHTML elements |

Element	Required Attribute(s)
applet	height, width
area	alt
base	href
basefont	size
bdo	dir
form	action
img	src, alt
map	id
meta	content
optgroup	label
param	name
script	type
style	type
textarea	cols, rows

For example, an inline image is valid only if it contains both the `src` and `alt` attributes, and a `form` element is valid only if it contains an `action` attribute.

Although the list of rules for well-formed and valid documents may seem long and onerous, these rules simply reflect good coding practice. You would not, for example, want to create an image map without an ID or an inline image without alternate text.

Inserting the DOCTYPE Declaration

To specify which DTD is used by an XML document, you add the following DOCTYPE declaration directly after the XML prolog

```
<!DOCTYPE root type "id" "url">
```

where *root* is the name of the root element of the document, *type* identifies the type of DTD (either PUBLIC or SYSTEM), *id* is an id associated with the DTD, and *url* is the location of an external file containing the DTD rules. For XHTML documents, you set the *root* value to html and the *type* value to PUBLIC.

Figure F-8 lists the complete DOCTYPE declarations for different versions of HTML and XHTML. Note that you can validate a document not only against different versions of XHTML 1.0, but even against different W3C specifications for HTML; this can be beneficial if you need to develop code for older browsers that do not support current standards. You can access the most recent versions of these DTDs on the W3C website.

Figure F-8	DTDs for different versions of HTML and XHTML

DTD	DOCTYPE
HTML 4.01 strict	`<!DOCTYPE html PUBLIC "-//W3C//DTD HTML 4.01//EN"` `"http://www.w3.org/TR/html4/strict.dtd">`
HTML 4.01 transitional	`<!DOCTYPE html PUBLIC` `"-//W3C//DTD HTML 4.01 Transitional//EN"` `"http://www.w3.org/TR/html4/loose.dtd">`
HTML 4.01 frameset	`<!DOCTYPE html PUBLIC "-//W3C//DTD HTML 4.01 Frameset//EN"` `"http://www.w3.org/TR/html4/frameset.dtd">`
HTML5	`<!DOCTYPE html>`
XHTML 1.0 strict	`<!DOCTYPE html PUBLIC "-//W3C//DTD XHTML 1.0 Strict//EN"` `"http://www.w3.org/TR/xhtml1/DTD/xhtml1-strict.dtd">`
XHTML 1.0 transitional	`<!DOCTYPE html PUBLIC` `"-//W3C//DTD XHTML 1.0 Transitional//EN"` `"http://www.w3.org/TR/xhtml1/DTD/xhtml1-transitional.dtd">`
XHTML 1.0 frameset	`<!DOCTYPE html PUBLIC "-//W3C//DTD XHTML 1.0 Frameset//EN"` `"http://www.w3.org/TR/xhtml1/DTD/xhtml1-frameset.dtd">`
XHTML 1.1	`<!DOCTYPE html PUBLIC "-//W3C//DTD XHTML 1.1//EN"` `"http://www.w3.org/TR/xhtml11/DTD/xhtml11.dtd">`
XHTML5	`<!DOCTYPE html>`

Setting the XHTML Namespace

As noted earlier, XHTML is only one of hundreds of XML vocabularies. In some situations, a document author may want to combine elements and attributes from different vocabularies in the same document. For example, a mathematician might want to create a single document that combines elements from both the XHTML and MathML vocabularies. Each element or attribute that belongs to a particular language is part of that language's **namespace**. There are two types of namespaces: default and local. For now, you will focus only on the default namespace. A **default namespace** is the namespace that is assumed to be applied, by default, to any element or attribute in the document. To declare a default namespace, you add the following `xmlns` (XML namespace) attribute to the *root* element of the document

```
<root xmlns="namespace">
```

where *namespace* is the namespace id. Every XML vocabulary has a unique namespace id. For example, if you wish to declare that the elements in your document belong to the XHTML namespace by default, you add the following attribute to the `html` element:

```
<html xmlns="http://www.w3.org/1999/xhtml">
```

The namespace id for XHTML looks like a URL but it is not treated as one by XML parsers. The id can actually be any string of characters as long as it uniquely identifies the document namespace. For XHTML 1.0, it was decided by the W3C to use *http://www.w3.org/1999/xhtml* as the unique identifier.

Even if you don't intend to combine different XML-based languages within the same document, it is still a good idea to add a namespace to an XHTML file to explicitly identify the XML vocabulary in use. In practical terms, though, an XHTML document is still interpretable by most browsers without a namespace.

Validating a File on the Web

Once you have created an XHTML or HTML document, you can check it for well formedness and validity using any one of the validators available on the web. One such validator is located at the W3C website: *https://validator.w3.org*. To use the validator:

1. Go to *https://validator.w3.org* in your browser.
2. Choose the location of your file:
   a. For a page on the web, click the Validate by URI tab and enter the address of the page.
   b. For a file on your computer, click the Validate by File Upload tab, click the Choose File button, then locate and select the file on your computer.
   c. For code you wish to enter directly, click the Validate by Direct Input tab and enter the markup code in text box.

3. Click the Check button to run the validator.

Figure F-9 shows part of an XHTML document that can be tested against the W3C validator.

| Figure F-9 | Contents of an XHTML file |

```
<?xml version="1.0" encoding="UTF-8" ?>

<!DOCTYPE html PUBLIC "-//W3C//DTD XHTML 1.0 Strict//EN"
    "http://www.w3.org/TR/xhtml1/DTD/xhtml1-strict.dtd">

<html xmlns="http://www.w3.org/1999/xhtml">
    <head>
        <meta http-equiv="Content-type" content="text/html;charset=UTF-8" />
        <title>Wizard Works</title>
        <link href="ww.css" rel="stylesheet" type="text/css" />
    </head>

    <body bgcolor="white">
        <div id="head">
            <img src="logo.jpg">
            <a href="#">Review Cart</a>
            <a href="#">Check Out</a>
        </div>
```

Callouts:
- XML prolog → `<?xml version="1.0" encoding="UTF-8" ?>`
- DTD for XHTML 1.0 strict → `<!DOCTYPE html PUBLIC ...>`
- XHTML 1.0 namespace
- meta element indicating the character encoding → `<meta http-equiv=...>`

When tested by the validator using the XHTML Strict DTD, the W3C validator returns the results shown in Figure F-10.

Figure F-10	Results for an invalid document

3 errors are found in the document

list and description of errors in the XHTML document

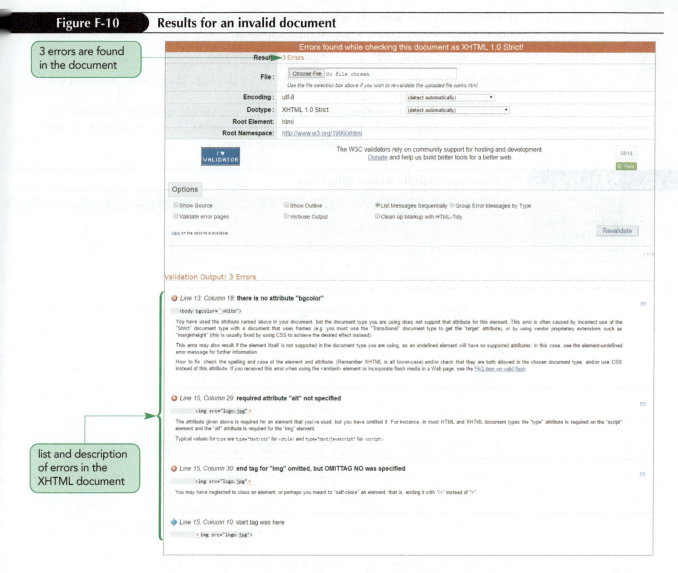

A total of three errors are reported by the validator. The first error is on Line 13:

Error Line 13, Column 18: there is no attribute "bgcolor"

```
<body bgcolor="white">
```

This is an error because there is no `bgcolor` attribute for the `body` element. Instead, the `bgcolor` attribute, used to define the background color, is a presentational attribute that has been deprecated in more recent versions of HTML and XHTML. To correct this error, you would have to remove the `bgcolor` attribute and use a CSS style to define the background color.

The next error is on Line 15:

Error Line 15, Column 29: required attribute "alt" not specified

```
<img src="logo.jpg">
```

This error occurs because the `alt` attribute is missing from the inline image. To correct this error, you would have to specify an alternate text for the inline image.

The third and final error also occurs on Line 15:

Error Line 15, Column 30: end tag for "img" omitted, but OMITTAG NO was specified

```
<img src="logo.jpg">
```

This error occurs because the improper syntax was used for the one-sided tag. The correct syntax for the inline image should appear as

```
<img src="logo.jpg" alt="Wizard Works" />
```

with "Wizard Works" used as the alternate text for the logo image and / added to the closing tag.

Once all of these corrections have been made, you should rerun the validator on the revised markup code to ensure no other errors exist. As shown in Figure F-11, the validator reports a successful test of the markup code.

Figure F-11	Page that successfully passes validation

document passes validation under the XHTML 1.0 Strict DTD

When your document passes the validation test, you might want to make a note of this fact in the body of your web page. The W3C provides code that you can paste into your document to let others know that your document matches all of the validation tests.

Conclusion

Browsers are very forgiving of lapses in syntax. In fact, this is one of the reasons that non-programmers were able to quickly create their own web pages in the early days of the web.

You may wonder if it is really important to validate a document and follow syntax rules when browsers are so accommodating. In fact, there are several good reasons to enforce syntax rules and follow good coding practices:

• Although many browsers accommodate variations in syntax, not all browsers do so and not always in the same way, which can result in varying display results when using different browsers. However, when you follow the syntax rules of the W3C, all browsers enforce those rules and in the same way.

• Web pages tend to be rendered more quickly when they use good syntax because browsers don't have to interpret poorly written code.

- If a browser renders one of your pages incorrectly, it is easier to debug the page if it is written in compliance with standard syntax. Many web developers do a validation check as part of the debugging process to locate errors in the code.
- In a working group where several people are tasked with maintaining the same website code, you need to have a common set of rules to avoid confusion and mistakes. So, for collaboration purposes, it is best to use the rules set down by the W3C.
- Even if you are writing your document in HTML, your business might also need to create XML-based documents. Given the similarity between the two markup languages, it is easier for everyone to use the same set of syntax rules.

Thus, even if you are writing your code in HTML rather than XHTML, it may be best to follow the syntax rules of XHTML. This does not mean you have to run a validation check every time or add a namespace or an XML prolog to your document, but you should use XHTML standards such as lowercasing element and attribute names, and you should always provide attribute values enclosed within quotes.

- If a browser renders one of your pages incorrectly, it is easier to debug the page that is written in compliance with standard syntax. Many web developers do a validation check as part of the debugging process to locate errors in the code.
- In a working group where several people are tasked with maintaining the same web site code, you need to have a common set of rules to avoid confusion and mistakes. So for collaboration purposes, it is best to use the rules set down by the W3C.
- Even if you are writing your document in HTML, your business might also need to create XML output. (Since the similarity between the two markup languages is such), it is easier for everyone to use the same set of syntax rules.

Thus, even if you are writing your code in HTML rather than XHTML, it may be best to follow the syntax rules of XHTML. This does not mean you have to run a validation check every time, or add a namespace or an XML prolog to your document, but you should use XHTML standards, such as lowercasing element and attribute names, and you should always provide attribute values enclosed within quotes.

GLOSSARY

!important CSS keyword that forces a particular style to override the default style sheet cascade. HTML 95

@charset CSS rule defining the character encoding used in a style sheet. HTML 84

@font-face CSS rule that defines a web font. HTML 106

@import CSS rule used to import a style sheet file into the current style sheet. HTML 96

@keyframe CSS rule that defines key frame styles used in an animation. HTML 623

@page CSS rule that defines the size and margins of the printed page. HTML 400

<a> HTML tag that marks a hypertext link to an external resource. HTML 46

<body> HTML tag that marks the document body. HTML 2

<cite> HTML tag that marks a citation. HTML 22

<em> HTML tag that marks emphasized text. HTML 22

<h1> HTML tag that marks a major heading. HTML 22

<head> HTML tag that marks the document head within an HTML file. HTML 2

<html> HTML tag that marks the beginning of the HTML document. HTML 2

<img> HTML tag that marks an image using the file specified in the src attribute. HTML 22

<li> HTML tag that marks a list item. HTML 46

<meta> HTML tag that marks metadata containing information about the document. HTML 2

<nav> HTML tag that marks a list of hypertext links used for navigation. HTML 46

<p> HTML tag that marks a document paragraph. HTML 22

<strong> HTML tag that marks text of major importance or seriousness. HTML 22

<title> HTML tag that marks the page title, which appears in the browser title bar or browser tab. HTML 2

<ul> HTML tag that marks an unordered list. HTML 46

3D transformation A transformation that involves three spatial axes. HTML 316

A

AAC. *See* Advanced Audio Coding

absolute path A folder path that starts from the root folder and processes down the entire folder structure. HTML 61

absolute positioning A layout technique that places an element at specified coordinates within its container element. HTML 224

absolute unit Units that are fixed in size regardless of the output devices. HTML 121

access key A single key on the keyboard that can be pressed in conjunction with another key to jump to a location on the web page. HTML 513

Accessible Rich Internet Application (ARIA) An HTML standard that assists screen readers in interpreting web page content. HTML 44

action HTML attribute that indicates the server program that processes a web form. HTML 500

active CSS pseudo-class that selects actively-clicked links. HTML 132

adaptive technology Technology that enables people with disabilities to use the web. HTML D2

addEventListener() method JavaScript method that listens for events as they propagate through the object hierarchy. HTML 830

Advanced Audio Coding A standard audio coding for all Apple products, as well as YouTube and several gaming systems. HTML 592

after CSS pseudo-element that selects page space directly after the element. HTML 132

alert() JavaScript method to display an alert dialog box in the browser window. HTML 667

align WEBVTT attribute that aligns the text within a track cue. HTML 600

alternate style sheet A style sheet that is not turned off by default and has a rel attribute value of "alternate stylesheet". HTML 944

altKey property JavaScript property that indicates whether the Alt key is pressed. HTML 830

American Standard Code for Information Interchange. *See* ASCII (American Standard Code for Information Interchange)

animation CSS style that applies a key frame animation to an object. HTML 623

animation-play-state CSS style that defines whether an animation is running or is paused. HTML 623

anonymous function A function without a name that can be used as the function definition within a method or another function. HTML 854

appendChild() JavaScript method that appends a specified node to a parent node. HTML 893

ARIA. *See* Accessible Rich Internet Application (ARIA)

array A collection of JavaScript values organized under a single name. HTML 736

array literal JavaScript syntax that defines an array using a comma-separated list of values within a set of square brackets. HTML 742

ASCII (American Standard Code for Information Interchange) The character set used for the English alphabet. HTML 33

assignment operator An operator that assigns a value to an item. HTML 704

assistive technology Technology that enables people with disabilities to use the web. HTML D2

associative array A group of items referenced not by an array index but by a descriptive text string or key. HTML 1073

asymmetric transition A transition in which the initial state to end state transition is not the reverse of the end state to initial state transition. HTML 634

attribute minimization Element attributes that do not require an attribute value. HTML 11

attribute name The name assigned to an attribute node. HTML 915

attribute node A node that represents an attribute associated with an element node. HTML 914

audio HTML element that embeds an audio file in the web page. HTML 586

augmented linear structure A linear structure in which each page contains an additional link to the opening page of the structure. HTML E2

B

background CSS property that defines all background options, including the use of multiple backgrounds. HTML 258

background-color CSS property that sets the background color. HTML 84

background-image CSS property that applies an image file to the element background. HTML 258

backtracking A regular expression technique in which the regular expression contains quantifiers such as the * or + characters, which forces the parser to examine each possible substring within a larger text string. HTML 1016

base object The fundamental JavaScript object whose methods are available to all objects. HTML 1109

before CSS pseudo-element that selects page space directly before the element. HTML 132

binary operator An operator that works with two operands. HTML 704

bitmap image An image format in which the image is comprised of pixels that can be marked with different colors. HTML 264

BOM. *See* browser object model

Boolean value A data type whose values are limited to true or false. HTML 694

border box model A layout model in which the width property refers to the width of the element's content, padding, and border spaces. HTML 191

border CSS property that adds a border around all sides of an element. HTML 258

border The part of the box model that surrounds the padding space. HTML 139

border-collapse CSS attribute that specifies which table borders are separated or collapsed into each other. HTML 435

border-image CSS property that defines an image file to create a graphic border. HTML 258

border-left CSS property that adds a border to the left edge of an element. HTML 258

border-radius CSS property that creates rounded corners with a specified radius. HTML 258

border-right CSS property that adds a border to the right edge of an element. HTML 258

box model A layout model in which element content is surrounded by padding, border, and margin spaces. HTML 139

box-shadow CSS property that adds a drop shadow to a block element. HTML 286

bracket notation An object property referenced using the *object*["*property*"] notation. HTML 1072

breakpoint A location in the program code where the browser will pause the program, allowing the programmer to determine whether an error has

already occurred in the script's execution. HTML 679

browser extension An extension to CSS supported by a specific browser. HTML 90

browser object An object that is part of the web browser. HTML 684

browser object model (BOM) A hierarchical structure that defines the relationship of the object within the web browser. HTML 684

browser style A style built into the web browser itself. HTML 87

bubbling phase The phase in the event model in which the event propagates up the object hierarchy to the root element. HTML 836

built-in object An object that is intrinsic to the JavaScript language. HTML 684

C

calculated style A style calculation that is based on all styles found within external style sheets, embedded styles, inline styles, and browser styles. HTML 951

calendar control A web form control for selecting date and time values. HTML 502

camel case A format where the initial word in a JavaScript property is lowercase but the first letter of each subsequent word is an uppercase letter. HTML 823

caption HTML element that marks a web table caption. HTML 434

caption-side CSS property that specifies the location (top or bottom) of the web table caption. HTML 435

capture phase The phase in the event model in which the event object moves down the object hierarchy, starting from the root element until it reaches the object that initiated the event. HTML 836

Cascading Style Sheets (CSS) A style sheet language supported by the W3C and used in web page design. HTML 32

case statement. *See* switch statement

CGI. *See* Common Gateway Interface

character class A regular expression pattern that limits the regular expression to a select group of characters. HTML 1010

character encoding The process by which the computer converts text into a sequence of bytes and then converts those bytes back into characters. HTML 17

character entity reference An HTML string that inserts a character based on a defined name. HTML 22

character set A collection of characters and symbols. HTML 33

check box A web form control used for selecting data limited to two possible values. HTML 502

checkbox HTML element that marks a check box control. HTML 528

child element An element contained within a parent element. HTML 108

child nodes The nodes contained within a specified node. HTML 895

clear CSS property that displays an element only when the left, right, or both floated objects have been cleared. HTML 170

client A device that receives network information or services. HTML 4

client-server network A network in which clients access information provided by one or more servers. HTML 4

client-side image map An image map that is defined within the web page and handled entirely by the web browser. HTML 324

client-side programming The programming environment in which program code is run locally on the user's computer with scripts that are downloaded from the server. HTML 668

client-side validation Validation that takes place in the user's browser. HTML 559

closing tag The tag that marks the end of the element content. HTML 2

codec A computer program that encodes and decodes streams of data. HTML 588

col HTML element that marks individual columns in a web table. HTML 458

colgroup HTML element that marks groups of columns in a web table. HTML 458

color CSS property that sets the text color. HTML 84

color gradient A background in which one color gradually blends into another color. HTML 296

color picker A web form control for choosing color values. HTML 502

color value A numeric expression that defines a color. HTML 98

color-stop A parameter of a color gradient that defines the extent of the color. HTML 286

colspan HTML attribute that indicates a table cell should cover several columns. HTML 434

command block A set of JavaScript commands enclosed within a set of curly braces. HTML 757

command button A web form button that runs a program. HTML 556

Common Gateway Interface (CGI) A server-based program, written in Perl, used for processing web form data. HTML 504

compare function A function used with the JavaScript sort() method to define a sorting order. HTML 748

comparison operator An operator that compares the value of one expression to another, returning a Boolean value indicating whether the comparison is true or not. HTML 760

compiler A software program that translates program code into machine language. HTML 669

conditional comment An Internet Explorer extension that encloses content that should only be run by particular versions of Internet Explorer. HTML 20

conditional expression An expression that is either true or false. HTML 770

conditional operator An operator used in an expression that returns one value if the condition is true and another if it is false. *Also called* ternary operator. HTML 775

conditional statement A statement that runs a command or command block only when certain circumstances are met. HTML 773

confirm() JavaScript method that creates a dialog box returning a value of true or false. HTML 854

console JavaScript host object used to access the contents of the browser's debugging console. HTML 1090

Constraint Validation API API used to perform validation within the browser. HTML 1029

constructor function JavaScript function that defines the properties and methods associated with the object type or class. HTML 1080

container An object that handles the packaging, transportation, and presentation of multimedia data. HTML 588

container collapse A layout challenge that occurs when an element contains only floated content and thus collapses in height. HTML 195

content box model A layout model in which the width property only refers to the width of the element content. HTML 191

content CSS property that inserts content into a page element. HTML 132

content-box CSS keyword that specifies the background extends only over the element content. HTML 258

contextual selector A selector that specifies the context under which a particular page element is matched. HTML 108

continue expression The Boolean expression in a for loop that must be true for the loop to continue. HTML 754

continue statement JavaScript statement that stops the processing of the commands in the current iteration of the loop and continues to the next iteration. HTML 790

control An object within a web form that allows users to interact with the form. HTML 502

controls HTML attribute that displays player controls for a multimedia clip. HTML 586

counter variable A variable within a for loop that changes value each time the loop is run. HTML 754

cover CSS keyword that specifies that the background image should completely cover the background. HTML 258

createElement() JavaScript method that creates an element node with the specified tag name. HTML 893

cross axis The flexbox axis that is perpendicular to the main axis. HTML 374

CSS at-rule CSS rule that directs how the browser should interpret and parse the CSS code. HTML 96

CSS pixel A pixel that is the fundamental unit in CSS measurements. HTML 355

CSS. *See* Cascading Style Sheets (CSS)

CSS3 The third, and most current version, of CSS. HTML 86

cursive A typeface that mimics handwriting with highly stylized elements and flourishes. HTML 116

cursor style CSS style that defines the cursor for a page element. HTML 830

customized object An object that is created by the programmer for use in an application. HTML 684

D

data attribute HTML attribute that stores customized data. HTML 476

data field The part of a web form in which data values are stored. HTML 503

data list A list of possible values that a form field can have. HTML 553

data type The type of information stored within a variable including numeric values, text strings, Boolean values, objects, and null values. HTML 694

datalist HTML element that defines a set of suggested field values. HTML 546

dataset object JavaScript object that is created from the data-* attributes associated with a page element. HTML 865

Date object JavaScript object used for storing date and time values. HTML 682

debugging The process of locating and fixing a programming error. HTML 677

declaring The process by which a variable is introduced and defined. HTML 693

decodeURIComponent() JavaScript method that decodes every URI character code with its character value. HTML 996

decrement operator A unary operator that decreases the value of the operand by 1. HTML 704

default namespace The namespace that is assumed to be applied to any element or attribute in the document. HTML F10

delimiter A character that marks the break between one substring and another. HTML 1003

deprecated The features and code from earlier HTML versions that have been phased out and are either no longer supported or developed. HTML 6

descendant element An element that descends from a parent element within the document hierarchy. HTML 108

description list A list of terms and matching descriptions. HTML 51

device pixel A pixel that refers to the actual physical pixel on a screen. HTML 355

device-pixel ratio A measure of the number of device pixels matched to a single CSS pixel. HTML 355

display CSS property that defines how an element should be laid out. HTML 170

do/while loop A program loop in which a stopping condition is tested right after the last command block is run. HTML 759

document body The part of an HTML file containing all of the content that will display in the web page. HTML 2

document fragment A node structure that is not part of the document's node tree. HTML 901

document head The part of an HTML file containing information about the document. HTML 2

document object An object that is part of the web page document. HTML 684

document object model (DOM) A hierarchical structure that defines the relationship of the object within the web document. HTML 684

document type declaration A processing instruction indicating the markup language used in the document. HTML 2

document type definition A collection of rules for an XML vocabulary that defines the content and structure of a valid document in that vocabulary. HTML F5

DOM. *See* document object model

domain name The server name portion of a URL. HTML 65

dot operator An object property referenced using the *object.property* notation. HTML 1072

drop cap A design element in which the initial letter in a body of text drops down into the text body. HTML 218

DTD file A text file in which a DTD is stored. HTML F5

DTD. *See* document type definition

dynamic pseudo-class A pseudo-class based on the actions of the user within the element. HTML 148

E

e-mail harvester An automated program that scans web pages for e-mail addresses. HTML 67

elastic layout A layout in which all measurements are expressed in em units and based on the default font size. HTML 177

element attribute The part of an element that provides information to the browser about the purpose of the element or how the element should be handled by the browser. HTML 11

element node A node that matches an element in the HTML file. HTML 892

element tag The fundamental building block of an HTML file, used to mark every document element. HTML 9

em unit CSS relative unit of length that expresses a size relative to the font size of the containing element. HTML 106

embedded content Content that is imported from another resource, often nontextual. HTML 36

embedded element An element containing embedded content such as graphic images, audio soundtracks, video clips, or interactive games. HTML 36

embedded object An object, such as a graphic image or media clip, that appears within a web page. HTML 589

embedded script A program script that is loaded within the HTML file. HTML 670

embedded style A style added to the head of an HTML file. HTML 87

empty element An element that is either nontextual or contains directives to the browser about how the page should be treated. HTML 9

ending tag The tag that marks the end of the element content. HTML 9

enumerable A property that is countable and thus accessible to `for...in` loops. HTML 1119

escape sequence A regular expression that begins with the backslash character \ to indicate that the character that follows should be interpreted as a character and not a command. HTML 1013

eval code Any code that is passed to the browser using the `eval()` function. HTML 1070

event Actions initiated by the user or the browser. HTML 812

event handler JavaScript property that controls how an object will respond to an event. HTML 815

event listeners JavaScript object that listens for events as they propagate through the capture, target, and bubbling phase of the event model. HTML 837

event model The programming model that describes how events and objects interact within the web page and web browser. HTML 836

event object JavaScript object that stores properties and methods associated with an event. HTML 811

Extensible Markup Language A language for designing specialized markup languages. HTML F2

extension The top level of a URL, indicating the general audience supported by the web server. HTML 65

external style A style created by the page author and placed into a CSS file and linked to the page. HTML 87

F

fantasy A highly ornamental typeface used for page decoration. HTML 116

field set A web form feature that groups fields that share a common characteristic or purpose. HTML 507

field The part of a web form in which data values are stored. HTML 503

fieldset HTML element that groups fields within a web form. HTML 500

FIFO. *See* first-in first-out

filter CSS property used to modify an object's color, brightness, contrast, or general purpose. HTML 310

first-in first-out (FIFO) A data structure principle in which the first item added to an array is the first one removed. HTML 750

first-of-type CSS pseudo-class that selects the first element type of the parent element. HTML 132

firstChild JavaScript property that returns the first child of the specified node. HTML 893

fixed grid A grid layout in which the widths of the columns and margins are specified in pixels with fixed positions. HTML 203

fixed layout A layout in which the size of the page and the page elements are fixed, usually using pixels as the unit of measure. HTML 176

flag The part of a regular expression that modifies the action of the regular expression. HTML 1008

flex CSS property that defines the size of the flex items and how they will grow or shrink in response to the changing size of the flexbox. HTML 372

flex-basis CSS property that provides the basis or initial size of the item prior to flexing. HTML 372

flex-flow CSS property that defines the orientation of the flexbox and whether items can wrap to a new line. HTML 372

flex-grow CSS property that specifies how fast the item grows above its basis size relative to other items in the flex box. HTML 372

flex-shrink CSS property that specifies how fast the item shrinks below its basis size relative to other items in the flex box. HTML 372

flexbox A box that contains items whose sizes automatically expand or contract to match the dimensions of the box. HTML 372

float CSS property that takes an object out of normal document flow and floats it on the left or right margin of its container element. HTML 170

floating A design technique in which an element is taken out of its default document position and placed along the left or right edge of its parent element. HTML 183

fluid grid A grid layout in which the widths of the columns and margins are specified in percentages. HTML 203

fluid layout A layout in which the size of the page elements are set using percentages. HTML 177

focus The state in which an element has been clicked by the user, making it the active control on the web form. HTML 566

font Definition of the style and appearance of each character in an alphabet. HTML 115

font stack A list of fonts defined in the font-family property. HTML 115

font-family CSS property that defines a font stack. HTML 106

font-size CSS property that sets the text size. HTML 106

for HTML attribute that associates a label with an input control. HTML 500

for loop A programming structure in which a set of commands is repeated based on the changing values of a counter variable. HTML 754

for…in loop A JavaScript structure that loops through all of the enumerable properties within an object. HTML 1106

forEach JavaScript method that loops through each item in an array, applying the commands in the command block. HTML 1106

form button A button on a web form that can be clicked to either run, submit, or reset the form. HTML 555

form HTML element that encloses a web form. HTML 500

fr unit CSS grid unit that represents a fraction of the available space left on the grid after all other rows and columns have attained their maximum allowable size. HTML 219

frameset DTD The DTD used by XHTML that supports frames and those HTML features that were deprecated in HTML5. HTML F6

framework A software package that provides a library of tools to design a website. HTML 204

function A collection of JavaScript commands that performs an action or returns a value. HTML 714

function code Any code placed within a function that must be called to be executed. HTML 1070

function declaration JavaScript syntax that declares a function using the *function*() statement. HTML 856

function operator JavaScript that declares a function as a variable's value. HTML 856

G

generic font A general description of a font face. HTML 115

get() HTML method applied to web forms that tells the browser to append the form data to the end of the URL specified by the action attribute. HTML 505

getElementById() JavaScript method that selects a web page element based on its ID value. HTML 682

getFullYear() JavaScript method that gets the 4-digit year value from a Date object. HTML 702

GIF (Graphic Interchange Format) The oldest bitmap image format, limited to 256 colors, but that also supports transparent colors and animated images. HTML 264

GIF. *See* GIF (Graphic Interchange Format)

global code Any code that lies outside of a function and is automatically executed when encountered by the browser. HTML 1070

global scope The scope of a variable that can be referenced anywhere within the JavaScript file. HTML 717

global variable A variable with global scope. HTML 717

Graphic Interchange Format. *See* GIF (Graphic Interchange Format)

grid cell A cell at the intersection of a grid row and grid column. HTML 220

grid column A column floated within a grid row. HTML 201

grid layout A layout that arranges the page within grid rows with grid columns floated inside those rows. HTML 201

grid row A row found within a grid layout. HTML 201

grouping element An element that organizes similar content into a distinct group, much like a paragraph groups sentences that share a common theme. HTML 26

H

H.264 A video codec that is the industry standard for high-definition video streams. HTML 602

hanging indent A layout in which the first line extends to the left of the block. HTML 126

hasAttribute() JavaScript method that returns a Boolean value indicating whether a node contains a specified attribute. HTML 915

hexadecimal number A number expressed in the base 16 numbering system. HTML 99

hidden field A web form field that is not displayed within the web form. HTML 536

hierarchical structure A website structure in which the home page links to pages dedicated to specific topics, which are linked to even more specific topics. HTML E2

host Any network device that is capable of sending and/or receiving data electronically. HTML 4

hotspot A region within an image that can be linked to a specific URL. HTML 324

hover CSS pseudo-class that selects links that are being hovered over. HTML 132

HSL color value Color defined by its hue, saturation, and lightness values. HTML 84

HTML (Hypertext Markup Language) A markup language that supports the tagging of distinct document elements and connecting documents through hypertext links. HTML 5

HTML 4.0 The fourth version of HTML, released in 1999, that provided support for multimedia, online commerce, and interactive scripts. HTML 5

HTML comment A descriptive note added to an HTML file that does not get rendered by a user agent. HTML 2

HTML. *See* HTML (Hypertext Markup Language)

HTML5 Shiv A script that provides support for HTML5 in older browsers. HTML 39

HTML5 The latest version of HTML, compatible with earlier HTML releases. HTML 5

HTTP. *See* Hypertext Transfer Protocol (HTTP)

hue The tint of a color, represented by a direction on the color wheel. HTML 99

hyperlink A link within a hypertext document that can be activated to access a data source. HTML 4

hypertext A method of organizing information in which data sources are interconnected through a series of hyperlinks that users activate to jump from one data source to another. HTML 4

Hypertext Markup Language. *See* HTML (Hypertext Markup Language)

Hypertext Transfer Protocol (HTTP) The protocol used by devices on the web. HTML 64

I

IANA. *See* Internet Assigned Numbers Authority (IANA)

IDE (Integrated Development Environment) A software package providing comprehensive coverage of all phases of the HTML development process. HTML 7

IDE. *See* IDE (Integrated Development Environment)

if else statement JavaScript conditional expression that runs a specified command if the condition is true and a different command if the condition is false. HTML 770

if statement JavaScript conditional expression that runs a specified command if the condition is true. HTML 770

iframe HTML element used to insert windows showing external content within a web page. HTML 619

image map Information that specifies the location and URLs associated within each hotspot within an image. HTML 324

increment operator A unary operator that increases the value of the operand by 1. HTML 704

index A number used with an array to distinguish one array value from another. HTML 741

inline element An element in which the content is placed in line with surrounding page content rather than starting on a new line. HTML 29

inline frames Windows within a web page that show external content. HTML 619

inline image An image that is placed, like text-level elements, in line with the surrounding content. HTML 37

inline style A style added as attributes of an HTML element. HTML 87

inline validation A technique in which invalid data from a web form is highlighted as it is entered by the user. HTML 547

innerHTML JavaScript method that returns or defines the HTML code contained within a web page element. HTML 682

input box A web form control for inserting text strings and numeric values. HTML 502

input HTML element that creates an input control for a web form. HTML 500

insertRule() JavaScript method that adds a style rule to a style sheet. HTML 936

inset CSS keyword that places a box shadow inside the element. HTML 286

instance *See* object instance

instantiating The act of creating an object based on an object class. HTML 1082

interactive element An element that allows for interaction between the user and the embedded object. *Also called* embedded element. HTML 36

Internet A wide area network incorporating an almost uncountable number of networks and hosts across the world. HTML 4

Internet Assigned Numbers Authority (IANA) The registration authority used to register the top levels of every domain name. HTML 65

Internet Explorer event model Event model used by the Internet Explorer browser prior to IE 9. HTML 851

interpreted language A computer language in which the program code is executed directly without requiring a compiler. HTML 669

ISO 8859-1 An extended version of the ASCII character set. HTML 33

J

JavaScript A programming language used for client-side programs. HTML 669

Joint photographic experts group. *See* JPEG (Joint Photographic Experts Group)

JPEG (Joint Photographic Experts Group) A bitmap image format that supports a palette of over 16 million colors, as well as file compression. HTML 264

JPEG. *See* JPEG (Joint Photographic Experts Group)

K

kerning A measure of the space between characters. HTML 106

key A descriptive text string used to reference object properties or items in an associative array. HTML 1073

key frames A series of images that are displayed in rapid succession to create the illusion of motion. HTML 634

kind HTML attribute that specifies the type of text track attached to a media clip. HTML 600

L

label HTML element that associates a text string with an input control. HTML 500

LAN. *See* Local area network (LAN)

last-in first-out (LIFO) A data structure principle in which the last item added to an array is the first one removed. HTML 750

last-of-type CSS pseudo-class that selects the last element type of the parent element. HTML 132

Latin-1 An extended version of the ASCII character set. HTML 33

layout viewport The part of the mobile layout containing the entire page content. HTML 352

leading A measure of the amount of space between lines of text, set using the line-height property. HTML 125

left CSS property that defines the left coordinates of an element placed using relative, absolute, or fixed positioning. HTML 224

legend HTML element that provides the text of a field set legend. HTML 500

letter-spacing CSS property that sets the space between letters. HTML 106

LIFO. *See* last-in first-out

lightness The brightness of a chosen color, ranging from 0% to 100%. HTML 99

line WEBVTT attribute that sets the vertical position of cue text. HTML 600

line-height CSS property that sets the height of a line. HTML 106

linear structure A website structure in which each page is linked with the pages that follow it and precede it. HTML E1

linear-gradient CSS property that creates a color gradient proceeding along a straight line. HTML 286

link CSS pseudo-class that selects unvisited links. HTML 132

list marker A symbol displayed alongside a list item. HTML 134

list-style-image CSS property that inserts an image for the list marker. HTML 132

list-style-type CSS property that defines the appearance of the list marker. HTML 132

load-time error A program error that occurs when the browser initially loads and reads the program code. HTML 677

local area network (LAN) A network confined to a small geographic area, such as within a building or department. HTML 4

local scope The scope of a variable that can only be referenced within the function in which the variable is defined. HTML 717

local storage object JavaScript object that stores data locally on the user's computer with no expiration date and thus can be accessed from previous browser sessions. HTML 1005

local variable A variable with local scope. HTML 717

location object JavaScript that stores the current location of the web document. HTML 1000

location.search JavaScript object that returns the query string portion of the current page's URL. HTML 996

logical error A program error that is free from syntax and executable mistakes but that results in an incorrect result. HTML 677

logical operator An operator that allows you to connect several Boolean expressions. HTML 760

Lorem ipsum Nonsensical improper Latin commonly used in page design as filler text. HTML 216

lossless compression File compression in which redundant data are removed to achieve a smaller file size. HTML 588

lossy compression File compression in which nonessential data are removed to achieve a smaller file size. HTML 588

Luhn Algorithm An algorithm developed in the 1960's to provide a quick validation check on an account number by ensuring that the sum of the digits in the number meet certain mathematical criteria. *Also called* Mod10 Algorithm. HTML 1041

M

`mailto` HTML communication scheme used to provide the URL for an e-mail link. HTML 46

main axis The central axis along which items within a flexbox are laid out. HTML 374

margin area The page section that contains the space between the printed content and the edges of the page. HTML 405

margin space The part of the box model that surrounds the element border, extending to the next element. HTML 139

`margin-top` CSS property that sets the margin space above the element. HTML 132

markup language A language that describes the content and structure of a document by tagging different document elements. HTML 5

`Math object` JavaScript object used for performing mathematical tasks and storing mathematical values. HTML 707

`Math.floor()` JavaScript method that rounds a numeric value down to the next nearest integer. HTML 702

matrix A data structure in which data values are arranged in a rectangular grid. HTML 745

`max` HTML attribute that specifies the maximum value from a range of possible field values. HTML 546

`max-width` CSS property that defines the maximum width of an element. HTML 170

`maximumFractionDigits` JavaScript parameter of the `toLocaleString()` method that sets the maximum number of fractional digits. HTML 971

media player A software program that decodes and plays multimedia content. HTML 589

media query Code used to apply specified style rules to a device based on the device type and the device features. HTML 342

metadata Content that describes the document or provides information about how the document should be processed by the browser. HTML 15

method An action that can be performed on an object. HTML 684

MIME type. *See* Multipurpose Internet Mail Extension

`min` HTML attribute that specifies the minimum value from a range of possible field values. HTML 546

`min-width` CSS property that defines the minimum width of an element. HTML 170

minifying The process of removing unnecessary characters from HTML and CSS files in order to increase processing speed. HTML 398

`minimumFractionDigits` JavaScript parameter of the `toLocaleString()` method that sets the minimum number of fractional digits. HTML 971

mobile device emulator A software program that duplicates the look and feel of a mobile device. HTML 359

Mobile first A design principle by which the overall page design starts with base styles that apply to all devices followed by style rules specific to mobile devices. HTML 350

Mod10 Algorithm *See* Luhn Algorithm

Modernizr A script that provides support for HTML5 in older browsers. HTML 39

modifier key The Alt, Ctrl, Shift, and Command keys on the keyboard. HTML 845

module A component of CSS3 that focuses on a particular design topic. HTML 86

modulus operator An operator that returns the integer remainder after dividing one integer by another. HTML 774

monospace A typeface in which each character has the same width, often used to display programming code. HTML 116

mouseenter Event that fires when the mouse pointer enters a page element. HTML 830

MP3. *See* MPEG-1 Audio Layer 3

MP4. *See* MPEG-4

MPEG-1 Audio Layer 3 A widely used format for digital audio players. HTML 592

MPEG-4 Proprietary video form developed by Apple based on the Apple QuickTime movie format. HTML 602

multidimensional array A JavaScript structure in which one array is nested within another. HTML 747

`multiple` HTML attribute that allows for multiple selections from a drop-down list. HTML 528

Multipurpose Internet Mail Extension An extension that provides a way of attaching nontextual content to e-mail messages. HTML 593

N

`name` HTML attribute that provides the name of a data field associated with an input control. HTML 500

named function A function that is given a name. HTML 856

named node map An unordered list of nodes that can be referenced by their names. HTML 930

namespace The part of a document that combines several vocabularies that define which part of the document belongs to which vocabulary. HTML F10

navicon A symbol, usually represented as three horizontal lines, used to hide menu items in mobile devices. HTML 394

navigation list An unordered list of hypertext links placed within the nav element. HTML 55

nested element An element contained within another element. HTML 9

nested list A list that is placed inside another list. HTML 50

network A structure in which information and services are shared among devices known as nodes or hosts. HTML 4

network node A network location that can access and share information and services. HTML 4

`nextSibling` JavaScript property that returns the next sibling of the specified node. HTML 893

`no-repeat` CSS keyword that specifies that no tiling should be done with the background image. HTML 258

node Any object within the HTML file. HTML 892

node list A list of nodes that references collections of objects. HTML 934

node tree The hierarchical structure of nodes within a document. HTML 892

nodeName JavaScript property that returns the name of a node. HTML 893

nodeValue JavaScript property that returns a node's value. HTML 893

nth-of-type CSS pseudo-class that selects the nth element type of the parent element. HTML 132

number HTML data type for an input control that creates a spin box control. HTML 546

numeric character reference An HTML string that inserts a character based on its code value. HTML 22

numeric value A data type for storing numbers. HTML 694

O

object An entity within the web browser or web page. HTML 684

object collections A group of objects. HTML 685

object detection Programming technique that uses an **if** structure to determine whether the browser supports a particular object, property, or method. HTML 852

object instance A specific object that is based on an object class. *Also called* instance. HTML 1082

object literal A custom object created by storing the properties of the object within a comma-separated list of *name:value* pairs enclosed within a set of curly braces. HTML 1062

object-based language A programming language that manipulates an object by changing a property or applying a method. HTML 684

Ogg (audio) An open source and royalty-free audio format that provides better sound quality than MP3. HTML 592

Ogg (video) An open source video format developed by the Xiph.org Foundation as an alternative to the MPEG-4 codec. HTML 602

onclick event handler JavaScript event handler that runs when a page object is clicked. HTML 810

one-sided element tag A tag used for empty elements, containing no closing tag. HTML 9

onload event handler JavaScript event handler that runs when the page is loaded by the browser. HTML 810

opacity A measure of the solidness of a color, ranging from 0 to 1. HTML 100

opacity CSS property that makes an object semi-transparent. HTML 286

opening tag The tag that marks the start of the element content. HTML 2

operand The variable or expression that operators act upon. HTML 704

operator A symbol used in JavaScript to act upon an item or variable within an expression. HTML 704

option button A web form control for selecting data from a small predefined list of options. *Also called* radio button. HTML 502

option HTML element that marks options from a selection list. HTML 528

ordered list A list that is used for items that follow some defined sequential order. HTML 48

orphans A property that limits the number of lines stranded at the bottom of a page. HTML 400

outline CSS property that draws a line around the selected elements. HTML 200

overflow CSS property that determines how the browser should handle content that exceeds the space allotted to the element. HTML 224

P

padding space The part of the box model that extends from the element content to the element border. HTML 139

padding-box CSS keyword that specifies the background extends through the padding space. HTML 258

page area The page section that contains the content of the document. HTML 405

page box The layout definition of the printed page. HTML 405

page-break-before CSS property that inserts page breaks before elements. HTML 400

page-break-inside CSS property that prohibits page breaks within an element. HTML 400

parallel array An array in which an item matches, or is parallel to, another entry in a different array. HTML 772

parameter A variable that is associated with a JavaScript function. HTML 714

parent element An element that contains one or more child elements. HTML 108

pattern HTML attribute that specifies the general pattern that characters in a field value must follow. HTML 546

patternMismatch JavaScript property that returns **true** if the value doesn't match the regular expression pattern. HTML 1026

Perl A programming language used with server-based programs. HTML 504

persistent style sheet The default style sheet that cannot be turned off and has a **rel** attribute value of "stylesheet". HTML 944

perspective CSS property and a function used in 3D transformations to measure how rapidly objects appear to recede or approach the viewer. HTML 310

pixel A single dot on the output device. HTML 122

placeholder A text string that appears within a form control, providing a hint about the kind of data that should be entered into the field. HTML 520

placeholder HTML attribute that inserts descriptive text into an input control. HTML 500

plug-in A software program accessed by the browser to provide a feature not native to the browser. HTML 589

PNG (Portable Network Graphic) A bitmap image format designed to replace the GIF format with a palette of a million colors. HTML 264

PNG. *See* PNG (Portable Network Graphic)

Portable Network Graphic. *See* PNG (Portable Network Graphic)

position WEBVTT attribute that sets the horizontal position of cue text. HTML 600

post method HTML method applied to web forms that tells the browser to send the form data in its own separate data stream. HTML 505

poster HTML attribute that displays a preview image of a video file. HTML 600

preferred style sheet A style sheet that can be turned off and on by the user and has a **title** attribute. HTML 944

presentational attribute An attribute that describes how page content should be rendered by the browser. HTML 36

presentational element An element that describes how page content should be rendered by the browser. HTML 36

preventDefault() JavaScript method that prevents the browser from performing its default response to an event. HTML 830

print style sheet A style sheet that formats the printed version of the web document. HTML 402

submit button A web form button that submits the form to the server for processing. HTML 556

submit HTML data type for an input control that creates a button used for submitting the form for processing. HTML 546

substring Strings of characters within a larger text string. HTML 1003

superclass The base object class within a prototype chain. HTML 1108

SVG (Scalable Vector Image) An XML markup language that can be used to create vector images. HTML 258

SVG. *See* SVG (Scalable Vector Image)

switch statement A JavaScript statement used to run different commands based on different values of a specified variable. *Also called* case statement. HTML 780

symmetric transition A transition in which the initial state to end state transition is the reverse of the end state to initial state transition. HTML 634

syntax The rules governing how a language should be used and interpreted. HTML 5

T

table HTML element that marks a web table. HTML 434

target phase The phase in the event model in which event reaches the target of the event object. HTML 836

target property JavaScript property that returns a reference to the object in which an event was initiated. HTML 811

tbody HTML element that marks the row(s) in a web table body. HTML 458

td HTML element that marks a cell containing table data. HTML 434

tel HTML communication scheme used to provide the URL for a telephone link. HTML 46

ternary operator. *See* conditional operator

text area box A web form control for entering text strings that may include several lines of content. HTML 502

text node A node that matches a text string contained within an element node. HTML 892

text string A data type for storing any group of characters enclosed within either double or single quotation marks. HTML 694

text-align CSS property that defines the horizontal alignment of the content of an element. HTML 106

text-level element An element within a grouping element that contains strings of the characters or page content. HTML 29

text-shadow CSS property that adds a drop shadow to a text string. HTML 286

textarea HTML element that marks a text area control. HTML 528

textContent JavaScript method that returns or defines the text contained within a web page element. HTML 682

tfoot HTML element that marks the row(s) in a web table footer. HTML 458

th HTML element that marks a cell containing a table header. HTML 434

thead HTML element that marks the row(s) in a web table header. HTML 458

Theora A royalty-free video codec that produces video streams that can be used with almost any container. HTML 602

this keyword JavaScript keyword that references the owner of an object or function. HTML 823

tiling A process by which a background image is repeated, filling up the background space. HTML 265

time-delayed command A JavaScript command that is run after a specific amount of time has passed. HTML 718

toLocaleDateString() JavaScript method that returns a text string containing the date using local conventions. HTML 682

toLocaleString() JavaScript method that formats a numeric value. HTML 971

toLocaleTimeString() JavaScript method that returns a text string containing the time using local conventions. HTML 682

top CSS property that defines the top coordinates of an element placed using relative, absolute, or fixed positioning. HTML 224

tr HTML element that encloses a table row. HTML 434

track HTML element that attaches a text track to a media clip. HTML 600

tracking A measure of the amount of space between words; set using the word-spacing property. HTML 125

transform CSS property used to rotate, rescale, skew, or shift a page object. HTML 310

transition A change in an object's style from an initial state to an ending state. HTML 624

transition CSS property that defines a transition between an initial state and an end state. HTML 622

transitional DTD The DTD used by XHTML that supports those HTML features that were deprecated in HTML5. HTML F6

typography The art of designing the appearance of characters and letters on a page. HTML 115

U

unary operator An operator that works with only one operand. HTML 704

Unicode The largest character set supporting up to 65,536 symbols that can be used with any of the world's languages. HTML 33

Uniform Resource Locator (URL) A standard address format used to link to a variety of resource documents. HTML 57

unordered list A list that is used for items that do not follow a defined sequential order. HTML 49

unstack The process of removing the last item from an array. HTML 750

update expression The expression in a for loop that updates the value of the counter variable each time through the loop. HTML 754

URI encoded character Character code used with URLs to replace characters that are not allowed in the query string. HTML 1020

URL. *See* Uniform Resource Locator (URL)

use strict JavaScript statement that specifies syntax rules should be strictly applied. HTML 667

user agent style A style built into the web browser itself. HTML 87

user-defined style A style defined by the user based on settings made in configuring the browser. HTML 87

UTF-8 The most common character encoding in present use. HTML 17

V

valid document A well-formed XML document that contains only those elements, attributes, and other features that have been defined for its XML vocabulary. HTML F5

validation The process of ensuring the user has supplied valid data. HTML 559

validator A program that tests code to ensure that it contains no syntax errors. HTML 7

`ValidityState` JavaScript object that stores the reason for failing form validation. HTML 1030

`value` HTML attribute that provides the default value for a data field. HTML 500

`value` JavaScript property that returns the field value from a web form control. HTML 970

`valueMissing` JavaScript property that returns `true` if a required value is missing. HTML 1026

vanishing point An effect of perspective in which parallel lines appear to converge to a point. HTML 317

`var` JavaScript keyword used to declare a variable. HTML 682

variable A named item in a program that stores a data value or an object. HTML 693

vector image An image format in which the lines and curves that comprise the image are based on mathematical functions. HTML 264

vendor prefix The prefix added to a browser extension. HTML 90

`video` HTML element that embeds a video file in a web page. HTML 600

viewport meta A meta tag used to set the properties of the layout viewport. HTML 342

viewport unit A relative unit of length that expresses a size relative to the width or height of the browser window. HTML 123

virtual keyboard A keyboard that exists as a software representation of a physical keyboard. HTML 514

`visited` CSS pseudo-class that selects previously-visited links. HTML 132

visual viewport The part of the mobile layout that displays the web page content that fits within a mobile screen. HTML 352

`VP8` An open source video codec used in Google's WebM video format. HTML 602

`VP9` A video codec developed by Google as a successor to VP8, offering the same video quality at half the download size. HTML 602

W

W3C. *See* World Wide Consortium (W3C)

WAN. *See* Wide area network (WAN)

watermark A translucent graphic that is part of the page content and that displays a message

that the content is copyrighted or in draft form or some other message directed toward the reader. HTML 267

WAV A commonly used format for Windows PC that is used for storing uncompressed audio. HTML 592

weakly typed language A programming language in which variables are not strictly tied to specific data types. HTML 695

web browser A software program that retrieves and displays web pages. HTML 5

web font A font in which the font definition is supplied to the browser in an external file. HTML 118

web form A web page design element in which users can enter data that can be saved and processed. HTML 502

Web Hypertext Application Technology Working Group (WHATWG) A group formed in 2004 to develop HTML5 as a rival version to XHTML 2.0. HTML 5

web page A document stored by a web server and accessed by a web browser. HTML 5

web safe font A font that is displayed mostly the same way in all operating systems and on all devices. HTML 116

web server A server that makes web pages accessible to the network. HTML 5

web table An HTML structure consisting of multiple rows with each row containing one or more table cells. HTML 436

WebM An open source format introduced by Google to provide royalty-free video and audio. HTML 602

WebVTT (Web Video Text Tracks) A text file format used for storing video text tracks. HTML 608

well-formed document An XML document that employs the correct syntax. HTML F3

WHATWG. *See* Web Hypertext Application Technology Working Group (WHATWG)

`while` **loop** A program loop in which the command block is run as long as a specified condition is met. HTML 758

white-space character An empty or blank character such as a space, tab, or line break. HTML 12

wide area network (WAN) A network that covers a wide area, such as several buildings or cities. HTML 4

widget An object within a web form that allows users to interact with the form. HTML 502

`widows` CSS property that limits the number of lines stranded at the top of a page. HTML 400

`width` CSS property that defines the width of an element. HTML 170

wildcard selector A selector that matches all elements. HTML 109

word A regular expression pattern that refers to any string of symbols consisting solely of word characters. HTML 1009

word character A characters in a regular expression that matches an alphabetical character, a digit, or the underscore character (_). HTML 1008

word cloud A chart of several words, in which each word's size is based on the frequency of use in a selected text. HTML 1057

World Wide Consortium (W3C) A group of web designers and programmers that set the standards or specifications for browser manufacturers to follow. HTML 5

World Wide Web (WWW) The totality of interconnected hypertext documents on the Internet. HTML 4

WWW. *See* World Wide Web (WWW)

X

XHTML (Extensible Hypertext Markup Language) A version of HTML in which syntax standards are strictly enforced. HTML 5

XHTML. *See* XHTML (Extensible Hypertext Markup Language)

XML parser A software program that checks an XML file for errors in syntax and content. HTML F3

XML vocabularies Markup languages developed using XML. HTML F2

XML. *See* Extensible Markup Language

INDEX

P

<p> tag, HTML 22, HTML 23, HTML 27, HTML B16

padding space, HTML 139, HTML 140–142

`padding-box` keyword, HTML 258

page area, HTML 405

page boxes, HTML 405

page break(s), HTML 415–421
  adding, HTML 415–416
  automatic, set by browsers, HTML 416
  preventing, HTML 416–418
  widows and orphans, HTML 418–419

page groups, HTML 27

page layout, HTML 169–256
  attributes, HTML C14–C15
  effective, HTML 222
  elastic, HTML 177
  fixed, HTML 176–177
  flexbox. *See* flexbox(es)
  flexible, image maps, HTML 329
  floating elements. *See* floating elements
  fluid, HTML 177
  grid layouts. *See* grid layouts
  positioning styles. *See* positioning styles
  responsive design, HTML 177

page names, HTML 406

`page` property, HTML 406–411

`@page` rule, HTML 400, HTML 405–414, HTML C4
  formatting hypertext links for printing, HTML 412–414
  page names and `page` property, HTML 406–411
  page pseudo-classes, HTML 406
  setting page size, HTML 405

page size, setting, HTML 405

page styles, creating and applying, HTML 407

page validation with XHTML, HTML F1–F13
  files on web, HTML F10–F12
  frameset DTD, HTML F5–F6

inserting DOCTYPE declaration, HTML F8–F9
  setting the XHTML namespace, HTML F9–F10
  strict DTD, HTML F5–F7
  transitional DTD, HTML F5–F6
  valid use of attributes, HTML F7–F8
  well-formed documents, HTML F2–F4

`page-break-after` property, HTML 415–416

`page-break-before` property, HTML 400, HTML 415–416

`page-break-inside` property, HTML 400

paragraphs, grouping content by, HTML 28

parallel arrays, HTML 772

<param> tag, HTML B16

parameters, HTML 714

parent elements, HTML 108

`pattern` attribute, HTML 546, HTML 562–563

pattern matching, validating data, HTML 1035–1036

`patternMismatch` property, HTML 1026

percent sign (%), JavaScript operators, HTML 704, HTML 705

Perl, HTML 504

perspective, HTML 317–320
  setting in 3D, HTML 318

`perspective()` function, HTML 317–320

`perspective` property, HTML 310, HTML 317, HTML 318

phone numbers, linking to, HTML 67–68

pipe (|)
  joining patterns, HTML 1014
  logical operators, HTML 761, HTML 771

pixels, HTML 122
  device and CSS, HTML 355

placeholder(s), HTML 524–525

`placeholder` attribute, HTML 500, HTML 524–525

plug-ins, HTML 589–590
  attributes, HTML 598–599
  as fallback options, HTML 599
  Section 508 guidelines, HTML D10–D11

plus sign (+), JavaScript operators, HTML 704, HTML 705

PNG (Portable Network Graphics), HTML 264

pointer events, HTML 832–836

`pop()` method, HTML 751, HTML 752

position, list markers, HTML 137, HTML 138–139

`position` attribute, HTML 600

positioning, setting background image position, HTML 267–268

positioning styles, HTML 224–246
  absolute positioning, HTML 227–230
  clipping elements, HTML 243–244
  fixed positioning, HTML 230
  inherited positioning, HTML 230
  overflow, HTML 240–242
  relative positioning, HTML 226–227
  stacking elements, HTML 244–245
  static positioning, HTML 226
  using, HTML 230–239

`post()` method, HTML 505

`poster` attribute, HTML 600

pound symbol (#), character encoding references, HTML 35

<pre> tag, HTML 27, HTML B16

precedence, styles, HTML 92

presentational attributes, HTML 36

presentational elements, HTML 36

`preventDefault()` method, HTML 819, HTML 830, HTML 841–842

print style(s), HTML 400–421
  formatting hyperlinks for printing, HTML 412–414
  media queries for printed output, HTML 403–405
  page breaks, HTML 415–421
  page names, HTML 406
  `page` property, HTML 406–411